Civilization in the West

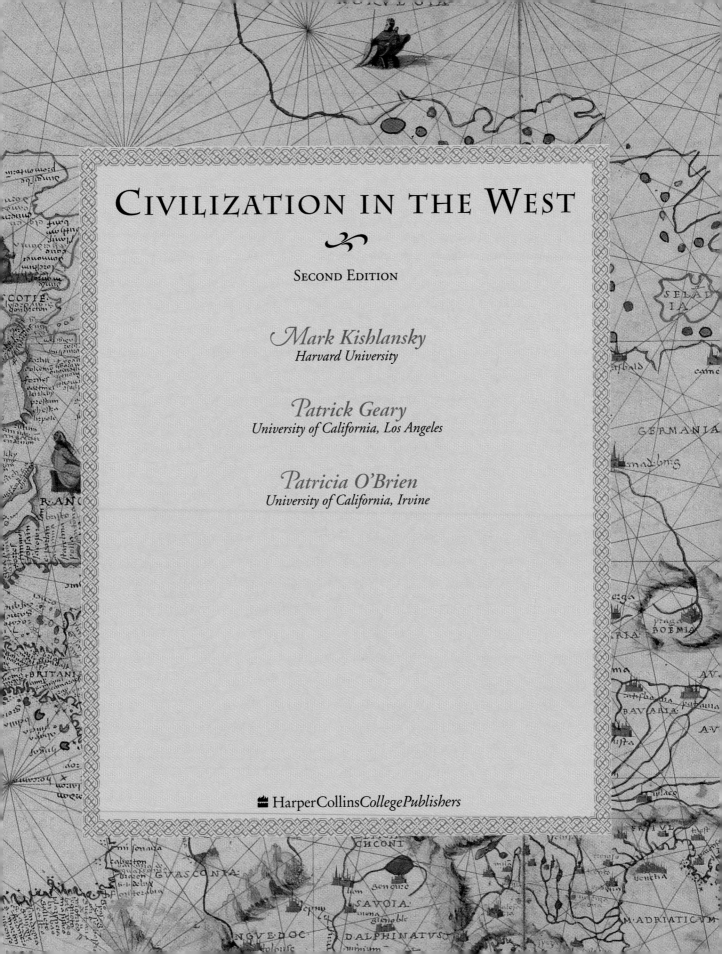

CIVILIZATION IN THE WEST

SECOND EDITION

Mark Kishlansky
Harvard University

Patrick Geary
University of California, Los Angeles

Patricia O'Brien
University of California, Irvine

HarperCollinsCollege*Publishers*

Executive Editor: Bruce Borland
Director of Development: Betty Slack
Developmental Editor: Barbara Muller
Text Designer and Art Manager: Alice Fernandes-Brown
Cover Designer: Mary McDonnell
Art Studio: Mapping Specialists Ltd. / Paul Lacy
Photo Researcher: Sandy Schneider
Electronic Production Manager: Alexandra Odulak
Manufacturing Manager: Alexandra Odulak
Electronic Page Makeup: Alice Fernandes-Brown / Molly Heron / Paul Lacy
Printer and Binder: RR Donnelley & Sons Company
Cover Printer: Coral Graphics Services, Inc.

Cover Illustration: Detail from *Allegory of Good Government: Effects of Good Government in the City* by Ambrogio Lorenzetti (ca.1285–1348). Scala/Art Resource, New York.

Photo credits appear on pp. C-4 through C-7.

For permission to use copyrighted material, grateful acknowledgment is made to the copyright holders on pp. C-1 through C-4, which are hereby made part of this copyright page.

Civilization in the West, Second Edition

Library of Congress Cataloging-in-Publication Data

Kishlansky, Mark A.
    Civilization in the west / Mark Kishlansky, Patrick Geary,
  Patricia O'Brien. —2nd ed.
      p.   cm.
    Includes bibliographical references (p.) and index.
    ISBN 0-673-99226-8 (student ed.)   —ISBN 0-673-99250-0
(instructor's ed.)
     1. Civilization, Western—History.   I. Geary, Patrick J., 1948– .
    II. O'Brien, Patricia, 1945– . III. Title.
CB245.K546   1995   94-22763
909'.09821—dc20   CIP

95 96 97 9 8 7 6 5 4 3 2

BRIEF CONTENTS

CONTENTS

CHAPTER 9   THE HIGH MIDDLE AGES 250

CHAPTER 10   THE LATER MIDDLE AGES, 1300–1500 288

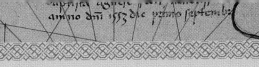

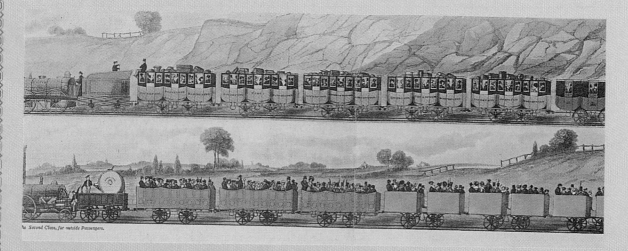

he Second Class, for outside Passengers.

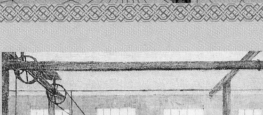

MAPS

CHARTS, TABLES, AND FIGURES

Documents

PREFACE

*I*n planning *Civilization in the West,* our aim was to write a book that students would *want* to read. Throughout our years of planning, writing, revising, rewriting, and meeting together, this was our constant overriding concern. Would students read our book? Would it be effective in conveying information while stimulating the imagination? Would it work for a variety of Western civilization courses with different levels and formats? It was not easy to keep this concern in the forefront throughout the long months of composition, but it was easy to receive the reactions of scores of reviewers to this simple question: "Would students *want* to read these chapters?" Whenever we received a resounding "No!" we began again—not just rewriting, but rethinking how to present material that might be complex in argument or detail or that might simply seem too remote to engage the contemporary student. Although all three of us were putting in long hours in front of word processors, we quickly learned that we were engaged in a teaching rather than a writing exercise. And though the work was demanding, it was not unrewarding. We hope that you will recognize and come to share with us the excitement and enthusiasm we felt in creating this text. We have enjoyed writing it, and we want students to enjoy reading it.

Judging from the reactions to our first edition, they have. We have received literally hundreds of cards and letters from adopters and users of *Civilization in the West.* The response has been both overwhelming and gratifying. It has also been constructive. Along with praise, we have received significant suggestions for making the next edition stronger. Topics such as the Crusades, the Enlightenment, and imperialism have been reorganized to present them more clearly. Subjects such as the ancient Hebrews, Napoleon, and German unification have been given more space and emphasis. New features have been added to freshen the book and keep abreast of current scholarship, and—most significantly—we have added over one hundred excerpts from primary sources to give students a feel for the concreteness of the past. We believe that this second edition of *Civilization in the West* not only preserves the much-praised quality of the first edition, but also enhances it.

Approach

We made a number of decisions early in the project that we believe contributed to our goal. First, we were *not* writing an encyclopedia of Western civilization. Information was not to be included in a chapter unless it related to the themes of that chapter. There was to be no information for information's sake, and each of us was called upon to defend the inclusion of names, dates, and events whenever we met to critique one another's chapters. We found, to our surprise, that by adhering to the principle that information included must contribute to or illustrate a particular point or dominating theme, we provided as much, if not more, material than books that habitually list names, places, and dates without any other context.

Second, we were committed to integrating the history of ordinary men and women into our narrative. We believe that isolated sections, placed at the end of chapters, that deal with the experiences of women or minority groups in a particular era profoundly distort historical experience. We called this technique *caboosing,* and whenever we found ourselves segregating women or families or the masses, we stepped back and asked how we might recast our treatment of historical events to account for a diversity of actors. How did ordinary men, women, and children affect the course of historical events? How did historical events affect the fabric of daily life for men and women and children from all walks of life? We tried to rethink critical historical problems of civilization as gendered phenomena. To assist us in this endeavor, we engaged two reviewers whose sole responsibility was to evaluate our chapters for the integration of these social groups into our discussion.

We took the same approach to the coverage of central and Eastern Europe that we did to women and minorities. Even before the epochal events of 1989 that returned this region to the forefront of international attention, we realized that in too many textbooks the Slavic world was treated as marginal to the history of Western civilization. Thus, with the help of a specialist reviewer, we worked to integrate more of the history of Eastern Europe into our text than is found in most others, and to do so in a way that presented these regions, their cultures and their institutions, as integral rather than peripheral to Western civilization.

To construct a book that students would *want* to read, we needed to develop fresh ideas about how to involve them with the material, how to transform them from passive recipients to active participants. We borrowed from computer science the concept of being "user-friendly." We wanted to find ways to stimulate the imagination of the student, and the more we experimented with different techniques, the more we realized that the most effective way to do this was visually. It is not true that contemporary students cannot be taught effectively by the written word; it is only true that they cannot be taught *as* effectively as they can by the combination of words and images. From the beginning, we realized that a text produced in full color was essential to the features we most wanted to use: the pictorial chapter openers; the large number of maps; the geographical tours of Europe at certain times in history; and the two-page special feature in each chapter, each with its own illustration.

Features

It is hard to have a new idea when writing a textbook—so many authors have come before, each attempting to do something more effective, more innovative than his or her predecessor. It is probably the case that somewhere there has been a text that has used a chapter-opening feature similar to the one we use here. What we can say with certainty is that nothing else we experimented with, no other technique we attempted, has had such an immediate and positive impact on our readers or has so fulfilled our goal of involving the students in learning as our *pictorial chapter openers*. An illustration—a painting, a photograph, a picture, an artifact, an edifice—appears at the beginning of each chapter, accompanied by text through which we explore the picture, guiding students across a canvas or helping them see in an artifact or a piece of architecture details that are not immediately apparent. It is the direct combination of text and image that allows us to achieve this effect, to "unfold" both an illustration and a theme. In some chapters we highlight details, pulling out a section of the original picture to take a closer look. In others we attempt to shock the viewer into the recognition of horror, or of beauty. Some chapter-opener images are designed to transport students back in time, to make them ask the question, "What was it like to be there?" All of the opening images have been chosen to illustrate a dominant theme within the chapter, and the dramatic and lingering impression they make helps reinforce that theme.

We have taken a similar image-based approach to our *presentation of geography*. When teachers of Western civilization courses are surveyed, no single area of need is cited more often than that of geographical knowledge. Students simply have no mental image of Europe, no familiarity with those geophysical features that are a fundamental part of the geopolitical realities of Western history. We realized that maps, carefully planned and skillfully executed, would be an important component of our text. To complement the standard map program of the text, we have added a special geographical feature. Six times throughout the book, we pause in the narrative to take a tour of Europe. Sometimes we follow an emperor as he tours his realm; sometimes we examine the impact of a peace treaty; sometimes we follow the travels of a merchant. Whatever the thematic occasion, our intention is to guide the student around the changing contours of the geography of Western history. In order to do this effectively, we have worked with our cartographer to develop small detailed maps to complement the overview map that appears at the beginning of each tour section. We know that only the most motivated students will turn back several pages to locate on a map a place mentioned in the text. Using small maps allows us to integrate maps directly into the relevant text, thus relieving students of the sometimes frustrating experience of attempting to locate not only a specific place on a map but perhaps even the relevant map itself. The great number of maps throughout the text, the specially designed tour-of-Europe geographical feature, and the ancillary programs of map transparencies and workbook exercises combine to provide the strongest possible program for teaching historical geography.

The third technique we have employed to engage students with historical subjects is the two-page *special feature* that appears in each chapter. These special features focus on a single event or personality chosen to enhance the student's sense that history is something that is real and alive. These features are written more dramatically and sympathetically, with a greater sense of wonder than would be appropriate in the body of the text. The prose style and the accompanying illustration are designed to captivate the reader. In this second edition we have written a number of new special features to keep the text fresh and to present a wider variety of historical experiences in this format. To help the student relate personally and directly to a historical event, we have highlighted figures such as Hypatia of Alexandria, Isabella of Castile, and nineteenth-century Zimbabwe political heroes Nehanda and Kagubi.

Finally, this second edition of *Civilization in the West* contains *selections from primary sources* designed to stimulate students' interest in history by allowing them to hear the past speak in its own voice. We have tried to provide a mixture of "canonical" texts along with those illustrating the lives or ordinary people in order to demonstrate the variety of materials that form the building blocks of historical narrative. Each selection is accompanied by an explanatory headnote that identifies author and work and provides the necessary historical context. Most of these extracts relate directly to discussions within the chapter, thus providing the student with a fuller understanding of a significant thinker or event.

There are many new features in our text, and much that is out of the ordinary. But there are important traditional aspects of the narrative itself that also require mention. *Civilization in the West* is a mainstream text in which most of our energies have been placed in developing a solid, readable narrative of Western civilization that integrates coverage of women and minorities into the discussion. We have highlighted personalities while identifying trends. We have spotlighted social history, both in sections of chapters and in separate chapters, while maintaining a firm grip on political developments. We hope that there are many things in this book that teachers of Western civilization will find valuable. But we also hope that there are things here with which you will disagree, themes that you can develop better, arguments and ideas that will stimulate you. A textbook is only one part of a course, and it is always less important than a teacher. What we hope is that by having done our job successfully, we will have made the teacher's job easier and the student's job more enjoyable.

Mark Kishlansky
Patrick Geary
Patricia O'Brien

Acknowledgments

୬

We want to thank the many conscientious historians who gave generously of their time and knowledge to review our manuscript. Their valuable critiques and suggestions have contributed greatly to the final product. We are grateful to the following:

Achilles Aavraamides
Iowa State University

Arthue H. Auten
University of Hartford

Sharon Bannister
University of Findlay

Patrick Bass
Mount Union College

Patrice Berger
University of Nebraska

Ronald S. Brockway
Regis University

Ronald G. Brown
Charles County Community College

Tim Crain
University of Wisconsin, Stout

Lorne E. Glaim
Pacific Union College

Sue Helder Goliber
Mount St. Mary's College

Manuel G. Gonzales
Diablo Valley College

Margaretta S. Handke
Mankato State University

Patricia Howe
University of St. Thomas

Alan M. Kirshner
Ohlone College

Bryan LeBeau
Creighton University

David B. Mock
Tallahassee Community College

Bruce K. O'Brien
Mary Washington College

Richard A. Oehling
Assumption College

Jack B. Ridley
University of Missouri, Rolla

Joanne Schneider
Rhode Island College

Steven C. Seyer
Lehigh County Community College

George H. Shriver
Georgia Southern University

We also acknowledge with gratitude the thoughtful evaluations and constructive suggestions of the historians who reviewed the first edition of this work.

Meredith L. Adams
Southwest Missouri State University

John W. Barker
University of Wisconsin

William H. Beik
Northern Illinois University

Lenard R. Berlanstein
University of Virginia

Raymond Birn
University of Oregon

Donna Bohanan
Auburn University

Werner Braatz
University of Wisconsin, Oshkosh

xxxiii

Thomas A. Brady, Jr.
University of Oregon

Anthony M. Brescia
Nassau Community College

Elaine G. Breslaw
Morgan State University

Daniel Patrick Brown
Moorpark College

Ronald A. Brown
Charles County Community College

Edward J. Champlin
Princeton University

Stephanie Evans Christelow
Western Washington University

Gary B. Cohen
University of Oklahoma

John J. Contreni
Purdue University

Samuel E. Dicks
Emporia State University

Frederick Dumin
Washington State University

Margot C. Finn
Emory University

Allan W. Fletcher
Boise State University

Elizabeth L. Furdell
University of North Florida

Thomas W. Gallant
University of Florida

Joseph J. Godson
Hudson Valley Community College

Eric Haines
Bellevue Community College

David A. Harnett
University of San Francisco

Paul B. Harvey, Jr.
Pennsylvania State University

Daniel W. Hollis
Jacksonville State University

Kenneth G. Holum
University of Maryland

Charles Ingrao
Purdue University

George F. Jewsbury
Oklahoma State University

Donald G. Jones
University of Central Arkansas

William R. Jones
University of New Hampshire

Richard W. Kaeuper
University of Rochester

David Kaiser
Carnegie-Mellon University

William R. Keylor
Boston University

Joseph Kicklighter
Auburn University

Charles L. Killinger, III
Valencia Community College

David C. Large
Montana State University

Lyle McAlister
University of Florida

Therese M. McBride
College of the Holy Cross

Roberta T. Manning
Boston College

Robert Moeller
University of California, Irvine

Pierce C. Mullen
Montana State University

Thomas F. X. Noble
University of Virginia

Dennis H. O'Brien
West Virginia University

Peter C. Piccillo
Rhode Island College

Theophilus Prousis
University of North Florida

Marlette Rebhorn
Austin Community College

John P. Ryan
Kansas City Kansas Community College

Steven Schroeder
Indiana University of Pennsylvania

Bonnie Smith
University of Rochester

Peter N. Stearns
Carnegie-Mellon University

Darryl B. Sycher
Columbus State Community College

Steven Vincent
North Carolina State University

Richard A. Voeltz
Cameron University

Eric Weissman
Golden West College

Each author also received invaluable assistance and encouragement from many colleagues, friends, and family members over the years of research, reflection, writing, and revising that went into the making of this text.

Mark Kishlansky wishes to thank Ann Adams, Robert Bartlett, Ray Birn, David Buisseret, Ted Cook, Frank Conaway, Constantine Fasolt, Katherine Haskins, Richard Hellie, Matthew Kishlansky, Donna Marder, Mary Beth Rose, Jeanne Thiel, and the staffs of the Joseph Regenstein Library and the Newberry Library.

Patrick Geary wishes to thank Mary Geary, Catherine Geary, and Anne Geary for their patience, support, and encouragement; he also thanks Anne Picard, Dale Schofield, and Hans Hummer for their able assistance throughout the project.

Patricia O'Brien thanks Jon Jacobson for his constant support and for sharing his specialized knowledge and his historical sense. She also wishes to thank Elizabeth Bryant for her encouragement and enthusiasm throughout the project and Robert Moeller for his keen eye for organization and his suggestions for writing a gendered history.

All the authors would also like to thank, though words are but a poor expression of our gratitude, Bruce Borland, Betty Slack, and Barbara Muller, the editors of our project. If ever authors have had more felicitous experiences with their editors than we have had with ours, they have been lucky indeed. The authors also extend sincere appreciation to Alice Fernandes-Brown and Alexandra Odulak, who contributed their skills and expertise to the design and production processes involved in the making of this book.

SUPPLEMENTS

❧

For Instructors

Instructor's Resource Manual

Prepared by Margot C. Finn of Emory University and David Mock of Tallahassee Community College, each chapter of this important resource manual contains a chapter summary, key terms, geographic and map items, and discussion questions.

Discovering Western Civilization Through Maps and Views

Created by Gerald Danzer, University of Illinois at Chicago—the recipient of the AHA's 1990 James Harvey Robinson Prize for his work in the development of map transparencies—this set of 140 four-color acetates is a unique instructional tool. It contains an introduction on teaching history through maps and a detailed commentary on each transparency. The collection includes cartographic and pictorial maps, views and photos, urban plans, building diagrams, and works of art.

Test Bank

Developed by John Paul Bischoff of Oklahoma State University, the Test Bank contains over 1200 multiple-choice, matching, and completion questions. Multiple-choice items are referenced by topic, text page number, and type (factual or interpretive).

TestMaster Computerized Testing System

This flexible, easy-to-master computer test bank includes all of the test items in the printed test bank. The TestMaster software allows you to edit existing questions and add your own items. Tests can be printed in several different formats and can include figures such as graphs and tables. Available for IBM and Macintosh computers.

QuizMaster

This new program enables you to design TestMaster generated tests that your students can take on a computer rather than in printed form. QuizMaster is available separately from TestMaster and can be obtained free through your sales representative.

Grades

This grade-keeping and classroom management software program maintains data for up to 200 students.

Transparencies

This set contains over 40 map transparencies drawn from the text.

For Students

Study Guide

Compiled by John Paul Bischoff of Oklahoma State University, this study guide is available in two volumes and offers for each text chapter a summary; a glossary list; and identification, multiple-choice, and critical-thinking questions.

SuperShell II Computerized Tutorial

Prepared by John Paul Bischoff of Oklahoma State University, this interactive program for IBM computers helps students learn major facts and concepts through drill and practice exercises and diagnostic feedback.

SuperShell II provides immediate correct answers, the text page number on which the material is discussed, and a running score of the student's performance on the screen throughout the session. This free supplement is available to instructors through their sales representative.

Mapping Western Civilization: Student Activities

Written by Gerald Danzer of the University of Illinois at Chicago, this free map workbook for students features exercises designed to teach students to interpret and analyze cartographic materials as historical documents. The instructor is entitled to a free copy of the workbook for each copy of the text purchased from HarperCollins.

TimeLink Computer Atlas of Western Civilization

This atlas, compiled by William Hamblin of Brigham Young University, is an introductory software tutorial and textbook companion. This Macintosh program covers material on European developments from 400 to 1500 A.D. Students can watch animated maps display geopolitical changes and study special topics, including the Anglo-Saxon migration to Britain and the Hundred Years' War.

ABOUT THE AUTHORS

Mark Kishlansky

Recently appointed Professor of History at Harvard University, Mark Kishlansky is among today's leading young scholars. Professor Kishlansky received his Ph.D. from Brown University. A Fellow of the Royal Historical Society and the Massachusetts Historical Society, his primary area of expertise is seventeenth-century English political history. Among his main publications are *Parliamentary Selection: Social and Political Choice in Early Modern England* and *The Rise of the New Model Army.* He has been the editor of the *Journal of British Studies* and was the recipient of the 1989 Most Distinguished Alumnus Award from SUNY Stony Brook.

Patrick Geary

Holding a Ph.D. in Medieval Studies from Yale University, Patrick Geary is a noted scholar and teacher. He is currently Director of the Center for Medieval and Renaissance Studies at the University of California, Los Angeles. Named outstanding undergraduate history teacher for the 1986–87 year at the University of Florida, Professor Geary has also held academic positions at the École des Hautes Études en Sciences Sociales, Paris; the Universität Wien; and Princeton University. His many publications include *Readings in Medieval History; Before France and Germany: The Creation and Transformation of the Merovingian World; Furta Sacra: Thefts of Relics in the Central Middle Ages;* and *Phantoms of Remembrance: Memory and Oblivion at the End of the First Millennium.*

Patricia O'Brien

As Director of the University of California Humanities Research Institute, Patricia O'Brien works to foster collaborative interdisciplinary research in the humanities. Her academic home is the Department of History at the University of California, Irvine, and she has held appointments at Yale University and at the École des Hautes Études en Sciences Sociales in Paris. Professor O'Brien is a specialist in modern French cultural and social history and has published widely on the history of crime, punishment, cultural theory, urban history, and gender issues. Representative publications include *The Promise of Punishment: Prisons in Nineteenth-Century France*; "The Kleptomania Diagnosis: Bourgeois Women and Theft in Late Nineteenth-Century France" in *Expanding the Past: A Reader in Social History*; and "Michel Foucault's History of Culture" in *The New Cultural History*, edited by Lynn Hunt.

CIVILIZATION IN THE WEST

SECOND EDITION

Single Volume Edition
0-673-99226-8

Volume I: Chapters
1-16 (to 1715)
0-673-99248-9

Volume II: Chapters
14-30 (1555-present)
0-673-99249-7

Volume A: Chapters
1-12 (to 1550)
0-673-99251-9

Volume B: Chapters
11-22 (1350-1815)
0-673-99252-7

Volume C: Chapters
22-30 (1789-present)
0-673-99253-5

From the Renaissance to the Present:
Chapters 11-30 (1350-present)
0-673-99254-3

Mark Kishlansky,
Harvard University

Patrick J. Geary,
University of California,
Los Angeles

Patricia O'Brien,
University of California,
Irvine

Bolstered by an eloquent, chronologically organized thematic narrative and a magnificent illustration program with full-color art and maps, *Civilization in the West, 2e,* masterfully recounts the human story of Western civilization. The second edition features greater thematic unity and a stronger chronological framework while it continues to examine the social, political, economic, and intellectual issues that have shaped civilization. New material includes enhanced coverage of religion and the Crusades, an updated look at Columbus, a separate section on the Enlightenment, and a thoroughly revised discussion of imperialism during the late nineteenth century. Pedagogically, primary source excerpts have been added in each chapter, while the popular chapter openers, "Special Feature" essays, and "Tours of Europe" have been retained from the successful first edition.

CHAPTER 6 THE TRANSFORMATION OF THE CLASSICAL WORLD

An illuminated manuscript illustrates Constantine's vision, in which he is told to fight under the sign of Christianity. The scene below shows his victory at the Mulvian Bridge.

INCREASED COVERAGE OF CHRISTIANITY

This material gives students a stronger, more coherent understanding of one of the primary monotheistic faiths of the Western tradition.

his new city, Constantine began to transform the empire into a Christian state and Christianity into a Roman state religion.

We will never know just what Constantine's conversion meant to him in personal terms. Its effects on the empire and on Christianity were obvious and enormous. Constantine himself continued to maintain cordial relations with representatives of all cults and to use ambiguous language that would offend no one when talking about "the deity." His successors were less broad-minded. They quickly reversed the positions of Christianity [...] pagan sacrifice was [...]

Cluniac and Cistercian Monasteries

INCREASED COVERAGE OF THE CRUSADES

This coverage allows students to more readily understand the legacy of this significant movement.

return to simplicity, separation from the rest of society, and a deeper internal spirituality. Chief among these groups were the Cistercians who, under the dynamic leadership of Bernard of Clairvaux (1090–1153), spread a rigorous, ascetic form of monasticism from England to the Vienna woods. The Cistercians built monasteries in the wilderness and discouraged the kinds of close ties with secular society established by the Cluniacs. They wished to avoid the crowds of pilgrims and the intense involvement with local affairs that characterized other types of monasticism. Paradoxically, by establishing themselves in remote areas, organizing their estates in an efficient manner, and gaining a great reputation for asceticism, the Cistercians became enormously wealthy and successful leaders in the economic changes taking place in the twelfth and thirteenth centuries.

The rural church not only served the lay population but worked to transform it. Although monks and bishops were spiritual warriors, most abhorred bloodshed among Christians and sought to limit the violence of aristocratic life. This attitude combined altruistic and selfish motives, since Church property was often the focus of aristocratic greed. The decline of public power and the rise of aristocratic autonomy and violence were particularly marked in southern France. There, beginning in the tenth century, churchmen organized the Peace of God and the Truce of God—movements that attempted to protect peasants, merchants, and clerics from aristocratic violence and to limit the times when warfare was allowed. During the eleventh century, the goals of warfare were shifted from attacks against other Christians to the defense of Christian society. This ... Crusades, those religious wars ... Europe's non-Christian

Crusaders: Soldiers of God

The Crusades left a complex and troubling legacy in world civilization. In order to direct noble violence away from Christendom, in 1095 Pope Urban II (1088–99) urged Western knights to use their arms to free the Holy Land from Muslim occupation. In return he promised to absolve them from all of the punishment due for their sins in this life or the next. Nobles and commoners alike responded with enormous enthusiasm, and soon gangs of looting peasants and organized bands of noble warriors both headed east. The commoners left a swath of destruction in their wake, and few mourned when they were destroyed by the Muslims. The nobles, composed primarily of second sons and lower nobility in search of land and fortune as well as salvation, were remarkably successful. After terrible hardships, the crusaders took Jerusalem in 1099 and established a Latin kingdom in Palestine. For over two centuries bands of Western warriors went on armed pilgrimage to defend this precarious kingdom.

The Latin kingdom of Jerusalem was the first experiment in European overseas colonialization. Its rulers, a tiny minority of Western knights who established a feudally structured monarchy modeled on the European society they had known, ruled a vastly larger population of Muslims and eastern Christians. Although the Christian rulers were not particularly harsh, they made little effort to absorb or even to understand the native population. Crusaders were uninterested in converting Muslims, and their efforts to impose Roman forms of Christian worship and organization alienated the indigenous Christian population of the kingdom. In art, culture, architecture, and social values, the crusaders remained Latins, absorbing only some lessons of military architecture, adopting some of the food and spices, and making some accommodation in their clothing and housing to the climate of the area. Otherwise, the Latin kingdom played a negligible role as a bridge between the eastern and western worlds. The Crusaders remained isolated, supported by the regular supplies brought by Italian merchants (for which cities such as Genoa and Pisa obtained valuable economic rights in the kingdom) and by periodic infusions of fighters in the form of individuals or as part of subsequent organized crusades.

The success of the First Crusade eluded subsequent expeditions. In the middle of the twelfth century, the erosion of the Latin kingdom alarmed Westerners, and the kings of France and Germany, Louis VII and Conrad III, responded Bernard of Clairvaux's call to take up the cross. The Second Crusade (1145–49) ended in

tion of educated Frenchmen who first read them. The book was officially banned and publicly burned, and a warrant was issued for Voltaire's arrest. The *Letters* dropped like a bombshell upon the moribund intellectual culture of the Church and the universities and burst open the complacent, self-satisfied Cartesian worldview. The book ignited in France a movement that would soon be found in nearly every corner of Europe.

Born in Paris in 1694 into a bourgeois family with court office, François-Marie Arouet, who later took the pen name Voltaire, was educated by the Jesuits, who encouraged his poetic talents and instilled in him an enduring love of literature. He was a difficult student, especially as he had already rejected the core of the Jesuits' religious doctrine. He was no less difficult as he grew and began a career as a poet and playwright. It was not long before he was imprisoned in the Bastille for penning verses that maligned the honor of the regent of France. Released from prison, he insulted a nobleman, who retaliated by having his servants publicly beat Voltaire. Voltaire issued a challenge for a duel, a greater insult than the first, given his low birth. Again he was sent to the Bastille and was only released on the promise that he would leave the country immediately.

Thus Voltaire found himself in Britain, where he spent two years learning English, writing plays, and enjoying his celebrity free from the dangers that celebrity entailed in France. When he returned to Paris in 1728, it was with the intention of popularizing

Britain to Frenchmen. He wrote and produced a number of plays and began writing the *Philosophical Letters*, a work that not only secured his reputation but also forced him into exile at the village of Cirey, where he moved in with the Marquise du Ch[aca]telet (1706–49).

The Marquise du Ch[aca]telet, though only twenty-seven at the time of her liaison with Voltaire, was one of the leading advocates of Newtonian science in France. She built a laboratory in her home and introduced Voltaire to experimental science. While she undertook the immense challenge of translating Newton into French, Voltaire worked on innumerable projects: poems, plays, philosophical and antireligious tracts (which she wisely kept him from publishing), and histories. It was one of the most productive periods of his life, and when the Marquise du Ch[aca]telet died in 1749, Voltaire was crushed.

Now past 50 years old, Voltaire began his travels. He was invited to Berlin by Frederick the Great, who admired him most of all the intellectuals of the age. The relationship between these two great egotists was predictably stormy and resulted in Voltaire's arrest in Frankfurt. Finally allowed to leave Prussia, Voltaire eventually settled in Geneva, where he quickly became embroiled in local politics and was none too politely asked to leave. He was tired of wandering and tired of being chased. His youthful gaiety and high spirits, which remained in Voltaire long past youth, were dealt a serious blow by the tragic earthquake in Lisbon in

Painting of a lively dinner conversation among philosophers. Voltaire, with raised arm, is shown seated to the left of Diderot.

INCREASED COVERAGE OF THE ENLIGHTENMENT

Enhanced, reorganized coverage of the Enlightenment enables students to see the role of this important set of attitudes and ideas in eighteenth-century culture.

Selections from primary sources (3-4 per chapter) stimulate students' interest in history by allowing them to hear the past speak in its own voice.

DECLARATION OF THE RIGHTS OF WOMAN AND CITIZEN

"Woman, wake up!" Thus did Olympe de Gouges (d. 1793), a self-educated playwright, address French women in 1791. Aware that women were being denied the new rights of liberty and property extended to all men by the Declaration of the Rights of Man and Citizen, Gouges composed her own Declaration of the Rights of Woman and Citizen, modeled on the 1789 document. Persecuted for her political beliefs, she foreshadowed her own demise at the hands of revolutionary justice in article 10 of her declaration. The Declaration of the Rights of Woman and Citizen became an important document in women's demands for political rights in the nineteenth century, and Gouges herself became a feminist hero.

ARTICLE I

Woman is born free and lives equal to man in her rights. Social distinctions can be based only on the common utility.

ARTICLE II

The purpose of any political association is the conservation of the natural and imprescriptible rights of woman and man; these rights are liberty, property, security, and especially resistance to oppression.

ARTICLE III

The principle of all sovereignty rests essentially with the nation, which is nothing but the union of woman and man; no body and no individual can exercise any authority which does not come expressly from it [the nation].

ARTICLE IV

Liberty and justice consist of restoring all that belongs to others; thus, the only limits on the exercise of the natural rights of woman are perpetual male tyranny;

these limits are to be reformed by the laws of nature and reason.

ARTICLE V

Laws of nature and reason proscribe all acts harmful to society; everything which is not prohibited by these wise and divine laws cannot be prevented, and no one can be constrained to do what they do not command.

ARTICLE VI

The law must be the expression of the general will; all female and male citizens must contribute either personally or through their representatives to its formation; it must be the same for all: male and female citizens, being equal in the eyes of the law, must be equally admitted to all honors, positions, and public employment according to their capacity and without other distinctions besides those of their virtues and talents.

ARTICLE VII

No woman is an exception; she is accused, arrested, and detained in cases determined by law. Women, like men, obey this rigorous law.

an estimated quarter of a million people to their deaths. The bureaucratized Reign of Terror was responsible for about forty thousand executions in a nine-month period, resulting in the image of the republicans as "drinkers of blood."

The Cult of the Supreme Being, a civic religion without priests or churches and influenced by ... nature, followed de-Christian... Notre Dame de Paris was ... eason, and the new religion

established its own festivals to undermine the persistence of Catholicism. The cult was one indication of the Reign of Terror's attempt to create a new moral universe of revolutionary values.

Women remained conspicuously absent from the summit of political power. After 1793, Jacobin revolutionaries, who had been willing to empower the popular movement of workers, turned against women's participation and denounced it. Women's associations were outlawed and the Society of Revolutionary

THE SOCIETY OF NATIONAL DEFENSE, SERBIA, 1911

The Society for National Defense (Narodna Odbrana) was a secret society formed by Serb nationalists. This group sought the liberation of Slavs through propaganda and subversive activities against Austria-Hungary, which had annexed Bosnia-Herzegovina in 1908. The Society for National Defense was a terrorist group, one of whose members was responsible for the assassination of the Austrian Archduke Ferdinand on 28 June 1914. Here the group spells out its program and speaks of a new kind of nationalism, one that it a "holy cause."

The Serbian people has endured during its existence many difficult and bitter days. Among these days is September 24, 1908, when Austria-Hungary illegally annexed Bosnia and Herzegovina. This day can be compared to the worst days of our past. It was especially painful for the Serbian people in that it came at a time when more fortunate peoples had already completed their national unification and had created large states, and when culture and freedom were presumed to be at their peak.

At such a time Austria-Hungary oppressed along with other peoples several million Serbs, whom she penalizes and seeks to alienate from us. They may not openly call themselves Serbs, and may not adorn their homes with the Serbian flag; they may not trade freely, cultivate their soil, erect Serbian schools, openly celebrate the feast of the patron saint [Slava], and may not sing of Kossowo or of Prince Marko and Milosch Obilitsch. Only such a state, only an Austria-Hungary, could carry through such an annexation. . . .

Today everywhere a new concept of nationalism has become prevalent. Nationalism (the feeling of nationality) is no longer a historical or poetical feeling, but the true practical expression of life. Among the French, Germans, and English, and among all other civilized peoples, nationalism has grown into something quite new; in it lies the concept of bread, space, air, commerce, competition in everything. Only among us is it still in the old form; that is, it is the fruit of spiritual suffering rather than of reasonable understanding and national advantage. If we speak of freedom and union, we parade far too much the phrases "breaking our chains" and "freeing the slaves"; we call far too much upon our former Serbian glory and think too little of the fact that the freeing of subjected areas and their union with Serbia are neces-

sary to our citizens, our merchants, and our peasants on the grounds of the most elementary needs of culture and trade, of food and space. If one were to explain to our sharp-eyed people our national task as one closely connected with the needs of everyday life, our people would take up the work in a greater spirit of sacrifice than is today the case. We must tell our people that the freedom of Bosnia is necessary, not just because of their feeling of sympathy with their brothers who suffer there, but also because of commerce and its connection with the sea; national union is necessary because of the stronger development of a common culture. The Italians welcome the conquest of Tripoli not just because of the glory to be won by the success of their arms, but especially because of the advantage they hope to gain by annexing Tripoli. Our people must adopt a more realistic attitude toward politics. We must show them how we would stand culturally and economically if we were united into one state and were in as favorable a position commercially as that of Timok in relation to the Adriatic. . . .

Along with the task of explaining to our people the danger threatening us from Austria, the *Narodna Odbrana* has also the other important tasks of explaining to them, while preserving our holy national memories, this new, healthy, fruitful conception of nationalism, and of convincing them to work for national freedom and unity. . . .

All in all, the *Narodna Odbrana* aims through its work to advance upon the enemy on the day of reckoning with a sound, nationally conscious, and internally reconciled Serbian people, a nation of Sokols, rifle clubs, heroes—in fact, the fear and terror of the enemy—reliant front-rank fighters and executors of Serbia's holy cause.

If this succeeds, all will be well for us; woe to us if we fail.

6 ↣ The Transformation of the Classical World

A Bride's Trousseau

Venus, assisted by mythical sea creatures and representations of *erotes*, or cupids, beautifies herself on the central panel of a magnificent silver chest that made up part of a fourth-century Roman bride's trousseau. On the top, the bride, Projecta, and her groom Secundus, are depicted within a wreath held by two more cupids. Along the base, Projecta, mirroring Venus, completes her own toilette while torchbearers and handmaidens perform for her the tasks the mythical beings attending to Venus. The iconography as well as the execution of this sumptuous object—composed of solid silver

with silver gilt and measuring almost two feet by one foot—testify to the high status of the bride and her deep attachment to the ancient classical traditions of Greco-Roman culture. Projecta and Secundus were Roman aristocrats, and their marriage was part of Roman rituals of class, wealth, and power as ancient as the goddess on the marriage chest.

And yet, within the thorough paganism of the symbolism and the lavish expense of the workmanship, the Latin inscription engraved on the rim across the front of the lid confronts the viewer with how utterly changed the Roman world has become. It reads, "Secundus and Projecta, live in Christ." In spite of the elaborate pagan symbolism of the casket, Secundus and Projecta were Christians. Yet they and their families and friends apparently saw nothing strange or improper about commemorating their marriage in the age-old manner of their pagan ancestors. A bride could live in Christ and still be Venus.

Such was the world of late antiquity. By the time Projecta married Secundus, the once persecuted Christian sect was now not only legal but rapidly on its way to becoming the established religion in the empire. Formerly a religion of hellenized Jews and freed slaves, it was attracting converts from among the highest classes of Roman society. And yet, while some stern religious teachers might condemn the ancient traditions of Roman religion, and while around the very time of Projecta's marriage the images of divine Victory were being removed from

the Roman Senate, aristocratic families, Christian as well as pagan, continued the ancient cultural traditions without a sense of betrayal or contradiction. Rome appeared as eternal and serene as Venus herself.

But the Projecta casket has more to tell us. It was found, along with over sixty other exquisite objects and seventy pounds of silver plate, on the Esquiline hill in Rome, where it had been hastily buried to hide it from some catastrophe. The probable catastrophe is not hard to guess: In 410, when Projecta would have been an elderly woman, the barbarian Visigoths sacked and pillaged Rome for three days, raping Roman women and looting them of such treasures as this.

And yet these barbarians were themselves Christians, while the city of Rome had remained, in spite of exceptions such as Projecta and Secundus, a pagan stronghold. Moreover, the Visigoths were no mere horde but, officially at least, a Roman army reacting in what had become a typical manner to the failure of the state to provide them with what they saw as their due. Such contrasts of paganism and Christianity, barbarity and Roman culture, were integral parts of a new Roman world, one characterized by radical transformations of Roman and barbarian culture that took place in the two centuries following the death of Marcus Aurelius in 180. Accelerating this process of change and transformation was the combination of events collectively referred to as the crisis of the third century.

₰ African Political Heroes and Resistance to the Scramble

Nehanda and Kagubi in prison awaiting execution, 1898

Often a country's political heroes are its generals and kings, its presidents and statesmen—men of power and accomplishment. Paintings and photgraphs of them emphasize grandeur and majesty, reflecting their larger-than-life importance. Two of the political heroes of contemporary Zimbabwe are very different, however. One is a short, aging woman of about sixty whose name was Nehanda. The other is a short middle-aged man of about forty-five called Kagubi. Both appear undistinguished: scruffy, unkempt, and barefoot. Yet both were executed on 27 April 1898 and buried with utmost secrecy. And although they died almost a century ago, their memory is alive in Zimbabwe and students are taught about them in history books. Why?

In 1889 Cecil Rhodes, the South African financier and politician, convinced that large deposits of gold existed in Zimbabwe, persuaded the British government to support his efforts to seize Zimbabwe and Zambia. He established a private chartered company known as the British South Africa Company (BSAC) and in 1890 invaded the eastern part of Zimbabwe. The people who lived here were Shona people, and conquering them seemed easy because they were politically fragmented into myriad little states with neither strong chiefs nor a military tradition. So easy was the conquest, indeed, that the settlers came to view the Shona with utter contempt.

One of the frequently stated purposes of European imperialism during the scramble for Africa was to carry "civilization" to the "primitive" peoples of Africa—to "bear the White Man's burden" so that the people could improve their lives. For the Shona, however, Rhodes' agents displayed little perceptible

civilization and much to be lamented. The Shona soon had a mass of grievances against the BSAC. Some of their land had been taken. They were forced to work for the settlers for little or no pay. They were compelled to pay taxes. Europeans took Shona women as concubines. Shona grievances grew steadily. Then, in 1896, their cattle herds were almost wiped out by a new disease, rinderpest, which the Italians who were occupying Eritrea had accidentally imported into Africa in the late 1880s and which was spreading southward. This seemed the last straw.

The Shona got the chance to make their complaints felt. At the end of 1895, most of the BSAC police force had gone over the border into the Transvaal to participate in the Jameson Raid on the Afrikaner state, and in 1896 they were still languishing in jail. With few police around, the Shona reasoned, the time was ripe for revolt against the BSAC. In June, the Shona rose in rebellion, and one hundred settlers were slain before the government knew what was occurring.

The BSAC could not believe that the disorganized Shona for whom they had such contempt were capable of such an uprising. But despite their lack of chiefs or a military tradition, they were. And when the company's officials investigated more closely, they were astounded to discover that the uprising, which came to be known as the *chimurenga*, was being organized and directed by the Shona religious leaders known as mediums. These were people who became possessed by spirits of Shona ancestors and articulated what the ancestors wanted the living to do. These people—obscure and seemingly unthreatening—were able not only to mobilize

the attack on the company, but, because of their very lack of notoriety in British eyes, to sustain it by spying on the company, distributing intelligence regarding company troop movements, and relaying messages across Shona country.

The result of the work of the spirit mediums was that the BSAC was unable to conquer the Shona quickly. The effort against the guerrilla war waged by the Shona took over fifteen months, almost bankrupting the company. Only in October 1897 did the company track down the leader of the rebellion, Kagubi, and his colleagues, including the important Nehanda. By then, however, the uprising had attracted so much negative publicity in Britain that the company was brought under greater control by the British government. Many of the abuses that had provoked the Shona to rebel were forbidden, and greater regularity in administration was instituted. The Shona had demonstrated to the company that there was a point beyond which the British could not go.

Seven decades later, in the 1970s, the African people again rose up, this time against the white government of Ian Smith, political heir to Cecil Rhodes, and this time successfully. They called their rebellion the "second *chimurenga*." When they finally won, the Africans needed a new group of patriotic heroes from their past about whom to teach in independant Zimbabwe's schools. Two of those chosen were Kagubi and Nehanda, scruffy and unkempt to be sure, but remembered as early patriots and martyrs, the memory of whose work against Rhodes was able to travel across the years and inspire Zimbabweans during the 1970s.

CHRONOLOGIES

These helpful features offer clear synopses of the progression of historical events in each chapter.

THE COLD WAR

1947	Marshall Plan starts U.S. aid to European countries
1947	Pro-Soviet governments established in Poland, Hungary, Bulgaria, and Romania
1948	Pro-Soviet government established in Czechoslovakia
1949	European states and United States form North Atlantic Treaty Organization (NATO)
1949	Federal Republic of Germany and German Democratic Republic established
1949	Soviet Union creates Council for Mutual Economic Assistance (Comecon)
1949	Soviet Union tests its first atomic bomb
1950–53	Korean War, ending with the partition of Korea
1953	United States and Soviet Union develop hydrogen bombs
1956	Hungarian uprising and subsequent repression by Soviet military forces
1957	The Netherlands, Belgium, Luxembourg, France, Italy, and West Germany form the European Economic Community (EEC), also called the Common Market
1957	Soviet Union launches first satellite, *Sputnik I*
1961	Berlin Wall built
1961–73	U.S. troops engaged in Vietnam
1962	Cuban missile crisis
1963	Soviet Union and United States sign Nuclear Test-Ban Treaty
1968	Prague Spring uprising in Czechoslovakia, quelled by Soviet Union

citizens paid for their inefficient and rigid planned economies dedicated to the development of heavy industry. In Eastern Europe and the Soviet Union, poverty was virtually eliminated, however, as the state subsidized housing, health care, and higher education, which were available to all.

Family Strategies

The pressures on European women and their families in 1945 were often greater than in wartime. Severe scarcity of food, clothes, and housing required careful management. Women who during the war held jobs in industry and munitions plants earned their own money and established their own independence. After the war, in victorious and defeated nations alike, women were moved out of the work force to make room for returning men. Changing social policies affected women's lives in the home and in the workplace and contributed to the politicization of women within the context of the welfare state.

Demography and Birth Control. Prewar concerns with a declining birthrate intensified after World War II. In some European countries, the birthrate climbed in the years immediately following the war, an encouraging sign to observers who saw in this trend an optimistic commitment to the future after the cessation of the horrors of war. The situation was more complicated in France and the United States, where the birthrates began to climb even before the war was over. Nearly everywhere throughout Europe, however, the rise in the birthrate was momentary, with the United States standing alone in experiencing a genuine and sustained "baby boom" until about 1960. In Germany and in Eastern Europe (Poland and Yugoslavia, for example), the costs of the war exacted heavy tolls on families long after the hostilities ended. On average, women everywhere were having fewer children by choice.

Technology had expanded the range of choices in family planning. In the early 1960s, the birth-control pill became available on the European and American markets, primarily to middle-class women. Europeans were choosing to have smaller families. The drop in the birthrate had clearly preceded the new technological interventions that included intrauterine devices (IUDs), improved diaphragms, sponges, and more effective spermicidal creams and jellies. The condom, invented a century earlier, was now sold to a mass market. Controversies surrounded the unhealthy side effects of the pill and the dangerous Dalkon shield, an IUD that had not been adequately tested before mar-

ed with some economic concessions but on the whole stressed common industrial and defense pursuits, employing ideological persuasion and military pressure to keep its reluctant partners in line. The slowed growth of the 1960s, the delay in development of con- ...nadequacy of basic foodstuffs, ...the costs that Eastern Bloc

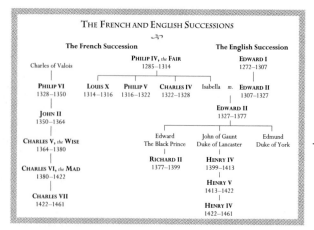

THE FRENCH AND ENGLISH SUCCESSIONS

The French Succession — **The English Succession**

PHILIP IV, *the* FAIR 1285–1314 / EDWARD I 1272–1307

Charles of Valois

PHILIP VI 1328–1350 / LOUIS X 1314–1316 / PHILIP V 1316–1322 / CHARLES IV 1322–1328 / Isabella *m.* EDWARD II 1307–1327

JOHN II 1350–1364

EDWARD II 1327–1377

CHARLES V, *the* WISE 1364–1380

Edward The Black Prince / John of Gaunt Duke of Lancaster / Edmund Duke of York

CHARLES VI, *the* MAD 1380–1422

RICHARD II 1377–1399 / HENRY IV 1399–1413

CHARLES VII 1422–1461

HENRY V 1413–1422

HENRY IV 1422–1461

DYNASTIC CHARTS

Redesigned for clarity, these effective charts trace the history of major European empires.

much less tied into international trade, with only the beginnings of a cloth industry and little to export except wool. At the start of the war Philip could rely on an income roughly three to five times greater than that of Edward. However, these inequalities mattered little because the French king had no means of harnessing the resources of his kingdom. His greater income was matched by greater expenses, and he had no easy way to raise extraordinary funds for war. In contrast, the English king could use Parliament as an efficient source of war subsidies. Edward could also extract great sums from taxes on wool exports. Even after the invasion of France, Philip had to rely on manipulation of the coinage, confiscation of Italian bankers' property, and a whole range of nuisance taxes to finance his campaigns.

War was expensive. In spite of chivalrous ideals, nobles no longer fought as vassals of the king but as highly paid mercenaries. The nature of this service differed greatly on the two sides of the Channel. In France, tactics and personnel had changed little since the twelfth century. The core of any army was the body of heavily armored nobles who rode into battle with their lords, supported by lightly armored knights. Behind them marched infantrymen recruited from

towns and armed with pikes. Although the French also hired mercenary Italian crossbowmen, the nobles despised them and never used them effectively.

In contrast, centuries of fighting with Welsh and Scottish enemies had transformed and modernized the English armies and their tactics. The great nobles continued to serve as heavily armored horsemen, but professional companies of foot soldiers raised by individual knights made up the bulk of the army. These professional companies consisted largely of pikemen and, most importantly, of longbowmen. Although it was not as accurate as the crossbow, the English longbow had a greater range. Moreover, when massed archers fired volleys of arrows into enemy ranks, they proved extremely effective against enemy pikemen and even lightly armored cavalry.

The first real test of the two armies came at the Battle of Crécy in 1346. There an overwhelmingly superior French force surrounded the English army. Massing their archers on a hill, the English rained arrows down on the French cavalry, which attacked in glorious but suicidal manner. Typical of the French chivalric behavior was that of King John of Bohemia, father of Charles IV, both of whom were fighting as mercenaries of the

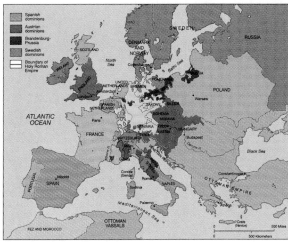

Spanish dominions
Austrian dominions
Brandenburg-Prussia
Swedish dominions
Boundary of Holy Roman Empire

The Peace of Westphalia, Europe 1648

their hostilities with one another, and soon the stage was set for a Continent-wide settlement.

A series of agreements, collectively known as the Peace of Westphalia, established the outlines of the political geography of Europe for the next century. Its focus was on the Holy Roman Empire, and it reflected Protestant successes in the final two decades of war. Sweden gained further territories on the Baltic, making it master of the north German ports. France, too, gained in territory and prestige. It kept the vital towns in the Lower Palatinate through which Spanish men and material had moved, and though it did not agree to come to terms with Spain immediately, France's fear of Spain was brought to an end. The Dutch gained state-hood and were given recognition by Spain and

through the power they had displayed in building and maintaining an overseas empire.

Territorial boundaries were reestablished as they had existed in 1624, giving the Habsburgs control of both Bohemia and Hungary. The independence of the Swiss cantons was now officially recognized, as were the rights of Calvinists to the protection of the Peace of Augsburg, which again was to govern the religious affairs of the empire. Two of the larger German states were strengthened as a counterweight to the emperor's power. Bavaria was allowed to retain the Upper Palatinate, and Brandenburg, which ceded some of its coastal territory to Sweden, gained territories in the east.

The emperor's political control over the German states was also weakened. German rulers were given

The Intellectual Reformation

There is nothing as powerful as an idea whose time has come. But the coming of ideas has a history as complex as the ideas themselves. In the early sixteenth century, reformers throughout western Europe preached new ideas about religious doctrine and religious practice. At first these ideas took the form of a sustained critique of the Roman Catholic church, but soon they developed a momentum of their own. Some reformers remained within traditional Catholicism; others moved outside and founded new Protestant churches. Whether Catholic or Protestant, wherever this movement for religious reform appeared it was fed by new ideas. But if new ideas were to supplant old ones, they had to be communicated—not only heard and repeated but accurately recorded and understood. This was made possible by the development of the technology of printing, which appeared in Germany in the late fifteenth century and rapidly spread across Europe in the succeeding decades. Yet printing was as much a result as it was a cause of the spread of ideas. The humanist call for a return to the study of the classics and for the creation of accurate texts, first heard in Italy, aroused scholars and leaders in all of the European states. Their appetite for manuscripts exhausted the abilities of the scribes and booksellers who reproduced texts. Printing responded to that demand.

The Print Revolution

The development of printing did not cause religious reform, but it is difficult to see how reform would have progressed in its absence. The campaign to change the doctrine and practice of Catholicism was waged through the press, with millions of flyers and pamphlets distributed across Europe to spread the new ideas. A third of all books sold in Germany between 1518 and 1525 were written by Luther. But the ways in which printing came to be used by religious reformers could hardly have been foreseen by the artisans, bankers, and booksellers who together created one of the true technological revolutions in Western history.

Printing was not invented. It developed as a result of progress made in a number of allied industries, of which papermaking and goldsmithing were the most important. Scholars and university students needed copies of manuscripts. Their need led to the development of a trade in bookselling that flourished in almost every university town. The process of reproduction was slowed by difficulties in obtaining the sheep and calf-

skins on which the manuscripts were written. It took the skins of 300 sheep to produce a single Bible. In the early fifteenth century, copyists began to substitute paper made from linen rags for the expensive vellum skins. A number of German artisans experimented with using movable metal type to make exact reproductions of manuscripts on paper. Paper took a better impression and provided an absolutely smooth surface, which was essential for pressing the image. In the 1450s, in Mainz, Johannes Gutenberg (ca. 1400–68) and his partners succeeded and published their famous Bibles.

The association of early printing with goldsmithing resulted from the high level of technical skill that was necessary to create the hard metal stamps from which the softer metal type was produced. Printing was an expensive business. The investment in type and in paper was considerable. Only the press itself was cheap. Any corn or wine press could be used to bring the long flat sheets of paper down upon a wooden frame filled with ink-coated metal type. Booksellers initially put up the capital needed to cast the stamps, mold the type, and buy the paper. They bound the printed pages and found the markets to distribute them. At first sales were slow. Printed books were considered inferior to handwritten manuscripts. Nor at first were printed books

Dates indicate the first occurrence of printing.

The Spread of Printing

CIVILIZATION IN THE WEST

1 ∿ THE FIRST CIVILIZATIONS

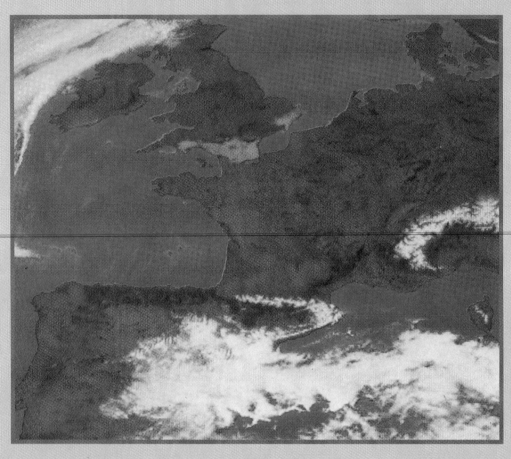

The Idea of Civilization

*T*he West is an idea. It is not visible from space. An astronaut viewing the blue-and-white terrestrial sphere can make out the form of Africa, bounded by the Atlantic, the Indian Ocean, the Red Sea, and the Mediterranean. Australia, the Americas, and even Antarctica are distinct patches of blue green in the darker waters that surround them. But nothing comparable separates Europe from Asia, East from West. Viewed from one hundred miles up, the West itself is invisible. Although astronauts can see the great Eurasian landmass curving around the Northern Hemisphere, the Ural Mountains—the theoretical boundary between East and West—appear but faintly from space. Certainly they are less impressive than the towering Himalayas, the Alps, or even the Caucasus. People, not geology, determined that the Urals should be the arbitrary boundary between Europe and Asia.

Even this determination took centuries. Originally, Europe was a name that referred only to central Greece. Gradually, Greeks extended it to include the whole Greek mainland and then the landmass to the north. Later, Roman explorers and soldiers carried Europe north and west to its modern boundaries. Asia too grew with time. Initially, Asia was only that small portion of what is today Turkey inland from the Aegean Sea. Gradually, as Greek explorers came to know of lands farther east, north, and south, they expanded their understanding of Asia to include everything east of the Don River to the north and the Red Sea to the south.

Western civilization is as much an idea as the West itself. Under the right conditions, astronauts can see the Great Wall of China snaking its way from the edge of the Himalayas to the Yellow Sea. No comparable physical legacy of the West is so massive that its details can be discerned from space. Nor are Western achievements rooted forever in one corner of the world. What we call Western civilization belongs to no particular place. Its location has changed since the origins of civilization, that is, the cultural and social traditions characteristic of the *civitas,* or city. "Western" cities appeared first outside what Europeans and Americans arbitrarily term "the West," in the Tigris and Euphrates river basins in present-day Iraq and Iran, a region we today call the Middle East. These areas have never lost their urban traditions, but in time other cities in North Africa, Greece, and Italy adapted and expanded this heritage in different ways. If we focus on this peculiar adaptation and expansion in this book, it is not because of some intrinsic superiority but only because the developments in Europe after the birth of Jesus become more significant than those of Egypt and Mesopotamia for understanding our contemporary culture.

Until the sixteenth century A.D., the western end of the Eurasian landmass—what we think of as western Europe—was the crucible in which disparate cultural and intellectual traditions of the Near East, the Mediterranean, and the north were smelted into a new and powerful alloy. Then "the West" expanded beyond the confines of Europe, carried by the ships of merchants and adventurers to India, Africa, China, and the Americas.

Western technology for harnessing nature, Western forms of economic and political organization, Western styles of art and music are—for good or ill—dominant influences in world civilization. Japan is a leading power in the Western traditions of capitalist commerce and technology. China, the most populous country in the world, adheres to Marxist socialist principles—a European political tradition. Millions of people in Africa, Asia, and the Americas follow the religions of Islam and Christianity. Both are monotheistic faiths that developed from Judaism in the cradle of Western civilization.

Many of today's most pressing problems are also part of the legacy of the Western tradition. The remnants of European colonialism have left deep hostilities throughout the world. The integration of developing nations into the world economy keeps much of humanity in a seemingly hopeless cycle of poverty as the wealth of poor countries goes to pay interest on loans from Europe and America. Western material goods lure millions of people from their traditional worlds into the sprawl of third world cities. The West itself faces a crisis. Impoverished citizens of former colonies flock to Europe and North America seeking a better life but often finding poverty, hostility, and racism instead. Finally, the advances of Western civilization endanger our very existence. Technology pollutes the world's air, water, and soil, and nuclear arms threaten the destruction of all civilization. And yet these are the same advances that allow us to lengthen life expectancy, harness the forces of nature, and conquer disease. It is the same technology that allows us to view our world from outer space.

How did we get here? In this book we attempt to answer this question. The history of Western civilization is not simply the triumphal story of progress, the creation of a better world. Even in areas in which we can see development—such as technology, communications, and social complexity—change is not always for the better. However, it would be equally inaccurate to view the course of Western civilization as a progressive decline from a mythical golden age of the human race. The roughly three hundred generations since the origins of civilization have bequeathed a rich and contradictory heritage to the present. Inherited political and social institutions, cultural forms, and religious and philosophical traditions form the framework within which the future must be created. The past does not determine the future, but it is the raw material from which the future will be made. To use this legacy properly, we must first understand it, not because the past is the key to the future, but because understanding yesterday frees us to create tomorrow.

Before Civilization

The human race was already ancient by the time civilization first appeared around 3500 years before the traditional date of the birth of Jesus. (Such dates are abbreviated B.C. for "before Christ"; A.D., the abbreviation of the Latin for "in the year of the Lord," is used to refer to dates after the birth of Jesus.) The first human-like creatures whose remains have been discovered date from as long as five million years ago. One of the best-known finds, nicknamed "Lucy" by the scientist who discovered her skeleton in 1974, stood only about four feet tall and lived on the edge of a lake in what is now Ethiopia. Lucy and her band did not have brains that were as well developed as those of modern humans. They did, however, use simple tools such as sticks, bone clubs, and chipped rocks, and they worked together to protect themselves and to find small animals, roots, and berries for food. Lucy lived to a considerable age—she was around twenty when she died. Although small and relatively weak compared with other animals, Lucy's species of creatures—neither fully apes nor human—survived for over four million years.

Varieties of the modern species of humans, *Homo sapiens* (thinking human), appeared well over one hundred thousand years ago and spread across the Eurasian landmass and Africa. The earliest *Homo sapiens* in Europe, the Neanderthal, differed little from us today. Although the term *Neanderthal* has gained a negative image in the popular imagination, these early humans were roughly the same size and had the same cranial capacity as we. They not only survived but even spread throughout much of Africa, Europe, and Asia during the last great ice age. To survive in the harsh tundra landscape, they developed a cultural system that enabled them to modify their environment. They knew how to make and use stone tools and lived in shelters they built from wood. Customs such as the burial of their dead with food offerings indicate that Neanderthals may have developed a belief in an afterlife. Thus they apparently had the capacity for carrying on intellectual activities such as abstract and symbolic thought. Although a bit shorter and heavier than most people today, they were clearly our close cousins.

No one knows why or how the Neanderthals were replaced by our subspecies, *Homo sapiens sapiens* (thinking thinking human), around forty thousand years ago. Whatever the reason and whatever the process—extinction, evolution, or extermination—this last arrival on the human scene was universally successful. All humans today—whether blond, blue-eyed Scandinavians, Australian aborigines, Africans, Japanese, or Native Americans—belong to this same subspecies. Differences in skin color, type of hair, and build are minor variations on the same theme. The identification of races, while selectively based on some of these physical variations, is, like civilization itself, a fact not of biology but of culture.

Early *Homo sapiens sapiens* lived in small kin groups of twenty or thirty, following game and seeking shelter in tents, lean-tos, and caves. We know little about the organization of this hunter-gatherer society. Although some contemporary historians have suggested that the Paleolithic era (ca. 600,000–10,000 B.C.) was a peaceful "golden age" in which women played a dominant

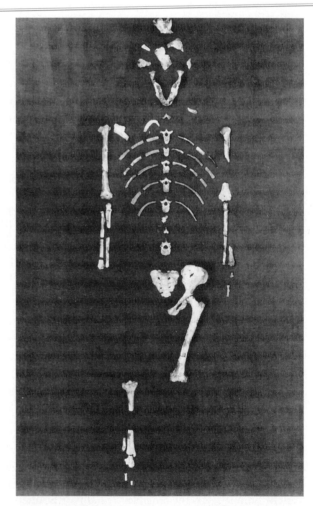

The remains of Lucy, the oldest known australopithecine, were found in East Africa. She is believed to have lived about four million years ago.

In this cave painting in northern Africa, animal magic evokes help from the spirit world in ensuring the prosperity of the cattle herd. A similar ceremony is still performed by members of the Fulani tribes in the Sahel, on the southern fringe of the Sahara.

role in social organization, no evidence substantiates this theory. Still, Paleolithic people worked together for hunting and defense and apparently formed emotional bonds based on more than sex or economic necessity. The skeleton of a man found a few years ago in Iraq, for example, suggests that although he was born with only one arm and was crippled further by arthritis, the rest of his community supported him and he lived to adulthood. Clearly his value to his society lay in something more than his ability to make a material contribution to its collective life. But even with this cooperation and socialization, life expectancy was very short. Most people died by age twenty, but even among those who survived into adulthood, most women were dead by thirty and most men by forty.

During the upper, or late, Paleolithic era (ca. 35,000–10,000 B.C.), culture, meaning everything about humans not inherited biologically, was increasingly determinant in human life. Paleolithic people were not on an endless and all-consuming quest to provide for the necessities of life. They spent less time on such things than we do today. Thus they found time to develop speech, religion, and artistic expression. Wall paintings, small clay and stone figurines of female figures, and finely decorated stone and bone tools indicate not just artistic ability but also abstract and symbolic thought. Presumably such figures had religious functions. Hunters may have painted images of animals to ensure that such species of game would always be plentiful. Figures of women may reflect concerns about human and animal fertility.

The arid wastes of Africa's Sahara may seem an unlikely place to find a continuous record of the civilizing of the West. Yet at the end of the last ice age, around 10,000 B.C., much of North Africa enjoyed a mild, damp climate and supported a diverse population of animals and humans. At Tassili-n-Ajjer in what is today Algeria, succeeding generations of inhabitants left over four thousand paintings on cliff and cave walls that date from ca. 6000 B.C. until the time of Jesus. Like a pictorial time line, these paintings show the gradual transformations of human culture.

The earliest cave paintings were produced by people who, like the inhabitants of Europe and the Near East, lived by hunting game and gathering edible plants, nuts, and fruit. The cave paintings include images of huge buffalo, now extinct, and other game animals as well as human figures apparently participating in ritual dances. Through this long period, humans perfected the making of stone tools, learned to work bone, antler, and ivory into weapons and utensils, and organized an increasingly complex society.

BEFORE CIVILIZATION

ca. 100,000 B.C.	*Homo sapiens*
ca. 40,000 B.C.	*Homo sapiens sapiens*
ca. 35,000–10,000 B.C.	**Late Paleolithic era (Old Stone Age)**
ca. 8000–6500 B.C.	**Neolithic era (New Stone Age)**
ca. 3500 B.C.	**Civilization begins**

Sometime around 5000 B.C., the artists at Tassili-n-Ajjer began to include in their paintings images of domesticated cattle and harnesslike equipment. Such depictions give evidence of the arrival in North Africa of two of the most profound transformations in human history: sedentarization, that is, the adoption of a fixed dwelling place, and the agricultural revolution. These fundamental changes in human culture began independently around the world and continued for roughly five thousand years. They appeared first around 10,000 B.C. in the Near East, then elsewhere in Asia around 8000 B.C. By 5000 B.C., the domestication of plants and animals was under way in Africa and what is today Mexico.

Around 10,000 B.C., many hunter-gatherers living along the coastal plains of what is today Syria and Israel and in the valleys and the hill country near the Zagros Mountains between modern Iran and Iraq began to develop specialized strategies that led, by accident, to a transformation in human culture. Near the Mediterranean coast, the close proximity of varied and productive ecosystems—the sea, coastal plains, hills, and mountains—encouraged people to practice what is called broad-spectrum gathering. That is, rather than constantly traveling in search of food, people stayed put and exploited the various seasonal sources of food, fish, wild grains, fruits, and game. In communities such as Jericho, people built and rebuilt their mud brick and stone huts over generations rather than moving on as had their ancestors. In the Zagros region, sedentary communities focused on single, abundant sources of food at specific seasons, such as wild sheep and goats in the mountains during summer and pigs and cattle in the lower elevations in winter. These people also harvested the wild forms of wheat and barley that grew in upland valleys.

No one really knows why settlement led to agriculture, which is, after all, a riskier venture than hunting and gathering. When humans focused on strains of plants and animals with naturally occurring recessive genetic traits that were advantageous to humans, they increased the risk that these varieties might be less hardy than others. Specialization in only a few such species of plants or animals could spell starvation if severe weather caused that crop to fail or if disease destroyed herds. Some scholars speculate that the push to take nature in hand came from population growth and the development of a political hierarchy that reduced the natural breaking away of groups when clans or tribes became too large for the natural resources of an area to support. In settled communities, infant mortality decreased and life expectancy rose. In part, these changes occurred because life in a fixed location was less exhausting than constant wandering for the very young and the very old. The killing of infants and the elderly decreased because young and old members of the tribe or community could be useful in simple agricultural tasks rather than the hindrance they might be in a community always on the move. Archaeologists working in Turkey have found the skeleton of an adult who had lived to maturity although his legs were so deformed that he could never have walked. That he was supported by his fellows and buried with respect when he died shows that he was valued in spite of his handicap. In a nomadic society, he would never have lived beyond infancy.

As population growth put pressure on the local food supply, gathering activities demanded more formal coordination and organization and led to the development of political leadership. This leadership and the perception of safety in numbers may have prevented the traditional breaking away to form other similar communities in the next valley, as had happened when population growth pressured earlier groups. In any case, settlement began to encourage the growth of plants such as barley and lentils and the domestication of pigs, sheep, and goats. People no longer simply looked for these favored species of plants and animals where they occurred naturally. Now they introduced them into other locations and favored them at the expense of plant and animal species not deemed useful. Agriculture had begun.

The ability to domesticate goats, sheep, pigs, and cattle and to cultivate barley, wheat, and vegetables changed human communities from passive harvesters of nature to active partners with it. The ability to expand the food supply in a limited region allowed the development of sedentary communities of greater size and complexity than those of the late hunter-gatherer period. These peoples of the Neolithic, or New Stone Age—approximately 8000–6500 B.C.—organized sizable villages. Jericho, which had been settled before the

Sculptured skulls found at Jericho date from between 7000 and 6000 B.C. They are actual human skulls whose faces have been reconstituted with molded and tinted plaster. Pieces of seashells represented the eyes.

agricultural revolution, grew into a fortified town complete with ditch, stone walls, and towers, and sheltered perhaps two thousand inhabitants. Çatal Hüyük in southern Turkey may have been even larger.

The really revolutionary aspect of agriculture was not simply that it ensured settled communities a food supply. The true innovation was that agriculture was portable. For the first time, rather than looking for a place that provided them with the necessities of life, humans could carry with them what they needed to make a site inhabitable. This portability also meant the rapid spread of agriculture throughout the region. Farmers in Çatal Hüyük cultivated varieties of plants that came from hundreds of miles away. In addition, the presence there of tools and statues made from stone not obtainable locally indicates that some trading with distant regions was taking place.

Agricultural societies brought changes in the form and organization of formal religious cults. Elaborate sanctuary rooms decorated with frescoes, bulls' horns, and sculptures of heads of bulls and bears indicate that structured religious rites were important to the inhabitants of Çatal Hüyük. At Jericho, human skulls covered with clay, presumably in an attempt to make them look as they had in life, suggest that these early settlers practiced ancestor worship. In these larger communities the bonds of kinship that had united small hunter-gatherer bands were being supplemented by religious organization, which helped control and regulate social behavior. The nature of this religion is a matter of speculation. Images of a female deity, interpreted as a guardian of animals, suggest the religious importance of women and fertility. An echo of these goddesses appears in a cave at Tassili-n-Ajjer. On one wall four females and one male appear in a painting with two bulls. The painting may depict a female guardian and her servants or priests.

Around 1500 B.C., a new theme appears on the cliff walls at Tassili-n-Ajjer. Now men herd horses and drive horse-drawn chariots. These innovations had only gradually reached the arid world of North Africa. They had developed over fifteen hundred years before in Mesopotamia (a name that means "between the rivers"), that featureless desert plain stretching to the marshes near the mouths of the Tigris and Euphrates rivers. Chariots symbolized a new, dynamic, and expansive phase in Western culture. Constructed of wood and bronze and used for transport and especially for aggressive warfare, they are symbolic of the culture of early river civilizations, the first civilizations in western Eurasia.

Mesopotamia: Between the Two Rivers

Need drove the inhabitants of Mesopotamia to create a civilization; nature itself offered little for human comfort or prosperity. The upland regions of the north receive most of the rainfall, but the soil is thin and poor. In the south, the soil is fertile but rainfall is almost nonexistent. There the twin rivers provide life-giving water, but also bring destructive floods that normally arrive at harvest time. Thus agriculture is impossible without irrigation. But irrigation systems, if not properly maintained, deposit harsh chemicals called alkaloids on the soil, gradually reducing its fertility. In addition, Mesopotamia's only natural resource is clay. It has no metals, no workable stone, no valuable minerals of use to ancient people. These very obstacles pressed the people to cooperative, innovative, and organized measures for survival. Survival in the region required planning and the mobilization of manpower

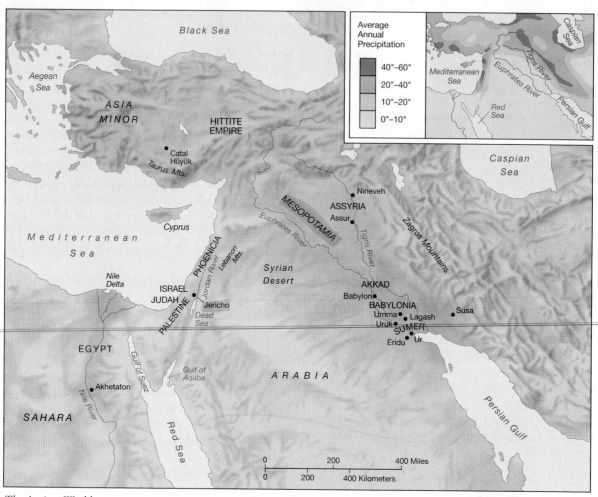

The Ancient World

possible only through centralization. Driven by need, they created a civilization. Mesopotamia

Until around 3500 B.C., the inhabitants of the lower Tigris and Euphrates lived in scattered villages and small towns. Then the population of the region, known as Sumer, began to increase rapidly. Small settlements became increasingly common; then towns such as Eridu and Uruk in what is now Iraq began to grow rapidly. These towns developed in part because of the need to concentrate and organize population in order to carry on the extensive irrigation systems necessary to support Mesopotamian agriculture. In most cases, the earlier role of particular villages as important religious centers favored their growth into towns. These towns soon spread their control out to the surrounding cultivated areas, incorporating the smaller towns and villages of the region. They also fortified themselves against the hostile intentions of their neighbors.

Nomadic peoples inhabited the arid steppes of Mesopotamia, constantly trading with and occasionally threatening settled villages and towns. Their menace was as ever-present in Near Eastern history as drought and flood. But nomads were a minor threat compared to the dangers posed by settled neighbors. As population growth increased pressure on the region's food supply, cities supplemented their resources by raiding their more prosperous neighbors. Victims sought protection within the ramparts of the settlements that had grown up around religious centers. As a result, the populations of the towns rose along with their towering temples, largely at the expense of the countryside. Between about 3500 and 3000 B.C., the population of Uruk quadrupled, increasing from ten to forty thousand. At the same time, the number of smaller towns and villages in the vicinity decreased rapidly. Other Mesopotamian cities, notably Umma, Eridu, Lagash, and Ur, developed along the same general lines. The growth of these cities established a precedent that would continue throughout history.

As villages disappeared, large agricultural areas were

abandoned. Regions previously irrigated by small natural waterways reverted to desert, while urban centers concentrated water supplies within their districts with artificial canals and dikes. By 3000 B.C., the countryside near the cities was intensively cultivated, while outlying regions slipped back into swampland or steppe. The city had become the dominant force in the organization of economy and society.

The Ramparts of Uruk

Cities did more than simply concentrate population. Within the walls of the city, men and women developed new technologies and new social and political structures. They created cultural traditions such as writing and literature. The pride of the first city dwellers is captured in a passage from the *Epic of Gilgamesh,* the first great heroic poem, which was composed sometime before 2000 B.C. In the poem, the hero Gilgamesh boasts of the mighty walls he had built to encircle his city, Uruk:

> *Go up and walk on the ramparts of Uruk*
> *Inspect the base terrace, examine the brickwork:*
> *Is not its brickwork of burnt brick?*
> *Did not the Seven Sages lay its foundations?*

Gilgamesh was justly proud of his city. In his day (ca. 2700 B.C.) these walls were marvels of military engineering, and even now their ruins remain a tribute to his age. Archaeologists have uncovered the remains of the ramparts of Uruk, which stretched over five miles and were protected by some nine hundred semicircular towers. In size and complexity they surpassed the great medieval walls of Paris, which were built some four thousand years later. These protective walls enclosed about two square miles of houses, palaces,

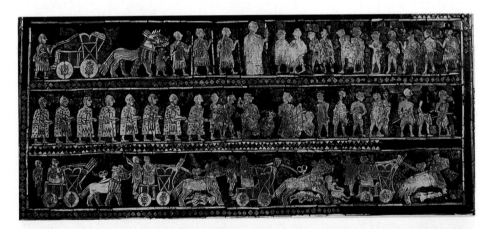

The Standard of Ur, made of shells, lapis lazuli, and limestone, was found at Ur. In the top panel, known as War, soldiers and horse-drawn chariots return victorious from battle. In the lower panel—Peace—the king celebrates the victory, captives are paraded before him, and the conquered people bring him tribute.

A Sumerian seal impression from Uruk shows a boat carrying two oarsmen, a priest, and a bull with an altar on its back.

workshops, and temples. For the first time, a true urban environment had appeared in western Eurasia, and Uruk was its first city.

Within Uruk's walls, the peculiar circumstances of urban life changed the traditional social structure of Mesopotamia. In Neolithic times, social and economic differences within society had been minimal. Urban immigration increased the power, wealth, and status of two groups. In the first group were the religious authorities responsible for the temples. The second consisted of the emerging military and administrative elites, such as Gilgamesh, who were responsible for the construction and protection of the cities. These two groups probably encouraged much of the migration to the cities. The decision to enter the city was not always voluntary; rather, it was usually forced by these ruling classes, who stood to gain the most from a concentration of population within the walls.

Whether they lived inside the city or on the farmland it controlled, Mesopotamians formed a highly stratified society that shared unequally in the benefits of civilization. Slaves, who did most of the unskilled labor within the city, were the primary victims of civilization. Most were prisoners of war, but some were people forced by debt to sell themselves or their children. Most of the remaining rural people were peasants who were little better than slaves. Having lost their freedom to the religious or military elite, they were reduced to working the land of others and depended on markets and prices out of their control. Better off were soldiers, merchants, and workers and artisans who served the temple or palace. At the next level were

landowning free persons. Above all of these were the priests responsible for temple services and the rulers. Rulers included the *ensi*, or city ruler, and the *lugal*, or king, the earthly representative of the gods. Kings were powerful and feared. The hero of the *Epic of Gilgamesh* is presented as a ruler so harsh that the gods created a wild man, Enkidu, to subdue him.

Urban life also redefined the role and status of women, who in the Neolithic period had enjoyed roughly the same roles and status as men. In cities, women tended to exercise private authority over children and servants within the household, while men controlled the household and dealt in the wider world. This change in roles resulted in part from the economic basis of the first civilization. Southern Mesopotamia has no sources of metal or stone. To acquire these precious commodities, trade networks were extended into Syria, the Arabian Peninsula, and even India. The primary commodities that Mesopotamians produced for trade were textiles, and these were largely produced by women captured in wars with neighboring city-states. Their menfolk were normally killed or blinded and used for menial tasks such as milling. The enslaved women employed in urban textile production constituted a dependent female population. Some historians suggest that the disproportionate numbers of low-status women in Mesopotamian cities affected the status of women in general. Although women could own property and even appear as heads of households, by roughly 1500 B.C. the pattern of patriarchal households predominated. Throughout Western history, while individual women might at times exercise great power, they did so largely in the private sphere. Public control of the house, the family, the city, and the state was largely in male hands.

Changes in society brought changes in technology. The need to feed, clothe, protect, and govern growing urban populations led to major technological and conceptual discoveries. Canals and systems of dikes partially harnessed water supplies. Farmers began to work their fields with improved plows and to haul their produce to town, first on sleds and ultimately on carts. These land-transport devices, along with sailing ships, made it possible not only to produce greater agricultural surplus but also to move this surplus to distant markets. Artisans used a refined potter's wheel to produce ceramic vessels of great beauty. Government officials and private individuals began to use cylinder seals, small stone cylinders engraved with a pattern, to mark ownership. Metalworkers fashioned gold and silver into valuable items of adornment and prestige. They also began to cast bronze, an alloy of copper and tin, which came into use for tools and weapons about 3000 B.C.

Perhaps the greatest invention of early cities was writing. As early as 7000 B.C., small clay or stone tokens with distinctive shapes or markings were being used to keep track of animals, goods, and fruits in inventories and bartering. By 3500 B.C., government and temple administrators were using simplified drawings—today termed pictograms—that were derived from these tokens, to assist them in keeping records of their transactions. A scribe molded a small lump of clay into a square. Holding it between his thumb and forefinger, he divided the smooth surface into a series of squares by scratching it with a sharp reed. He then drew his pictograms within each square. In the dry, hot Mesopotamian air these lumps of clay dried quickly into firm tablets. If accidentally hardened by fire, they became virtually indestructible. Thousands have survived in the ruins of Mesopotamian cities.

The first tablets were written in Sumerian, a language related to no other known tongue. Each pictogram represented a single sound, which corresponded to a single object or idea. In time, these pictograms developed into a true system of writing. The drawings themselves became smaller and more abstract and were arranged in straight lines. Since the scribe first pressed the triangle-shaped writing instrument into the clay and then drew it across the square, this writing took on its characteristic wedge, or "cuneiform," shape (from the Latin *cuneus,* wedge). Finally, scribes took a radical step. Rather than simply using pictograms to indicate single objects, they began to use cuneiform characters

An early Sumerian clay tablet found in Iraq records the barley rations allotted in a five-day week to forty workmen.

to represent concepts. For example, the pictogram for "foot" could also mean "to stand." Ultimately, pictograms came to represent sounds divorced from any particular meaning.

The implications of the development of cuneiform writing were revolutionary. Since symbols were liberated from meaning, they could be used to record any language. Over the next thousand years, scribes used these same symbols to write not only in Sumerian but also in the other languages of Mesopotamia, such as Akkadian, Babylonian, and Persian. The earliest extant clay tablets are little more than lists of receipts. Later, tablets were used to preserve contracts, maintain administrative records, and record significant events, prayers, myths, and proverbs. Writing soon allowed those who had mastered it to achieve greater centralization and control of government, to communicate over enormous distances, to preserve and transmit information, and to express religious and cultural beliefs. Writing reinforced memory, consolidating and expanding the achievements of the first civilization and transmitting them to the future. Writing was power, and for much of subsequent history a small minority of merchants and elites and the scribes in their employ wielded this power. In Mesopotamia, this power served to increase the strength of the king, the servant of the gods.

Gods and Mortals in Mesopotamia

Uruk had begun as a village like any other. Its rise to importance resulted from its significance as a religious site. A world of many cities, Mesopotamia was also a world of many gods, and Mesopotamian cities bore the imprint of the cult of their gods.

The gods were like the people who worshiped them. They lived in a replica of human society, and each god had a particular responsibility. Every object and element from the sky to the brick or the plow had its own active god. The gods had the physical appearance and personalities of humans as well as human virtues and vices, but always to an exaggerated extent. Like humans, they lived in a stratified society. The hundreds of ordinary divinities were overshadowed by greater gods like Nanna and Ufu, who were the protectors of Ur and Sippar. Others, such as Inanna, or Ishtar, the goddess of love, fertility, and wars, and her husband Dumuzi, were worshiped throughout Mesopotamia. Finally, at the top of the pantheon were the gods of the sky, the air, and the rivers. The sky god was An, whose temple was in Uruk. Enki was god of earth and waters, and Enlil was the supreme ruler of the air.

Mesopotamians believed that the role of mortals was to serve the gods and to feed them through sacrifice. Towns had first developed around the gods' temples for this purpose. By around 2500 B.C., although military lords and kings had gained political power at the expense of the temple priests, the temples still controlled a major portion of economic resources. They owned vast estates where peasants cultivated wheat, barley, vegetable gardens, and vineyards and tended flocks of sheep and herds of cattle and pigs. The produce from temple lands and flocks supported the priests, scribes, artisans, laborers, farmers, teamsters, smiths, and weavers who operated these complex religious centers. At Lagash, for example, the temple of the goddess Bau owned over eleven thousand acres of land. The king held one-quarter of this land for his own use. The priests divided the remainder into individual plots of about thirty-five acres, each to be cultivated for the support of the temple workers or rented out to free peasants. At a time when the total population was approximately forty thousand, the temple employed more than twelve hundred workers of various sorts, supervised by an administrator and an inspector appointed by the priests. The temple of Bau was only one of twenty temples in Lagash—and not the largest or most wealthy among them.

Temples dominated the city's skyline as they dominated the city's life. Square, rectangular, or oval, they consisted of the same essential elements. Worshipers entered through a vestibule that opened onto a spacious courtyard dominated by an altar. Here sacrifices were offered to the idol of the god. Spreading out from the courtyard was a maze of smaller chambers, which provided housing for the priests and storage facilities for the accumulated offerings brought to feed the god. By around 2000 B.C., a ziggurat, or tiered tower, dedi-

The southwestern side of the ruins of the ziggurat of Ur. On top of a main platform fifty feet high, two successively smaller stages were built. The top stage was a temple containing a religious shrine. Ramplike stairways led up to the shrine from the ground.

cated to the god stood near many temples. The great Ziggurat of Ur, for example, measured nearly two thousand square feet at its base and originally stood more than 120 feet high. Ziggurats were constructed of mud bricks and covered with baked bricks set in bitumen, and they were often ornamented with elaborate multicolored mosaics. Today their weathered remains are small hills rising unexpectedly from the Iraqi plain. It is easy to see why people of a later age thought that the people who had built the ziggurats wanted a tower that would reach to heaven—the origin of the biblical story of the Tower of Babel.

Although Mesopotamians looked to hundreds of personal divinities for assistance, they did not attempt to establish personal relationships with their great gods. They believed that these gods were little interested in humans and casual contact with them was dangerous. However, since they assumed that the gods lived in a structured world that operated rationally, they believed that mortals could deal with them and enlist their aid by following the right rituals. Rites centered on the worship of idols. The gods were thought to be present if their idols showed the appropriate features, clothing, ornaments, and equipment and if they were cared for in the proper manner. The most important care was feeding. At the temple of Uruk, the gods were offered two meals a day, each consisting of two courses served in regal quantity and style. The offerings were left before the idol so that it could consume their immaterial essence. Then the meals were served to the priests. The surplus of the vast amounts of food brought to the temple was distributed among the temple staff and servants.

Through the proper rituals, a person could buy the god's protection and favor. Still, mortal life was harsh and the gods offered little solace to the great issues of human existence. This attitude is powerfully presented in the *Epic of Gilgamesh,* which, while not an accurate picture of Mesopotamian religion, still conveys much of the values of this civilization. In this popular legend Gilgamesh, king of Uruk, civilizes the wild man Enkidu, who had been sent by the gods to temper the king's harshness. Gilgamesh and Enkidu become friends and undertake a series of adventures. However, even their great feats cannot overcome death. Enkidu displeases the gods and dies. Gilgamesh then sets out to find the magic plant of eternal life with which to return his friend from the somber underworld. On his journey he meets Ut-napishtim, the Mesopotamian Noah, who recounts the story of the Great Flood and tells him where to find the plant. Gilgamesh follows Ut-napishtim's advice and is successful but loses the plant on his

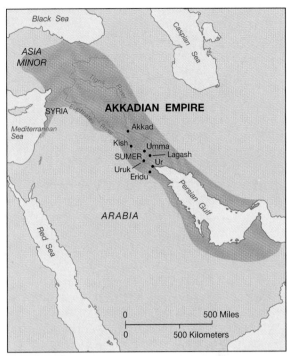

Akkad Under Sargon

journey home. The message is that only the gods are immortal, and the human afterlife is at best a shadowy and mournful existence. In Mesopotamian society, this earthly life alone was considered worth living, and one had to accomplish all that one could in it.

Sargon and Mesopotamian Expansion

The temple was one center of the city; the palace was the other. As representative of the city's god, the king was the ruler and highest judge. Like people in other strata of society, the king held privileges and responsibilities appropriate to his position. He was responsible for the construction and maintenance of religious buildings and the complex system of canals that maintained the precarious balance between swamp and arid steppe. Finally, he commanded the army, defending his community against its neighbors and leading his forces against rival cities.

The cultural and economic developments of early Mesopotamia occurred within the context of almost constant warfare. From around 3000 B.C. until 2300 B.C., the rulers of Ur, Lagash, Uruk, and Umma fought among themselves for control of Sumer (their name for the southern region of Mesopotamia). While their urban and political traditions were similar, the region

This bronze head, dating from around 2300 B.C., was found at Nineveh. It is sometimes identified as Sargon, king of Akkad. Later invaders mutilated the nose and eyes, apparently making a political statement.

had no political, linguistic, or ethnic unity. The population was a mixture of Sumerians and Semites—peoples speaking Semitic languages related to modern Arabic or Hebrew—all jealously protective of their cities and gods and eager to extend their domination over their weaker neighbors.

The extraordinary developments in this small corner of the Middle East might have remained isolated phenomena were it not for Sargon (ca. 2334–2279 B.C.), king of Akkad and the most important figure in Mesopotamian history. During his long reign of fifty-five years, Sargon built on the conquests and confederacies of the past to unite, transform, and expand Mesopotamian civilization. Born in obscurity, after his death he was worshiped as a god. Sargon was the son of a priestess and an unknown father. A legend similar to that of Moses says that Sargon's mother placed him in a reed basket and set him adrift on the Euphrates. In his youth he was the cupbearer to the king of Kish. Later, he overthrew his master and conquered Uruk, Ur, Lagash, and Umma. This made him lord of Sumer.

Such glory had satisfied his predecessors, but not Sargon. Instead he extended his military operations east across the Tigris, west along the Euphrates, and north into modern Syria, thus creating the first great multiethnic empire state in the West.

The Akkadian state, so named by contemporary historians for Sargon's capital at Akkad, consisted of a vast and heterogeneous collection of city-states and territories. Sargon attempted to rule it by transforming the traditions of royal government. First, he abandoned the traditional title of king of Kish in favor of "King of the Four Regions," a title emphasizing the universality of his rule. Second, rather than eradicating the traditions of conquered cities, he allowed them to maintain their own institutions but replaced many of their autonomous ruling aristocracies with his own functionaries. He also reduced the economic power of local temples in favor of his supporters, to whom he apparently distributed temple property. At the same time, however, he tried to win the loyalty of the ancient cities of Sumer by naming his daughter high priestess of the moon-god Nanna at Ur. He was thus the first in a long tradition of Near Eastern rulers who sought to unite his disparate conquests into a true state.

Sargon did more than just conquer cities. Although a Semite, he spread the achievements of Sumerian civilization throughout his vast state. In the Akkadian pantheon, Sumerian and Semitic gods were venerated equally, and similar gods from various traditions were merged into the same divinities. Akkadian scribes used cuneiform to write the Semitic Akkadian language, thus continuing the tradition of literate administration begun by the Sumerians. So important did Sargon's successors deem his accomplishments that they ordered him worshiped as a god.

The Akkadian nation-state proved as ephemeral as Sargon's cultural accomplishments were lasting. All Mesopotamian states tended to undergo a rapid rise under a gifted military commander, then began to crumble under the internal stresses of dynastic disputes and regional assertions of autonomy. Thus weakened, they could then be conquered by other expanding states. First Ur, under its Sumerian king and first law-codifier, Shulgi (2094–2047 B.C.), and then Amoritic Babylonia, under its great ruler Hammurabi (1792–1750 B.C.), assumed dominance in the land between the rivers. From about 2000 B.C. on, the political and economic centers of Mesopotamia were in Babylonia and in Assyria, the region to the north at the foot of the Zagros Mountains.

THE CODE OF HAMMURABI

The society revealed in the Code of Hammurabi was a complex world of landed aristocrats, merchants, and simple workers and shopkeepers. Its economy functioned on a complex system of credit relationships binding the various members of the society together, as seen in the following selections.

If a merchant lent grain at interest, he shall receive sixty *qu* of grain per *jur* as interest [= 20 percent rate of interest]. If he lent money at interest, he shall receive one-sixth shekel six *se* (i.e., one-fifth shekel) per shekel of silver as interest.

If a seignior who incurred a debt does not have the money to pay it back, but has the grain, the merchant shall take grain for his money with its interest in accordance with the ratio fixed by the king.

If a seignior gave money to another seignior for a partnership, they shall divide equally in the presence of god the profit or loss which was incurred.

If a woman wine seller, instead of receiving grain for the price of a drink, has received money by the large weight and so has made the value of the drink less than the value of the grain, they shall prove it against that wine seller and throw her into the water.

If an obligation came due against a seignior and he sold the services of his wife, his son, or his daughter, or he has been bound over to service, they shall work in the house of their purchaser or obligee for three years, with their freedom reestablished in the fourth year.

If an obligation came due against a seignior and he has accordingly sold [the services of] his female slave who bore him children, the owner of the female slave may repay the money which the merchant paid out and thus redeem his female slave.

Hammurabi and the Old Babylonian Empire

In the tradition of Sargon, Hammurabi expanded his state through arms and diplomacy. He expanded his power south as far as Uruk and north to Assyria. In the tradition of Shulgi, he promulgated an important body of law, known as the Code of Hammurabi. In the words of its prologue, this code sought

> *To cause justice to prevail in the country*
> *To destroy the wicked and the evil,*
> *That the strong may not oppress the weak.*

As the favored agent of the gods, the king held responsibility for regulating all aspects of Babylonian life, including dowries and contracts, agricultural prices and wages, commerce and money lending, and even professional standards for physicians and architects. Hammurabi's code thus offers a view of many aspects of Babylonian life, although always from the perspective of the royal law. This law lists offenses and prescribes penalties, which vary according to the social status of the victim and the perpetrator. The code creates a picture of a prosperous society composed of three legally defined social strata: a well-to-do elite, the mass of the population, and slaves. Each group had its own rights and obligations in proportion to its status. Even slaves enjoyed some legal rights and protection, could marry free persons, and might eventually obtain freedom.

Much of the code seeks to protect women and children from arbitrary and unfair treatment. Husbands ruled their households, but they did not have unlimited authority over their wives. Women could initiate their own court cases, practice various trades, and even hold public positions. Upon marriage, husbands gave their fathers-in-law a payment in silver or in furnishings. The father of the wife gave her a dowry over which she had full control. Some elite women personally controlled great wealth.

The law code held physicians, veterinarians, architects, and boat builders to standards of professional behavior. If a physician performed a successful eye operation on a member of the elite, the code specified that he receive ten shekels of silver. However, if the physician caused the loss of the eye, he lost his hand. Builders of houses had to repair any damages caused if their structures collapsed. If a free person died in the collapse, the builder had to pay with his life.

The Code of Hammurabi was less a royal attempt to restructure Babylonian society than an effort to reorganize, consolidate, and preserve previous laws in order to maintain the established social and economic order. What innovation it did show was in the extent of such punitive measures as death or mutilation. Penalties in earlier codes had been primarily compensation in silver or valuables. Hammurabi's extensive use of the law of retaliation was an assertion of royal authority in maintaining justice.

Law was not the only area in which the Old Babylonian kingdom began an important tradition. In order to handle the economics of business and government administration, Babylonians developed the most sophisticated mathematical system known prior to the fifteenth century A.D. Babylonian mathematics was based on a numerical system from one to sixty (today we still divide hours and minutes into sixty units). Babylonian mathematicians devised multiplication

BETWEEN THE TWO RIVERS	
ca. 3500 B.C.	Pictograms appear
ca. 3000–2316 B.C.	War for control of Sumer
ca. 2700 B.C.	Gilgamesh
ca. 2334–2279 B.C.	Sargon
1792–1750 B.C.	Hammurabi
ca. 1600 B.C.	Hittites destroy Old Babylonian state
ca. 1286 B.C.	Battle of Kadesh

tables and tables of reciprocals that allowed quick calculations of all products from one to fifty-nine with each of the numbers from two to fifty-nine. They also devised tables of squares and square roots, cubes and cube roots, and other calculations needed for computing such important figures as compound interest. Babylonian mathematicians developed an algebraic system and solved linear and quadratic equations for such practical purposes as determining the shares of inheritance for several sons or the wages to be paid for a variety of workers employed for several days. Similar tables of coefficients made possible the calculation of areas of various geometric figures as well as the amounts of standard building materials needed for buildings in these shapes. Although Babylonian mathematicians were not primarily interested in theoretical problems and were seldom given to abstraction, their technical proficiency indicates the advanced level of sophistication with which Hammurabi's contemporaries could tackle the problems of living in a complex society.

For all its successes, Hammurabi's state was no more successful than those of his predecessors at defending itself against internal conflicts or external enemies. Despite his efforts, the traditional organization inherited from his Sumerian and Akkadian predecessors could not ensure orderly administration of a far-flung collection of cities. Hammurabi's son lost over half of his father's kingdom to internal revolts. Weakened by internal dissension, the kingdom fell to a new and potent force in Western history, the Hittites.

From their capital of Hattushash (modern Bogazköy in Turkey), the Hittites established a centralized state based on agriculture and trade in the metals mined from the ore-rich mountains of Anatolia and exported to Mesopotamia. Perfecting the light horse-drawn war chariot, the Hittites expanded into northern Meso-

A seven-foot-high diorite stele, dating from about 1750 B.C., is inscribed with the law code of Hammurabi. The relief at the top shows Hammurabi standing at left in the presence of the sun-god, perhaps explaining his code of laws.

potamia and along the Syrian coast. They were able to destroy the Babylonian state around 1600 B.C. Unlike the Sumerians and the Semitic nomads, Akkadians, and Babylonians, the Hittites were an Indo-European people, speaking a language that was part of a linguistic family that includes most modern European languages as well as Persian, Greek, Latin, and Sanskrit. The Hittites' gradual expansion south along the coast was checked at the battle of Kadesh around 1286 B.C., when they encountered the army of an even greater and more ancient power—the Egypt of Ramses II.

The Gift of the Nile

Like that of the Tigris and Euphrates valleys, the rich soil of the Nile Valley can support a dense population. There, however, the similarities end. Unlike the Mesopotamian, the Nile floodplain required little effort to make the land productive. Each year the river flooded at exactly the right moment to irrigate crops and to deposit a layer of rich, fertile silt. South of the last cataracts, the fertile region called Upper Egypt is about eight miles wide and is flanked by high desert plateaus. Near the Mediterranean in Lower Egypt, the Nile spreads across a lush, marshy delta more than one hundred miles wide. Egypt knew only two environments, the fertile Nile Valley and the vast wastes of the Sahara surrounding it. This inhospitable and largely uninhabitable region limited Egypt's contact with outside influences. Thus while trade, communication, and violent conquest characterized Mesopotamian civilization, Egypt knew self-sufficiency, an inward focus in culture and society, and stability. In its art, political structure, society, and religion, the Egyptian universe was static. Nothing was ever to change.

The earliest sedentary communities in the Nile Valley appeared on the western margin of the Nile Delta around 4000 B.C. In villages such as Merimda, which had a population of over ten thousand, huts constructed of poles and adobe bricks huddled together near wadis—fertile river beds that were dry except during the rainy season. Farther south, in Upper Egypt, similar communities developed somewhat later but achieved an earlier political unity and a higher level of culture. By around 3200 B.C., Upper Egypt was in contact with Mesopotamia and had apparently borrowed something of that region's artistic and architectural traditions. During the same period, Upper Egypt developed a pictographic script.

These cultural achievements coincided with the political centralization of Upper Egypt under a series of kings. Probably around 3150 B.C., King Narmer or one of his predecessors in Upper Egypt expanded control over the fragmented south, uniting Upper and Lower Egypt and establishing a capital at Memphis on the border between these two regions. For over twenty-five hundred years, the Nile Valley, from the first cataract to the Mediterranean, enjoyed the most stable civilization the Western world has ever known.

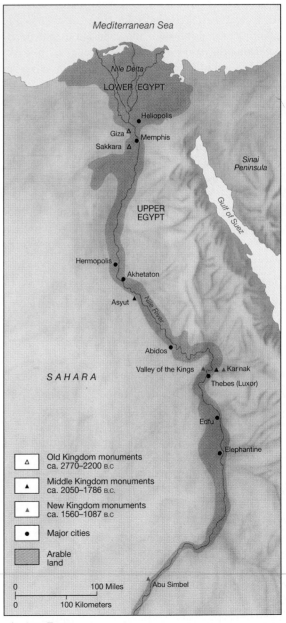

Ancient Egypt

Tending the Cattle of God

Historians divide the vast sweep of Egyptian history into thirty-one dynasties, regrouped in turn into four periods of political centralization: pre- and early dynastic Egypt (ca. 3150–2770 B.C.), the Old Kingdom (ca. 2770–2200 B.C.), the Middle Kingdom (ca. 2050–1786 B.C.), and the New Kingdom (ca. 1560–1087 B.C.). The time gaps between kingdoms were periods of disruption and political confusion termed intermediate periods. While minor changes in social, political, and cultural life certainly occurred during these centuries, the changes were less significant than the astonishing stability and continuity of the civilization that developed along the banks of the Nile.

Divine kingship was the cornerstone of Egyptian life. Initially, the king was the incarnation of Horus, a sky and falcon god. Later, the king was identified with the sun god Ra (subsequently known as Amen-Re, the great god), as well as with Osiris, the god of the dead. As divine incarnation, the king was obliged above all to care for his people. It was he who ensured the annual flooding of the Nile, which brought water to the parched land. His commands preserved *maat,* the ideal state of the universe and society, a condition of harmony and justice. In the poetry of the Old Kingdom, the king was the divine herdsman, while the people were the cattle of god:

> *Well tended are men, the cattle of god.*
> *He made heaven and earth according to their desire*
> *and repelled the demon of the waters . . .*
> *He made for them rulers (even) in the egg,*
> *a supporter to support the back of the disabled.*

Unlike the rulers in Mesopotamia, the kings of the Old Kingdom were not warriors but divine administrators. Protected by the Sahara, Egypt had few external enemies and no standing army. A vast bureaucracy of literate court officials and provincial administrators assisted the god-king. They wielded wide authority as religious leaders, judicial officers, and, when necessary, military leaders. A host of subordinate overseers, scribes, metalworkers, stonemasons, artisans, and tax collectors rounded out the royal administration. At the local level, governors administered provinces called *nomes,* the basic units of Egyptian local government.

Women of ancient Egypt were more independent and involved in public life than were those of Mesopotamia. Egyptian women owned property, conducted their own business, entered legal contracts, and brought lawsuits. They also had an integral part in religious rites. They were not segregated from men in their daily activities and shared in the economic and professional life of the country at every level except one: women were apparently excluded from formal education. The professional bureaucracy was open only to those who could read and write. As a result, the primary route to public power was closed to women, and the bureaucratic machinery remained firmly in the hands of men.

The role of this bureaucracy was to administer estates, collect taxes, and channel revenues and labor toward vast public works projects. These construction projects focused on the king. He lived in the royal city of Memphis in the splendor of a *Per-ao,* or "great house," from which comes the word *pharaoh,* the Hebrew term for the Egyptian king. During the Old and Middle Kingdoms, more imposing than the great house of the living king were the pyramid temple-tomb complexes of his ancestors. The vast size and superb engineering of these structures remain among the marvels of human creation.

The founder of the Old Kingdom, King Zoser, who was a rough contemporary of Gilgamesh, built the first of these pyramid temples, the Step Pyramid at Sakkara. The pyramid tombs were only part of elaborate religious complexes at whose center were temples housing royal statues. Within the temples priests and servants performed rituals to serve the dead kings just as they had served the kings when they were alive. Even death did not disrupt the continuity so vital to Egyptian civilization. The cults of dead kings reinforced the monarchy, since veneration of past rulers meant veneration of the kings' ancestors. The pyramids thus strengthened the image of the living king by honoring the physical remains of his predecessors.

Building and equipping the pyramids focused and transformed Egypt's material and human resources. Artisans had to be trained, engineering and transportation problems solved, quarrying and stone-working techniques perfected, and laborers recruited. In the Old Kingdom, whose population has been estimated at perhaps 1.5 million, more than seventy thousand workers at a time were employed in building these great temple-tombs. No smaller work force could have built such a massive structure as the Great Pyramid of Khufu (ca. 2600 B.C.), which stood 481 feet high and contained almost six million tons of stone. In comparison, the great Ziggurat of Ur rose only some 120 feet above the Mesopotamian plain. The pyramids were constructed by peasants working when the Nile was in flood and they could not till the soil. Although actual construction was seasonal, the work was unending. No sooner was one complex completed than the next was begun.

Feeding these masses of laborers absorbed most of the country's agricultural surplus. Equipping the temples and pyramids provided a constant demand for the highest-quality luxury goods, since royal tombs and temples were furnished as luxuriously as palaces. Thus the construction and maintenance of these vast complexes focused the organization and production of Egypt's economy and government.

Democratization of the Afterlife

In the Old Kingdom, future life was available through the king. The graves of thousands of his attendants and servants surrounded his temple. All the resources of the kingdom went to maintaining existing cults and establishing new ones. All the wealth, labor, and expertise of the kingdom thus flowed into these temples, reinforcing the position of the king. Like the tip of a pyramid, the king was the summit, supported by all of society.

Gradually, however, the absolute power of the king declined. The increasing demands for consumption by the court and the cults forced agricultural expansion into areas where returns were poor, thus decreasing the flow of wealth. As bureaucrats increased their efforts to supply the voracious needs of living and dead kings and their attendants, they neglected the maintenance of the economic system that supplied these needs. The royal government was not protecting society; the "cattle of god" were not being well tended. Finally, tax-exempt religious foundations, established to ensure the perpetual cult of the dead, received donations of vast amounts of property and came to rival the power of the king. This removed an ever-greater amount of the country's wealth from the control of the king and his agents. Thus the wealth and power of the Egyptian kings declined at roughly the time that Sargon was expanding his Akkadian state in Mesopotamia. By around 2200 B.C., Egyptian royal authority collapsed entirely, leaving political and religious power in the hands of provincial governors.

After almost two hundred years of fragmentation, the governors of Thebes in Upper Egypt reestablished centralized royal traditions, but with a difference. Kings continued to build vast temples, but they did not resume the tremendous investments in pyramid complexes on the scale of the Old Kingdom. The bureaucracy was opened to all men, even sons of peasants, who could master the complex pictographic writing. Private temple-tombs proliferated and with them new pious foundations. These promised eternal care by which anyone with sufficient wealth could enjoy a comfortable afterlife.

The memory of the shortcomings of the Old Kingdom introduced a new ethical perspective expressed in the literature written by the elite. For the first time, the elite voiced the concern that justice might not always be served and that the innocent might suffer at the

The Egyptian Book of the Dead *contained spells to aid the souls of the dead in achieving immortality in the afterlife. This portion shows the deceased being judged by the god Osiris.*

A HOMESICK EGYPTIAN

The story of Sinuhe, an Egyptian of the Middle Kingdom (ca. 2050–1786 B.C.), was among the most popular stories in Egyptian history. Sinuhe fled into exile but, in spite of his prosperity among foreigners, longed for his home. In the following passage Sinuhe, who has been summoned to return to the Pharaoh, tells of his reception.

I found his majesty upon the Great Throne in a recess of fine gold. When I was stretched out upon my belly, I knew not myself in his presence, although this god greeted me pleasantly. I was like a man caught in the dark: my soul departed, my body was powerless, my heart was not in my body, that I might know life from death.

Then his majesty said: "Lift him up. Let him speak to me." Then his majesty said: "Behold thou art come. Thou hast trodden the foreign countries and made a flight. But now elderliness has attacked thee; thou hast reached old age. It is no small matter that thy corpse be properly buried; thou shouldst not be interred by bowmen. Do not, do not act thus any longer: for thou dost not speak when thy name is pronounced!" Yet I was afraid to respond, and I answered it with the answer of one afraid: "What is it that my lord says to me? I should answer it, but there

is nothing that I can do: it is really the hand of a god."

Then his majesty said: "He shall not fear. He has no title to be in dread. He shall be a courtier among the nobles, He shall be put in the rank of the courtiers. Proceed to the inner chambers of the morning toilet, in order to make his position."

There was constructed for me a pyramid-tomb of stone in the midst of the pyramid-tombs. The stone-masons who hew a pyramid-tomb took over its ground-area. The outline draftsmen designed in it; the chief sculptors carved in it, and the overseers of works who are in the necropolis made it their concern. My statue was overlaid with gold, and its skirt was of fine gold. It was his majesty who had it made. There is no poor man for whom the like has been done. So I was under the favor of the king's presence until the day of mooring had come.

---

hands of royal agents. In the story of Sinuhe, a popular tale from around 1900 B.C., an official of Amenemhet I (d. 1962 B.C.) flees Egypt after the death of his king. He fears that through false reports of his actions he will incur the wrath of Amenemhet's son, Senusert I. Only in his old age, after years in exile, does Sinuhe dare to return to his beloved Egypt. There, through the intercession of the royal children, Senusert receives him honorably and grants him the ultimate favor, his own pyramid-tomb. In the "Tale of the Eloquent Peasant," a peasant is constantly mistreated by royal officials. Although he, like Sinuhe, ultimately receives justice, the moral is clear. The state system at times failed in its responsibility to safeguard maat. Still, these stories, in the end, reaffirm the existing system.

The greater access to power and privilege in the Middle Kingdom benefited foreigners as well as Egyptians. Assimilated Semites rose to important adminis-

trative positions. By around 1600 B.C., when the Hittite armies were destroying the state of Hammurabi's successors, large bands of Semites had settled in the eastern Delta, setting the stage for the first foreign conquest of Egypt. A series of kings referred to by Egyptian sources as "rulers of foreign lands," or *Hyksos*, overran the country and ruled the Nile Valley as far south as Memphis. These foreigners adopted the traditions of Egyptian kingship and continued the tradition of divine rule, even using names compounded with that of the sun god, Ra.

The Hyksos kings introduced their military technology and organization into Egypt. In particular, they brought with them the light horse-drawn war chariot. This mobile fighting platform—manned by warriors armed with bows, bronze swords of a type previously unknown in Egypt, and lances—transformed Egyptian military tactics. These innovations remained even after

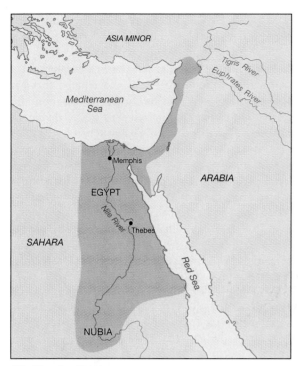

The Egyptian Empire

the Hyksos were expelled by Ahmose I (1552–1527 B.C.), the Theban founder of the Eighteenth Dynasty, with whose reign the New Kingdom began.

The Egyptian Empire

Ahmose did not stop with the liberation of Egypt. He forged an empire. He and his successors used their newfound military might to extend the frontiers of Egypt south up the Nile beyond the fourth cataract and well into Nubia, solidifying Egypt's contacts with other regions of Africa. To the east they absorbed the caravan routes to the Red Sea, from which they were able to send ships to Punt (probably modern Somalia), the source of the myrrh and frankincense needed for funeral and religious rituals. Most important was the Egyptian expansion into Canaan and Syria. Here Egyptian chariots crushed their foes as kings pressed on as far as the Euphrates. Thutmose I (1506–1494 B.C.) proclaimed: "I have made the boundaries of Egypt as far as that which the sun encircles."

Thutmose's immediate successors were his children, Thutmose II (1494–1490 B.C.) and Hatshepsut

(1490–1468 B.C.), who married her brother. Such brother-sister marriages, although not unknown in polygamous Egyptian society, were rare. After the death of Thutmose II, Hatshepsut ruled both as regent for her stepson Thutmose III (1490–1468 B.C.) and as co-ruler. She was by all accounts a capable ruler, preserving stability and even personally leading the army on several occasions to protect the empire. However, the traditions of male leadership were such that Hatshepsut could not present a public image as a female monarch. In royal inscriptions and in pictures, she had herself portrayed in the formal rigid pose and dress of a king, including a false beard.

In spite of the efforts of Hatshepsut and her successors, the Egyptian empire was never as grand as its kings proclaimed. Many of the northern expeditions were raids rather than conquests. Still, the expanded political frontiers meant increased trade and unprecedented interaction with the rest of the ancient world. The cargo excavated from the wreck of a ship that sank off the coast of what is now Turkey around 1350 B.C. vividly portrays the breadth of international exchange in the New Kingdom. The nationality of the ship, its origins, and its destination are unknown, but it carried a cargo of priceless and exotic merchandise from around the Mediterranean world. From distant Cyprus came copper ingots. Tin ingots probably originated in the Hittite state in what are now parts of Afghanistan and Turkey. In the ship's hold lay numerous jars from Canaan and vases from Greece. When it sank, the ship was carrying Canaanite glass ingots, jewelry, and jars of ointment; ebony from Nubia; pottery from Cyprus; weapons from Egypt, Greece, and Syria; cylinder seals from Mesopotamia or Syria; raw ivory; and a mass of damaged Egyptian gold jewelry probably intended for scrap.

The lost ship was probably not a merchant vessel in the modern sense; private merchants were virtually unknown in the Egyptian empire. Instead, most precious commodities circulated through royal ventures or as gifts and tribute. The ship may well have been carrying tribute to the king, for in the New Kingdom as in the Old, the ruler, as the incarnation of the great god Amen-Re, was the pinnacle of the political and economic order.

Religion was both the heart of royal power and its only limiting force. Although the king was the embodiment of the religious tradition, he was also bound by that tradition, as it was interpreted by an ancient and powerful system of priesthoods, pious foundations, and

This painted limestone head of Hatshepsut was originally from a statue. She is shown wearing the crown of Egypt and the stylized beard that symbolized royalty and was often seen on the statues and death masks of pharaohs.

cults. The intimate relationship between royal absolutism and religious cult culminated in the reign of Amenhotep IV (1364–1347 B.C.), the most controversial and enigmatic ruler of the New Kingdom, who challenged the very basis of royal religious control. In a calculated break with over one thousand years of Egyptian religious custom, Amenhotep attempted to abolish the cult of Amen-Re along with all of the other traditional gods, their priesthoods, and their festivals. In their place he promoted a new divinity, the sun-disk god Aten. Amenhotep moved his capital from Thebes

to a new temple city, Akhetaton (near the modern village of Tel al-'Amarna) and changed his own name to Akhenaten ("it pleases Aten").

Akhenaten has been called the first monotheist, a reformer who sought to revitalize a religion that had decayed into superstition and magic. Yet his monotheism was not complete. The god Aten shared divine status with Akhenaten himself. Akhenaten attacked other cults, especially that of Amen-Re, to consolidate royal power and to replace the old priesthoods with his own family members and supporters. In his artistic policies, he broke with the past, but again the break was limited. Official portraiture, which depicted Akhenaten with a long, thin face, a swollen stomach, and large thighs, was no more "realistic" than the earlier tradition. Instead, Akhenaten appeared as both man and woman, an image of his counterpart Aten, the godhead who was father and mother of all creation.

Still, in attempting to reestablish royal divinity, Akhenaten did temporarily transform the aesthetics of Egyptian court life. Traditional archaic language gave way to the everyday speech of the fourteenth century B.C. Wall paintings and statues showed people in the clothing that they actually wore rather than in stylized parade dress. This new naturalism rendered the king at once more human and more divine. It differentiated him from the long line of preceding kings, emphasizing his uniqueness and his royal power.

The strength of royal power was so great that during his reign Akhenaten could command acceptance of his radical break with Egyptian stability. However, his ambitious plan did not long survive his death. His innovations annoyed the Egyptian elite, while his abolition of traditional festivals alienated the masses. His son-in-law, Tutankhamen (1347–1337 B.C.), the son of Akhenaten's predecessor, was a child when he became king upon Akhenaten's death. Under the influence of his court advisors, probably inherited from his father's reign, he restored the ancient religious traditions and abandoned the new capital of Akhetaton for his father's palace at Thebes. Something of the relaxed artistic style introduced by Akhenaten survived in the art of Tutankhamen's reign. However, the religious themes and objects found in the young king's tomb—which was unearthed by the English archaeologist Howard Carter in 1922—show a complete return to the old ways within a few years of Akhenaten's death. (See "Discovering the Pharaohs," pp. 24–25.)

Return to the old ways meant return to the old problems. Powerful pious foundations controlled fully 10 percent of the population. Dynastic continuity ended after Tutankhamen and a new military dynasty seized the throne. These internal problems provided an opportunity for the expanding Hittite state in Asia Minor (now Turkey) to expand south at the expense of Egypt. Ramses II (1289–1224 B.C.) checked the Hittite expansion at the battle of Kadesh, but the battle was actually a draw. Eventually, Ramses and the Hittite king Hattusilis III signed a peace treaty whose terms included nonaggression and mutual defense. Archaeologists have found copies of the treaty, both in Hattushash and in Egypt. Written in Egyptian, Hittite, and the international diplomatic language of Akkadian, the agreement marked the failure of both states to unify the Fertile Crescent, the region stretching from the Persian Gulf northwest through Mesopotamia and down the Mediterranean coast to Egypt.

The Gift of the Nile

ca. 3150–2770 B.C.	Predynastic and early dynastic Egypt
ca. 2770–2200 B.C.	Old Kingdom
ca. 2600 B.C.	Pyramid of Khufu
ca. 2050–1786 B.C.	Middle Kingdom
ca. 1560–1087 B.C.	New Kingdom
1552–1527 B.C.	Ahmose I
1506–1494 B.C.	Thutmose I
1494–1490 B.C.	Thutmose II
1490–1468 B.C.	Hatshepsut
1364–1347 B.C.	Amenhotep IV (Akhenaten)
1347–1337 B.C.	Tutankhamen
1289–1224 B.C.	Ramses II

The mutual standoff at Kadesh did not long precede the disintegration of both Egypt and the Hittite state. Within a century, states large and small along the Mediterranean coast from Anatolia to the Delta and from the Aegean Sea in the west to the Zagros Mountains in the east collapsed or were destroyed in what seems to have been a general crisis of the civilized world. The various raiders, sometimes erroneously called the "Sea Peoples," who struck Egypt, Syria, the Hittite state, and elsewhere were not the primary cause of the crisis. It was rather internal political, economic, and social strains within both Egypt and the Hittite state that provided the opportunity for various groups—including Anatolians, Greeks, Israelites, and others—to raid the ancient centers of civilization. In the ensuing confusion, the small Semitic kingdoms of Syria and Canaan developed a precarious independence in the shadow of the great powers.

Between Two Worlds

City-based civilization was an endangered species throughout antiquity. Just beyond the well-tilled fields of Mesopotamia and the fertile delta of the Nile lay the world of Semitic tribes of seminomadic shepherds and traders. Of course, not all Semites were nonurban. Many had formed part of the heterogeneous population of the Sumerian world. Sargon's Semitic Akkadians and Hammurabi's Amorites created great Mesopotamian nation-states, adopting the ancient Sumerian cultural traditions. Along the coast of Canaan other Semitic groups established towns that

A relief from the ruins of the temple of Aten at Tel al-'Amarna shows the pharaoh Akhenaten, Queen Nefertiti, and one of their daughters adoring the god Aten in the form of the sun's disk. The Aten sends down tiny hands to accept the libations of the royal pair.

❧ Discovering the Pharaohs

The English archaeologist Howard Carter had been searching the Valley of the Kings, near Thebes, for the tomb of Tutankhamen for five fruitless years. Years later, he described the events of 26 November 1922, the day that culminated his quest:

> With trembling hands I made a tiny breach in the upper left-hand corner of the door. Darkness and blank space, as far as an iron testing-rod could reach, showed that whatever lay beyond was empty, and not filled like the passage we had just cleared. Candle tests were applied as a precaution against possible foul gases, and then, widening the hole a little, I inserted the candle and peered in, Lord Carnarvon, Lady Evelyn Herbert and A. R. Callender standing anxiously beside me to hear the verdict. At first I could see nothing, the hot air escaping from the chamber causing the candle flame to flicker, but presently, as my eyes grew accustomed to the light, details of the room within emerged slowly from the mist, strange animals, statues, and gold—everywhere the glint of gold. For the moment—an eternity it must have seemed to the others standing by—I was struck dumb with amazement, and when Lord Carnarvon, unable to stand the suspense any longer, inquired anxiously, "Can you see anything?" it was all I could do to get out the words, "Yes, wonderful things."

The "wonderful things" Carter saw were over five thousand priceless objects, including translucent alabaster jars and cups, painted wooden caskets, life-size wooden statues of the king, four chariots, three large couches in the forms of animals, a golden throne, a shrine encased in thick sheet-gold, and a great number of smaller jars, boxes, baskets, and other burial offerings spread through four underground rooms. The burial chamber itself contained the shrine housing the remains of the king, its seals intact. Inside the shrine was another gilt shrine, and within it a third, and a fourth, each more exquisite and precious. Within the last lay the yellow quartzite sarcophagus that held the king's mummified remains in three coffins. The first was of gilded wood; the second, gilded wood with glass paste; the third, 450 pounds of solid gold. The tomb of Tutankhamen, the only royal tomb known to have escaped ancient grave robbers, remains the most spectacular archaeological discovery of all time.

As spectacular as it was, Carter's discovery was not the most important in the history of Egyptology. Actually, Carter's find would have been impossible without a more significant breakthrough that had occurred exactly 100 years earlier and that took place not on the banks of the Nile in Egypt but on those of the Seine in France. Carter was able to discover Tutankhamen's tomb only because an earlier scholar had discovered the secret of Egyptian hieroglyphics. Over the following century, archaeologists, historians, and philologists (scholars who study language) had pieced together the history of ancient Egypt and Tutankhamen's role in it.

The story begins in 1798 when Napoleon Bonaparte invaded Egypt with a view to adding this ancient land to the French Republic. He took with him not just soldiers but also a Commission of Science and Arts composed of over one hundred scientists, engineers, and mathematicians. During their three-year occupation of Egypt, they and their commander were captivated by the splendor of Egypt's ancient monuments. They mapped and sketched hundreds of temples, pyramids, and ruins and brought back to France thousands of objects, many covered with intriguing but unreadable hieroglyphics. Back in France, members of the commission worked for years studying, classifying, and publishing the first comprehensive and systematic survey of Egyptian antiquities. Still the hieroglyphics, and with them the rich history of ancient Egypt, remained a mystery.

The mystery was solved in 1822 by the young scholar Jean François Champollion (1790–1832). Champollion had already mastered Latin, Greek, Hebrew, Syriac, Ethiopic, Arabic, Persian, Sanskrit, and Coptic when, at age eighteen, he began to devote himself to cracking the mystery of

Egyptian writing. His key was a basalt fragment discovered at Rachid (in English, Rosetta) on the west branch of the Nile in 1799 by Napoleon's commission. The stone contains three inscriptions. The uppermost is written in hieroglyphics; the second in what is called demotic, the simplified common script of ancient Egypt; and the third in Greek. Champol-

lion guessed that the three inscriptions might all contain the same text. He spent the next fourteen years working from the Greek to the demotic and finally to the hieroglyphics until he had deciphered the whole text and uncovered the basics of ancient Egyptian writing. In 1822 he reported his great discovery to the French Academy of Inscriptions. Champollion's discovery remains the most significant event in Egyptology, and he accomplished it without ever setting foot on Egyptian soil.

In the following century, scholars translated thousands of inscriptions and texts, identifying and dating monuments, tombs, and objects and gradually compiling a full and accurate picture of Egyptian history, including the reign of the rather obscure Tutankhamen. By the beginning of the twentieth century, archaeologists knew that he had been the successor of Akhenaten, that he had restored the cult of Amen-Re and the other traditional gods, that he had moved his court back to Thebes, and that he had probably been buried in the nearby Valley of the Kings. In 1906 a British archaeologist working in the valley came across a series of scattered finds that included objects containing hieroglyphic inscriptions pointing to Tutankhamen. An American Egyptologist at the Metropolitan Museum in New York recognized these as the remains of a ritual funeral banquet performed for Tutankhamen. Armed with all of this knowledge accumulated over decades, Carter began a systematic search for the lost tomb. On 26 November 1922, his search ended.

were modeled on those of Mesopotamia and that were involved in the trade between Egypt and the north. But the majority of Semitic peoples continued to live a life radically different from that of the people of the flood-plain civilizations. From these, one small group, the Hebrews, emerged to establish a religious and cultural tradition unique in antiquity.

A Wandering Aramaean Was My Father

Sometime after 2000 B.C., small Semitic bands under the leadership of patriarchal chieftains spread into what is today Syria, Lebanon, Israel, and Palestine. These bands lived on the edge of civilization. They criss-crossed the Fertile Crescent, searching for pasture for their flocks. Occasionally they participated in the trade uniting Mesopotamia and the towns of the Mediter-ranean coast. For the most part, however, they pitched their tents on the outskirts of towns only briefly, mov-ing on when their sheep and goats had exhausted the supply of pasturage. The biblical patriarch Abraham was typical of these chieftains. The story of his migra-tion from Ur to Haron and then to Hebron—as described in the Book of Genesis, chapters 11–12—conforms to the general pattern of such wandering groups. Semitic Aramaeans and Chaldeans brought with them not only their flocks and families, but Mesopotamian culture as well.

Later Hebrew history records such Mesopotamian traditions as the story of the flood (Genesis, chapters 6–10), legal traditions strongly reminiscent of those of Hammurabi, and the worship of the gods on high places. Stories such as that of the Tower of Babel (Gen-esis, chapter 11) and the Garden of Eden (Genesis, chapters 2–4) likewise have a Mesopotamian flavor, but with a difference. For these wandering shepherds, urban culture was a curse. In the Hebrew Bible (the Christian Old Testament), the first city was built by Cain, the first murderer. The Tower of Babel, probably a ziggurat, was a symbol not of human achievement but of human pride.

At least some of these wandering Aramaeans, among them Abraham, as the Hebrews later described him, also rejected the gods of Mesopotamia. Religion among these nomadic groups focused on the specific divinity of the clan. In the case of Abraham, this was the god El, the highest god of the Canaanites, the inhabitants of the coastal regions that would later be Lebanon, Pales-tine, and Israel. Abraham and his successors were not monotheists. They did not deny the existence of other gods. They simply believed that they had a personal pact with their own god.

The Kingdoms of Israel and Judah

In its social organization and cultural traditions, Abraham's clan was no different from its neighbors. These independent clans were ruled by a senior male (hence the Greek term *patriarch*—"rule by the father"). Women, whether wives, concubines, or slaves, were treated as distinctly inferior, virtually as property. As a nonliterate society, these nomadic people had little access to the learned traditions of the Fertile Crescent. Indeed, nothing marked them for any greatness. They became significant only in retrospect, and not in the Palestine of the patriarchs but in the Egypt of the pharaohs.

Some of Abraham's descendants must have joined the steady migration from Canaan into Egypt that took place during the Middle Kingdom and the Hyksos period. Although initially well treated, after the expul-sion of the Hyksos in the sixteenth century B.C., many of the Semitic settlers in Egypt were reduced to slavery. Around the thirteenth century B.C., a small band of Semitic slaves numbering less than one thousand left Egypt for Sinai and Canaan under the leadership of Moses. The memory of this departure, known as the Exodus, became the formative experience of the descendants of those who had taken part and those who later joined them. Moses, a Semite who carried an Egyptian name and who, according to tradition, had been raised in the royal court, was the founder of the Israelite people (so named for Israel, a name given the patriarch Jacob).

During the years that they spent wandering in the desert and then slowly conquering Canaan, the Israelites forged a new identity and a new faith. From the Midianites of the Sinai Peninsula they adopted the god Yahweh as their own. Although composed of vari-ous Semitic and even Egyptian groups, the Israelites adopted the oral traditions of the clan of Abraham as their common ancestor and identified his god, El, with Yahweh. They interpreted their extraordinary escape from Egypt as evidence of a covenant with this god, a treaty similar to those concluded between the Hittite kings and their dependents.

The Hebrew tradition of exodus embodied two themes: The first concerns what Yahweh had done: "I am Yahweh your God, who brought you out of Egypt, out of the house of bondage" (Exodus 20:2). The second theme—which is embodied in the Ten Commandments, the basis of Mosaic law—prescribes how Israel should respond. Unlike the conditional laws of Hammurabi's code (if. . . , then . . .) the law of Yahweh was absolute: "Thou shall not . . ." More than simply commands, the laws are ethical claims made by Yahweh on his people. Thus Yahweh was to be the Israelites' exclusive god; they were to make no alliances with any others. They were to preserve peace among themselves, and they were obligated to serve Yahweh with arms. Finally, each generation was under the moral obligation to renew the covenant as God's chosen people.

Inspired by their new identity and their new religion, the Israelites swept into Canaan. Taking advantage of the vacuum of power left by the Hittite-Egyptian standoff following the battle of Kadesh, they destroyed or captured the cities of the region. In some cases the local populations welcomed the Israelites, abandoned or overthrew their local leaders, and accepted the religion of Yahweh. In other places, the indigenous peoples were slaughtered, down to the last man, woman, and child.

A King Like All the Nations

During its first centuries, Israel was a loosely organized confederation of tribes whose only focal point was the religious shrine at Shiloh. This shrine, in contrast with the temples of other ancient peoples, housed no idols, but only a chest known as the Ark of the Covenant, which contained the law of Moses and mementos of the Exodus. At times of danger temporary leaders would lead united tribal armies. The power of these leaders, called judges in the Hebrew Bible, rested solely on their personal leadership qualities. This "charisma" indicated that the spirit of Yahweh was with the leader. Yahweh alone was the ruler of the people.

By the eleventh century B.C., this disorganized political tradition placed the Israelites at a disadvantage in fighting their neighbors. The Philistines, who dominated the Canaanite seacoast and had expanded inland, posed the greatest threat. By 1050 B.C., the Philistines had defeated the Israelites, captured the Ark of the Covenant, and occupied most of their territory. Many Israelites clamored for "a king like all the nations" to lead them to victory. To consolidate their forces, the Israelite religious leaders reluctantly established a kingdom. Its first king was Saul and its second was David.

David (ca. 1000–962 B.C.) and his son and successor, Solomon (ca. 961–922 B.C.), brought the kingdom of Israel to its peak of power, prestige, and territorial expansion. David defeated and expelled the Philistines, subdued Israel's other enemies, and created a united state that included all of Canaan from the desert to the sea. He established Jerusalem as the political and reli-

A relief on a basalt obelisk (ca. 830 B.C.) depicts Jehu, a king of Israel, making obeisance to the Assyrian monarch Shalmaneser III. This is the oldest identified portrait of an Israelite.

THE KINGDOM OF ISRAEL

Hebrew scriptures preserve two accounts of the establishment of the monarchy and the selection of Saul by Samuel as the first king (ca. 1020 B.C.). The first, from 1 Samuel 9, is favorable to the monarchy, describing how Saul was privately anointed by Samuel. The second, from 1 Samuel 8, is hostile to the monarchy, suggesting that by desiring a king the people of Israel were rejecting the traditional leadership of God alone.

1 Samuel 9:10

The Lord revealed to Samuel: "Tomorrow about this time I will send to you a man from the land of Benjamin, and you shall anoint him to be prince over my people Israel. He shall save my people from the hand of the Philistines; for I have seen the affliction of my people because their cry has come to me" . . . Then Samuel took a vial of oil and poured it on his head and kissed him and said, "Has not the Lord anointed you to be prince over his people Israel? And you shall reign over the people of the Lord and you will save them from the hand of their enemies round about."

1 Samuel 8

All the elders of Israel gathered together and came to Samuel at Ramah, and said to him . . . "Appoint for us a king to govern us like all the nations". . . And Samuel prayed to the Lord. And the Lord said to Samuel, "Hearken to the voice of the people in all that they say to you; for they have not rejected you, but they have rejected me from being king over them". . . So Samuel told all the words of the Lord to the people who were asking for a king from him. He said, "These will be the ways of the king who will reign over you: He will take your sons and appoint them to his chariots and to be his horsemen, and to run before his chariots; and he will appoint for himself commanders of thousands and commanders of fifties, and some to plow his ground and to reap his harvest, and to make his implements of war and the equipment of his chariots. He will take your daughters to be perfumers and cooks and bakers. He will take the best of your fields and vineyards and olive orchards and give them to his servants. He will take the tenth of your grain and of your vineyards and give it to his officers and to his servants . . . And in that day you will cry out because of your king, whom you have chosen for yourselves; but the Lord will not answer you in that day."

But the people refused to listen to the voice of Samuel; and they said, "No! but we will have a king over us, that we also may be like all the nations, and that our king may govern us and go out before us and fight our battles."

From the Holy Bible, Revised Standard Version.

---

gious capital. No longer would the Ark of the Covenant rest in the tents of Israel's nomadic ancestors. Solomon went still further, building a magnificent temple complex to house the Ark and to serve as Israel's national shrine. Just as they transformed the worship of Yahweh from rural cult to urban religion, David and Solomon restructured Israel from a tribal to a monarchical society. The old tribal structure remained only as a religious tradition. Solomon centralized land divisions, raised taxes, and increased military service in order to strengthen the monarchy.

The cost of this transformation was high. Originally the kingship was intended to be a holy office instituted by and subordinate to Yahweh, who was understood to have made an everlasting covenant with David as fulfillment of the promise of a nation to Abraham. However, under David, and especially under Solomon, the kingdom grew more tyrannical as it grew more powerful. Solomon behaved like any other king of his time. He contracted marriage alliances with neighboring princes and allowed his wives to practice their own cults. He demanded extraordinary taxes and services from his people to pay for his lavish building projects. When he was unable to pay his Phoenician creditors for supplies and workers, he deported Israelites to work as slaves in Phoenician mines.

In order to protect the covenant with Yahweh from the demands of the kings, religious leaders known as prophets, operating outside the royal power structures, criticized kings and their professional temple prophets, calling the people of Israel and its leaders to an accounting. They explained historical events in terms of the faithfulness of the Israelites to their covenant with Yahweh. The prophets were independent of royal

A terra-cotta plaque from Babylon shows a harp of the type used by the Israelites.

control and spoke out constantly against any ruler whose immorality compromised the terms of the covenant. They called upon rulers and people to reform their lives and to return to Yahweh. Some prophets were killed. Still they persisted, establishing a tradition of religious opposition to royal absolutism, a tradition which, like monotheism itself, is an enduring legacy.

Not surprisingly, the united kingdom did not survive Solomon's death. The northern region, demanding that aspirants to the throne should be tested for their faithfulness to Yahweh, broke off to become the kingdom of Israel with its capital in Shechem. The south, the kingdom of Judah, continued the tradition of David from his capital of Jerusalem. These small, weak kingdoms did not long maintain their independence. Beginning in the ninth century B.C., a new Mesopotamian power, the Assyrians, began a campaign of conquest and unprecedented brutality throughout the Near East. The Hebrew kingdoms were among their many victims. In 722 B.C., the Assyrians destroyed the kingdom of Israel and deported thousands of its people to upper Mesopotamia. Judah escaped destruction for just over a century by submitting to Assyria and becoming a dependent client state. In 586 B.C., the kingdom of Judah was conquered by Assyria's destroyers, the New Babylonian Empire under King Nebuchadnezzar II (604–562 B.C.). The temple of Solomon was destroyed, Jerusalem was burned, and Judah's elite were deported to Babylon.

During the years of exile in Babylon, intense study of the Torah, or law, took the place of temple worship. In synagogues, or houses of study, the exiles rethought the meaning of their covenant in light of the destruction of their kingdom and the temple. Increasingly, Yahweh was understood to be not one god among many but rather the one universal God, creator and ruler of the universe. Although Yahweh might be described in human terms, he was so beyond human understanding that he could not be depicted in any image.

Although beyond all earthly powers, Yahweh intervened in human history to accomplish his goals. He

In this gypsum bas-relief panel, Israelite refugees are seen sadly departing their home city of Lachish after its subjugation by the Assyrians in 701 B.C. The sculpture was commissioned by the tyrant Sennacherib to commemorate his victory.

BETWEEN TWO WORLDS

ca. 1050 B.C.	**Philistines defeat the Israelites**
ca. 1000–961 B.C.	**David, king of Israel**
ca. 961–922 B.C.	**Solomon, king of Israel**
722 B.C.	**Assyrians destroy kingdom of Israel**
604–562 B.C.	**Nebuchadnezzar II**
586 B.C.	**Nebuchadnezzar II conquers kingdom of Judah**

had formed a covenant with Abraham and renewed it with Moses and David. In the future, Yahweh would triumph through a servant whose fidelity, sufferings, and humility would be the instruments of that divine triumph. Whether this suffering servant was understood either as an individual or as those exiles who remained faithful to Yahweh, the belief was central to the exilic tradition.

The Babylonian captivity ended some fifty years later when the Persians, who had conquered Babylonia, allowed the people of Judah to return to their homeland and rebuild their temple. Those who returned did so with a new understanding of themselves and their covenant, an understanding that developed into Judaism. The fundamental figures in this transformation were Ezra and Nehemiah (fifth and fourth centuries B.C.). These important Jewish emissaries of the Persian king came to Judaea (formerly the kingdom of Judah) to revive piety by emphasizing the Torah. Ezra and Nehemiah were particularly concerned with keeping Judaism uncontaminated by other religious and cultural influences. They condemned those who had remained in Judaea and who had intermarried with foreigners during the exile. Only the exiles who had remained faithful to Yahweh and who had avoided foreign marriages could be the true interpreters of the Torah. This new, increasingly complex system of separatism and national purity, reinforced through teaching in synagogues, came to characterize the Jewish religion in the post-exilic period.

Among its leaders were a group known as Pharisees, zealous adherents to the Torah, who produced a body of oral law termed the Mishnah, or second law, by which the law of Moses was to be interpreted and safeguarded. In subsequent centuries this oral law, along with its interpretation, developed into the Talmud. Pharisees believed in resurrection and in spirits such as angels and devils, and they held some of the prophetic

books to be part of the Torah. A group of conservative, aristocratic priests and landowners called Sadducees opposed what they saw as innovations made by the Pharisees. They accepted only the first five books of the Bible as Torah and rejected such Pharisaic beliefs as resurrection.

Both traditions reinterpreted the covenant tradition within the realities of existence in a small dependent region within a great empire. The Pharisees and much of the populace believed that a messiah, or savior, would arise as a new David to reestablish Israel's political independence. Among the priestly elite, the hope for a Davidic messiah was seen as more universal: a priestly messiah would arise and bring about the kingdom of glory. Some Jews actively sought political liberation from the Persians and their successors. Others were content to cooperate with a succession of foreign rulers while preserving ritual and social purity and awaiting the messiah. Still others, such as the Essenes, withdrew into isolated communities to await the fulfillment of the prophecies.

Nineveh and Babylon

The Assyrian state that destroyed Israel accomplished what no other power had ever achieved. It tied together the floodplain civilizations of Mesopotamia and Egypt. But the Assyrian state was not just larger than the nation-states that had preceded it; it differed in nature as well as in size. The nation-states of Akkadia, Babylonia, the Hittites, and even the Egyptian empire were essentially diverse collections of city-states. Each preserved its own institutions and cultural traditions while diverting its economic resources to the capital. The Assyrian Empire was an integrated state in which conquered regions were reorganized and remade along the model of the central government. By the middle of the seventh century B.C., the Assyrian Empire stretched from the headwaters of the Tigris and Euphrates rivers to the Persian Gulf, along the coast from Syria to beyond the Delta, and up the Nile to Thebes. Now the ancient gods of Sumer were worshiped in the sanctuaries of Memphis.

The Assyrian plain north of Babylonia had long been the site of a small Mesopotamian state threatened by seminomads and great powers such as the Babylonians and later the Hittites. When King Assur-dan II mounted the throne in 934 B.C., his country was, as he himself later said, exhausted. Gradually he and his successors began to strengthen the state against its enemies

The Ishtar Gate (ca. 600 B.C.), built at Babylon during the New Babylonian Empire. The lions and fantastic dragons that flank the gateway are made of brilliantly glazed bricks.

and to allow its population to rebuild its agricultural and commercial base. The Assyrian army, forged by constant warfare into a formidable military machine, began to extend the frontiers of the kingdom in the manner of so many earlier Mesopotamian empires: both toward the Mediterranean and down the twin rivers toward the Persian Gulf. However, like its predecessors, within a century this empire seemed destined for collapse.

Rapid growth and unprecedented wealth had created a new class of noble warriors who were resented and mistrusted by the petty nobility of the old heartland of the Assyrian kingdom. The old nobility demanded a greater share in the imperial wealth and a more direct role in the administration of the empire. When the emperors ignored their demands, they began a long and bitter revolt that lasted from 827 B.C. until 750 B.C. This internal crisis put Assyria at the mercy of its external enemies, who seemed on the verge of destroying the Assyrian state. Instead, the revolt paved the way for the ascension of Tiglath-pileser III (746–727 B.C.), the greatest empire builder of Mesopotamia since Sargon. Tiglath-pileser and his successors transformed the structure of the Assyrian state and expanded its empire. They created a model for empire that would later be copied by Persia, Macedonia, and Rome. In the sense that the Assyrians not only conquered but created an administrative system by which to rule, theirs was the first true empire.

From his palace at Nineveh, Tiglath-pileser combined all of the traditional elements of Mesopotamian statecraft with a new religious ideology and social system to create the framework for a lasting multiethnic imperial system. This system rested on five bases: a transformed army, a new military-religious ideology, a novel administrative system, a social policy involving large-scale population movements, and the calculated use of massive terror.

The heart of Tiglath-pileser's program was the most modern army the world had ever seen. In place of traditional armies of peasants and slaves supplied by great aristocrats, he raised professional armies from the conquered lands of the empire and placed them under the command of Assyrian generals. The Assyrian army was also the first to use iron weapons on a massive scale. The bronze swords and shields of their enemies were no match for the stronger iron weapons of the Assyrians. Assyrian armies were also well balanced, including not only infantry, cavalry, and chariots, but also engineering units for constructing the siege equipment needed to capture towns. Warfare had become a science.

In addition to the professional army, Tiglath-pileser created the most developed military-religious ideology of any ancient people. Kings had long been agents of the gods, but Ashur, the god of the Assyrians, had but one command: Enlarge the empire! Thus warfare was the mission and duty of all, a sacred command paralleled through the centuries in the cries of "God wills it" of the Christian crusaders and the "God is great" of Muslims.

Tiglath-pileser restructured his empire, both at home in Assyria and abroad, so that revolts of the sort that had nearly destroyed it would be less possible. Within Assyria, he increased the number of administrative districts, thus decreasing the strength of each. This reduced the likelihood of successful rebellions launched by dissatisfied governors. Outside Assyria proper, the king liquidated traditional leaders whenever possible and appointed Assyrian governors or at least assigned loyal overseers to protect his interests. Even then he did not allow governors and overseers unlimited authority or discretion; instead, he kept close contact with local administrators through a system of royal messengers.

In order to shatter regional identities, which could lead to separatist movements, Tiglath-pileser deported and resettled conquered peoples on a massive scale. He sent thirty thousand Syrians to the Zagros Mountains and moved eighteen thousand Aramaeans from the Tigris to Syria. Thousands must have died of exhaustion, hunger, and thirst during these forced marches of men, women, and children. The survivors, cut off from their homelands by hundreds of miles and surrounded by people speaking different languages and practicing different religions, posed no threat to the stability of the empire.

Finally, in the tradition of his Assyrian predecessors, Tiglath-pileser and his successors maintained control of conquered peoples through a policy of unprecedented cruelty and brutality. One, for example, boasted of once having flayed an enemy's chiefs, using their skins to cover a great pillar he erected at their city gate, on which he impaled his victims. The enemy officers were treated more kindly—he simply cut off their arms and legs.

Ironically, while the imperial military and administrative system created by the Assyrians became in time the blueprint for future empires, its very ferocity led to its downfall. The hatred inspired by such brutality led to the destruction of the Assyrian Empire at the hands of a coalition of its subjects. In what is today Iran, Indo-European tribes coalesced around the Median dynasty. Egypt shook off its Assyrian lords under the leadership of the pharaoh Psamtik I (664–610 B.C.). In Babylon, which had always proven difficult for the

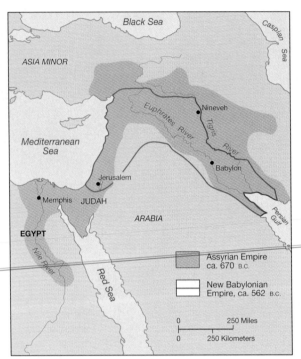

The Assyrian and New Babylonian Empires

Assyrians to control, a new Aramaean dynasty began to oppose Assyrian rule. In 612 B.C., the Medes and Babylonians joined forces to attack and destroy Nineveh. Once more, the pattern begun by Sargon—imperial expansion, consolidation, decay, and destruction—was repeated.

However, the lessons that the Assyrians taught the world were not forgotten by the Babylonians, who modeled their imperial system on that of their predecessors, even while harkening back to traditions of the Old Babylonian kingdom of Hammurabi. Administration of the New Babylonian Empire, which extended roughly over the length of the Tigris and west into Syria and Canaan, owed much to Assyrian tradition. The Code of Hammurabi once more formed the fundamental basis for justice. Babylonian kings restored and enriched temples to the Babylonian gods, and temple lands, administered by priests appointed by the king, played an important role in Babylonian economy and culture. Babylonian priests, using the mathematical methods developed during the Old Babylonian kingdom, made important advances in mathematical astronomy, laying the foundation for subsequent exact studies of heavenly bodies.

Under King Nebuchadnezzar II, the city of Babylon reached its zenith, covering some five hundred acres and containing a population of over one hundred thousand, more than twice the population of Uruk at its height. The city walls, counted among the seven wonders of the world by the later Greeks, were so wide that two chariots could ride abreast on them. And yet this magnificent fortification was never tested. In 539 B.C., a Persian army under King Cyrus II (ca. 585–ca. 529 B.C.), who had ousted the Median dynasty in 550 B.C., slipped into the city through the Euphrates riverbed at low water and took the city by surprise.

• • •

The legacy of the first three thousand years of civilization is more than a tradition of imperial conquest, exploitation, and cruelty. It goes beyond a mere catalog of discoveries, inventions, and achievements, impressive as they are. The legacy includes the basic structure of Western civilization. The floodplain civilizations and their neighbors provided the first solutions to problems of social and political organization and complex government. They built what we now recognize to have been the first cities, city-states, nation-states, and finally multinational empires. They attacked the problems of uneven distribution of natural resources through irrigation, long-distance trade, and communication. Their religious traditions, from polytheism to monotheism, provided patterns for subsequent Western religious traditions. Mesopotamian astronomy and mathematics and Egyptian engineering and building were fundamental for future civilizations. The immediate successors of these civilizations, however, would be to the west of the great river valleys, in the mountainous peninsulas and scattered islands of southern Europe.

Suggestions for Further Reading

General Reading

Cambridge Ancient History, Vol. 1, Part 1 (Cambridge: Cambridge University Press, 1970). Contains essays on every aspect of ancient civilizations.

* A. Bernard Knapp, *The History and Culture of Ancient Western Asia and Egypt* (Chicago: Dorsey Press, 1987). A good general survey of the entire period.

* Gerda Lerner, *The Creation of Patriarchy* (New York: Oxford University Press, 1986). A study of gender and politics in antiquity by a leading feminist historian.

* Barbara Lesko, "Women of Egypt and the Ancient Near East" in Renate Bridenthal, Claudia Koonz, and Susan Stuart, eds., *Becoming Visible,* 2d ed. (Boston: Houghton Mifflin, 1987). A general survey of women in ancient civilizations.

Before Civilization

* Lewis R. Binford, *In Pursuit of the Past* (New York: Thames & Hudson, 1988). A general introduction to prehistoric archaeology, intended for a general audience, by an expert.

Peter Ucko and G. W. Dimbleby, *The Domestication and Exploitation of Plants and Animals* (Chicago: Aldine, 1969). Technical essays on the origins of domestication.

Mesopotamia: Between the Two Rivers

Hans J. Nissen, *The Early History of the Ancient Near East, 9000–2000 B.C.* (Chicago: University of Chicago Press, 1988). An up-to-date survey of early Mesopotamia.

* A. L. Oppenheim, *Ancient Mesopotamia,* 2d ed. (Chicago: University of Chicago Press, 1977). Another general introduction by an expert.

* Georges Roux, *Ancient Iraq* (New York: Penguin Books, 1980). A very readable general introduction intended for a broad audience.

Morris Silver, *Economic Structures of the Ancient Near East* (New York: B&N Imports, 1985). A controversial analysis of ancient Near Eastern economy.

* O. Neugebauer, *The Exact Sciences in Antiquity* (New York: Dover, 1970). A series of technical essays on ancient mathematics and astronomy.

The Gift of the Nile

H. Frankfort, *Ancient Egyptian Religion* (New York: Harper & Row, 1961). A classic study of Egyptian religion.

* B. B. G. Trigger et al., *Ancient Egypt: A Social History* (Cambridge: Cambridge University Press, 1983). A current survey of ancient Egyptian social history by a group of experts.

Between Two Worlds

John Bright, *A History of Israel,* 3d ed. (Louisville, KY: Westminster John Knox Press, 1981). A standard history of the Israelites until the middle of the second century B.C.

* Henry Jackson Flanders, Robert Wilson Crapps, and David Anthony Smith, *People of the Covenant: An Introduction to the Old Testament,* 3d ed. (New York: Oxford University Press, 1988). A balanced introduction to Hebrew and Jewish history that draws on both Jewish and Christian scholarship.

A. T. Olmstead, *History of Assyria* (Chicago: University of Chicago Press, 1975). The fundamental survey of the Assyrian Empire.

H. W. F. Saggs, *Everyday Life in Babylonia and Assyria* (New York: Putnam, 1965). A readable account of Babylonian and Assyrian society.

*Paperback edition available.

Hecuba and Achilles

*T*he wrath of the great warrior Achilles is the
subject of Homer's *Iliad,* the first and greatest
epic poem of Greece, written shortly after 750 B.C.
Angered by a perceived slight to his honor, Achilles
sulks in his tent while the other Achaeans, or
Greeks, fight a desperate and losing battle against
their enemies, the defenders of the city of Troy.
Only after his friend Patroclus is slain by the Trojan
prince Hector does Achilles return to the battle to
avenge his fallen comrade and propel the Achaeans
to victory. Near the end of the epic, after he has
slain Hector in hand-to-hand combat, Achilles ties
his foe's body to the back of his chariot and drags it
three times around Patroclus's tomb to appease his
friend's spirit. The gods are horrified at this demeaning treatment of the body of one who had always
been faithful in his sacrifices. Zeus, the chief god,
sends his messenger Iris to Hector's mourning parents—his father, Priam, king of Troy, and his mother, Hecuba. Iris urges them to ransom their son's
body from Achilles. Moved by the message, Priam
goes to Achilles' tent to plead for Hector's body.
Achilles, moved by pity and grief for his own father
and for Patroclus, grants the old king his request,
and Priam returns in sorrow to Troy, bearing the
body of his son for burial.

The first portions of this episode are brilliantly
rendered on the side of the sixth-century B.C.
hydria, or water pitcher, shown here. At the center,
Achilles leaps into his chariot. The naked body of
Hector stretches below him, and the chariot rushes
around the *tumulus,* or burial mound, of Achilles'
friend, represented by the white hill to the right.
Above it, the small winged spirit of Patroclus watch-
es. In death he is a pale reflection, a shade of his former self, still attired in the clothing and arms of a
warrior. But even as Achilles carries out his deed of
vengeance, Iris, the winged messenger of Zeus,
rushes to Hector's parents, who are shown under a
columned portico, which represents Troy. Typically,
the artist has taken some liberty with the story. It
is not the grieving father the artist has chosen to
feature but rather Hecuba, Hector's disconsolate
mother. In a vivid manner, totally alien to previous
artistic traditions, the Greek artist, like the Greek
poet, has captured the essentials of human tragedy.

For all its violent action, the *Iliad* is concerned
less with what people do than with how they face
the great moments of their life, their time of suffering, their time of death. Hector had died well and in
so doing won immortal fame from his enemies, the
Greeks. Achilles eventually acted well, and in his
encounter with Priam faced the universal elements
of human destiny: life, love, suffering, endurance,
death. Such sentiments, expressed by Homer,
became an enduring heritage of Greek civilization
and, through it, the civilization of the West. In the
small, fragile, and violent communities of Greek-
speakers spread across the Mediterranean, citizen
soldiers first struggled with these and other fundamental issues that have set the agenda for the West
to the present day.

Greece in the Bronze Age to 700 B.C.

Early in the *Iliad* Homer pauses to list the captains and ships of the besieging forces. The roll call of heroes and their homelands is more than a literary device. It is the distant echo of a vanished world, the world of "the goodly citadel of Athens, wealthy Corinth, Knossos, and Gortys of the great walls, and the established fortress of Mycenae." The poet lived in an age of illiterate warrior herdsmen, of impoverished, scattered, and sparsely populated villages. Still, in the depths of this "Dark Age"—roughly from 1200 to 700 B.C.—the distant memory of a time of rich palaces, teeming cities, and powerful kings lived on. Homer and his contemporaries could not know that these confused memories were of the last great Bronze Age (ca. 3500–1200 B.C.) civilization of the Mediterranean. Still less could they have imagined that at the very time when they were singing of the wrath of Achilles and the lost glory of his age, they were also preparing the foundations of a far greater and lasting civilization, that of classical Greece.

Unlike the rich floodplains of Mesopotamia and Egypt, Greece is a stark world of mountains and sea. The rugged terrain of Greece, only 10 percent of which

A marble statue of a seated harp player from the Cyclades Islands, dating from the third millennium B.C. The statue is executed in great detail despite the primitive tools at the sculptor's disposal.

is flat, and the scores of islands that dot the Aegean and Ionian seas favor the development of small, self-contained agricultural societies. The Greek climate is uncertain, constantly threatening Greek farmers with failure. While temperature remains fairly constant, rainfall varies enormously from year to year, island to island, valley to valley. Arid summers alternate with cool, wet winters. Greek farmers struggled to produce the Mediterranean triad of grains, olives, and wine, which first began to dominate agriculture around 3000 B.C. Wheat, barley, and beans were the staples of Greek life. Chickpeas, lentils, and bread, supplemented with olive oil, wine, and cheese, filled the stomachs of Greek farmers and townspeople. Only on rare holidays did ordinary folk see fish or perhaps some mutton on their tables. When the rains came too soon or too late, even bread and beans might be missing. The constant fluctuations in climate and weather from region to region helped break down the geographical isolation by forcing isolated communities to build contacts with a wider world in order to survive.

Islands of Peace

To Homer, the Greeks were all Achaeans no matter whether they came from the Greek mainland, the islands in the Aegean Sea, or the coast of Asia Minor. Since the late nineteenth century, archaeologists have discerned three fairly distinct late Bronze Age cultures—the Cycladic, the Minoan, and the Mycenaean—that flourished in the Mediterranean prior to the end of the twelfth century B.C.

The first culture appeared on the Cyclades, the rugged islands strewn across the bottom of the Aegean from the Greek mainland to the coast of Asia Minor. As early as 2500 B.C., artisans in small settlements on the islands of Naxos and Melos developed a high level of metallurgical and artistic skill. Veins of lead and silver run through the hills of the Cyclades. Local people perfected techniques of working these metals, methods that later traveled both north to the mainland and south to Crete. The most impressive and enigmatic remains of the Cycladic culture (ca. 3000–ca. 1550 B.C.) are marble figurines, both male and female, found in large numbers in graves on the mainland, the islands themselves, and in Asia Minor. These severe geometrical figures presumably had a religious significance that is now unknown.

Cycladic society was not concentrated into towns, nor apparently was it particularly warlike. Many of the largest Cycladic settlements were unfortified. Cycladic

Greece in the Bronze Age

Cycladic culture
ca. 2500 B.C.–ca. 1900 B.C.

Minoan culture
ca. 2000 B.C.–ca. 1400 B.C.

Mycenaean culture
ca. 1600 B.C.–ca. 1100 B.C.
(boundary represents 1250 B.C.)

religion, to judge from fragments of large clay statues of female figures found in a temple on the island of Ceos, focused on female deities, perhaps fertility goddesses.

This early Bronze Age society faded slowly and imperceptibly, but not before influencing its neighbors, especially Crete, the large Mediterranean island to the south. There, beginning around 2500 B.C., developed a remarkably sophisticated centralized civilization termed Minoan after the legendary King Minos.

Knowledge of Minoan civilization burst upon the modern world suddenly in 1899. In that year the English archaeologist Sir Arthur Evans made the first of a series of extraordinary archaeological discoveries at Knossos, the legendary palace of Minos. Since then, additional centers have been found on the southern and eastern coasts of the island as well as at Chania in the northwest. Crete's location between the civilizations of the Fertile Crescent and the barbarian worlds of the north and west made the island a natural point

of exchange and amalgamation of cultures. Still, during the golden age of Crete, roughly between 2000 and 1550 B.C., the island developed unique traditions. Great palace complexes were constructed at Knossos, Phaistos, Hagia Triada, and elsewhere on the island. They appear as a maze of storerooms, workrooms, and living quarters clustered around a central square. Larger public rooms may have existed at an upper level, but all traces of them have disappeared. The walls of these palaces still display frescoes that present a vivid image of Cretan life in the late Bronze Age. Some frescoes depict crowds of prosperous Cretans watching as court ladies dance under olive trees or as male and female athletes practice the deadly sport of vaulting over the backs of ferocious bulls. Other wall paintings show aristocratic women, elaborately clothed in sumptuous dresses that leave their breasts exposed, engaged in conversation while the athletic spectacle unfurls before them.

In the Toreador Fresco from the Cretan Palace of Minos, dating from about 1500 B.C., one daring wasp-waisted athlete vaults over the back of a charging bull while another holds the bull by the horns. The bull played a major role in Minoan religious symbolism.

Palace bureaucrats, using a unique form of syllabic writing known as Linear A, controlled agricultural production and distribution as well as the work of skilled artisans in their surrounding areas. A well-maintained road system connected the cities across the island, especially between Knossos, the capital, and Phaistos in the south, which may have been a winter palace. Towns with well-organized street plans, drainage systems, and clear hierarchies of elite and lesser homes dotted the landscape.

Like other ancient civilizations, Minoan Crete was a strongly stratified system in which the vast peasantry paid a heavy tribute in olive oil and other produce. Tribute or taxes flowed to local and regional palaces and ultimately to Knossos, which stood at the pinnacle of a four-tier network uniting the island. To some extent, the palace elites redistributed this wealth back down the system through their patterns of consumption. However, the abundance of luxury imports at Knossos, Phaistos, and elsewhere indicate that much of the wealth amassed by the elite was consumed by the great numbers of palace servants and artisans or went abroad to pay for the Egyptian and Syriac luxury goods, Italian metal, and Baltic amber found in abundance in the ruins.

Though the system may have been exploitative, it was not militaristic. None of the palaces or towns of Crete was fortified. The delicate and naturalistic frescoes and statues never depict warriors, weapons, or battles. Nor was the cult of the ruler particularly emphasized. The throne room at Knossos is modest, and none of its decorations suggest the sort of royal aggrandizement typical in the Mesopotamian, Hittite, or Egyptian worlds. Monumental architecture and sculpture designed to exalt the ruler and to overwhelm the commoner is entirely absent from Crete. A key to this unique social tone may be Cretan religion, and with it the unusually high status of women. Although male gods received veneration, Cretans particularly worshiped female deities, whose cults were centered in some twenty-five caves scattered across the island. Here and at the palaces, bulls and bulls' horns as well as the double-headed ax, or *labris,* played an important—if today mysterious—role in the worship of these gods. Chief among the female deities was the mother goddess, who was the source of good and evil. One must, however, be careful not to paint too idyllic an image of Cretan religion. Children's bones found in excavations of the palace of Knossos show traces of butchering and the removal of slices of flesh. Other hints at human sacrifice have been found at Archanes, immediately behind the Knossos palace.

Although evidence such as the frequent appearance of women participating in or watching public ceremonies and the widespread worship of female deities cannot lead to the conclusion that Minoan society was a form of matriarchy, it does suggest that Minoan civilization differed considerably from the floodplain civilizations of the Near East and the societies developing on the mainland. At least until the fourteenth century B.C., Cretan society was truly unique. Both men and women seem to have shared important roles in religious and public life and together built a structured society without the need for vast armies or warrior kings.

Around 1450 B.C., a wave of destruction engulfed all of the Cretan cities except Knossos, which finally met destruction around 1375 B.C. The causes of this catastrophe continue to inspire historical debate. Some argue that a natural disaster such as an earthquake or the eruption of a powerful volcano on Thera was responsible for the destruction. More likely, given the martial traditions of the continent and their total absence on Crete, the destruction was the work of mainland Greeks taking control of Knossos and other Minoan centers. An Egyptian tomb painting from the fifteenth century B.C. graphically illustrates the transition. An ambassador in Cretan dress was overpainted by one wearing a kilt characteristic of that worn by mainland Greeks. Around this same time, true warrior graves equipped with weapons and armor begin to appear on Crete and at Knossos for the first time. Following this violent conquest, only Knossos and Phaistos were rebuilt, presumably by Greek lords who had eliminated the other political centers on the island. A final destruction hit Knossos around 1200 B.C.

Mainland of War

The contrast between the islands and the Greek mainland was particularly marked. Around 1600 B.C., a new and powerful warrior civilization arose on the Peloponnesus at Mycenae. The only remains of the first phase of this civilization are thirty graves found at the bottom of deep shafts arranged in two circles, but they tell of a rich, powerful, and warlike elite. The delicate gold ornaments, bronze swords, spearheads, knives, axes, armor, and utensils that fill the graves emphasize the warrior lives of their occupants. By 1500 B.C., mainland Greeks were using huge *tholoi,* or beehive-shaped tombs, for royal burials. These structures were magnificent achievements of architecture and masonry, far beyond anything seen previously in Europe. The largest, found at Mycenae and erroneously called the Treasury of Atreus after a character of Greek myth, is forty-eight feet in diameter and forty-three feet from the floor to its vaulted ceiling. This great vault, capped by a stone weighing over one hundred tons, was the largest vault in the world for over sixteen hundred years, surpassed only by Roman architects at the height of the Roman Empire. Over fifty such tombs have been found on the Greek mainland, as have the remains of over five hundred villages and great palaces at Mycenae, Tiryns, Athens, Thebes, Gla, and Pylos. This entire civilization, which encompassed not only the Greek mainland but also parts of the coast of Asia Minor, is called Mycenaean, although there is no evidence that the city of Mycenae actually ruled all of Greece.

The Mycenaeans quickly adopted artisanal and architectural techniques from neighboring cultures, especially from the Hittites and from Crete. However, the Mycenaeans incorporated these techniques into a distinctive tradition of their own. Unlike the open Cretan palaces and towns, Mycenaean palaces were strongly walled fortresses. From these palaces Mycenaean kings, aided by a small military elite, organized and controlled the collection of taxes and tribute from subordinate towns and rural districts. Through their palace administrators, they controlled the production of bronze, the weaving of woolen cloth, and the extensive maritime trade in agricultural produce with other regions.

A bronze dagger blade showing a lion hunt in inlaid gold and silver, dating from around 1500 B.C., was found at the Citadel of Mycenae.

Mycenaean administrators also adopted the Linear A script of Crete, transforming it to write their own language, a Greek dialect, in a writing known as Linear B. Linear B appears to have been used almost exclusively for record keeping in palaces—indicating amounts of tribute, the organization of workers, and the quantities of weapons, sheep, and slaves engaged in various religious and palace duties.

The Dark Age

Mycenaean domination did not last for long. Around 1200 B.C., many of the mainland and island fortresses and cities were sacked and totally destroyed. In some areas, such as Pylos, the population fell to roughly 10 percent of what it had been previously, while in others, such as Patras, population grew but remained dispersed. Centralized government, literacy, urban life, civilization itself disappeared from Greece for over four hundred years. Why and how this happened is one of the great mysteries of world history.

The Lion Gate at Mycenae. On a stone slab atop a huge lintel, two lions face each other across a sacred column of the type found at Knossos on Crete. The heads, now lost, were made of separate pieces of metal or stone.

In later centuries the Greeks believed that following the Trojan War, new peoples, especially the Dorians, had migrated into Greece, destroying Mycenae and most of the other Achaean cities. More recently, some historians have argued that catastrophic climatic change, volcanic eruptions, or some other natural disaster wrecked the cities and brought famine and tremendous social unrest in its wake. Neither theory is accurate. No single invasion or natural disaster caused the collapse of the civilizations of late Bronze Age Greece. Mycenaean Greece was destroyed neither by barbarian invaders nor by acts of God. It self-destructed. Its disintegration was part of the widespread crisis affecting the eastern Mediterranean in the twelfth century B.C. (see chapter 1, p. 23). The pyramid of Mycenaean lordship, built by small military elites commanding maritime commercial networks, was always threatened with collapse. Overpopulation, the fragility of the agrarian base, the risks of overspecialization in cash crops such as grain in Messenia and in sheep raising in Crete, and rivalry among states—all made Mycenaean culture vulnerable. The disintegration of the Hittite empire and the near-collapse of the Egyptian empire disrupted Mediterranean commerce, exacerbating hostilities among Greek states. As internal warfare raged, the delicate structures of elite lordship disappeared in the mutual sackings and destructions of the palace fortresses. The Dark Age poet Hesiod (ca. 800 B.C.), though writing about his own time, probably got it about right:

> *Father will have no common bond with son*
> *Neither will guest with host, nor friend with friend*
> *The brother-love of past days will be gone. . . .*
> *Men will destroy the towns of other men.*

With the collapse of the administrative and political system on which Mycenaean civilization was built, the tiny elite that had ruled it vanished as well. Some of these rulers probably migrated to the islands, especially Cyprus, and the eastern Mediterranean. Others took to piracy, alternately raiding the coast from Anatolia to Egypt and serving as mercenaries in foreign armies. What later Greeks remembered as the Trojan War may have been a cloudy recollection of the last raids of freebooters along the edge of the collapsing Hittite empire. From roughly 1200 until 800 B.C., the Aegean world entered what is generally termed the Dark Age, a confused and little-known period during which Greece returned to a more primitive level of culture and society.

GREECE IN THE BRONZE AGE

ca. 2500 B.C.	**Beginning of Minoan civilization in Crete**
ca. 2000–1500 B.C.	**Golden Age of Crete**
ca. 1600 B.C.	**Beginning of Mycenaean civilization in Greece**
ca. 1450 B.C.	**Cretan cities, except Knossos, destroyed**
ca. 1375 B.C.	**Knossos destroyed**
ca. 1200–700 B.C.	**Greek Dark Age**
ca. 1200 B.C.	**Mycenaean sites in Greece destroyed; Knossos destroyed again**
ca. 1100–1000 B.C.	**Writing disappears from Greece**

In the wake of the Mycenaean collapse, bands of northerners moved slowly into the Peloponnesus while other Greeks migrated out from the mainland to the islands and the coast of Asia Minor. As these tribal groups merged with the indigenous populations, they gave certain regions distinctive dialectic and cultural characteristics. Thus the Dorians settled in much of the Peloponnesus, Crete, and southwest Asia Minor. Ionians made Attica, Euboea, and the Aegean islands their home, while a mixed group called Aeolians began to migrate to central and northwest Asia Minor. As a result, from the eleventh century B.C., both shores of the Aegean became part of a Greek-speaking world. Still later, Greeks established colonies in what are today Ukraine, Italy, North Africa, Spain, and France. Throughout its history, Greece was less a geographical than a cultural designation.

Everywhere in this world, between roughly 1100 and 1000 B.C., architecture, urban traditions, and even writing disappeared along with the elites whose exclusive benefit these achievements had served. The Greece of this Dark Age was much poorer, more rural, and more simply organized. It was also a society of iron-workers. Iron began to replace bronze as the most common metal for ornaments, tools, and weapons. At first this was a simple necessity. The collapse of long-distance trade deprived Greeks of access to tin and copper, the essential ingredients of bronze. Gradually, however, the quality of iron tools and weapons began to improve as smiths learned to work hot iron into a primitive steel.

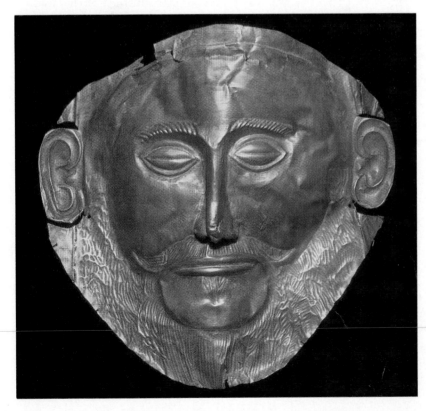

A golden funeral mask (ca. 1500 B.C.) found in the royal tombs of Mycenae. The mask may be the likeness of Agamemnon, the king of Mycenae in the Homeric epics.

Hector and Andromache

The Trojan hero Hector is almost as central to the Iliad *of Homer as is Achilles. Unlike the latter, Hector is a dutiful, reliable support to his city and to Andromache, who is not only his wife but his closest and dearest companion. The description of their last meeting is one of the great expressions of the heroic ethos and of the bonds of man and woman in that culture.*

At last his own generous wife came running to meet him,
Andromache, the daughter of high-hearted Eëation . . .
She came to him there, and beside her went an attendant carrying
the boy in the fold of her bosom, a little child, only a baby,
Hector's son, the admired, beautiful as a star shining . . .
Andromache, stood close beside him, letting her tears fall,
and clung to his hand and called him by name and spoke to him:
"Dearest, your own great strength will be your death, and you
have no pity on your little son, nor on me, ill-starred, who soon
    must be your widow". . .
Then tall Hector of the shining helm answered her: "All these
things are in my mind also, lady; yet I would feel deep shame
before the Trojans, and the Trojan women with trailing garments,
if like a coward I were to shrink aside from fighting . . .
But it is not so much the pain to come of the Trojans
that troubles me . . . as the thought of you, when some bronze-
armored Achaian leads you off, taking away your day of liberty in
tears; and in Argos you must work at the loom of another". . .
Then taking up his dear son he tossed him about in his arms and
 kissed him, and lifted his voice in prayer to Zeus and the other immortals:
"Zeus, and you other immortals, grant that this boy, who is my
son, may be as I am, pre-eminent among the Trojans,
great in strength, as I am, and rule strongly over Ilion;
And someday let them say of him: 'He is better by far than his father,'
as he comes from the fighting; and let him kill his enemy
and bring home the blooded spoils, and delight the heart of his mother."

From the *Iliad* of Homer, Book VI.

What little is known of this period must be gleaned from archaeology and from two great epic poems written down around 750 B.C., near the end of the Dark Age. The archaeological record is bleak. Pictorial representation of humans and animals almost disappears. Luxury goods and most imports are gone from tombs. Gold ornaments and jewelry are so rare that they may have come from some Mycenaean hoard found by Dark Age Greeks rather than from contemporary arti-sans. Pottery made at the beginning of the Dark Age shows little innovation, crudely imitating forms of Mycenaean production.

Gradually, beginning in the eleventh century B.C., things began to change a bit. New geometric forms of decoration begin to appear on pottery. New types of iron pins, weapons, and decorations appeared that owe little or nothing to the Mycenaean tradition. Cultural changes accompanied these material changes. Around the middle of the eleventh century B.C., Greeks in some locations stopped burying their dead and began to practice cremation. Whatever the meaning of these changes, they signaled something new on the shores of the Aegean.

The two epic poems the *Iliad* and the *Odyssey* hint at this something new. The *Iliad* is the older poem, dating probably to the second half of the eighth century B.C. The *Odyssey* dates from perhaps fifty years later. Traditionally ascribed to Homer, these epics were actually the work of oral bards, or performers who composed as they chanted, weaving the tale of traditional lines and expressions as they went along. The world in which the action of the Homeric epics takes place was already passing away when the poems were composed, but the world described is not really that of the late Bronze Age. Although the poems explicitly harken back to the Mycenaean age, much of the description of life, society, and culture actually reflects Dark Age conditions.

Thus Homer's heroes were petty kings, chieftains, and nobles, whose position rested on their wealth, measured in land and flocks, on personal prowess, on networks of kin and allies, and on military followings. The Homeric hero Odysseus is typical of these Dark Age chieftains. In the *Iliad* and the *Odyssey* he is king of Ithaca, a small island off the west coast of Greece. He had inherited his kingship from his father, but he derived his real authority from his skills as a speaker and warrior. To the Homeric poets he was "goodly Odysseus" as well as "the man of wiles" and "the waster of cities." He retained command of his men only as long as he could lead them to victory in raids against their neighbors, which formed the most honorable source of wealth. Odysseus describes his departure for home after the fall of Troy with pride:

> The wind that bore me from Ilios brought me . . . to Ismarus, whereupon I sacked their city and slew the people. And from the city we took their wives and much goods, and divided them among us, that none through me might go lacking his proper share.

Present, the king was judge, gift giver, lawgiver, and commander. But when he was absent, no legal or governmental institutions preserved his authority. Instead the nobility—lesser warriors who were constantly at odds with the king—sought to take his place. In the *Odyssey* only their mutual rivalry saves Odysseus's wife, Penelope, from being forced to marry one of these haughty aristocrats eager to replace the king.

These nobles—warriors wealthy enough to possess horses and weapons—lived to prove their strength and honor in combat against their equals, which was the one true test of social value. The existence of chieftains such as Odysseus was a threat to their honor, and by the eighth century B.C., the aristocracy had eliminated kings in most places. Ranking beneath these proud warriors, as a shadowy mass, was the populace. Some of this group, like Odysseus's faithful servants who aided him in defeating his enemies upon his return home, were slaves. Most were shepherds or farmers too mired down in the laborious work of subsistence agriculture to participate in the heroic lifestyle of their social betters. Still, even the populace were not entirely excluded from public life. Odysseus's son Telemachus summoned an assembly of the people to listen to his complaints against the noble suitors of his mother. This does not mean that the assembly was particularly effective. They listened to both sides and did nothing. Still, a time was coming when changes in society would give a new and hitherto unimagined power to the silent farmers and herdsmen of the Dark Age.

From the Bronze Age civilizations, speakers of Greek had inherited distant memories of an original, highly organized urban civilization grafted onto the rural, aristocratic warrior society of the Dark Age. Most importantly, this common, dimly recollected past gave all Greek-speaking inhabitants of the Mediterranean world common myths, values, and identity.

A vase painting of farmers harvesting olives. Olive oil was an important commodity in Greek commerce.

In this vase painting, a man drives two oxen pulling a plowshare while another farmer scatters seed in the furrows.

Archaic Greece, 700–500 B.C.

Between roughly 800 and 500 B.C., extraordinary changes took place in the Greek world. The descendants of the farmers and herdsmen of Homer's Dark Age brought about a revolution in political organization, artistic traditions, intellectual values, and social structures. In a burst of creativity forged in conflict and competition, they invented politics, invented abstract thought, invented the individual. Greeks of the Archaic Age (ca. 700–500 B.C.) set the agenda for the rest of Western history.

The first sign of radical change in Greece was a major increase in population in the eighth century B.C. In Attica, for example, between 780 and 720 B.C. the population increased perhaps sevenfold. Similar rapid population growth occurred throughout the Greek world. The reasons for this extraordinary increase are obscure, but it may have resulted from a shift from herding to agriculture. In any case, the consequences were enormous. First, population increase meant more villages and towns, greater communication among them, and thus the more rapid circulation of ideas and skills. Second, the rising population placed impossible demands on the agricultural system of much of Greece, overcrowding the land and forcing many farmers into poverty and many others into migration. Third, it led to greater division of labor and, with an increasingly diverse population, to fundamental changes in political systems. The old structure of loosely organized tribes and chieftains became inadequate to deal with the more complex nature of the new society.

The multiplicity of political and social forms developing in the Archaic Age set the framework in which developed the first flowering of Greek culture. Economic and political transformations laid the basis for intellectual advance by creating a broad class with the prosperity to enjoy sufficient leisure for thought and creative activity. At the same time, literacy and local pride allowed the new citizen populations of the Greek cities to participate in intellectual and cultural activities in an unprecedented manner. Finally, maritime relations brought people and ideas from around the Greek world together, cross-fertilizing artists and intellectuals in a way never before seen.

Ethnos and Polis

In general, two forms of political organization developed in response to the population explosion of the eighth century B.C. On the mainland and in much of the western Peloponnesus, people continued to live in large territorial units called *ethne* (sing. *ethnos*). In each ethnos people lived in villages and small towns scattered across a wide region. Common customs and a common religion focusing on a central religious sanctuary united them. The ethnos was governed by an elite, or *oligarchy* (meaning "rule by the few") made up of major landowners who met from time to time in one or another town within the region. This form of government, which had its roots in the Dark Age, continued to exist throughout the classical period.

A much more innovative form of political organization, which developed on the shores of the Aegean and on the islands, was the *polis* (pl. *poleis*), or city-state. Initially, *polis* meant simply "citadel." Villages clustered around these fortifications, which were both protective structures and cult centers for specific deities. These high fortified sites—*acropolis* means "high citadel"—were sacred to specific gods: in Athens and Sparta, to Athena; in Argos and Samos, to Hera; at Corinth and Thermon, to Apollo. In addition to protection, the polis offered a marketplace, or *agora,* where farmers and artisans could trade and conduct business. The rapid population growth of the eighth century B.C. led to the fusion of these villages and the formation of real towns. Each town was independent, each was ruled by a monarch or an oligarchy, and each controlled the surrounding region, the inhabitants of which were on an equal footing with the townspeople. At times of political or military crisis, the rulers might summon an assembly of the free males of the community to the agora to participate in or to witness the decision-making process. In the following centuries, these city-states became the center for that most dramatic Greek experiment in government—democracy.

The general model of the polis may have been borrowed from the eastern Mediterranean Phoenicians, the merchant society responsible for much of the contact Greeks of the eighth century B.C. had with the outside world. On the other hand, by 800 B.C. the Greeks themselves had a permanent trading post at Al Mina on the Syrian coast and thus were in direct contact with the traditions of the Near East. The Phoenicians were certainly the source of an equally important innovation that appeared in Greece at the same time: the reintroduction of writing. The Linear B script, which the Mycenaeans had used exclusively for administrative and bureaucratic purposes, had entirely disappeared, along with the complex palace systems that it had served. Sometime in the eighth century B.C., Greeks adopted the Phoenician writing system. But this time the purpose was not primarily central administrative record keeping. From the start this writing system was intended for private, personal use and was available to virtually anyone. In a society fascinated with the oral traditions of the heroic past, it is no surprise that the Greeks radically transformed the Phoenician system, making its Semitic characters into arbitrary sounds and adding vowel notation in order to record poetry. Soon this writing system was being used to indicate ownership of objects, to record religious and secular vows, and even to entertain.

Within the polis, political power was not the monopoly of the aristocracy. The gradual expansion of the politically active population resulted largely from the demands of warfare. In the Dark Age, warfare had been dominated by heavily armed mounted aristocrats

A Corinthian vase showing hoplites marching into battle.

who engaged their equals in single combat. In the Archaic Age, such individual combat between aristocratic warriors gave way to battles decided by the use of well-disciplined ranks of infantrymen called *phalanges* (sing. *phalanx*). Properly disciplined, the phalanx could withstand attacks of better-equipped aristocratic warriors. And while few Greeks could afford costly weapons, armor, and horses, between 25 and 40 percent of the landowners could provide the shields, lances, and bronze armor needed by the infantrymen, or *hoplites.* These foot soldiers developed their own warrior pride, equal to but differing from that of the aristocrat. In the words of Tyrtaeus, a poet of the mid-seventh century B.C., the hoplite was to "stand near and take the enemy, strike with long spear or sword, set foot by foot, lean shield on shield, crest upon crest, helmet on helmet." The democratization of war led gradually to the democratization of political life. Those who brought victory in the phalanx were unwilling to accept total domination by the aristocracy in the agora. Growing demands of the common people, combined with demographic expansion and economic changes, created enormous social and political tensions throughout the Greek world. The rapid growth of the urban population, the increasing impoverishment of the rural peasantry, and the rise of a new class of wealthy merchant commoners were all challenges that traditional forms of government failed to meet. Everywhere traditional aristocratic rule was being undermined, and cities searched for ways to resolve this social conflict. No one solution emerged, and one of the outstanding achievements of archaic Greece was the almost limitless variety of political forms elaborated in its city-states.

Colonists and Tyrants

Colonization and tyranny were two intertwined results of the political and social turmoil of the seventh century B.C. Population growth, changes in economy, and opposition to aristocratic power led Greeks to seek change externally through emigration and internally through political restructuring.

Late in the eleventh century B.C., Greeks began to migrate to new homes on the islands and along the coast of Asia Minor, in search of commercial advantages or a better life. Many of these communities, such as Rhodes, Miletus, Ephesus, and Erythrae, probably renewed older Greek traditions from the Mycenaean period. By the eighth century B.C., Greeks had pushed still farther east in search of sources for bronze. Euboeans established a permanent trading community at Al Mina in northern Syria, and Greeks established themselves in other eastern towns such as Tarsus.

Beginning around 750 B.C., a new form of colonization began in the western Mediterranean. The impetus for this expansion was not primarily trade, but rather the need to reduce population pressure at home. The first noteworthy colony, Cumae near Naples, was founded by emigrants from Euboea. Soon other cities sent colonists to southern Italy and Sicily. Chalcis founded Messina, Corinth founded Syracuse, and Achaea founded Sybaris, to name a few. Before long, these colonies themselves became mother cities, sending out parties to found still other colonies. Around 700 B.C., similar colonies appeared in the northeast in Thrace, on the shores of the Black Sea, and as far as the mouth of the Don River.

Colonists were not always volunteers. At Thera, for example, young men were chosen by lot to colonize Cyrene. The penalty for refusing to participate was death and confiscation of property. According to tradition, Sparta sent illegitimate sons to found Tarentum, and other cities forced political dissidents to emigrate. Usually colonists included only single males, the most volatile portion of the community. Colonies were thus a safety valve to release the pressures of population growth and political friction.

Although colonies remained attached culturally to their mother cities, they were politically independent. The men who settled them were warriors as well as farmers or traders and they carved out their new cities at the expense of the local population. Intermarriage was the norm, but so was the conquest and enslavement of much of the original population, followed by a gradual absorption of natives into Greek civilization.

Colonization relieved some of the population pressure on Greek communities, but it did not solve the problem of political conflict. As opposition to entrenched aristocracies grew, first in Argos, then at Corinth, Sicyon, Elis, Mytilene, and elsewhere, individuals supported by those opposed to aristocratic rule seized power. These rulers were known as *tyrants,* a term that originally meant the same as "king." In the course of the later sixth century B.C., *tyrant* came to designate those who had achieved supreme power without benefit of official position. Often, this rise to power came through popularity with hoplite armies. However, the term *tyrant* did not carry the negative connotation associated with it today. Early tyrants were generally welcomed by their fellow citizens and played a crucial role in the destruction of aristocratic government and the creation of civic traditions.

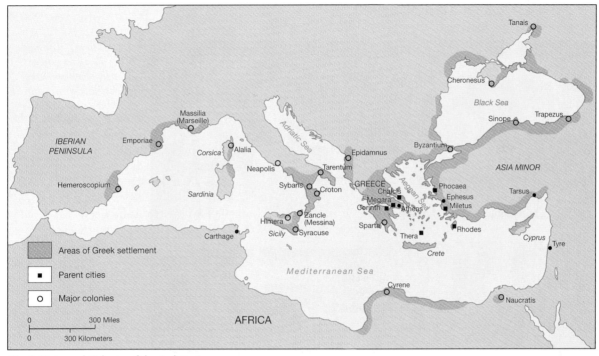

Greek Cities and Colonies of the Archaic Age

Generally, tyrants were motivated not so much by great civic spirit as by the desire to win and maintain power. Still, to this end they weakened the power of entrenched aristocratic groups, promoted the prosperity of their supporters by protecting farmers and encouraging trade, undertook public works projects, founded colonies, and entered marriage alliances with rulers of other cities, which provided some external peace. Although they stood outside the traditional organs of government, tyrants were frequently content to govern through them, leaving magistracies and offices intact but ensuring that through elections these offices were filled with the tyrant's supporters. Thus at Corinth, Mytilene, Athens, and elsewhere, tyrants preserved and even strengthened constitutional structures as a hedge against the return to power of aristocratic factions.

The great weakness of tyrannies was that they depended for their success on the individual qualities of the ruler. Tyrants tended to pass their powers on to their sons and, as tyrannies became hereditary, cities came to resent incompetent or excessively harsh heirs' arbitrary control of government. This process seldom took more than three generations. As popular tyranny gave way to harsh and arbitrary rule, opposition brought on civil war and the deposition or abdication of the tyrant. Gradually, tyranny acquired the meaning it bears today, and new forms of government emerged.

Still, in spite of the bitter memory Greek tyranny left in people's minds, in many cities tyrants had for a time solved the crisis of political order and had cleared the way for broader participation in public life than had ever before been known.

Greek commerce expanded along with the colonies. In the painting on the interior of the Arkesilas Cup, dating from around 560 B.C., the king of Cyrene, a Greek colony in North Africa, is shown supervising the preparation of hemp or flax for export.

A detail from a vase made in the fourth century B.C. in Sicily shows courtesans entertaining guests with music at a symposium, or drinking party.

Gender and Power

Military, political, and cultural life in the city-states became more democratic, but this democratization did not extend to women. Greek attitudes toward gender roles and sexuality were rigid. Except in a few cities, and in certain religious cults, women played no public role in the life of the community. They were isolated in the portions of the home reserved for them and remained firmly under male control throughout their lives, passing from the authority of their fathers to that of their husbands. Women were to be good mothers and obedient wives, not partners or close friends. For the most part friendship existed only between members of the same sex, and this friendship was often intensely sexual. Thus bisexuality was the norm in Greek society, although neither Greek homosexuality nor heterosexuality were the same as they are in modern society. Rather, both coexisted and formed a part of a sexuality of domination by those considered superior in age, rank, or sex over others. Mature men took young boys as their lovers, helped educate them, and inspired them by word and deed to grow into ideal warriors and citizens. We know less about such practices among women, but teachers such as Sappho of Lesbos (ca. 610–ca. 580 B.C.) formed similar bonds with their pupils, even while preparing them for marriage.

Those women who were in public life were mostly slaves, frequently prostitutes. These ranged from impoverished streetwalkers to *hetairai*—educated, sophisticated courtesans who entertained men at *symposia* (sing. *symposion*), or male banquets, which were the centers of cultural and social life. Many female slaves were acquired by collecting and raising infant daughters who had been abandoned by impoverished families or those who simply did not want any more daughters. Greek society did not condemn or even question infanticide, prostitution, and sexual exploitation of women and slave boys. These practices formed part of the complex and varied social systems of the developing city-states.

Gods and Mortals

Greeks and their gods enjoyed an ambivalent, peculiar, almost irreverent relationship. On the one hand, Greeks made regular offerings to the gods, pleaded with them for help, and gave them thanks for assistance. On the other hand, the gods were thoroughly human, sharing in an exaggerated manner not only human strengths and virtues but also weaknesses and vices.

Greeks offered sacrifices to the gods on altars, which were raised everywhere—in homes, in fields, in sacred groves. Normally, the priests responsible for these rituals were lay people, often political and military leaders, but no group had the sort of monopoly on the cult of the gods enjoyed by Mesopotamian and Egyptian priests. Beginning in the Dark Age, cities dedicated open-air altars to the gods, often on the acropolis. In time, these altars were enclosed within temples. However, unlike the temples of other societies, Greek temples were houses of the gods, not centers of ritual. The earliest temples were constructed of wood or brick. Around 700 B.C., the first stone temples appeared, and shortly afterward the Greek temple achieved its classic form. The so-called Doric temple consisted of an oblong or rectangular room covered by a pitched roof and circled by columns. These temples, which housed a statue of the god, were otherwise largely empty. Although dedicated to the gods, temples reflected the wealth and patriotism of the city. They stood as monuments to the human community rather than to the divine.

On special occasions, festivals celebrated at sanctuaries honored the gods of the city with processions, athletic contests, and feasts. Some of these celebrations were local, some involved the whole polis or ethnos, while others drew participants from all of the Greek world. The two greatest pan-Hellenic (meaning "all Greek," from *Hellas,* the Greek word for Greece) sanctuaries were Olympia and Delphi. Because both were remote from centers of political power, they were insulated from interstate rivalry and provided neutral ground on which hostile neighbors could meet in peace.

Olympia was the main sanctuary of Zeus and had been a cult site since the Bronze Age. Beginning in 776 B.C., every four years, wars and conflicts were temporarily suspended while athletes from the whole Greek world met at Olympia to participate in contests in honor of Zeus. Initially, the sports included only footraces and wrestling. In the sixth century B.C., horse races and other events were added and the games at Olympia grew in importance. (See "The Agony of Athletics," pp. 50–51.) The religious nature of the contests lowered neither their heated interstate rivalry nor the violence with which they were pursued. Wrestling in particular could be deadly, since matches continued until one participant signaled that he had had enough. Many wrestlers chose death rather than defeat. Victors were seen as the ideals of human society, the perfect triumph of body and soul, and Olympic victors were treated as national heroes. As Greek culture slowly spread through the Mediterranean world, so did participation in the Olympics, which continued for over one thousand years, ending only in A.D. 393.

Delphi, the site of the shrine of Apollo, god of music, archery, medicine, and prophecy, was the second pan-Hellenic cult center. Like Olympia, Delphi drew athletes from the whole Greek world to its athletic contests. However, Delphi's real fame lay in its oracle, or spokeswoman for the god Apollo. From the eighth century B.C., before undertaking any important decision such as establishing a colony, beginning a war, or even contracting a marriage, individuals and representatives of distant cities traveled to Delphi to ask Apollo's advice. In the turbulent seventh and sixth centuries B.C., Apollo was the acknowledged expert on justice. Through his oracle he guided petitioners seeking purification from the guilt attached to shedding others' blood and reconciliation with their fellow citizens. For a stiff fee, visitors were allowed to address questions to the god through a female medium. She entered a trance state and uttered a reply, which lay priests at the shrine then put into verse form and transmitted to the petitioner. The ambiguity of the Delphic replies was legendary. Petitioners had to interpret the answers they received as best they could.

A vase painting showing the Pythia, the priestess of Delphi, seated on her tripod. She holds a branch of the laurel plant, which is sacred to her patron, the god Apollo. The petitioner standing at right will most likely receive an enigmatic reply to his question.

❧ The Agony of Athletics

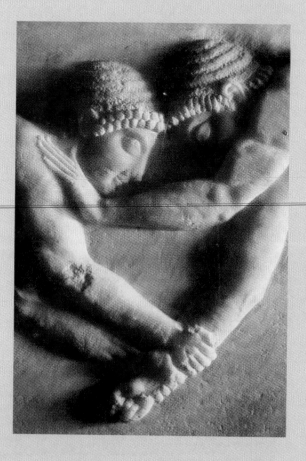

The Greeks did not play sports. Our word *play* is related to the Greek word *pais* (child), and there was nothing childish about Greek athletics. The Greek word was *agonia,* and our modern derivation, *agony,* hits closer to the mark. From Homeric times, sports were a deadly serious affair. Poets, philosophers, and statesmen placed athletic victories above all other human achievements. "There is no greater glory for a man, no matter how long his life," proclaimed Homer, "than what he achieves with his hands and feet."

Athletic contests took place within a religious context, honoring the gods but glorifying the human victors. By 500 B.C., there were fifty sets of games across the Greek world held at regular intervals. Among the most prestigious contests were the so-called Crown Games at Delphi, Corinth, and Nemea; the most important were those held every four years as part of the cult of Zeus at Olympia. The most important event of the Olympic Games was the 192-meter race, or *stade,* from which comes the word *stadium.* So important was victory in this event that the name of the victor provided the basic system of Greek dating. Years were reckoned from the last Olympiad and were recorded as "three years after Epitelidas of Sparta won the stade" (577 B.C.), or "the year in which Phanias of Pellene won the stade" (512 B.C.). In time, other events were added to the Olympics—other footraces (including one in which the contestants wore armor), throwing of the discus and javelin, the long jump, horse races, and chariot races. The *pankration* combined wrestling and boxing in a no-holds-barred contest. The pentathlon included five events: discus, jumping, javelin, running, and wrestling.

The serious nature of sport was equaled by its danger. One inscription from a statue erected at Olympia reads simply, "Here he died, boxing in the stadium, having prayed to Zeus for either the crown or death." The most celebrated pankration hero was Arrichion, who won but died in victory. Although his opponent was slowly strangling him, Arrichion managed to kick his adversary in such a way as to force the ball of his ankle free from its socket. The excruciating pain caused the opponent to signal defeat just as Arrichion died, victorious.

The ultimate disgrace was not injury or even death, but defeat. As one contemporary author put it, "In the Olympic Games you cannot just be beaten and then depart, but first of all, you will be disgraced not only before the people of Athens or Sparta or Nicopolis but before the whole world." Greeks did not honor good losers, only winners. As Pindar, the great lyric poet who celebrated victorious athletes, wrote, "As they the losers returned to their mothers no laughter sweet brought them pleasure, but they crept along the backroads, avoiding their enemies, bitten by misfortune."

If failure was bitter, victory was sweet indeed. Victors received enduring fame and enormous fortune. Poets composed odes in their honor, and crowds hurried to meet them on their return home. Most games carried considerable cash prizes. At the four big games, winners received only crowns of olive or laurel leaves, but their home cities gave them more-substantial gifts. Athens, for example, paid Olympic victors the equivalent of five hundred bushels of grain. This fabulous sum put the winner—for one year at least—in the ranks of the wealthiest Athenians. Most cities granted winners public honors and allowed them to eat at public expense for the rest of their lives. Thus the best athletes were essentially professionals, traveling from game to game. The Thasian boxer and pankratiast Theogenes claimed to have won over thirteen hundred victories during a professional career that spanned more than two decades. After his death he received the ultimate accolade: he was worshiped in Thasos as a god.

Competition among cities to field winning athletes was as sharp as the competition among the athletes themselves. Cities hired coaches, often themselves former Olympic champions, and actively recruited athletes from rival neighboring cities. The colony of Croton in Italy, for example, won the stade 44 percent of the time between 588 B.C. and 484 B.C. Then Croton's leading sprinter, Astylos, was lured to Syracuse and won three races, including the stade, for that city. Croton never again achieved

an Olympic victory. Presumably its best athletes had been bought off.

In keeping with the rest of male-dominated Greece, only men were allowed to participate in or attend the Olympic Games. Separate games dedicated to Zeus's wife, Hera, were held for unmarried women at Olympia. Women competed only in footraces over a shortened track. While men competed naked, their bodies rubbed down with olive oil, in the Heraia women wore a short tunic. Victors in the Heraia did not receive the same honors as their male counterparts, but at least one woman found an indirect way to win a victory at the male Olympics. Cynisca, the daughter of a Spartan king, entered a team of horses in the race, encouraged, the story goes, by her brother, who wanted to show that victory in these events "required no excellence but was a victory of money and expense." Whatever her motivation, Cynisca was certainly proud of her achievement. Following the victory won for her by her male driver, she erected a statue of herself at Olympia with an inscription that read:

Sparta's kings were fathers and brothers of mine,
But since with my chariot and storming horses I,
   Cynisca,
Have won the prize, I place my effigy here
And proudly proclaim
That of all Grecian women I first bore the crown.

The Greeks' passion for games is unique in antiquity, and the progressive interest of Romans and "barbarians" in athletics was a sure sign of their absorption of Greek culture. Perhaps the best explanation of the place of athletics in the Greek world was that the single athlete, standing alone and naked and striving with all his being for excellence, was the purest expression of the individualism that animated Hellenic society.

Though gods were petitioned, placated, and pampered, they were not privileged or protected. Unlike the awe-inspiring gods of the Mesopotamians and Egyptians, the traditional Greek gods, inherited from the Dark Age, were represented in ways that showed them as all too human, vicious, and frequently ridiculous. Zeus was infamous for his frequent rapes of boys and girls. His lust was matched only by the fury of his jealous wife, Hera. According to one story, a visitor to Athens asked why its citizens so often used the exclamation "by Zeus." The answer came back, "Because so many of us are." Other gods received equally irreverent treatment. Poseidon, god of earthquakes, water, and the sea, was powerful and dangerous as well as brutal, arbitrary, and vindictive. Dionysus, a popular god of emotional religion and wine, was frequently drunk. The Greek gods were immortal, superhuman in strength, and able to interfere in human affairs. But in all things, they reflected the values and weaknesses of the Greek mortals, who could bargain with them, placate them, and even trick them.

Religious cults were not under the exclusive control of any priesthood or political group. Thus, there were no official versions of stories of gods and goddesses. This is evident both from Greek poetry, which often presents contradictory stories of the gods, and from pottery, which bears pictorial versions of myths that differ greatly from written ones. Although centers such as Delphi were universal religious sites, drawing visitors from the whole Greek world and even beyond, no one group or sacred site enjoyed a monopoly on access to the gods. Like literacy and government, the gods belonged to all.

Myth and Reason

The glue holding together the individual and frequently hostile Greek poleis and ethne scattered throughout the Mediterranean was their common stock of myths and a common fascination with the Homeric legends. Stories of gods and heroes, told and retold, were fashioned into *mythoi* (myths, literally, "formulated speech"), which explained and described the world both as it was and as it should be. Myths were told about every city, shrine, river, mountain, and island. Myths explained the origins of cities, festivals, the world itself. Why are there seasons? Because Persephone, a daughter of Zeus, had been carried off by Hades, god of the dead, and for four months each year she had to dwell in his dark kingdom. What is the place of humans in the cosmos? They stand between beasts and gods because Prometheus tricked Zeus and gave men fire with which they cook their food and offer the bones and fat of sacrificial animals to the gods. Why is there evil and misfortune? Because, Greek men explained, in revenge for Prometheus's trickery, Zeus offered man Pandora (the name means "all gifts"), the first woman, whose beauty hid her evil nature. By accepting this gift, humans brought evil and misfortune on themselves.

Such stories were more than simply fanciful explanations of how things came to be. Myths sanctioned and supported the authority of social, political, and religious traditions. They presented how things had come to be in a manner that prescribed how they were to remain. The stories of Prometheus and Pandora, for example, defined the ambivalent relationship between gods and humans, the evil nature of women, and the ritual role of fire and sacrifice to the gods.

As important as these myths were, they were not immutable. Archaic Greeks constantly reworked ancient myths, retelling them, adjusting their content and thus their meanings. Pandora began as evil. "Whoever trusts a woman is trusting himself to a thief." But in another version of the myth, Pandora is curious rather than evil. She opens a jar given her by Zeus that contained all evils and thereby unintentionally releases them into the world. As colonists traveled to the far shores of the Mediterranean, their mythic heroes moved with them. New legends told of the travels of Heracles, Apollo, and other gods and heroes to Sicily, Italy, and beyond. In the process of revising and retelling, myths became a powerful and dynamic tool for reasoning about the world.

Archaic Greeks showed a similar combination of veneration and liberty in dealing with the Homeric legends. Young Greeks were urged to model themselves on the example of the ancients as described in the *Iliad* and the *Odyssey*. Increasingly, however, thoughtful Greeks approached the heroic ideals of these epics with a sense of detachment and criticism. Military values were still important, but the ancient aristocratic values were no longer universally accepted. Some mothers might tell their sons as they marched off to war, "Return with your shield or on it"—that is, victorious or dead—but Archilochus, a seventh-century B.C. lyric poet, could take a very different view of shields and honor:

A perfect shield bedecks some Thracian now;
I had no choice, I left it in a wood.
Ah, well, I saved my skin, so let it go!
A new one's just as good.

ALL THINGS CHANGE

The thought of Heraclitus of Ephesus is preserved entirely in fragmentary, oracular-like aphorisms. These brief statements nevertheless convey a sense of his reflections on the nature of the universe.

1. It is wise to hearken, not to me, but to my Word, and to confess that all things are one.
2. Though this Word is true evermore, yet men are as unable to understand it when they hear it for the first time as before they have heard it at all. For, though all things come to pass in accordance with this Word, men seem as if they had no experience of them, when they make trial of words and deeds such as I set forth, dividing each thing according to its kind and showing how it truly is. But other men know not what they are doing when awake, even as they forget what they do in sleep. . . .
3. Cold things become warm, and what is warm cools; what is wet dries, and the parched is moistened. . . .
4. You cannot step twice into the same river; for fresh waters are ever flowing in upon you. . . .
5. Homer was wrong in saying: "Would that strife might perish from among gods and men!" He did not see that he was praying for the destruction of the universe; for if his prayer were heard, all things would pass away.

The new, open examination of traditional values extended into all areas of investigation. By the sixth century B.C., a number of Ionian Greeks began to investigate the origins and nature of the universe, not in terms of myth or religion, but by observation and rational thought. Living on the coast of Asia Minor, these Ionians were in contact with the ancient civilizations of Mesopotamia and learned much from the Babylonian traditions of astronomy, mathematics, and science. However, their primary interest went beyond observing and recording to speculating. They were the first philosophers—intellectuals who sought natural explanations for the world around them.

Thales of Miletus (ca. 625–ca. 547 B.C.) regarded water as the fundamental substance of the universe. For Anaximander (610–ca. 527 B.C.), the primary substance was matter—eternal and indestructible. It was Anaximenes of Miletus (fl. ca. 545 B.C.) who regarded air as the primary substance of the universe. Heraclitus of Ephesus (ca. 540–ca. 480 B.C.) saw the universe not as one unchanging substance but rather as change itself. For him, the universe is constantly in flux, changing like a flickering fire. One cannot step into the same river twice, Heraclitus taught, because no flowing stream is ever the same from one moment to another. Thus it is with the world. All is constantly in a state of becoming, not in a static state of being. And yet this constant change is not random. The cosmic tension between stability and flux is regulated by laws that human reason can determine. The universe is rational.

The significance of such speculative thought was not in the conclusions reached, but rather in the method employed. The Ionian philosophers no longer spoke in myth but rather in plain language. They reached their conclusions through observation and rational thought in which religion and the gods played no direct role. As significant as their original speculations was the manner in which these philosophers were received. Although as late as the fourth century B.C., intellectuals still occasionally fell prey to persecution, by the sixth century B.C., much of Greek society was ready to tolerate such nonreligious, rational teaching, which in other times and places would have been thought scandalous or atheistic.

Art and the Individual

Archaic Greeks borrowed from everywhere and transformed all that they borrowed. Just as they adopted and adapted the Phoenician alphabet and Mesopotamian science, they took Near Eastern and Egyptian painting and sculpture and made them their own. During the Dark Age, the Mycenaean traditions of art had entirely disappeared. Pottery showed only geometric decorations; sculpture was unknown. Gradually, from the ninth century B.C., stylized human and animal figures began to appear within the tightly composed geometric patterns. As Greek traders increased their contacts with the Near East, lions, griffins, and other strange beasts began to appear on vases, jugs, vials, and other pottery containers. But by the eighth century B.C., such exotic subjects had given way to the Greek passion for human images taken from their own myths and legends. The preferred technique was the so-called black figure style,

The François Vase is a large krater, a vessel for mixing wine. It comes from the Greek colonies of Sicily and dates from around 570 B.C. The krater is decorated with bands on which are depicted martial and mythological scenes.

ARCHAIC GREECE

ca. 780–720 B.C.	**Population increase in Greece**
776 B.C.	**First Olympic Games held**
ca. 750–700 B.C.	**Greeks develop writing system based on Phoenician model; Greeks begin colonizing western Mediterranean**
ca. 700–500 B.C.	**Archaic Age of Greece**
ca. 700 B.C.	**First stone temples appear in Greece**
ca. 650 B.C.	**Cypselus breaks rule of Bacchiads in Corinth; rules city as tyrant**
594 B.C.	**Solon elected chief archon of Athens; institutes social and political reforms**
586 B.C.	**Death of Periander ends tyrants' rule in Corinth**
499 B.C.	**Ionian cities revolt**

developed first at Corinth. Subjects were painted in black silhouette on red clay and then details were cut with a sharp point so that the background could show through. As the popularity of these mythic and heroic scenes increased, so too did the artists' technical competence. Unlike Egyptian and Syrian artisans, who were largely content within a static tradition of representation, the Greeks competed with one another to overcome technical problems of perspective and foreshortening. They also experimented with techniques of portraying long and complicated narratives on individual vases. Masters of the technique were proud of their skills and eager to proclaim their accomplishments. From the sixth century B.C., many of the finest examples were signed, sometimes, as in the case of the François vase shown here, by both the potter or the owner of the pottery shop and the painter. Such masterpieces celebrated not only the heroes of the past but also the artist as individual and as the interpreter of culture no less original than the poet.

Greek sculpture underwent a similar dramatic development. The earliest and most common subject of Archaic sculpture was the standing male nude, or *kouros,* figure, which was in wide demand as a grave monument, a statue dedicated to a god, or even a cult statue of a male deity. In Egypt, seventh-century B.C. Greeks had seen colossal statues and had learned to work stone. They brought these techniques home, improved on them by using iron tools (the Egyptians knew only bronze ones), and began to create their own human images. The kouros was a relatively easy figure to carve. Essentially, the sculptor began with a prism-shaped block of stone about 6 feet by 1 foot by 1½ feet. Applying a system of widely accepted ratios, the artist then carved it into a recognizable three-dimensional human form. The rigidly formulaic position of the kouros—standing, arms by the sides, looking straight ahead, left foot extended—followed Egyptian tradition and left little room for originality. Thus sculptors sought to give their statues originality and individuality, not as representations of individuals, but as the creations of the individual sculptor. To this end, they experimented with increasingly natural molding of limbs and body and began signing their works. Thus, as in vase painting, Greek sculpture reflected the importance of the individual, not in its subject matter, but in its creator. The widely popular kouros figures left little room for experimentation with more complex problems of composition and action. Their female counterparts, *korai,* followed similarly rigid traditions to which sculptors added female attributes. In the korai figures it was the clothing rather than the anatomy that allowed some scope to the artist's talents.

The real challenges in sculpture, as in poetry and vase painting, came in the portrayal of narrative in decorations on monuments, primarily temples. Unlike kouroi, which were usually private commissions intended to adorn the tombs of aristocrats, these public buildings were constructed as expressions of civic pride and were accessible to everyone. Here the creativity and dynamism of Greek cities could be paralleled in stone. Figures such as the Calf-Bearer (ca. 590 B.C.) and the Rampin Horseman (ca. 560 B.C.) from the Athenian acropolis are daring in the complexity of composition and the delicacy of execution. These are statues that tell stories. In the former, a master farmer carries a calf to be sacrificed to Athena. The two gentle heads and the cross formed by the farmer's hands and the calf's legs are individual traits without precedent in ancient art.

The Calf-Bearer was commissioned for the temple of Athena, which was destroyed by the Persians in 480 B.C. when they captured Athens and burned the Acropolis.

In the latter, the earliest-known Greek equestrian statue, the rider's head is turned naturally, possibly peeking out from behind the head of his mount. The horseman wears a wreath of parsley, probably an indication that he had won the prize in a race held in connection with a religious feast. Both statues surpass the monotony

Head and upper torso of the Rampin Horseman.

and anonymity of tradition. Although formally intended for religious purposes, these figures serve not only the gods and the aristocratic elite but the whole community.

A Tale of Three Cities

The political, social, and cultural transformations that occurred in the Archaic Age took different forms across the Greek world. No community or city-state was typical of Greece. The best way to understand the diversity of Archaic Greece is to examine three very different cities that by the end of the sixth century B.C. had become leading centers of Greek civilization. Corinth, Sparta, and Athens present something of the spectrum of political, cultural, and social models of the Hellenic world. Corinth, like many cities, developed into a commercial center in which the assembly of citizens was dominated by an oligarchy. Sparta developed into a state in which citizenship was radically egalitarian but restricted to a small military elite. In Athens, the Archaic Age saw the foundations of an equally radical democracy.

Wealthy Corinth

Corinth owed its prosperity to its privileged site, dominating both a rich coastal plain and the narrow isthmus connecting the Peloponnesus to the mainland. In the eighth century B.C., as Greeks turned their attention to the west, Corinthians led the way. Corinthian pottery appeared throughout western Greece and southern Italy. Corinthian trade led to colonization, and settlers from Corinth founded Syracuse and other cities in Sicily and Italy. These colonies reduced the population pressure on the city and provided markets for its grain and manufactured goods, primarily pottery and textiles. Even more important to Corinthian prosperity was its role in the transport of other cities' products from east to west. By carrying goods across the isthmus and loading them onto other ships, merchants could avoid the long and dangerous passage around the Peloponnesus. Duties imposed on other cities using this unique passage added to Corinthian wealth from agriculture and its own commerce.

The precise details of early Corinthian government are uncertain. Still, it appears that in Corinth as in many other cities, a tyranny replaced a ruling clan and in time this tyranny ended with an oligarchic government. Until the middle of the seventh century B.C., Corinth and its wealth were ruled in typical Dark Age fashion by an aristocratic clan known as the Bacchiads. There were approximately two hundred members of this clan, all of whom claimed descent from the mythical hero Heracles. Corinth began its rise under this aristocratic rule, and individual Bacchiads led colonizing expeditions to Italy and Sicily. However, the increasing pressures of population growth, rapidly expanding wealth, and dramatic changes in the economy produced social tensions that the traditional aristocratic rulers were unable to handle. As in cities throughout the Greek world, these tensions led to the creation of a new order.

The early history of Corinth is obscure, but apparently around 650 B.C. a revolution led by a dissident Bacchiad named Cypselus (ca. 657–627 B.C.) and supported by non-Bacchiad aristocrats and other Corinthians broke the Bacchiads' grip on the city. The revolution led to the establishment of Cypselus as tyrant. Cypselus and his son Periander (ca. 627–586 B.C.) seem to have been generally popular with most Corinthians. As Periander himself said, "The safety of the tyrant is better guarded by the goodwill of the citizens than by the spears of a bodyguard."

In Corinth, as in many other cities, the tyrants restructured taxes, relying primarily on customs duties,

Two Faces of Tyranny

The spectrum of tyrannies in Archaic Greece is shown in the lives of Periander of Corinth and Peisistratus of Athens. The description of Periander is that of Herodotus; the description of Peisistratus comes from the Athenian Constitution, one of over a hundred constitutions compiled by Aristotle and his students between 328 and 325 B.C. as part of the research for his Politics.

Now Periander at the first was of milder mood than his father; but after he had held converse by his messengers with Thrasybulus the despot of Miletus, he became much more blood-thirsty than Cypselus. For he sent a herald to Thrasybulus and enquired how he should most safely so order all matters as best to govern his city. Thrasybulus led the man who had come from Periander outside the town, and entered into a sown field; where, while he walked through the corn and plied the herald with still-repeated questions about his coming from Corinth, he would ever cut off the tallest that he saw of the stalks, and cast away what he cut off, till by so doing he had destroyed the best and richest of the crop; then, having passed through the place and spoken no word of counsel, he sent the herald away . . . . But Periander understood what had been done, and perceived that Thrasybulus had counseled him to slay those of his townsmen who stood highest, and with that he began to deal very evilly with his citizens. For whatever act of slaughter or banishment Cypselus had left undone, that did Periander bring to accomplishment.

From Herodotus, *The Histories,* Book V, ch. 92.

The factions were three: one was the part of the Men of the Coast . . . and they were thought chiefly to aim at the middle form of constitution; another was the party of the Men of the Plain, who desired the oligarchy . . . third was the party of the Hillmen, which had appointed Peisistratus over it, as he was thought to be an extreme advocate of the people. And on the side of this party were also arrayed, from the motive of poverty, those who had been deprived of the debts due to them, and, from the motive of fear, those who were not of pure descent . . . Peisistratus inflicted a wound on himself with his own hand and then gave out that it had been done by the members of the opposite factions, and so persuaded the people to give him a bodyguard . . . He was given the retainers called Club-Bearers, and with their aid he rose against the people and seized the Acropolis . . .

Peisistratus's administration of the state was . . . moderate, and more constitutional than tyrannic; he was kindly and mild in everything, and in particular he was merciful to offenders, and moreover he advanced loans of money to the poor for their industries, so that they might support themselves by farming. In doing this he had two objects, to prevent their stopping in the city and make them stay scattered about the country and to cause them to have a moderate competence and be engaged in their private affairs, so as not to desire nor to have time to attend to public business.

From Aristotle, Athenian Constitution.

which were less of a burden on the peasantry. Around 600 B.C., Periander began construction of a causeway across the isthmus on which ships could be hauled from the Aegean to the western Mediterranean. In this way merchant vessels (and warships) could enter the Gulf of Corinth without having to unload. This causeway eventually became a major source of Corinth's wealth. Periander also attacked conspicuous consumption on the part of the aristocracy. He forbade women to wear expensive clothes and jewelry. He introduced laws against idleness and put thousands of Corinthians to work in extensive building programs. He erected temples and sent colonists to Italy. Under his leadership the Corinthian fleet developed into the most powerful naval force in the Adriatic and Aegean seas. Under its tyrants, Corinth led the Greek world in the production of black figure pottery, which spread throughout the Mediterranean. A great seaport, Corinth also became known as the center of prostitution, and a popular saying ran, "Not every man has the luck to sail to Corinth," implying both that not everyone would be fortunate enough to enjoy its pleasures and that not everyone had the luck to survive such a trip without considerable expense.

Greek merchant ships such as this one shown on a painted vase transported goods all over the Mediterranean.

The tyrants also laid the foundation for broader political participation. Cypselus divided the population into eight tribes, based not on traditional ethnic divisions but on arbitrary groupings by region. All of Corinth was divided into three large regions. The population of each region was distributed among each of the eight tribes. This assignment prevented the emergence of political factions based on regional disputes. Ten representatives from each tribe formed a council of eighty men. Under the tyrants, this council was largely advisory and provided a connection between the autocratic rulers and the citizens.

In Corinth as elsewhere, the strength or weakness of tyranny rested on the abilities and personality of individual tyrants. The benefits they brought their cities could not entirely overcome the negative impression made by the arbitrary nature of their rule. Thus their popularity declined rapidly. Cypselus had been a beloved liberator. His son Periander, in spite of his accomplishments, was remembered for his cruelty and violence. To later Greeks, Periander was the originator of the brutal, arbitrary rule later considered typical of repressive tyranny. Shortly after Periander's death in 586 B.C., a revolt killed his successor and tyranny in Corinth ended.

The new government continued the tribal and council system established by Cypselus. From the sixth century B.C. until its conquest by Macedonia in 338 B.C., Corinth was ruled by an oligarchy. Although an assembly of the *demos,* or adult males, met occasionally, actual government was in the hands of eight deliberators, or *probouloi,* and nine other men from each tribe, who together formed the council of eighty. How council members and probouloi were selected is unknown. Presumably they were elected for very long periods, if not for life, and the council tended to be self-perpetuating. Still, the oligarchs who made up the council avoided the kind of exclusive and arbitrary tendencies that had destroyed both the Bacchiads and the tyrants. They were remarkably successful in maintaining popular support among the citizens and provided a reliable and effective government.

Thus Corinth flourished, a city more open to commerce and wealth than most, moderate in its political institutions and eager for stability. As one fourth-century B.C. poet wrote:

[There] lawfulness dwells, and her sister,
Safe foundation of cities,
Justice, and Peace, who was bred with her;
They dispense wealth to men.

Martial Sparta

At the beginning of the eighth century B.C., the Peloponnesus around Sparta and Laconia faced circumstances similar to those of Corinth and other Greek communities. Population growth, increasing disparity between rich and poor, and an expanding economy created powerful tensions. However, while Corinthian society developed into a complex mix of aristocrats, merchants, artisans, and peasants, ruled by an oligarchy, the Spartan solution presented a rigid two-tiered social structure. By the end of the Archaic Age, a small, homogeneous class of warriors called *homoioi,* or equals, ruled a vast population of state serfs, or *helots.* The two classes lived in mutual fear and mistrust. Spartans controlled the helots through terror and ritual murder. The helots in turn were "an enemy constantly waiting for the disasters of the Spartans." And yet, throughout antiquity the Spartans were the Greeks most praised for their courage, simplicity of life, and service to the state.

War was the center of Spartan life, and war lay at the origin of the Spartans' extraordinary social and political organization. In the eighth century B.C., the Spartans conquered the fertile region of Messenia and compelled the vanquished Messenians to turn over one-half of their harvests. The spoils were not divided equally, but went to increase the wealth of the aristocracy, thus creating resentment among the less privileged. Early in the seventh century B.C., the Spartans attempted a similar campaign to take the plain of Thyreatis from the city of Argos. This time they were not so fortunate; they were defeated, and resentment of the ordinary warriors toward their aristocratic leaders flared into open conflict. The Messenians seized upon this time as a moment to revolt, and for a time Sparta was forced to fight at home and abroad for its very existence. In many cities, such crises gave rise to tyrants. In Sparta, the crisis led to radical political and social reforms that transformed the polis into a unique military system.

The Spartans attributed these reforms to the legendary lawgiver Lycurgus (seventh century B.C.). Whether or not Lycurgus ever existed and was responsible for all of the reforms, they saved the city and ended its internal tensions at the expense of abandoning the mainstream of Greek development. Traditionally, Greeks had placed personal honor above communal concerns. During the crisis of the second Messenian war, Spartans of all social ranks were urged to look not to individual interest but to *eunomia,* good order and obedience to the laws, which alone could unite Spar-

tans and bring victory. Faced with certain defeat as the only alternative, Spartans answered the call and became the first Greeks to elevate duty and patriotism above individual interest. United, the Spartans crushed the Messenians. In return for obedience, poor citizens received equality before the law and benefited from a land distribution that relieved their poverty. Conquered land, especially that in Messenia, was divided and distributed to Spartan warriors. However, the Spartan warriors were not expected to work the land themselves. Instead, the state reduced the defeated Messenians to the status of helots and assigned them to individual Spartans. While this system did not erase all economic inequalities among the Spartans (aristocrats continued to hold more land than others), it did decrease some of the disparity. It also provided a minimum source of wealth for all Spartan citizens and allowed them to devote themselves to full-time military service.

This land reform was coupled with a political reform that incorporated elements of monarchy, oligarchy, and democracy. The state was governed by two hereditary kings and a council of elders, the *gerousia.* The two royal families probably represented the combination of differing groups that had formed the Spartan polis at some earlier date. Their authority in peacetime was limited to familial and religious affairs. In war, they commanded the army and held the power of life and death.

In theory at least, the central institution of Spartan government was the gerousia, which was composed of thirty men at least sixty years of age and included the two kings. The gerousia directed all political activity, especially foreign affairs, and served as high court. Members were elected for life by the assembly, or *apella,* which was composed of all equals over the age of thirty and which approved decisions of the gerousia. However, this approval, made by acclamation, could easily be manipulated, as could the course of debate within the gerousia itself. Wealth, cunning, and patronage were more important in the direction of the Spartan state than were its formal structures.

Actual administration was in the hands of five magistrates termed *ephors.* Ephors were not members of the gerousia and often came from fairly obscure backgrounds. However, their powers were extremely broad. They presided over joint sessions of the gerousia and apella. They held supreme authority over the kings during wartime and acted as judges for noncitizens. Finally, the ephors controlled the *krypteia,* or secret police, a band of youths who practiced state terrorism as part of their rite of passage to the status of equal. On the orders of the ephors, the krypteia assassinated, intrigued, arrested powerful people, and terrorized helots. Service in this corps was considered a necessary part of a youth's education.

The key to the success of Sparta's political reform was an even more radical social reform that placed everyone under the direct supervision and service of the state from birth until death. Although admiring aristocratic visitors often exaggerated their accounts of Spartan life, the main outlines are clear enough. Eunomia was the sole guiding principle, and service to the state came before family, social class, and every other duty or occupation.

Spartan equals were made, not born. True, only a man born of free Spartan parents could hope to become an equal, but birth alone was no guarantee of admission to this select body, or even of the right to live. Elsewhere in Greece, parents were free to decide whether children should be raised or abandoned. In Sparta, public officials examined infants and decided whether they were sufficiently strong to be allowed to live or should be exposed on a hillside to die. From birth until age seven, a boy lived with his mother, but then he entered the state education system, or *agoge,* living in barracks with his contemporaries and enduring thirteen years of rigorous military training. Harsh discipline and physical deprivation were essential parts of this training, which was intended to teach men to endure pain and to conquer in battle.

At age twelve, training with swords and spears became more intense, as did the rigors of the lifestyle. Boys were given only a single cloak to wear and slept on thin rush mats. They were encouraged to supplement their meager diet by stealing food, although if caught they were severely whipped, not for the theft but for the failure. All of this they were expected to endure in silence.

Much of the actual education of the youths was entrusted to accomplished older warriors who selected boys as their homosexual lovers. Such relationships between youths and adults were the norm throughout Greece, although in Sparta they were more important than elsewhere. Not only did the lover serve as tutor and role model, but in time the two became a fighting team, each inspiring the other to show the utmost valor. Ultimately, the older warrior would even help his young lover select a wife.

At age twenty, Spartan youths were enrolled in the krypteia. Each was sent out into the countryside with nothing but a cloak and a knife and forbidden to return until he had killed a helot. This finishing school for killers kept helots in a constant state of terror and gave ephors a deadly efficient mechanism for enforcing their will.

If a youth survived the rigors of his training until age thirty, he could at last be incorporated into the rank of equals, provided he could pass the last obstacle. He had to be able to furnish a sufficient amount of food from his own lands for the communal dining group to which he would be assigned. This food might come from inherited property or, if he had proved himself an outstanding warrior, from the state. Those who passed this final qualification became full members of the assembly, but they continued to live with the other warriors. Now they could marry, but family life in the usual sense was nonexistent. To symbolize the furtive nature of marriage, the prospective groom acted out a ritual abduction of his bride. Thereafter he would slip out occasionally at night to sleep with her.

Although their training was not as rigorous as the education of males, Spartan women were given an upbringing and allowed a sphere of activity unknown elsewhere in Greece. Girls, like boys, were trained in athletic competition and, again like them, competed naked in wrestling, footraces, and spear throwing. This training was based not on a belief in the equality of the sexes but simply on the desire to improve the physical stamina and childbearing abilities of Spartan women. Women were able to own land and to participate widely in business and agricultural affairs, the reason being that since men were entirely involved in military pursuits, women were expected to look after economic and household affairs. When a foreign woman commented that Spartan women were the only women who could rule men, a Spartan wife replied, "With good reason, for we are the only women who bring forth men."

Few Lacedaemonians (as Spartans were also called) ever became equals. Not only were there far more helots than Spartans, but many inhabitants of the region, termed *perioikoi,* or peripherals, although they were free citizens of their local communities, were not allowed into the agoge. Others were washed out, unable to endure the harsh life, and still others lacked the property qualifications to supply their share of the communal meals. Thus, for all the trappings of egalitarianism, equality in Sparta was the privilege of a tiny minority.

The total dedication to military life was reinforced by a deliberate rejection of other activities. Prior to the eighth century B.C., Sparta had participated in the general cultural and economic transformations of the

Greek world. Legend even made Sparta the birthplace of music. However, from the time of the second Messenian war, Sparta withdrew from the mainstream of Greek civilization. Equals could not engage in crafts, trade, or any other forms of economic activity. Because Sparta banned silver and gold coinage, it could not participate in the growing commercial network of the Greek world. Although a group of free citizens of subject towns could engage in such activities, the role of Sparta in the economic and cultural life of Greece was negligible after the seventh century B.C. Militarily, Sparta cast a long shadow across the Peloponnesus and beyond, but the number of equals was always too small to allow Sparta both to create a vast empire and to maintain control over the helots at home. Instead, Sparta created a network of alliances and nonaggression pacts with oligarchic neighbors. In time this network came to be known as the Peloponnesian League.

Democratic Athens

Athens enjoyed neither the advantage of a strategic site such as Corinth's nor that of the rich plains of Sparta. However, the "goodly citadel of Athens" was one of the few Mycenaean cities to have escaped destruction at the start of the Dark Age. Gradually, Athens united the whole surrounding region of Attica into a single polis, by far the largest in the Greek world. Well into the seventh century B.C., Athens followed the general pattern of the polis seen in Corinth and Sparta. Like other Dark Age communities, Athens was ruled by aristocratic clans, particularly the Alcmaeonids. Only the members of these clans could participate in the *areopagus,* or council, which they entered after serving a year as one of the nine *archons,* magistrates who were elected yearly. Until the seventh century B.C., Athens escaped the social pressures brought on by population growth and economic prosperity that led to civil strife, colonialism, and tyranny elsewhere. This was due largely to its relative abundance of arable land and its commercial prosperity, based on the export of grain.

By the late seventh century B.C., however, Athens had begun to suffer from the same class conflict that had shaken other cities. Newly rich merchants and artisans of the middle classes resented the aristocratic monopoly on political power. Poor farmers were angry because, far from participating in the growing prosperity, they were being forced into debt to the wealthy. When they were unable to pay their debts, they or their children were sold as slaves by their creditors. Sometime around 630 B.C., an aristocrat named Cylon

attempted to seize power as tyrant. His attempt failed, but when he was murdered by one of the Alcmaeonids, popular revulsion drove the Alcmaeonids from the city. A decade of strife ensued as aristocratic clans, wealthy merchants, and farmers fought for control of the city. Violence between groups and families threatened to tear the community apart. In 621 B.C., the Athenians granted a judge, Draco, extraordinary powers to revise and systematize traditional laws concerning vengeance and homicide. His restructuring of procedures for limiting vengeance and preventing bloodshed were harsh enough to add the term *draconian* to the Western legal vocabulary. When asked why death was the most common penalty he imposed, Draco explained that minor offenses merited death and he knew of no more severe penalty for major ones. Still, these measures did nothing to solve the central problems of political control. Finally, in 594 B.C., Solon (ca. 630–ca. 560 B.C.), an aristocratic merchant, was elected chief archon and charged with restructuring the city's government. Solon based his reform on the ideal of eunomia, as had the Spartans, but he followed a very different path to secure good order.

In Sparta, Lycurgus had begun with a radical redistribution of land. In Athens, Solon began with the less extreme measure of eliminating debt bondage. Athenians who had been forced into slavery or into sharecropping because of their debts were restored to freedom. A law forbade mortgaging free men and women as security for debts. Athenians might be poor, but they would be free. This free peasantry formed the basis of Athenian society throughout its history.

Solon also reorganized the rest of the social hierarchy and broke the aristocracy's exclusive control of the areopagus by dividing the society into four classes based on wealth rather than birth and opening the post of archon to the top two classes. He further weakened the areopagus by establishing a council of four hundred members, drawn from all four classes, to which citizens could appeal decisions of the magistrates.

Although Solon's reforms established the framework for a resolution of Athens's social tensions, they did not entirely succeed. Solon himself did not consider his new constitution perfect, only practical. Asked if he had given the Athenians the best laws that he could give them, he answered, "The best that they could receive." Resistance from the still-powerful aristocracy prompted some Athenians to urge Solon to assume the powers of a tyrant in order to force through his reforms. He refused, but after his death, Peisistratus (d. 527 B.C.), an aristocrat strongly supported by the peasants against his own class, hired a mercenary force to seize control of the city. After two abortive attempts, Peisistratus ruled as tyrant from 545 B.C. until his death.

With his bodyguard firmly established on the acropolis, Peisistratus might have governed the city, for a while at least, as an absolute tyrant. Instead, he—and later his son Hippias (d. 490 B.C.), who succeeded him until 510 B.C.—continued to rule through Solon's constitution but simply ensured that the archons elected each year were their agents. Thus the Athenian tyrants strengthened Solon's constitution even while they further destroyed the powers of the aristocracy.

Peisistratus and Hippias drew their support from the demos—the people at large—rather than from an aristocratic faction. They claimed divine justification for their rule and made a great show of devotion to the Athenian gods. At one point, Peisistratus even dressed a very tall, beautiful girl to look like the goddess Athena, patron of the city, and had her driven into town in a chariot while heralds went before her announcing that Athena herself was supporting him. He also promoted annual festivals, and in so doing began the great tradition of Athenian literature. At the festival of Athena, professional reciters of *rhapsoidiai* (epic poetry) recited large portions of the *Iliad* and the *Odyssey.* During a festival in honor of Dionysus, actors performed the first tragedies and comedies. The tyrants also directed a series of popular nationalistic public works programs that beautified the city, increased national pride, and provided work for the poor. They rebuilt the temple of Athena on the acropolis, for which both the statues of the Rampin Horseman and the Calf-Bearer were commissioned. The tyrants also constructed a system of terra-cotta pipes by which clear mountain water was brought into the agora, and they built public halls and meeting places. These internal measures were accompanied by support for commerce and export, particularly of grain. The tyrants introduced the silver "owl" coin, which became the first international Greek currency. Soon Athens was challenging Corinth as the leading commercial power and trading in grain as far away as the Black Sea.

Peisistratus was firm. His son Hippias was harsh. Still, even Hippias enjoyed the support of the majority of the citizens of both popular and aristocratic factions. Only after the assassination of his younger brother did Hippias become sufficiently oppressive to drive his opponents into exile. Some of these exiles obtained the

An Athenian silver coin called a tetradrachm, *dating from the fifth century B.C. The owl is the symbol of the goddess Athena.*

assistance of Sparta and returned to overthrow Hippias in 510 B.C. Hippias's defeat ended the tyrants' rule in Athens and won for Sparta an undeserved reputation as the opponent of all tyranny.

Following the expulsion of Hippias, some aristocrats attempted to return to the "good old days" of aristocratic rule. However, for more than eighty years, Athenians had been accustomed to Solon's constitution and were unwilling to give it up. Moreover, the tyrants had created a fierce sense of nationalistic pride among all ranks of Athenians, and most were unwilling to turn over government to only a few. Thus, when the aristocrats made their bid to recover power, their primary opponent, Cleisthenes (ca. 570–ca. 507 B.C.), "made the demos his faction" and pushed through a final constitutional reform that became the basis for Athenian democracy.

The essence of Cleisthenes' reform lay in his reorganization of the major political units by which members of the council were selected. Previously, each citizen had belonged to one of four tribes, further broken down into twelve brotherhoods, or *phratries,* which were administrative and religious units. In a manner similar to that of Cypselus in Corinth, Cleisthenes reshuffled these phratries into thirty territorial units, or *demes,* comprising urban, inland, or coastal regions. These thirty units in turn were grouped into ten tribes, each consisting of one unit from each of the urban, inland, and coastal regions. The tribes elected the members of the council, military commanders, jurors, and magistrates. As in Corinth, this reorganization destroyed the traditional kin-based social and political pattern and integrated people of differing social, economic, and regional backgrounds. Aristocrats, merchants, and poor farmers had to work together to find common ground for political action, both regionally and nationally. With this new, integrated democracy and its strong sense of nationalism, Athens emerged from the Archaic Age as the leading city of the Hellenic world.

Neither Corinth, Sparta, nor Athens was a typical archaic Greek city—there was no such thing. However, each faced similar problems: deep conflict between old aristocratic families and wider society, growing population pressure, and threats from within and without. Their solutions—a period of tyranny in Corinth and Athens followed by oligarchy in the former and radical democracy in the latter or, in the case of Sparta, the creation of a small but egalitarian military elite—suggest the spectrum of alternatives from which cities across the Greek world sought to meet these challenges.

The Coming of Persia and the End of the Archaic Age

By the end of the sixth century B.C., the products of Greek experimentation were evident throughout the Mediterranean. Greek city-states had resolved the crises of class conflict. Greek merchants and artisans had found ways to flourish despite poor soil and uncertain climate. Greek philosophers, poets, and artists had begun to celebrate the human form and the human spirit. Still, these achievements were the product of small, independent, and relatively weak communities on the fringe of the civilized world. The Greeks' insignificance and isolation had kept them out of the sphere of interest of the great floodplain empires to the east.

In the second half of the sixth century B.C., all this changed. The Persian Empire, under its dynamic king, Cyrus II, began a process of conquest and expansion west into Asia Minor. The Persian Empire, which eventually reached from what is today western Turkey to India, was an extraordinary amalgam of the ancient imperial traditions of Mesopotamia, the dynamic Zoroastrian religion of the supreme deity Ahura Mazda, and a willingness to tolerate wide varieties of religious and cultural traditions. Cyrus granted the provinces of his empire great autonomy and preserved local forms of government wherever possible, being careful only to impose governors, or satraps, loyal to him and his Achaemenid dynasty. In keeping with this tradition, when he absorbed Ionia and the kingdom of Lydia on the coast of Asia Minor, he put tyrants loyal to Persia to rule over these Greek communities, and for a few decades these centers of Greek culture and thought accepted foreign control. In 499 B.C., the passion for democracy that had swept much of mainland Greece reached Ionia. Cities such as Miletus, Ephesus, Chios, and Samos revolted, expelled their Persian-appointed tyrants, established democracies, and sent ambassadors to the mainland to seek assistance. Eretria and Athens, two mainland cities with Ionian roots, responded, sending ships and men to aid the Ionian rebels. Athenian interests were more than simple solidarity with their Ionian cousins. Athens depended on grain from the Black Sea region and felt its direct interests to lie with the area. The success of the revolt was short-lived. The puny Greek cities were dealing with the largest empire the West had yet known. By 500 B.C., the Persian Empire included Asia Minor, Mesopotamia, Palestine, and Egypt, uniting all the peoples from the Caucasus to the Sudan.

The giant Persian Empire responded slowly, but with force, to the Greek revolt. King Darius I (522–486 B.C.) gathered a vast international force from throughout his empire and set about to recapture the rebellious cities. The war lasted five years and ended in a Persian victory. By 494 B.C., the Persians had retaken the cities of the coast and nearby islands. In the cities deemed most responsible for the revolt, the population was herded together and the boys were castrated and made into royal eunuchs. The girls were sent to Darius's court, the remainder of the population was sold into slavery, and the towns were burnt to the ground. Once the rebels had been disposed of, Darius set out to punish their supporters on the mainland, Eretria and Athens. With the same meticulous planning and deliberate pace, the Persian king turned his vast armies toward the Greek mainland.

3 ~ Classical and Hellenistic Greece, 500–100 B.C.

Alexander at Issus

*W*ar with Persia opened and closed the centuries of Greek glory. The invasion of the Greek mainland by Darius I in 490 B.C. pitted the greatest empire the West had ever known against a few small, mutually suspicious states. His failure created among the Greeks a new belief in the superiority of the Greek world over the barbarian and of free men over Eastern despots. Darius III (336–330 B.C.) suffered a far more devastating defeat than his ancestor at the hands of Alexander the Great (336–323 B.C.) and a combined Greek army 157 years later. Darius I had lost his pride, but

Darius III lost his empire and, shortly afterward, his life.

Alexander had announced his expedition as a campaign to punish the Persians for their invasion of Greece over a century and a half earlier. Greeks rightly viewed Alexander's victory at Issus in 333 B.C. as the beginning of the end for the Persians, and it was long celebrated by Greek poets and artists. The most famous of these was Philoxenus of Eretria, whose paintings marked the high point of Greek pictorial art. His masterpiece, like all other Greek paintings executed on wood, is long vanished. However, sometime in

the first century B.C., a wealthy Roman commissioned a mosaic copy of the painting for his villa at Pompeii in southern Italy. The mosaic—measuring some sixteen feet by eight feet and containing a million and a half stones, each the size of a grain of rice—is itself a masterpiece. It is also a faithful copy of Philoxenus's painting, which a Roman critic had characterized as "surpassed by none."

Alexander, with reckless disregard for his own safety, had led his right wing across a small stream at a gallop and routed the Persians' left flank. At the same time the Persian center, which consisted of

Greek mercenaries, managed to push Alexander's center back into the stream. Finally, Alexander and his right wing swung left, cutting Darius's Greeks to pieces, scattering his Persian guard, and forcing Darius to flee for his life.

In muted tones of red, brown, black, and yellow, Philoxenus brings all the skills developed through two centuries of Greek art to capture this most dramatic moment of the battle. The action takes place on a dusty and barren plain. The only landscape features are a lone dead tree and a forest of spears. Bold foreshortening, first used in the previous century, renders the rear of the horse in the center almost three-dimensional as it runs in blind fury toward Darius's chariot. Although the entire scene is wildly chaotic, each man and each mount is portrayed as an individual, with his own expression of emotion and his own part to play in the violent action.

The young Alexander, his hair blowing free and his eye fixed not on Darius but on his greater destiny, exudes the reckless courage and violence for which he was so famous. And yet he is not the center of the composition. That place of honor goes to Darius, whose kindly, tortured face looks back as his horses pull his chariot to safety. His hand stretches out in helpless sympathy toward the young Persian who has thrown himself

between his king and Alexander, taking through his chest the spear that the Greek king had intended for the Persian ruler.

The effect of the painting is at once heroic and disconcerting. Who is the hero of the battle? Is it the wild-eyed Alexander in his moment of victory, or is it the aged Persian monarch, whose infinite sadness at his moment of defeat is not for himself but for his young aide, who has given his life so that Darius might live? The picture here is no simple juxtaposition of civilization against barbarity. Greeks fought on both sides at Issus, just as they had in the Persian wars of the fifth century B.C. Nor did Alexander's warriors despise their Persian enemies.

Alexander told Darius's mother, captured after the battle, that he felt no personal bitterness toward her son. By the fourth century B.C., Greeks had learned that right and wrong, good and evil, civilized and barbarian were not simple issues. In the past century and a half, they had seen many wars, many leaders, and many defeats. Greek intellectuals had explored the complexity of human existence, agreeing with the philosopher Socrates that the unexplored life was not worth living. Greek dramatists had taught that suffering brought wisdom. Philoxenus's depictions of Darius and Alexander reflect the same complexity. Who is the hero here? Who is the man of wisdom?

Learning to ask these questions was a painful education for Greeks of the fifth and fourth centuries B.C. The victories over the Persian forces of Darius and his successors brought an unprecedented period of political and cultural freedom and creativity, but also deadly rivalry between Athens and Sparta, the leaders of the victorious Greeks. Democratic Athens transformed its wartime alliance into an empire, and only a generation after Athenian and Spartan troops had faced the Persians, they fought each other in a long and futile war, which left the Greek world exhausted and easy prey for the ambitious Macedonian dynasty.

War and Politics in the Fifth Century B.C.

The vast Persian army moving west in 490 B.C. threatened the fruits of three centuries of Greek political, social, and cultural experimentation. The shared ideal of freedom within community and the common bond of language and culture seemed no basis on which to build an effective resistance to the great Persian Empire. Moreover, Darius I was not marching against the Greeks as such. Few Greek states other than Athens had supported the Ionians against their Persian conquerors. Many Greeks saw the Persians as potential allies or even rulers preferable to their more powerful Greek neighbors and rivals within their own states. Separated by political traditions, intercity rivalries, and cultural differences, the Greeks did not feel any sense of national or ethnic unity. Particular interest, rather than patriotism or love of freedom, determined which cities opposed the Persian march. In the end, only Eretria, a badly divided Athens, and the small town of Plataea were prepared to refuse the Persian king's demand for gifts of earth and water, the traditional symbols of submission.

The Persian Wars

Initially, the Persian campaign followed the pattern established in Ionia. In the autumn of 490 B.C., Darius quickly destroyed the city of Eretria and carried off its population in captivity. The victorious Persian forces, numbering perhaps twenty thousand infantrymen and mounted archers, then landed at the Bay of Marathon, one of the few locations in Attica where horses could pasture that late in the year. Even with around six hundred Plataeans, the total Athenian force was no more than half that of its enemies, but the Greeks were better armed and commanded the hills facing the Marathon plain on which the Persian troops had massed. The Athenians also benefited from the leadership of Miltiades (ca. 544–489 B.C.), an experienced soldier who had served Darius and who knew the Persian's strengths and weaknesses. For over a week the two armies faced each other in a battle of nerves. Growing dissension in the Athenian ranks finally led the Greek generals to make a desperate and unexpected move. Abandoning the high ground, the Athenian hoplites rushed in disciplined phalanxes over almost a mile of open fields and then attacked the amazed Persian forces at a run. Although the Persians broke through the center of the Greek lines, the Athenians routed the Persian flanks

The plain of Marathon. The Greek hoplites lined up in the foothills at the left for the decisive battle against the Persian invaders in 490 B.C.

and then turned in, enveloping the invaders in a deadly trap. In a few hours it was all over. Six thousand Persians lay dead, while fewer than two hundred Athenians were buried in the heroes' grave that still marks the Marathon plain. The Persians retreated to their ships and sailed for the Bay of Phalerum near Athens, hoping to attack the city itself before its victorious troops could return. However, the Athenians, though exhausted from the battle, rushed the twenty-three miles home in under eight hours, beating the Persian fleet. When the Persians learned that they had lost the race, they turned their ships for Asia.

The almost miraculous victory at Marathon had three enormous consequences for Athens and for Greece in general. First, it established the superiority of the hoplite phalanx as the finest infantry formation in the Mediterranean world. Not only Athenians but all Greeks were thereafter convinced of the superiority of their soldiers. Second, Greeks expanded this belief in military superiority to a faith in the general superiority of Greeks over the "barbarians" (those who spoke other languages). Finally, by proving the value of the citizen army, the victory of the Athenians solidified and enhanced the democratic reforms of Cleisthenes.

Common citizens were determined that the victory won by the hoplite phalanx at Marathon should not be lost to an aristocratic faction at home. To guard against this danger, the Athenian assembly began to practice ostracism, ten-year exile without loss of property, imposed on those who threatened to undermine the constitution of Cleisthenes. Each year every Athenian citizen had the opportunity to write on a potsherd (in Greek, *ostrakon*) the name of the man he most wished to leave Attica. If at least six thousand citizens voted, the state sent the individual receiving the most votes into temporary exile. No charges or accusations had to be made, much less proven. Anyone who had offended the Athenians or who, by his prominence, seemed a threat to democracy could be ostracized. Aristides (ca. 530–ca. 486 B.C.), known as "The Just" and a hero of the battle of Marathon, was ostracized in 482 B.C. During the vote, an illiterate farmer, taking him for an ordinary citizen, approached Aristides and asked him to write the name Aristides on a potsherd for him. When asked if Aristides had done him any wrong, the farmer replied, "None at all, nor do I know him. I am just tired of hearing everyone call him 'The Just.'" Aristides complied and, gaining the most votes, sadly left Attica.

At the same time, Athenians also began to select their chief officers not simply by direct election but by lot. This practice prevented any individual from rising

This ostrakon was found in the Athenian agora. It was used to cast a vote to choose a person who would be ostracized—banished from Athens for a period of ten years. The name on the first line is Themistocles.

to power by creating a powerful faction. Themistocles (ca. 528–462 B.C.), the son of a noble father and a non-Greek mother, took the lead in using the tools of ostracism and selection by lot to hold the aristocratic factions at bay. He also used his influence to convince Athens to fortify its harbor at Piraeus and to invest in a powerful fleet as protection against the inevitable return of the Persians.

Occupied by problems elsewhere in their vast empire and the unexpected death of Darius I in 486 B.C., the Persians paid little attention to Greece for six years. After Darius's death, his son Xerxes (486–465 B.C.), probably more interested in securing the western frontier of his empire than avenging his father's loss at Marathon, began to amass foodstuffs, weapons, and armies for a land assault on his Greek enemies. In response to these preparations, Greek cities began to attempt to close ranks against the invaders. Still, however, many Greek communities saw their neighbors as greater threats than the Persians. Some states—including Thebes, Argos, and Thessaly—more or less willingly allied with the Persians against Athens or Sparta. More distant cities such as Syracuse refused assistance except on their own terms, and north of the Peloponnesus only Athens, Plataea, and a few other small states were willing to fight. Sparta was prepared to defend itself and its league but was not interested in campaigns far from home. Finally, in 481 B.C., when the Persian invasion was imminent, representatives of what a contemporary called "the Greeks who had the best thoughts for Greece" met in Sparta to plan resistance. The allies agreed that the Spartans would take command of the combined land and sea forces, which probably totaled roughly 35,000 helots, 5,000 hoplites, and 378 ships.

Although larger than those mustered by Athens against Darius, the Greek forces were puny compared with Xerxes' estimated two hundred thousand infantry and one thousand light and highly maneuverable Ionian and Phoenician ships. The Spartan commanders sought a strategic point at which the numerical superiority of the Persian forces would be neutralized. The choice fell on the narrow pass of Thermopylae and the adjacent Euboean strait. While a select force of hoplites held the pass, the Greek fleet, following a strategy devised by Themistocles, harried the larger Persian one. Neither action produced a Greek victory, but none could have been expected.

At Thermopylae, the Greeks held firm for days against wave after wave of assaulting troops ordered forward by an amazed and outraged Xerxes. Finally, Greek allies of the Persians showed them a narrow mountain track by which they were able to attack the Greek position from the rear. Seeing that all was lost, the Spartan king Leonidas (490–480 B.C.) sent most of his allies home. Then he and his three hundred Spartan equals faced certain death with a casual disdain characterized by the comment made by one Spartan equal. Told that when the Persians shot their arrows, they were so numerous that they hid the sun, the Spartan replied, "Good. If the Persians hide the sun, we shall have our battle in the shade." The epitaph raised later by the Spartan state to Leonidas and his men read simply, "Go tell the Spartans, you who read: we took their orders, and are dead." Dead they were, but they had bought precious time for the Greek allies.

While the Persian troops were blocked at Thermopylae, their fleet was being battered by fierce storms in the Euboean straits and harassed by the heavier Greek ships. Here the Greeks learned that in close quarters, they could stand up to Xerxes' Phoenician navy. This lesson proved vital a short time later. While the Persian army burned Athens and occupied Attica, Themistocles lured the fleet into the narrow strait between Salamis and the mainland. There the slower Greek vessels bottled up the larger and vastly more numerous enemy ships and cut them to pieces.

After Salamis, Xerxes lost his appetite for fighting Greeks. Without his fleet, he could not supply a vast army far from home in hostile territory. Leaving a force to do what damage it could, he led the bulk of his forces back to Persia. At Athenian urging, the Greek allies under Leonidas's kinsman Pausanias (d. ca. 470 B.C.) met the Persians at Plataea in 479 B.C. Once more hoplite discipline and Greek determination meant more than numerical superiority. That night the Spartan king dined in the splendor of the captured tent of the defeated Persian commander. Athenian sea power and Spartan infantry had proven invincible. Soon the Athenians were taking the offensive, liberating the Ionian cities of Asia Minor and, in the process, laying the foundations of an Athenian empire every bit as threatening to their neighbors as that of Xerxes.

The Athenian Empire

Sparta, not Athens, should have emerged as the leader of the Greek world after 479 B.C. The Spartans, after all, had provided the crucial military force and leadership, and Sparta had emerged unscathed from the Persian wars. However, the constant threat of a helot revolt and the league members' desire to go their separate ways left Sparta too preoccupied with internal problems to fill the power vacuum left by the Persian defeat. Nor did Spartan values encourage international ambitions. Sparta's militarism at home did not translate into military expansion abroad.

Athens, on the other hand, was only too ready to take the lead in bringing the war home to the Persians. With Sparta out of the picture, the Athenian fleet was the best hope of liberating the Aegean from Persians and pirates. Athenian propaganda emphasized the Persian menace and Ionian solidarity. In 478 B.C. Athens accepted control of what historians have come to call

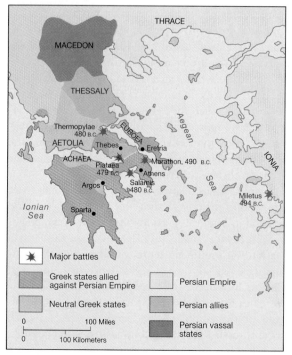

The Persian Wars

The Two Faces of Athenian Democracy

Early in the Peloponnesian War, Thucydides summarized the virtues of Athenian democracy in the speech he ascribes to Pericles in honor of those who died in the first year of the war. By 416 B.C., the sixteenth year of the Peloponnesian War, Athenian imperialism no longer even paid lip service to the ideals of democracy or freedom. Thucydides illustrates this in his reconstructed debate between representatives of the Spartan colony of Melos, which had attempted to remain neutral, and representatives of the Athenians, who demanded their surrender and enslavement.

Pericles' Funeral Oration

Our constitution is called a democracy because power is in the hands not of a minority but of the whole people. When it is a question of settling private disputes, everyone is equal before the law; when it is a question of putting one person before another in positions of public responsibility, what counts is not membership of a particular class, but the actual ability which the man possesses. No one, so long as he has it in him to be of service to the state, is kept in political obscurity because of poverty.

The Melian Debate

Athenians: You know as well as we do that, when these matters are discussed by practical people, the standard of justice depends on the equality of power to compel and that in fact the strong do what they have the power to do and the weak accept what they have to accept.

Melians: And how could it be just as good for us to be the slaves as for you to be the masters?
Athenians: You, by giving in, would save yourselves from disaster; we by not destroying you, would be able to profit from you.
Melians: So you would not agree to our being neutral, friends instead of enemies, but allies of neither side?
Athenians: No, because it is not so much your hostility that injures us; it is rather the case that, if we were on friendly tems with you, our subjects would regard that as a sign of weakness in us, whereas your hatred is evidence of our power.

Ultimately the Melians rejected Athens's demands, and shortly after the Athenians captured the city, they executed all the men and sold the women and children as slaves.

From Thucydides, *The Peloponnesian War.*

---

the Delian League, after the island of Delos, a religious center that housed the league's treasury. Athens and some of the states with navies provided ships; others contributed annual payments to the league. Initially, the league pursued the war against the Persians, not only driving them back along the Aegean and the Black seas, but also supporting rebels in the Persian Empire as far away as Egypt. At the same time, Athens hurriedly rebuilt its defensive fortifications, a move correctly interpreted by Sparta and other states as directed more against them than against the Persians.

Athens's domination of the Delian League assured its prosperity. Attica, with its fragile agriculture, depended on Black Sea wheat, and the league kept these regions under Athenian control. Since Athens received not only cash "contributions" from league members but also one-half of the spoils taken in battle, the state's public coffers were filled. The new riches made possible the reconstruction of the city that was burned by the Persians into the most magnificent city of Greece.

The league was too vital to Athenian prosperity to stand and fall with the Persian threat. The drive against the Persian Empire began to falter after a league expedition to Egypt in 454 B.C. ended in total defeat. Discouraged by this and other setbacks, the Athenian Callias, acting for the league, apparently concluded a treaty of peace with Persia in 449 B.C., making the alliance no longer necessary. For a brief moment it appeared that the Delian League might disband. But it was too late. The league had become an empire and Athens's allies were its subjects.

The Athenian empire was an economic, judicial, religious, and political union held together by military might. Athens controlled the flow of grain through the Hellespont to the Aegean, ensuring its own supply and heavily taxing cargoes to other cities. Athens controlled the law courts of member cities and used them to repress anti-Athenian groups. Major cases were brought to Athens itself, where large politicized democratic juries ensured that the Athenian demos, or people, would emerge as winners. Everywhere the goddess Athena received official worship as the patroness of Ionia. The goddess, through her temples, owned great amounts of land leased out to Athenians. Rich and poor citizens alike acquired territory throughout the empire. The rich took over vast estates confiscated from local opponents of Athenian dominance, while the poor replaced hostile populations in the colonies.

Control over this empire depended on the Athenian fleet to enforce cooperation. Athenian garrisons were established in each city, and "democratic" puppet governments ruled according to the wishes of the garrison commanders. Revolt, resignation from the league, or refusal to pay the annual tribute resulted in brutal suppression. The whole population of one rebellious city in Euboea was expelled and replaced with Athenian colonists. Athens sold the population of another into slavery. Persian tyranny had hardly been worse than Athenian imperialism.

Private and Public Life in Athens

During the second half of the fifth century B.C., Athens, enriched by tribute from its over 150 subject states, was a vital, crowded capital drawing merchants, artisans, and laborers from throughout the Greek world. At its height, the total population of Athens and surrounding Attica numbered perhaps 350,000, although probably fewer than 60,000 were citizens, that is, adult males qualified to own land and participate in Athenian politics. Over one-quarter of the total population were slaves. Historians have often described Athens as a slave-based society, and certainly slavery was a fundamental institution throughout its history. Ever since the reforms of Solon had prohibited debt bondage, great landowners, unable to force ordinary free men to work their estates, had turned to slave labor. Slaves were also vital in mining and other forms of craft and industrial work. In addition, most citizen households, even modest ones, boasted at least one or two domestics.

Greek slaves were not distinguished by race, ethnicity, or physical appearance. Anyone could become a slave. Prisoners of war, foreigners who failed to pay taxes, victims of pirate raids, all could end up on the auction blocks of the ancient world. Pirates even captured the great philosopher Plato while he was traveling from Sicily to Athens and sold him into slavery in Egypt. Only a payment by his family saved him from an obscure life in the household of some wealthy Egyptian.

Slaves were as much the property of their owners as land, houses, cattle, and sheep. Many masters treated their slaves well. After all, the cost of a slave was higher than the annual wage of a skilled free man. However, masters were under no obligation to treat their slaves kindly. Beatings, tattooing, starvation, and shackling were all common means of enforcing obedience. The bodies of male and female slaves were always at the disposition of their masters, who could use them as they wished or hand them over to others.

Still, the variety of slave experience was enormous. Rural slaves generally fared worse than urban ones, and those who worked the mines led the most appalling lives, literally worked to death. Others worked side by side with their masters in craft shops or even set up their own businesses, from which they were allowed to keep some of their profit to ultimately purchase their freedom. One slave left an estate worth over 33,000 drachmas (the equivalent of 165 years' salary for an ordinary free man), which included slaves of his own!

Roughly half of Athens's free population were foreigners—*metoikoi*, or metics. These were primarily Greek citizens of the tributary states of the empire, but they might also be Lydians, Phrygians, Syrians, Egyptians, Phoenicians, or Carians. The number of metics increased after the middle of the fifth century B.C., both because of the flood of foreigners into the empire's capital and because Athenian citizenship was restricted to persons with two parents who were of citizen families. Under these rules, neither Cleisthenes, the great reformer of the sixth century B.C., nor Themistocles, the architect of the victory against Persia, both of whose mothers had been foreigners, could have been Athenian citizens.

Metics could not own land in Attica, nor could they participate directly in politics. They were required to have a citizen protector and to pay a small annual tax. Otherwise, they were free to engage in every form of activity. The highest concentration of metics was found in the port of Piraeus, where they participated in commerce, manufacturing, banking, and skilled crafts. Educated metics also contributed to the intellectual and cultural life of the city. One of the wealthiest and most influential residents of Athens in the late fifth century B.C. was Cephalas of Syracuse. The great historian of the Persian wars, Herodotus, was a foreigner from Halicarnassus.

More than half of those born into citizen families were entirely excluded from public life. These were the women, who controlled and directed the vital sphere of

A small clay plaque discovered in Corinth shows workmen laboring in a pit quarrying clay for the pottery industry, which brought prosperity to the city. Refreshments, in the jar at the center, are being lowered to the workers.

the Athenian home, but who were considered citizens only for purposes of marriage, transfer of property, and procreation. During the Archaic period, aristocratic women had enjoyed some independence. However, the triumph of democracy reduced the public role of all women to that of breeder and property conduit. From birth to death, every female citizen lived under the protection of a male guardian, either a close relative such as father or brother, or a husband or son. Women spent almost their entire lives in the inner recesses of the home, emerging only for funerals and a very few religious festivals. Fathers arranged marriages, the purposes of which are abundantly clear from the ritualized exchange of words sealing the betrothal:

> "I give this woman for the procreation of legitimate children."
> "I accept."
> "And [I give a certain amount as] dowry."
> "I am content."

A wife had no control over her dowry, which passed to her son. In the event of divorce or the death of her husband, the woman and her dowry returned to her father. Should a woman's father die without a will or an heir, his closest male relative could demand her as his wife and thus claim the inheritance, even if the woman was already married to someone else.

An honorable Athenian woman stayed at home and managed her husband's household. Wealthy women directed the work of servants and slaves. In modest homes women were expected to participate along with the slaves in domestic chores such as spinning and in rearing children. Only the poorest citizens sent their wives and daughters to work in the marketplace or the fields. Even the most casual contact with other men was strictly forbidden without permission, although men were expected to engage in various sorts of extramarital affairs. In the words of one Athenian male, "Hetairai we have for our pleasure, mistresses for the refreshment of our bodies, but wives to bear us legitimate children and to look after the house faithfully."

Within the home, Athenian women were vital, if subordinate, partners. The household, as Athenians never tired of repeating, was the foundation of all society. Thus the role of women was indeed important. The public sphere was entirely closed to them, although even some men realized the potential for resentment. A woman in one of Euripides' tragedies describes her status:

> We women are the most unfortunate creatures.
> Firstly with an excess of wealth it is required
> For us to buy a husband and take for our bodies
> A master; for not to take one is even worse....
> What they say of us is that we have a peaceful time
> Living at home, while they do the fighting in war.
> How wrong they are! I would very much rather stand
> Three times in the front of battle than bear one child.

Male control over women may have resulted in part from fear. Women were identified with the forces of nature, which included both positive forces such as fertility and life and negative forces such as chaotic irrationality, which threatened civilization. These two poles were epitomized by the cult of Dionysus. He was the god of wine, life blood, and fertility, but he was also the deity whose female devotees, the *maenads,* were portrayed as worshiping him in a state of frenzied savagery that could include tearing children and animals limb from limb.

The male citizens of fifth-century B.C. Athens were free to an extent previously unknown in the world. But Athenian freedom was freedom in community, not freedom from community. The essence of their freedom lay in their participation in public life, especially self-government, which was their passion. This participation always occurred within a complex network of familial, social, and religious connections and obligations. Each person belonged to a number of groups: a deme, a tribe, a family, various religious associations, and occupational groups. Each of these communities placed different and even contradictory demands on its members. The impossibility of satisfying all of these

A Greek vase painting showing women weaving on a loom.

solemn occasions, as many as six thousand citizens might convene in the *pnyx,* the meeting place of the assembly. They also made up the large juries, always composed of several hundred citizens, who decided legal cases less on law than on the political merits of the case and the quality of the orators who pleaded for each side. Such large bodies were too unwieldy to deal with the daily tasks of government. Thus, control of these tasks fell to the council, or *boule,* composed of five hundred members selected by lot by the tribes; the magistrates, who were also chosen by lot; and ten military commanders or generals, the only major office-holders elected rather than chosen at random.

Paradoxically, the resolute determination of Athenian democrats to prevent individuals from acquiring too much power helped to create a series of extraconstitutional power brokers. Since most offices were filled by lot and turned over frequently, real political leadership came not from officeholders but from generals and from popular leaders. These so-called demagogues, while at times holding high office, exercised their power through their speaking skills, informal networks, and knowledge of how to get things done. They acquired this knowledge through their willingness to serve for long periods in various capacities on commit-

demands, of responding to the special interests of each, forced citizens to make hard choices, to set priorities, and to balance conflicting obligations. This process of selection was the essence of Athenian freedom, a freedom that, unlike that of the modern world, was based not on individualism but on a multitude of collectivities. The sum of these overlapping groupings was Athenian society, in which friends and opponents alike were united.

Unity did not imply equality. Even in fifth-century B.C. Athens, not all Athenians were socially or economically equal. Most were farmers who looked to military service as a means of increasing their meager income. Others engaged in trade or industry, although metics, with their commercial contacts in their cities of origin, dominated much of these activities in Athens. However, the aristocracy was still strong, and most of the popular leaders of the century came from the ranks of old wealth and influence. They used their wealth to attract supporters from the poorer ranks of the citizenry. Still, sovereignty lay not with these aristocrats but with the demos—the people.

In theory the adult male citizens of Athens were Athens's sovereigns. Since the time of Solon, they had formed the *ekklesia,* or assembly. On particularly

The interior of a black figure kylix, *or drinking cup, dating from about 540 B.C., is decorated with a scene of the god of wine, Dionysus, reclining in a boat. He is surrounded by dolpins and bunches of grapes.*

tees, as unpaid government workers, and in minor elected offices. Demagogues tended to be wealthy aristocrats who could afford to put in the time demanded by these largely voluntary services. Governing an empire demanded skill, energy, and experience, but Athenian democracy was formally run by amateurs. Small wonder that the city's public life was dominated by these popular leaders.

Although many demagogues competed for power and attracted the support of the people, the Athenian demos was not kind to its heroes. Ten years after the Greek victory at Salamis in 480 B.C., Athens ostracized Themistocles, whose leadership there had saved Athens. Mistrusted by many of his co-citizens, he ended his days, ironically, in the service of the Persian king. Cimon (ca. 510–451 B.C.), the son of the Marathon hero Miltiades, helped destroy Themistocles and succeeded him as the most influential leader of the city. As long as he lavished his wealth on the populace and led Athenian armies to victory against the Persians, Cimon remained popular. He also fought to hold the Athenian empire together when the island of Thasos attempted to secede in 465 B.C. However, his luck ran out three years later. In 462 B.C., Cimon led an army to assist Sparta in suppressing a revolt of its helots. The Spartans, fearing that he was actually planning to plot with the helots against them, sent him and his army home in disgrace. This disgrace was fatal, and Athens ostracized Cimon upon his return.

For the next thirty years, one individual dominated Athenian public life: the general Pericles (ca. 495–429 B.C.). Although not an original thinker, he was a great orator and a successful military commander, who proved to be the man most able to win the confidence of Athens and to lead it during the decades of its greatest glory. The Athenian political system of radical democracy reached its zenith under the leadership of Pericles, even while its imperial program drew it into a long and fatal war against Sparta, the only state powerful enough to resist it.

Pericles and Athens

Pericles was descended from the greatest aristocratic families of Athens. Nevertheless, as one ancient author put it, he "took his side, not with the rich and the few, but with the many and the poor." Pericles acquired intimate knowledge of government through long service on various public works projects, projects that provided lucrative income to poorer citizens who had supplemented their incomes as oarsmen before being idled by the peace of Callias of 449 B.C. Pericles was

A bust of Pericles.

also president of the commission responsible for constructing the great ivory-and-gold statue of Athena that stood in the Parthenon, the main temple in Athens. He served on the commission that built the Lyceum, the city exercise center, and the Parthenon itself. These enormous projects won him a great popular following while giving him an intimate knowledge of public finance and the details of Athenian government. He enhanced his position further through his great powers of persuasion. His speaking ability was described by an opponent, Thucydides, son of Melesias (d. ca. 410 B.C.). When asked by the king of Sparta whether he or Pericles was the better wrestler, Thucydides was said to have replied that while he could throw Pericles, the latter was so eloquent that he could easily convince those who had seen him thrown that he had not fallen but rather had won the match.

Pericles had been a young supporter of Themistocles and had commissioned the dramatist Aeschylus to write a play glorifying Themistocles at the time of his ostracism. Pericles never ruled Athens. As a general he could only carry out the orders of the ekklesia and the boule, and as a citizen he could only attempt to persuade his fellows. Still he was largely responsible for the extension of Athenian democracy to all free citizens. Under his influence, Athens abolished the last property requirements for officeholding. He convinced the state to pay those who served on juries, thus making it possible for even the poorest citizens to participate in this important part of Athenian government. But he was also responsible for a restriction of citizenship to those whose mothers and fathers had been Athenians. Such a law would have denied citizenship to many of the most illustrious Athenians of the sixth century B.C., including his own ancestors. By adopting such a measure, Athens was closing the door to persons of talent and energy who might have been of great service to the city in the future. The law also prevented citizens of Athens's subject states from developing a real stake in the fate of the empire.

Pericles had been an opponent of the aristocratically oriented Cimon at home and disputed Cimon's foreign policy, which saw Athens and Sparta as "yoke mates" against Persia. Pericles had little fear of Persia, but shared Cimon's view that the Athenian empire had to be preserved at all costs. This policy ultimately drew Athens into deadly conflict with Sparta. The first clash between the two great powers came around 460 B.C. Megara, which lay between the Peloponnesus and Attica, withdrew from the Spartan alliance and sought Athens's assistance against nearby Corinth in a border dispute. The Athenians, eager to add Megara to their empire, went to their assistance. Soon Sparta and Aegina entered the fray, but Athens emerged victorious, checking Sparta and absorbing Megara, Aegina, and Boeotia. However, in 446 B.C., after the Athenian defeat in Egypt, Megara and Boeotia rebelled and Sparta invaded the disputed region. Unable to face this new threat at home after their disastrous loss abroad, in 445 B.C. the Athenians, under the leadership of Pericles, concluded a peace treaty with Sparta whereby Athens abandoned all of its continental possessions. The treaty was meant to last for thirty years. It held for fourteen.

The two great powers were eager to preserve the peace, but the whole Greek world was a tinderbox ready to burst into flame. The spark came from an unexpected direction. In 435 B.C., Corinth and its colony Corcyra on the Adriatic Sea came to blows and Corcyra sought the assistance of Athens. Athens had never had much interest or involvement in the west, but it did not want the Corinthian fleet, vital to the Spartan alliance, augmented by absorbing the ships of Corcyra. Therefore the Athenians agreed to a defensive alliance with Corcyra and assisted it in defeating its enemy. This assistance infuriated Corinth, an ally of Sparta, and in 432 B.C. the Corinthians convinced the

Spartans that Athenian imperial ambitions were insatiable. In the words of the great historian of the war, Thucydides (d. ca. 401 B.C.), "What made war inevitable was the growth of Athenian power and the fear which this caused in Sparta." The next year, Sparta invaded Attica. The Peloponnesian War, which would destroy both great powers, had begun.

The Peloponnesian War

The Peloponnesian War was actually a series of wars and rebellions. Athens and Sparta waged two devastating ten-year wars, from 431 B.C. to 421 B.C. and then again from 414 B.C. to 404 B.C. At the same time, cities in each alliance took advantage of the wars to revolt against the great powers, eliciting terrible vengeance from both Athens and Sparta. Within many of the Greek city-states, oligarchs and democrats waged bloody civil wars for control of their governments. Moreover, between 415 and 413 B.C., Athens attempted to expand its empire in Sicily, an attempt that ended in disaster. Before it was over, the Peloponnesian War had become an international war, with Persia entering the fray on the side of Sparta. In the end, there were no real victors, only victims.

Initially, Sparta and Athens both hoped for quick victory. Sparta's strength was its army, and its strategy was to invade Attica, devastate the countryside, and force the Athenians into an open battle. Given the Spartan infantry's strength, numbers, and skill, such a battle could only end in an Athenian defeat. Pericles urged Athens to adopt a strategy of conserving its hoplite forces while exploiting its naval strength. Athens was a naval power and, with its empire and control of Black Sea grain, could hold out for years behind its fortifications, the great wall linking Athens to its port of Piraeus. At the same time, the Athenian fleet could launch raids along the coast of the Peloponnesus, thus bringing the war home to the Spartans. Pericles hoped in this way to outlast the Spartans. In describing the war, Thucydides uses the same word for "survive" and "win."

The first phase of the war, called the Archidamian War after the Spartan king Archidamus (431–427 B.C.), was indecisive. Sparta pillaged Attica but could not breach the great wall or starve Athens. In 430 B.C., the Spartans received unexpected help in the form of plague, which ravaged Athens for five years. By the time it ended in 426 B.C., as much as one-third of the Athenian population had died, including Pericles. Still Athens held out, establishing bases encircling the Peloponnesus and urging Spartan helots and allies to revolt.

At Pylos in 425 B.C., the Athenian generals Cleon and Demosthenes captured a major force of Spartan equals. The Spartans offset this defeat by capturing the city of Amphipolis on the northern Aegean. The defeated Athenian commander, Thucydides, was exiled for his failure and retired to Spartan territory to write his great history of the war. Exhausted by a decade of death and destruction, the two sides contracted peace in 421 B.C. Although Athens was victorious in that its empire was intact, the peace changed nothing and tensions festered for five years.

After the peace of 421 B.C., Pericles' kinsman Alcibiades (ca. 450–404 B.C.) came to dominate the demos. Well-spoken, handsome, and brave—but also vain, dissolute, and ambitious—Alcibiades led the city into disaster. Although a demagogue who courted popular support, he despised the people and schemed to overturn the democracy. His personal life, perhaps typical of privileged young Athenian aristocrats, had little room for the traditional religious or patriotic values of the city. In 415 B.C. he urged Athens to expand its empire west by attacking Syracuse, the most prosperous Greek city of Sicily, which had largely escaped the devastation of the Archidamian War. The expedition went poorly and Alcibiades, accused at home of having profaned one of the most important Athenian religious cults, was ordered home. Instead, he fled to Sparta, where he began to assist the Spartans against Athens. The Sicilian expedition ended in disaster. Athens lost over two hundred ships and fifty thousand men. At the same time, Sparta resumed the war, this time with naval support provided by Persia.

Suddenly Athens was fighting for its life. Alcibiades soon abandoned Sparta for Persia and convinced the Athenians that if they would abandon their democracy for an oligarchy, Persia would withdraw its support of Sparta. In 411 B.C., the desperate Athenian assembly established a brutal oligarchy controlled by a small faction of antidemocratic conspirators. Alcibiades' promise proved hollow and the war continued. Athens reestablished its democracy, but the brief oligarchy left the city bitterly divided. The Persian king renewed his support for Sparta, sending his son Cyrus (ca. 424–401 B.C.) to coordinate the war against Athens. Under the Spartan general Lysander (d. 395 B.C.), Sparta and its allies finally closed in on Athens. Lysander captured the Athenian fleet in the Hellespont, destroyed it, killed three thousand Athenian prisoners, and severed Athens's vital grain supply. Within months Athens was entirely cut off from the outside world and starving. In 404 B.C., Sparta accepted Athens's unconditional surrender. Athens's fortifications came down, its empire

The Delian League and the Peloponnesian War

vanished, and its fleet, except for a mere twelve ships, dissolved.

The Peloponnesian War showed not only the limitations of Athenian democracy but the potential brutality of oligarchy as well. More ominously, it demonstrated the catastrophic effects of disunity and rivalry among the Greek cities of the Mediterranean.

Athenian Culture in the Hellenic Age

Most of what we today call Greek is actually Athenian: throughout the Hellenic age (the fifth and early fourth centuries B.C., as distinct from the Hellenistic period of roughly the later fourth through second centuries B.C.), the turbulent issues of democracy and oligarchy, war and peace, hard choices and conflicting obligations found expression in Athenian culture even as the glory of the Athenian empire was manifested in art and architecture. The great dramatists Aeschylus, Sophocles, and Euripides were Athenian, as were the sculptor Phidias, the Parthenon architects Ictinus and Callicrates, and the philosophers Socrates and Plato. To Athens came writers, thinkers, and artists from throughout the Greek world.

The Examined Life

A primary characteristic of Athenian culture was its critical and rational nature. In heated discussions in the assembly and the agora, the courtroom and the private symposium, Athenians and foreigners drawn to the city no longer looked to the myths and religion of the past for guidance. Secure in their identity and protected by the openness of their radical democracy, they began to examine past and present and to question the foundations of traditional values. From this climate of inquiry emerged the traditions of moral philosophy and its cousin, history.

The Ionian interest in natural philosophy—the explanation of the universe in rational terms—continued throughout the fifth century B.C. But philosophers began also to turn their attention to the human world, in particular to the powers and limitations of the individual's mind and the individual's relationship with society. By the end of his life, the philosopher Heraclitus (see chapter 2, p. 53) had become intrigued with the examination of the rational faculties themselves rather than what one could know with them. In part, this meant a search for personal, inner understanding that would lead to proper action within society, in other words, to the search for ethics based on reason. In part, too, such an inquiry led to a study of how to formulate arguments and persuade others through logic.

In the political world of fifth-century B.C. Athens, rhetoric—the art of persuasion—was particularly important, because it was the key to political influence. Ambitious would-be successors to Pericles and Alcibiades were prepared to pay well to learn the art of persuasion. Teachers called Sophists ("wise people") traveled throughout Greece offering to provide an advanced education for a fee. Although the sophistic tradition later gained a negative reputation, teachers such as Gorgias (ca. 485–ca. 380 B.C.) and Protagoras (ca. 490–421 B.C.) trained young men not only in the art of rhetoric but also in logic. By exercising their students' minds with logical puzzles and paradoxical statements, the Sophists taught a generation of wealthy Greeks the powers and complexities of human reason.

Socrates (ca. 470–399 B.C.) was considered by many of his contemporaries as but one more Sophist, but he himself reacted against what he saw as the amoral and superficial nature of sophistic education. Although as a young man he had been interested in natural philosophy, he abandoned this tradition in favor of the search for moral self-enlightenment urged by Heraclitus. "Know thyself" was Socrates' plea. An unexamined life, he argued, was not worth living. Socrates refused any pay for his teaching, arguing that he had nothing to teach. He knew nothing, he said, and was superior to the Sophists only because he recognized his ignorance while they professed wisdom.

Socrates' method infuriated his contemporaries. He would approach persons with reputations for wisdom or skill and then, through a series of disarmingly simple questions, force them to defend their beliefs. The inevitable result was that in their own words the outstanding Sophists, politicians, and poets of the day demonstrated the inadequacy of the foundations of

This statuette is a realistic portrait of the philosopher Socrates, who was celebrated for his mind rather than his physical endowments. Our verbal portraits of Socrates and his ideas come to us from Plato and Xenophon.

SOCRATES THE GADFLY

Plato's Apology *presents an account of Socrates' defense of his role in Athenian society, continually driving his fellow citizens to examine their assumptions.*

And now, Athenians, I am not arguing in my own defense at all, as you might expect me to do, but rather in yours in order that you may not make a mistake about the gift of the god to you by condemning me. For if you put me to death, you will not easily find another who, if I may use a ludicrous comparison, clings to the state as a sort of gadfly to a horse that is large and well-bred but rather sluggish because of its size, so that it needs to be aroused. It seems to me that the god has attached me like that to the state, for I am constantly alighting upon you at every point to arouse, persuade, and reproach each of you all day long. You will not easily find anyone else, my friends, to fill my place; and if you are persuaded by me, you will spare my life. You are indignant, as drowsy persons are when they are awakened, and, of course, if you are persuaded by Anytus, you could easily kill me with a single blow, and then sleep on undisturbed for the rest of your lives, unless the god in his care for you sends another to arouse you.

From Plato, *Apology*.

---

their beliefs. While his opponents were left in confusion and outrage, Socrates' young followers, who included many of the sons of the aristocracy, delighted in seeing their elders so humiliated and embarrassed.

Since Socrates refused to commit any of his teaching to writing, we have no direct knowledge of the content of his instruction. We know of him only from the conflicting reports of his former students and opponents. One thing is certain, however. While demanding that every aspect of life be investigated, Socrates never doubted the moral legitimacy of the Athenian state. Condemned to death in 399 B.C. on the trumped-up charges of corrupting the morals of the Athenian youth and introducing strange gods, he rejected the opportunity to escape into exile. For seventy years, he argued, he had accepted the laws of Athens. Now he must accept their sentence, for by rejecting the laws of the city, he would in fact be guilty of the charges against him. Rather than reject Athens and its laws, he drank the fatal potion of hemlock given him by the executioner.

The philosophical interest in human choices and social constraints found echo in the historical writing of the age. Herodotus (ca. 484–ca. 420 B.C.), the first historian, was one of the many foreigners who found in Athens the intellectual climate and audience he needed to write an account of the Persian Wars of the preceding generation. His book of inquiries, or *historia,* into the origins and events of the conflict between Greeks and Persians is the first true history. Herodotus had traveled widely in the eastern Mediterranean, collecting local stories and visiting famous temples, palaces, and cities. In his study he presents a great panorama of the civilized world at the end of the sixth century B.C. His descriptions range from the peoples of the Persian Empire to the construction of the great pyramids (he reports that sixteen hundred talents of silver were paid for supplies of radishes, onions, and leeks for the workers who built the pyramid of Khufu). The story builds gradually to the heroic clash between the ancient civilizations of the East and the Greeks. Herodotus does not hesitate to repeat myths, legends, and outrageous tales. His faith in the gods is strong and he believes that the gods intervene in human affairs. Still, he is more than just a good storyteller or a chronicler of legends. Often, after reporting conflicting accounts he will conclude, "Both stories are told and the reader may take his choice between them." In other cases, after recounting a particularly far-fetched account heard from local informants, he comments, "Personally, I think this story is nonsense."

As he explains in his introduction, Herodotus's purpose in writing was twofold. First, he sought to preserve the memory of the past by recording the achievements of both Greeks and Orientals. Second, he set out to show how the two came into conflict. It was this concern to explain, to go beyond mere storytelling, that earned Herodotus the designation of "the father of history." Still, his understanding of cause and effect was fairly simple. He believed that wars arise from grievances and retribution. Thus the Persian Wars appear rather like large-scale feuds, the origins of which are lost in myth. At the same time, Herodotus is less interested in the mythic dimensions of the conflict than in the human, and his primary concern is the action of individuals under the press of circumstances. Ultimately, the Persian Wars become for Herodotus the conflict between freedom and despotism, and he describes with passion how different Greek states chose between the two. The choice, as he phrased it, was "to live in a rugged land and rule or to cultivate rich plains and be slaves."

The story of the Peloponnesian War was recorded by a different sort of historian, one who focused more narrowly on the Greek world and on political power. Through oral interviews and reading, Herodotus painstakingly recovered information about the events he described. Thucydides had been an Athenian general and a major actor in the first part of the Peloponnesian War. He began his account at the very outbreak of the conflict, thus writing a contemporary record of the war rather than a history of it. As Herodotus is called the father of history, Thucydides might be called the first social scientist.

Neither myth nor religion nor morality takes center stage in Thucydides' account of what he saw from the outset to be "a great war and more worth writing about than any of those which had taken place in the past." For him, the central subject is human society in action. His passion is the open, self-conscious political life characteristic of the Greek polis, and his view of the give-and-take of politics shows a strong debt to the sophistic tradition. Thucydides views the Greek states as acting out of rational self-interest. His favorite device for showing the development of such policies is the political set speech, in which two opposing leaders attempt to persuade their fellow citizens on the proper course of action. Thucydides was seldom actually present at the events he describes. Even when he was, he could not have transcribed the speakers' exact words. Rather, he attempted to put into the mouths of the speakers "whatever seemed most appropriate to me for each speaker to say in the particular circumstances." Although fictitious by modern standards, these speeches penetrate to the heart of the tough political choices facing the opposing forces. This hard-nosed approach to political decisions continues to serve as a model to historians and practitioners of power politics.

Still, morality is always just below the surface of Thucydides' narrative. Even as he unflinchingly chronicles the collapse of morality and social order in the face of political expediency, he recognizes that this process will destroy his beloved Athens. In his account of the second phase of the war, Athens acts with the full arrogance of a tyrant. Its overwhelming pride leads it to attack and destroy its weaker neighbors and ultimately to invade Sicily, with all the disastrous consequences of that campaign. The consequences of political self-interest, devoid of other considerations, follow their own natural course to disaster and ruin. In the later, unfinished chapters (Thucydides died shortly after Athens's final defeat), the Peloponnesian War takes on the characteristics of a tragedy. Here Thucydides, the ultimate political historian, shows the deep influence of the dominant literary tradition of his day, Greek drama.

Athenian Drama

Since the time of its introduction by Peisistratus in the middle of the sixth century B.C., drama had become popular, not only in Athens, but throughout the Greek world. Plays formed part of the annual feast of Dionysus and dealt with mythic subject matter largely taken from the *Iliad* and the *Odyssey*. As the dramatist Aeschylus said, "We are all eating crumbs from the great table of Homer." Three types of plays honored the Dionysian festival. Tragedies dealt with great men who failed because of flaws in their natures. Their purpose was, in the words of the philosopher Aristotle, to effect "through pity and terror the correction and refinement of passions." Comedies were more directly topical and political. They parodied real Athenians, often by name, and amused even while making serious points in defense of democracy. Somewhere between tragedies and comedies, satyr plays remained closest to the Dionysian cult. In them lecherous drunken satyrs—mythical half-man, half-goat creatures—interact with gods and men as they roam the world in search of Dionysus.

Athenian drama became more secular and less mythic as dramatists began to deal with human topics explosive in their immediacy and timeless in their portrayal of the human condition. Only a handful of the hundreds of Greek plays written in the fifth century B.C. survive. The first of the great Athenian tragedians whose plays we know is Aeschylus (525–456 B.C.), a veteran of Marathon and an eyewitness of the battle of Salamis. His one surviving trilogy, the *Oresteia,* traces the fate of the family of Agamemnon, the Greek commander at Troy. The three plays of the trilogy explore the conflicting obligations of filial respect and vengeance, which ultimately must be settled by rational yet divinely sanctioned law. Upon his return from Troy, the victorious Agamemnon is murdered by his unfaithful wife Clytemnestra. Orestes, his son, avenges his father's murder by murdering Clytemnestra, but in so doing incurs the wrath of the Furies, avenging spirits who pursue him for killing his mother. The conflict of duties and loyalties cannot be resolved by human means. Finally, Orestes arrives at the shrine of Apollo at Delphi, where the god purifies him from the pollution of the killing. Then, at Athens, Athena rescues Orestes, creating the Athenian law court and transforming the Furies into the Eumenides, the kindly guardian spirits of Athens.

The mature plays of Aeschylus's younger contemporary, Sophocles (496–406 B.C.), are tragedies in which religion plays a less important role. Instead, Sophocles sought to express human character. Although the Athenian audience knew the stories on which he based his plays, his plots move in a natural pace. He shows how humans make decisions and carry them out, constrained by their pasts, their weaknesses, and their vices, but free nonetheless. Sophocles' message is endurance, acceptance of human responsibility and, at the same time, of the ways of the gods, who overrule people's plans. The heroine of *Antigone* is the sister of Polynices, exiled son of King Oedipus of Thebes. Polynices has died fighting his city and Creon, its new ruler, commands under penalty of death that Polynices' body be left unburied. This would mean that his soul would never find rest, the ultimate punishment for a Greek. Antigone, with a determination and courage equal to her love for her brother, buries Polynices and is entombed alive for her crime. Here the conflict between the state, which claims the total obedience of its people, and the claims of familial love and religious piety meet in tragic conflict. Creon, warned by a prophet that he is offending heaven, orders Antigone's release, but it is too late. Rather than wait for death, she has already hanged herself.

Sophocles was the most successful of the fifth-century B.C. tragedians, and in the next century his plays came to be considered the most "classic" of the tragedies. His younger contemporary, Euripides (485–406 B.C.), was far more original and daring in his subject matter and treatment of human emotions. Unlike the stately dramas of Aeschylus and the deliberate progressions of Sophocles, Euripides' plays abound in plot twists and unexpected, violent outbursts of passion. His characters are less reconciled to their fates and less ready to accept the traditional gods:

Does someone say that there are gods in heaven?
There are not, there are not—unless one choose
To follow old tradition like a fool.

Euripides' women were often wronged and seldom accepted their lot. Medea, the central figure of his most famous tragedy, made it possible for the adventurer Jason to complete his quest for the mythical Golden Fleece. Abandoning her land in the east, she returns with the hero, bears his children, and settles with him at Corinth. Jason hopes to marry the daughter of the king, his only child, but must send Medea away. He tries to reason with her and she pretends to agree. Instead, she murders the Corinthian princess and her own children by Jason before escaping in a magical chariot drawn by dragons. Passion, not reason, rules Euripides' world.

Neither passion nor reason, but politics rules the world of Greek comedy. Rather than the timelessness of the human condition, Athenian comic playwrights focused their biting satire on the political and social issues of the moment. Notably, the comic genius Aristophanes (ca. 450–ca. 388 B.C.) used wit, imagination, vulgarity, and great poetic sensitivity to attack everything that offended him in his city. In his plays he mocks and ridicules statesmen, philosophers, rival playwrights, and even the gods. His comedies are full of outrageous twists of plot, talking animals, obscene jokes and puns, and mocking asides. And yet Aristophanes was a deeply patriotic Athenian, dedicated to the democratic system and equally dedicated to the cause of peace. In his now-lost *Babylonians,* written around 426 B.C. as Athenians struggled to recover from the plague and Cleon continued to pursue the bloody war against Sparta, he mocks Cleon and the Athenian demagogues while portraying the cities of the Delian League as slaves forced to grind grain at a mill. In *Lysistrata,* written in 411 B.C. after Athens had once more renewed the war, the women of Greece force their men to make peace by conspiring to refuse them sex as long as war continues. Through the sharp satire and absurd plots of his plays, Aristophanes communicates his sympathy for ordinary people, who must match wits with the charlatans and pompous frauds who attempt to dominate Athens's public life.

The Human Image

The humanity in Greek drama found its parallel in art. In the late sixth century B.C., a reversal of the traditional black figure technique had revolutionized vase painting. Artists had begun to outline scenes on unfired clay and then fill in the background with black or brown glaze. The interior details of the figures were also added in black. The result was a much more lifelike art, a lighter, more natural coloring, and the possibility of more perspective, depth, and molding. The drinking cup shown here, signed by Douris, one of the finest fifth-century B.C. vase painters, exemplifies this fluidity and naturalness. The subject matter is erotic: a mature man is offering a handsome youth money for sex. The execution is masterful. The two figures interact and yet balance each other, exactly filling the circular space of the cup's interior. Douris has captured the animation of the two figures' faces and their naturally expressive gestures as they bargain, as well as the fine detail of their musculature and clothing.

Sculpture reflected the same development toward balance and realism contained within an ideal of human form. The finest bronzes and marbles of the fifth century B.C. show freestanding figures whose natural vigor and force, even when they are engaged in strenuous exertion, are balanced by the placidity of their faces and their lack of emotion. The tradition established by the Athenian sculptor Phidias (ca. 500–ca. 430 B.C.) sought a naturalism in the portrayal of the human figure, which remained ideal rather than individual. Even explicitly commemorative statues, dedicated for victories in games or battle, showed people as they participated in the larger context of humanity.

The greatest sculptural program of the fifth century B.C. was that produced for the Athenian acropolis. The reconstruction of the acropolis, which had been destroyed by the Persians, was the culmination of Athenian art. Originally, the Athenians had not planned to rebuild its temples. However, Pericles decided to use the tribute collected from the Delian League to launch an enormous building project, which transformed the Athenian acropolis into the greatest complex of buildings in the ancient world. A first-century A.D. author who had visited all the great cities of the Mediterranean remarked, "They seem to have within them some everlasting breath of life and an ageless spirit intermingled with their composition."

The acropolis complex was so designed that a visitor was guided to see it in the proper order and perspective. One entered through the monumental Propylaea, or gateway, a T-shaped structure approached by a flight of steps. From the top of the steps, one could glimpse both Phidias's great bronze statue of Athena Promachos in the center of the acropolis and, to the right, the Parthenon. As visitors entered the acropolis itself, they passed on the right the small temple of Athena as Victory. This small temple, built slightly later than the Parthenon, looks out toward Salamis. It was constructed in the Ionic style, or order, an architectural tradition distinguished chiefly by the simple but fluid patterns of flowers and scrolls on its capitals, patterns borrowed from Oriental architecture. Continuing on the Sacred Way, one saw on the left the delicate Ionic Erechtheum, which housed the oldest Athenian cults. On the right, visitors were overawed by the Parthenon, a monument as much to Athens as to Athena.

Even today, the ruined temple seems a rectangular embodiment of order, proportion, and balance, an effect achieved through irregularity, illusion, and variation. The Parthenon is the most perfect example of the Doric order, an austerely beautiful building tradition reminiscent of earlier wooden structures. Every surface, from the floor to the columns to the horizontal beams, curves slightly. The spacing of the columns varies and each leans slightly inward. Those at the rear are larger than those at the front to compensate for the effect of viewing them from a greater distance. Just as the idealization of Athenian statues leaves the viewer with the impression of seeing a perfect individual, the illusion of flatness, regularity, and repetition in the Parthenon is the intended effect of an optical illusion.

An illusion, too, was the sense of overwhelming Athenian superiority and grandeur the acropolis was intended to convey. By the time the Erechtheum was completed in 406 B.C., the Athenian empire was all but destroyed, the city's population devastated, and its democracy imperiled. Two years later Athens surrendered unconditionally to Sparta.

A fifth-century B.C. drinking cup in terra-cotta from Attica in Greece. The cup, depicting a man and a youth, is signed by Douris. Over two hundred extant vases are ascribed to him.

The ruins on the Acropolis of Athens are dominated by the Parthenon (far right). At the left is the temple of Athena as Victory.

The intellectual and artistic accomplishments of Athens were as enduring as its empire proved ephemeral. Writers and artists alike focused their creative energies on human existence, seeking a proper proportion, order, and meaning, a blend of practical and the ideal, which Athens's political leaders tragically lacked.

From City-States to Macedonian Empire, 404–323 B.C.

The Peloponnesian War touched every aspect of Greek life. The war brought changes to the social and political structures of Greece by creating an enduring bitterness between elites and populace and a distrust of both democracy and traditional oligarchy. The mutual exhaustion of Athens and Sparta left a vacuum of power in the Aegean. Finally, the war raised fundamental questions about the nature of politics and society throughout the Greek world.

Politics After the Peloponnesian War

Over the decades-long struggle, the conduct of war and the nature of politics had changed, bringing new problems for victor and vanquished alike. Lightly armed professional mercenaries willing to fight for anyone able to pay gradually replaced hoplite citizen soldiers as the backbone of the fighting forces. Just as the rise of hoplite phalanxes in the sixth century B.C. had weakened oligarchies, the rise of these poorer warriors weakened the political importance of hoplites in favor of those who could pay and outfit rootless mercenaries. The rise of mercenary armies meant trouble for democracies such as Athens as well as for Sparta with its class of equals.

As war became professional and protracted, it became more brutal. When the Spartans and their band of allies captured Plataea in 427 B.C., they slaughtered all the men, enslaved the women, and razed the city. Despite Cleon's urgings, Athens refused to treat Mytilene in the same way when it captured that city in the same year. But by 416 B.C., when Athens captured Melos, it did not hesitate to treat its citizens as Sparta had dealt with those of Plataea. Lysander's slaughter of Athenian prisoners of war in 405 B.C. was business as usual. The moment of Greek unity experienced during the second Persian war was forgotten in the horrors of the Peloponnesian conflict.

Victory left Sparta no more capable of assuming leadership in 404 B.C. than it had been in 478 B.C. Years of war had reduced the population of equals to less than three thousand. The city could no longer maintain its traditional isolation from the outside world. Sparta could not control the Greek world without a powerful fleet, but ships and crews were costly and could be maintained only by taxing its empire or by accepting subsidies from Persia. Greedy and ambitious Spartans began to accumulate much of the wealth that poured in as booty and tribute from throughout the Aegean, while other equals lost the land they needed to maintain their place in society.

The Spartans also proved extremely unpopular imperialists. As reward for Persian assistance, Sparta returned the Ionian cities to Persian control. Elsewhere it established hated oligarchies to rule in a way favorable to Sparta's interests. In Athens, a brutal tyranny of thirty men took control in 404 B.C. With Spartan support, they executed fifteen hundred democratic leaders and forced five thousand more into exile. The Thirty Tyrants evoked enormous hatred and opposition. Within a year the exiles recaptured the city, restored democracy, and killed or expelled the tyrants.

Similar opposition to Spartan rule emerged throughout the Greek world, shattering the fragile peace created by Athens's defeat. For over seventy years the Greek world boiled in constant warfare. Mutual distrust, fear of any city that seemed about to establish a position of clear superiority, and the machinations of the Persian Empire to keep Greeks fighting each other produced a constantly shifting series of alliances.

Persia turned against its former ally when Sparta supported an unsuccessful attempt by Cyrus to unseat his brother Artaxerxes II. Soon the unlikely and unstable alliance of Athens, Corinth, Argos, Thebes, and Euboea, financed by Persia, entered a series of vicious wars against Sparta. Rapidly shifting alliances and mutual hostility ensured that there was no real victor. The first round ended in Spartan victory, due to the shifting role of Persia, whose primary interest was the continued disunity of the Greeks. By 377 B.C., however, Athens had reorganized its league and with Thebes as ally was able to break Spartan sea power. The decline of Sparta left a power vacuum soon filled by Thebes. Athens, concerned by this new threat, shifted alliances, making peace with its old enemy. However, Spartan military fortunes had so declined that when Sparta attacked Thebes in 371 B.C., its armies were destroyed and Spartan power broken. The next year Thebes invaded the Peloponnesus and freed Messenia, the foundation of Sparta's economic prosperity. Sparta never recovered. Deprived of its economic base, its body of equals reduced to a mere eight hundred, and its fleet gone, Sparta never regained its historic importance.

Theban hegemony was short-lived. Before long the same process of greed, envy, and distrust that had devastated the other Greek powers destroyed Thebes. In 355 B.C., when Thebes attempted to conquer the small state of Phocis, its enemies seized Delphi and used the vast treasure that had accumulated there over the years as gifts to Apollo to hire mercenaries. These professionals gradually wore down the Theban forces over the course of ten years. During the same time, Athens's reconstituted league disintegrated as members opposed Athenian attempts once more to convert a free association of states into an empire. By the 330s, all of the Greek states had proven themselves incapable of creating stable political units larger than their immediate polis.

Philosophy and the Polis

The failure of Greek political forms, oligarchy and democracy alike, profoundly affected Athenian philosophers. Plato (ca. 428–347 B.C.), an aristocratic student of Socrates, grew up during the Peloponnesian War and had witnessed the collapse of the empire, the brutality of the Thirty Tyrants, the execution of Socrates, and the revival of the democracy and its imperialistic ambitions. From these experiences he developed a hatred for Athenian democracy and a profound distrust of ordinary people's ability to tell right from wrong. Disgusted with public life, Plato left Attica for a time and traveled in Sicily and Italy, where he encountered different forms of government and different philosophical schools. Around 387 B.C., he returned to Athens and opened the Academy, a school to provide Athenian youth with what he considered to be knowledge of what was true and good for the individual and the state.

Plato chose a most unlikely literary form for transmitting his teachings. He used the dialogue, in the form of discussions between his teacher, Socrates, and a variety of students and opponents, to develop his ideas. While Plato shared with his mentor the conviction that human actions had to be grounded in self-knowledge, Plato's philosophy extended much further. His arguments about the inadequacy of all existing forms of government and the need to create a new form of government through the proper education of elite philosopher rulers were part of a complex understanding of the universe and the individual's place in it. (See "The First Utopia," pp. 86–87.)

Plato argued that true knowledge is impossible as long as it focuses on the constantly changing, imperfect world of everyday experience. Human beings can have real knowledge only of that which is eternal, perfect, and beyond the experience of the senses—the realm of what Plato calls the Forms. When we judge that individuals or actions are true or good or beautiful, we do so not because these particular persons or events are truly virtuous, but because we recognize that they participate in some way in the Idea, or Form, of truth or goodness or beauty. Consistent with Socrates' insistence on looking within oneself, Plato argues that we recognize these Forms, not in the object itself, but within our memories of a previous existence when our spirits or souls had direct contact with the universe of the Forms. Thus all knowledge is recollection, and everything exists only to the extent to which it participates in the Forms.

The evils of the world, and in particular the vices and failures of government and society, result from ignorance of the truth. Most people live as though chained in a cave in which all they can see are the shadows cast by a fire on the walls. In their ignorance, they mistake these flickering, imperfect images for reality. Their proper ruler must be a philosopher, one who is not deceived by the shadows. The philosopher's task is to break their chains and turn them toward the source of the light so that they can see the world as it really is. Ultimately, the philosopher will lead them from the cave to see the ultimate source of light—the sun outside. Truth will make them free.

Plato's idealist view (in the sense of the Ideas, or Forms) of knowledge dominated much of ancient philosophy. His greatest student, Aristotle (384–322 B.C.), however, rejected this view in favor of a philosophy rooted in the natural world. Aristotle came from a medical family of northern Greece and, although a student in Plato's Academy for almost twenty years, he never abandoned observation for speculation. Systematic investigation and explanation characterize Aristotle's vast work, and his interests ranged from biology to statecraft to the most abstract philosophy. In each field, he employed essentially the same method. He observed as many individual examples of the topic as possible and from these specific observations extracted general theories. His theories—whether on the nature of matter, the species of animals, the working of the human mind, ethics, or the proper form of the state—are distinguished by clarity of logical thinking, precision in the use of terminology, and respect for the world of experience. While ready to acknowledge his debt to Plato and other thinkers whose books he collected and read with great interest, he remained steadfastly opposed to Plato's Forms. For Aristotle, understanding of this world remains basic, and no valid theory can make it unintelligible.

Aristotle brought this approach to the question of life in society. He defined humans as "political animals," that is, animals particularly characterized by life

A Roman copy of a Greek statue of Aristotle. Many ancient Greek sculptures are known to us only through Roman copies.

in the polis. He analyzed over 150 city constitutions in order to find what contributed to their successes and failures. Unlike Plato, he did not regard any particular form of government as ideal. Rather, he concluded that the type of government ultimately mattered less than the balance between narrow oligarchy and radical democracy. Consistent with his belief that "virtue lies in a mean," he advocated governments composed of citizens who were neither extremely wealthy nor extremely poor. Moderation was the key to stability and justice.

Aristotle's teaching had little effect on his most famous student, Alexander, the son of King Philip of Macedon. Nor apparently did Aristotle's firsthand observation of this traditional hereditary monarchy in northern Greece influence the philosopher's understanding of the realities of Greek politics. And yet, during the very years that Aristotle was teaching, the vacuum created by the failure of the Greek city-states was being filled by the dynamic growth of the Macedonian monarchy that finally ended a century of Greek warfare, and with it the independence of the Greek city-states.

✌ The First Utopia

If the Greeks were fixated on good government, it might be because they had seen so many examples of bad. The bewildering variety of political forms that replaced the tyrants of the sixth century B.C. had proved no better than the evil they had sought to correct. By the end of the fourth century B.C., Lysander's brutal rule disillusioned many about the advantages of the Spartan mixture of monarchy, oligarchy, and democracy. The oligarchy of Corinth and the federalism of Thebes proved no better. And the radical democracy of Athens had brought disaster not only to the city but to all of Greece.

Aristotle and Plato each tackled the problem according to his own philosophical inclinations. Aristotle, ever the empiricist, collected over 150 city constitutions, which he hoped to analyze in order to discover the best form of government. His teacher Plato would have thought such an exercise a waste of time. To Plato, all existing constitutions were bad. No place had the perfect form of government. He thus set about in his *Republic* to describe the constitution of "no place" (in Greek, *utopia,* a term coined over eighteen hundred years later), the ideal government. In his description, Plato tackles the ultimate problem of politics: how should the state be ordered? His answer is a disturbing and fascinating image of a just society, created by a philosopher-king and ruled by a hand-picked body of Guardians.

Plato's ideal state resembles the Greek polis in size. A relatively small, territorially limited state is all that he can imagine. It is populated by four groups of people: slaves, artisans, auxiliaries, and Guardians. The first group is implied but never discussed. Plato, like any other Greek, could not have imagined a society existing without slave labor. Most of the citizens are farmers, artisans, and tradesmen, each specializing in that form of economic activity for which he or she is most suited. They are the only property owners in the republic, form the basis of its prosperity, and lead lives much like those of the ordinary citizens of a Greek polis, except that they have no role in defense or government.

The third group—in part self-perpetuating, in part recruited from the most promising children of the second—are the auxiliaries, who devote themselves exclusively to protecting the state from internal and external dangers. Auxiliaries are made, not born, and the program of education outlined by Plato is the critical ingredient in his ideal state. Boys and girls destined to be auxiliaries (equality of the sexes is fundamental in the republic) must be trained to know what is true and good and must be protected from lies and deception. Thus Plato bans poets and dramatists from his educational program. After all, Homer, Hesiod, Aeschylus, and Sophocles clothe fictions about the immorality of the gods and men in language of great beauty. Instead, the auxiliaries will be taught music and lyric poetry to instill in them a love of the harmony and order of the world. They also undertake physical training appropriate for soldiers, which not only prepares them for battle but, like music, develops the proper harmony of body and soul.

The auxiliaries must be free of private interests or ambitions, which would distract them from the needs of the state. Thus, they must live without private property or private family. Their needs are to be provided for by the artisan class, making it unnecessary and impossible for the auxiliaries to amass anything of their own. Because family concerns might distract them from their duty, they must live in a garrisonlike arrangement. Rulers would select appropriate male and female auxiliaries to mate and produce the best offspring. The children of such unions would be brought up together, regarding themselves and the adult auxiliaries as one large family identical with the state.

The best of these children, distinguished by their intellectual and moral ability, are to be selected as rulers, or Guardians. They undergo further education in the exact sciences and logic to train them to recognize the fundamental principles on which all truth depends. Finally, at the age of thirty-five, after years of study, a Guardian undertakes the hard task of governing, which Plato sees as a process of sharing with those less fortunate the enlightenment that education has given them. Plato did not consider his republic an exercise in imagination. He firmly believed that it was practical and possible. The best means by which to establish it was through a philosopher-king, a ruler in whom "political power and philosophy meet together."

Plato's contemporaries as well as subsequent generations have been at once fascinated and horrified by this ideal state. For many, the idea of total equality of the sexes was too absurd to consider. For others, the abolition of the family or the banning of poetry went beyond the realm of reason. Aristotle thought that the effects of such a system would be the opposite of those Plato intended, creating dissension and rebellion rather than reducing them. Modern readers praise or condemn Plato's republic because it smacks of communism, thought control, and totalitarianism. The modern social philosopher Karl Popper, for example, has termed Plato's political demands "purely totalitarian and antihumanitarian," and considers Plato the most determined enemy of freedom ever known. Goaded by Plato's challenge, political theorists ever since have taken up the task of devising their own image of the perfect society, seeking their own answer to Plato's challenge, "Where shall we find justice?"

Herodotus was unique among classical authors in his refusal to consider Greek customs superior to those of non-Greeks. In the following passage, he tells a story to prove his point.

If it were proposed to all nations to choose which seemed best of all customs, each, after examination made, would place its own first; so well is each persuaded that its own are by far the best. It is not therefore to be supposed that any, save a madman, would turn such things to ridicule. I will give this one proof among many from which it may be inferred that all men hold this belief about their customs: When Darius was king, he summoned the Greeks who were with him and asked them what price would persuade them to eat their fathers' dead bodies. They answered that there was no price for which they would do it.

Then he summoned those Indians who are called Callatiae, who eat their parents, and asked them (the Greeks being present and understanding by interpretation what was said) what would make them willing to burn their fathers at death. The Indians cried aloud, that he should not speak of so horrid an act. So firmly rooted are these beliefs; and it is, I think, rightly said in Pindar's poem that use and wont is lord of all.

From Herodotus, *The Histories*, Book III.

The Rise of Macedon

The polis had never been the only form of the Greek state. Alongside the city-states of Athens, Corinth, Syracuse, and Sparta were more decentralized ethne ruled by traditional hereditary chieftains and monarchs. Macedonia, in the northeast of the mainland, was one such ethnos. Its kings, chosen by the army from within a royal family, ruled in cooperation with nobles and clan leaders. Kings enhanced their position by marrying a number of wives from among the families of powerful supporters and allies. The Macedonian people spoke a Greek dialect and Macedonian kings and elite identified with Greek culture and tradition. However, constant rivalry for the throne, relative impoverishment, and loose organization prevented the Macedonians from playing much of a role in the events and achievements of the fifth and sixth centuries B.C. Macedonia had, however, long served as a buffer between the barbarians to the north and the Greek mainland, and its tough farmers and pastoralists were geared to constant warfare. As Athens, Sparta, and Thebes fought each other to mutual exhaustion, Macedonia under King Philip II (359–336 B.C.) moved into the resulting power vacuum.

Philip was called by a contemporary the greatest man Europe had ever produced. If political acumen and military skill are the only criteria, he deserves the title. These Philip had in abundance, but his ambition exceeded them both. During his twenties he murdered his way to the throne (the usual Macedonian proce-

dure) and set about consolidating his position at home and strengthening his influence abroad through military and diplomatic means. Philip showed a particular genius for rapidly organizing and leading armies and for conducting complex multiple campaigns each year. He secured his borders against northern barbarians and captured the northern coast of the Aegean, including the gold and silver mines of Mount Pangaeus, which gave him a ready source of money for his campaigns. Then he turned his attention to the south.

In 346 B.C., Philip intervened in the war between Thebes and Phocis, ending that conflict but forcing himself into the center of Greek affairs. From then on he was relentless in his efforts to swallow up one Greek state after another. In spite of the powerful oratory of the Athenian statesman Demosthenes (384–322 B.C.), who recognized Philip's threat, the Greek states resisted uniting against Philip, and one by one they fell. In 338 B.C., Philip achieved a final victory at Chaeronea and established a new league, the League of Corinth. However, unlike all those that had preceded it, this league was no confederation of sovereign states. It was an empire ruled by a king and supported by wealthy citizens whose cooperation Philip rewarded well. This new model of government, a monarchy drawing its support from a wealthy elite, became a fixture of the Mediterranean world for over two thousand years.

Philip's success was based on his powerful military machine, which combined both Macedonian military tradition and the new mercenary forces that had emerged over the past century in Greece. The heart of his army was the infantry, which was trained in the use of pikes some fourteen feet long—four feet longer than those of the Greek hoplites. Tribesmen from the Macedonian hills formed the core of this fighting force. Allies and Greek mercenaries, paid for with Mount Pangaeus gold, could swell their ranks to armies of over forty thousand. Macedonian phalanxes moved forward in disciplined ranks, pushing back their foes, whose shorter lances could not reach the Macedonians. When the enemy were contained, the Macedonian cavalry charged from the flank and cut them to pieces. The cavalry, composed of nobles and tribal chieftains, lived in close proximity to the king and felt tremendous personal loyalty to Philip. Known as the Royal Companions, they were the elite of Macedon and the greatest beneficiaries of Philip's conquests.

No sooner had Philip subdued Greece than he announced a campaign against Persia. He intended to lead a combined Greek force in a war of revenge and conquest to punish the great empire for its invasion of Greece 150 years earlier and its subsequent involvement in the Greek world. Before he could begin, however, he met the fate of his predecessors. At the age of forty-six he was cut down by an assassin's knife, leaving his twenty-year-old son, Alexander (336–323 B.C.), to

lead the expedition. Within thirteen years Alexander had conquered the world.

The Empire of Alexander the Great

Alexander was less affected by his teacher, the philosopher Aristotle, than he was by the poet Homer. Envisioning himself a new Achilles, Alexander sought to imitate and surpass that legendary warrior and hero of the *Iliad*. Shortly after moving his troops across the Hellespont from Europe to Asia, Alexander visited Troy, where he lay a wreath on the supposed tomb of his hero and took from a temple weapons said to have belonged to Achilles. These he had carried before him in all of his battles.

Alexander's military genius, dedication to his troops, reckless disregard for his own safety, and ability to move both men and supplies across vast distances at great speed inspired the war machine developed by Philip and led it on an odyssey of conquest that stretched from Asia Minor to India. In 334 B.C., the first year of his campaign, Alexander captured the Greek cities of Asia Minor. Then he continued east. At Gordium, according to legend, he confronted an ancient puzzle, a complex knot tied to the chariot of the ancient king of that city. Whoever could loosen the

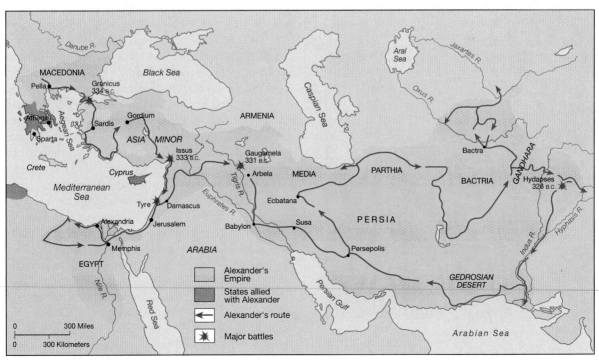

The Empire of Alexander the Great

knot, the legend said, would become master of Asia. Alexander solved that puzzle, as he did all of his others, with his sword. Two months later he defeated the Persian king Darius III at Issus and then headed south toward the Mediterranean coast and Egypt. After his victories there, he turned again to the north and entered Mesopotamia. At Gaugamela in 331 B.C., he defeated Darius a second, decisive time. Shortly after, Darius was murdered by the remnants of his followers. Alexander captured the Persian capital of Persepolis with its vast treasure and became the undisputed ruler of the vast empire.

The conquest of Persia was not enough. Alexander pushed on, intending to conquer the whole world. His armies marched east, subduing the rebellious Asian provinces of Bactria and Sogdiana. He negotiated the Khyber Pass from what is now Afghanistan into the Punjab, crossed the Indus River, and defeated the local Indian king. Everywhere he went he reorganized or founded cities, entrusting them to loyal Macedonians and other Greeks and settling them with veterans of his campaigns, and then pushed on toward the unknown. Beyond Bucephala on the Hydaspes River, in what is

CLASSICAL GREECE

525–456 B.C.	**Aeschylus**
ca. 500–ca. 430 B.C.	**Phidias**
496–406 B.C.	**Sophocles**
490 B.C.	**Battle of Marathon**
485–406 B.C.	**Euripides**
ca. 484–ca. 420 B.C.	**Herodotus**
480 B.C.	**Battles of Thermopylae and Salamis**
478 B.C.	**Athens assumes control of Delian League**
ca. 470–399 B.C.	**Socrates**
ca. 460–430 B.C.	**Pericles dominates Athens**
ca. 450–ca. 388 B.C.	**Aristophanes**
431–421; 414–404 B.C.	**Peloponnesian War**
ca. 428–347 B.C.	**Plato**
384–322 B.C.	**Aristotle**
384–322 B.C.	**Demosthenes**
338 B.C.	**Philip of Macedon defeats Athens**
336–323 B.C.	**Reign of Alexander the Great**

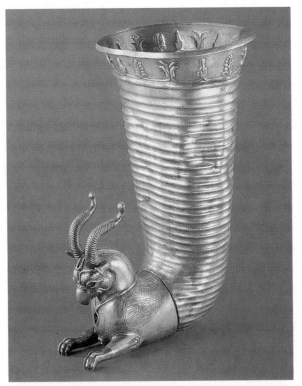

A partially gilded silver rhyton, *or drinking vessel, is an example of Persian art. A horned griffin forms the base and lotus buds encircle the rim. Treasures such as this were looted from the Persians by Alexander's conquering army.*

now Pakistan, his Macedonian warriors finally halted. Worn out by years of bloody conquest and exhausting travel, they refused to go farther, even if Alexander himself were to lead them. "If there is one thing above all others a successful man should know," their spokesman told him, "it is *when to stop*." Furious but impotent, Alexander turned south, following the Indus River to its mouth in the hope that it might turn out to be an extension of the Nile encircling the earth. Upon reaching the Indian Ocean he at last turned west, leading his army across the barren Gedrosia desert and finally back to Persepolis in 324 B.C. No mortal had ever before accomplished such a feat. Even in his own lifetime, Alexander was venerated as a god.

Alexander is remembered as a greater conqueror than ruler, but his plans for his reign, had he lived to complete them, might have won him equal fame. Unlike his Macedonian followers, who were interested mainly in booty and power, he recognized that only by merging local and Greek peoples and traditions could he forge a lasting empire. Thus, even while founding cities on the Greek model throughout his empire, he carefully respected the local social and cultural traditions of the conquered peoples. In fact, after his return from India, he executed many Macedonian governors found guilty of misrule or corruption. Alexander enlist-

ALEXANDER CALLS A HALT

❧

The second century A.D. historian Arrian, drawing on earlier accounts and his own sense of Alexander, re-creates the exchange between Alexander and his trusted officer Coenus, which led Alexander at last to abandon his relentless easterly march of conquest.

Alexander: I observe, gentlemen, that when I would lead you on a new venture you no longer follow me with your old spirit. I have asked you to meet me that we may come to a decision together: are we, upon my advice, to go forward, or, upon yours, to turn back? . . . With all that [has been] accomplished, why do you hesitate to extend the power of Macedon—*your* power—to the Hyphasis and the tribes on the other side? Are you afraid that a few natives who may still be left will offer opposition?. . .

For a man who *is* a man work, in my belief, if it is directed to noble ends, has no object beyond itself . . . Our ships will sail round from the Persian Gulf to Libya as far as the Pillars of Hercules, whence all Libya to the eastward will soon be ours, and all Asia too, and to this empire there will be no boundaries but what God Himself has made for the whole world.

Coenus: I judge it best to set some limit to further enterprise. You know the number of Greeks and Macedonians who started upon this campaign, and you can see how many of us are left today . . . Every man of them longs to see his parents again, if they yet survive, or his wife, or his children . . . Do not try to lead men who are unwilling to follow you; if their heart is not in it, you will never find the old spirit or the old courage. Consent rather yourself to return to your mother and your home. Once there, you may bring good government to Greece and enter your ancestral house with all the glory of the many victories won in this campaign, and then, should you so desire it, you may begin again and undertake a new expedition against these Indians of the East, or if you prefer, to the Black Sea or to Carthage and the Libyan territories beyond . . . Sir, if there is one thing above all others a successful man should know, it is *when to stop.*

From Arrian, *The Campaigns of Alexander,* Book V.

---

ed elite units of Persian youths to be trained in Macedonian-style warfare and traditions. At the same time he encouraged marriages between his companions and the daughters of local elites. In one mass ceremony at Susa thousands of his warriors married Persian women. Alexander himself led the way, marrying Darius's daughter Stateira just as he had previously married Roxane, daughter of the king of Bactria. Whether his program of cultural and social amalgamation could have succeeded is a moot point. In 323 B.C., two years after his return from India, he died at Babylon at the age of thirty-two.

The empire did not long outlive the emperor. Vicious fighting soon broke out among his generals and his kin. Alexander's wife Roxane and son Alexander IV (323–317 B.C.) were killed, as were all other members of the royal family. The various units of the empire broke apart into separate kingdoms and autonomous cities, in which each ruler attempted to continue the political and cultural tradition of Alexander in a smaller sphere. Alexander's empire became a shifting kaleidoscope of states, kingdoms, and cities, dominated by priest-kings, native princelings, and ter-

ritorial rulers, all vying to enhance their positions while preserving a relative balance of power. By 275 B.C., three large kingdoms dominated Alexander's former domain. The most stable was Egypt, which Ptolemy I (323–285 B.C.), one of Alexander's closest followers, acquired upon Alexander's death and which he and his descendants ruled until Cleopatra VII (51–30 B.C.) was defeated by the Roman Octavian in 31 B.C. In the east, the Macedonian general Seleucus (246–226 B.C.) captured Babylon in 312 B.C., and he and his descendants ruled a vast kingdom reaching from what is today western Turkey to Afghanistan. Whittled away in the east by both the Greek kingdom of Bactria and the non-Greek Parthians and in the west by the Greek Attalids in Pergamum, the Seleucid kingdom gradually shrank to a small region of northern Syria before it fell to Rome in 64 B.C. After fifty years of conflict, Antigonus Gonatas (276–239 B.C.), the grandson of another of Alexander's commanders, secured Macedon and Greece. His Antigonid successors ruled the kingdom until it fell to the Romans in 168 B.C.

Alexander's conquests transformed the political map of southern Europe, western Asia, and Egyptian Africa.

They swept away or absorbed old traditions of government, brought Greek traditions of urban organization, and replaced indigenous ruling elites with hellenized dynasties. Within this vast region, rulers encouraged commercial and cultural contact, enriching their treasuries and creating a new form of Greek culture. Still, Alexander's successors never developed the interest or ability to integrate this Greek culture and the more ancient indigenous cultures of their subjects. Ultimately, this failure proved fatal for the Hellenistic kingdoms.

The Hellenistic World

Although vastly different in geography, language, and custom, the Hellenistic kingdoms (so called to distinguish them from the Hellenic civilization of the fifth and early fourth centuries B.C.) shared two common traditions. First, great portions of the Hellenistic world, from Asia Minor to Bactria and south to Egypt, had been united at various times by the Assyrian and Persian empires. During these periods they had absorbed much of Mesopotamian civilization and in particular the administrative traditions begun by the Assyrian Tiglath-pileser. Thus the Hellenistic kings ruled kingdoms already accustomed to centralized government and could rely on the already existing machinery of tax collection and administration to control the countryside. For the most part, however, these kings had little interest in the native populations of their kingdoms beyond the amount of wealth that they could extract from them. Hellenistic monarchs remained Greek, and they lavished their attentions on the newly created Greek cities, which absorbed vast amounts of the kingdoms' wealth.

These cities and their particular form of Greek culture were the second unifying factor in the Hellenistic world. In the tradition of Alexander himself, the Ptolemys, Seleucids, and Antigonids cultivated Greek urban culture and recruited Greeks for their most important positions of responsibility. Alexander had founded over thirty-five cities during his conquests. The Seleucids established almost twice as many throughout their vast domain, even replacing the ancient city of Babylon with their capital, Seleucia, on the Tigris. In Egypt the Ptolemys replaced the ancient capital of Memphis with the new city of Alexandria. These cities became the centers of political control, economic consumption, and cultural diffusion throughout the Hellenistic world.

Urban Life and Culture

The Hellenistic kingdoms lived in a perpetual state of warfare with one another. Kings needed Greek soldiers, merchants, and administrators and competed with their rivals in offering Greeks all the comforts of home. Hellenistic cities were Greek in physical organization, constitution, and language. Each had an agora, or marketplace, that would not have been out of place in Attica. They boasted temples to the Greek gods and goddesses, theaters, baths, and most importantly, a *gymnasion,* or combination sports center and school. In the gymnasion young men competed in Greek sports and absorbed Greek poetry and philosophy just as did their cousins on the Peloponnesus. Sophocles' tragedies played to enthusiastic audiences in an enormous Greek theater in what is today Ai Khanoum on the Oxus River in Afghanistan, and the rites of Dionysus were celebrated in third-century B.C. Egypt with processions of satyrs, maenads, free wine for all, and a golden phallus 180 feet long. Since these Greeks were drawn from throughout the Greek-speaking world, in time a universal Greek dialect, *koine,* became the common language of culture and business like the Latin of the medieval West, the German of the Habsburg empire, or basic English in much of the world today.

For all their Greek culture, Hellenistic cities differed fundamentally from Greek cities and colonies of the past. Not only were they far larger than any earlier Greek cities, but their government and culture were different from those of other cities or colonies. Colonies had been largely independent poleis. The Hellenistic cities were never politically sovereign. The regional kings maintained firm control over the cities, even while working to attract Greeks from the mainland and the islands to them. On the one hand, this policy weakened the political significance of Greek life and culture. Politics was no longer the passion that it had been in the fifth and early fourth centuries B.C. In each city a council elected from among the Greek inhabitants was largely self-governing in domestic matters. However, while these cities were in theory democracies, kings firmly controlled city government, and participation in the city councils and magistracies became the affair of the wealthy.

On the other hand, the Hellenistic cities were much less closed than were the traditional poleis of the Hellenic world. There, citizenship had been largely restricted by birth, and social identity had been determined by deme, tribe, and family. In the new cities of the east, Greeks from all over were welcomed as soldiers and administrators regardless of their city of origin. By

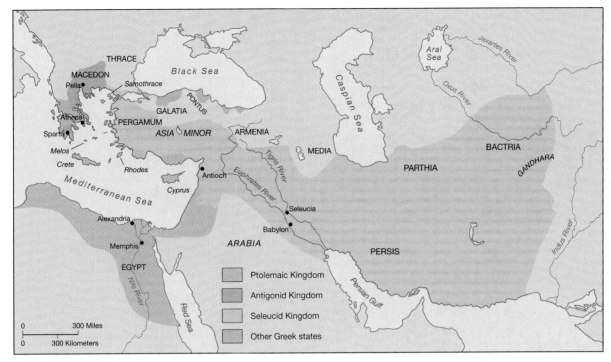

The Hellenistic Kingdoms

the second century B.C., Greeks no longer identified themselves by their city of origin but as "Hellenes," that is, Greeks. Moreover, to a limited extent, native elites could, through the adoption of Greek language, culture, and traditions, become Greek themselves—an achievement that had been impossible for the metics of Athens, Corinth, or Sparta.

The great social and geographical mobility possible in the new cities extended to women as well as men. No longer important simply as transmitters of citizenship, women began to assume a greater role in the family, in the economy, and in public life. Marriage contracts, particularly in Ptolemaic Egypt, emphasized the theoretical equality of husband and wife. In one such contract, the wife was granted "mastery in common with (her husband) over all their possessions." The husband and wife were further enjoined to take no concubines or male or female lovers. The penalty for the husband was loss of the wife's dowry; for the wife, the punishment was divorce.

Since women could control their own property, many engaged in business and some became wealthy. Wealth translated into civic influence and power. Phyle, a woman of the first century B.C. from Priene in Asia Minor, spent vast sums on a reservoir and aqueducts to bring water to her city. She was rewarded with high political office, as was a female archon in Histria on the Black Sea in the second century B.C.

The most powerful women in Hellenistic society were queens, especially in Egypt, where the Ptolemys adopted the Egyptian tradition of royal marriages between brothers and sisters. Four of the first eight Ptolemys married sisters in order to eliminate foreign dynastic influences in court. Arsinoë II (ca. 316–270 B.C.) ruled as an equal with her brother-husband Ptolemy II (286–246 B.C.) She inaugurated a tradition of powerful female monarchs that ended only with Cleopatra VII, the last independent ruler of Egypt, who successfully manipulated the Roman generals Julius Caesar (100–44 B.C.) and Mark Antony (81–30 B.C.) to maintain Egyptian autonomy.

Just as monarchs competed with one another in creating Greek cities, they vied in making their cities centers of Greek culture. Socially ambitious and newly wealthy citizens supported poets, philosophers, and artists as a means of demonstrating their status. Queens, in particular, patronized poets and dramatists, and cities and wealthy individuals endowed gymnasia and libraries. The largest library was in Alexandria in Egypt, where the Ptolemys established the Mouseion, or Museum, as the house of the muses, the goddesses of the arts and literature. In time the library at Alexandria housed half a million book-rolls, including all of the great classics of Greek literature. In order to acquire still more, ships arriving in Alexandria were boarded and searched for books to copy. Generations of poet-scholars edited and commented on the classics, in the process inventing literary criticism and preserving much of what is known about classical authors.

Hellenistic writers were not simply book collectors or critics. They developed new forms of literature, including the romance, which often recounted imaginary adventures of Alexander the Great, and the pastoral poem, which the Sicilian Theocritus (ca. 310–250 B.C.) developed out of popular shepherd songs. Callimachus (ca. 305–ca. 240 B.C.), the cataloger of the library in Alexandria and royal tutor, was the acknowledged (and envied) master of the short, witty epigram. With equal skill he could poke fun at himself as a frustrated lover of boys and parties or move the reader with touching poems on his deceased friends.

Political rivalry also encouraged architectural and artistic rivalry, as kings competed for the most magnificent Hellenistic cities. Temples, porticoes, and public buildings grew in size and ornamentation. Architects experimented with multitiered buildings, combining traditional Doric and Ionian orders. In the Seleucid kingdom, the more flamboyant Corinthian order with its luxuriantly foliated capitals was especially popular. The Seleucid king Antiochus IV (176–165 B.C.) completed in the Corinthian order the great temple of Olympian Zeus in Athens, until Roman times the largest building in Europe.

Hellenistic architects not only developed more elaborate and monumental buildings, they also combined these buildings in harmonious urban ensembles. New cities presented unprecedented opportunities for urban planners, and Hellenistic rulers provided the funds to undertake major urban renewal projects in older cities. In cities such as Rhodes and Pergamum, planners incorporated their constructions into the terrain, using natural hills and slopes to create elegant terraced vistas.

Freestanding statues and magnificent murals and mosaics adorned the public squares, temples, and private homes of Hellenistic cities. While artists continued the traditions of the Hellenic age, they displayed more freedom in portraying tension and restlessness as well as individuality in the human form. Little remains of Hellenistic painting, although Roman mosaics such as that of Alexander at Issus suggest the virtuosity with which mural painters managed multifigure compositions, perspective, and realistic portrayal of landscapes. Sculptors also demonstrated their skill in the portrayal of drapery tightly folded or falling naturally across the human form. The *Nike* (Victory) from Samothrace (ca. 200 B.C.) and the Aphrodite from Melos, known more commonly as the Venus de Milo (ca. 120 B.C.), are supreme examples of Hellenistic sculptural achievement.

The Nike, *or* Winged Victory, *was found in fragments on the island of Samothrace in the Aegean Sea in 1863. The head and arms were never discovered. The statue is now in the Louvre in Paris.*

Hellenistic Philosophy

Philosophy, too, flourished in the Hellenistic world, but in directions different from those initiated by Plato and Aristotle, who were both deeply committed to political involvement in the free polis. Instead, Cynics, Epicureans, and Stoics turned inward, advocating types of morality less directly tied to the state and society. These philosophies appealed to the rootless Greeks of the Hellenistic east who were no longer tied by bonds of religion or patriotism to any community. Each philosophy was as much a way of life as a way of thought and offered different answers to the question of how the individual, cut loose from the security of traditional social and political networks, should deal with the whims of fate.

The Cynic tradition, established by Antisthenes (ca. 450–ca. 350 B.C.), a pupil of Socrates, and Diogenes of Sinope (d. ca. 320 B.C.), taught that excessive attachment to the things of this world was the source of evil and unhappiness. Individual freedom comes through renunciation of material things, society, and pleasures. The more one has, the more one is vulnerable to the whims of fortune. The Cynics' goal was to reduce their possessions, connections, and pleasures to the absolute minimum. "I would rather go mad than enjoy myself," Antisthenes said. The story was told that once, while Diogenes was sunning himself, Alexander the Great came to see the philosopher and, standing before him, offered to do for him anything that he desired. "Stand out of my sun," was Diogenes' reply.

Like the Cynics, the Epicureans sought freedom, but from pain rather than from the conventions of ordinary life. Epicurus (341–270 B.C.) and his disciples have often been attacked for their emphasis on pleasure ("You need only possess perception and be made of flesh, and you will see that pleasure is good," Epicurus wrote), but this search for pleasure was not a call to sensual indulgence. Pleasure must be pursued rationally. Today's pleasure can mean tomorrow's suffering. The real goal is to reduce desires to that which is simple and attainable. Thus Epicureans urged retirement from politics, retreat from public competition, and concentration instead on friendship and private enjoyment. Epicurus's garden became a tranquil retreat for himself and his disciples. For Epicurus, reason properly applied illuminates how best to pursue pleasure. The universe is entirely material, consisting of atoms, and the gods

have no interest or role in this world. Alone, humans must search for their pleasure through reason, which will make them free. The traditional image of the Epicurean as an indulgent sensualist is a gross caricature. As Epicurus advised one follower, an Epicurean "revels in the pleasure of the body—on a diet of bread and water."

The Stoics also followed nature, but rather than leading them to retire from public life, it led them to greater participation in it. Just as the universe is a system in which stars and planets move according to fixed laws, so too is human society ordered and unified. As the founder of Stoicism, Zeno (ca. 335–ca. 263 B.C.), expressed it, "All men should regard themselves as members of one city and people, having one life and order." Every person has a role in the divinely ordered universe, and all roles are of equal value. True happiness consists in freely accepting one's role, whatever it may be, while unhappiness and evil result from attempting to reject one's place in the divine plan. Stoic virtue consists in applying reason to one's life in such a way that one knowingly lives in conformity to nature. Worldly pleasures, like worldly pain, have no particular value. Both are to be accepted and endured.

All three philosophical traditions emphasized the importance of reason and the proper understanding of nature. Hellenistic understanding of nature was one area in which Greek thinkers were influenced by the ancient Oriental traditions brought to them through the conquests of Alexander. Particularly for mathematics, astronomy, and engineering, the Hellenistic period was a golden age.

Mathematics and Science

Ptolemaic Egypt became the center of mathematical studies. Euclid (ca. 300 B.C.), whose *Elements* was the fundamental textbook of geometry until the twentieth century, worked there, as did his student Apollonius of Perga (ca. 262–ca. 190 B.C.), whose work on conic sections is one of the greatest monuments of geometry. Both Apollonius and his teacher were as influential for their method as for their conclusions. Their treatises follow rigorous logical proofs of mathematical theorems, which established the form of mathematical reasoning to the present day. Archimedes of Syracuse (ca. 287–212 B.C.) corresponded with the Egyptian mathematicians and made additional contributions to geometry—such as the calculation of the approximate value of pi—as well as to mechanics, arithmetic, and engineering. Archimedes was famous for his practical application of engineering, particularly to warfare, and

A Hellenistic bronze statue of a veiled dancer from the third century B.C. The figure is a remarkable example of the effect created by the treatment of flowing draperies, which was a hallmark of the art of the Hellenistic period.

legends quickly grew up about his marvelous machines with which he helped Syracuse defend itself against Rome. Although it was not true, as reported, that the rumor of him on the city's walls was sufficient to cause the Roman fleet to flee in terror, such traditions indicate the esteem in which applied science was held in the Hellenistic world.

Many mathematicians, such as Archimedes and Apollonius, were also mathematical astronomers, and the application of their mathematical skills to the exact data collected by earlier Babylonian and Egyptian empirical astronomers greatly increased the understanding of the heavens and earth. Archimedes devised a means of measuring the diameter of the sun, and Eratosthenes of Cyrene (ca. 276–194 B.C.) calculated the circumference of the earth to within two hundred miles. Aristarchus of Samos (ca. 270 B.C.) theorized that the sun and fixed stars were motionless and that the earth moves around the sun. His theory, unsupported by mathematical evidence and not taking into account the elliptical nature of planetary orbits or their nonuniform speeds, was rejected by contemporaries. Hipparchus of Nicea (ca. 146–127 B.C.) offered an alternative theory, placing the earth at the center of the universe. Backed by more mathematically acceptable arguments, his system remained, with slight adjustments made three hundred years later by Ptolemy of Alexandria, the dominant theory until the sixteenth century.

Like astronomy, Hellenistic medicine combined theory and observation. In Alexandria, Herophilus of Chalcedon (ca. 335–ca. 280 B.C.) and Erasistratus of Ceos (ca. 250 B.C.) conducted important studies in human anatomy. The Ptolemaic kings provided them with condemned prisoners whom they dissected alive and thus were able to observe the functioning of the organs of the body. The terrible agonies inflicted on their experimental subjects were considered to be justified by the argument that there was no cruelty in causing pain to guilty men to seek remedies for the innocent.

For all of the vitality of the Hellenistic civilization, these cities remained parasites on the local societies. No real efforts were made to merge the two and to develop a new civilization. Some ambitious members of the indigenous elites tried to adopt the customs of the Greeks, while others plotted insurrection. The clearest example of these conflicting tensions was that of the Jewish community. Early in the second century B.C., a powerful Jewish faction, which included the High Priest of Yahweh, supported hellenization. With the assistance of the Seleucid king, this faction set up a gymnasion in Jerusalem where Jewish youths and even priests began to study Greek and participate in Greek culture. Some even underwent painful surgery to reverse the effects of circumcision so that they could pass for Greeks in naked athletic contests. This rejection of tradition infuriated a large portion of the Jewish population. When the Seleucids finally attempted to introduce pagan cults into the temple in 167 B.C., open rebellion broke out and continued intermittently until the Jews gained independence in 141 B.C.

This violent opposition was repeated elsewhere from time to time, especially in Egypt and Persia, where, as in Judaea, old traditions of religion and monarchy provided rallying points against the transplanted Greeks. In time the Hellenistic kingdoms' inability to bridge the gap between Greek and indigenous populations proved fatal. In the East, the non-Greek kingdom of Parthia replaced the Seleucids in much of the old Persian empire. In the West, continuing hostility between kingdoms and within kingdoms prepared the way for their progressive absorption by the new power to the west: Rome.

• • •

In the fifth century B.C., the rugged slopes, fertile plains, and arid islands of the Greek world gave rise to characteristic forms of social, political, and cultural organization that have reappeared in varying forms wherever Western civilization has taken root. In Athens, which emerged from the ruins of the Persian invasion as the most powerful and dynamic state in the Hellenic world, the give-and-take of a direct democracy challenged men to raise fundamental questions about the relationship between individual and society, freedom and absolutism, gods and mortals. At the same time, this society of free males excluded the majority of its inhabitants—women, foreigners, and slaves—from participation in government and fought a long and ultimately futile war to hold together an exploitative empire.

The interminable wars among Greek states ultimately left the Greek world open to conquest by a powerful, semi-Greek monarchy that went on to spread Athenian culture throughout the known world. Freed from the particularism of individual city-states, Hellenistic culture became a universal tradition emphasizing the individual rather than the community of family, tribe, or religious association. And yet this universal Hellenistic cultural tradition remained a thin veneer, hardly assimilated into the masses of the ancient world. Its proponents, except for Alexander the Great, never sought a real synthesis of Greek and barbarian tradition. Such a synthesis would begin only with the coming of Rome.

Suggestions for Further Reading

General Reading

John Boardman, Jasper Griffin, and Oswyn Murray, *Greece and the Hellenistic World* (New York: Oxford University Press, 1988). An excellent, up-to-date survey of Greek history by a series of experts.

* Michel M. Austin and Pierre Vidal-Naquet, *Economic and Social History of Ancient Greece* (Berkeley, CA: University of California Press, 1977). An excellent survey of Greek society.

Cambridge Ancient History, 2d ed., Vols. 5 (1989) and 7 (1984). Contains essays on most aspects of Greek history.

* Simon Hornblower, *The Greek World, 479–323 B.C.* (New York: Routledge, Chapman & Hall, 1983). An up-to-date survey concentrating on political history.

War and Politics in the Fifth Century B.C.

John Manuel Cook, *The Persian Empire* (New York: Schocken Books, 1983). The standard history of Persia from the perspective of history and archaeology.

R. Meiggs, *The Athenian Empire* (New York: Oxford University Press, 1979). The standard account.

P. J. Rhodes, *The Athenian Empire* (1985). A short summary.

* A. H. M. Jones, *Athenian Democracy* (Baltimore, MD: Johns Hopkins University Press, 1957). A collection of essays by a major traditional historian.

* M. I. Finley, *Democracy Ancient and Modern,* 2d ed. (New Brunswick, NJ: Rutgers University Press, 1985). A valuable essay on Athenian democracy by a leading historian of antiquity.

W. R. O'Connor, *The New Politicians of Fifth-Century Athens* (Princeton, NJ: Princeton University Press, 1971). Reappraises the demagogues within the context of Athenian political life.

A. W. Gomme, *Historical Commentary on Thucydides,* 5 vols. (New York: Oxford University Press, 1945–80). The fundamental study of the sources.

G. E. M. de St. Croix, *The Origins of the Peloponnesian War* (Ithaca, NY: Cornell University Press, 1972). An interpretation of the Peloponnesian War broader than the title indicates.

* David M. Schaps, *Economic Rights of Women in Ancient Greece* (New York: Columbia University Press, 1979). An examination of the roles of women in Greek society, focusing on property rights.

* W. K. Lacey, *The Family in Classical Greece* (Ithaca, NY: Cornell University Press, 1984). Ordinary life in the Greek world.

Renate Bridenthal and Claudia Koonz, eds., *Becoming Visible: Women in European History,* 2d ed. (Boston: Houghton Mifflin, 1988). Includes essays on women in classical Greece.

* Yvon Garlan, *Slavery in Ancient Greece* (Ithaca, NY: Cornell University Press, 1988). A recent study of Greek slavery.

Athenian Culture in the Hellenic Age

* W. K. C. Guthrie, *History of Greek Philosophy,* Vol. 3 (New York: Cambridge University Press, 1971). Covers the Sophists.

I. Crombie, *An Examination of Plato's Doctrines,* 2 vols. (Atlantic Highlands, NJ: Humanities Press International, 1963). A safe guide into works on Plato.

* G. E. R. Lloyd, *Aristotle: The Growth and Structure of His Thought* (New York: Cambridge University Press, 1968). A developmental approach to Aristotle.

W. Burkert, *Greek Religion* (Cambridge, MA: Harvard University Press, 1985). General survey of the topic.

* J. Boardman, *Greek Art,* 3d ed. (New York: Thames & Hudson, 1985). A handbook introduction by period.

* Simon Goldhill, *Reading Greek Tragedy* (New York: Cambridge University Press, 1986). A general introduction to Athenian tragedy.

From City-States to Macedonian Empire, 404–323 B.C.

G. Cawkwell, *Philip of Macedon* (Boston: Faber & Faber, 1978). A political biography of the Macedonian king.

* A. B. Bosworth, *Conquest and Empire* (New York: Cambridge University Press, 1988). A scholarly but readable account of Alexander the Great.

R. L. Fox, *Alexander the Great* (New York: Dial, 1973). Lively recent biography.

The Hellenistic World

* R. W. Walbank, *The Hellenistic World* (Cambridge, MA: Harvard University Press, 1981). General overview.

P. M. Fraser, *Ptolemaic Alexandria* (New York: Oxford University Press, 1972). Especially good on Hellenistic literature in Egypt.

A. A. Long, *Hellenistic Philosophy* (Wolfeboro, NH: Longman Publishing Group, 1974). On Hellenistic thought.

* J. J. Pollitt, *Art in the Hellenistic Age* (New York: Cambridge University Press, 1986). A recent survey.

J. Barnes et al., *Science and Speculation* (New York: Cambridge University Press, 1982). A collection of papers on Hellenistic science.

*Paperback edition available.

4 ❧ EARLY ROME AND THE ROMAN REPUBLIC, 800–31 B.C.

Eternal Rome

*F*ive miles from its mouth, the Tiber River snakes in a lazy S around the first highlands that rise from the marshes of central Italy. These weathered cliffs, separated by tributary streams, look down on the river valley that broadens to over a mile and a half wide, the first and only natural ford for many miles. Only three promontories, the Capitoline, Palatine, and Aventine, are separate hills. The others, the Quirinal, Viminal, Caelian, Oppian, and Esquiline, are actually spurs of the distant Apennines. Gradually the pastoral villages founded on these hills spread down to the valleys between them, united, and grew to a city whose name for over two thousand years was synonymous with empire.

Rome wasn't built in a day. The earliest Roman villages were found on the Palatine—from whose heights the picture was taken—which remained throughout Rome's history the favored residential area. Here Latin shepherds first erected their crude huts and republican senators later built their homes. Still later, emperors built their increasingly splendid residences on its slopes until the term *palace* became synonymous with the seat of royalty. The Capitoline with its steep cliffs, which begin at the extreme left of the photograph, served as an acropolis, the religious center of the community. Here was found the Capitol, which contained not only temples but also the state archives and the city mint beside the temple of Juno the Admonisher, Juno Moneta (hence our word *money*). The Capitol, so the Romans thought, was indestructible, and it became a symbol of the eternal city. As Romans established colonies across Italy and throughout the Mediterranean, the colonies too had their hill temples, their so-called capitols.

The area shown in the center of the photograph, between the Palatine and Capitoline, was originally a low, marshy burial ground. In the seventh century B.C., Etruscan kings drained the marshes, making it possible to pave the area between the hills and turn it into a public meeting place, or *forum.* The Forum became the heart of the city. Through it ran the Sacred Way, the road that cuts diagonally from left to right in the photograph. At the south end, to the right of the photograph, was the marketplace, which bustled with shops and businesses. To the north, where the domed church of Saints Luca and Magartina now stands, was the Comitium, the meeting place of the citizens' assembly. Here the king and, in republican times, the popular assembly conducted political busi-

ness. Just below it still stands the Curia, the meeting place of the Roman Senate, which survived because it was converted into a Christian church in the seventh century A.D.

Here too temples and monuments rose to meet religious and public needs. Perhaps the most ancient structure was the circular temple of Vesta, the hearth goddess, the surviving columns of which can be seen in the lower center of the photograph. In this temple consecrated virgins, the most honored women of Rome, tended the sacred fire, the symbol of the life of Rome. The ruins of the virgins' magnificent residence fill the lower right of the photograph. Just above it stood the royal residence, the Regia, which during the republic came to be the quarters of one of Rome's chief priests, the *pontifex maximus.* To the lower right stood the temple to the twin gods Castor and Pollux, who were credited with bringing victory in the early days of the republic against Rome's Latin neighbors. In time, still other temples joined these, for honoring the gods and honoring Rome were one.

As Rome grew from a simple city to an empire, the Forum reflected these changes. Simple Etruscan architecture gave way to the Greek style of building. Marble replaced brick and stucco.

Near the Curia, a golden milestone marked the point from which all distances were measured and to which all roads of the empire led. The turmoil of the last years of the republic also left its mark. In the center of the picture, the semicircular brown stone ruin is all that remains of the temple of the Divine Julius, erected on the spot where Julius Caesar's remains were cremated after his murder on the Ides of March. After his death, Caesar received divine honors; he was the first Roman to be so treated by his city. Next to the temple stands all that remains of the monumental arch of Caesar's adopted son Octavian, known to history as Augustus, the first and greatest of the Roman emperors.

By the time of Caesar and Augustus, Rome had replaced its Forum, just as it had replaced its republican constitution. Caesar had begun and Augustus completed new forums, known collectively as the Forum of the Caesars, which lay beyond the trees at the top of the picture. Their successor Trajan (A.D. 98–117) would build a still greater one just beyond it. Still, for centuries of Romans and for the Western societies that succeeded them, the narrow space encompassing the Capitoline, the Palatine, and the Forum was the epicenter of the city and the world.

Italy's First Civilization

Etruscan civilization was the first great civilization to emerge in Italy. The Etruscans have long been regarded as a people whose origins, language, and customs are shrouded in mystery. Actually, the mystery is more apparent than real. The Greek historian Herodotus thought that the Etruscans had emigrated from Lydia in Asia Minor, and many historians, noting similarities between Etruscan and Eastern traditions, have subsequently accepted the thesis of eastern origins. A second ancient tradition, reported by the Greek scholar Dionysius of Halicarnassus (ca. 20 B.C.), is that the Etruscans did not emigrate from anywhere but rather had always been in western Italy. In recent years, archaeologists have demonstrated that this latter thesis is probably correct. The earliest materials from Etruscan sites indicate no break with the civilization of pre-Italic Villanovan Italy but rather a gradual development from it. Probably, just as in the Aegean, an indigenous cultural tradition was overwhelmed by the chaos of the twelfth-century B.C. crisis and the migration of Indo-Europeans from the north. This tradition shares much with Eastern civilizations, such as the importance of underworld gods, fertility cults, and the high status of women. Some scholars even speak of a common Mediterranean civilization submerged for a time but reemerging transformed centuries later.

The Etruscan language is commonly seen as the second great mystery. Unlike the early Minoan writing, which was found to be early Greek written in an unknown script, Etruscan is written in an alphabet derived from that of Greece. Still, despite the derivation of the alphabet, the Etruscan language appears unrelated to any other language and even today some of the extant Etruscan texts remain incompletely deciphered. Bilingual inscriptions and careful analysis, however, have made it possible to read many of the extant Etruscan texts, and in the process the mysteries of the Etruscans have become much less mysterious.

Etruscan civilization coalesced slowly in Etruria over the course of the seventh century B.C. from diverse regional and political groups sharing a similar cultural and linguistic tradition. In the mid-sixth century B.C., in the face of Greek pressure from the south, twelve of these groups united in a religious and military confederation. Over the next hundred years, the confederation expanded north into the Po Valley and south to Campania, creating a loose Etruscan alliance that included almost all of the peninsula. Cities, each initially ruled by a king, were the centers of Etruscan civilization, and everywhere the Etruscans spread they either improved upon existing towns or founded new ones. Towns in the north included Bologna, Parma, Modena, Ravenna, Milan, and Mantua; in the south, there were Nola, Nuceria, Pompeii, Sorrento, and Salerno. The Etruscan confederation remained a loose one and, unlike that of the Carthaginians, never developed into a centralized empire. Etruscan kings assumed power in conquered towns, but between the sixth and

Etruscan tombs were furnished with the familiar objects of everyday life. The square columns of this tomb are adorned with stucco reliefs of cooking utensils, tools, bedding, and weapons. Charon, the guardian of the entrance to Hades, is depicted along with his three-headed dog, Cerberus.

fifth centuries B.C., Etruscan kingship gave way to oligarchic governments, much as Greek monarchies did a bit earlier. In the place of kings, aristocratic assemblies selected magistrates, often paired together or combined into "colleges" to prevent individuals from seizing power. These republican institutions provided the foundation for later Roman republican government.

The remnants of an ancient civilization, the Etruscans retained throughout their history social and cultural traditions long since vanished elsewhere in the Mediterranean. Society divided sharply into two classes, lords and servants. The lords' wealth was based on the rich agricultural regions of Etruria, where grain grew in abundance, and on the equally rich deposits of copper and iron. The vast majority of the population were actual slaves, working the lands and mines of the aristocracy.

The aristocrats were aggressive and imaginative landowners. They developed hydraulic systems for draining marshes, produced wine famous throughout the Mediterranean, and put their slaves to work in mines and in smelting. Still, they were largely absentee landlords, spending much of their time in the towns that characterized Etruscan civilization. These cities, with their massive walls, enclosed populations of as many as twenty thousand. Etruscans built largely in wood, so little remains of their houses, temples, and public buildings. However, their extensive cemeteries have preserved a vivid image of Etruscan life. In the tombs of Caere and other Etruscan settlements, the dead were buried in family chamber tombs which recall the homes of the living. These were furnished with the wares of everyday life, including benches, beds, ornaments, utensils, and vessels and platters of Etruscan and Corinthian manufacture. The walls of the more sumptuous tombs are decorated with lively, brilliantly colored scenes of feasting, processions, and activities of daily life.

The most striking aspect of Etruscan life to Greek contemporaries and to later Romans was the elevated status of Etruscan women. The decorations and furnishings of tombs, inscriptions, and reports by contemporaries indicate that, as in the much earlier Minoan civilization, women played an active, public role in society. Unlike honorable Greek women, Etruscan women took part in banquets, reclining beside their male companions on couches from which they ate. They attended and even occasionally presided over dances, concerts, and sporting events. Women, as wives and mothers, were also active in political life. When a

king died, his successor had to be designated and consecrated by the Etruscan queen to establish his legitimacy. Greeks such as Aristotle regarded the public behavior of Etruscan women as lewd. The great philosopher accused them of lying under the same cloak with men at banquets. To later Romans, the political role of women such as Tullia, wife of King Lucius Tarquin (Tarquin the Proud), the Etruscan king of Rome, was equally shocking. The Roman historian Livy (59 B.C.–A.D. 17) claims that when Tullia first recognized her husband as king, he was so shocked that he sent her home. In truth, he was surely grateful.

While the Etruscans were consolidating their hegemony in western Italy, they were at the same time establishing their maritime power. From the seventh to the fifth centuries B.C., Etruscans controlled the Italian coast of the Tyrrhenian Sea as well as Sardinia, from which their ships could reach the coast of what is today France and Spain. Attempts to extend farther south into Greek southern Italy and toward the Greek colonies on the modern French coast brought the Etruscans and the Greeks into inevitable conflict. Etruscan cities fought sporadic sea battles against Greek cities in the waters of Sicily as well as off the coasts of Corsica and Etruria. Common hostility toward the Greeks as well as complementary economic interests soon brought the Etruscans into alliances with Carthage. Toward the end of the sixth century B.C., Etruscan cities—including Rome—signed a series of pacts with Carthage that created military alliances against the Phocaeans and Syracuse. Etruscan fleets were victorious over the Phocaeans, driving them from Corsica, but they were no match for Syracuse. In 474 B.C., shortly after the battle of Himera, the Syracusan fleet destroyed that of the Etruscans off Cumae. Cumae marked the beginning of Etruscan decline. Through the fifth century B.C., Etruscan cities lost control of the sea to the Greeks. Around the same time, Celts from north of the Alps invaded and conquered the Po Valley. And to the south, Etruscans saw their inland territories progressively slipping into the hands of their former subjects, the Romans.

These Romans had learned and profited from their domination by the Etruscans as well as from their dealings with Greek and Carthaginian civilizations. From these early civilizations on the western shores of the Mediterranean Sea, Rome had begun to acquire the commercial, political, and military expertise to begin its long development from a small city to a great empire.

From City to Empire, 509–146 B.C.

What manner of people were these who, from obscure origins, came to rule an empire? Their own answer would have been simple: They were farmers and soldiers, simple people accustomed to simple, straightforward actions. Throughout their long history, Romans liked to refer to the clear-cut models provided by their semilegendary predecessors: Cincinnatus the farmer, called away to the supreme office of dictator in time of danger, then returning to his plow; Horatius Cocles, the valiant warrior who held back an Etruscan army on the Tiber bridge until it could be demolished and then, despite his wounds, swam across the river to safety; Lucretia, the wife who chose death after dishonor. These were myths, but they were important myths to Romans, who preferred concrete models to abstract principles.

Later Romans liked to imagine the history of their city as one predestined by the gods for greatness. Some liked to trace the origins of Rome to Romulus and Remus, twin sons of the war god Mars and a Latin princess. According to legend, the children, after having been thrown into the Tiber River, were raised by a she-wolf. Other Romans, having absorbed the Homeric traditions of Greece, taught that the founder of Rome was Aeneas, son of the goddess of love, Aphrodite, and the Trojan Anchises, who had wandered west after the fall of Troy. All agreed that Rome had been ruled by kings who underwent a steady decline in ability and morals until the last, Tarquin the Proud, was expelled by outraged Latins. These legends tell much about the attitudes and values of later Romans. They tell nothing about the origins of the city, its place in the Latin and Etruscan worlds, and its rise to greatness.

Latin Rome

Civilization in Italy meant Etruria to the north and Greater Greece to the south. In between lay Latium, a marshy region punctured by hills on which a sparse population could find protection from disease and enemies. This population was an amalgam of aboriginal Ligurians and the more recently arrived Latins and Sabines, who lived a pastoral life in small scattered villages.

The Alban hills south of the Tiber were a center of Latin population. Sometime in the eighth century B.C., roughly forty Latin villages formed a loose confederation, the Alban League, for military and religious purposes. Not long after, in the face of an expanding Etruscan confederation from the north and Sabine penetration from the east, the Albans established a village on the steep Palatine hill to the north. The Palatine was one of several hills overlooking a natural ford on the Tiber; it constituted the first high ground some fourteen miles from the sea. The strategic importance of the site, as well as its relatively healthy climate above the disease-ridden marshes, made it a natural location for a settlement. This Alban village, called Roma Quadrata, was soon joined by other Latin and Sabine settlements on nearby hills. By the end of the eighth century B.C., seven Latin villages that clustered along the route from the Tiber to Alba had formed a league for mutual defense and shared religious cults.

Early Roman society was composed of households; clans, or *gentes;* and village councils, or *curiae* (sing. *curia*). The male head of each household, the *paterfamilias,* had power of life and death over its members and was responsible for the proper worship of the spirits of the family's ancestors, on whom continued prosperity depended. Within some villages, these families were grouped into gentes, which claimed descent from a semimythical ancestor.

Male members of village families formed councils, which were essentially religious organizations but also provided a forum for public discussion. These curiae tended to be dominated by gentes, but all males could participate, including those who belonged to the plebs, that is,

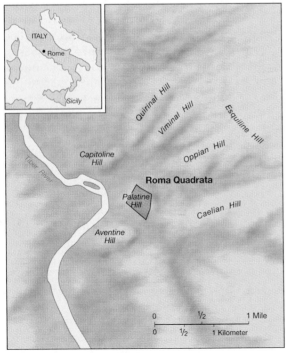

Ancient Rome

families not organized into gentes. Initially the distinction between plebeian families and those families grouped into gentes was one of custom rather than economic, social, or political importance. Only later did the leaders of the gentes call themselves patricians ("descendants of fathers") and claim superiority to the plebs.

Important plebeian and patrician families increased their power through a system of clientage, which remained a fundamental aspect of social and political organization throughout Roman history. Clients were free men who depended on the protection of a more powerful individual or family and who owed various services, including political support, in return for this protection.

Villages themselves grouped together for military and voting purposes into ethnic *tribus*, or tribes, each composed of a number of curiae. Each individual curia supplied a contingent of infantry and each tribe cooperated to supply a unit of horsemen to the Roman army.

Assemblies of all members of the curiae expressed approval of major decisions, especially declaration of war and the selection of new kings, and thus played a real if limited political role. More powerful although less formal was the role of the Senate (assembly of elders), which was composed of heads of families. The Senate's power derived from the individual importance of its members and from its role in selecting a candidate for king, who was then presented to the assembly of the curiae for approval.

Kings served as religious leaders, the primary means of communication between gods and men. In time, kings attained some political and judicial authority, but through the early Latin period royal power remained fundamentally religious and limited by the Senate, curiae, gentes, and families.

The seven villages that made up primitive Rome developed independently of their Etruscan and Greek neighbors. Initially, Romans lived in thatched huts, tended their flocks on the hillsides, and maintained their separate village identities. By the seventh century B.C. they had begun fortifications and other structures indicating the beginnings of a dynamic civic life. This independent course of development changed in the middle of the seventh century B.C., when the Etruscans overwhelmed Latium and absorbed it into their civilization. Under its Etruscan kings, Rome first entered civilization.

Etruscan Rome

The Etruscans introduced in Latium and especially in Rome their political, religious, and economic traditions. Etruscan city organization partially replaced

Latin tribal structures. Etruscan kings and magistrates ruled Latin towns, increasing the power of traditional Latin kingship. The kings were not only religious leaders, directing the cults of their humanlike gods, but also led the army, served as judges, and held supreme political power. In Rome a series of Etruscan kings, notably Tarquin the Elder and Servius Tullius, used the city's location on the Tiber ford as a strategic position from which to control Latium to the south. As Latium became an integral part of the Etruscan world, the Tiber became an important commercial route, carrying the agricultural produce of Latium throughout Etruria and bringing to Rome the products of Etruscan and Greek workshops. For the first time, Rome began to enter the wider orbit of Mediterranean civilization. The town's population swelled with the arrival of merchants and artisans.

As Rome's importance grew, so did its size. Surrounding villages were added to the original seven, as were the Sabine colonies on the Quirinal and Capitoline hills. Etruscan engineers drained the marshes into a great canal flowing to the Tiber, thus opening the lowlands between the hills to settlement. This in turn allowed them to create and pave the Forum. The Etruscans were also builders, constructing a series of vast fortifications encircling the town. Under Etruscan

On the Etruscan sarcophagus of Larthia Scianti, a matron reclines as at a banquet. Much of our knowledge of this first Italian civilization comes from the elaborate paintings and statuary found in Etruscan cemeteries.

influence, the fortified Capitoline hill, which served much like a Greek acropolis, became the cult center with the erection of the temple to Jupiter, the supreme god; Juno, his consort; and Minerva, an Etruscan goddess of craftwork similar to Athena. In its architecture, religion, commerce, and culture, Latin Rome was deeply indebted to its Etruscan conquerors.

As important as the physical and cultural changes brought by the Etruscans was their reorganization of the society. As in Greece, this restructuring was tied to changes in the military. The Etruscans had learned from the Greeks the importance of hoplite tactics, and King Servius Tullius (578–534 B.C.) introduced this system of warfare into Rome. This led to the abolition of the earlier curia-based military and political system in favor of one based only on property holding. Weakening the traditional Latin social units, the king divided Roman society into two groups. Those landowners wealthy enough to provide armed military service were organized into five *classis* (from which the word *class* is derived), ranked according to the quality of their arms and hence their wealth. Each class was further divided into military units called centuries. This military reorganization had fundamental political importance as well. Members of these centuries constituted the centuriate assembly, which replaced the older curial assemblies for such vital decisions as the election of magistrates and the declaration of war.

The constitution and operation of this centuriate assembly ensured control by the most conservative forces within the society. Small centuries of wealthy, well-armed cavalrymen and fully armed warriors outnumbered the more modestly equipped but numerically greater centuries. Likewise, men over the age of forty-seven, though in a minority, controlled over half of the centuries in each class. Since votes were counted not by individuals but by centuries, this ensured within the assembly the domination of the rich over the poor, the elder over the younger. The remainder of the society was the *infra classem*, those literally "under class," who owned no property and were thus excluded from military and political activity.

With this military and political reorganization came a reconstruction of the tribal system. Servius Tullius abolished the old tribal organization in favor of geographically organized tribes into which newcomers could easily be incorporated. Henceforth, while the family remained powerful, involvement in public life was based on property and geography. Latins, Sabines, Ligurians, and Etruscans could all be active citizens of the growing city.

While the old tribal units and curiae declined, divisions between the patricians and the plebeians grew more distinct. During the monarchy the patricians came to compose an upper stratum of wealthy nobles. They forbade marriage outside their own circle, forming a closed, self-perpetuating group that monopolized the Senate, religious rites, and magisterial offices. Although partially protected by the kings, the plebeians, whether they were rich or poor, were pressed into a second-class status and denied access to political power.

When the Etruscans came to Rome, they found it a small collection of wood and reed villages only beginning to develop into an urban center. In less than two centuries, they transformed it into a prosperous, unified urban center that played an important role in the economic and political life of central Italy. They laid the foundations of a free citizenry, incorporating Greek models of military and social organization. The transformations brought about by the Etruscan kings became an enduring part of Rome. The Etruscans themselves did not. Just as the hoplite revolution in Greece saw the end of most Hellenic monarchies, around the traditionally reported date of 509 B.C. the Roman patricians expelled the last king, Tarquin the Proud, and established a republic (from the Latin *res publica*, "public property," as opposed to *res privata*, "private property of the king").

Rome and Italy

Always the moralizers, later Roman historians made the expulsion of King Tarquin the dramatic result of his son's lust. According to legend, Sextus, the son of Tarquin, raped Lucretia, a virtuous Roman matron. She told her husband of the crime and then took her own life. Outraged, the Roman patricians were said to have driven the king and his family from the city. Actually, monarchy was giving way to oligarchic republics across Etruria in the sixth century B.C. Rome was hardly exceptional. However, the establishment of the Roman republic coincided roughly with the beginning of the Etruscan decline, allowing the city of Rome to assert itself and to develop its Latin and Etruscan traditions in unique ways. This development took place within an atmosphere of internal dissension and external conquest.

The patrician oligarchy had engineered the end of the monarchy, and patricians dominated the offices and institutions of the new republic at the expense of the plebs who, in losing the king, lost their only defender.

Governmental institutions of the early republic developed within this context of patrician supremacy.

Characteristic of republican institutions was that at every level, power was shared by two or more equals elected for fixed terms. This practice of shared power was intended to ensure that magistrates would consult with each other before making decisions and that no individual could achieve supreme power at any level. Replacing the king were the two consuls, each elected by the assembly for a one-year term. Initially only the consuls held the *imperium,* the supreme power to command, to execute the law, and to impose the death penalty. Only in moments of grave crisis might a consul, with the approval of the Senate, name a single dictator with extraordinary absolute power for a very brief period, never more than six months. In time other magistracies developed to perform specialized functions. *Praetors,* who in time also exercised the imperium, administered justice, and defended the city in the absence of the consuls. *Quaestors* controlled finances. *Censors* assigned individuals their places in society, determined the amount of their taxes, filled vacancies in the Senate, and negotiated contracts for public construction projects. A variety of military commanders directed wars against neighboring cities and peoples under the imperium of the consuls. In all their actions these officeholders consulted with each other and with the Senate, which was composed of roughly three hundred powerful former magistrates. The centuriate assembly functioned as the legislative organ of the state, but it continued to be dominated by the eldest and wealthiest members of society.

During the early republic, wealthy patricians, aided by their clients, monopolized the Senate and the magistracies. Successful magistrates rose through a series of increasingly important offices, which came to be known as the *cursus honorum,* to the position of consul. Censors selected from among former magistrates in appointing new senators, thus ensuring that the Senate would be dominated by the patrician elite. Patricians also controlled the system of priesthoods, which they held for life. With political and religious power came economic power. The poorer plebs in particular found themselves sinking into debt to wealthy patricians, losing their property, and with it the basis for military service and political participation. In the courtroom, in the temple, in the assembly, and in the marketplace, plebeians found themselves subjected to the whims of an elite from which they were excluded.

The plebs began to organize in response to patrician control. On several occasions in the first half of the

By the middle of the second century B.C., the Roman republic had evolved to the point where private citizens could cast private ballots. This Roman coin of 137 B.C. features a Roman voter dropping a stone tablet into a voting urn.

fifth century B.C., the whole plebeian order withdrew a short distance from the city, refusing to return or to serve in the military until conflicts with the patricians were resolved. In time the plebs created their own assembly, the Council of the Plebs, which enacted laws binding on all plebeians. This council founded its own temples and elected magistrates called tribunes, whose persons were declared sacred to the gods. The tribunes protected the plebs from arbitrary patrician power. Anyone harming the tribunes, whether patrician or plebeian, could be killed by the plebs without trial. With their own assembly, magistracies, and religious cults, the plebeians were well on the way to creating a separate republic. This conflict between the plebeians and the patricians, known as the Struggle of Orders, threatened to tear Roman society apart, just as pressure from hostile neighbors placed Rome on the defensive.

Roman preeminence in Latium had ended with the expulsion of the last king. The Etruscan town of Veii just north of the Tiber began launching periodic attacks against Rome. To the south, the Volscians had begun to expand north into the Litis and Trerus valleys. The inability of the patricians to meet this military pressure alone ultimately forced them to a compromise with the plebeians. One of the first victories won by the plebs, around 450 B.C., was the codification of basic Roman law, the Law of the Twelve Tables, which recog-

THE TWELVE TABLES

The recording of the Twelve Tables in 449 B.C. was a great victory for the plebs both because it curbed the exercise of arbitrary power by patrician magistrates and because it established the principle of equality before the law.

TABLE I. PRELIMINARIES TO AND RULES FOR A TRIAL

If plaintiff summons defendant to court, he shall go. If he does not go, plaintiff shall call witness thereto. Then only shall he take defendant by force.

If defendant shirks or takes to his heels, plaintiff shall lay hands on him . . .

For a landowner, a landowner shall be surety; but for a proletarian person, let any one who is willing be his protector . . .

When parties make a settlement of the case, the judge shall announce it. If they do not reach a settlement, they shall state the outline of their case in the meeting place or Forum before noon . . .

TABLE III. EXECUTION; LAW OF DEBT

When a debt has been acknowledged, or judgment about the matter has been pronounced in court, thirty days must be the legitimate time of grace. After that, the debtor may be arrested by laying on of hands. Bring him into court. If he does not satisfy the judgment, or no one in court offers himself as surety in his behalf, the creditor may take the defaulter with him. He may bind him either in stocks or in fetters . . . The debtor, if he wishes, may live on his own. If he does not live on his own, the person [who shall hold him in bonds] shall give him one pound of grits for each day . . .

TABLE IV. RIGHTS OF HEAD OF FAMILY

Quickly kill . . . a dreadfully deformed child.

TABLE VI. GUARDIANSHIP; SUCCESSION

Females shall remain in guardianship even when they have attained their majority . . . except Vestal Virgins.

Conveyable possessions of a woman under guardianship of agnates cannot be rightfully acquired by [long-term possession], save such possessions as have been delivered up by her with a guardian's sanction . . .

TABLE IX. PUBLIC LAWS

Laws of personal exception [i.e., bills of attainder] must not be proposed; cases in which the penalty affects the person of a citizen must not be decided except through the greatest assembly and through those whom the censors have placed upon the register of citizens . . .

TABLE XI. SUPPLEMENTARY LAWS

Intermarriage shall not take place between plebeians and patricians.

---

nized the basic rights of all free citizens. As important as the specific provisions of the law—which covered private, criminal, sacred, and public matters—was the fact that it was written and posted publicly. Thus anyone, not only patrician magistrates, could have access to it. Around the same time, the state began to absorb the plebeian political and religious organizations intact. Gradually, priesthoods, magistracies, and thus the Senate opened to plebeians. The consulship was the last prize finally won by the plebs in 367 B.C. In 287 B.C., as the result of a final secession of the plebs, the decisions of the plebeian assembly became binding on all citizens, patrician and plebeian alike.

Bitter differences at home did not prevent patricians and plebs from presenting a united front against their enemies abroad. External conquest deflected internal hostility and profited both orders. By the beginning of the fourth century B.C., the united patrician-plebeian state was expanding its rule both north and south. Roman legions, commanded by patricians but formed of the whole spectrum of property-owning Romans, reestablished Roman preeminence in Latium and then began a series of wars that brought most of Italy under Roman control. In 396 B.C., Roman forces captured and destroyed Veii and shortly after conquered the rest of southern Etruria. In the south, Roman and Latin forces turned back the Volscians. In 390 B.C., Rome suffered a temporary setback at the hands of the Gauls, or Celts, of northern Italy, who raided south and sacked much of the city before being bought off with a large tribute payment. Even this event had a silver lining. The damage to Rome was short-lived, but the Gauls had dealt a deathblow to the Etruscan cities of the north, clearing the way for later Roman conquest. A last-ditch effort by the Latins to preserve their autonomy was crushed in 338 B.C., and by 295 B.C. Rome had secured its rule as far north as the Po Valley. In the south, Roman infantry and persistence proved the equal of professional Greek armies. Rome won a war of attrition against a series of Hellenistic commanders, the

last of whom was the Greek king Pyrrhus of Epirus (319–272 B.C.). Pyrrhus, regarded as the greatest tactician of his day, won a series of victories that proved more costly to him than to his Roman opponents. In 275 B.C., after losing two-thirds of his troops in these "Pyrrhic victories," he withdrew to Sicily. By 265 B.C., Rome had absorbed the Hellenistic cities of the south.

The Roman conquest benefited patrician and plebeian alike. While the patricians acquired wealth and power, the plebeians received a prize of equal value: land. After the capture of Veii, for example, the poor of Rome received shares of the conquered land. Since landowning was a prerequisite for military service, this distribution created still more peasant soldiers for further expeditions. Some citizens received land in organized colonies similar to those of Greece, while others received individual plots spread about the conquered territories. Still, while the constant supply of new land did much to diffuse the tensions between orders, it did not actually resolve them. Into the late third century B.C., debt and landlessness remained major problems creating tensions in Roman society. Probably not more

A relief of a Roman war galley. The deck is crowded with infantrymen. Galleys were usually rowed by slaves while the soldiers remained fresh for the task of subduing enemy ships.

than one-half of the citizen population owned land by 200 B.C.

The Roman manner of treating conquered populations, radically different from anything seen before, also contributed to Rome's success. In war, no one could match the Roman legions for ruthless, thorough destruction. Yet no conquerors had ever shown themselves so generous in victory. After Rome crushed the Latin revolt of 338 B.C., virtually all of the Latins were incorporated into the Roman citizenry. Later colonies founded outside Latium were given the same status as Latin cities. Other more-distant conquered peoples were considered allies and required to provide troops but no tribute to Rome. In time, they too might become citizens. In its wars against the Hellenistic cities of the south, Rome took pains to portray itself as defending Greek civilization against the barbarism of marauding mercenary armies.

The implications of these measures were revolutionary. By extending citizenship to conquered neighbors and by offering the future possibility to allies, Rome tied their fate to its own. Rather than potentially subversive subjects, conquered populations became strong supporters. Thus, in contrast to the Hellenistic cities of the east, where Greeks jealously guarded their status from the indigenous population, Rome's colonies acted as magnets, drawing local populations into the Roman cultural and political orbit. In time a fortunate few who cooperated with Rome might—with luck, talent, and money—share the benefits of Roman citizenship. Greeks were scandalized by the Roman tradition of giving citizenship even to freed slaves. By the end of the fourth century B.C., some of the sons of these freedmen were finding a place in the Senate. Finally, in all of its wars of conquest, Rome claimed a moral mandate. Romans went to great lengths to demonstrate that theirs were just wars, basing their claims on alleged acts of aggression by their enemies, on the appeal to Rome by its allies, and, increasingly, by presenting themselves as the preservers and defenders of Greek traditions of freedom. Both the political and the propagandistic measures proved successful. Between 265 B.C. and 91 B.C., few serious revolts shook the peace and security of Italy south of the Po.

Benevolent treatment of the conquered spurred further conquest. Since subject cities and peoples did not pay tribute, the only way for Rome to benefit from its conquests or to exercise its authority was to demand and use troops. These troops aided still further conquests, which brought the spoils of war to them as well as to Rome. By 264 B.C., all of Italy was united under Roman hegemony. Roman expansion finally brought Rome into conflict with the great Mediterranean power of the west, Carthage.

Rome and the Mediterranean

Since its earliest days, Rome had allied itself with Carthage against the Greek cities of Italy. The zones of interest of the two cities had been quite separate. Carthage was a sea empire, while Rome was a land-based power without a navy. The Greeks, aspiring to power on land and sea, posed a common threat to both Rome and Carthage. However, once Rome had conquered the Greek cities to the south, it became enmeshed in the affairs of neighboring Sicily, a region with well-established Carthaginian interests. There, in 265 B.C., a group of Italian mercenary pirates in Messina, threatened by Syracuse, requested Roman assistance. The Senate refused but the plebeian assembly, eager for booty, exercised its newly won right to legislate for the republic and accepted. Shortly afterward the Romans invaded Sicily, and Syracuse turned to its old enemy, Carthage, for assistance. The First Punic War had begun.

The First Punic War, which lasted from 265 to 241 B.C., was a costly, brutal, and drawn-out affair which Rome won by dint of persistence and methodical calculation rather than strategic brilliance. Rome invaded and concluded an alliance with Syracuse in 263 B.C. The war rapidly became a sea war. Rome had little previous naval experience but quickly learned the rules of the game, then rewrote them to its own advantage. Taking a wrecked Carthaginian ship as a model, Roman builders constructed twenty fast ships propelled by roughly two hundred oarsmen to ram and sink opposing ships. Rome also built one hundred larger ships with crews of three hundred, manned by Roman allies. Unaccustomed to fighting at sea, Roman engineers turned sea battles into land battles by placing on their ships heavy gangplanks that could be dropped onto enemy ships. The gangplanks were equipped with a heavy iron spike to secure them to the enemy's deck. This allowed a contingent of legionnaires to march onto the enemy ship and fight as though on dry land.

With these innovations, the Romans won impressive initial victories but still could not deliver a knockout blow either in Sicily or North Africa for over twenty years. Warfare and Mediterranean storms took their toll of opposing fleets. Finally, in 241 B.C., Rome forced the Carthaginian commander, Hamilcar Barca (ca. 270–229 B.C.), to surrender simply because the

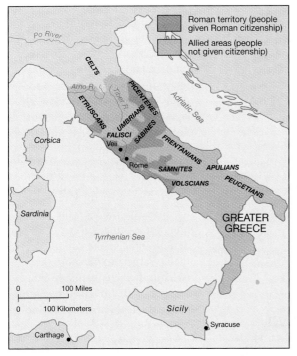

Rome in 264 B.C.

The map legend reads:

Roman territory (people given Roman citizenship)

Allied areas (people not given citizenship)

the Senate that he was simply trying to raise funds to pay off Carthage's indemnity.

Carthaginian successes in Spain, led after Hamilcar's death by his son-in-law Hasdrubal (d. 221 B.C.) and his son Hannibal (247–183 B.C.), finally provoked Rome to war in 218 B.C. As soon as this Second Punic War had begun, Hannibal began an epic march north out of Spain, along the Mediterranean coast, and across the Alps. In spite of great hardships, he was able to transport over 23,000 troops and approximately eighteen war elephants into the plains of northern Italy. (See "Hannibal's Elephants," pp. 114–115.)

Hannibal's brilliant generalship brought victory after victory to the Carthaginian forces. In the first engagement, on the Trebia River in the Po Valley, the Romans lost twenty thousand men, two-thirds of their army. Carthaginian success encouraged the Gauls to join the fight against the Romans. Initially, Italian, Etruscan, and Greek allies remained loyal, but after Rome's catastrophic defeats at Lake Trasimene in Etruria in 217 B.C., and especially at Cannae in 216 B.C., a number of Italian colonies and allies, and especially the cities of Capua and Syracuse, went over to the enemy. In the east, Philip V of Macedon (238–179 B.C.) made a treaty with Carthage in the hope of taking Illyria (today the coast of Croatia) from a defeated Rome.

As commanders chosen by the patrician-dominated Senate failed to stop the enemy, the Roman plebs became increasingly dissatisfied with the way the oligarchy was conducting the war. However, popular pressure to appoint new commanders did little to alleviate the situation. In 217 B.C., following the battle of Lake Trasimene, the Senate named the capable general Quintus Fabius Maximus (d. ca. 203 B.C.) dictator. He used delaying tactics successfully to slow the Carthaginians, thus earning the title *Cunctator,* or Delayer. The popular assembly, impatient for a decisive victory, elected a second dictator, thus effectively canceling the position of Quintus Fabius Maximus. The next year, popular pressure forced the election of Gaius Terentius Varro as consul. Varro quickly led the army to the greatest defeat in Roman history, at Cannae. There Hannibal surrounded and annihilated Varro's numerically superior army.

Three things saved the Roman state. First, while some important allies and colonies defected, the majority held firm. Rome's traditions of sharing the fruits of victory with its allies, extending the rights of Roman citizenship, and protecting central and southern Italy against its enemies proved stronger than the appeals of

Romans could afford to build one more fleet than he. Carthage paid a huge indemnity and abandoned Sicily. Syracuse and Messina became allies of Rome. In a break with tradition, Rome obligated the rest of Sicily to pay a true tribute in the form of a tithe (one-tenth) of their crops. Shortly after that, Rome helped itself to Sardinia as well, from which it again demanded tribute, not simply troops. Rome had established an empire.

During the next two decades Roman legions kept busy in the north, defeating the Ligurians on the northwest coast, the Celtic Gauls south of the Alps, and the Illyrians along the Adriatic coast. At the same time, Carthage fought a bitter battle against its own mercenary armies, which it had been unable to pay off after its defeat. Carthage then began the systematic creation of an empire in Spain. Trade between Carthage and Rome reached the highest level in history, but trade did not create friendship. The two former enemies maintained a wary peace. On both sides, powerful leaders saw the treaty of 241 B.C. as just a pause in a fight to the death. Hamilcar Barca had his nine-year-old son Hannibal swear to be Rome's eternal enemy. Fearful and greedy Romans insisted that Carthage had to be destroyed for the security of Rome. They were particularly disturbed by the growth of Carthage's Spanish empire, even though Hamilcar Barca assured

❧ Hannibal's Elephants

towerlike structure from which archers could shoot down on the massed infantry. However, like modern tanks, the primary importance of the beasts was the enormous shock effect created by a charge of massed war elephants. Still, they often created more problems than they solved.

Indian princes had used elephants in warfare for centuries. When Alexander the Great crossed the Indus in 326 B.C., the Indian king Porus came within an ace of defeating the Greek conqueror, thanks largely to his more than two hundred elephants. In 302 B.C., Seleucus I received five hundred war elephants from an Indian king as part of a peace treaty. The next year these animals contributed greatly to Seleucus's victory over Antigonus at Ipsus, which made possible the creation of his separatist kingdom in Syria. Thereafter Seleucid kings used elephants as an integral part of their military and even attempted, without much success, to breed elephants in Syria.

The Ptolemys, too, used elephants in Egypt, but lacking access to Indian animals, they had to be content with the smaller African forest elephant. The great African bush elephant, the largest land animal and a far greater beast than either the forest or the Indian elephant, remained unknown to the Western world until the nineteenth century. The Ptolemys sent large-scale hunting parties into Ethiopia to capture forest elephants. Captured animals were trained and driven by Indians. In battles between Seleucids and Ptolemys, however, the larger Indian elephants usually brought victory.

"What do you get when you cross an Alp with an elephant?" Hannibal hoped that the answer was "Rome." Elephants were the most spectacular, extravagant, and unpredictable element in ancient warfare. Since the time of Alexander the Great, Hellenistic kings and commanders tried to use the great strength, size, and relative invulnerability of these animals to throw opposing infantry into confusion and flight. Elephants' unusual smell and loud trumpeting also panicked horses not accustomed to these strange beasts, wreaking havoc with cavalry units. Mahouts, or drivers, who were usually Indians, controlled and directed the animal from a seat on the elephant's neck. Normally each elephant carried a small,

The Romans first experienced the terror of elephant charges in their war against Pyrrhus in the south of Italy. They next encountered them in the Punic wars. The Carthaginians had learned to use elephants around the middle of the third century B.C., capturing them in the Atlas Mountains of North Africa and putting them to good use in Spain. When Hannibal decided to invade Italy via the Alps, he naturally wanted to take along these formidable beasts.

This was easier said than done. In 217 B.C., Hannibal set out from Carthago Nova and some weeks later arrived at the Rhone River with an army that included roughly 38,000 infantry, 8,000 cavalry, and 37 elephants. Ferrying the pachyderms across the river was a major undertaking, since the frightened animals refused to walk onto rafts. Finally, the Carthaginians lashed together a series of rafts, the first two on dry land, the others forming a pontoon into the river. The sides were piled with earth so that the elephants could not see that they were not walking on dry land. Their Indian mahouts led them a few at a time to the end rafts, which were then cut free and towed across the river by boats. Most of the animals, seeing water on all sides, remained terrified but still. Others panicked, upsetting the rafts, falling into the river, and drowning their mahouts. Once in the water, however, most of the elephants were able to swim to the far shore.

As difficult as the river crossing was, it paled in comparison with the problems of crossing the Alps. As Hannibal moved slowly up the valley of the Arc, his troops were under constant harassment from local Celtic tribes eager to ambush them at every occasion. From high up in the passes, the Celts showered down rocks, throwing the pack animals into confusion and causing them to hurl themselves off the narrow paths. Landslides carried away portions of the track and, as Hannibal advanced, the path became too narrow for elephants and eventually even for horses and mules. Engineers had to rebuild paths, taking up valuable time. Great boulders had to be cleared away by heating them and then pouring vinegar into crevices to cause them to explode. At the top of the pass, new snow forced a three-day halt while a new road wide enough for the elephants to descend was constructed down the more precipitous Italian side of the mountain. During this time the elephants were without fodder and suffered enormously. Finally, after fifteen days, Hannibal's depleted troops reached the fertile plains of the Po Valley. He had lost almost half of his infantry and cavalry since reaching the Rhone and more than half of his elephants.

Was it worth it? In his first major encounter with the Romans at the Trebia River, Hannibal split his elephants into two groups to protect the wings of his infantry. The beasts were a major factor in the devastating defeat inflicted on the Romans. However, shortly after, the cold and snow killed all but one of the animals. This lone survivor became Hannibal's personal command post. The great Punic victories at Lake Trasimene and Cannae were won without the assistance of the pachyderm shock force. In 207 B.C., Hannibal's brother Hasdrubal (d. 207 B.C.) entered Italy with ten elephants, but at the battle of Metaurus they panicked, stampeded, and did more harm to the Carthaginians than to the Romans.

The next time Hannibal faced a Roman army with his full contingent of war elephants was at Zama. There his eighty animals proved a bitter disappointment. Ordered to charge, many of the elephants panicked at the sound of trumpets and horns, wheeled about, and went raging into the massed African cavalry arrayed on the Punic side. Some elephants did charge, but with limited effect. The Romans had learned to take aim at the mahouts, killing them and leaving the animals without direction. The Romans also allowed the elephants to charge past, then attacked their flanks with javelins and their legs with swords. Finally, the Roman commander had taken the precaution of leaving wide paths between his formations. Many of the animals simply charged down these paths and disappeared into the open fields beyond the Roman lines.

The Romans themselves made little use of elephants in warfare. These exotic beasts better suited the inflated egos of Eastern kings than the practical minds of Roman generals. The Romans preferred the disciplined advance of a well-trained cohort of Roman legionnaires to the charge of a war elephant. It was with these steadfast and resolute infantrymen rather than with raging elephants that they won an empire.

POLYBIUS DESCRIBES THE SACK OF NEW CARTHAGE

In the following selection, the Greek historian Polybius, who was a close friend of the adopted grandson of Scipio Africanus, describes the Roman capture of New Carthage (Carthago Nova) in Spain in 210 B.C. during the Second Punic War. Before a siege, Romans offered their enemies generous terms, but once the siege was begun, they offered none. The passage shows the combination of brutality and thoroughness with which the Romans liquidated those who defied them.

Scipio, when he judged that a large enough number of troops had entered the town, let loose the majority of them against the inhabitants, according to the Roman custom; their orders were to exterminate every form of life they encountered, sparing none, but not to start pillaging until the word was given to do so. This practice is adopted to inspire terror, and so when cities are taken by the Romans you often see not only the corpses of human beings but dogs cut in half and the dismembered limbs of other animals, and on this occasion the carnage was especially frightful because of the large size of the population.

Scipio himself with about 1,000 men pressed on toward the citadel. Here [the Carthaginian commander] Margo at first put up some resistance, but as soon as he knew for certain that the city had been captured he sent a message to plead for his safety, and handed over the citadel. Once this had happened the signal was given to stop the slaughter and the troops then began to pillage the city. When darkness fell . . . Scipio . . . recalled the rest of his troops from the private houses of the city and ordered them through the military tribunes to collect all the spoils in the marketplace, each maniple bringing its own share . . . Next day all the booty . . . was collected in the marketplace, where the military tribunes divided it among their respective legions, according to the Roman custom . . . All those who have been detailed to collect the plunder then bring it back, each man to his own legion, and after it has been sold, the tribunes distribute the proceeds equally among all.

From Polybius, *The Rise of the Roman Empire.*

Hannibal. Although victorious time and again, without local support Hannibal could not hold the terrain and cities he won. New allies such as Syracuse, which fell in 212 B.C., were forcibly returned to the Roman camp. Fabius resumed his delaying tactics, and gradually Hannibal's victories slipped from his hands.

The second reason for Rome's survival was the tremendous social solidarity all classes and factions of its population showed during these desperate years. In spite of the internal tensions between patricians and plebeians, their ultimate dedication to Rome never faltered. Much of this loyalty was due to the Roman system of strong family and patronage ties. Kinsmen and clients answered the call of their patriarchs and patrons to bounce back repeatedly from defeat. Roman farmer-soldiers stood firm.

The final reason for Rome's ultimate success was Publius Cornelius Scipio (236–184 B.C.), also known as Scipio the Elder, a commander who was able to force Hannibal from Italy. Scipio, who earned the title Africanus for his victory, accomplished this not by attacking Hannibal directly, but by taking the war home to the enemy, first in Spain and then in Africa. In 210 B.C. Scipio arrived in Spain and rapidly captured the city of Carthago Nova (New Carthage, now Cartagena). Within four years he destroyed Punic power in Spain. Riding the crest of popular enthusiasm at home, he raised a new army and in 204 B.C. sailed for Africa. His victories there drew Hannibal home, where at Zama in 202 B.C. the Roman commander destroyed the Carthaginian army. Zama put an end to both the Second Punic War and Carthaginian political power. Saddled with a huge indemnity, forced to abandon all of its territories and colonies to Rome, and reduced to a small portion of the North African coast, Carthage had become in effect a Roman subject.

But still this humiliating defeat was not enough for Rome. While some Roman senators favored allowing Carthage to survive as a means of keeping the Roman plebs under senatorial control, others demanded destruction. Chief among them was the censor Marcus Porcius Cato, known as Cato the Elder (234–149 B.C.), who ended every speech with *Delenda est Carthago,* "Carthage must be destroyed." Ultimately, trumped-up reasons were found to renew the war in 149 B.C. In contrast to the desperate, hard-fought campaigns of the Second Punic War, the Third was an unevenly matched slaughter. In 146 B.C., Scipio Aemilianus (184–129 B.C.), or Scipio the Younger, the adopted grandson of Scipio the Elder, overwhelmed Carthage and sold its few survivors into slavery. As a symbolic act of final destruction, he then had the site razed, plowed, and cursed. Carthage's fertile hinterland became the property of wealthy Roman senators.

In the same year that Carthage was destroyed, Roman armies destroyed Corinth, a second great center of Mediterranean commerce. This victory marked the culmination of Roman imperialist expansion east into the Greek and Hellenistic world that had begun with the conquest of Illyria. This expansion was not simply the result of Roman imperialist ambitions. The Hellenistic states, in their constant warring and bickering, drew Rome into their conflicts against their neighbors. Greek states asked the Roman Senate to arbitrate their disputes. Pergamum requested military assistance against Macedonia. Appealing to Rome's claims as "liberator," cities pressed the Senate to preserve their freedom in the face of aggressive expansion by their more powerful neighbors. In a series of intermittent, uncoordinated, and sporadic engagements, Rome did intervene, though its real focus was on its life-and-death struggle with Carthage. Roman intentions may not have been conquest, but Roman intervention upset the balance of power in the Hellenistic world. Although Rome became a major player in the eastern Mediterranean more by chance than by design, it rapidly became the winner. The price of Roman arbitration, intervention, and protection was loss of independence. Gradually the Roman shadow fell over the eastern Mediterranean.

The treaty Philip V of Macedon concluded with Carthage during the Second Punic War provided an initial excuse for war, one seized upon more eagerly by the plebeian assembly than by the Senate. Shortly after its victory at Zama, Rome provoked Philip to war and then easily defeated him in 197 B.C., proclaiming the freedom of the Greek cities and withdrawing from Greece. In 189 B.C., the Seleucid Antiochus III (223–187 B.C.) of Syria suffered the same fate, and Rome declared the Greek cities in Asia Minor he had controlled free. The Greeks venerated the Roman commander, Titus Quinctius Flamininus (228–174 B.C.), as a god—the first Roman to be accorded this Eastern honor. In reality, the control of the cities lay in the hands of local oligarchs favorable to Rome. In 179 B.C., Philip's son Perseus (179–168 B.C.) attempted to stir up democratic opposition to Rome within the cities. This time Rome responded more forcefully. The Macedonian kingdom was divided into four republics governed by their own senates and magistrates selected from among the local aristocrats. In Epirus, seventy cities were destroyed and 150,000 people sold into slavery. This harsh punishment prompted other Greek cities to react with panic even to the mere threat of Roman retribution. When the citizens of Rhodes heard that the Senate was contemplating declaring war on them, they quickly executed all of their anti-Roman fellows.

The final episode of Rome's expansionist drama unfolded during the Third Punic War. When Rome resumed its war with Carthage in 149 B.C., several Greek cities attempted once more to assert their autonomy from the hated oligarchies established by Rome. Retribution was swift. The Roman legions crushed the rebel forces and, as an example to all, Corinth was razed as thoroughly as was Carthage. Vast booty from wealthy Corinth poured into Rome while the survivors found themselves enslaved in the homes and estates of Roman victors.

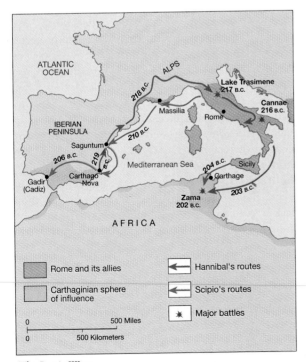

The Punic Wars

THE ROMAN REPUBLIC

509 B.C.	**Expulsion of last Etruscan king; beginning of Roman republic**
ca. 450 B.C.	**Law of the Twelve Tables**
396 B.C.	**Rome conquers southern Etruria**
295 B.C.	**Rome extends rule north to Po Valley**
265–241 B.C.	**First Punic War**
264 B.C.	**All of Italy under Roman control**
218–202 B.C.	**Second Punic War**
149–146 B.C.	**Third Punic War; Carthage is destroyed**

In the west, in northern Italy, Spain, and Africa, Roman conquest had been direct and complete. Tribal structures had been replaced with Roman provinces governed by former magistrates or proconsuls. In the east, Rome preferred to work through the existing political hierarchies. Still, Rome cultivated its image as protector of Greek liberties against the Macedonian and Seleucid monarchies and preferred indirect control to annexation. Its power was no less real for being indirect.

By 146 B.C., the Roman republic controlled the whole rim of the Mediterranean from Rhodes in the east across Greece, Dalmatia, Italy, southern Gaul, Spain, and North Africa. Even Syria and Egypt, although nominally independent, had to bow before Roman will. This subjugation had been graphically demonstrated in 168 B.C., when the Seleucid Antiochus IV (175–164 B.C.) invaded the kingdom of the Egyptian ruler Ptolemy VI (180–145 B.C.) and besieged Alexandria. The Ptolemys had long before made a treaty with Rome, and the Senate sent an envoy to Antiochus with written instructions to withdraw immediately from Egypt. The king replied that he would like to consult his advisers before making a decision. The Roman envoy immediately drew a circle around Antiochus, ordering him to give an answer before he stepped out of the ring. Such directness was unknown in the world of Hellenistic diplomacy. After a moment's hesitation, the deeply shocked Antiochus replied that he would do whatever the Romans demanded. Perseverance and determination had brought Rome from obscurity to the greatest power the West had ever known. The republic had endured great adversity. It would not survive prosperity.

Republican Civilization

Territorial conquest, the influx of unprecedented riches, and exposure to sophisticated Hellenistic civilization ultimately overwhelmed earlier Roman civilization. This civilization had been created by stubborn farmers and soldiers who valued above all else authority, simplicity, and piety. This unique culture was the source of strength that led Rome to greatness, but its limitations prevented the republic from resolving its internal social tensions and the external problems caused by the burden of empire.

Farmers and Soldiers

The ideal Roman farmer was not the great estate owner of the Greek world, but the smallholder, the dirt farmer of central Italy. A typical farm might be as little as ten acres worked by the owner and his family. Such farms produced grain and beans and raised hogs for family consumption. In addition, Roman farmers cultivated vineyards and olive groves for cash crops. But the most important crop of Roman farms was citizens. "From farmers come the bravest men and the sturdiest soldiers," wrote Cato the Elder.

Nor was the ideal Roman soldier the gallant cavalryman but rather the solid foot soldier. Cavalry, composed of wealthy citizens who made up the elite equestrian order (from the Latin *equus,* horse), and especially allies, provided reconnaissance and protected Roman flanks. However, the main fighting force was the infantry. Sometime in the early republic the Greek phalanx was transformed into the Roman legion, a flexible unit composed of thirty companies of 120 men each. Legions maneuvered in three rows of squares of men, each containing 120 soldiers. The first row engaged the enemy, first with javelins, and then with short swords. As men in the first row tired, members of the second and eventually the third could step in to relieve them. Likewise, the whole square could move back in formation, its place taken by a fresh unit that could keep up the pressure on the enemy. Such tactics demanded less virtuoso military ability than solid discipline.

Constant training, careful preparation, and painstaking execution characterized every aspect of Roman military expeditions. Wars were won as much by engineering feats as by feats of arms. Engineers constructed bridges, siege machines, and catapults. By the time of the late republic, Roman armies on the march could construct identical camps each night, quickly

One of a series of Roman mosaics illustrating tasks appropriate to the months of the year. Here two laborers are using an olive press with a horizontal screw for the December olive pressing.

building a strong square fort 2,150 feet on a side. Within each camp, every unit had exactly the same location for its quarters, as did the commander and paymaster. The chain of command was rigidly maintained, from the commander—a Roman consul—through military tribunes and centurions, two of whom commanded each company of 120 men. Even the slaughter and pillage that followed the capture of an enemy city were carried out with firm Roman discipline. When Scipio the Elder took Carthago Nova in 210 B.C., he ordered his troops to exterminate every form of life they encountered, sparing none, and not to start pillaging until ordered to do so. After the citadel had fallen, the order went out to stop killing and start pillaging. Half of the army collected the spoils and brought them to a central location while the other half stood guard. The military tribunes then distributed the booty among their legions.

These solid, methodical troops, the backbone of the republican armies that conquered the Mediterranean, were among the victims of that conquest. The pressures of constant international warfare were destroying the farmer-soldiers whom the traditionalists loved to praise. When the Roman sphere of interest had been confined to central Italy, farmers could do their planting in spring, serve in the army during the summer

months, and return home to care for their farms in time for harvest. When Rome's wars became international expeditions lasting for years, many soldiers, unable to work their lands while doing military service, had to mortgage their farms in order to support their families. When they returned they often found that during their prolonged absences they had lost their farms to wealthy aristocratic moneylenders. While aristocrats amassed vast landed estates worked by imported slaves, ordinary Romans and Italians lacked even a family farm capable of supporting themselves and their families. Without land, they and their sons were excluded from further military service and sank into the growing mass of desperately poor, disenfranchised citizens.

Typical of such soldiers in many ways was Spurius Ligustinus, an ordinary soldier who by 177 B.C. had served twenty-two years in foreign campaigns. Born on a minuscule Sabine farm, he had entered the army and served two years in Macedonia against Philip V, then immediately reenlisted to serve in Spain. During a third enlistment he fought in Aetolia and was promoted to centurion. Later he served in three additional Spanish campaigns. Ligustinus held the rank of chief centurion four times and was thirty-four times rewarded for bravery. When he was well past fifty years of age, his sole means of support besides the military was the half-acre farm inherited from his father, from which he was expected to support six sons and two daughters. For such men and their families, the benefits of conquest must have seemed illusory indeed.

The Roman Family

In Roman tradition, the paterfamilias was the master of the family—which in theory included his wife, children, and slaves—over whom he exercised the power of life and death. This authority lasted as long as he lived. Only at his death did his sons, even if long grown and married, achieve legal and financial independence. The family was the basic unit of society and of the state. The authority of the paterfamilias was the foundation of this essentially patriarchal society and the key to its success.

Although not kept in seclusion as in Greece, Roman women theoretically never exercised independent power in this male-dominated world. Before marriage, a Roman girl was subject to the authority of her father. When she married, her father traditionally transferred legal guardianship to her husband, thus severing her bonds to her paternal family. A husband could divorce his wife at will, returning her and her dowry to her father. Wives did exercise real though informal authority within the family. Part of this authority came from their role in the moral education of their children and the direction of the household. Part also came from their control over their dowries. Widows might exercise even greater authority in the raising of their children.

Paternal authority over children was absolute. Not all children born into a marriage became members of the family. The Law of the Twelve Tables allowed defective children to be killed for the good of the family. Newborn infants were laid on the ground before the father, who decided whether the child should be raised. By picking up a son, he accepted the child into the family. Ordering that a daughter be nursed similarly signified acceptance. If there were too many mouths to feed or the child was simply unwanted, the father could command that the infant be killed or abandoned. Abandoned children might be adopted by childless couples. Frequently, if they survived at all, it was as slaves or prostitutes.

Nor were all sons born into Roman families. Romans made use of adoption for many purposes. Families without heirs could adopt children. Powerful political and military figures might adopt promising young men as their political heirs. These adopted sons held the same legal rights as the natural offspring of the father and thus were integral members of his family. Some adoptions even took place posthumously. An important Roman might name a younger man as his adopted son in his will.

Slaves, too, were members of the family. On the one hand, slaves were property without personal rights. On the other, they might live and work alongside the free members of the family, worship the family gods, and enjoy the protection and endure the authority of the paterfamilias. In fact, the authority of the paterfamilias was roughly the same over slave and free members of the family. If he desired, he could sell the free members of the family into slavery. Even freed slaves remained obligated to their former owner throughout life. They owed him special respect and could never oppose him

in lawsuits or other conflicts, under penalty of returning to servitude.

The center of everyday life for the Roman family was the *domus,* the family house, whose architectural style had developed from Etruscan traditions. Early Roman houses, even of the wealthy and powerful, were simple, low buildings well suited to the Mediterranean climate, constructed around an open courtyard, or *atrium.* Cato the Elder described the home of the great general Manius Curius, who had driven Pyrrhus from Italy, as a small, plain dwelling, and this simplicity predominated through the second century B.C. The house looked inward, presenting nothing but blank walls to the outside world. Visitors entered through the front door into the atrium, a central courtyard containing a collecting pool into which rainwater for household use flowed from the roof through terra-cotta drains. Originally, the atrium not only provided sunlight but allowed smoke from the hearth to escape. In niches or on shelves stood wax or terra-cotta busts of ancestors and statues of the household gods. The walls, constructed of blocks of stone, were often painted in bands of different colors in imitation of polychrome marble. Around the atrium, openings gave onto workrooms, storerooms, bedrooms, offices, and small dining rooms.

In the wake of imperial conquests, the Roman family and its environment began to change in ways disturbing to many of the oligarchy. Some women, perhaps in imitation of their more liberated Hellenistic sisters, began to take a more active role in public life. One example is Cornelia, a daughter of Scipio Africanus, who bore her husband twelve children, only three of whom survived to maturity. After her husband's death in 154 B.C., she refused to remarry, devoting herself instead to raising her children, administering their inheritance, and directing their political careers.

Some married women, too, escaped the authority of their husbands. Fewer and fewer fathers transferred authority over their daughters to their husbands. Instead, daughters remained under their father's authority as long as he lived. This meant that upon the

The progress of a Roman son. At left the baby nurses while the proud father looks on. The toddler in his father's arms soon gives way to the young boy playing with a donkey and cart. The maturing youth is seen at right reciting his lessons.

The atrium of the House of the Silver Wedding in Pompeii. The pool in the floor caught the rainwater that entered through the opening in the high roof.

father's death, they became independent persons, able to manage their own affairs without the consent of or interference by their husbands. Although some historians believe that sentimental bonds of affection may have increased between many husbands and wives and parents and children as legal bonds loosened, it also meant that the wife's relationship to her children was weakened. Roman mothers had never been legally related to their children. Wives and mothers were not fully part of their husband's families. Thus their brothers' families, not their own children, were their natural heirs. Just as adoption created political bonds, marriage to daughters sealed alliances between men. However, when these alliances fell apart or more advantageous ones presented themselves, fathers could force their daughters to divorce their husbands and to marry someone else. Divorce became increasingly common in the second century B.C. More and more, wives were temporary visitors in their husband's homes.

Homes grew in size, wealth, and complexity for those who participated in the wealth of empire. With increasing prosperity, the atrium became more elegant, intended to impress visitors with the wealth of the family and its traditions. The water basin became a reflecting pool, often endowed with a fountain and surrounded by towering columns. In many cases a second open area, or *peristyle,* appeared behind the first. The wealthy surrounded the atrium and peristyle with glass-enclosed porticoes and decorated their walls with frescoes, mosaics, and paintings looted from Hellenistic cities of the East. Furniture of fine inlaid woods, bronze, and marble and Eastern carpets and wall hangings increased the exotic luxury of the patrician domus.

Not every Roman family could afford its own domus, and in the aftermath of the imperial expansion, housing problems for the poor became acute. In Rome and other towns of Italy, shopkeepers lived in small houses attached to their shops or in rooms behind their workplaces. Peasants forced off their land and crowded into cities found shelter in multistory apartment buildings, an increasingly common sight in the cities of the empire. In these cramped structures, families crowded into small, low rooms about ten feet square. All the families shared a common enclosed courtyard. These apartment buildings and shops were not hidden away from the homes of the wealthy. In Roman towns throughout Italy, simple dwellings, luxurious mansions, shops, and apartment buildings existed side by side. The rich and the poor rubbed shoulders every day, producing a friction that threatened to burst into flame.

Roman Religion

Romans worshiped many gods, the more the better. Every aspect of daily life and work was the responsibility of individual powers, or *numina.* Every man had his genius or personal *numen,* just as every woman had her *juno.* Each family had its household powers, the *lares familiares,* whose proper worship was the responsibility of the paterfamilias. The *Vesta* was the spirit of the hearth-fire. The *lares* were the deities of farmland, the domus, and the guardians of roads and travelers. The *penates* guarded the family larder or storage cupboard. These family spirits exercised a binding power, a *religio,* upon the Romans, and the pious Roman householder

A bronze statuette of a lar, a Roman household god representing an ancestral spirit. In some houses, such statuettes were placed in miniature shrines fashioned after Roman temples. At mealtimes bits of food were burned as offerings to the ancestors.

recognized these claims and undertook the *officia,* or duties, to which the spirits were entitled.

These basic attitudes of religion, piety, and office lay at the heart of Roman reverence for order and authority. They extended to other traditional Roman and Latin gods such as Jupiter, the supreme god; Juno, his wife; Mars, the god of war; and the two-faced Janus, spirit of gates and new beginnings. This piety extended also to the anthropomorphic Etruscan gods for whom temples were erected on the Capitoline hill, and to the Greek deities whom the Romans absorbed along with the Hellenic world.

Outside the household, worship of the gods and the reading of the future in the entrails of sacrificed animals, the flight of birds, or changes in weather were the responsibilities of colleges of priests. Roman priests did not, as did those in the Near East, form a special caste but rather were important members of the elite who held priesthoods in addition to other public offices. Religion was less a matter of personal relationship with the gods than a public, civic activity binding society together. State-supported cults with their colleges of priests, Etruscan- and Greek-style temples, and elaborate ceremonies were integral parts of the Roman state and society. The world of the gods reflected that of mortals.

As the Roman mortal world expanded, so did the divine. Romans were quick to identify foreign gods with their own. Thus Zeus became Jupiter, Hera became Juno, and Aphrodite became Venus. Whenever possible, Romans interpreted foreign cults in familiar Roman terms. This *interpretatio romana* allowed for the incorporation of conquered peoples into the Roman religious world, which was one with the state. It also made possible the introduction of Roman gods into newly conquered regions, where shrines and temples to indigenous gods could be rededicated to the gods of Rome under their local names.

Still, the elasticity of Roman religion could stretch just so far. With the empire came not only the cults of Zeus, Apollo, and Aphrodite to Rome but that of Dionysus as well. Unlike the formal public cults of the other Greek deities, which were firmly in the control of authorities, that of Dionysus was largely outside state control. Women, in the tradition of the maenads, controlled much of the ecstatic and overtly sexual rituals associated with the god. Moreover, these rituals took place in secret, open only to the initiates of the god. Following the Second Punic War, the cult of Dionysus, known in Latin as Bacchus, spread rapidly in Italy, drawing thousands of devotees from all social orders. To the members of the oligarchy everything about the cult seemed to threaten traditional Roman values: it was Greek; it was dominated by women; most significantly, its rituals were secret. At these rites, or *Bacchanalia,* men and women were rumored to engage in every kind of sexual act. The Roman Senate was ready to believe anything about this rapidly spreading cult. As Titus Livius, or Livy (59 B.C.–A.D. 17), a later Roman moralist and historian, put it:

> The corruption was not confined to one kind of evil, the promiscuous violation of free men and of women; the cult was also a source of false witnesses, forged documents and wills, and perjured evidence, dealing also in poisons and in wholesale murders among the devotees, and sometimes ensuring that not even the bodies were found for burial.

In 186 B.C., the Senate decreed the cult of Bacchus a conspiracy and ordered an inquiry. The consul Spurius Postumius Albinus, acting on the dubious testimony of a former prostitute, began a brutal persecution. Rituals were banned, priests and adherents arrested, and

A detail from a wall painting in the Villa Item (Villa of the Mysteries) near Pompeii. A female satyr suckles a young goat while another plays the panpipes. At right a young woman recoils before the apparition of Dionysus and Ariadne and the symbols of the mysteries, which are depicted on the adjacent wall.

rewards offered to informants who provided lurid and fanciful accounts of what had taken place at the Bacchanalia. Panic spread throughout Italy as thousands of devotees fled in fear of their lives. Others took their own lives in despair. Hundreds of people were imprisoned and greater numbers were executed. The Senate ordered all shrines to Bacchus destroyed and Bacchanalia banned throughout Italy. Perhaps more than any other episode, the suppression of the Bacchic cult showed the fear that the oligarchy felt about the changes sweeping Roman civilization.

Republican Letters

As Rome absorbed foreign gods, it also absorbed foreign letters. From the Etruscans the Romans adopted and adapted the alphabet, the one in which most Western languages are written to this day. Early Latin inscriptions are largely funeral monuments and some public notices such as the Law of the Twelve Tables. The Roman high priest responsible for maintaining the calendar of annual feasts also prepared and updated annals—short accounts of important religious and secular events of each year—which he put on public display outside his home. Important treaties, records of booty, and decrees of the Senate found their way onto inscriptions as well. However, prior to the third century B.C., apart from extravagant funerary eulogies carefully preserved within families, Romans had no apparent interest in writing or literature as such. The birth of Latin letters began with Rome's exposure to Greek civilization.

Early in the third century B.C., Greek authors had begun to pay attention to expanding Rome. The first serious Greek historian to focus on this new western power was Timaeus (ca. 356–ca. 260 B.C.), who spent most of his productive life in Athens. There he wrote a history of Rome up to the Pyrrhic war, interviewing Roman and Greek witnesses in order to gain an understanding of this Italian city that had defeated a Hellenistic army. Polybius (ca. 200–ca. 118 B.C.), the greatest of the Greek historians to record Rome's rise to

A memorial sculpture of Cato the Elder and his wife. Cato defended the ancient Roman traditions even as he himself was deeply influenced by the changes sweeping Rome.

power, gathered his information firsthand. As one of a thousand eminent Greeks deported to Rome for political investigation, he became a close friend of Scipio Aemilianus and accompanied him on his Spanish and African campaigns. Polybius became a strong supporter of Roman expansion. His history of the Punic and eastern wars, in the tradition of Thucydides, searches for truth in eyewitness testimony, in the writings of earlier authors, and in the personal experience of the author. Polybius's history is both the culmination of the traditions of Greek historiography and its transformation, since it centers on the rise of a non-Greek power to rule "almost the whole inhabited world."

At the same time that Greeks began to take Rome seriously, Romans themselves became interested in Greece and in particular in the international Hellenistic culture of the eastern Mediterranean. The earliest Latin literary works were clearly adaptations if not translations of Hellenistic genres and texts. Still, they indicated an independence typically Roman. Although Polybius dated the Roman interest in things Greek from the fall of Syracuse in 212 B.C., by 240 B.C. plays in the Greek tradition were said already to have been performed in Rome. The earliest extant literary works—ironically in light of the sober image of the Roman farmer-soldier—are the plays of Plautus (ca. 254–184 B.C.) and Terence (186–159 B.C.), lightly adapted translations of Hellenistic comedies.

Scheming servants, mistaken identities, bedroom farces, young lovers, and lecherous elders make up the plots of the Roman plays. What is most remarkable about these comedies, however, is the extent to which their authors experimented with and transformed Greek literature. Plautus in particular, while maintaining superficially the Greek settings of his plays, actually creates a world more Roman than Greek. References to Roman laws, magistrates, clients, and social situations abound, as do humorous derogatory comments on Greek mores. Terence, though remaining closer to Greek models, romanized his material through the creation of an elegant, natural style. Although criticized by many at the time, his plays rapidly became classics of Latin writing, influencing subsequent generations of Latin authors who worked to create a literary language separate from but equal to Greek.

Determined soldier-farmers, disciplined by familial obligations and their piety toward the gods and the Roman state, spread Roman rule throughout the Mediterranean world. Confident of their military and governmental skills and lacking pretensions to great skill in arts, literature, and the like, they were eager to absorb the achievements of others, even while adapting them to their own needs.

The Price of Empire, 146–121 B.C.

Rome's rise to world power within less than a century profoundly affected every aspect of republican life. Magistrates operating far from senatorial control in conquered provinces exercised power and found opportunities for enrichment never before seen. Successful commanders, honored and even deified by eastern cities, felt the temptation to ignore the strict requirements of senatorial accountability. There were fortunes to be made in the empire, and these fortunes distanced the oligarchy ever further from ordinary Roman citizens. A cynical saying circulating in the later republic summed up the situation well. During the time of a provincial command, it was said, one had to make three fortunes: the first to pay off the bribes it took to get the office, the second to pay off the jury that would investigate corruption after the command had expired, and a third to live on for the rest of one's life. Thus provincial commanders enriched themselves through extortion, collusion with dishonest government contractors and tax collectors, and wholesale bribe taking. Ordinary citizens, aware of such abuses, felt increasingly threatened by the wealthy and powerful. The old traditions of the farmer-soldier, the paterfamilias, the pious venerator of the gods, and the plain-speaking Latin dissolved before the vast new horizons, previously unimagined wealth, alien culture, and unprecedented opportunities of empire.

In the second century B.C., Romans found themselves in a dilemma as the old and the new exerted equal pressures. These tensions led to almost a century of bitter civil strife and ultimately to the disintegration of the republic. The complex interaction of these tensions can best be seen in the life of one man, Marcus Porcius Cato.

Cato the Elder is often presented as the preserver of the old traditions, in contrast to Scipio Aemilianus, destroyer of Carthage and proponent of Hellenism in the Roman world. True, as censor fighting against conspicuous consumption and as self-conscious defender of the past, Cato cast himself in the mold of the traditional Roman. And Scipio, with his love of Hellenism and his political career defined more by personal achievement than traditional magistracies, represented

CATO'S SLAVES

The two sides of Cato's personality are strikingly shown in his treatment of slaves. The following description is within the generally admiring portrait of the old Roman by Plutarch (ca. A.D.46–after 119), who leaves it to the reader to decide whether "these acts are to be ascribed to the greatness or pettiness of his spirit."

He [Cato] himself says that he never wore a suit of clothes which cost more than a hundred drachmas; and that, when he was general and consul, he drank the same wine which his workmen did and that the meat or fish which was bought in the meat-market for dinner did not cost above thirty *asses*. All which was for the sake of the commonwealth, that so his body might be the hardier for the war. Having a piece of embroidered Babylonian tapestry left him, he sold it; because none of his farmhouses were so much as plastered. Nor did he ever buy a slave for above fifteen hundred drachmas; as he did not seek for effeminate and handsome ones, but able sturdy workmen, horse keepers and cow-herds; and these he thought ought to be sold again, when they grew old, and no useless servants fed in the house. In short, he reckoned nothing a good bargain which was superfluous; but whatever it was he bought for a farthing, he would think it a great price, if you had no need of it; and was for the purchase of lands for sowing and feeding rather than grounds for sweeping and watering.

Some imputed these things to petty avarice, but others approved of them, as if he had only the more strictly denied himself for the rectifying and amending of others. Yet certainly, in my judgment, it marks an over-rigid temper for a man to take the work out of his servants as out of brute beasts, turning them off and selling them in their old age, and thinking there ought to be no further commerce between man and man than whilst there arises some profit by it. We see that kindness or humanity has a larger field than bare justice to exercise itself in; law and justice we cannot, in the nature of things, employ on others than men; but we may extend our goodness and charity even to irrational creatures; and such acts flow from a gentle nature, as water from an abundant spring.

From Plutarch, *The Lives of the Noble Grecians and Romans.*

a new type of Roman. But if the division between old and new, between Cato and Scipio, had been so clear-cut, the dilemma of republican Rome would not have been so great. As it was, Cato reflected in himself this contradictory clash of values. Like the two-faced god Janus whom he invoked in all his undertakings, Cato was the stern censor, the guardian and proponent of traditional Roman virtue, as well as the new Roman of shrewd business acumen, influence, and power unimaginable to the simple farmers he professed to admire.

Cato was born in the Latin town of Tusculum in 234 B.C. and grew to maturity on a family estate in Sabine territory. Although he boasted that he had spent his entire youth in frugality, rigor, and industry, his was a moderately wealthy family of Roman citizens. He came of age just at the start of the Second Punic War and distinguished himself in campaigns against Hannibal in Italy and Syracuse in Sicily. In between campaigns he became even more famous for his eloquence in pleading legal cases. His talents, matched by his drive and energy, brought him to the attention of a number of powerful members of the senatorial aristocracy, under whose patronage he came to Rome. There he began to rise through the offices of military tribune, quaestor, and ultimately consul and censor.

This first-generation senator became the spokesman for the traditional values of Rome, for severity and simplicity, for honesty and frugality in private and public life. Never known for his personal charm or tact, Cato was constantly embroiled in controversy. He saved his particular venom for those who enriched themselves with the spoils of conquest, who adopted Greek traditions of culture, and who displayed their new wealth and culture in fine furniture, expensive clothes, and gangs of Greek slaves. He made a great show of his own frugality, glorifying his simple farm life and the care he took in the management of his estates and of his extended familia, and working his fields side by side with his slaves. He despised senators who were profiting from the expansion of the empire to become involved in trade, and supported legislation to keep senators out of commerce. In public office Cato was equally frugal, drinking the same cheap wine as his men when on military campaigns and boasting of how little public money he spent. He ridiculed Greek philosophy and education, warning his son that the Romans would be destroyed once they were infected with Greek learning. Cato presented himself as the epitome of the old Roman farmer-soldier, a man of simplicity and traditional values.

Actually, Cato, as much as anyone else, was deeply involved in the rapid changes brought about by the empire. He may have worked along with his slaves and shared their table, but as soon as they grew old he sold them to the state to avoid having to support them, something no conscientious paterfamilias would ever have done. Although he led the battle to prevent senators from participating in commerce, he was perhaps the first of that body to diversify his holdings and investments. He bought up land, hot baths, and mineral deposits. He invested his surpluses in maritime commerce, being careful to use middlemen to circumvent his own laws. He also grew rich through moneylending, not only to merchants but also to slaves. Although he avoided conspicuous consumption himself, as consul and censor he was responsible for many of the sumptuous building projects in Rome through which ordinary Romans first experienced the luxuries of the Hellenistic world. While scorning Greek culture, his extant writings and speeches show how deeply indebted he was to Greek literature. Even in his own day he was called the Roman Demosthenes, and he worked bits of Greek authors even into his attacks on Greek civilization.

Cato was neither duplicitous nor hypocritical. He was simply typical. Many senators agreed with him that the old values were slipping away and with them the foundation of the republic. Many feared that personal ambition was undermining the power of the oligarchy. And yet these same people could not resist exploiting the changed circumstances for their own benefit.

• • •

Rome had come a long way since its origin as an outpost of the Alban League. At first overshadowed by its more civilized neighbors to the north and south, it had slowly and tenaciously achieved independence from and then domination over its more ancient neighbors. It is difficult to point to particular Roman ideas, institutions, or techniques that made this possible. Virtually all of these were absorbed or adapted from the Etruscans, Greeks, and others with whom Rome came into contact. Rome's great success was largely due to Roman authoritarianism as well as to its genius for creative adaptation, flexibility, and thoroughness, and its willingness to give those it conquered a stake in Roman victory. Until the middle of the second century B.C., this formula had served the republic well. After the final destruction of Carthage, however, an isolated and fearful oligarchy appeared unwilling or unable to broaden the base of those participating in the Roman achievement. The result was a century of conflict and civil war that destroyed the republican empire.

Suggestions for Further Reading

Primary Sources

Many of the works of Polybius, Livy, Cato, Caesar, Cicero, and other Roman authors are available in English translation from Penguin Books. The first volume—*Roman Civilization, Selected Readings,* Vol. I: *The Republic* (1951), by Naphtali Lewis and Meyer Reinhold—contains a wide selection of documents with useful introductions.

The Western Mediterranean to 509 B.C.

B. H. Warmington, *Carthage,* rev. ed. (New York: F. A. Praeger, 1969). A basic introduction.

Massimo Pallottino, *The Etruscans* (Bloomington, IN: Indiana University Press, 1975). A general introduction to Etruscan history, language, and civilization.

From City to Empire, 509–146 B.C.

Leon Homo, *Primitive Italy and the Beginnings of Roman Imperialism* (Philadelphia: Century Bookbindery, 1968). A classic introduction to early Italian history.

Michael Crawford, *The Roman Republic* (Cambridge, MA: Harvard University Press, 1978). A modern survey of the republican period, emphasizing political history.

* John Boardman, Jasper Griffin, and Oswyn Murray, *The Roman World* (New York: Oxford University Press, 1988). A balanced collection of essays on all aspects of Roman history and civilization.

* P. A. Brunt, *Social Conflicts in the Roman Republic* (New York: Norton, 1971). Analyzes the continuing struggle between patricians and plebeians until the end of the republic.

Keith Hopkins, *Conquerors and Slaves* (New York: Cambridge University Press, 1978). A sociological study of the effects of slavery on imperial society and government.

* Mary Beard and Michael Crawford, *Rome in the Late Republic* (Ithaca, NY: Cornell University Press, 1985). A short interpretative essay on the crisis of the late republic.

Republican Civilization

Suzanne Dixon, *The Roman Mother* (Norman, OK: University of Oklahoma Press, 1988). A balanced view of Roman mothers in law and in society.

* Erich S. Gruen, *The Hellenistic World and the Coming of Rome,* 2 vols. (Berkeley, CA: University of California Press, 1984). A detailed history of the Hellenistic world, presenting Rome's gradual and unintended rise to dominance in it.

Geza Alfoldy, *The Social History of Rome* (Berlin: Walter de Gruyter, 1988). A survey of Rome that emphasizes the relationship between social structure and politics.

The Price of Empire, 146–121 B.C.

Alan E. Astin, *Cato the Censor* (New York: Oxford University Press, 1978). An excellent biography of Cato that also analyzes his writings.

*Paperback edition available.

5 ❧ IMPERIAL ROME, 27 B.C.–A.D. 192

Competitive Consumption

Romans loved to party, and they loved to see their heroes party as well. In this first-century mosaic, Heracles, the strong-man warrior hero, has challenged Dionysus, the god of wine, to a drinking contest. The god, typically portrayed as a pale-skinned, soft youth, has given up while the sun-burned, muscular hero, his body tanned by his exertions in the sun, drains the last cup and receives the laurel wreath of victory. This was a contest with which wealthy Romans—themselves reclining at a banquet in the chamber that was decorated with this mosaic—could easily identify. Were they not like Heracles, powerful warriors and men of action, able not only to defeat enemies in battle but even in leisure? It was the good life, pursued with the same determination and competitiveness that had created and sustained an empire.

Opulence, leisure, and sensual pleasure were the counterpoint to the discipline, hardship, and valor so valued by earlier generations of Romans. How-ever, this new lifestyle was not restricted to the members of the ancient patrician families that had so long dominated Roman society and government. The empire seemed to offer such pleasures to every-one, regardless of background, who was willing and able to cooperate with the imperial system spreading across the Mediterranean world. Ambitious soldiers, clever merchants—even dutiful and enterprising slaves—hoped to drink from the cups of Dionysus and Heracles, even if it meant subverting and destroying the republican system.

The fall of the republic meant a recognition that its traditions could no longer sustain and inspire the people who counted, both in Rome and beyond. Across the empire, from the cold mists of Britain to the burning deserts of Arabia, the same cultural val-ues and the same idea of success drew local elites into the imperial system. This image of a divine drinking bout could have come from anywhere; in fact, it graced a villa in Antioch-on-the-Orontes (the modern Turkish city of Antakya).

It also mattered little that Dionysus and Heracles were figures of Greek mythology—the Romans had appropriated Greek culture as thoroughly as they had the Greek cities and states of the Hellenistic world. Having conquered Greece, so the saying went, the Romans were in turn conquered by its culture, although this culture was less that of abstract Greek philosophy than a taste for Greek literature and wine.

Of course, few inhabitants of the empire could realistically expect to imitate the leisure and conspic-uous consumption of gods and heroes. For the vast majority of the population, survival, not luxury, was the often-elusive goal. The demands of the imperial machinery of armies, bureaucrats, and wealthy landowners drew off the surplus production of mil-lions of slaves and ordinary peasants and laborers. But this had been the case before the coming of Rome in most of the Mediterranean world, and in many places arbitrary rule, violence, and discord had made the lives of the poor even worse. Thus the image of an expansionist Roman imperial system is only half of the reality. The other half was the fre-quent demands placed on Rome to intervene in local affairs, to settle disputes for neighbors and client states, and to establish the Roman peace.

The fundamental problem, never resolved by Rome, was how to sustain an empire built on tradi-tional Roman virtues in a world that increasingly rejected them. War-hardened Heracles could defeat a soft Dionysus at his own game, but how much wine could Heracles consume before he, too, was as soft and helpless as the god?

The Price of Empire

Roman victory defeated the republic. Roman conquest of the Mediterranean world and the establishment of the Roman Empire spelled the end of the republican system. Roman society could not withstand the tensions caused by the enrichment of the few, the impoverishment of the many, and the demands of the excluded populations of the empire to share in its benefits. Traditional Roman culture could not survive the attraction of Hellenistic civilization with its wealth, luxuries, and individualistic values. Finally, Roman government could not restrain the ambitions of its oligarchs or protect the interests of its ordinary citizens. The creation of a Mediterranean empire brought in its wake a century of revolutionary change before stable new social, cultural, and political forms emerged in the Roman world.

Winners and Losers

Rome had emerged victorious in the Punic and Macedonian wars against Carthage and Macedon, but the real winners were the members of the oligarchy—the *optimates,* or "the best," as they called themselves—whose wealth and power had grown beyond all imagining. These optimates included roughly three hundred senators and magistrates, most of whom had inherited wealth, political connections, and long-established clientages. Since military command and government of the empire were entrusted to magistrates who were answerable only to the Senate, of which they were members, the empire was essentially their private domain. Their combination of landed wealth, political experience, and social ties placed them at the pinnacle of Roman society.

But new circumstances created new opportunities for many others. Italian merchants, slave traders, entrepreneurs, and bankers, many of lowly origin, poured into the cities of the east in the wake of the Roman legions. These newly enriched Romans constituted a second elite and formed themselves into a separate order, that of the *equites,* or equestrians, distinguished by their wealth and honorific military service on horseback, but connected with the old military elite. Since the Senate did not create a government bureaucracy to administer the empire, equestrian tax farmers became essential to provincial government. Companies of these publicans, or tax collectors, purchased the right to collect rents on public land, tribute, and customs duties from provincials. Whatever they collected beyond the amount contracted for by Roman officials was theirs to keep. Publicans regularly bribed governors and commanders to allow them to gouge the local populations with impunity and on occasion even obtained Roman troops to help them make their collections. Gradually, some of these "new men," their money "laundered" through investments in land, managed to achieve lower magistracies and even move into the senatorial order. Still, the upper reaches of office were closed to all but a tiny minority. By the end of the Punic wars, only some twenty-five families could hope to produce consuls.

The losers in the wars included the vanquished who were sold into slavery by the tens of thousands, the provincials who bore the Roman yoke, the Italian allies who had done so much for the Romans, and even the citizen farmers, small shopkeepers, and free artisans of the republic. All four groups suffered from the effects of empire, and over the next century all resorted to vio-

This relief shows mounted Roman equites, led by musicians, proceeding to a temple for sacrificial rites. As Roman power expanded, Roman religion was increasingly influenced by Greek ideas and by eastern mystery cults such as those of Mithras, Isis, and Serapis.

Roman slaves sifting grain. Roman victories in the Punic and Macedonian wars brought in a huge influx of slaves from the conquered lands. Slaves were pressed into service on the estates and plantations of wealthy landowners.

lence against the optimates. The slaves revolted first. Thousands of them, captured in battle or taken after victory, flooded the Italian and Sicilian estates of the wealthy. Estimates vary, but in the first century B.C., the slave population of Italy was probably around two million, fully one-third of the total population. This vastly expanded slave world overwhelmed the traditional role of slaves within the Roman *familia*. Rural slaves on absentee estates enjoyed none of the protections afforded traditional Roman servants. Cato sold off his slaves who reached old age; others simply worked them to death. Many slaves, born free citizens of Hellenistic states, found such treatment unbearable. In 135 B.C., a small group of particularly badly mistreated slaves in Sicily took up arms against their masters. Soon other slaves joined, ultimately swelling the ranks of the rebels to over two hundred thousand. It took the Roman state three years to crush the revolt.

A generation later slaves revolted in southern Italy and, between 104 and 101 B.C., again in Sicily. This time the cause was more specific. The Senate had passed a decree freeing enslaved citizens of Roman allies, but Sicilian slave owners blocked implementation of the order in Sicily. The rebel ranks quickly swelled to over thirty thousand, and only a full-scale military campaign was able to defeat them.

The most serious slave revolt occurred in Italy between 74 and 71 B.C. Gladiators—professional slave fighters trained for Roman amusement—revolted in Capua. Under the competent leadership of the Thra-

cian gladiator Spartacus, over one hundred thousand slaves took up arms against Rome. Ultimately eight legions, more troops than had met Hannibal at Zama, were needed to put down the revolt.

All slave revolts were doomed to failure. The revolutionaries lacked a unified goal, organization, discipline, and strategy. Some wanted freedom to return home. Others sought to establish themselves as autonomous kings with slaves of their own. Still others wished simply to avenge themselves against their masters. Their desperate struggles proved unequal to the numerical and military superiority of the disciplined legions, and retribution was always terrible. After the defeat of Spartacus, crucified rebels lined the road from Rome to Naples.

Revolts profoundly disturbed the Roman state, all the more because it was not just slaves who revolted. In many cases poor free peasants and disgruntled provincials rose up against Rome. The most significant provincial revolt was that of Aristonicus, the illegitimate half brother of Attalus III (ca. 138–133 B.C.) of Pergamum, a Roman client state. Attalus had left his kingdom to Rome at his death. In an attempt to assert his right to the kingdom, Aristonicus armed slaves and peasants and attacked the Roman garrisons. The hellenized cities of Asia Minor remained loyal to Rome, but this provincial uprising, the first of many over the centuries, lasted more than three years, from 133 to 130 B.C. In 88 B.C., Mithridates VI (120–63 B.C.), the king of Pontus, led an uprising against Roman soldiers, merchants, businessmen, and publicans in Asia Minor.

The revolt spread to Greece and tens of thousands of Romans died at the hands of poor freemen.

Revolts by slaves and provincials were disturbing enough. Revolts by Rome's Italian allies were much more serious. After the Second Punic War, these allies, on whose loyalty Rome had depended for survival, found themselves badly treated and exploited. Government officials used state power to undermine the position of the Italian elites. At the same time Roman aristocrats used their economic power to drive the Italic peasants from their land, replacing them with slaves. Some reform-minded Romans attempted to defuse tensions by extending citizenship to the allies, but failure of this effort led to a revolt at Fregellae, south of Rome, in 125 B.C. A broader and more serious revolt took place between 91 and 89 B.C. after the Senate blocked an attempt to extend citizenship to the allies. During this so-called Social War (from *socii,* the Latin word for allies), almost all the Italian allies rose against Rome. These revolts differed from those in the provinces in that the Italian elites as well as the masses aligned themselves against the Roman oligarchy. Even some ordinary Roman citizens joined the rebel forces against the powerful elite.

Optimates and Populares

The despair that could lead ordinary Roman citizens to armed rebellion grew from the social and economic consequences of conquests. While aristocrats amassed vast landed estates worked by cheap slaves, ordinary Romans often lacked even a family farm capable of supporting themselves and their families. Many found their way to Rome, where they swelled the ranks of the unemployed. Huddled into shoddily constructed tenements, they lived off the public subsidies. While many senators bemoaned the demise of the Roman farmer-soldier, few were willing to compromise their own privileged position to help. In the face of the oligarchy's unwillingness to deal with the problem, in 133 B.C. the tribune Tiberius Gracchus (ca. 163–133 B.C.) attempted to introduce a land-reform program that would return citizens to agriculture. Gracchus was the first of the *populares,* political leaders appealing to the masses. His motives were probably a mixture of compassion for the poor, concern over the falling numbers of citizens who had the minimum land to qualify for military service, and personal ambition. Over the previous century, great amounts of public land had illegally come into

A bedroom from a villa at Boscoreale, about one mile north of Pompeii, that was buried by the Vesuvius eruption of A.D. 79. The well-preserved wall paintings show bucolic scenes and architectural vistas.

The Reforms of Tiberius Gracchus

In the following passage, the romanized Greek Appian of Alexandria (ca. A.D. 95–ca. 165), drawing on earlier but now lost records, describes the positions of the two factions in the dispute over the land reform Tiberius Gracchus introduced in 133 B.C.

Tiberius Sempronius Gracchus, an illustrious man, eager for glory, a most powerful speaker, and for these reasons well known to all, delivered an eloquent discourse while serving as tribune, lamenting the fact that the Italians, a people so valiant in war and related in blood to the Romans, were declining little by little into pauperism and paucity of numbers without any hope of remedy. He inveighed against the multitude of slaves as useless in war and never faithful to their masters, and adduced the recent calamity brought upon the masters by their slaves in Sicily . . . After speaking thus he again brought forward the law providing that nobody should hold more than 500 *iugera* of public domain. But he added a provision to the former law, that [two] sons of the occupiers might each hold one-half that amount and that the remainder should be divided among the poor by three elected commissioners, who should be changed annually.

This was extremely disturbing to the rich because, on account of the commissioners, they could no longer disregard the law as they had done before; nor could they buy from those receiving allotments, because Gracchus had provided against this by forbidding such sales. They collected together in groups, and made lamentation, and accused the poor of appropriating their fields of long standing, their vineyards, and their buildings. Some said they had paid the price of the land to their neighbors. Were they to lose the money with the land? Others said the graves of their ancestors were in the ground, which had been allotted to them in the division of their fathers' estates. Others said that their wives' dowries had been expended on these estates, or that the land had been given to their own daughters as dowry . . . All kinds of wailing and expressions of indignation were heard at once. On the other side were heard the lamentations of the poor—that they were being reduced from competence to extreme poverty, and from that to childlessness, because they were unable to rear their offspring. They recounted the military services they had rendered, by which this very land had been acquired, and were angry that they should be robbed of their share of the common property . . . Emboldened by numbers and exasperated against each other they kindled incessant disturbances, and waited eagerly for the voting of the new law, some intending to prevent its enactment by all means, and others to enact it at all costs.

---

private hands. With the support of reform-minded aristocrats and commoners, Gracchus proposed a law that would limit the amount of public land an individual could hold to about 312 acres. He also proposed a commission to distribute to landless peasants the land recovered by the state as a result of the law. Because many senators who illegally held vast amounts of public land strongly opposed the measure, it faced certain failure in the Senate. Gracchus therefore took it to the plebeian assembly. Since 287 B.C., the measures of the assembly had been binding on all society and only the ten elected tribunes could veto its decisions. Here Gracchus's proposal was assured of support by the rural poor who flocked to Rome to vote for it. When the

aristocratic optimates, hoping to preserve their position, influenced one of the other nine tribunes to oppose the law, Gracchus had him deposed by the assembly, a move that shocked many senators. Senators, bound by custom and tradition, found Gracchus's maneuver to avoid the Senate and his unprecedented deposition of a tribune novel and deeply disturbing. The law passed, and a three-person commission to distribute land was established. However, Gracchus's maneuvering lost him many of his aristocratic supporters, who feared that a popular democracy led by a demagogue was replacing the senatorial oligarchy.

Also in 133 B.C., Gracchus introduced another bill that provided that the royal treasury of the kingdom of

Pergamum, bequeathed to Rome by Attalus III, be used to help citizens receiving land to purchase livestock and equipment. These laws, which challenged the Senate's traditional control over finance and foreign affairs, deeply disturbed the conservative elite, but as long as Gracchus held office, he was protected from any sort of attack by the traditional immunity accorded tribunes. It was no secret, however, that the Senate planned to prosecute him as soon as his one-year term expired. To escape this fate, he appealed to the assembly to reelect him for an unprecedented second consecutive term. To his opponents, this appeal smacked of an attempt to make himself sole ruler, a democratic tyrant on the Greek model. A group of senators and their clients, led by one of Gracchus's own cousins, broke into the assembly meeting at which the election was to take place and murdered the tribune and three hundred of his supporters.

The optimates in the Senate could eliminate Tiberius Gracchus, but they could not so easily eliminate the movement he had led. In 123 B.C., his younger brother, Gaius Sempronius Gracchus (153–121 B.C.), became tribune and during his two one-year terms initiated an even broader and more radical reform program. Tiberius had been concerned only about poor citizens. Gaius attempted to broaden the citizenry and to shift the balance of power away from the Senate. Alarmed by the revolt at Fregellae, he attempted to extend citizenship to all Latins and improve the status of Italian allies by extending to them the right to vote in the assembly. In order to check the power of senatorial magistrates in the provinces, he transferred to the equestrians the right to investigate provincial corruption. This move brought the wealthy equestrian order into politics as a counterbalance to the Senate. Gaius also improved the supply and distribution of grain in Rome and other Italian cities to benefit the urban poor. He reestablished his brother's land-distribution project, extended participation to Latins and Italians, and encouraged colonization as a means to provide citizens with land. Finally, in order to protect himself and his party from the anticipated reaction of the Senate and to prepare to avenge his brother's death, he pushed through a law stipulating that only the people could condemn a citizen to death.

Gaius's program was extraordinary for several reasons. In the first place, it was exactly that, a program, the first comprehensive attempt to deal with the problems facing Roman society. Secondly, it proposed a basic shift of power, drawing the equestrian order for the first time into the political arena opposite the Senate and making the assembly rather than the Senate the initiator of legislation. Finally, it offered a solution to the problem of the allies that, although rejected at the time, was finally adopted some twenty years later. In the short run, however, Gaius's program was a failure. In 121 B.C., he failed to be reelected for a third term and thus lost the immunity of the tribunate. Recalling the fate of his brother, he armed his supporters. Once more the Senate acted, ordering the consul to take whatever measures he deemed necessary. Gaius and some three thousand of his supporters died.

The deaths of Tiberius and Gaius Gracchus marked a new beginning in Roman politics. Not since the end of the monarchy had a political conflict been decided with personal violence. The whole episode provided a model for future attempts at reform. Reformers would look not to the Senate or the aristocracy but to the people, from whom they would draw their political power. The experience of the Gracchi also provided a model for repression of other reform programs: violence.

The End of the Republic

With the Gracchi dead and the core of their reforms dismantled, the Senate appeared victorious against all challengers. At home, the masses of ordinary Roman citizens and their political leadership were in disarray. The conquered lands of North Africa and the Near East filled the public coffers as well as the private accounts of Roman senators and publicans.

In reality, Rome had solved neither the problem of internal conflict between rich and poor nor that of how to govern its enormous empire. The apparent calm ended when revolts in Africa and Italy exposed the fragility of the Senate's control and ushered in an ever increasing spiral of violence and civil war.

The Crisis of Government

In 112 B.C., the Senate declared war against Jugurtha (ca. 160–104 B.C.), the king of a North African client state who, in his war against a rival, had killed some Roman merchants in the Numidian city of Cirta. The war dragged on for five years amid accusations of corruption, incompetence, and treason. Finally in 107 B.C., the people elected as consul Gaius Marius (157–86 B.C.), a "new man" who had risen through the tribunate, and entrusted him with the conduct of the war. In order to raise an army, Marius ignored property qualifications and enlisted many impoverished Romans and armed them at public expense. Although recruiting of landless citizens had probably taken place before, no one had done it in such an overt and massive manner. Senators looked on Marius's measure with great suspicion, but the poor citizen recruits, who had despaired of benefiting from the land reforms proposed by the Gracchi, looked forward to receiving a grant of land at the end of their military service.

Marius quickly defeated Jugurtha in 106 B.C. In the next year Celtic and Germanic barbarians crossed the Alps into Italy and, although technically disqualified from further terms, Marius was elected consul five times between 104 and 100 B.C. to meet the threat. During this period he continued to recruit soldiers from among the poor and on his own authority extended citizenship to allies. Marius promised land to his impoverished soldiers but after his victory in 101 B.C. the Senate refused to provide veterans with farms. As a result, Marius's armies naturally shifted their allegiance away from the Roman state and to their popular commander. Soon this pattern of loyalty became the norm. Politicians forged close bonds with the soldiers of their armies. Individual commanders, not the state or the Senate, ensured that their recruits received their pay, shared in the spoils of victory, and obtained land upon their retirement. In turn, the soldiers became fanatically devoted to their commanders. Republican armies had become personal armies, potent tools in the hands of ambitious politicians.

The outbreak of the Social War in 91 B.C. marked the first use of these armies in civil war. Both Marius and the consul Lucius Cornelius Sulla (138–78 B.C.) raised armies to fight the Italians, who were pacified only after Roman citizenship was extended to all Italians in 89 B.C. The next year Mithridates VI (120–63 B.C.), the king of Pontus, took advantage of the Roman preoccupation in Italy to invade the province of Asia. As soon as the Italian threat receded, Sulla, as the representative of the optimates, raised an army to fight Mithridates. As leader of the populares, who favored reform, Marius attempted to have Sulla relieved of command. Sulla marched on Rome, initiating a bloody civil war. In the course of this war Rome was occupied three times—once by Marius and twice by Sulla. Each commander ordered mass executions of his opponents and confiscated their property, which he then distributed to his supporters.

Ultimately Sulla emerged victorious and ruled as dictator from 82 to 79 B.C., using this time to shore up senatorial power. He doubled the size of the Senate to six hundred, filling the new positions with men drawn from the equites. He reduced the authority of tribunes and returned jury courts from the equites to the senators. In order to weaken the military power of magistrates, he abolished the practice of assigning military commands to praetors and consuls. Rather, they were to be held by proconsuls, or former magistrates, who would serve for one year as provincial governors.

In 79 B.C., his reforms in place, Sulla stepped down to allow a return to oligarchic republican rule. Although his changes bought a decade of peace, they did not solve the fundamental problems dividing optimates and populares. If anything, his rule had proven that the only real political option was a dictatorship by a powerful individual with his own army. During the last generation of the republic, idealists continued their hopeless struggle to prop up the dying republican system while more forward-thinking generals fought among themselves for absolute power.

The Civil Wars

Marcus Tullius Cicero (106–43 B.C.) reflected the strengths and weaknesses of the republican tradition in the first century B.C. Although cultivated, humane, and dedicated to the republican constitution, he was also ambitious, blind to the failings of the optimates, a poor judge of character, and out of touch with the political realities of his time. Like Cato in an earlier age, he was a "new man," the son of a wealthy equestrian who provided his children with the best possible education both in Rome and in Athens and Rhodes. In Greece, Cicero developed a lifelong attachment to Stoic philosophy and developed the oratory skills necessary for a young Roman destined for public life. After returning to Rome he quickly earned a reputation for his skills as a courtroom orator. At the same time he began his climb up the political ladder by championing popular causes while protecting the interests of the wealthy and soliciting the assistance of young optimates. Cicero identified firmly with the elite, hoping that the republic could be saved through the harmonious cooperation of the equestrian and senatorial orders. Neither group was interested in following his program, but most considered him a safer figure than military strongmen like Sulla, who sought high office. In 63 B.C. Cicero was elected consul, the first "new man" to hold the office in over thirty years. The real threat to the existence of the republic was posed by the ambitions of powerful military commanders—Pompey (106–48 B.C.), Crassus (ca. 115–53 B.C.), and Julius Caesar (100–44 B.C.).

CICERO ON JUSTICE AND REASON

In his De Legibus *(On the Laws), Cicero recast the Stoic tradition of the universal laws of nature into a dialogue modeled on Plato's dialogue by the same name. In it, Cicero defends the belief that true justice must be based on reason, which, accessible to all persons, could be the solution to the evils facing the Roman republic and a guide in the governance of its empire.*

But the most foolish notion of all is the belief that everything is just which is found in the customs or laws of nations. Would that be true, even if these laws had been enacted by tyrants? . . . Justice is one; it binds all human society, and is based on one Law, which is right reason applied to command and prohibition . . . But if Justice is conformity to written laws and national customs, and if, as the same persons claim, everything is to be tested by the standard of utility, then anyone who thinks it will be profitable to him will, if he is able, disregard and violate the laws. It follows that Justice does not exist at all, if it does not exist in Nature, and if that form of it which is based on utility can be overthrown by that very utility itself. And if nature is not to be considered the foundation of Justice, that will mean destruction of the virtues on which human society depends, for where then will there be a place for generosity, or love of country, or loyalty, or the inclination to be of service to others or to show gratitude for favors received? For these virtues originate in our natural inclination to love our fellowmen, and this is the foundation of Justice . . . but if the principles of Justice were founded on the decrees of peoples, the edicts of princes, or the decisions of judges, then Justice would sanction robbery and adultery and forgery of wills, in case these acts were approved by the votes or decrees of the populace.

From Marcus Tullius Cicero, *De Legibus.*

Marcus Tullius Cicero, the famous statesman and orator, fought throughout his career to save the dying Roman republic.

Pompey and Crassus, both protégés of Sulla, rose rapidly and unconstitutionally through a series of special proconsular commands by judicious use of fraud, violence, and corruption. Pompey first won public acclaim by commanding a victorious army in Africa and Spain. Upon his return to Rome in 70 B.C., he united with Crassus, who had won popularity for suppressing the Spartacus rebellion. Together they worked to dismantle the Sullan constitution to the benefit of the populares. In return, Pompey received an extraordinary command over all of the coasts of the Mediterranean, in theory to suppress piracy but actually to give him control over all of the provinces of the empire. When in 66 B.C., King Mithridates of Pontus again attacked Greece, Pompey assumed command of the provinces of Asia. His army not only destroyed Mithridates but continued on, conquering Armenia, Syria, and Palestine, acquiring an impressive retinue of client kings and increasing the income from the provinces by some 70 percent.

While Pompey was extending the frontiers of the empire to the Euphrates, Crassus, whose wealth was legendary—"No one should be called rich," he once observed, "who is not able to maintain an army on his

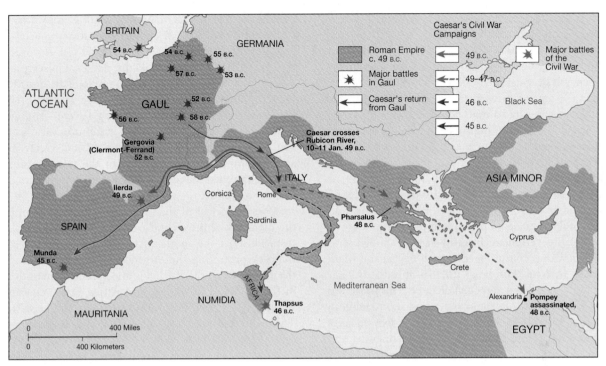

The Career of Julius Caesar

income"—was consolidating his power. He allied himself with Julius Caesar, a young, well-connected orator from one of Rome's most ancient patrician families, who nevertheless promoted the cause of the populares. The Senate feared the ambitious and ruthless Crassus, and it was to block the election of Crassus' candidate Catiline (Lucius Sergius Catilina, ca. 108–62 B.C.) to the consulate in 63 B.C. that the Senate elected Cicero instead. Catiline soon joined a conspiracy of Sullan veterans and populares, but Cicero quickly uncovered and suppressed the conspiracy and ordered Catiline's execution.

When Pompey returned from Asia in triumph in 62 B.C., he expected to find Italy convulsed with the Catiline revolt and in need of a military savior in the tradition of Sulla. Instead, thanks to Cicero's quick action, all was in order. Although he never forgave Cicero for stealing his glory, Pompey disbanded his army and returned to private life, asking only that the Senate approve his organization of the territories he had conquered and grant land to his veterans. The Senate refused. In response Pompey formed an uneasy alliance with Crassus and Caesar. This alliance was known as the first triumvirate, from the Latin for "three men." Caesar was elected consul in 59 B.C. and the following year received command of the province of Cisalpine Gaul in northern Italy.

Pompey and Crassus may have thought that this command would remove the ambitious young man from the political spotlight. Instead, Caesar, who has been called with only some exaggeration "the sole creative genius ever produced by Rome," used his province as a staging ground for the conquest of a vast area of western Europe to the mouth of the Rhine. His brilliant military skills beyond the Alps and his dedication to his troops made him immensely popular with his legions. His ability for self-promotion ensured that this popularity was matched at home, where the populares eagerly received news of his Gallic wars. In 53 B.C. Crassus died leading an army in Syria, leaving Pompey and the popular young Caesar to dispute supreme power. As word of Caesar's military successes increased his popularity at Rome, Pompey's suspicion of his younger associate also increased. Finally, in 49 B.C., Pompey's supporters in the Senate relieved Caesar of his command and ordered him to return to Italy.

Return he did, but not as commanded. Rather than leave his army on the far side of the Rubicon River—which marked the boundary between his province of Cisalpine Gaul and Italy—as ordered, he marched on Rome at the head of his legions. This meant civil war, a vicious bloodletting that convulsed the whole Mediterranean world. In 48 B.C., Caesar defeated Pompey in northern Greece, and Pompey was assassinated shortly thereafter in Egypt. Still the wars went on between Pompey's supporters and Caesar until 45 B.C., when with all his enemies defeated, Caesar returned to Rome. There, unlike Sulla, he showed his opponents clemency as he sought to heal the wounds of war and to undertake an unprecedented series of reforms. He enlarged the Senate to nine hundred and widened its representation, appointing soldiers, freedmen, provincials, and above all wealthy men from the Italian towns. He increased the number of magistracies to broaden participation in government, founded colonies at Carthage and Corinth, and settled veterans in colonies elsewhere in Italy, Greece, Asia, Africa, Spain, and Gaul. Still, he made no pretense of returning Rome to republican government. In early 44 B.C., though serving that year as consul together with his general Mark Antony (Marcus Antonius) (ca. 81–30 B.C.), Caesar had himself declared perpetual dictator. This move was finally too much for some sixty die-hard republican senators. On March 15, a group led by two enemies whom Caesar had pardoned, Cassius Longinus and Marcus Junius Brutus, assassinated him as he entered the senate chamber.

Cicero rejoiced when he heard of the assassination, which was clear evidence of his political naïveté. The republic was dead long before Caesar died, and the assassination simply returned Rome to civil war, a civil

This silver coin was struck to commemorate the assassination of Julius Caesar. Two daggers flank a cap symbolizing liberty. The legend reads "The Ides of March." On the other side is a profile of Brutus.

war that destroyed Cicero himself. Mark Antony, Marcus Lepidus (d. 12 B.C.), another of Caesar's generals, and Caesar's grand-nephew and adopted son Octavian (63 B.C.–A.D. 14), who took the name of his greatuncle, soon formed a second triumvirate to destroy Caesar's enemies. After a bloody purge of senatorial and equestrian opponents, including Cicero, Antony and Octavian set out after Cassius and Brutus, who had fled into Macedonia. At Philippi in 42 B.C. Octavian and Antony defeated the armies of the two assassins (or, as they called themselves, liberators), who preferred suicide to capture.

After the defeat of the last republicans at Philippi, the members of the second triumvirate began to look suspiciously at one another. Antony took command of the east, protecting the provinces of Asia Minor and the Levant from the Parthians and bleeding them dry in the process. Lepidus received Africa, and Octavian was left to deal with the problems of Italy and the west.

Initially Octavian had cut a weak and unimposing figure. He was only eighteen when he was named adopted son and heir in Caesar's will. He had no military or political experience and was frequently in poor health. Still, he had the magic of Caesar's name with which to inspire the army, he had a visceral instinct for politics and publicity, and he combined these with an absolute determination to succeed at all costs. Aided by more competent and experienced commanders, notably Marcus Agrippa (ca. 63–12 B.C.), and Gaius Maecenas (ca. 70–8 B.C.), he began to consolidate his power at the expense of his two colleagues. Lepidus attempted to gain a greater share in the empire but found that his troops would not fight against Octavian. He was forced out of his position and allowed to retire in obscurity, retaining only the honorific title of *pontifex maximus*.

Antony, to meet his ever growing demand for cash, became dependent on the Ptolemaic ruler of Egypt, the clever and competent Cleopatra VII (51–30 B.C.). For her part, Cleopatra manipulated Antony in order to maintain the integrity and independence of her kingdom. Octavian seized the opportunity to portray Antony as a traitor to Rome, a weakling controlled by an Oriental woman who planned to move the capital of the empire to Alexandria. Antony's supporters replied with propaganda of their own, pointing to Octavian's humble parentage and his lack of military ability. The final break came in 32 B.C. Antony, for all his military might, could not attack Italy as long as the despised Cleopatra was with him. Nor could he abandon her without losing her essential financial support. Instead, he tried to lure Octavian to a showdown in Greece. His

THE END OF THE REPUBLIC

135–81 B.C.	**Revolts against the republic**
133–121 B.C.	**Gracchi reform programs**
107 B.C.	**Gaius Marius elected consul**
91–82 B.C.	**Social War and civil war (Marius vs. Sulla)**
82–79 B.C.	**Sulla rules as dictator**
79–27 B.C.	**Era of civil wars**
63 B.C.	**Cicero elected consul First triumvirate (Pompey, Crassus, Caesar)**
59 B.C.	**Caesar elected consul**
45 B.C.	**Caesar defeats Pompey's forces**
44 B.C.	**Caesar is assassinated Second triumvirate (Mark Antony, Lepidus, Octavian)**
42 B.C.	**Octavian and Mark Antony defeat Cassius and Brutus at Philippi**
31 B.C.	**Octavian defeats Mark Antony and Cleopatra at Actium**
27 B.C.	**Octavian is declared Augustus**

philosophy, particularly *The Republic* and *The Laws,* in conscious imitation of Plato's concern for the proper order of society. For Cicero, humans and gods are bound together in a world governed not simply by might but by justice. The universe, while perhaps not fully intelligible, is nonetheless rational, and reason must be the basis for society and its laws.

These same concerns for virtue are evident in the writings of the great historians of the late republic, Sallust (86–ca. 34 B.C.) and Livy (59 B.C.–A.D. 17). Sallust was a supporter of Julius Caesar, who had written his own stylistically powerful histories of the Gallic and civil wars. For him as well as for his younger contemporary Livy, the chaos of civil war was the direct result of moral corruption and decline that followed the successes of the empire. For Sallust, the moral failing was largely that of the Senate and its members, who trampled the plebs in their quest for power and personal glory. Livy, who was much more conservative, con-

plan misfired. Agrippa forced him into a naval battle off Actium in 31 B.C. in which Antony was soundly defeated. He and his Egyptian queen committed suicide and Octavian ruled supreme in the Roman Empire.

The Good Life

Mere survival was a difficult and elusive goal through the last decades of the republic. Still, some members of the elite sought more. They tried to make sense of the turmoil around them and formulate a philosophy of life to provide themselves with a model of personal conduct. By now Rome's elite were in full command of Greek literature and philosophy, and they naturally turned to the Greek tradition to find their answers. However, they created from it a distinctive Latin cultural tradition. The most prominent figure in the late republic is Cicero, who combined his active life as lawyer and politician with an abiding devotion to Stoic philosophy. In Stoicism's belief in divine providence, morality, and duty to one's allotted role in the universe, he found a rational basis for his deeply committed public life. In a series of written dialogues, Cicero presented Stoic values in a form that created a Latin philosophical language freed from slavish imitation to Greek. He also wrote a number of works of political

A statue of a patrician exhibiting busts of his ancestors in a funeral procession. Roman portrait sculpture developed on Hellenistic Greek models.

demned plebeian demagogues as well as power-hungry senators. Only those aristocratic conservatives who, like Cato, had stood for the ancient Roman traditions merited praise. In the second century B.C. the Greek historian Polybius had been fascinated with the rise of the Roman republic to world supremacy. A century later the Roman historians were even more fascinated with its decline.

A different kind of morality dominated the work of Lucretius (ca. 100–55 B.C.), the greatest poet of the late republic. Just as Cicero had molded Stoicism into a Roman civic philosophy, Lucretius presented Epicurean materialist philosophy as a Roman alternative to the hunger for power, wealth, and glory. In his great poem *On the Nature of Things,* Lucretius presents the Epicurean's thoroughly physical understanding of the universe. He describes its atomic composition, the evolution of man from brutish beginnings to civilization, and the evil effects not only of greed and ambition but also of religion. All that exists is material reality. Religion, whether the state-supported cults of ancient Rome or the exotic cults introduced from the east, plays on mortals' fear of death, a fear that is irra-tional and groundless. "Death is nothing to us," Lucretius writes. "It is only the natural fulfillment of life. A rational, proportional enjoyment of life is all that matters. Sorrow and anxiety come from but an ignorant emotionalism."

Emotion was precisely the goal of another poetic tradition of the late republic, that of the "neoteric" or new-style poets, especially Catullus (ca. 84–ca. 54 B.C.). Avoiding politics or moralistic philosophy, these poets created short, striking lyric poems which, although inspired by Hellenistic poetry, combine polished craftsmanship with a direct realism that is without precedent. Roughly two dozen of Catullus's poems are addressed to his lover, whom he calls Lesbia. Mostly poems of rejection and disillusion, they are both artful and direct, a cry from the heart, but from a very sophisticated heart:

> *My lady says that she wants to marry no one so much as me,*
> *Not even should Jupiter himself ask her.*
> *So says she. But what a woman says to her eager lover*
> *Should be written in the wind and rushing water.*

One of the most striking differences between this Latin poetry and its Greek antecedents is the reality and individuality of the persons and relationships expressed. Catullus's poems follow the complex twists and turns of his real affair with Lesbia, who was in reality the cultured, emancipated, and wealthy Clodia, wife of the consul Metellus Celer. Lesbia and the other individuals in Catullus's poems are both very real persons and universal representatives of humanity. Such poetry could exist only because the late republic produced women sufficiently educated and independent to appreciate it.

The same interest in the individual affected the way artists of the late republic borrowed from Greek art. Since Etruscan times, Romans had commemorated their ancestors in wax or wooden busts displayed in the atria of their homes. Hellenistic artists concentrated on the ideal, but Romans cherished the individual. The result was a portraiture that caught the personality of the individual's face, even while portraying him or her as one of a type. Statues of the ideal nude, the armored warrior, or the citizen in his simple toga followed the proportions and conventions of Hellenistic sculpture. The heads however, created in hard, dry style, are as unique and personal as the characters who live in Catullus's lyric poems. We see in them the strengths and weaknesses, the stresses and the privileges, that marked the last generation of the Roman republic.

A lifelike portrait bust of a Roman matron

The Augustan Age

It took Octavian two years following his victory at Actium in 31 B.C. to eliminate remaining pockets of resistance and to work out a system to reconcile his rule with Roman constitutional traditions and yet not surrender any of his power. That power rested on three factors: his immense wealth, which he used to secure support; his vast following among the surviving elites as well as among the populares; and his total command of the army. It also rested on the exhaustion of the Roman people, who were eager, after decades of civil strife, to return to peace and stability. Remembering the fate of Julius Caesar, however, Octavian had no intention of rekindling opposition by establishing an overt monarchy. Instead, in 27 B.C., as he himself put it in the autobiographical inscription he had erected outside his mausoleum years later, he returned the republic from his own charge to the Senate and the people of Rome. In turn the Senate decreed him the title of *Augustus,* meaning "exalted."

What this meant was that Augustus, as he was now called, continued to rule no less strongly than before, but he did so not through any autocratic office or title–he preferred to be called simply the "first citizen," or *princeps*—but by preserving the form of the traditional Roman magistracies. For four years he rested his authority on consecutive terms as consul, and after 23 B.C. held a life position as tribune. The Senate granted him proconsular command of the provinces of Gaul, Spain, Syria, and Egypt, the major sources of imperial wealth and the locations of more than three-quarters of the Roman army. Later the Senate declared his *imperium,* or command, of these "imperial" provinces superior to that of any governors of other provinces. Thus Augustus, through the power of the plebeian office of tribune, stood as the permanent protector of the Roman people. As simultaneously either consul or proconsul, he held the command of the army and the basis of the ancient patrician authority. He was the first and greatest emperor.

These formalities deceived no one. Augustus's power was absolute. However, by choosing not to exercise it in an absolutist manner, he forged a new constitutional system that worked well for himself and his successors. By the end of his extraordinarily long reign of forty-one years, few living could remember the days of the republic and fewer still mourned its passing. Under Augustus and his successors, the empire enjoyed two centuries of stability and peace, the *Pax Romana.*

The Empire Renewed

Cicero had sought in vain a concord of the orders, a settlement of the social and political frictions of the empire through the voluntary efforts of a public-minded oligarchy. What could not happen voluntarily, Augustus imposed from above, reforming the Roman state, society, and culture.

Key to Augustus's program of renewal was the Senate, which he made, if not a partner, then a useful subordinate in his reform. He gradually reduced the number of senators, which had grown to over a thousand, back down to six hundred. In the process he eliminated the unfit and incompetent as well as the impoverished and those who failed to show the appropriate *pietas* toward the princeps. At the same time he made membership hereditary, although he continued to appoint individuals of personal integrity, ability, and wealth to the body. Under Augustus and his successors,

This idealized marble portrait statue of the emperor Augustus addressing his army was found in the Villa of Livia, wife of Augustus, at Prima Porta in Rome. The carvings on his breastplate recall a diplomatic incident during his reign.

access to the Senate became easier and more rapid than ever before, and the body was constantly renewed by the admission of wealthy sons of provincials and even of freed slaves. Most conspicuous among the "new men" to enter the Senate under Augustus were the wealthy leaders of Italian cities and colonies. These small-town notables formed the core of Augustus's supporters and worked most closely with him to renew the Roman elite.

Augustus also shared with the Senate the governance of the empire, although again not on an equal footing. The Senate named governors to the peaceful provinces, while Augustus named commanders to those frontier "imperial" provinces where were stationed most of the legions. Senators themselves served as provincial governors and military commanders. The Senate also functioned as a court of law in important cases. Still in all, the Senate remained a creature of the emperor, seldom asserting itself even when asked to do so by Augustus or his successors and competing within its own ranks to see who could be first to do the emperor's bidding. "Men fit for slaves!" was how Augustus's successor Tiberius disgustedly described senators.

Augustus undertook an even more fundamental reform of the equites, those wealthy businessmen, bankers, and tax collectors who had vied with the senatorial aristocracy since the reforms of Tiberius Gracchus. After Actium many equites found themselves proscribed—sentenced to death or banishment—and had their property confiscated. Augustus began to rebuild their ranks by enrolling a new generation of successful merchants and speculators, who became the foundation of his administration. Equestrians formed the backbone of the officer corps of the army, of the treasury, and of the greatly expanded imperial administration. The equestrian order was open at both ends. Freedmen and soldiers who acquired sufficient wealth moved into the order, and the most successful and accomplished equestrians were promoted into the Senate. Still, the price for a renewed equestrian order was its removal from the political arena. No longer was provincial tax collection farmed out to companies of equestrian publicans, nor were they allowed a role in executive or judicial deliberations. For most, these changes were a small price to pay for security, standing, and avenues to lucrative employment. Small wonder that emperors often had difficulty persuading the most successful equites to give up their positions for the more public but less certain life of a senator.

The land crisis had provoked much of the unrest in the late republic, and after Actium, Augustus had to satisfy the needs of the loyal soldiers of his sixty legions.

Drawing on his immense wealth, acquired largely from the estates of his proscripted enemies, he pensioned off thirty-two legions, sending them to colonies he purchased for them throughout the empire. The remaining twenty-eight legions became a permanent professional army stationed in imperial provinces. In time the normal period of enlistment became fixed at twenty years, after which time Augustus provided the legionnaires with land and enough cash to settle among the notables of their colonies. After A.D. 5 the state assumed the payment of this retirement bonus. Augustus also enrolled over one hundred thousand noncitizens into auxiliary units stationed in the imperial provinces. Auxiliaries served for twenty-five years and upon retirement were rewarded with colonies and Roman citizenship. Finally, Augustus established a small, elite unit, the praetorian guard, in and around Rome as his personal military force. Initially, the praetorians protected the emperors. In later reigns, they would make them.

These measures created a permanent solution to the problem of the citizen-soldier of the late republic. Veteran colonies—all built as model Roman towns with their central forum, baths, temples, arenas, and theaters as well as their outlying villas and farms—helped romanize the far provinces of the empire. These colonies, unlike the independent colonies of Greece in an earlier age, remained an integral part of the Roman state. Thus romanization and political integration went hand in hand, uniting through peaceful means an empire first acquired by arms. Likewise, ambitious provincials, through service as auxiliaries and later as citizens, acquired a stake in the destiny of Rome.

Not every citizen, of course, could find prosperity in military service and a comfortable retirement. The problem of urban poverty in Rome continued to grow. By the time of Augustus, the capital city had reached a population of perhaps 600,000 people. A tiny minority relaxed in the comfortable homes built on the Palatine. Tens of thousands more crammed into wooden and brick tenements and jostled each other in the crowded, noisy streets. (See "Living in Rome," pp. 144–145.) Employment was hard to find, since free labor had difficulty competing against slaves. The emperors, their power as tribunes making them protectors of the poor, provided over 150,000 resident citizens with a basic dole of wheat brought from Egypt. They also built aqueducts to provide water to the city. In addition, they constructed vast public recreation centers. These included both the sumptuous baths—which were combination bathing facilities, health clubs, and brothels—and arenas such as the Colosseum, where fifty thousand spectators could watch gladiatorial displays, and the Circus Maximus, where a quarter of the city's population could gather at once to watch chariot races. Such mass gatherings replaced the plebeian assemblies of the republic as the occasions on which the populace could express its will. Few emperors were foolish enough to ignore the wishes of the crowd roared out in the Circus.

Divine Augustus

Augustus's renewal of Rome rested on a religious reform. In 17 B.C. he celebrated three days of sacrifices, processions, sacred games, and theater performances known as the secular games. Although celebrations marking the beginning of each one-hundred-year generation, or *saeculum,* had been a part of ancient Roman tradition, Augustus revived the games and expanded them to mark the beginning of a new age. After the death of Lepidus in 12 B.C., he assumed the office of pontifex maximus and used it to direct a reinvigoration of Roman religion. He restored numerous temples and revived ancient Roman cults that had fallen into neglect during the chaos of the civil wars. He established a series of public religious festivals, reformed priesthoods, and encouraged citizens to participate in the traditional cults of Rome. His goals in all these religious reforms were twofold. After decades of public authority controlled by violence and naked aggression, he was determined to restore the traditions of Roman piety, morality, sacred order, and faith in relationship between the gods and Roman destiny. An equally important goal was Augustus's promotion of his own cult. His adoptive father, Julius Caesar, had been deified after his death, and Augustus benefited from this association with a divine ancestor. His own genius, or guiding spirit, received special devotion in temples throughout the West dedicated to "Rome and Augustus." In the East, citizens and noncitizens alike worshiped him as a living god. In this manner the emperor became identical with the state, and the state religion was closely akin to emperor worship. After his death Augustus and virtually all of the emperors after him were worshiped as official deities in Rome itself.

Closely related to his fostering of traditional cults was Augustus's attempt to restore traditional Roman virtues, especially within the family. Like the reformers of the late republic, he believed that the declining power of the paterfamilias was at the root of much that was wrong with Rome. To reverse the trend and to restore the declining population of free Italians, Augustus attempted to encourage marriage, procreation, and the firm control of husbands over wives. He imposed penalties for those who chose not to marry and bestowed rewards on those who produced large families. He enacted laws to prevent women from having extramarital affairs and even exiled his own daughter and granddaughter for promiscuity.

Augustus's call for a return to ancient virtue echoed that of leading figures of the late republic, in particular Cicero. The story is told that Augustus himself, although he had been partially responsible for Cicero's proscription and death, recognized the merit of his philosophy. He once came upon one of his grandchildren reading Cicero. The child, knowing that Cicero had been his grandfather's enemy, attempted to hide the book. Augustus took it, looked through it, and returned it, saying, "My child, this was a learned man and a lover of his country."

Augustus actively patronized those writers who shared his conservative religious and ethical values and who might be expected to glorify the princeps, and he used his power to censor and silence writers he considered immoral. Chief among the favored were the poets Virgil (70–19 B.C.) and Horace (65–8 B.C.). Both came from provincial and fairly modest origins, although both received excellent educations. Each lost his property in the proscriptions and confiscations during the

This fourth-century mosaic depicts gladiatorial combatants, some of whom are identified by name. Roman gladiators were lionized by society much as sports stars are today. Some who began as slaves became men of wealth and substance.

✎ Living in Rome

In spite of its magnificent temples, palaces, and forums, the Rome of the empire had more in common with the teeming cities of the third world—Nairobi or Calcutta—than with the modern capitals of Washington, Paris, or London. The narrow, twisted streets; the din of hawkers, animals, and shoppers; the stench of garbage and sewage; and above all, the teeming masses of the desperately poor made Rome a nightmare for those not rich enough to isolate themselves in the luxury of a Palatine mansion.

At its height in the second century, the population of Rome and Ostia, its port, numbered well over a million. Feeding, housing, employing, and maintaining even a minimum of sanitation for so many people were almost beyond the ability of the Roman state. The poor crowded together in dark, dank apartment buildings thrown up with little care and in constant danger of collapse. In his biting satire on life in Rome, the poet Juvenal (ca. A.D. 55–after 127) complained of the constant fear that Roman tenements would come crashing down on their inhabitants. Even if the buildings did not collapse, they were likely to catch fire from one of the many poorly protected fireplaces tended by each family. Fires were frequent, and the fire brigade organized under Augustus could do little to stop fire from racing through the crowded buildings. In A.D. 64 a disastrous fire (rumored to have been started by the Emperor Nero) swept from the area of the Circus Maximus near the Palatine hill through the city. Tacitus described the fire: "There were no residences fenced with masonry or temples surrounded by walls, or anything else to act as an obstacle. The blaze in its fury ran through the level portions of the city, rose to the hills, then again devastated the lower places." When it was over, of the fourteen districts of the city, only four remained undamaged. Three had been leveled; in seven there remained only a few shattered, half-burned relics of houses.

While catastrophes on so grand a scale were infrequent, daily life held sufficient terrors for most inhabitants. The city was filthy. Although the streets were mostly paved, they were thick with mud in rainy weather and dust in dry weather. To this were added garbage, animal excrement, and human sewage illegally dumped from tenement windows. The *cloaca maxima,* or great sewer, could accommodate only a small portion of the city's wastes, and in any case it flowed into the Tiber, which was polluted with garbage, offal of slaughtered animals, and every sort of waste. By law, sewage was to be carried outside the city limits and dumped into foul-smelling pits that ringed Rome, pushed back year to year as the suburban slums expanded with the city's growth.

During their short lives (urban men could hope to live to an average age of perhaps twenty-six, women to twenty-three), Rome's masses were constantly engaged in a desperate search for food. The famous "bread and circuses" provided by the emperors were too little and reached only a fraction of the urban poor. Only about one-third of Roman families received the monthly ration of thirty-three kilograms of wheat, hardly enough to sustain them. Even these had to find some sort of income with which to supplement their diet with oil, beans, cheese, fruits, and meat, as well as to pay for rent and clothing.

Since Rome had virtually no industry, the majority of the middle classes supported themselves by

working to transport the vast quantities of foodstuffs and other necessities the city consumed each day. The poor, if they found work at all, did so in menial service positions, often in public enterprises such as baths.

Competition for even the most humble positions was keen and, in order to protect their jobs, Roman workers of all levels organized into colleges, or guilds—trade associations with social and religious functions. These guilds protected members from unauthorized competition, set salaries, and at the same time provided the city government with a means of policing its vast population. Guilds ranged from teachers, physicians, scribes, and shippers, to sewer cleaners and muleteers. Over twenty specialized guilds in the public baths encompassed such workers as bath attendants, masseuses, and even armpit-hair pluckers.

Their meager incomes protected by their guilds and their precarious diets supplemented by the public dole, Rome's masses lived their short lives in a condition exceeded in wretchedness only by that of the worst slaves. When they died, not even a pauper's grave awaited them. Their remains were simply dumped into the sewage pits beyond the city's walls.

civil wars, but their poetry eventually won them the favor of Augustus. In time Horace received a comfortable estate at Licenza, east of Rome. Virgil's family estates were returned to him, and he received a villa at Nola and houses in Rome and Naples. In return, through their poetry in praise of the emperor, Horace and Virgil conferred immortality on Augustus.

Horace celebrated Augustus's victory at Actium, his reform of the empire, and reestablishment of the ancient cults that had brought Rome divine favor. In Horace's poems, Augustus is almost a god. His deeds are compared to those of the great heroes of Roman legend and judged superior. Interspersed with the poems praising Augustus are poems of great beauty praising the love of both boys and girls and the enjoyment of wine and music. To Horace, the glories of the new age inaugurated by Augustus with the secular games of 17 B.C. included not only the splendor of empire but also the enjoyment of privileged leisure.

Virgil began his poetic career with pastoral poems celebrating the joys of rural life and the bitterness of the loss of lands in the civil wars. By 40 B.C. he was turning to greater themes. In his fourth *Eclogue,* he announced the birth of a child, a child who would usher in a new golden age. This prophetic poem may have anticipated the birth of a son to Octavian's sister and Mark Antony; it may simply have been an expression of hope for renewal. Later, under the patronage of Maecenas and Augustus, Virgil turned directly to glorify Augustus and the new age. The ultimate expression of this effort was the *Aeneid,* an epic consciously intended to serve for the Roman world the role of the Homeric poems in the Greek.

As he reworked the legend of Aeneas—a Trojan hero who escaped the destruction of the city, wandered throughout the Mediterranean, and ultimately came to Latium—Virgil presented a panoramic history of Rome and its destiny. Unlike the Homeric heroes Achilles and Odysseus, who were driven by their own search for glory, Aeneas is driven by his piety, that is, his duty toward the gods and his devotion to his father. Aeneas must follow his destiny, which is the destiny of Rome, to rule the world in harmony and justice. In the midst of his wanderings, Aeneas (like Odysseus before him) enters the underworld to speak with his dead father. Here he sees a vision of Rome's greatness to come. He sees the great heroes of Rome, including Augustus, "son of a god," and he is told of the particular mission of Rome:

> Let others fashion in bronze more lifelike, breathing images
> Let others (as I believe they will) draw living faces from marble
> Others shall plead cases better and others will better
> Track the course of the heavens and announce the rising stars.
> Remember, Romans, your task is to rule the peoples
> This will be your art: to teach the habit of peace
> To spare the defeated and to subdue the haughty.

The finest of the poets who felt the heavy hand of Augustus's disfavor was Ovid (43 B.C.–A.D. 17), the great Latin poet of erotic love. In *Art of Love* and *Amores,* he cheerfully preaches the art of seduction and adultery. He delights in poking irreverent fun at everything from the sanctity of Roman marriage to the seri-

A relief from the Ara Pacis (Altar of Peace), which was erected between 13 and 9 B.C. to commemorate Augustus's victories in Gaul and Spain. Mother Earth is shown surrounded by symbols of fruitfulness—children, fruit, flowers, and livestock.

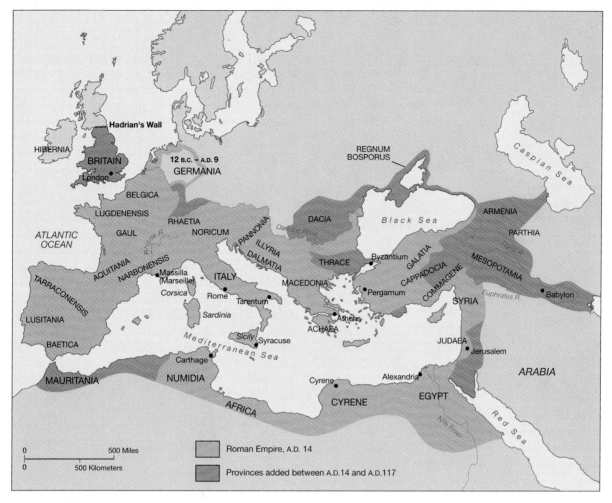

The Roman Empire, A.D. *14 and 117*

ous business of warfare. In his great *Metamorphoses,* a series of artfully told myths, he parodies the heroic epic, mocking with grotesque humor the very material Virgil used to create the *Aeneid.* By A.D. 8 Augustus had had enough. He exiled the witty poet to Tomis, a miserable frontier post on the Black Sea. There Ovid spent the last nine years of his life, suffering from the harsh climate, the constant danger of nomadic attacks, and, most of all, the pain of exile from the center of the civilization he loved. Exactly what offense he had committed is not clear. Perhaps for Augustus what was most intolerable was that, in spite of the emperor's efforts to foster an immortal poetic tradition glorifying the Roman virtues, Ovid was clearly appreciated by his contemporaries as the greatest poet of the age.

Augustus's Successors

Horace and Virgil may have made Augustus's fame immortal. His flesh was not. The problem of succession occupied him throughout much of his long reign

and was never satisfactorily solved. Since the princeps was not a specific office but a combination of offices and honors held together by military might and religious aura, formal dynastic succession was impossible. Instead Augustus attempted to select a blood relative as successor, include him in his reign, and have him voted the various offices and dignities that constituted his own position.

Unfortunately, Augustus outlived all of his first choices. His nephew and adopted son Marcellus, to whom he married his only child, Julia, died in 23 B.C. He then married Julia to his old associate Agrippa and began to groom him for the position, but Agrippa died in 12 B.C. Lucius and Gaius, the sons of Julia and Agrippa, also died young. Augustus's final choice, his stepson Tiberius (A.D. 14–37) proved to be a gloomy and unpopular successor but nevertheless a competent ruler under whom the machinery of the empire functioned smoothly. The continued smooth functioning of the empire even under the subsequent members of Augustus's family—the mad Gaius, also known as

THE ROMAN EMPIRE

Julio-Claudian Period	**Augustus**
	(27 B.C.–A.D. 14)
	Tiberius (A.D. 14–37)
	Caligula (37–41)
	Claudius (41–54)
	Nero (54–68)
Year of the Four Emperors, A.D. 69	
Flavian Period, A.D. 69–96	**Vespasian (69–79)**
	Titus (79–81)
	Domitian (81–96)
Antonine Period, 96–193	**Trajan (98–117)**
	Hadrian (117–138)
	Marcus Aurelius (161–180)
	Commodus (180–192)

Caligula (37—41); the bookish but competent Claudius (41–54); and initially under Nero (54–68)—is a tribute to the soundness of Augustus's constitutional changes and the vested interest that the descendants of Augustus's military and aristocratic supporters had in them.

Nero was, however, more than even they could bear. Profligate, vicious, and paranoid, Nero divided his time between murdering his relatives and associates—including his mother, his aunt, his wife, his tutors, and eventually his most capable generals—and squandering his vast wealth on mad attempts to gain recognition as a great poet, actor, singer, and athlete. (When he competed in games, other contestants wisely lost.) Finally, in A.D. 68, the exasperated commanders in Gaul, Spain, and Africa revolted. Once more war swept the empire. Nero slit his own throat (one of his last sentences was "Dead, and so great an artist!"), and in the next year, the "Year of the Four Emperors," four men in quick succession won the office only to lose their lives just as quickly. Finally, in 70, Vespasian (A.D. 69–79), the son of a "new man" who had risen through the ranks to the command in Egypt, secured the principate and restored order.

The first emperors had rounded off the frontiers of the empire, transforming the client states of Cappadocia, Thrace, Commagene, and Judaea in the east and Mauritania in North Africa into provinces. Claudius (A.D. 41–54) presided over the conquest of Britain in

A.D. 43. These emperors introduced efficient means of governing and protecting the empire, and tied together its inhabitants—roughly fifty million in the time of Augustus—in networks of mutual dependence and common interest. Augustus established peaceful relations with the Parthian Empire, which permitted unhampered trade between China, India, and Rome. In the west, after a disastrous attempt to expand the empire to the Elbe ended in the loss of three legions in A.D. 9, the frontier was fixed at the Rhine. The northern border stopped at the Danube. The deserts of Africa, Nubia, and southern Arabia formed the southern borders of what in the first century A.D. many saw as the "natural" boundaries of the empire.

When Vespasian's troops fought their way into Rome in vicious hand-to-hand street fighting, the populace watched with idle fascination. The violence of A.D. 69, unlike that of the previous century, involved mostly professional legions and their commanders. The rest of the empire sat back to watch. In a few restive regions of the empire, some Gauls, the Batavians along the Rhine, and die-hard Jewish rebels tried to use the momentary confusion to revolt, but by and large the empire remained stable. This stability was the greatest achievement of Augustus and his immediate successors.

The emperors of the Flavian dynasty—Vespasian and his sons and successors Titus (79–81) and Domitian (81–96)—were stern and unpretentious provincials who restored the authority and dignity of their office, although they also did away with much of the trappings of republican legitimacy that Augustus and his immediate successors had used. They solidified the administrative system, returned the legions to their fairly permanent posts, and opened the highest reaches of power as never before to provincial elites. After the Flavian emperors, the Antonines (96–193)—especially Trajan (98–117), Hadrian (117–138), and Antoninus Pius (138–161)—ruled for what has been termed "the period in the history of the world during which the human race was most happy and prosperous."

The Pax Romana

Not all was peaceful during this period. Trajan initiated a new and final expansion of the imperial frontiers. Between 101 and 106 he conquered Dacia (modern Romania). He resumed war with the Parthians, conquering the provinces of Armenia and Mesopotamia by 116. During the second century, the Palestinian Jews revolted in 115–117 and again in 132–135. The emperor Hadrian put down this second revolt and expelled the surviving Jews from Judaea. Along both the eastern and western frontiers legions had to contend with sporadic border incidents. However, within these borders a system of Roman military camps, towns, and rural estates constituted a remarkably heterogeneous and prosperous civilization.

Administering the Empire

The imperial government of this vast empire was as oppressive as it was primitive. Taxes, rents, forced labor service, military levies and requisitions, and outright extortion weighed heavily on its subjects. Still, fewer than one thousand officials ever held direct official command within the empire at any time. These were largely the governors and officials of the senatorial provinces, but even they had little direct control over the daily lives of the governed. The daily exercise of government fell to local elites, the army, and members of the imperial household.

To a considerable extent, the inhabitants of the empire continued to be governed by the indigenous elites whose cooperation Rome won by giving them broad autonomy. Thus Hellenistic cities continued to manage their own affairs under the supervision of essentially amateur Roman governors. Local town councils in Gaul, Germany, and Spain supervised the collection of taxes, maintained public works projects, and kept the peace. In return for their participation in Roman rule, these elites received Roman citizenship, a prize that carried prestige, legal protection, and the promise of further advancement in the Roman world.

In those imperial provinces controlled directly by the emperor the army was much more in evidence, and the professional legions were the ultimate argument of imperial tax collectors and imperial representatives, or *procurators*. Moreover, as the turmoil of the Year of the Four Emperors amply demonstrated, the military was the ultimate foundation of imperial rule itself. Still, soldiers were as much farmers as fighters. Legions usually remained in the same location for years, and veterans' colonies sprang up around military camps. These settlements created a strong Roman presence and blurred the distinction between army post and town.

Finally, much of the governing of the empire was done by the vast households of the Roman elite, particularly that of the princeps. Freedmen and slaves from the emperor's household often governed vast regions, oversaw imperial estates, and managed imperial factories and mines. These slaves and former slaves were loyal, competent, and easily controlled. The vast, powerful, and efficient imperial household was also a means of social and economic advancement. Proximity to the emperor brought power and status, regardless of birth. The descendants of the old Roman nobility might look down their noses at imperial freedmen, but they obeyed their orders.

The empire worked because it rewarded those who worked with it and left alone those who paid their taxes and kept quiet. Local elites, auxiliary soldiers, and freedmen could aspire to rise to the highest ranks of the power elite. Seldom has a ruling elite made access to its ranks so open to those who cooperated with it. As provincials were drawn into the Roman system, they were also drawn into the world of Roman culture. Proper education in Latin and Greek, the ability to hold one's own in philosophical discussion, the absorption of Roman styles of dress, recreation, religious cults, and life itself, all were essential for ambitious provincials. Thus, in the course of the first century A.D., the disparate portions of the empire competed not to free themselves from the Roman yoke, but to become Roman themselves.

The Origins of Christianity

The same openness that permitted the spread of Latin letters and Roman baths to distant Gaul and the shores of the Black Sea provided paths of dissemination for other distinctly un-Roman religious traditions. For many in the empire, the traditional rituals offered to the household gods and the state cults of Jupiter, Mars, and the other official deities were insufficient foci of religious devotion. Many educated members of the elite were actually vague monotheists, believing in a supreme deity even while convinced that the ancient traditional cults were essential aspects of patriotism, the cornerstone of the piety necessary to preserve public order. Many others in the empire sought personal, emotional bonds with the divine world.

As noted in chapter 4, in the second century B.C. the Roman world had been caught up in the emotional cult of Dionysus—an ecstatic, personal, and liberating religion entirely unlike the official Roman cults. Again in the first century A.D., so-called mystery cults—that is, religions promising immediate, personal contact with a deity that would bring immortality—spread throughout the empire. Some were officially introduced into Rome as part of its open polytheism. These included the Anatolian Cybele or great mother-goddess cult, which was present in Rome from the late third

A painting from Herculaneum depicts priests of the cult of Isis, an Egyptian goddess of procreation and birth. By the time of the empire, many Romans had turned from the spiritually unrewarding state religion to Eastern mystery cults.

century B.C. Devotees underwent a ritual in which they were bathed in the blood of a bull or a ram, thereby obtaining immortality. The cult of the Egyptian goddess Isis spread throughout the Hellenistic world and to Rome in the republican period. In her temples, staffed by Egyptian priests, water from the Nile was used in elaborate rites to purify initiates. From Persia came the cult of Mithras, the ancient Indo-Iranian god of light and truth who, as bringer of victory, found special favor with Roman soldiers and merchants eager for success in this life and immortality beyond the grave. Generally Rome tolerated these alien cults as long as they could be assimilated, or at least reconciled in some way, into the cult of the Roman gods and the genius of the emperor.

With one religious group this assimilation was impossible. As we saw in chapter 1, the Jews of Palestine had long refused any accommodation with the polytheistic cults of the Hellenistic kingdoms or with Rome. Roman conquerors and emperors, aware of the problems of their Hellenistic predecessors, went to considerable lengths to avoid antagonizing this small

and unusual group of people. When Pompey seized Jerusalem in 63 B.C., he was careful not to interfere in Jewish religion and even left Judaea under the control of the Jewish high priest. Later, Judaea was made into a client kingdom under the puppet Herod. Jews were allowed to maintain their monotheistic cult and were excused from making sacrifices to the Roman gods.

Still, the Jewish community remained deeply divided about its relationship with the wider world and with Rome. At one end of the spectrum were the Sadducees. They were willing to work with Rome and even adopt some elements of Hellenism, as long as the services in the temple could continue.

At the other end of the spectrum were the Hasidim, those who rejected all compromise with Hellenistic culture and collaboration with foreign powers. Many expected the arrival of a messiah, a liberator who would destroy the Romans and reestablish the kingdom of David. One party within the Hasidim were the Pharisees, who practiced strict dietary rules and rituals to maintain the separation of Jews and Gentiles (literally, "the peoples," that is, all non-Jews). The most prominent figure in this movement was Hillel (ca. 30 B.C.–A.D. 10), a Jewish scholar from Babylon who came to Jerusalem as a teacher of the law. He began a tradition of legal and scriptural interpretation which, in an expanded version centuries later, became the Talmud. Hillel was also a moral teacher who taught peace and love, not revolt. "Whatever is hateful to you, do not to your fellow man: this is the whole Law; the rest is mere commentary," he taught. He also looked beyond the Jewish people and was concerned with the rest of humanity. "Be of the disciples of Aaron; loving peace and pursuing peace; loving mankind and bringing them near to the Torah."

For all their insistence on purity and separation from other peoples, the Pharisees did not advocate violent revolt against Rome. They preferred to await divine intervention. Another group of Hasidim, the Zealots, were less willing to wait. After A.D. 6, when Judaea, Samaria, and Idumaea were annexed and combined into the province of Judaea administered by imperial procurators, the Zealots began to organize sporadic armed resistance to Roman rule. As ever, armed resistance was met with violent suppression. Through the first century A.D., clashes between Roman troops and Zealot revolutionaries grew more frequent and more widespread.

The already complex landscape of the Jewish religious world became further complicated by the brief career of Joshua ben Joseph (ca. 6 B.C.–A.D. 30), known to history as Jesus of Nazareth and to his followers as Jesus the Messiah, or the Christ. Jesus came from Galilee, an area known as a Zealot stronghold. However, while Jesus preached the imminent coming of the kingdom, he did so in an entirely nonpolitical manner. He was, like many popular religious leaders, a miracle worker. When people flocked around him to see his wonders, he preached a message of peace and love of God and neighbor. His teachings were entirely within the Jewish tradition and closely resembled those of Hillel—with one major exception. While many contemporary religious leaders announced the imminent coming of the messiah, Jesus informed his closest followers, the apostles and disciples, that he himself was the messiah.

For roughly three years Jesus preached in Judaea and Galilee, drawing large, excited crowds. Many of his followers pressed him to lead a revolt against Roman authority and reestablish the kingdom of David, even though he insisted that the kingdom he would establish was not of this world. Other Jews saw his claims as blasphemy and his assertion that he was the king of the Jews, even if a heavenly one, as a threat to the status quo. Jesus became more and more a figure of controversy, a catalyst for violence. Ultimately the Roman procurator, Pontius Pilate, decided that he posed a threat to law and order. Pilate, like other Roman magistrates, had no interest in the internal religious affairs of the Jews. However, he was troubled by anyone who

Spoils From the Temple in Jerusalem, *a marble relief from the Arch of Titus. The arch was begun by Titus's father, the emperor Vespasian, to commemorate Titus's victory over the Jews in A.D. 78.*

had the potential for causing political disturbances, no matter how unintentionally. Pilate ordered Jesus scourged and put to death by crucifixion, a common Roman form of execution for slaves, pirates, thieves, and noncitizen troublemakers.

The cruel death of this gentle man ended the popular agitation he had stirred up, but it did not deter his closest followers. They soon announced that three days after his death he had risen and had appeared to them numerous times over the next weeks. They took this resurrection as proof of his claims to be the messiah and confirmation of his promise of eternal life to those who believed in him. Soon a small group of his followers, led by Peter (d. ca. A.D. 64), formed another Jewish sect, preaching and praying daily in the temple. New members were initiated into this sect, soon known as Christianity, through baptism, a purification rite in which the initiate was submerged briefly in flowing water. They also shared a ritual meal in which bread and wine were distributed to members. Otherwise, they remained entirely within the Jewish religious and cultural tradition, and hellenized Jews and pagans who wished to join the sect had to observe strict Jewish law and custom.

Christianity spread beyond its origin as a Jewish sect because of the work of one man, Paul of Tarsus (ca.

A Roman tombstone inscribed with some of the earliest examples of Christian symbols. The anchor represents hope, while the fish recall Jesus' words "I will make you fishers of men."

A.D. 5–ca. 67), a follower of the Hillel school and an early convert to Christianity. Although Paul was an observant Jew, he was part of the wider cosmopolitan world of the empire and from birth enjoyed the privileges of Roman citizenship. He saw Christianity as a separate tradition, completing and perfecting Judaism but intended for the whole world. Non-Jewish converts, he convinced Peter and most of the other leaders, did not have to become Jews. The Christian message of salvation was to be preached to all nations and people of all estates, for "there is neither Jew nor Greek, slave nor free, male or female, for all are one in Christ Jesus."

Paul set out to spread his message, crisscrossing Asia Minor and Greece and even traveling to Rome. Wherever he went, Paul won converts and established churches, called *ecclesiae,* or assemblies. Everywhere Paul and the other disciples went they worked wonders, cast out demons, cured illnesses, and preached. In his preaching and his letters to the various churches he had established, Paul elaborated the first coherent system of theology, or beliefs, of the Christian sect. His teachings, while firmly rooted in the Jewish historical tradition, were radically new. God had created the human race, he taught, in the image of God and destined it for eternal life. However, by deliberate sin of the first humans, Adam and Eve, humans had lost eternal life and introduced evil and death into the world. Even then God did not abandon his people but began, through the Jews, to prepare for their eventual redemption. That salvation was accomplished by Jesus, the son of God, through his faith, a free and unmerited gift of God to his elect. Through faith, the Christian ritual of baptism, and participation in the church, men and women can share in the salvation offered by God.

How many conversions resulted from Paul's theological message and how many resulted from the miracles he and the other disciples worked will never be known. People of the ancient world believed firmly in the power of demons—the supernatural spirits of various types who influenced humans for good or ill. Christian preachers were recognized as having power over spirits, and people who could cast out demons were considered worth listening to. A third factor certainly played a part in the success of conversions. That was the courage Christians showed in the face of persecution.

Even the tolerance and elasticity of Rome for new religions could be stretched only to a point. The Christians' belief in the divinity of their founder was no problem. Their offer of salvation to those who participated in their mysteries was only normal. But their

Peter Announces the Good News

The following passage, attributed to the apostle Peter in the book of Christian scripture known as the Acts of the Apostles, is probably a close approximation of the earliest Christian preaching. In it, Jesus is presented as the new Moses.

Men of Israel, why do you stare at us, as though by our own power or piety we had made him [a paralytic who has just been cured] walk? The God of Abraham and of Isaac and of Jacob, the God of our fathers, glorified his servant Jesus, whom you delivered up and denied in the presence of Pilate, when he had decided to release him. But you denied the Holy and Righteous One, and asked for a murderer to be granted to you, and killed the Author of life, whom God raised from the dead. To this we are witnesses. And his name, by faith in his name, has made this man strong whom you see and know; and the faith which is through Jesus has given the man this perfect health in the presence of you all.

And now, brethren, I know that you acted in ignorance, as did also your rulers. But what God foretold by the mouth of all the prophets, that his Christ should suffer, he thus fulfilled. Repent therefore, and turn again, that your sins may be blotted out, that times of refreshing may come from the presence of the Lord, and that he may send the Christ appointed for you, Jesus, whom heaven must receive until the time for establishing all that God spoke by the mouth of his holy prophets from of old.

Moses said, "The Lord God will raise up for you a prophet from your brethren as he raised me up. You shall listen to him in whatever he tells you. And it shall be that every soul that does not listen to that prophet shall be destroyed from the people." And all the prophets who have spoke, from Samuel and those who came afterwards, also proclaimed these days.

You are the sons of the prophets and of the covenant which God gave to your fathers, saying to Abraham, "And in your posterity shall all the families of the earth be blessed." God, having raised up his servant, sent him to you first, to bless you in turning every one of you from your wickedness.

From Acts 3: 12–26. The Holy Bible, Revised Standard Version.

---

stubborn refusal to acknowledge the existence of the other gods and to participate in the cult of the genius of the emperor was intolerable. Judaism, which accepted these same tenets, was generally tolerated because it was not actively seeking to convert others. Christianity was an aggressive and successful cult, attracting followers throughout the empire. This was not religion, it was subversion. Beginning during Nero's reign, Roman officials sporadically rounded up Christians, destroyed their sacred scriptures, and executed those who refused to sacrifice to the imperial genius. But instead of decreasing the cult's appeal, persecution only aided it. For those who believed that death was birth into a new and better life, martyrdom was a reward, not a penalty. Christian men, women, and children suffered willingly, enduring unto death the most gruesome tortures Roman cruelty could devise. The strength of their convictions convinced others of the truth of their religion.

As numbers of Christians increased in the face of persecution, the organization and teaching of this new faith began to evolve. Initially, the followers of Jesus had assumed that the end of the world was very near, and thus no elaborate organizational structure was needed. As time went on, a hierarchy developed within the various communities established by Paul and the other apostles. The leader of each community was the bishop, an office derived from the priestly leader of the Jewish synagogue who was responsible both for charity and the Torah. Assisted by *presbyters* (priests), deacons, and deaconesses, bishops assumed growing responsibilities as expectations for the second coming receded. These responsibilities included presiding over the eucharist, or ritual meal, that was the center of Christian worship, as well as enforcing discipline and teaching.

Jesus had left no body of sacred texts, but Christian teaching focused on the Gospels, accounts of Jesus' life written toward the end of the first century; letters, or Epistles; and narratives and visionary writings by his early disciples and their immediate successors. In their preaching, bishops connected these texts to the tradition of Jewish Scriptures, explaining that the life of

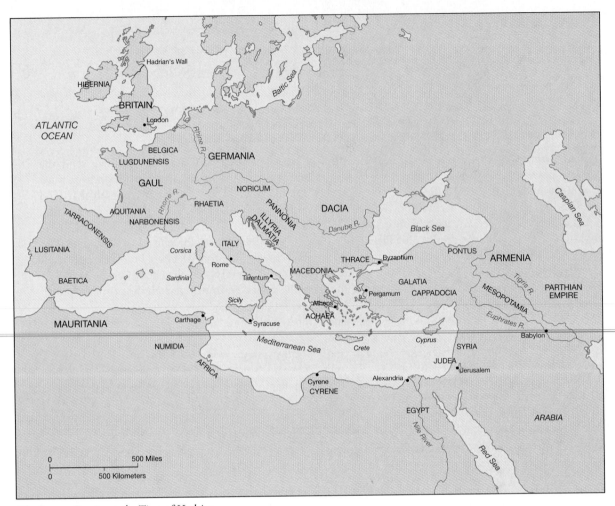

The Roman Empire at the Time of Hadrian

Jesus was the completion and fulfillment of the Jewish tradition. Over centuries, certain Gospels, Epistles, and one book of revelation came to be regarded as authoritative and, together with the version of Jewish Scripture in use in Greek-speaking Jewish communities, constituted the Christian Bible.

The teaching responsibility of the bishop took on increasing importance in the course of the second and third centuries, as the original Christian message began to be challenged from the outside on moral and intellectual grounds and debated from within by differing Christian interpreters. Hellenistic moral philosophers and Roman officials condemned Christianity as immoral and, because of its rejection of the cult of the emperor and the gods of Rome, atheistic. Neoplatonists found the teachings of Christianity philosophically naive and they mocked Christian teachers as "wool seekers, cobblers, laundry workers, and the most illiterate and rustic yokels."

Even with the Christian community, different groups interpreted the essential meaning of the new faith in contradictory ways. Monatists, for example, argued that Christians were obligated to fast and abstain from marriage until the Second Coming. Dualist Gnostics interpreted the Christian message as a secret wisdom, or *gnosis,* which, combined with baptism, freed men and women from their fates. Jesus, they taught, was no real man but only appeared in human form to impart to select followers this secret wisdom in opposition to Yahweh, the god of the material world.

Bishops took up the challenge of refuting external charges and settling internal debates. They met pagan attacks with their enemies' own weapons, both showing the exemplary morality of Christians by the standards of Stoic ethics and using Neoplatonic philosophical traditions to interpret the Christian message. Their leading role in defending the faith and determining what was correct, or orthodox, belief raised the importance of bishops' authority. By the end of the first century, *episcopal* (from the Greek word for bishop) authority was understood to derive from their status as successors of the apostles. Bishops of those churches established directly by the apostles in Jerusalem, Antioch, Alexandria, and Rome—termed *patriarchates*—claimed special authority over other, less ancient communities.

Gradually, the exalted position of the bishop and his assistants led to a distinction between the clergy—that is, those who served at the altar—and the laity, the rank and file of Christians. At the same time, women, who had played central roles in Jesus' ministry, were excluded from positions of authority within the clergy. In this process, the Christian community came to resemble closely the Roman patriarchal household, a resemblance that increased the appeal of the new sect to nonbelievers.

Although Christianity spread rapidly through the eastern Mediterranean in the first and second centuries, it remained in the eyes of the empire's rulers as only a minor irritation characterized by one cultured senator as "nothing but a degenerate sort of cult carried to extravagant lengths." Its fundamental role in the transformation of the Roman world would not become clear until the third and fourth centuries.

A Tour of the Empire

Each town in the sprawling empire, from York in the north of Britain to Dura Europus on the Euphrates, was a center of Roman culture, or *Romanitas,* in provinces still closely tied to local provincial traditions. Each boasted a forum, where locals conducted business and government affairs. Each had an arena for gladiatorial games; baths; a racetrack; and a theater where Greek and Latin plays entertained the populace. Temples to the Capitoline Jupiter and to the deified emperors adorned the cities. Aqueducts brought fresh water from distant springs into the heart of the cities. Local property owners made up the senate or curia of each town in imitation of that of Rome. These included both wealthy provincials who had tied their future to Rome and retired veterans whose pensions made them immediately part of the local gentry. Local aristocrats competed with each other in their displays of civic duty, often constructing public buildings at their own expense, dedicating statues or temples to the emperor or influential patrons, and endowing games and celebrations for the amusement of their communities.

Connecting these towns was a network of well-maintained roads frequented by imperial administrators, merchants, the idle rich, and soldiers. Beginning in 120 the roads of the empire saw a most unusual traveler: the emperor Hadrian (117–138), who traveled

them to conduct an extraordinary inspection of the length and breadth of his empire.

Hadrian, the adopted son and heir of Trajan, had received an excellent Greek education and was an accomplished writer, poet, connoisseur, and critic. Still, he had spent most of his early career as a successful field commander and administrator in Dacia and the lower Danube. This region, newly conquered by Trajan, presented particular security problems. The great Pannonian plain was a natural invasion route into southern and western Europe. The Danube, while broad, was easily crossed by barbarian raiders and made for a long and poorly defensible frontier. Years of military experience in the region had made Hadrian very aware of the potential weaknesses of the vast Roman borders, and his primary interest was to inspect those military commands most critical for imperial stability.

Thus he set out west, traveling first through the provinces of Gaul, prosperous and pacific regions long integrated into the Roman world. Gaul was known for its good food, its pottery manufacture, and its comfortable if culturally slightly backward local elites. Much of Gaul's prosperity came from supplying the legions guarding the Rhine-Danube frontier, and it was across the Rhine toward Germany, where the legions faced the barbarians of "Free Germany," that Hadrian was head-

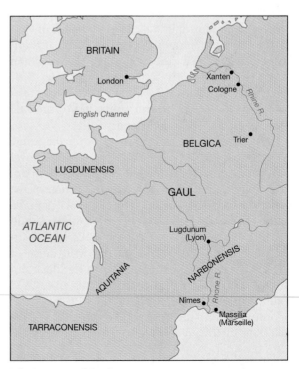

The Provinces of Gaul

Spain

Roman villas, ranging from simple country farmhouses to vast mansions with over sixty rooms. Over a hundred towns and villages were large enough to boast walls, ranging from London, with a population of roughly thirty thousand, to numerous settlements of between two thousand and ten thousand.

No sooner had he put things straight in Britain than Hadrian returned to Gaul, paused in Nîmes in the south, and then headed south toward his native Spain. By the second century A.D., Spain was even more thoroughly romanized than most of Gaul, having been an integral part of the empire since the Second Punic War. It was also far richer. Spanish mines yielded gold, iron, and tin, and Spanish estates produced grain and cattle. Since the reign of Vespasian, the residents of Spanish communities had been given some of the rights of Roman citizens, thus making them eligible for military service, a value even greater to the empire than Spain's mineral wealth. Problems with military service brought Hadrian to Spain. The populace was becoming increasingly resistant to conscription, a universal phenomenon, and Hadrian's presence strengthened the efforts of recruiters.

ed. Legions stationed at Xanten, Cologne, and Trier were far removed from the Mediterranean world that formed the heart of the empire. The dark forests, cold winters, and crude life made Germany a hardship post. Hadrian threw himself into the harsh camp life of Germany in order to bolster discipline and combat-readiness. He shared rough field rations, long marches, and simple conditions with his troops, improving their equipment even while demolishing creature comforts such as dining rooms, covered walks, and ornamental gardens erected by their commanders.

From Germany, Hadrian traveled down the Rhine through what is today Holland and then crossed over to Britain. Here too defense was utmost on his mind. Celts from the unconquered northern portion of the island had been harassing the romanized society to the south. The emperor ordered the erection of a great wall over fifty miles long across Britain from coast to coast. The most critical eastern half of this wall, much of which still stands, was built of stone ten feet thick and fifteen feet high, while the western half was constructed of turf. Battlements, turrets, and gates, as well as garrison forts, extended the length of the wall. South of the wall, Roman Britain was studded with hundreds of

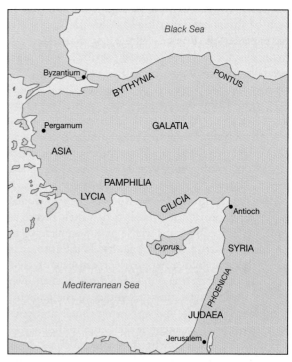

Asia

From Spain, the emperor may have crossed the Strait of Gibraltar to deal personally with a minor revolt of Moorish tribes in Mauritania, a constant low-level problem with these seminomadic peoples living on the edge of the desert. In any event, he soon set sail for the provinces of Asia. Here he was in the heart of the Hellenistic world so central to the empire's prosperity. Its great cities were centers of manufacture and its ports the vital links in Mediterranean trade. As in Hellenistic times, these cities were the organizing principle of the region, with local senates largely self-governing and rivalries among cities preventing the creation of any sort of provincial identities. Thus in Asia Hadrian worked with individual communities, showering honors and privileges on the most cooperative, checking no doubt on the financial affairs of others, and founding new communities in the Anatolian hinterland. The last activity was particularly important because, for all of the civilized glory of urban Asia, the rural areas remained strongly tied to traditions that neither Greeks nor Romans had managed to weaken. The empire remained two worlds: one urban, hellenized, mercantile, and collaborationist; the other rural, traditional, exploited, and potentially separatist.

In 125, Hadrian left Asia for Greece, where he participated in traditional religious rituals. Greek culture continued to be vital for Rome, and by participating in the rituals of Achaia and Athens the emperor placed himself in the traditions of the legendary Heracles and Philip of Macedon. He no doubt also seized the opportunity to audit the accounts of provincial governors and procurators, whose reputation for misuse of their powers was infamous. Finally, in 127 Hadrian returned to Rome via Sicily, a prosperous amalgam of Greek and Latin cultures dominated by vast senatorial estates, or *latifundia,* stopping to climb Mount Etna, it was said, to see the colorful sunrise.

This restless emperor spent less than twelve months in Rome before setting out again, this time for Africa. There, as in Germany, his concern was the discipline and preparedness of the troops guarding the rich agricultural areas and thriving commercial centers of the coast from the marauding nomads on the edges of the desert. Shortly after that, he was again in Athens to dedicate public works projects he had undertaken as well as an altar to himself—like all emperors in the East, Hadrian was venerated as a living god. From Greece he headed east, again crossing Asia and this time moving into Cappadocia and Syria. His concerns

Italy and Greece

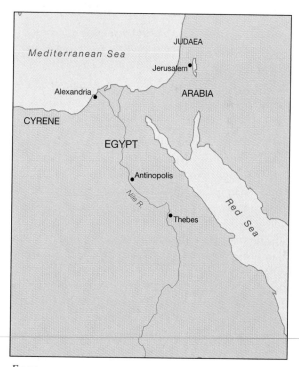

Egypt

A Roman bronze corn ticket from the time of the Antonines. Free corn, along with free admission to the games, was a privilege of every citizen of the city of Rome under the empire.

here were again defense, but against a powerful civilized Parthian empire, not barbarian tribes. Hadrian renewed promises of peace and friendship with the Parthian king, even returning the latter's daughter, whom Trajan had captured in the last Parthian war.

Moving south, Hadrian stopped in Jerusalem, where he dedicated a shrine to Jupiter Capitolinus on the site of the destroyed Jewish temple before heading to Egypt for an inspection trip up the Nile. Egypt remained the wealthiest Roman province and the most exploited. Since Augustus, Egypt had been governed directly by the imperial household, its agricultural wealth from the Nile Delta going to feed the Roman masses. At the same time Alexandria continued to be one of the greatest cultural centers of the Roman world. This culture, however, was a fusion of Greek and Egyptian traditions, constantly threatening to form the basis for a

nationalist opposition to Roman administrators and tax collectors. Hadrian sought to defuse this powder keg by disciplining administrators and by founding a new city, Antinopolis, which he hoped would create a center of loyalty to Rome.

Hadrian finally returned to the imperial residence on the Palatine in 131. He had spent over ten years on the road and had no doubt done much to strengthen and preserve the *Pax Romana,* or Roman peace. Still, to the careful observer the weaknesses of the empire were as evident as its strengths. The frontiers were vast and constantly tested by a profusion of hostile tribes and peoples. Roman citizens from Italy, Gaul, and Spain were increasingly unwilling to serve in such far-flung regions. As a result, the legions were manned by progressively less romanized soldiers, and their battle readiness and discipline, poorly enforced by homesick officers, declined dangerously. In the more civilized eastern provinces, corrupt local elites, imperial governors, and officials siphoned off imperial revenues destined for the army to build their personal fortunes. Also, in spite of centuries of hellenization and Roman administration, city and countryside remained culturally and politically separated. Early in the second century, such problems were no more than small clouds on the horizon, but in the following century they would grow into a storm that would threaten the very existence of the empire.

The Culture of Antonine Rome

Annius Florus, a poet friend of Hadrian, commenting on the emperor's exhausting journeys, wrote:

> *I do not want to be Caesar,*
> *To walk about among the Britons,*
> *To endure the Scythian hoar-frosts.*

To which Hadrian replied:

> *I do not want to be Florus,*
> *To walk about among taverns,*
> *To lurk about among cook-shops.*

Like the other members of his dynasty, Hadrian enjoyed an easy familiarity with men of letters, and like other men of letters of the period, Florus was a provincial, an African drawn from the provincial world to the great capital. Another provincial, Rome's greatest historian, Cornelius Tacitus (ca. 56–ca. 120), recorded the history of the first century of the empire. Tacitus wrote

A relief from the Column of Marcus Aurelius depicts Germans loyal to Rome executing rebel Germans while Roman cavalrymen look on.

to instruct and to edify his generation and did so in a style characterized by irony and a sharp sense of the differences between public propaganda and the realities of power politics. He was also unique in his ability to portray noble opposition to Roman rule. His picture of Germanic and British societies served as a warning to Rome against excessive self-confidence and laxity.

Tacitus's contemporaries Plutarch (ca. 46–after 119) and Suetonius (ca. 69–after 122) were biographers rather than historians. Plutarch, who wrote in Greek, composed *Parallel Lives,* a series of character studies in which he compared eminent Greeks with eminent Romans. His purpose was to portray public virtue and to show how philosophical principles could be integrated into lives of civic action. Suetonius also wrote biographies, using anecdotes to portray character. Suetonius's biographies of the emperors fall short of the literary and philosophical qualities of Plutarch's character studies and far short of Tacitus's histories. Suetonius delighted in the rumors of private scandals that surrounded the emperors and used personal vice to explain public failings. Still, the portraits Suetonius created remained widely popular through the centuries, while Tacitus's histories fell out of fashion.

In the later second century, Romans in general preferred the study and writing of philosophy, particularly Stoicism, over history. The most influential Stoic philosopher of the century was Epictetus (ca. 55–135), a former slave who taught that man could be free by the control of his will and the cultivation of inner peace. Like the early Stoics, Epictetus taught the universal brotherhood of humankind and the identity of nature and divine providence. He urged his pupils to recognize that dependence on external things was the cause of unhappiness and that therefore they should free themselves from reliance on material possessions, public esteem, and all other things prized by the worldly. Each individual would find happiness by adapting himself to his own particular expression of nature and by accepting with indifference the advantages and disadvantages that this role entailed.

The slave's philosophy found its most eager pupil in an emperor. Marcus Aurelius (161–180) reigned during a period when the stresses glimpsed by Hadrian were beginning to show in a much more alarming manner. Once more the Parthians attacked the eastern frontier, while in Britain and Germany barbarians struck across the borders. In 166 a confederation of barbarians known as the Marcomanni crossed the Danube and raided as far south as northern Italy. A plague brought west by troops returning from the Parthian front ravaged the whole empire. Like his predecessor Hadrian, Aurelius felt bound to endure the Scythian hoar-frosts rather than luxuriate in the taverns of Rome. He spent virtually the whole of his reign on the Danubian frontier, repelling the barbarians and shoring up the empire's defenses.

Throughout his reign Aurelius found consolation in the Stoic philosophy of Epictetus. In his soldier's tent at night he composed his *Meditations,* a volume of philosophical musings. Like the slave, the emperor sought freedom from the burden of his office in his will and in the proper understanding of his role in the divine order. He called himself to introspection, to a constant awareness, under the glories and honors heaped upon him by his entourage, of his true human nature: "A poor soul burdened with a corpse."

Aurelius played his role well, dying in what is today Vienna, far from the pleasures of the capital. His Stoic philosophy did not, however, serve the empire well. For all his emphasis on understanding, Aurelius badly misjudged his son Commodus (180–192), who succeeded him. Commodus, whose chief interest was in being a gladiator, saw himself the incarnation of Heracles and appeared in public clad as a gladiator and as consul. As Commodus sank into insanity, Rome was once more convulsed with purges and proscriptions. Commodus's assassination in 192 did not end the violence. The *Pax Romana* was over.

• • •

The haphazard conquest of the Mediterranean world threw Roman republican government, traditional culture, and antagonistic social groups into chaos. The result was a century and a half of intermittent violence and civil war before a new political and social order headed by an absolute monarch established a new equilibrium. During the following two centuries, a deeply hellenized Roman civilization tied together the vast empire by incorporating the wealthy and powerful of the Western world into its fluid power structure while brutally crushing those who would not or could not conform. The binding force of the Roman Empire was great and would survive political crises in the third century as great as those that had brought down the republic three hundred years before.

Suggestions for Further Reading

Primary Sources

Major selections of the works of Caesar, Cicero, Tacitus, Plutarch, Suetonius, and Marcus Aurelius are available in English translation from Penguin Books. The second volume by Naphtali Lewis and Meyer Reinhold, *Roman Civilization Selected Readings,* Vol. II: *The Empire* (1951), contains a wide selection of documents with useful introductions.

The Price of Empire

* Mary Beard and Michael Crawford, *Rome in the Late Republic* (Ithaca, NY: Cornell University Press, 1985). An analysis of the political processes of the late republic as part of the development of Roman society, not simply the decay of the republic.

* E. Badian, *Roman Imperialism in the Late Republic* (Ithaca, NY: Cornell University Press, 1968). A study of the contradictory forces leading to the development of the empire.

The End of the Republic

Ronald Syme, *The Roman Revolution,* 2d ed. (New York: Oxford University Press, 1960). A classic study of the social groups who made up the party of Augustus.

E. S. Gruen, *The Last Generation of the Roman Republic* (Berkeley, CA: University of California Press, 1973). A controversial recent analysis of the politics of the late republic.

D. Stockton, *Cicero: A Political Biography* (London: Oxford University Press, 1971). A biography of the great orator in the context of the end of the republic.

The Augustan Age

G. W. Bowersock, *Augustus and the Greek World* (New York: Oxford University Press, 1965). A cultural history of the Augustan Age.

D. A. West and A. J. Woodman, *Poetry and Politics in the Age of Augustus* (New York: Cambridge University Press, 1984). The cultural program of Augustus.

J. B. Campbell, *The Emperor and the Roman Army* (New York: Oxford University Press, 1984). Essential for understanding the military's role in the Roman Empire.

Richard Duncan-Jones, *The Economy of the Roman Empire,* 2d ed. (New York: Cambridge University Press, 1982). A series of technical studies on Roman wealth and its economic context and social applications.

The Pax Romana

Fergus Millar, *The Roman Empire and Its Neighbors,* 2d ed. (New York: Holmes & Meier, 1981). A collection of essays surveying the diversity of the empire.

* Peter Garnsey and Richard Saller, *The Roman Empire: Economy, Society, and Culture* (Berkeley, CA: University of California Press, 1987). A topical study of imperial administration, economy, religion, and society, arguing the coercive and exploitative nature of Roman civilization on the agricultural societies of the Mediterranean world.

Fergus Millar, *The Emperor in the Roman World* (Ithaca, NY: Cornell University Press, 1977). A study of emperors, stressing their essential passivity, responding to initiatives from below.

Philippe Ariès and Georges Duby, eds., *History of Private Life.* Vol. 1: *From Pagan Rome to Byzantium* (Cambridge, MA: Harvard University Press, 1986). Essays on the interior, private life of Romans and Greeks by leading French and British historians.

* Judith P. Hallett, *Fathers and Daughters in Roman Society & the Elite Family* (Princeton, NJ: Princeton University Press, 1984). A study of indirect power exercised by elite women in the Roman world as daughters, mothers, and sisters.

* Ramsay MacMullen, *Paganism in the Roman Empire* (New Haven, CT: Yale University Press, 1981). A description of the varieties and levels of pagan religion in the Roman world.

Jane F. Gardner, *Women in Roman Law and Society* (Bloomington, IN: Indiana University Press, 1986). A study of the extent of freedom and power over property enjoyed by Roman women.

Edward Champlin, *Fronto and Antonine Rome* (Cambridge, MA: Harvard University Press, 1980). A cultural history of Antonine court life through the letters of the second century's greatest rhetorician.

* Joseph Jay Deiss, *Herculaneum: Italy's Buried Treasure* (New York: Harper and Row, 1985). A vividly written and well-illustrated introduction to Herculaneum for a general audience.

*Paperback edition available.

6 ✺ THE TRANSFORMATION OF THE CLASSICAL WORLD

A Bride's Trousseau

*V*enus, assisted by mythical sea creatures and representations of *erotes,* or cupids, beautifies herself on the central panel of a magnificent silver chest that made up part of a fourth-century Roman bride's trousseau. On the top, the bride, Projecta, and her groom, Secundus, are depicted within a wreath held by two more cupids. Along the base, Projecta, mirroring Venus, completes her own toilette while torchbearers and handmaidens perform for her the tasks of the mythical beings attending to Venus. The iconography as well as the execution of this sumptuous object—composed of solid silver with silver gilt and measuring almost two feet by one foot—testify to the high status of the bride and her deep attachment to the ancient classical traditions of Greco-Roman culture. Projecta and Secundus were Roman aristocrats, and their marriage was part of Roman rituals of class, wealth, and power as ancient as the goddess on the marriage chest.

And yet, within the thorough paganism of the symbolism and the lavish expense of the workmanship, the Latin inscription engraved on the rim across the front of the lid confronts the viewer with how utterly changed the Roman world has become. It reads, "Secundus and Projecta, live in Christ." In spite of the elaborate pagan symbolism of the casket, Secundus and Projecta were Christians. Yet they and their families and friends apparently saw nothing strange or improper about commemorating their marriage in the age-old manner of their pagan ancestors. A bride could live in Christ and still be Venus.

Such was the world of late antiquity. By the time Projecta married Secundus, the once persecuted Christian sect was now not only legal but rapidly on its way to becoming the established religion in the empire. Formerly a religion of hellenized Jews and freed slaves, it was attracting converts from among the highest classes of Roman society. And yet, while some stern religious teachers might condemn the ancient traditions of Roman religion, and while around the very time of Projecta's marriage the images of divine Victory were being removed from the Roman Senate, aristocratic families, Christian as well as pagan, continued the ancient cultural traditions without a sense of betrayal or contradiction. Rome appeared as eternal and serene as Venus herself.

But the Projecta casket has more to tell us. It was found, along with over sixty other exquisite objects and seventy pounds of silver plate, on the Esquiline hill in Rome, where it had been hastily buried to hide it from some catastrophe. The probable catastrophe is not hard to guess: In 410, when Projecta would have been an elderly woman, the barbarian Visigoths sacked and pillaged Rome for three days, raping Roman women and looting them of such treasures as this.

And yet these barbarians were themselves Christians, while the city of Rome had remained, in spite of exceptions such as Projecta and Secundus, a pagan stronghold. Moreover, the Visigoths were no mere horde but, officially at least, a Roman army reacting in what had become a typical manner to the failure of the state to provide them with what they saw as their due. Such contrasts of paganism and Christianity, barbarity and Roman culture, were integral parts of a new Roman world, one characterized by radical transformations of Roman and barbarian culture that took place in the two centuries following the death of Marcus Aurelius in 180. Accelerating this process of change and transformation was the combination of events collectively referred to as the crisis of the third century.

The Crisis of the Third Century

From the reign of Septimius Severus (193–211) to the time of Diocletian (284–305), both internal and external challenges shook the Roman Empire. The empire survived, but its social, political, and economic structures were radically transformed.

Sheer size was a fundamental problem for the empire. Haphazard expansion in many regions—to the north and west for instance—overextended the frontiers. The manpower and resources needed to maintain this vast territory strained the economic system of the empire. Like a thread stretched to the breaking point, the thin line of border garrisons and forts was ready to snap.

The economic system itself was part of the reason for this strain on resources. For all of its commercial networks, the economy of the empire remained tied to agriculture. To the aristocrats of the ancient world, agriculture was the only honorable source of wealth. Thus the prosperous Roman citizen bought slaves and land, not machinery. The goal of the successful merchant was to liquidate his commercial assets, buy estates, and rise into the leisured landholding elite. As a result, liquid capital either for investment or taxation was always scarce.

The lack of sophistication in commercial and industrial business practice characterized the financial system of the empire as well. Government had always been conducted on the cheap. The tax system of the empire had never been very efficient at tapping into the real wealth of the aristocracy. Each individual city made its own collective assessments. Individuals eager to win the gratitude of their local communities were expected to provide essential services from their own pockets. Even with the vast wealth of the empire at its disposal, the government never developed a system of public debt—that is, a policy of borrowing against future revenues. As a result, the only way to solve short-term cash-flow problems was to debase the coinage by using more copper and less silver. This practice became epidemic in the third century, when the price of a bushel of wheat rose over 200 percent.

The failure of the empire to develop a stable political base complicated its economic problems. In times of emergency, imperial control relied on the personal presence and command of the emperor. As the empire grew, it became impossible for this presence to be felt everywhere. Moreover, the empire never developed either a regular system of imperial succession or an adequate power base. Control of the army, which was the ultimate source of imperial power, was possible only as long as the emperor was able to lead his armies to victory.

Enrich the Army and Scorn the Rest

Through much of the late second and third centuries, emperors failed dismally to lead their armies to victory. The pressure on the borders was temporarily halted by Marcus Aurelius but it resumed under his successors. The barely romanized provincials in the military bore the brunt of these attacks. When the emperors selected by the distant Roman Senate failed to win victory, front-line armies unhesitatingly raised their own commanders to the imperial office. These commanders, such as the Pannonian general Septimius Severus, set about restructuring the empire in favor of the army. They opened important administrative posts to soldiers, expanded the army's size, raised military pay, initiated expensive building programs in frontier settlements, and in general introduced authoritarian military discipline throughout society. To finance these costly measures, the new military government confiscated senatorial wealth, introduced new forms of taxation, and increasingly debased the coinage.

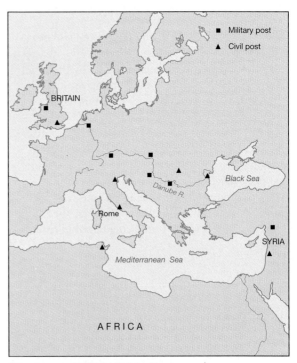

The Career of Publius Helvius Pertinax

The old senatorial elite and the people living in the more civilized regions of the empire thought these measures disastrous. Soldiers in the provinces welcomed the changes. With their first rise in real income, soldiers could improve their standard of living while in service and buy their way into provincial elites upon retirement. At long last they were allowed to marry even while on active service. Free-spending soldiers and imperial extravagance helped the bleak settlements on the edges of military camps grow into prosperous cities with all the comforts of the older parts of the empire.

For the first time capable soldiers could hope to rise to the highest levels of public power regardless of their birth. One extraordinarily successful soldier was Publius Helvius Pertinax. Born the son of a freed slave in the north of Italy (Liguria) in 126, he abandoned a career as a schoolteacher to enter the military. His rise to the top of the military and bureaucratic ladder began in Syria. From Syria he was promoted to a post in Britain. He then returned to the Continent and served in the Danubian region during the Marcomannian wars in both civil and military capacities for approximately ten years. By the time he was fifty, his success as a military commander won for him the office of consul. He then held a series of military, civil, and proconsular positions in Syria, Britain, Italy, and Africa before returning to Rome. When the emperor Commodus was murdered in 192, the palace guard proclaimed Pertinax emperor—the first emperor who had not come from the privileged senatorial class.

Soon, however, the military control of the empire turned into a nightmare even for the provinces and their armies. Exercising their newly discovered power, armies raised and then destroyed pretender after pretender, offering support to whichever imperial candidate promised them the greatest riches. Pertinax, the first of these soldier-emperors, set the precedent. Less than three months after becoming emperor he was murdered by his soldiers. The army's incessant demands for higher pay led emperors to lower the amount of silver in the coins with which the soldiers were paid. But the less the coins were worth, the more of them were necessary to purchase goods. And the more goods cost, the less valuable was the salary of the soldiers. Wages doubled but the price of grain tripled in the third century. Thus soldiers were worse off at the end of the period than at the beginning. Such drastic inflation wrecked the economic stability of the empire and spurred the army on to greater and more impossible demands for raises. Emperors who could not meet the demands were killed by their troops. In fact, the

This cameo was made to the order of Shapur I after the capture of Valerian during the great battle near Antioch in A.D. 260. The symbolic scene has Shapur seizing Valerian simply by grasping his hand.

army was much more effective at killing emperors than enemies. Between 235 and 284, seventeen of the twenty more or less legitimate emperors were assassinated or killed in civil war.

The crisis of the third century did not result only from economic and political instability within the empire. Rome's internal imperial crises coincided with an increase of attacks from outside the empire. In Africa, Berber tribes harassed the frontiers. The Sassanid dynasty in Persia threatened Rome's eastern frontier. When the emperor Valerian (253–260) attempted to prevent the Persian king of kings Shapur I from seizing Roman Mesopotamia and Armenia, he was captured and held prisoner for the rest of his life. Valerian became such a curiosity that after his death his skin was reportedly stuffed and kept on display for centuries in a Persian temple.

The greatest danger to Rome came not from the south or east, but rather from the west. There, along the Rhine, various Germanic tribes known collectively as the Franks and the Alemanni began raiding expeditions into the empire. Along the lower Danube and in southern Russia, the Gothic confederation raided the Balkans and harassed Roman shipping on the Black Sea.

An Empire on the Defensive

The central administration of the empire simply could not deal effectively with the numerous barbarian attacks. Left on their own, regional provincial commanders at times even headed separatist movements.

Provincial aristocrats who despaired of receiving any help from distant Rome often supported these pretenders. One such commander was Postumus, whom the armies of Spain, Britain, and Gaul proclaimed emperor. His nine-year separatist reign (ca. 258–268) was the longest and most stable of that of any emperor, legitimate or otherwise, throughout this whole troubled period.

Political and military instability had devastating effects on the lives of ordinary people. Citizenship had been extended to virtually all free inhabitants of the empire in 212, but that right was a formality given simply to enlarge the tax base, since only citizens paid inheritance taxes. In reality the legal and economic status of all but the richest declined. Society became sharply divided into the privileged *honestiores*—senators, municipal gentry, and the military—and the increasingly burdened *humiliores*—everyone else. The humiliores suffered the most from the tax increases because unlike the honestiores they could neither bribe their way out of them nor intimidate tax collectors with private armies. They were also frequent targets of extortion by the military and of violence perpetrated by bandits.

It was the impossible burden of taxation that drove many individuals into banditry. Such crime had long been endemic to the Roman Empire, and slave and peasant bandits, rustlers, and even pirates played an ambivalent role in society. Often they terrorized the countryside, descending from the hills to attack villages or travelers. However, at times they also protected peasants from greedy tax collectors and military commanders. In Gaul and Spain, peasants and local leaders organized armed resistance movements to withstand the exorbitant demands of tax collectors. Although these resistance movements, termed *Bacaudae*, were always ruthlessly crushed, they continued to reappear—a sure sign of the desperation of ordinary people. In the first centuries of the empire bandits operated primarily in peripheral areas recently and poorly subjugated to Roman rule. In the late second and third centuries they became an increasing problem in Italy itself.

The most famous of the bandits was Bulla the Lucky, who headed a band of over 600 men and plundered Italy during the reign of Septimius Severus. No simple thief, Bulla was more like a Roman Robin Hood. He often robbed his prisoners of only a portion of their goods, which he distributed to the needy. He detained skilled artisans and made use of their skills, then let them go with a parting gift. On one occasion he captured the centurion charged with hunting him down and, dressed in the official robes of a Roman magistrate, summoned the centurion in his own "court." The centurion, his head shaved like a slave, was brought before Bulla and told: "Carry this message back to your masters: let them feed their slaves so that they might not be compelled to turn to a life of banditry."

Bulla lived and died outside the law, but as the third century progressed, such lawlessness increasingly became the law. The life of Maximinus the Thracian, known as Little Big Man (173–238), typifies this change. He began life as a shepherd, then drifted into rustling; but he also protected the local community. Later he entered the Roman army, where his extraordinary physical size and skills caught the attention of Septimius Severus, who promoted him to centurion. Maximinus rose quickly through the ranks and in 235 was proclaimed emperor at Mainz by a mutinous army, which had overthrown the grandson of Septimius Severus. Although he reigned only a bit more than two years, Maximinus's career showed how fluid the boundaries between legitimate violence and banditry had become during the third century.

This relief shows landowners collecting rents from peasants. The peasantry, displaced by slaves, congregated in the capital and formed a poverty-stricken urban underclass.

Tacitus on the Germans

At the end of the first century A.D. Tacitus wrote a brief account of the Germanic peoples living beyond the frontiers, in part to inform Romans about this neighboring people and in part to criticize the morals and practices of Roman society. In general, his information, although selective and filtered through Roman culture, appears quite accurate.

They pick their kings on the basis of noble birth, their general on the basis of bravery. Nor do their kings have limitless or arbitrary power, and the generals win favor by the example they set if they are energetic, if they are distinguished, if they fight before the battle-line, rather than by the power they wield. But no one except the priests is allowed to inflict punishment with death, chains, or even flogging, and the priests act not, as it were, to penalize and at the command of the general, but, so to speak, at the order of the god, who they believe is at hand when they are waging war . . . The nobles make decisions about lesser matters, all freemen about things of greater significance, with this priviso, nonetheless, that those subjects, of which ultimate judgment is in the hands of the mass of people, receive preliminary consideration among the nobles . . . When the crowd thinks it opportune, they sit down fully armed. Silence is demanded by the priests, who then also have the right of compulsion. Soon the king or the chieftains are heard, in accordance with the age, nobility, glory in war, and eloquence of each, with the influence of persuasion being greater than the power to command. If a proposal has displeased them, they show their displeasure with a roar; but if it has won favor, they bang their *frameae* [spears] together; the most prestigious kind of approval is praise with arms . . . There is an obligation to undertake the personal feuds as well as the friendships of one's father or blood-relative; but the feuds do not continue without possibility of settlement, for even murder is atoned for by a specific number of cattle and sheep and the entire family accepts the settlement, with advantage to the community, since feuds are the most dangerous when joined with freedom.

From Tacitus, *Germany.*

The Barbarian World

Compounding the internal violence that threatened to destroy the Roman Empire were the external attacks of the Germanic barbarians. These attacks reflected changes within the Germanic world as profound as those within the empire. Between the second and fifth centuries the Germanic world was transformed from a mosaic of small, decentralized agricultural tribes into a number of powerful military tribal confederations capable of challenging Rome itself. We cannot understand the impact of the barbarians on the empire without understanding the social and political organization and the transformation of these people living beyond the frontier.

The Germanic peoples typically inhabited small villages organized into patriarchal households, integrated into clans, which in turn composed tribes. The boundaries between each of these groups were fluid, and central government was extremely weak. For the most part, clans governed themselves, and except in war tribal leaders had little authority over their followers. In the second century many tribes had kings, but they were religious rather than political leaders.

Germanic communities lived by farming, but cattle raising and especially warfare carried the highest social prestige. Men measured their status by the number of cattle they owned and by their martial ability. Women took care of agricultural chores and household duties. Like the number of cattle, the number of wives showed a man's social position. Polygyny was common among chiefs.

Warfare defined social groupings and warriors dominated public life. Only within the clan was fighting inappropriate. But rival clans within the same tribe dealt with one another brutally. Conflict took the form of the feud, and each act of aggression was repaid in kind. If an individual within a clan had a grievance with an individual within another clan, all his kinsmen were obliged to assist him. Thus a single incident could result in a continuous escalation of acts of revenge. Murder piled upon murder as sons and brothers retaliated for each act of vengeance.

Clans in other tribes were fair game for raiding and conquering. The wars that resulted formed the normal mechanisms by which wealth circulated among tribes, either as booty or as gifts exchanged to conclude peace. Individuals, clans, and tribes built their reputations on warfare. The more successful a tribe was in warfare, the more clans it attracted and the greater its position became in the barbarian world.

The practice of feuding, especially within the tribe, had enormous costs. Families were decimated, and strong warriors who were needed to defend the tribe from outside attack faced constant danger from members of their own tribe. Thus tribal leaders attempted to reduce hostilities by establishing payments called *wergeld* in place of the blood vengeance demanded in reparation for crimes. Such wergeld, normally paid in cattle or slaves, was voluntary, since the right of vengeance was generally recognized, and the unity of the tribe remained precarious.

Tribes also attempted to reinforce unity through religious cults involving shared myths of common ancestry and rituals intended to underline group cohesion. Drinking was the most important of these rituals. When not fighting, Germanic warriors spent much of their time drinking beer together at the table of their war leader. Because it provided the most ready means of preserving grain, beer was a staple of Germanic diet. Communal beer drinking was also a way of uniting potentially hostile neighbors. Not surprisingly, it could also lead to drunken brawls that reopened the very feuds drinking bouts were intended to end. These feuds could in turn lead to the hiving off of irreconcilable factions, which might in time form their own tribes.

In contrast to the familial structure of barbarian society stood another warrior group that cut across kindred and even tribal units. This was the warrior band, called in Latin the *comitatus*. Some young warriors formed personal bonds with particularly able leaders and pledged them absolute loyalty. In return the leaders were obligated to lead their warriors to victory and to share with them the spoils of war. These warrior societies, far from being the basic units of a larger tribal military force, were organized for their own plunder and fighting. While they might be a valuable aid in intertribal warfare, they could also shatter the fragile peace by conducting raids on neighbors, thus bringing whole tribes into internal conflict. Although nontribal, successful comitatus could form the nuclei of new tribes. Successful warrior leaders might draw sufficient numbers of followers and conquer so many other groups that in time the band would become a new tribe.

This intratribal and intertribal violence produced a rough equilibrium of power and wealth as long as small Germanic tribes lived in isolation. The presence of the Roman Empire, felt both directly and indirectly in the barbarian world, upset this equilibrium. Unintention-

An ivory plaque portraying Stilicho, a Vandal by birth, who rose to be Master of Soldiers and Consul of Rome. He is shown here in the patrician robes of a consul and carrying the weapons of a soldier, suggesting his dual role.

ally, Rome itself helped transform the Germanic tribes into the major threat to the imperial system.

The direct presence of Roman merchants extended only about a hundred miles beyond the frontiers into "free Germany." However, the attraction of Roman luxury goods and the Romans' efforts to establish friendly Germanic buffer zones along the borders drew even distant tribes into the Roman imperial system. Across the barbarian world, tribal leaders and comitatus leaders sought the prestige that Roman goods brought them. Roman provincial commanders encouraged these leaders to enter into commercial arrangements with the Romans. In exchange for their cattle, which the Romans needed for their troops, the Germanic leaders received gold and grain. This outside source of wealth greatly increased economic disparity within Germanic society. In addition, some leaders made treaties with Rome, thus receiving the advantage of Roman support, which other tribal leaders lacked. In return for payments of gold and foodstuffs, chieftains of these "federated" tribes agreed to oppose tribes hostile to Rome and to prevent young hotheads of their own tribes from raiding across the frontier. Some chiefs supplied warriors for the Roman army. Others even led their comitatus into Roman service. By the late third century the Roman army included Franks, Goths, and Saxons serving as far away from their homes as Egypt. Such "imperial Germans" moved back and forth between the Roman and barbarian worlds, using each as a foundation for increased power in the other and obscuring the cultural and political differences between the two.

The inherent attraction of Roman material civilization and the Romans' policy of supporting "their" barbarians tended to upset Germanic society and to accentuate political, social, and economic differences within tribal units. This in turn led to the formation of pro- and anti-Roman factions, which further splintered barbarian tribes. New and powerful groups appeared, older tribal units vanished, and new forms of military organization came to predominate.

The effects of contact between barbarians and Romans reached far and wide throughout the empire and beyond the frontier. Along the Rhine and Danube, the result was the so-called West Germanic Revolution. In order to survive in a time of constant warfare, tribes had to become armies. The armies needed a united and effective leadership. Among most of the western Germanic peoples, the tradition of the older tribal king was abandoned. A new kind of nonroyal chieftain emerged as the war leader of the people and as the representative of the war god Woden. In the later second and third centuries the turmoil resulted in the formation of new tribes and tribal confederations—the Marcomanni, the Alemanni, and the Franks. By the end of the second century this internal barbarian transformation spilled over into the empire in the form of the Marcomannian wars and the Saxon, Frankish, and Alemannic incursions into the western provinces.

Around the same time, along the Oder and Vistula rivers to the north, a group later known as the Goths began their slow consolidation around a royal family. The Goths were unique in that their kings exercised more military authority than was usual for a Germanic tribe. These kings formed the nucleus of a constantly changing barbarian group. A Goth was not necessarily a biological descendant of the small second-century tribe living along the shore of the Baltic. Anyone who fought alongside the Gothic king was a Goth.

Between the second and fourth centuries, the bearers of this Gothic royal tradition began to filter to the south and east, ultimately transferring their model of barbarian organization to the area of present-day Kiev in Ukraine. This move was not so much a physical migration of thousands of people across Europe as the gradual confederation under Gothic leadership of various Germanic, Slavic, and Scythian peoples living around the Black Sea. By the early third century this Gothic confederation was strong enough to challenge Roman supremacy in the region. These first Gothic wars in the east were even more devastating than were the later wars in the west.

The Empire Restored

By the last decades of the third century, the empire seemed in danger of crumbling under combined internal and external pressure. That it did not was largely due to the efforts of the soldier-emperor Aurelian (270–275), who was able to repulse the barbarians, restore the unity of the empire, and then set about stabilizing the internal imperial structure. Although Aurelian was assassinated, his successors were able to build on his efforts. Restoration came to fruition under Diocletian (284–305), who summed up and solidified the transformations made under his predecessors. However, the restored empire under Diocletian bore little resemblance to the Roman Empire of the first and second centuries.

Diocletian the God-Emperor

Diocletian, a Dalmatian soldier who had risen through the ranks to become emperor, completed the process of stabilization and reorganization of the imperial system begun by Aurelian. The result was a regime that in some ways increased imperial power and in other ways simply did away with the pretenses that had previously masked the emperor's true position.

No longer was the emperor *princeps,* or "first citizen." Now he was *dominus,* or "lord," the term of respect used by slaves in addressing their masters. He also assumed the title of *Iovius,* or Jupiter, thus claiming divine status and demanding adoration as a living god. Diocletian emphasized the imperial cult and the autocratic power of the emperor, but he did not grasp this power exclusively for himself. He recognized that the empire was too large and complex for one man to rule. To solve the problem, he divided the empire into eastern and western parts, each part to be ruled by both an augustus and a junior emperor, or caesar. Diocletian was augustus in the east, supported by his caesar, Galerius. In the west the rulers were the augustus Maximian and his caesar, Constantius.

The tetrarchy was an attempt to regulate the succession. Here, the emperors Diocletian and Maximian are depicted with their caesars—Constantius of the west and Galerius of the east—who were their respective sons-in-law.

In theory this tetrarchy, or rule by four, provided for regular succession. The caesars, who were married to daughters of the augusti, were to succeed them. The new system also made revolts and assassinations less likely to be successful, since a person would have to kill all four rulers in order to seize power. Although from time to time subsequent emperors would rule alone, Diocletian's innovation proved successful and enduring. The empire was divided administratively into eastern and western parts until the death of Julius Nepos, the last legitimate emperor in the west, in 480.

In addition to this constitutional reform, Diocletian enacted or consolidated a series of measures to improve the functioning of the imperial administration. He reorganized and expanded the army, approximately doubled the number of provinces, separated their military and civil administration, and greatly increased the number of bureaucrats to administer them. He attempted to stem runaway inflation by increasing the amount of silver in coins and fixing maximum prices and wages throughout the empire. He restructured the imperial tax system, basing it on payments in goods and produce in order to distribute the burden more equitably on all citizens and to avoid problems of currency debasement.

The pillar of Diocletian's success was his victorious military machine. He was effective because, like the barbarian chieftains who had turned their tribes into armies, he militarized society and led this military society to victory. Like Diocletian himself, his soldiers were drawn from marginal provincial regions. They showed tremendous devotion to their god-emperor. By the time of Diocletian's reign, a career such as that of Pertinax (p. 165) had become the rule for emperors rather than the exception.

The career of Aurelius Gaius, an obscure provincial officer, is typical of that of soldiers of Diocletian's army. Gaius was born in a Galatian village in what is today Turkey. Like many other young men from his village, he sought his fortune by entering military service in a Danubian legion that traditionally drew recruits from Galatia. He served in infantry and cavalry units in Pannonia and then in Gaul near Strasbourg, advancing through the ranks from simple recruit to cavalryman, adjutant, and finally centurion in Diocletian's personal guard. He traveled the length and breadth of the empire with Diocletian. Six times he fought outside the empire in campaigns that penetrated the Gothic kingdom, Persia, North Africa, and Numidia.

Compared to that of Pertinax, Gaius's career reflects the differences between successful careers at the end of the second century and those at the end of the third. Unlike Pertinax, Gaius served his entire career within the military. Diocletian had largely ended the tradition of mixing civil and military offices, a measure that perhaps prevented undue military meddling in civil government but that also cut off most bureaucrats from the army, the real source of power. Second, Gaius's military service took him to an even wider range of provinces than did that of Pertinax. However, as remarkable as the regions in which he served are the places he apparently never visited. Except for a short time in Strasbourg, Gaius spent no time in Gaul and never visited Britain. The extreme west of the empire was increasingly irrelevant to the interests of central

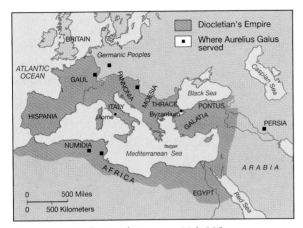

The Empire Under Diocletian, A.D. 284–305

government. Neither did Gaius visit Italy and Greece, the centers of the old classical world. For him, as for Diocletian, the periphery of the empire had become its center; the center was increasingly marginal to the program of the empire.

Some aspects of Diocletian's program, such as the improvement of the civil administration and the military, were successful. Others, such as the reform of silver currency and wage and price controls, were dismal failures. One effect of the fiscal reforms was to bind *colons,* or hereditary tenant farmers, to their lands, since they were forbidden to leave the villages where they were registered to pay their taxes. In this practice lay the origins of European serfdom. Another effect was the gradual destruction of the local city councils, since their members—the *decurions*—were held personally responsible for the payment of local assessments whether or not they could be collected from the other inhabitants. In time this led to the dissolution of local civil government.

All of these measures were designed to marshal the entire population in the monumental task of preserving *Romanitas.* Central to this task was the proper reverential attitude toward the divine emperors who directed it. One group seemed stubbornly opposed to this heroic effort: the Christians. In 298 an incident occurred that seemed to confirm their subversive attitude. At a sacrifice in the presence of Diocletian, the Roman priests were unable to obtain the desired favorable omens, and they attributed their failure to the presence of Christians, who were crossing themselves to ward off demons. Such blasphemous conduct—it might be compared, for instance, to desecrating the flag at a public assembly—led to the beginning of the

Great Persecution, which formally began in 303 and lasted sporadically until 313. Although unevenly pursued across the empire, it resulted in the destruction of churches, the burning of copies of Christian scriptures, the exclusion of Christians from access to imperial courts, and the torture, maiming, and death of hundreds of Christians who refused to sacrifice to the pagan gods.

Constantine, the Emperor of God

In 305, in the midst of the Great Persecution, Diocletian and his co-augustus Maximian took the extraordinary step of abdicating in favor of their caesars, Galerius and Constantius. This abdication was intended to provide for an orderly succession. Instead, the sons of Constantius and Maximian, Constantine (306–337) and Maxentius (306–312), drawing on the prejudice of the increasingly barbarian armies toward hereditary succession, set about wrecking the tetrarchy. In so doing they plunged the empire once more into civil war as they fought over the western half of the empire.

Victory in the west came to Constantine in 312, when he defeated and killed Maxentius in a battle at the Mulvian Bridge outside Rome. Constantine attributed his victory to a vision telling him to paint a ☧ on the shields of his soldiers. For pagans this symbol indicated the solar emblem of the cult of the Unconquered Sun. For Christians it was the Chi-Rho, ☧, formed from the first two letters of the Greek word for Christ. The next year, in Milan, Constantine rescinded the persecution of Christians and granted Christian clergy the same privileges enjoyed by pagan priests. Constantine himself was not baptized until near death, a common practice in antiquity. However, during his reign Christianity grew from a persecuted minority to the most favored cult in the empire.

Almost as important as Constantine's conversion to Christianity was his decision to establish his capital not in Rome, with its strong association with the cult of the traditional gods, nor in Milan or Trier, the military capitals of the west, but in Byzantium, a city founded by Greek colonists on the narrow neck of water connecting the Black Sea to the Mediterranean. He transformed and enriched this small town, calling it the New Rome. Later it was known as Constantinople, the city of Constantine. For the next eleven centuries Constantinople served as the heart of the Roman and then the Byzantine world. Even to barbarians, it was known simply as "the City," a title once held by Rome. From

An illuminated manuscript illustrates Constantine's vision, in which he is told to fight under the sign of Christianity. The scene below shows his victory at the Mulvian Bridge.

his new city, Constantine began to transform the empire into a Christian state and Christianity into a Roman state religion.

We will never know just what Constantine's conversion meant to him in personal terms. Its effects on the empire and on Christianity were obvious and enormous. Constantine himself continued to maintain cordial relations with representatives of all cults and to use ambiguous language that would offend no one when talking about "the deity." His successors were less broad-minded. They quickly reversed the positions of Christianity and paganism. In 341 pagan sacrifice was banned, and by 355 the temples had been closed and the death penalty for sacrificing to the gods had been decreed, although not enforced. In 357 the altar of Victory, on which senators had offered incense since the time of Augustus, was removed from the Senate.

While paganism was being disestablished, Christianity was rapidly becoming the established religion. Conversion in no way meant a break with the theocratic consolidation initiated by Diocletian. On the contrary, Constantine was one of the most ruthless and ambitious emperors Rome had ever known. He sought in the Christian cult exactly the kind of support Diocletian had

A painting of Christ from a catacomb ceiling. The catacombs were underground passages near Rome used by the early Christians as cemeteries, for funeral and memorial services, and as places of refuge during times of persecution.

RELIGIOUS TOLERATION AND PERSECUTION

In 313 Constantine and Licinius met at Milan and agreed on an empire-wide policy of religious toleration. The first selection is from the "Edict of Toleration" and the so-called "Edict of Milan" (actually a directive probably issued to eastern governors shortly after by Licinius). The second, from the Theodosian Code, published by Emperor Theodosius in 395, ends toleration, both of Arianism and of pagan practices, reversing the status of persecutor and persecuted.

Observing that freedom of worship should not be denied, but that each one should be given the right in accordance with his conviction and will to adhere to the religion that suits his preference, we had already long since given orders both to the Christians . . . to maintain the faith of their own sect and worship . . .

When I, Constantine Augustus, and I, Licinius Augustus, met under happy auspices in Milan . . . we considered that first of all regulations should be drawn up to secure respect for divinity, to wit: to grant both to the Christians and to all men unrestricted right to follow the form of worship each desired, to the end that whatever divinity there be on the heavenly seat may be favorably disposed and propitious to us and all those placed under our authority. Accordingly, with salutary and most upright reasoning, we resolved on adopting this policy, namely that we should consider that no one whatsoever should be denied freedom to devote himself either to the cult of the Christians or to such religion as he deems best suited for himself, so that the highest divinity, to whose worship we pay allegiance with free minds, may grant us in all things his wonted favor and benevolence.

. . .

I, 2. It is Our will that all the peoples who are ruled by the administration of Our Clemency shall practice that religion which the divine Peter the Apostle transmitted to the Romans, as the religion which he introduced makes clear even unto this day . . . According to the apostolic discipline and the evangelic doctrine, we shall believe in the single Deity of the Father, the Son, and the Holy Spirit, under the concept of equal majesty and of the Holy Trinity.

We command that those persons who follow this rule shall embrace the name of Catholic Christians. The rest, however, whom We adjudge demented and insane, shall sustain the infamy of heretical dogmas, their meeting places shall not receive the name of churches, and they shall be smitten first by divine vengeance and secondly by the retribution of Our own initiative, which we shall assume in accordance with the divine judgment.

X, 2. Superstition shall cease, the madness of sacrifices shall be abolished. For if any man in violation of the law of the sainted Emperor, Our father, and in violation of this command of Our Clemency, should dare to perform sacrifices, he shall suffer the infliction of a suitable punishment and the effect of an immediate sentence.

---

looked for in a return to Jupiter and the traditional gods. Constantine made enormous financial contributions to Christian communities to repay them for their losses during persecutions. He erected rich churches on the model of Roman basilicas, or administrative buildings, and converted temples into Christian places of worship. He gave bishops the authority to act as magistrates within the Christian community. Once the particular objects of persecution, bishops became favored courtiers. Constantine attempted to make himself the de facto head of the Church. He even presided at the council of the whole church held in Nicaea in 325. Constantine and

his successors, with the exception of his nephew Julian (361–363)—who attempted unsuccessfully both to reestablish paganism and to promote traditional Hellenism—sought to use the cult of the one God to strengthen their control over the empire.

Although imperial control over Christianity was strong, it was not total. One of the most powerful Christian successors to Constantine, Theodosius I (347–395), met his match in the person of the equally determined bishop of Milan, Ambrose (339–397). In 390, the emperor, angered by riots in the Greek city of Thessalonica, ordered a general massacre of the population. Ambrose dared to excommunicate, or ban, the emperor from his church in Milan until Theodosius did public penance for his act of brutality. Many feared that Ambrose would be the next victim of imperial wrath, but finally the emperor acquiesced, acknowledging that even he was subject to the rule of God as interpreted by the bishops. The confrontation between bishop and emperor later became an oft-cited precedent church leaders used to define the relationship between religious and secular authority.

Although imperial support was essential to the spread of Christianity in the fourth century, other factors encouraged conversion as well. Christian miracles—particularly that of exorcism, or casting out of demons—won many converts. The ancient world was filled with daimons, supernatural creatures whose power for good or ill no one doubted. Every village had its possessed persons—madmen and women, troubled youths, and hate-filled citizens. Much of traditional pagan ritual was aimed at dealing with the spirits bedeviling such people. Wandering Christian preachers seemed more competent than others to deal with these tormentors, proving that their God was more powerful than the spirits and that their message was worthy of a hearing.

Over the course of the fourth century, the number of Christians rose from five to thirty million. Imperial support, miracles, and preaching could not, by themselves, account for this phenomenal growth. Physical coercion played a large part. The story was told, for example, of the conversion of the town of Gaza under its first bishop, Porphyry, around 400. Although the account is largely fictional, it describes what must have been a fairly typical progression in the process of conversion. Porphyry arrived to find a pagan city. He began to make converts almost at once through the force of his miracles. His prayers to God ended a drought, aided a woman in childbirth, and expelled demons. The eloquence of his preaching struck his opponents dumb. Enormous imperial gifts enriched the local church. Then finally, upon imperial command, all of the local temples were destroyed and "a great number" of leading pagans who refused conversion were tortured to death. The remaining pagan population converted. Whether or not the story is true, it illustrates the essential role that naked force often played in the process of conversion. This suited church leaders such as Porphyry who, when questioned about the value of conversions resulting from terror, is said to have quoted St. Paul: "Whether falsely or truly, Christ is preached, and I rejoice in that." Conversion—by whatever method—also suited the emperors, who saw a unified cult as an essential means of bolstering their position.

Imperial Christianity

The religion to which Constantine converted had matured institutionally and intellectually since its origins as a reform movement within Judaism. By the late third century, Christian communities existed throughout the empire, each headed by a bishop considered divinely guided and answerable only to his flock and to God. These bishops replaced pagan philosophers as sources of wisdom and authority. (See "The Stainless Star of Wisdom's Discipline," pp. 176–177.) In the west, the bishop of Rome, termed the pope, had acquired the position of first among equals, a position at times acknowledged by the eastern patriarchates as well out of respect for the successor of Peter and Paul and bishop of the ancient capital. However, the Church as a whole was divided on fundamental questions of belief, and the growing importance of Christianity in the Roman Empire added to the gravity of these divisions. The two most contentious issues were, in the Greek-speaking regions of the empire, the nature of Christ, and in the Latin-speaking provinces, the extent to which individuals could earn their salvation through their own virtue.

Divinity, Humanity, and Salvation

Jesus, the savior or Christ, was at the heart of Christian belief, but individual Christian communities interpreted the nature of Christ differently as they attempted to reconcile their faith to the intellectual traditions of late antiquity. Christian Scriptures spoke of the Father, the Son, and the Spirit. Yahweh was generally accepted as the Father and Christ as the Son, and the Spirit was understood to be the continuing presence of God sent by Jesus after his resurrection and ascension.

Generally, Christians saw God as a Trinity, at once one and three. But the relationship among the three was a source of endless debate, particularly for Greek-speaking Christians attempting to reconcile their faith with the Neoplatonic ideas of successive emanations from God to creation, which were incorporated into the Christian understanding of the Trinity. Was Christ just a man, chosen by God as a divine instrument, or was he God, and if so, had he simply appeared to be human? These were not trivial or academic questions

The creation of Eve, from a fourth-century sarcophagus. Adam lies asleep on the ground, God the Father is seated at the left, and God the Son places his hand on Eve's head.

for Christians, since the possibility of salvation depended on their answer. Throughout the eastern half of the empire, ordinary people were ready to fight not only with words but even with weapons to defend their positions.

Throughout the so-called Christological controversies—which began in the early third century and continued through the fifth—two extremes presented Christ as either entirely human or entirely God, with centrists attempting to hold a middle ground. At one extreme were the Monarchians, who emphasized the oneness of God by arguing that the three represented three activities although God possessed only one substance, and the Gnostics, who argued that Jesus had only appeared to be human but in reality was only divine. On the other extreme were the Adoptionists, who explained that Jesus was a man to whom God sent his spirit at baptism.

The first Christian intellectual to undertake a systematic exposition of the Trinity was the great Alexandrine theologian Origen (185–254). In all of his teachings, Origen moved Christian teaching from a literal to a symbolic understanding of Scripture and gave it a sound philosophical foundation by synthesizing the Neoplatonic tradition with Christianity. His trinitarian teachings insisted on the co-eternality of the Son with the Father but, drawing as he did on Neoplatonic ideas of emanations, he seemed to subordinate the Son to the Father and to make the Spirit a creation of the Son. In the generations following Origen, the controversy continued, particularly between those who taught the equality of the persons of the Trinity and those who,

like the Alexandrine theologian Arius (ca. 250–336), insisted that Jesus was not equal to God the Father. By the time of Constantine, the issue threatened to destroy the unity of Christianity, and at the emperor's command the bishops of the entire Church assembled at Nicaea in 325 to settle the controversy. At the emperor's urging, the council condemned the teachings of Arius and adopted the term *homousion,* "of one being," to describe the equality of the Father and the Son.

The Council of Nicaea did not end the Christological controversy. For almost a century, Arians continued to win adherents to their denial of the divinity of Christ, even among the Christian emperors who succeeded Constantine. Before the Arian tradition finally died out within the empire, missionaries spread it to the barbarian Goths beyond the frontiers. Similarly, at the other extreme, Monophysites in Egypt and Syria argued that Christ had only one nature—the divine. A century after Nicaea another council was held at Chalcedon in 451 to resolve the issue. Following the recommendation of the bishop of Rome, Pope Leo I (440–461), the bishops at Chalcedon agreed that in the one God there were three divine persons, the Father, the Son, and the Spirit. However, the second person of the Trinity, the Son, had two natures, one fully human, the other fully divine. The Chalcedon formulation established the orthodox, or "right-believing," position, and the full weight of the imperial machinery worked to impose it on all. In Egypt and Palestine, the decree was greeted with outrage: mobs of monks and laity rioted in the streets to oppose the "unclean synod of Chalcedon." Two centuries later, the ease with which Islam was able to conquer these regions from the empire resulted in part from their deep alienation from Orthodox teachings imposed by Constantinople.

Although a western bishop had provided the formula for Chalcedon, Latin Christians were not as deeply concerned with the Christological debates as were the easterners. For westerners, the great question was less the nature of God than the mechanism of salvation, and the role of humans in the salvational process.

These concerns grew directly from the monumental transformations in Christianity following the conversion of Constantine and the absorption of Christianity into the imperial machine. As the ranks of Christians were swelled by people converting for political or social expediency, two groups, the Donatists and the Pelagians, taught that salvation was the right of only a small, elite minority who held themselves above the imperfect lives of the masses.

The Stainless Star of Wisdom's Discipline

Public philosophers were prized citizens of every ancient city. These austere teachers, distinguished by their black robes, were courted by the wealthy as tutors of their sons and by the powerful for the benefit of their wisdom. But in the early fifth century, Alexandria, long famed for its great museum and rival schools, boasted a philosopher with a difference: Hypatia (ca. 370–415), a woman famed for her wisdom and described by one supporter as "mother, sister, teacher, benefactress in all things." Her controversial career and terrible death summarize the complexity and factionalism of late antiquity.

As was the case with many other professional philosophers, Hypatia's father had been a renowned philosopher before her, specializing in astronomy, mathematics, divination, and Neoplatonic philosophy. Hypatia wrote commentaries on mathematical and astronomical treatises, and she edited and annotated Ptolemy's *Almagest,* the classic textbook of Greek astronomy. However, she won her greatest praise—and her greatest criticism—for her practice of philosophy. Popular teachers are often controversial, and as a pagan, as a woman, and as a philosopher in the turbulent world of late antiquity, Hypatia was the center of more than her share. But philosophers were more than teachers in antiquity. Because of their deep learning, their detachment from the concerns of daily life, and their eloquence, they were allowed and even expected to play a public role, advising, admonishing, and reconciling the powerful.

Hypatia's defenders and detractors came from the ranks of both Christians and pagans. Her former student Synesius of Cyrene, who ended his life as a bishop, was her strongest supporter, describing her as "the lady who rightfully presides over the mysteries of philosophy," while her rival, the pagan philosopher Damascius, considered her a huckstering Cynic ready to teach any philosophy to anyone who wanted it. The truth, as usual, was probably somewhere in between, although certainly much of the controversy surrounding her came less from her teaching than her sex.

Women teachers and philosophers were a comparative rarity, and even for some admirers, her beauty and her independence (she never married) tempted them to expect more from her than philosophy. According to one tradition, she disabused a love-struck student by throwing the ancient equivalent of a used sanitary napkin at him, saying, "This is what you are in love with, young man—nothing that is beautiful."

Controversial because of her sex and her teaching, she was even more so because she remained the most publicly admired and consulted pagan philosopher in an increasingly Christian city. Although Christians were in the majority in Alexandria by 400, they were an insecure majority and one prone to violence. Disagreements often ended in street fighting and rioting. To make matters worse, bands of fanatical monks often poured into the city from the nearby desert monasteries to take part in these violent confrontations. In 415, riots broke out as Christians—with the encouragement of the new patriarch, or archbishop, of Alexandria, Cyril (ca. 377–444)—sought to expel the city's large Jewish population. Cyril, always a firebrand and not hesitant to see his supporters turn to violence if it would further his cause, soon ran afoul of the prefect of the city, Orestes, who opposed the violence against the Jews. Monks in town to support the Christians accused Orestes of supporting sacrifice to the ancient gods—a capital offense—and one monk attempted to stone the prefect as he rode through the city.

Orestes was exonerated of the charge of paganism and his supporters quickly arrested the monk who had struck the prefect. After a speedy trial he was tortured to death. Cyril was outraged and appealed to the emperor, claiming that the executed monk was a martyr. But even moderate Christians found Cyril's appeal groundless and he was forced to abandon it.

When tensions ran high in ancient cities, philosophers often provided the means of breaking an impasse and tipping the scales in one direction or another. It was they who traditionally used their eloquence and wisdom to persuade those in power to act as they should. According to reports, Hypatia, although known as an even-handed teacher of both Christians and pagans, was a close associate of Orestes and was known to have his ear and those of the other members of Alexandria's power elite. The sight of the wealthy and powerful coming and going at her house to seek her advice infuriated Cyril's supporters, who thought that their bishop, not a pagan philosopher, should play the role of guide and advisor in the city. A rumor spread "among the Church people" that she had used her occult wisdom to bewitch Orestes and prevent a reconciliation between the prefect and the patriarch. During the solemn season of Lent, their animosity heightened by the fasting, a mob of monks stopped Hypatia's carriage in the streets, dragged her out, stripped her naked, then took her to a nearby church where they cut her to pieces and threw her remains into a fire.

Hypatia's murder meant more than simply the destruction of a brilliant woman by an ignorant, puritanical mob. It was more than just another violent confrontation between the pagan and Christian worlds. It was the end of a kind of urban culture in which the philosopher, the man or woman of learning, enjoyed a position of public respect and authority. Henceforth, respect and authority would come not from learning but from God.

The Donatists had developed in North Africa as a response to the political shifts within Christian leadership in the early fourth century. During the last persecutions many Christians and even bishops had collaborated with Roman authorities, handing over sacred Scriptures to be burned. Disturbed by the ease with which these traitors (our word *traitor* comes from the Latin verb *tradere,* "to hand over") had returned to positions of power in the Church under Constantine and by the growth of political conversions, the Donatists insisted that the Church had to be pure and that its ministers had to be blameless. Thus they argued that baptisms and ordinations performed by these traitors were invalid. The visible Church on earth had to be as perfect as the invisible one, and only the Donatists had preserved this purity. When, not surprisingly, the imperial government rejected these elitist claims and attempted to suppress the sect, the North African Donatists took up arms in a revolt against the imperial system and especially its Orthodox bishops.

The Pelagians also held themselves to a higher standard than that of ordinary Christians, who accepted sin as an inevitable part of human life. Pelagians believed rather that human nature had been so created that people could achieve perfection in this life. God's will, like the will of the emperor, was absolute. Moreover, humans had both the duty and the ability to obey it. Like the Donatists, Pelagians believed that members of the true Church perfected themselves by the force of their own wills, thus making a radical break with the compromising world in which they lived.

The primary opponent of both the Donatists and the Pelagians was Augustine of Hippo (354–430), a convert to Christianity who, more than any other individual, set the course of Western Christianity and political philosophy for the next thousand years. Born into a well-off North African family in the town of Tagaste, he was quickly drawn into the good life and upward mobility open to bright young provincials in the fourth century. In his *Confessions,* the first psychological autobiography, Augustine describes how his skills in rhetoric took him to the provincial capital of Carthage and then on to Rome and finally Milan, the western imperial residence, where he gained fame as one of the foremost rhetoricians of the empire.

Connections as well as talent contributed to his rise to fame. Although his mother was a Christian, he was not baptized at birth, and while in Carthage he joined the Manichees, a materialist, dualist sect that taught that good and evil were caused by two different ultimate principles and that rejected the notion of spiritual reality. As protégé of the Manichees, Augustine

gained introductions to the leading pagan aristocrats of his day.

While in Milan, Augustine came into contact with kinds of people he had never encountered in Africa, particularly with Neoplatonists and Christians. The most important of these was Ambrose, bishop of Milan. The encounter with a spiritual philosophy and a Christianity compatible with it profoundly changed the young professor. After a period of agonized searching, Augustine converted to the new religion. With characteristic enthusiasm, he embraced Christianity as wholeheartedly as he had previously embraced his career. Abandoning his Italian life, he returned to the North African town of Hippo to found a monastery where he could devote himself to reading the Scrip-

A detail from a painting by the fourteenth-century artist Simone Martini shows Augustine of Hippo, author of the Confessions.

LOVE IN THE TWO CITIES

Augustine took more than fourteen years to write his great masterpiece, The City of God. *Initially he intended to write simply a defense of Christianity from the charge that the disasters of his age, culminating in the sack of Rome in 410, resulted from Rome abandoning its traditional gods. In time the work grew into a wide-ranging inquiry into the nature of human society. In the following passage he summarizes his fundamental conclusion that human society and divine society are based on fundamentally different foundations—the one on selfishness and the desire for domination, the other on justice and love.*

What we see, then, is that two societies have issued from two kinds of love. Worldly society has flowered from a selfish love which dared to despise God, whereas the communion of saints is rooted in a love of God that is ready to trample on self. In a word, this latter relies on the Lord, whereas the other boasts that it can get along by itself. The city of man seeks the praise of men, whereas the heights of glory for the other is to hear God in the witness of conscience. The one lifts up its head in its own boasting; the other says to God: "Thou art my glory, thou liftest up my head." (Psalm 3:4)

In the city of the world, both the rulers themselves and the people they dominate are dominated by the lust for domination; whereas in the City of God all citizens serve one another in charity, whether they serve by the responsibilities of office or by the duties of obedience. The one city loves its leaders as symbols of its own strength; the other says to its God: "I love thee, O Lord, my strength." (Psalm 17:2). Hence, even the wise men in the city of man live according to man, and their only god has been the goods of their bodies or of the mind or of both, though some of them have reached a knowledge of God, "they did not glorify him as God or give thanks but became vain in their reasonings, and their senseless minds have been darkened. For while professing to be wise" (that is to say, while glorying in their own wisdom, under the domination of pride), "they have become fools, and they have changed the glory of the incorruptible God for an image made like to corruptible man and to birds and four-footed beasts and creeping things" (meaning that they either led their people, or imitated them, in adoring idols shaped like these things), "and they worshipped and served the creature rather than the Creator who is blessed forever." (Romans 1:21–25). In the City of God, on the contrary, there is no merely human wisdom, but there is a piety which worships the true God as He should be worshiped and has as its goal that reward of all holiness whether in the society of saints on earth or in that of angels of heaven, which is "that God may be all in all." (1 Corinthians 15:28.)

From St. Augustine, *The City of God.*

---

tures. However, his neighbors were determined to harness the intellectual talents of their brilliant native son. When their bishop died, they forcibly seized Augustine and made him their bishop.

Augustine spent the remainder of his life as bishop of this small provincial town, but his reputation as spokesperson for the Christian tradition spread throughout the empire. As a professor of rhetoric he had become an expert in debate, and much of his episcopal career was spent in refuting opponents such as Donatists and Pelagians within the Church as well as dealing with traditional pagans who blamed the problems of the empire on the new religion. Christians, they claimed, had abandoned the traditional gods and the traditional Roman virtues and justice that had made Rome great.

In responding to these attacks, Augustine elaborated a new Christian understanding of human society and the individual's relationship to God, which dominated Western thought for the next fifteen centuries. He rejected the elitist attempt of the Donatists and Pelagians to identify the true Church with any earthly community. Likewise he rejected the claim of pagans that the Roman tradition was the embodiment of true virtue. Instead he argued that the true members of God's elect necessarily coexisted in the world with sinners. No earthly community, not even the empire or the visible Church, was the true "city of God." Earthly society participated in the true Church, the "city of God," through the sacraments and did so quite apart from the individual worthiness of the recipients or even of the ministers of these rites. Belief that the presence of sinners within the Church blocked the plan of salvation or that responsibility for salvation lay with the individual was to deny the omnipotence of God.

Thus neither the Donatist sect nor the Pelagian community nor even the imperial Church was essential for salvation. Those to be saved were not identified

A gold plaque from a sixth-century Syrian reliquary. The subject is Simeon Stylites on his pillar; the snake represents the vanquished devil. Clients could consult the holy man by climbing up the ladder on the left.

lives. Elsewhere, particularly in the desert of Syria, the model of the monk remained the individual hermit. The Syrian desert, unlike that of Egypt, was particularly suitable for such an ascetic life. Here the desert was milder, an individual could find food in wild roots and water in rain pools, and villages were never too far off. Moreover, the life of the wandering hermit was closely connected to traditional seminomadic lifestyles in the Fertile Crescent. But the Christian hermits who appeared across Syria in late antiquity were unlikely to be mistaken for Bedouin. The Christian hermits were wild men and women who came down from the mountainsides and galvanized the attention of their contemporaries by their lifestyles. Their lives were characterized by the most extreme forms of self-mortification and radical rejection of civilization. The most famous of the hermits, Simeon Stylites (ca. 390–459), spent thirty-six years perched at the top of a pillar fifty feet high. Two women, Marana and Cyra, lived forty-two years chained in a small open-roofed enclosure.

Such people of God, rejecting civilized life in the most overt and radical ways, nevertheless met very real social and cultural needs of the population. Their lack of ties to human society made them the perfect arbitrators in the constant disputes that threatened to disrupt village life. They were "individuals of power," whose proven ability to cast out demons and work miracles made them ideal community patrons at a time when traditional power brokers of the village were being lured away to imperial service or provincial cities. The greatest of these holy people, like Simeon Stylites, received as visitors not only local peasants but also emperors and empresses who eagerly sought their advice. In an age of individualism, the Syrian hermits were, along with the emperors, the most prominent examples of individuals who had risen above humanity and who stood (literally in the case of the pillar dwellers) somewhere between the divine and the human.

Unlike the eastern monks, the Syrian hermits of the fourth and fifth centuries had few parallels in the west. Hermits did inhabit the caves and forests of Italy and Gaul, and pious women found solitude as recluses even in the center of Rome. But these westerners did not establish themselves either as independent sources of religious power or as political power brokers. Their monasticism remained a personal religious commitment. When one Roman woman was asked why she remained shut up in her cell, she replied, "I am on a journey." When asked where she was going, she answered simply, "To God."

A Parting of the Ways

Those who remained in "the world" at the end of the fourth century could hardly take so serene a view of life. Christians and pagans might differ in their explanations for the ills that had befallen the empire but none could deny their severity. The vulnerability of the Constantinian system became clear shortly after 376 when the Huns, a nomadic horse-riding people from central Asia, swept into the Black Sea region and threw the entire barbarian world once more into chaos. The Huns quickly destroyed the Gothic confederation and absorbed many of the peoples who had constituted the Goths. Others sought protection in the empire. The Visigoths, as they came to be known, were the largest of these groups, and their fate illustrated how precarious existence could be for all the occupants of the imperial frontier. Driven from their lands and thus from their food supply, the Visigoths turned to the empire for assistance. But the Roman authorities treated them as brutally as had the Huns, forcing some to sell their children into slavery in return for morsels of dog flesh. In despair the Visigoths rose up against the Romans, and against all odds their desperate rebellion succeeded. They annihilated an imperial army at Adrianople in 378, and the emperor Valens himself was killed. His successor, Theodosius, was forced to allow the Visigoths to settle along the Danube and to be governed by their own leaders despite the fact that they lived within the boundaries of the empire.

Theodosius's treaty with the Visigoths set an ominous precedent. Never before had a barbarian people been allowed to settle as a political unit within the empire. Within a few years, the Visigoths were again on the move, traveling across the Balkans into Italy under the command of their chieftain Alaric (ca. 370–410). In 410 they captured Rome and sacked it for three days, an event that sent shock waves throughout the entire empire. Rome had been sacked before, but ever since the Celtic sack of Rome in 390 B.C., the sacking had always been done by Romans. The symbolic effect of the Visigoths' victory far exceeded the amount of real damage, which was relatively light. Only after Alaric's death did the Visigoths leave Italy, ultimately settling in Spain and southern Gaul with the approval of the emperor.

The Barbarization of the West

Rome did not fall. It was transformed. Romans participated in and even encouraged this transformation. Roman accommodation with the Visigoths set the pattern for subsequent settlement of barbarians in the western half of the empire. By this time, barbarians made up the bulk of the imperial army, and commanders were frequently themselves barbarians. However, these barbarian troops had been integrated into existing Roman military structures. Indeed, these so-called imperial Germans had often proven even more loyal to Rome than the Roman provincial populations they were to protect. In the late fourth and fifth centuries, emperors accepted whole barbarian peoples as integral parts of the Roman army and settled them within the empire. Usually the emperors diverted a percentage of tax revenues from the region's estates in order to support these "guests."

The Visigothic kingdom in southern Gaul and Spain was typical in this respect. Alaric's successor, Ataulf, was extremely eager to win the approval of the emperor. He married Galla Placidia, the daughter of Emperor Theodosius and the sister of Emperor Honorius, in a Roman ceremony in Narbonne in 414. Soon

afterward he established a government at Bordeaux directed by Gallo-Roman aristocrats. Although his opponents soon assassinated him, his successors concluded a treaty with Constantinople in which the Visigoths were recognized as a legitimate, established political presence within the empire. This so-called kingdom of Toulouse endured for almost a century. South of the Pyrenees, the Gothic kingdom of Toledo continued for almost three hundred years.

The Visigoths were not the only powerful barbarian people to challenge the empire. The Vandals, who had entered the empire in 406, crossed over into Africa, the richest region of the western empire, and quickly conquered it. Avowed enemies of the empire, the Vandals used their base in North Africa to raid the European coastline and attack Roman shipping. In 455 they sacked Rome much more thoroughly than had the Goths forty-five years earlier.

Another threat appeared in the 430s, when the Huns, formerly Roman allies, invaded the empire under their charismatic leader Attila (ca. 406–453). Although defeated in Gaul by a combined army of barbarians under the command of the Roman general Flavius Aetius in 451, they turned toward Italy and penetrated as far as Rome. There they were stopped not by the rapidly disintegrating imperial forces but by the bishop of Rome, Pope Leo I, who met Attila before the city's gates. What transpired between the two is not known, but Attila's subsequent withdrawal from Italy

The Vandals crossed into North Africa from Spain and founded a state centered on Carthage. This mosaic of the late fifth or early sixth century shows a prosperous Vandal lord leaving his villa. His costume is typical of barbarians.

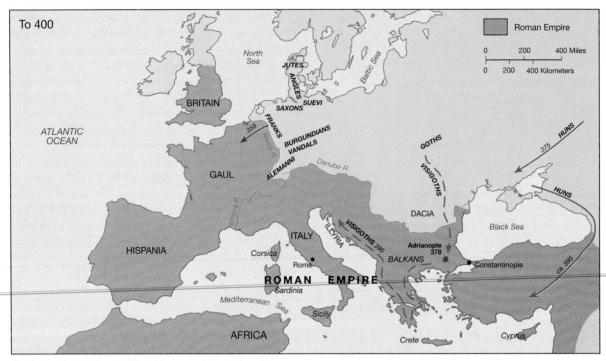

Barbarian Migrations and Invasions

vastly increased the prestige of the papacy. Now not only were popes successors of Saint Peter and bishops of the principal city of the west, but they were replacing the emperor as protector of the city. The foundations of the political power of the papacy were established.

The confederation of the Huns collapsed after the death of Attila in 453, but imperial power did not revive in Italy. A series of incompetent emperors were pushed aside by barbarian generals who assumed power in the peninsula and sought recognition from Zeno, the emperor in the east. However, after the death of the last legitimate western emperor, Julius Nepos, in 480, Zeno conferred the title of patrician on the Ostrogothic king Theodoric. In 489 Theodoric invaded Italy with imperial blessing and established himself as ruler of Italy.

In Theodoric's kingdom, the Roman and Ostrogothic institutions remained separate, united only at the top in the person of Theodoric. To his barbarians Theodoric was king; to the Romans he was patrician and military commander in the west. In reality, imperial presence had ceased to exist in Italy.

In Gaul, between the Seine and the Loire, the Roman general Flavius Aetius and, after his death, the general Syagrius continued to represent some imperial presence. But the armies that Aetius and Syagrius commanded consisted entirely of barbarians—particularly of Visigoths and Franks—and they represented the interests of local aristocratic factions rather than those of Constantinople. So thoroughly barbarized had these last Roman commanders become in their military command and political control that the barbarians referred to Syagrius as "king of the Romans." Ultimately, in 486, Syagrius was defeated and replaced by the Frank Clovis, son of his military commander Childeric, probably with the blessing of the emperor.

Britain met a similar fate. Abandoned by Roman legions around 407, the Romano-Celtic population in this province concluded a treaty with bands of Saxons and Angles to protect Britain from other barbarian raiders. As had happened elsewhere in the empire, the barbarians came as federated troops and stayed as rulers. Gradually, during the fifth century, Germanic warrior groups conquered much of the island. The Anglo-Saxons pushed the native inhabitants to the west and the north. There, as the Cornish and the Welsh (in Anglo-Saxon, Welsh means simply "enemy"), they preserved the Christian religion but largely lost their other Roman traditions.

The establishment of barbarian kingdoms within the Roman world meant the end of the western empire as a political entity. However, the emperors of the east

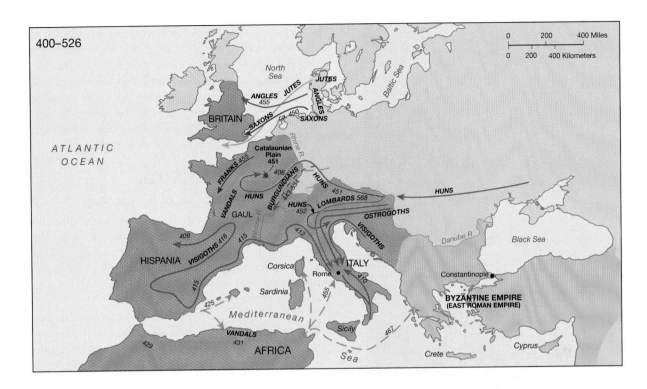

and west continued to pretend that all these barbarian peoples, with the exception of the Vandals, were Roman troops commanded by loyal Roman officers who happened to be of barbarian origin. Following the precedent established with the Visigoths, the emperors gave their kings or war leaders official status within the empire as Roman generals or patricians. They generally rewarded their leaders by redirecting to them imperial taxes from areas where they were settled. Occasionally emperors granted them portions of abandoned lands or existing estates. Local Roman elites considered these leaders rude and uncultured barbarians who nevertheless could be made to serve these elites' own interests more easily than better educated imperial bureaucrats.

As a result, the aristocracy of the west, the *maiores,* viewed the decay of the civil government without dismay. This decay was due largely to the poverty of the imperial treasury. In the fifth century the entire public revenues of the west amounted to little more than the annual incomes of a few wealthy private aristocrats. Managing to escape both taxation and the jurisdiction of public officials, these individuals carved out for themselves vast estates, which they and their families controlled with private armies and which they governed as virtually autonomous lordships. Ordinary freemen, pressed by the remnants of imperial taxation and by barbarians, were forced into accepting the protection and hence control offered by these aristocrats, who thereby came to control whole villages and districts.

The primary source of friction between barbarians and provincial elites was religion. Many Goths had converted to Christianity around the time that the Huns had destroyed the Gothic confederation. However, they had chosen the Arian form of Christianity in order to appease the Arian emperors Constantius and Valens. But the Goths and most other barbarian peoples held to the Arian form of faith long after it had been abandoned in the empire. Thus, wherever the barbarians settled, they were met with distrust and hostility from the orthodox clergy. In southern Gaul and Italy this hostility created serious difficulties because during the fifth century bishops had assumed many of the traditional duties and powers held by provincial Roman administrators.

Although during the fifth century the western aristocracy had largely given up on the civil administration, these wealthy landowners increasingly identified with the episcopacy. In Gaul, bishops were regularly selected from members of the greatest Gallo-Roman senatorial families, establishing veritable episcopal dynasties. In Italy and Spain too, bishops were drawn

A jeweled eagle brooch from the Cesena treasure, a collection of Ostrogothic artifacts found near Ravenna and dating from the time of Theodoric.

part this transition took place with less disturbance of the local social or political scene than was once thought. During the fifth century the imperial presence simply faded away as barbarian kings came to rule in the name of the emperor. After 480, the emperor resided exclusively in the east. The last western emperors disappeared without serious opposition either from western aristocrats or from their eastern colleagues.

The Hellenization of the East

The eastern half of the empire, in contrast to the west, managed to survive and even to prosper in the fifth and sixth centuries. In the east, beginning in 400, the trends toward militarization and barbarization of the administration were reversed, the strength of the imperial government was reaffirmed, and the vitality and integrity of the empire were restored.

Several reasons account for the contrast between east and west. First, the east had always been more urbanized and civilized than the west. It had an old tradition of civil control that antedated the Roman Empire itself. When the decay of Roman traditions allowed regionalism and tribalism to arise in the west, the same decay brought in the east a return to Hellenistic traditions. Second, the east had never developed the tradition of public poverty and private wealth characteristic of the west. In the east tax revenues continued to support an

from the landed aristocracy. These bishops, most of whom were elected after long years of outstanding secular leadership, served as the primary protectors and administrators of their communities, filling the vacuum left by the erosion of other civil offices. They, more than either local civil officials or the Bacaudae, were successful in representing the community before imperial tax collectors or barbarian chieftains.

Thus, in spite of the creation of the barbarian kingdoms, cultural and political leadership at the local level remained firmly in the hands of the aristocracy. Aristocratic bishops, rather than hermits, monopolized the role of mediators of divine power just as their lay brothers, in cooperation with barbarian military leaders, monopolized the role of mediators of secular power.

Barbarian military leaders needed local ties by which to govern the large indigenous populations over whom they ruled. They found cooperation with these aristocrats both necessary and advantageous. Thus while individual landowners might have suffered in the transition from Roman to barbarian rule, for the most

On this medallion from Spain, the emperor Theodosius is presented as a godlike figure detached from the struggles of ordinary people.

administrative apparatus, which remained in the hands of civilians rather than barbarian military commanders. Moreover, the local aristocracies in the eastern provinces never achieved the wealth and independence of their western counterparts. Finally, Christian bishops, frequently divided over doctrinal issues, never managed to monopolize either sacred power, which was shared by itinerant holy men and monks, or secular power, which was wielded by imperial agents. Thus, under the firm direction of its emperors, especially Theodosius and later Zeno, the eastern empire not only survived but prepared for a new expansionist phase under the emperor Justinian.

• • •

The divergence in religious power between east and west was characteristic of the growing differences between the two halves of the Roman Empire at the close of late antiquity. The profound crises—military, social, and economic—that had shaken the empire and the barbarian world in the course of the third century, left the west transformed. The new imperial system, based on an absolute ruler and an authoritarian Christianity, held the Roman world together for a few more centuries. Ultimately, however, the two halves of the old Mediterranean empire drifted in different directions as each formed a new civilization from Roman and indigenous traditions.

The east remained more firmly attached not only to Roman traditions of government but also to the much more ancient traditions of social complexity, urban life, and religious culture that stretched back to the dawn of civilization. The emperors continued to rule from Constantinople for another thousand years, but the extent of their authority gradually shrank to little more than the city itself. Furthermore, their empire was so profoundly hellenized in nature that it is properly called Byzantine (from the original name of Constantinople) rather than Roman.

The west experienced a transformation even more profound than that of the east. The triple heritage of late Roman political and military forms, barbarian society, and Christian culture coalesced into a new civilization that was perhaps less the direct heir of antiquity than was that of the east, but was all the more dynamic for its distinctiveness. In culture, politics, and patterns of urban and rural life, the west and the east had gone separate ways, and their paths diverged ever more in the centuries ahead.

Suggestions for Further Reading

The Crisis of the Third Century

* A. H. M. Jones, *The Later Roman Empire, 284–602: A Social, Economic and Administrative Survey,* 2 vols. (Baltimore: The Johns Hopkins University Press, 1986). The standard detailed survey of late antiquity by an administrative historian.

* Peter Brown, *The World of Late Antiquity,* A.D. *150–750* (New York: Harcourt Brace Jovanovich, 1971). A brilliant essay on the cultural transformation of the ancient world.

E. A. Thompson, *The Early Germans* (Oxford: Oxford University Press, 1965). An important social and economic view of Germanic society.

The Empire Restored

* Ramsay MacMullen, *Paganism in the Roman Empire* (New Haven, CT: Yale University Press, 1981). A sensible introduction to the varieties of Roman religion in the imperial period.

T. D. Barnes, *The New Empire of Diocletian and Constantine* (Cambridge, MA: Harvard University Press, 1982). A current examination of the transformations brought about under these two great emperors.

Imperial Christianity

* Ramsay MacMullen, *Christianizing the Roman Empire (100–400)* (New Haven, CT: Yale University Press, 1984). A view of Christianity's spread from the perspective of Roman history.

W. H. C. Friend, *The Rise of Christianity* (London: Darton, Longman and Todd, 1984). A panoramic survey of Christianity from its origins to the seventh century.

* Peter Brown, *Power and Persuasion in Late Antiquity: Towards a Christian Empire* (Madison, WI: University of Wisconsin Press, 1992). A highly readable yet penetrating account of the growth of episcopal power within the political culture of the later Roman Empire.

* David Knowles, *Christian Monasticism* (New York: McGraw-Hill, 1969). A very readable introduction by a great historian of monastic history.

A Parting of the Ways

* Judith Herrin, *The Formation of Christendom* (Princeton, NJ: Princeton University Press, 1987). A history of the transformed Mediterranean world, east and west, to 800 from the perspective of a noted Byzantinist.

* Herwig Wolfram, *History of the Goths* (Berkeley, CA: University of California Press, 1988). An ethnologically sensitive history of the formation of the Gothic peoples.

*Paperback edition available.

7 ✣ THE CLASSICAL LEGACY IN THE EAST: BYZANTIUM AND ISLAM

From Temple to Mosque

*F*irst a temple dedicated to the Syriac god Hadad and then to the Roman god Jupiter, later the Christian church of St. John, and finally a mosque, the Great Mosque of Damascus in Syria bears testimony to the great civilizations that have followed one another in the Near East. Like the successive houses of worship, each civilization rose upon the ruins of its predecessor, incorporating and transforming the rich legacy of the past into a new culture. Little of the pagan and Christian structures is visible, although the mosque owes much to both, as does the civilization it represents.

Nothing remains of the pre-Roman structure. In the first century A.D. the Romans rebuilt the temple to include an outer enclosure 1233 by 1000 feet with four monumental gateways. In the interior was a porticoed court marked by four corner towers. Monumental portals, or gateways, in the east and west walls provided access to this inner court through triple doorways. In the center of the court stood a structure housing the statue of Jupiter.

Around the time of Constantine, the temple was converted into a Christian church dedicated to Saint John the Baptist. Apparently, a portion of the interior por-

ticoed court, which measured roughly 517 by 318 feet, was enclosed to provide a space for worshipers. Two of the four towers were raised to serve as bell towers. For a time after Damascus fell to the Arabs in 635, Christians and Muslims shared the church. Initially there were only a few Muslims, who required no more than a small place in the exterior courtyard.

However, the Muslim population of the city grew rapidly, and by 705 Damascus was the capital of a vast, expanding Muslim empire, which would soon stretch from the Pyrenees to the Indus River. The caliph al-Walid (705–715) wanted a place of prayer befitting his capital's glory. He invited the Christian community to choose a site for another church. When they refused, he expelled

Roman, Empire. Although the caliphate and the Byzantine Empire were bitter enemies, the Christian emperor loaned the caliph Byzantine artists to create the mosaics. Even today, the surviving Barada mosaics show Damascus as it appeared to al-Walid's Byzantine artists: a rich, verdant valley of palaces and houses.

The Christian antecedents of the mosque did not entirely disappear. During the preliminary work, an underground chapel was said to have been found, containing a chest with a human head. On the chest was written, "This is the head of John, son of Zacharias." Al-Walid had the sacred relic placed under one of the pillars and a monument erected over it. To this day the shrine survives in the mosque, a symbol of the links between Judaism, Christianity, and Islam.

This moment of artistic and religious cooperation was brief. Only a few years later, in 717, al-Walid's successor subjected Constantinople to the most fearful siege it would endure for five hundred years. Still, the continuity of religious worship and the common taste for classical art show how deeply both the caliphate and the empire were bound together in the common heritage of late antiquity, of which both were the true heirs.

them and hired Greek architects to adapt the structure to Muslim worship. They demolished the interior walls of the church, leaving only the ancient walls of the porticoed court and the tower at each of the four corners. These four Christian towers became the first minarets, towers from which Muslim religious leaders call the faithful to prayer five times each day. Within the ancient walls, the courtyard was surrounded by porticoes on three sides and by the facade of the sanctuary on the fourth side.

Al-Walid wanted his mosque to be the most magnificent in his empire, and he determined to employ the finest artists in the world to cover its walls with mosaics. The supreme center of mosaic art was Constantinople, capital of the Byzantine, or eastern

The Byzantines

At the end of the fifth century A.D., the eastern empire of Theodosius and Zeno had escaped the fate that its western counterpart had suffered at the hands of the Germanic peoples. Wealthier and more urbanized than the west, its population had also been accustomed to centralized government for more than a thousand years. Still, the long-term survival of the eastern empire seemed far from certain. Little unified the empire of Constantinople. The population of the capital split into rival political factions whose violent conflicts often threatened the stability of the government. These rival groups, organized militarily and politically, controlled the Circus, or Hippodrome, where the games and char-

iot races that were the obsession of the city's population took place. These factions took their names, the Greens and the Blues, from their Circus colors. When these two factions joined forces with the army, they were powerful enough to create or destroy emperors. Beyond Constantinople, the empire's population consisted of the more or less hellenized peoples of Asia Minor, Armenians, Slavs, Arabs, Syrians, Egyptian Copts, and others. Unlike western Europe, the east was still a world of cities, which were centers of commerce, industry, and Hellenistic culture. But the importance of these urban centers began to decline in favor of the rural peasant world, which not only fed the empire and was the source of its great wealth but also provided the generations of tough soldiers necessary to protect the empire from its enemies.

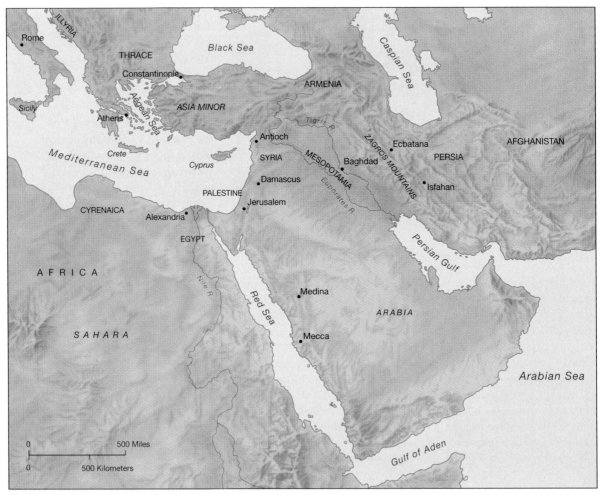

The Eastern Mediterranean

A mosaic from the church of San Vitale in Ravenna. The Emperor Justinian, along with secular and ecclesiastical officials, is shown bringing an offering to the church. The halo around his head signifies the sacred nature of the imperial office.

Finally, the eastern empire was more divided than unified by its Christianity. Rivalry among the great cities of Antioch, Alexandria, Jerusalem, Rome, and Constantinople was expressed in the competition among their bishops or patriarchs. The official "right teaching," or orthodox, faith of Constantinople and its patriarch was bitterly opposed by "deviant," or heterodox, bishops of other religious traditions, around which developed separatist ethnic political movements. In Syria and Egypt in particular, theological disagreements about the nature of God had become rallying points of political opposition. By the time of Justinian (527–565), emperors were obsessed with maintaining absolute authority and imposing uniformity on their empire.

Justinian and the Creation of the Byzantine State

Strong-willed, restless, and ambitious, Justinian is remembered as "the emperor who never slept." Although his goals were essentially conservative, he transformed the very foundations of the imperial state, its institutions and its culture. He hoped to restore the territory, power, and prestige of the ancient Roman Empire, but his attempts to return to the past created a new world. With the assistance of his dynamic wife Theodora, his great generals Belisarius and Narses, his brilliant jurist Tribonian, his scientists Anthemius of Tralles and Isidorus of Miletus, and his brutally efficient administrator and tax collector John of Cappadocia, he remade the empire.

Spurred on by the ambitious Theodora, in 532 Justinian checked the power of the Circus factions by brutally suppressing a riot that left thirty thousand dead in the capital city. Belisarius and Narses recaptured North Africa from the Vandals, Italy from the Ostrogoths, and part of Spain from the Visigoths, restoring for one last moment some of the geographical unity of the empire of Augustus and Constantine. Tribonian revised and organized the existing codes of Roman law into the Justinian Code, a great monument of Western jurisprudence that remains today the foundation of most of Europe's legal systems. Anthemius and Isidorus combined their knowledge of mathematics, geometry, kinetics, and physics to build the Church of the Holy Wisdom (Hagia Sophia) in Constantinople, one of the largest and most innovative churches ever constructed. This structure was as radical as it was simple. In essence it is a huge rectangle, 230 by 250 feet, above which a

THE JUSTINIAN CODE

In 533 the commission appointed by the Emperor Justinian completed the Digest, *the most important section of his great Code, the most influential legal text in European history. In his preface, Justinian explains his reason for ordering the codification and reveals the image of imperial power that would be the cornerstone of the Byzantine state for almost a thousand years.*

IN THE NAME OF OUR LORD JESUS CHRIST. THE EMPEROR CAESAR FLAVIUS JUSTINIANUS, CONQUEROR OF THE ALEMANNI, GOTHS, FRANKS, GERMANS, ANTES, ALANI, VANDALS, AND AFRICANS, PIOUS, HAPPY, AND GLORIOUS, CONQUEROR AND VANQUISHER, TO YOUNG MEN DESIROUS OF LEARNING THE LAW, GREETING.

Imperial majesty should not only be adorned with military might but also graced by laws, so that in times of peace and war alike the state may be governed aright and so that the Emperor of Rome may not only shine forth victorious on the battlefield, but may also by every legal means cast out the wickedness of the perverters of justice, and thus at one and the same time prove as assiduous in upholding the law as he is triumphant over his vanquished foes.

This double objective we have achieved with the blessing of God through our utmost watchfulness and foresight. The barbarian races brought under our yoke know well our military achievements; and Africa also and countless other provinces bear witness to our power having been after so long an interval restored to the dominion of Rome and to our Empire by our victories which we have gained through the inspiration of Divine guidance. Moreover, all these peoples are now also governed by laws which we ourselves have promulgated or compiled.

When we had elucidated and brought into perfect harmony the revered imperial constitutions which were previously in confusion, we turned our attention to the immense mass of ancient jurisprudence. Now, by the grace of Heaven, we have completed this work of which even we at one time despaired like sailors crossing the open sea.

From Justinian, *The Digest of Roman Law. Theft, Rapine, Damage and Insult.*

---

vast dome 100 feet in diameter rises to a height of 180 feet and seems to float, suspended in air. As spectacular but not as well appreciated were the achievements of John of Cappadocia, who was able to squeeze the empire's population for the taxes to pay for these conquests, reforms, and building projects. Justinian may have been referring to more than just his new church when, upon entering it for the first time, he compared himself to the biblical builder of the first temple in Jerusalem, declaring, "Solomon, I have vanquished thee!"

Ultimately, Justinian's spectacular achievements came at too high a price. He left his successors an empire virtually bankrupt by the costs of his wars and his building projects, bitterly divided by his attempts to settle religious controversies, and poorly protected on its eastern border, where the Sassanid Empire was a constant threat. Most of Italy and Spain soon returned to barbarian control. In 602 the Sassanid emperor Chosroes II (d. 628) invaded the empire, capturing Egypt, Palestine, and Syria and threatening Constantinople itself. In a series of desperate campaigns, the emperor Heraclius (610–641) turned back the tide and crushed the Sassanids, but it was too late. A new power, Islam, had emerged in the deserts of Arabia. This new power was to challenge and ultimately absorb both the Sassanids and much of the eastern Roman Empire. As a result, the east became increasingly less Roman and more Greek or, specifically, more Byzantine.

For over seven hundred years the Byzantine Empire played a major role in Western history. From the seventh through tenth centuries, when most of Europe was too weak and disorganized to defend itself against the expansion of Islam, the Byzantines stood as the bulwark of Christianity. When organized government had virtually disappeared in the west, the Byzantine Empire provided a model of a centralized bureaucratic state ruled according to principles of Roman law. When, beginning in the fourteenth century, western Europeans began once more to appreciate the heritage of Greek and Roman art and literature, they turned to Constantinople. There the manuscripts of Greek writers such as Plato and Homer had been preserved and studied and were available to contribute to a rebirth of classical culture in the west. When the Slavic north, caught between the Latin Christians and the Muslims,

The interior of Hagia Sophia. The building was converted into a mosque after the Ottoman conquest of 1453. The magnificent mosaics were painted over to conform to Islamic religious dictates against representing the human figure.

sought its cultural and religious orientation, it looked to the liturgical culture of Byzantine orthodoxy. Perhaps most importantly, when urban civilization had all but disappeared from the rest of Europe, Greeks and Latins could still look "to the City," *eis tēn polin,* or as the Turks pronounced it, *Istanbul.*

Emperors and Individuals

The classic age of Byzantine society, roughly from the eighth through the tenth centuries, has been described as "individualism without freedom." The Byzantine world was intensely individualistic—unlike the Roman, which emphasized public and private associations; unlike the western barbarian kingdoms, in which hierarchical gradations connected everyone, from peasant to king; and unlike the communal society of Islam. But Byzantine individualism did not lead to a great amount of individual initiative or creativity. Still less

did it imply individual freedom of action within the political sphere, a concept that hardly existed for the vast majority of the empire's population. Instead, Byzantine individualism meant that individuals and small family groups stood as isolated units in a society characterized, until the mid-eleventh century, by the direct relationship between an all-powerful emperor and citizens of all ranks.

In part this individualism resulted from the Byzantine form of government. The Byzantine state was, in theory and often in fact, an autocracy. Since the time of Diocletian, all members of society were subjects of the emperor, who alone was the source of law. How a person became emperor remained, as it had been in the Roman Empire, more a question of military power than of constitutional succession. Although in theory emperors were elected by the senate, army, and people of Constantinople, in practice emperors generally selected their own successors and had them crowned in their own lifetimes.

As long as the empire remained a civilian autocracy, it was even possible for a woman to rule, either as regent for a minor son or as sovereign. Thus Irene (780–802), widow of Leo IV (725–780), ruled as regent for her son Constantine VI (780–797). However, when her son reached his majority, she had him blinded and deposed and ruled alone from 797 to 802, not merely as the *basilissa,* or wife of the emperor, but as the *basileus,* or emperor itself. In the eleventh century the empire was ruled for a time by two sisters: Zoe (1028–34), daughter of one emperor and widow of another, and Theodora (1042–56), who was dragged out of a church by an enthusiastic mob and proclaimed empress.

The Empress Irene, widow of Leo IV, was the only woman to rule the Byzantine Empire in her own right. As regent during the minority of her son, she reestablished the worship of icons. In 802 Irene was dethroned and exiled to Lesbos.

This ivory panel, one-half of a diptych, celebrates the Lampadius family. The bottom scene depicts chariot races in the Hippodrome at Constantinople. The stone pillar in the middle is a hieroglyphic-covered obelisk brought from Egypt.

Male or female, emperors were above and beyond their subjects, often quite literally. In the tenth century a mechanical throne was installed in the main audience room. The throne would suddenly lift the emperor high above the heads of astonished visitors. Like God the Father, with whom he was closely identified in imperial propaganda, the emperor was separated from the people by an unbridgeable gulf. For great lords and peasants alike, the only proper attitude toward such a ruler was adoration and abject humility.

Thus the traditional corporate bodies of the Roman Empire wasted away or became window dressing for the imperial cult. The senate, which had received the rights and privileges of the Roman Senate in 359, gradually ceased to play any autonomous role. Long before its powers were officially abolished in the ninth century, the senate had become simply a passive and amorphous body of prominent people called upon from time to time to participate in public ceremonies. Sena-

tors were present when important foreign ambassadors were received. Senatorial acclamation of new emperors was always a part of the imperial coronation ceremony. But such roles were simply part of an elaborate ritual emphasizing the dignity and power of the emperor.

The Circus factions, which in the sixth century had the power to make or break emperors, met the same fate as the corportate bodies of the Roman Empire. From autonomous political groups, the Circus factions too gradually became no more than participants in imperial ceremonies. By the tenth century, the Greens and the Blues were simply officially constituted groups whose role was to praise the emperor by mouthing traditional formulas on solemn occasions. The Hippodrome games became aristocratic pastimes. Chariot races, increasingly amateurish, ended in the early thirteenth century. By the end of that century the great Hippodrome was nearly deserted except for occasional games of polo played by young aristocrats.

While the emperor was the source of all authority, the actual administration of the empire was carried out by a vast bureaucracy composed of military and civilian officers. The empire was divided into roughly twenty-five provinces, or *themes*. The soldiers in each theme, rather than being full-time warriors, were also farmers. Each soldier received a small farm from which to support himself and his family. Soldiers held their farms as long as they served in the army. When a soldier retired or died, his farm and his military obligation passed to his eldest son. These farmer-soldiers were the backbone of both the imperial military and the economic system. They not only formed a regular locally based native army, but they also kept much of Byzantine agriculture in the hands of free peasants rather than great aristocrats. The themes were governed by military commanders, or *stratēgoi,* who presided over both civilian and military bureaucrats. Although virtually all-powerful in their provinces, stratēgoi could be appointed, removed from office, or transferred at the whim of the emperor.

In contrast to the military command of the themes, the central administration, which focused on the emperor and the imperial family, was wholly civil. The most important positions at court were occupied by eunuchs, castrated men who offered a number of advantages to imperial administration. Eunuchs often directed imperial finance, served as prime ministers, directed the vast bureaucracy, and even undertook military commands. Because they could not have descendants, there was no danger that they would attempt to turn their offices into hereditary positions or that they would plot and scheme on behalf of their children. Moreover, since the sacred nature of the emperor

A tenth-century Greek manuscript of the gospel from Constantinople is decorated with a drawing of laborers in a vineyard. Such illustrated texts often recorded the daily activities of ordinary people, including plowing, fishing, farming, and sheep shearing.

required physical perfection, eunuchs could not aspire to replace their masters on the throne. Finally, although at times their influence with the emperor made them immensely powerful, eunuchs were at once feared and despised by the general population. Thus there was little likelihood that they would build autonomous power bases outside of imperial favor. One Byzantine historian described the powerful eunuch John the Orphanotrophos (mid–eleventh century) by saying that "nothing at all escaped his notice nor did anyone even try to do so, for everyone feared him and all dreaded his vigilance." The extensive use of eunuchs was one of the keys to the survival of absolutist authority in the empire. While many eunuchs promoted the interests of their brothers and nephews, they were less dangerous than ambitious aristocrats. They preserved imperial authority at a time when both Islamic and Latin states were experiencing a progressive erosion of central power to the benefit of ambitious aristocratic families.

A godlike emperor and a centralized bureaucracy left little room for the development of the hierarchies of private patronage, lordship, and group action that were characteristic of western Europe. In the Byzantine Empire, aristocrat and peasant were equal in their political powerlessness. Against the emperor and the bureaucracy, no extended kin group or local political unit offered security or comfort. Thus Byzantine society tended to be organized at the lowest level, that of the nuclear family. This structure was imprinted even on the physical landscape of Byzantine cities. Single-family dwellings replaced the public spaces and buildings of antiquity. Public assemblies and communal celebrations either disappeared or were absorbed into the ritual of imperial dignity. Daily life focused on the protective enclosure of the private home, which served as both shelter and workplace. Professional and craft associations continued to exist as they had in antiquity. However, like everything else in Byzantium, these were not autonomous professional groups intended to protect the interests of their members. Instead, they were

promoted and controlled by imperial officials in order to regulate and tax urban industry.

The countryside, which was the backbone of Byzantine prosperity into the eleventh century, was also a world with limited horizontal and vertical social bonds. Villages were the basic elements in the imperial system. The village court handled local affairs and tax assessments, but it in turn dealt directly with the imperial bureaucracy. Occasionally villages might unite against imperial tax collectors, but normally villagers dealt with each other and with outside powers as wary individuals. This attitude was an outgrowth of agricultural techniques practiced in Greece and Asia Minor, where a peasant's prosperity depended not on teamwork but rather on individual effort. Most peasants, whether they were landowners, peasant soldiers, or renters on great estates, survived on the labor of their own family and perhaps one or two slaves. In the eleventh century, tax records indicated only three types of peasants, distinguished according to their equipment: those with two yoke of cattle, those with one, and those with none. Large cooperative undertakings as in Islamic lands or the use of communal equipment as became the rule in the west was unknown. Individual families worked their own fields, which were usually enclosed with protective stone or brick walls. Byzantine peasants would have agreed with the neighbor in Robert Frost's poem "Mending Wall," who says, "Good fences make good neighbors."

Like the villages, Byzantine towns were isolated. The mountainous terrain of Greece and Asia Minor contributed to this isolation, cutting off ready overland communication among communities and forcing them to turn to the sea. In this respect Constantinople was ideally situated to develop into the greatest commercial center of the West, at its height boasting a population of over one million. Because of Constantinople's strategic location on the Bosporus, that slim ribbon of water uniting the Black and Mediterranean seas, all of the products of the empire and those of the Slavic, Latin,

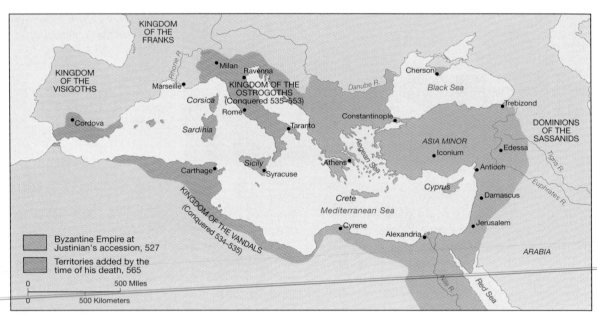

The Byzantine Empire Under Justinian

and Islamic worlds, as well as Oriental goods arriving overland from central Asia, had to pass through the city. Silks, spices, and precious metals were loaded onto ships at Trebizond and then transported south to Constantinople. Baltic amber, slaves, and furs from the Slavic world were carried down the Dnepr River to the Black Sea and then to Constantinople. There, all goods passing north or south had to be unloaded, assessed, and subjected to a flat import-export tariff of 10 percent.

The empire's cities were centers for the manufacture of luxury goods in demand throughout the Islamic and Christian worlds. The secret of silk manufacture had been smuggled out of China by a Christian monk who had hidden silkworms in his pilgrim's staff during his journey home. Imperial workshops in Constantinople and closely regulated workshops in Corinth and Thebes produced fine silks, brocades, carpets, and other luxury products marketed throughout the Mediterranean. These goods were also subject to the state's customary 10 percent tax.

As vital as maritime commerce was to the empire, most Byzantines hated the sea. They feared it as a source of constant danger from Muslim and Christian pirates. They dreaded its sudden storms and hidden dangers. When they did travel by ship, they prayed to their sacred icons and tried to sail, as one Byzantine put it, "touching the shore with an oar." Moreover, particularly among the elite, commerce was considered

demeaning. The story is told that when one ninth-century emperor learned that his wife owned a ship, he ordered it and its cargo burned. Never great mariners, Byzantines were largely content to allow others—first Syrians and Slavs and later Italians—to monopolize the empire's commerce.

A Foretaste of Heaven

The cultural cement that bound emperor and subjects together was Orthodox Christianity. The Islamic capture of Alexandria, Jerusalem, and Antioch had removed the centers of regional religious particularism from the empire. The barbarian domination of Italy had isolated Rome and reduced its influence. These two processes left Constantinople as the only remaining patriarchate in the empire and thus the undisputed center of Orthodox Christianity. However, like virtually every other aspect of Byzantine society and culture, the patriarch and the Orthodox faith he led were subordinated to the emperor. Although in theory patriarchs were elected, in reality emperors appointed them. Patriarchs in turn controlled the various levels of the Church hierarchy, which included metropolitans, bishops, and the local clergy. This ecclesiastical structure reflected the organization of the state bureaucracy, which it reinforced. Local priests were drawn from the peasant society of which they were a part. They were expected to be married and to live much like their neighbors. Bishops, metropolitans, and patriarchs were recruited from monasteries and remained celibate. They were, so to speak, spiritual eunuchs who represented the emperor. In rare instances a patriarch might threaten to excommunicate an emperor, as the patriarch Polyeuct did to Emperor John Tzimisces (969–976) when he proposed to marry his predecessor's wife Theophano, but such threats could seldom be carried out with impunity. Generally the Church supported the emperor and the imperial cult.

The essence of Orthodox religion was the liturgy, or ceremonies, of the Church, which provided, it was said, a foretaste of heaven. Adoration of God and veneration of the emperor were joined as the cornerstone of imperial propaganda. Ecclesiastical and court processions assured that everything and everyone was in the proper place and that order and stability reigned in this world as a reflection of the eternal order of the next. This confirmation, in churches and in court, of stability and permanence in the face of possible crisis and disruption calmed and reassured the liturgically oriented society. The effects of Byzantine ceremonial reached far beyond the Byzantines themselves. According to Russian sources, when the prince of Kiev sent observers to report on the manners of worship in Islamic, Latin, and Greek societies, the effect of the Byzantine liturgy was overpowering: "We knew not whether we were in heaven or on earth, for on earth there is no such splendor or such beauty." So strong was the impression made by the rituals of the Church that the prince decided to invite Byzantine clergy to instruct his people.

The one aspect of religious life not entirely under imperial control was monasticism. Since the time of the desert fathers, monastic communities had been an essential part of Christianity. From the sixth century on, numerous monastic communities were founded throughout the empire, and by the eleventh century there were at least three hundred monasteries within the walls of Constantinople alone. Following the Muslim invasions of the eleventh century, Anatolia became the major center of monastic life outside the city. Monasteries were often wealthy and powerful. Moreover, their religious appeal, often based on the possession of miracle-working religious images, or icons, posed an independent source of religious authority at odds with the imperial centralization of all aspects of Byzantine life. To the faithful, icons were not simply representations or reminders of Jesus and the saints: they had a real if intermediary relationship with the person represented, and as such themselves merited veneration and, some argued, adoration.

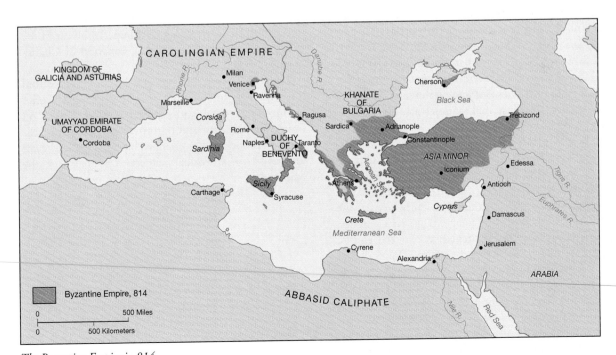

The Byzantine Empire in 814.

In this manuscript illustration, an icon is being destroyed while priests try to persuade Leo V to abandon his iconoclast policies.

Beginning with Emperor Leo III, the Isaurian (717–741), the military emperors who had driven back Islam sought to curtail the independence of monastic culture, and particularly the cult of icons that was an integral part of it. These emperors and their supporters, termed *iconoclasts* (literally, "breakers of images"), objected to the mediating role of sacred images in worship. While the iconoclasts may have been influenced by Jewish and Islamic prohibitions of images, they were also fighting the sort of decentralization in religion that the imperial bureaucracy prevented in government. Monasteries, with their miracle-working icons, became the particular object of imperial persecution. Monasteries were closed and their estates confiscated. Monks, termed by one emperor "idolaters and lovers of darkness," were forced to marry. Everywhere imperial agents painted over frescoes in churches and destroyed icons, statues, and illustrated manuscripts. The defenders of icons—*iconodules,* or image venerators—were imprisoned, tortured, and even executed. Most bishops, the army, and much of the non-European population of the empire supported the iconoclast emperors, but monks, the lesser clergy, and the majority of the populace—particularly women—violently resisted the destruction of their beloved images. For over a century, the iconoclast dispute threatened to tear the empire apart. The first phase, which began in 726, ended in 787, when a council summoned by the Empress Irene confirmed the adoration of images. After her deposition in 802, a milder iconoclastic persecution revived until the Empress Theodora (842–858), who ruled during the minority of her son, ended the persecution and restored image veneration in 843. Monasteries reopened and regained much of their former wealth and prestige. Images were brought out of hiding and new ones created, and icons resumed their role in the eastern Christian church. The longest-lasting effect of the iconoclastic struggle was in Byzantium's relations with the West. Christians in western Europe—particularly the popes of Rome—never accepted the iconoclast position. The popes considered the iconoclast emperors heretics and looked increasingly to the Frankish Carolingian family for support against them and the Lombards of Italy. In this manner the Franks first entered Italian politics and began, with papal support, to establish themselves as a rival imperial power in the west, which culminated in the coronation of Charlemagne in 800.

Between the sixth and ninth centuries, the reduced but still vital Roman Empire in the east developed a distinctive political and cultural tradition based on imperial absolutism and buttressed by a powerful religious tradition and an effective bureaucracy that dealt directly with individual subjects on behalf of the emperor.

The Rise of Islam

Recite: in the name of your Lord,
The Creator Who created man from clots of blood!
Recite: Your Lord is the Most Bounteous One,
Who taught by the pen,
Taught mankind things they did not know.

This command to recite, to reveal God's will, communicated directly by God, launched an obscure merchant in the Arabian city of Mecca on a career that would transform the world. Through faith, Abu al-Qasim Muhammad ibn 'Abd Allah ibn 'Abd al-Muttalib ibn Hashim (ca. 570–632), or more simply Muhammad, united the tribes of the Arabian peninsula and propelled them on an unprecedented mission of conquest. Within a century of Muhammad's death, the world of *Islam*—a word that means "submission to the will of God"—included all of the ancient Near East and extended from the Syr Darya River in Asia south into the Indian subcontinent, west across the African coast to the Atlantic, north through Spain, and along the Mediterranean coast to the Rhone River. Just as their faith combined elements of traditional Arab worship with Christianity and Judaism, the Arabian conquerors and their subject populations created a vital civilization from a mix of Arabian, Roman, Hellenistic, and Sassanid traditions, a civilization characterized from its inception by a multiplicity of forms in which these various elements were combined with the religious traditions of the prophet Muhammad.

Arabia Before the Prophet

Although Arabs did not appear in written sources as such before the ninth century B.C., their ancestors had played an important—if supporting—role in Near Eastern history for thousands of years. In the Egyptian Old Kingdom, the incense trees of southern Arabia had drawn Egyptians to the region, then known as the land of Punt. Trade routes between the Fertile Crescent and Egypt had crossed northern Arabia for just as long, drawing its inhabitants into contact with civilization. By the sixth century A.D., Arabic-speaking peoples from the Arabian peninsula had spread through the Syrian Desert as far north as the Euphrates.

Those who lived on the fringes of the Byzantine and Sassanid empires had been largely absorbed into the cultural and political spheres of these two great powers. The northern borders of Arabia along the Red Sea formed Roman provinces that even produced an emperor, Philip the Arab (244—249). Hira, to the south of the Euphrates, became a Sassanid puppet principality that, although largely Christian, often provided the Persians with auxiliaries. At times the Sassanid Empire also controlled Bahrain on the Persian Gulf, as well as Yamama and the Yemen, both vital in the spice trade. Within both empires the distinction between

Arab and non-Arab populations was blurred. Except for a common language and a hazy idea of common kinship, nothing differentiated Arabs from their neighbors.

Southern Arabia, with a relatively abundant rainfall and fertile soils, was an agricultural region long governed by monarchs. Here was the kingdom of Saba, the Sheba of the Bible, which had existed since the tenth century B.C. During the fifth century A.D. the kings of the Yemen had extended their influence north over the Bedouin tribes of central Arabia in order to control and protect the caravan trade between north and south. However, in the late sixth century A.D. Ethiopian and then Persian conquerors destroyed the Arabian kingdom of the Yemen and absorbed it into their empires. The result was a power vacuum that left central Arabia and its trade routes across the deserts in confusion.

The interior of the Arabian peninsula was much less directly affected by the great empires to the north or the Arabian kingdoms to the south. Waterless steppes and seas of shifting sand dunes had long defeated Roman, Persian, and Sassanid efforts to control the Arabic Bedouin. These nomads roamed the peninsula in search of pasturage for their flocks. Theirs was a life of independence, simplicity, and danger.

Although they acknowledged membership in various tribes, the Bedouin's real allegiance was to much more narrow circles of lineages and tenting groups. As in the Germanic tribes of Europe, kin relationships rather than formal governmental systems protected individuals through the obligation for vengeance and blood feud. In the words of a pre-Islamic poet, "Blood for blood—wiped out were the wounds, and those who had gained a start in the race profited not by their advantage." Tribal chieftains, called sheikhs, chosen from ruling families, had no coercive power, either to right wrongs or to limit feuds. They served only as arbitrators and executors of tribal consensus. The patriarch of each family held final say over his kin. He could ignore the sheikh and go his own way with his flocks and herds, wives and slaves.

The individual was unimportant in Bedouin society. Private land ownership was unknown, and flocks and herds were often held in common by kindreds. The pastoral economy of the Bedouin provided meat, cheese, and wool. Weapons, ornaments, women, and livestock could be acquired through exchange at the market towns that developed around desert oases. More commonly these goods and women were taken in raids against other tribes, caravans, and settlements or by exacting payments from weaker neighbors in return

A Persian miniature shows the Ka'bah in Mecca, the most sacred of Muslim shrines, surrounded by visiting pilgrims.

Rivalry and feuding among tribes could be set aside at a mutually accepted neutral site, which might grow up around a religious sanctuary. A sanctuary, or *haram,* which was often on the border between tribal areas, was founded by a holy man not unlike the Christian holy men of the Syrian Desert. The holy man declared the site and surrounding area neutral ground on which no violence could take place. Here enemies could meet under truce to settle differences under the direction of the holy man or his descendants. Merchant communities sprang up within the safety of these sites, since the sanctuary gave them and their goods protection from their neighbors.

Mecca was just such a sanctuary, around whose sacred black rock, or Ka'bah, a holy man named Qusayy established himself and his tribe, the Quraysh, as its guardians sometime early in the sixth century. In the next century Mecca grew into an important center under the patronage of the Quraysh, who made it the center of a commercial network. Through religious, diplomatic, and military means they organized camel caravans that could safely cross the desert from the Yemen in the south to Iran and Syria in the north. During the early seventh century, when increased hostilities between the Byzantine and Sassanid empires severed the direct trading links between the empires, the Quraysh network became the leading commercial organization in northern Arabia. Still, its effectiveness remained tied to the religious importance of Mecca and the Ka'bah. When Muhammad, a descendant of Qusayy, began to recite the monotheistic message of Allah, his preaching was seen as a threat to the survival of his tribe and his city.

for protection. Raids, however, yielded much more than mere booty. Often launched in defense of family honor, they were the means of increasing prestige and glory in this warrior society. Prizes won in battle were lightly given away as signs of generosity and marks of social importance.

Some of the Arabs of the more settled south, as well as inhabitants of towns along caravan routes, were Christian or Jewish. As farmers or merchants, these groups were looked down upon by the nomadic Bedouin, most of whom remained pagan. Although they recognized some important gods, and even a high god usually called Allah, Bedouin worshiped local tribal deities often thought of as inhabiting a sacred stone or spring. Worship involved gifts and offerings and played only a small part in nomadic life. Far more important was commitment to the tribe, expressed through loyalty to the tribal cult and through unity of action against rival tribes.

Muhammad, Prophet of God

More is known about Muhammad's life than about that of Moses, Jesus, Buddha, or any of the other great religious reformers of history. Still, Muhammad's early years were quickly wrapped in a protective cloak of pious stories by his followers, making it difficult to discern truth from legend. A member of a lesser branch of the Quraysh, Muhammad was an orphan raised by relatives. At about age twenty he became the business manager for Khadijah, a wealthy widow whom he later married. This marriage gave him financial security among the middle ranks of Meccan merchants. During this time he may have traveled to Syria on business and heard the preaching of Christian monks. He certainly became familiar with Judaism through contact with Jewish traders. In his thirties, he began to devote an

THE QUR'AN

The following passages from the Qur'an express the central importance of the revelation of Allah, compassion for Jews and Christians as sharers in the belief in the one God, and the condemnation of polytheistic idolaters.

In the Name of Allah, the Compassionate, the Merciful

This Book is not to be doubted. It is a guide to the righteous, who have faith in the unseen and are steadfast in prayer; who bestow in charity a part of what We give them; who trust what has been revealed to you [Muhammad] and to others before you, and firmly believe in the life to come. These are rightly guided by their Lord; these shall surely triumph.

As for the unbelievers, whether you forewarn them or not, they will not have faith. Allah has set a seal upon their hearts and ears; their sight is dimmed and a grievous punishment awaits them . . .

Men, serve your Lord, who has created you and those who have gone before you, so that you may guard yourselves against evil; who has made the earth a bed for you and the sky a dome, and has sent down water from heaven to bring forth fruits for your sustenance. Do not knowingly set up other gods besides Him . . .

Believers, Jews, Christians, and Sabaeans [ancient rulers of Yemen believed to be monotheists]—whoever believes in Allah and the Last Day and does what is right—shall be rewarded by their Lord; they have nothing to fear or to regret . . .

Yet there are some who worship idols, bestowing on them the adoration due to Allah (though the love of Allah is stronger in the faithful). But when they face their punishment the wrongdoers will know that might is His alone and that Allah is stern in retribution. When they face their punishment the leaders will disown their followers, and the bonds which now unite them will break asunder. Those who followed them will say: "Could we but live again, we would disown them as they have disowned us not."

Thus Allah will show them their own works. They shall sign with remorse, but shall never come out of Hell.

From Qur'an, sura 2.

---

increasing amount of time to meditation, retiring to the barren, arid mountains outside the city. There, in the month of Ramadan in the year 610, he reported a vision of a man, his feet astride the horizon. The figure commanded: "O Muhammad! Thou art the Messenger of God. Recite!"

Khadijah, to whom he confided his revelation in fear and confusion, became his first convert. Within a year he began preaching openly. His early teachings stressed the absolute unity of God, the evils of idolatry, and the threat of divine judgment. Further revelations to Muhammad were copied word for word in what came to be the Qur'an, or Koran. These messages offered Arabs a faith founded on a book. In their eyes, this faith was both within the tradition of and superior to the Christianity and Judaism of their neighbors. The Qur'an was the final revelation and Muhammad the last and greatest prophet. To Muslims—the term *Muslim* means "true believer"—Muhammad is simply the Prophet.

Allah's revelation emphasized, above all, his power and transcendence. The duty of humans is worship. The prayers of Islam, in contrast with those of Christianity and Judaism, are essentially prayers of praise, seldom prayers of petition. This reverential attitude places little premium on scriptural interpretation or theological speculation. Muslims regard the whole Qur'an as the exact and complete revelation of God, literally true, and forming a unified whole, though revelations contained in it came at various times throughout the Prophet's life. It is the complete guide for secular and religious life, the fundamental law of conduct for Islamic society. The Prophet emphasized constantly that he was simply God's messenger and that he merited no special veneration or worship. For this reason Muslims have always rejected the label *Muhammadan,* which nonbelievers often apply to them. Muslims are not followers of Muhammad but of the God of Abraham and Jesus, who chose to make the final and complete revelation of his power and his judgment through the Prophet.

Initially, such revelations of divine power and judgment neither greatly bothered nor influenced Mecca's merchant elite. Muhammad's earliest followers, such as his cousin 'Ali ibn Abi (ca. 600–661), came from his own clan and from among the moderately successful members of the Meccan community—the "nearly haves" rather than the "have nots," as one scholar put

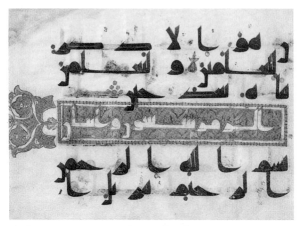

Arabic manuscripts were decorated with intricate geometric designs. This page from an eighth- or ninth-century copy of the Qur'an illustrates the elegance and formality of the Kufic form of Arabic calligraphy. Vowel marks appear as dots of various colors.

it. Elite clans such as the Umayya, who controlled the larger Quraysh tribe, saw little to attract them to the upstart. But soon Muhammad began to insist that those who did not accept Allah as the only God were damned, as were those who continued to venerate the sorts of idols on which Mecca's prosperity was founded. With this proclamation, toleration gave way to hostility. Muhammad and his followers were ostracized, and even persecuted.

Around 620, some residents of Medina, a smaller trading community populated by rival pagan, Jewish, and Islamic clans and racked by internal political dissension, approached the Prophet and invited him to govern the community in order to end the factional squabbles. Rejected at home, Muhammad answered their call. On 24 September 622, Muhammad and one supporter secretly made their way from Mecca to Medina. This short journey of less than three hundred miles, known as the Hijra, was destined to change the world.

The Hijra marks the beginning of the Islamic dating system in the way that the birth of Jesus begins the Christian. The Hijra was the Prophet's first step—or steps—in the shift from preaching to action. He organized his followers from Mecca and Medina into the Umma, a community that transcended the old bonds of tribe and clan. He set about turning Medina into a haram like Mecca, with himself as founding holy man and the Umma as his new family. But this was not to be a haram, or indeed a family like any other. Muhammad was not merely a sheikh whose authority rested on consensus. He was God's messenger, and his authority was

absolute. His goal was to extend this authority far beyond his adopted town of Medina to Mecca, and ultimately to the whole Arab world.

First he gained firm control of Medina at the expense of its Jewish clans. He had expected these monotheists to embrace his teachings. Instead, they rejected the unlettered Arab's attempt to transform Judaic and Christian traditions into an Arab faith. Rejection was their undoing. The Prophet expelled them in the name of political and religious unity. Those not expelled were executed.

Muhammad then used this unified community to attack the Quraysh where they were most vulnerable—in their protection of camel caravans. The inability to destroy the upstarts or protect its trading network cost the Quraysh tribe much of its prestige. More and more members of Meccan families and local tribes converted to Islam. In 629, Muhammad and 10,000 warriors marched on Mecca and captured the city in a swift and largely bloodless campaign.

During the three years between Muhammad's triumphant return to Mecca and his death, Islam moved steadily toward becoming the major force in the Arabian peninsula. The divine revelations increasingly took on legal and practical dimensions as Muhammad was forced to serve, not just as Prophet, but as political leader of a major political and economic power. The Umma had become a sort of supertribe, open to all individuals who would accept Allah and his Prophet. The invitation extended to women as well as to men.

Islam brought a transformation of the rights of women in Arabian society. This did not mean that they achieved equality with men any more than they did in any premodern civilization, east or west. Men continued to dominate Islamic society, in which military prowess and male honor were valued. Women remained firmly subordinate to men, who could have up to four wives, could divorce them at will, and often kept women segregated from other men. When in public, Islamic women in many regions adopted the Syriac Christian practice of wearing a veil that covers all of the face but the eyes. Islam did, however, forbid female infanticide, a common practice in pre-Islamic society. Brides, and not their fathers or other male relatives, received the dowry from their husbands, thus making marriage more a partnership than a sale. All wives had to be treated equally. If a man was unable to do so, he had to limit himself to a single wife. Islamic women acquired inheritance and property rights and gained protection against mistreatment in marriage. Although they remained second-class in status, at least women had a status, recognized and protected within the Umma. (See "Harems and Gynaiconites," pp. 204–205.)

The rapid spread of Islam within the Arab world can be explained by a number of religious and material factors. Perhaps most attractive, though actually least important, was the sensuous vision of the afterlife promised to believers. Paradise is presented as a world of refreshing streams and leafy bowers, where redeemed men lie upon divans, eat exotic foods served by handsome youths, and are entertained by beautiful virgins called Houris, created especially for them by Allah. Probably more compelling than the description of heaven was the promise of the torments awaiting nonbelievers on the day of judgment. "For the wrong-doers we have prepared a fire which will encompass them like the walls of a pavilion. When they cry out for a drink they shall be showered with water as hot as melted brass, which will scald their faces. Evil shall be their drink, dismal their resting-place." But as central as these otherworldly considerations were, the concrete attractions of Islam in this world were equally important. These included both economic prosperity and the opportunity to continue a lifestyle of raiding and warfare in the name of Allah.

Muhammad won over the leaders of the Quraysh by making Mecca the sacred city of Islam and by retaining the Ka'bah, cleansed of idols, as the center of Islamic pilgrimage. Not unlike the Roman courtiers of Constantine's day who rapidly adopted Christianity, the once disdainful elite now rushed to convert and reestablish their preeminent position within the community. The rapid rehabilitation of old families such as the Umayyads greatly disturbed many of Muhammad's earliest followers, especially those from Medina whose timely invitation had been essential in launching the Prophet's career.

Muhammad's message spread to other tribes through diplomatic and occasionally military means. The divisive nature of Bedouin society contributed to

A manuscript illustration showing a party of Muslim pilgrims on their way to Mecca. Every able Muslim man is required to make the pilgrimage once in his lifetime.

Harems and Gynaiconites

"Lay injunctions on women kindly," Muhammad is reputed to have said in his farewell address to his followers. "You have taken them only as a trust from God." Islamic teachers did not share with many Christian monks and clerics the notion of woman as the source of evil and sin, the weak temptress and daughter of Eve. Nevertheless, Islamic society was unambiguously male-oriented. Women were firmly excluded from public view and, in normal circumstances, from public roles. As in pre-Islamic times, Muslims practiced resource polygyny, much like the Germanic tribes in Europe. Although most men could afford only one wife, the rich and powerful might have several wives (the Qur'an limited the number to four) and numerous concubines and slave women. Muslim conquerors adopted the tradition of veiling women. To safeguard them better, the women were often kept in a harem, a secure and secluded section of the home or palace, where they were watched over by trustworthy eunuchs.

If Byzantines did not remark much on the treatment of women in Islam, it is probably because their own traditions were not very different. Although polygyny was not officially permitted, the practice of veiling women was first popular among the Christians of Syria and was adopted by the Muslims after the conquest. As for the harem, the institution, if not the name, existed in Byzantium as well. The imperial court had its *gynaiconites,* or women's section. Most women seldom left their homes. A Byzantine jurist, describing an earthquake in 1068, remarked with surprise that after the quake women who normally stayed secluded in the interior rooms of their houses "forgot their innate shame" and ran out into the street.

Every rule has its exceptions. In Islam individual women, particularly the mothers of powerful commanders, could exercise considerable indirect power. Al-Khayzuran was a servant in the caliph's household when she bore al-Mahdi, the caliph's son, two boys. After al-Mahdi became caliph in 755, he freed her and married her. She soon became the most important figure in his administration.

Byzantine women could also wield enormous power either in their own right as empress or through their sons and husbands. Anna Dalassena, mother of the emperor Alexius I Comnenus, managed the bureaucracy for her son. Her granddaughter, Anna Comnena, wrote that her father Alexius "took upon himself the wars against the barbarians and whatever battles and combats pertained to them, while he entrusted to his mother the complete management of civil affairs." These were, however, exceptions to normal practice. Women normally had no access to public power, and for every Al-Khayzuran or Anna Dalassena there were thousands of women cut off from the public sphere.

Muslim women, when they did act in public, did so at a decided disadvantage. In matters of inheritance and in witnessing and giving testimony, women, even if free, were valued at one half of a man. Byzantines were also reluctant to allow women to participate in public affairs. In the ninth century Emperor Leo VI (886–912) forbade women to act as witnesses in contracts because "the power to act as witness in the numerous assemblies of men with which they mingle, as well as taking part in public affairs, gives them the habit of speaking more freely than they ought, and, depriving them of the morality and reserve of their sex, encourages them in the exercise of boldness and wickedness, which, to some extent, is even insulting to men."

Subordination, seclusion, and control over women were for both societies a primary means of showing masculine honor and prestige. Byzantines, and especially Muslims, were shocked that Latin Christian women appeared in public, talked to men, and at times exercised "masculine" power. Crusaders and their wives and mistresses were a particular scandal to Muslims. One reported with horror that "the Franks have no trace of jealousy or feeling for the point of honor. One of them may be walking along with his wife, and he meets another man, and this man takes his wife aside and chats with her privately, while the husband stands apart for her to finish her conversation; and if she takes too long he leaves her alone with the companion and goes away." A later Muslim visitor to France concluded that "in France women are of higher station than men, so that they do what they wish and go where they please; and the greatest lord shows respect and courtesy beyond all limits to the humblest of women." To be delivered from such scandal, one Muslim visitor to Europe "prayed to God to save us from the wretched state of these infidels who are devoid of manly jealousy and are sunk in unbelief."

his success. Frequently, factions within other tribes turned to Muhammad for mediation and support against their rivals. In return for his assistance, petitioners accepted his religious message. Since the Qur'an commanded Muslims to destroy idol worship, conversion provided the occasion for holy wars (jihads) of conquest and profitable raids against their still-pagan neighbors. Converts showed their piety by sending part of their spoils as alms to Medina. The Qur'an permitted Christians and Jews living under the authority of Islamic communities to continue to practice their faith, but they were forced to pay a head tax shared among members of the Umma.

The Spread of Islam

Muhammad died in the summer of 632 after a short illness, leaving no successor and no directions concerning the leadership of the Umma. Immediately his closest and most influential followers selected Abu Bakr (632–634), the fourth convert to Islam, to be caliph, or successor of the Prophet. Abu Bakr and, after his death two years later, the caliph 'Umar (634–644) faced formidable obstacles. Within the Umma, tensions between the early Medina followers of the Prophet and the Meccan elite were beginning to surface. A more

critical problem was that the tribes that had accepted the Prophet's leadership believed that his death freed them from their treaty obligations. Now they attempted to go their own ways. Some sent emissaries to announce that, while they would remain Muslims, they would no longer pay alms. Others attempted to abandon Islam altogether.

To prevent the collapse of the Umma, Abu Bakr launched a war of reconversion. Purely by chance, this war developed into wars of conquest that reached far beyond the Arab world. Commanded by Khalid ibn al-Walid (d. 642), the greatest early Islamic general, Muslim forces defeated tribe after tribe and brought them back into the Umma. But long-term survival demanded expansion.

Since Muslims were forbidden to raid fellow believers and raids were an integral part of Bedouin life, the only way to keep recently converted Bedouin in line was to lead them on military expeditions against non-Muslims. Khalid and his armies were people of the desert, and they used this sea of sand as the British Empire would later use the oceans in the nineteenth century. Arab armies could move men and supplies quickly across the arid wastes, crush their enemies, and then retreat back into the desert, beyond the reach of Byzantine and Sassanid forces. Under Abu Bakr, Mus-

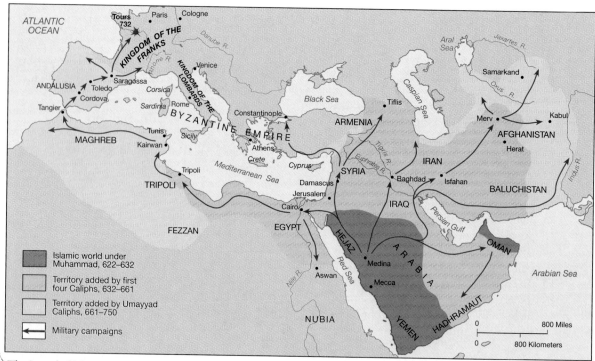

The Spread of Islam

lim expansion covered all of Arabia. Under ʿUmar, Islam conquered Iran, Iraq, Syria, and Egypt.

The swift and total collapse of the Sassanid Empire and the major portion of the Byzantine Empire astounded contemporaries, not least the Muslims themselves. Their success seemed to be irrefutable proof that Muhammad's message was from God. By 650 Islam stretched from Egypt to Asia Minor, from the Mediterranean to the Indus River.

Of course, there were other factors that contributed to the Muslims' phenomenal success. Protracted wars between the Byzantine and Sassanid empires and internal divisions within the Byzantine world helped. For over a decade, Egypt, Palestine, and Syria had been under Persian control. Although eventually reconquered by the Byzantine emperor Heraclius, these provinces had not yet recovered from the decades of warfare, and within them a whole generation had grown up with no experience of Byzantine government.

In addition, the reimposed Byzantine yoke was widely resented because of profound cultural differences between Greeks and the inhabitants of Syria, Iraq, and Egypt. Many looked on the Byzantines not as the liberators but as the enemy. Syria and Egypt had always been different from the rest of the Roman world. Although their great cities of Antioch and Alexandria had long been centers of Hellenistic learning and culture, the hinterlands of each enjoyed ancient cultural traditions totally alien to those of their urban neighbors. In Syria, this rural society was Aramaic- and Arabic-speaking. In Egypt, it was Coptic. With the steady decay of urban life and the rising demands on the rural economy, these local traditions rose to greater prominence. Eventually these traditions coalesced around religious customs sustained by liturgies in the vernacular and sharply at odds with the Orthodox Christianity of Constantinople.

These profound cultural, ethnic, and social antagonisms were largely fought out in the sphere of doctrine, particularly over the nature of Jesus the Christ. The form of Christianity that the emperors sought to impose, defined at the Council of Chalcedon in 451, insisted that Jesus was only one person but had two complete natures, one fully human, the other entirely divine. Such a distinction rested less on the language of the New Testament than on the Greek philosophical tradition. To the Syrian and Egyptian communities, this position was heresy. "Anathema to the unclean Synod of Chalcedon!" wrote one Egyptian monk. Closer to the Jewish tradition of the transcendence of God, the Syriac and Egyptian Monophysite (meaning "one nature") Christians insisted that Jesus had but a single nature and that it was divine.

The two groups vented their intense hatred of each other in riots, murders, and vicious persecutions directed by zealous emperors. As a result, for many Christians of the Near East, the arrival of the Muslims, whose beliefs about the unity and transcendence of God were close to their own and who promised religious toleration and an end to persecution, was seen initially as a divine blessing.

Many Christians and Jews in Syria, Palestine, Egypt, and North Africa shared this view of the Muslim conquest as liberation rather than enslavement. Jews and Christians may have been second-class citizens in the Islamic world, but at least they had a defined place. Conquered populations were allowed to practice their religion in peace. Their only obligation was to pay a head tax to their conquerors, a burden considerably less onerous than the money exacted by Byzantine tax collectors.

The Byzantines' defeat of the Sassanids indirectly facilitated the Muslims' conquest of Iraq. When the Bedouin realized that the Persians were too weakened to protect their empire against raiders, they intensified their attacks. Soon, recent converts to Islam, too late to profit from the conquests of Syria and Egypt, were spearheading the conquest. By 650 the great Sassanid Empire had disappeared and the Byzantine Empire had lost Egypt, Syria, Mesopotamia, Palestine, portions of Asia Minor, and much of North Africa. During the reigns of Constantine IV (668–685) and Leo III (717–741), Constantinople itself fought for its own survival against besieging Muslim fleets. Each time it survived only through the use of a secret weapon, so-called Greek fire, an explosive liquid that burst into flame when sprayed by siphons onto enemy ships. Although the city itself survived, the Muslim conquests left the once-vast empire a small state reduced to little more than Greece, western Asia Minor, southern Italy, and the Balkans.

Authority and Government in Islam

Conquering the world for Islam proved easier than governing it. What had begun as a religious movement within Arabian society had created a vast multinational empire in which Arabs were a tiny minority. Nothing in the Qurʾan, nothing in Arabian experience, provided a blueprint for empire. Thus, the Muslims' ability to consolidate their conquests is even more remarkable than the conquests themselves. Within the first decades

The terrifying weapon known as Greek fire is turned on an enemy during a naval battle. This early example of chemical warfare was a mixture of unknown ingredients that ignited and burned furiously when it came into contact with water. The sailors in the illustration are using it like a flamethrower.

following the death of the Prophet, two models of governance emerged, models that continue to dominate Islamic politics to the present.

The first model was that of pre-Islamic tribal authority. The Umma could be considered a supertribe, governed by leaders whose authority came from their secular power as leaders of the superior military and economic elements within the community. This model appealed particularly to Quraysh and local tribal leaders who had exercised authority before Muhammad. The second model was that of the authority exercised by the Prophet. In this model, the Umma was more than a supertribe, and its unity and purity had to be preserved by a religiously sanctioned rule exercised by a member of the Prophet's own family. This model was preferred by many of the more recent converts to Islam, especially the poor. Governance under each of the two models was attempted successively in the seventh and eighth centuries.

Regardless of their disagreements on the basis of political authority, both groups adopted the administrative systems of their conquered lands. Byzantine and Sassanid bureaucracy and government, only slightly adjusted, became the models for government in the Islamic world until the twentieth century. In Syria and Egypt, Byzantine officials and even churchmen were incorporated into the government, much as had been the case in Europe following the Germanic conquests. For example, John of Damascus (ca. 676–ca. 754), a Christian theologian venerated as a saint, served as the caliph's chief councillor. His faithfulness to the Islamic government and opposition to Byzantine imperial iconoclasm earned him the title of "cursed favorer of Saracens [Muslims]" from the Byzantine emperor.

Likewise, the Muslims left intact the social structures and economic systems of the empires they conquered. Lands remained in the hands of their previous owners. Only state property or, in the Sassanid Empire,

that of the Zoroastrian priesthood, became common property of the Muslim community. The monastery of Saint Catherine on Mount Sinai, founded by the emperor Justinian around 540, for example, survived without serious harm and still shelters Orthodox monks today.

The division of the spoils of conquest badly divided the Umma and precipitated the first crises in the caliphate. Under 'Umar, two groups received most of the spoils of the conquests. First were the earliest followers of the Prophet, who received a disproportionate share of revenues. Second were the conquerors themselves, who were often recent converts from tribes on the fringes of Arabia. After 'Umar's death, his successor 'Uthman (d. 656), a member of the powerful Umayya clan of Mecca, attempted to consolidate control over Islam by Quraysh elite. He began to reduce the privileges of early converts in favor of the old Meccan elite. At the same time, he demanded that revenue from the provinces be sent to Medina. The result was rebellion, both within Arabia and in Egypt. 'Uthman's only firm support lay in distant Syria, ruled by members of his own clan. Abandoned at home and abroad, he was finally murdered as he sat reading the Qur'an in his home.

In spite of 'Uthman's unpopularity, his murder sent shockwaves throughout the Umma. The fate of his successor, Muhammad's beloved son-in-law and nephew 'Ali (656–661), had an even more serious effect on the future of Islam. Although chosen as fourth caliph, 'Ali was immediately charged with complicity in 'Uthman's murder and strongly opposed by the Umayyad commander of Syria. To protect himself, 'Ali moved the caliphate from Arabia to Iraq. There he sought the support of underprivileged recent converts by stressing the equality of all believers and the religious role of the caliph, who was to be less governor and tax collector than spiritual guide of Islam.

'Ali's spiritual appeal could not make up for his political weakness. At home and abroad his support gradually crumbled as the Quraysh and their Syrian supporters gained the upper hand. In 661 'Ali was murdered by supporters of his Umayyad rivals. Still, the memory of the "last orthodox caliph" remained alive in the Islamic world, especially in Iraq and Iran. Centuries later, a tradition developed in Baghdad that legitimate leadership of Islam could come only from the house of 'Ali. Adherents of this belief developed into a political and religious sect known as Shi'ism. Although frequently persecuted as heretical by the majority of Muslims, Shi'ism remains a potent minority movement within the Islamic world today.

The immediate effect of 'Ali's death, however, was the triumph of the old Quraysh and in particular the Umayyads, who established at Damascus in Syria a caliphate that lasted a century. The Umayyads made no attempt to base their rule on spiritual authority. Instead, they ruled as secular leaders, attempting to unite the Islamic empire through an appeal to Arab unity. Profits from this state went entirely to the Quraysh and members of Arabian tribes who formed the backbone of the early Umayyad army, monopolized high administration, and acquired rich estates throughout the empire.

The Umayyads extended the Islamic empire to its farthest reaches. In the north, armies from Syria marched into Anatolia and were only stopped in 677 by the Byzantine fleet before Constantinople itself. In the east, Umayyad armies pressed as far as the Syr Darya River on the edge of the Chinese T'ang empire. In the south and southwest, Umayyad progress was even more successful. After the conquest of the Mediterranean coast of Africa, the general Tariq ibn Ziyad (d. ca. 720) in 711 crossed the strait separating Morocco from Spain near the Rock of Gibraltar (the name comes from the Arabic *jabal Tariq,* "Tariq's mountain"). He quickly conquered virtually the entire peninsula. Soon raiding parties had ventured as far north as the Loire Valley in what is today France. There they were halted by the Frankish commander Charles Martel in 732. Much of Spain, however, remained part of the Dar al-Harab (the House of Islam) until 1492.

The Umayyad caliphate's external success in conquering failed to extend to its dealings with the internal tensions of the Umma. The Umayyads could not build a stable empire on the twin foundations of a tiny Arabian elite and a purely secular government taken over from their Byzantine predecessors. Arabs, as well as Jews, Zoroastrians, and Christians, converted in great numbers. Not all Muslim commanders looked favor-

ably on such conversions. Far from practicing "conversion by the sword," as was often the case in Christian missionary activity, Muslim leaders at times even discouraged the spread of Islam among the non-Arabs they had conquered. The reason was simple. Christians and Jews had to pay the head tax imposed upon them. If they converted, they no longer paid the tax. In time, this growing population of non-Arab Muslims began to demand a share in the empire's wealth.

Not only were the numbers of Muslims increasing, so also was their fervor. Growing numbers of devout Muslims—Arabs and non-Arabs alike—were convinced that leadership had to be primarily spiritual and that this spiritual mandate was the exclusive right of the family of the Prophet. Ultimately, a coalition of dissatisfied Persian Muslims and Arabian religious reformers united under the black banners of the descendants of Muhammad's paternal uncle, 'Abbas (566–ca. 653). In 750 this group overthrew the Umayyads everywhere but in Spain and established a new caliphate in favor of the 'Abbasids.

With the fall of the Umayyad caliphate, Arabs lost control of Islam forever. The 'Abbasids attempted to govern the empire according to religious principles. These were found in the Qur'an and in the *sunnah,* or

A fifteenth-century Persian miniature showing the Tigris River flooding parts of Baghdad, the 'Abbassid capital.

practices established by the Prophet, and preserved first orally and then in the *hadith,* or traditions, which were somewhat comparable to the Christian Gospels. This new empire was to be a universal Muslim commonwealth in which Arabs had no privileged position. "Whoever speaks Arabic is an Arab," ran a popular saying. The 'Abbasids had risen to power as "the group of the saved," and they hoped to make the moral community of Islam the cornerstone of their government, with obedience to 'Abbasid authority an integral part of Islamic belief.

The institutional foundations of the new caliphate, however, like those of the Umayyads, remained firmly in the ancient empires they had conquered. The great caliph Mansur (754–775) moved the capital from Damascus to Baghdad, an acknowledgment of the crucial role of Iraqi and Iranian military and economic strength. The city, a few miles from the ruins of Ctesiphon on the Tigris River, was largely constructed from building stones hauled by slaves from the old city to the new. In the same manner, the 'Abbasids constructed an autocratic imperial system on the model of their Persian predecessors. With their claims to divine sanction as members of the "holy family" and their firm control of the military, increasingly composed of slave armies known as Mamluks, the 'Abbasids governed the Islamic empire at its zenith.

Ultimately, however, the 'Abbasids were no more successful than the Umayyads in maintaining authority over the whole Muslim world. By the tenth century, local military commanders, termed *emirs,* took control of provincial governments in many areas while preserving the fiction that they were appointed by the 'Abbasid caliphs. The caliphs maintained the symbolic unity of Islam while the emirs went their separate ways. The majority of Muslims accepted this situation as a necessary compromise. In contrast to the Shi'ites, who continued to look for a leader from the family of 'Ali, the Sunnis, as they came to be known, remain to the present the majority group of Muslims. The Sunnis had no fixed theory of government or succession to the caliphate. Instead, they accepted the events of history in a practical manner, secure in the truth of the hadith: "My Umma will never agree upon an error."

In the west the 'Abbasids could not maintain even a facade of unity. Supporters of 'Ali's family had never accepted the 'Abbasid claims to be the legitimate spiritual leaders of the Islamic community. These Shi'ites launched sporadic revolts and separatist movements. The most successful was that of 'Ubayd Allah the Fatimid (d. 934), who claimed to be the descendant of

'Ali and rightful leader of Islam. In 909, with the support of North African seminomadic Berbers, he declared himself caliph in defiance of the 'Abbasids at Baghdad. In 969 'Ubayd's Fatimid successors conquered Egypt and established a new city, Cairo, as the capital of their rival caliphate. By the middle of the eleventh century, the Fatimid caliphate controlled all of North Africa, Sicily, Syria, and western Arabia.

In Umayyad Spain, although the Muslim population remained firmly Sunni, the powerful emir 'Abd ar-Rahman III (891–961) took a similar step. In 929 he exchanged his title for that of caliph, thus making his position religious as well as secular. Everywhere the political and religious unity of Islam was being torn apart.

The arrival in all three caliphates of Muslim peoples not yet integrated into the civilization of the Mediterranean world accelerated this disintegration. From the east, Seljuk Turks, long used as slave troops, entered Iraq and in 1055 conquered Baghdad. Within a decade they had conquered Iran, Syria, and Palestine as well. Around the same time Moroccan Berbers conquered much of North Africa and Spain, while Bedouin raided freely in Libya and Tunisia. These invasions by Muslims from the fringes of the Islamic commonwealth had catastrophic effects on the Islamic world. The Turks, unaccustomed to commerce and to the administrative traditions of the caliphate, divided their empire among their war leaders, displacing traditional landowners and disrupting commerce. The North African Berbers and Bedouin destroyed the agricultural and commercial systems that had survived successive Vandal, Byzantine, and Arabian invasions.

Islamic Civilization

The Islamic conquest of the seventh century brought peace to Iraq and Iran after generations of struggle and set the stage for a major agricultural recovery. In the tradition of their Persian predecessors, the caliphs organized vast irrigation systems, which made Mesopotamia the richest agricultural region west of China. Peasants and slaves raised dates and olives in addition to wheat, barley, and rice. Sophisticated hydraulics and scientific agriculture brought great regions of Mesopotamia and the Mediterranean coast into cultivation for the first time in centuries.

By uniting the Mediterranean world with Arabia and India, the 'Abbasid empire created the greatest trade network ever seen. Muslim merchants met in busy, bustling ports on the Persian Gulf and the Red Sea. There they traded silk, paper, spices, and horses

Arab astronomers made many advances. They perfected the astrolabe, an instrument used to observe and calculate the positions of heavenly bodies.

the majority language, Arabic vocabulary and structure transformed the traditional language. While 'Abassid political unity was falling apart, this new civilization was reaching its first great synthesis. As desert conquerors, the Arabs might have been expected to destroy or ignore the heritage of Persian and Hellenistic culture. Instead, they became its protectors and preservers. As early as the eighth century, caliphs collected Persian, Greek, and Syriac scientific and philosophical works and had them translated into Arabic. Legal scholars concerned with the authenticity of hadith used Greek rationalist methods to distinguish genuine from spurious traditions. Religious mystics called Sufis blended Neoplatonic and Muslim traditions to create new forms of religious devotion. The medical writings of Hippocrates and Galen circulated widely in the Islamic world, and Muslim physicians were by far the most competent and respected in the West through the fifteenth century. Mathematics and astronomy were both practical and theoretical fields. Muslim intellectuals introduced the so-called Arabic numerals from India and by the tenth century had perfected the use of decimal fractions and algebra. Although theoretical astronomy was limited to reforming rather than recasting Ptolemaic theory, Muslim astronomers absorbed and continued the highly accurate traditions of Mesopotamian planetary observation. The tables they compiled were more accurate than those known in the Byzantine and Latin worlds.

Although most Islamic scientists were professional physicians, astronomers, or lawyers, they were also deeply concerned with abstract philosophical questions, particularly those raised by the works of Plato and Aristotle, which had been translated into Arabic. Many sought to reconcile Islam with this philosophical heritage in the same manner that Origen and Augustine had done for Christianity. Ya'qub al-Kindi (d. 873), the first Arab philosopher, noted that "The truth . . . must be taken wherever it is to be found, whether it be in the past or among strange peoples." The Persian physician Ibn Sina (980–1037), known in the West as Avicenna, wrote over a hundred works on all aspects of science and philosophy. He compiled a vast encyclopedia of knowledge in which he attempted to synthesize Aristotelian thought into a Neoplatonic view of the universe. In the next century the Cordoban philosopher Ibn Rushd (1126–98), called Averroës in the West, went still further, teaching an authentic Aristotelian philosophy stripped of Neoplatonic mystical trappings. His commentaries on Aristotle were enormously influential even outside the Islamic world. For

from China for silver and cotton from India. Gold from the Sudan was exchanged for iron from Persia. Carpets from Armenia and Tabaristan, in what is now Iran, were traded, and from western Europe came slaves. Much of these luxury goods found their way to Baghdad, known as the marketplace for the world.

Baghdad and other Muslim cities were marketplaces for ideas as well as for merchandise. Within a few generations, descendants of Bedouin established themselves in the great cities of the ancient Near East and absorbed the traditions of Persian, Roman, and Hellenistic civilizations. However, unlike the Germanic peoples of western Europe, who quickly adopted the Latin language and Roman Christianity, the Muslims recast Persian and Hellenistic culture in an Arabic form. Even in Iran, where Farsi, or Persian, survived as

As heirs to the great medical learning of Hellenistic civilization, easterners, Muslim and Christian alike, had nothing but contempt for western medical and surgical practices, especially as employed by crusaders. Even if exaggerated, the following description, written by Usama ibn Munqidh, a highly educated and cultured twelfth-century emir or military commander who had firsthand knowledge of Latin crusaders, conveys the gulf that separated Arabian and western medical practice.

The ruler of Munaitira [a crusader fortress in what is now Lebanon] wrote to my uncle asking him to send a doctor to treat some of his followers who were ill. My uncle sent a Christian called Tabit. After only ten days he returned and we said, "You cured them quickly!" This was his story: "They took me to see a knight who had an abscess on his leg, and a woman with consumption. I applied a poultice to the leg, and the abscess opened and began to heal. I prescribed a cleansing and refreshing diet for the woman. Then there appeared a Frankish doctor, who said: 'This man has no idea how to cure these people!' He turned to the knight and said: 'Which would you prefer, to live with one leg or to die with two?' When the knight replied that he would prefer to live with one leg, he sent for a strong man and a sharp axe. They arrived, and I stood by to watch. The doctor supported the leg on a block of wood,

and said to the man: 'Strike a mighty blow, and cut cleanly!' And there, before my eyes, the fellow struck the knight one blow, and then another, for the first had not finished the job. The marrow spurted out of the leg, and the patient died instantaneously. Then the doctor examined the woman and said: 'She has a devil in her head who is in love with her. Cut her hair off!' This was done, and she went back to eating her usual Frankish food, garlic, and mustard, which made her illness worse. 'The devil has got into her brain,' pronounced the doctor. He took a razor and cut a cross on her head, and removed the brain so that the inside of the skull was laid bare. Then he rubbed [it] with salt; the woman died instantly. At this juncture, I asked whether they had any further need of me, and as they had none I came away, having learnt things about medical methods that I never knew before."

Christian philosophers of the thirteenth century, Averroës was known simply as "the Commentator."

At the same time that Muslim thought and culture was at its most creative, Islam faced invasion from a new and unaccustomed quarter: Constantinople. In the tenth and early eleventh centuries, the Byzantines pressed the local rulers of northern Syria and Iraq in a series of raids that reached as far as the border of Palestine. At the end of the eleventh century, western Europeans, encouraged and supported by the Byzantines, captured Jerusalem and established a Western-style kingdom in Palestine that survived for over a century. Once more, Constantinople was a power in the Mediterranean world.

The revelations to the prophet Muhammad led to one of the greatest transformations the world has ever known. Islam forged a united Arabian people who went on to conquer more of Asia, Africa, and Europe than had any military empire in history. This conquest in the name of Allah created a vast religious and commercial zone in which ideas and cultures flowed as freely as silks and spices. The Arabians soon lost political control of the Islamic movement, but their religious

tradition and its emphasis on worship of the one God remains an enduring legacy in world civilization.

The Byzantine Apogee and Decline, 1000–1453

During the tenth and eleventh centuries, Byzantium dominated the Mediterranean world for the last time. Imperial armies under the Macedonian dynasty (867–1059) began to recover some lands lost to Islam during the previous two centuries. Antioch was retaken in 969, and for over a century Byzantine armies operated in Syria and pushed to the border of Palestine. By the middle of the eleventh century, Armenia and Georgia, which had formed independent principalities, had been reintegrated into the empire. To the west, Sicily remained in Muslim hands, but southern Italy, which had been subject to Muslim raids and western barbarian occupation, was secured once more. Byzantine fleets recaptured Crete, cleared the Aegean of Muslim pirates, and reopened the vital commercial sea routes.

THE BYZANTINE EMPIRE AND THE RISE OF ISLAM

527–565	**Reign of Justinian**
610	**Muhammad's vision**
662	**The Hijra, Muhammad's journey from Mecca to Medina**
726–787	**First phase of iconoclast dispute**
732	**Muslim advance halted by Franks**
750	**'Abbasids overthrow Umayyads; take control of Muslim world**
802–843	**Second phase of iconoclast dispute**
843	**Empress Theodora ends iconoclast persecution; restores image veneration**
867–1059	**Macedonian dynasty rules Byzantine Empire; begins recovering lands from Muslims**
1054	**Schism splits churches of Rome and Constantinople**
1071	**Robert Guiscard captures Sicily and southern Italy; Battle of Manzikert; Seljuk Turks defeat Byzantines**
1099	**First Crusade establishes Latin kingdom in Jerusalem**
1221	**Genghis Khan leads Mongol army into Persia**
1453	**Constantinople falls to Ottomans**

To the north, missionaries spread Byzantine culture as well as the Christian religion among the Slavic peoples beyond the frontiers of the empire. The most important missionaries were the brothers Cyril (ca. 827–869) and Methodius (ca. 827–885), who preached to the Khazars and the Moravians. They also invented the Cyrillic alphabet, which they used to translate the Bible and other Christian writings into Slavic. Their missionary activities laid the foundation for the conversion of Serbia, Bulgaria, and Russia. In 1018 Basil II (976–1025) destroyed the Bulgarian kingdom and brought peace to the Balkan peninsula.

The conquests of the Macedonian dynasty laid the foundation for a short-lived economic prosperity and cultural renaissance. Conquered lands, particularly Anatolia, brought new agricultural wealth. Security of the sea fostered a resurgence of commerce, and customs duties enriched the imperial treasury. New wealth financed the flourishing of Byzantine art and literature. However, just as in the spheres of Byzantine liturgy and court ceremonial, the goal of Byzantine art was not to reflect the transient "reality" of this world but rather the permanent, classic values inherited from the past. Thus, rarely in Byzantine art, literature, or religion was innovation appreciated or cultivated. The language, style, and themes of classical Greek literature, philosophy, and history completely dominated Byzantine culture. Only in rare works such as the popular epic *Digenis Akrites* does something of the flavor of popular Byzantine life appear. The title of the work means roughly "the border defender born of two peoples," for the hero, Basil, was the son of a Muslim father and a Christian Greek mother. The epic consists of two parts, one describing the exploits of the hero's father, a Muslim emir or general, and the other describing the exploits of the hero, Digenis Akrites, as he fights both Muslims and bandits. The portrayal of the hero's battles, his encounters with wild beasts and dragons, and his heroic death, as well as descriptions of his intelligence, learning, and magnificent palace, are at once part of the Western epic tradition and a reflection of life on the edge of the empire. *Digenis Akrites* is unique for its close relation to popular oral traditions of Byzantine society.

Another picture of Byzantine life was created by cultivated authors who were able to master completely their ancient models and to fashion within these inherited forms of literature compelling works of enduring value. One such author was the historian and imperial courtier Michael Psellus (1018–ca. 1078). His firsthand descriptions of rampaging mobs in Constantinople, hounding their enemies "like wild beasts," his acute analyses of imperial politics, and his descriptions of the inner workings of court intrigues bring to life Byzantine society at its height.

The Disintegration of the Empire

In all domains, however, the successes of the Macedonian emperors set the stage for serious problems. Rapid military expansion and economic growth allowed new elites to establish themselves as autonomous powers and to position themselves between the imperial administration and the people. The constant demand for troops always exceeded the supply of traditional salaried soldiers. In the eleventh century, emperors began to grant imperial estates to great magnates in return for military service. These grants, termed *pronoia,* often included immunity from imperial taxation and the right to certain administrative activities traditionally carried out by the central government. The practice created in effect a largely independent landed military aristocracy that stood between the peasantry and the imperial government. This policy weakened the centralized state and reduced its income from taxes.

As generals became dissatisfied with the civilian central administration, they began to turn their armies against the emperors, launching over thirty revolts in as many years. To defend itself against both the Muslims without and the generals within, the central government, composed of intellectuals, eunuchs, and urban aristocrats, had to spend vast sums on mercenary armies. These armies, composed largely of Armenians, Germans, and Normans, soon began to plunder the empire they were hired to protect. Further danger came from other, independent Normans who, under their commander Robert Guiscard (ca. 1015–85), conquered Byzantine Bari and southern Italy and then Muslim Sicily. Soon Guiscard was threatening the empire itself. The hostility between military aristocracy and imperial administration largely destroyed the tradition of civilian government. "Do not wish to be a bureaucrat," one general advised his son. "It is not possible to be both a general and a comedian."

Under increasing pressure from local magnates on the one hand and desperate imperial tax collectors on the other, villages began to make deals with powerful patrons who would represent them in return for the surrender of their independence. Through the eleventh and twelfth centuries, the Byzantine peasantry passed from the condition of individualism without freedom to collectivism without freedom. Through the same process landlords and patrons acquired the means to exercise a political role, which ended the state's monopoly on public power.

At the same time that civil war and external pressure were destroying the provincial administration, Byzantine disdain for commerce was weakening the empire's ability to control its income from customs duties. Initially the willingness to turn over commerce to Italians and others posed few problems. Those engaged in actual commerce were for the most part citizens of the empire and were in any case subject to the 10 percent tariffs. However, in the tenth and eleventh centuries, merchants of Amalfi, Bari, and then Venice came to dominate Byzantine commerce. Venetian merchant fleets could double as a powerful navy in times of need, and by the eleventh century the Venetians were the permanent military and commercial power in the Mediterranean. When Robert Guiscard and his Nor-

mans threatened the empire, the emperors had to turn to the Venetians for protection and were forced to cede them major economic privileges. The Venetians acquired the right to maintain important self-governing communities in major ports throughout the empire and were allowed to pay lower tariffs than the Byzantines paid.

In 1071, the year that Robert Guiscard captured the last Byzantine city in Italy, the empire suffered an even more disastrous defeat in the east. At Manzikert in Anatolia the emperor Romanus IV (1067–71) and his unreliable mercenary army fell to the Seljuk Turks, who captured Romanus. The defeat at Manzikert sealed the fate of the empire. Anatolia was lost and the gradual erosion of the empire in both the west and the east had begun.

The Conquests of Constantinople and Baghdad

At the end of the eleventh century, the Comnenian dynasty (1081–1185) briefly halted the political and economic chaos of the empire. Rather than fighting the tendency of the centralized state to devolve into a decentralized aristocratic one, Alexius I Comnenus (1081–1118) tied the aristocracy to his family, thus making it an instrument of imperial government. In the short run the process was successful. He expanded the use of pronoia to strengthen loyal aristocrats, and he granted them offices in the central administration that had been traditionally reserved for eunuchs. He stabilized Byzantine currency, which was the international exchange medium in the Islamic and Christian worlds and which had been dangerously devalued by his predecessors. Still, by the late twelfth century, the empire was a vulnerable second-rate power caught between Latin Europe and Islam.

Initially, the Christian West was a more deadly threat than the Islamic East. In the eleventh century, after more than five hundred years of economic and political weakness, western Europe was beginning to reach parity with Byzantium. Robert Guiscard and his Normans, who had conquered Sicily and southern Italy, were typical examples of the powerful, militaristic aristocracy developing in the remains of the old western empire. This military threat from the west was paralleled by a religious one. In the centuries that Rome had been largely cut off from Constantinople, western Christianity had developed a number of rituals and beliefs differing from Orthodox practice. This parting of the ways had already appeared during the iconoclas-

The Byzantine emperor Alexius I Comnenus appealed to the West for help in fighting the Muslims.

tic controversies of the eighth and ninth centuries. In the eleventh century it was directed by an independent and self-assertive papacy in Rome, which claimed supreme authority throughout Christendom. Disagreements between the patriarchs of Constantinople and the popes of Rome prevented cooperation between the two Christian worlds and led to further deterioration of relationships between Greeks and Latins. These disagreements came to a head in 1054, when the papal representative, or legate, Cardinal Humbert (ca. 1000–61) met with the patriarch of Constantinople, Michael Cerularius (ca. 1000–59), to negotiate ecclesiastical control over southern Italy and Sicily. Humbert was arrogant and demanding, Michael Cerularius haughty and uncompromising. Acting beyond his authority, Humbert excommunicated the patriarch and all his followers. The patriarch responded in kind, excommunicating Humbert and all connected with him. This formal excommunication was lifted in the 1960s, but the schism, or split, between the churches of Rome and Constantinople continues today.

Excommunication was probably the least of the dangers the Byzantines faced from the west. The full fury of this ignorant, greedy, and violent western society reached the empire when, after the defeat at Manzikert, the emperor Alexius called on western Christians for support against the Muslims. To his horror, adventurers of every sort eager to conquer land and wealth in the name of the cross flooded the empire. In the penetrating and often cynical biography of her father, Alexius's daughter Anna (ca. 1083–1148) describes how, as quickly as possible, Alexius hurried these crusaders (from the Latin *cruciata*, "marked with a cross") on to Palestine before they could turn their violence against his empire. Even while recognizing that the crusaders were uncouth and barbarous, the Byzantines had to admit that the Latins were effective. Despite enormous hardships, the First Crusade was able to take advantage of division in the Muslim world to conquer Palestine and establish a Latin kingdom in Jerusalem in 1099.

The crusaders' initial victories and the growth of Latin wealth and power created in Constantinople a temporary enthusiasm for western European styles and customs. The Byzantines soon realized, however, that the Latin kingdom posed a threat not only to Islam but to themselves as well. While crusaders threatened Byzantine territories, Venetian merchants imposed a stranglehold on Byzantine trade. When emperors granted other Italian towns concessions equal to those of the Venetians, they found that they had simply amplified their problems. Anti-Latin sentiment reached the boiling point in 1183. In the riots that broke out in that year, Italians and other westerners in Constantinople were murdered and their goods seized. Just twenty-one years later, in 1204, a wayward crusade, encouraged by Venice, turned aside from its planned expedition to Palestine to capture a bigger prize—Constantinople. After pillaging the city for three days—the Byzantine survivors commented that even the Saracens would have been less cruel—the westerners established one of their own as emperor and installed a Venetian as patriarch.

The Byzantines did manage to hold on to a portion of their empire centering on Nicaea, and before long the Latins fell to bickering among themselves. In 1261 the ruler of Nicaea, Michael Palaeologus (ca. 1224–82), recaptured Constantinople with the assistance of the Genoese and had himself crowned emperor in the Hagia Sophia. Still, the empire was fatally shattered, its disintegration into autonomous lordships complete. The restored empire consisted of little more

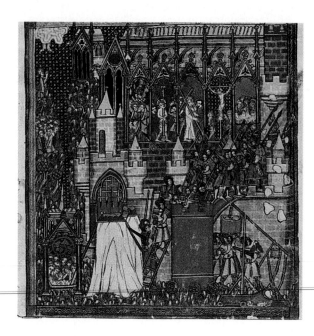

The battle of Jerusalem is illustrated in this twelfth-century manuscript. Events in the life of Jesus are shown at the top, as in stained-glass windows. Crusaders storm the walls while siege engines hurl stones at the defenders.

From the ruins of the Seljuk kingdom arose a variety of small Turkish principalities, or emirates. After the collapse of the Mongol empire, one of these emirates, the Ottoman, began to expand at the expense of both the weakened Byzantine and the Mongol-Seljuk empires. In the next centuries the Ottomans expanded east, south, and west. Around 1350, they crossed into the Balkans as Byzantine allies but soon took over the region for themselves. By 1450 the Ottoman stranglehold on Constantinople was complete. The final scene of the conquest, long delayed but inevitable, occurred three years later.

For Greeks and for Italian intellectuals of the Renaissance, the conquest of Constantinople by the Ottomans was the end of an imperial tradition that reached back to Augustus. But Mehmed the Conqueror (1452–81) could as easily be seen as its restorer. True, the city was plundered by the victorious army. But this was simply the way of war in the fifteenth century. The city, its palaces, and its religious edifices fared better under the Turks than they had under its previous Christian conquerors. The Latins had placed a prostitute on the patriarch's throne in the Hagia Sophia. Mehmed, after purging the church of its Christian

than the district around Constantinople, Thessalonica, and the Peloponnesus. Bulgarians and Serbs had expanded far into the Greek mainland. Most of the rich Anatolian regions had been lost to the Turks, and commercial revenues were in the hands of the Genoese allies. The restored empire's survival for almost two hundred years was due less to its own prerogative than to the internal problems of the Islamic world.

The caliphs of Baghdad, like the emperors of Constantinople, succumbed to invaders from the barbarous fringes of their empire. In 1221 the Mongol prince Temujin (ca. 1162–1227), better known to history as Genghis Khan (Universal Ruler), led his conquering army into Persia from central Asia. From there, a portion of the Mongols went north, invading Russia in 1237 and dividing it into small principalities ruled by Slavic princes under Mongol control. In 1258 a Mongol army captured Baghdad and executed the last 'Abbasid caliph, ending a five-hundred-year tradition. The Mongol armies then moved west, shattering the Seljuk principalities in Iraq, Anatolia, and Syria and turning back only before the fierce resistance of the Egyptian Mamluks.

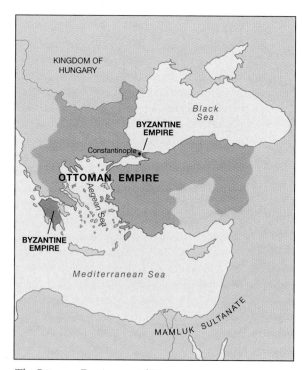

The Ottoman Empire, ca. 1450

trappings, rededicated it to the worship of the one God. Once more Constantinople, for centuries a capital without a country, was the center of a great Mediterranean empire. In the following centuries, Ottoman rule stretched from the gates of Vienna to the Caspian Sea and from the Persian Gulf to the Strait of Gibraltar. The legacy of absolutism, of imperial government, and of cultural pluralism inherited from Sassanid Persia and imperial Rome survived until the beginning of the twentieth century.

* * *

Although often deadly enemies, the Byzantine and Islamic worlds were both genuine heirs of the great eastern empires of antiquity. The traditions of the Assyrian, Alexandrian, Persian, and Roman empires lived on in their cities, their bureaucracies, and their agricultural and commercial systems. Both also shared the monotheistic religious tradition that had emerged from Judaism. In their schools and libraries, they preserved and transmitted the literary and scientific heritage of antiquity. Through Islam, the legacy of the West reached the Far East. Through Byzantium, the peoples of the Slavic world became heirs of the caesars. The inhabitants of western Europe long viewed these two great civilizations with hostility, incomprehension, and fear. Still, in the areas of culture, government, religion, and commerce, the West learned much from its eastern neighbors.

Suggestions for Further Reading

The Byzantines

George Ostrogorsky, *History of the Byzantine State* (Rutgers, NJ: Rutgers University Press, 1969). The standard one-volume history of Byzantium.

Cyril Mango, *Byzantium: The Empire of New Rome* (New York: Scribner's, 1980). An imaginative and provocative reevaluation of the Byzantine world.

Joan M. Hussey, *The Orthodox Church in the Byzantine Empire* (New York: Oxford University Press, 1986). An introduction to Orthodox Christianity.

* Dimitri Obolensky, *The Byzantine Commonwealth: Eastern Europe, 500–1453* (Crestwood, NY: St. Vladimir's Seminary Press, 1983). Relates Byzantium to the Slavic world.

* J. W. Barker, *Justinian and the Later Roman Empire* (Madison, WI: University of Wisconsin Press, 1975). A survey of Justinian's reign intended for a general public.

Speros Vryonis, Jr., *Byzantium and Europe* (New York: Harcourt Brace Jovanovich, 1967). A survey of the relationship between Byzantium and the West.

A. A. Vasiliev, *History of the Byzantine Empire* (Madison, WI: University of Wisconsin Press, 1952). A classic survey of Byzantine history by a great Russian scholar.

Alexander Kazhdan and Giles Constable, *People and Power in Byzantium* (Washington, DC: Dumbarton Oaks, 1982). An imaginative and controversial analysis of Byzantine culture by a Russian Byzantinist and a western medievalist.

The Rise of Islam

* Albert Hourani, *A History of the Arab Peoples* (New York: Warner Books, 1992). A clear and thoughtful survey of Arab history for nonspecialists.

* Bernard Lewis, *The Arabs in History* (New York: Harper & Row, 1966). A well-written general introduction by an authority.

* Hugh Kennedy, *The Prophet and the Age of the Caliphates* (White Plains, NY: Longman, 1986). A valuable summary of the early political history of Islam.

* John L. Esposito, *Women in Muslim Family Law* (Syracuse, NY: Syracuse University Press, 1982). A general introduction to the topic, with historical material in the first two chapters.

G. E. Von Grunebaum, *Classical Islam: A History, 600–1258* (Chicago: Aldine, 1970). A general introduction to early Islamic history.

Aziz Al-Azmeh, *Arabic Thought and Islamic Societies* (London: Routledge, Chapman & Hall, 1986). A demanding but valuable introduction to Islamic intellectual history.

Roy P. Mottahedeh, *Loyalty and Leadership in an Early Islamic Society* (Princeton, NJ: Princeton University Press, 1980). An important introduction to the social values and structures of western Iran and southern Iraq in the tenth and eleventh centuries.

Bernard Lewis, ed., *Islam and the Arab World* (New York: Knopf, 1976). An illustrated collection of essays on Islamic history and culture.

* Bernard Lewis, *The Muslim Discovery of Europe* (New York: W. W. Norton, 1985). Views of the West by Muslim travelers.

The Byzantine Apogee and Decline, 1000–1453

* Michael Agold, *The Byzantine Empire, 1025–1204.* (White Plains, NY: Longman, 1985). A solid recent survey of the Byzantine Empire prior to the capture of Constantinople by the Latins.

* P. M. Holt, *The Age of the Crusades: The Near East from the Eleventh Century to 1517.* (White Plains, NY: Longman, 1986). An excellent up-to-date survey of the political history of the Near East in the later Middle Ages.

*Paperback edition available

8 ❧ THE WEST IN THE EARLY MIDDLE AGES, 500–900

The Chapel at the Waters

The Palatine Chapel in Aachen, now a small German city near the Belgian border, expresses a fascination with the traditions of the Roman past infused with the creativity of a new epoch. These two strands of tradition and change describe Europe during the early Middle Ages, generally the period between 500 and 900. Aachen was a favorite residence of the Frankish king Charles the Great, or Charlemagne (768–814), who often came there to enjoy its natural hot springs. In time it came to be his primary residence and the capital of his vast kingdom, which stretched from central Italy to the mouth of the Rhine River. Around 792 Charlemagne, a descendant of barbarian warriors, commissioned an architect to design a palace as complex as his residence—one that would rival the great Roman and Byzantine buildings of Italy and Constantinople.

Royal agents scoured Europe for Roman ruins from which columns, precious marble, and ornaments could be salvaged and reused. From these ancient stones, masons raised a complex of audience rooms, royal apartments, baths, and quarters for court officials. The whole ensemble was intentionally reminiscent of the Lateran Palace in Rome, which had been the residence of the emperors before being given to the popes.

The central building of Charlemagne's palace complex was the chapel, a symmetrical octagon 300 feet on its principal axes, modeled on San Vitale in Ravenna. The choice of model was significant. Ravenna had been the former capital of Roman Italy and of Theodoric the Great, the Ostrogothic king whom Charlemagne greatly admired. Although modeled on Roman buildings, the Palatine Chapel was admirably suited to the glorification of Charlemagne.

The building was divided into three tiers. The first tier on the ground floor held the sanctuary, where priest and people met for worship. The topmost tier, supported by ancient Roman pillars shipped to Aachen from Rome and Ravenna, represented the heavens. Between the two was a gallery connected by a passage to the royal residence. On this gallery sat the king's throne. From his seat, Charlemagne could look down upon the religious services being conducted below. Looking up to where he sat, worshipers were constantly reminded of the king's intermediary position between ordinary mortals and God.

This architectural design boldly asserted that Charlemagne was more than a barbarian king. By 805, when the chapel was dedicated, he had made good this assertion. As a contemporary chronicler wrote, while in Rome in the year 800:

> On the most holy day of Christmas, when the king rose from prayer in front of the shrine of the blessed apostle Peter to take part in the Mass, Pope Leo placed a crown on his head, and he was hailed by the whole Roman people. . . . He was now called Emperor and Augustus.

Thus, to Charlemagne and to his supporters, this coronation ceremony revived the Roman Empire in the west. Charlemagne, with his vast empire and his imperial palace, was a true successor of the ancient Roman emperors. Like his chapel in Aachen (long after known as Aix-la-Chapelle, "the chapel at the waters"), this empire was built on the remains of Roman tradition, onto which were grafted a vigorous tradition of Germanic kinship and society. According to the Byzantines, who looked on Charlemagne and his imperial coronation with alarm, the western empire could not be revived because it had never really ended. According to them, the death in 480 of the last western emperor, Julius Nepos, had ended the division of the empire. Since then the Byzantine emperors had pretended that they ruled both east and west. Charlemagne's claims, made through the ceremony in Rome and more subtly in the imperial architecture of his palace, represented to them not a revival of the empire but a threat to its existence.

open arms. In addition, in the midst of the reconquest a new and terrible disease appeared throughout the Mediterranean world. The plague killed about one-third of Europe's population in the next two centuries.

The destruction of Italy by war and disease paved the way for its conquest by the Lombards. As allies in Justinian's army, some members of this Germanic tribe from along the Danube had learned firsthand of the riches of Italy. In 568 the Lombard people left the Carpathian basin to their neighbors, the Avars, and invaded the exhausted and war-torn Italian peninsula. By the end of the sixth century, the Ostrogoths had disappeared and the Byzantines retained only the boot of Italy and a narrow strip stretching from Ravenna to Rome. The Byzantine presence in Rome was weak. By default, the popes—especially Gregory the Great (590–604)—became the defenders and governors of the city. Gregory organized the resistance to the Lombards, fed the population during famines, and comforted his people through the dark years of plague and warfare. As a vigorous political and spiritual leader, he laid the foundations of the medieval papacy.

The Lombards were more brutal and less sophisticated than their Ostrogothic predecessors. They had little use for Roman administrative tradition. Instead they divided Italy into military districts under the control of dukes whose authority replaced that of Roman bureaucrats. But it is an ill wind indeed that blows no one good. The Lombards largely eliminated the Roman tax system under which Italians had long suffered. Moreover, they were less concerned with preserving their own cultural traditions than were the Ostrogoths, even in the sphere of religion. Initially the Lombards were Arians, but in the early seventh century the Lombard kings and their followers accepted orthodox Christianity. This conversion paved the way for the unification of the society. Italy may have been less civilized under the Lombards than under the Goths or Romans, but life for the vast majority of the population was probably better than it had been for centuries.

Rather than accepting a divided society (as did the Ostrogoths) or merging into an orthodox Roman culture (as did the Lombards), the Visigoths of Gaul and Spain sought to unify the indigenous population of their kingdom through law and religion. Roman law deeply influenced Visigothic law codes and formed an enduring legal heritage to the West. Religious unity was a more difficult goal. The kings' repeated attempts to force conversion to Arianism failed and created tension and mistrust. This mistrust proved fatal. In 507

Gallo-Roman aristocrats supported the Frankish king Clovis in his successful conquest of the Visigothic kingdom of Toulouse. Defeat drove the Visigoths deeper into Spain, where they gradually forged a unified kingdom based on Roman administrative tradition and Visigothic kingship.

Spain was a rich country, and its Visigothic kings profited accordingly. Cordoban leather, olive oil, and grain cultivated on vast estates still owned by the Romans were exported throughout the known world. Greek, Jewish, and Syrian merchants crowded into the ports of the kingdom and carried its products as far as Ireland to the northwest and Palestine in the east. This prosperity benefited Spain's rulers, filling royal coffers with gold, since some of the Roman tax system survived. Both the Franks to the north and the Muslims to the south eyed Spain's riches greedily.

The long-sought-after religious unity was finally achieved when King Recared (586–601) and the Gothic aristocracy embraced orthodox Christianity. This conversion further blurred the differences between Visigoths and Roman provincials in the kingdom. It also initiated an unprecedented use of the Church and its ideology to strengthen the monarchy. Visigothic kings modeled themselves after the Byzantine emperors, proclaimed themselves new Constantines, and used Church councils—held regularly at Toledo—as governing assemblies. Still, Visigothic distrust, which was directed toward anyone who was different, continued. It focused especially on the considerable Jewish population, which had lived in Spain since the diaspora, or dispersion, in the first century of the Roman Empire. Almost immediately after Recared's conversion, he and his successors began to enact a series of anti-Jewish measures, culminating in 613 with the command that all Jews accept baptism or leave the kingdom. Although this mandate was never fully carried out, the virulence of the persecution of the Jews grew through the seventh century. At the same time rivalry within the aristocracy weakened the kingdom and left it vulnerable to attack from without.

In 711 Muslims from North Africa invaded and quickly conquered the Visigothic kingdom. While some remnants of the Visigoths held on in small kingdoms in the northwest, most of the population quickly came to terms with their new masters. Jews rejoiced in the religious toleration brought by Islam, and many members of the Christian elite converted to Islam and retained their positions of authority under the new regime. (See "The Jews in the Early Middle Ages," pp. 224–225.)

The Anglo-Saxons: From Pagan Conquerors to Christian Missionaries

The motley collection of Saxons, Angles, Jutes, Frisians, Suebians, and others who came to Britain as federated troops and stayed on as rulers did not coalesce into a united kingdom until almost the eleventh century. Instead, these Germanic warriors carved out small kingdoms for themselves, enslaving the Romanized Britons or driving them into Wales. Although independent, these little kingdoms—varying from five to as many as eleven at different times—maintained some sort of identity as a group. The king of the dominant kingdom was accorded the honorific title of Bretwalda, or "Wide Ruler." Other kings looked to him as first among equals and sought his advice and influence in their dealings with one another. Unlike the Goths, none of these peoples had previously been integrated into the Roman world. Thus, rather than fusing Roman and Germanic traditions, they eradicated the former. Although the ruined walls of Roman cities such as London, Gloucester, and Carlisle continued to offer some protection to a handful of people, urban life disappeared, and with it the Roman traditions of administration, taxation, and culture.

In their place developed a world whose central values were honor and glory, whose primary occupation was fighting, and whose economic system was based on plunder and the open-handed distribution of riches. In many ways this Anglo-Saxon world resembled the heroic age of ancient Greece. This was a society dominated by petty kings and their aristocratic war leaders. These invaders were not, like the Goths, just a military elite. They also included free farmers who replaced the Romanized British peasantry, introducing their language, agricultural techniques, social organization, and folkloric traditions to the southeastern part of the island. These ordinary settlers, much more than the kings and aristocrats, were responsible for the gradual transformation of Britain into England—the land of the Angles.

The Anglo-Saxons were pagans, and, although Christianity survived, the relationship between conquered and conquerors did not provide a climate conducive to conversion. Christianity came instead from without. The conversion of England resulted from a two-part effort. The first originated in Ireland, the most western society of Europe and the one in which Celtic traditions had survived with few changes for over a thousand years. Ireland had never been part of the Roman Empire and thus had never adapted the forms of urban life and centralized, hierarchical government or religion characteristic of Britain and the continent. In the fifth century, merchants and missionaries introduced to Ireland an eastern, monastic form of Christianity, which adapted easily to the rural, tribal organization of Irish society. Although Irish Christianity was entirely orthodox in its beliefs, the isolation of Ireland led to the development of numerous practices at odds with those common to Constantinople and Rome. Thus, while Ireland had important bishops, the most influential churchmen were powerful abbots of strict, ascetic monasteries, closely connected with tribal chieftains, who directed the religious life of their regions. Around 565 the Irish monk Columba (521–597) established a monastery on the island of Iona off the coast of Scotland. From there, wandering Irish monks began to convert northern Britain.

This gilded copper plate, one of the Lombard treasures, was part of a helmet decoration. The Lombard king Agilulf (590–615) is shown receiving tribute from his conquered subjects. On either side of the king are winged victories carrying signs saying VICTURIA.

❧ The Jews in the Early Middle Ages

ויאמר הסוחר רימני אשר תכתוב על הכיס אותותי׃ את שמי ואת שם אבותי׃
כי הרואים בזה ישלומו וסרמה׃ ויאמר הנע כתב מי חפצך׃ שוך׃

The intolerance and persecution of Jews by the Visigoths was the exception rather than the rule in early medieval Europe. Since the diaspora, Jews had settled throughout the West, primarily in towns. In Italy, Rome, Ravenna, and Pavia had important communities. In the Frankish kingdom Jews were particularly numerous in the southern cities of Lyon, Vienne, Arles, Marseille, and Narbonne, although Jewish communities could be found in more northern towns such as Orléans, Soissons, Nantes, Aachen, and Frankfurt. In contrast with later practice, Jews appeared no different from their Christian neighbors. They spoke the same language, wore no distinctive clothing, and occupied no designated section of town, or ghetto. Although they worshiped in their synagogues and studied in their yeshivas, they otherwise were very much integrated into the fabric of society.

Some Jews owned rural estates where they cultivated vineyards and farms alongside their Christian neighbors. Jewish farmers and landowners were particularly common in the areas of Vienne, Mâcon, and Arles, where they appear in records of land transactions buying, selling, and exchanging property with individuals and Christian churches. However, most Jews were merchants or practiced other urban professions such as goldsmithing and medicine. Some acted as tax collectors and emissaries for lay and ecclesiastical lords. The reasons for these specializations were obvious. First, Jewish communities in the West maintained ties with other Jews in the Byzantine and Muslim worlds, exchanging letters on religious and legal affairs and traveling back and forth. Second, sporadic attacks on Jews did occur. In the sixth century, for example, the Frankish king Chilperic (561–584) attempted to force Jews in his kingdom to be baptized. Thus Jews concentrated in occupations that allowed them to move easily and quickly in time of danger. Finally, the lack of interest on the part of their Christian neighbors in trade and the disappearance of Syriac and Greek merchants in the seventh century left long-distance commerce almost entirely in the hands of Jews. Royal documents speak frequently of "Jews and other merchants," possibly implying that Gentile merchants were an unimportant minority.

Jewish merchants traveled widely—from Scandinavia to Iran, India, and even as far as China—exporting western slaves, furs, and weapons and returning with such exotic luxuries as spices and silks. Trade was important to western monarchs, not only for supplies of luxuries, but also for the tariff income it provided. In the ninth century Jewish merchants were so vital to the empire of Louis the Pious that he granted them special privileges and took them under his royal protection. A palace official, the master of the Jews, was responsible for protecting the Jews throughout the empire, and appeals against them to the king usually were settled in the Jews' favor. Not everyone was equally pleased with the tolerance shown this non-Christian minority. Bishop Agobard of Lyon (799–840) complained bitterly to Louis about his policy of tolerance. The bishop was particularly disturbed by the fact that, while few Jews could be persuaded to convert, in the area of Lyon many Christians found the sermons of rabbis preferable to those of their priests and conversions to Judaism were becoming frequent.

The most celebrated conversion was that of Bodo, a young Frankish aristocrat raised in Louis's palace and educated in his school. In 838, while on what he pretended was a pilgrimage to Rome, he converted to Judaism, sold his entourage into slavery, married a young Jewish woman, and fled to Saragossa in Muslim Spain. From there he wrote scathing attacks on the immorality and doctrinal ignorance of the Christian clergy he had known in Aachen. Fourteen clerics there, he claimed, held fourteen different opinions on their faith. Disgusted by what he considered to be the ignorance and idolatry of Christianity, he saw his conversion as a return to the worship of the one true God.

Christian churchmen were scandalized by Bodo and embarrassed by their inability to convert Jews through peaceful persuasion, but they were powerless to do anything about the situation. Traditional Christian doctrine asserted that the conversion of the Jews would be one of the signs of the end of the world. Until then they had the right to toleration. Moreover, the early medieval world was one of many peoples, laws, and traditions. In a society in which different people in the same towns, and even the same households, might live according to Roman, Frankish, Gothic, or Burgundian law, Jews were but one more group with a distinct identity. Kings refused to limit the civil and religious rights of their Jewish subjects, forbade Christians to baptize Jewish slaves, and in general protected them as valued members of society.

The second effort at Christianizing Britain began with Pope Gregory the Great. In 596 he sent the missionary Augustine (known as Augustine of Canterbury to distinguish him from the bishop of Hippo) to attempt to convert the English. Augustine arrived in the southeast kingdom of Kent, where the pagan King Ethelbert—encouraged by his wife Bertha, a Christian Frankish princess—gave him permission to preach. Augustine laid the foundations for a hierarchical, bishop-centered church based on the Roman model. In time, Ethelbert and much of his kingdom accepted Christianity, and Augustine was named archbishop of Canterbury by the pope. Augustine had similar success in nearby Essex and established a second bishopric at London shortly before his death in 604.

As Irish missionaries spread south from Iona and Roman missionaries moved north from Canterbury, their efforts created in England two opposing forms of orthodox Christianity. One was Roman, episcopal, and hierarchical. The other was Celtic, monastic, and decentralized. The Roman and Celtic churches agreed on basic doctrines. However, each had its own calendar of religious feasts and its own rituals. These differences posed serious problems since they existed not only in the same society but sometimes even within the same family. For example, a wife who followed Roman custom might be fasting and abstaining from meat during the season of penance that preceded Easter, while her husband who followed the Celtic calendar—according to which Easter came earlier—was already feasting and celebrating. It was precisely this situation that led King

Oswy of Northumbria (d. 670), the Bretwalda, to call an episcopal meeting, or synod, in 664 at Whitby to settle the issue. After hearing arguments from both sides, Oswy accepted the customs of the Roman Church—allying himself and ultimately all of Anglo-Saxon England with the centralized, hierarchical form of Christianity, which could be used to strengthen his monarchy.

During the century-and-a half following the Synod of Whitby, Anglo-Saxon Christian civilization blossomed. Contact with the Continent, and especially with Rome, increased. The monasteries of Monkwearmouth and Jarrow became centers of learning, culminating in the writings of Bede (673–735), the greatest scholar of his century. Bede probably never set foot outside the monasteries of Monkwearmouth, to which he had been given as a child of seven, and Jarrow, which he entered in 681. Bede's knowledge of natural science, rhetoric, chronology, scripture, and especially history spread his fame throughout the West. His history of the English church and people is the finest historical work of the early Middle Ages. His influence lives on today, for he was the scholar responsible for the popularization of dating history from before or after the birth of Jesus.

By the eighth century, England was no longer a mission land but had itself begun to send out Christian missionaries. From around 700, descendants of the Anglo-Saxon conquerors started traveling to "Old Saxony" (the region of the Continent from which their ancestors had originally come), as well as to other parts of the Germanic world, to convert their still-pagan

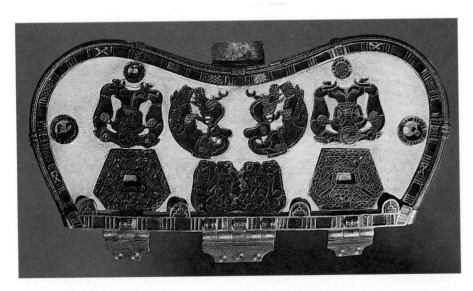

This purse lid, decorated with gold and garnets, is one of the treasures of the seventh-century burial site of an East Anglian king at Sutton Hoo in Suffolk, England.

FROM SLAVE TO QUEEN

Queen Balthild (d. ca. 680), an Anglo-Saxon woman captured and sold into slavery in Francia, became the wife of Clovis II, king of Neustria and Burgundy (639–657). Her career, including her regency for her son Clothar III and eventual forced retirement to the monastery she had founded at Chelles, is typical of the complex role and reputation early medieval queens enjoyed. This laudatory account, which was probably written by a nun at Chelles, hints that Balthild had been forced into the convent by those opposed to her political role.

Divine Providence called her from across the seas. She, who came here as God's most precious and lofty pearl, was sold at a cheap price. Erchinoald, a Frankish magnate and most illustrious man, acquired her, and in his service the girl behaved most honorably. She gained such happy fame that, when the said lord Erchinoald's wife died, he hoped to unite himself to Balthild, that faultless virgin, in a matronal bed. But when she heard this, she fled and most swiftly took herself out of his sight. Thereafter it happened, with God's approval, that Balthild, the maid who escaped marriage with a lord, came to be espoused to Clovis, son of the former king Dagobert. Thus by virtue of her humility she was raised to a higher rank.

She acted as a mother to the princes, as a daughter to priests, and as a most pious nurse to children and adolescents. She distributed generous alms to everyone. She guarded the princes' honor by keeping their intimate counsels secret. In accordance with God's will, her husband King Clovis migrated from the body and left his sons with their mother. Immediately after him her son Clothar took up the kingdom of the Franks, maintaining peace in the realm. Then, to promote peace, by command of Lady Balthild with the advice of the other elders, the people of Austrasia accepted her son Childeric as their king and the Burgundians were united with the Franks. And we believe, under God's ordinance, that these three realms then held peace and concord among themselves because of Lady Balthild's great faith. She proclaimed that no payment could be exacted for receipt of a sacred rank. Moreover, she ordained that yet another evil custom should cease, namely that many people determined to kill their children rather than nurture them, for they feared to incur the public exactions which were heaped upon them by custom, which caused great damage to their affairs.

It was her holy intention to enter the monastery of religious women which she had built at Chelles. But the Franks delayed much for love of her and would not have permitted this to happen except that there was a commotion made by the wretched Bishop Sigobrand whose pride among the Franks earned him his mortal ruin. Indeed, they formed a plan to kill him against her will. Fearing that the lady would act heavily against them, and wish to avenge him, they suddenly relented and permitted her to enter the monastery.

From The Life of the Blessed Queen Balthild.

cousins. Until the late eighth and ninth centuries, when new waves of Germanic invaders known as Vikings began to destroy Anglo-Saxon civilization, England furnished the Continent with many of its leading thinkers and scholars.

The Franks: An Enduring Legacy

The name Frank means "fierce" or "free." In fact, in their early history most Franks were virtual slaves of the Romans. In the fourth century A.D., various small Germanic tribes along the Rhine River coalesced into a loose confederation known as the Franks. A significant group of them, the Salians, made the mistake of attacking Roman garrisons and were totally defeated. The Romans resettled the Salians in a largely abandoned region of what is now Belgium and Holland. There they formed a buffer to protect Roman colonists from other Germanic tribes and provided a ready supply of recruits for the Roman army. During the fourth and fifth centuries, these Salian Franks and their neighbors assumed an increasingly important role in the military defense of Gaul and began to spread out of their "reservation" into more settled parts of the province. Although many high-ranking Roman officers of the fourth century were Franks, most were neither con-

TWO MISSIONARIES

Bede (ca. 672–735) described in detail the two missionary movements in England. The first, led by Augustine of Canterbury, represented Roman traditions to which Bede himself was firmly attached. The second, led by Aidan (d. 651), represented the Irish traditions Bede opposed. And yet he wrote vivid and contrasting descriptions of the character and styles of the two men.

Those [British bishops] summoned [by Augustine] to this council first visited a wise and prudent hermit and enquired of him whether they should abandon their own Traditions and Augustine's demand. He answered: "If he is a man of God, follow him." "But how can we be sure of this?" they asked. "Our Lord says, Take my yoke upon you and learn of Me, for I am meek and lowly of heart," he replied. "Therefore if Augustine is meek and lowly in heart, it shows that he bears the yoke of Christ himself, and offers it to you. But if he is haughty and unbending, then he is not of God, and we should not listen to him. Arrange that he and his followers arrive first at the place appointed for the conference. If he rises courteously as you approach, rest assured that he is the servant of Christ and do as he asks. But if he ignores you and does not rise, then, since you are in the majority, do not comply with his demands."

The Bishops carried out his suggestion, and it happened that Augustine remained seated in his chair. Seeing this, they became angry, accusing him of pride and taking pains to contradict all that he said . . . saying among themselves that if he would not rise to greet them in the first instance, he would have even

less regard for them once they submitted to his authority.

Later, Bede describes Aidan's approach to spreading the word of God:

He never sought or cared for any worldly possessions, and loved to give away to the poor who chanced to meet him whatever he received from kings or wealthy folk. Whether in town or country, he always travelled on foot unless compelled by necessity to ride; and whatever people he met on his walks, whether high or low, he stopped and spoke to them. If they were heathen, he urged them to be baptized; and if they were Christians, he strengthened their faith, and inspired them by word and deed to live a good life and to be generous to others. . . . He cultivated peace and love, purity and humility; he was above anger and greed, and despised pride and conceit; he set himself to keep as well as to teach the laws of God, and was diligent in study and prayer. He used his priestly authority to check the proud and powerful.

From Bede, *A History of the English Church and People.*

querors nor members of the military elite but rather soldier-farmers who settled beside the local Roman peoples they protected.

In 486, Clovis, leader of the Salian Franks and commander of the barbarized Roman army, staged a successful coup (possibly with the approval of the Byzantine emperor), defeating and killing Syagrius, the last Roman commander in the west. Although Clovis ruled the Franks as king, he worked closely with the existing Gallo-Roman aristocracy as he consolidated his control over various Frankish factions and over portions of Gaul and Germany held by other barbarian kingdoms. Clovis's early conversion to orthodox Christianity helped ensure the effectiveness of this Gallo-

Roman cooperation. Like other barbarian kings allied with Theodoric the Ostrogoth, Clovis may have been at least nominally an Arian. However, urged on by his wife Clotilda, he embraced orthodox Christianity. His religious conversion was very much in the tradition of Constantine. Clovis converted to orthodox Christianity in the hope that God would give him victory over his enemies and that his new faith would win the support of the Roman aristocracy in Gaul. The king's baptism convinced many of his subjects to convert as well, paving the way for the assimilation of Franks and Romans into a new society. This Frankish society became the model for European social and political organization for over a thousand years.

The Horseman's Stone of Hornhausen, a seventh-century relief from a Frankish tomb. The horseman with lance and shield rides above a two-headed serpent. Pictorial stones such as this are found mainly in Sweden.

The mix of Frankish warriors and Roman aristocrats spread rapidly across western Europe. Clovis and his successors absorbed the Visigothic kingdom of Toulouse, the Thuringians, and the kingdom of the Burgundians. They also expanded Frankish hegemony through what is now Bavaria and south of the Alps into northern Italy. Unlike other barbarian kingdoms such as those of the Huns or Ostrogoths, which evaporated almost as soon as their great founders died, the Frankish synthesis was enduring. Although the dynasty established by Clovis—called the Merovingian after a legendary ancestor—lasted only until the mid-eighth century, the Frankish kingdom was the direct ancestor of both France and Germany.

After Clovis's death in 511, his kingdom was divided among his four sons. This decision to fragment his lands probably resulted from a compromise agreement among his sons, his Germanic warriors, and his Roman advisors. For the next two hundred years, the heart of the Frankish kingdom—the region between the Rhine and Loire rivers—was often divided into the kingdoms of Neustria, Burgundy, and Austrasia, each ruled by a Merovingian king. The outlying regions of Aquitaine and Provence to the south and Alemania, Thuringia, and Bavaria to the east were governed by Frankish dukes appointed by the kings. Still, the Frankish world was never as divided as Anglo-Saxon England. In the early eighth century a unified Frankish kingdom reemerged as the dominant force in Europe.

With the establishment of the barbarian kingdoms, the theoretical unity of the western empire was forever destroyed. Within each of these smaller polities, rulers and ruled began forging from their complex Roman and Germanic traditions a new cultural synthesis.

Living in the New Europe

The substitution of Germanic kings for imperial officials made few obvious differences in the lives of most inhabitants of Italy, Gaul, and Spain. The vast majority of Europeans were poor farmers whose lives centered on their villages and fields. For these people the seasons in the agricultural year, the burdens of rent and taxation, and the frequent poor harvests, food shortages, famines, and epidemics were more important than empires and kingdoms. Nevertheless, fundamental, if imperceptible, changes were transforming ordinary life.

These changes took place at every level of society. The slaves and semifree peasants of Rome gradually began to form new kinds of social groups and to practice new forms of agriculture as they merged with the Germanic warrior-peasants. Elite Gallo-Roman landowners came to terms with their Frankish conquerors, and these two groups began to coalesce into a single unified aristocracy. In the same way that Ger-

Cast of a signet ring that belonged to Childeric, king of the Salian Franks (ca. 457–482). The inscription CHILDERICI REGIS *surrounds the portrait of the king.*

manic and Roman society began to merge, Germanic and Roman traditions of governance united between the sixth and eighth centuries to create a powerful new kind of medieval kingdom.

Creating the European Peasantry

Three fundamental changes transformed rural society during the early Middle Ages. First, Roman slavery virtually disappeared. Next, the household emerged as the primary unit of social and economic organization. Finally, Christianity spread throughout the rural world.

Economics, not ethics, destroyed Roman slavery. In the kind of slavery typical of the Roman world, large gangs of slaves were housed in dormitories and directed in large-scale operations by overseers. This form of slavery demanded a highly organized form of estate management and could be quite costly since slaves had to be fed and housed year-round. Since slaves did not

always reproduce at a rate sufficient to replace themselves, the supply had to be replenished from without. However, as the empire ceased to expand, the supply of fresh slaves dwindled. As cities shrank, many markets for agricultural produce disappeared, making market-oriented, large-scale agriculture less profitable. Enterprising landlords in the west sold off some of their slaves to the east, particularly to the Muslims. Furthermore, the Germanic societies that settled in the west had no tradition of gang slavery.

As a result, from the sixth through the ninth centuries owners abandoned the practice of keeping gang slaves in favor of the less complicated practice of establishing slave families on individual plots of land. The slaves and their descendants cultivated these plots, made annual payments to their owners, and cultivated the undivided portions of the estate, the fruits of which went directly to the owner. Thus slaves became something akin to sharecroppers. Gradually they began to intermarry with colons and others who, though nominally free, found themselves in an economic situation much like that of slaves. By the ninth century, the distinction between slaves who had acquired traditional rights to their farms, or manses, and free peasants who held and worked manses belonging to others was blurred. By the tenth and eleventh centuries, peasant farmers throughout much of Europe were subject to the private justice of their landlords, no matter whether their ancestors had been slave or free. Although they were not slaves in the classical sense, the peasantry had fused into a homogeneous unfree population.

The division of estates into separate peasant holdings contributed to the second fundamental transformation of European peasant society: the formation of the household. Neither the Roman tradition of slave agriculture nor the Germanic tradition of clan organization had encouraged the household as the basic unit of society. When individual slaves and their spouses were placed on manses, which they and their children were expected to cultivate, the household became the basic unit of Western economy.

However, the household was more than an economic unit. It was also the first level of government. The head of the household, whether slave or free, male or female—women, particularly widows, were often heads of households—exercised authority over its other members. This authority made the householder a link in the chain of the social order, which stretched from the peasant hovel to the royal court.

Households became the basic form of peasant life. Not all peasants, however, could expect to establish

This seventh-century relief, found at Gondorf on the Moselle River, exemplifies the eclectic Merovingian culture. The griffins in the corners show Germanic influence; the beaded border recalls late antique art. The doves on the shoulders of the bearded figure may indicate that it represents Christ.

"The labors of the months" was a popular motif in medieval art. This illustration from the Astronomical Notices *was found in Salzburg. The annual round of agricultural tasks, such as sowing and reaping and grape picking, is depicted along with scenes of hunting and hawking.*

their own households. The number of manses was limited, a factor that condemned many men and women to life within the household of a more fortunate relative or neighbor. On one ninth-century estate, for example, 43 percent of the peasant households contained more than one adult male. Some of these unmarried men lived with relatives or wealthier peasants until they could be established in their own households. Many others spent their whole lives as servants in the house of another peasant.

Peasant life centered on the house, the village, and the field. In the Mediterranean world, peasants constructed their houses of fieldstone. In the north, they built their houses of wood. Often these structures consisted simply of two or three rooms shared by both the human and animal members of the household. Archaeologists can often distinguish the areas of human and animal habitation in such houses only by the relatively higher frequency of animal dung in one section than in another. The hovel was heated by the body warmth of

the cattle and sheep and by a hearth fire. Smoke escaped, not through a chimney, but through a hole in the roof.

The rhythm of peasant life was tied to the agricultural cycle, which had changed little since antiquity. January and February were the dormant months, when the family huddled together from the cold and tried to survive on the previous harvest. They lived on coarse bread made from the previous year's grain, onions and leeks, and nuts gathered from the forest. They drank wine or, in the north, a thick beer, which was a major source of protein. On special occasions they might enjoy a bit of pork. In March, they trimmed the vines for the growing season. Cattle were put out to pasture in April. In May peasants cut the fodder needed by the lord's horses. June meant plowing, July haying, and August harvesting. In September and October grapes were harvested and winter grain (an innovation of perhaps the eighth century) was planted. In November the new wine was stored in barrels, the grain was milled, and the pigs (the primary source of meat for peasants) were allowed into the forest to gorge themselves on nuts and grubs. December was slaughter month, and then the family faced another winter. Although women and men worked together on the harvest, normally peasants divided labor into male and female tasks. Husbands and sons tended to the work in the fields. Wives and daughters cared for chickens, prepared the dark bread that was the staple of the peasant diet, and spun and wove wool and flax to make clothing.

Occasionally peasants used new tools or technical innovations in their labor. Some lords established water mills for grinding grain on their estates. Here and there peasants used heavy plows capable of cutting and turning the heavy clay soil of northern Europe. Some farsighted lords had their peasants fertilize the fields with lime to restore the soil, but ninth-century peasants resented the extra labor that this recent innovation required. Technological progress was sporadic and uneven, and agricultural returns were correspondingly low.

In fact, returns were much lower than they had been in antiquity. Careful Roman landlords, using better tools and coordinating the work of their slaves more efficiently, were accustomed to harvesting eight times as much grain as they had sown. Frankish estates were doing well if they recorded harvests of three or four to one. In some years, no more grain was harvested than the seed necessary to plant the following June. Peasants had to choose between starving through the winter or eating the seed and starving the following year. Actually, the choice was not theirs, but rather that of their aristocratic lords, whose noble lifestyle they were forced to support.

Peasant culture, like peasant society, experienced a fundamental transformation during the early Middle Ages. During this period the peasantry became Christian. In antiquity Christianity had been an urban phenomenon. The term for the rural population—*pagans,* that is, the inhabitants of the countryside (*pagus*)—had long been synonymous with "unbelievers." The spread of Christianity throughout the rural world began in earnest in the sixth century, when bishops and monks began to replace the peasants' traditional agrarian cults with Christian feasts, rituals, and beliefs. In sixth-century Gaul, for example, peasants regularly held a three-day celebration beside a mountain lake into which they threw food and valuable objects as an offering to the local god. The local bishop was unable to convince them to abandon the practice. Instead, he built a church on the spot in honor of Saint Hilary of Poitiers. The church contained relics of the saint. Peasants continued to travel to the lake to celebrate the feast, but the purpose of the feast was to honor Saint Hilary.

Christianity penetrated more deeply into rural society with the systematic establishment of parishes, or rural churches. By the ninth century this parish system began to cover Europe. Bishops founded parish churches in the villages of large estates, and owners were obligated to set aside one-tenth of the produce of their estates for the maintenance of the parish church. The priests who staffed these churches came from the local peasantry and received a basic education in Latin and in Christian ritual from their predecessors and from their bishops. The continuing presence of priests in each village had a profound effect on the daily lives of Europe's peasants. Christian ritual came to be a regular part of peasant life.

Creating the European Aristocracy

At the same time that a homogeneous peasantry was emerging from the blend of slaves and free farmers, a homogeneous aristocracy was evolving out of the mix of Germanic and Roman traditions. In Germanic society, the elite had owed its position to a combination of inherited status and wealth, perpetuated through military command. Families who produced great military commanders were thought to have a special war-luck granted by the gods. The war-luck bestowed on men and women of these families a near-sacred legitimacy.

This legitimacy made the aristocrats largely independent of their kings. In times of war, kings might command, but otherwise the extent to which they

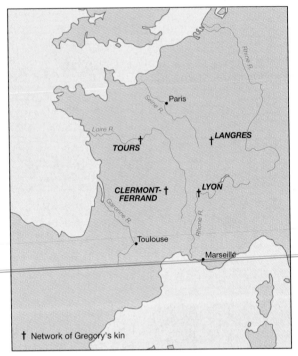

The Episcopal Kin of Gregory of Tours

could be said to govern aristocrats was minimal. The earliest Frankish laws, which prescribe wergeld, or payments, for offenses in place of unlimited blood feuds, do not mention aristocrats. The reason is probably that the kings had no recognized authority to command aristocrats to forego their right to settle disputes among themselves. The freedom of the aristocracy meant freedom from royal governance.

The Roman aristocracy was based on inheritance of land rather than leadership. During the third and fourth centuries Roman aristocrats' control of land extended over the persons who worked that land. At the same time, great landowners were able to free themselves from provincial government.

Like their Germanic counterparts, Roman aristocrats acquired a sacred legitimacy, but within the Christian tradition. They monopolized the office of bishop and became identified with the sacred and political traditions associated with the Church. The family of the Gallo-Roman bishop and historian Gregory of Tours (539–594) exemplifies this aristocratic tradition. By the time he took office in 573, 13 of the previous 18 bishops of Tours had come from his family. In addition he was related to generations of bishops from Langres, Lyon, Clermont-Ferrand, and elsewhere

In Spain and Italy, the religious differences separating Arians and orthodox Christians impeded the fusion of the Germanic and Roman aristocracies. In Gaul, the conversion of Clovis and his people facilitated the rapid blending of the two worlds. North of the Loire River, where most of the Franks had settled, Roman aristocrats soon became Franks. By the mid-sixth century the descendants of Bishop Remigius of Reims, who had baptized Clovis, had Frankish names and considered themselves Franks. Still, the Roman aristocratic tradition of great landholders became an integral part of the identity of the Frankish elite.

In the late sixth century, this northern Frankish aristocracy found its own religious identity and legitimacy in the Irish monasticism introduced by Saint Columbanus (543–615) and other wandering monks. At home in Ireland, these monks had been accustomed to working not with kings but with leaders of clans. In Gaul the monks worked closely with the Frankish aristocrats, who encouraged them to build monasteries on the aristocrats' estates. Eventually these monasteries amassed huge land-holdings and became major economic and political centers headed by aristocrats who had abandoned secular life for the cloister. The abbots and abbesses who headed the monasteries were venerated after their deaths as saints and miracle workers. Their descendants drew on the inherited prestige of being members of the "family of saints" in the same way that earlier aristocrats had claimed legitimacy as carriers of war-luck.

South of the Loire River, conditions were decidedly different. Here Irish monasticism was less important than episcopal office. The few Frankish and Gothic families who had settled in the south were rapidly absorbed into the Gallo-Roman aristocracy, which drew its prestige from control of local religious and secular power. Latin speech and Roman culture distinguished these "Romans," regardless of their ancestry.

Aristocratic life was similar whether north or south of the Loire, in Anglo-Saxon England, Visigothic Spain, or Lombard Italy. Aristocratic family structures were loosely knit clans that traced descent from important ancestors through either the male or the female line. Clans jealously guarded their autonomy against rival clans and from royal authority.

The aristocratic lifestyle focused on feasting, on hospitality, and on the male activities of hunting and warfare. In southern Europe, great nobles lived in spacious villas (an inheritance of Roman tradition), often surrounded by solid stone fortifications. In the north, Frankish and Anglo-Saxon nobles lived in great wooden halls, richly decorated but lacking fortifications. In winter, both kinds of lordly residences were the centers of banqueting and drinking bouts. Here important aristocrats gathered their supporters; entertained them at extravagant banquets; fed them vast stores of food, wine, and beer; and lavished on them gifts of jewelry, weapons, and fine horses. At the nobles' residences they received their rivals, planned their alliances, and settled their disputes.

During the fall and winter months, aristocratic men spent much of their time hunting deer and wild boar in their forests. Hunting was not merely sport. Essentially it was preparation for war, the activity of the summer months. As soon as the snows of winter began to melt and roads became passable, aristocrats gathered their retainers and marched to war. The enemy varied. It might be rival families with whom feuds were nursed for generations. It might be raiding parties from a neighboring region. Or the warriors might join a royal expedition led by the king and directed against a rival kingdom. Whoever the enemy, warfare brought the promise of booty and, as important, glory.

This scene is from the lid of the Franks Casket, a whalebone box that was made in the north of England at the beginning of the eighth century. The carving depicts Egil the Archer defending his home. The other sides of the box are carved with a mixture of Christian and pagan scenes.

Within this aristocratic society women played a wider and more active role than had been the case in either Roman or barbarian antiquity. In part women's new role was due to the influence of Christianity, which recognized the distinct—though always inferior—rights of women. Christianity fought against the barbarian tradition of allowing chieftains numerous wives and recognized women's right to lead a cloistered religious life. In addition, the combination of Germanic and Roman familial traditions permitted women to participate in court proceedings, to inherit and dispose of property, and, if widowed, to serve as tutors and guardians for their minor children. Finally, the long absence of men at the hunt, at the royal court, or on military expeditions left wives in charge of the domestic scene for months or years at a time.

The religious life in particular opened to aristocratic women possibilities of autonomy and authority previously unknown in the West. Women administered large and wealthy institutions and even exercised this authority over mixed monasteries, in which men and women lived in separate quarters but recognized the rule of the abbess. For example, Saint Hilda of Whitby (614–680), an Anglo-Saxon princess, established and ruled a religious community that included both women and men. This community was one of the most important in England. Five monks of Whitby later became bishops, and kings and aristocrats regularly traveled to the monastery to ask Hilda's advice. It was in Hilda's community that the Synod of Whitby took place, and Hilda played an active role advising the king and assembled bishops.

Governing Europe

The combination in the early Middle Ages of the extremes of centralized Roman power and fragmented barbarian organization produced a wide variety of governmental systems. At one end of the spectrum were the politically fragmented Celtic and Slavic societies. At the other end were the Frankish kingdoms that descendants of Clovis, drawing on the twin heritages of Roman institutions and Frankish tradition, attempted to rule.

Rulers and aristocrats both needed and feared each other. Kings had emerged out of the Germanic aristocracy and could rule only in cooperation with aristocrats. Aristocrats were primarily concerned with maintaining and expanding their own spheres of control and independence. They perceived royal authority over them or their dependents as a threat. Still, they

needed kings. Strong kings brought victory against external foes and thus maintained the flow of booty to the aristocracy. Aristocrats in turn redistributed the spoils of war among their followers to preserve the bonds of warrior society. Thus, under capable kings aristocrats were ready to cooperate, not as subjects but as partners.

Gregory of Tours provides an account that illustrates the nature of the relationship between king and aristocrat. Clovis was dividing up the booty after his victory at Soissons when the bishop of the city approached and asked him to return a large pitcher. Clovis wished to do so and asked his warriors to grant him the pitcher over and above Clovis' normal share of the spoils. All agreed except for one Frank, who struck the pitcher with his battle-ax, declaring, "You shall have none of this booty except your fair share." Clovis did nothing to this warrior until the annual military muster the following March. When he came to the man who had struck the pitcher, he berated him for the poor condition of his weapons and threw his ax to the ground. As the man bent over to pick it up, Clovis used his own ax to split open the man's head. "That," he said, "is for what you did to my pitcher in Soissons."

This story illustrates both the strength and the weakness of early medieval monarchs. Clovis was the most powerful Frankish king before the eighth century, yet even he was unable to redress a blatant affront to his authority except under very specific circumstances. As the successors of Germanic war leaders and late Roman generals, kings were primarily military commanders. During campaigns and at the annual "Marchfield," when the free warriors assembled, the king was all-powerful. At those times he could cut down his enemies with impunity. At other times the king's role was strictly limited. His direct authority extended only over the members of his household and his personal warrior band.

The king's role in administering justice was similarly ambivalent. He was not the source of law, which was held to be simply the customs of the past, nor was he responsible for enforcing this customary law. Enforcement was the duty of individuals and families. Only if they wished did they bring their grievances to the king or his agents for arbitration or judgment. However, even though kings could not formally legislate, they effectively molded law and legal procedure by collecting, selecting, clarifying, and publishing customary laws. Again Clovis presents a model for such legislative activity in the compilation of Salic law made during his reign. Anglo-Saxon and Visigothic kings of the seventh through tenth centuries did the same.

As heirs of Roman governmental tradition, kings sought to incorporate these traditions into their roles. By absorbing the remains of local administration and taxation, kings acquired nascent governmental systems. Through the use of written documents, Roman scribes expanded royal authority beyond the king's household and personal following. Tax collectors continued to fill royal coffers with duties collected in markets and ports.

Finally, by assuming the role of protector of the Church, kings acquired the support of educated and experienced ecclesiastical advisors and the right to intervene in disputes involving clergy and laity. Further, as defenders of the Church, kings could claim a responsibility for the preservation of peace and the administration of justice—two fundamental Christian (but also Roman) tasks. Early medieval kings had no fixed capitals from which they governed. Instead they were constantly on the move, supervising their kingdoms and consuming the produce of their estates. The arrival of the king and his entourage was a major event long remembered in a region. A chronicler writing years later recalled the arrival in Burgundy (eastern France) of the Frankish king Dagobert I (623–638): "The profound alarm that his coming caused among the Burgundian bishops, magnates and others of consequence was a source of general wonder; but his justice brought great joy to the poor."

Since kings could not be everywhere at once, they were represented locally by aristocrats who enjoyed royal favor. In the Frankish world these favorites were called *counts* and their districts *counties.* In England royal representatives were termed *ealdormen* and their regions were known as *shires.* Whether counts or ealdormen, these representatives were military commanders and judicial officers drawn from aristocratic families close to the king. Under competent and effective kings, partnership with these aristocratic families worked well. Under less competent rulers and during the reigns of minors, these families often managed to turn their districts into hereditary, almost autonomous regions. The same thing happened when rival members of the royal house sought supporters against their cousins and brothers. The sphere of royal authority shrank or expanded, in large measure in response to the individual qualities of the king. The personality of the king mattered far more than the institution of kingship did.

Thus, at both ends of the social spectrum, Germanic and Roman traditions and institutions were combining to create a new society, organized not by nationality or ethnicity but by status and united by shared religious values and political leadership.

The Carolingian Achievement

The Merovingian dynasty initiated by Clovis presided over the synthesis of Roman and Germanic society. It was left to the Carolingians who followed to forge a new Europe. In the seventh century, members of the new aristocracy were able to take advantage of royal minorities and dynastic rivalries to turn themselves into virtual rulers of their small territories. By the end of the century the kings had become little more than symbolic figures in the Frankish kingdoms. The real power was held by regional strongmen called dukes. The most successful of these aristocratic factions was that led by Charles Martel (ca. 688–741) and his heirs, known as the Carolingians.

This family had risen to prominence in the seventh century in Austrasia by controlling the office of mayor of the palace, the highest court official who advised the king as spokesman for the aristocracy. The Carolingians increased their influence by marrying their sons to daughters of other aristocratic families. In the late seventh century they extended their control to include Neustria and Burgundy as well as Austrasia. By the second quarter of the eighth century Charles Martel, while not king, was the acknowledged ruler of the Frankish kingdom.

Charles Martel was ruthless, ambitious, and successful. He crushed rivals in his own family, subdued competing dukes, and united the Frankish realm. He was successful in part because he molded the Frankish cavalry into the most effective military force of the time. His heavily armored mounted warriors used the newly introduced stirrup to keep themselves steady on their mounts. The warriors were extremely effective, but also costly. Martel financed them with property confiscated from his enemies and from the Church. In return for oaths of absolute fidelity, he gave his followers (or vassals) estates, which they held as long as they served him faithfully. With this new army he practiced a scorched-earth policy against his opponents that left vast areas of Provence and Aquitaine desolate for decades.

Charles Martel looked beyond military power to the control of religious and cultural institutions. He supported Anglo-Saxon missionaries, such as Boniface (ca. 680–755), who were trying to introduce on the Continent the Roman form of Christianity they knew in England. This hierarchical style of Christianity served Carolingian interests in centralization—especially since Charles appointed his loyal supporters as bishops and abbots. Missionaries and Frankish armies worked hand in hand to consolidate Carolingian rule.

The ecclesiastical policy that proved most crucial to later Carolingians was Charles's support of the Roman papacy. Charles caught the attention of Pope Gregory III (731–741) in 732, after defeating a Muslim force near Tours that had attempted to continue the northward expansion of Islam. A few years later, when the pope needed protection from the Lombards to maintain his central Italian territories, he sought and obtained help from the Frankish leader.

The alliance with the papacy solidified during the lifetime of Charles's son Pippin (ca. 714–768). Pippin inherited his father's power. However, since he was not of the royal Merovingian family, he had no more right to supreme authority than any other powerful aristocrat. Pippin needed more than the power of a king: he needed the title. No Frankish tradition provided a precedent by which a rival family might displace the Merovingians. Pippin turned instead to the pope. Building on his increasingly close relationship with the papacy and the Frankish church dominated by his supporters, Pippin sought legitimacy in religious authority. In a carefully orchestrated exchange between Pippin and Pope Zacharias (741–752), the latter declared that the individual who exercised the power of king ought also to have the title. Following this declaration, the last Merovingian was deposed, and in 751 a representative of the pope anointed Pippin king of the Franks.

The alliance between the new dynasty and the papacy marked the first union of royal legitimacy and ecclesiastical sanction in European history. Frankish, Gothic, and Anglo-Saxon kings had been selected on secular criteria. Kings combined royal descent with military power. Now the office of king required the active participation of the Church. The new Frankish kingship led Europe into the first political, social, and cultural restructuring of the West since the end of the Roman Empire.

Charlemagne and the Renewal of the West

Pippin's son Charlemagne was the heir of the political, religious, and social revolutions begun by his grandfather and father. Charlemagne was a large man, over six feet tall, with piercing eyes, a robust physique, and a restless spirit. To his intimates he was a generous lord constantly surrounded by friends, whether at table consuming vast quantities of wine and roast meat, in the baths in Aachen (where he often swam with more than a hundred courtiers), or on the march with his Frankish army. To his enemies he was the man of iron—the grim and invincible warrior clad head to foot in steel, sweeping all before him. He was a conqueror, but he was also a religious reformer, a state builder, and a patron of the arts. As the leader of a powerful, united Frankish kingdom for over forty years, Charlemagne changed the West more profoundly than anyone since Augustus.

Almost every spring Charlemagne assembled his Frankish armies and led them against internal or external enemies. He subdued the Aquitainians and Bavarians. He conquered the kingdom of the Lombards and assumed the title of King of the Lombards. He crushed the Saxons, annexed the Spanish region of Catalonia, and destroyed the vast Pannonian kingdom of the Avars. In wars of aggression, his armies were invincible. The heavy cavalry first employed by Charles Martel simply mowed down the more lightly armored and equipped enemy. Moreover, Charlemagne's logistical support was unmatched in the early Middle Ages. His ability to ship men and supplies down the Danube River enabled him to capture the enormous hoard of gold the Avars had amassed from raids and annual payments by the Byzantines. As Einhard, Charlemagne's counselor and advisor, boasted, "These Franks, who

This bronze equestrian statue of a king dates from the ninth century. The rider wears the typical Frankish attire of hose, tunic, and long riding cloak. The subject is often identified as Charlemagne.

CHARLEMAGNE AND THE ARTS

According to Charlemagne's biographer Einhard (ca. 770–840), the emperor not only fostered education for others but himself took an active interest in studies. In the following passage Einhard describes the king's own educational program, the breadth of his interests and the mixed results he achieved. The description should be read with some caution, however. For example, Charlemagne's interest in astronomy and his practice of keeping writing materials in his bed (presumably to record his dreams) may be more of an indication of his interest in astrology and divination than of his interest in the liberal arts.

Charles had the gift of ready and fluent speech, and could express whatever he had to say with the utmost clearness. He was not satisfied with command of his native language merely, but gave attention to the study of foreign ones, and in particular was such a master of Latin that he could speak it as well as his native tongue; but he could understand Greek better than he could speak it. He was so eloquent, indeed, that he might have passed for a teacher of eloquence. He most zealously cultivated the liberal arts, held those who taught them in great esteem, and conferred great honors upon them. He took lessons in grammar of the deacon Peter of Pisa, at that time an aged man. Another deacon, Albin of Britain, sur-named Alcuin, a man of Saxon extraction, who was the greatest scholar of the day, was his teacher in other branches of learning. The King spent much time and labor with him studying rhetoric, dialectics, and especially astronomy; he learned to reckon, and used to investigate the motions of the heavenly bodies most curiously, with an intelligent scrutiny. He also tried to write, and used to keep tablets and blanks in bed under his pillow, that at leisure hours he might accustom his hand to form the letters; however, as he did not begin his efforts in due season, but late in life, they met with ill success.

From Einhard, *The Life of Charlemagne.*

---

until then had seemed almost paupers, now discovered so much gold and silver in the palace and captured so much previous booty in their battles, that it could rightly be maintained that they had in all justice taken from the Huns [Avars] what these last had unjustly stolen from other nations."

War booty fueled Charlemagne's renewal of European culture. As a Christian king he considered it his duty to reform the spiritual life of his kingdom and to bring it into line with his concept of the divinely willed order. To achieve this goal he needed a dedicated and educated clergy. In the previous three centuries, secular schools had disappeared and Frankish monasteries had ceased to be centers of learning. Most of the native clergy were poorly educated and indifferent in their observance of the rules of religious life.

Creating a reformed, educated clergy was an effort every bit as complex and demanding as organizing the army. Charlemagne recruited leading intellectuals from England, Spain, Ireland, and Italy to the royal court to lead a thorough educational program. The architect of his cultural reform, Alcuin of York (ca. 732–804), directed a school for young lay and ecclesiastical aristocrats in the king's palace and encouraged the king to finance a wide variety of educational programs. Charle-magne supported schools in great monasteries such as Fulda and St. Gall for the training of young clerics and laymen. These schools needed books. Charlemagne's educational reformers scoured Italy for fading copies of works by Virgil, Horace, and Tacitus with the same determination that his builders hunted antique marbles and columns for his chapel. Alcuin and others corrected and copied classical texts corrupted by generations of haphazard transmission. The earliest extant manuscripts of virtually all the classics of Roman antiquity date from the late eighth or early ninth century. Caroline minuscule—the new style of handwriting developed to preserve these texts—was so clear and easily readable that during the Renaissance, humanists (mistakenly thinking that these manuscripts dated from Roman times) adopted it as their standard script. It remains essentially the form of printing common today—this book is printed in a version of Caroline minuscule.

The first decades of educational reform produced little that was new, but the reformers of this era laid the necessary foundation for what has been called the Carolingian Renaissance. Their successors in the ninth century built on this foundation to make creative contributions in theology, philosophy, historiography, and

Charlemagne's Empire, 814

to some extent in literature. For the first time since Augustine, the West produced a really first-class theologian and philosopher, John Scotus Erigena (ca. 810–ca. 877), who mastered Greek and created a unique and influential synthesis of Neoplatonic philosophy.

The pursuit of learning was not a purely clerical affair. In the later ninth century, great aristocrats were highly literate and collected their own personal libraries. Count Everard of Friuli, who died in 866, left an estate that included over fifty books, among them works by Augustine, histories, biographies of saints' lives, and seven law books. Elite women participated fully in the Carolingian Renaissance. One example is the noblewoman Dhuoda, who composed a manual of instruction for her son. Her writings show her to be a woman of deep piety and learning familiar with the Bible and the works of Augustine, Gregory the Great, other theologians, and some classical authors.

Educational reform went hand in hand with reform of ecclesiastical institutions. Charlemagne and his son Louis the Pious (814–840) worked to establish the Benedictine rule as the norm for monastic life. They also tried to ensure that parish clergy were competent and committed to serving the needs of the people. The goal was the formation of a purified and organized cler-gy performing its essential role of celebrating Christian ritual and praying for the Frankish king. At the same time, the monasteries were to provide competent clerics to serve the royal administration at every level. These reforms were expensive. The fiscal reorganization of ecclesiastical institutions was as far-reaching as their cultural reform. For the first time, Frankish synods or councils made tithing mandatory, specifying that one-tenth of all agricultural harvests were to go to the maintenance of church buildings, the support of the clergy, and the care of the poor. Monasteries grew rich with donations of land and slaves captured in battle. Monastic estates were reorganized, records of dues and revenues revised for greater efficiency, and dependent workers shifted around to maximize productivity.

Carolingian Government

Charlemagne well knew that conquest alone could not unify his enormous kingdom with its vast differences in languages, laws, customs, and peoples. The glue that held it together was loyalty to him and to the Roman Church.

In the tradition of his father and grandfather, Charlemagne appointed counts throughout Europe.

The counts were members of the great Frankish families who had been loyal to Charlemagne's family for generations. Thus he created what might be termed an "imperial aristocracy"—truly international in scope. These counts supervised the royal estates in their counties and each spring led the local military contingent, which included all the free men of the county. Counts also presided over local courts, which exercised jurisdiction over the free persons of the county. The king maintained his control over the counts by sending teams of emissaries, or *missi dominici,* composed of bishops and counts to examine the state of each county.

Charlemagne recognized that while his representatives might be drawn from Frankish families, he could not impose Frankish legal and cultural traditions on all his subjects. The only universal system that might unify the kingdom was Roman Christianity. Unity of religious practices, directed by the reformed and educated clergy, would provide spiritual unity. Furthermore, since the clergy could also participate in the administration of the kingdom, they could guarantee administrative unity as well. Carolingian monarchs did not intend the enriched and reformed Church to be independent of royal authority; it was rather to be an integral part of the Carolingian system of government. However, at least some of the educated clerics and lay aristocrats who participated in the system formed a clear political ideology based on Augustinian concepts of Christian government. They attempted to educate Charlemagne and his successors to the duties of a king: maintaining peace and providing justice.

The mobile palace was the center of Carolingian government. It included the royal household and ecclesiastical and secular aristocrats who directed the various activities of the central administration. Within this palace the king held his own court. There, too, clerics maintained written records, produced official records of royal grants or decisions called diplomas, and prepared capitularies, which were written instructions for the implementation of royal directives at the local level.

Carolingian government was no modern bureaucracy or state system. The laymen and clerics who served the king were tied to him by personal oaths of loyalty rather than by any sense of dedication to a state or nation. Still, the attempts at governmental organization were far more sophisticated than anything that the West had seen for four centuries or would see again for another four. The system of counts and missi provided the most effective system of government prior to the thirteenth century and served as the model for subsequent medieval rulers.

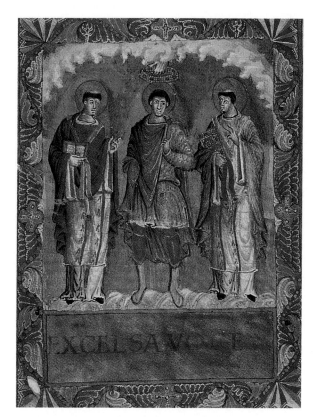

In this illustration from the Coronation Sacramentary of Charles the Bald, Emperor Charlemagne is shown flanked by Pope Gelasius and Pope Gregory the Great.

The size of Charlemagne's empire approached that of the old Roman Empire in the west. Only Britain, southern Italy, and parts of Spain remained outside Frankish control. With the reunification of most of the West and the creative adaptation of Roman traditions of culture and government, it is not surprising that Charlemagne's advisors began to compare his empire to that of Constantine. This comparison was accentuated by Charlemagne's conquest of Lombard Italy and his protection of Pope Leo III—a role traditionally played by the Byzantine emperors. At the end of the eighth century the throne in Constantinople was held by a woman. Irene (752–802) was powerful and capable, but western male leaders considered her unfit for such an office by reason of her sex. All these factors finally converged in one of the most momentous events in Western political history: Charlemagne's imperial coronation on Christmas Day in the year 800.

A page from the Lindisfarne Gospels (ca. 700) showing stylized human and animal representations.

new Western art. The artistic traditions of the barbarian world consisted almost entirely of the decoration of small, portable objects such as weapons, jewelry, and, after conversion, manuscripts. Although some Mediterranean motifs penetrated northward, barbarian art was essentially nonrepresentational and consisted primarily of elaborate interlaced geometric forms of great sophistication and fine craftsmanship. When animal and human forms did appear, as in the Lindisfarne Gospels, produced around 700, or the magnificent Book of Kells, created by Irish monks around a century later, they were transformed into intricate patterns of decoration.

For Charlemagne and his reformers, such abstract art was doubly inappropriate. Not only was it too distant from the Roman heritage that they were trying to emulate, but it could not be used for instruction or propaganda. Therefore Charlemagne invited Italian and Byzantine artists and artisans to his kingdom to teach a form of representational art that would educate

Historians debate the precise meaning of this event, particularly since Charlemagne was said to have remarked afterward that he would never have entered St. Peter's Basilica in Rome had he known what was going to happen. Presumably he meant that he wished to be proclaimed emperor by his Frankish people rather than by the pope, since this is how he had his son Louis the Pious acclaimed emperor in 813. Moreover, Charlemagne apparently saw his title of emperor more as a reflection of his accomplishments than as a political title indicating the foundation of his authority.

Nevertheless, the imperial coronation of 800 subsequently took on great significance. Louis attempted to make his imperial title the sole basis for his rule, and for the next thousand years Germanic kings traveled to Rome to receive the imperial diadem and title from the pope. In so doing they inadvertently strengthened papal claims to enthrone—and at times to dethrone—emperors.

Carolingian Art

The same creative adaptation of the classical heritage that gave birth to a new Western empire produced a

Illustration of Christ, attended by angels, from the Book of Kells.

Europe in the Ninth Century

as well as decorate. However, these southern traditions were no more slavishly followed by northern artists than were Roman political traditions by Charlemagne's government.

Instead, the artistic styles from the East were transformed. The synthesis of Mediterranean and northern artistic traditions produced a dynamic, plastic style of representation in which figures seem intensely alive and active. These figures—which appear in manuscript illuminations, frescoes, ivories, and bas-reliefs—are often arranged in narrative cycles that engage the mind as well as the eye. The Utrecht Psalter is the consummate masterpiece of this tradition. Each psalm is accompanied by a crowded, complex visual interpretation of the text in which verbal and visual metaphors move from scene to scene. In its arrangement and use of classical allusions, the whole work is clearly intended to echo classical antiquity. And yet the execution breathes with a dramatic vision and reality beyond any

of its numerous classical models and is fully equal to the religious themes it represents. In art, as in every other sphere, the Carolingian rebirth was actually a new birth.

A Tour of Europe in the Ninth Century

The Carolingian empire stretched from the Baltic Sea to the Adriatic and linked, through a network of commerce and exchange, the Germanic and Slavic worlds of the north, the Islamic world of Spain and the Near East, and the Mediterranean world of Byzantium. Carolingian kings rebuilt roads, bridges, and ports to facilitate trade. Charlemagne also reformed Western currency, abandoning gold coinage in favor of the more easily obtainable and liquid silver.

Silver was the medium of exchange at the northern ports of Durstede near the mouth of the Rhine and Quentovic near what is now Etaples. It was here that Frankish merchants haggled with Anglo-Saxon and Danish traders over cloth, furs, and amber from the Baltic. Merchants along the Slavic frontier and down the Danube River dealt primarily in human commodities. Great slave trains passed from these regions into the Rhine region. In Verdun young boys were castrated at "eunuch factories" before being sent down the Rhone River to the cities of lower Provence, where they were sold to Muslim agents from Spain and North Africa. Jewish and Greek merchants supplied the Frankish church and aristocracy with luxury goods from Constantinople and the East. The travels of a merchant in the early ninth century might begin with a short trip from Quentovic to the English coast and then continue clockwise around the Frankish world.

England

A continental visitor in England would be well treated. In 796 Charlemagne had written to King Offa of Mercia (757–796), offering English merchants protection in his kingdom and agreeing that "our men, if they suffer any injustice in your dominion, are to appeal to the judgment of your equity, lest any disturbance should arise." Offa, the only king Charlemagne referred to as "brother," ruled a prosperous southeast England and was acknowledged as a leader by other Anglo-Saxon rulers. His success was based partly on military actions against the Welsh. He had led raids deep into Wales and had constructed a great dike 25 feet high and 150 miles long along the entire length of the Welsh frontier. Charlemagne's letter indicates, though, that Mercia's prosperity was also based on extensive trading with the Continent, a trade in which Anglo-Saxon woolens and silver were exchanged for wine, oil, and other products of the Continent.

Mercian supremacy did not last beyond the rule of Offa. In the constant warfare among Anglo-Saxon kingdoms during the first half of the ninth century, Mercia fell to Wessex. The cycle of rise and fall of little kingdoms might have continued had the Vikings not come onto the scene. These Scandinavian raiders had been harassing the coast since 786. They did not pose a serious threat to England, however, until 865, when a great Viking army interested in conquest landed north of the Humber River. All but one of the Anglo-Saxon kingdoms were destroyed. Three kings were killed and a fourth was forced to abdicate.

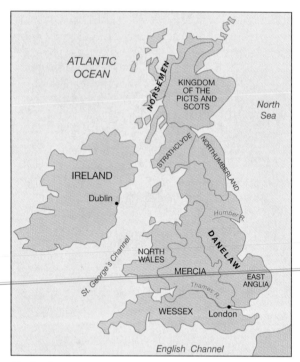

England

The surviving king, Alfred of Wessex (870–899), reorganized his army, established a network of fortifications, created a navy, and thus temporarily halted the Viking conquest. Still, he realized that his military achievement could be consolidated only by the transformation of his political base. Few of Alfred's contemporaries saw him as the savior of England. He had first to win the loyalty of people in his own kingdom and then attract that of Anglo-Saxons outside his kingdom.

Alfred won support by reforming the legal and cultural foundations of his kingdom. His legal reforms aimed to reassure subjects of the various Anglo-Saxon kingdoms of equal treatment. At the same time they emphasized the importance of oaths of loyalty and the gravity of treason. Alfred further reassured Anglo-Saxon nobles by arranging marriage alliances with influential noble families. Finally, Alfred inaugurated a religious and cultural program to extend literacy and learning so that his people might better understand and follow God's word. Alfred and his reformers used the vernacular Anglo-Saxon because at this time Latin was almost entirely unknown in England. Alfred encouraged the translation of the greatest books of the Christian tradition into Anglo-Saxon. He even translated some of the books himself.

By the time Alfred died in 899, southern England was united under Wessex leadership. Eastern England north of the Thames River was occupied and colonized by Danes. In this region, known as the Danelaw, the Vikings settled as farmers and slowly merged with the local population.

Scandinavia

Scandinavians in England were merchants as well as raiders. They traded furs, amber, and fish for English silver and cloth. A merchant interested in the northern trade might depart England from the town of York and travel down the Ouse and the Humber rivers to the North Sea. To make this passage, a merchant might sail with a Scandinavian merchant-Viking in his longboat. These magnificent ships, over seventy feet long, were fast, flexible, and easily maneuvered. They allowed Scandinavians to cross the ocean to America and to navigate the shallow rivers of Europe. A merchant's journey would begin with passage across the English Channel, followed by a two-day sail north along the coast of the Jutland Peninsula to the mouth of the Eider River. From here merchants could take advantage of the newly established trade route that crossed the Jutland Peninsula to Hedeby at the head of the Slie Fjord on the Baltic Sea, thus avoiding the long and dangerous sea voyage around the Skaw, the northern-most point of the Jutland Peninsula. After a few days a serious trader would press on, passing the Swedish archipelago, out past the islands of Oland and Gotland, through the narrow strait where Stockholm now stands, to Birka, the greatest port of Scandinavia. In Birka, Danes, Swedes, Franks, Frisians, Anglo-Saxons, Balts, Greeks, and Arabs met and carried on their international trade.

Like England, Scandinavia had long been an area of Frankish commercial and political interest. The Saxons had previously formed a buffer between the Scandinavians and the Frankish world, but Charlemagne's conquests had brought the two societies into direct contact.

Scandinavian society resembled the Germanic society of the first century. It was composed of three social classes. At the top were wealthy chiefs, or *jarlar* (earls), who had numerous servants, slaves, and free retainers. At the bottom were thralls, or bondsmen. In between were peasant freeholders, who formed the majority of the population. Scandinavians lived mainly for personal glory and war booty. Military ability and political cunning were equally prized, in women as well as men. In this society women enjoyed considerable freedom and authority that shocked more "civilized" observers from other cultures. An Arab merchant who visited

Hedeby in 950 reported that women could claim the right to divorce whenever they wished. In the ninth century, however, internal developments began to threaten the traditional independence of Scandinavian men and women, contributing to the Scandinavian expansion into the rest of Europe.

Scandinavian kings were traditionally selected by groups of earls and exercised positions more as firsts among equals than as rulers. Around the end of the eighth century, however—possibly in imitation of Frankish and Anglo-Saxon royalty—Scandinavian kings began to consolidate power at home and to look to the wealthy Anglo-Saxon and Frankish worlds as sources of booty and glory. Earls and royal pretenders, threatened or displaced by the kings, also began to go "viking," or raiding, in order to replace abroad what they had lost at home.

The directions in which Northmen went viking depended on the regions of Scandinavia from which they came. Swedes looked east, trading with the Slavic world and Byzantium. Norwegians looked to Ireland and Scotland, and later to Greenland, Iceland, and North America. The Danes tended to focus on England and the Frankish empire.

Swedish merchant-Vikings, known as the Rus', traveled down the Volga, Dvina, and Dnepr rivers as far as the Black and Caspian seas in search of furs and slaves.

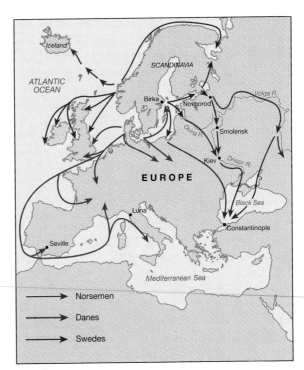

Scandinavia

There they met the trading routes of the Byzantine Empire and the caliphate of Baghdad. Rus'-fortified trading settlements at Novgorod, Smolensk, and Kiev became the nuclei of a Slavic-Scandinavian political unit to which the Rus' eventually gave their name: Russia.

Norwegians began their viking in Europe's western islands in the late eighth century. Ireland, which until then had been undisturbed either by Roman or Germanic invaders, was the first victim. Norwegians also raided south along the coast of the Frankish kingdom, Spain, and even into the Mediterranean region, where they raided Provence, North Africa, and Italy. In Italy a wily Norwegian plundered the city of Luna (which he mistook for Rome) by a ruse so bold that it captured the imagination of even the Franks. Unable to take the town by storm, the commander had his men inform the Italians that the Norwegian leader had died. Since he had been a Christian, they wished him to receive a Christian burial. When the chieftain's body was brought into the city by his "mourning" followers, he suddenly rose from the dead and killed the bishop, and then he and his men sacked the town.

The political consolidation in Norway under Harold Finehair (860–933) culminated in 872 and led more Norwegians to go viking. Earls who objected to Harold's consolidation went abroad to maintain their freedom. Some settled in the Faroe Islands, while others colonized Iceland.

The southernmost Scandinavians, the Danes, were most intimately familiar with the Frankish and Anglo-Saxon realms. During the reigns of Charlemagne's successors, Danish viking progressed from scattered raids against wealthy monasteries or trading towns like Durstede to organized expeditions and finally to massive conquests. Some of these Vikings, led by Danish kings, colonized whole areas, such as Northumbria and the region of the mouth of the Seine River. It was this region that later became known as Normandy—land of the Northmen.

The Slavic World

A merchant in Scandinavia might join an expedition of Swedish Rus' to cross the Baltic Sea and enter the Slavic world in search of ermine and slaves. The Carolingians' effects were felt, both in merchant activity and in the presence of imperialist armies and missionaries. The Slavic world of the ninth century was a rapidly changing amalgam of Germanic and Slavic peoples whose ultimate orientation—north to Scandinavia, east to Constantinople, or west to Aachen—was an open question.

In antiquity and the early Middle Ages distinctions between Slavic and Germanic peoples were hazy, and the development of Slavic society and culture was quite similar to that of the Germans. In the sixth century, Slavic tribes had begun to filter west. In the seventh century, a Frank named Samo (d. ca. 660) organized a brief but powerful confederation of Slavs in the area between the Sudeten Mountains and the eastern Alps. For a time this confederation resisted both the Avars and the Merovingians.

In the following century the Great Moravian empire developed out of Slavic tribes along the March River. Both the Byzantine and the Carolingian empires sought to bring Moravia into their spheres of influence. In the middle of the ninth century Frankish, Italian, and Greek missionaries began to compete to organize a Christian church in this Slavic empire. In 852 a Slavic prince particularly suspicious of the Franks turned to the Greeks. He encouraged the missionary efforts of Cyril and Methodius, who enjoyed the encouragement of both the Byzantines and the papacy. Through their translation of liturgical texts into Slavonic (for which they probably invented the Cyrillic script used today in Russia), they not only laid the basis for a Slavic church but also began a tradition of Slavic literacy.

The promising beginning made by the two missionary brothers was short-lived, since the Franks feared an independent Slavic church. In 864 the Carolingian king Louis the German (843–876) conquered Moravia. Methodius, who had been appointed arch-

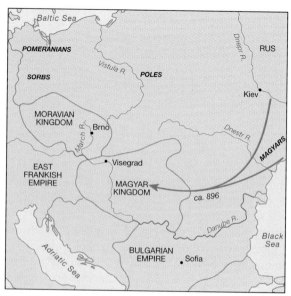

The Slavic World

bishop of Moravia and Pannonia by the pope, was imprisoned in a German monastery for the rest of his life. The Frankish hegemony lasted only a few decades. In 895 a new steppe people, the Magyars, or Hungarians, swept into Pannonia as had the Huns and Avars before them. These new invaders destroyed the Franks' puppet Moravian empire and split the Slavic world in two. The south Slavs in what is now the Balkans were cut off from the northern Slavs in what is now Poland, Russia, and Ukraine.

The Magyar kingdom proved a greater threat to the Franks than the Slavs or Avars. The Magyars not only conquered Pannonia as far as the Enns River, they also raided deep into the Carolingian empire. For fifty years swift bands of Magyar horsemen crossed the Alps and pillaged the Po Valley, terrorizing the eastern portions of the empire and even striking as far west as modern Burgundy.

Muslim Spain

The Slavic world was not only in contact with the Christian societies of Byzantium and the West. Muslim merchants used Arab gold to buy furs and slaves from Rus' traders at settlements along the Dnepr River. A Spanish merchant might depart from Kiev and, to avoid the Magyars, travel down the Dnepr to the Black Sea past Constantinople, and then across the length of the Mediterranean to Al-Andalus, as the Muslims called Spain. After the disintegration of the Umayyad caliphate (see pp. 209–210), the last Umayyad, 'Abd ar-Rahman I (731–788), made his way to Spain, where in 756 he established an independent emirate. Under the centralized control of the Umayyad emirs, the economic and cultural life of urban Spain, which had stagnated under the Visigoths, experienced a renaissance as vital as that taking place across the Pyrenees in the Frankish empire.

To secure the emirate, 'Abd ar-Rahman and his successors had to overcome internal division and external aggression. The Spanish population included an elite minority of Arabs, recently arrived Syrians, North African Berbers, converted Spaniards, Christian Spaniards, and Jews. In addition, Frankish aggression and Scandinavian Vikings continually harassed Al-Andalus.

In the short run, 'Abd ar-Rahman secured control by brute force. Relying on a professional army composed mainly of slaves, the emirs crushed revolts mounted by various Muslim factions. They strengthened a series of semi-autonomous districts, or marches, commanded by military governors as buffers against

Spain

the Frankish kingdom to the north. Finally, they established a line of guard posts along the coast to protect themselves against the Northmen.

In the long run, the emirs sought stability in religion and law. They presented themselves as the champions and protectors of Islam, assuming in 926 the titles of "caliph," "commander of the believers," and "defender of the religion of God." In this way they built a religious foundation for their rule. Likewise, they cultivated the study and application of Islamic law as a source of justice and social order.

The economic prosperity of Al-Andalus was based on an enlightened system of agriculture that included the introduction of oranges, rice, sugarcane, and cotton from the eastern Mediterranean. Complementing agriculture was a renewed urban life bolstered by vigorous trade to the north, east, and south. From the later ninth century this trade was supplemented by raiding expeditions into Italy and southern Gaul. In the ninth and tenth centuries, Spain was the most prosperous region of Europe and one of the wealthiest areas of the Muslim world.

In this climate of security and prosperity developed the most sophisticated and refined culture in the West. Arabic poetry and art developed in a manner exactly the opposite of that in the Carolingian world. Poetry, visual art, and architecture deemphasized

An example of the animal style common in the Celtic-Germanic art of the early Middle Ages, this wooden animal head is the terminal of a post from a seventh-century Viking ship.

physical forms and encouraged abstraction and meditation. Meditation drew the individual away from the reality of objects and images toward the unseen divinity. Such abstract, contemplative art did not develop in western Christendom for centuries.

After the Carolingians: From Empire to Lordships

Alien, dynamic, and potentially threatening neighbors surrounded the Carolingian kingdom. To the west was Anglo-Saxon England; to the east were the Slavic and Byzantine worlds. Scandinavia lay to the north, and Al-Andalus threatened to the south. In the later ninth and tenth centuries, the Frankish kingdom collapsed, owing in part to the actions of these neighbors, but primarily to the kingdom's own internal weaknesses.

Charlemagne, despite his imperial title, had remained dependent on his traditional power base, the

Frankish aristocracy. For them, learned concepts of imperial renovation meant little: they wanted wealth and power. Under Charlemagne, the empire's prosperity and relative internal peace had resulted largely from continued successful expansion at the expense of neighbors. Its economy had been based on plunder and the redistribution of booty among the aristocracy and wealthy churches. As wars of conquest under Charlemagne gave place to defensive actions against Magyars, Vikings, and Saracens, the supply of wealth dried up. Aristocratic supporters had to be rewarded with estates within the empire. Aristocrats thus became enormously wealthy and powerful. Count Everard, whose library was mentioned earlier (p. 238), left his sons estates scattered from Friuli in northern Italy to what is now Belgium.

Competition among Charlemagne's descendants as well as grants to the aristocracy weakened central authority. By fate rather than by design, Charlemagne had bequeathed a united empire to his son Louis the Pious (814–840). Charlemagne had intended to follow Frankish custom and divide his estate among all his sons, but only Louis survived him. Louis' three sons, in contrast, fought one another over their inheritance, and in 843 they divided the empire among them. The eldest son, Lothair (840–855), who inherited his father's imperial title, received an unwieldy middle portion that stretched from the Rhine River south through Italy. Louis the German (840–876) received the eastern portions of the empire. The youngest son, Charles the Bald (840–877), was allotted the western portions. In time the western kingdom became France and the eastern kingdom became the core of Germany. The middle kingdom, which included what are now Holland, Belgium, Luxembourg, Lorraine (or Lotharingia, from *Lothair*), Switzerland, and northern Italy, remained a disputed region into the twentieth century.

The disintegration of the empire meant much more than its division among Charlemagne's heirs. In no region were his successors able to provide the degree of peace and public control that he had established. The Frankish armies, designed for wars of aggression, were too clumsy and slow to deal with the lightning raids of Northmen, Magyars, and Saracens. The constant need to please aristocratic supporters made it impossible for kings to prevent aristocrats from absorbing free peasants and churches into their economic and political spheres. Increasingly, these magnates were able to transform the offices of count and bishop into inherited familial positions. They also determined who would reign in their kingdoms and sought kings who posed no threat to themselves.

The Division of Charlemagne's Empire

Most aristocrats saw this greater autonomy as their just due. Only dukes, counts, and other local lords could organize resistance to internal and external foes at the local level. They needed both economic means and political authority to provide protection and maintain peace. These resources could be acquired only at the expense of royal power. Thus, during the late ninth and tenth centuries much of Europe found its equilibrium at the local level as public powers, judicial courts, and military authority became the private possession of wealthy families. Charlemagne's empire had become a patchwork of local lordships.

Ultimately, new royal families emerged from among these local leaders. The family of the counts of Paris, for example, gained enormous prestige from the fact that they had led the successful defense of the city against the Vikings from 885 to 886. For a time they alternated with Carolingians as kings of the West Franks. After the ascension of Hugh Capet in 987, they entirely replaced the Carolingians.

In a similar manner, the eastern German kingdom, which was divided into five great duchies, began to elect non-Carolingians as kings. In 919 the dukes of this region elected as their king Duke Henry of Saxony (919–936), who had proven his abilities fighting the Danes and Magyars. Henry's son, Otto the Great (936–973), proved to be a strong ruler who subdued

the other dukes and definitively crushed the Magyars. In 962 Otto was crowned emperor by Pope John XII (955–964), thus reviving the empire of Charlemagne, although only in its eastern half. However, the dukes of this eastern kingdom chafed constantly at the strong control the Ottonians attempted to exercise at their expense. Although the empire Otto reestablished endured until 1806, he and his successors never matched the political or cultural achievements of the Carolingians.

By the tenth century, the early medieval kingdoms, based on inherited Roman notions of universal states and barbarian traditions of charismatic military leadership, had all ended in failure. After the demise of the Carolingian empire, the West began to find stability at a more local but also more permanent level. The local nature of Western society did not mean, however, that the Roman and Carolingian traditions were forgotten. Carolingian religious reform, classical learning, and political ideology were preserved in the following centuries.

Church reform took on new life in 909 with the foundation of the monastery of Cluny in eastern France. Cluniac monks, drawn from the lesser aristocracy, were God's shock troops, fighting evil with their

This magnificent jeweled crown was made for Otto I. The small portrait represents King Solomon.

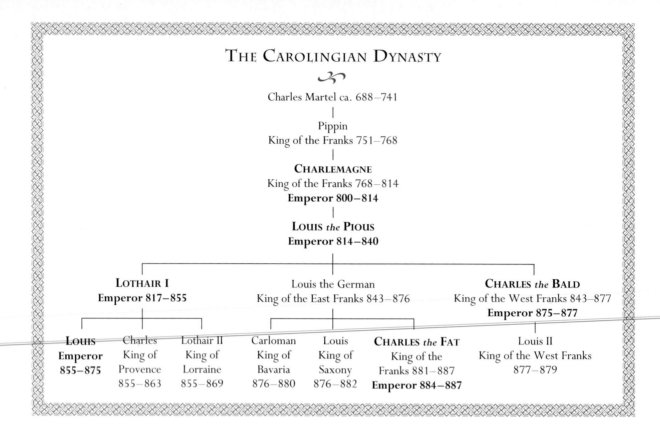

THE CAROLINGIAN DYNASTY

Charles Martel ca. 688–741

Pippin
King of the Franks 751–768

CHARLEMAGNE
King of the Franks 768–814
Emperor 800–814

LOUIS *the* **PIOUS**
Emperor 814–840

LOTHAIR I	Louis the German	**CHARLES** *the* **BALD**
Emperor 817–855	King of the East Franks 843–876	King of the West Franks 843–877
		Emperor 875–877

LOUIS	Charles	Lothair II	Carloman	Louis	**CHARLES** *the* **FAT**	Louis II
Emperor	King of	King of	King of	King of	King of the	King of the West Franks
855–875	Provence	Lorraine	Bavaria	Saxony	Franks 881–887	877–879
	855–863	855–869	876–880	876–882	**Emperor 884–887**	

prayers with the same vigor that their secular cousins fought the enemy with their swords. Cluny, inspired by the monastic program of Louis the Pious and granted immunity from secular interference, became the center of an extraordinary expansion of Benedictine monasticism throughout the West.

The revival of classical learning begun in Carolingian schools, although hampered by the new wave of invasions that began in the later ninth century, continued in centers such as St. Gall, Auxerre, and Corvey. During the late ninth and tenth centuries, western Christian civilization spread north and east. By the year 1000 Scandinavia, Poland, Bohemia, and even Hungary had become Christian kingdoms with national churches whose bishops were approved by the pope. Among the aristocracy, just as all restraints on this warrior elite seemed to have been thrown off, a gradual process of transformation of their material and mental world began. Encouraged by Cluniac monasticism and by episcopal exhortations, nobles began to consider limiting their violence against one another and placing it instead in the service of Christendom.

•••

According to a ninth-century legend, Charlemagne once dreamed that he was visited by a sword-carrying spirit from the other world. The sword, a gift to the emperor from God, bore on its blade four Germanic words: *Rhat, Radoleiba, Nasg,* and *Enti.* The next day Charlemagne explained to his courtiers that the dream was a prophecy of the future. *Rhat* was the assistance God had given Charlemagne in conquering his enemies. *Radoleiba* indicated how, under Charlemagne's son, all of this would quickly dissipate. *Nasg* foretold the greed of his grandsons, who would allow their followers to plunder the Church and spread poverty through the land. *Enti* indicated the end, either of his royal family or of the world.

The anonymous author of this legend recognized that although the Magyar, Viking, and Saracen raids contributed to the disintegration of the Carolingian empire, their role was secondary. The internal dynamics of the Frankish world and its unresolved social and political tensions were the essential causes for the collapse of the Carolingian synthesis.

In the long run, however, the Carolingian synthesis left a powerful and enduring legacy. At the start of the Middle Ages in the West, a variety of Germanic kingdoms experimented with a whole spectrum of ways to reconcile the twin elements of barbarian and Roman tradition. The Ostrogoths attempted to preserve the two as separate entities and soon vanished. The Visigoths sought unification through coercion and found themselves isolated and weakened. In England, Germanic invaders sought to replace Roman traditions entirely. Only the Franks found a lasting means of amalgamating Roman and Germanic societies.

The key elements of this synthesis were orthodox Christianity, Roman administration, and Frankish military kingship. Between 500 and 800 these three elements coalesced into a vital new civilization. Although the political structure created by Charlemagne did not survive his grandsons, the Frankish model proved enduring in every other respect. The cultural renaissance laid the foundation of all subsequent European intellectual activities. The alliance between Church and monarchy provided the formula for European kings for almost a thousand years. The administrative system with its central and local components, its counts and its missi, its diplomas and capitularies, provided the model for later medieval government in England and on the Continent. The idea of the Carolingian empire, the symbol of European unity, has never entirely disappeared from the West.

Suggestions for Further Reading

The Making of the Barbarian Kingdoms, 500–750

Roger Collins, *Early Medieval Europe: 300–1000* (Basingstoke: Macmillan Education, 1991). A brief survey of the barbarian kingdoms in late antiquity and the early Middle Ages, with an emphasis on political history.

* Herwig Wolfram, *History of the Goths* (Berkeley, CA: University of California Press, 1987). An outstanding study of the formation of the Goths in late antiquity.

Thomas Burns, *The Ostrogoths* (Bloomington, IN: Indiana University Press, 1984). A recent study of Italy under the Goths.

Edward James, *The Origins of France From Clovis to the Capetians, 500–1000* (London: Macmillan, 1982). A brief survey of the Franks, with special attention to the archaeological sources.

* Patrick J. Geary, *Before France and Germany: The Origins and Transformation of the Merovingian World* (New York: Oxford University Press, 1988). A study of the Merovingians from the perspective of late Roman traditions.

* James Campbell, ed., *The Anglo-Saxons* (Oxford: Phaidon, 1982). A collection of essays on Anglo-Saxon England by an outstanding group of archaeologists and historians.

Living in the New Europe

Suzanne Fonay Wemple, *Women in Frankish Society: Marriage and the Cloister, 500–900* (Philadelphia: University

of Pennsylvania Press, 1981). A pioneering study of women in the early Middle Ages.

* David Herlihy, *Medieval Households* (Cambridge, MA: Harvard University Press, 1985). An important survey of medieval peasant society.

The Carolingian Achievement

* Rosamond McKitterick, *The Frankish Kingdoms Under the Carolingians, 751–987* (New York: Longman, 1983). A very detailed study of Carolingian history, with an emphasis on intellectual developments.

* Heinrich Fichtenau, *The Carolingian Empire: The Age of Charlemagne* (Toronto: University of Toronto Press, 1957). A classic reevaluation of the weaknesses of the Carolingian empire.

Pierre Riche, *Daily Life in the World of Charlemagne* (Philadelphia: University of Pennsylvania Press, 1978). A look at the lives of men and women in the ninth century by a leading French scholar.

A Tour of Europe in the Ninth Century

* Peter Sawyer, *The Age of the Vikings* (New York: St. Martin's Press, 1971). A good introduction to Scandinavian history.

* Geoffrey Barraclough, ed., *Eastern and Western Europe in the Middle Ages* (New York: Harcourt Brace Jovanovich, 1970). Essays by specialists on Eastern Europe and its relationship to the West.

Roger Collins, *Early Medieval Spain: Unity in Diversity, 400–1000* (New York: St. Martin's Press, 1983). A balanced recent survey of Visigothic and Islamic Spain.

W. Montgomery Watt, *A History of Islamic Spain* (Edinburgh: Edinburgh University Press, 1965). An intelligent introduction to Spain under Islam for the nonspecialist.

After the Carolingians: From Empire to Lordships

* Heinrich Fichtenau, *Living in the Tenth Century: Studies in Mentalities and Social Orders* (Chicago: University of Chicago Press, 1990). A brilliant evocation of the quest for order on the Continent following the dissolution of the Carolingian empire.

* Georges Duby, *The Early Growth of the European Economy: Warriors and Peasants From the Seventh to the Twelfth Century* (Ithaca: Cornell University Press, 1974). An imaginative survey of the economic and social forces forming in Europe in the early Middle Ages.

* Timothy Reuter, *Germany in the Early Middle Ages, 800–1056* (New York: Longman, 1991). A readable, original survey of early German history by a British scholar thoroughly knowledgeable of current German scholarship.

*Paperback edition available.

9 ❧ THE HIGH MIDDLE AGES

The Royal Tombs at Fontevrault

*I*n the monastic church of Fontevrault, a double monastery of monks and nuns in western France ruled by a powerful abbess, reposes the most powerful and influential woman of the twelfth century, Eleanor of Aquitaine (1122–1204), heiress of one of the greatest principalities of France, wife of two kings, and mother of two more. The lifesize polychrome figure, executed shortly after her death, reclines peacefully, her hands holding a book, her head, surrounded by a wimple and surmounted by a crown, resting on a pillow. The serenity of her repose masks the turbulence of her life. Beside her lie the two most important men in her life: her husband Henry II of England (1154–89) and their son Richard the Lion-Hearted (1189–99). The paths that brought Eleanor, Henry, and Richard to Fontevrault tell much about the world of the High Middle Ages.

Eleanor's father, Duke William X of Aquitaine, had inherited a great but troubled principality built by the military, diplomatic, and dynastic skills of his ancestors at a time when lordship, not kingship or religion, had been the key to power in France. William's death had left fifteen-year-old Eleanor, the most coveted heiress in Europe, in the care of the French king Louis VI. He promptly married her to secure her vast holdings in the south and west. The marriage was a disaster from every perspective. The behavior of the lively young queen and her ladies scandalized the timid, austere, and pious Louis and his clerical advisors, particularly when she accompanied her husband on the ill-fated Second Crusade. Even worse, Eleanor failed to provide Louis with a male heir. Such a failure was always considered the fault of the wife, and Louis divorced her in 1152. Eleanor promptly married Duke Henry of Normandy, thereby uniting the west of France. She also bore Henry eight children, four of them boys, much to the chagrin of her former husband. When Henry became King Henry II of England in 1154, together they ruled a vast region of Europe, from Scotland to south-central France, often called the Angevin Empire.

Eleanor and Henry directed the most vibrant, exciting, and creative court in Europe—a court that moved constantly about the Angevin Empire. However, Eleanor felt most at home in her native Poitiers. Her court became a center of literary production, and her patronage was responsible for the flourishing of French romances and Provençal love lyrics.

In time Eleanor's problems with Henry became even more serious than those she had had with Louis. Henry was one of the greatest figures in the development of English royal power, and he attempted to rule his wife's lands with an iron hand. At the same time he sought to exclude his sons from real authority. The sons in turn spent much of their time in revolt against their father, often with the assistance of their mother. However, Henry was too smart to divorce his wife and thus lose her vast estates. Instead he attempted to force her into the convent at Fontevrault. When she refused, he imprisoned her. For fourteen years, Queen Eleanor remained under lock and key. But it was Henry who entered Fontevrault first: he died on the Continent in 1189 in the midst of a rebellion led by Richard and King Philip Augustus of France. Henry was hastily buried at nearby Fontevrault because the traditional burial place of his family was in revolt.

Henry's heir and opponent, Eleanor's beloved son Richard the Lion-Hearted, freed her on his father's death. While her son pursued dreams of chivalric glory on crusade or on the battlefield, she governed the vast Angevin realm single-handedly. When the Duke of Austria took Richard hostage on his return from the Third Crusade, it was Eleanor who collected the ransom that paid for his liberty. Richard died in 1199 while besieging a small and insignificant castle. On his deathbed he asked to be buried at Henry's feet at Fontevrault, in repentance for having betrayed his father.

Eleanor then worked as best she could to support her youngest son John as king of England and to preserve the dynastic network of her family. When King Philip Augustus, the son of her former husband, wanted to marry Eleanor's granddaughter Blanche of Castille to his son, the future Louis VIII, Eleanor, although in her late seventies, made the arduous winter journey across the Pyrenees to Castile in order to fetch the bride. Worn out by her exertions, in 1202 Eleanor freely retired to the monastery where Henry had attempted to send her over a quarter of a century before. She died there peacefully in 1204.

Eleanor's life spanned the age of feudal lordships and the creation of the medieval state. Her youth was spent in a world in which great feudal nobles like her father had dominated public life. Her middle years saw western Europe find its own voice as it developed a vibrant culture and international vision under the domination of vast, eclectic interlocking lordships, principalities, and kingships such as the Angevin Empire. But she lived on into a world dominated by kings such as Philip Augustus, who relied on a growing world of merchants, bankers, professional soldiers, and bureaucrats to create a smaller but more cohesive and ultimately more powerful centralized monarchy. Eleanor was at home in the first world, and she helped to create and dominate the second. The third was alien to her, and her death at Fontevrault came in good time.

The Countryside

From the tenth through the thirteenth centuries, enormous transformations re-created the rural landscape. The most significant of these changes concerned the peasantry, but these changes are difficult to chronicle, since until the nineteenth century, the majority of the common people left no written record of their lives. What we know of them was recorded by a tiny literate elite whose interest in the masses was primarily either economic or judicial. To this elite, the lives, work, and aspirations of these peasants were worth recording only to the extent that the information could improve the collection of rents, tithes, and taxes, or if it could better control the potential threat of peasants to the established order. With few exceptions, the only medieval peasants whose voices we hear are those who were forced to testify before the court of a secular lord or an ecclesiastical inquisitor.

In this medieval farmstead newly cut from the forest, men beat acorns out of the trees for the pigs to eat while horses wearing collars pull the plow. Note the fenced-in vegetable garden at the right.

By the tenth century the population of Europe was growing, and with this population growth came new forms of social organization and economic activity. Between the years 1000 and 1300 Europe's population almost doubled, from approximately 38 million to 74 million. Various reasons have been proposed for this growth. Perhaps the end of the Viking, Magyar, and Saracen raids left rural society in relative peace to live and reproduce. The decline of slavery meant that individual peasant families could live and bear children without constraints imposed by masters. Gradually improving agricultural techniques and equipment lessened somewhat the constant danger of famine. Possibly, too, a slowly improving climate increased agricultural yields. None of these explanations is entirely satisfactory. Whatever the cause of the population growth, it changed the face of Europe.

During the tenth century the great forests that had covered most of Europe began to be cut back as population spread out from the islands of cultivation that had characterized the ninth century into the wilderness. In the north of Germany and in what is now Holland, beginning around 1100, enterprising peasants began to drain marshes—a slow process of creating new land that would continue into the 1900s. This progress was not linear everywhere. In England, for example, forests actually gained on plowland after the Norman Conquest of 1066. However, by the mid-twelfth century the acrid smoke from slash-and-burn clearing of the forest could be smelled all across Europe.

The Peasantry: Serfs and Freemen

The peasants who engaged in the opening of this internal frontier were the descendants of the slaves, unfree farmers, and petty free persons of the early Middle Ages. In the east along the frontier of the Germanic empire, in the Slavic world, in Scandinavia, in southern Gaul, in northern Italy, and in the reconquered portions of Christian Spain, the peasants were free persons who owned land, entered into contracts with magnates, and remained responsible for their own fates. In the course of the eleventh century, across much of northwestern Europe and in particular in France, the various gradations in social status disappeared and the peasantry formed a homogeneous social category loosely described as serfdom. While serfs were not slaves in a legal sense, their degraded status, their limited or nonexistent access to public courts of law, and their enormous dependency on their lords left them in a situation similar to that of those Carolingian slaves who settled on individual farmsteads in the ninth century.

Each year peasants had to hand over to their lords certain fixed portions of their meager harvests. In addition, they were obligated to work a certain number of days the *demesne,* or reserve of the lord, the produce of which went directly to him for his use or sale. Finally, they were required to make ritual payments symbolizing their subordination.

Most peasants led lives of constant insecurity. They were inadequately housed, clothed, and fed; subject to the constant scrutiny of their lords; and defenseless against natural or man-made disasters. Their homes offered little protection from the elements. Most homes were small shacks constructed of mud and wood, with one or two rooms inhabited by the entire family and their most precious domestic animals. Roofs were so low that village gossips would often lift up an eave to listen in on their neighbors—hence the origin of the term *eavesdrop.* These huts must have been extremely dark and sooty. They usually had no windows, and until the sixteenth century they had no chimneys: instead, smoke from the open hearth was allowed to escape through a hole in the roof. It is small wonder that tuberculosis and other lung diseases were endemic.

Across Europe, peasant houses were clustered in villages on manors or large estates. This was due in part to the peasants' need for security and companionship against the dangers and terrors of a hostile world. However, in some parts of Europe the clustering was the result of their lord's desire to keep a close eye on his labor supply. Beginning in the tenth century in central Italy and elsewhere, lords forced peasants to abandon isolated farmsteads and traditional villages and to move into small fortified settlements. In these new villages peasants were obligated to settle disputes in the lord's court, to grind their grain in the lord's mill, and to bake their bread in the lord's oven—all primary sources of revenue for the lord. At the center of the village was the church, often the only stone or brick building in the village. Until the thirteenth century, even the lord's castle was often simply a wooden structure similar to an American frontier fort. The same sort of monopoly enforced on the lords' mills and ovens applied to the church. Villagers had to contribute a tenth of their revenues to the church and to make donations in order to receive the sacraments. In some villages these payments may have actually gone to the church; usually they went to the lord as well.

Each morning men went out to work in the fields, which surrounded the village. In some villages each peasant householder held thin strips of widely scattered land, while pasturage and woodland were exploited in common. While this arrangement may have been inefficient from the perspective of time lost traveling to work different plots of land, such an open-field system allotted all peasant households a portion of all different sorts of land. In addition, the physical separation of the plots provided families insurance against total loss of crops due to sudden storms or other localized disasters. In other villages, each household tended a unified parcel of land. These closed fields generally corresponded with greater divergences in wealth within the village and encouraged more independence.

While the men plowed and worked the fields, women took charge of the domestic tasks. These included wool carding, spinning, weaving, caring for the family's vegetable garden, bearing and raising children, and brewing the thick souplike beer that was a primary source of carbohydrates in the peasant diet. During harvest women worked in the fields alongside the men.

Beer, black bread, beans, cabbage, onions, and cheese made up the typical peasant fare. Meat was a rarity. Cattle and sheep were too precious to slaughter, and what little meat peasants ate came from the herds of pigs left free to forage in nearby forests for acorns and grubs. Only in northern Europe, where inadequate winter fodder necessitated culling herds each winter, did peasants occasionally enjoy beef. Inadequate agricultural methods and inefficient storage systems left the peasantry in constant threat of famine. A bad year could send mobs of desperate peasants roaming the land in search of food. In the mid-eleventh century the archbishop of Trier was on his way to church with his mounted retinue when he was stopped by a crowd of starving beggars. He offered them money but they refused it, forcing him and his entourage to dismount and watch in disbelief while the crowd ripped the horses apart and devoured them.

The expansion of arable land offered new hope and opportunities to peasants. As rapid as it was, population growth between the tenth and twelfth centuries did not keep up with the demand for laborers in newly settled areas of Europe. Thus labor was increasingly in demand and lords were often willing to make special arrangements with groups of peasants in order to encourage them to bring new land under cultivation. From the beginning of the twelfth century, peasant villages acquired from their lord the privilege to deal with him and his representatives collectively rather than individually. Villages purchased the right to control petty courts and to limit fines imposed by the lord's representative; peasants acquired protection from arbitrary demands for labor and extraordinary taxes.

These good times did not last forever. During the late twelfth and thirteenth centuries, the labor market gradually stagnated. Europe's population—particularly in France, England, Italy, and western Germany—began to reach a saturation point. As a result, lay and ecclesiastical lords found that they could profit more by hiring cheap laborers than by demanding customary services and payments from their serfs. They also found that their serfs were willing to pay for increased privileges.

Peasants could purchase the right to marry without the lord's consent, to move to neighboring manors or to nearby towns, and to inherit. They acquired personal freedom from their lord's jurisdiction, transformed their servile payments into payments of rent for their manses, purchased their own land, and commuted their labor services into annual or even one-time payments. In other words, they began to purchase their freedom. This free peasantry benefited the emerging states of western Europe, since kings and towns could extend their legal and fiscal jurisdictions over these persons and their lands at the expense of the nobility. Governments thus encouraged the extension of freedom and protected peasants from their former masters. By the fourteenth century, serfs were a rarity in many parts of western Europe.

This is not to say that these freed serfs and their descendants necessarily gained prosperity. Freedom often meant freedom from the protection that lords had provided. It meant the freedom to fail, and even to starve. Some peasants acquired their own lands and prospered, while others moved to towns to make their fortune. Still others sank into the ranks of landless beggars. Nevertheless, free peasants were increasingly able to involve themselves in the emerging world of cash-crop farming and to tie into a growing trend toward agricultural specialization. Northern Germany and Sicily focused on grain production; the river valleys of France and Germany focused on vineyards. Areas around emerging towns concentrated on truck gardening to supply produce for these growing urban centers. Clever and successful peasants acquired land, employed their own workers, and established a level of wealth equivalent at times to that of the lesser nobility. On the other hand, by the fourteenth century bands of unsuccessful landless and starving peasants, expelled from rented property by lords seeking to cut labor costs, began to roam the countryside, occasionally becoming the source of political and social turmoil.

Even as western serfs were acquiring a precious though fragile freedom, the free peasantry in much of eastern Europe and Spain were losing it. In much of the Slavic world through the eleventh century, peasants lived in large, roughly territorial communes of free families. Gradually, however, princes, churches, and aristocrats began to build great landed estates. By the thirteenth century—under the influences of western and Byzantine models and of the Mongols, who dominated much of the Slavic world from 1240—lords began to acquire political and economic control over the peasantry. The process was gradual, however, and was not completed until the sixteenth century. In Hungary during the twelfth century, free peasants and unfree servants merged to form a stratum of serfs subordinated to the emerging landed aristocracy and to the lesser nobility composed of free warriors. A similar process took place in parts of Spain. In all these regions, the decline of the free peasantry accompanied the decline of public authority to the benefit of independent nobles. The aristocracy rose on the backs of the peasantry.

The Aristocracy: Fighters and Breeders

Beginning in the late tenth century, writers of legal documents began to employ an old term in a novel manner to designate certain powerful free persons who belonged neither to the old aristocracy nor to the peasantry. The term was *miles*. In classical Latin, *miles* meant "soldier." As used in the Middle Ages, we would translate it as "knight." Initially, a knight was simply a mounted warrior—the term said nothing about his social status. Some knights were serfs, and in Germany knights remained a distinctly lower social group well into the thirteenth century. However, in France, northern Italy, England, and much of Spain, beginning in the eleventh century, the term *knight* (in French, *chevalier;* in Spanish, *caballero*) worked its way up the social ladder. By the end of the twelfth century even kings such as Richard the Lion-Hearted of England identified themselves as part of a knightly, or *chivalric,* world. A term that originally described a function had come to designate a lifestyle.

The center of this lifestyle was northern France. From there, the ideals of knighthood, or chivalry, spread out across Europe, influencing aristocrats as far east as Byzantium. The essence of the knightly lifestyle was fighting. Through warfare this aristocracy had maintained or acquired its freedom, and through warfare it justified its privileges. The origins of this small elite (probably nowhere more than 2 percent of the population) were diverse. Many were descended from the old aristocracy of the Carolingian age. In the region of Burgundy in eastern France, for example, by the twelfth century approximately forty-one families were considered "noble." These families, or "houses," had sprung from six great clans of the Carolingian period. They traced descent through the male line. Inheritance was usually limited to the eldest sons, and daughters were given a dowry but did not share in inheritance. Younger sons had to find service with some great lord or live in the households of their older brothers. Even the eldest sons who became heads of these households could not freely dispose of family property without consulting their kinsmen.

Such noble families, proud of their independence and ancestry, maintained their position through complex kin networks, mutual defense pacts with other nobles, and control of castles. This control gave them the ability to dominate the surrounding countryside. By the twelfth century nobles lived safely behind castle walls, often even independent of the local counts, dukes, and kings. This lesser nobility absorbed control of such traditionally public powers as justice, peace, and taxation.

For the sons of such nobles, preparation for a life of warfare began early, often in the entourage of a maternal uncle or a powerful lord. Boys learned to ride, to handle heavy swords and shields, to manage a lance on horseback, and to swing an axe with deadly accuracy. They also learned more-subtle but equally important lessons about honor, pride, and family tradition. The feats of ancestors or heroes, sung by traveling minstrels at the banqueting table on long winter nights, provided models of knightly action. In *The Song of Roland*—a legend loosely based on the exploits of an eighth-century count in Charlemagne's army who was killed in an ambush as the Franks crossed the Pyrenees from Spain—they learned the importance of loyalty and fierce dedication to duty and the dangers of pride and reckless faith in one's own sword. In the legends of King Arthur, they learned the disasters that weak leadership could bring to a band of warriors or to a whole country. The culmination of this education for English and French nobles came in a ceremony of knighting. An adolescent from age sixteen to eighteen received a sword from an older, experienced warrior. No longer a boy, he now became a youth, ready to enter the world of fighting for which he had trained.

A youth was a noble who had been knighted but who had not married or acquired land, either through inheritance or as a reward from a lord for service, and thus had not yet established his own "house." The length of time one remained a youth varied enormously. It could easily extend into one's thirties or beyond. During this time the knight led the life of a warrior. He joined in promising military expeditions and amused

Manuscript illustration showing an aide arming a man for fighting on foot.

himself with tournaments, mock battles that often proved as deadly as the real thing. A knight could win an opponent's horses and armor as well as renown. Drinking, gambling, and lechery were other common activities. This was an extraordinarily dangerous lifestyle. Many youths did not survive to the next stage in a knight's life—that of acquiring land, wife, honor, and his own following of youths. The basic plot outline of most medieval romances is in essence the dream of every young knight: kill an older opponent, marry his wife, acquire his lands, and found a house.

The period between childhood and maturity was no less dangerous for noblewomen than for men. Marriages were the primary forms of alliances between noble houses, and the production of children was essential to the continued prosperity of the family. Thus daughters were raised as breeders, married at around age sixteen, and then expected to produce as many children as possible. Given the primitive knowledge of obstetrics, bearing children was even more dangerous than bearing a lance. Many noblewomen died in childbirth, often literally exhausted by frequent successive births. Although occasionally practiced, contraception was condemned both by the Church and by husbands eager for offspring, and even the natural contraceptive effects of nursing were not available to noblewomen, who normally gave their infants to wet nurses to suckle.

In this martial society, the political and economic status of women declined considerably. Because they were considered unable to participate in warfare, in northern Europe women were also frequently excluded from inheritance, estate management, courts, and public deliberations. Although a growing tradition of "courtliness" glorified the status of aristocratic women in literature, women were actually losing ground in the real world. Some noblewomen did control property and manage estates, but usually such roles were possible only for widows who had borne sons and who could play a major part in raising them. Such women were not uncommon. If a noblewoman was able to bear children successfully, she stood an excellent chance of surviving her husband, who was probably at least fifteen years her senior and whose military pursuits placed him in constant danger. Such a role was not likely to endear her to her male contemporaries. For all their martial valor, medieval men feared women and female sexuality. They mistrusted this representative of another lineage who was essential to the continuance of their own. Both secular tradition and Christian teaching portrayed women as devious, sexually demanding temptresses often responsible for the corruption and downfall of men. Many men felt threatened by this aggressive sexual stereotype. They resented the power wielded by wealthy widows and abbesses.

The noble lifestyle for men and women demanded specific virtues. A knight and his lady were to be "gentle," a term that meant simply "of good birth." Men were to be "preu," or powerful fighters. Both men and women were praised for graciousness—open-handed generosity to their followers or retainers. To maintain a lifestyle of conspicuous consumption required wealth, and wealth meant land. The nobility was essentially a society of heirs who had inherited not only land but also the serfs who worked their manors. Lesser nobles acquired additional property from great nobles and from ecclesiastical institutions in return for binding contracts of mutual assistance. This tradition was at least as old as the Carolingians, who granted their followers land in return for military service. In later centuries counts and lesser lords continued this tradition, exchanging land for support. Individual knights became vassals of lay or ecclesiastical magnates, swearing fealty or loyalty to the lord and promising to defend

A knight and a lady in a fifteenth-century garden. The ideals of chivalry and courtly love glorified women in literature and song, but in real life the subordinate status of women reflected the values of a martial society.

and aid him. Normally this oath included serving a certain number of days in the lord's military expeditions, guarding his castles, escorting him, and providing other military services. In some regions the knight also underwent a ritual of homage whereby he placed his hands in the hands of the lord and acknowledged himself the man (in French, *homme*) of the lord, ready to serve him as far as his freedom permitted. In return the lord swore to protect his vassal and granted him a means of support by which the vassal could maintain himself while serving his lord. Usually this grant, termed a *fief,* was a parcel of productive land and the serfs and privileges attached to it. The vassal and his heirs had the right to hold the fief as long as they were able to provide the service demanded for it. Should they ever be unable to continue, or should their lineage die out, the fief returned to the lord.

Individual lords often had considerable numbers of vassals, who might also be the vassals of other lay and secular lords. These networks formed vital social and political structures. In some unusual situations—as in England immediately after the Norman Conquest and in the Latin Kingdom of Jerusalem, founded following the First Crusade in 1099—these structures of lords and vassals constituted systems of hierarchical government. Elsewhere individuals often held fiefs from and owed service to more than one lord; not all of the individuals in a given county or duchy owed their primary obligation to the count or duke. Usually most of a noble's land was owned outright rather than held in fief, thus making the feudal bond less central to a noble's status. As a result, these bonds—anachronistically called feudalism by French lawyers of the sixteenth and seventeenth centuries—constituted just one more element of a social system tied together by kinship, regional alliances, personal bonds of fealty, and the surviving elements of Carolingian administration inherited by counts and dukes. Outside Germany, Hungary, and a few regions such as Normandy and Anjou, the society of the eleventh and twelfth centuries was one of intensely local autonomous powers in which public order and political authority were spread as widely as ever in European history.

The Church: Saints and Monks

The religious needs of the peasantry remained those that their pre-Christian ancestors had known: fertility of land, animals, and women; protection from the ravages of climate and the warrior elite; and supernatural cures for the ailments and disabilities of their harsh life. The cultural values of the nobility retained the essentials of the Germanic warrior ethos, including family honor, battle, and display of status. The rural church of the High Middle Ages met the needs of both, although it subtly changed them in the process.

Most medieval people, whether peasants or lords, lived in a world of face-to-face encounters, a world in which abstract creeds counted for little and in which interior state and external appearance were rarely distinguished. In this world, religion primarily meant action, and the essential religious actions were the liturgical celebrations performed by the clergy. Many of the parish priests who celebrated the eucharist, performed baptisms, solemnized marriages, and conducted funerals were peasants who had received only rudimentary instruction from their predecessors and whose knowledge of Latin and theology was minimal. But these intellectual factors would become significant only centuries later. The essential qualification was that priests could perform the rites of the Church. What contemporaries complained about was not the clergy's ignorance but its greed and immorality. Ordinary lay people wanted priests who would not extort them by selling the sacraments and would not seduce their wives and daughters. They wanted priests who would not leave the village for months or years at a time to seek clerical advancement elsewhere rather than remaining in the village performing the rituals necessary to keep the supernatural powers well disposed toward men and women in the community.

The most important of these supernatural powers was not some distant divinity but the saints—local, personal, and even idiosyncratic persons. During their lives saintly men and women had shown that they enjoyed special favor with God. After their deaths, they continued to be the link between the divine and the

This gold-plated statue contains the skull of Saint Foy, a young girl who was martyred during the last Roman persecution of the Christians in 303. The image illustrates the medieval veneration of the physical relics of the saints.

SAINT FRANCIS OF ASSISI ON HUMILITY AND POVERTY

By 1223 Francis of Assisi's desire to lead a life of radical poverty and simplicity in conformity with the life of Jesus in the Gospels had inspired thousands to follow his example, and he was obligated to prepare a rule by which his order of Friars Minor would be governed. This simple rule emphasizes his fundamental concerns of humility and poverty.

1. This is the rule and way of living of the minorite brothers: namely to observe the holy Gospel of our Lord Jesus Christ, living in obedience, without personal possessions, and in chastity. Brother Francis promises obedience and reverence to our lord pope Honorius, and to his successors who canonically enter upon their office and to the Roman Church. And the other brothers shall be bound to obey brother Francis and his successors.

2. If any persons shall wish to adopt this form of living and shall come to our brothers, they shall send them to their provincial ministers. . . . The ministers shall say unto them the word of the holy Gospel, to the effect that they shall go and sell all that they have and strive to give it to the poor. But if they shall not be able to do this, their good will is enough. . . . And those who have now promised obedience shall have one gown with a cowl, and another, if they wish it, without a cowl. And those who are compelled by necessity, may wear shoes. . . .

3. I firmly command all the brothers by no means to receive coin or money, of themselves or through an intervening person. But for the needs of the sick and for clothing the other brothers, the ministers alone and the guardians shall provide through spiritual friends, as it may seem to them that necessity demands.

4. Those brothers to whom God has given the ability to labor, shall labor faithfully and devoutly. . . . As a reward, they may receive for themselves and their brothers the necessaries of life, but not coin or money, and this humbly, as becomes the servants of God and the followers of most holy poverty.

5. The brothers shall appropriate nothing to themselves, neither a house, nor a place, nor anything; but as pilgrims and strangers in this world, in poverty and humility, serving God, they shall confidently go seeking for alms. Nor need they be ashamed, for the Lord made Himself poor for us in this world. . . .

6. I firmly command all the brothers not to have suspicious relations or to take counsel with women. And, with the exception of those whom special permission has been given by the Apostolic Chair, let them not enter nunneries. Neither may they become fellow godparents with men or women, lest from this cause a scandal may arise among the brothers or concerning brothers.

From *The Rule of St. Francis of Assisi.*

---

earthly spheres. Through their bodies, preserved as relics in the monasteries of Europe, they continued to live among mortals even while participating in the heavenly court. Thus they could be approached just like local earthly lords and, like them, be won over through offerings, bribes, oaths, and rituals of supplication and submission. Just as peasants who surrendered their liberty to a lord by entering his special *familia* could expect the lord's protection, so too could petitioners enter the *familia* of a saint, become the saint's serf, and thus expect the saint's supernatural assistance.

Saints were approached directly. Petitioners pilgrimaged to a saint's tomb and kept vigil there, praying, fasting, and beseeching the saint's protection. These tombs were normally found in monasteries, the "cities of God" that dotted the landscape. As houses of the saints, monasteries orchestrated and controlled the places and times by which the laity could have access to these patrons. As the recipients of gifts to the saints, made in expectation of or in gratitude for supernatural assistance, monastic communities became wealthy and powerful institutions. Every community had its own local saints, either early martyrs of the region or saints whose remains had been transported there. In addition there were regional and national pilgrimages to saints such as Saint Fides and Saint Denis in France, Saint

Stephen in Hungary, and Saint Theodosij in Kiev. Finally, there were the great international pilgrimages to Saint James of Compostela in Spain, to the tombs of the martyrs in Rome, and the greatest one of all: to the empty sepulcher of Jesus in Jerusalem.

Monasteries did more than orchestrate the cult of the special category of the dead who were the saints. They were also responsible for the cult of the ordinary dead, for praying for the souls of ordinary mortals. In particular, monastic communities commemorated and prayed for those members of noble families who, through donations of land, had become especially associated with the monastic community. It was widely believed in the eleventh century that the devil himself

had complained that the monastery of Cluny was capable of snatching the souls of dead sinners from him through the power of its prayers. Association with such monasteries through gifts and exchanges of property, and particularly through burial in the monastic cemetery, provided the surest means of continuing noble families' honor and prestige into the next world. Across Europe noble families founded monasteries on their own lands or invited famous abbots to reorganize existing monasteries. These monasteries formed integral parts of the institutional existence of families. They continued the ritual remembrance of the family, providing it with a history and forming an important part of its material as well as spiritual prestige.

VISIONS LIKE A FLAME

In a society that generally took very seriously Saint Paul's admonition that women were "to be silent in the assembly," few women dared to preach or teach, and fewer still were heeded by the rest of society. The great exception in the twelfth century was Hildegard of Bingen (1098–1179), a nun from the Rhine region who spent her life first in a small, walled-in cloister beside the Benedictine Abbey of Disibodenberg and then in the monastery of Rupertsberg that she founded in 1150. From earliest childhood she had experienced visions, but only in 1141 did she feel inspired to report them. In time, her extraordinary visions and the religious insights they contained were confirmed by the leading churchmen of her day, including Pope Eugenius III, who urged her to publish "all that she had learned from the Holy Spirit." Still later, after fifty years in the cloister, she set out on preaching missions and for twelve years addressed lay and clerical congregations up and down the Rhine. Her influence reached still further afield through her letters to emperors, bishops, and popes sternly admonishing them for their failings. The following passage is from her first visionary work, Scivias, *or "Know the Ways," in which she described her first visions.*

In the year 1141 of the incarnation of Jesus Christ the Son of God, when I was forty-two years and seven months of age, a fiery light, flashing intensely, came from the open vault of heaven and poured through my whole brain. Like a flame that is hot without burning it kindled all my heart and all my breast, just as the sun warms anything on which its rays fall. And suddenly I could understand what such books as the Psalter, the Gospel and other catholic volumes both of the Old and New Testament actually set forth; but I could not interpret the words of the text; nor could I divide up the syllables; nor did I have any notion of the cases or tenses.

Ever since I was a girl—certainly from the time I was five years old right up to the present—in a won-

derful way I had felt in myself (as I do even now) the strength and mystery of these secret and marvelous visions. Yet I revealed this to no one except for a very few people and the religious who lived in the same community as I; but right up until the time when God in his grace wished it to be revealed, I suppressed it beneath strict silence. The visions which I saw I did not perceive in dreams nor when asleep nor in a delirium nor with the eyes or ears of the body. I received them when I was awake and looking around with a clear mind, with the inner eyes and ears, in open places according to the will of God. But how this could be, it is difficult for us mortals to seek to know.

Supported by both peasants and nobles, Benedictine monasteries reached their height in the eleventh and twelfth centuries. Within their walls developed a religious culture that was one of the greatest achievements of the Middle Ages. Entry into a monastery was usually reserved for young nobles, whose families entrusted them to the monastery at the age of seven. There they were to remain until the end of their lives, first as novices in the religious culture of the monastery and later as mature monks and nuns—the professionals in the dance of medieval religion. The essence of the monastic life was the passionate pursuit of God. The goal was not simply salvation but perfection, and this required discipline of the body through a life of voluntary chastity and poverty and discipline of the spirit through obedience and learning. The Benedictine's life moved to the rhythm of the divine office, the ancient series of eight hours each day when the monks put aside work, study, or rest and assembled in the monastic church for the communal chanting of prayers, psalms, and hymns. Some of the prayers were fixed. Others varied according to the liturgical calendar and corresponded to the events in the history of salvation and the life of Christ. From matins—recited after midnight—until compline—the last evening prayer— the monks praised God and asked his aid and that of his saints on behalf of themselves, their secular patrons, their families, and all of society.

Proper participation in this communal liturgy required an education closely in tune with the needs of monastic prayer. Its essence was the *lectio divina,* or the process of reading and studying the Old and New Testaments, for which the study of pagan classics and the writings of the Church Fathers was essential. Reading and studying were active, physical pursuits. Monks and nuns read out loud, the murmur of their voices filling the monastery even when they read in their own rooms or cells. Study did not mean primarily logical analysis. Rather it was a system that combined the tools of grammar, memorization, and word association. It emphasized imaginative description, concordance of scriptural passages related only by similar words, and the application of such "scientific" methods as the allegorical meanings of stones, parts of the body, animals, and so on. Such methods were culled from ancient and medieval scientific texts. This study was combined with the allegorical analysis developed by Origen and the early Church Fathers to produce a distinctive, nonrational but extremely powerful form of intellectual and emotional spirituality. Far from denying the physical and erotic side of human nature, the monastic tradition saw in erotic love a metaphor of divine love. The most popular scriptural text in monastic study was the Song of Songs—a remarkable love poem in the Old Testament that never once mentions God.

Monasteries were communities of professional prayers and therein found their social justification. They were also enormously rich and powerful social and political institutions. The monastery of Cluny, in saving souls through prayer, became the first international organization of monastic centers. Cluny had abbeys and dependent communities, called priories, throughout Europe. The abbots of Cluny were among the most powerful and influential people in Europe during the eleventh and twelfth centuries—considered as equals with kings, popes, and emperors. In order to remain in form for the strenuous liturgical commemoration of living and dead patrons, Cluniac monks largely abandoned the tradition of manual work, leaving such mundane activities to their thousands of serfs and lay agents.

Hildegard of Bingen's fiery vision as represented by a manuscript illuminator supervised by Hildegard herself.

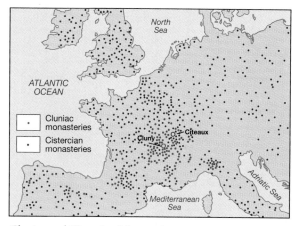

Cluniac and Cistercian Monasteries

The Cluniac monks' comparative luxury and concentration on liturgy to the neglect of other spiritual activities led some monastic reformers to call for a return to simplicity, separation from the rest of society, and a deeper internal spirituality. Chief among these groups were the Cistercians who, under the dynamic leadership of Bernard of Clairvaux (1090–1153), spread a rigorous, ascetic form of monasticism from England to the Vienna woods. The Cistercians built monasteries in the wilderness and discouraged the kinds of close ties with secular society established by the Cluniacs. They wished to avoid the crowds of pilgrims and the intense involvement with local affairs that characterized other types of monasticism. Paradoxically, by establishing themselves in remote areas, organizing their estates in an efficient manner, and gaining a great reputation for asceticism, the Cistercians became enormously wealthy and successful leaders in the economic changes taking place in the twelfth and thirteenth centuries.

The rural church not only served the lay population but worked to transform it. Although monks and bishops were spiritual warriors, most abhorred bloodshed among Christians and sought to limit the violence of aristocratic life. This attitude combined altruistic and selfish motives, since Church property was often the focus of aristocratic greed. The decline of public power and the rise of aristocratic autonomy and violence were particularly marked in southern France. There, beginning in the tenth century, churchmen organized the Peace of God and the Truce of God—movements that attempted to protect peasants, merchants, and clerics from aristocratic violence and to limit the times when warfare was allowed. During the eleventh century, the goals of warfare were shifted from attacks against other Christians to the defense of Christian society. This redirection produced the Crusades, those religious wars of conquest directed against Europe's non-Christian neighbors.

Crusaders: Soldiers of God

The Crusades left a complex and troubling legacy in world civilization. In order to direct noble violence away from Christendom, in 1095 Pope Urban II (1088–99) urged Western knights to use their arms to free the Holy Land from Muslim occupation. In return he promised to absolve them from all of the punishment due for their sins in this life or the next. Nobles and commoners alike responded with enormous enthusiasm, and soon gangs of looting peasants and organized bands of noble warriors both headed east. The commoners left a swath of destruction in their wake, and few mourned when they were destroyed by the Muslims. The nobles, composed primarily of second sons and lower nobility in search of land and fortune as well as salvation, were remarkably successful. After terrible hardships, the crusaders took Jerusalem in 1099 and established a Latin kingdom in Palestine. For over two centuries bands of Western warriors went on armed pilgrimage to defend this precarious kingdom.

The Latin kingdom of Jerusalem was the first experiment in European overseas colonization. Its rulers, a tiny minority of Western knights who established a feudally structured monarchy modeled on the European society they had known, ruled a vastly larger population of Muslims and eastern Christians. Although the Christian rulers were not particularly harsh, they made little effort to absorb or even to understand the native population. Crusaders were uninterested in converting Muslims, and their efforts to impose Roman forms of Christian worship and organization alienated the indigenous Christian population of the kingdom. In art, culture, architecture, and social values, the crusaders remained Latins, absorbing only some lessons of military architecture, adopting some of the food and spices, and making some accommodation in their clothing and housing to the climate of the area. Otherwise, the Latin kingdom played a negligible role as a bridge between the eastern and western worlds. The crusaders remained isolated, supported by the regular supplies brought by Italian merchants (for which cities such as Genoa and Pisa obtained valuable economic rights in the kingdom) and by periodic infusions of fighters in the form of individuals or as part of subsequent organized crusades.

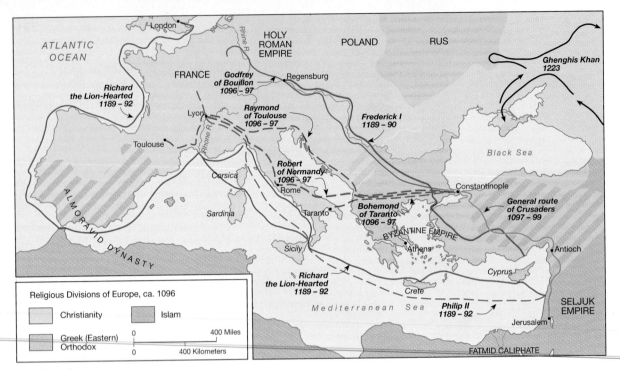

The Crusades

The success of the First Crusade eluded subsequent expeditions. In the middle of the twelfth century, the erosion of the Latin kingdom alarmed Westerners, and the kings of France and Germany, Louis VII and Conrad III, responded to Bernard of Clairvaux's call to take up the cross. The Second Crusade (1145–49) ended in defeat and disaster at the hands of the Seljuk Turks in Asia Minor.

In 1187 the Kurdish Muslim commander, Saladin, defeated the Latin Kingdom at the battle of Hattin and reconquered Jerusalem. Emperor Frederick Barbarossa and the kings of France and England, Philip II Augustus and Richard the Lion-Hearted, responded with the Third Crusade (1187–92). Frederick drowned in Anatolia, and Richard and Philip quarreled to such a point that Philip abandoned the crusade and returned to France. Richard failed to recapture Jerusalem but signed a peace treaty with Saladin. On his way home, the English king was captured and imprisoned in Austria until his mother, Eleanor, could raise a king's ransom to buy his freedom.

The Fourth Crusade (1201–04) never even made it to Palestine. Rather, it was sidetracked with Venetian encouragement into capturing and sacking the Byzantine capital of Constantinople. The Fifth Crusade (1217–21), organized by Pope Innocent III and manned primarily by nobles from Austria and Hungary, was unsuccessful. It failed after the crusaders refused an offer by the sultan al-Kamil to exchange the rich seaport of Damietta in return for the holy city of

Jerusalem and the rest of the Latin kingdom. The Sixth Crusade (1228–29) was led by the Holy Roman Emperor Frederick II, who regained Jerusalem through a peace treaty with the Muslims. This treaty angered the pope and led to Frederick's excommunication from the Catholic church. In 1244 the Muslims once again seized Jerusalem. This inspired King Louis IX of France to lead the Seventh Crusade (1248–54). This crusade ended when Louis and many of his men were defeated and captured by the Muslims. Louis was freed after a large ransom was paid. In 1270 he led the Eighth Crusade against the Muslims. Louis died from a plague soon after arriving in Tunis in northern Africa.

Although military failures, the Crusades appealed particularly to younger sons and knights who hoped to acquire in the East the status that constricting lineages denied them in the West. Other such holy wars were directed against the Muslims in Spain, the Slavs in eastern Europe, and even against heretics and political opponents in France and Italy.

The Crusades—glorified in the nineteenth century by European imperialists, who saw them as the model for Europe's expansion into the East—were brutal and vicious. The crusaders were often motivated as much by greed as by piety. Some began with the wholesale slaughter of Jews in Europe and ended with equally bloody massacres in Palestine. When Jerusalem was taken in 1099, eyewitnesses reported that blood ran ankle deep in the old city. Scalping and head-hunting were practiced by both sides, as was the indiscriminate

In one sense, the Third Crusade was a tilting match between Saladin and Richard the Lion-Hearted. In this fanciful illustration, Saladin, at right, is being unhorsed by Richard.

killing of captives. By the end of the thirteenth century, the military failure of the Crusades, the immorality of many of the participants, and doubts about the spiritual significance of such wars contributed to their decline. So too did the rise of centralized monarchies, whose rulers, with few exceptions, viewed the Crusades as wasteful and futile distractions. Although later preachers from time to time urged kings and nobles to take up the cross against the infidel, the age of the Crusades passed with the age of the independent warrior aristocracy.

In the first third of the eleventh century, a French bishop, Adalbero of Laon (d. 1030), described the ideal structure of society as composed of three groups: those who worked, those who fought, and those who prayed. Adalbero identified the workers as the peasants, the fighters as the king, and the prayers as the bishops. Not long after, monastic writers adopted but adjusted his schema. The workers remained the peasants, but the fighters became the nobles and the prayers become the monks. While there were always people who did not fit neatly into either of these systems, in the eleventh and twelfth centuries most Europeans did fall roughly into one of these categories. Peasants, lords, and monks made up the great majority of Europe's population and lived together in mutual dependence, sharing involvement with the rhythm of the agrarian life. From the later part of the twelfth century, however, this rural world became increasingly aware of a different society—the citizens of the growing cities and towns of Europe. These citizens had no place in the simplistic tripartite scheme of Adalbero. They moved to a different rhythm than that of Adalbero's society–commerce and manufacture.

Medieval Towns

Monastic preachers liked to remind their listeners that according to the Bible, Cain had founded the first town after killing his brother Abel. For monks, nobles, and peasants, the town was an anomaly–a center of commerce and manufacture populated by people who did not fit well into the traditional social structure that was promoted by representatives of the rural aristocratic order. Towns seemed somehow immoral and perverse, but at the same time fascinating. Monks saw the city as the epitome of evil from which they had fled, and yet in the twelfth century new monasteries were being established in or near towns, while older monasteries established on the outskirts of towns found themselves being incorporated into growing urban areas. Nobles disdained urban society for its lack of respect for aristocracy and its disinterest in their cult of violence. Still, as rude warriors were transformed into courtly nobles, these nobles were drawn to the luxuries provided by urban merchants and became indebted to urban moneylenders in order to maintain their "gracious" lifestyles. For many peasants, towns were refuges from the hopelessness of their normal lives. "Town air makes one free," they believed, and many serfs fled the land to try their fortunes in the nearby towns. Clearly, something was very different about the urban communities that emerged, first in Italy, then in the Low Countries and across Europe in the later eleventh and twelfth centuries.

Italian Communes

Urban life had never ceased to be an essential ingredient in Italy, which had maintained its urban traditions and ties with the Mediterranean world since antiquity. Urban populations had shrunk in late antiquity and were dominated by their bishops, who exercised secular and ecclesiastical lordship. However, the towns of the Italian peninsula had continued to play commercial and political roles and to attract not only runaway serfs but even nobles, who maintained fortified towers within the town walls.

The coastal cities of Amalfi, Bari, Genoa, and especially Venice had continued to play important roles in

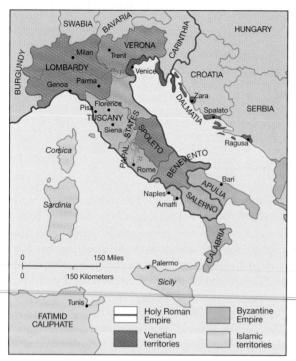

Italian Towns and Cities, ca. 1000

commerce both with the Byzantines and with the new Muslim societies. For Venice, this role was facilitated by its official status as a part of the Byzantine Empire, which gave it access to Byzantine markets. The geographical isolation of most of these cities from prosperous hinterlands gave them an additional advantage as commercial centers. With nothing of their own to trade but perhaps salt and, in Venice, glass, they were forced to serve as go-betweens for the transport of eastern spices, silks, and ivories. These goods were exchanged for western goods such as iron, slaves, timber, grain, and oil. In order to protect their merchant ships, Italian coastal cities developed their own fleets, and by the eleventh century they were major military forces in the Mediterranean. Venice's fleet became the primary protector of the Byzantine Empire and was thereby able to win more favorable commercial rights than those enjoyed by Greek merchants.

As the merchants of the Italian towns penetrated the markets at the western end of the great overland spice routes connecting China, India, and central Asia with the Mediterranean, they established permanent merchant colonies in the East. When expedient, they did not hesitate to use military force to win concessions. In 1088, for example, the Venetians sacked the capital of Tunis in North Africa in order to force concessions to their merchants.

The Crusades, armed pilgrimages for pious northern nobles, were primarily economic opportunities for the Italians, who had no scruples about trading with Muslims. Furthermore, only the Italians had the ships and the expertise to transport the crusaders by sea. This mode of transportation offered the crusaders hope of success, since every Crusade but the first that had followed an overland route had ended in failure. Moreover, the ships of the Italian cities were the only means of supplying the crusading armies once they were in Palestine. The crusaders paid the Italian merchants handsomely for their assistance. They also granted them economic and political rights in the Palestinian port cities such as Tyre and Acre, where both the Venetians and the Genoese had their own quarters governed by their own laws. The culmination of this relationship between the northern crusaders and the Italians was the Fourth Crusade, which, short on funds, was sidetracked by the Venetians into capturing and sacking Constantinople. As noted in Chapter 7 (see p. 215), the Byzantine Empire never recovered from this disaster, and Venice emerged as the undisputed Mediterranean power.

By the thirteenth century, Italian merchants had spread far beyond the Mediterranean. The great merchant banking houses of Venice, Florence, and Genoa had established offices around the Mediterranean and Black seas; south along the Atlantic coast of Morocco; east into Armenia and Persia; west to London, Bruges, and Ghent; and north to Scandinavia. Some individual merchants, the Venetian Marco Polo (1254–1324), for example, traded as far east as China.

These international commercial operations required more sophisticated systems of commercial law and credit than the West had ever known. Italian merchants developed the practices of double-entry bookkeeping, limited-liability partnership, commercial insurance, and international letters of exchange. Complex commercial affairs also required the development of a system of credit and interest-bearing loans, an idea abhorrent to traditional rural societies. Since usury, or borrowing and lending at credit, was regarded as making money by manipulating time, which belonged only to God, churchmen condemned the practice. They considered it a form of simony, the buying and selling of spiritual goods. In spite of ecclesiastical prohibitions, bankers found ways of hiding interest payments in contracts, thus allowing lender and seller to participate in

In this illustration from a fourteenth-century manuscript, the Venetian merchant Marco Polo (1254–1324), with his father and uncle, is seen departing from Venice for points east in 1271. Marco traveled as far as China and did not return home to Venice until twenty-four years later.

the growing world of credit-based transactions. Long before the emergence of the Protestant work ethic, Italian capitalists had developed the tools of modern business.

Just as significant as the international trade networks established by these traders were the cultural and institutional infrastructures that made these far-flung operations possible. The most basic of these was a mentality that considered commerce an honorable occupation. Since antiquity, aristocratic culture had considered only warfare and agriculture as worthy pursuits. Even the great commercial operations of the Roman world tended to be in the hands of equestrians and freedmen. The strength of the Italian towns was that they were able to throw off this rural, aristocratic value system. By the ninth century, even the doge, or duke, of Venice had invested much of his wealth in commercial operations. By the later tenth and eleventh centuries, this passion for commerce had spread from the seacoasts to the towns throughout Italy, and from there to cities such as Marseille, Barcelona, and others in southern Europe. Urban dwellers generally found nothing ignoble in commerce and banking. By the twelfth century wealthy citizens, whether descended

from successful merchants or from landed aristocrats, were indifferently termed *magnates*. The rest of the town's population was called *populars*. The difference between the two was essentially economic. Since commercial activity offered a means of social mobility, the two could act in close accord, particularly when dealing with urban lords or outside powers. In the eleventh and early twelfth centuries, many Italian towns bought off or expelled their traditional lords such as counts and bishops, thus allowing the magnates and populars of these cities to create their own governing institutions or communes.

During the twelfth and thirteenth centuries, Italy played host to a bewildering variety of experiments in self-government as urban populations banded together in communes of citizens who sought to govern themselves. These relatively small communities of citizens (the largest was approximately one hundred thousand adults) developed a keen sense of patriotism, local pride, and fierce independence reminiscent of the ancient Greek city-states. They manifested this pride in artistic and architectural competition as individual cities and their citizens sought to surpass each other in the construction of beautiful plazas, town halls, and sumptuous urban palaces. The communes also sought to control every aspect of civic life: prices, markets, weights and measures, sanitation, and medical care. Who might wear what forms of dress and jewelry? How many inches of lace might the wife of a merchant wear on her dress? Could an ordinary citizen wear a cloak trimmed with sable? Might Christian women wear earrings, or were these reserved for Jews? Such questions were considered appropriate topics of public legislation.

The unity and patriotism the Italian cities showed the rest of the world was matched in intensity by the violence of their internal disputes. Every adult male was expected to participate in government, usually in his free time and at the expense of his private business activities. This involvement was intensely partisan as magnates disputed among themselves and with the ordinary populace for control of the town. These conflicts frequently turned violent as citizens took sides on wider issues of Italian and European politics.

Within many towns, the magnates formed their own corporation—the society of knights—to protect their privileged position. Families of nobles and magnates, whose cultural values were similar to those of the rural aristocracy, competed with each other for honor and power. Often they erected lofty towers on their urban palaces, both for prestige and for defense against their neighbors. Feuds fought between noble families and their vassals in city streets were frequent events in Italian towns.

Opposing the magnates were popular corporations—the society of the people—which sought to rein in the violent and independent-minded nobles. These popular organizations could include anyone who was not a member of the society of knights, although in reality the organizations were dominated by the prominent leaders of craft and trade associations, or guilds. In many towns, the society of the people was organized both by residential district and by guild and sought to prevent the formation of special interest groups or conspiracies within the commune. To enforce its measures, the society had its own elected officers and its own military, headed by a "captain of the people," who might command as many as one thousand troops against the magnates.

In order to tip the scales in their favor, differing parties frequently invited outside powers into local affairs. The greatest outside contenders for power in the Italian cities were the Germanic empire and the papacy. Most towns had an imperial faction (named Ghibelline after Waiblingen castle, which belonged to the family of Frederick II) bitterly opposed by a papal faction (in

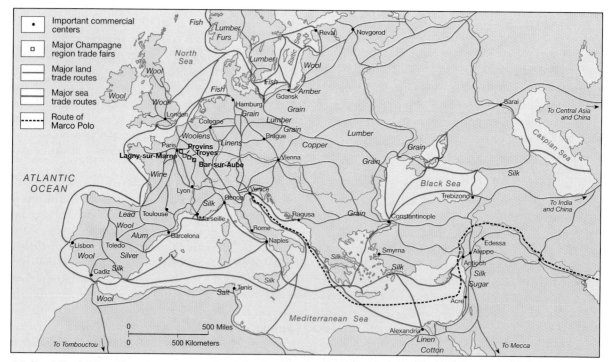

Medieval Trade Networks

time called Guelph after the Welf family, which opposed Frederick's family). In time, the issues separating Guelphs and Ghibellines changed, and the Guelphs became the party of the wealthy eager to preserve the status quo, while those out of power rallied to the Ghibelline cause.

In order to maintain civic life in spite of these conflicts, cities established complex systems of government in which officers were selected by series of elections and lotteries designed to prevent any one faction from seizing control. Sovereignty lay with the *arengo,* or assembly, which comprised all adult male citizens. Except in very small communes, this body was too large to function efficiently, so most communes selected a series of working councils. The great council might be as large as 400; an inner council had perhaps 24 to 40 members. Generally, executive authority was vested in consuls, whose numbers varied widely and who were chosen from various factions and classes. When these consuls proved unable to overcome the partisan politics of the factions, many towns turned to hiring *podestas,* nonpolitical professional city managers from outside the community. These normally were magnates from other communes who had received legal educations and who served for relatively short periods. In Modena, for example, they served six months. They were required to bring with them four judges, twenty-four cavalrymen, and sergeants and grooms to help maintain order. They could not have any relatives in Modena, could not leave town without permission of the great council, and could not eat or drink with local citizens lest they be drawn into factional conflicts. Their salaries were paid every two months, the last third not being handed over until after a final audit of their term. Only by such stringent means could the commune hope to keep partisan politics from corrupting their podesta!

Northern Towns

The Mediterranean ("mid-earth") Sea was so named because, to the Greeks and Romans, it seemed to be in the middle of the world. In this sense, there were other "mediterranean" seas to the north. The Baltic and North seas and the English Channel tied together the peoples of Scandinavia, Lithuania, northern Germany, Flanders, and England. Scandinavian fish and timber, Baltic grain, English wool, and Flemish cloth circulated around the edges of these lands, linking them in a common economic network. Here, as in the south, there developed urban merchant and manufacturing communities linked by sea routes—distinguished from the surrounding countryside by the formation of a distinctly urban commercial mentality.

The earliest of these interrelated communities were the cloth towns of Flanders, Brabant, and northern France. Chief among these cloth towns were Ghent, Bruges, Ypres, Flanders and England and the wool-exporting towns of England, particularly London. Both Flanders and England had been known for their cloth production since Roman times. In the eleventh century Flanders, lacking the land for large-scale sheep grazing and facing a growing population, began to specialize in the production of high-quality cloth made from English wool. At the same time England, which experienced an economic and population decline following the Norman Conquest, began to export the greater part of its wool to Flanders to be worked. The production of wool cloth began to develop from a cottage occupation into Europe's first major industry.

Woolen manufacture was a natural for such a transformation. The looms required to manufacture heavy wool cloth were large and expensive and the skills needed to produce the cloth were complex. No less than thirteen separate steps were required to turn raw wool into finished cloth, and each step demanded special expertise, chemicals such as dyes and color fixers, and equipment. The need for water both to power looms and to wash the cloth during production tended to concentrate cloth manufacture along waterways. Finally, as competition increased, only centralization and regulation of manufacture could ensure quality control and thus enhance marketability. Moreover, wool cloth was a necessity of life throughout Europe, and the growing population provided the first large-scale market for manufactured goods since the disintegration of the Roman Empire.

For all of these reasons, by the late eleventh century the traditional image of medieval cloth production had been transformed. No longer did individual women sit in farmhouses spinning and weaving. Now manufacture was concentrated in towns and men replaced women at the looms. Furthermore, production was closely regulated and controlled by a small group of extremely wealthy merchant-drapiers (cloth makers)

Concentration of capital, specialization of labor, and increase of urban population created vibrant, exciting cities essentially composed of three social orders. At the top were wealthy patricians—the merchant-drapiers. Their agents traveled to England and purchased raw wool, which they then distributed to weavers and other master artisans. These artisans—often using equipment rented from the patricians—carded, dyed, spun, and wove the wool into cloth. Finally, the finished cloth was returned to the patricians, whose agents then marketed it throughout Europe. Through their control of raw materials, equipment, capital, and distribution, the merchant-drapiers controlled the cloth trade, and thus the economic and political life of the Flemish wool towns. Through their closed associations, or guilds, they controlled production and set standards, prices, and wages. They also controlled communal government by monopolizing urban councils. In wealth and power, the merchant-drapiers were almost indistinguishable from the great nobles with whom they often intermarried.

At the bottom of urban society were the unskilled and semiskilled artisans, called "blue nails" because constant work with dye left their fingers permanently stained. These workers led an existence more precarious than that of most peasants. Employed from week to week, paid barely living wages, and entirely dependent on the woolen industry for their livelihood, they often hovered on the edge of subsistence. In the early fourteenth century, the temporary interruption of grain shipments from northern Germany to Ypres left thousands dead of starvation. Small wonder that from the thirteenth century on, "blue nails" were increasingly hostile to patricians. Sporadic rebellions and strikes spread across Flanders, Brabant, and northern France. Everywhere they were ruthlessly suppressed. The penalty for organizing a strike was death.

Between the patricians and the workers stood the masters—the skilled artisans who controlled the day-to-day production of cloth and lesser crafts. Masters organized into guilds with which they regulated every aspect of their trades and protected themselves from competition. The masters often leased their looms or other equipment from the merchant-drapiers and received from them raw materials and wages to be distributed to their workers. If the hope of the common artisan was someday to move up into the rank of master, masters hoped to amass sufficient capital to pur-

As towns grew, the numbers and types of jobs grew as well. In this fifteenth-century Flemish manuscript illumination, a guild master of the dyer's guild supervises as men of the guild dye cloth.

chase their own looms and perhaps someday move up into the rank of patrician.

Tying together the northern and southern commercial worlds were the great fairs of Champagne. Six times during the year the towns of Champagne—particularly Troyes and Provins—swelled with exotic crowds of merchants from Flanders, England, Scandinavia, Germany, Brabant, Spain, and Italy. Rich and poor from the surrounding countryside also poured into the towns, as merchants from north and south met to bargain and trade under the protection of the local counts.

Representing Flanders were agents of the merchant-drapiers of each town, whose carefully inspected and regulated products carried the prestige and financial prosperity of their communities. Cloth was known by the name of the town in which it was made, and thus quality control was a corporate rather than an individual issue. From Italy came merchants of the great Italian trading companies to purchase northern cloth for resale throughout the Mediterranean. Often these Italians were young merchants whose trips were financed by wealthy capitalists who had entered into a limited-liability contract with the young adventurers for the duration of the journey.

Southern merchants brought silks, sugar, salt, alum (a chemical essential in cloth manufacture), and, most important, spices to trade at the fairs. Medieval cooks gloried in the use of spices—most cooks knew over two hundred of them. The liberal use of exotic spices may have served as a preservative, and spices probably hid the taste of half-rotten food. But primarily the use of spices was a part of the conspicuous consumption by which the rich could display their wealth and status.

In addition to the trade in cloth and spices, leather from Spain, iron from Germany, copper and tin from Bohemia, salted or smoked fish and furs from Scandinavia, and local wines, cheeses, and foodstuffs also changed hands under the watchful eyes of fair officials. The officials supervised weights, measures, and currency exchanges. The fair staff also provided courts to settle disagreements among merchants. These great international exchanges connected the financial and marketing centers of the south with the manufacturing and trading communities of the north, tying the north to the south more effectively than any system since the political institutions of the Roman Empire.

Urban Culture

The urban world of the twelfth and thirteenth centuries created forms of religious and cultural expression particularly suited to it. During the eleventh century, cathedrals had become centers of learning as young clerics sought training in schools established by bishops. Initially these urban schools in Germany, Italy, France, and England were similar to centers of monastic education. However, unlike monks, young men who attended the cathedral schools received an education aimed more at participation in the affairs of the world than in the worship of God. They learned the skills of writing and computation and received the legal training that allowed them to rise to positions of prominence in an increasingly literate and complex urban world. Basic education consisted of the study of the trivium—grammar, rhetoric, and logic, the first three of the seven liberal arts, which had formed the basis of Roman liberal education. In some cathedral schools students went on to study the quadrivium—the mathematical disciplines of geometry, theory of numbers, astronomy, and musical harmonies. In Italy students traveled to Ravenna and Bologna to study Roman law.

In the late eleventh and early twelfth centuries, the pace of urban intellectual life quickened. The combination of population growth, improved agricultural productivity, political stability, and educational interest culminated in what has been called the "renaissance of the twelfth century." Bologna and Paris became the undisputed centers of the new educational movements. Bologna specialized in the study of law. There, from the eleventh century, a number of important teachers began to make detailed, authoritative commentaries on the *Corpus iuris civilis*—the sixth-century compilation of law prepared on the order of the Roman emperor Justinian. In the next century the same systematic study was applied to Church law, culminating in the *Decretum Gratiani,* or "Concord of Discordant Canons," prepared around 1140 in Bologna by the monk Gratian. The growing importance of legal knowledge in politics, international trade, and Church administration drew students from across Europe to Bologna. There they organized a *universitas,* or guild of students, the first true university. In Bologna law students, many of them adults from wealthy merchant or aristocratic backgrounds, controlled every aspect of the university from the selection of administrators to the exact length of professors' lectures. Professors and administrators were firmly subject to the guild's control and were fined if they broke any of the regulations.

North of the Alps, Paris became the center for study of the liberal arts and of theology during the twelfth century. The city's emergence as the leading educational center of Europe resulted from a convergence of factors. Paris was the center of an important cathedral school as well as of a monastic school, that of the Victorines on the left bank of the Seine River. In the twelfth century it became the capital of the French kings, who needed educated clerics, or clerks, for their administration. Finally, in the early twelfth century, students from across Europe flocked to Paris to study with the greatest and most original intellect of the century, Peter Abelard (1079–1142).

Brilliant, supremely self-assured, and passionate, Abelard arrived in Paris in his early twenties and quickly took the intellectual community by storm. He ridiculed the established teachers, bested them in open debate, and established his own school, which drew the best minds of his day. Abelard's intellectual method combined the tools of legal analysis perfected in Bologna with Aristotelian logic and laid the foundation of what has been called the Scholastic method. Logical reasoning, Abelard believed, could be applied to all problems, even those concerning the mysteries of faith.

So great was Abelard's reputation that an ambitious local cleric engaged him to give private instructions to his brilliant niece, Heloise. Soon Abelard and Heloise were having an affair and all of Paris was singing the love song he composed for her. When Heloise became pregnant, the two were secretly married. Fearing harm to his clerical career, Abelard refused to make the marriage public, preferring to protect his position rather than Heloise's honor. Her outraged uncle hired thugs who broke into Abelard's room and castrated him. After Abelard recovered from his mutilation, he and Heloise each entered monasteries. Abelard spent years as the abbot of a small monastery in Brittany. In 1136 he returned to teach in Paris, where he quickly drew new attacks, this time led by Bernard of Clairvaux, who accused him of heresy. Abelard was convicted by a local council and forced to burn some of his own works. He sought protection from his persecutors in the monastery of Cluny, where he died in 1142.

Although Abelard himself met tragedy in his personal and professional life, the intellectual ferment he had begun in Paris continued long after him. By 1200 education had become so important in the city that the

This illustration from a fourteenth-century manuscript shows Henry of Germany delivering a lecture to university students in Bologna.

universitas was granted a charter by King Philip Augustus, who guaranteed its rights and immunities from the control of the city. Unlike that at Bologna, the University of Paris remained a corporation of professors rather than of students. It was organized like other guilds into masters; bachelors, who were similar to journeymen in other trades; and students, who were analogous to apprentices.

Students began their studies at around age fourteen or fifteen in the faculty of arts. After approximately six years they received a bachelor of arts degree, which was a prerequisite of entering the higher faculties of theology, medicine, or law. After additional years of reading and commenting on specific texts under the supervision of a master, students received the title of master of arts, which gave them the license to teach anywhere within Christian Europe.

Though these years were filled with study, students also enjoyed a spirited life that revolved around the taverns and brothels that filled the student district, or Latin Quarter. Drunken brawls were frequent and relationships between students and townspeople were often strained because students enjoyed legal immunity from city laws. In 1229 a fight between students and a tavern owner over their bill erupted into general rioting and street battles that left many students and citizens dead or injured. Furious at the government for having

sent in soldiers to quell the riot, the masters dissolved the university for six years and threatened never to return to Paris. Masters and students migrated to Oxford, Reims, Orléans, and elsewhere, greatly aiding the development of these other intellectual centers. In 1231 most of the masters' demands were finally met and the teachers returned to Paris secure in their rights of self-governance.

The intellectual life of the universities was in its way as rough-and-tumble as any student brawl. Through the thirteenth and fourteenth centuries it was dominated by a pagan philosopher already dead for a thousand years. The introduction of the works of Aristotle into the West between 1150 and 1250 created an intellectual crisis every bit as profound as that of the Newtonian revolution of the seventeenth century or the Einsteinian revolution of the twentieth century. For centuries Western thinkers had depended on the Christianized Neoplatonic philosophy of Origen and Augustine. Aristotle was known in the West only through his basic logical treatises, which in the twelfth century had become the foundation of intellectual work, thanks in large part to the work of Peter Abelard. Logic, or dialectic, was seen as the universal key to knowledge, and the university system was based on its rigorous application to traditional texts of law, philosophy, and Scripture.

The Scholastic theologian Thomas Aquinas was influenced by Plato (at lower right) and Aristotle (at lower left), as well as by many early Christian thinkers (shown above him). The Islamic philosopher Averroës is shown lying vanquished at his feet.

Beginning in the late twelfth century, Christian and Jewish scholars began translating Aristotle's treatises on natural philosophy, ethics, and metaphysics into Latin. Suddenly Christian intellectuals who had already accepted the Aristotelian method were brought face to face with Aristotle's conclusions: a world without an active, conscious God; a world in which everything from the functioning of the mind to the nature of matter could be understood without reference to a divine creator. Further complicating matters, the texts arrived not from the original Greek, but normally through Latin translations of Arabic translations. These translations were accompanied by learned commentaries by Muslim and Jewish scholars, especially by Averroës, the greatest Aristotelian philosopher of the twelfth century.

As the full impact of Aristotelian philosophy began to reach churchmen and scholars, reactions varied from condemnation to whole-hearted acceptance. At one extreme, in 1210 Church authorities forbade the teaching of Aristotle's philosophy in Paris, a prohibition the professors ignored. At the other extreme, Parisian scholars such as Siger de Brabant (ca. 1235–ca. 1281) eagerly embraced Aristotelian philosophy as interpreted by Averroës, even when these teachings varied from Christian tradition. To many people it appeared that there were two irreconcilable kinds of truth, one knowable through divine revelation, the other through human reason.

One Parisian scholar who refused to accept this dichotomy was Thomas Aquinas (1225–74), a professor of theology and the most brilliant intellect of the High Middle Ages. Although an Aristotelian who recognized the genius of Averroës, Aquinas refused to accept the possibility that human reason, which was a gift from God, led necessarily to contradictions with divine revelation. Aquinas's great contribution, contained in his *Summa Against the Gentiles* (1259–64) and in his incomplete *Summa of Theology* (1266–73), was to defend the integrity of human reason and to reconcile it with divine revelation. Properly applied, the principles of Aristotelian philosophy could not lead to error, he argued. However, human reason unaided by revelation could not always lead to certain conclusions. Questions about such matters as the nature of God, creation, and the human soul could not be resolved by reason alone. In developing his thesis, Aquinas recast Christian doctrine and philosophy, replacing their Neoplatonic foundation with an Aristotelian base. Although not universally accepted in the thirteenth century (in 1277 the bishop of Paris condemned many of his teachings as heretical), in time Aquinas's synthesis came to dominate Christian intellectual life for centuries.

Aquinas was a member of a new religious order, the Dominicans, who along with the Franciscans appeared in response to the social and cultural needs of the new urbanized, monetized European culture. Benedictine monasticism was ideally suited to a rural, aristocratic world; it had little place in the bustling cities of Italy, Flanders, and Germany. In these commercial urban environments, Christians were more concerned with the problems of living in the world than with escaping from it. Lay persons and clerics alike were concerned

An altarpiece depicting Saint Francis of Assisi with six scenes from his life. His hands show the stigmata—symbolic marks that represent the wounds Christ received on the cross.

with the growing wealth of ecclesiastical institutions. Across southern Europe individual reformers attacked the wealthy lifestyles of monks and secular clergy as un-Christian. Individual monks might take vows of poverty, but monasteries themselves were often very wealthy. Torn between their own involvement in a commercial world and an inherited Christian-Roman tradition that looked upon commerce and capital as degrading, reformers called for a return to what they imagined to have been the life of the primitive Church, one that emphasized both individual and collective poverty. The poverty movement attracted great numbers of followers, many of whom added to their criticisms of traditional clergy a concern over clerical morality and challenges about the value of sacraments and the priesthood. Although many reformers were condemned as heretics and sporadically persecuted, the reform movement continued to grow and threatened to destroy the unity of western Christendom.

The people who preserved the Church's unity were inspired by the same impulses, but they channeled their enthusiasm into reforming the Church from within. Francis of Assisi (1182–1226), the son of a prosperous Italian merchant, rejected his luxurious life in favor of one of radical poverty, simplicity, and service to others. He was a man of extraordinary simplicity, humility, and joy, and his piety was in keeping with his character. As he wandered about preaching repentance, he drew great numbers of followers from all ranks, especially from the urban communities of Italy. Convinced of the importance of obedience, Francis asked the pope to approve the way of life he had chosen for himself and his followers. The pope, recognizing that in Francis the impulses threatening the Church might be its salvation, granted his wish. The Order of Friars Minor, or Franciscans, grew by thousands, drawing members from as far away as England and Hungary.

Francis insisted that his followers observe strict poverty, both individually and collectively. The order could not own property, nor could its members even touch money. They were expected to beg for food each day for their sustenance. They were to travel from town to town, preaching, performing manual labor, and serving the poor. In time the expansion of the order and its involvement in preaching against heresy and in education brought about compromises with Francis' original ideals. The Franciscans needed churches in which to preach, books with which to study, and protection from local bishops. Most of the friars accepted these changes. These, the so-called conventuals, were bitterly opposed by the spirituals, or rigorists, who sought to maintain the radical poverty of their founder. In the fourteenth century this conflict led to a major split in the order, and ultimately to the condemnation of the spirituals as heretics.

The order of friars founded by Dominic (1170–1221) also adopted a rule of strict poverty, but the primary focus of the Dominicans was on preaching to the society of the thirteenth century. This order, which emphasized intellectual activity, concentrated on preaching against heresies and on higher education. Thus the Dominicans too gravitated toward the cities of western Europe, and especially toward its great universities. These new orders of preachers, highly educated, enthusiastic, and eloquent, began to formulate for the urban laity of Europe a new vision of Christian society—a society not only of peasants, lords, and monks, but also of merchants, artisans, and professionals. At the same time, their central organizations and their lack of direct ties to the rural aristocracies made them the favorite religious orders of the increasingly powerful centralized monarchies.

The Invention of the State

The disintegration of the Carolingian state in the tenth century left political power fragmented among a wide variety of political entities. In general these were of two types. The first, the papacy and the empire, were elective, traditional structures that claimed universal sovereignty over the Christian world, based on a sacred view of political power. The second, largely hereditary and less extravagant in their religious and political pretensions, were the limited kingdoms that arose within the old Carolingian world and on its borders.

The Universal States: Empire and Papacy

The Frankish world east of the Rhine River had been less affected than the kingdom of the West Franks by the onslaught of Vikings, Magyars, and Saracens. The eastern Frankish kingdom, a loose confederacy of five great duchies—Saxony, Lorraine, Franconia, Swabia, and Bavaria—had preserved many of the Carolingian religious, cultural, and institutional traditions. In 919, Duke Henry I of Saxony (919–936) was elected king, and his son Otto I (936–973) laid the foundation for the revival of the empire. Otto inflicted a devastating defeat on the Magyars in 955, subdued the other dukes, and tightened his control over the kingdom. He accomplished this largely through the extensive use of bishops and abbots, whom he appointed as his agents and sources of loyal support. In 951, in order to prevent a southern German prince from establishing himself in northern Italy, Otto invaded and conquered Lombardy. Eleven years later he entered Rome, where he was crowned emperor by the pope.

Otto, known to history as "the Great," had established the main outlines of German imperial policy for the next three hundred years. These were conflict with the German aristocracy, reliance on bishops and abbots as imperial agents, and preoccupation with Italy. His successors, both in his own Saxon dynasty (919–1024) and in the succeeding dynasties, the Salians (1024–1125) and the Staufens (1138–1254), continued this tradition. Magnates elected the German kings, who were then consecrated as emperors by the pope. Royal fathers generally were able to bring about the election of their sons, and in this manner they attempted to turn the kingship into a hereditary office. However, the royal families could not manage to produce male heirs in each generation, and thus the magnates continued to exercise real power in royal elections. Because of this elective tradition, German emperors were never

The Empire of Otto the Great, ca. 963

able to establish effective control over the German magnates outside their own duchies.

The magnates' ability to expand their own power and autonomy at the expense of their Slavic neighbors to the east also contributed to the weakness of the German monarchy. In the 1150s for example, Henry the Lion (ca. 1130–95), Duke of Bavaria and Saxony, carved out an autonomous principality in the Slavic areas between the Elbe and the Vistula, founding the major trading towns of Lübeck and Rostock. It was the goal of every great aristocratic family to extend its own independent lordship. In order to counter such aristocratic power, emperors looked to the Church, both for the development of the religious cult of the emperor as "the anointed of the Lord" and as a source of reliable military and political support. While the offices of count and duke had become hereditary within the great aristocracy, the offices of bishop and abbot remained public charges to which the emperor could appoint loyal supporters. Since these ecclesiastics had taken vows of celibacy, the emperor did not fear that they would attempt to pass their offices on to their children. Moreover, churchmen tended to be experienced, educated administrators who could assist the emperor in the administration of the empire. Like the Carolingians, the Saxon and Salian emperors needed a purified, reformed Church free of local aristocratic control to serve the interests of the emperor. This imperial church system was the cornerstone of the empire.

Those laymen the emperor could count on, particularly from the eleventh century on, were trusted household serfs whom the kings used as their agents. Although unfree, these ministerials were entrusted with important military commands and given strategic castles throughout the empire. Despised by the free-born nobility, they tended at first to be loyal supporters of the emperor. In the twelfth century, they took on the chivalric ideals of their aristocratic neighbors and benefited from conflicts between emperor and pope to acquire their autonomy. As old noble families died out, ministerial families replaced them as a new hereditary aristocracy.

Otto the Great had entered Italy to secure his southern flank. His successors became embroiled in Italian affairs until in the thirteenth century they abandoned Germany altogether. As emperors, they had to be crowned by the pope. This was possible only if they controlled Rome. Moreover, the growing wealth of northern Italian towns was an important source of financial support if Lombardy could be controlled. Finally, the preoccupation with Italy was a natural outcome of the nature of this empire. Imperial claims to universal sovereignty continued the Carolingian tradition of empire. An imperial office without Italy was unthinkable. Thus the emperors found themselves drawn into papal and Italian politics, frequently with disastrous results. Germany became merely a source of men and material with which to fight the Lombard towns and the pope. From the eleventh through the thirteenth centuries, emperors granted German princes autonomy in return for this support.

The early successes of this imperial program created the seeds of its own destruction. Imperial efforts to reform the Church resulted in a second, competing claimant to universal authority—the papacy. In the later tenth and early eleventh centuries, emperors had intervened in papal elections, deposed and replaced

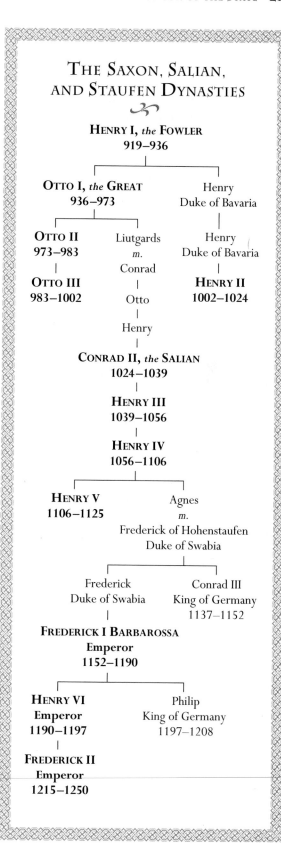

corrupt popes, and worked to ensure that bishops and abbots within the empire would be educated, competent churchmen. The most effective reformer was Emperor Henry III (1039–56), an effective and devout emperor who took seriously his role as the anointed of the Lord to reform the Church, both in Germany and in Rome. When three rivals claimed the papacy, Henry called a synod that deposed all three and installed the first of a series of German popes. The most effective was Henry's own cousin, Leo IX (1049–54), who traveled widely in France, Germany, and Italy. Leo condemned simony, that is, the practice of buying Church offices, and fostered monastic reforms such as that of Cluny. He also encouraged the efforts of a group of young reformers drawn from across Europe.

In the next decades, these new, more radical reformers began to advocate a widespread renewal of the Christian world, led not by emperors but by popes. These reformers pursued an ambitious set of goals. They sought to reform the morals of the clergy, and in particular to eliminate married priests. They tried to free churches and monasteries from lay control both by forbidding lay men and women from owning churches and monasteries and by eliminating simony. They particularly condemned "lay investiture," or the practice by which kings and emperors appointed bishops and invested them with the symbols of their office. Finally, they insisted that the pope, not the emperor, was the supreme representative of God on earth and as such had the right to exercise a universal sovereignty. Had not Christ said to Peter, the first bishop of Rome: "To you I shall give the keys of the kingdom of heaven; and whatsoever you shall bind on earth shall be bound also in heaven, and whatsoever you shall loose upon earth will be loosed also in heaven"?

Every aspect of the reform movement met with strong opposition throughout Europe. However, its effects were most dramatic in the empire because of the central importance there of the imperial church system. Henry III's son Henry IV (1056–1106) clashed head-on with the leading radical reformer and former protégé of Leo IX, Pope Gregory VII (1073–85), over the emperor's right to appoint and to install or invest bishops in their offices. This investiture controversy changed the face of European political history. The contest was fought not simply with swords but with words. Legal scholars for both sides searched Roman and Church law for arguments to bolster their claims, thus encouraging the revival of legal studies at Bologna. For the first time, public opinion played a crucial role in politics, and both sides composed carefully worded propaganda tracts aimed at secular and religious audiences. Gradually, the idea of the separate spheres of church and state emerged for the first time in European political theory.

The actual course of the conflict was erratic and in the end weakened both the empire and the papacy. In 1075 Henry IV, supported by many German bishops, attempted to depose Gregory. Gregory excommunicated and deposed Henry, freed the German nobility from their obligations to him, and encouraged them to rebel. As anti-imperial strength grew, Henry took a desperate gamble. Crossing the Alps in the dead of winter in 1077, he arrived before the castle of Canossa in northern Italy, where Gregory was staying. Dressed as a humble penitent, Henry stood in the snow asking the pope for forgiveness and reconciliation. As a priest, the pope could not refuse, and he lifted the excommunication. Once more in power, Henry began again to appoint bishops. Again in 1080 Gregory excommunicated and deposed him. This time the majority of the German nobles and bishops remained loyal to the emperor, and Henry marched on Rome. Deserted by most of his clergy, Gregory had to flee to the Normans in southern Italy. He died in Salerno in 1085, his last words being "I have loved justice and hated iniquity, therefore I die in exile."

Henry did not long enjoy his victory. Gregory's successors rekindled the opposition to Henry and even convinced Henry's own son to join in the revolt. The conflict ended in 1122, when Emperor Henry V (1106–25) and Pope Calixtus II (1119–24) reached an agreement known as the Concordat of Worms. This agreement differentiated between the royal and the spiritual spheres of authority and allowed the emperors a limited role in episcopal election and investiture. The compromise changed the nature of royal rule in the empire, weakening the emperors and contributing to the long-term decline of royal government in Germany.

The decline that began with the investiture controversy continued as emperors abandoned political power north of the Alps in order to pursue their ambitions in Italy. Frederick I Barbarossa (1152–90) spent much of his reign attempting to reimpose imperial authority and to collect imperial incomes from the rich towns of northern Italy. For this he needed the support of the German princes, and he granted them extraordinary privileges in return for their cooperation south of the Alps. In 1156, for example, he gave Henry Jasomirgott (ca. 1114–77) virtual autonomy in the newly created duchy of Austria. Still, the combined efforts of the Lombard towns and the papacy were too much for Frederick and his armies to win a decisive victory. By the time of Frederick's death in Germany in 1190—he

Henry IV kneeling at Canossa to ask Abbot Hugh of Cluny and Countess Matilda of Tuscany to intercede for him with Pope Gregory VII.

ley that formed the nucleus of the Papal States. Moreover, in every corner of Europe bishops and clergy were, at least in theory, agents of papal programs. The elaboration of systematic canon law encouraged by the papal reformers as a weapon in the investiture controversy created a system of courts and legal institutions more sophisticated than that of any secular monarch. Church courts claimed jurisdiction over all clerics regardless of the nature of the legal problem, and over all baptized Christians in such fundamental issues as legitimacy of marriages, inheritances, and oaths. During the pontificate of Innocent III (1198–1216), the papacy reached the height of its powers. Innocent made and deposed emperors, excommunicated kings, summoned a crusade against heretics in the south of France, and placed whole countries such as England and France under interdict, that is, the suspension of all religious services when rulers dared to contradict him. Still he found time to support Francis of Assisi and Dominic, and in 1215 to call the Fourth Lateran Council, which culminated the reforms of the past century and had a lasting effect on the spiritual life of clergy and laity alike.

At the council, more than twelve hundred assembled bishops and abbots, joined by great nobles from across Europe, defined fundamental doctrines such as the nature of the eucharist, ordered annual confession of sins, and detailed procedures for the election of bishops. They also mandated a strict lifestyle for clergy and forbade their participation in judicial procedures in which accused persons had to undergo painful ordeals, such as grasping a piece of red-hot iron and carrying it a prescribed distance, to prove their innocence. More ominously, the council also mandated that Jews wear special identifying markings on their clothing—a sign of the increasing hostility Christians felt toward the Jews in their midst.

During the thirteenth century the papacy continued to perfect its legal system and its control over clergy throughout Europe. However, politically the popes were unable to assert their claims to universal supremacy. This was true both in Italy, where the communes in the north and the kingdom of Naples in the south resisted direct papal control, and in the emerging kingdoms north of the Alps, where monarchs successfully intervened in Church affairs. The old claims of papal authority rang increasingly hollow. When Pope Boniface VIII (1294–1303) attempted to prevent the French king Philip IV (1285–1314) from taxing the French clergy, boasting that he could depose kings "like servants" if necessary, Philip proved him wrong. Philip's agents hired a gang of adventurers who kidnapped the

drowned crossing a river while on a crusade—the emperor was more a feudal lord than a sovereign, and in Italy his authority was disputed by the papacy and the towns. Frederick's successors continued his policy of focusing on Italy with no better success. In 1230 Frederick II (1215–50) conceded to each German prince sovereign rights in his own territory. From the thirteenth to the nineteenth century these princes ruled their territories as independent states, leaving the office of emperor a hollow title.

The investiture controversy ultimately compromised the authority of the pope as well as that of the emperor. First, the series of compromises beginning with the Concordat of Worms established a novel and potent tradition in Western political thought: the definition of separate spheres of authority for secular and religious government. Secondly, while in the short run popes were able to exercise enormous political influence, from the thirteenth century they were increasingly unable to make good their claims to absolute authority.

Papal power was based on more than Scripture. Over the centuries, the popes had acquired large amounts of land in central Italy and in the Rhone Val-

pope, plundered his treasury, and released him a broken, humiliated wreck. He died three weeks later. The French king who had engineered Boniface's humiliation represented a new political tradition much more limited but ultimately more successful than either the empire or the papacy—the medieval nation-state.

The Nation-States: France and England

The office of king was a less pretentious and more familiar one than that of emperor. As the Carolingian world disintegrated, a variety of kingdoms had appeared in France, Italy, Burgundy, and Provence. Beyond the confines of the old Carolingian world, kingship was well established in England and northern Spain. In Scandinavia, Poland, Bohemia, and Hungary powerful chieftains were consolidating royal power at the expense of their aristocracies. The claims of kings were much more modest than those of emperors or popes. Kings lay claim to a limited territory and, while the king was anointed and thus a "Christus" (from the Greek word for sacred oil), kings were only one of many representatives of God on earth. Finally, kings were far from absolute rulers. During the tenth and eleventh centuries, the powers of justice, coinage, taxation, and military command, once considered public, had been usurped by aristocrats and nobles. Kings needed the support of these magnates and often—as in the case of France—these dukes and counts were wealthier and more powerful than the kings. Still, between the tenth and fourteenth centuries some monarchies, especially those of France and England, developed into vigorous, powerful, centralized kingdoms. In the process they gave birth to what has become the modern state.

In 987, when Hugh Capet was elected king of the West Franks, no one suspected that his successors would become the most powerful rulers of Europe, for they were relatively weak magnates whose only real power lay in the region between Paris and Orléans. The dukes of Normandy, descendants of Vikings whose settlement had been recognized by Frankish kings, ruled their duchy with an authority of which the kings could only dream. Less than a century later, Duke William of Normandy expanded his power even more by conquering England. In the twelfth century, the English kings ruled a vast collection of hereditary lands on both sides of the English Channel called the Angevin Empire, territories much richer than those ruled by the French king. The counts of Flanders also ruled a prosperous region much better unified than the French king's small

PROMINENT POPES AND RELIGIOUS FIGURES OF THE HIGH MIDDLE AGES

1049–1054*	Pope Leo IX
1073–1085	Pope Gregory VII
1088–1099	Pope Urban II
1098–1179	Hildegard of Bingen
1119–1124	Pope Calixtus II
1170–1221	Saint Dominic
1182–1226	Saint Francis of Assisi
1198–1216	Pope Innocent III
1225–1274	Saint Thomas Aquinas
1294–1303	Pope Boniface VIII

*Dates for popes are dates of reign.

territory in the area around Paris. In the south, the counts of Poitou, who were also dukes of Aquitaine, were building up a powerful territorial principality in this most Romanized region of the kingdom. In Anjou an ambitious aristocratic family consolidated to form a virtually independent principality.

Biology and bureaucracy created the medieval French monarchy. Between 987 and 1314, every royal descendant of Hugh Capet (after whom the dynasty was called the Capetian) left a male heir—an extraordinary record for a medieval family. During the same period, by comparison, the office of emperor was occupied by men from no less than nine families. By simply outlasting the families of their great barons, the Capetian kings were able to absorb lands when other families became extinct. This success was not just the result of luck. Kings such as Robert the Pious (996–1031) and Louis VII (1137–80) risked excommunication in order to divorce wives who had not produced male heirs. In 1152 Louis had his marriage with the richest heiress of the twelfth century, Eleanor of Aquitaine (1122–1204), annulled in part because she had given him no sons. With the annulment he also lost the chance to absorb her territories of Aquitaine and Poitou. A few months later Eleanor married Count Henry of Anjou (1133–89), who two years later became King Henry II of England. Imagine Louis's chagrin when, with Henry, Eleanor produced four sons, in the process making the English kings the greatest magnates in France!

The Capetians' long run of biological luck, combined with the practice of having a son crowned during his father's lifetime and thus being firmly established before his father's death, was only part of the explanation for the Capetian success. The Capetians also wisely used their position as consecrated sovereigns to build a power base in the Île-de-France (the region around Paris) and among the bishops and abbots of the kingdom, and then to insist on their feudal rights as the lords of the great dukes and counts of France. It was this foundation that Philip II (1180–1223), the son of Louis VII by his third wife, used to create the French monarchy.

Philip II was known to posterity as Augustus or "the aggrandizer" because through his ruthless political intrigue and brilliant organizational sense he more than doubled the territory he controlled and more than quadrupled the revenue of the French crown. (See "The Paris of Philip Augustus," pp. 280–281.) Through marriage he acquired Vermandois, the Amienois, Artois, and Valois. He later absorbed Flanders and set the stage for the absorption of the great county of Toulouse by his son Louis VIII (1223–26) in the aftermath of the Albigensian Crusade launched by Pope Innocent III. Philip's greatest coup, however, was the confiscation of all the continental possessions of the English king John (1199–1216), the son of Henry II and Eleanor of Aquitaine. Although sovereign in England, as lord of Normandy, Anjou, Maine, and Touraine, John was technically a vassal of King Philip. When John married the fiancée of one of his continental vassals, the outraged vassal appealed to Philip in his capacity as John's lord. Philip summoned John to appear before the royal court, and when John refused to do so, Philip ordered him to surrender all of his continental fiefs. This meant war, and one by one John's continental possessions fell to the French king. Philip's victory over John's ally, the emperor Otto IV (1198–1215), at Bouvines in 1214 sealed the English loss of Normandy, Maine, Anjou, Poitou, and Touraine (see map, p. 282).

As important as the absorption of these vast regions was the administrative system Philip organized to govern them. Using members of families from the old royal demesne, he set up administrative officials called baillis and seneschals—salaried nonfeudal agents who collected his revenues and represented his interests. The baillis, who were drawn from common families and who often had received their education at the University of Paris, were the foundation of the French bureaucracy, which grew in strength and importance through the thirteenth century. By governing the regions of France according to local traditions but always with an eye to the king's interests, these bureaucrats did more than anyone else to create a stable, enduring political system.

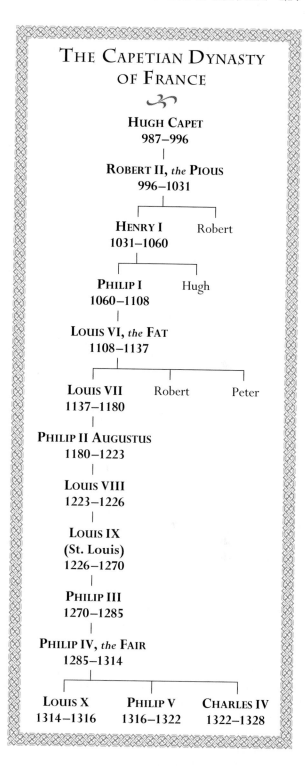

THE CAPETIAN DYNASTY OF FRANCE

HUGH CAPET
987–996

ROBERT II, the PIOUS
996–1031

HENRY I   Robert
1031–1060

PHILIP I   Hugh
1060–1108

LOUIS VI, the FAT
1108–1137

LOUIS VII   Robert   Peter
1137–1180

PHILIP II AUGUSTUS
1180–1223

LOUIS VIII
1223–1226

LOUIS IX
(St. Louis)
1226–1270

PHILIP III
1270–1285

PHILIP IV, the FAIR
1285–1314

LOUIS X   **PHILIP V**   **CHARLES IV**
1314–1316   **1316–1322**   **1322–1328**

Philip's grandson Louis IX (1226–70) fine-tuned this administrative machine and endowed it with the aura of sanctity. Louis was as perfect an embodiment of medieval Christian virtue as Saint Francis of Assisi,

❧ The Paris of Philip Augustus

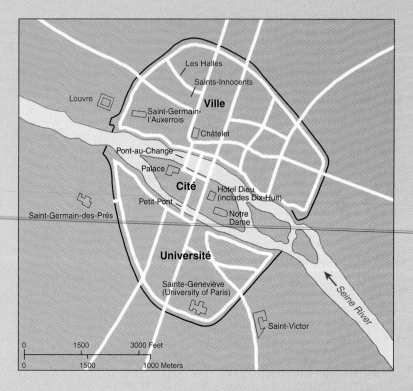

Returning to Paris after his victory over the emperor Otto IV at Bouvines in July 1214 Philip Augustus was met before the city walls by crowds of townspeople, who spread flowers in his path and led him in triumph into his city. The people danced, clergy and students chanted, bells rang, and the homes and churches of the city overflowed with flowers. The rejoicing, which continued for seven days and nights, was a celebration of the king and the city that he had created.

Prior to his reign, Paris had been just one of several royal residences. Philip made it his capital, enriched it, and transformed it. During his reign the population of the city doubled, from approximately 25,000 to over 50,000 inhabitants, making it the most populous city north of the Alps. Philip paved the city's principal streets and built aqueducts to replace those built by the Romans, which had been long in ruins. Shortly before leaving on a crusade in 1192, he ordered construction of a new city wall,

protected by 76 towers and pierced by 14 gates. To guard against the English down the river, Philip also constructed a fortification, the Louvre, just outside the new walls. Within these walls, which eventually enclosed some 618 acres, developed a complex combination of commercial, political, and cultural life unique in Europe.

Paris was actually three cities in 1214: the ancient island of the *cité*, with its royal and episcopal functions; the *ville*, the commercial center of Paris, on the right bank; and the *université*, the intellectual center of Europe, on the left. Philip left his mark on each.

The cité continued its ancient function as the religious and political center of Paris. The island was divided between the two lords of the city, the king and the bishop. At the eastern end, surrounded by a warren of smaller churches and clerical residences, stood the cathedral. Notre Dame had been in the process of reconstruction since 1163, its soaring Gothic vaulting rising from its older Romanesque pillars. By the first quarter of the thirteenth century, work had begun on the west facade and the great rose window was under way. Across the entire facade stretched the gallery of the kings—28 imposing statues of biblical rulers who looked across the cathedral square to the western end of the island and the palace of the king of France.

The palace consisted of a round stone tower and a chapel dedicated to Saint Nicholas, both of which dated to the early eleventh century. Here Philip had established the royal court and permanently fixed his archives and accounting office. Here he resided when in Paris, and here he housed his family, retainers, chaplains, and chancery personnel. To the palace came Philip's baillis to report on their annual activities. For the first time, the French monarchy had a fixed seat of government.

The royal precincts on the cité were linked with the ville on the right bank by the Grand-Pont, a bridge covered with the houses of money changers. At the end of the bridge stood a small tower, or châtelet, protecting access to the cité. It was in the ville that in 1183 Philip constructed the first permanent Paris market, Les Halles, which remained the principal Paris market until the 1960s. The buildings consisted of two large sheds surrounded by walls pierced with great doors out of which merchants and artisans sold their products. Around Les Halles rose the residences and workshops of the tailors, blacksmiths, goldsmiths, shoemakers, coopers, tanners, cartwrights, furriers, potters, carpenters, and other tradespeople. With few exceptions these craft workers occupied post-and-beam structures crowded together so closely that often their upper stories touched, forming arches over the narrow, twisting streets. Near Les Halles was the great cemetery of the Saints-Innocents, the most squalid and bizarre quarter of Paris. The primary cemetery of Paris for centuries, the site was used as an informal market, the favorite meeting place for thieves, charlatans, and prostitutes. Here dogs tore at half-buried corpses while lovers met for a few moments of pleasure. Philip had walled the cemetery in 1187, but the walls had accomplished little more than providing security for clandestine activities.

The episcopal quarter of the cité was connected to the predominantly clerical left bank by the Petit-Pont. At the end of this bridge stood another châtelet, which protected access to the cité and which also served as a prison. In the previous century, the left bank had become the intellectual center of Europe. Its schools, those of the monasteries of Saint-Germain-des-Prés and Saint-Victor, and especially the school established on Mont Sainte Geneviève, attracted students from as far away as Germany, England, Italy, Hungary, and Scandinavia. Philip's new wall enclosed only Mont Sainte Geneviève, which had become the nucleus of the corporation of masters that formed the University of Paris. Students and masters, reassured by the physical security of the new walls and the political security afforded by Philip's charters for the university, flocked to the area. By 1219 they were so numerous that they grouped themselves into four "nations," divisions of the university population according to their countries of origin.

The crowded, jostling atmosphere in the university was similar to that in the ville, but on the left bank the crowds consisted of students, teachers, their servants (the latter "nearly all thieves" as one alumnus later recalled), and wandering clerics, or goliards, who lived by their wits on the fringe of the university. Prosperous students rented rooms from local landlords and amused themselves in the numerous taverns. Generous benefactors were beginning to establish charitable foundations, or colleges, in which poor clerics might find room and board. Already in existence were the colleges of Dix-huit, Saint-Honoré, and Saint-Thomas du Louvre. The most famous, founded by Louis IX's chaplain Robert de Sorbon, would not be established until 1257.

A great and vibrant capital, Philip's Paris was also dangerous, filthy, and smelly. Twice during Philip's reign flooding destroyed both the Grand-Pont and the Petit-Pont. In 1196 Philip had had to seek refuge from rising water on Mount Saint Geneviève. Although Philip had paved the principal streets, the others remained virtually open sewers. Crowded conditions were ideal breeding grounds for infectious diseases of all sorts, and hospitals such as the Hôtel Dieu probably did more to incubate and spread disease than to contain it. Despite its dangers, crime, and lack of sanitation, Paris was alive, exciting, teeming with new people and new ideas. In the thirteenth century Paris became what it would continue to be—the vibrant heart of the French nation.

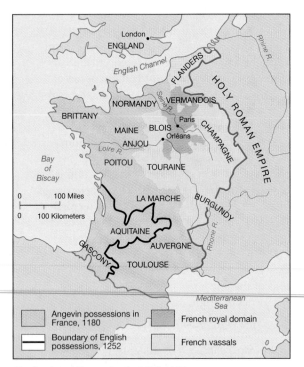

England and France in the Mid-1200s.

the threat of Boniface VIII (see pp. 277–278), he could rely on subjects and agents for whom the king of France and not the pope was sovereign.

The growth of royal power transformed the traditional role of the aristocracy. As the power and wealth of kings increased, the ability of the nobility to maintain their independence decreased. Royal judges undermined lords' control over the peasantry. Royal revenues enabled kings to hire warriors rather than relying on traditional feudal levies. At the same time, the increasing expenses of the noble lifestyle forced all but the wealthiest aristocrats to look for sources of income beyond their traditional estates. Increasingly they found this in royal service. Thus, in the thirteenth century the nobility began to lose some of its independence to the state.

A very different path brought the English monarchy to a level of power similar to that of the French kings by the end of the thirteenth century. While France was made by a family and its bureaucracy, the kingdom originally forged by Alfred and his descendants was transformed by the successors of William the Conqueror, using its judges and its people, often in spite of themselves.

When King Edward the Confessor (1042–66) died, three claimants disputed the succession. Anglo-Saxon sources insist that Edward and his nobles chose Earl Harold Godwinson (ca. 1022–66) over Duke William of Normandy and the Norwegian king Harold III (1045–66). William insisted that Edward had designated him and that years before, when Earl Harold had been shipwrecked on the Norman coast and befriended by the duke, he had sworn an oath to assist William in gaining the crown. Harold of Norway and William sailed for England. Harold Godwinson defeated the Norwegian's army and killed the king, but he met his end shortly after on the bloody field of Hastings, and William secured the throne.

William's England was a small, insular kingdom that had been united by Viking raids little more than a century before. Hostile Celtic societies bordered it to the north and west. Still, it had important strengths. First, the king of the English was not simply a feudal lord, a first among equals—he was a sovereign. Secondly, Anglo-Saxon government had been participatory, with the free men of each shire taking part in court sessions and sharing the responsibilities of government. Finally, the king had agents, or reeves, in each shire (shire reeves, or sheriffs) who were responsible for representing the king's interests, presiding over the local court, and collecting royal taxes and incomes. This ability to

who died in the year of Louis's coronation. Generous and pious, but also brave and capable, Louis took seriously his obligation to provide justice for the poor and protection for the weak. A disastrous crusade in 1248, which ended in his capture and ransom in Egypt, convinced Louis that his failure was punishment for his sins and those of his government. When he returned to France, he dispatched investigators to correct abuses by baillis and other royal officials and restored property unjustly confiscated by his father's agents during the Albigensian Crusade. In addition, he established a permanent central court in Paris to hear appeals from throughout the kingdom. Although much of the work was handled by a growing staff of professional jurists, Louis often became involved personally. As one of his advisors recalled years later, "In summer, after hearing mass, the king often went to the wood of Vincennes, where he would sit down with his back against an oak, and make us all sit round him. Those who had any suit to present could come to speak to him without hindrance from an usher or any other person."

In 1270 Louis attempted another crusade and died in an epidemic in Tunis. The good will and devotion that he won from his subjects was a precious heritage that his successors were able to exploit for centuries. When his grandson Philip the Fair (1285–1314) faced

In a key panel of the Bayeux Tapestry, woven not long after the Battle of Hastings to present William the Conqueror's version of the events, William Godwinson swears to William that he will assist him in gaining the crown of England

raise money was the most important aspect of the English kingship for William the Conqueror and his immediate successors, who remained thoroughly Continental in interest, culture, and language (the first English king to speak English fluently was probably King John). England was seen primarily as a source of revenue. To tap this wealth, the Norman kings transformed rather than abolished Anglo-Saxon governmental traditions, adding Norman feudalism and administrative control to Anglo-Saxon kingship.

William preserved English government while replacing Anglo-Saxon officers with his continental vassals, chiefly Normans and Flemings. He rewarded his supporters with land confiscated from the defeated Anglo-Saxons, but he was careful to give out land only in fief. In contrast to continental practice, where many lords owned vast estates outright, in England all land was held directly or indirectly of the king. Because he wanted to know the extent of his new kingdom and its wealth, William ordered a comprehensive survey of all royal rights. The recorded account, known as the Domesday Book, was the most extensive investigation of economic rights since the late Roman tax rolls had been abandoned by the Merovingians.

Since William and his successors concentrated on their continental possessions and spent little time in England, they needed an efficient system of controlling the kingdom in their absence. To this end they developed the royal court, an institution inherited from their Anglo-Saxon predecessors, into an efficient system of fiscal and administrative supervision. The most important innovation was the use of a large checkerboard, or exchequer, which functioned like a primitive computer to audit the returns of their sheriffs. Annual payments were recorded on long rolls of parchment called pipe rolls, the first continuous accounting system in Europe. The use of extensive written records and strict accounting produced the most efficient and prosperous royal administration in Europe.

Almost two decades of warfare over the succession in the first half of the twelfth century greatly weakened royal authority, but Henry II (1154–89), reestablished central power by reasserting his authority over the nobility and through his legal reforms. Using his continental wealth and armies, he brought the English barons into line, destroyed private castles, and reasserted his rights to traditional royal incomes. He strengthened royal courts by expanding royal jurisdiction at the expense of Church tribunals and of the courts owned by feudal lords.

Henry's efforts to control the clergy led to one of the epic clashes of the investiture controversy. The archbishop of Canterbury, Thomas à Becket (ca. 1118–70), although a personal friend of Henry, who had made him first chancellor and then archbishop, refused to accept the king's claim to jurisdiction over clergy. In

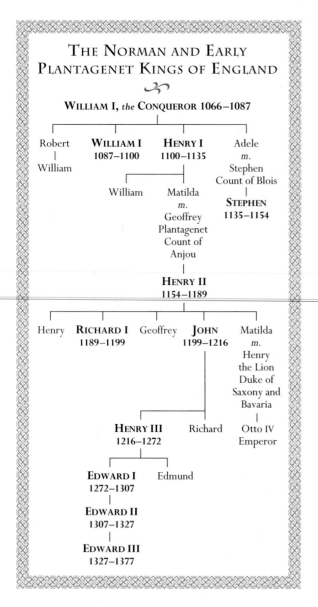

THE NORMAN AND EARLY PLANTAGENET KINGS OF ENGLAND

WILLIAM I, *the* **CONQUEROR 1066–1087**

Robert — **WILLIAM I** 1087–1100 — **HENRY I** 1100–1135 — Adele *m.* Stephen Count of Blois

William

William — Matilda *m.* Geoffrey Plantagenet Count of Anjou

STEPHEN 1135–1154

HENRY II 1154–1189

Henry — **RICHARD I** 1189–1199 — Geoffrey — **JOHN** 1199–1216 — Matilda *m.* Henry the Lion Duke of Saxony and Bavaria

HENRY III 1216–1272 — Richard — Otto IV Emperor

EDWARD I 1272–1307 — Edmund

EDWARD II 1307–1327

EDWARD III 1327–1377

feudal ones was even more successful, laying the foundation for a system of uniform judicial procedures through which royal justice reached throughout the kingdom: the common law. In France, royal agents observed local legal traditions but sought always to turn them to the king's advantage. In contrast, Henry's legal system simplified and cut through the complex tangle of local and feudal jurisdictions concerning land law. Any free person could purchase, for a modest price, a letter, or writ, from the king ordering the local sheriff to impanel a jury to determine if that person had been recently dispossessed of an estate, regardless of that person's legal right to the property. The procedure was swift and efficient. If the jury found for the plaintiff, the sheriff immediately restored the property, by force if necessary. While juries may not have meted out justice, they did resolve conflicts, and they did so in a way that protected landholders. These writs became enormously successful and expanded the jurisdiction of royal courts into areas previously outside royal jurisdiction.

Henry's son John may have made the greatest contribution to the development of the English state by losing Normandy and most of his other continental lands. Loss of these territories forced English kings to concentrate on ruling England, not their continental territories. Moreover, John's financial difficulties, brought about by his unsuccessful wars to recover his continental holdings, led him to such extremes of fiscal extortion that his barons, his prelates, and the townspeople of London revolted. In June 1215 he was forced to accept the "great charter of liberties," or Magna Carta, a conservative feudal document demanding that the king respect the rights of his vassals and of the burghers of London. The great significance of the document was its acknowledgment that the king was not above the law.

John and his weak, ineffective son Henry III (1216–72), although ably served by royal judges, were forced by their failures to cede considerable influence to the great barons of the realm. Henry's son Edward I (1272–1307) was a strong and effective king who conquered Wales, defended the remaining continental possessions against France, and expanded the common law. He found that he could turn baronial involvement in government to his own advantage. By summoning his barons, bishops, and representatives of the towns and shires to participate in a "parley" or "parliament," he could raise more funds for his wars. Like similar

spite of his friendship with the king, Becket, who had been educated at Paris, was deeply influenced by the papal reform movement and had a great sense of the dignity of his office. For six years Becket lived in exile on the Continent and infuriated Henry by his stubborn adherence to the letter of Church law. He was allowed to return to England in 1170, but that same year he was struck down in his own cathedral by four knights eager for royal favor. The king did penance but, unlike the German emperors, ultimately preserved royal authority over the Church.

Henry's program to assert royal courts over local and

THE GREAT CHARTER

Faced with defeat abroad at the hands of the French king Philip Augustus and baronial revolt at home, in 1215 King John was forced to sign the Magna Carta, the "great charter" guaranteeing the traditional rights of the English nobility. Although a conservative document, in time it was interpreted as the guarantee of the fundamental rights of the English people.

John, by the grace of God king of England, lord of Ireland, duke of Normandy and of Aquitaine, and count of Anjou, to his archbishops, bishops, abbots, earls, barons, justiciars, foresters, sheriffs, reeves, ministers, and all his bailiffs and faithful men, greeting. Know that, through the inspiration of God, for the health of our soul and [the souls] of all our ancestors and heirs, for the honour of God and the exaltation of Holy Church, and for the betterment of our realm, by the counsel of our venerable fathers . . . of our nobles . . . and of our other faithful men—

1. We have in the first place granted to God and by this our present charter have confirmed, for us and our heirs forever, that the English Church shall be free and shall have its rights entire and its liberties inviolate. . . . We have also granted to all freemen of our kingdom, for us and our heirs forever, all the liberties hereinunder written, to be had and held by them and their heirs of us and our heirs.

2. If any one of our earls or barons or other men holding of us in chief dies, and if when he dies his heir is of full age and owes relief [that heir] shall have his inheritance for the ancient relief . . . .

6. Heirs shall be married without disparagement.

7. A widow shall have her marriage portion and inheritance immediately after the death of her husband and without difficulty; nor shall she give anything for her dowry or for her marriage portion or for her inheritance— which inheritance she and her husband were holding on the day of that husband's death. . . .

8. No widow shall be forced to marry so long as she wishes to live without a husband; yet so that she shall give security against marrying without our consent if she holds of us, or without the consent of her lord if she holds of another. . . .

12. Scutage or aid shall be levied in our kingdom only by the common counsel of our kingdom, except for ransoming our body, for knighting our eldest son, and for once marrying our eldest daughter; and for these [purposes] only a reasonable aid shall be taken. The same provision shall hold with regard to the aids of the city of London. . . .

17. Common pleas shall not follow our court, but shall be held in some definite place. . . .

20. A freeman shall be amerced for a small offence only according to the degree of the offence; and for a grave offence he shall be amerced according to the gravity of the offence, saving his contenement [sufficient property to guarantee sustenance for himself and his family]. And a merchant shall be amerced in the same way, saving his merchandise; and a villein in the same way, saving his wainage [harvested crops necessary for seed and upkeep of his farm]. . . .

39. No freeman shall be captured or imprisoned or disseised [dispossessed of his estates] or outlawed or exiled or in any way destroyed, nor will we go against him or send against him, except by the lawful judgment of his peers or by the law of the land. . . .

54. No one shall be seized or imprisoned on the appeal of a woman for the death of any one but her husband. . . .

From the Magna Carta.

Edward I presiding over a session of Parliament. Edward expanded the institution to include representatives of the boroughs and shires.

an exacting system of accounting, increased the power of the English monarchy. By 1300, France, with its powerful royal bureaucracy, and England, with its courts and accountants, were the most powerful states in the West.

• • •

In 1300 Pope Boniface VIII extended a plenary indulgence (the remission of all punishment due people's sins) to those who visited the churches of Rome during that year. It was a jubilee year, an extraordinary celebration to occur once every century. There was much to celebrate. By 1300 Europe had achieved a level of population density, economic prosperity, cultural sophistication, and political organization greater than at any time since the Roman Empire. Across Europe, a largely free peasantry cultivated a wide variety of crops, both for local consumption and for growing commercial markets, while landlords sought increasingly rational approaches to estate management and investment. In cities and ports, merchants, manufacturers, and bankers presided over an international commercial and manufacturing economy that connected Scandinavia to the Mediterranean Sea. In schools and universities, students learned the skills of logical thinking and disputation while absorbing the traditions of Greece and Rome in order to prepare themselves for careers in law, medicine, and government. In courts and palaces, nascent bureaucracies worked to expand the rule of law over recalcitrant nobles, to keep the peace, and to preserve justice. Finally, after almost a thousand years of political, economic, and intellectual isolation, western Europe had become once more a dominant force in world civilization.

Spanish, Hungarian, and German assemblies of the thirteenth century, these assemblies were occasions to consult, to present royal programs, and to extract extraordinary taxes for specific projects. They were also opportunities for those summoned to petition the king for redress of grievances. Initially, representatives of the shires and towns attended only sporadically. However, since the growing wealth of the towns and countryside made their financial support essential, these groups came to anticipate that they had a right to be consulted and to consent to taxation.

Through a system of royal courts and justices employing local juries and a tradition of representative parliaments, this forced self-government, coupled with

Suggestions for Further Reading

The Countryside

* Georges Duby, *Rural Economy and Country Life in the Medieval West* (Columbia, SC: University of South Carolina Press, 1968). An authoritative survey of medieval agriculture and society.

* Lynn White, Jr., *Medieval Technology and Social Change* (New York: Oxford University Press, 1966). Imaginative essays on the social impact of technology in the Middle Ages.

* Georges Duby, *The Knight, the Lady, and the Priest: The Making of Modern Marriage in Medieval France* (New York:

Pantheon Books, 1984). A short study of the conflict between lay and religious social values in medieval France.

* Georges Duby, *The Chivalrous Society* (Berkeley, CA: University of California Press, 1978). Essays on the French aristocracy by the leading medieval historian.

Ronald C. Finucane, *Soldiers of the Faith: Crusaders and Moslems at War* (New York: St. Martin's Press, 1984). A critical reappraisal of the Crusades for general readers.

Medieval Towns

* Robert S. Lopez, *The Commercial Revolution of the Middle Ages, 950–1350* (New York: Cambridge University Press, 1971). An excellent survey of medieval commercial history.

* Daniel Waley, *The Italian City-Republics* (New York: McGraw-Hill, 1969). A brief and highly readable account of Italian towns.

* Helene Wieruszowski, *The Medieval University* (Princeton, NJ: Van Nostrand, 1966). A short history of medieval universities.

* R. W. Southern, *Western Society and the Church in the Middle Ages* (New York: Penguin Books, 1990). A well-written account of the medieval Church for a general public.

The Invention of the State

* Joseph R. Strayer, *On the Medieval Origins of the Modern State* (Princeton, NJ: Princeton University Press, 1970). A very brief but imaginative account of medieval statecraft by a leading historian of French institutions.

* John W. Baldwin, *The Government of Philip Augustus: Foundations of French Royal Power in the Middle Ages* (Berkeley, CA: University of California Press, 1986). A detailed but important study of the crucial reign of Philip II.

* Horst Fuhrmann, *Germany in the High Middle Ages, c. 1050–1200* (New York: Cambridge University Press, 1986). A fresh synthesis of German history by a leading German historian.

Bryce Lyon, *A Constitutional and Legal History of Medieval England*, 2d ed. (New York: W. W. Norton, 1980). A detailed account of the making of the medieval English constitution.

M. T. Clanchy, *England and Its Rulers, 1066–1272* (New York: B & N Imports, 1983). A good recent survey of English political history.

*Paperback edition available.

10 ✒ The Later Middle Ages, 1300–1500

Webs of Stone and Blood

Like a delicate basket of woven stone, the Gothic vaulting in the choir of Saint Vitus Cathedral in Prague encloses and unifies the sacred space over which it floats. In a similar manner, the great aristocratic families of the fourteenth and fifteenth centuries spun webs of estates, hereditary principalities, and fiefs across Europe. In art as in life, dynamic individuals reshaped the legacy of the past into new and unexpected forms.

In France, where Gothic architecture originated in the twelfth century, architects had long used stone springers and vaults, but only to emphasize verticality and lift the eyes of the faithful to the heavens. Through the thirteenth and fourteenth centuries, French architects vied with one another to raise their vaults ever higher but never rethought the basic premise of their design. Peter Parler (1330–99), the architect of Saint Vitus, approached the design of his cathedral in a novel way. He used intersecting vaults not simply for height but to bind together the interior space of the edifice in a net of intersecting stone arches. This ability to rethink the architectural heritage of the past marked Peter Parler as the greatest architectural genius of the fourteenth century. Emperor Charles IV (1355–78), the head of the most successful web-spinning aristocratic family of the late Middle Ages, recognized Parler's talent and enlisted him in making his Bohemian capital one of the most splendid cities of Europe.

Along with his innovations in architecture, Peter Parler also opened new directions in sculpture. Again breaking with French tradition, in which sculptors sought to present their subjects as ideal types, Parler concentrated on realism and individual portraiture in his work. The carved heads of Bohemia's kings, queens, prelates, and princes that peer down from the ambulatory of Saint Vitus are real people, with their blemishes, their virtues, and their vices marked in their faces. This interest in the individual was entirely appropriate in the late fourteenth century—a time when kings and peasants, saints and heretics, lords and merchants sought to make their mark by stepping out of their traditional roles. The characters of the age had personalities as marked as Parler's individualistic sculptures. Their epithets tell much: John "the Valiant" of Brittany; Philip "the Bold" of Burgundy; his son John "the Fearless"; the Habsburg John "the Parricide"; Charles II "the Bad" of Navarre; Pedro IV "the Cruel" of Aragon; Charles VI "the Mad" of France. Powerful and ambitious men and women fought for political dominance, religious visionaries and preachers announced new and daring revelations, and thinkers and artists broke with hallowed philosophical and literary traditions. Parler had no doubt about his own importance in this age of individuals. His own portrait bust looks down from the cathedral beside those of kings and queens.

Parler was born into a well-known family of stonemasons near the German town of Württemberg. He learned his craft from his father but at a young age surpassed the elder Parler, not simply in the execution of stone constructions, but in their design. A century earlier a young man of such recognized talent would almost certainly have gravitated from his native Swabia to France, then the cultural center of Europe. However, although French language, styles, and tradition continued to inspire Europeans everywhere throughout the fourteenth century, by mid-century France was increasingly troubled by dynastic problems, war, economic decline, and the ravages of disease. It was no longer the magnet that drew the greatest artists, architects, and thinkers. Thus, at the age of twenty-three the brilliant and ambitious young architect looked to the east rather than to the west and cast his lot with the splendid court of Charles IV, king of Bohemia and soon to be Holy Roman Emperor. Charles invited Parler to complete his great Prague cathedral, which had been begun by a French architect and modeled on the great cathedrals of France. With Charles's patronage, Parler modified the building program to incorporate his original vision of architecture and portraiture. He went on to direct the construction of churches, bridges, and towers in Prague and throughout Bohemia. Within a generation Parler's students had spread his refinement of Gothic architecture and sculpture throughout the Holy Roman Empire—to Austria, Bavaria, Swabia, Alsace, Poland, and Italy. Parler, the weaver of stone, and Charles, the weaver of politics, were emblematic of their age.

Politics as a Family Affair

Like those of his architect, Charles's roots were in the Rhineland and his cultural inspiration in France. The ancestral estates of his family, the house of Luxembourg, lay on the banks of the Moselle River. Between 1250 and 1350, the Luxembourg family greatly expanded its political and geographical powers by involving itself in the dynastic politics of the decaying Holy Roman Empire. At the height of his power, Charles controlled a patchwork of lands that included Luxembourg, Brabant, Lusatia, Silesia, Moravia, Meissen, and Brandenburg. His daughter married Richard II of England. A son succeeded him in Bohemia and another obtained the Hungarian crown.

Such fragmented and shifting territorial bases were typical of the great families of the fourteenth and fifteenth centuries. Everywhere, family politics threatened the fragile institutional developments of the thirteenth century. Aristocrats competed for personal power and used public office, military command, and taxing power for private ends. What mattered was neither territorial boundaries nor political divisions but marriage alliances, kinship, and dynastic ambitions.

The Struggle for Central Europe

In addition to the Luxembourgs, four other similarly ambitious families competed for dominance in the empire. First were the Wittelsbachs, the chief competitors of the Luxembourgs. The Wittelsbachs had originated in Bavaria but had since spread across Europe. In the west the Wittelsbachs had acquired Holland, Hainaut, and Frisia, while in the east they temporarily held Tyrol and Brandenburg. Next were the Habsburgs, allies of the Luxembourgs, who had begun as a minor comital family in the region of the Black Forest. They expanded east, acquiring Austria, Tyrol, Carinthia, and Carniola. When Rudolf I of Habsburg (1273–91) was elected emperor in 1273, Otakar II, king of Bohemia (1253–78) and head of the powerful Premysl family, dismissed Rudolf as "poor." Compared with the Premysls, perhaps he was. At its height, the Premysl family controlled not only Bohemia but also Moravia, Austria, and a miscellany of lands stretching from Silesia in the north to the Adriatic Sea. Finally, the house of Anjou—descendants of Charles of Anjou, the younger brother of the French king Louis IX, who had become king of Naples—created a similar eastern network. Charles's son Charles Robert secured election as king of Hungary in 1310. His son Louis (1342–82) added the crown of

Poland (1370–82) to the Hungarian crown of Saint Stephen. The protracted wars and maneuvers that these families conducted for dominance in the empire resembled nothing so much as the competition that had taken place three centuries earlier for dominance in feudal France.

For over a century, not only great princes but also monks, adventurers, and simple peasants streamed into the kingdoms and principalities of eastern Europe. Since the early thirteenth century, the Teutonic orders had used the sword to spread Christianity along the Baltic coast. By the early fourteenth century these knight-monks had conquered Prussia and the coast as far east as the Narva River (now well within Russia) where they reached the borders of the Christian principality of Novgorod. The pagan inhabitants of these regions had to choose between conversion and expulsion. When they fled, their fields were turned over to land-hungry German peasants. Long wagon trains of pioneers snaked their way across Germany from the Rhineland, Westphalia, and Saxony to this new frontier. In the Baltic lands they were able to negotiate advantageous contracts with their new lords, guaranteeing them greater freedom than they had known at home.

By the fifteenth century religious and secular German lords had established a new agrarian economy, modeled on western European estates, in regions previously unoccupied or sparsely settled by the indigenous Slavic peoples. This economy specialized in the cultivation of grain for export to the west. Each fall fleets of hundreds of ships sailed from the ports of Gdansk and Riga to ports in the Netherlands, England, and France. Returning flotillas carried Flemish cloth and tons of salt for preserving food to places as far as Novgorod. The influx of Baltic grain into Western Europe caused a decline in domestic grain prices and a corresponding economic slump for landlords throughout the fourteenth and fifteenth centuries.

Farther south, the Christian kingdoms of Poland, Bohemia, and Hungary beckoned different sorts of westerners. Newly opened silver and copper mines in Bohemia, Silesia, southern Poland, and Hungarian Transylvania needed skilled miners, smelters, and artisans. Many were recruited from the overpopulated regions of western Germany. East-west trade routes developed to export these metals, giving new life to the Bohemian towns of Prague and Brno, the Polish cities of Kraków and Lvov, and Hungarian Buda and Bratislava. Trade networks reached south to the Mediterranean via Vienna, the Brenner Pass, and Venice. To the north, trade routes extended to the Elbe River and the trading towns of Lübeck and Bremen.

The silver-mining community at Kutná Hora near Prague, ca. 1490.

The Bavarian towns of Augsburg, Rothenburg, and Nuremberg flourished at the western end of this network. To the east, Lvov became a great trading center connecting southern Russia with the west.

The wealth of eastern Europe, its abundant land, and its relative freedom attracted both peasants and merchants. The promise of profitable marriages with eastern royalty drew ambitious aristocrats. Continually menaced by one another and by the aggressive German aristocracy to the west, the royal families of Poland, Hungary, and Bohemia were eager to make marriage alliances with powerful aristocratic families from farther afield. Through such a marriage, for example, Charles Robert of Anjou became king of Hungary after the extinction of that realm's ancient royal dynasty. Similarly Charles Robert's son Louis inherited the Polish crown in 1370 after the death of Casimir III, the last king of the Polish Piast dynasty. Nobles of the east-

ern European kingdoms were pleased to confirm the election of such outsiders. The elections prevented powerful German nobles from claiming succession to the Bohemian, Hungarian, and Polish thrones. At the same time, the families of the western European aristocracy did not have sufficiently strong local power bases to challenge the autonomy of the eastern nobility. For the outsiders, eastern alliances meant the expansion of family power and the promise of glory.

Charles IV (1347–78) was typical of these restless dynasts. His grandfather, Emperor Henry VII (1308–13), had arranged for his son, John of Luxembourg, to marry Elizabeth (d. 1330), the Premysl heiress of Bohemia, and thus acquire the Bohemian crown in 1310. John was king in name only. He spent most of his career fighting in the dynastic wars of the empire and of France. However, by mastering the intricate politics of the decaying Holy Roman Empire, he arranged the deposition of the Wittelsbach emperor Louis IV (1314–47) and in 1346 secured the election of Charles as king of the Romans, or heir of the empire. The following year the Bohemian crown passed to Charles.

Although born in Prague and deeply committed to what he called "the sweet soil of my native land," Charles had spent most of his youth in France, where he was deeply influenced by French culture. However, upon his return to Prague in 1333 he rediscovered his Czech cultural roots. As king of Bohemia, he worked to make Prague a cultural center by combining French and Czech traditions. He imported artisans, architects, and artists such as Peter Parler to transform and beautify his capital. In 1348 he founded a university in Prague, the first in the empire, modeled on the University of Paris. Keenly interested in history, Charles provided court historians with the sources necessary to write their histories of the Bohemian kingdom. "It is to the great profit of the state that young princes be taught history," he wrote, "lest through ignorance they should become degenerate inheritors of an ancient greatness."

Charles took a more active role in this cultural renewal than perhaps any European king since Alfred of England, fostering a literary renaissance in both Latin and Czech. Although he had forgotten his native Czech during his long stay in France, he soon learned to read and write it, along with French, German, Italian, and Latin. He authored a number of religious texts, fostered the use of the Czech language in religious services, and initiated a Czech translation of the Bible. He even composed his own autobiography, perhaps the first lay person to do so in medieval Europe.

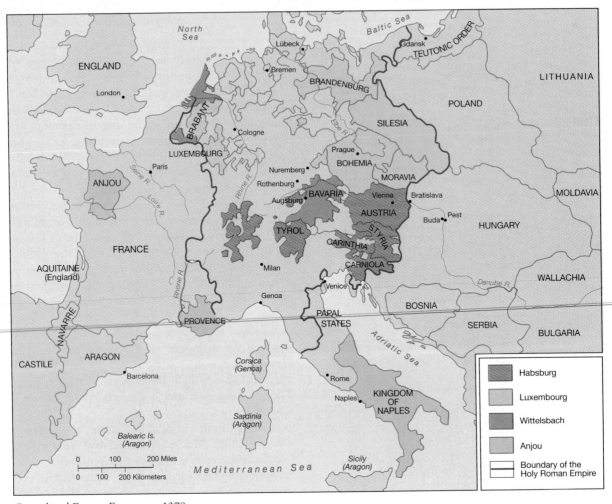

Central and Eastern Europe, ca. 1378

The effects of Charles's cultural policies were far-reaching, but in directions he never anticipated. His interests in Czech culture and religious reform bore unexpected fruit during the reign of his son Sigismund, king of Germany (1410–37), Bohemia (1419–37), and Hungary (1387–1437), and Holy Roman Emperor (1433–37). During Sigismund's reign Czech religious and political reformers came into open conflict with the powerful German-speaking minority in the University of Prague. Led by the theologian Jan Hus (ca. 1372–1415), this reform movement ultimately challenged the authority of the Roman Church and became the direct predecessor of the great reformation of the sixteenth century.

Even while building up his beloved city of Prague, Charles was dismantling the Holy Roman Empire. By the fourteenth century, the title of emperor held little political importance, although as an honorific title it was still bitterly contested by the great families of the empire. Charles sought to end such disputes and at the same time to solidify the autonomy of the kingdoms,

such as Bohemia, against the threats of future imperial candidates. In 1356 he issued the "Golden Bull," an edict that officially recognized what had long been the reality, namely, that the various German princes and kings were autonomous rulers. The bull also established the procedure by which future emperors would be elected. Thereafter, the emperor was chosen by seven great princes of the empire without the consultation or interference of the pope—a tradition of interference that dated to the coronation of Charlemagne. The procedure made disputed elections less likely, but it acknowledged that the office itself was less significant.

The same process that sapped the power of the emperor also reduced the significance of the princes. The empire fragmented into a number of large kingdoms and duchies such as Bohemia, Hungary, Poland, Austria, and Bavaria in the east and over sixteen hundred autonomous principalities, free towns, and sovereign bishoprics in the west. The inhabitants of these territories, often ruled by foreigners who had inherited sovereign powers through marriage, organized themselves into estates—political units of knights, burghers, and clergy—to present a united front in dealing with their prince. The princes in turn did not enjoy any universally recognized right to rule and were forced to negotiate with their estates for any powers they actually enjoyed.

The disintegration of the empire left political power east of the Rhine widely dispersed for over five hundred years. While this meant that Germany did not become a nation-state until the nineteenth century, decentralization left late medieval Germany as a fertile region of cultural and constitutional creativity. In this creative process the office of emperor played no role. After the Habsburg family definitively acquired the imperial office in 1440, the office of emperor ceased to have any role in Germany. Rather, the office became one of the building blocks of the great multinational Habsburg empire of central Europe, an empire that survived until 1918.

A Hundred Years of War

The political map of western Europe was no less a patchwork quilt of family holdings than was the empire. On the Iberian Peninsula, the gradual Christian reconquest bogged down as the three Christian monarchies of Castile, Aragon, and Portugal largely ignored the remaining Muslim kingdom of Granada. Instead, dynastic rivalries, expansionist adventures in Sicily and Italy, internal revolts of nobility and peasants, and futile wars against one another commanded the energy and attention of the Christian kingdoms. Only when Ferdinand of Aragon married Isabella of Castile in 1469 did something like a unified Spain begin to emerge from this world of familial rivalries.

North of the Pyrenees, the situation was even more critical. The same kinds of familial rivalries that destroyed the empire as a political entity threatened to overwhelm the feudal monarchies of France and England in the fourteenth and fifteenth centuries. In both kingdoms, weakening economic climates and demographic catastrophe exacerbated dynastic crises and fierce competition. The survival of the English and French monarchies was due to luck, to a longer tradition of bureaucratic government, and—in the minds of contemporaries—to the hand of God.

Three long-simmering disputes triggered the series of campaigns collectively termed the Hundred Years' War. The first issue was conflicting rights to Gascony in southern France. Since the mid-thirteenth century, the kings of England had held Gascony as a fief of the French king. Neither monarchy was content with this arrangement, and for the next 75 years kings quarreled constantly over sovereignty in the region.

The second point of contention was the close relationship between England and the Flemish cloth towns. These manufacturing centers were the primary customers for English wool. Early in the fourteenth century, Flemish artisans rose up in a series of bloody revolts against the aristocratic cloth dealers who had long monopolized power. The count of Flanders and the French king supported the wealthy merchants, while the English sided with the artisans.

The final dispute concerned the royal succession in France. Charles IV (1322–28), the son of Philip IV, the Fair, died without an heir. The closest descendant of a French king was the grandson of Philip the Fair, King Edward III of England (1327–77). Edward, however, was the son of Philip's daughter Isabella. The French aristocracy, which did not want an English king to inherit the throne and unite the two kingdoms, pretended that according to ancient Frankish law, the crown could not pass through a woman. Instead, they preferred to give the crown to a cousin of the late king, Philip VI (1328–50), who became the first of the Valois kings of France. At first the English voiced no objection to Philip's accession, but in 1337, when the dispute over Gascony again flared up and Philip attempted to confiscate the region from his English "vassal" Edward III, the English king declared war on Philip. Edward's stated goal was not only to recover Gascony but also to claim the crown of his maternal grandfather.

Though territorial and dynastic rivalry were the triggers that set off the war, its deeper cause was chivalry. The elites of Europe were both inspired by and trapped in a code of conduct that required them not only to maintain their honor by violence but also to cultivate violence to increase that honor. This code had been appropriate in a period of weak kingship, but by the late thirteenth century, the growth of courts and royal power in France and in England left little room for private vengeance and vendettas. Nobles were now more often royal retainers than knights errant traveling about the countryside righting wrongs. Government was increasingly an affair of lawyers and bureaucrats, and war an affair of professionals. Yet kings and nobles alike still agreed with the sentiment expressed by a contemporary poet: "The glory of princes is in their pride and in undertaking great peril." By the fourteenth century only war provided sufficient peril.

Edward III of England and his rival Philip VI of France both epitomized the chivalrous knight. Both gloried in luxurious living and conspicuous consumption. Captivated by the romantic tales of King Arthur and the Round Table, in 1344 Edward organized a four-day-long round table celebration to which he invited the most outstanding nobles in England. A contemporary noted: "Among the knights continuous joustings took place for three days; the best melody was made by the minstrels, and various joyous things; to these were given changes of clothing; to these gifts abounded; these were enriched with plenty of gold and silver." A few years later Edward organized the Order of the Garter, a select group of nobles who were to embody the highest qualities of chivalry. For a ruler like Edward, obsessed with knightly glory, war with France was the ideal way to win honor and fame.

In spite of his chivalric ideals, Edward was practical when it came to organizing and financing his campaigns. Philip shared Edward's ideals but lacked his rival's practicality and self-assurance. Before his elevation to the throne, Philip had been a valiant and successful warrior, fond of jousting, tournaments, and lavish celebrations. After his coronation he continued to act like a figure from a knightly romance, surrounding himself with aristocratic advisors who formed the most

brilliant court of Europe, dispensing the royal treasure to his favorites, and dreaming of leading a great crusade to free the Holy Land. However, as the first French king in centuries elected rather than born into the right of succession, Philip treated the magnates from whose ranks he had come with excessive deference. He hesitated to press them for funds and deferred to them on matters of policy even while missing opportunities to raise other revenue from towns and merchants. Finally, although a competent warrior, Philip was no match in strategy or tactics for his English cousin.

Still, the sheer size and wealth of France should have made it the favorite in any war with England. Its population of roughly 16 million made it by far the largest and most densely populated kingdom in Europe. The north of France was a major cereal producer. Vineyards around Bordeaux, Paris, Beaune, and Auxerre produced wines sold throughout western Europe. Paris, the largest city north of the Alps, was a center of commerce as well as an intellectual capital. The Flemish cloth towns, subdued by Philip in 1328, were the most industrialized area of Europe. England, by contrast, was a relatively small, sparsely populated kingdom. Its total population was under 5 million and its economy

In this scene from Thomas Malory's Morte d'Arthur, *Galahad, who will occupy the vacant seat at the Round Table, is introduced to King Arthur and his knights.*

THE FRENCH AND ENGLISH SUCCESSIONS

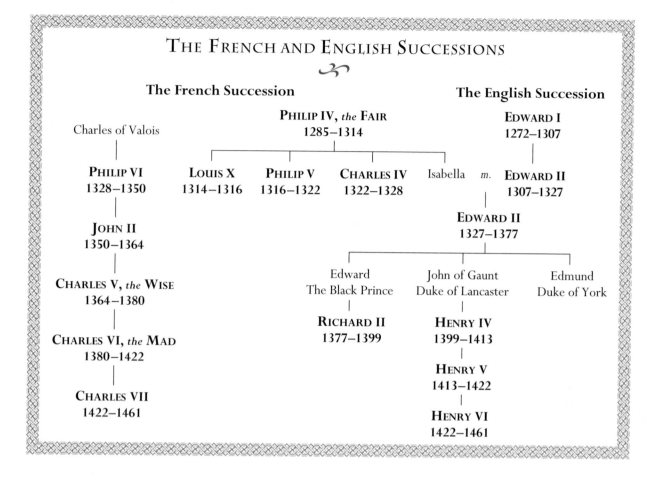

The French Succession

The English Succession

Charles of Valois

PHILIP IV, *the* **FAIR**
1285–1314

EDWARD I
1272–1307

PHILIP VI
1328–1350

LOUIS X
1314–1316

PHILIP V
1316–1322

CHARLES IV
1322–1328

Isabella   *m.*   **EDWARD II**
1307–1327

JOHN II
1350–1364

EDWARD II
1327–1377

Edward
The Black Prince

John of Gaunt
Duke of Lancaster

Edmund
Duke of York

CHARLES V, *the* **WISE**
1364–1380

RICHARD II
1377–1399

HENRY IV
1399–1413

CHARLES VI, *the* **MAD**
1380–1422

HENRY V
1413–1422

CHARLES VII
1422–1461

HENRY VI
1422–1461

---

much less tied into international trade, with only the beginnings of a cloth industry and little to export except wool. At the start of the war Philip could rely on an income roughly three to five times greater than that of Edward. However, these inequalities mattered little because the French king had no means of harnessing the resources of his kingdom. His greater income was matched by greater expenses, and he had no easy way to raise extraordinary funds for war. In contrast, the English king could use Parliament as an efficient source of war subsidies. Edward could also extract great sums from taxes on wool exports. Even after the invasion of France, Philip had to rely on manipulation of the coinage, confiscation of Italian bankers' property, and a whole range of nuisance taxes to finance his campaigns.

War was expensive. In spite of chivalrous ideals, nobles no longer fought as vassals of the king but as highly paid mercenaries. The nature of this service differed greatly on the two sides of the Channel. In France, tactics and personnel had changed little since the twelfth century. The core of any army was the body of heavily armored nobles who rode into battle with their lords, supported by lightly armored knights. Behind them marched infantrymen recruited from towns and armed with pikes. Although the French also hired mercenary Italian crossbowmen, the nobles despised them and never used them effectively.

In contrast, centuries of fighting against Welsh and Scottish enemies had transformed and modernized the English armies and their tactics. The great nobles continued to serve as heavily armored horsemen, but professional companies of foot soldiers raised by individual knights made up the bulk of the army. These professional companies consisted largely of pikemen and, most importantly, of longbowmen. Although it was not as accurate as the crossbow, the English longbow had a greater range. Moreover, when massed archers fired volleys of arrows into enemy ranks, they proved extremely effective against enemy pikemen and even lightly armored cavalry.

The first real test of the two armies came at the Battle of Crécy in 1346. There an overwhelmingly superior French force surrounded the English army. Massing their archers on a hill, the English rained arrows down on the French cavalry, which attacked in glorious but suicidal manner. Typical of the French chivalric behavior was that of King John of Bohemia, father of Charles IV, both of whom were fighting as mercenaries of the

French king. Although he was totally blind, John requested and received the privilege of commanding the vanguard of the first French division. He had his men tie their horses together and lead him into battle so that he might strike a blow. The next day his body and those of all his men were found on the field, their mounts still bound together.

The English victory was total. By midnight they had repelled 16 assaults, losing only one hundred men while killing over three thousand French. The survivors, including Philip VI, fled in disorder. Strangely enough, the French learned nothing from the debacle. In 1356 Philip's successor, John II (1350–64), rashly attacked an English army at Poitiers and was captured. In 1415 the French blundered in a different way at Agincourt. This time most of the heavily armored French knights dismounted and attempted to charge the elevated English position across a soggy, muddy field. Barely able to walk and entirely unable to rise again if they fell, all were captured. Out of fear that his numerically inferior English army would be overwhelmed if the French recovered their breath, the English king ordered over fifteen hundred French nobles and three thousand ordinary soldiers killed. He kept over a thousand of the greatest nobles for ransom. English losses were less than one hundred.

Pitched battles were not the worst defeats for the French. More devastating were the constant raiding and systematic destruction of the French countryside by the English companies. The relief effort launched by Pope Benedict XII (1334–42) in 1339 gives some idea of the scale of destruction. Papal agents, sent to aid victims of the English invasion, paid out over 12,000 pounds—the equivalent of one-third of the English annual royal income—to peasants in just one region of northern France. The funds distributed were simple charity and far from adequate compensation. Villagers estimated that their actual losses were perhaps seven times greater than what they received.

Raiding and pillaging continued for decades, even during long truces between the French and English kings. During periods of truce unemployed free companies of French and English mercenaries roamed the countryside, supporting themselves by banditry while awaiting the renewal of more-formal hostilities. As one chronicler recalled, "From the Loire to the Seine and from there to the Somme, nearly all the fields were left for many years, not merely untended but without people capable of cultivating them, except for rare patches of soil, for the peasants had been killed or put to flight." Never had the ideals of chivalric conduct been so far distant from the brutal realities of warfare.

The battle of Agincourt (1415) was one of the great battles of the Hundred Years' War. The heavily armored French cavalry met defeat at the hands of a much smaller force of disciplined English pikemen and longbowmen.

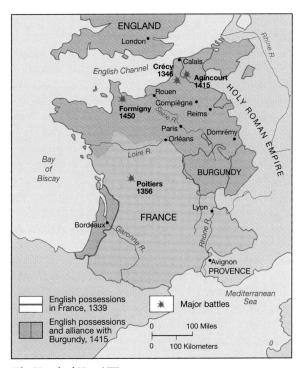

The Hundred Years' War

peared. French kings repeatedly seized the assets of Italian merchant bankers in order to finance the war. Such actions made the Italians, who had been the backbone of French commercial credit, extremely wary about extending loans in the kingdom. The kings then turned to French and Flemish merchants, extorting from them forced loans that dried up capital that might otherwise have been returned to commerce and industry. Politically and economically, France seemed doomed.

The flower of French chivalry did not save France. Instead, at the darkest moment of the long and bloody struggle, salvation came at the hands of a simple peasant girl from the county of Champagne. By 1429 the English and their Burgundian allies held virtually all of northern France, including Paris. Now they were besieging Orléans, the key to the south. The heir to the French throne, the dauphin, was the weak-willed and uncrowned Charles VII (1422–61). To him came Joan of Arc (1412–31), a simple, illiterate but deeply religious girl who bore an incredible message of hope. She claimed to have heard the voices of saints ordering her to save Orléans and have the dauphin crowned according to tradition at Reims.

The French kings were powerless to prevent such destruction, just as they were unable to defeat the enemy in open battle. Since the kings were incapable of protecting their subjects or of leading their armies to victory, the "silken thread binding together the kingdom of France," as one observer put it, began to unravel, and the kingdom so painstakingly constructed by the Capetian monarchs began to fall apart. Not only did the English make significant territorial conquests, but the French nobles began behaving much as those in the Holy Roman Empire, carving out autonomous lordships. Private warfare and castle building, never entirely eradicated even by Louis IX and Philip IV, increased as royal government lost its ability to control the nobility. Whole regions of the kingdom slipped entirely from royal authority. Duke Philip the Good of Burgundy (1396–1467) allied himself with England against France and profited from the war to form a far-flung lordship that included Flanders, Brabant, Luxembourg, and Hainaut. By the time of his death, he was the most powerful ruler in Europe. Much of the so-called Hundred Years' War was actually a French civil war.

During this century of war the French economy suffered even more than the French state. Trade routes were broken and commerce declined as credit disap-

A fifteenth-century portrait of Joan of Arc. The Maid of Orléans was tried for heresy and executed in 1431. Later, in 1456, Pope Calixtus III pronounced her innocent. Pope Benedict XV formally declared her a saint in 1920.

Charles and his advisers were more than skeptical about this brash peasant girl who announced her divinely ordained mission to save France. Finally convinced of her sincerity, if not of her ability, Charles allowed her to accompany a relief force to Orléans. The French army, its spirit buoyed by the belief that Joan's simple faith was the work of God, defeated the English and ended the siege. This victory led to others, and on 16 July 1429 Charles was crowned king at Reims.

After the coronation, Joan's luck began to fade. She failed to take Paris, and in 1431 she was captured by the Burgundians, who sold her to the English. Eager to get rid of this troublesome peasant girl, the English had her tried as a heretic. Charles did nothing to save his savior. After all, the code of chivalry did not demand that a king intervene on behalf of a mere peasant girl, even if she had saved his kingdom. She was burned at the stake in Rouen on 30 May 1431.

Despite Joan's inglorious end, the tide had turned. The French pushed the English back toward the coast. In the final major battle of the war, fought at Formigny in 1450, the French used a new and telling weapon to defeat the English—gunpowder. Rather than charging the English directly as they had done so often before, they mounted cannon and pounded the English to bits. Gunpowder completed the destruction of the chivalric traditions of warfare begun by archers and pikemen. By 1452 English continental holdings had been reduced to the town of Calais. Although the English kings continued to call themselves kings of France until the eighteenth century, it was a hollow title. The continental warfare of more than a century was over.

Though war on the Continent had ended, warfare in England was just beginning. In some ways, the English monarchy had suffered even more from the Hundred Years' War than had the French. At the outset, English royal administration had been more advanced than the French. The system of royal agents, courts, and parliaments had created the expectation that the king could preserve peace and provide justice at home while waging successful and profitable wars abroad. As the decades dragged on without a decisive victory, the king came to rely on the aristocracy, enlisting its financial assistance by granting these magnates greater power at home. War created powerful and autonomous aristocratic families with their own armies. Under a series of weak kings these families fought among themselves. Ultimately they took sides in a civil war to determine the royal succession. For thirty years, from 1455 to 1485, supporters of the house of York, whose badge was the white rose, fought the rival house of Lancaster, whose symbol was the red rose, in the sort of dynastic struggle that would not have seemed out of place in the disintegrating German empire. The English Wars of the Roses, as the conflict came to be called, finally

A fourteenth-century manuscript illustration shows bankers counting gold coins. Italian banks helped finance armies on both sides of the Hundred Years' War, and the two largest banking firms were bankrupted when Edward III of England failed to repay their loans.

ended in 1485 when Henry Tudor of the Lancasterian faction defeated his opponents. He inaugurated a new era as Henry VII (1485–1509), the first king of the Tudor dynasty.

By the end of the fifteenth century, England and France had survived with their central monarchial institutions largely intact, although their aristocracies still shared an important role in the exercise of power.

Life and Death in the Later Middle Ages

The violence and pageantry of late medieval warfare played out against a backdrop of extraordinary social upheaval. By the end of the thirteenth century, population growth in the West had strained available resources to the breaking point. All arable land was under cultivation, and even marginal moorland, rocky mountainsides, and arid plains were being pressed into service to feed a growing population. At the same time, kings and nobles demanded ever higher taxes and rents to finance their wars and extravagant lifestyles. The result was a precarious balance in which a late frost, a bad harvest, or hungry mercenaries could mean disaster. Part of the problem could be alleviated by importing grain from the Baltic or from Sicily, but this solution carried risks of its own. Transportation systems were too fragile to ensure regular supplies, and their rupture could initiate a cycle of famine, disease, and demographic collapse. Population began to decline slowly around 1300, and the downturn became catastrophic within the next fifty years. In the period between 1300 and 1450, Europe's population fell by more than 30 percent. It did not recover until the seventeenth century.

Dancing with Death

Between 1315 and 1317 the first great famine of the fourteenth century, triggered by crop failures and war, struck Europe. People died by the thousands. Urban workers, because they were chronically undernourished, were particularly hard hit. In the Flemish cloth town of Ypres, whose total population was less than twenty thousand, the town ordered the burial of 2,794 paupers' corpses within a five-month period. Although this was the greatest famine in medieval memory, it was not the last. The relatively prosperous Italian city of Pistoia, for example, recorded 16 different famines and food shortages in the fourteenth and fifteenth centuries.

Disease accompanied famine. Crowded and filthy towns, opposing armies with their massed troops, and overpopulated countrysides provided fertile ground for the spread of infectious disease. Moreover, the greatly expanded trade routes of the thirteenth and fourteenth centuries that carried goods and grain between the East and the West also provided highways for deadly microbes. At Pistoia again, local chroniclers of the fourteenth and fifteenth centuries reported fourteen years of sickness, fevers, epidemic, and plague.

Between 1347 and 1352, from one-half to one-third of Europe's population died from a virulent combination of bubonic, septicemic, and pneumonic plague known to history as the Black Death. The disease, carried by the fleas of infected rats, traveled the caravan routes from central Asia. It arrived in Messina, Sicily, aboard a merchant vessel in October 1347. From there the Black Death spread up the boot of Italy and then into southern France, England, and Spain. By 1349 it had reached northern Germany, Portugal, and Ireland. The following year the Low Countries, Scotland, Scandinavia, and Russia fell victim.

Plague victims died horribly. Soon after being bitten by an infected flea, they developed high fever, began coughing, and suffered excruciatingly painful swellings in the lymph nodes of the groin or armpits. These swellings were known as buboes, from which the disease took its name. In the final stages the victims began to vomit blood. The bubonic form of the disease usually killed within five days. The septicemic form, which attacked the blood, was more swift and deadly. Those infected by the airborne, pneumonic form usually died in less than three days; in some cases, within a matter of hours.

The plague was all the more terrifying because its cause, its manner of transmission, and its cure were totally unknown until the end of the nineteenth century. Preachers saw the plague as divine punishment for sin. Ordinary people frequently accused Jews of causing it by poisoning drinking water. The medical faculty of Paris announced that it was the result of the conjunction of the planets Saturn, Jupiter, and Mars, which caused a corruption of the surrounding air.

Responses to the plague were equally varied. Across Europe terrified people thought that by joining penitential groups that prayed, fasted, and even whipped themselves, they could turn away divine wrath through self-mortification. Others thought it best to abandon themselves to pleasure, either out of despair or in the hope that a pleasant life of eating and drinking would in some way ward off the terror of the plague. In many

THE BLACK DEATH IN FLORENCE

Giovanni Boccaccio set his Decameron *in Florence at the height of the Black Death. His eyewitness description of the plague is the most graphic account of the disease and its effects on society.*

I say, then, that the sum of thirteen hundred and fifty-eight years had elapsed since the fruitful Incarnation of the Son of God, when the noble city of Florence, which for its great beauty excels all others in Italy, was visited by the deadly pestilence. Some say that it descended upon the human race through the influence of the heavenly bodies, others that it was a punishment signifying God's righteous anger at our iniquitous way of life. But whatever its cause, it had originated some years earlier in the East, where it had claimed countless lives before it unhappily spread westward, growing in strength as it swept relentlessly on from one place to the next. . . . Against these maladies, it seemed that all the advice of physicians and all the power of medicine were profitless and unavailing. . . . Some people were of the opinion that a sober and abstemious mode of living considerably reduced the risk of infection. They therefore formed themselves into groups and lived in isolation from everyone else. . . . Others took the opposite view, and maintained that an infallible way of warding off this appalling evil was to drink heavily, enjoy life to the full, go round singing and merrymaking, gratifying all of one's cravings whenever the opportunity offered, and shrug the whole thing off as one enormous joke. . . . There were many other people who steered a middle course between the two already mentioned, neither restricting their diet to the same degree as the first group, nor indulging so freely as the second in drinking and other forms of wantonness, but simply doing no more than satisfy their appetite. Instead of incarcerating themselves, these people moved about freely, holding in their hands a posy of flowers, or fragrant herbs, or one of a wide range of spices, which they applied at frequent intervals to their nostrils, thinking it an excellent idea to fortify the brain with smells of that particular sort, for the stench of dead bodies, sickness, and medicines seemed to fill and pollute the whole of the atmosphere.

Some people pursuing what was possibly the safer alternative callously maintained that there was no better or more efficacious remedy against the plague than to run away from it. . . .

Of the people who held these various opinions, not all of them died. Nor, however, did they all survive. On the contrary, many of each different persuasion fell ill here, there, and everywhere, and having themselves, when they were fit and well, set an example to those who were as yet unaffected, they languished away with virtually no one to nurse them. This scourge had implanted so great a terror in the hearts of men and women that brothers abandoned brothers, uncles their nephews, sisters their brothers, and in many cases wives deserted their husbands. But even worse, and almost incredible, was the fact that fathers and mothers refused to nurse and assist their own children, as though they did not belong to them.

From Giovanni Boccaccio, *The Decameron.*

German towns terrified Christian citizens looked for outside scapegoats and slaughtered the Jewish community. Cities, aware of the risk of infection although ignorant of its process, closed their gates and turned away outsiders. Individuals with means fled to country houses or locked themselves in their homes to avoid contact with others. (See "A Room of One's Own," pp. 302–303.) Nothing worked. The Italian author Giovanni Boccaccio (1313–75) remarked on the wide range of opinions on how to deal with the plague, "Of the people who held these various opinions, not all of them died. Nor, however, did they all survive."

As devastating as the first outbreak of the plague was, its aftershocks were even more catastrophic. Once established in Europe, the disease continued to return roughly once each generation. Pistoia, for example, which probably lost roughly two-thirds of its population in 1348, suffered recurrences in 1389; in 1393; in 1399 when one-half of the population died; and again in 1410, 1416, 1418, 1423, 1436, and 1457. The rueful call "Bring out your dead" resounded for centuries in European cities. The last outbreak of the plague in Europe was the 1771 epidemic in Moscow that killed 60,000.

A page from the fourteenth-century psalter and prayer book of Bonne of Luxembourg, Duchess of Normandy. The three figures of the dead shown here contrast with three living figures on the facing page of the psalter to illustrate a moral fable.

The Black Death, along with other epidemics, famines, and war-induced shortages, affected western much more than eastern Europe. The culminating effect of these disasters was a darker, more somber vision of life than that of the previous centuries. This vision found its expression in the Dance of Death, an increasingly popular image in art. Naked, rotting corpses dance with great animation before the living. The latter, depicted in the dress of all social orders, are immobile, surprised by death, reluctant but resigned.

Although no solid statistics exist from the fourteenth century, the plague certainly killed more people than all of the wars and famines of the century. It was the greatest disaster ever to befall Europe. The Black Death touched every aspect of life, hastening a process of social, economic, and cultural transformation already under way. The initial outbreak shattered social and economic structures. Fields were abandoned, workplaces stood idle, international trade was suspended. Traditional bonds of kinship, village, and even reli-

gion were broken by the horrors of death, flight, and failed expectations. "People cared no more for dead men than we care for dead goats," wrote one survivor. Brothers abandoned brothers, wives deserted husbands, and terror-stricken parents refused to nurse their own children. Nothing had prepared Europe for this catastrophe, no teaching of the Church or its leaders could adequately explain it, and in spite of desperate attempts to fix the blame on Jews or strangers, no one but God could be held responsible. Survivors stood alone and uncertain before a new world. Across Europe, moralists reported a general lapse in traditional ethics, a breakdown in the moral codes. The most troubling aspect of this breakdown was what one defender of the old order termed "the plague of insurrection" that spread across Europe. This plague was brought on by the dimming of the hopes held by the survivors of the Black Death.

The Plague of Insurrection

Initially, even this darkest cloud had a silver lining. Lucky survivors of the plague soon found other reasons to rejoice. Property owners, when they finished burying their dead, discovered that they were far richer in land and goods. At the other end of the social spectrum, the plague had eliminated the labor surplus. Peasants were suddenly in great demand. For a time at least, they were able to negotiate substantially higher wages and an improved relationship with landlords. An English thresher who before 1349 had been paid around three pence a day could hope to earn 25 percent more after the plague.

These hopes were short-lived. The rise in expectations produced by the redistribution of wealth and the labor shortage created new tensions. Landlords sought laws forcing peasants to accept preplague wages and tightened their control over serfs in order to prevent them from fleeing to cities or other lords. At the same time, governments attempted to benefit from laborers' greater prosperity by imposing new taxes. In cities, where the plague had been particularly devastating, the demographic decline sharply lowered demand for goods and thus lowered the need for manufacturing and production of all kinds. Like rural landowners, master craftsmen sought legislation to protect their incomes. New laws reduced production by restricting access to trades and increased masters' control over the surviving urban laborers. Social mobility, once a characteristic of urban life, slowed to a halt. Membership in guilds became hereditary, and young apprentices or journeymen had little hope of ever rising to the level of independent master craftsmen.

✃ A Room of One's Own

Through most of history, men and women lived and died in public, under the scrutiny of family, friends, and neighbors. Solitude and privacy, far from being considered desirable privileges, were dire punishments self-inflicted by ascetic hermits or imposed by society on its outcasts. Nowhere is this rejection of isolation more obvious than in the arrangement of physical space within which people lived. Throughout the Middle Ages, peasant families crowded into single-room cottages not only out of financial necessity but also out of a desire for intimacy. Lords resided in castles whose living quarters were no more private. Monks shared communal dormitories, and even bishops and abbots slept surrounded by their clerics.

Living in such a corporate world, medieval people thought of themselves first as members of a group—a *familia*—whether of kin, of members of a household, of a religious order, of a merchant society, or of a warrior band. People aspired less to self-expression and personal fulfillment than to conformity to a model, such as that of the ideal knight, monk, merchant, or Christian.

If life meant playing a role, then success demanded a constant audience. Medieval homes reflected the different types of audiences and the different degrees of intimacy to which they were admitted. Typically, houses in fourteenth-century towns had three types of space corresponding to three levels of intimacy. The ground-floor vestibule served as workshop or salesroom for artisans. For wealthy families it was where the public was received. Beyond or above the vestibule were the rooms devoted to family activities, to which friends and intimates were invited. On the third level was the bedroom or bedrooms.

The center of privacy and intimacy was the bedroom, a place of repose and sleep, but also the space where one's most intimate guests might be entertained and where the family's most valued treasures were kept. The distinction between bedroom and public room might be fairly arbitrary. Often private portions of a wealthy house or castle consisted of a large room that could be divided by movable wooden partitions into a public hall and a more intimate chamber. Both spaces were used for banquets and entertaining, the latter reserved for honored guests. At night the chamber might serve as the bedroom of the master and mistress of the house, but in some castles it was the sleeping room only for the lord, his warriors, and their concubines. Wives and children slept in communal chambers of their own.

Dominating the bedroom was the bed, and it was a poor family indeed that did not own at least a bed frame and a straw mattress. Beds were often huge by modern standards, ranging from five to twelve feet in width. The bed consisted of three parts. First was the frame, made of oak or pine. Often the frame was high enough for a small cot to be stored under it. The mattress, made of cloth and stuffed with straw or wool, was placed on top of straw piled up in the frame. The wealthy might be able to afford a mattress stuffed with feathers. Finally, the bed had a variety of cushions and pillows, sheets, and a canopy that could be drawn, making the bed virtually a room within a room.

The size of the bed was not just for display: often it was occupied by the whole family. One prosperous Italian peasant who died in 1406 shared his vast bed with his wife and three children. In fifteenth-century France, all the children of a family often shared a single bed. A French theologian, worried about the potential for incest, prayed that it would "please God that it should be the custom in France for children to sleep alone in small beds, or at worst brothers together and sisters or others together, as is the custom in Flanders."

Even if people did choose to sleep in their beds alone or only with their spouses, they normally kept one or more servants in their bedchambers, both to have help readily at hand and to keep an eye on them.

Only gradually, beginning around the fourteenth century, as states and communal governments sought greater control over subjects and citizens, did first families and then individuals begin to carve out their own space away from the prying eyes of outsiders or even more intimate companions. The number of bedrooms in houses and castles increased. Monasteries were renovated so that each monk or nun could occupy a single cell. Intellectuals added "thinking rooms" to their homes, where they might read, write, and meditate in solitude. This creation of private space within which a person could be truly alone with his or her own activities, thoughts, and emotions was an essential component of the development of a sense of the individual. Isolated within the confines of a room of their own, people could begin to explore the ultimate privacy—the interior of their own minds.

These new tensions led to violence when kings added their demands for new war taxes to the landlords' and masters' attempts to erase the peasants' and workers' recent gains. The first revolts took place in France, where peasants and townspeople, disgusted with the incompetence of the nobility in their conduct of the war against England, feared that their new wealth would be stolen from them by corrupt and incompetent aristocrats.

In 1358, in order to ransom King John II from the English, the French government attempted to increase taxes on the peasantry. At the same time, local nobles increased their rents and demands. Peasants in the area of Beauvais, north of Paris, fearing they would lose the modest level of prosperity they had gained over the previous ten years, rebelled against their landlords. The revolt—known as the Jacquerie for the archetypical French peasant, Jacques Bonnehomme—was a spontaneous outburst directed against the nobility, whom the peasants saw as responsible for all their ills. Without real leadership or program, peasants attacked as many nobles as they could find, killing them along with their wives and children and burning their homes and castles. The peasants' brutality deeply shocked the upper classes, whose own violence was constrained within the

bounds of the chivalric code. One chronicler reported in horror, "Among other evil deeds, they killed a knight and quickly began to roast him before the eyes of his wife and children. After ten or twelve had raped the noble lady, they wanted to force her to eat her husband's flesh. They then put her to death horribly." Because the Church largely supported the power structure, the uprising was also strongly anticlerical. Churches were burned and priests killed. Success bred further attacks, and the disorganized army of peasants began to march south toward Paris, killing, looting, and burning everything associated with the despised nobility.

In the midst of this peasant revolt, Etienne Marcel (ca. 1316–58), a wealthy Parisian cloth merchant, led an uprising of Parisian merchants who sought to take control of royal finances and force fiscal reforms on the dauphin, the future Charles V. Although initially the rebels were primarily members of the merchant and guild elite, Marcel soon enlisted the support of the radical townspeople against the aristocracy. He even made overtures to the leaders of the Jacquerie to join forces. For a brief time it appeared that the aristocratic order in France might succumb. However, in the end peasant and merchant rebels were no match for professional armies. The Jacquerie met its end at Meaux, outside

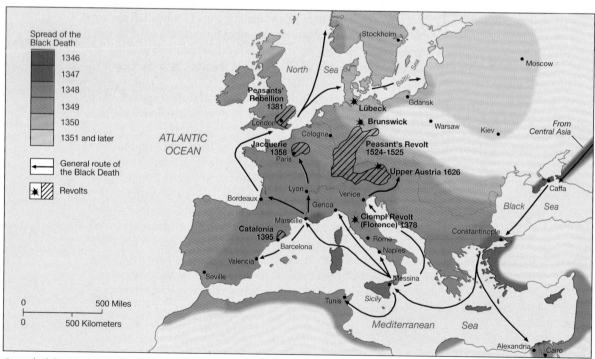

Spread of the Black Death

Amid the disasters of the Hundred Years' War and the Black Death, the fourteenth century witnessed numerous peasant revolts. This manuscript illustration shows armed rioters ransacking the house of a wealthy Paris merchant.

Paris, where an aristocratic force cut the peasants to pieces. Survivors were systematically hunted down and hung or burned alive. The Parisian revolt met a similar fate. Aristocratic armies surrounded the city and cut off its food supply. Marcel was assassinated and the dauphin Charles regained the city.

The French revolts set the pattern for similar uprisings across Europe. Rebels were usually relatively prosperous peasants or townspeople whose economic situations were threatened by aristocratic attempts to turn back the clock to the period before the Black Death. In 1381 English peasants, reacting to new and hated taxes, rose in a less violent but more coordinated revolt known as the Great Rebellion. Peasant revolts took place in the northern Spanish region of Catalonia in 1395 and in Germany throughout the fourteenth and fifteenth centuries. The largest was the great Peasant's Revolt of 1524. Although always ruthlessly suppressed, European peasant uprisings continued until the peasant rebellion of 1626 in upper Austria. These outbursts did not necessarily indicate the desperation of Europe's peasantry, but they did reflect the peasants' new belief that they could change their lives for the better through united action.

Urban artisans imitated the example of their rural cousins. Although there had been some uprisings in the Flemish towns before the Black Death, revolts of townspeople picked up momentum in the second half of the fourteenth century. In general, the town rebels were not the destitute urban poor any more than the peasant rebels had been the landless rural poor. Instead they were generally independent artisans and small tradesmen who wanted to break the control of the powerful guilds. The one exception to this pattern was the Ciompi revolt of 1378 in Florence. There the wool workers rioted and forced recognition of two guilds of laborers alongside the powerful guilds of masters. The workers and artisans controlled city government until 1382, when mercenaries hired by the elite surrounded the workers' slums and crushed them in bloody house-to-house fighting. In spite of the brutal suppression and ultimate failure of popular revolts, they became permanent, if intermittent, features on the European social landscape. The line from the Jacquerie runs to the storming of the Bastille 431 years later, and beyond.

Living and Dying in Medieval Towns

Population decline, war, and class conflict in France and the Low Countries fatally weakened the vitality of the commercial and manufacturing system of northwestern Europe. These same events reduced the market for Italian goods and undermined the economic strength of the great Italian cities. The Hundred Years' War bankrupted many of Florence's greatest banking houses, such as the Bardi and Peruzzi, who lent to both French and English kings. Commercial activity declined as well. While in the 1330s Venice had sent between four and nine trading galleys to Flanders each year, by the 1390s the city was sending only three to five. Genoa, which earlier had led in the trade with the cloth towns of the north, saw the economic activity of its port decline by roughly one-third to one-half during the same period. While Italians did not disappear from northern cities, they no longer held a near monopoly on northern trade.

These setbacks for the Italians worked to the advantage of German towns in the disintegrating empire. Along the Baltic Sea, in Scandinavia, and in northern

Germany, towns such as Lübeck, Lüneburg, Visby, Bremen, and Cologne formed a commercial and political alliance to control northern trade. During the second half of the fourteenth century, this Hanseatic League—the word *Hansa* means "company"—monopolized the northern grain trade and forced Denmark to grant its members exclusive rights to export Scandinavian fish throughout Europe. Hanseatic merchants established colonies from Novgorod to London and Bruges, and even to Venice. They carried dried and salted fish to Prague and supplied grain from Riga to England and France.

English towns also profited from the decline of Flanders and France. The population decline of the fourteenth century led many English landowners to switch from traditional farming to sheep raising, since pasturing sheep required few workers and promised cash profits. While surviving peasants were driven off

A fifteenth-century manuscript illustration of a street in a medieval French town shows (left to right) a tailor, a furrier, a barber, and a druggist.

the land and forced to beg for a living, lords produced more wool than ever before. However, instead of exporting the wool to Flanders to be made into cloth, the English began to make cloth themselves. Protected by high tariffs on imports and low duties on exports, England had become a major exporter of finished cloth by the middle of the fifteenth century.

The new social and economic circumstances of European towns accentuated the gulf between rich and poor. The streets and markets of fifteenth-century towns bustled with the sights and sounds of rich Hanseatic merchants, Italian bankers, and prosperous local tradesmen. The back alleys and squatter settlements on the edges of these towns teemed with a growing mass of desperate and despairing workers and their families. The combination of economic depression, plague, and rural crisis deepened the misery of the growing population of urban poor. Driven both by mounting compassion for the urban poor and by a growing fear of the violent potential of this ever-increasing population, medieval towns developed novel systems to deal with poverty. The first was public assistance; the second was social control and repression.

Traditionally, charity had been a religious act that focused more on the soul of the giver than on the effect on the life of the recipient. The same had been true of charitable organizations such as confraternities and hospitals. Confraternities were pious religious organizations of lay people and clergy who ministered to the poor and sick. Hospitals were all-purpose religious institutions providing lodging for pilgrims, the elderly, and the ill. By the fourteenth century, such pious institutions had become inadequate to deal with the growing numbers of poor and ill. Towns began to assume control over a centralized system of public assistance. New, specialized institutions appeared for the care of different categories of the poor, including the ill, women in childbirth, the aged, orphans, and travelers. Pesthouses were founded in which plague victims could be isolated. Hospitals also distributed food to the poor. In 1403 the hospital of the Holy Spirit in Cologne supported over fourteen hundred paupers per week. Seventy years later that number had grown to almost five thousand.

Although men and women who had taken religious vows staffed these institutions, city governments contributed to their budgets and oversaw their finances. Cities also attempted to rationalize the distribution of charity according to need and merit. Antwerp, for example, established a centralized relief service, which distributed badges to those deemed worthy of public assistance. Only those who presented their badges

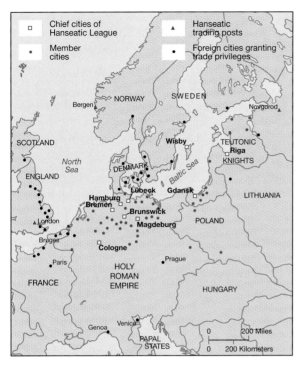

The Hanseatic League

could receive food. This system spread throughout Europe in the fourteenth century.

At the same time that towns began to organize public assistance, they attempted to control more strictly the activities of the urban poor. In the fourteenth century, Nuremberg forbade begging to everyone except those who had received a special license. In Strasbourg, blind beggars organized an official "Confraternity of Strasbourg Beggars" on the model of other professional guilds, with its own officers, regulations, and membership requirements. Many towns, fearing wandering professional beggars and landless peasants, allowed them to remain only three days before being expelled.

One consequence of poverty was increased crime. Fear of the poor led to repressive measures and harsh punishments. Traditionally, in much of Europe crimes such as robbery, larceny, and even manslaughter had been punishable by fines and payments to the victim or the victim's heirs. Elsewhere, as in France and England, where corporal punishment had been the normal penalty for major crimes, hanging, blinding, and the loss of a hand or foot had been the most common punishments. During the later Middle Ages, gruesome forms of mutilation and execution became common for a long list of offenses. Petty larceny was punished with whipping, cutting off ears or thumbs, branding, or expulsion. In some towns, robbery of an amount over threepence was punished with death. Death by hanging might be replaced by more savage punishments such as breaking on the wheel. In this particularly brutal torture the prisoner's limbs and back were first broken with a wagon wheel. Then the criminal was tied to the wheel and left on a pole to die. Drowning, boiling, burning, and burial alive—a particularly common punishment for women—were other frequently used methods of execution

The frequency of such punishments increased with their severity. In Augsburg, until the middle of the thirteenth century executions were so rare that the city did not even have a public executioner before 1276. However, in the following two centuries, the city fathers increased executions in an attempt to control what they perceived as an ever-rising crime rate, largely attributed to the growing masses of the poor. In 1452 the skulls of 250 hanged persons were found in pits on the gallows hill. At the same time the bodies of 32 thieves twisted in the wind above.

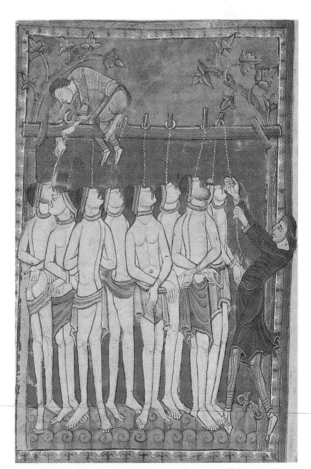

A twelfth-century portrayal of a mass hanging of thieves who had invaded a church

The Spirit of the Later Middle Ages

The Dance of Death and the gallows were not the only images of later medieval life. The constant presence of death made life more precious. Europeans celebrated life with a vigor and creativity characterized by a growing sense of individuality, independence, and variety. During the fourteenth century, the Church failed to provide unified spiritual and cultural leadership to Europe. The institutional division of the Church was paralleled by divisions over how to lead the proper Christian life. Many devout Christians developed independent lifestyles intended to bring them closer to God without reliance on the Church hierarchy. They elaborated beliefs branded by the Church as heresy. Others called into question the philosophical bases of theological speculation developed since the time of Abelard and Aquinas. Finally, the increasing pluralism of European culture gave rise to new literary traditions that both celebrated and criticized the medieval legacy of Christianity, chivalry, and social order.

Christendom Divided

The universal empire as well as its traditional competitor, the universal Church, declined in the later Middle Ages. The papacy never recovered from the humiliating defeat Pope Boniface VIII suffered at the hands of King Philip the Fair in 1303. The ecclesiastical edifice created by the thirteenth-century popes was shaken to its foundations, first by becoming a virtual appendage of the French monarchy, and then by a dispute that for over forty years gave European Christians a choice between two, and finally three, claimants to the chair of Saint Peter.

In 1305 the College of Cardinals elected as pope the bishop of Bordeaux. The new pope, who took the name Clement V (1305–14), was close to Philip IV of France and had no desire to meet the fate of his predecessor, Pope Boniface VIII. Thus Clement took up residence, not in Rome, but in the papal city of Avignon on the east bank of the Rhone River. Technically, Avignon was a papal estate within the Holy Roman Empire. Actually, with France just across the river, the pope at Avignon was under French control.

For the next seventy years, French popes and French cardinals ruled the Church. The traditional enemies of France, as well as religious reformers who expected leadership from the papacy, looked on this situation with disgust. The Italian poet Petrarch (1304–74) denounced what he termed the "Babylonian captivity" of the papacy in especially bitter tones:

> Now I am living in France, in the Babylon of the West. The sun in its travels sees nothing more hideous than this place on the shores of the wild Rhone. Here reign the successors of the poor fishermen of Galilee; they have strangely forgotten their origin.

Although Petrarch went on to accuse the popes and their courtiers of every possible crime and sin, the Avignon popes were no worse than any other great lords of the fourteenth century. In pursuit of political and financial rewards, they had simply lost sight of their roles as religious leaders.

The popes of Avignon were more successful in achieving their financial goals than in winning political power. Although they attempted to follow an independent course in international affairs, their French orientation eroded their influence in European politics, especially in the Holy Roman Empire. Pope John XXII (1316–34), one of the most unpleasant and argumentative persons ever to hold the chair of Peter, tried to block the election of the Wittelsbach Louis of Bavaria as emperor. Louis ignored the pope, invaded Italy, and was proclaimed emperor by the people of Rome. In 1338 the German electors solemnly declared that the imperial office was held directly from God and did not require papal confirmation—a declaration later upheld in the Golden Bull. No longer could the popes exert any direct influence in the internal affairs of Europe's states.

Frustrated politically, the Avignon popes concentrated on perfecting the legal and fiscal system of the Church and were enormously successful in concentrating the vast financial and legal power of the Church in the papal office. From the papal court, or curia, they created a vast and efficient central bureaucracy whose primary role was to increase papal revenues.

Revenues came from two main sources. The less lucrative but ultimately more important source was the sale of indulgences. The Church had long taught that sinners who repented might be absolved of their sins and escape the fires of hell. However, they still had to suffer temporary punishment. This punishment, called penance, could take the form of fasting, prayer, or performance of some good deed. Failing to do penance on earth, absolved sinners would have to endure a period in purgatory before they could be admitted to heaven. However, since the saints had done more penance than

A WOMAN BEFORE THE INQUISITION

In 1320 Jacques Fournier (ca. 1280–1342), bishop of Pamiers in France and the future pope Benedict XII, interrogated the villagers of Montaillou in southern France about their involvement in the Cathar heresy, a dualist religion present in the region since the eleventh century, whose members were called "the good Christians." The following excerpt is from the testimony of Béatrice de Planissoles, a member of the lower nobility and a prominent inhabitant of the village.

Twenty-six years ago during the month of August, I was the wife of the late knight Bérenger de Roquefort, castellan of Montaillou. The late Raimond Roussel was the intendant and the stewart of our household which we held at the castle of Montaillou. He often asked me to leave with him and to go to Lombardy with the good Christians who are there, telling me that the Lord had said that man must quit his father, mother, wife, husband, son and daughter and follow him, and that he would give him the kingdom of heaven. When I asked him, "How could I quit my husband and my sons?" he replied that the Lord had ordered it and that it was better to leave a husband and sons whose eyes rot than to abandon him who lives for eternity and who gives the kingdom of heaven.

When I asked him, "How is it possible that God created so many men and women if many of them are not saved?" he answered that only the good Christians will be saved and no others, neither religious nor priests, nor anyone except these good Christians. Because, he said, just as it is impossible for a camel to pass through the eye of a needle, it is impossible for those who are rich to be saved. This is why the kings and princes, prelates and religious, and all those who have wealth, cannot be saved, but only the good Christians. . . . He also told me that all spirits sinned at the beginning with the sin of pride, believing that they could know more and be worth more than God, and for that they fell to earth. These spirits later take on bodies, and the world will not end before all of them have been incarnated into the bodies of men and women. Thus it is that the soul of a newborn child is as old as that of an old man.

He also said that the souls of men and women who were not good Christians, after leaving their bodies, enter the bodies of other men and women a total of nine times. If in these nine bodies they do not find the body of a good Christian, the soul is damned. If on the contrary, they find the body of a good Christian, the soul is saved.

I asked him how the spirit of a dead man or woman could enter the mouth of a pregnant woman and from there into the mouth of the fruit that she carries in her womb. He answered that the spirit could enter the fruit of the woman's womb by any part of her body.

Thus he urged me to leave with him so that we could go together to the good Christians, mentioning various noble women who had gone there. Alesta and Serena, women of Châteauverdun, painted themselves with colors which made them appear foreign, so that they could not be recognized and went to Toulouse. When they arrived at an inn, the hostess wanted to know if they were heretics and gave them live chickens, telling them to prepare them because she had things to do in town, and left the house. [Cathars avoided killing and eating animals.] When she had returned she found the chickens still alive and asked them why they had not prepared them. They responded that if the hostess would kill them, they would prepare them but that they would not kill them. The hostess heard that and went to tell the inquisitors that two heretics were in her establishment. They were arrested and burned. When it was time to go to the stake, they asked for water to wash their faces, saying that they would not go to God painted thusly.

I told Raimond that they would have done better to abandon their heresy than to allow themselves to be burned, and he told me that the good Christians did not feel fire because fire with which they are burned cannot hurt them.

The Great Schism

who took the name of Urban VI (1378–89). Once elected, Urban attempted to reform the curia, but he did so in a most undiplomatic way, insulting the cardinals and threatening to appoint sufficient non-French bishops to their number to end French control of the curia. The cardinals soon left Rome and announced that because the election had been made under duress it was invalid and that Urban should resign. When he refused they held a second election and chose a Frenchman, Clement VII (1378–94), who took up residence in Avignon. The Church now had two heads, both with reasonable claims to the office.

The chaos created by this so-called Great Schism divided western Christendom. In every diocese, when a bishop died his successor had to be appointed by the pope. But by which pope? To whom did taxes go? Who received the income from the sale of indulgences or benefices? Did appeals in the church courts go to Rome or to Avignon? More significantly, since each pope excommunicated the supporters of his opponent, everyone in the West was under a sentence of excommunication. Could anyone be saved?

Communities were divided. When the city of Bruges officially accepted the Avignon pope, many citizens left their homes and professions to live in cities loyal to Rome. Not surprisingly, countries tended to side with one or the other contender for political reasons. France recognized Clement. France's traditional enemies, England and the empire, recognized Urban. England's traditional enemy, Scotland, accepted Clement. Most of Italy sided with Urban, but the Angevin kingdom of Naples and Sicily recognized Clement, as did most of Spain.

Nothing in Church law or tradition offered a solution to this crisis. Nor did unilateral efforts to settle the crisis succeed. Twice France invaded Italy in an attempt to eliminate Urban but failed both times. Professors at the University of Paris argued that both popes should abdicate, but neither was willing to do so. Moreover, the situation perpetuated itself. When Urban and Clement died, cardinals on both sides elected successors. By the end of the fourteenth century, France and the empire were exasperated with their popes and even the cardinals were determined to end the stalemate.

Church lawyers argued that a general council alone could end the schism. Both popes opposed this "conciliarist" argument because it suggested that an assembly of the Church rather than the pope held supreme authority. However, in 1408 cardinals from both sides summoned a council in the Italian city of Pisa. The council deposed both rivals and elected a new pope. But this solution only made matters worse, since nei-

was required to make up for the temporal punishments due them, they had established a treasury of merit—a sort of spiritual bank account. The pope was the "banker" and could transfer some of this positive balance to repentant sinners in return for some pious act such as contributing money to build a new church. These so-called indulgences could be purchased for one's own use or to assist the souls of family members already in purgatory. Papal "pardoners" working on commission used high-pressure sales pitches to sell indulgences across Europe.

The second and major source of papal income was the sale of Church offices, or benefices. Popes claimed the right to appoint bishops and abbots to all benefices and to collect a hefty tax for the appointment. The system encouraged pluralism, that is, individuals could acquire numerous ecclesiastical benefices scattered across Europe in the same way that lay lords held multiple fiefs and territories from France to Poland. Like the pope, papal appointees often viewed their offices merely as sources of income, leaving pastoral duties, when they were performed at all, to hired local clergy.

In 1377 Pope Gregory XI (1370–78) returned from Avignon to Rome but died almost immediately upon arrival. Thousands of Italians, afraid that the cardinals would elect another Frenchman, surrounded the church where they were meeting and demanded an Italian pope. The terrified cardinals elected an Italian,

ther rival accepted the decision of the council. Europe now had to contend with not two popes but three, each claiming to be the true successor of Saint Peter.

Six years later the Council of Constance managed a final solution. There, under the patronage of the emperor-elect Sigismund (1410–37), cardinals, bishops, abbots, and theologians from across Europe met to resolve the crisis. Their goal was not only to settle the schism but also to reform the Church to prevent a recurrence of such a scandal. The participants at Constance hoped to restructure the Church as a limited monarchy in which the powers of the pope would be controlled through frequent councils. The Pisan and Avignon popes were deposed. The Roman pope, abandoned by all of his supporters, abdicated. Before doing so, however, he formally convoked the council in order to preserve the tradition that a general council had to be called by the pope. Finally, the council elected as pope an Italian cardinal not aligned with any of the claimants. The election of the cardinal, who took the name Martin V (1417–31), ended the schism.

The relief at the end of the Great Schism could not hide the very real problems left by over a century of papal weakness. The prestige of the papacy had been permanently compromised. Everywhere the Church had become more national in character. The conciliarist demand for control of the Church, which had ended the schism, lessened the power of the pope. Moreover, during the century between Boniface VIII and Martin V, new religious movements had taken root across Europe, movements which the political creatures who had occupied the papal office could neither understand nor control. The Council of Constance, which brought an end to the schism, also condemned Jan Hus, the leader of the Czech reform movement and the spiritual founder of the Protestant reformation of the sixteenth century. The disintegration of the Church loomed ever closer as pious individuals turned away from the organized Church and sought divine help in personal piety, mysticism, or even magic.

Discerning the Spirit of God

When Joan of Arc first appeared before the dauphin in 1429, he feared that she was a witch. Only a physical examination by matrons, which determined that she was a virgin, persuaded him otherwise—witches were believed to have had intercourse with the devil. In 1431 the English burned Joan as a heretic. For the two years between 1429 and 1431 and long after, many venerated her as a saint. Everyone in the late Middle Ages was familiar with witches, saints, and heretics. Distinguishing among them was often a matter of perspective.

In this illustration from a fifteenth-century chronicle, Jan Hus, wearing a heretic's hat, is shown being burned at the stake.

A LETTER TO BABBO

Catherine of Siena was not only a mystic, experiencing and reporting extraordinary visions and subsisting on the Eucharist and bitter herbs. She was also an outspoken advisor and critic of the leading figures of her day, including Pope Gregory XI, whom she criticized and cajoled to reform his own behavior and to return from Avignon to Rome. In the following letter, this poor woman from the slums of Siena admonishes Gregory, whom she calls "my sweetest Babbo" (a child's name for father) for advancing his own family and favorites at the cost of the Church and warns him it would be better to resign than to misuse his authority.

Most sweet and holy Father, your wretched and poor daughter, Catherine, in Christ sweet Jesus recommends herself to you in His precious Blood with desire to see you a manly man without any fear or carnal love for yourself or for your blood relatives. I realize in the sweet presence of God that nothing so much as this checks your good and holy desire and so hinders the honor of God and the exaltation and reform of the Holy Church. Therefore my soul longs with inestimable love that God in his infinite mercy will take from you each passion and all tepidity of heart and will reform you into another man by rekindling in you an ardent and burning desire, for in no other way can you fulfill the will of God and the desires of His servants. Alas, my sweetest Babbo, pardon my presumption in what I have said and am saying—the sweet and primal Truth forces me. This is His will, Father; he demands this of you. He demands that you require justice in the multitude of iniquities committed by those nourished and sheltered in the garden of the Holy Church; He declares that beasts should not receive men's food. Because He has given you authority and because you have accepted it, you ought to use your virtue and power. If you do not wish to use it, it might be better for you to resign what you have accepted; it would give more honor to God and health to your soul.

Accusations of witchcraft were relatively rare in the Middle Ages. The age of witch-hunts occurred in the sixteenth and seventeenth centuries. During the Middle Ages magic existed in a wide variety of forms, but its definition was fluid and its practitioners were not always considered witches. Alchemists and astrologers held honored places in society, while simple practitioners of folk religion, medicine, and superstition were condemned—particularly when they were poor women.

Witches, believed to have made a contract with the devil, were condemned as a type of heretic and were persecuted like other heretics. Only at the end of the fifteenth century, with the publication of the *Witches' Hammer*, a great handbook for inquisitors, did the European witch craze begin in earnest. Earlier, authorities had been more fearful of those people who sought their own pacts, not with the devil, but with God.

Even as Europeans were losing respect for the institutional Church, people everywhere were seeking closer and more intimate relationships with God. Distrusting the formal institutions of the Church, lay persons and clerics turned to private devotions and mysticism to achieve union with the divine. They developed their own forms of devotion based on translations of the Bible into their native languages. They looked for a direct relationship with God, thus minimizing the importance of the Church hierarchy. Most of these, like the Beguines and Beghards of northern Europe, stayed within the Church. Others, among them many female mystics, maintained an ambiguous relationship with the traditional institutions of Christianity. A few, such as the Brethren of the Free Spirit, broke sharply with it.

In the fourteenth and fifteenth centuries, a great many pious laymen and women chose to live together in order to strive for spiritual perfection without entering established religious orders. The female Beguines and male Beghards of northern cities often formed miniature towns-within-towns. The Brethren of the Common Life in the Rhineland and Low Countries dedicated themselves to preaching, charity, and a pious life. In the early fifteenth century an unknown member of the Brethren wrote the *Imitation of Christ,* a book of spiritual direction that continues to be the most widely read religious text after the Bible.

Christians of the later Middle Ages sought to imitate Christ and venerated the Eucharist, or communion wafer, which the Church taught was the actual body of Christ. Male mystics focused on imitating Christ in his poverty, his suffering, and his humility. The Spiritual Franciscans made radical poverty the cornerstone of their belief and the yardstick by which to judge Christian action. The furor between the Spiritual Franciscans and the more moderate Conventuals led Pope John XXII to condemn radical poverty in 1323 and to begin persecuting the Spirituals as heretics. As the wealth and luxury of the Church hierarchy increased, so did the spiritual reaction against it.

Women developed their own form of piety, which focused not on wealth and power but on spiritual nourishment, particularly as provided by the Eucharist. For women mystics, radical fasting became preparation for the reception of the Eucharist, often described in highly emotional and erotic terms. After a long period of fasting, Lukardis of Oberweimar (d. 1309) had a vision in which Christ appeared to her as a handsome youth and blew into her mouth. In the words of her biographer, "She was infused with such sweetness and such inner fruition that she felt as if drunk." From the age of twenty-three, Catherine of Siena (d. 1380) subsisted entirely on the Eucharist, cold water, and bitter herbs that she sucked and then spat out. She wrote of the importance of the Eucharist, "We must attach ourselves to the breast of Christ crucified, which is the source of charity, and by means of that flesh we draw milk." For these and other pious women, fasting and devotion to the Eucharist did not mean rejection of the body. Rather these were attempts to use their senses to approach perfect union with God, who was for them both food and drink.

Only a thin line separated the saint's heroic search for union with God from the heretic's identification with God. The radical Brethren of the Free Spirit believed that God was all things and that all things would return to God. Such pantheism denied the possibility of sin, punishment, and the need for salvation. Members of the sect were hunted down, and many were burned as heretics. Local bishops and clergy often confused Beguines, Beghards, and Brethren of the Common Life with adherents of the Free Spirit movement. The specter of the Inquisition, the ecclesiastical court system charged with ferreting out heretics, hung over all such communities.

When unorthodox Christians were protected by secular lords, the ecclesiastical courts were powerless. This was the case with John Wycliffe (ca. 1330–84), an Oxford theologian who attacked the doctrinal and political bases of the Church. He taught that the value of the sacraments depended on the worthiness of the priest administering them, that Christ was present in the Eucharist only in spirit, that indulgences were useless, and that salvation depended on divine predestination rather than individual merit. Normally these teachings would have led him to the stake. But he had also attacked the Church's right to wealth and luxury, an idea whose political implications pleased the English monarchy and nobility. Wycliffe's own exemplary manner of life and his teaching that the Church's role in temporal affairs should be severely limited made him an extremely popular figure in England. Thus he was allowed to live and teach in peace. Only under Henry V (1413–22) were Wycliffe's followers, known as Lollards, vigorously suppressed by the state.

Before this condemnation took place, however, Wycliffe's teachings reached the kingdom of Bohemia through the marriage of Charles IV's daughter Anne of Bohemia to the English king Richard II. Anne took with her to England a number of Bohemian clerics, some of whom studied at Oxford and absorbed the political and religious teachings of Wycliffe, which they then took back to Bohemia. In Prague some of Wycliffe's less radical teachings took root among the theology faculty of the new university. Wycliffe's ideas were particularly popular with Czech professors of theology, who were demanding not only a reform of religious teaching and practice but also a reduction of the influence of German professors in the University of Prague. The leading proponent of Wycliffe's teachings in Prague was Jan Hus (1373–1415), an immensely popular young master and preacher. Although Hus rejected Wycliffe's ideas about the priesthood and the sacraments, he and other Czech preachers attacked indulgences and demanded a reform of Church liturgy and morals. They grafted these religious demands onto an attack on German dominance of the Bohemian kingdom. These attacks outraged both the Pisan pope John XXIII (1410–15) and the Bohemian king

Wenceslas IV (1378–1419), who favored the German faction. The pope excommunicated Hus, and the king expelled the Czech faculty from the university. Hus was convinced that he was no heretic and that a fair hearing would clear him. He therefore agreed to travel to the Council of Constance under promise of safe conduct from the emperor-elect Sigismund to defend his position. There he was tried on a charge of heresy, convicted, and burned at the stake.

News of Hus's execution touched off a revolt in Bohemia. Unlike the peasant revolts of the past, however, this revolt had broad popular support throughout all levels of Czech society. Peasants, nobles, and townspeople saw the attack on Hus and his followers as an attack on Czech independence and national interest by a Church and an empire controlled by Germans. The rebels slaughtered the largely German city council and defeated an army sent by emperor-elect Sigismund to crush the revolt. Soon a radical faction known as the Taborites was demanding the abolition of private property and the institution of a communal state. Although moderate Hussites and Bohemian Catholics combined to defeat the radicals in 1434, most of Bohemia remained Hussite through the fifteenth century. The sixteenth-century reformer Martin Luther declared himself a follower of Jan Hus.

THE LATER MIDDLE AGES, 1300–1500

1305–1377	Babylonian Captivity (Avignon papacy)
1337–1452	Hundred Years' War
1347–1352	Black Death spreads throughout Europe
1358	Jacquerie revolt of French peasants
	Etienne Marcel leads revolt of Parisian merchants
1378	Ciompi revolt in Florence
1380	Death of Catherine of Siena
1378–1417	Great Schism divides Christianity
1381	Great Rebellion of English peasants
1409–1410	Council of Pisa
1414–1417	Council of Constance ends Great Schism
1415	Jan Hus executed
1431	Death of Joan of Arc
1455–1485	English Wars of the Roses

William of Ockham and the Spirit of Truth

The critical and individualistic approach that characterized religion during the later Middle Ages was also typical of the philosophical thought of the period. The delicate balance between faith and reason taught by Aquinas and other intellectuals in the thirteenth century disintegrated in the fourteenth. As in other areas of life, intellectuals questioned the basic suppositions of their predecessors, directing intellectual activity away from general speculations and toward particular, observable reality.

The person primarily responsible for this new intellectual climate was the English Franciscan William of Ockham (ca. 1300–49). Ockham was no ivory-tower intellectual. He was a dedicated Spiritual Franciscan, whose defense of radical poverty led to his excommunication by the cantankerous Pope John XXII. Excommunication drove Ockham to the court of John's enemy, the Emperor Louis IV, where he became a dedicated propagandist for the imperial cause. There he developed a truly radical political philosophy. Imperial power, Ockham argued, derived not from the pope but from the people. People are free to determine their own form of government and to elect rulers. They can make

their choice directly, as in the election of the emperor by electors who represent the people, or implicitly, through continuing forms of government. In either case, government is entirely secular. Neither popes nor bishops nor priests have any role.

Ockham went still further. He denied the absolute authority of the pope, even in spiritual matters. Rather, Ockham argued, parishes, religious orders, and monasteries should send representatives to regional synods that in turn would elect representatives to general councils. Both laypersons and clergy would serve on these councils, which were to act rather like parliaments, tempering papal absolutism.

As radical as Ockham's political ideas were, his philosophical outlook was even more extreme and exerted a more direct and lasting influence. The Christian Aristotelianism that developed in the thirteenth century had depended on the validity of general concepts, called universals, which could be analyzed through the use of logic. Aquinas and others who studied the eternity of the world, the existence of God, the nature of the soul, and other philosophical questions believed that people could reach general truths by abstracting universals from particular, individual cases. Ockham argued that universals were merely names, no more than convenient tags for discussing individual things. Universals had no connection with reality and could not be used to reason from particular observations to general truths. This radical nominalism (from the Latin *nomen,* "name") thus denied that human reason could aspire to certain truth. For Ockham and his followers, philosophical speculation was essentially a logical, linguistic exercise, not a way to certain knowledge. Ockham died in 1349, a victim of the plague, but his political and philosophical teachings lived on. His ideas on Church governance by a general council representing the whole Christian community offered the one hope for a solution to the Great Schism that erupted shortly after his death. Conciliarists like Pierre d'Ailly (1350–1420) and Jean de Gerson (1363–1429) drew on Ockham's attack on papal absolutism to propose an alternative church. The Council of Constance, which ended the schism, was the fruit of Ockham's political theory, as were the various organizational structures of the Protestant churches of the sixteenth century.

Just as Ockham's political theory dominated the later fourteenth century, his nominalist philosophy won over the philosophical faculties of Europe. Since he had discredited the power of Aristotelian logic to increase knowledge, the result was, on the one hand, a decline in abstract speculation, and on the other hand, a greater interest in scientific observation of individual phenomena. In the next generation Parisian professors trained in the tradition of Ockham, laid the foundation for scientific studies of motion and the universe that led to the scientific discoveries of the sixteenth and seventeenth centuries.

Vernacular Literature and the Individual

Just as the religious and philosophical concerns of the later Middle Ages developed within national frameworks and criticized accepted authority from the perspective of individual experience, so too did the vernacular (as opposed to Latin) literatures of the age begin to explore the place of the individual within an increasingly complex society. Across Europe, authors reviewed the traditional values of society with a critical eye, reworking and transforming traditional literary genres into statements both personal and profound.

In Italy, a trio of Tuscan poets, Dante Alighieri (1265–1321), Francesco Petrarch (1304–74), and Giovanni Boccaccio (1313–75), not only made Italian a literary language but composed in it some of the greatest literature of all time. Dante, the first and greatest of the three, was born into a modest but respectable Flo-

rentine family, and after receiving an excellent education entered the public life of his city. At the same time he began writing poetry and quickly acquired a reputation for his ability to express in love lyrics a new sensitivity and individual expression. In 1301 he fell victim to the viciousness of Florentine politics and was exiled from his beloved city for the remainder of his life. For two decades he traveled through Italy, residing in the courts of friendly princes and writing philosophical treatises and literary works, which culminated in his *Divine Comedy,* written during the last years of his life.

The Divine Comedy is a view of the whole Christian universe, populated with people from antiquity and from Dante's own day. The poem is both a sophisticated summary of philosophical and theological thought at the beginning of the fourteenth century and an astute political commentary on his times. The poet sets this vision within a three-part poetic journey through hell (*Inferno*), purgatory (*Purgatorio*), and heaven (*Paradiso*). In each part Dante adopts a poetic style appropriate to the subject matter. His journey through hell to witness the sufferings of the damned is described in brutal, immediate language that makes one almost feel the agony of the condemned, each of whom receives an eternal punishment appropriate to his or her sins. The violent conquerors Alexander the Great and Attila the Hun, for example, wallow for all eternity in boiling blood as punishment for spilling the blood of so many others. In purgatory, Dante meets sinners whose punishments will someday end. These he describes in a language of dreams and imagination, of nostalgic recollections cast in a misty landscape of the memory. On a ledge populated by hoarders and wasters, for example, the poet hears but does not see Hugh Capet, founder of the French Capetian dynasty, who describes a vision of his greedy descendants who devastate Italy to gain riches. Dante describes paradise in a symbolic language that is nonphysical and nonrepresentational. In the face of transcendent perfection, human imagery and poetry fail. In his final vision, he sees the reflected light of a mystical rose in which the saints are ranked. These include both religious leaders such as Bernard of Clairvaux and political leaders such as Emperor Henry VII, grandfather of Charles IV. *The Divine Comedy* is Dante's personal summary of all that is good and bad in medieval culture and politics.

English literature emerged from over two centuries of French cultural domination with the writings of William Langland (ca. 1330–95) and Geoffrey Chaucer (ca. 1343–1400). Both presented images of contemporary society with a critical and often ironic view. In *Piers Plowman* Langland presents society from

A miniature painted by Guglielmo Giraldi to illustrate canto VIII of Dante's Inferno *shows Dante and Virgil being ferried across the River Styx by the boatman Phlegyas.*

the perspective of the peasantry. Chaucer's work is much more sophisticated and wide-ranging, weaving together the whole spectrum of late medieval literature and life.

Chaucer was born into a London merchant family and spent a long and successful career as a courtier, serving English aristocrats and finally the king both in England and on the Continent. His travels brought him into contact with the literary and philosophical traditions of all of Europe, and he mastered every genre, always molding them with wit and imagination into something new.

Dante had set his great poem within a vision of the other world. Chaucer placed his tales in the mouths of a group of thirty pilgrims traveling to the tomb of Thomas à Becket at Canterbury. The pilgrims represent every walk of life and spectrum of society: a simple knight, a vulgar miller, a lawyer, a lusty widow, a merchant, a squire, a physician, a nun, her chaplain, and a monk, among others. Each pilgrim is at once strikingly individual and representative of his or her profession or station in life. The tales that they tell are drawn from

folklore, Italian literature, the lives of the saints, courtly romance, and religious sermons. However, Chaucer plays with the tales and their genres in the retelling. He uses them to contrast or illuminate the persons and characters of their tellers as well as to comment in subtle and complex ways on the literary, religious, and cultural traditions of which they are part. His knight, for example, tells a tale of chivalric love taken from Boccaccio. However, in Chaucer's version, the tale becomes both more real and vivid and more humorous as he plays with the traditional genre of courtly love poetry. The Wife of Bath, a forceful woman who has survived five husbands, argues for the superiority of married life over celibacy, particularly when the wife controls the marriage. Her tale, which takes a form common in religious sermons, continues her argument. It is a retelling of a fairy tale in which a woman is released from a spell by a knight. She offers him the choice of having her ugly and faithful or beautiful and free to bestow her favors where she will. The knight courteously leaves the decision to her and is rewarded by her promise to be both fair and faithful. In his mastery of the whole heritage of medieval culture and his independent use of this heritage, Chaucer proved himself the greatest English writer before Shakespeare.

Much of Italian and English literature drew material and inspiration from French, which continued into the fifteenth century to be the language of courtly romance. In France, literature continued to project an unreal world of allegory and nostalgia for a glorious if imaginary past. Popular literature, developed largely in the towns, often dealt with courtly themes, but with a critical and more realistic eye.

In this literary world appeared a new and extraordinary type of poet, a woman who earned her living with her pen, Christine de Pisan (1364–ca. 1430). Married at sixteen and widowed at twenty-five, Christine was left virtually impoverished with the responsibility for supporting herself, her three children, her mother, and a niece. Rather than remarrying, she decided to earn her way as an author—an unheard-of decision for a woman of the fourteenth century. Beginning her education from scratch, she absorbed history and literature and began writing the sorts of conventional love poems popular with the French aristocracy. From there she moved to autobiographical poetry in which she described how fortune had changed her life. Her success was immediate and tremendous. Kings, princes, and aristocrats from England to Italy bought copies of her works and tried to attract her to their courts.

As a professional woman of letters, Christine fought the stereotypical medieval image of women as weak,

Christine de Pisan presenting a manuscript of her poems to Isabeau of Bavaria, the wife of King Charles VI of France.

sexually aggressive temptresses. With wit and reason she argued that women could be virtuous and showed the fallacies of traditional antifeminist preaching, poetry, and belief. She appealed to women to develop their own sense of self-worth directly from experience and not to rely on the advice of men who, no matter how well read, could not have any direct, accurate knowledge of the meaning of being a woman. In her *Hymn to Joan of Arc,* she saluted her famous contemporary for her accomplishments: bringing dignity to women, striving for justice, and working for peace in France.

Though Christine de Pisan was the exception rather than the rule, her life and writing epitomized the new possibilities and new interests of the fifteenth century. They included an acute sense of individuality, a willingness to look for truth not in the clichés of the past but in actual experience, and a readiness to defend one's views with tenacity. Although an heir of the medieval world, Christine, like her contemporaries, already embodied the attitudes of a new age.

That new age was reflected in a second tradition in fifteenth-century France, that of realist poetry. Around 1453, just as the English troops were enduring a final battering from the French artillery, Duke Charles of Orléans (1394–1465) organized a poetry contest. Each contestant was to write a ballad that began with the contradictory line, "I die of thirst beside the fountain." The duke, himself an outstanding poet, wrote an entry that embodied the traditional courtly themes of love and fortune:

I die of thirst beside the fountain,
Shaking from cold and the fire of love;
I am blind and yet guide the others;
I am weak of mind, a man of wisdom;
Too negligent, often cautious in vain,
I have been made a spirit,
Led by fortune for better or for worse.

An unexpected and very different entry came from the duke's prison. The prisoner-poet, François Villon (1432–ca. 1464), was a child of the Paris streets, an impoverished student, a barroom brawler, a killer, and a thief who spent much of his life trying to escape the gallows. He was also the greatest realist poet of the Middle Ages. His entry read:

I die of thirst beside the fountain,
Hot as fire, my teeth clattering,
At home I am in an alien land;
I shudder beside a glowing brazier,
Naked as a worm, gloriously dressed,
I laugh and cry and wait without hope,
I take comfort and sad despair,
I rejoice and have no joy,
Powerful, I have no force and no strength,
Well received, I am expelled by all.

The duke focused on the sufferings of love; the thief on the physical sufferings of the downtrodden. The two poets represent the contradictory tendencies of literature in the later Middle Ages. From Prague to Paris, everywhere vernacular languages had come into their own. Poets used their native tongues to express a spectrum of sentiments and to describe a spectrum of emotions and values. The themes and ideas expressed ranged from the polished, traditional values of the aristocracy, trying to maintain the ideals of chivalry in a new and changed world, to the views of ordinary people, by turns reverent or sarcastic, joyful or despondent.

• • •

Late in life, Christine de Pisan relinquished her independence to enter a convent. Charles of Orléans was so moved by Villon's poetry that he released him from prison. The pope and the Hussites came to terms. King Charles VII ordered a new investigation into Joan of Arc, which absolved her—posthumously—of the charge of heresy. The religious, political, and cultural systems of the later Middle Ages remained sufficiently flexible to absorb the contradictory tendencies that they had created. This flexibility would not last. In the next century the political, religious, and cultural landscapes of Europe would be transformed by the new impulses born in the later Middle Ages.

The fourteenth and fifteenth centuries saw demographic collapse brought on by plague and accentuated by overpopulation and the ravages of warfare. They saw the transformation of the masses of the poor from the objects of Christian charity to the objects of fear and mistrust. During these centuries, warfare in France, England, Italy, and elsewhere evolved from elite battles to devastating professional campaigns of mass destruction capable of leaving whole countries in ruins for decades. Peasants fought for survival; aristocrats and wealthy merchants fought for greater power, prestige, and wealth on an international scale. Family alliances and merchant companies bound Europe together in a web of blood and money.

As the inherited forms of social and political organization strained to absorb these new conditions, individuals sought their own answers to the problems of life and death, using the legacy of the past, but using it in novel and creative ways. Dynasts created new principalities without regard for ancient allegiances. Mystics and heretics sought God without benefit of traditional religious hierarchies, and poets and philosophers sought personal expression outside the confines of inherited tradition.

The legacy of the later Middle Ages was a complex and ambiguous one. The thousand years of synthesis of classical, barbarian, and Christian traditions did not disappear. The bonds holding this world together were not yet broken. But the last centuries of the Middle Ages bequeathed a critical detachment from this heritage expressed in the revolts of peasants and workers, the preaching of radical religious reformers, and the poems of mystics and visionaries.

Suggestions for Further Reading

General Reading

Daniel Waley, *Later Medieval Europe* (London: Longman, 1975). A brief introduction with a focus on Italy.

Margaret Aston, *The Fifteenth Century: The Prospect of Europe* (New York: W. W. Norton, 1968). A general survey of the fifteenth century.

* Johan Huizinga, *The Waning of the Middle Ages* (New York: St. Martin's Press, 1954). An old but still powerful interpretation of culture and society in the Burgundian court in the later Middle Ages.

Robert Bartlett, *The Making of Europe: Conquest, Colonization, and Cultural Change, 950–1350* (Princeton: Princeton University Press, 1993). A comparative study of Europe's expansion into the Celtic, Islamic, and Slavic worlds in the later Middle Ages.

Politics as a Family Affair

Francis Dvornik, *The Slavs in European History and Civilization* (New Brunswick, NJ: Rutgers University Press, 1962). A masterful introduction to the history of eastern Europe.

* Geoffrey Barraclough, ed., *Eastern and Western Europe in the Middle Ages* (New York: Harcourt Brace Jovanovich, 1970). An excellent collection of essays on various aspects of eastern European history.

Joachim Leuschner, *Germany in the Late Middle Ages* (Amsterdam: Elsevier, 1980). An introduction to late medieval German history.

Richard W. Kaeuper, *War, Justice and Public Order: England and France in the Later Middle Ages* (Oxford: Oxford University Press, 1988). A fine analysis of the effects of war on England and France.

* C. T. Allmand, *The Hundred Years War: England and France at War, c. 1300–c. 1450* (New York: Cambridge University Press, 1988). A recent, brief introduction to the Hundred Years' War by a British historian.

* Régine Pernoud, *Joan of Arc, by Herself and Her Witnesses* (New York: Stein & Day, 1966). Contemporary writings by and about Joan of Arc.

Life and Death in the Later Middle Ages

* Philip Zieger, *The Black Death* (New York: Harper & Row, 1969). A reliable introduction to the plague in the fourteenth century.

H. A. Miskimin, *The Economy of Early Renaissance Europe, 1300–1460* (New York: Cambridge University Press, 1975). An accessible introduction to the economic history of the later Middle Ages.

* P. Dollinger, *The German Hansa* (Stanford, CA: Stanford University Press, 1970). A brief history of the Hansa intended for the nonspecialist.

* Edith Ennen, *The Medieval Town* (New York: North-Holland, 1979). A brief history of medieval cities by a German specialist.

* Georges Duby, ed., *A History of Private Life.* Volume 2, *Revelations of the Medieval World* (Cambridge, MA: Harvard University Press, 1988). A series of provocative essays on the origins of privacy and the individual.

Bronislaw Geremek, *The Margins of Society in Late Medieval Paris,* tr. Jean Birrell (Cambridge: Cambridge University Press, 1987). A landmark study of the urban poor in the late Middle Ages.

* Michel Mollat and Philippe Wolff, *The Popular Revolutions of the Late Middle Ages* (London: Allen & Unwin,1973). An accessible history of late medieval revolts, focusing on those of medieval cities.

The Spirit of the Later Middle Ages

* Geoffrey Barraclough, *The Medieval Papacy* (New York: W. W. Norton, 1968). A brief overview of the papacy.

Yves Renouard, *The Avignon Papacy (1305–1403)* (Hamden, CT: Archon Books, 1970). A readable account of the Avignon popes.

* Heiko A. Oberman, *The Harvest of Medieval Theology* (Cambridge, MA: Labyrinth Press, 1963). A technical but rewarding account of late medieval theology.

Howard Kaminsky, *A History of the Hussite Revolution* (Berkeley, CA: University of California Press, 1967). The best account of the Hussite movement.

Gordon Leff, *Heresy in the Later Middle Ages* (Manchester: Manchester University Press, 1967). A survey of heretical movements in the fourteenth and fifteenth centuries.

* Caroline Walker Bynum, *Holy Feast and Holy Fast: The Religious Significance of Food to Medieval Women* (Berkeley, CA: University of California Press, 1987). An imaginative and scholarly examination of the role of food in the spirituality of medieval women.

E. F. Chaney, *François Villon in His Environment* (Oxford: Oxford University Press, 1946). An old but still valuable study of Villon and his world.

H. S. Bennett, *Chaucer and the Fifteenth Century* (Oxford: Oxford University Press, 1961). An accessible historical introduction to Chaucer.

John Freccero, *Dante and the Poetics of Conversion* (Cambridge, MA: Harvard University Press, 1986). A serious and rewarding study of Dante by an acknowledged master.

*Paperback edition available.

11 ❧ THE ITALIAN RENAISSANCE

A Civic Procession

*I*t is 25 April 1444, the day Venice celebrates its patron, Saint Mark, with a procession through the square that bears his name. Processions are a common form of civic ritual by which a community defines itself. The special features that identify Venice for its citizens are all on display. City flags and emblems are mounted on poles, and clothes bear the insignia of various orders and groups. The procession re-creates all forms of communal life. Here are the religious orders (the white-clad broth-ers of the Confraternity of Saint John are passing before us now), and the civic leaders can be seen just behind them. Musicians entertain both marchers and onlookers. A band files by on the right. The procession is orderly, but it is by no means con-trived. It is not staged, as would be a modern cere-mony, and this is evident in the relaxed attitude of ordinary citizens who gather in the middle of the square. There is no apparent drama to observe, and they walk and talk quite naturally. So, too, do the participants. In the lower left-hand corner of the painting, some friars are reading music; at the lower right, members of the confraternity carry their candles negligently.

Yet this painting, *The Procession of the Relic of the Holy Cross* (1496) by Gentile Bellini (ca. 1429–1507), was commissioned to commemorate a miracle rather than a civic procession. On the evening before Saint Mark's day, a visiting merchant and his son were touring the square when the boy fell and cracked his skull. The doctors who treated him regarded the case as hopeless and prepared the father for his son's death. The next morning, the Brothers of the Confraternity of Saint John paraded their relic of a piece of the cross on which Jesus was crucified. The merchant approached the golden altarpiece containing the relic, dropped to his knees, and prayed that Saint Mark would miraculously cure his son. He is the red-clad figure kneeling just to the right of center, where the line of brothers breaks. The next day the boy revived.

The Brothers of Saint John commissioned Bellini to commemorate this event. He came from the most distinguished family of painters in Venice. His father, Jacopo, had studied in Florence and had brought his sons into his workshop as young boys. Until the age of thirty, Gentile worked on his father's commissions, learning the difficult craft of painting. Art was a family business in fifteenth-century Italy. The large workshops, with their master and apprentices, turned out vast canvasses with assembly-line precision. The master created the composition and sketched it; his skilled assistants, like the Bellini brothers, worked on the more complex parts; and young apprentices painted backgrounds. The master was first and foremost a businessman, gaining commissions to sustain his family and his workers. The Bellinis were connected to the Confraternity of Saint John, and it was only natural that Gentile would receive this lucrative contract.

Although *The Procession of the Relic of the Holy Cross* was designed to re-create a central moment in the history of the confraternity, it is not the confraternity that dominates the picture. Miracles were part of civic life, and each town took pride in the special manifestations of heavenly care that had taken place within it. Thus it is Venice that is the centerpiece of Bellini's canvas. Dominating the painting is the Basilica of San Marco, with its four great horses over the center portico and the winged lion—the city's symbol—on the canopy above. The procession emanates from the duke's palace to the right of the church, and the great flags of the city are seen everywhere. By the end of the fifteenth century, Venice was one of the greatest powers on earth, the center for international trade and finance. Home to the largest concentration of wealthy families anywhere in Europe, it could well afford the pomp and splendor of its processions. The achievements of God and the achievements of humans blend together in this painting as they blended together in that era of remarkable accomplishments that historians call the Renaissance.

Renaissance Society

Perhaps the most surprising result of the Black Death was the way in which European society revived itself in the succeeding centuries. Even at the height of the plague, a spirit of revitalization was evident in the works of artists and writers. Petrarch (1304–74), the great humanist poet and scholar, was among the first to differentiate the new age in which he was living from two earlier ones: the classical world of Greece and Rome, which he admired, and the subsequent Dark Ages, which he detested. This spirit of self-awareness is one of the defining characteristics of the Renaissance. "It is but in our own day that men dare boast that they see the dawn of better things," wrote Matteo Palmieri (1406–75). Like many others, Marsilio Ficino (1433–99), a Florentine physician and philosopher who translated Plato and dabbled in astrology, dubbed his times a golden age: "This century, like a golden age, has restored to light the liberal arts, which were almost extinct: grammar, poetry, rhetoric, painting, sculpture, architecture, and music." The Renaissance was a new age by self-assertion. In that self-assertion, wave after wave of artistic celebration of the human spirit found its wellspring and created a legacy that is still vibrant 500 years later.

What was the Renaissance? A French word for an Italian phenomenon, *renaissance* literally means "rebirth." The word captures both the emphasis on humanity that characterized Renaissance thinking and the renewed fascination with the classical world. But the Renaissance was an age rather than an event. There is no moment at which the Middle Ages ended, and late medieval society was artistically creative, socially well developed, and economically diverse. Yet eventually the pace of change accelerated, and it is best to think of the Renaissance as an era of rapid transitions. Encompassing the two centuries between 1350 and 1550, it passed through three distinct phases. The first, from 1350 to 1400, was characterized by a declining population, the uncovering of classical texts, and experimentation in a variety of art forms. The second phase, from 1400 to 1500, was distinguished by the creation of a set of cultural values and artistic and literary achievements that defined Renaissance style. The large Italian city-states developed stable and coherent forms of government, and the warfare between them gradually ended. In the final period, from 1500 to 1550, invasions from France and Spain transformed Italian political life, and the ideas and techniques of Italian writers and artists radiated to all points of the Continent. Renaissance ideas and achievements spread throughout western Europe and were particularly important in Holland; but they are best studied where they first developed, on the Italian peninsula.

The Environment

The Italian peninsula differed sharply from other areas of Europe in the extent to which it was urban. By the late Middle Ages nearly one in four Italians lived in a town, in contrast to one in ten elsewhere. Not even the plague did much to change this ratio. There were more Italian cities and more people in them. By 1500, seven of the ten largest cities in the West were in Italy. Naples, Venice, and Milan, each with a population of more than one hundred thousand, led the rest. But not every city was a great metropolis, and it was the numerous smaller towns, with populations nearer to one thousand, that gave the Italian peninsula its urban character. Cities also served as convenient centers of judicial and ecclesiastical power.

Cities acted as central places around which a cluster of large and small villages was organized. Urban areas, especially the small towns, provided markets for the agricultural produce of the countryside and for the manufactured goods of the urban craftsmen. It was in the cities that goods and services changed hands. This allowed for the specialization in agricultural and industrial life that increased both productivity and wages. Cities also caught the runoff of rural population, especially the surplus of younger sons and daughters who could not be accommodated on the farms. Cities grew by migration rather than by natural increase, and immigrants flooded into them. Thus the areas surrounding a city were critical to its prosperity and survival. The urban system was a network of cities encompassed by towns and encircled by rural villages. Florence, the dominant city in the region of Tuscany, exemplifies this relationship. Though it possessed two-thirds of its region's wealth, Florence contained only 14 percent of the regional population. The surrounding countryside was agriculturally rich because marketing costs were low and demand for foodstuffs high. Smaller cities channeled their local produce and trade to Florence.

Though cities may have dominated Renaissance Italy, by present standards they were small in both area and population. Despite the city's wealth, great banks, magnificent palaces, and piazzas, a person could walk across fifteenth-century Florence in less than half an hour. In 1427 its population was 37,000, only half its pre-plague size. Most Italian cities contained large fields for agricultural production, and within the outer

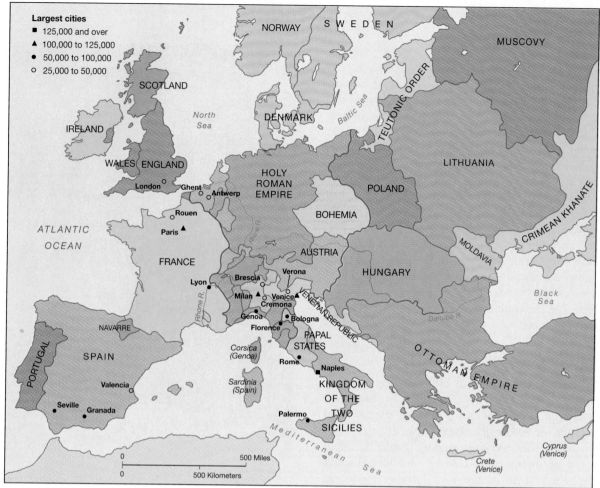

Largest Cities in Western Europe, ca. 1500

walls of Florence were gardens and fields of grain. Inside the inner city walls the people crowded together into tightly packed quarters. The intensity of the stench from raw sewage, rotting foodstuffs, and animals being brought to slaughter was equaled only by the din made by hoofs and wooden cartwheels on paving stones.

Urban populations were organized far differently from rural ones. On the farms, the central distinctions involved ownership of land. Some farmers owned their estates outright and left them intact to their heirs. Others were involved in a sharecropping system by which absentee owners of land supplied working capital in return for half of the farm's produce. A great gulf in wealth separated owners from sharecroppers. But within the groups the gaps were not as great. There were gradations, but these were ordinarily temporary conditions that bad harvests, generous dowries, or divided inheritances balanced out over time.

In the city, however, distinctions were based first on occupation, which largely corresponded to social position and wealth. Cities began as markets, and the priv-ilege to participate in the market defined citizens. City governments provided protection for consumers and producers by creating monopolies through which standards for craftsmanship were maintained and profits for craftsmen were guaranteed. These monopolies were called guilds or companies. Each large city had its own hierarchy of guilds. At the top were the important manufacturing groups—clothiers, metalworkers, and the like. Just below them were bankers, merchants, and the administrators of civic and Church holdings. At the bottom were grocers, masons, and other skilled workers. Roughly speaking, all of those within the guild structure, from bottom to top, lived comfortably. Yet the majority of urban inhabitants were not members of guilds. Many managed to eke out a living as wage laborers; many more were simply destitute. As a group, these poor constituted as much as half of the entire population. Most were dependent upon civic and private charity for their survival.

The disparities between rich and poor were overwhelming. The concentration of wealth in the hands of an ever-narrowing group of families and favored guilds characterized every large city. One reason for this was the extreme instability of economic life. Prices and wages fluctuated wildly in response to local circumstance. After an epidemic of plague, wages climbed and the prices of consumer goods tumbled. A bad harvest sent food prices skyrocketing. Only those able to even out these extreme swings by stockpiling goods in times of plenty and consuming them in times of want were safe. Capital, however initially accumulated, was the key to continued wealth. Monopolies ensured the profitability of trade and manufacturing, but only those with sufficient capital could engage in either. In Florence, for example, 10 percent of the families controlled 90 percent of the wealth, with an even more extreme concentration at the top. The combined wealth of the richest 100 Florentine families was greater than the combined wealth of 87 percent of the city's population.

Production and Consumption

This concentration of wealth and the way in which it was used defined Renaissance economy. Economic life is bound up in the relationship between resources and desires, or, as economists would have it, supply and demand. The late medieval economy, despite the development of international banking and long-distance trade, was still an economy of primary producers: between 70 and 90 percent of Europe's population was involved in subsistence agriculture. Even in Italy, which contained the greatest concentration of urban areas in the world, agriculture predominated. The manufacture of clothing was the only other significant economic activity. Moreover, most of what was produced was for local consumption rather than for the marketplace. The relationship between supply and demand was precisely measured by the full or empty stomach. Even in good times, more than 80 percent of the population lived at subsistence level with food, clothing, and shelter their only expenses. Thus, when we discuss the market economy of the Renaissance, we are discussing the circumstances of the few rather than the many.

The defining characteristic of the early Renaissance economy was population change. Recurring waves of plague kept population levels low for more than a century. In the century between 1350 and 1450, one in every six years was characterized by an unusually high mortality rate. At the end of this period, for example, Florence's population was only a quarter of what it had been at the beginning. This dramatic reduction in population depressed economic growth. Until 1460 the major sectors of the economy were stagnant. The gen-

Cloth making was a major contributor to European economic growth during the Middle Ages. In this 1470 portrait of Cloth Merchants' Street in Bologna, a tailor (center) measures a prospective client.

eral economy did not revive until the sustained population increase toward the end of the fifteenth century. Until then, in both agriculture and manufacturing, supply outstripped demand.

On the farms, overabundance resulted from two related developments, the concentration of surviving farmers on the best land and the enlargement of their holdings. In the shops, finished products outnumbered the consumers who survived the epidemics. Overproduction meant lower prices for basic commodities, and the decline in population meant higher wages for labor. The result was that at the lowest levels of society survivors found it easier to earn their living and even to create a surplus than had their parents. For a time the lot of the masses improved.

But for investors, such economic conditions meant that neither agriculture nor cloth making were particularly attractive. Expensive investments in land or equipment for sharecropping were paid back in inexpensive grain. High wages for the few surviving skilled workers brought a return only in cheap cloth. In such circumstances, consumption was more attractive than investment. It was not merely the perceived shortage in profitable investments that brought on the increase in conspicuous consumption during the fifteenth century. In the psychological atmosphere created by unpredictable, swift, and deadly epidemics, luxurious living seemed an appropriate response. Moreover, although tax rates increased, houses and personal property remained exempt, making luxury goods attractive investments. Even those at the lowest levels of society eagerly purchased whatever their meager means permitted.

For these reasons, the production and consumption of luxuries soared. By the middle of the fourteenth century, Florence was known for its silks and jewelry as much as for its cloth. Venice became a European center for the glass industry, especially for the finely ground glass that was used in eyeglasses. Production of specialty crops like sugar, saffron, fruits, and high-quality wine expanded. International trade increasingly centered on acquiring Eastern specialities, resulting in the serious outflow of gold and silver that enriched first the Byzantine and then the Ottoman emperors.

The Experience of Life

Luxury helped improve a life that for rich and poor alike was short and uncertain. Nature was still people's most potent enemy. Renaissance children who survived infancy found their lives governed by parentage and by sex. In parentage the great divide was between those who lived with surplus and those who lived at subsistence. The first category encompassed the wealthiest bankers and merchants down to those who owned their own farms or engaged in small urban crafts. The vast majority of urban and rural dwellers comprised the second category. About the children of the poor we know very little other than that their survival was unlikely. If they did not die at birth or shortly afterward, they might be abandoned—especially if female—to the growing number of orphanages in the cities, waste away from lack of nutrition, or fall prey to ordinary childhood diseases for which there were no treatments. Eldest sons were favored; younger daughters were disadvantaged. In poor families, however, this favoritism meant little more than early apprenticeship to day labor in the city or farm labor in the countryside. Girls were frequently sent out as domestic servants far from the family home.

Children of the wealthy had better chances for survival than did children of the poor. For children of the wealthy, childhood might begin with "milk parents,"

life in the home of the family of a wet nurse who would breast-feed the baby through infancy. Only the very wealthy could afford a live-in wet nurse, which would increase the child's chances of survival. Again, daughters were more likely to be sent far from home and least likely to have their nursing supervised. The use of wet nurses not only emancipated parents from the daily care of infants, it also allowed them to resume sexual relations. Nursing women refrained from sex in the belief that it affected their milk.

During the period between weaning and apprenticeship, Renaissance children lived with their families. There was no typical Renaissance family. Nuclear families—parents and their children under one roof—were probably more common than extended families, which might include grandparents and other relatives. But the composition of the family changed over the course of the life cycle and included times in which married children or grandparents were present and other times when a single parent and small children were the only members. Moreover, even nuclear families commonly contained stepparents and stepchildren as well as domestic servants or apprentices. Thus a child returning to the parental household was as likely to form emotional bonds with older siblings as with parents.

The family was an economic unit as well as a grouping of relatives. Decisions to abandon children, to send them away from the household when very young, or to

Old Man with a Child *by the Florentine painter Domenico del Ghirlandaio (1449–94).*

ON THE FAMILY

Leon Battista Alberti wrote a number of important tracts that set out the general principles of a subject, including On Architecture, *which was considered the basic text for three hundred years. His writings on the family bring insight into the nature of a patriarchal, male-dominated institution.*

They say that in choosing a wife one looks for beauty, parentage, and riches. . . . Among the most essential criteria of beauty in a woman is an honorable manner. Even a wild, prodigal, greasy, drunken woman may be beautiful of feature, but no one would call her a beautiful wife. A woman worthy of praise must show first of all in her conduct, modesty, and purity. Marius, the illustrious Roman, said in that first speech of his to the Roman people: "Of women we require purity, of men labor." And I certainly agree. There is nothing more disgusting than a coarse and dirty woman. Who is stupid enough not to see clearly that a woman who does not care for neatness and cleanliness in her appearance, not only in her dress and body but in all her behavior and language, is by no means well mannered? How can it be anything but obvious that a bad-mannered woman is also rarely virtuous? We shall consider elsewhere the harm that comes to a family from women who lack virtue, for I myself do not know which is the worse fate for a family, total celibacy or a single dishonored woman. In a bride, therefore, a man must first seek beauty of mind, that is, good conduct and virtue.

In her body he must seek not only loveliness, grace, and charm but must also choose a woman who is well made for bearing children, with the kind of constitution that promises to make them strong and big. There's an old proverb, "When you pick your wife, you choose your children." All her virtues will in fact shine brighter still in beautiful children. It is a well-known saying among poets: "Beautiful character dwells in a beautiful body." The natural philosophers require that a woman be neither thin nor very fat. Those laden with fat are subject to coldness and constipation and slow to conceive. They say that a woman should have a joyful nature, fresh and lively in her blood and her whole being. They have no objections to a dark girl. They do reject girls with a frowning black visage, however. They have no liking for either the undersized or the overlarge and lean. They find that a woman is most suited to bear children if she is fairly big and has limbs of ample length. They always have a preference for youth, based on a number of arguments which I need not expound here, but particularly on the point that a young girl has a more adaptable mind. Young girls are pure by virtue of their age and have not developed any spitefulness. They are by nature modest and free of vice. They quickly learn to accept affectionately and unresistingly the habits and wishes of their husbands.

From Leon Battista Alberti, *On the Family*

take in domestic servants were based on economic calculations. In the competition for scarce resources, the way in which children were managed might determine the survival of the family unit. Sons could expect to be apprenticed to a trade, probably between the ages of ten and thirteen. Most, of course, learned the crafts of their fathers, but not necessarily in their father's shop. By adolescence these fortunate boys, who might have had some rudimentary schooling, were earning token wages that contributed to family income. Sons inherited the family business and its most important possessions—tools of the trade or beasts of labor for the farm. Inheritance customs varied. In some places only the eldest son received the equipment of the family occupation; in others, like Tuscany, all the sons shared it.

Still, in the first fifteen years of life, these most-favored children would have spent between one-third and one-half of their time outside the household in which they had been born.

Expectations for daughters centered on their chances of marriage. For a girl, dowry was everything. If a girl's father could provide a handsome one, her future was secure; if not, the alternatives were a convent, which would take a small bequest, or a match lower down the social scale, where the quality of life deteriorated rapidly. Daughters of poor families entered domestic service in order to have a dowry provided by their masters. The dowry was taken to the household of the husband. There the couple resided until they established their own separate family. If the

Detail from a fifteenth-century Florentine painted wedding chest shows a procession of young people participating in a ductio ad maritum, *the installation of a new bride in her husband's home.*

husband died, it was to his parental household that the widow returned.

Women married in late adolescence, usually around the age of twenty. Among the wealthy, marriages were perceived as familial alliances and business transactions rather than love matches. The dowry was an investment on which fathers expected a return, and while the bride might have some choice, it was severely limited. Compatibility was not a central feature in matchmaking. Husbands were, on average, ten years older than their wives and likely to leave them widows. In the early fifteenth century, about one-fourth of all adult women in Florence were widows, many without prospects of remarriage.

Married women lived in a state of nearly constant pregnancy. Alessandra Strozzi, whose father was one of the wealthiest citizens of Florence, married at the age of sixteen, gave birth to eight children in ten years, and was widowed at the age of twenty-five. Not all pregnancies produced children. The rates of miscarriages and stillbirths were very high, and abortions and infanticide were not unknown. Only among the families who hovered between surplus and subsistence is there any evidence of attempts to control pregnancies. These efforts, which relied upon techniques like the rhythm method and withdrawal, were not particularly effective. The rhythm method was especially futile because of the misunderstanding of the role of women in conception. It was not yet known that the woman contained an egg that was fertilized during conception. Without this knowledge it was impossible to understand the cycle of ovulation. Practically speaking, family size was limited on the one end by late marriages and on the other by early deaths.

Life experiences differed for males. Men married later—near the age of twenty-five on the farms, nearer the age of thirty in the cities—because of the cost of setting up in trade or on the land. Late marriage meant long supervision under the watchful eye of father or master, an extended period between adolescence and adulthood. The reputation that Renaissance cities gained for homosexuality and licentiousness must be viewed in light of the advanced age at which males married. The level of sexual frustration was high, and its outlet in ritual violence and rape was also high.

The establishment of one's own household through marriage was a late rite of passage, considering the expectations of early death. Many men, even those with families, never succeeded in setting up separately from their fathers or elder brothers. Men came of age at thirty but were thought to be old by fifty. Thus for men marriage and parenthood took place in middle age rather than in youth. Valued all their lives more highly than their sisters, male heads of households were the source of all power in their domiciles, in their shops, and in the state. They were responsible for overseeing every aspect of the upbringing of their children, even choosing wet nurses for their infants and spouses for their daughters. But their wives were essential partners who governed domestic life. Women labored not only at the hearth, but in the fields and shops as well. Their economic contribution to the well-being of the family was critical, both in the dowry they brought at marriage and in the labor they contributed to the household. If their wives died, men with young children remarried quickly. While there were many bachelors, there were few widowers.

In most cases death came suddenly. Epidemic diseases, of which plague was the most virulent, struck with fearful regularity. Even in the absence of a serious outbreak, there were always deaths in town and country attributable to the plague. Epidemics struck harder at the young—children and adolescents, who were the majority of the population—and hardest in the summer months, when other viruses and bacteria weakened the population. Influenza must have been the second largest cause of death, though in the absence of proper records we can only guess. Medical treatment was more likely to hasten death than to prolong life. Lorenzo de' Medici's physician prescribed powdered pearls for the Florentine ruler's gout. After that Lorenzo complained more of stomach pains than of gout. Marsilio Ficino, in his popular medical tract "How to Prolong Your Life," recommended drinking liquefied gold during certain phases of the moon. Such remedies revealed a belief in the harmony of nature and the healing power of rare substances. They were not silly or superstitious, but they were not effective either. Starvation was rare, less because of food shortage than because the seriously undernourished were more likely to succumb to disease than to famine. In urban areas, the government would intervene to provide grain from public storehouses at times of extreme shortage; in the countryside large landholders commonly exercised the same function.

The Quality of Life

Though life may have been difficult during the Renaissance, it was not unfulfilling. Despite constant toil and frequent hardship, people of the Renaissance had reason to believe that their lives were better than those of their ancestors and that their children's lives would be better still. On the most basic level, health improved and, for those who survived plague, life expectancy increased. Better health was related to better diet. Improvement came from two sources, the relative surplus of grain throughout the fifteenth century and the wider variety of foods consumed. Bread remained the most widely consumed foodstuff, but even subsistence consumers were beginning to supplement their diet with meat and dairy products. There was more pork and lamb in the diet of ordinary people in the fifteenth century than there would be for the next four hundred years. At the upper levels of society, sweet wine and citrus fruits helped offset the lack of vegetables. This diversification of diet resulted from improvements in transportation and communication, which brought more goods and services to a growing number of towns in the chain that linked the regional centers to the rural countryside.

But the towns and cities contributed more than consumer goods to Renaissance society. They also introduced a new sense of social and political cohesiveness. The city was something to which people belonged. In urban areas they could join social groups of their own choosing and develop networks of support not possible in rural environments. Blood relations remained the primary social group. Kin were the most likely source of aid in times of need, and charity began at home. Kin groups extended well beyond the immediate family, with both cousins and in-laws laying claim to the privileges of blood. The urban family could also depend upon the connections of neighborhood. In some Italian cities, wealth or occupation determined housing patterns. In others, like Florence, rich and poor lived side by side and identified themselves with their small administrative unit and with their local church. Thus they could participate in relationships with others both above and below them in the social scale. From their superiors they gained connections that helped their families; from their inferiors they gained devoted clients. The use of both in such important functions as godparenting demonstrates how the urban family built a complex set of social relations.

As in the Middle Ages, the Church remained the spatial, spiritual, and social center of people's lives. There was not yet any separation between faith and reason. The Church provided explanations for both the mysterious and the mundane. It offered comfort in this life and in the life to come. In it were performed the rituals of baptism, marriage, and burial that measured the passage of life. The Church was also the source of the key symbols of urban society. The flags of militia troops, the emblems of guilds, the regalia of the city itself were all adorned by recognizably religious symbols. The Church preserved holy relics, like the piece of the true cross in Venice, that were venerated for their power to protect the city or to endow it with particular skills and resources. Through its holy days as much as through its rituals, the Church helped channel leisure activities into community celebrations.

A growing sense of civic pride and individual accomplishment were underlying characteristics of the Italian Renaissance, enhanced by the development of social cohesion and community solidarity that both Church and city-state fostered. It is commonly held that the Renaissance was both elitist and male dominated, that it was an experience separate from that of the society at large. There can be no question that it was the rich who commissioned works of art and that it was the highly skilled male craftsmen who executed them. But neither lived in a social vacuum. The Renaissance was not the result of the efforts of a privileged few. Family values that permitted early apprenticeships in surrogate households and that emphasized the continuity of crafts from one generation to the next made possible the skilled artists of the Renaissance cities. The stress on the production of luxury goods placed higher value upon individual skills and therefore upon excellence in workmanship. Church and state sought to express social values through representational art. One of the chief purposes of wall murals was to instruct the unlettered in religion, to help them visualize the central episodes in Christian history and thus increase the pleasure they derived from their faith. The grandiose architecture and statuary that adorned central places were designed to enhance civic pride, nurture loyalty, and communicate the protective power of public institutions.

For ordinary people the world of the Renaissance was not much different than the world of the Middle Ages. Although urban areas grew, providing a wider variety of occupations and a varied material life, most people continued to scratch a meager living from the soil. The crucial difference from generation to generation was the degree of infectious diseases and the rate of rising or falling population. For the lucky ones there was surplus, for the unfortunate there was dearth. Within these confines men were privileged over women, having greater security and status and monopolizing power. But the tightly knit organization of family life protected the weak and the poor, while the church provided faith, hope, and charity.

Renaissance Art

In every age, artistic achievement represents a combination of individual talent and predominant social ideals. Artists may be at the leading edge of the society in which they live, but it is the spirit of that society that they capture in word or song or image. Artistic disciplines also have their own technical development. Individually, Renaissance artists were attempting to solve problems of perspective and three-dimensionality that had defeated their predecessors. But the particular techniques or experiments that interested them owed as much to the social context as they did to the artistic one. For example, the urban character of Italian government led to the need for civic architecture—public buildings on a grand scale. The celebration of individual achievement led to the explosive growth of portraiture. Not surprisingly, major technological breakthroughs were achieved in both areas. Nor should we underestimate the brilliance of the artists themselves. To deny genius is to deprecate humanity. What we need to explain is not the existence of a Leonardo or a Michelangelo but their coexistence.

This relationship between artist and social context was all the more important in the Renaissance, when artists were closely tied to the crafts and trades of urban society and to the demands of clients who commissioned their work. Although it was the elite who patronized art, it was skilled tradesmen who produced it. Artists normally followed the pattern of any craftsman, an apprenticeship begun as a teenager and a long period of training and work in a master's shop. This form of education gave the aspiring artist a practical rather than a theoretical bent and a keen appreciation for the business side of art. Studios were identified with particular styles and competed for commissions from clients, especially the Church. Wealthy individuals commissioned art as investments, as marks of personal distinction, and as displays of public piety. They got what they paid for, usually entering into detailed contracts that stipulated the quality of materials and the amount of work done by the master. Isabella d'Este (1474–1539), one of the great patrons of Renaissance artists, wrote hundreds of letters specifying the details of the works she commissioned. She once sent an artist threads of the exact dimensions of the pictures she had ordered. Demand for art was high. The vast public-works projects needed buildings, the new piazzas (public squares) and palazzos (private houses) needed statuary, and the long walls of churches needed murals.

The survival of so many Renaissance masterpieces allows us to reconstruct the stages by which the remarkable artistic achievements of this era took place. Although advances were made in a variety of fields during the Renaissance, the three outstanding areas were architecture, sculpture, and painting. While modern artists would consider each a separate discipline, Renaissance artists crossed their boundaries without hesitation. Not only could these artists work with a variety of materials, their intensive and varied apprenticeships taught them to apply the technical solutions of one field to the problems of another. Few Renaissance artists confined themselves to one area of artistic expression, and many created works of enduring beauty in more than one medium. Was the greatest achievement of Michelangelo his sculpture of David, his paintings on the ceiling of the Sistine Chapel, or his design for the dome of Saint Peter's? Only a century of interdisciplinary cross-fertilization could have prepared the artistic world for such a feat.

An Architect, a Sculptor, and a Painter

The century that culminated in Michelangelo's extraordinary achievements began with the work of three Florentine masters who deeply influenced one another's development, Brunelleschi (1377–1446), Donatello (1386–1466), and Masaccio (1401–28). In the Renaissance, the dominant artistic discipline was architecture. Buildings were the most expensive investment patrons could make, and the technical knowledge necessary for their successful construction was immense. Not only did the architect design a building, he also served as its general contractor, its construction supervisor, and its inspector. Moreover, the architect's design determined the amount and the scale of the statuary and decorative

Florence Cathedral was begun by Arnolfo di Cambio in 1296. The nave was finished about 1350 and the dome, designed by Brunelleschi, was added in the 1420s. This view shows the dome and the apse end of the cathedral.

paintings to be incorporated. By 1400 the Gothic style of building had dominated western Europe for over two centuries. Its pointed arches, vaulted ceilings, and slender spires had simplified building by removing the heavy walls formerly thought necessary to support great structures. Gothic construction permitted greater height, a characteristic especially desirable in cathedrals, which stretched toward the heavens. But though the buildings themselves were simplified, the techniques for erecting them became more complex. By the fifteenth century, architects had turned their techniques into an intricate style. They became obsessed by angular arches, elaborate vaultings and buttresses, and long, pointed spires.

It was Brunelleschi who decisively challenged the principles of Gothic architecture by recombining its basic elements with those of classical structures. His achievement was less an innovation than a radical synthesis of old and new. Basing his designs on geometric principles, Brunelleschi reintroduced planes and spheres as dominant motifs. His greatest work was the dome on the cathedral in Florence, begun in 1420. His design was simple but bold. The windows at the base of the dome of the cathedral illustrate Brunelleschi's geometric technique. Circular windows are set inside a square of panels, which in turn are set inside a rectangle. The facades are dominated by columns and rounded arches, proportionally spaced from a central perspective. Brunelleschi is generally credited with having been the first Renaissance artist to have understood and made use of perspective, though it was immediately put to more dramatic effect in sculpture and painting.

The sculptor's study was the human form in all of its three-dimensional complexity. The survival of Roman and Hellenistic pieces, mostly bold and muscular torsos, meant that the influence of classical art was most direct in sculpture. Donatello translated these classical styles into more naturalistic forms. His technique is evident in the long flowing robes that distinguish most of his works. Donatello sculpted the cloth, not in the stylized angularity of the past in which the creases were as sharp as sword blades, but in the natural fashion in which cloth hung. Donatello also revived the freestanding statue, which demanded greater attention to human anatomy because it was viewed from many angles. *Judith Slaying Holofernes* (1455) is an outstanding example of Donatello's use of geometric proportion and perspective. Each side of the piece captures a different vision of Judith in action. In addition, Donatello led the revival of the equestrian statue, sculpting the Venetian captain-general Gattamelata for a public

Donatello's bronze statue Judith Slaying Holofernes *symbolized the Florentines' love of liberty and hatred of tyranny.*

the illusion that a flat surface has three dimensions. Masaccio worked with standard Christian themes, but he brought an entirely novel approach to them all. In an adoration scene he portrayed a middle-aged Madonna and a dwarfish baby Jesus; in a painting of Saint Peter paying tribute money he used his own likeness as the face of one of the Apostles. His two best-known works are *The Expulsion of Adam and Eve* (ca. 1427) and *The Holy Trinity* (1425). In *The Expulsion of Adam and Eve* Masaccio has left an unforgettable image of the fall from grace in Eve's primeval anguish. Her deep eyes and hollow mouth are accentuated by casting the source of light downward and shading what otherwise would be lit. In *The Holy Trinity,* Masaccio provides the classic example of the use of linear perspective. In the painting, the ceiling of a Brunelleschi-designed temple recedes to a vanishing point beyond the head of God, creating the simultaneous illusion of height and depth.

Renaissance Style

By the middle of the fifteenth century, a recognizable Renaissance style had triumphed. Florence continued to lead the way, though ideas, techniques, and influences had spread throughout the Italian peninsula and even to the north and west. The outstanding architect of this period was Leon Battista Alberti (1404–72), whose treatise *On Building* (1452) remained the most influential work on the subject until the eighteenth century. Alberti consecrated the geometric principles laid down by Brunelleschi and infused them with a humanist spirit. He revived the classical dictum that a building, like a body, should have an even number of supports and, like a head, an odd number of openings. This furthered precise geometric calculations in scale and design. But it was in civic architecture that Alberti made his most significant contributions. Here he demonstrated how classical forms could be applied to traditional living space by being made purely decorative. His facade of the Palazzo Rucellai uses columns and arches not as building supports, but as embellishments that give geometric harmony to the building's appearance.

No sculptor challenged the preeminence of Donatello for another fifty years, but in painting there were many contenders for the garlands worn by Masaccio. The first was Piero della Francesca (ca. 1420–92) who, though trained in the tradition of Masaccio, broke new ground in his concern for the visual unity of his paintings. From portraits to processions to his stunning fresco *The Resurrection* (ca. 1463), Piero concen-

square in Padua. This enormous bronze horse and rider (1445–50) borrowed from surviving first- and second-century Roman models but relied upon the standpoint of the viewer to achieve its overpowering effect. This use of linear perspective was also a characteristic of Donatello's dramatic works, like the breathtaking altar scenes of the miracles of Saint Anthony in Padua, which resemble nothing so much as a canvas cast in bronze.

These altar scenes clearly evince the unmistakable influence of the paintings of Masaccio. Although he lived less than thirty years, Masaccio created an enduring legacy. His frescoes in the Brancacci Chapel in Florence were studied and sketched by all of the great artists of the next generation, who unreservedly praised his naturalism. What most claims the attention of the modern viewer is Masaccio's shading of light and shadow and his brilliant use of linear perspective to create

Botticelli's Primavera *(Spring), also called "Garden of Venus." Venus, in the center, is attended by the three Graces and by Cupid, Flora, Chloris, and Zephyr. Botticelli's figures have a dreamlike quality, an unreality highlighted by their beautiful faces and lithe figures.*

trated upon the most technical aspects of composition. He was influenced by Alberti's ideas about the geometry of form, and it is said that his measurements and calculations for various parts of *The Resurrection* took more time than the painting itself. Another challenger was Sandro Botticelli (1445–1510), whose classical themes, sensitive portraits, and bright colors set him apart from the line of Florentine painters with whom he studied. His mythologies *The Birth of Venus* and *Spring* (both ca. 1478) depart markedly from the naturalism inspired by Masaccio. Botticelli's paintings have a dreamlike quality, an unreality highlighted by the beautiful faces and lithe figures of his characters.

Botticelli's concern with beauty and personality is also seen in the paintings of Leonardo da Vinci (1452–1519), whose creative genius embodied the Renaissance ideal of the "universal man." Leonardo's achievements in scientific, technical, and artistic endeavors read like a list of all of the subjects known during the Renaissance. His detailed anatomical drawings and the method he devised for rendering them, his botanical observations, and his engineering inventions (including models for the tank and the airplane) testify to his unrestrained curiosity. His paintings reveal the scientific application of mathematics to matters of proportion and perspective. The dramatic fresco *The Last Supper* (ca. 1495–98), for example, takes the traditional scene of Christ and his disciples at a long table and divides it into four groups of three, each with its own separate action, leaving Christ to dominate the center of the picture by balancing its two sides. Leonardo's

Leonardo da Vinci's La Gioconda, *or* Mona Lisa.

THE RENAISSANCE MAN

Giorgio Vasari celebrated the creativity of the artists who made Italy the center of cultural activity in the later Middle Ages. His commemoration of their achievements through the medium of biographies helped to create the aura that still surrounds Renaissance art.

The most heavenly gifts seem to be showered on certain human beings. Sometimes supernaturally, marvelously, they all congregate in one individual. Beauty, grace, and talent are combined in such bounty that in whatever that man undertakes, he outdistances all other men and proves himself to be specially endowed by the hand of God. He owes his pre-eminence not to human teaching or human power. This was seen and acknowledged by all men in the case of Leonardo da Vinci, who had, besides the beauty of his person (which was such that it has never been sufficiently extolled), an indescribable grace in every effortless act and deed. His talent was so rare that he mastered any subject to which he turned his attention. Extraordinary strength and remarkable facility were here combined. He had a mind of regal boldness and magnanimous daring. His gifts were such that his celebrity was worldwide, not only in his own day, but even more after his death, and so will continue until the end of time.

Leonardo was frequently occupied in the preparation of plans to remove mountains or to pierce them with tunnels from plain to plain. By means of levers, cranes, and screws, he showed how to lift or move great weights. Designing dredging machines and inventing the means of drawing water from the greatest depths were among the speculations from which he never rested. Many drawings of these projects exist which are cherished by those who practice our arts. . . .

Leonardo, with his profound comprehension of art, began many things that he never completed, because it seemed to him that perfection must elude him. He frequently formed in his imagination enterprises so difficult and so subtle that they could not be entirely realized and worthily executed by human hands. His conceptions were varied to infinity. In natural philosophy, among other things, he examined plants and observed the stars—the movements of the planets, the variations of the moon, and the course of the sun. . . .

From Giorgio Vasari, *Lives of the Most Eminent Painters, Sculptors, and Architects.*

---

psychological portrait *La Gioconda* (1503–06), popularly called the Mona Lisa, is quite possibly the best-known picture in the Western world.

From Brunelleschi to Alberti, from Masaccio to Leonardo da Vinci, Renaissance artists placed a unique stamp upon visual culture. By reviving classical themes, geometric principles, and a spirit of human vitality they broke decisively from the dominant medieval traditions. Art became a source of individual and collective pride, produced by masters but consumed by all. Cities and wealthy patrons commissioned great works of art for public display. New buildings rose everywhere, adorned with the statues and murals that still stand as a testimony to generations of artists.

Michelangelo

The artistic achievements of the Renaissance culminated in the creative outpourings of Michelangelo Buonarroti (1475–1564). It is almost as if the age itself had produced a summation of how it wished to be remembered. Uncharacteristically, Michelangelo came from a family of standing in Florentine society and gained his apprenticeship over the opposition of his father. He claimed to have imbibed his love of sculpture from the milk of his wet nurse, who was the wife of a stonecutter. In 1490 Michelangelo gained a place in the household of Lorenzo de' Medici, thus avoiding the long years of apprenticeship during which someone else's style was implanted upon a young artist.

In 1496 Michelangelo moved to Rome. There his abilities as a sculptor brought him a commission from a French cardinal for a religious work in the classical style, which Michelangelo named the *Pietà*. Although this was his first attempt at sculpting a work of religious art, Michelangelo would never surpass it in beauty or composition. The *Pietà* created a sensation in Rome, and by the time that Michelangelo returned to Florence in 1501, at the age of twenty-six, he was already acknowledged as one of the great sculptors of his day. He was immediately commissioned to work on an enormous block of marble that had been quarried near-

The creation of Adam and Eve, a detail from Michelangelo's frescoes on the ceiling of the Sistine Chapel. The Sistine frescoes had become obscured by dirt and layers of varnish and glue applied at various times over the years. In the 1980s they were cleaned to reveal their original colors.

ly a half-century before and had defeated the talents of a series of carvers. He worked continuously for three years on his *David* (1501–04), a piece that completed the union between classical and Renaissance styles. Michelangelo's giant nude gives eloquent expression to his belief that the human body is the "mortal veil" of the soul.

Although Michelangelo always believed himself to be primarily a sculptor, his next outstanding work was in the field of painting. In 1508 Pope Julius II commissioned Michelangelo to decorate the small ceremonial chapel that had been built next to the new papal residence. The initial plan called for figures of the twelve apostles to adorn the ceiling, but Michelangelo soon launched a more ambitious scheme: to portray, in an extended narrative, human creation and those Old Testament events that foreshadowed the birth of Christ. Everything about the execution of the Sistine Chapel paintings was extraordinary. First, Michelangelo framed his scenes within the architecture of a massive classical temple. In this way he was able to give the impression of having flattened the rounded surface on which he worked. Then, on the two sides of the central panels, he represented figures of Hebrew prophets and pagan Sybils as sculptured marble statues. Finally, within the center panels came his fresco scenes of the events

of the creation and of human history from the Fall to the Flood. His representations were simple and compelling: the fingers of God and Adam nearly touching; Eve with one leg still emerging from Adam's side; the half-human snake in the temptation are all majestically evocative.

The *Pietà,* the *David,* and the paintings of the Sistine Chapel were the work of youth. Michelangelo's crowning achievement—the building of Saint Peter's—was undertaken at the age of seventy-one. The purpose of the church was to provide a suitable monument for the grave of Saint Peter. The basework had already been laid, and drawings for the building's completion had been made thirty years earlier by Donato Bramante. Michelangelo altered these plans in an effort to bring more light within the church and provide a more majestic facade outside. His main contribution, however, was the design of the great dome, which centered the interior of the church on Saint Peter's grave. More than the height, it is the harmony of Michelangelo's design that creates the sense of the building thrusting upward like a Gothic cathedral of old. The dome on Saint Peter's was the largest then known and provided the model, in succeeding generations, for Saint Paul's Cathedral in London and the U.S. Capitol building in Washington, D.C.

Renaissance art served Renaissance society. It reflected both its concrete achievements and its visionary ideals. It was a synthesis of old and new, building upon classical models, particularly in sculpture and architecture, but adding newly discovered techniques and skills. Demanding patrons like Pope Julius II, who commonly interrupted Michelangelo's work on the Sistine Chapel with criticisms and suggestions, fueled the remarkable growth in both the quantity and quality of Renaissance art. When Giorgio Vasari (1511–74) came to write his *Lives of the Great Painters, Sculptors, and Architects* (1550), he found over two hundred artists worthy of distinction. But Renaissance artists did more than construct and adorn buildings or celebrate and beautify spiritual life. Inevitably their work expressed the ideals and aspirations of the society in which they lived, the new emphasis upon learning and knowledge; upon the here and now rather than the hereafter; and most importantly, upon humanity and its capacity for growth and perfection.

Renaissance Ideals

Renaissance thought went hand in glove with Renaissance art. Scholars and philosophers searched the works of the ancients to find the principles on which to build a better life. They scoured monastic libraries for forgotten manuscripts, discovering among other things Greek poetry and history, the works of Homer and Plato, and Aristotle's *Poetics*. Their rigorous application of scholarly procedures for the collection and collation of these texts was one of the most important contributions of those Renaissance intellectuals who came to be known as humanists. Humanism developed in reaction to an intellectual world that was centered on the Church and dominated by otherworldly concerns. Humanism was secular in outlook, though by no means was it antireligious.

Humanists celebrated worldly achievements. Pico della Mirandola's *Oration on the Dignity of Man* (1486) is the best known of a multitude of Renaissance writings influenced by the discovery of the works of Plato. Pico believed that people could perfect their existence on earth because humans were divinely endowed with the capacity to determine their own fate. "O highest and most marvelous felicity of man! To him it is granted to have whatever he chooses, to be whatever he wills."

Thus humanists studied and taught the humanities—the skills of disciplines like philology, the art of language, and rhetoric, the art of expression. Although they were mostly laymen, humanists applied their learning to both religious and secular studies. Humanists were not antireligious. Although they reacted strongly against Scholasticism (see chapter 14), they were heavily indebted to the work of medieval churchmen, and most were devoutly religious. Nor were they hostile to the Church. Petrarch, Leonardo Bruni, and Leon Battista Alberti were all employed by the papal court at some time in their careers, as was Lorenzo Valla, the most influential of the humanists. Their interest in human achievement and human potential must be set beside their religious beliefs. As Petrarch stated quite succinctly: "Christ is my God; Cicero is the prince of the language I use."

Humanists and the Liberal Arts

The most important achievements of humanist scholars centered on ancient texts. It was the humanists' goal to discover as much as had survived from the ancient world and to provide texts of classical authors that were as full and accurate as possible. Although much was already known of the Latin classics, few of the central works of ancient Greece had been uncovered. Humanists preserved this heritage by reviving the study of the Greek language and by translating Greek authors into Latin. After the fall of Constantinople in 1453, Italy became the center for Greek studies as Byzantine scholars fled the Ottoman conquerors. Humanists also introduced historical methods in studying and evaluating texts, establishing principles for determining which of many manuscript copies of an ancient text was the oldest, the most accurate, and the least corrupted by copyists. This was of immense importance in studying the writings of the ancient Fathers of the Church, many of whose manuscripts had not been examined for centuries. The humanists' emphasis upon the humanistic disciplines fostered new educational ideals. Along with the study of theology, logic, and natural philosophy that had dominated the medieval university, humanist scholars stressed the importance of grammar, rhetoric, moral philosophy, and history. They believed that the study of these "liberal arts" should be undertaken for its own sake. This gave a powerful boost to the ideal of the perfectability of the individual that appeared in so many other aspects of Renaissance culture.

Humanists furthered the secularization of Renaissance society through their emphasis on the study of the classical world. The rediscovery of Latin texts during the later Middle Ages spurred interest in all things ancient. Petrarch, who is rightly called the father of humanism, revered the great Roman rhetorician Cicero above all others. For Petrarch, Cicero's legacy was eloquence. He stressed this in his correspondence with the leading scholars of his day and taught it to those who would succeed him. From 1350 to 1450, Cicero was the dominant model for Renaissance poets and orators. Petrarch's emphasis upon language led to efforts to recapture the purity of ancient Latin and Greek, languages that had become corrupted over the centuries. The leading humanist in the generation after Petrarch was Leonardo Bruni (1370–1444), who was reputed to be the greatest Greek scholar of his day. He translated both Plato and Aristotle and did much to advance mastery of classical Greek and foster the ideas of Plato in the late fifteenth century.

The study of the origins of words, their meaning and their proper grammatical usage, may seem an unusual foundation for one of the most vital of all European intellectual movements. But philology was the humanists' chief concern. This can best be illustrated by the work of Lorenzo Valla (1407–57). Valla was brought up in Rome, where he was largely self-educated, though according to the prescriptions of the Floren-

A miniature portrait of Petrarch is seen within the illuminated initial A *in a manuscript of the poet's treatise* De remediis utriusque fortunae *(Remedies Against Fortune).*

tine humanists. Valla entered the service of Alfonso I, king of Naples, and applied his humanistic training to affairs of state. The kingdom of Naples bordered on the Papal States, and its kings were in continual conflict with the papacy. The pope asserted the right to withhold recognition of the king, a right that was based upon the jurisdictional authority supposedly ceded to the papacy by the Emperor Constantine in the fourth century. This so-called Donation of Constantine had long been a matter of dispute, and its authenticity had been challenged frequently in the Middle Ages. But those challenges were made on political grounds, and the arguments of papal supporters were as strenuous as those of papal opponents. Valla settled the matter definitively. Applying historical and philological critiques to the text of the Donation, Valla proved that it could not have been written earlier than the eighth century, 400 years after Constantine's death. He exposed words and terms that had not existed in Roman times, like *fief* and *satrap,* and thus proved beyond doubt that the Donation was a forgery and papal claims based upon it were without merit.

Valla's career demonstrates the impact of humanist values on practical affairs. Although humanists were scholars, they made no distinction between an active and a contemplative life. A life of scholarship was a life of public service. They saw their studies as means of improving themselves and their society—"Man is born in order to be useful to man." This civic humanism is best expressed in the writings of Leon Battista Alberti (1404–72), whose treatise *On the Family* (1443) is a classic study of the new urban values, especially prudence and thrift. Alberti extolled the virtues of "the fatherland, the public good, and the benefit of all citizens." An architect, a mathematician, a poet, a playwright, a musician, and an inventor, Alberti was one of the great virtuosi of the Renaissance.

Alberti's own life might have served as a model for the most influential of all Renaissance tracts, Baldesar Castiglione's *The Courtier* (1528). While Alberti directed his lessons to the private lives of successful urban families, Castiglione (1478–1529) directed his to the public life of the aspiring elite. In Castiglione's view, the perfect courtier was as much born as made: "Besides his noble birth I would have the Courtier endowed by nature not only with talent and beauty of person and feature, but with a certain grace and air that shall make him at first sight pleasing." Everything that the courtier did was to maintain his pleasing grace and his public reputation. *The Courtier* was an etiquette book, and in it Castiglione prescribed every detail of

Portrait of Baldesar Castiglione *by Raphael.*

organ of Florentine government that had responsibility for war and diplomacy. Here Machiavelli received his education in practical affairs. His special interest was in the militia, and he was an early advocate of organizing and training Florentine citizens to defend the city rather than hiring mercenaries. He drafted position papers on the tense international situation that followed the French invasion of Italy in 1494. Machiavelli devoted all his energies and his entire intellect to his career. He was a tireless correspondent, and he began to collect materials for various tracts on military matters. He also planned out a prospective history in which to celebrate the greatness of the Florentine republic that he served.

But as suddenly as Machiavelli rose to his position of power and influence, he fell from it. The militia that he had advocated and in part organized was soundly defeated by the Spaniards, and the Florentine republic fell. Machiavelli was summarily dismissed from office in 1512 and was imprisoned and tortured the following year. Released and banished from the city, he retired to a small country estate and turned his restless

the education necessary for the ideal state servant, from table manners to artistic attainments. Although each talent was to be acquired through careful study and application, it was to be manifested with *sprezzatura,* a natural ease and superiority that was the essence of the gentleman.

Machiavelli and Politics

At the same time that Castiglione was drafting a blueprint for the idealized courtier, Niccolò Machiavelli (1469–1527) was laying the foundation for the realistic sixteenth-century ruler. No Renaissance work has been more important or more controversial than Machiavelli's *The Prince* (1513). Its vivid prose, its epigrammatic advice—"Men must either be pampered or crushed"—and its clinical dissection of power politics have attracted generation after generation of readers. With Machiavelli begins the science of politics.

Machiavelli came from an established Florentine family and entered state service as an assistant to one of his teachers, who then recommended him for the important office of secretary to the Council of Ten, the

Portrait of Niccolò Machiavelli, who expounded his theory of statecraft in The Prince.

THE LION AND THE FOX

❧

Niccolò Machiavelli wrote The Prince *in 1513 while he was under house arrest. It is one of the classics of Western political theory in which the author separates the political from the moral.*

Everyone understands how praiseworthy it is in a prince to keep faith, and to live uprightly and not craftily. Nevertheless we see, from what has taken place in our own days, that princes who have set little store by their word, but have known how to overreach men by their cunning, have accomplished great things, and in the end got the better of those who trusted to honest dealing.

Be it known, then, that there are two ways of contending—one in accordance with the laws, the other by force; the first of which is proper to men, the second to beasts. But since the first method is often ineffectual, it becomes necessary to resort to the second. A prince should, therefore, understand how to use well both the man and the beast. . . . But inasmuch as a prince should know how to use the beast's nature wisely, he ought of beasts to choose both the lion and the fox; for the lion cannot guard himself from the toils, nor the fox from wolves. He must therefore be a fox to discern toils, and a lion to drive off wolves.

To rely wholly on the lion is unwise; and for this reason a prudent prince neither can nor ought to keep his word when to keep it is hurtful to him and the causes which led him to pledge it are removed. If all men were good, this would not be good advice, but since they are dishonest and do not keep faith with you, you in return need not keep faith with them.

From Niccolò Machiavelli, *The Prince.*

---

energies to writing. Immediately he began work on what became his two greatest works, *The Prince* and the *Discourses on Livy* (1519).

Machiavelli has left a haunting portrait of his life in exile, and it is important to understand how intertwined his studies of ancient and modern politics were.

> On the coming of evening, I return to my house and enter my study; and at the door I take off the day's clothing, covered with mud and dust, and put on garments regal and courtly; and reclothed appropriately, I enter the ancient courts of ancient men, where, received by them with affection, I feed on that food which only is mine and which I was born for. For four hours of time I do not feel boredom, I forget every trouble, I do not dread poverty, I am not frightened by death; entirely I give myself over to them.

In this state of mind *The Prince* was composed.

The Prince is a handbook for a ruler who would establish a lasting government. It attempts to set down principles culled from historical examples and contemporary events to aid the prince in attaining and maintaining power. By study of these precepts and by their swift and forceful application, Machiavelli believed that the prince might even control fortune itself. *The Prince* is purely secular in content and philosophy. Where the medieval writer of a manual for princes would have stressed the divine foundations of the state, Machiavelli asserted the human bases: "The chief foundations on which all states rest are good laws and good arms." What made *The Prince* so remarkable in its day, and what continues to enliven debate over it, is that Machiavelli was able to separate all ethical considerations from his analysis. Whether this resulted from cynicism or from his own expressed desire for realism, Machiavelli uncompromisingly instructed the would-be ruler to be half man and half beast—to conquer neighbors, to murder enemies, and to deceive friends. Steeped in the humanist ideals of fame and *virtù*—a combination of virtue and virtuosity, of valor, character, and ability—he sought to reestablish Italian rule and place government upon a stable, scientific basis that would end the perpetual conflict among the Italian city-states.

The careers of Lorenzo Valla and Niccolò Machiavelli both illustrate how humanists were able to bring the study of the liberal arts into the service of the state. Valla's philological studies had a vital impact on diplomacy; Machiavelli's historical studies were directly applicable to warfare. Humanists created a demand for learning that helps account for the growth of universities, the spread of literacy, and the rise of printing. They also created a hunger for knowledge that characterized intellectual life for nearly two centuries.

The Politics of the Italian City-States

Like studs on a leather boot, city-states dotted the Italian peninsula. They differed in size, shape, and form. Some were large seaports, others small inland villages; some cut wide swaths across the plains, others were tiny islands. The absence of a unifying central authority in Italy, resulting from the collapse of the Holy Roman Empire and the papal schism, allowed ancient guilds and confraternities to transform themselves into self-governing societies. By the beginning of the fifteenth century the Italian city-states were the center of power, wealth, and culture in the Christian world.

This dominion rested on several conditions. First, Italy's geographical position favored the exchange of resources and goods between the East and the West. Until the fifteenth century, and despite the crusading efforts of medieval popes, the East and the West fortified each other. A great circular trade had developed, encompassing the Byzantine Empire, the North African coastal states, and the Mediterranean nations of western Europe. The Italian peninsula dominated the circumference of that circle. Its port cities, Genoa and Venice especially, became great maritime powers through their trade in spices and minerals. Second, just beyond the peninsula to the north lay the vast and populous territories of the Holy Roman Empire. There the continuous need for manufactured goods, especially cloths and metals, was filled by long caravans that traveled from Italy through the Alps. Milan specialized in metal crafts. Florence was a financial capital as well as a center for the manufacture of fine luxury goods. Finally, the city-states and their surrounding areas were agriculturally self-sufficient.

Because of their accomplishments, we tend to think of these Italian city-states as small nations. Even the term *city-state* implies national identity. Each city-state governed itself according to its own rules and customs, and each defined itself in isolation from the larger regional or tribal associations that once prevailed. Indeed, the struggles of the city-states against one another speak eloquently of their local self-identification. Italy was neither a nation nor a people.

The Five Powers

Although there were dozens of Italian city-states, by the early fifteenth century five had emerged to dominate the politics of the peninsula. In the south was the kingdom of Naples, the only city-state governed by a hereditary monarchy. Its politics were mired by conflicts over its succession, and it was not until the Spaniard Alfonso I of Aragon (1442–58) secured the throne in 1443 that peace was restored. Bordering Naples were the Papal States, whose capital was Rome but whose territories stretched far to the north and lay on both sides of the spiny Apennine mountain chain that extends down the center of the peninsula. Throughout the fourteenth and early fifteenth centuries, the territories under the nominal control of the Church were largely independent and included such thriving city-states as Bologna, Ferrara, and Urbino. Even in Rome the weakened papacy had to contend with noble families for control of the city.

The three remaining dominant city-states were clustered together in the north. Florence, center of Renaissance culture, was one of the wealthiest cities of Europe before the devastations of the plague and the sustained economic downturn of the late fourteenth century. The city itself was inland and its main waterway, the Arno, ran to the sea through Pisa, whose subjugation in 1406 was a turning point in Florentine history. Nominally Florence was a republic, but during the fifteenth century it was ruled in effect by its principal banking family, the Medici.

To the north of Florence was the duchy of Milan, the major city in Lombardy. It too was landlocked, cut off from the sea by Genoa. But Milan's economic life was oriented northward to the Swiss and German towns beyond the Alps, and its major concern was preventing foreign invasions. The most warlike of the Italian cities, Milan was a despotism, ruled for nearly two centuries by the Visconti family.

The last of the five powers was the republic of Venice. Ideally situated at the head of the Adriatic Sea, Venice became the leading maritime power of the age. Until the fifteenth century, Venice had been less interested in securing a landed empire than in dominating a seaborne one. Its outposts along the Greek and Dalmatian coasts, and its favored position in Constantinople, were the source of vast mercantile wealth. The republic was ruled by a hereditary elite—headed by an elected doge, who was the chief magistrate of Venice—and a variety of small elected councils.

The political history of the Italian peninsula during the late fourteenth and early fifteenth centuries is one of unrelieved turmoil. Wherever we look, the governments of the city-states were threatened by foreign invaders, internal conspiracies, or popular revolts. By the middle of the fifteenth century, however, two trends were apparent amid this political chaos. The first was the consolidation of strong centralized governments within the large city-states. These took different forms but yielded a similar result—internal political stability. The return of the popes to Rome after the Great Schism restored the pope to the head of his temporal estates and began a long period of papal dominance over Rome and its satellite territories. In Milan, one of the great military leaders of the day, Francesco Sforza (1401–66), seized the reins of power. The succession of King Alfonso I in Naples ended a half-century of civil war. In both Florence and Venice the grip that the political elite held over high offices was tightened by placing greater power in small advisory councils and, in Florence, by the ascent to power of the Medici family. This process, known as the rise of signorial rule, made possible the establishment of a balance of power within the Italian peninsula.

It was the leaders of the Italian city-states who first perfected the art of diplomacy. Constant warfare necessitated continual alliances, and by the end of the fourteenth century the large city-states had begun the practice of keeping resident ambassadors at the major seats of power. This enhanced communication, a principal challenge in Renaissance diplomacy, and also provided leaders with accurate information about the conditions of potential allies and enemies. Diplomacy was both an offensive and a defensive weapon. This was especially so because the city-states hired their soldiers as contract labor. These mercenary armies, whose leaders were known as *condottieri* from the name of their contract, were both expensive and dangerous to maintain. If they did not bankrupt their employers, they might desert them or, even worse, turn on them.

Venice: A Seaborne Empire

Water was the source of the prosperity of Venice. Located at the head of the Adriatic Sea, the city is formed by a web of lagoons. Through its center snakes the Grand Canal, whose banks were lined with large and small buildings that celebrated its civic and mercantile power. At the Piazza San Marco stood the vast palace of the doge, elected leader of the republic, and the Basilica of Saint Mark, a domed church built in the Byzantine style. At the Rialto were the stalls of the bankers and moneylenders, less grand perhaps but no less important. Here, too, were the auction blocks for the profitable trade in European slaves, eastern European serfs, and battlefield captives who were sold into service in Egypt or Byzantium. On the eastern edge of the island city was the Arsenal, erected in the twelfth century to house the shipbuilding and arms manufacturing industries. Three centuries later it was the indus-

trial marvel of the world, where the Venetian great galleys were constructed with assembly-line precision.

Its prosperity based on trade rather than conquest, Venice enjoyed many natural advantages. Its position at the head of the Adriatic permitted access to the raw materials of both the East and the West. The rich Alpine timberland beyond the city provided the hardwoods necessary for shipbuilding. The hinterland population were steady consumers of grain, cloth, and the new manufactured goods—glass, silk, jewelry, and cottons—that came pouring onto the market in the later Middle Ages.

But the success of Venice owed more to its own achievements than to these rich inheritances. "It is the most triumphant city I have ever seen," wrote the Frenchman Philippe de Commynes at the end of the fifteenth century. The triumph of the Venetian state was the triumph of dedicated efficiency. The heart of its success lay in the way in which it organized its trade and its government. The key to Venetian trade was its privileged position with the Byzantine Empire. Through a treaty with the Byzantines, Venetian traders gained a competitive edge in the spice trade with the East. Venetians were the largest group of resident Europeans in Constantinople, and their personal contacts with eastern traders were an important part of their success. The spice trade was so lucrative that special ships were built to accommodate it. These galleys were constructed at public expense and doubled as the Venetian navy in times of war. By controlling these ships, the government strictly regulated the spice trade. Goods imported into or exported from Venice had to be carried in Venetian ships and be consigned by Venetian merchants. The trade in spices was carefully organized in other ways as well. Rather than allow the wealthiest merchants to dominate it, as they did in other cities, Venice specified the number of annual voyages and sold shares in them at auction based on a fixed price. This practice allowed big and small merchants to gain from the trade and encouraged all merchants to find other trading outlets.

Like its trade, Venetian government was also designed to disperse power. Although it was known as the Most Serene Republic, Venice was not a republic in the sense that we use the word; it was rather an oligarchy—a government administered by a restricted group. Political power was vested in a Great Council whose membership had been fixed at the end of the thirteenth century. All males whose fathers enjoyed the privilege of membership in the Great Council were registered at birth in the "Book of Gold" and became members of the Great Council when adults. There

A view of the original Rialto bridge in Venice, painted by Carpaccio in 1494, when Venice was at the height of its imperial power.

were no further distinctions of rank within this nobility, whose members varied widely in wealth and intermarried freely with other groups in the society. From the body of the Great Council, which numbered about twenty-five hundred at the end of the fifteenth century, was chosen the Senate—a council about one-tenth the size, whose members served a one-year term. It was from the Senate that the true officers of government were selected: the doge, who was chosen for life; and members of a number of small councils, who administered affairs and advised the doge. Members of these councils were chosen by secret ballot in an elaborate process by which nominators were selected at random. Terms of office on the councils were extremely short in order to limit factionalism and to prevent any individual from gaining too much power. Venetian-style republicanism was admired throughout Europe.

With its mercantile families firmly in control of government and trade, Venice created an overseas empire in the east during the thirteenth and fourteenth centuries. Naval supremacy, based largely on technological advances that made long-distance and winter voyages possible, allowed the Venetians to offer protection to strategic outposts in return for either privileges or tribute. But in the fifteenth century, Venice turned to the west. In a dramatic reversal of its centuries-old policy, it began a process of conquest in Italy, an empire on terra firma, as Venetian islanders called it. There were several reasons for this new policy. First, the Venetian navy was no longer the unsurpassed power that it once had been. More importantly, mainland expansion offered new opportunities for Venice. Not all Venetians were traders, and the new industries that were being developed in the city could readily benefit from control of mainland markets. So could those Venetian nobles employed to administer the conquered lands. They argued persuasively that the supply of raw materials and foodstuffs on which Venetian trade ultimately depended should be secured by the republic itself. Most decisively of all, opportunity was knocking. In Milan, Visconti rule was weakening and the Milanese territories were ripe for picking.

Venice reaped a rich harvest. For the first half of the fifteenth century, the Most Serene Republic engaged in unremitting warfare. Its successes were remarkable. It pushed out to the north to occupy all the lands between the city and the Habsburg territories; it pushed to the east until it straddled the entire head of the Adriatic; and it pushed to the west almost as far as Milan itself. Venetian victories resulted from both the traditional use of hired mercenaries and from the Venetians' own ingenuity at naval warfare. Although Venice was creating a landed empire, the course of expansion, especially in Lombardy, was along river routes. At the Arsenal were built new oared vessels armed with artillery for river sieges. Soon the captured territories were paying for continued expansion. The western conquests in particular brought large populations under Venetian control which, along with their potential as a market, provided a ready source of taxation. By the end of the fifteenth century, the mainland dominions of Venice were contributing nearly 40 percent of the city's revenue at a cost far smaller than that of the naval empire a century earlier. Venice had become the most powerful city-state in Italy.

Florence: Spinning Cloth into Gold

"What city, not merely in Italy, but in all the world . . . is more proud in its palazzi, more bedecked with churches, more beautiful in its architecture, more imposing in its gates, richer in its piazzas, happier in its wide streets, greater in its people, more glorious in its citizenry, more inexhaustible in wealth, more fertile in its fields?" So boasted the humanist Coluccio Salutati (1331–1406) in 1403 during one of the most calamitous periods in Florentine history. Salutati's boastings were not unusual; the Florentines' mythical view of their homeland as savior of Christianity and as heir to the republican greatness of Rome was everywhere apparent. And it seemed to be most vigorously expressed in the city's darkest moments.

Florentine prosperity was built on two foundations: money and wool. Beginning in the thirteenth century, Florentine bankers were among the wealthiest and most powerful in the world. Initially their position was established through support of the papacy in its long struggle with the Holy Roman Empire. Florentine financiers established banks in all the capitals of Europe and the East, though their seats in Rome and Naples were probably most important. In the Middle Ages bankers had served more functions than simply handling and exchanging money. Most were also tied to mercantile adventures and underwrote industrial activity. So it was in Florence, where international bankers purchased high-quality wool to be manufactured into the world's finest woven cloth. At its height before the plague, the cloth industry employed nearly thirty thousand workers, providing jobs at all levels of society, from the rural women who spun the wool into yarn at piecework wages to the highly paid weavers and dyers whose skills made Florentine cloth so highly prized.

The activities of both commerce and cloth manufacture depended on external conditions, and thus the wealth of Florence was potentially unstable. In the mid-fourteenth century instability came with the plague that devastated the city. Nearly 40 percent of the entire population was lost in the single year 1348, and recurring outbreaks continued to ravage the already weakened survivors. Loss of workers and loss of markets seriously disrupted manufacturing. By 1380 cloth production had fallen to less than a quarter of pre-plague levels. On the heels of plague came wars. The property of Florentine bankers and merchants abroad was an easy target. Thirty years of warfare with Milan, interrupted by only a single decade of peace (1413–23), resulted in total bankruptcy for many of the city's leading commercial families. More significantly, the costs of warfare, offensive and defensive, created a massive public debt. Every Florentine of means owned shares in this debt, and the republic was continually

Painted terra-cotta bust of Lorenzo de' Medici by Andrea del Verrocchio.

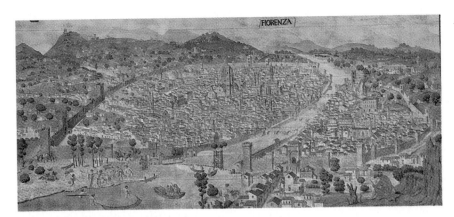

A view of Florence in 1490.

devising new methods for borrowing and staving off crises of repayment. Small wonder that the republic turned for aid to the wealthiest banking family in Europe, the Medici.

The ability of the Medici to secure a century-long dynasty in a government that did not have a head of state is just one of the mysteries surrounding the history of this remarkable family. Cosimo de' Medici (1389–1464) was one of the richest men in Christendom when he returned to the city in 1434 after a brief exile. His leading position in government rested upon supporters who were able to gain a controlling influence on the Signoria, the ruling Council in Florence's republican form of government. Cosimo built his party carefully, recruiting followers among the craftsmen whom he employed and even paying delinquent taxes to maintain the eligibility of his voters. Most importantly, emergency powers were invoked to reduce the number of citizens qualified to vote for the Signoria until the majority were Medici backers.

Cosimo was a practical man. He raised his children along humanist principles and was a great patron of artists and intellectuals. He collected books and paintings, endowed libraries, and spent lavishly on his own palace, the Palazzo Medici, which after his death was transformed into the very center of Florentine cultural life. Cosimo's position as an international banker brought him into contact with the heads of other Italian city-states and enabled him to negotiate peace treaties.

It was Cosimo's grandson Lorenzo (1449–92) who linked the family's name to that of the age. Lorenzo was trained to office as if he had been a prince rather than a citizen of a republic. His own father ruled for five years and used his son as a diplomat in order to acquaint him with the leaders of Europe. Diplomacy was Lorenzo's greatest achievement. He held strong humanist values instilled in him by his mother, Lucrezia Tornabuoni,

who organized his education. He wrote poetry and drama, and even entered competitions for architectural designs. But Lorenzo's chief contribution to artistic life as it reached its height in Florence was to facilitate its production. He brought Michelangelo and other leading artists to his garden; he brought Pico della Mirandola and other leading humanists to his table. He secured commissions for Florentine artists throughout the Italian peninsula, ensuring the spread of their influence and the continued regeneration of artistic creativity in Florence itself.

Lorenzo was generally regarded as the leading citizen of Florence, and this was true both in terms of his wealth and his influence. He did not rule from high office, though he maintained the party that his grandfather had built and even extended it through wartime emergency measures. His power was based on his personality and reputation, a charisma enhanced when he survived an assassination attempt in which his brother was killed. His diplomatic abilities were the key to his survival. Almost immediately after Lorenzo came to power, Naples and the papacy began a war with Florence, a war that was costly to the Florentines in both taxation and lost territory. In 1479 Lorenzo traveled to Naples and personally convinced the Neapolitan king to sign a separate treaty. This restored the Italian balance of power and ensured continued Medici rule in Florence. Soon Lorenzo even had a treaty with the pope that allowed for the recovery of lost territories and the expansion of Florentine influence. But two years after his death, the Italian peninsula was plunged into those wars that turned it from the center of European civilization into one of its lesser satellites.

The End of Italian Hegemony, 1450–1527

In the course of the Renaissance, western Europe was Italianized. For a century the city-states dominated the trade routes that connected the East and the West. Venetian and Genoese merchants exchanged spices and minerals from the Black Sea to the North Sea, enriching the material life of three continents. They brought wool from England and Spain to the skilled craftsmen in the Low Countries and Florence. Italian manufactures such as Milanese artillery, Florentine silk, and Venetian glass were prized above all others. The ducat and the florin, two Italian coins, were universally accepted in an age when every petty prince minted his own money. The Italian peninsula exported culture in the same way that it exported goods. Humanism quickly spread across the Alps, aided by the recent invention of printing (which the Venetians soon dominated), while Renaissance standards of artistic achievement were known worldwide and everywhere imitated. The city-states shared their technology as well. The compass and the navigational chart, projection maps, double-entry bookkeeping, eyeglasses, the telescope—all profoundly influenced what could be achieved and what could be hoped for. In this spirit Christopher Columbus—a Genoese seaman—successfully crossed the Atlantic under the Spanish flag, and Amerigo Vespucci—a Florentine merchant—gave his name to the newly discovered continents.

But it was not in Italy that the rewards of innovation or the satisfactions of achievement were enjoyed. There the seeds of political turmoil and military imperialism,

combined with the rise of the Ottoman Turks, were to reap a not-unexpected harvest. In 1454 the five powers agreed to the Peace of Lodi. This established two balanced alliances, one between Florence and Milan, the other between Venice and Naples. These states, along with the papacy, pledged mutual nonaggression, a policy that lasted for nearly forty years. But the Peace of Lodi did not bring peace. It only halted the long period in which the major city-states struggled against one another. Under cover of the peace, the large states continued the process of swallowing up their smaller neighbors and creating quasi-empires. This was a policy of imperialism as aggressive as that of any in the modern era. Civilian populations were overrun, local leaders exiled or exterminated, tribute money taken, and taxes levied. Each of the five states either increased its mainland territories or strengthened its hold upon them.

By the end of the fifteenth century the city-states eyed one another greedily and warily. Each expected the others to begin a peninsula-wide war for hegemony and took the steps that ultimately ensured the contest. Perhaps the most unusual aspect of the imperialism of the city-states was that it had been restricted to the Italian peninsula. Each of the major powers shared the dream of recapturing the glory that was Rome. Although the Venetians had expanded abroad, their acquisitions had not come through conquest or occupation. In their Greek and Dalmatian territories, local law and custom continued to govern under the benevolent eye of Venetian administrators. But in their mainland territories, the Venetians were as ruthless as the Florentines were in Pisa or as Cesare Borgia was in Romagna when he consolidated the Papal States by fire and sword. Long years of siege and occupation had militarized the Italian city-states. Venice and Florence balanced their budgets on the backs of their captured territories, Milan had been engaged in constant war for decades, and even the papacy was militarily aggressive.

And the Italians were no longer alone. The most remarkable military leader of the age was not a Renaissance *condottiere* but an Ottoman prince, Mehmed II (1451–81), who conquered Constantinople and Athens and threatened Rome itself. The rise of the Ottomans (whose name is derived from that of Osman, their original tribal leader) is one of the most compelling stories in world history. Little more than a warrior tribe at the beginning of the fourteenth century, 150 years later the Ottomans had replaced stagnant Byzantine rule with a virile and potent empire. First they gobbled up towns and cities in a wide arc around Constantinople. Then they fed upon the Balkans and

Italy, 1494

THE SIEGE OF CONSTANTINOPLE

Mehmed II (1432–1481) was one of the great military geniuses of world history. He consolidated the expansion of the Ottoman Empire in Asia Minor and in 1453 organized the siege of Constantinople. He personally directed the combined land and naval assault and brilliantly improvised the tactics that led to the fall of the city. The fall of Constantinople to the Ottomans was a watershed. Kritovoulos was a Greek who entered the service of Mehmed II, probably after the siege. Though he was not an eyewitness of the fall of Constantinople, he gathered numerous accounts together in composing his history. In this selection he refers to the defenders of the city as Romans because Constantinople was what remained of the Roman Empire.

Sultan Mehmed considered it necessary in preparation for his next move to get possession of the harbor and open the Horn for his own ships to sail in. So, since every effort and device of his had failed to force the entrance, he made a wise decision, and one worthy of his intellect and power. It succeeded in accomplishing his purpose and in putting an end to all uncertainties.

He ordered the commanders of the vessels to construct as quickly as possible glideways leading from the outer sea to the inner sea. . . . He brought up the ships and placed large cradles under them, with stays against each of their sides to hold them up. And having under-girded them well with ropes, he fastened long cables to the corners and gave them to the soldiers to drag, some of them by hand, and others by certain machines and capstans.

So the ships were dragged along very swiftly. And their crews, as they followed them, rejoiced at the event and boasted of it. Then they manned the ships on the land as if they were on the sea. Some of them hoisted the sails with a shout, as if they were setting sail, and the breeze caught the sails and bellied them out. Others seated themselves on the benches, holding the oars in their hands and moving them as if rowing. And the commanders, running along by the sockets of the masts with whistlings and shouting, and with their whips beating the oarsmen on the benches, ordered them to row. The ships, borne along over the land as if on the sea, were some of them being pulled up the ascent to the top of the hill while others were being hauled down the slope into the harbor, lowering the sails with shouting and great noise.

It was a strange spectacle, and unbelievable in the telling except to those who actually did see it—the sight of ships borne along on the mainland as if sailing on the sea, with their crews and their sails and all their equipment. I believe this was a much greater feat than the cutting of a canal across at Athos by Xerxes, and much stranger to see and to hear about.

The Romans, when they saw such an unheard-of thing actually happen, and warships lying at anchor in the Horn—which they never would have suspected—were astounded at the impossibility of the spectacle, and were overcome by the greatest consternation and perplexity. They did not know what to do now, but were in despair. In fact they had left unguarded the walls along the Horn for a distance of about thirty stadia, and even so they did not have enough men for the rest of the walls, either for defense or for attack, whether citizens or men from elsewhere. Instead, two or even three battlements had but a single defender.

And now, when this sea-wall also became open to attack and had to be guarded, they were compelled to strip the other battlements and bring men there. This constituted a manifest danger, since the defenders were taken away from the rest of the wall while those remaining were not enough to guard it, being so few.

From Kritovoulos, *The History of Mehmed the Conquerer.*

---

the eastern kingdoms of Hungary and Poland. By 1400 they were a presence in all the territory that stretched from the Black Sea to the Aegean. By 1450 they were its master.

Venice was most directly affected by the Ottoman advance. Not only was its favored position in eastern trade threatened, but during a prolonged war at the end of the fifteenth century, the Venetians lost many of their most important commercial outposts. Ottoman might closed off the markets of eastern Europe. Islands in the Aegean Sea and seaports along the Dalmatian coast fell to the Turks in alarming succession. By 1480 Venetian naval supremacy was a thing of the past. (See "The Fall of Constantinople," pp. 346–347.)

✌ The Fall of Constantinople

The prayers of the devout were fervent on Easter Sunday in 1453. The Christians of Constantinople knew that it was only a matter of time before the last remaining stronghold of the Byzantine Empire came under siege. For decades the ring of Ottoman conquests had narrowed around this holy city until it alone stood out against the Turkish sultan. Constantinople, the bridge between Europe and Asia, was tottering. The once teeming center of Eastern Christianity had never recovered from the epidemics of the fourteenth century, and now dwindling revenues matched the dwindling population.

Perhaps it was this impoverishment that had kept the Turks at bay. Constantinople was still the best-fortified city in the world. Shaped like the head of a

horse, it was surrounded by water on all but one side, and that side was protected by two stout rings of walls separated by a trench lined with stones. No cannon forged in the West could dent these battlements, and no navy could hope to force its way through the narrow mouth of the Golden Horn. Thus an uneasy peace existed between sultan and emperor. It was shattered in 1451 with the accession of a new sultan, the nineteen-year-old Mehmed II. Mehmed's imagination was fired by the ancient prophecies that a Muslim would rule the East. Only Constantinople was a fitting capital for such an empire, and Mehmed immediately began preparations for its conquest.

In 1452 Mehmed had constructed a fortress at the narrow mouth of the Bosporus and demanded tribute from all ships that entered the Golden Horn. The Byzantine emperor sent ambassadors to Mehmed to protest this aggression. Mehmed returned their severed heads. When the first Venetian convoy refused to lower its sails, Mehmed's artillery efficiently sank one of the galleys with a single shot. The Turks now controlled access to the city for trade and supplies. An attack the following spring seemed certain.

The emperor appealed far and wide for aid: to the Venetians and Genoese to protect their trade and to the pope to defend Christianity. The Europeans were willing, but as yet they were unable. They did not think that the Ottomans could assemble an army before summer. By then an Italian armada could dislodge the Ottoman fortress and reinforce the city with trained fighting men.

But they hadn't reckoned with Mehmed. While the Italians bickered over the cost of the expedition and Christians everywhere made ready to celebrate Holy Week, the Ottomans assembled a vast army of fighters and laborers and a huge train of weapons and supplies. Among them was the largest cannon ever cast, with a 26-foot barrel that shot a 1200-pound ball. Fifty teams of oxen and 200 men took two months to pull it in place.

Mehmed's forces—which eventually numbered more than 150,000, of which 60,000 were soldiers—assembled around the walls of Constantino-ple on 5 April. During the next week a great flotilla sailed up the Bosporus and anchored just out of reach of the Byzantine warships in the Golden Horn. A census taken inside the city revealed that there were only 7000 able-bodied defenders—about 5000 Greek residents and 2000 foreigners, mostly Genoese and Venetians. These Italians were the only true soldiers among them.

Though the defenders were vastly outnumbered, they still held the military advantage. As long as their ships controlled the entrance to the Golden Horn, they could limit the Ottoman attack to only one side of the city, where all of the best defenders could be massed. The Byzantines cast a boom—an iron chain supported by wooden floats—across the mouth of the Horn to forestall a naval attack. By the middle of April, the Turks had begun their land assault. Each day great guns pounded the walls of the city, and each night residents worked frantically to repair the damage. Everyone con-tributed. Old women wove baskets in which chil-dren carried stones. Monks and nuns packed mud and cut branches to shore up the breaches in the wall. The Turks suffered heavily each time they attempted to follow a cannon shot with a massed charge, but the attack took its toll among the defenders as well. No one was safe from the flam-ing arrows and catapulted stones flung over the city's walls. Choking black smoke filled the air as the huge cannon shook the foundations of the city and treated its stout stone walls as if they were plaster. Nevertheless, for the first month of siege the defenders held their own.

The stubborn defense of the city infuriated Mehmed. As long as there was only one point of attack, the defenders could resist indefinitely. The line of assault had to be extended, and this could only be done by sea. With the boom effectively impregnable and with Italian seamen superior to the Turks, the prospects seemed dim. But what could not be achieved by force might be achieved by intel-ligence. Mehmed devised a plan to carry a number of smaller ships across land and then to float them

behind the Christian fleet. Protected by land forces, the ships could be used as a staging point for anoth-er line of attack. Thousand of workmen built huge wooden rollers, which were greased with animal fat. Under cover of darkness and the smoke of cannon fire, 72 ships were pulled up the steep hills and pushed down into the sea. Once they were safely anchored, a pontoon bridge was built and cannon were trained on the seaward walls of the city.

By now the city had withstood siege for nearly six weeks without any significant reinforcement. At the end of May there was a sudden lull. A messenger from the sultan arrived to demand surrender. The choice was clear. If the city was taken by force, the customary three days of unrestricted pillage would be allowed; but if it yielded, the sultan pledged to protect the property of all who desired to remain under his rule. The emperor replied feebly that no one who had ever laid siege to Constantinople had enjoyed a long life. He was ready to die in defense of his capital.

On 30 May the final assault began. Mehmed knew that his advantage lay in numbers. First he sent in waves of irregular troops, mostly captured slaves and Christians, who suffered great losses and were finally driven back by the weakened defenders. Next, better-trained warriors attacked and widened the breaches made by the irregulars. Finally came the crack Janissaries, the sultan's elite warriors, disci-plined from birth to fight. It was the Janissaries who found a small door left open at the base of the wall. In they rushed, quickly overwhelming the first line of defenders and battering their way through the weaker second walls. By dawn the Ottoman flag was raised over the battlements and the sack of Constan-tinople had begun.

There was no need for the customary three days of pillage. By the end of the first day there was noth-ing left worth taking. The churches and monasteries had been looted and defaced, the priests and nuns murdered or defiled, and thousands of civilians had been captured to be sold into slavery. Large areas of the city smoldered from countless fires. The bastion of Eastern Christendom was no more.

The Italian city-states might have met this challenge from the east had they been able to unite in opposing it. Successive popes pleaded for holy wars to halt the advance of the Turks, which was compared in officially inspired propaganda to an outbreak of plague. The fall of Constantinople in 1453 was an event of epochal proportions for Europeans, many believing that it fore-shadowed the end of the world. "A thing terrible to relate and to be deplored by all who have in them any spark of humanity. The splendor and glory of the East has been captured, despoiled, ravaged and completely sacked by the most inhuman barbarians," the Venetian doge was informed. Yet it was Italians rather than Ottomans who plunged the Italian peninsula into those wars from which it never recovered.

The Wars of Italy (1494–1529) began when Naples, Florence, and the Papal States united against Milan. At first this alliance seemed little more than another shift in the balance of power. But rather than call upon Venice to redress the situation, the Milanese leader, Ludovico il Moro, sought help from the French. An army of French cavalry and Swiss mercenaries, led by Charles VIII of France (1483–98), invaded the Italian peninsula in 1494. With Milanese support the French swept all before them. Florence was forced to surrender Pisa, a humiliation that led to the overthrow of the Medici and the establishment of French sovereignty. The Papal States were next to be occupied, and within a year Charles had conquered Naples without engaging the Italians in a single significant battle. Unfortunately, the Milanese were not the only ones who could play at the game of foreign alliances. Next, it was the turn of the Venetians and the pope to unite and call upon the services of King Ferdinand of Aragon and the Holy Roman Emperor. Italy was now a battleground in what became a total European war for dynastic supremacy. The city-states used their foreign allies to settle old scores and to extend their own mainland empires. At the turn of the century Naples was dismembered. In 1509 the pope conspired to organize the most powerful combination of forces yet known against Venice. All of the "terra firma" possessions of the Most Serene Repub-lic were lost, but by a combination of good fortune and skilled diplomacy Venice itself survived. Florence was less fortunate, becoming a pawn first of the French and then of the Spanish. The final blow to Italian hegemo-ny was the sack of Rome in 1527, when German mer-cenaries fulfilled the fears of what the "infidels" would do to the Holy City.

Surveying the wreckage of the Italian wars, Machi-avelli ended *The Prince* with a plea for a leader to emerge to restore Italian freedom and re-create the unity of the ancient Roman republic. He concluded with these lines from Petrarch:

> *Then virtue boldly shall engage*
> *And swiftly vanquish barbarous rage,*
> *Proving that ancient and heroic pride*
> *In true Italian hearts had never died.*

The revival of "ancient and heroic pride" fueled the Italian Renaissance. The sense of living in a new age, the spirit of human achievement, and the curiosity and wonderment of writers and artists all characterized the Renaissance. The desire to re-create the glories of Rome was not Machiavelli's alone. It could be seen in the palaces of the Italian aristocracy; in the papal rebuilding of the Holy City; and in the military ambi-tions of princes. But the legacy of empire, of "ancient and heroic pride," had passed out of Italian hands.

Suggestions for Further Reading

General Reading

Ernst Breisach, *Renaissance Europe, 1300–1517* (New York: Macmillan, 1973). A solid survey of the political histo-ry of the age.

* Denys Hay, *The Italian Renaissance* (Cambridge: Cam-bridge University Press, 1977). An elegant interpretive essay. The best first book to read.

* John Stephens, *The Italian Renaissance : The Origins of Intellectual and Artistic Change Before the Reformation* (New York: Longman, 1990). A recent survey of the period with up-to-date interpretations of major issues.

* P. Burke, *Culture and Society in Renaissance Italy* (Princeton, NJ: Princeton University Press, 1987). A good introduction to social and intellectual developments.

* Eugenio Garin, ed., *Renaissance Characters* (Chicago: University of Chicago Press, 1991). Studies of prototypical Renaissance figures from courtiers to courtesans, by leading historians.

Renaissance Society

* M. Aston, *The Fifteenth Century: The Prospect of Europe* (London: Thames and Hudson, 1968). A concise survey of continental history; well written and well illustrated.

* J. R. Hale, *Renaissance Europe: The Individual and Soci-ety* (Berkeley: University of California Press, 1978). A lively study that places the great figures of the Renaissance in their social context.

* Carlo Cippola, *Before the Industrial Revolution: European Society and Economy, 1000–1700* (New York: Norton, 1976). A sweeping survey of social and economic developments across the centuries.

* Harry Miskimin, *The Economy of Early Renaissance Europe, 1300–1460* (Englewood Cliffs, NJ: Prentice Hall, 1969). A detailed scholarly study of economic development.

* D. Herlihy & C. Klapiche-Zuber, *The Tuscans and Their Families* (New Haven, CT: Yale University Press, 1985). Difficult but rewarding study of the social and demographic history of Florence and its environs.

* Christiane Klapiche-Zuber, *Women, Family, and Ritual in Renaissance Italy* (Chicago: University of Chicago Press, 1985). A sparkling collection of essays on diverse topics in social history from wet-nursing to family life.

* Margaret L. King, *Women of the Renaissance* (Chicago: University of Chicago Press, 1991). Most recent study by a leading women's historian.

Renaissance Art

* Michael Baxandall, *Painting and Experience in Fifteenth Century Italy* (Oxford: Oxford University Press, 1972). A study of the relationship between painters and their patrons, of how and why art was produced.

Frederick Hartt, *History of Italian Renaissance Art* (Englewood Cliffs, NJ: Prentice Hall, 1974). The most comprehensive survey, with hundreds of plates.

* Michael Levey, *Early Renaissance* (London: Penguin Books, 1967). A concise survey of art; clearly written and authoritative.

* Rudolph Wittkower, *Architectural Principles in the Age of Humanism* (New York: Norton, 1971). A difficult but rewarding study of Renaissance architecture.

* Roberta Olson, *Italian Renaissance Sculpture* (New York: Thames and Hudson, 1992). Well illustrated and easy to read. The best introduction to the subject.

* Linda Murray, *High Renaissance and Mannerism* (London: Thames and Hudson, 1985). The best introduction to late Renaissance art.

* Howard Hibbard, *Michelangelo* (New York: Harper & Row, 1974). A compelling biography of an obsessed genius.

Renaissance Ideals

* Hans Baron, *The Crisis of the Early Italian Renaissance* (Princeton, NJ: Princeton University Press, 1966). One of the most influential intellectual histories of the period.

* Ernst Cassirer, ed., *The Renaissance Philosophy of Man* (Chicago: University of Chicago Press, 1948). An outstanding selection of writings from the leading Renaissance humanists.

* George Holmes, *The Florentine Enlightenment, 1400–1450,* 2d ed. (Oxford: Clarendon Press, 1992). A new edition of the best study of intellectual developments in Florence.

Donald R. Kelley, *Renaissance Humanism* (Boston: Twayne Publishers, 1991). A thorough account of humanist thought by a leading intellectual historian.

Albert Rabil, ed., *Renaissance Humanism* (Philadelphia: University of Pennsylvania Press, 1988). A multi-authored, multivolume collection of essays on humanism with all of the latest scholarship.

* Quentin Skinner, *Machiavelli* (Oxford: Oxford University Press, 1981). A brief but brilliant life.

The Politics of the Italian City-States

* Lauro Martines, *Power and Imagination: City-States in Renaissance Italy* (New York: Alfred A. Knopf, 1979). An important interpretation of the politics of the Italian powers.

* Frederic C. Lane, *Venice: A Maritime Republic* (Baltimore, MD: Johns Hopkins University Press, 1973). A complete history of Venice that stresses its naval and mercantile developments.

* Gene Brucker, *Renaissance Florence,* 2d ed. (Berkeley: University of California Press, 1983). The best single-volume introduction to Florentine history.

* J. R. Hale, *Florence and the Medici* (London: Thames and Hudson, 1977). A compelling account of the relationship between a city and its most powerful citizens.

*Paperback edition available.

12 ❧ THE EUROPEAN EMPIRES

Ptolemy's World

For over a thousand years, educated Europeans thought of the world as it had been described by Ptolemy in the second century. Most of their knowledge came from guesswork rather than observation. The world was a big place when you had to cross it on foot or by four-legged beast, or in small rickety vessels that hugged the shoreline as they sailed. Those without education lived in a world bounded by their farm or their village and thought of neighboring cities as faraway places. There were few experiences to pass from generation to generation, and those that were handed down changed from fact to fancy in the retelling. The people of the Renaissance probably knew less for certain about the planet they inhabited than had the Greeks, and the Greeks knew precious little. But lack of knowledge did not cause confusion. People who lived at the end of the fifteenth century knew enough to conduct their affairs and to dream their dreams.

The map here depicts the image of the world that Ptolemy bequeathed, the world that the Renaissance inherited with Ptolemy's calculations and writings. The first thing to notice is that it is shaped like a sphere. Though popular myth, confirmed by common sense, held that the world was flat and that one could theoretically fall off its edges, educated Europeans understood that it was spherical. Ptolemy had portrayed the earth as an irregular semicircle divided into degrees of longitude, beginning with 0° in the west, where Europe was situated, and progressing to 180° in the east. His construction of latitude was less certain, for less was known (then as now) about the extreme north and south. But Ptolemy did locate an equator, somewhat off center, and he portrayed as accurately as he could what was known of the European landmass. Scandinavia in the north and England and Ireland, set off from the Continent and from each other, are readily visible. The contours of Spain in the southwest are clear, though distorted. As the ancient world centered on the Mediterranean (literally, "in the middle of the earth") it was the area most accurately reconstructed. Italy, Greece, and Asia Minor are easily recognizable, while France and Spain stretch out of shape like taffy. The size of the Mediterranean is grossly overestimated, its coastline occupying nearly a quarter of the map.

Africa, too, is swollen. It spans the too-wide Mediterranean and then balloons out to cover the entire southern hemisphere. Its eastern portions stretch into Asia, though so little is certain that they are labeled *terra incognita*—unknown lands. Europe, Africa, and Asia are the only continents. They are watered by a single ocean whose name changes with the languages of its neighboring inhabitants. Most remarkable of all is the division of the earth's surface. Land covers three-quarters of it. This was the world as it was known in 1400, and this was why the ensuing century would be called the age of exploration.

European Encounters

There were many reasons why this map of the world changed in the early sixteenth century. It was an age of exploration in many ways. Knowledge bequeathed from the past created curiosity about the present. Technological change made long sea voyages possible, and the demands of commerce provided incentives. Ottoman expansion on the southern and eastern frontiers of the Continent threatened access to the goods of the East on which Europeans had come to rely. Spices were rare and expensive, but they were not merely luxuries. While nobles and rich merchants consumed them lavishly to enhance their reputations for wealth and generosity, spices had many practical uses. Some acted as preservatives, others as flavorings to make palatable the rotting foodstuffs that were the fare of even the wealthiest Europeans. Others were used as perfumes to battle the noxious gases that rose from urban streets and invaded homes and workplaces. The drugs of the East, the nature of which we can only guess at, helped soothe chronic ill health. The demand for all of these "spices" continued to rise at a greater rate than their supply. There was more than a fortune to be made by anyone who could participate in the trade.

Eastern spices were expensive. Most European manufactured goods had little utility in the East. Woven wool, which was the staple of western industry, was too heavy to be worn in eastern climes. Both silk and cotton came from the East and were more expertly spun there. Even western jewelry relied upon imported stones. While metalwork was an attractive commodity for export, the dilemma of the arms trade was as acute then as it is now. Providing Ottomans or other Muslims with weapons to wage holy wars against Christian Europe posed problems of policy and morality. And once the Ottomans began to cast great bronze cannon of their own, European arms were less eagerly sought. Western gold and silver flowed steadily east. As supplies of precious metals dwindled, economic growth in Europe slowed. Throughout the fifteenth century, ever larger amounts of western specie were necessary to purchase ever smaller amounts of eastern commodities. Europe faced a severe shortage of gold and silver, a shortage that threatened its standard of living and its prospects for economic growth. The search was on to discover new sources of gold.

A Passage to India

It was the Portuguese who made the first dramatic breakthroughs in exploration and colonization. Perched on the southwestern tip of Europe, Portugal was an agriculturally poor and sparsely populated nation. Among its few marketable commodities were fish and wine, which it traded with Genoese and Venetian galleys making their voyages to northern Europe. Portugal's North African trade was more lucrative, but extended warfare between Christians and Muslims had made it unreliable. The Portuguese had long been sea explorers, especially in the Atlantic Ocean, where they had established bases in the Azores and Madeira islands. Their small ships, known as caravels, were ideal for ocean travel, and their navigators were among the most skillful in the world. Yet they were unable to participate in the lucrative Mediterranean trade in bullion and spices until the expanding power of the Ottomans threatened the traditional eastern sea routes.

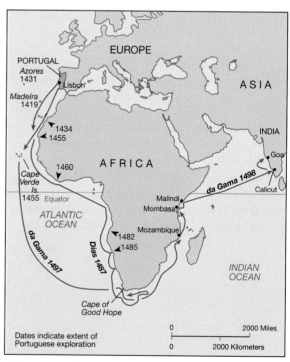

Portuguese Explorations

In the early fifteenth century, the Portuguese gained a foothold in northern Africa and used it to stage voyages along the continent's unexplored western coast. Like most explorers, the Portuguese were motivated by an unselfconscious mixture of faith and greed. Establishing southern bases would enable them to surround their Muslim enemies while also giving them access to the African bullion trade. The Portuguese navigator Bartolomeu Dias (ca. 1450–1500) summarized these goals succinctly: "To give light to those who are in darkness and to grow rich." Under the energetic leadership of Prince Henry the Navigator (1394–1460), the Portuguese pushed steadily southward. Prince Henry studied navigational techniques, accumulated detailed accounts of voyages, and encouraged the creation of accurate maps of the African coastline. What was learned on one trip was applied to the next. Soon the Portuguese were a power in the West African trade in slaves and gold ore. Black slaves became a staple of the African voyages, with nearly 150,000 slaves imported in the first fifty years of exploration. Portugal became the first European nation in which black slavery was common. Most slaves were used as domestics and laborers in Portugal; others were sent to work the lucrative sugar plantations that Prince Henry had established on the island of Madeira.

Prince Henry's systematic program paid off in the next generation. By the 1480s Portuguese outposts had reached almost to the equator, and in 1487 Bartolomeu Dias rounded the tip of Africa and opened the eastern African shores to Portuguese traders. The aim of these enterprises was access to Asia rather than Africa. Dias might have reached India if his crew had not mutinied and forced him to return home. A decade later Vasco da Gama (ca. 1460–1524) rounded the Cape of Good Hope and crossed into the Indian Ocean. His journey took two years, but when he returned to Lisbon in 1499 laden with the most valuable spices of the East, Portuguese ambitions were achieved. Larger expeditions followed, one of which, blown off course, touched the South American coast of Brazil. Brazil was soon subsumed within the Portuguese dominions.

The Portuguese came to the East as traders rather than as conquerors. Building on their experience in West Africa, they developed a policy of establishing military outposts to protect their investments and subduing native populations only when necessary. Their achievements resulted more from determination than from technological superiority, though their initial dis-

Prince Henry the Navigator made no voyages himself. He spent his life directing exploration along the western coast of Africa from his base at Sagres, at the extreme southwestern tip of Portugal.

plays of force, like da Gama's attack on Calicut in 1503, terrified the Asian rulers who controlled the spice trade. Throughout the East the Portuguese took advantage of local feuds to gain allies, and they established trading compounds that were easily defensible. The Portuguese general Alfonso de Albuquerque (1453–1515) understood the need for strategically placed garrisons and conquered the vital ports of the Middle East and India. By the first decade of the sixteenth century, the Portuguese were masters of a vast empire, which spanned both the eastern and western coasts of Africa and the western shores of India. Most importantly, the Portuguese controlled Ceylon and Indonesia, the precious Spice Islands from which came cloves, cinnamon, and pepper. Almost overnight, Lisbon became one of the trading capitals of the world, tripling in population between 1500 and 1550.

This sixteenth-century map of Java and the Moluccas shows European traders bartering for spices. At the upper left, a ship laden with the rich cargo sails for markets in Europe.

It was northern Europe that was to harvest what Portugal had sown. The long voyages around Africa were costly and dangerous. Portugal produced no valuable commodities and had to exchange bullion for spices. Moreover, the expense of maintaining a far-flung empire ate into the profits of trade at the same time that the increased volume necessary to make the voyages worthwhile drove down spice prices. Between 1501 and 1505, over eighty ships and seven thousand men sailed from Portugal to the East. This vast commitment was underwritten by Flemish, German, and Italian bankers. Soon Antwerp replaced Lisbon as the marketplace for Asian spices. Ironically, it was in the accidental discovery of Brazil rather than in Asia that the Portuguese were rewarded for the enterprise of their explorers.

Mundus Novus

While most of Portugal's resources were devoted to the Asian trade, those of the Spanish kingdom came to be concentrated in the New World. Though larger and richer than its eastern neighbor, Spain had been segmented into a number of small kingdoms and principalities and divided between Christians and Muslims. Not until the end of the fifteenth century, when the crowns of Aragon and Castile were united and the Muslims expelled from Granada, could the Spanish concentrate their resources. By then they were far behind in establishing commercial enterprises. With Portugal dominating the African route to India, Queen Isabella of Castile was persuaded to take an interest in a western route by a Genoese adventurer, Christopher Columbus (ca. 1446–1506). That interest resulted in one of the greatest accidents of history. (See "Isabella of Castile," pp. 356–357.)

Like all well-informed people of his day, Columbus believed that the world was round. By carefully calculating routes and distances, he concluded that a western track would be shorter and less expensive than the path that the Portuguese were breaking around Africa. Columbus's conclusions were based partly on conventional knowledge and partly on his own self-assurance. All were wholly erroneous. He misjudged the size of the globe by 25 percent and the distance of the journey by 400 percent. But he persevered against all odds. Columbus sailed westward into the unknown in 1492, and on 12 October he landed in the Bahamas, on an island that he named San Salvador. He had encountered a *Mundus Novus,* a New World.

Initially, Columbus's discovery was a disappointment. He had gone in search of a western passage to the Indies and he had failed to return to Spain laden with eastern spices. Despite his own belief that the islands he

A woodcut depicting Christopher Columbus's landing on the island of Hispaniola.

A MOMENTOUS DISCOVERY

Christopher Columbus seemingly needs no introduction. His name has forever been associated with the European discovery of the New World, although the meaning of that discovery has been continually contested. In the summer of 1492, Columbus sailed west from the Canary Islands believing that he would reach the coast of China. Instead he landed on an island in the Caribbean. This passage, from a letter addressed to the royal treasurer of Spain, contains his first impressions of the people he encountered.

A Letter addressed to the noble Lord Raphael Sanchez, Treasurer to their most invincible Majesties, Ferdinand and Isabella, King and Queen of Spain, by Christopher Columbus, to whom our age is greatly indebted, treating of the islands of India recently discovered beyond the Ganges, to explore which he had been sent eight months before under the auspices and at the expense of their said Majesties.

The inhabitants of both sexes in this island, and in all the others which I have seen, or of which I have received information, go always naked as they were born, with the exception of some of the women, who use the covering of a leaf, or small bough, or an apron of cotton which they prepare for that purpose. None of them are possessed of any iron, neither have they weapons, being unacquainted with, and indeed incompetent to use them, not from any deformity of body (for they are well-formed), but because they are timid and full of fear.

They carry however in lieu of arms, canes dried in the sun, on the ends of which they fix heads of dried wood sharpened to a point, and even these they dare not use habitually; for it has often occurred when I have sent two or three of my men to any of the villages to speak with the natives, that they have come out in a disorderly troop, and have fled in such haste at the approach of our men, that the fathers forsook their children and the children their fathers. This timidity did not arise from any loss or injury that they had received from us; for, on the contrary, I gave to all I approached whatever articles I had about me, such as cloth and many other things, taking nothing of theirs in return: but they are naturally timid and fearful. As soon however as they see that they are safe, and have laid aside all fear, they are very simple and honest, and exceedingly liberal with all they have; none of them refusing any thing he may possess when he is asked for it, but on the contrary inviting us to ask them. They exhibit great love towards all others in preference to themselves: they also give objects of great value for trifles, and content themselves with very little or nothing in return.

Such are the events which I have briefly described. Farewell.

Lisbon, the 14th of March.
CHRISTOPHER COLUMBUS,
Admiral of the Fleet of the Ocean.

Christopher Columbus, *Letter from the First Voyage* (1493).

---

had discovered lay just off the coast of Japan, it was soon apparent that he had found an altogether unknown landmass. Columbus's own explorations and those of his successors continued to focus on discovering a route to the Indies. This was all the more imperative once the Portuguese succeeded in finding the passage around Africa. Rivalry between the two nations intensified after 1500, when the Portuguese began exploring the coast of Brazil. In 1494 the Treaty of Tordesillas had confined Portugal's right to the eastern route to the Indies as well as to any undiscovered lands east of an imaginary line fixed west of the Cape Verde Islands. This entitled Portugal to Brazil; the Spanish received whatever lay west of the line. At the time few doubted that Portugal had the better of the bargain.

But Spanish-backed explorations soon proved the value of the new lands. Using the Caribbean islands as a staging ground, successive explorers uncovered the vast coastline of Central and South America. In 1513 Vasco Núñez de Balboa (1475–1517) crossed the land passage in Panama and became the first European to view the Pacific Ocean. The discovery of this ocean refueled Spanish ambitions to find a western passage to the Indies.

In 1519 Ferdinand Magellan (ca. 1480–1521), a Portuguese mariner in the service of Spain, set sail in pursuit of Columbus's goal of reaching the Spice Islands by sailing westward. His voyage, which he did not live to complete, remains the most astounding of the age. After making the Atlantic crossing, Magellan resupplied his fleet in Brazil. Then his ships began the long southerly run toward the tip of South America,

✒ Isabella of Castile

"It is bittersweet to reign" was the motto of her predecessor, Henry IV. It was also the legacy of Isabella of Castile. She was beloved in life and revered after death; indeed, until recently there was a movement to have her canonized as a saint in the Catholic church. Her achievements were staggering. Her reign ended nearly a half century of internecine and dynastic warfare in Castile. Through her marriage to Ferdinand of Aragon she united the two largest kingdoms on the Spanish peninsula. With their combined resources, Isabella and Ferdinand were able to accomplish what their predecessors had only dreamed of for 500 years: the final reconquest of Spanish lands held by the Moors. By her financial support to a Genoese explorer named Christopher Columbus, Isabella gained for Castile title to the richest discovery in history.

But these accomplishments were not without cost. For Isabella, a united Spain was a Catholic Spain. The reconquista was conducted as a holy war of Christian against Muslim. It was as brutal as it was successful. Isabella was directly involved in planning the military campaign and attending to the details of logistics and strategy. She ended centuries of religious diversity by expelling both the Muslims and the Jews. She also accepted the need to purify Catholicism and encouraged the work of the Inquisition in examining the beliefs of converts known as conversos. This resulted in the exile or execution of thousands of former Muslims and Jews and blackened forever the reputation of the Spanish church.

Isabella of Castille was not raised to rule. She had two older brothers and was given a "woman's" education as a child. While her brother Alfonso struggled with Latin and French, she was taught only Castilian. While he learned to wield a sword, she learned to manipulate a needle. Isabella mastered sewing and the decorative arts of needlepoint and embroidery. Even as queen she sewed Ferdinand's shirts as a mark of respect and wifely devotion. But if she accepted the education that was offered to her, she had a streak of independence as well. She loved to hunt and refused to give up horses for donkeys as befitted a noblewoman. She also refused to accept the husband that her half-brother Henry IV had chosen for her. Isabella was a valuable pawn in the international game of diplomacy. She had a reputation for great beauty—her strawberry-blond hair and turquoise eyes were uncommon and much admired in Spain—and this, plus the fact that she had been named heir to the Castilian throne in 1468, brought a number of suitors. Henry betrothed her to Alfonso of Portugal, but Isabella had set her heart on Ferdinand of Aragon. In 1469 the two teenagers eloped, setting off a succession crisis in Castile and ultimately a civil war for the crown in which Isabella triumphed.

Ferdinand and Isabella enjoyed three decades of a happy marriage. Despite their travels, they were nearly inseparable. They ruled their kingdoms as partners and shared the joys and sorrows of their days. They endured the death of their only son, Juan, in 1497 and of his sister Isobel the following year. Three girls outlived their mother, but the eldest, Isabella's heir, Juana, had exhibited such erratic behavior that she was widely believed mentally incompetent. Her claims to the throne were ultimately set aside. Their youngest daughter, Catherine, the queen's favorite, was married to an English prince in 1501. Her mother would not live to see her divorced by Henry VIII.

At the time of their marriage, neither Ferdinand nor Isabella could have known that the union of their crowns was the first step in making Spain the most powerful nation in Europe. The two economies were complementary: Aragon with its long Mediterranean coastline was mercantile and Castile with its vast plain and fertile valleys was agricultural. Both were to benefit by the reconquest of Granada, which joined Spain's Atlantic and Mediterranean seaboards in the southeast. Isabella herself directed the military campaign. During eight years of battle she guided Christian forces from the front, organizing supplies, reinforcements, and arms. She took special care of the wounded, setting up hospital tents that she visited. "The dead weigh on me heavily," she confessed to Ferdinand, "but they could not have gone better employed." Isabella was present at the siege of Granada, viewing the battlements personally and receiving the surrendered keys to the city on 2 January 1492.

The conquest of Granada drove the Muslims south into North Africa. It completed one part of the queen's program for religious unity. The second part was accomplished by decree. In April 1492 all Jews were given three months to depart the Spanish kingdoms. They were prohibited from removing arms, horses, or precious metal, making them not only homeless, but destitute. From the beginning of her reign, Isabella had persecuted the Jewish minority in her realm. They were made to wear distinguishing badges and denied civil rights that they had long enjoyed. At the same time, the work of the Spanish Inquisition under the direction of the zealous Cardinal Tomás de Torquemada had increased anti-Semitic tensions within Castile. Using threats and torture, Torquemada exposed loyal *conversos* as secret Jewish agents. He encouraged confiscation of *converso* property and attacks against Jewish communities. Although the queen at first intervened to maintain civic order, she, too, believed that the Jews constituted a disloyal fifth column within her state. But as long as she was at war with the Muslims, she needed Jewish financiers and administrators.

Once the war had ended, expulsion followed. Paradoxically, the first of these representatives of the old wealth of Castile boarded ship on the same day as a Genoese explorer, Christopher Columbus, set sail under the Castilian flag to uncover the new wealth of Castile. Columbus had approached Isabella twice before, but on both occasions his proposals had been rejected. Isabella's councillors were opposed both to Columbus's plan of sailing west to reach the Indies and to the concessions he demanded should he be successful. Although crown finances were depleted by the war and Isabella did not wish to bargain with an Italian adventurer, she realized that she would risk little to gain much. The decision was the most important of her reign. Through the discoveries made by Columbus and his successors, Castile reaped the greatest windfall in European history.

though he had no idea of the length of the continent. Suppressing mutinies and overcoming shipwrecks and desertions, Magellan finally found the straits that still bear his name. This crossing was the most difficult of all; the 300 miles took thirty-eight terrifying days to navigate.

The Pacific voyage was equally remarkable. The sailors went nearly four months without taking on fresh food or water. Survival was miraculous. "We drank yellow water and often ate sawdust. Rats were sold for half a ducat a piece."

When Magellan finally reached land, in the Philippines, his foolhardy decision to become involved in a local war cost him his life. It was left to his navigator, Sebastian Elcano (ca. 1476–1526), to complete the journey. In 1522, three years and one month after setting out, Elcano returned to Spain with a single ship and 18 survivors of the crew of 280. But in his hold were spices of greater value than the cost of the expedition, and in his return was practical proof that the world was round.

The circumnavigation of Magellan and Elcano brought to an end the first stage of the Spanish exploration of the New World. Columbus's dreams were realized, but the vastness of the Pacific Ocean made a western passage to the Indies uneconomical. In 1529 the Spanish crown relinquished to the Portuguese its claims to the Spice Islands for a cash settlement. By then, trading spices was less alluring than mining gold and silver.

The Spanish Conquests

At the same moment that Magellan's voyage closed one stage of Spanish exploration, the exploits of Hernando Cortés (1485–1547) opened another. The Spanish colonized the New World along the model of their reconquest of Spain. Individuals were given control over land and the people on it in return for military service. The interests of the crown were threefold: to convert the natives to Christianity; to extend sovereignty over new dominions; and to gain some measure of profit from the venture. The colonial entrepreneurs had a singular interest—to grow rich. By and large, the colonizers came from the lower orders of Spanish society. Even the original captains and governors were drawn from groups, like younger sons of the nobility, that would have had little opportunity for rule in Castile. They undertook great risks in expectation of great rewards. Ruthlessness and greed were their universal qualities.

Thus many of the protective measures taken by the crown to ensure orderly colonization and fair treatment

of the natives were ineffective in practice. During the first decades of the sixteenth century, Spanish captains and their followers subdued the Indian populations of the Caribbean islands and put them to work on the agricultural haciendas that they had carved out for themselves. As early as 1498, Castilian women began arriving in the New World. Their presence helped change the character of the settlement towns from wild frontier garrisons to civilized settlements. Younger daughters of the lesser nobility, guided and guarded by chaperones, came to find husbands among the successful conquistadores. Some of these women ultimately inherited huge estates and participated fully in the forging of Spanish America.

Life on the hacienda, even in relative ease with a Castilian wife and family, did not always satisfy the ambitions of the Spanish colonizers. Hernando Cortés was one such conquistador. Having participated in the conquest of Cuba, Cortés sought an independent command to lead an expedition into the hinterland of Central America, where a fabulous empire was rumored to exist. Gathering a force of 600 men, Cortés sailed across the Gulf of Mexico in 1519; established a fort at Vera Cruz, where he garrisoned 200 men; and then sank his boats so that none of his company could turn back. With 400 soldiers, he began his quest. The company marched 250 miles through steamy jungles and over rugged mountains before glimpsing the first signs of the great Aztec civilization. The Aztec empire was a

This drawing shows the Spanish invaders and their Indian allies attacking the temple at Tenochtitlán.

THE HALLS OF MONTEZUMA

Bernal Díaz del Castillo (ca. 1492–1581) was one of the soldiers who accompanied Hernán Cortés on the conquest of the Aztecs. Díaz wrote The True History of the Conquest of New Spain *to refute what he regarded as inaccurate accounts of the conquest. In this passage he describes the Aztec gods from a Christian point of view and shows how difficult it was for the Europeans to understand the different cultures they were encountering.*

Then Cortés said to Montezuma . . . "Your Highness is indeed a great prince, and it has delighted us to see your cities. Now that we are here in your temple, will you show us your gods?"

Montezuma replied that he would first have to consult with his priests. After he had spoken with them, he bade us enter a small tower room, a kind of hall where there were two altars with very richly painted planks on the ceiling. On each altar there were two giant figures, their bodies very tall and stout. The first one, to the right, they said was Uichilobos, their god of war. It had a very board face with monstrous, horrible eyes, and the whole body was covered with precious stones, gold, and pearls that were stuck on with a paste they make in this country out of roots. The body was circled with great snakes made of gold and precious stones, and in one hand he held a bow and in the other some arrows. A small idol standing by him they said was his page; he held a short lance and a shield rich with gold and precious stones. Around the neck of Uichilobos were silver Indian faces and things that we took to be the hearts of these Indians, made of gold and decorated with many precious blue stones. There were braziers with copal incense, and they were burning in them the hearts of three Indians they had sacrificed that day. All the walls and floor were black with crusted blood, and the whole place stank.

To the left stood another great figure, the height of Uichilobos, with the face of a bear and glittering eyes made of their mirrors, which they call *tezcal*. It was decorated with precious stones the same as Uichilobos, for they said that the two were brothers. This Tezcatepuca was the god of hell and had charge of the souls of the Mexicans. His body was girded with figures like little devils, with snakelike tails. The walls were so crusted with blood and the floor was so bathed in it that in the slaughterhouses of Castile there was no such stink. They had offered to this idol five hearts from the day's sacrifices. . . .

Our captain said to Montezuma, half laughingly, "Lord Montezuma, I do not understand how such a great prince and wise man as yourself can have failed to come to the conclusion that these idols of yours are not gods, but evil things—devils is the term for them. . . .

The two priests with Montezuma looked hostile, and Montezuma replied with annoyance, "Señor Malinche, if I had thought that you would so insult my gods, I would not have shown them to you. We think they are very good, for they give us health, water, good seedtimes and weather, and all the victories we desire. We must worship and make sacrifices to them. Please do not say another word to their dishonor."

From Bernal Díaz, *The True History of the Conquest of New Spain* (1552–68)

---

loose confederation of native tribes that the Aztecs had conquered during the previous century. They were ruled by the emperor Montezuma II (1502–20) from his capital at Tenochtitlán, a marvelous city built of stone and baked clay in the middle of a lake. Invited to an audience with the Aztec emperor, Cortés and his men saw vast stores of gold and silver.

The conquest of the Aztecs took nearly a year. Nearly one hundred thousand natives from the tribes that the Aztecs had conquered supported the Spanish assault. Cortés's cavalry terrified the Aztecs. They had never seen horses or iron armaments. Cortés also benefitted from the Aztec practice of taking battlefield captives to be used in religious sacrifices. This allowed many Spanish soldiers, who would otherwise have been killed, to be rescued and to fight again.

By 1522 Cortés was master of an area larger than all of Spain. But the cost in native lives was staggering. In thirty years a population of approximately 25 million had been reduced to less than 2 million. Most of the loss was due to exposure to European diseases like smallpox, typhoid, and measles, against which the natives were helpless. Their labor-intensive system of agriculture could not survive the rapid decrease in population, and famine followed pestilence.

This tragic sequence was repeated everywhere the Europeans appeared. In 1531 Francisco Pizarro (ca. 1475–1541) matched Cortés's feat when he conquered the Peruvian empire of the Incas. This conquest vastly extended the territory under Spanish control and became the true source of profit for the crown when a huge silver mine was discovered in 1545 at Potosí in what is now southern Bolivia. The gold and silver that poured into Spain in the next quarter century helped support Spanish dynastic ambitions in Europe. During the course of the sixteenth century, over two hundred thousand Spaniards migrated across the ocean. Perhaps one in ten were women who married and set up families. In succeeding generations these settlers created huge haciendas built on the forced labor of black African slaves, who proved better able to endure the rigors of mining and farming than did the natives.

The Legacy of the Encounters

By the seventeenth century, long-distance trade had begun to integrate the regions of the world into a single marketplace. Slaves bought in Africa mined silver in South America. The bullion was shipped to Spain,

where it was distributed across Europe. Most went to Amsterdam to settle Spanish debts, Dutch bankers having replaced the Italians as the paymasters of Europe. From Holland the silver traveled east to the Baltic Sea—the Dutch lifeline where vital stores of grain and timber were purchased for home consumption. Even more of this African-mined Spanish silver, traded by the Dutch, was carried to Asia to buy spices in the Spice Islands, cottons in India, and silk in China. Millions of ounces of silver flowed from South America to Asia via the European trading routes. On the return voyage, Indian cottons were traded in Africa to purchase slaves for the South American silver mines.

Gold, God, and glory neatly summarized the motives of the European explorers. Perhaps it is not necessary to delve any further. The gold of Africa and the silver of South America enriched the western nations. Christian missions arose wherever the European empires touched down: among Africans, Asians, and Native Americans. And glory there was in plenty. The feats of the European explorers were recounted in story and song. The *Lusiads* (1572) by Luiz de Camões (ca. 1524–80), one of the greatest works of Portuguese literature, celebrated the new age. "They were men of no ordinary stature, equally at home in war and in dangers of every kind: they founded a new kingdom among distant peoples, and made it great." In the

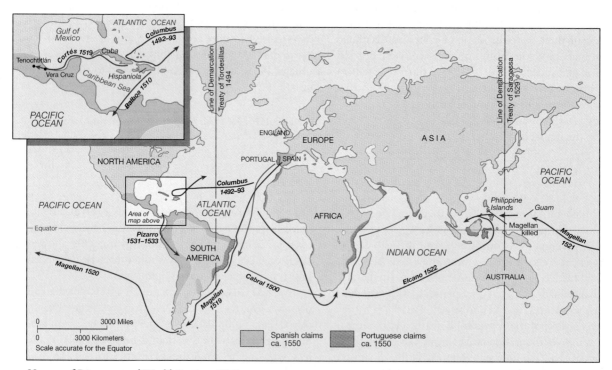

Voyages of Discovery and World Empires, 1550

This French navigator has come ashore to use an early navigating instrument in order to avoid the inaccurate readings obtained on a rolling deck.

achievement of exploration and conquest the modern world had finally surpassed the ancients. "Let us hear no more then of Ulysses and Aeneas and their long journeyings, no more of Alexander and Trajan and their famous victories. My theme is the daring and renown of the Portuguese, to whom Neptune and Mars alike give homage."

The feats of exploration were worthy of celebration. In less than fifty years, tenacious European seafarers found passages to the east and continents to the west. In doing so they overcame terrors both real and imagined. Hazardous journeys in uncharted waters took their toll in men and ships. The odds of surviving a voyage of exploration were no better than those of surviving an epidemic of plague. Nearly two-thirds of da Gama's crew perished on the passage to India. The 40 men that Columbus left on Hispaniola, almost half his company, disappeared without trace. Only one of the five ships that set out with Magellan in 1519 returned to Spain. "If you want to learn how to pray, go to sea" was a Portuguese proverb that needed no explanation.

However harsh was reality, fantasy was more terrifying still. Out of sight of land for three months, da Gama's crew brooded over the folk wisdom of the sea: that the earth was flat and the ships would fall off its edge; that the green ocean was populated by giant monsters. As they approached the equator, they feared that the water would become so hot it would boil them alive and the sun so powerful it would turn their skin black. Sailors to the New World expected to find all manner of horrible creations. Cyclopes and headless one-legged torsos were popularized in drawings, while cannibals and giants were described in realistic detail by the earliest voyagers. No wonder mutiny was a constant companion of exploration.

Yet all of these inhibitions were overcome. So too were those over which the explorers had more control. The expansion of Europe was a feat of technology. Advances in navigational skills, especially in dead reckoning and later in calculating latitude from the position of the sun, were essential preconditions for covering the distances that were to be traveled. So were the more sophisticated ship designs. The magnetic compass and the astrolabe were indispensable tools. New methods for the making of maps and charts, and the popular interest in them, fueled both ambitions and abilities. It was a mapmaker who named the newly found continents after Amerigo Vespucci (1451–1512), the Italian explorer who voyaged to Brazil for the Portuguese. It may have been an accident that Columbus found the New World, but it was no coincidence that he was able to land in the same place three more times.

Riches and converts, power and glory, all came in the wake of exploration. But in the process of exploring new lands and new cultures, Europe also discovered itself. It learned something of its own aspirations. Early Portuguese voyagers went in quest of the mythical Prester John, a saintly figure who was said to rule a heaven on earth in the middle of Africa. The first children born on Madeira were named Adam and Eve, though this slave plantation of sugar and wine was an unlikely Garden of Eden. The optimism of those who searched for the fountain of youth in the Florida swamps was not only that they would find it there, but that a long life was worth living.

Contact with the cultures of the New World also forced a different kind of thinking about life in the old one. The French essayist Michel de Montaigne (1533–92) was less interested in the perceptions of Native Americans than he was of his own countrymen when he recorded this encounter: "They have a way in their language of thinking of men as halves of one another. They noticed among us some men gorged to the full with things of every sort while their other halves were beggars at their doors. They found it strange that these poverty stricken halves should suffer such injustice." The supposed customs of strange lands also provided the setting for one of the great works of English social criticism, Sir Thomas More's *Utopia* (1516).

Europe also discovered and revealed a darker side of itself in the age of exploration. Accompanying the boundless optimism and assertive self-confidence that made so much possible was a tragic arrogance toward and callous disregard of native races. Portuguese travelers described Africans as "dog-faced, dog-toothed people, satyrs, wild men, and cannibals." Such attitudes helped justify enslavement. The European conquests were both brutal and wasteful. The Dominican priest Bartolomé de Las Casas (1474–1566) championed the cause of the native inhabitants at the court of the Spanish kings. His *Apologetic History of the Indies* (1550) highlighted the complexity of native society even as he witnessed its destruction. The German artist Albrecht Dürer (1471–1528) marveled at the "subtle ingenuity of the men in those distant lands" after viewing a display of Aztec art.

But few Europeans were so enlightened about native society. Although Europeans encountered heritages that were in some ways richer than their own, only the most farsighted westerners could see that there was more value in the preservation of these heritages than in their demolition. The Portuguese spice trade did not depend upon the indiscriminate destruction of eastern ports. The obliteration of millions of Aztecs and Incas was not a necessary result of the fever for gold and silver. The destruction was wanton. It revealed the rapaciousness, greed, and cruelty of the Portuguese and Spanish conquerors. These were the impulses of the Crusades rather than of the Renaissance. The Iberian *reconquista*—the holy war against the Muslims by which the Iberian Peninsula was won back into Christian hands—was replayed throughout South America with tragic results.

Europe in 1500

Just as the map of the world was changing as a result of the voyages of exploration, so the map of Europe was changing as a result of the activities of princes. The early sixteenth century was the age of the prince, the first great stage of nation building that would last for the next three hundred years. The New Monarchies, as they are sometimes called, consolidated territories that were divided culturally, linguistically, and historically. The states of Europe are political units, and they were forged by political means: by diplomacy, by marriage, and most commonly by war. The national system that we take for granted when thinking about Europe is a relatively recent development. Before we can observe its beginnings, we must first have a picture of Europe as it existed in 1500. At that time it was composed of nearly five hundred distinct political units.

Europe is a concept. Like all concepts, it is difficult to define. The vast plain that stretches from the Netherlands to the steppes of Russia presents few natural barriers to migration. Tribes had been wandering across this plain for thousands of years, slowly settling into the more fertile lands to practice their agriculture. Only in the south did geographical forces stem the flow of humanity. The Carpathian Mountains created a basin for the settlement of Slavic peoples that extended down to the Black Sea. The Alps provided a boundary for French, Germanic, and Italian settlements. The Pyrenees defined the Iberian Peninsula, with a mixture of African and European peoples.

Eastern Boundaries

In the East, three great empires had created the political geography that could be said to define a European boundary: the Mongol, the Ottoman, and the Russian. During the early Middle Ages, Mongol warriors had swept across the Asian steppes and conquered most of central and southern Russia. By the sixteenth century the Mongol empire was disintegrating, its lands divided into a number of separate states called khanates. The khanate of the Crimea, with lands around the northern shores of the Black Sea, created the southeastern border of Europe.

The Ottoman territories defined the southern boundary. By 1450 the Ottomans controlled all of Byzantium and Greece, dominating an area from the Black Sea to the Aegean. Fifty years later they had conquered nearly all the lands between the Aegean and the Adriatic seas. A perilous frontier was established on the Balkan Peninsula. There the principalities of Moldavia, Wallachia, Transylvania, and Hungary held out against the Ottomans for another quarter century before being overrun.

The Russian state defined the eastern boundary of Europe. Russia too had been a great territorial unit in the Middle Ages, centered at Kiev in the west and stretching eastward into Asia. The advance of the Mon-

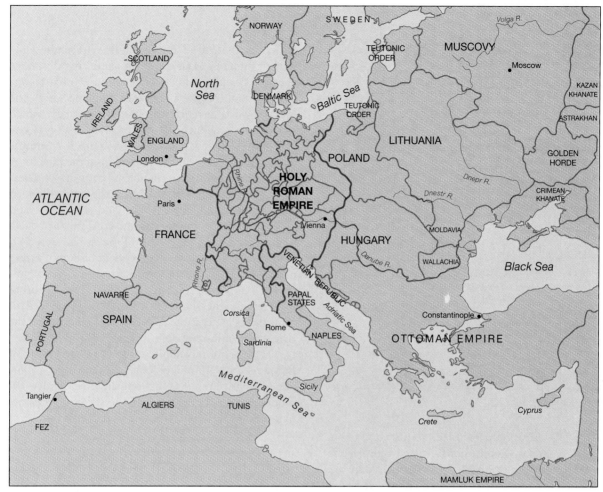

Europe in 1500

gols in the thirteenth century had contracted the eastern part of Russia, and its western domains had disintegrated under the practice of dividing the ruling prince's inheritance among his sons. In 1500 Europe reached as far east as the principality of Muscovy. There the heritage of East and West mingled. In some periods of history Russia's ties with the West were most important; at other times Russia retreated into isolation from Europe.

The northern borders of eastern Europe centered on the Baltic Sea, one of the most important trading routes of the early modern era. On the northern coasts lay the Scandinavian nations of Sweden, Norway, and Denmark. These loosely confederated nations had a single king throughout the fifteenth century. Denmark, the southernmost of the three, was also the richest and most powerful. It enjoyed a favorable trading position on both the North and Baltic seas and social and economic integration with the Germanic states on its border. On the southern side of the Baltic Sea lay the

dominions of the Teutonic Knights, physically divided by the large state of Poland-Lithuania. The Teutonic territories, in the valuable Baltic region of Prussia, had been colonized by German crusaders in the thirteenth century.

Poland-Lithuania comprised an enormous territory that covered the length of Europe from the Baltic to the Black Sea. The crowns of these two nations had been joined at the end of the fourteenth century, and their dynastic history was tied up with the nations of Bohemia and Hungary to their west and south. While Bohemia was increasingly drawn into the affairs of central Europe, Hungary remained more eastern in orientation. This was partly because the Bohemians gave nominal allegiance to the Holy Roman Emperor and partly because the Ottoman conquests had engulfed a large part of the Hungarian territories. At the end of the fifteenth century, Poland, Lithuania, Bohemia, and Hungary were all ruled by the same family, the Jagiellons.

Eastern Europe

Mongols and Ottomans to the south, Russians in the east, Scandinavia in the north, Poland-Lithuania in the center, and Hungary in the west: such were the contours of the eastern portion of Europe. Its lands were, on the whole, less fertile than those farther west, and its climate was more severe. It was a sparsely populated region. Its wealth lay in the Baltic fisheries, in the Hungarian and Bohemian silver mines, and in the enormous Russian forests, where wood and its by-products were plentiful. Except in the southern portions of Poland and central Bohemia, the region was agriculturally poor. The eastern territories had been resettled during the population crisis of the early fourteenth century. Then native Slavs were joined by German colonizers from the West and Asian conquerors from the East. This clash of races did much to define the political history of eastern Europe.

Central Europe

The middle of the continent was defined by the Holy Roman Empire and occupied almost entirely by Germanic peoples. In length the empire covered the territory from the North and Baltic seas to the Adriatic and the Mediterranean, where the Italian city-states were located. In width it stretched from Bohemia to Burgundy. Politically, central Europe comprised a bewildering array of principalities, Church lands, and free

towns. By the end of the fifteenth century, the Holy Roman Empire was an empire in name only. The large states of Brandenburg, Bohemia, and Bavaria resembled the political units of the east. In the south, the Alps provided an effective physical boundary, which allowed the Archduchy of Austria and the Swiss Confederation to follow their own separate paths. Stretching across the center of the empire, from the Elbe River to the North Sea, were a jumble of petty states. Great cities like Nuremberg and Ulm in the south, Bremen and Hamburg in the north, and Frankfurt and Cologne in the west were free municipalities. Large sections of the northwestern part of the empire were governed by the Church through resident bishops. Further to the west were the prosperous Low Countries: Holland and its port of Amsterdam, Brabant and its port of Antwerp. In the southwest, the empire extended in some places as far as the Rhone River and included the rich estates of Luxembourg, Lorraine, and Burgundy.

The riches of the empire made it the focal point of Europe. Nearly 15 million people lived within its borders. Its agriculture varied from the olive- and wine-producing areas in the southwest to the great granaries in its center. Rich mineral deposits and large reserves of

Central Europe

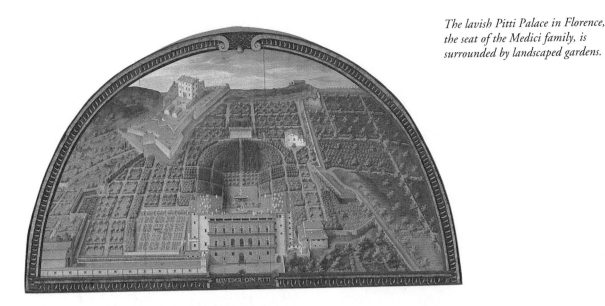

The lavish Pitti Palace in Florence, the seat of the Medici family, is surrounded by landscaped gardens.

timber made the German lands industrially advanced. The European iron industry was centered here, and the empire was the arms manufacturer for the western world. The empire was also a great commercial center, heir to the Hanseatic League of the Middle Ages. Its northern and western ports teemed with trade, and its merchants were replacing the Italians as the leading international bankers.

Like the empire, the Italian peninsula was divided into a diverse collection of small city-states. During the course of the fifteenth century, five of these had emerged as most powerful (see chapter 11). In the north were Florence, Venice, and the Duchy of Milan. In the south was Rome, spiritual center of Catholicism and residence of the pope. Although Roman and papal government were separate jurisdictions, in fact their fates were bound together. Papal lands stretched far to the north of Rome, and wars to defend or expand them were Roman as well as papal ventures. The kingdom of Naples—the breadbasket of the Mediterranean—occupied the southernmost part of Italy and included the agriculturally rich island of Sicily.

The West

The Iberian Peninsula, the French territories, and the British Isles formed the westernmost borders of Europe. Separated from France in the north by the Pyrenees, the Iberian Peninsula is surrounded by the Atlantic Ocean and the Mediterranean Sea on the west and east. But neither its protective mountain barrier nor its ample coastlines was its most significant geo-graphical feature during its formative period. Rather, it was the fact that Iberia is separated from North Africa only by the easily navigable Strait of Gibraltar. During the Middle Ages the peninsula was overrun by North African Muslims, whom the Spanish called Moors. From the eighth to the fifteenth centuries, Iberian history was dominated by the reconquista—the recapture and re-Christianization of the conquered territories. This reconquest was finally completed in 1492, when the Moors were pushed out of Granada and the Jews were expelled from Spain. At the end of the fifteenth century, the Iberian Peninsula contained several separate kingdoms. The most important were Portugal on the western coast—the only Continental nation to have the same borders in 1500 as it does today—Aragon, with its Mediterranean ports of Barcelona and Valencia; and Castile, the largest of the Iberian states. The marriage of King Ferdinand of Aragon and Queen Isabella of Castile in 1469 had joined the crowns of Aragon and Castile, but the two kingdoms remained separate.

The remnants of ancient Gaul were also favored by a maritime location. Like those of Iberia, French coasts are located along the Mediterranean Sea and the Atlantic Ocean. France's eastern boundaries touched the empire; its southern mountain border touched Spain. To the northwest, Britain was less than thirty miles from France across the English Channel. Toward the end of the fifteenth century, France was still divided into many smaller fiefs. The royal domain centered on Paris and extended to Champagne in the east and Normandy in the west. South of this area, however, from Orléans to Brittany, were principalities that had

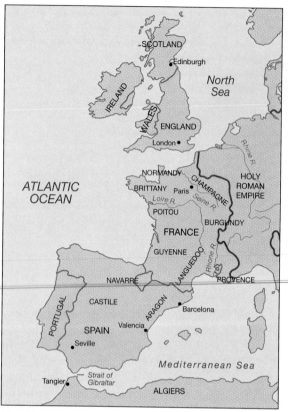

Western Europe

political and geographical forms. Huge states in the east, tiny principalities in the center, emerging nations in the west, all seemingly had little in common. There was as yet no state system and no clear group of dominant powers. The western migration of the Germanic peoples appeared to be over, but their consolidation was as yet unimagined. The Iberians struggled to expel the Moors, the Hungarians to hold back the Ottomans. Everywhere one looked there was fragmentation and disarray. Yet in less than half a century the largest empire yet known in the West would be formed. States would come to be consolidated and dynasties established all over the Continent. And with the rise of the state would come the dream of dominion, an empire over all of Europe.

The Formation of States

It was Machiavelli who identified the prince as the agent of change in the process of state formation. He believed that the successful prince could bring unity to his lands, security to his borders, and prosperity to his subjects. The unsuccessful prince brought nothing but ruin.

A process as long and as complex as the formation of nations is not subject to the will of individuals. Factors as diverse as geography, population, and natural resources are all decisive. So too are the structures through which human activity is channeled. The ways in which families are organized and wealth is transmitted from generation to generation can result in large estates with similar customs or small estates with varying ones. The manner in which social groups are formed and controlled can mean that power is centralized or dispersed. The beliefs of ordinary people and the way they practice them can define who is a part of a community and who is not. All these elements and many others have much to do with the way in which European states began to take shape at the end of the fifteenth century. Despite these complexities, we should not lose sight of the simple truth of Machiavelli's observations. In the first stages of the consolidation of European nations, the role of the prince was crucial.

Indeed, in the middle of the fifteenth century there were many factors working against the formation of large states in Europe. The most obvious involved simple things like transportation and communication. The distance that could be covered quickly was very small. In wet and cold seasons, travel was nearly impossible. The emperor Charles V sat in Burgundy for two months awaiting a favorable wind to take him to his

long been contested between England and France. Nor was the rich central plain yet integrated into the royal domain. Agriculturally, French lands were the richest in Europe. France enjoyed both Mediterranean and Atlantic climates, which suited the growing of the widest variety of foodstuffs. Its population of approximately 13 million was second only to that of the empire.

Across the Channel lay Britain (comprising England, Scotland, and Wales) and Ireland. Britain had been settled by an array of European colonizers—Romans, Danes, Angles, and Saxons—before being conquered in the eleventh century by the French Normans. From that time, it was protected by the rough waters of the English Channel and the North Sea and allowed to develop a distinct cultural and political heritage. Wales to the west and Scotland to the north were still separate nations at the beginning of the sixteenth century. Both were mountainous lands with harsh climates and few natural advantages. They were sparsely populated. Though Ireland, too, was sparsely populated, it contained several rich agricultural areas especially suited for dairying and grazing.

In 1500 Europe exhibited a remarkable diversity of

newly inherited kingdom of Spain. Similarly, directives from the center of the states to the localities were slow to arrive and slower still to be adopted. Large areas were difficult to control and to defend. Distinct languages or dialects also made for difficulties in communication. Only the most educated could use Latin as a common written language. Separate languages contributed to separate cultures. Customary practices, common ancestry, and shared experiences helped define a sense of community through which small states defined themselves.

To these natural forces that acted to maintain the existence of small units of government were added invented ones. To succeed, a prince had to establish supremacy over a number of rivals. For the most part, states were inherited. In some places it was customary to follow the rule of primogeniture—inheritance by the eldest son. In others, estates were split among sons, or among children of both sexes. Some traditions, like those of the French, excluded inheritance through women; others, like the Castilian, treated women's claims as equal to men's. Short lives meant prolonged disputes about inheritance. Rulers had to defend their thrones from any number of rivals with strong claims to legitimacy.

So, too, did rulers have to defend themselves from the ambitions of their mightiest subjects. Dukes could dream only one dream. The constant warfare of the European nobility was one of the central features of the later Middle Ages. To avoid resort to arms, princes and peers entered into all manner of alliances, using their children as pawns and the marriage bed as the chessboard. Rulers also faced independent institutions within their states, powerful organizations that had to be won over or crushed. The long process of taming the Church was well advanced by the end of the fifteenth century and about to enter a new stage. Fortified towns presented a different problem. They possessed both the manpower and wealth necessary to raise and maintain armies. They also jealously guarded their privileges. Rulers who could not tax their towns could not rule their state. Finally, most kingdoms had assemblies that represented the propertied classes, especially in matters of taxation. Some, like the English Parliament and the Spanish Cortes, were strong; others, like the Imperial Diet and the French Estates-General, were weak. But everywhere they posed an obstacle to the extension of the power of princes.

In combination, these factors slowed and shaped the process of state formation. But neither separately nor

The stone-walled castles of the Middle Ages were rendered obsolete by the introduction of artillery. This painting of the siege of Ribodane in France (ca. 1480) shows the bombards (left) battering down the castle walls.

together were they powerful enough to overcome it. The fragmentation of Europe into so many small units of government made some consolidation inevitable. There were always stronger and weaker neighbors, always broken successions and failed lines. The practice of dynastic marriage meant that smaller states were continually being inherited by the rulers of larger ones. If the larger state was stable, it absorbed the smaller one. If not, the smaller state would split off again to await its next predator or protector. As the first large states took shape, the position of smaller neighbors grew ever more precarious.

This was especially true by the end of the fifteenth century because of the increase in the destructive power of warfare. Technological advances in cannonry and in the skills of gunners and engineers made medieval fortifications untenable. The fall of Constantinople was as much a military watershed as it was a political one. Gunpowder decisively changed battlefield tactics. It made heavy armor obsolete and allowed for the development of a different type of warfare. Lightly armored horses and riders could not only inflict more damage upon one another, but they were now mobile enough to be used against infantry. Infantry armed with long pikes or small muskets became the crucial components of armies that were growing ever larger. Systems of supply were better, sources of small arms were more available, and the rewards of conquest were more tangible. What could not be inherited or married could be conquered.

Eastern Configurations

The interplay of factors that encouraged and inhibited the formation of states is most easily observed in the eastern parts of Europe. There the different paths taken by Muscovy and Poland-Lithuania stand in contrast. At the beginning of the sixteenth century, the principality of Muscovy was the largest European political unit. Muscovy had established itself as the heir to the ancient state of Russia through conquest, shrewd political alliances, and the good fortune of its princes to be blessed with long reigns. Muscovy's growth was phenomenal. Under Ivan III, "the Great" (1462–1505), Muscovy expanded to the north and west. During a long series of wars it annexed Novgorod and large parts of Livonia and Lithuania. Its military successes were almost unbroken, but so too were its diplomatic triumphs. Ivan the Great preferred pacification to conquest, though when necessary he could conquer with great brutality. Between 1460 and 1530, Muscovy

increased its landed territory by 1.5 million square miles.

A number of factors led to the rise of Muscovy. External threats had diminished. First, the deterioration of the Mongol empire that had dominated south-central Russia allowed Ivan to escape the yoke of Mongol rule that the Russian princes had worn for centuries. Second, the fall of Constantinople made Muscovy the heir to eastern Christendom, successor to the Roman and Byzantine empires. Ivan's marriage to Sophia, niece of the last emperor of Byzantium, cemented this connection. Sophia brought both Italian craftsmen and Byzantine customs to the Russian court, helping Ivan open his contacts with the wider world.

Territorial conquests and the decline of Byzantium were not the only important features of the consolidation of the Muscovite state. Ivan the Great was fortunate in having no competitors for his throne. He was able to use other social groups to help administer the new Muscovite territories without fear of setting up a rival to power. Ivan extended the privileges of his nobility and organized a military class who received land as a reward for their fidelity. He also developed a new theory of sovereignty that rested on divine rather than temporal power. Traditionally, Russian princes ruled their lands by patrimony. They owned both estates and occupants. Ivan the Great extended this principle to cover all lands to which there was an ancient Russian claim and combined it with the religious authority of the Orthodox church. Both he and his successors ruled with the aid of able Church leaders who were normally part of the prince's council.

What made the expansion of Muscovy so impressive is that land once gained was never lost. The military and political achievements of Ivan the Great were furthered by his son Vasili and his more famous grandson Ivan IV, "the Terrible" (1533–84). Ivan IV defeated the Mongols on his southeastern border and incorporated the entire Volga river basin into Muscovy. But his greatest ambition was to gain a port on the Baltic Sea and establish a northern outlet for commerce. His objective was to conquer Livonia. Nearly three decades of warfare between Muscovy and Poland-Lithuania—with whom Livonia had allied itself—resulted in large territorial gains, but Muscovy always fell short of the real prize. And Ivan's northern campaigns seriously weakened the defense of the south. In 1571 the Crimean Tartars advanced from their territories on Muscovy's southwestern border and inflicted a powerful psychological blow when they burned the city of Moscow. Although the Tartars were eventually driven off Mus-

A delegation of Russian boyars bearing gifts visited the Holy Roman Emperor Maximilian II in 1576 in order to seek his aid against Poland-Lithuania.

covite soil, expansion in both north and south was at an end for the next 75 years.

By the reign of Ivan IV, Muscovite society was divided roughly into three groups: the hereditary nobility known as the boyars, the military service class, and the peasantry who were bound to the land. There was no large mercantile presence in Muscovy and its urban component remained small. The boyars, who were powerful landlords of great estates, owed little to the tsar. They inherited their lands and did not necessarily benefit from expansion and conquest. Members of the military service class, on the other hand, were bound to the success of the crown. Their military service was a requirement for the possession of their estates, which were granted out of lands gained through territorial expansion. Gradually the new military service class grew in power and prestige, largely at the expense of the older boyars. Ivan IV used members of the military service class as legislative advisors and elevated them in his parliamentary council (the Zemsky Sobor), which also contained representatives of the nobility, clergy, and towns.

Unlike his grandfather, Ivan IV had an abiding mistrust of the boyars. They had held power when he was a child, and it was rumored that his mother had been poisoned by them. It was in his treatment of the boyars that he earned the nickname "the Terrible." During his brutal suppression of supposed conspiracies, several thousand families were massacred by Ivan's own orders and thousands more by the violent excesses of his agents. Ivan constantly imagined plots against himself, and many of the men who served him met horrible deaths. He also forcibly relocated boyar families, stripping them of their lands in one place but granting them new lands elsewhere. This practice made their situation similar to that of the military service class, who owed their fortunes to the tsar.

All of these measures contributed to the breakdown

of local networks of influence and power and to a disruption of local governance. But they also made possible a system of central administration, one of Ivan IV's most important achievements. He created departments of state to deal with the various tasks of administration, and this resulted in more efficient management of revenues and of the military. Ivan IV promoted the interests of the military service class over those of the boyars, but he did not destroy the nobility. New boyars were created, especially in conquered territories, and these new families owed their positions and loyalty to the prince. Both the boyars and the military benefited from Ivan's policy of binding the great mass of people to the land. Russian peasants had few political or economic rights in comparison to those of western peasants, but during the early sixteenth century even the meager rights Russian peasants had were curtailed. The right of peasants to move from the estate of one lord to that of another was suspended, all but binding the peasantry to the land. This serfdom made possible the prolonged absence of military leaders from their estates and contributed to the creation of the military-service class. But it also made imperative the costly system of coercing agricultural and industrial labor. In the long term, serfdom retarded the development of the Muscovite economy by removing incentive from large landholders to make investments in commerce or to improve agricultural production.

The growth of an enlarged and centralized Muscovy stands in contrast to the experiences of Poland-Lithuania during the same period. At the end of the fifteenth century, Casimir IV (1447–92) ruled the kingdom of Poland and the grand duchy of Lithuania. His son Vladislav II ruled Bohemia (1471–1516) and Hungary (1490–1516). Had the four states been permanently consolidated they could have become an effective barrier to Ottoman expansion in the south and Russian expansion in the east. But the union of crowns had never been the union of states. The union of crowns had taken place over the previous century by political alliances, diplomatic marriages, and the consent of the nobility. Such arrangements kept peace among the four neighbors, but it kept any one of them from becoming a dominant partner.

While the Polish-Lithuanian monarchs enjoyed longevity similar to that of the Muscovites, those who ruled Hungary and Bohemia were not so fortunate: by the sixteenth century a number of claimants to both crowns existed. The competition was handled by diplomacy rather than war. The accession of Vladislav II, for example, was accompanied by large concessions, first to the Bohemian towns and later to the Hungarian nobility. The formal union of the Polish and Lithuanian crowns in 1569 also involved the decentralization of power and the strengthening of the rights of the nobility in both countries. In the end, the states split apart. The Russians took much of Lithuania, the Ottomans

much of Hungary. Bohemia, which in the fifteenth century had been ruled more by its nobles than its king, was absorbed into the Habsburg territories after 1526.

There were many reasons why a unified state did not appear in east-central Europe. In the first place, external forces disrupted territorial and political arrangements, and wars with the Ottomans and the Russians absorbed resources. Second, the princes faced rivals to their crowns. Although Casimir IV was able to place his son on the thrones of both Bohemia and Hungary, he managed to do so against the powerful claims of the Habsburg princes, who continued to intrigue against the Jagiellons. These contests for power necessitated concessions to leading citizens, which decreased the ability of the princes to centralize their kingdoms or to effect real unification among them. The nobility of Hungary, Bohemia, and Poland-Lithuania all developed strong local interests that increased over time. In Bohemia, Vladislav II was king in name only, and even in Poland the nobility won confirmation of its rights and privileges from the monarchy. War, rivalries for power, and a strong nobility prevented any one prince from dominating this area as the princes of Muscovy dominated theirs.

The Western Powers

Just as in the east, there was no single pattern to the consolidation of the large western European states. They, too, were internally fragmented and externally imperiled. While England had to overcome the ruin of decades of civil war, France and Spain faced the challenges of invasion and occupation. Western European princes struggled against powerful institutions and individuals within their states. Some they conquered, others they absorbed. Each nation formed its state differently: England by administrative centralization, France by good fortune, and Spain by dynastic marriage. Yet in 1450 few imagined that any one of these states would succeed.

The Taming of England. Alone among European states, England suffered no threat of foreign invasion during the fifteenth century. This island fortress might easily have become the first consolidated European state were it not for the ambitions of the nobility and the weakness of the crown. For thirty years the English aristocracy fought over the spoils of a helpless monarch. The Wars of the Roses (1455–85), as they came to be called, were as much a free-for-all among the English peerage as they were a contest for the throne between the houses of Lancaster and York. At their cen-

A miniature painted by a Krakow artist about 1510 depicts the final act of the coronation rite. The king in majesty is surrounded by his court while a Te Deum *is sung. The knights in the foreground bear the standards of Poland and Lithuania.*

ter was an attempt by the dukes of York to wrest the crown from the mad and ineffective Lancastrian king Henry VI (1422–61). All around the edges was the continuation of local and family feuds that had little connection to the dynastic struggle.

Three decades of intermittent warfare had predictable results. The houses of Lancaster and York were both destroyed. Edward IV (1461–83) succeeded in gaining the crown for the House of York, but he was never able to wear it securely. When he died, his children, including his heir, Edward V (1483), were placed in the protection of their uncle Richard III (1483–85). It was protection that they did not survive. The two boys disappeared, reputedly murdered in the Tower of London, and Richard declared himself king. Richard's usurpation led to civil war, and he was killed by the forces of Henry Tudor at the battle of Bosworth Field in 1485. By the end of the Wars of the Roses the monarchy had lost both revenue and prestige, and the aristocracy had stored up bitter memories for the future.

It was left to Henry Tudor to pick up the pieces of the kingdom. As legend has it, he picked up the crown off a bramble bush. The two chief obstacles to his determination to consolidate the English state were the power of the nobility and the poverty of the monarchy. No English monarch had held secure title to the throne for over a century. Henry Tudor, as Henry VII (1485–1509), put an end to this dynastic instability at once. He married Elizabeth of York, in whose heirs would rest the legitimate claim to the throne. Their children were indisputable successors to the crown. He also began the long process of taming his overmighty subjects. Traitors were hung and turncoats rewarded. He and his son Henry VIII (1509–47) adroitly created a new peerage, which soon was as numerous as the old feudal aristocracy. These new nobles owed their titles and loyalty to the Tudors. They were favored with offices and spoils and were relied upon to suppress both popular and aristocratic rebellions. Henry VIII was even more ruthless than his father. He preferred the chopping block to the peace treaty. In 1450 there were nine English dukes; by 1525 there were only two. With both carrot and stick, the Tudors tamed the peerage.

The financial problems of the English monarchy were not so easily overcome. In theory and practice an English king was supposed to live "of his own," that is, off the revenues from his own estates. In normal circumstances, royal revenue did not come from the king's subjects. The English landed classes had established the principle that only on extraordinary occasions were they to be required to contribute to the maintenance of

Holbein's last portrait of Henry VIII, painted in 1542. Henry made England into one of the world's greatest naval powers but embroiled the kingdom in a series of costly foreign wars. He married six times in an effort to produce a legitimate male heir.

government. This principle was defended through their representative institution—the Parliament. When the kings of England wanted to tax their subjects, they had first to gain the assent of Parliament. Although Parliaments did grant requests for extraordinary revenue, especially for national defense, they did so grudgingly. The English landed elites were not exempt from taxation, but they were able to control the amount of taxes they paid.

The inability of the crown to extract its living from its subjects made it more dependent on the efficient management of its own estates. Thus English state building depended upon the growth of centralized institutions that could oversee royal lands and collect royal customs. Gradually, medieval institutions like the Exchequer were supplanted by newer organs that were better able to adjust to modern methods of accounting, record keeping, and enforcement. Henry sent ministers

LAST WORDS

Anne Boleyn was the second wife of Henry VIII and the mother of Elizabeth I. Henry's desire to have a son and his passion for Anne resulted in his divorce from Catherine of Aragon and England's formal break with the Roman Catholic church. When Anne bore only a daughter, she too became dispensable. She was convicted of adultery and incest and executed in 1536. Here are her last words.

Good friends, I am not come here to excuse or to justify myself, for as much as I know full well that aught that I could say in my defense doth not appertain unto you, and that I could draw no hope of life from the same. But I come here only to die, and thus to yield myself humbly to the will of the King my lord. And if in my life I did ever offend the King's grace, surely with my death I do now atone for the same. And I blame not my judges, nor any other manner of person, nor anything save the cruel law of the land by which I die. But be this, and be my faults as they may, I beseech you all, good friends, to pray for the life of the King my sovereign lord and yours, who is one of the best princes on the face of the earth, and who hath always treated me so well that better could not be; wherefore I submit to death with a good will, humbly asking pardon of the world.

Anne Boleyn, scaffold speech.

to view and value royal lands. He ordered the cataloging and collection of feudal obligations. Ship cargoes were inspected thoroughly and every last penny of customs charged. Whether Henry's reputation for greed and rapacity was warranted, it was undeniable that he squeezed as much as could be taken from a not very juicy inheritance. His financial problems limited both domestic and foreign policy.

It was not until the middle of the next reign that the English monarchy was again solvent. As a result of his dispute with the papacy, Henry VIII confiscated the enormous wealth of the Catholic church, and with one stroke solved the crown's monetary problems (see chapter 13). But the real contribution that Henry and his chief minister, Thomas Cromwell (ca. 1485–1540), made to forming an English state was the way in which this windfall was administered. Cromwell accelerated the process of centralizing government that had begun under Edward IV. He divided administration according to its functions by creating separate departments of state, modeled upon courts. These new departments were responsible for record keeping, revenue collection, and law enforcement. Each had a distinct jurisdiction and a permanent, trained staff. Cromwell coordinated the work of these distinct departments by expanding the power of the Privy Council, which included the heads of these administrative bodies. Through a long evolution, the Privy Council came to serve as the king's

executive body. Cromwell also saw the importance of Parliament as a legislative body. Through Parliament, royal policy could be turned into statutes that had the assent of the political nation. If Parliament was well managed, issues that were potentially controversial could be defused. Laws passed by Parliament were more easily enforced locally than were proclamations issued by the king. By the end of Henry VIII's reign, the English monarchy was strong enough to withstand the succession of a child king, precisely the circumstance that had plunged the nation into civil war a century earlier.

The Unification of France. Perhaps the most remarkable thing about the unification of France is that it took place at all. The forces working against the consolidation of a French state were formidable. France was surrounded by aggressive and powerful neighbors with whom it was frequently at war. Its greatest nobles were semi-independent princes who were constant rivals for the throne and consistent opponents of the extension of royal power. The French people were deeply suspicious of the pretensions of the monarchy. Provincialism was not simply negative; it was a fierce pride of and loyalty toward local customs and institutions that had deep roots within communities. Furthermore, France was splintered by profound regional differences. The north and south were divided by culture and by language (the *langue d'oc* in the south and the *langue d'oïl* in the north). As late as the fifteenth century, a French king needed a translator to communicate with officials from his southern lands.

The first obstacles that were overcome were the external threats to French security. For over a century, the throne of France had been contested by the kings of England. The so-called Hundred Years' War, which was fought intermittently between 1337 and 1453, originated in a dispute over the inheritance of the French crown and English possessions in Gascony in southern France (see chapter 10). The war was fought on French soil, and by the early fifteenth century English conquests in north-central France extended from Normandy to the borders of the Holy Roman Empire. Two of the largest French cities, Paris and Bordeaux, were in English hands.

The problems posed by the Hundred Years' War were not just those of victory and defeat. The struggle between the kings of England and the kings of France allowed French princes and dukes, who were nominally vassals of the king, to enhance their autonomy by making their own alliances with the highest bidder. When the English were finally driven out of France in the middle of the fifteenth century, the kings of France came into a weakened and divided inheritance.

Nor was England the only threat to the security of the French monarchy. On France's eastern border, in a long arching semicircle, were the estates of the dukes of Burgundy. The dukes of Burgundy and the kings of France shared a common ancestry—both were of the House of Valois. Still, the sons of brothers in one generation were only cousins in the next, and the two branches of the family grew apart. The original Burgundian inheritance was in the southeast, centered at Dijon. A good marriage and good fortune brought to the first duke the rich northern province of Flanders. For the next hundred years, the aim of the dukes of Burgundy was to unite their divided estates. While England and France were locked in deadly embrace, Burgundy systematically grew. It absorbed territory from both the Holy Roman Empire and France. To little pieces gained through marriages were added little pieces taken through force. As the second half of the fifteenth century began, the court of the duke of Burgundy was the glittering jewel of Europe, the heir of the Italian Renaissance. Wealthy and powerful, it stood poised to achieve what had once only been dreamed: the unification of the Burgundian lands. The conquest of Lorraine finally connected the ducal estates in one long, unbroken string.

But it was a string stretched taut. The power of Burgundy threatened its neighbors in all directions. Both France and the empire were too weak to resist its expansion, but the confederation of Swiss towns to the southwest of Burgundy was not. Fearing a Burgundian advance against them, a number of independent Swiss towns pooled their resources to raise a large army. In a series of stunning military victories, Swiss forces repelled the Burgundians from their lands and demolished their armies. Charles the Bold, the last Valois duke of Burgundy, fell at the Battle of Nancy in 1477. His estates were quickly dismembered. France recovered its ancestral territories, including Burgundy, and through no effort of its own was now secure on its eastern border.

The king most associated with the consolidation of France was Louis XI (1461–83). He inherited an estate exhausted by warfare and civil strife. More by chance than by plan he vastly extended the territories under the dominion of the French crown and, more importantly, subdued the nobility. Louis XI was as cunning as he was peculiar. In an age in which royalty was expressed through magnificence, Louis sported an old felt hat and a well-worn coat. His enemies constantly underestimated his abilities, which earned him the nickname "the Spider." But during the course of his

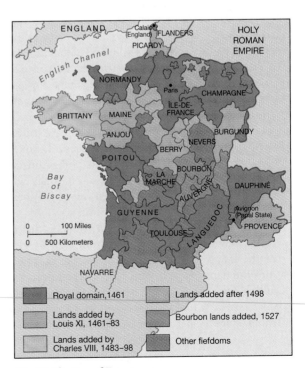

The Unification of France

THE KINGDOM OF FRANCE

Claude de Seyssel (ca. 1450–1519) was a legal scholar and professor at the University of Turin. He came from the duchy of Savoy, a small state that mixed French and Italian peoples and culture. Seyssel thus learned about the French monarchy as an outsider and wrote The Monarchy of France *as a book of counsel for French kings. In this passage he explains and defends the Salic law, which prohibited legitimate title to the French throne from passing through a woman. The legal documents that supposedly established Salic law were fakes.*

Without going too deeply into the disputes of the philosophers, we may presuppose three kinds of political rule: monarchy under a single person, aristocracy under a certain number of the better sort, and democracy the popular state. Of these, according to the true and most widespread opinion, monarchy is the best if the prince is good and has the sense, the experience, and the good will to govern justly. That rarely comes to pass, however, because with such authority and license it is hard to follow the right course and hold fairly the balance of justice. The second state seems the more reasonable and praiseworthy since it is more lasting, better founded, and easier to bear, being comprised of the persons selected by the assembly or a part of them. Such persons are, moreover, subject to corruption and change, at least to the extent that, when there are several bad and inadequate men among them, the better sort, being their superiors, can repress their boldness and thwart their unreasonable enterprises. As to the popular state, it has always been turbulent, dangerous, and hostile to the better sort. Nevertheless, the aristocratic state is often transformed into oligarchy, a monopoly by covetous and ambitious folk, who, though chosen as the wisest and most prudent of the people to rule and to govern the people well, care only for their particular profit. So when all is said, none of these states can possibly be perpetual, for ordinary in the course of time they get worse, especially when they go on growing, so that often one [by disorder] rises from the other.

The first special trait that I find good is that this realm passes by masculine succession and, by virtue of the law which the French call Salic, cannot fall into the hands of a woman. This is excellent, for by falling into the feminine line it can come into the power of a foreigner, a pernicious and dangerous thing, since a ruler from a foreign nation is of a different rearing and condition, of different customs, different language, and a different way of life from the men of the lands he comes to rule. He ordinarily, therefore, wishes to advance those of his nation, to grant them the most important authority in the handling of affairs, and to prefer them to honors and profits. Moreover, he always has more love for and faith in them and so conforms more to their customs and ways than to the customs of the land to which he has newly come, whence there always follows envy and dissension between the natives and the foreigners and indignation against the princes, as has often been seen by experience, and is seen all the time. When the succession goes from male to male, the heir is always certain and is of the same blood as those who formerly ruled, so the subjects have the very same love and reverence for him as for his predecessors. Even though he be related only distantly and the dead king have daughters, yet without deviation or scruple the people turn to him as soon as the other has ceased to be, and there is no disturbance or difficulty. So it went at the death of King Charles VIII and of King Louis XII recently deceased. Although in former times there were great quarrels and differences on such occasions, which brought great wars, persecutions, and desolations to the realm, nevertheless, these differences were not the reason for the troubles but the pretext, although well known to be frivolous and ill founded. In the end matters must have been redressed and so established that there can never again be dissensions and difficulties on this score. [In order to demonstrate what I said about the perfection of the monarchy of France I have included in this account] the state of France as it is now, joining the old laws, customs, and observances with the new and more recent.

From Claude de Seyssel, *The Monarchy of France* (1515).

reign, Louis XI gradually won back what he had been forced to give away. Years of fighting both the English and each other left the ranks of the French aristocracy depleted. As blood spilled on the battlefields, the stocks of fathers and sons ran low. Estates, to which no male heirs existed, fell forfeit to the king. In this manner, the crown absorbed Anjou and Maine in the northwest and Provence in the south. More importantly, Louis XI ultimately obtained control of the two greatest independent fiefs, Brittany and Orléans. He managed this feat by arranging the marriage of his son Charles to the heiress of Brittany and of his daughter Jeanne to the heir of Orléans. When in 1527 the lands of the duke of Bourbon fell to the crown, the French monarch ruled a unified state.

The consolidation of France was not simply the result of the incorporation of diverse pieces of territory into the domain of the king. More than in any other state, the experience in France demonstrated how a state could be formed without the designs of a great leader. Neither Louis XI nor his son Charles VIII (1483–98) were nation builders. Louis's main objective was always to preserve his estate. His good fortune saved him from the consequences of many ill-conceived policies. But no amount of luck could make up for Louis's failure to obtain the Burgundian Low Countries for France after the death of Charles the Bold in 1477. The marriage of Mary of Burgundy to Maximilian of Habsburg was one of the great turning points in European history. It initiated the struggle for control of the Low Countries that endured for over two centuries.

These long years of war established the principle of royal taxation that was so essential to the process of state building in France. It enabled the monarchy to raise money for defense and for consolidation. Because of the strength of the nobles, most taxation fell only on the commoners, the so-called third estate. The *taille* was a direct tax on property from which the nobility and clergy were exempt. The *gabelle* was a consumption tax on the purchase of salt in most parts of the kingdom, and the *aide* was a tax on a variety of commodities, including meat and wine. These consumption taxes were paid by all members of the third estate no matter how poor they might be. Although there was much complaint about taxes, the French monarchy established a broad base for taxation and a high degree of compliance long before any other European nation.

Along with money went soldiers, fighting men necessary to repel the English and to defend the crown against rebels and traitors. Again the French monarchy

was the first to establish the principle of a national army, raised and directed from the center but quartered and equipped regionally. From the nobility were recruited the cavalry, from the towns and countryside the massive infantry. Fortified towns received privileges in return for military service to the king. Originally towns were required to provide artillery, but constant troubles with the nobility had led the kings of France to establish their own store of heavy guns. The towns supplied small arms, pikes, and swords, and later pistols and muskets. By the beginning of the sixteenth century, the French monarch could raise and equip an army of his own.

Taxation and military obligation demanded the creation and expansion of centralized institutions of government. This was the most difficult development in the period of state formation in France. The powers of royal agents were constantly challenged by the powers of regional nobles. It is easy to exaggerate the extent of the growth of central control and to underestimate the enduring hold of regional and provincial loyalties. Even the crown's absorption of estates did not always end local privileges and customs. France was not a nation and was hardly a state by the opening of the sixteenth century. But despite continued regional autonomy, a beginning had been made.

The Marriages of Spain. Before the sixteenth century there was little prospect of a single nation emerging on the Iberian Peninsula. North African Muslims, called Moors, occupied the province of Granada in the south, while the stable kingdom of Portugal dominated the western coast. The Spanish peoples were divided among a number of separate states. The two most important were Castile, the largest and wealthiest kingdom, and Aragon, which was composed of a number of quasi-independent regions, each of which maintained its own laws and institutions. Three religions and four languages (not including dialects) widened these political divisions. Furthermore, the different states had different outlooks. Castile was, above all, determined to subjugate the last of Islamic Spain and to convert its large Jewish population to Christianity. Aragon played in the high-stakes game for power in the Mediterranean, claiming sovereignty over Sicily and Naples and exercising that sovereignty whenever it could.

A happy teenage marriage brought together the unhappy kingdoms of Castile and Aragon. When Ferdinand of Aragon and Isabella of Castile secretly exchanged wedding vows in 1469, both their homelands were rent by civil war. In Castile, Isabella's brother, Henry IV (1454–74), struggled unsuccessfully against the powerful Castilian nobility. In Aragon, Ferdinand's father, John II (1458–79), faced a revolt by the rich province of Catalonia on one side and the territorial ambitions of Louis XI of France on the other. Joining the heirs together increased the resources of both kingdoms. Ferdinand took an active role in the pacification of Castile, while Castilian riches allowed him to defend Aragon from invasion. In 1479 the two crowns were united and the Catholic monarchs, as they were called, ruled the two kingdoms jointly. But the unification of the crowns of Castile and Aragon was not the same as the formation of a single state between them. Local privileges were zealously guarded, especially in Aragon, where the representative institutions of the towns—the Cortes—were aggressively independent. Their attitude is best expressed in the oath of the townsmen of Saragossa: "We accept you as our king provided you observe all our liberties and laws; and if not, not." The powerful Castilian nobility never accepted Ferdinand as their king and refused him the crown after Isabella's death.

But Ferdinand and Isabella (1479–1516) took the first steps toward forging a Spanish state. Their most notable achievement was the final recovery of the lands that had been conquered by the Moors. For centuries the Spanish kingdoms had fought against the North African Muslims, who had conquered large areas of the southern peninsula. The reconquista was characterized by short bursts of warfare followed by long periods of wary coexistence. By the middle of the fifteenth century, the Moorish territory had been reduced to the province of Granada, but civil strife in Castile heightened the possibility of a new Moorish offensive. "We no longer mint gold, only steel," was how a Moorish ruler replied to Isabella's demand for the traditional payment of tribute money. The final stages of the reconquista began in 1482 and lasted for a decade. The struggle was waged as a holy war and was financed in part by grants from the pope and the Christian princes of Europe. It was a bloody undertaking. The Moorish population of nearly half a million was reduced to one hundred thousand before the town of Granada finally fell and the province was absorbed into Castile.

The reconquista played an important part in creating a national identity for the Christian peoples of Spain. In order to raise men and money for the war effort, Ferdinand and Isabella mobilized their nobility

and town governments and created a central organization to oversee the invasion. Ferdinand was actively involved in the warfare, gaining the respect of the hostile Castilian nobles in the process. The conquered territories were used to reward those who had aided the effort, though the crown maintained control and jurisdiction over most of the province. But the idea of the holy war also had a darker side and an unanticipated consequence. The Jewish population that had lived peacefully in both Castile and Aragon became another object of hostility. Many Jews had risen to prominence in government and in skilled professions. Others, who had accepted conversion to Christianity and were known as *conversos,* had become among the most powerful figures in Church and state.

Both groups were now attacked. The conversos fell prey to a special Church tribunal created to examine their sincere devotion to Catholicism. This was the Spanish Inquisition, which, though it used traditional judicial practices—torture to gain confessions, public humiliation to show contrition, and burnings at the stake to maintain purity—used them on a scale never before seen. Thousands of conversos were killed, and many more families had their wealth confiscated to be used for the reconquista. In 1492 the Jews themselves were expelled from Spain. Though the reconquista and the expulsion of the Jews inflicted great suffering upon victims and incalculable loss to the Castilian economy, both events enhanced the prestige of the Catholic monarchs.

In many ways, Ferdinand and Isabella had trodden the paths of the medieval monarchy. They relied upon personal contact with their people more than upon the use of a centralized administration. They frequently dispensed justice personally, sitting in court and accepting petitions from their subjects. Quite remarkably, they had no permanent residence and traveled the length and breadth of their kingdoms. Isabella is said to have visited every town in Castile, and it is entirely possible that a majority of the population of both kingdoms actually saw their monarchs at one time or another. Queen Isabella was venerated in Castile, where women's right to inheritance remained strong. Ferdinand's absences from Aragon were always a source of contention between him and the Cortes of the towns, yet he was careful to provide regents to preside in his absence and regularly returned to visit his native kingdom. He was not an absentee monarch.

The joint presence of Ferdinand and Isabella in the

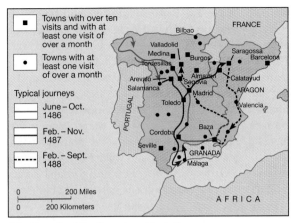

The Travels of Ferdinand and Isabella

Aragon had separate councils, they were organized similarly and had greater contact than before. Charles V realized the importance of Spain, especially of Castile, in his empire. He learned Castilian and spent more time there than in any other part of his empire, calling it "the head of all the rest." Like Ferdinand and Isabella he traveled throughout Castile and Aragon; but unlike them he established a more permanent bureaucratic court, modeled on that of Burgundy, and placed able Spaniards at the head of its departments. This smoothed over the long periods when Charles was abroad, especially the thirteen years between 1543 and 1556.

Yet neither his personal efforts to rule as a Spanish monarch, nor those of his able administrators were the most important factor in uniting the Spanish kingdoms of Iberia. Rather it was the fact that Charles V brought Spain to the forefront of European affairs in the sixteenth century. Spanish prowess, whether in arms or in culture, became a source of national pride that helped erode regional identity. Gold and silver from the New World helped finance Charles's great empire. Whether or not he dreamed of uniting all of Europe under his rule, Charles V fulfilled nearly all of the ancient territorial ambitions of the Spanish kingdoms. In Italy he prosecuted Aragonese claims to Sicily and Naples; in the north he held on firmly to the kingdom of Navarre, which had been annexed by Ferdinand and which secured Spain's border with France. In the south he blocked off Ottoman and Muslim expansion. The reign of Charles V ushered in the dawn of Spain's golden age.

The Dynastic Struggles

The formation of large states throughout Europe led inevitably to conflicts among them. Long chains of marriages among the families of the European princes meant that sooner or later the larger powers would lay claim to the same inheritances and test the matter by force. Thus the sixteenth century was a period of almost unrelieved general warfare that took the whole of the Continent as its theater. Advances in technology made war more efficient and more expensive. They also made it more horrible. The use of artillery against infantry increased the number of deaths and maiming injuries, as did the replacement of the arrow by the bullet. As the size of armies increased, so did casualties.

provinces of Spain was symbolic of the unity that they wished to achieve. Despite the great obstacles, they were intent on bringing about a more permanent blending. Ferdinand made Castilian the official language of government in Aragon and even appointed Castilians to Aragonese posts. He and Isabella actively encouraged the intermarriage of the two aristocracies and the expansion of the number of wealthy nobles who held land in both kingdoms. A single coinage, stamped with the heads of both monarchs, was established for both kingdoms. Nevertheless, these measures did not unify Spain or erase the centuries' long tradition of hostility among the diverse Iberian peoples.

It was left to the heirs of Ferdinand and Isabella to forge together the Spanish kingdoms, and the process was a painful one. The hostility to a foreign monarch that both the Castilian nobility and the Aragonese towns had shown to Ferdinand and Isabella increased dramatically at the accession of their grandson, who became the Emperor Charles V (1516–56). Charles had been born and raised in the Low Countries, where he ruled over Burgundy and the Netherlands. Through a series of dynastic accidents, he became heir to the Spanish crown with its possessions in the New World and to the vast Habsburg estates that included Austria. Charles established his rule in Spain gradually. For a time he was forced to share power in Castile and to suppress a disorganized aristocratic rebellion.

Because of his foreign obligations, Charles was frequently absent from Spain. During those periods he governed through regents and royal councils that did much to centralize administration. Though Castile and

The sixteenth-century army of the Ottoman Turks under Suleiman the Magnificent was the most feared military power in the West. Most of the Ottoman soldiers were cavalry, armed only with bows, lances, and swords, but the Turks also possessed cannon and other modern weapons.

Nearly sixty thousand men met at Marignano in 1515, where it took 30 French cavalry charges and 28 consecutive hours of battle before the Swiss infantry was driven from the field. The slaughter of French nobility at Pavia in 1525 was the largest in a century, while the Turkish sultan Suleiman the Magnificent recorded the burial of 24,000 Hungarian soldiers after the battle of Mohacs in 1526.

Power and Glory

The frequency with which offensive war was waged in the sixteenth century raises a number of questions about the militaristic values of the age. Valor remained greatly prized—a Renaissance virtue inherited from the crusading zeal and chivalric ideals of the Middle Ages.

Princes saw valor as a personal attribute and sought to do great deeds. Ferdinand of Aragon and Francis I of France (1515–47) won fame for their exploits in war. Charles the Bold and Louis II of Hungary were less fortunate: their battlefield deaths led to the breakup of their states. Wars were fought to further the interests of princes rather than the interests of national sovereignty or international Christianity. They were certainly not fought in the interests of their subjects. States were an extension of a prince's heritage: what rulers sought in battle was a part of the historical and familial rights that defined themselves and their subjects. The wars of the sixteenth century were dynastic wars.

Along with desire came ability. The New Monarchs were capable of waging war. The very definition of their states involved the ability to accumulate territories and to defend them. Internal security depended upon locally raised forces or hired mercenaries. Both required money, which was becoming available in unprecedented quantities as a result of the increasing prosperity of the early sixteenth century and the windfall of gold and silver from the New World. Professional soldiers, of whom the Swiss and Germans were the most noteworthy, sold their services to the highest bidders. Developments in transport and supply enabled campaigns to take place far from the center of a state. Finally, communications were improving. The need for knowledge about potential rivals or allies had the effect of expanding the European system of diplomacy. Resident agents were established in all the European capitals, and they had a decisive impact upon war and peace. Their dispatches formed the most reliable source of information about the strengths of armies or the weaknesses of governments, about the birth of heirs or the death of princes.

Personality also played a part in the international warfare of the early sixteenth century. The three most consistent protagonists—Charles V, Francis I, and Henry VIII—were of similar age and outlook. Each came unexpectedly to his throne in the full flush of youth, eager for combat and glory. The three were self-consciously rivals, each jealous of the other's successes, each triumphant in the other's failures. Henry VIII and Francis I held wrestling bouts when they met in 1520. Francis I challenged Charles V to single combat after the French king's humiliating imprisonment in Madrid in 1526. As the three monarchs aged together, their youthful wars of conquest matured into strategic warfare designed to maintain a continental balance of power.

A portrait of Emperor Charles V.

The Italian Wars

The struggle for supremacy in Europe in the sixteenth century pitted the French House of Valois against the far-flung estates of the Habsburg empire. Yet the wars took place in Italy. The rivalries among the larger Italian city-states proved fertile ground for the newly consolidated European monarchies. Both French and Spanish monarchs had remote but legitimate claims to the kingdom of Naples in southern Italy. In 1494 the French king, Charles VIII, took up an invitation from the ruler of Milan to intervene in Italian affairs. His campaign was an unqualified, if fleeting, success. He marched the length of the Iberian Peninsula, overthrew the Medici in Florence, forced the pope to open the gates of Rome, and finally seized the crown of Naples. The occupation was accomplished without a single great battle and lasted until the warring Italian city-states realized that they had more to fear from the French than from one another. Once that happened, Charles VIII beat a hasty retreat. But the French appetite for Italian territory was not sated. Soon a deal was struck with Ferdinand of Aragon to divide the kingdom of Naples in two. In the end, Spain wound up with all of Naples and France was left with nothing but debts and grievances.

Thus, when Francis I came to the French throne and Charles V to the Spanish, Naples was just one of several potential sources of friction. Not only had Ferdinand betrayed the French in Naples, he had also broken a long-standing peace on the Franco-Spanish border by conquering the independent but French-speaking kingdom of Navarre. Francis could be expected to avenge both slights. Charles, on the other hand, was the direct heir of the dukes of Burgundy. From his childhood he had longed for the restoration of his

The Italian Wars

the Holy Roman Emperor, and it soon appealed for Imperial troops to help repel the French invaders. Milan was strategically important to Charles V, as it was the vital link between his Austrian and Burgundian possessions. Almost as soon as he took up the imperial mantle, Charles V was determined to challenge Francis I in Italy.

The key to such a challenge was the construction of alliances among the various Italian city-states and most especially with England, whose aid both Charles and Francis sought to enlist in the early 1520s. Henry VII had found foreign alliances a ready source of cash, and he was always eager to enter into them as long as they did not involve raising armies and fighting wars. Henry VIII was made of sterner stuff. He longed to reconquer France and to cut a figure on the European scene. Despite the fact that his initial Continental adventures had emptied his treasury without fulfilling his dreams, Henry remained eager for war. He was also flattered to find himself the object of attention by both Valois and Habsburg emissaries. Charles V made two separate trips to London, while Henry crossed the Channel in 1520 to meet Francis I in one of the gaudiest displays of conspicuous consumption that the century would witness, appropriately known as the Field of the Cloth of Gold.

The result of these diplomatic intrigues was an alliance between England and the Holy Roman Empire. English and Burgundian forces would stage an invasion of northern France while Spanish and German troops would again attempt to dislodge the French forces from Italy. The strategy worked better than anyone could have imagined. In 1523 Charles's forces gained a foothold in Milan by taking the heavily fortified town of Pavia. Two years later Francis was ready to strike back. At the head of his own royal guards, he massed Swiss mercenaries and French infantry outside Pavia and made ready for a swift assault. Instead, a large imperial army arrived to relieve the town, and in the subsequent battle the French suffered a shattering defeat. Francis I was captured.

The victory at Pavia, which occurred on Charles V's twenty-fifth birthday, seemingly made him master of all of Europe. His ally Henry VIII urged an immediate invasion and dismemberment of France and began raising an army to spearhead the attack. But Charles's position was much less secure than it appeared. The Ottomans threatened his Hungarian territories, and the Protestants threatened his German lands. He could not afford a war of conquest in France. His hope now was to reach an agreement with Francis I for a lasting

ancestral lands, including Burgundy itself, which had been gobbled up by Louis XI after the death of Charles the Bold. Competition between Francis and Charles became all the more ferocious when Charles's grandfather, the Holy Roman Emperor Maximilian I (1486–1519), died in 1519. Both monarchs launched a vigorous campaign for the honor of succeeding him.

For nearly a century the Holy Roman Emperor had come from the Austrian ruling family, and there was little reason to believe that Charles V, who now inherited the Habsburg lands in Austria and Germany, would not also succeed to this eminent but empty dignity. Nevertheless, the electors were willing to be bribed by French agents who supported Francis's candidacy, and even by English agents who supported Henry VIII. Charles spent the most of all, and his eventual election not only aggravated the personal animosity among the monarchs, but added another source of conflict in Italy. When Louis XII (1498–1515) succeeded Charles VIII as king of France, he had laid claim to the duchy of Milan through an interest of his wife's, though he was unable to enforce it. Francis I proved more capable. In 1515 he stunned all of Europe by crushing the vaunted Swiss mercenaries at the battle of Marignano. But the duchy of Milan was a territory under the protection of

The Field of the Cloth of Gold, the lavish setting for the meeting between Henry VIII and Francis I in June 1520. The fountain in the foreground provides free wine for all.

European peace, and for this purpose the French king was brought in captivity to Madrid.

It is doubtful that there was ever any real chance for peace between Habsburg and Valois after the battle of Pavia. Francis's personal humiliation and Charles's military position were both too strong to allow for a permanent settlement in which Habsburgs ruled in Milan and Naples. But it was neither political nor personal considerations that were the source of another thirty years of continuous European warfare. Rather it was Charles's demand that Burgundy be returned to him. Although Francis was hardly in a position to bargain, he held out on this issue for as long as possible and secretly prepared a disavowal of the final agreement before it was made. By the Treaty of Madrid in 1526, Francis I yielded Burgundy and recognized the Spanish conquest of Navarre and Spanish rule in Naples. The agreement was sealed by the marriage of Francis to Charles's sister, Eleanor of Portugal. But marriage was not sufficient security for such a complete capitulation. To secure his release from Spain, Francis was required to leave behind as hostages his seven- and eight-year-old sons until the treaty was fulfilled. For three years the children languished in Spanish captivity.

No sooner had he set foot upon French soil than Francis I renounced the Treaty of Madrid. Despite the threat that this posed to his children, Francis argued that the terms had been extracted against his will, and he even gained the approval of the pope for violating his oath. Setting France on a war footing, he began seeking new allies. Henry VIII, disappointed with the meager spoils of his last venture, switched sides. So too did a number of Italian city-states, including Rome. Most importantly, Francis I entered into an alliance with the Ottoman sultan, Suleiman the Magnificent (1520–66), whose armies were pressing against the southeastern borders of the Holy Roman Empire. In the year following Pavia, the Ottomans secured an equally decisive triumph at Mohács, captured Budapest, and threatened Vienna, the eastern capital of the Habsburg lands. Almost overnight Charles V had been turned from hunter into hunted. The Ottoman threat demanded immediate attention in Germany, the French and English were preparing to strike in the Low Countries, and the Italian wars continued. In 1527 Charles's unpaid German mercenaries stormed through Rome, sacked the papal capital, and captured the pope. Christian Europe was mortified.

The struggle for European mastery ground on for decades. The Treaty of Cateau-Cambrésis in 1559 brought to a close sixty years of conflict. In the end the French were no more capable of dislodging the Habsburgs from Italy than were the Habsburgs of forcing the Ottomans out of Hungary. The great stores of silver that poured into Castile from the New World were consumed in the fires of Continental warfare. In 1557 both France and Spain declared bankruptcy to avoid foreclosures by their creditors. For the French, the Italian wars were disastrous. They seriously undermined the state's financial base, eroded confidence in the monarchy, and thinned the ranks of the ruling nobility. The adventure begun by Charles VIII in search of glory brought France nearly to ruin. It ended with fitting irony. After the death of Francis I, his son Henry II (1547–59) continued the struggle. Henry never forgave his father for abandoning him in Spain, and he sought revenge on Charles V, who had been his jailer. He regarded the Treaty of Cateau-Cambrésis as a victory and celebrated it with great pomp and pageantry. Among the feasts and festivities were athletic competitions for the king's courtiers and attendants. Henry II entered the jousting tournament and was killed there.

• • •

Charles V died in his bed. The long years of war made clear that the dream to dominate Europe could only be a dream. He split apart his empire and granted to his brother, Ferdinand I (1558–64), the Austrian and German lands and the mantle of the Holy Roman Empire. To his son Philip II (1556–98) he ceded the Low Countries, Spain and the New World, Naples, and his Italian conquests. In 1555 Charles abdicated all of his titles and retired to a monastery to live out his final days. The cares of an empire that once stretched from Peru to Vienna were lifted from his shoulders. Beginning with his voyage to Castile in 1517, he had made ten trips to the Netherlands, nine to Germany, seven to Italy, six to Spain, four to France, two to England, and two to Africa. "My life has been one long journey," he told those who witnessed him relinquish his crowns. On 21 September 1558, he finally rested forever.

Suggestions for Further Reading

General Reading

* G. R. Potter, ed., *The New Cambridge Modern History*. Vol. I, *The Renaissance, 1493–1520* (Cambridge: Cambridge University Press, 1957). Comprehensive survey of political history written by renowned scholars.

* Denys Hay, *Europe in the Fourteenth and Fifteenth Centuries* (London: Longman, 1966). A good first survey of political history.

* Eugene Rice, *The Foundations of Early Modern Europe, 1460–1559* (New York: Norton, 1970). An outstanding synthesis.

European Encounters

C. R. Boxer, *The Portuguese Seaborne Empire, 1415–1825* (London: Hutchinson, 1968). The best history of the first of the explorer nations.

Felipe Fernandez-Armesto, *Before Columbus: Exploration and Colonization from the Mediterranean to the Atlantic, 1229–1492* (London: Macmillan, 1987). A comprehensive survey. Difficult but rewarding.

Felipe Fernandez-Armesto, *Columbus* (Oxford: Oxford University Press, 1991). The best of the new studies. Reliable, stimulating, and up-to-date.

* Samuel Morrison, *Christopher Columbus, Mariner* (New York: New American Library, 1985). A biography by an historian who repeated the Columbian voyages.

* Kirkpatrick Sale, *The Conquest of Paradise : Christopher Columbus and the Columbian Legacy* (New York: Plume Publishers, 1991). An entertaining and infuriating account. Very readable and very controversial.

* Dan O'Sullivan, *Age of Discovery, 1400–1550* (London: Longman, 1984). Best short synthetic work.

Valerie Flint, *The Imaginative Landscape of Christopher Columbus* (Princeton, NJ: Princeton University Press, 1992). A study of what Columbus and his contemporaries knew about the geography of the world.

* Lyle McAlister, *Spain and Portugal in the New World, 1492–1700* (Minneapolis: University of Minnesota Press, 1984). The most up-to-date history of the great South American empires.

* J. H. Parry, *The Age of Reconnaissance* (New York: New American Library, 1963). A survey of technological and technical changes that made possible the European discovery of America.

* J. H. Elliott, *The Old World and the New, 1492–1650* (Cambridge: Cambridge University Press, 1970). A brilliant look at the reception of knowledge about the new world by Europeans.

* A. W. Crosby, *The Columbian Exchange: Biological and Cultural Consequences of 1492* (Westport, CT: Greenwood Press, 1972). An argument about the medical consequences of the transatlantic encounter.

Europe in 1500

N. J. G. Pounds, *An Historical Geography of Europe, 1500–1800* (Cambridge: Cambridge University Press, 1979). A remarkable survey of the relationship between geography and history.

* Daniel Waley, *Later Medieval Europe* (London: Longman, 1985). A good brief account.

The Formation of States

J. H. Shennan, *The Origins of the Modern European State, 1450–1725* (London: Hutchinson, 1974). An analytic account of the rise of the state.

Bernard Guenée, *States and Rulers in Later Medieval Europe* (London: Basil Blackwell, 1985). An engaging argument about the forces that helped shape the state system in Europe.

* Norman Davies, *God's Playground: A History of Poland.* Vol. 1, *The Origins to 1795* (New York: Columbia University Press, 1982). The best treatment in English of a complex history.

* Orest Subtelny, *Ukraine: A History* (Toronto: University of Toronto Press, 1988). A compendious history of a people and their domination by their neighbors—from the earliest times to the twentieth century.

* Richard Pipes, *Russia Under the Old Regime* (London: Weidenfeld and Nicolson, 1974). A majesterial account.

* Robert O. Crummey, *The Formation of Muscovy, 1304–1613* (London: Longman, 1987). The best one-volume history.

J. R. Lander, *Government and Community, England, 1450–1509* (Cambridge, MA: Harvard University Press, 1980). A comprehensive survey of the late fifteenth century.

* S. B. Chrimes, *Henry VII* (Berkeley: University of California Press, 1972). A traditional biography of the first Tudor.

* C. D. Ross, *The Wars of the Roses* (London: Thames and Hudson, 1976). The best one-volume account.

* G. R. Elton, *Reform and Reformation, England, 1509–1558* (Cambridge, MA: Harvard University Press, 1977). A survey by the dean of Tudor historians.

Richard Vaughan, *Valois Burgundy* (Hampden, CT: Shoe String Press, 1975). An engaging history of a vanished state.

* Paul M. Kendall, *Louis XI: The Universal Spider* (New York: Norton, 1971). A highly entertaining account of an unusual monarch.

* R. J. Knecht, *French Renaissance Monarchy* (London: Longman, 1984). A study of the nature of the French monarchy and the way it was transformed in the early sixteenth century.

John Lynch, *Spain, 1516–1598: From Nation State to World Empire* (Cambridge, MA: Blackwell, 1992). The most up-to-date survey.

* L. P. Harvey, *Islamic Spain, 1250 to 1500* (Chicago: University of Chicago Press, 1990). A detailed political history of Islamic rule in Spain before the reconquista.

* J. H. Elliot, *Imperial Spain, 1469–1716* (New York: Mentor, 1963). Still worth reading for its insights and examples.

The Dynastic Struggles

* J. R. Hale, *War and Society in Renaissance Europe* (Baltimore, MD: Johns Hopkins University Press, 1986). Assesses the impact of war on the political and social history of early modern Europe.

M. F. Alvarez, *Charles V* (London: Thames and Hudson, 1975). An accessible biography of the most remarkable man of the age.

* R. J. Knecht, *Francis I* (Cambridge: Cambridge University Press, 1982). A compelling study by the leading scholar of sixteenth century France.

* J. J. Scarisbrick, *Henry VIII* (Berkeley: University of California Press, 1968). The definitive biography.

*Paperback edition available.

13 ✢ THE REFORM OF RELIGION

Sola Scriptura

*I*n the beginning was the word, and the word was with God, and the word was God." In no other period of European history was this text of the apostle John so appropriate. Men and women shared a consuming desire to hear and to read the Word of God as set down in the Bible. In the early sixteenth century, Europeans developed an insatiable appetite for the Bible. Scriptures rolled off

printing presses in every shape and form, from the great vellum tomes of Gutenberg pictured here to pocket Bibles that soldiers carried into battle. They came in every imaginable language. Before 1500 there were fourteen complete Bibles printed in German, four each in Italian, French, and Spanish, one in Czech, and even one in Flemish. There were hundreds more editions in Latin, the official

Vulgate Bible first translated by Saint Jerome in the fourth century. Whole translations and editions of the Bible were only part of the story. Separate sections, especially the Psalms and the first books of the Old Testament, were printed by the thousands. There were twenty-four French editions of the Old Testament before an entirely new translation appeared in 1530. When Martin Luther began his own German translation of the Bible in 1522, it immediately became an international best-seller. In twenty-five years it went into 430 editions. It is estimated that one million German Bibles were printed in the first half of the sixteenth century—a time when Europe had a German-speaking population of about 15 million people, 90 percent of whom were illiterate.

Bible owning was no fad. It was but one element in a new devotional outlook that was sweeping the Continent and that would have far-reaching consequences for European society during the next 150 years. A renewed spirituality was everywhere to be seen. It was expressed in a desire to change the traditional practices and structures of the Roman church. It was expressed in a desire to have learned and responsible ministers to tend to the needs of their parishioners. It was expressed in a desire to establish godly families, godly cities, and godly kingdoms. Sometimes it took the form of sarcasm and bitter denunciations; sometimes it took the form of quiet devotion and pious living. The need for reform was everywhere felt; the demand for reform was everywhere heard. It came from within the Roman church as much as from without.

The inspiration for reform was based on the Word of God. Scholars, following humanist principles,

worked on biblical translations in an attempt to bring a purer text to light. Biblical commentary dominated the writings of churchmen as never before. Woodcut pictures depicting scenes from the life of Jesus or from the Old Testament were printed in untold quantities for the edification of the unlettered. For the first time common people could, in their own dwellings, contemplate representations of the lives of the saints. Many of the Bibles that were printed in vernacular—that is, in the languages spoken in the various European

states rather than in Latin—were interleaved with illustrations of the central events of Christian history. Preachers spoke to newly aware audiences and relied on biblical texts to draw out their message. Study groups, especially in urban areas, proliferated so that the literate could read and learn together. Bible reading became a part of family life, one which mothers and fathers could share with their children and their servants. *Sola Scriptura*—by the word alone—became the battle cry of religious reform.

The Intellectual Reformation

There is nothing as powerful as an idea whose time has come. But the coming of ideas has a history as complex as the ideas themselves. In the early sixteenth century, reformers throughout western Europe preached new ideas about religious doctrine and religious practice. At first these ideas took the form of a sustained critique of the Roman Catholic church, but soon they developed a momentum of their own. Some reformers remained within traditional Catholicism; others moved outside and founded new Protestant churches. Whether Catholic or Protestant, wherever this movement for religious reform appeared it was fed by new ideas. But if new ideas were to supplant old ones, they had to be communicated—not only heard and repeated but accurately recorded and understood. This was made possible by the development of the technology of printing, which appeared in Germany in the late fifteenth century and rapidly spread across Europe in the succeeding decades. Yet printing was as much a result as it was a cause of the spread of ideas. The humanist call for a return to the study of the classics and for the creation of accurate texts, first heard in Italy, aroused scholars and leaders in all of the European states. Their appetite for manuscripts exhausted the abilities of the scribes and booksellers who reproduced texts. Printing responded to that demand.

The Print Revolution

The development of printing did not cause religious reform, but it is difficult to see how reform would have progressed in its absence. The campaign to change the doctrine and practice of Catholicism was waged through the press, with millions of flyers and pamphlets distributed across Europe to spread the new ideas. A third of all books sold in Germany between 1518 and 1525 were written by Luther. But the ways in which printing came to be used by religious reformers could hardly have been foreseen by the artisans, bankers, and booksellers who together created one of the true technological revolutions in Western history.

Printing was not invented. It developed as a result of progress made in a number of allied industries, of which papermaking and goldsmithing were the most important. Scholars and university students needed copies of manuscripts. Their need led to the development of a trade in bookselling that flourished in almost every university town. The process of reproduction was slowed by difficulties in obtaining the sheep and calf-skins on which the manuscripts were written. It took the skins of 300 sheep to produce a single Bible. In the early fifteenth century, copyists began to substitute paper made from linen rags for the expensive vellum skins. A number of German artisans experimented with using movable metal type to make exact reproductions of manuscripts on paper. Paper took a better impression and provided an absolutely smooth surface, which was essential for pressing the image. In the 1450s, in Mainz, Johannes Gutenberg (ca. 1400–68) and his partners succeeded and published their famous Bibles.

The association of early printing with goldsmithing resulted from the high level of technical skill that was necessary to create the hard metal stamps from which the softer metal type was produced. Printing was an expensive business. The investment in type and in paper was considerable. Only the press itself was cheap. Any corn or wine press could be used to bring the long flat sheets of paper down upon a wooden frame filled with ink-coated metal type. Booksellers initially put up the capital needed to cast the stamps, mold the type, and buy the paper. They bound the printed pages and found the markets to distribute them. At first sales were slow. Printed books were considered inferior to hand-written manuscripts. Nor at first were printed books

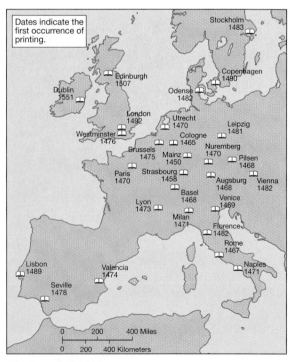

The Spread of Printing

An early print shop. The man at the right operates the screw press while an apprentice (center) stacks the printed sheets. The men at the left are setting type for the next impression.

less expensive. Bibles like those printed by Gutenberg were major investments, equivalent to purchasing a house today. Many printing shops quickly went bankrupt as they misjudged their markets and were unable to pay back their loans.

Still, once it was begun, printing spread like wildfire. By 1480, over 110 towns had established presses, most in Italy and Germany. After that the pace quickened. By the beginning of the sixteenth century, Venice and Paris were the centers of the industry, with the Paris presses producing over three hundred new titles annually. Most of the early printed works were either religious or classical. Bibles, church service books, and the commentaries of the church fathers were most common. Cicero topped the list of classical authors.

What is most amazing about the printing revolution is how rapidly printing came to be a basic part of life. In the first forty years after the presses began, perhaps as many as twenty million books were produced and distributed. Printing changed the habits of teachers and students, and therefore the possibilities of education. It altered the methods by which the state conducted its business. It affected both legal training and legal proceedings. Compilations of laws could now be widely distributed and more uniformly enforced. Printing had a similar effect on the development of scientific study. The printing press popularized the discoveries of the New World and contributed to the reproduction of more accurate charts and maps, which in turn facilitated further discovery. Printing also helped standardize language—both Latin and vernacular—by frequent repetition of preferred usage and spelling. Perhaps most importantly, printing created an international intellectual community whose ideas could be dispersed the length and breadth of the Continent. The printing press enhanced the value of ideas and of thinking. Nothing could be more central to the reform of religion.

Christian Humanism

Many of the ideas that spread across Europe as the result of the printing revolution originated in Italian humanism (see chapter 11). The revival of classical literature, with its concern for purity in language and eloquence in style, was one of the most admired achievements of the Renaissance. Students from all over Europe who descended upon Italian universities to study medicine and law came away with a strong dose of philology, rhetoric, moral philosophy, and the other liberal arts. Their heads were filled with the new learning. By the beginning of the sixteenth century, the force of humanism was felt strongly in northern and western Europe, where it was grafted to the dominant strains of traditional theological teaching. The combination was a new and powerful intellectual movement known as Christian humanism.

Although the humanism of the north differed from that of the Italian city-states, this is not to say that northern humanists were Christians and Italian humanists were not. But Italian intellectual interests were in secular subjects, especially in mastering classical languages and in translating classical texts. Italian humanists had established techniques for the recovery of accurate texts and had developed principles for compiling the scholarly editions that now poured forth from the printing presses. Christian humanists applied these techniques to the study of the authorities and texts of the Church. Most of the new humanists had been trained in Italy, where they devoted themselves to the mastery of Greek and Latin. They had imbibed the idea that scholars, using their own critical faculties, could establish the authority of texts and the meaning of words. Building upon the patient work of their predecessors and the advantages offered by printing, this new generation of humanists brought learning to educated men and women throughout Europe.

Christian humanism was a program of reform rather than a philosophy. It aimed to make better Christians through better education. Humanists were especially interested in the education of women. "For what is more fruitful than the good education and order of women, the one half of all mankind," wrote Thomas More (1478–1535). Humanists helped found schools for girls and advocated that they be trained in the same subjects as boys. Thomas More raised his daughters to be among the educated elite of England, and they enjoyed international renown. The Spanish humanist Juan Luis Vives (1492–1540) wrote *The Instruction of a Christian Woman* (1523), a handbook for women of the elite orders commissioned by Catherine of Aragon. Renowned women scholars even held places at Italian universities. Humanist educational principles posed an implicit challenge to Roman Catholicism. Schools had once been the monopoly of the Church, which used them to train clergymen. The Church had founded them and kept them afloat in good times and in bad. Literacy itself had been preserved over the centuries so that the gospel could be propagated.

By the sixteenth century these purposes had been transformed. Schools now trained many who were not destined for careers in the Church, and literacy served the needs of the state, the aristocracy, and the merchant classes. More importantly, as the humanists perfected their techniques of scholarship, the Church continued to rely upon traditional methods of training and traditional texts. The dominant manner of teaching at the schools and universities was known as Scholasticism. Passages of biblical texts were studied through the commentaries of generations of church fathers. Rote memorization of the opinions of others was more highly valued than critical thinking. Argument took place by formal disputation of questions on which the church fathers disagreed. Disputed questions became more and more obscure. Even if Scholastics did not debate the question "How many angels can dance on the head of a pin?" it seemed to many humanists that they might as well have. The Vulgate Bible was used throughout western Christendom. It was now a thousand years old.

The Humanist Movement

Many humanist criticisms of Church teaching focused on its failure to inspire individuals to live a Christian life. Humanist writers were especially scathing about popular practices that bordered on superstition, like pilgrimages to holy places or the worship of relics from the early history of the Church. Such beliefs became the butt of popular humor: "If the fragments [of the Lord's Cross] were joined together they would seem a full load for a freighter. And yet the Lord carried his whole cross." Christian humanists wanted to inspire Christians. As the great Dutch humanist Desiderius Erasmus observed, "To be learned is the lot of only a few; but no one is unable to be a Christian, no one is unable to be pious." This ironic strain in humanist writing is most closely associated with Erasmus, but it is also visible in the humanist social criticism of Sir Thomas More's *Utopia*. (See "Utopia," pp. 390–391.)

Christian humanism was an international movement. The humanists formed the elite of the intellectual world of the sixteenth century, and their services were sought by princes and peers as well as by the most distinguished universities. In fact, the New Monarchs supported the humanists and protected them from their critics. Marguerite of Navarre, sister of Francis I, was an accomplished writer who frequently interceded on behalf of the leading French humanists. Ferdinand of Aragon, Henry VIII, and the Holy Roman Emperors Maximilian I and Charles V all brought humanists to their courts and aided their projects. Maria of Hungary and Mary and Elizabeth Tudor were trained in humanist principles and participated in humanist literary achievements. This support was especially important for educational reform. Under the influence of the French humanist Jacques Lefevre d'Étaples (ca. 1455–1536), Francis I established the College de France; under the direction of Cardinal Jiménez de Cisneros,

A DUTCH WIT

In Praise of Folly (1500) was a witty satire on the abuses to be found in the Catholic church. Desiderius Erasmus wrote it on a lark to be presented to his friend, Sir Thomas More, on whose name its Greek title puns. It was probably the first best-seller of the age of printing.

These various forms of foolishness so pervade the whole life of Christians that even the priests themselves find no objection to admitting, not to say fostering, them, since they do not fail to perceive how many tidy little sums accrue to them from such sources. But what if some odious philosopher should chime in and say, as is quite true: "You will not die badly if you live well. You are redeeming your sins when you add to the sum that you contribute a hearty detestation of evil doers: then you may spare yourself tears, vigils, invocations, fasts, and all that kind of life. You may rely upon any saint to aid you when once you begin to imitate his life."

As for the theologians, perhaps the less said the better on this gloomy and dangerous theme, since they are a style of man who show themselves exceeding supercilious and irritable unless they can heap up six hundred conclusions about you and force you to recant; and if you refuse, they promptly brand you as a heretic—for it is their custom to terrify by their thunderings those whom they dislike. It must be confessed that no other group of fools are so reluctant to acknowledge Folly's benefits toward them, although I have many titles to their gratitude, for I make them so in love with themselves that they seem to be happily exalted to the third heaven, whence they look down with something like pity upon all other mortals, wandering about on the earth like mere cattle.

From Erasmus, In Praise of Folly.

---

the University of Alcala was founded in Spain. Throughout northern Europe, professorships in Greek and Latin were endowed at universities to help further the study of classical languages.

The centerpiece of humanist reforms was the translation of Christian texts. Armed with skills in Greek and Latin, informed by scholars of Hebrew and Aramaic, humanist writers prepared new editions of the books of the Bible and of the writings of the early church fathers. Their favorite method was side-by-side translation. The Polyglot—literally "many languages"—Bible that was produced in 1522 at the University of Alcala took a team of scholars fifteen years to complete. They gathered together copies of all known biblical manuscripts and rigorously compared their texts. They established the principle that inconsistencies among Latin manuscripts were to be resolved by reference to Greek texts, and difficulties in Greek texts by reference to Hebrew texts. The result was six elegantly printed volumes that allowed scholars to compare the texts. The Old Testament was printed in three parallel columns of Hebrew, Latin Vulgate, and Greek. The New Testament was printed in double columns, with the Greek text on one side and the Vulgate on the other. The Greek edition of the Bible and its establishment as a text superior to the Vulgate caused an immediate sensation throughout humanist and Church circles.

The Wit of Erasmus

Although the Polyglot Bible contained the first completed Greek edition of the New Testament, it was not the first published one. That distinction belongs to the man whose name is most closely associated with the idea of Christian humanism: Desiderius Erasmus of Rotterdam (ca. 1466–1536). Orphaned at an early age, Erasmus was educated by the Brothers of the Common Life, a lay brotherhood that specialized in schooling children and preparing them for a monastic life. Marked out early by his quick wit, pleasant though strong personality, and extraordinary intellectual gifts, Erasmus entered a monastery and was then allowed to travel to pursue his studies, first in France and then in England.

In England Erasmus learned of new techniques for instructing children both in classical knowledge and in Christian morals, and he became particularly interested in the education of women. He dedicated a number of his later writings to women patrons who were accomplished humanist scholars. While in England, Erasmus decided to compose a short satire on the lines of his conversations with Thomas More, extolling what was silly and condemning what was wise. The result was *In Praise of Folly* (1509), a work that became one of the first best-sellers in publishing history.

❧ Utopia

"It is a general rule that the more different anything is from what people are used to, the harder it is to accept." So warned the imaginary traveler Raphael Hythloday as he described Utopia, a fabulous society he had visited in the New World. Utopian society was different indeed. In Utopia, all property was held in common; there were no social classes; families were extended to include grandparents, in-laws, and flocks of children; and all work and most social activities were regulated by the state. Utopians were rarely tempted to sin. Everyone wore the same practical clothes to abolish vanity: "No matter how delicate the thread, they say a sheep wore it once and still was

nothing but a sheep." Everyone ate the same food in large common halls to abolish jealousy: "A man would be stupid to take the trouble to prepare a worse meal at home when he had a sumptuous one near at hand in the hall." To abolish greed, Utopians scorned gold and silver: "Criminals who are to bear through life the mark of some disgraceful act are forced to wear golden rings on their ears, golden bands on their fingers, golden chains around their necks, and even golden crowns on their heads." Utopians lived harmoniously in planned cities, honored their elders, cared for their sick, and brought up their children to love learning and respect hard work. They led "a life as free of anxiety and as full of joy as possible."

There were many ways in which Christian humanists attempted to instruct their contemporaries to lead a joyful life. None has proved more enduring than the imaginary community Sir Thomas More created in Utopia, a social satire so convincing that a Catholic priest sought to become its bishop and sea travelers tried to learn its location. More's creation has proven so compelling that it has given its name to the entire genre of dreamworlds that followed in its wake. His vision of a carefully planned and permanently contented society has passed into our language, but in a way that would not have pleased the author. Now the term *utopian* has a wistful ring. It is a label for impractical ideals that will never come to pass, a name for well-meaning but misguided daydreams. For More, as for his generation of humanists, the goal of teaching Christians to lead a Christian life was neither wistful nor impractical.

Sir Thomas More was a London lawyer by vocation but a humanist scholar by avocation. His father had practiced law and planned a similar career for his son. But Thomas's stay at Oxford University coincided with the first flush of humanist enthusiasm there, especially in the study of Greek. More proved so exceptionally able that his father removed him to London in fear that reading Greek would turn him away from Catholicism. More proved as able at law school as he had at the university, and he was soon singled out as one of the best lawyers of his day. But in his spare time he continued to study the classics and became part of the growing humanist circle in London. There he met Erasmus, who was to become his lifelong friend.

Erasmus left a vivid portrait of More. "His complexion is fair, his face being rather blond than pale; his hair is auburn inclining to black, his eyes a bluish grey. It is a face more expressive of pleasantry than of gravity or dignity. He seems to be born and made for friendship, his extraordinary kindness and sweetness of temper are such as to cheer the dullest spirit."

More wrote *Utopia* in 1516, before he embarked upon the public career that would result in his becoming Chancellor of England, Speaker of the House of Commons, Privy Councilor and companion to Henry VIII, and finally a victim of the king's divorce and assumption of the title Supreme Head of the Church of England. More's life ended on the chopping block, and his death was mourned by humanists throughout Europe.

The community that More described in *Utopia* combined Plato's republic with a Christian monastery and was based on travelers' tales of the New World. But More's Utopia resembled nothing so much as England. The real and the imaginary, the serious and the absurd intermingle to disguise the author's point of view. *Utopia* is written in the form of a dialogue in which the author pretends to be one of the characters. On a visit to Antwerp, the character More is introduced to an imaginary traveler named Raphael Hythloday. During a long evening, Hythloday relates a tale of a remarkable society that he encountered on his voyages. Utopia is a self-sufficient island, protected from invasion by the sea and thus able to develop its social customs without interference.

Hythloday contrasts the practices of the Utopians with those of contemporary Europeans and refutes the character More's objections that such arrangements are impractical. For example, whereas European peasants and artisans work fourteen hours a day, Utopians work for only six. But all Utopians work. There are no idle aristocrats with their marauding retainers, no priests or monks or nuns, no beggars unable to find jobs. Moreover, there is no surplus of workers in one field and shortage in another. For two years each Utopian works on a farm. After that, Utopians work at a craft according to the needs of the city. Both males and females are educated to be of service to their community. Women are trained in less strenuous but no less essential trades like weaving or spinning. The populations of cities are strictly controlled so that there is neither poverty nor homelessness. In their spare time Utopians engage in uplifting activities such as music, gardening, or artistic pursuits. Severe punishment awaits transgressors, but in contrast to the European practice of executing thieves, Utopian criminals are enslaved so that they can work for the restitution of the wrongs that they committed. Even as slaves they live well, with good food and much leisure. Although they do not have the benefit of Christian religion, the Utopians believe in a single divinity as well as an afterlife, and their worship is simple and natural.

More's *Utopia* was written in Latin, but the name of the island and its cities are all Greek words. For More's humanist friends, the joke was plain. *Utopia* means "nowhere" in Greek, and Hythloday means "peddler of nonsense." Humanist interest in the New World and in the strange native customs of the Native Americans made it a logical setting for an idealized community. But Utopia was a model for a Christian community, one in which the seven deadly sins had all been abolished and replaced by a life led according to the Golden Rule, a place where people attempted to do unto others what they wished done unto themselves. By ironic contrast with the unfulfilling life led by Europeans—grasping for riches, dominated by vanity, motivated by pride—the peaceful and simple life of the Utopians held great attraction. By contrasting the success of heathen Utopians with the failure of Christian Europeans, More called upon his contemporaries to reform their own lives. The purpose of *Utopia* was not to advocate the abolition of wealth and property or the intervention of the state in the affairs of the individual but to demonstrate that a society founded upon good principles would become a good society. A society that dedicated itself to Christian principles would become truly Christian.

An engraving of Erasmus by the German master Albrecht Dürer. The title, the date, and the artist's name appear in Latin behind the philosopher. The Greek inscription reads: "His writings depict him even better."

Before his visit to England, Erasmus had worked solely on Latin translations, but he came to realize the importance of recovering the Greek texts of the early church fathers. At the age of thirty, he began the arduous task of learning ancient Greek and devoted his energies to a study of the writings of Saint Jerome, the principal compiler of the Vulgate, and to preparing an edition of the Greek text of the Bible. Erasmus's New Testament and his edition of the writings of Saint Jerome both appeared in 1516. Coming from the pen of the most renowned intellectual in Europe, they were an immediate success.

Erasmus devoted his life to restoring the direct connection between the individual Christian and the textual basis of Christian doctrine. Although he is called the father of biblical criticism, Erasmus was not a theologian. He was more interested in the practical impact of ideas than in the ideas themselves. His scathing attacks upon the Scholastics, popular superstition, and the pretensions of the traditionalists in the Church and the universities all aimed at the same goal: to restore the experiences of Christ to the center of Christianity.

Many of Erasmus's popular writings were how-to books—how to improve one's manners, how to speak Latin properly, how to write letters—he even propounded 22 rules on how to lead a Christian life. Although his patrons were the rich and his language was Latin, Erasmus also hoped to reach men and women lower down the social order, those whom he believed the Church had failed to educate. "The doctrine of Christ casts aside no age, no sex, no fortune or position in life. It keeps no one at a distance." He hoped that his biblical translations would comfort others in the same way that they had comforted him. "I would to God that the plowman would sing a text of the Scripture at his plow and that the weaver would hum [it] to the tune of his shuttle. I wish that the traveler would expel the weariness of his journey with this pastime. I wish that all communication of the Christian would be of the Scriptures."

The Lutheran Reformation

On the surface, the Roman Catholic church appeared as strong as ever at the end of the fifteenth century. The growth of universities and the spread of the new learning had helped create a better-educated clergy. The printing press proved an even greater boon to the Church than it had to the humanists by making widely available both instructional manuals for priests and up-to-date service books for congregations. The prosperity of European societies enhanced the prosperity of the Church. In Rome successive late medieval popes had managed to protect Church interests in the wake of the disintegration of the autonomous power of the Italian city-states. This was a remarkable feat. Popes had become first diplomats and then warriors in order to repel French and Spanish invaders. Although Rome had been invaded, it had never been conquered. And it was more beautiful than ever, as the greatest artists and artisans of the Renaissance had built and adorned its churches. Pilgrims came in the hundreds of thousands to bask in its glory. On the surface all was calm.

Yet everywhere in Europe the cry was for reform. Reform the venal papacy and its money-sucking bishops. Reform the ignorant clergy and the sacrilegious priests. Raise up the fallen nuns and the wayward friars. Wherever one turned, one saw abuses. Parish livings were sold to the highest bidder to raise money. This was simony. Rich appointments were given to the kinsmen of powerful Church leaders rather than to those most qualified. This was nepotism. Individual clergymen accumulated numerous positions whose responsibilities they could not fulfill. This was pluralism. Some priests who took the vow of chastity lived openly with their concubines. Some mendicants who took the vow of poverty dressed in silk and ate from golden plates.

Yet the cry for reform that pierced the states of Europe at the beginning of the sixteenth century was a cry not so much of anguish as of hope. It came at a moment when people from all walks of life demanded greater spiritual fulfillment and held those whose vocation it was to provide such fulfillment to higher standards of achievement. It was expectation rather than experience that powered the demands for reform.

The Spark of Reform

Europe was becoming more religious. The signs of religious fervor were everywhere. Cities hired preachers to expound the gospel. Pilgrims to the shrines of saints clogged the roadways every spring and summer. It is estimated that 140,000 people visited the relics at Aachen on one day in 1496. Rome remained the greatest attraction, but pilgrims covered the Continent. The shrine of the apostle Saint James at Compostela in Spain was believed to cure the ill. Endowments of masses for the dead increased. Henry VII of England provided money for ten thousand masses to be said for his soul. Even moderately well-to-do city merchants might bequeath funds for several hundred. The chantries, where such services were performed, became overburdened by this "arithmetical piety," as there were neither enough priests nor enough altars to supply the demand.

People wanted more from the Church than the Church could possibly give them. Humanists condemned visits to the shrines as superstitious; pilgrims demanded that the relics be made more accessible. Reformers complained of pluralism; the clergy complained that they could not live on the salary of a single office. In one English diocese, 60 percent of all parish incomes were inadequate to live on. Civic authorities demanded that the established Church take greater responsibility for good works; the pope demanded that civic authorities help pay for them.

Contradiction and paradox dominated the movements for reform. Although the most vocal critics of the Church complained that its discipline was too lax, for many ordinary people its demands were too rigorous. The obligations of penance and confession weighed heavily upon them. Church doctrine held that sins had to be washed away before the souls of the dead could enter heaven. Until then they suffered in purgatory. Sins were cleansed through penance—the performance of acts of contrition assigned after confession. Despite the rule that confession must be made at least annually, it is doubtful if many Catholics entered the confessional for years on end. This is not to say that they were unconcerned about their sins or did not desire to do penance for them. Rather, it was the ordeal of the confession itself that kept many people away. "Have you skipped mass? Have you dressed proudly? Have you thought of committing adultery? Have you insulted or cursed your parents? Have you failed to offer prayers, give alms, and endow masses for departed parents?" These were just a few of the uncomfortable questions that priests were instructed to pose in confession. In towns merchants were asked about their trading practices, shopkeepers about the quality of their goods. Magistrates were questioned about their attitudes to the clergy, intellectuals about their attitudes to the pope.

Thus it is hardly surprising that the sale of indulgences became a popular substitute for penance and confession. An indulgence was a portion of the treasury of good works performed by righteous Christians throughout the ages. They could be granted to those who desired to atone for their sins. Strictly speaking, an indulgence supplemented penance rather than substituted for it. It was effective only for the contrite—for sinners who repented of their sins. But as the practice of granting indulgences spread, this subtle distinction largely disappeared. Indulgences came to be viewed as pardons and the gift given to the Church in return as payment. "So soon as coin in coffer rings, the soul from purgatory springs." Indulgences were bought by the living to cleanse the sins of the dead, and some people even bought indulgences in anticipation of sins they had not yet committed.

By the sixteenth century, to limit abuses by local Church authorities, only the pope, through his agents, could grant indulgences. And their sale had become big business. Indulgences were one of the first items printed on Gutenberg's press. Popes used special occasions to offer an indulgence for pilgrimages to Rome or for contributions to special papal projects. Other indulgences were licensed locally, usually at the shrines of saints or at churches that contained relics. This was one reason why pilgrimages became increasingly popular. Frederick III, "the Wise" (1463–1525), ruler of Saxony, was one of the largest collectors of relics in Europe. At its height, his collection contained 17,000 different

) ihr deutschen merck et mich recht/
Des heiligen Vaters Papstes Knecht/
bin ich/vnd br ing euch jst allein/
Zehn tausent vnd neun hundert carein/
jnab vnd Ablaß von einer Sünd/
Vor euch/ewer Elter n/Weib vnd Kind/
sol ein jeder gewehret sein
So viel jhr teg t ins Kästelein/
So bald der Gilden im Becken klingt/
Jm hug die Seel im Himel jpringt/

An anonymous caricature of Johann Tetzel, whose sale of an indulgence inspired Martin Luther's Ninety-five Theses. Tetzel answered with 122 theses of his own but was rebuked and disowned by the Catholics.

items, including a branch of Moses' burning bush, straw from Christ's manger, and 35 fragments of the true cross. Together, his relics carried remission for sins that would otherwise have taken over a quarter of a million years in purgatory to be cleansed.

The indulgence controversy was a symptom rather than a cause of the explosion of feelings that erupted in the small German town of Wittenberg in the year 1517. In that year the pope was offering an indulgence to help finance the rebuilding of Saint Peter's Basilica in Rome. The pope chose Prince Albert of Brandenburg (1490–1545) to distribute the indulgence in Germany, and Albert hired the Dominican friar Johann Tetzel (ca. 1465–1519) to preach its benefits. Tetzel offered little warning about the theological niceties of indulgences to those who paid to mitigate their own sins or alleviate the suffering of their ancestors whose souls resided in purgatory.

Enthusiasm for the indulgence spread to the neighboring state of Saxony, where Frederick banned its sale. His great collection of relics carried their own indulgences, and Tetzel offered unwelcome competition. But Saxons flocked into Brandenburg to make their purchases. By the end of October, Tetzel was not very far from Wittenberg Castle, where Frederick's relics were housed. On All Saints' Day the relics would be opened to view and, with the harvest done, one of the largest crowds of the year would gather to see them. On the night before, Martin Luther (1483–1546), a professor of theology at Wittenberg University, posted on

the door of the castle church 95 theses attacking indulgences and their sale.

Aside from the timing of Luther's action, there was nothing unusual about the posting of theses. In the Scholastic tradition of disputation, scholars presented propositions, or theses, for debate and challenged all comers to argue with them in a public forum. Luther's theses were controversial, but—as that was the whole point of offering them for discussion—they were meant to be. Only circumstance moved Luther's theses from the academic to the public sphere. Already there was growing concern among clergy and theologians about Tetzel's blatant sale of indulgences. Hordes of purchasers believed that they were buying unconditional remission of sin. In the late summer and early fall of 1517, the frenzy to buy indulgences had reached gold-rush proportions, and individual priests and monks began to sound the alarm: an indulgence without contrition was worthless.

Luther's theses focused this concern and finally communicated it beyond the walls of the church and university. The theses were immediately translated into German and spread throughout the Holy Roman Empire by humanists who had long criticized practices such as the sale of indulgences as superstitious. Prospective buyers became wary; past purchasers became angry. They had been duped again by the Church, by the priests who took their money and by the Italian pope who cared nothing for honest, hard-working Germans. But Prince Albert and the pope needed the income. They could not stand by while sales collapsed and anticlerical and antipapal sentiment grew. Luther and his theses would have to be challenged.

Martin Luther's Faith

Martin Luther was not a man to challenge lightly. Although he was only an obscure German professor, he had already marked himself out to all who knew him. In his youth Luther was an exceptionally able student whose father sent him to the best schools in preparation for a career in law. But Martin had his own ideas about his future, which were made more vivid when he was nearly struck by lightning. Against the wishes of his father, he entered an Augustinian monastery, wholeheartedly followed the strict program of his order, and was ordained a priest in 1507. Intellectually gifted, he went on to study at the university, first at Erfurt and then at Wittenberg, where he received his doctorate and was appointed to the theology faculty in 1512.

A professor at the age of twenty-nine, he also served as priest at the castle church, where he preached each week. He attracted powerful patrons in the university and gained a reputation as an outstanding teacher. He began to be picked for administrative posts and became overseer of eleven Augustinian monasteries. His skills in disputation were so widely recognized that he was sent to Rome to argue a case on behalf of his order. Each task he was given he fulfilled beyond expectation; at every step he proved himself ready to go higher.

In all outward appearances, Luther was successful and contented. But beneath this tranquil exterior lay a soul in torment. As he rose in others' estimation, he sank in his own. Through beating and fasting he mortified his flesh. Through vigil and prayer he nourished his soul. Through study and contemplation he honed his intellect. Still he could find no peace. Despite his devotion, he could not erase his sense of sin; he could not convince himself that the righteousness God demanded of him was a righteousness he could achieve. "I was one who terribly feared the last judgment and who nevertheless with all my heart wished to be saved."

Knowledge of his salvation came to Luther through study. His internal agonies led him to ponder over and over again the biblical passages that described the right-

eousness of God. In the intellectual tradition in which he had been trained, that righteousness was equated with law. The righteous person either followed God's law or was punished by God's wrath. It was this understanding that tormented him. "I thought that I had to perform good works till at last through them Jesus would become a friend and gracious to me." But no amount of good works could overcome Luther's feelings of guilt for his sins. Like a man caught in a net, the more he struggled the more entangled he became. For years he wrestled with his problem. Almost from the moment he began lecturing in 1512 he searched for the key to the freedom of his own soul.

Even before he wrote his Ninety-five Theses, Luther had made the first breakthrough by a unique reading of the writings of Saint Paul. "I pondered night and day until I understood the connection between the righteousness of God and the sentence 'The just shall live by faith.' Then I grasped that the justice of God is the righteousness by which through grace and pure mercy, God justifies us through faith. Immediately I felt that I had been reborn and that I had passed through wide open doors into paradise!" Finally he realized that the righteousness of God was not a burden that humans carried, but a gift that God bestowed. It could not be earned by good works but was freely given. It was this belief that fortified Luther during his years of struggle with both civil and Church powers.

Over the next several years, Luther refined his spiritual philosophy and drew out the implications of his newfound beliefs. His religion was shaped by three interconnected tenets. First came justification by faith alone—*sola fide*. An individual's everlasting salvation came from faith in God's goodness rather than from the performance of good works. Sin was ever present and inescapable. It could not be washed away by penance, and it could not be forgiven by indulgence. Second, faith in God's mercy came only through the knowledge and contemplation of the Word of God—*sola scriptura*. All that was needed to understand the justice and mercy of God was contained in the Bible, the sole authority in all things spiritual. Reading the Word, hearing the Word, expounding upon and studying the Word—this was the path to faith, and through faith to salvation. Finally, all who believed in God's righteousness and had achieved their faith through the study of the Bible were equal in God's eyes. No longer was it necessary for men and women to renounce their worldly existence and take up a life consumed by spiritual works. Neither pope nor priest, neither monk nor nun could achieve a higher level of spirituality than the most ordinary citizen. The priesthood was of all believ-

Martin Luther.

LUTHER ON MARRIAGE

Martin Luther wrote thousands of pages of theological and devotional literature in establishing a new religious movement. His simple style and everyday examples made his message accessible to hundreds of thousands of ordinary people. In this selection from his tract On Good Works *(1520), he compares the relationship of the husband and wife to that of the Christian and Christ.*

We can understand this whole matter [of good works] by an obvious human example. When husband and wife are fond of one another and live together in love and in confidence in one another, and each believes truly in the other, who shall teach them how they should act, what they should do or leave undone, say or not say, think or not think? Their own insight tells them all that need be, and more too. There is no distinction in their "works" for one another. They do the long, hard, and heavy tasks as willingly as the slight and easy things, and moreover they act with glad, peaceful, and secure hearts and are altogether free and unconstrained. But when doubt comes they begin to ask what is best, and begin to distinguish between their acts in order to gain the other's favor, and go about with troubled and heavy hearts, perhaps well-nigh in despair or driven to downright desperation.

So the Christian who lives in confidence toward God knows what things he should do, and does all gladly and freely, not with a view to accumulating merit and good works, but because it is his great joy to please God and to serve him without thought of reward, contented if he but do God's will. On the contrary, he who is not at one with God, or is in doubt, will begin to be anxious how he may satisfy God and justify himself by his works. He runs off on a pilgrimage to St. James of Compostella, to Rome, to Jerusalem—here, there, anywhere; prays to St. Bridget, or some other saint, fasts this day and that, confesses here and confesses there, asks this man and that, but finds no peace.

From Martin Luther, *On Good Works.*

---

ers. Each followed his or her own calling in life and found his or her own faith through Scripture. Ministers and preachers were valuable because they could help others learn God's Word. But they could not confer faith.

Luther's spiritual rebirth and the theology that developed from it posed a fundamental challenge to the Roman Catholic church. The doctrine of justification by faith alone called into question the Church's emphasis upon the primacy of works—that is, receiving the sacraments administered by the priests and performing acts of charity and devotion. The doctrine that faith was achieved through Scripture weakened the mediating power of the Church by making salvation an individual rather than a collective event. The doctrine of the equality of all believers struck at the vast establishment of religious houses as well as the spiritual hierarchy of the Church from the lowest priest to the pope. Although for centuries the Roman Catholic church had met doctrinal challenges and had absorbed many seemingly unorthodox ideas, Luther's theology could not be among them. It struck too deeply at the roots of belief, practice, and structure. If Luther was right, then the Roman Catholic church must be wrong.

Yet for all of the transforming power of these appar-

ently simple ideas, it was not Luther alone who initiated the reform of religion. His obsession with salvation was based on the same impulse that had made indulgences so popular. Before Luther, countless thousands strove for salvation. Justification by faith alone provided an alternative to the combination of works and faith that many Roman Catholics found too difficult to fulfill. Luther's insistence that faith comes only through the study of the Word of God was facilitated by the new learning and the invention of printing. The printing press prepared the ground for the dissemination of his thought as much as it disseminated it. This was a result of the Renaissance. Luther's hope for the creation of a spiritual elite, confirmed in their faith and confident of their salvation, readily appealed to the citizens of hundreds of German towns who had already made of themselves a social and economic elite. This was a result of the growth of towns. The idea of the equality of all believers meant that all were equally responsible for fulfilling God's commandments. This set secular rulers on an equal footing with the pope at a moment in Western history when they were already challenging papal power in matters of both Church and state. This was a result of the formation of states. For all of the painful soul-searching by which he came to his shattering insight, there was embodied in Luther the culmination of changes of which he was only dimly aware.

Lutheranism

The first to feel the seriousness of Luther's challenge to the established order was the reformer himself. The head of his order, a papal legate, and finally the Emperor Charles V all called for Luther to recant his views on indulgences. Excommunicated by Pope Leo X in 1521, Luther was ordered by Charles V to appear before the diet, or assembly, in Worms. The emperor demanded that Luther retract his teachings. Infuriatingly, Luther replied that, if he could be shown the places in the Bible that contradicted his views, he would gladly change them. "I cannot and I will not retract anything, since it is neither safe nor right to go against conscience. I cannot do otherwise." In fact, during the three years between the posting of his theses and his appearance before the emperor, Luther came to conclusions much more radical than his initial attack on indulgences. Preparing to contend with papal representatives about the pope's right to issue indulgences, Luther came to believe that the papacy was a human rather than a divine invention. Therefore he denounced both the papacy and the general councils of the Church. In his *Address to the Christian Nobility of the German Nation* (1520), he called upon the princes to take the reform of religion into their own hands. No longer was there hope of compromise. Charles V declared Luther an enemy of the empire. In both Church and state he was now an outlaw.

But Luther had attracted powerful supporters as well as powerful enemies. Prince Frederick III of Saxony consistently intervened on his behalf, and the delicate international situation forced Luther's chief antagonists to move more slowly than they might have wished. The pope hoped first to keep Charles V off the imperial throne and then to maintain a united front with the German princes against him. Charles V, already locked in his lifelong struggle with the French, needed German military support and peace in his German territories. These factors consistently played into Luther's hands.

While pope and emperor were otherwise occupied, Luther refined his ideas and thus was able to hold his own in the theological debates in which he won important converts. More importantly, as time passed Luther's reputation grew, not only in Germany, but all over Europe. Between 1517 and 1520 he published 30 works, all of which achieved massive sales. Yet Luther alone could not sustain what came to be called

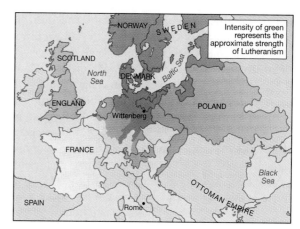

The Spread of Lutheranism

Lutheranism. The Roman Catholic church had met heresy before and knew how to deal with it. What turned Luther's theology into a movement—which after 1529 came to be known as Protestantism—was the support he received among German princes and within German cities.

There were many reasons that individual princes turned to Luther's theology. First and foremost was sincere religious conviction. Matters of the hereafter were a pressing concern in a world in which the average life span was thirty years and nearly all natural phenomena were inexplicable. And they were more pressing still among the educated elites inspired by the new learning and confident of their power to reason critically. Yet there were secular reasons as well. The formation of large states had provided a model for civil government. On a smaller scale, German princes worked to centralize their administration, protect themselves from predatory neighbors, and increase their revenues. They had long suffered under the burden of papal exactions. Taxes and gifts flowed south to a papacy dominated by Italians. Luther's call for civil rulers to lead their own churches meant that civil rulers could keep their own revenues.

The Reformation spread particularly well in the German cities, especially those the emperor had granted the status of freedom from the rule of any prince. Once Protestant ideas were established, entire towns adopted them. The cities had long struggled with the tension of the separate jurisdictions of state and Church. Much urban property was owned by the Church and thus exempt from taxation and law enforcement, and the clergy constituted a significant proportion of urban populations. Reformed religion stressed the equality of clergy and laity, and thus the indisputable power of civil authorities. Paradoxically, it was because the cities contained large numbers of priests that Luther's ideas reached them quickly. Many of his earliest students served urban congregations and began to develop doctrines and practices that, though based on Luther's ideas, were adapted to the circumstances of city life. The reform clergy became integrated into the life of the city in a way that the Catholic clergy had not. They married the daughters of citizens, became citizens themselves, and trained their children in the guilds. Moreover, the imperial free cities were also the center of the printing trade and home to many of the most noted humanists who were initially important in spreading Luther's ideas.

Luther's message held great appeal for the middle orders in the towns. While it was necessary for the leader of a state to support reform if it was to survive, in the cities it was the petty burghers, lesser merchants, tradesmen, and artisans who led the movements that ultimately gained the approval of city governments. These groups resented the privileges given to priests and members of religious orders who paid no taxes and were exempt from the obligations of citizenship. The level of anticlericalism, always high in Germany, was especially acute in cities that were suffering economic difficulties. Pressure from ordinary people and petty traders forced town leaders into action. The evangelism of reforming ministers created converts and an atmosphere of reform. Support from members of the ruling oligarchy both mobilized these pressures and capitalized upon them. Town governments secured their own autonomy over the church, tightening their grip upon the institutions of social control and enhancing the social and economic authority of their members. Once Protestant, city governments took over many of the religious houses, often converting them into schools or hostels for the poor. Former monks were allowed to enter trades and to become citizens. Former nuns were encouraged to marry. Luther himself married an ex-nun after the dissolution of her convent.

Religious reform appealed to women as well as men, but it affected them differently. Noblewomen were among the most important defenders of Protestant reformers, especially in states in which the prince opposed it. Marguerite of Navarre (1492–1549), sister of Francis I, frequently intervened with her brother on behalf of individual Lutherans who fell afoul of Church authorities. She created her own court in the south of France and stocked it with both humanists and Protestants. Her devotional poem *Mirror of the Sinful Soul* (1533) inspired women reformers and was translated

A portrait of Marguerite de Valois, queen of Navarre, the cultured and talented sister of King Francis I.

into English by Elizabeth I. Mary of Hungary (1505–58) served a similar role in the Holy Roman Empire. Sister of both Charles V and Ferdinand I, queen of Hungary and later regent of the Netherlands, she acted as patron to Hungarian reformers. Although Mary was more humanist than Protestant, Luther dedicated an edition of the Psalms to her, and she read a number of his works. Her independent religious views infuriated both of her brothers. Bona (1493–1558), wife of Sigismund I of Poland, was especially important in eastern reform. An Italian by birth, Bona was a central figure in spreading both Renaissance art and humanist learning in Poland. She became one of the largest independent landowners in the state and initiated widespread agricultural and economic reforms. Her private confessor was one of Poland's leading Protestants.

Luther's reforms also offered much to women who were not so highly placed in society. The doctrine of the equality of all believers put men and women on an equal spiritual footing, even if it did nothing to break the male monopoly of the ministry. But the most important difference that Protestantism made to ordinary women was in the private rather than the public sphere. Family life became the center of faith when salvation was removed from the control of the Church. Luther's marriage led him to a deeper appreciation of the importance of the wife and mother in the family's spirituality. "Next to God's word there is no more precious treasure than holy matrimony."

By following humanist teaching on the importance of educating women of the upper orders and by encouraging literacy, the reformers did much that was uplifting. Girls' schools were founded in a number of German cities, and townswomen could use their newly acquired skills in their roles as shopkeepers, family accountants, and teachers of their children. But there were losses as well as gains. The attack on the worship of saints, and especially of the Virgin Mary, removed female images from religion. Protestantism was male dominated in a way that Catholicism was not. Moreover, the emphasis upon reading the Bible tended to reinforce the image of women as weak and inherently sinful. The dissolution of the convents took away from women the one institution that valued their gender and allowed them to pursue a spiritual life outside marriage.

A medal struck in 1580 by a Protestant sect called the Polish Brethren shows a crude human representation of Christ.

The Spread of Lutheranism

By the end of the 1520s, the Holy Roman Empire was divided between cities and states that accepted reformed religion and those that adhered to Roman Catholicism. Printing presses, traveling merchants, and hordes of students who claimed—not always accurately—to have attended Luther's lectures or sermons spread the message. Large German communities across northern Europe, mostly founded as trading outposts, became focal points for the penetration of reformist ideas. In Livonia the Teutonic Knights established a Lutheran form of worship that soon took hold all along the shores of the Baltic. Lutheran-inspired reformers seized control of the Polish port city of Gdansk, which they held for a short time, while neighboring Prussia officially established a Lutheran church. Polish translations of Luther's writings were disseminated into Poland-Lithuania, and Protestant communities were established as far south as Krakow.

Merchants and students carried Luther's ideas into Scandinavia, but there the importance of political leaders was crucial. Christian III (1534–59) of Denmark had been present at the Diet of Worms when Luther made his famous reply to Charles V. Christian was deeply impressed by the reformer, and after a ruinous civil war, he confiscated the property of the Catholic church in Denmark and created a reformed religion under Luther's direct supervision.

Paradoxically, Lutheranism came to Sweden as part of an effort to throw off the yoke of Danish dominance. Here, too, direct connection with Luther provided the first impulses. Olaus Petri (1493–1552) had studied at Wittenberg and returned to preach Lutheran doctrine among the large German merchant community in Stockholm. He was a trained humanist who used both Erasmus's Greek New Testament and Luther's German one to prepare his Swedish translation (1526). When Gustav I Vasa (1523–60) led a successful uprising against the Danes and became king of Sweden, he encouraged the spread of Protestant ideas and allowed Petri to continue his Swedish translations of the mass and the Lutheran service. Under the protection of the monarchy, Lutheranism flourished in Scandinavia, where it remains the dominant religion to this day.

Luther's impact extended into central Europe. Bohemia had had a reforming tradition of its own that antedated Luther. Although the teachings of Jan Hus (1373–1415) had been condemned by the Catholic church, Hussitism was in fact the all but established religion in most parts of Bohemia. Ferdinand was bound by law to allow its moderate practice. Hussites had already initiated many of the reforms insisted upon by Luther: the mass was said in Czech, and the Bible had been translated into the vernacular. Most importantly, the laity took the wine as well as the bread at communion. Hussites believed that communion in both forms was mandated by the Bible. This was the real issue that separated them from Roman Catholics, for the Hussites refused to accept the traditional view that the authority of either the pope or the general council of the Church could alter God's command. On all these issues, Hussites and Lutherans shared a common program. But the Hussites were conservative in almost everything else. While the German communities in Bohemia accepted the core of Lutheran doctrine, most Czechs rejected justification by faith alone and maintained their own practices.

As important as Protestant ideas were in northern and central Europe, it was in the Swiss towns of the Holy Roman Empire that they proved most fertile. Here was planted the second generation of reformers, theologians who drew radical new conclusions from Luther's insights. In the east, Huldrych Zwingli (1484–1531) brought reformed religion to the town of Zurich. Educated at the University of Basel and deeply influenced by humanist thought early in his career, Zwingli was a preacher among the Swiss mercenary troops that fought for the empire. In 1516 he met Erasmus in Basel and under his influence began a study of the Greek writings of the church fathers and of the New Testament. Zwingli was also influenced by reports of Luther's defiance of the pope, for his own antipapal views were already developing. Perhaps most decisively for his early development, in 1519 Zwingli was stricken by plague. In his life-and-death struggle he came to a profoundly personal realization of the power of God's mercy.

These experiences became the basis for the reform theology Zwingli preached in Zurich. He believed that the Church had to recover its earlier purity and to reject the innovations in practices brought in by successive popes and general councils. He stressed the equality of believers, justification by faith alone, and the sufficiency of the gospel as authority for church practice. He attacked indulgences, penance, clerical celibacy, prayers to the Virgin, statues and images in churches, and a long list of other abuses. He also stressed that the mass was to be viewed as a commemorative event rather than one which involved the real presence of Christ. He preferred to call the service the Lord's Supper. His arguments were so effective that the town council adopted them as the basis for a reform of religion.

The principles Zwingli preached quickly spread to neighboring Swiss states. He participated in formal religious disputations in both Bern and Basel. In both places his plea for a simple, unadorned religious practice met widespread approval. Practical as well as theo-logical, Zwingli's reforms were carried out by the civil government with which he allied himself. This was not the same as the protection that princes had given to Lutherans. Rather, in the places that came under Zwingli's influence there was an important integration of church and state. Zwingli organized a formal military alliance of the Protestant Swiss towns. For him, the Bible carried a social message, and it is fitting that he died on the battlefield defending the state. He stressed the divine origins of civil government and the importance of the magistrate as an agent of Christian reform: "A church without the magistrate is mutilated and incomplete." This theocratic idea—that the leaders of the state and the leaders of the church were linked together—became the basis for further social and political reform.

The Protestant Reformation

By the middle of the 1530s, Protestant reform had entered a new stage. Luther did not intend to form a new religion; his struggle had been with Rome. Before he could build, he had to tear down—his religion was one of protest. Most of his energy was expended in attack and counterattack. The second generation of reformers faced a different task. The new reformers were the church builders who had to systematize doctrine for a generation that had already accepted religious reform. Their challenge was to draw out the logic of reformed ideas and to create enduring structures for reformed churches. The problems they faced were as much institutional as doctrinal. How was the new church to be governed in the absence of the traditional hierarchy? How could discipline be enforced when members of the reformed community went astray? What was the proper relationship between the community of believers and civil authority? Whatever the failings of the Roman Catholic church, it had ready answers to these critical questions. The first generation of reformers had thrown out the stagnant bathwater of ecclesiastical abuses; it was left to the second generation to discover if they had thrown out the baby and the bathtub as well.

Geneva and Calvin

The Reformation came late to Geneva. In the sixteenth century Geneva was under the dual government of the Duchy of Savoy, which owned most of the surrounding rural areas, and the Catholic bishop of the town, who

The Eternal Decree

John Calvin was born in France but led the Reformation in the Swiss town of Geneva. He was one of the leaders of the second generation of reformers, whose task was to refine the structure of church doctrine. Calvinism was propounded in the Institutes of the Christian Religion *(1534), from which this section on the doctrine of predestination is taken.*

We must be content with this—that such gifts as it pleased the Lord to have bestowed upon the nature of man he vested in Adam; and therefore when Adam lost them after he had received them, he lost them not only from himself but also from us all. . . . Therefore from a rotten root rose up rotten branches, which sent their rottenness into the twigs that sprang out of them; for so were the children corrupted in their father that they in turn infected their children. . . .

And the apostle Paul himself expressly witnesseth that therefore death came upon all men, because all men have sinned and are wrapped in original sin and defiled with the spots thereof. And therefore the very infants themselves, since they bring with them their own damnation from their mothers' womb, are bound not by another's but by their own fault. For although they have not as yet brought forth the fruits of their own iniquity, yet they have the seeds thereof inclosed within them; yea, their whole nature is a certain seed of sin, therefore it cannot but be hateful and abominable to God. . . .

Predestination we call the eternal decree of God, whereby he has determined with himself what he wills to become of every man. For all are not created to like estate; but to some eternal life and to some eternal damnation is foreordained. Therefore as every man is created to the one or the other end, so we say that he is predestinate either to life or to death.

From John Calvin, *Institutes of the Christian Religion.*

---

was frequently a Savoy client. The Genevans also had their own town council, which traditionally struggled for power against the bishop. By the 1530s the council had gained the upper hand. The council confiscated Church lands and institutions, secularized the Church's legal powers, and forced the bishop and most of his administrators to flee the city. War with Savoy inevitably followed, and Geneva would certainly have been crushed into submission had it not been for its alliance with neighboring Bern, a potent military power among the Swiss towns.

Geneva was saved and was free to follow its own course in religious matters. Under Zwingli's influence, Bern had become Protestant, and it might have been expected that Geneva would adopt this model even though French rather than German was the predominant language of the city. Some Protestant preachers arrived in Geneva to propagate reformed religion, and after a public disputation the town council abolished the mass. In 1536 the adult male citizens of the city voted to become Protestant. But as yet there was no reformer in Geneva to establish a Protestant program and no clear definition of what that program might be.

Martin Luther had started out to become a lawyer and ended up a priest. John Calvin started out to become a priest and ended up a lawyer. The difference tells much about each man. Calvin (1509–64) was born in France, the son of a bishop's secretary. His education was based on humanist principles, and he learned Greek and Hebrew, studied theology, and received a legal degree from the University of Orléans. Around the age of twenty he converted to Lutheranism. He described the experience as "unexpected," but it had predictable results. Francis I had determined to root Protestants out of France, and Calvin fled Paris. Persecution of Protestants continued in France, and one of Calvin's close friends was burned for heresy. These events left an indelible impression upon him. In 1535 he left France for Basel, where he wrote and published the first edition of his *Institutes of the Christian Religion* (1536), a defense of French Protestants against persecution. Directed to Francis I, it set out "the whole sum of godliness and whatever it is necessary to know of the doctrine of salvation." Calvin returned briefly to France to wind up his personal affairs and then decided to settle in Strasbourg, where he could retire from public affairs and live out his days as a scholar.

TEMPLE DE LYON, NOMMÉ PARADIS.

This painting depicts a Calvinist service in Lyon, France, in 1564. The sexes are segregated, and the worshipers are seated according to rank. An hourglass times the preacher's sermon.

To Calvin, providence guided all human action. He could have no better evidence for this belief than what happened next. War between France and the Holy Roman Empire clogged the major highways to Strasbourg. Soldiers constantly menaced travelers, and Protestants could expect the worst from both sides. Thus Calvin and his companions detoured around the armies and passed through Geneva. How Calvin's presence there came to be known remains a mystery, but when Guillaume Farel (1489–1565), one of Geneva's leading Protestant reformers, heard of it, he quickly made his way to the inn where Calvin was staying. Farel implored Calvin to remain in Geneva and lead its reformation. Calvin was not interested. Farel tried every means of persuasion he knew until, in exasperation, Farel declared that God would curse Calvin's retirement if, Calvin wrote, "I should withdraw and refuse to help when the necessity was so urgent. By this imprecation I was so terror-struck that I gave up the journey that I had undertaken." For a quarter of a century, Calvin labored to bring order to the Genevan church.

Calvin's greatest contributions to religious reform came in church structure and discipline. He had stud-ied the writings of the first generation of reformers and accepted without question justification by faith alone and the biblical foundation of religious authority. Like Luther and Zwingli he believed that salvation came from God's grace. But more strongly than his predecessors he believed that the gift of faith was granted only to some and that each individual's salvation or damnation was predestined before birth. "We call predestination God's eternal decree. For all are not created in equal condition; rather, eternal life is foreordained for some, eternal damnation for others." The doctrine of predestination was a traditional one, but Calvin emphasized it differently and brought it to the center of the problem of faith. "Many are called but few are chosen," Calvin quoted from the Bible. Those who were predestined to salvation, "the elect," were obliged to govern; those who were predestined to damnation were obliged to be governed. Thus, for the church that Calvin erected, discipline was the central concern.

Calvin structured the institution of the Genevan church in four parts. First were the pastors who preached the Word to their congregations. There were fewer than ten pastors in Geneva in the early 1540s and fewer than twenty by the time of Calvin's death—a far cry from the five hundred priests who administered the sacraments there under Catholicism. While the pastors preached, the doctors, the second element in Calvin's church, studied and wrote. The doctors were scholars who mastered the difficult portions of the Bible and who increased the stock of learned pastors by their teaching. In the beginning Calvin was the only Genevan doctor, but after he helped to establish the University of Geneva in 1559, there was a ready supply of learned theologians.

Pastors and doctors made up the top tier of the official church; deacons and elders the lower. Deacons, the third element in Calvin's four-part structure, were laymen chosen by the congregation to oversee the institutions of social welfare run by the church. These included the hospitals and schools that cared for the sick and the poor and instructed the young. The last element was the elders of the church, who were its governors in all moral matters. They were the most controversial part of Calvin's establishment and the most fundamental. They had the power to discipline. Chosen from among the elite of the city, the 12 elders enforced the strict Calvinist moral code that extended into all aspects of private life. The elders and the pastors met each week in a body known as the consistory to examine violations of God's laws; for them was reserved the ultimate sanction of excommunication. Offenses ranged from trivial superstitions—a woman wrapping a walnut containing a spider around the neck of her sick husband—to cases of blasphemy. Sexual offenses were the most common. Adultery and fornication were vigorously suppressed, and prostitutes, who had nearly become a recognized guild in the early sixteenth century, were expelled from Geneva.

The structure that Calvin gave to the Genevan church soon became the basis for reforms throughout the Continent. The Calvinist church was self-governing, independent of the state, and therefore capable of surviving and even flourishing in a hostile environment. Expanded in several subsequent editions, *The Institutes of the Christian Religion* became the most influential work of Protestant theology. It had begun as an effort to extend Protestantism to France, and Calvin never abandoned hope that his homeland would be converted. Waves of Calvinist-educated pastors returned to France in the mid-sixteenth century and established churches along Calvinist lines. Calvinism spread north to Scotland and the Low Countries, where it became the basis for Dutch Protestantism, and east to Poland, where it flourished in Lithuania and Hungary. It reached places untouched by Luther and revitalized reform where Lutheranism had been sup-

pressed. Perhaps its greatest impact was in Britain, where the Reformation took place not once but twice.

The English Reformation

The king of England wanted a divorce. Henry VIII had been married to Catherine of Aragon (1485–1536) as long as he had been king, and she had borne him no male heir to carry on his line. Catherine of Aragon had done her duty: in ten years she had given birth to six children and endured several miscarriages. Yet only one daughter, Mary, survived. Nothing so important as the lack of a male heir could happen by accident, and Henry came to believe that it was God's punishment for his marriage. Catherine had been married first to Henry's older brother, who had died as a teenager, and there was at least one scriptural prohibition against marrying a brother's wife. A papal dispensation had been provided for the marriage, and now Henry wanted a papal dispensation for an annulment. For three years his case ground its way through the papal courts. Catherine of Aragon was the aunt of the Emperor Charles V, and the emperor had taken her side in the controversy. With imperial power in Italy at its height, the pope was content to hear all of the complex legal and biblical precedents argued at leisure.

By 1533 Henry could wait no longer. He had already impregnated Anne Boleyn (ca. 1507–36), one of the ladies-in-waiting at his court. If the child—which Henry was certain would be a boy—was to be legitimate, a marriage would have to take place at once. Legislation was prepared in Parliament to prevent papal interference in the decisions of England's courts, and Thomas Cranmer (1489–1556), archbishop of Canterbury, England's highest ecclesiastical officer, agreed to annul Henry's first marriage and celebrate his second. This was the first step in a complete break with Rome. Under the guidance of Thomas Cromwell (ca. 1485–1540), the English Parliament passed statute after statute that made Henry supreme head of the church in England and owner of its vast wealth. Monasteries were dissolved and a Lutheran service was introduced. England's first reformation came as a result of the "King's Great Matter." On 7 September 1533, Anne Boleyn gave birth not to the expected son, but to a daughter, the future Queen Elizabeth I.

Henry's reformation was an act of state, but the English Reformation was not. There was an English tradition of dissent from the Roman church that stretched back to the fourteenth century and that had survived even the most determined efforts to suppress it. Anticlericalism was especially virulent in the towns,

Pope Clement VII's confirmation of the title Defender of the Faith, given to Henry VIII by Pope Leo X in recognition of Henry's attack on Luther and his defense of the teachings of the Church.

the lost Lollard program and found many recruits in London and the northern port towns.

Protestantism grew slowly in England because it was vigorously repressed. Like Francis I and Charles V, Henry VIII viewed actual attacks on the established church as potential attacks on the established state. The consolidation of the Tudor monarchy was too recent for him not to be concerned with its stability. Henry had earned the title "Defender of the Faith" from the pope in 1521 for authoring an attack on Luther. Bonfires of Lutheran books lit the English skies. Small groups of Protestants at Cambridge and Oxford universities were sniffed out and hunted down by Henry's agents. Some made public recantations; some fled to the Continent; one—Thomas Bilney—went to the stake. The first published English translation of the New Testament, made by William Tyndale in 1525, had to be smuggled into England. As sensitivity to the abuses of the Church grew and Lutheran ideas spread, official censorship and persecution sharpened.

Henry's divorce unleashed a groundswell of support for religious change. The king's own religious beliefs remained a secret, but Anne Boleyn and Thomas Cromwell sponsored Lutheran reforms and Thomas Cranmer put them into practice. Religion was legislated through Parliament, and the valuable estates of the Church were sold to the gentry. These practices found favor with both the legal profession and the landed elites and made Protestantism more palatable among these conservative groups. It was in the reign of Edward VI (1547–53), Henry's son by his third wife, that the

where citizens refused to pay fees to priests for performing services like burial. And humanist ideas flourished in England, where Thomas More, John Colet, and a host of others supported both the new learning and its efforts to reform spiritual life. The English were as susceptible as other Europeans to Luther's ideas, which crossed the Channel with German merchants and English travelers. Luther's attack on ritual and the mass and his emphasis on Scripture and faith echoed

An allegorical painting of Edward VI triumphing over the pope, shown lying at the King's feet. To Edward's left is his Privy Council; his father, Henry VIII, gestures to the young king from his deathbed.

The burning of Archbishop Cranmer at Oxford.

central doctrinal and devotional changes were made. Although they were Protestant in tenor, there remained compromises and deliberate ambiguities. The chantries were abolished, and with them masses for the dead. Church service was now conducted in English, and the first two English prayer books were created. The mass was reinterpreted along Zwinglian lines and became the Lord's Supper, the altar became the communion table, and the priest became the minister. Preaching became the center of the church service, and concern over the education of learned ministers resulted in commissions to examine and reform the clergy.

Beginning in the 1530s, state repression turned against Catholics. Those who would not swear the new oaths of allegiance or recognize the legality of Henry VIII's marriage suffered for their beliefs as the early Protestants had suffered for theirs. Thomas More and over forty others paid with their lives for their opposition. Others took up arms against the government, marrying economic and political grievances to religious ones. An uprising in the north in 1536, known as the Pilgrimage of Grace, posed the most serious threat to the English Crown since the Wars of the Roses. Gentry and common people opposed the dissolution of the monasteries and feared for provision for their spiritual needs. Henry's ability to suppress the Pilgrimage of Grace owed more to his political power than to the conversion of his governing classes to Protestantism. Edward VI's government faced a similar uprising in

1549 when it attempted to introduce a new and more Protestant prayer book. Catholicism continued to flourish in England, surviving underground during the reigns of Henry and Edward and reemerging under Mary I (1553–58).

Mary Tudor was her mother's child. The first woman to rule England, she held to the Catholic beliefs in which Catherine of Aragon had raised her, and she vowed to bring the nation back to her mother's church. When Edward VI died, the English ruling elite opted for political legitimacy rather than religious ideology in supporting Mary against a Protestant pretender to the throne. The new queen was as good as her word. She reestablished papal sovereignty, abolished Protestant worship, and introduced a crash program of education in the universities to train a new generation of priests. The one thing that Mary could not achieve was restoration of monastic properties and Church lands: they had been scattered irretrievably and any attempt at confiscation from the landed elite would surely have been met with insurrection. Mary had to be content with reestablishing orthodoxy. She fought fire with fire. Catholic retribution for the blood of their martyrs was not long in coming. Cranmer and three other bishops were burned for heresy, and over 270 others, mostly commoners, were consigned to the flames.

Nearly eight hundred Protestants fled the country rather than suffer a similar fate. These Marian exiles, as they came to be called, settled in a number of reformed communities, Zurich, Frankfurt, and Geneva among them. There they imbibed the second generation of Protestant ideas, especially Calvinism, and from there they began a propaganda campaign to keep reformed religion alive in England. It was the Marian exiles who were chiefly responsible for the second English reformation, which began in 1558 when Mary died and her half-sister, Elizabeth I (1558–1603), came to the throne.

Under Elizabeth, England returned to Protestantism. The rapid reversals of established religion were more than disconcerting to laity and clergy alike. Imagine the experience of ordinary churchgoers. For all their lives they had prayed to the Virgin Mary for aid and comfort. One day all images of the Virgin disappeared from the church. The Latin mass was replaced by a whole new English service. Then the Latin mass returned and back came the images of the Virgin. Five years later the Virgin was gone again and the English service was restored. Imagine the plight of a clergyman who questioned the vow of chastity in the 1540s. Prohibited from marrying under Henry VIII, he was encouraged to marry under Edward VI. When Mary came to the throne, he had to put his wife aside and deny the legitimacy of his children. At Elizabeth's accession he was married again—if he could find his wife and if she had not taken another husband. The Elizabethan reforms put an end to these uncertainties.

But what was reestablished was not what had come before. Even the most advanced reforms during Edward's reign now seemed too moderate for the returning exiles. Against Elizabeth's wishes the English church adopted the Calvinist doctrine of predestination and the simplification (but not wholesale reorganization) of the structure of the church. But it did not become a model of thoroughgoing reformation. The Thirty-nine Articles (1563) continued the English tradition of compromising points of disputed doctrine and of maintaining traditional practices wherever possible. The Calvinism that the exiles learned abroad was more demanding than the Calvinism that the queen practiced at home.

The Reformation of the Radicals

Schism breeds schism. That was the stick with which Catholic church and civil authorities beat Luther from the beginning. By attacking the authority of the established church and flouting the authority of the established state, he was fomenting social upheaval. It was a charge to which he was particularly sensitive. He insisted that his own ideas buttressed rather than subverted authority, especially civil authority, under whose protection he had placed the Church. As early as 1525, peasants in Swabia appealed to Luther for support in their social rebellion. They based some of their most controversial demands, such as the abolition of tithes and labor service, on biblical authority. Luther offered them no comfort. "Let every person be subject to the governing authorities with fear and reverence," he quoted from the Bible while instructing rebels to lay down their arms and await their just rewards in heaven.

But Luther's ideas had a life of their own. He clashed with Erasmus over free will and with Zwingli over the mass. Toward the end of his life he felt he was holding back the floodgates against the second generation of Protestant thinkers. Time and again serious reformers wanted to take one or another of his doctrines further than he was willing to go himself. The water was seeping in everywhere.

The most dangerous threat to the establishment of an orthodox Protestantism came from groups who were described, not very precisely, as Anabaptists. *Anabaptist* was a term of abuse. Although it identified people who practiced adult baptism—literally, "baptism again"— the label was mainly used to tar religious opponents with the brush of extremism. For over a hundred years it defined the outcast from the Protestant fold. New ideas were branded Anabaptist to discredit them; religious enthusiasts were labeled Anabaptists to expel them. Catholics and Protestants both used the term to describe what they were not, and thereby defined what they were.

Anabaptists appeared in a number of German and Swiss towns in the 1520s. Taking seriously the doctrine of justification by faith, Anabaptists argued that only believers could be members of the true church of God. Those who were not of God could not be members of his church. While Catholics, Lutherans, and Calvinists incorporated all members of society into the church, Anabaptists excluded all but true believers. As baptism was the sacrament through which entry into the church took place, Anabaptists reasoned that it was a sacrament for adults rather than infants. Although this practice was as much symbolic as substantive, it was a practice that horrified others. Infant baptism was a core doctrine for both Catholics and Protestants. It was one of only two sacraments that remained in reformed religion. It symbolized the acceptance of Christ, and without it eternal salvation was impossible. Luther, Zwingli, and Calvin agreed that infant baptism was biblical in

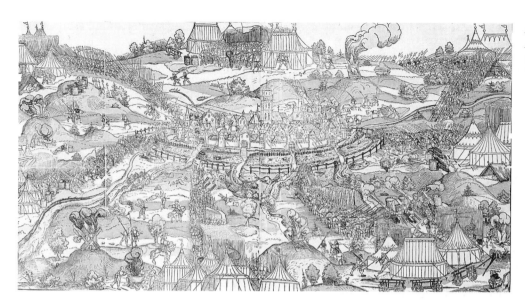

A woodcut of the Anabaptist strong-hold of Münster in Westphalia.

origin and all wrote vigorously in its defense. It was a doctrine with practical import. Unbaptized infants who died could not be accepted in heaven, and infant mortality was appallingly common.

Thus the doctrine of Anabaptism posed a psychological as well as a doctrinal threat to the reformers. But the practice of adult baptism paled in significance to many of the other conclusions that religious radicals derived from the principle of *sola scriptura*—by the Word alone. Some groups argued the case that since true Christians were only those who had faith, all others must be cast out of the church. These true Christians formed small separate sects. Many believed that their lives were guided by the Holy Spirit, who directed them from within. Both men and women could give testimony of revelations that appeared to them or of mystical experiences. Some went further and denied the power of civil authority over true believers. They would have nothing to do with the state, refusing to pay taxes, perform military obligations, or give oaths: "The Sword must not be used by Christians even in self-defense. Neither should Christians go to law or undertake magisterial duties." Some argued for the community of goods among believers and rejected private property. Others literally followed passages in the Old Testament that suggested polygamy and promiscuity.

Wherever they settled, these small bands of believers were persecuted to the brutal extent of the laws of heresy. Catholics burned them, Protestants drowned them, and they were stoned and clubbed out of their communities. Although Anabaptists were never a large group within the context of the Protestant churches, they represented an alternative to mainstream views—whether Lutheran or Calvinist—that was both attractive and persistent. There was enough substance in their ideas and enough sincerity in their patient sufferings that they continued to recruit followers as they were driven from town to town, from Germany into the Swiss cities, from Switzerland into Bohemia and Hungary.

There, on the eastern edges of the Holy Roman Empire, the largest groups of Anabaptists finally settled. Although all practiced adult baptism, only some held goods in common or remained pacifist. Charismatic leaders such as Balthasar Hubmaier (1485–1528) and Jacob Hutter (d. 1536) spread Anabaptism to Moravia in southern Bohemia, where they converted a number of the nobility to their views. They procured land for their communities, which came to be known as the Moravian Brethren. The Moravian Anabaptists ultimately split on the question of pacifism when the advancing Turkish armies posed the problem starkly. Anabaptists remained a target of official persecution, and Hubmaier, Hutter, and a number of other leaders met violent deaths. But the Moravian communities were able to survive and to spread their movement throughout Hungary and Poland. Independent groups existed in England and throughout northwest Europe, where Menno Simons (1496–1561), a Dutch Anabaptist, spent his life organizing bands of followers who came to be known as Mennonites.

The Catholic Reformation

Like a rolling wave, Protestant reform slapped up across the face of Europe, but the rock of the Roman Catholic church endured. Although pieces of the universal church crumbled away in northern Germany, Switzerland, Bohemia, Scandinavia, England, and Scotland, the dense mass remained in southern Germany, Italy, Poland-Lithuania, Spain, France, and Ireland. Catholics felt the same impulses toward a more fulfilling religious life as did Protestants and complained of the same abuses of clerical, state, and papal powers. But the Catholic response was to reform the Church from within. A new personal piety was stressed, which led to the founding of additional spiritual orders. The ecclesiastical hierarchy became more concerned with pastoral care and initiated reforms of the clergy at the parish level. The challenge of converting other races, Asians and Native Americans especially, led to the formation of missionary orders and to a new emphasis on preaching and education. Protestantism itself revitalized Catholicism. Pope and emperor met the challenge of religious reform with all of the resources at their disposal. If anything, Roman Catholicism was stronger at the end of the era of religious reformation than it had been at the beginning.

The Spiritual Revival

The quest for individual spiritual fulfillment dominated later medieval Roman Catholicism. Erasmus, Luther, and Zwingli were all influenced by a Catholic spiritual movement known as the New Piety. It was propagated in Germany by the Brethren of the Common Life, a lay organization that stressed the importance of personal meditation upon the life of Christ. *The Imitation of Christ* (1427) the central text of the New Piety, commonly attributed to Thomas à Kempis (1379–1471), was among the most influential works of the later Middle Ages, with 70 editions printed before 1500. The Brethren taught that a Christian life should be lived according to Christ's dictates as expressed in the Sermon on the Mount. They instructed their pupils to lead a simple ascetic life with personal devotion at its core. These were the lessons that the young Erasmus found so liberating and the young Luther so stifling.

The New Piety, with its emphasis on a simple personal form of religious practice, was a central influence upon Christian humanism. It is important to realize that humanism developed within the context of Catholic education and that many churchmen embraced the new learning and supported educational reform or patronized works of humanist scholarship. The Polyglot Bible, the first new translation project of the sixteenth century, was organized by Cardinal Jiménez de Cisneros (1436–1517), Archbishop of Toledo and Primate of Spain. The greatest educational reformer in England, John Colet (1467–1519), was dean of Saint Paul's, London's cathedral church. Without any of his famed irony, Erasmus dedicated his Greek Bible to the pope. Although they set out to reform education and to provide better texts through which Christian learning could be accomplished, the leading Christian humanists remained within the Catholic Church even after many of their criticisms formed the basis of Protestant reforms.

This combination of piety and humanism imbued the ecclesiastical reforms initiated by Church leaders. Archbishop Jiménez de Cisneros, who also served as Inquisitor-General of the Spanish Inquisition, undertook a wide-ranging reorganization of Spanish religious life in the late fifteenth century. He tackled the Herculean task of reforming the parish clergy in his diocese. He emphasized the need for priests to explain the gospel to their congregations and to instruct children in Church doctrine. Jiménez de Cisneros also initiated reforms in the religious houses, especially within his own Franciscan order. Although not every project was successful, Jiménez de Cisneros's program took much of the sting out of Protestant attacks on clerical abuse, and there was never a serious Protestant movement in Spain.

The most influential reforming bishop was Gian Matteo Giberti (1495–1543) of Verona. Like Jiménez de Cisneros, Giberti believed that a bishop must be a pastor rather than an administrator. After a period of service in Rome, Giberti returned to live in his diocese and made regular visits to all of its parishes. Using his own frugal life as an example, Giberti rigorously enforced vows, residency, and the pastoral duties of the clergy. "The priests in this diocese are marked men; the unworthy are removed from their offices; the jails are full of their concubines; sermons for the people are preached incessantly and study is encouraged," came the report after one of his tours. He founded almshouses to aid the poor and orphanages to house the homeless. In Verona, Giberti established a printing

Heavenly Vision

✦

Teresa of Ávila was a Carmelite nun whose life became a model of spirituality for Spanish Catholics in the seventeenth century. She founded a number of monasteries and convents and wrote popular devotional literature. Her autobiography was published after her death.

My love of, and trust in, our Lord, after I had seen Him in a vision, began to grow, for my converse with Him was so continual. I saw that, though He was God, He was man also; that He is not surprised at the frailties of men; that He understands our miserable nature, liable to fall continually, because of the first sin, for the reparation of which He had come. I could speak to Him as a friend, though He is my Lord, because I do not consider Him as one of our earthly lords, who affect a power they do not possess, who give audience at fixed hours, and to whom only certain persons may speak. If a poor man have any business with these, it will cost him many goings and comings, and currying favour with others, together with much pain and labour before he can speak to them. Ah, if such a one has business with a king! Poor people, not of gentle blood, cannot approach him, for they must apply to those who are his friends; and certainly these are not persons who tread the world under their feet; for they who do this speak the truth, feat nothing, and ought to fear nothing; they are not courtiers, because it is not the custom of a court, where they must be silent about those things they dislike, must not even dare to think about them, lest they should fall into disgrace.

O my Lord! O my King! who can describe Thy Majesty? It is impossible not to see that Thou art Thyself the great Ruler of all, that the beholding of Thy Majesty fills men with awe. But I am filled with greater awe, O my Lord, when I consider Thy humility and the love Thou hast for such as I am. We can converse and speak with Thee about everything whenever we will; and when we lose our first fear and awe at the vision of Thy Majesty, we have a greater dread of offending Thee—not arising out of the fear of punishment, O my Lord, for that is as nothing in comparison with the loss of Thee!

From *The Life of St. Theresa* (1611).

---

press, which turned out editions of the central works of Roman Catholicism, especially the writings of Augustine.

The most important indication of the reforming spirit within the Roman church was the foundation of new religious orders in the early sixteenth century. Devotion to a spiritual life of sacrifice was the chief characteristic of the lay and clerical orders that had flourished throughout the Middle Ages. In one French diocese, the number of clergy quadrupled in the last half of the fifteenth century, and while entrants to the traditional orders of Franciscans and Dominicans did not rise as quickly, the growth of lay communities like the Brethren of the Common Life attested to the continuing appeal of Catholic devotionalism.

Devotionalism was particularly strong in Italy, where a number of new orders received papal charters. The Capuchins were founded by the Italian peasant Matteo de Bascio (ca. 1495–1552). He sought to follow the strictest rule of the life of Saint Francis of Assisi, a path that even the so-called Observant Franciscans had found too arduous. Bascio won admiration for his charitable works among the poor and the victims of the plague in the late 1520s and ultimately secured approval for the establishment of a small community devoted to penance and good works. In contrast, the Theatines were established by a group of well-to-do Italian priests who also wished to lead a more austere devotional existence than was to be found in the traditional orders. Like the Capuchins, they accepted a life of extreme poverty, in which even begging was only a last resort. Their small house in Rome became a center for intellectual spirituality that nurtured two subsequent popes. Throughout Italy, spiritual groups coalesced, some to become permanent orders like the Capuchins and Theatines, some to remain loose affiliations.

This spiritual revival spread all over Catholic Europe and was not limited to male orders. In Spain, Saint Teresa of Ávila (1515–82) led the reform of the

Carmelites. From an early age she had had mystical visions and had entered a convent near her home. But her real spiritual awakening came when she was forty. She believed that women had to withdraw totally from the world around them in order to achieve true devotion. Against the wishes of the male superiors of her order, she founded a convent to put her beliefs into practice and began writing devotional tracts like *The Way of Perfection* (1583). Teresa was ultimately granted the right to establish convents throughout Castile, and she supervised the organization of 16 religious houses for women. In 1535 Angela Merici (ca. 1474–1540) established another female order. The Ursulines were one of the most original of the new foundations, composed of young unmarried girls who remained with their families but lived chaste lives devoted to the instruction of other women. The group met together monthly and submitted to the discipline of a superior, but otherwise they rejected both the cloistered monastic life and vows. The Ursuline movement, begun in northern Italy, spread into France and helped provide women with education and with moral role models.

Loyola's Pilgrimage

At first sight Saint Ignatius Loyola (1491–1556) appears an unlikely candidate to lead one of the most vital movements for religious reform in the sixteenth century. The thirteenth child of a Spanish noble family, Loyola trained for a military life in the service of Castile. He began his career as an administrative official and then became a soldier. In 1521 he was one of the garrison defenders when the French besieged Pamplona. A cannonball shattered his leg, and he was carried home for a long enforced convalescence. There he slowly and carefully read the only books in the castle, a life of Christ and a history of the saints. His reading inspired him. Before he had sought glory and renown in battle. But when he compared the truly heroic deeds of the saints to his own vainglorious exploits, he decided to give his life over to spirituality.

Loyola was not a man to do things by halves. He resolved to model his life on the sufferings of the saints about whom he had read. He renounced his worldly goods and endured a year-long regimen of physical abstinence and spiritual nourishment in the town of Manresa. He deprived himself of food and sleep for long periods and underwent a regimen of seven hours of daily prayer, supplemented by nearly continuous religious contemplation. "But when he went to bed, great enlightenment, great spiritual consolations often came to him, so that he lost much of the time he had

A Spanish wood carving showing St. Ignatius Loyola, the founder of the Society of Jesus.

intended for sleeping." During this period of intense concentration he first began to have visions, which later culminated in a mystical experience in which Christ called him directly to his service.

Like Luther, Loyola was tormented by his inability to achieve grace through penance, but unlike Luther he redoubled his efforts. At Manresa, Loyola encountered *The Imitation of Christ,* which profoundly influenced his conversion. He recorded the techniques he used during this vigil in *The Spiritual Exercises,* which became a handbook for Catholic devotion. In 1523, crippled and barefoot, he made a pilgrimage to Jerusalem, where he intended to stay and battle the infidel. But he was dissuaded from this course and returned to Spain intent upon becoming a priest.

By this time, Loyola had adopted a distinctive garb that attracted both followers and suspicion. Twice the Spanish ecclesiastical authorities summoned him to be examined for heresy. In 1528 he decided to complete his studies in France. Education in France brought with it a broadening of horizons that was so important in the movement that Loyola was to found. He entered the same college that Calvin had just left, and it is more than likely that he came into contact with the Protestant and humanist ideas that were then in vogue. Given his own devotional experiences, Protestantism held little attraction. While in France, Loyola and a small group of his friends decided to form a brotherhood after they became priests. They devoted themselves to the cure of souls and took personal vows of poverty, chastity, and obedience to the pope. On a pilgrimage to Rome, Loyola and his followers again attracted the attention of ecclesiastical authorities. Loyola explained his mission to them and in 1540 won the approval of Pope Paul III to establish a new holy order, the Society of Jesus.

Loyola's Society was founded at a time when the spiritual needs of the church were being extended beyond the confines of Europe. Loyola volunteered his followers, who came to be known as Jesuits, to serve in the remotest parts of the world, and this offer was soon accepted. One disciple, Francis Xavier (1506–52), was sent to Portugal, where he embarked on an expedition to the East. For ten years Xavier made converts to Catholicism in the Portuguese port cities in the East, and then in India and Japan. Other Jesuits became missionaries to the New World, where they offered Christian consolation to the Native American communities. By 1556 the Society of Jesus had grown from ten to a thousand and Loyola had become a full-time administrator in Rome.

Loyola never abandoned the military images that had dominated his youth. He thought of the world as an all-consuming struggle between the forces of God and Satan: "It is my will to conquer the whole world and all of my enemies." He enlisted his followers in military terms. The Jesuits were "soldiers of God" who served "beneath the banner of the Cross." Loyola's most fundamental innovation in these years was the founding of schools to train recruits for his order. Jesuit training was rigorous. The period of the novitiate was extended and a second period of secular education was added. Since they were being prepared for an active rather than a contemplative life, Jesuits were not cloistered during their training. At first Loyola wanted to train only those who wished to be missionaries. When this proved impractical, Jesuit schools were opened to the laity and lay education became one of the Jesuits' most important functions. Loyola lived to see the establishment of nearly a hundred colleges and seminaries and the spread of his order throughout the world. He died while at prayer.

The Counter-Reformation

The Jesuits were both the culmination of one wave of Catholic reform and the advance guard of another.

They combined the piety and devotion that stretched from medieval mysticism through humanism, diocesan reforms, and the foundations of new spiritual orders. But they also represented an aggressive Catholic response that was determined to meet Protestantism head on and repel it. This was the Church Militant. Old instruments like the Inquisition were revived, and new weapons like the Index of prohibited books were forged. But the problems of fighting Protestantism were not only those of combating Protestant ideas. Like oil and water, politics and religion failed to combine. The emperor and the hierarchy of the German church, where Protestantism was strong, demanded thoroughgoing reform of the Catholic church; the pope and the hierarchy of the Italian church, where Protestantism was weak, resisted the call. As head of the Catholic church, the pope was distressed by the spread of heresy in the lands of the empire. As head of a large Italian city-state, the pope was consoled by the weakening of the power of his Spanish rival. Brothers in Christ, pope and emperor were mortal enemies in everything else. Throughout the Catholic states of Germany came the urgent cry for a reforming council of the Church. But the voices were muffled as they crossed the Alps and made their way down the Italian peninsula.

At the instigation of the emperor, the first serious preparations for a general council of the Church were made in the 1530s. The papacy warded it off. The complexities of international diplomacy were one factor—the French king was even less anxious to bring peace to the empire than was the pope—and the complexities of papal politics were another. The powers of a general council in relation to the powers of the papacy had never been clarified. Councils were usually the product of crises, and crises were never the best times to settle constitutional matters. Hard cases make bad law. After the advent and spread of Protestantism, successive popes had little reason to believe that in this gravest crisis of all a council would be mindful of papal prerogatives. In fact, Catholic reformers were as bitter in their denunciations of papal abuses as were Protestants. The second attempt to arrange a general council of the Church occurred in the early 1540s. Again the papacy warded it off.

These factors ensured that when a general council of the Church did finally meet, its task would not be an easy one. The emperor wanted the council in Germany; the pope wanted it in Italy. The northern churches, French and German alike, wanted reforms of the papacy; the papacy wanted a restatement of orthodox doctrine. The Spanish church wanted reform along the principles set down by Jiménez de Cisneros—for

Fishing for Souls *(1614) by Adriaen van de Velde. This allegorical painting shows Protestants (on the left) and Catholics (on the right) vying for the souls of Christians. In the water, parties from both banks try to drag naked men and women into their boats. Overhead, uniting them all, shines the unheeded rainbow of God.*

example, that bishops must be made resident in their dioceses. The papacy needed bishops to serve as administrators in Rome. Many princes whose states were divided among Catholics and Protestants wanted compromises that might accommodate both. Ferdinand I, King of Bohemia, saw the council as an opportunity to bring the Hussites back into the fold. He wanted to allow the laity to take communion in both kinds and the clergy to marry. Charles V and the German bishops wanted the leading Protestant church authorities to offer their own compromises on doctrine that might form a basis for reuniting the empire. The papacy wanted traditional Church doctrine reasserted.

The general council of the Church that finally met in Trent from 1545 to 1563 thus had nearly unlimited potential for disaster. It began in compromise—Trent was an Italian town under the government of the emperor—but ended in total victory for the views of the papacy. For all of the papacy's seeming weaknesses—the defections of England and the rich north German territories cut into papal revenues and Italy was under Spanish occupation—an Italian pope always held the upper hand at the council. Fewer than a third of the delegates came from outside Italy. The French looked upon the council suspiciously and played only a

minor role, and the emperor forbade his bishops to attend after the council moved to Bologna. While 270 bishops attended one or another of the council's sessions, 187 of them were Italians.

Yet for all of these difficulties, the councillors at Trent made some real progress. They corrected a number of abuses, of which the sale of indulgences was the most substantive. They formulated rules for the better regulation of parish priests and stressed the obligation of priests and bishops to preach to their congregations. Following the work of Jiménez de Cisneros and Giberti, they emphasized the pastoral function of the clergy. On the heels of the success of the Jesuits, they ordered seminaries to be founded in all dioceses where there was not already a university so that priests could receive sufficient education to perform their duties. They prepared a new modern and uniform Catholic service and centralized and updated the Index of prohibited books to include Protestant writings from all over the Continent.

The Council of Trent made no concessions to Protestants, moderate or radical. The councillors attempted to turn back every doctrinal innovation of the previous forty years. Although Protestant theologians attended one of the council's sessions, their views were totally repudiated and efforts at compromise, which were supported by a number of Catholics on the council, were rejected. The councillors upheld justification by faith and works over justification by faith alone. They confirmed the truth of Scripture and the traditions of the Church against Scripture alone. They declared the Vulgate the only acceptable text of the Bible and encouraged vast bonfires of Greek and Hebrew Scriptures in an effort to undo the great scholarly achievements of the humanists. They reaffirmed the seven sacraments and the doctrine of the miracle of the Eucharist. They upheld clerical celibacy. The redefinition of traditional Roman Catholicism drew the doctrinal lines clearly and ended decades of confusion. But it also meant that the differences between Catholics and Protestants could now be settled only by the sword.

The Empire Strikes Back

Warfare dominated the reform of religion almost from its beginning. The burnings, drownings, and executions by which both Catholics and Protestants attempted to maintain religious purity were but raindrops compared to the sea of blood that was shed in sieges and on battlefields beginning in the 1530s. Neither side was capable of waging an all-out war against the other, but they fought intermittently for twenty-five years. The Catholic divisions were clear. The Holy Roman Empire continued to be engaged in the west with its archenemy France, and in the south with the ever-expanding Ottoman Empire. Charles V needed not only peace within his own German realms, but also positive support for his offensive and defensive campaigns. He could never devote his full resources to suppressing Protestant dissent.

Yet there was never a united Protestant front to suppress. The north German towns and principalities that accepted Lutheranism in the 1520s had had a long history of warfare among themselves. Princes stored up grievances from past wars and contested inheritances; cities stored up jealousies from commercial rivalries and special privileges. Added to this was the division between Luther and Zwingli over doctrinal issues that effectively separated the German and Swiss components of the Reformation from each other. Each faction formed its own political league, and the division almost certainly cost Zwingli his life in 1531, when Zurich was left to stand by itself against imperial allies.

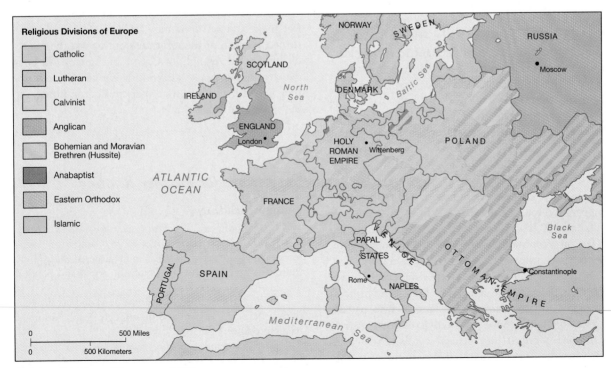

Religious Divisions of Europe, ca. 1555

THE REFORMATION AND THE COUNTER-REFORMATION

1517	Luther writes his Ninety-five Theses
1521	Luther is excommunicated and declared an enemy of the empire; Henry VIII receives title Defender of the Faith
1523	Zwingli expounds his faith in formal disputation
1533	Henry VIII divorces Catherine of Aragon, marries Anne Boleyn, and breaks with the church of Rome
1536	Calvin publishes *Institutes of the Christian Religion*
1540	Loyola receives papal approval for Society of Jesus
1545–1563	Council of Trent
1553	Mary I restores Catholicism in England
1563	Elizabeth I enacts the Thirty-nine articles, which restores Protestantism to England

Although both the Protestant and the Catholic sides were internally weak, it was the greater responsibilities of Charles V that allowed for the uneasy periods of peace. Each pause gave the Protestant reformers new life. Lutheranism continued to spread in the northern part of the Holy Roman Empire, and Zwinglian reform in the south. Charles V asked the papacy to convoke a general council and the Protestants to stop evangelizing in new territories. But Protestant leaders were no more capable of halting the spread of the Reformation than were Catholics. Thus each violation of each uneasy truce seemed to prove treachery. In 1546, just after Luther's death, both sides raised armies in preparation for renewed fighting. In the first stage of war, Charles V scored a decisive victory, capturing the two leading Protestant princes and conquering Saxony and Thuringia, the homeland of Lutheran reform.

Charles V's greatest victories were always preludes to his gravest defeats. The remaining Protestant princes were driven into the arms of the French, who placed dynastic interests above religious concerns. Again Europe was plunged into general conflict, with the French invading the German states from the west, the Turks from the south, and the Protestant princes from the north. Charles V, now an old and broken man, was forced to flee through the Alps in the dead of winter and was brought to the bargaining table soon after. Through the Peace of Augsburg in 1555, the emperor agreed to allow the princes of Germany to establish the religion of their people. Protestant princes would govern Protestant states, Catholic princes Catholic states. The Peace of Augsburg ended forty years of religious struggle in Germany.

• • •

In 1547 the then-victorious Charles V stood at the grave of Martin Luther. Luther had been buried in the shadow of the church in which he had been baptized, and now other shadows darkened his plot. Imperial troops were masters of all Saxony and were preparing to turn back the religious clock in Luther's homeland. The emperor was advised to have Luther's body exhumed and burned to carry out twenty-five years too late the Edict of Worms that had made Luther an outlaw from church and state. But Charles V was no longer the self-confident young emperor who had been faced down by the Saxon monk on that long-ago day. Popes had come and gone, and his warrior rivals Francis I and Henry VIII were both dead. He alone survived. He had little stomach for the petty revenge that he might now exact upon the man who more than any other had ruined whatever hope there might have been for a united empire dominant over all of Europe. "I do not make war on dead men," Charles declared as he turned away from the reformer's grave. But the ghosts of Luther and Zwingli, of Calvin and Ignatius of Loyola were not so easily laid to rest. For another century they would haunt a Europe that could do nothing else but make war on dead men.

Suggestions for Further Reading

General Reading

* G. R. Elton, ed., *The New Cambridge Modern History.* Vol. II, *The Reformation, 1520–1559* (Cambridge: Cambridge University Press, 1958). A multiauthored study of the Protestant movement, with sections on social and political life.

* Owen Chadwick, *The Reformation* (London: Penguin Books, 1972). An elegant and disarmingly simple history of religious change.

* Euan Cameron, *The European Reformation* (Oxford: Oxford University Press, 1991). The most up-to-date survey of the Reformation period. Difficult but rewarding.

* Steven Ozment, *The Age of Reform, 1250–1550* (New Haven, CT: Yale University Press, 1980). An important interpretation of an epoch of religious change.

The Intellectual Reformation

Lucien Febvre and Henri Martin, *The Coming of the Book* (Atlantic Highlands, NJ: Humanities Press, 1976). A study of the early history of bookmaking.

* E. Eisenstein, *The Printing Revolution in Early Modern Europe* (Cambridge: Cambridge University Press, 1983). An abridged edition of a larger work that examines the impact of printing upon European society.

R. W. Scribner, *For the Sake of Simple Folk* (Cambridge: Cambridge University Press, 1981). A study of the impact of the reformation on common people. Especially good on the iconography of reform.

* Richard Marius, *Thomas More* (New York: Alfred A. Knopf, 1984). A recent reinterpretation of the complex personality of England's greatest humanist.

* Roland Bainton, *Erasmus of Christendom* (New York: Charles Scribner's Sons, 1969). Still the best starting point and most compelling biography.

Richard L. DeMolen, *Erasmus* (New York: St. Martin's Press, 1974). Selections from Erasmus's writings.

The Lutheran Reformation

* Francis Oakley, *The Western Church in the Later Middle Ages* (Ithaca, NY: Cornell Univeristy Press, 1979). A study of the spiritual and intellectual state of the Roman Catholic church on the eve of the Reformation.

* Hajo Holborn, *A History of Modern Germany,* Vol. I, *The Reformation* (New York: Alfred Knopf, 1964). A widely respected account in a multivolume history of Germany. Especially strong on politics.

* Roland Bainton, *Here I Stand* (New York: New American Library, 1968). The single most compelling biography of Luther.

* John Dillenberger, *Martin Luther: Selections from His Writings* (New York: Doubleday, 1961). A comprehensive selection from Luther's vast writings.

* Heiko Oberman, *Luther, Man Between God and the Devil* (New York: Doubleday, 1992). English translation of one of the best German biographies of Luther. Sets Luther within the context of late medieval spirituality.

* Bernd Moeller, *Imperial Cities and the Reformation* (Durham, NC: Labyrinth Press, 1982). A central work that defines the connection between Protestantism and urban reform.

* Alister E. McGrath, *Reformation Thought: An Introduction,* 2d ed. (New York: Basil Blackwell, 1993). A useful general work that explains the central doctrines of the Protestant Reformation, from Luther to the radical reformers.

Lyndal Roper, *The Holy Household: Women and Morals in Reformation Augsburg* (Oxford: Oxford University Press, 1989). The best work to show the impact of the Reformation on family life and women.

R. Po-chia Hsia, ed., *The German People and the Reformation* (Ithaca, NY: Cornell University Press, 1988). A collection of essays exploring the social origins of the Reformation.

G. R. Potter, *Huldrych Zwingli* (New York: St. Martin's Press, 1977). A difficult but important study of the great Swiss reformer.

The Protestant Reformation

E. William Monter, *Calvin's Geneva* (London: John Wiley & Sons, 1967). A social and political history of the birthplace of Calvinism.

T. H. L. Parker, *John Calvin: A Biography* (Philadelphia: The Westminster Press, 1975). The classic study.

* William Bousma, *John Calvin* (Oxford: Oxford University Press, 1987). A study that places Calvin within the context of the social and intellectual movements of the sixteenth century.

* John Dillenberger, *John Calvin: Selections from His Writings* (New York: Doubleday, 1971). A comprehensive collection.

* J. J. Scarisbrick, *Henry VIII* (Berkeley: University of California Press, 1968). The classic biography of the larger-than-life monarch.

* A. G. Dickens, *The English Reformation,* 2d ed. (London: Batsford, 1989). The classic study of reform in England, newly updated.

* Rosemary O'Day, *The Debate on the English Reformation* (London: Methuen, 1986). A survey of conflicting views by eminent scholars.

George H. Williams, *The Radical Reformation* 2d ed. (Kirksville, MO: Sixteenth Century Journals Publishers, 1992). The most comprehensive synthesis of the first generation of radical Protestants, now brought up to date.

Claus-Peter Clasen, *Anabaptism, A Social History, 1525–1618* (Ithaca, NY: Cornell University Press, 1972). An important study of the Anabaptist movement.

* Steven Ozment, *Protestants: The Birth of a Revolution* (New York: Doubleday, 1992). An accessible study of the origins of Protestant beliefs and the impact of Protestant ideas among ordinary people.

The Catholic Reformation

Jean Delumeau, *Catholicism Between Luther and Voltaire,* (Philadelphia: Westminster Press, 1977). An important reinterpretation of the Counter-Reformation.

* John C. Olin, *The Autobiography of St. Ignatius Loyola* (New York: Harper & Row, 1974). The best introduction to the founder of the Jesuits.

* A. D. Wright, *The Counter-Reformation* (New York: St. Martin's Press, 1984). A comprehensive survey.

* A. G. Dickens, *The Counter Reformation* (London: Thames and Hudson, 1968). An excellent introduction, handsomely illustrated.

*Paperback edition available.

14 ✌ Europe at War, 1555–1648

The Massacre of the Innocents

"War is one of the scourges with which it has pleased God to afflict men," wrote Cardinal Richelieu (1585–1642), the French minister who played no small part in spreading the scourge. War was a constant of European society and pene-trated to its very core. It dominated all aspects of life. It enhanced the power of the state; it defined gender roles; it consumed lives and treasure and commodities ravenously. War affected every member of society from combatants to civilians. There were no innocent bystanders. Grain in the fields was destroyed because it was food for soldiers; houses were burned because they provided shelter for soldiers. Civilians were killed for aiding the enemy or holding out against demands for their treasure and supplies. Able-bodied men were taken forcibly to serve as conscripts, leaving women to plant and harvest as best as they could.

There was nothing new about war in the middle of the sixteenth century. The early part of the century had witnessed the dynastic struggle between the Habsburgs and the House of Valois as well as the beginnings of the religious struggle between Catholics and Protestants. But the wars that dominated Europe from 1555 to 1648 brought together the worst of both of these conflicts. War was fought on a larger scale, it was more brutal and more expensive, and it claimed more victims, civilians and combatants alike. During this century war extended throughout the Continent. Dynastic strife, rebellion, and international rivalries joined together with the ongoing struggle over religion. Ambition and faith were an explosive mixture. The French endured forty years of civil war; the Spanish, eighty years of fighting with the Dutch. The battle for hegemony in the east led to dynastic strife for decades on end as Poles, Russians, and Swedes pressed their rival claims to each other's crowns. Finally, in 1618, these separate theaters of war came together in one of the most brutal and terrifying episodes of destruction in European history, the Thirty Years' War.

Neither the ancient temple nor the Roman costume can conceal the immediacy of the picture here. It is as painful to look at now as it was when it was created over 350 years ago. Painted by Nicolas Poussin (1594–1665) at the height of the Thirty Years' War, *The Massacre of the Innocents* remains a horrifying composition of power, terror, and despair. The cruel and senseless slaughter of the innocent baby that is about to take place is echoed throughout the canvas. Between the executioner's legs can be seen a mother clasping her own child tightly and anticipating the fall of the sword. In the background on the right, another mother turns away from the scene and carries her infant to safety. In the foreground strides a mother holding her dead child. She tears at her hair and cries in anguish. To a culture in which the image of mother and child—of Mary and Jesus—was one of sublime peacefulness and inexpressible joy, the contrast could hardly be more shocking.

The picture graphically displays the cruelty of the soldier, the helplessness of the child, and the horror of the mother. By his grip on the mother's hair and his foot on the baby's throat, the warrior shows his brute power. The mother's futile effort to stop the sword illustrates her powerlessness. She scratches uselessly at the soldier's back. Naked, the baby boy raises his hands as if to surrender to the inevitable, as if to reinforce his innocence.

To study Europe at war, we must enter into a world of politics and diplomacy, of issues and principles, of judgment and error. We must talk about armies in terms of their cost and numbers, of generals in terms of their strategy and tactics, and of battles in terms of winners and losers. There can be no doubt that the future of Europe was decisively shaped by this century of wholesale slaughter during which dynastic and religious fervor finally ran its course. The survival of Protestantism, the disintegration of the Spanish empire, the rise of Holland and Sweden, the collapse of Poland and Muscovy, the fragmentation of Germany—these were all vital transformations whose consequences would be felt for centuries. We cannot avoid telling this story, untangling its causes, narrating its course, or revealing its outcome. But neither should we avoid facing its reality. Look again at the painting by Poussin.

The Crises of the Western States

"Un roi, une foi, une loi"—one king, one faith, one law. This was a prescription that members of all European states accepted without question in the sixteenth century. Society was an integrated whole, equally dependent upon monarchical, ecclesiastical, and civil authority for its effective survival. A European state could no more tolerate the presence of two churches than it could the presence of two kings. But the Reformation had created two churches.

In Germany, where the problem first arose, the Peace of Augsburg (1555) enacted the most logical solution. The religion of the ruler was to be the religion of the subjects. Princes, town governments, and bishops would determine faith. Not surprisingly, this was a policy more convenient for rulers than for the ruled. Sudden conversions of princes, a hallmark of Protestantism, threw the state into disarray. Those closely identified with Catholicism and those who firmly believed in its doctrines had no choice but to move to a neighboring Catholic community and begin again. Given the dependence of ordinary people upon networks of kin and neighbors, enforced migration was devastating. Protestant minorities in Catholic states suffered the same fate. The enmity between the two groups came as much from bitter experience as from differences of belief.

Thus compromises that might have brought Protestants back into a reformed Catholic church were doomed from the start. Doomed too was the practical solution of toleration. To the modern mind, toleration seems so logical that it is difficult to understand why it took over a century of bloodshed before it came to be grudgingly accepted by those countries most bitterly divided. But toleration was not a practical solution in a society that admitted no principle of organization other than one king, one faith. In such a world, toleration was more threatening than warfare. Pope Clement VIII (1592–1605) described liberty of conscience as "the worst thing in the world." Those who advocated limited forms of toleration were universally despised. Those occasions during which toleration was a reluctant basis for a cease-fire were moments for catching breath before resuming the struggle for total victory. Only Poland-Lithuania, Hungary, and a few German states experimented with religious toleration during the sixteenth century.

The crises of the western European states that stretched from the middle of the sixteenth century to the middle of the seventeenth were as much internal and domestic as they were external and international. In France, a half-century of religious warfare sapped the strength of both the monarchy and the nation. In Spain, the protracted revolt of the Netherlands drained men, money, and spirit from the most powerful nation in Europe. Decades of intermittent warfare turned the golden age of Spain to lead and hastened the decline of the Spanish empire. Each crisis had its own causes and its own history. Yet it was no coincidence that they occurred together or that they starkly posed the conflict between the authority of the state and the conscience of the individual. The century between the Peace of Augsburg (1555) and the Peace of Westphalia (1648) was the century of total war.

The French Wars of Religion

No wars are more terrible than civil wars. They tear at the very fabric of society, rending its institutions and destroying the delicate web of relationships that underlie all communal life. The nation is divided; communities break into factions; families are destroyed. Civil wars are wars of passion. Issues become elevated into causes and principles that form the rallying cry of heroic self-sacrifice or wanton destruction. Civil wars feed on themselves. Each act of war becomes an outrage to be revenged, each act of revenge a new outrage. Passions run deep, and however primitive, the rules for the civilized conduct of war are quickly broken. The loss of lives and property is staggering, but the loss of communal identity is greater still. Generations pass before societies recover from their civil wars. Such was the case with the French wars of religion.

Protestantism came late to France. It was not until after Calvin reformed the church in Geneva and began to export his brand of Protestantism that French society began to divide along religious lines. By 1560 there were over two thousand Protestant congregations in France, whose membership totaled nearly 10 percent of the French population. Calvin and his successors concentrated their efforts on large provincial towns and had their greatest success among the middle ranks of urban society, merchants, traders, and artisans. They also found a receptive audience among aristocratic women, who eventually converted their husbands and their sons.

The wars of religion, however, were brought on by more than the rapid spread of Calvinism. Equally important was the vacuum of power that had been created when Henry II (1547–59) died in a jousting tournament. Surviving Henry were his extraordinary widow, Catherine de Médicis, three daughters, and

Religious Divisions in France

participants, each side in the struggles had different objectives. Catherine wanted peace and was willing to accept almost any strategy for securing it. War weakened the state and weakened loyalty to the monarch. At first she negotiated with the Bourbons, but she was ultimately forced to accept the fact that the Guises were more powerful. The Guises wanted to suppress Protestantism and eliminate Protestant influence at court. They were willing to undertake the task with or without the king's express support.

Once the wars began, the leading Protestant peers fled the court, but the position of the Guises was not altogether secure. Henry Bourbon, king of Navarre, was the next in line to succeed to the throne should Charles IX and his two brothers die without male heirs. Henry had been raised in the Protestant faith by his mother, Jeanne d'Albret, whose own mother, Marguerite of Navarre, was among the earliest protectors of the French Protestants. The objectives of the Huguenots, as the French Calvinists came to be called, were less clear-cut. The townsmen wanted the right to practice their faith, the clergy wanted the right to preach and make converts, and the nobility wanted

four sons, the oldest of whom, Francis II (1559–60), was only fifteen. Under the influence of his beautiful young wife, Mary, Queen of Scots, Francis II allowed the Guise family to dominate the great offices of state and to exclude their rivals from power. The Guises controlled the two most powerful institutions of the state, the army and the Church.

The Guises were staunchly Catholic, and among their enemies were the Bourbons, princes of the blood with a direct claim to the French throne but also a family with powerful Protestant members. The revelation of a Protestant plot to remove the king from Paris provided the Guises with an opportunity to eliminate their most potent rivals. The Bourbon duc de Condé, the leading Protestant peer of the realm, was sentenced to death. But five days before Condé's execution, Francis II died and Guise power evaporated. The new king, Charles IX (1560–74), was only ten years old and firmly under the grip of his mother, Catherine de Médicis, who now declared herself regent of France. (See "The Monstrous Regiment of Women," pp. 420–421.)

Condé's death sentence convinced him that the Guises would stop at nothing to gain their ambitions. Force would have to be met with force. Protestants and Catholics alike raised armies, and in 1562 civil war erupted. Because of the tangle of motives among the

Catherine de Médicis was the daughter of Lorenzo de' Medici of the Florentine ruling family.

❦ The Monstrous Regiment of Women

"To promote a woman to bear rule, superiority, dominion or empire above any realm, nation, or city is repugnant to nature, contumely to God, and the subversion of good order, of all equity and justice." So wrote the Scottish theologian John Knox (1513–72) in *The First Blast of the Trumpet Against the Monstrous Regiment of Women* (1558). Although he made his points more emphatically than many others, Knox was only repeating the commonplace notions of his day. He could quote Aristotle and Aquinas as well as a host of secular authorities to demonstrate female inadequacies: "Nature, I say, doth paint them forth to be weak, frail, impatient, feeble, and foolish." He could quote Saint Paul along with the ancient Fathers of the Church to demonstrate the "proper" place of women—"Man is not of the woman, but the woman of the man."

But no stacking up of authorities, no matter how numerous or revered, could erase the fact that all over Europe in the sixteenth century women could and did rule. In the Netherlands, Mary, Queen of Hungary (1531–52), and Margaret of Parma (1559–67) were successful regents. Jeanne d'Albret (1562–72) was queen of the tiny state of Navarre, territory claimed by both France and Spain but kept independent by this remarkable woman. Catherine de Médicis (1560–89), wife of one king of France and mother of three others, was the effective ruler of that nation for nearly thirty years. Mary, Queen of Scots (1542–87), was the nominal ruler of Scotland almost from her birth. England was ruled by two very different women, the Catholic Mary I (1553–58) and her Protestant half-sister Elizabeth I (1558–1603).

The problems faced by this long list of queens and regents were more than just the ordinary cares of government. The belief that women were inherently inferior in intelligence, strength, and character was so pervasive that for men like Knox, a woman ruler was almost a contradiction in terms. Yet this was not the view taken by everyone, and female rule had its defenders as well as its detractors. One set of objections was overcome by the traditional medieval theory of the two bodies of the monarch. This argument was developed to reconcile the divine origins and functions of monarchs with their very real human frailties. In the theory of the two bodies, there was the body natural and the body politic. Both were joined together in the person of the ruler, but the attributes of each could be separated. Rule of a woman did nothing to disrupt this notion. In fact, it made it easier to argue that the frailties of the body natural of a woman were in no way related to the strengths of the body politic of a monarch.

While such ideas might help a female ruler win the acceptance of her subjects, they did little to invigorate her own sense of her role. Female rulers often strained against the straitjacket that definitions of gender placed them in. When angered, Elizabeth I would proclaim that she had more courage than her father, Henry VIII, "though I am only a woman." Mary, Queen of Scots, once revealed that her only regret was that she "was not a man to know what life it was to lie all night in the fields or to walk with a buckler and a broadsword." Some queens assumed masculine traits, riding in armor or leading forces to battle. Elizabeth's presence in armor at the threat of the landing of the Spanish Armada was viewed as one of the heroic moments of her reign. Other women rulers combined characteristics that were usually separated by gender definitions. Margaret of Parma was considered one of the most accomplished horse riders of her day. After leading her courtiers through woods and fields at breakneck speed, she would then attend council meetings and work on her needlepoint. Mary, Queen of Scots, loved hawking, a traditional kingly sport, in the Scottish wilds. After relishing the hawk's destruction of its prey, she liked to negotiate matters of state by beginning with tears and entreaties and ending with accusations and threats. The effect was more than disconcerting.

Women were no more or less successful as rulers than were men. Women's achievements, like men's, depended upon strength of character and the circumstances of the times. All the women rulers of the sixteenth century had received outstanding educations. Whether raised Catholic or Protestant, each was trained in Latin as well as modern languages, in the liberal arts, and in fine arts. Mary and Elizabeth Tudor of England wrote poetry and played musical instruments with considerable accomplishment. Mary, Queen of Scots, who was raised at the court of France, was considered particularly apt at learning, praise not often accorded a foreigner by the French. Catherine de Médicis, orphaned as an infant, was raised in convents and instructed in the new learning by Italian nuns. It was said that her political instincts were in her blood: Machiavelli had dedicated *The Prince* to her father. Marguerite of Navarre chose one of the leading French humanists to supervise the training of her daughter, Jeanne d'Albret.

Mary, Queen of Scots, was the only one of these female rulers born to rule. She was the sole survivor of her father, who died shortly after her birth. Mary and Elizabeth Tudor came to their thrones after the death of their younger brother Edward VI; Mary of Hungary and Margaret of Parma came to theirs as princesses of the House of Habsburg. The rule of Catherine de Médicis was the most unexpected of all. Her vigorous husband, Henry II, died during a jousting tournament, and her eldest son, Francis II, husband of Mary, Queen of Scots, died the following year. Instead of retirement as a respected queen dowager (the widow of a previous king) Catherine de Médicis was forced into the vortex of French politics to protect the rights of her ten-year-old son, Charles IX.

For most of these queens and regents, marriage was of central importance to their position. Both Mary, Queen of Hungary, and Mary, Queen of Scots, married kings whose reigns were exceedingly brief. Lewis of Hungary died at the battle of Mohács in 1526, just four years after Mary had become his queen. Mary, Queen of Scots, was widowed even sooner, and throughout the rest of her remarkable career schemed to remarry. To strengthen her claim to the throne of England, she married the Scottish Lord Darnley. When he proved unsatisfactory to her plans, she plotted his murder and then married one of his assassins. When this husband died, she sought a match with a powerful English lord who might help her capture Elizabeth's throne. These intrigues finally led to her execution in England in 1587. Mary Tudor married Philip II of Spain in hope of reestablishing Catholicism in England through a permanent alliance with the most powerful Catholic state in Europe. Her dreams went unfulfilled when she failed to produce an heir, and the throne passed to her sister, Elizabeth, who, alone among the women rulers of the period, did not marry.

Unfortunately, the accomplishments of women rulers did little to dispel prejudices against women as a whole or to alter the definition of gender roles. Except for Mary, Queen of Scots, whose principal achievement was to provide an heir to the English throne, all the queens and regents of the sixteenth century were successful rulers. Margaret of Parma steered the careful middle course in the conflict between Spain and the Netherlands. She opposed the intervention of the Duke of Alba, and, had her advice been followed, the eighty years of war between Spain and the Netherlands might have been avoided. Catherine de Médicis held the crown of France on the heads of her sons, navigated the treacherous waters of civil war, and provided the model for religious toleration that finally was adopted in the Edict of Nantes. Elizabeth I of England became one of the most beloved rulers in that nation's history. A crafty politician who learned to balance the factions at her court and who turned the aristocracy into a service class for the crown, she brought nearly a half-century of stability to England at a time when the rest of Europe was in flames.

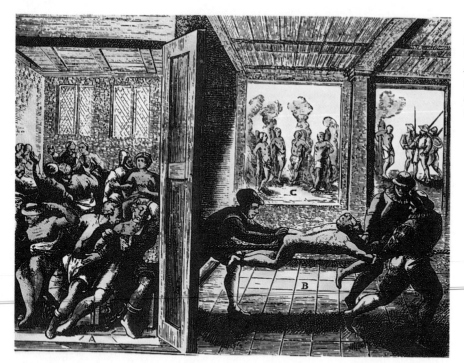

This scene depicts the mistreatment of French Catholics by the Protestants in the town of Angoulême. They were deprived of all nourishment, dragged over a taut rope, and then slowly roasted at the stake.

their rightful place in local government. Almost from the beginning, the Huguenots were on the defensive, fighting to preserve what they already had and to avoid annihilation.

The inconclusive nature of the early battles might have allowed for the pragmatic solution sought by Catherine de Médicis had it not been for the assassination of the duc de Guise in 1563 by a Protestant fanatic. This act added a personal vendetta to the religious passions of the Catholic leaders. They encouraged the slaughter of Huguenot congregations and openly planned the murder of Huguenot leaders. Protestants gave as good as they got. In open defiance of Valois dynastic interests, the Guises courted support from Spain, while the Huguenots imported Swiss and German mercenaries to fight in France. Noble factions and irreconcilable religious differences were pulling the government apart.

By 1570 Catherine was ready to attempt another reconciliation. She announced her plans for a marriage between her daughter Margaret and Henry of Navarre, a marriage that would symbolize the spirit of conciliation between the crown and the Huguenots. The marriage was to take place in Paris during August 1572. The arrival of Huguenot leaders from all over France to attend the marriage ceremony presented an opportunity of a different kind to the Guises and their supporters. If leading Huguenots could be assassinated in Paris, the Protestant cause might collapse and the truce that

the wedding signified might be turned instead into a Catholic triumph.

Saint Bartholomew was the apostle that Jesus described as a man without guile. Ironically, it was on his feast day that the Huguenots who had innocently come to celebrate Henry's marriage were led like lambs to the slaughter. On 24 August 1572 the streets of Paris ran red with Huguenot blood. Although frenzied, the slaughter was inefficient. Henry of Navarre and a number of other important Huguenots escaped the carnage and returned to their urban strongholds. In the following weeks the violence spread from Paris to the countryside and thousands of Protestants paid for their beliefs with their lives. Until the French Revolution, no event in French history would evoke as much passion as the memory of the Saint Bartholomew's Day Massacre.

One King, Two Faiths

The Saint Bartholomew's Day Massacre was a transforming event in many ways. In the first place, it prolonged the wars. A whole new generation of Huguenots now had an emotional attachment to the continuation of warfare: their fathers and brothers had been mercilessly slaughtered. By itself the event was shocking enough. But in the atmosphere of anticipated reconciliation created by the wedding, it screamed out for revenge. And the target for retaliation was no longer limited to the Guises and their followers. By accepting the results of the massacre, the monarchy sanctioned it and spilled Huguenot blood on itself. For over a decade Catherine de Médicis had maintained a distance between the crown and the leaders of the Catholic movement. That distance no longer existed.

Nor could the Huguenots continue to maintain the fiction that they were fighting against the king's evil advisors rather than against the king. After Saint Bartholomew's Day, Huguenot theorists began to develop the idea that resistance to a monarch whose actions violated divine commandments or civil rights was lawful. For the first time, Huguenot writers provided a justification for rebellion. Perhaps most importantly, a genuine revulsion against the massacres swept the nation. A number of Catholic peers now joined with the Huguenots to protest the excesses of the crown and the Guises. These Catholics came to be called *politiques* from their desire for a practical settlement of the wars. They were led by the duc d'Anjou, next in line to the throne after Henry III (1574–89) became king.

Against them, in Paris and a number of other towns, the Catholic League was formed, a society that pledged its first allegiance to religion. The League took up where the Saint Bartholomew's Day Massacre left off, and the slaughter of ordinary people who unluckily professed the wrong religion continued. Matters grew worse in 1584, when Anjou died. With each passing year it was becoming apparent that Henry III would produce no male heir. After Anjou's death, the Huguenot Henry of Navarre was the next in line for the throne. Catholic Leaguers talked openly of altering the royal succession and began to develop theories of lawful resistance to monarchical power. By 1585, when the final civil war began—the war of the three Henrys, named for Henry III, Henry Guise, and Henry of Navarre—the crown was in the weakest possible position. Paris and the Catholic towns were controlled by the League, the Protestant strongholds by Henry of Navarre. King Henry III could not abandon his capital or his religion, but neither could he gain control of the Catholic party. The extremism of the Leaguers kept the politiques away from court, and without the politiques, there could be no settlement.

In December 1588 Henry III summoned Henry Guise and Guise's brother to a meeting in the royal bedchamber. There they were murdered by the king's order. The politiques were blamed for the murders—revenge was taken on a number of them—and Henry III was forced to flee his capital. Paris was still firmly in the hands of the League, and Henry was in danger of becoming a king without a country. He made a pact with Henry of Navarre, and together royalist and Huguenot forces besieged Paris. All supplies were cut off from the city and only the arrival of a Spanish army prevented its fall. In 1589 Catherine de Médicis died, her ambition to reestablish the authority of the monarchy in shambles, and in the same year a fanatic priest gained revenge for the murder of the Guises by assassinating Henry III.

Painting of the Saint Bartholomew's Day Massacre. The massacre began in Paris on 24 August 1572, and the violence soon spread throughout France.

Now Henry of Navarre came into his inheritance. After nearly thirty years of continuous civil war, it was certain that a Huguenot could never rule France. The League had already proclaimed a Catholic rival as king, and the pope excommunicated Henry of Navarre and absolved France from loyalty to him. If Henry was to become king of all France, he would have to become a Catholic king. It is not clear when Henry made the decision to accept the Catholic faith—"Paris is worth a mass," he reportedly declared—but he did not announce his decision at once. Rather he strengthened his forces, tightened his bonds with the politiques, and urged his countrymen to expel the Spanish invaders. He finally made his conversion public and in 1594 was crowned Henry IV (1589–1610). A war-weary nation was willing to accept the sincerity of its new king rather than endure a seemingly endless struggle. Even the Leaguers were exhausted. Their claimant to the throne had died, and they were now seen as rebels rather than patriots. War had sapped both their treasuries and their spirit. Most of the leading peers on both sides were nearly bankrupt, and Henry IV was willing to pay large cash settlements to all those who would return to their estates and pledge allegiance to him.

Resistance to the reestablishment of the monarchy continued for several years, but Henry IV was a strong and capable ruler. He declared war on Spain to unite his nation against foreign aggression, and he carefully reestablished the balance of aristocratic factions at his court. The League collapsed, and moderate Catholics rallied around the king. Although Huguenots and Calvinists everywhere were shocked by Henry's conversion, they were hardly in a position to wage a successful war against their former leader. Henry's accession gave them their first real hope for an enduring settlement with the crown.

In 1598 Henry proclaimed the Edict of Nantes, which granted limited toleration to the Huguenots. It was the culmination of decades of attempts to find a solution to the existence of two religions in one state. It was a compromise that satisfied no one, but it was a compromise that everyone could accept. One king, two faiths was as apt a description of Henry IV as it was of the settlement. Yet neither Henry's conversion nor the Edict of Nantes stilled the passions that had spawned and sustained the French wars of religion. Sporadic fighting between Catholics and Huguenots continued, and fanatics on both sides fanned the flames of religious

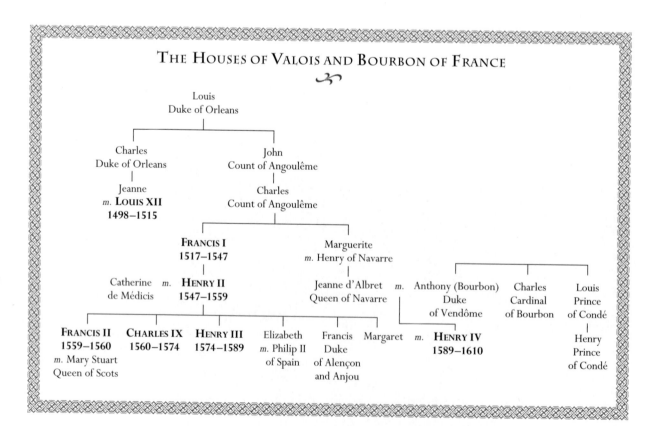

THE HOUSES OF VALOIS AND BOURBON OF FRANCE

The Edict of Nantes (1598) was a milestone in the development of religious toleration in Europe. It was granted by King Henry IV to the Huguenots at the end of the French wars of religion. The Edict of Nantes established the rights of Protestants and was in effect for nearly a century.

We ordain that the Catholic, Apostolic and Roman religion shall be restored and re-established in all places and districts of this our kingdom and the countries under our rule, where its practice has been interrupted, so that it can be peacefully and freely practiced there, without any disturbance or hindrance. We forbid very expressly all persons of whatever rank, quality or condition they may be, under the aforesaid penalties, to disturb, molest or cause annoyance to clerics in the celebration of the Divine worship. . . .

And in order not to leave any cause for discords and disputes between our subjects, we have permitted and we permit those of the so-called Reformed religion to live and dwell in all the towns and districts of this our kingdom and the countries under our rule, without being annoyed, disturbed, molested or constrained to do anything against their conscience, or for this cause to be sought out in their houses and districts where they wish to live, provided that they conduct themselves in other respects according to the provisions of our present Edict. . . .

From the Edict of Nantes.

Henry IV renounced Protestantism and embraced the Roman Catholic Church to gain the throne of France, saying, "Paris is worth a mass."

hatred. Henry IV survived eighteen attempts on his life before he was finally felled by an assassin's knife in 1610, but by then he had reestablished the monarchy and brought a semblance of peace to France.

The World of Philip II

By the middle of the sixteenth century, Spain was the greatest power in Europe. The dominions of Philip II (1556–98) of Spain stretched from the Atlantic to the Pacific; his continental territories included the Netherlands in the north and Milan and Naples in Italy. In 1580 Philip became king of Portugal, uniting all the states of the Iberian Peninsula. With the addition of Portugal's Atlantic ports and its sizable fleet, Spanish maritime power was now unsurpassed. Spain was also a great cultural and intellectual center. The fashions and tastes of its golden age dominated all the courts of Europe.

Great power meant great responsibilities, and few monarchs took their tasks more seriously than did Philip II. Trained from childhood for the cares of office, he exceeded all expectations. Philip II earned his reputation as "King of Paper" by maintaining a grueling work schedule. Up at eight and at mass soon afterwards, he met with his advisers and visitors on official business until noon. After a brief lunch, he began the real business of the day, the study of the mountains of

THE FRENCH WARS OF RELIGION

1559	Death of Henry II
1560	Protestant duc de Condé sentenced to death
1562	First battle of wars of religion
1563	Catholic duc de Guise assassinated; Edict of Amboise grants limited Protestant worship
1572	Saint Bartholomew's Day massacre
1574	Accession of Henry III
1576	Formation of Catholic League
1584	Death of duc d'Anjou makes Henry of Navarre heir to throne
1585	War of the three Henrys
1588	Duc de Guise murdered by order of Henry III
1589	Catherine de Médicis dies; Henry III assassinated
1594	Henry IV crowned
1598	Edict of Nantes

papers that his empire generated. Although summaries were prepared of the hundreds of documents he handled each day, Philip II frequently read and annotated the longer originals. No detail was too small to escape his attention. His work day often lasted ten hours or longer. Even when he was traveling, his secretaries carried huge chests of state papers that Philip studied in his carriage and annotated on a portable desk that always accompanied him.

There was good reason why this slightly stooped king appeared as if he had the weight of the world on his shoulders. In the Mediterranean, Spain alone stood out against the expansion of Ottoman power. The sultan's navy continually threatened to turn the Mediterranean into a Turkish lake, while his armies attempted to capture and hold Italian soil. All Europe shuddered at the news of each Ottoman advance. Popes called for holy wars against the Turks, but only Philip heeded the cry. From nearly the moment that he inherited the Spanish crown, he took up the challenge of defending European Christianity. For over a decade Philip maintained costly coastal garrisons in North Africa and Italy and assembled large fleets and larger armies to discourage or repel Turkish invasions. This sparring could not go on indefinitely, and in 1571 both sides prepared for a decisive battle. A combined Spanish and Italian force of over three hundred ships and eighty thousand men met an even larger Ottoman flotilla off the coast of Greece. The Spanish naval victory at Lepanto was con-

sidered one of the great events of the sixteenth century, celebrated in story and song for the next three hundred years. Although the Turks continued to menace the Mediterranean islands, Lepanto marked the end of Ottoman advances.

If Philip II saw himself as a Christian monarch fending off the advance of the infidel, he also saw himself as a Catholic monarch fending off the spread of heresy. There can be no doubt of Philip's personal devotion to Catholicism or of his oft-expressed conviction "I would prefer to lose all my dominions and a hundred lives if I had them rather than be lord over heretics." The lives that were to be lost in battling heretics were numbered not in hundreds, but in hundreds of thousands. Philip II came to the throne at just the moment that Calvinism began its rapid growth in northern Europe. He supported the Catholic cause in France throughout the civil wars, sending money, advisers, and ultimately an army to relieve Paris. His ambassadors urged Catherine de Médicis and her sons to take the most repressive measures against the Huguenots, including the Saint Bartholomew's Day Massacre.

Philip was equally aggressive against English Protestants. For a brief time he had been king in England through his marriage to Mary I (1553–58). He encouraged Mary's efforts to restore the Catholic church in England and supported her policies of repression. When Mary died and Elizabeth I (1558–1603) rejected his marriage proposal, his limited rule in England came to an end. From then on, England and Spain entered a long period of hostility. English pirates raided Spanish treasure ships returning to Europe, and Elizabeth covertly aided both French and Dutch Protestants. Finally, in 1588, Philip decided upon invasion. A great

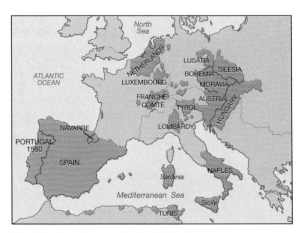

The Habsburg Empire Under Philip II

This painting by an unknown artist depicts the clash between the Spanish and English fleets during the Armada invasion in 1588.

fleet set sail from the Portuguese coast to the Netherlands, where a large Spanish army stood waiting to be conveyed to England.

The Spanish Armada comprised over 130 ships, many of them the pride of the Spanish and Portuguese navies. They were bigger and stronger than anything possessed by the English, whose forces were largely merchant vessels hastily converted for battle. But the English ships were faster and more easily maneuverable in the unpredictable winds of the English Channel. They also contained guns that could easily be reloaded for multiple firings, while the Spanish guns were designed to discharge only one broadside before hand-to-hand combat ensued. With these advantages the English were able to prevent the Armada from reaching port in the Netherlands and to destroy many individual ships as they were blown off course. The defeat of the Spanish Armada was less a military than a psychological blow to Philip II: he could more easily replace ships than restore confidence in Spanish power.

The Burgundian Inheritance

This confidence was all the more necessary when Philip II faced the gravest crisis of his reign: the revolt of the Netherlands. Although Philip's father, Charles V, had amassed a great empire, he had begun only as the duke of Burgundy. Charles's Burgundian inheritance encompassed a diverse territory in the northwestern corner of Europe. The 17 separate provinces of this territory were called the Netherlands, or the Low Countries, because of the flooding that kept large portions of them under water. The Netherlands was one of the richest and most populous regions of Europe, an international leader in manufacturing, banking, and commerce. Antwerp and Amsterdam were bustling port cities with access to the North Sea; inland were the prosperous industrial towns of Ghent and Brussels. The preeminence of the Netherlands was all the more remarkable because the provinces themselves were divided geographically, culturally, and linguistically. Rivers, lakes, and flooded plains separated the southern provinces, where French was the background and language of the inhabitants, from the northern ones, where Germans had settled and Dutch was spoken. Charles V attempted to unify the provinces by removing them from the jurisdiction of the Holy Roman Empire and establishing a separate regency under his eldest son, Philip II. Thus the future of the Netherlands was tied to Spain and the New World when Philip II set sail for Castile in 1559 to claim the crown of Spain

Although Philip II had every intention of returning to the Low Countries, in fact the Netherlands had seen

REVOLT OF THE NETHERLANDS

1559	Margaret of Parma named regent of the Netherlands
1566	Calvinist iconoclasm begins revolt
1567	Duke of Alba arrives in Netherlands and establishes Council of Blood
1568	Protestant Count Egmont executed
1572	Protestants capture Holland and Zeeland
1573	Alba relieved of his command
1576	Sack of Antwerp; pacification of Ghent
1581	Catholic and Protestant provinces split
1585	Spanish forces under Alexander Farnese take Brussels and Antwerp
1609	Twelve Years' Truce

the last of their king. Philip left his half-sister, Margaret of Parma, as regent, providing her with a talented group of Spanish administrators to carry out policies that were to be formulated in Madrid. As Philip's own grasp on the affairs of the Netherlands loosened, so did the loyalty of the native nobility to the absent monarch. The resentments that built up were traditional ones—hostility to foreigners, distrust of royal advisers, and contempt for policies that lacked understanding of local conditions. All of these discontents came together over Philip's religious policies.

The Low Countries had accepted the Peace of Augsburg in a spirit of conciliation in which it was never intended. Here Catholics, Lutherans, Anabaptists, and Calvinists peaceably coexisted. As in France, this situation changed dramatically with the spread of Calvinism. The heavy concentration of urban populations in the Low Countries provided the natural habitat for Calvinist preachers, who made converts across the entire social spectrum. As Charles V, Holy Roman Emperor, he may have made his peace with Protestants, but as Charles I, king of Spain, he had not. Charles V had maintained the purity of the Spanish Catholic church through a sensible combination of reform and repression.

Philip II intended to pursue a similar policy in the Low Countries. With papal approval he initiated a scheme to reform the hierarchy of the Church by expanding the number of bishops, and he invited the Jesuits to establish schools for orthodox learning. Simultaneously, he strengthened the power of the Inquisition and ordered the enforcement of the decrees of the Council of Trent. The Protestants sought the protection of their local nobility who—Catholic or Protestant—had their own reasons for opposing Provincial nobility, and magistrates resented both the policies that were being pursued and the fact that they disregarded local autonomy. Town governors and noblemen refused to cooperate in implementing the new laws. Leading Protestants like Prince William of Orange, one of the largest landholders in the Netherlands, and Count Egmont, an outstanding military leader, urged Margaret to adopt a policy of toler-

A prosperous Dutch trader in the East Indies poses with his wife on a hill near the port of Batavia (now Jakarta, Indonesia).

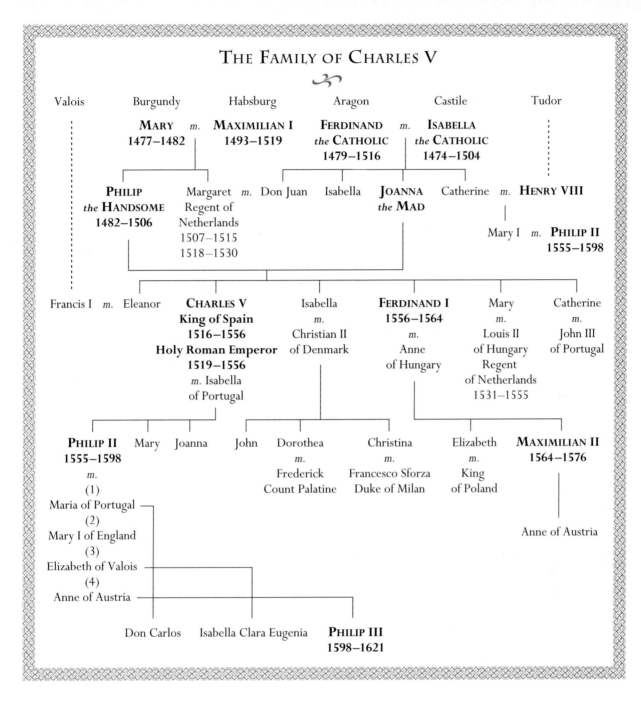

THE FAMILY OF CHARLES V

| Valois | Burgundy | Habsburg | Aragon | Castile | Tudor |

MARY 1477–1482 *m.* **MAXIMILIAN I** 1493–1519   **FERDINAND** *the* **CATHOLIC** 1479–1516 *m.* **ISABELLA** *the* **CATHOLIC** 1474–1504

PHILIP *the* **HANDSOME** 1482–1506   Margaret *m.* Don Juan   Isabella   **JOANNA** *the* **MAD**   Catherine *m.* **HENRY VIII**
Regent of Netherlands 1507–1515 1518–1530

Mary I *m.* **PHILIP II** 1555–1598

Francis I *m.* Eleanor   **CHARLES V** King of Spain 1516–1556 Holy Roman Emperor 1519–1556 *m.* Isabella of Portugal   Isabella *m.* Christian II of Denmark   **FERDINAND I** 1556–1564 *m.* Anne of Hungary   Mary *m.* Louis II of Hungary Regent of Netherlands 1531–1555   Catherine *m.* John III of Portugal

PHILIP II 1555–1598 *m.*
(1) Maria of Portugal
(2) Mary I of England
(3) Elizabeth of Valois
(4) Anne of Austria

Mary   Joanna   John   Dorothea *m.* Frederick Count Palatine   Christina *m.* Francesco Sforza Duke of Milan   Elizabeth *m.* King of Poland   **MAXIMILIAN II** 1564–1576

Anne of Austria

Don Carlos   Isabella Clara Eugenia   **PHILIP III** 1598–1621

---

ation along the lines of the Peace of Augsburg and made clear that they would resign from office rather than support anything else.

The Revolt of the Netherlands

The passive resistance of nobles and magistrates was soon matched by the active resistance of the Calvinists. Unable to enforce Philip's policy, Margaret and her advisers agreed to a limited toleration. But in the sum-

mer of 1566, before it could be put into effect, bands of Calvinists unleashed a storm of iconoclasm in the provinces, breaking stained glass windows and statues of the Virgin and the saints, which they claimed were idolatrous. Catholic churches were stormed and turned into Calvinist meeting houses. Local authorities were helpless in the face of determined Calvinists and apathetic Catholics; they could not protect Church property. Iconoclasm gave way to open revolt. Fearing social rebellion, even the leading Protestant noblemen took part in suppressing these riots.

CANNIBALS

Michel de Montaigne (1533–92) came from a wealthy family in the Bordeaux region of France and ultimately inherited the chateau from which his name derives. Before his early retirement he worked in the legal profession. His Essays *(1572–88) combined humanist learning with the new philosophy of skepticism. The following excerpt, from "Of Cannibals," shows both his penetrating intelligence and his detached observation of the world around him.*

These nations, then, seem to me barbarous in this sense, that they have been fashioned very little by the human mind, and are still very close to their original naturalness. The laws of nature still rule them, very little corrupted by ours; and they are in such a state of purity that I am sometimes vexed that they were unknown earlier, in the days when there were men able to judge them better than we. I am sorry that Lycurgus and Plato did not know of them; for it seems to me that what we actually see in these nations surpasses not only all the pictures in which poets have idealized the golden age and all their inventions in imagining a happy state of man, but also the conceptions and the very desire of philosophy. . . .

For the rest, they live in a country with a very pleasant and temperate climate, so that according to my witnesses it is rare to see a sick man there; and they have assured me that they never saw one palsied, bleary-eyed, toothless, or bent with age. They are settled along the sea and shut in on the land side by great high mountains, with a stretch about a hundred leagues wide in between. They have a great abundance of fish and flesh which bear no resemblance to ours, and they eat them with no other artifice than cooking.

They have their wars with the nations beyond the mountains, further inland, to which they go quite naked, with no other arms than bows or wooden swords ending in a sharp point, in the manner of the tongues of our boar spears. It is astonishing what firmness they show in their combats, which never end but in slaughter and bloodshed; for as to routs and terror, they know nothing of either.

Each man brings back as his trophy the head of the enemy he has killed, and sets it up at the entrance to his dwelling. After they have treated their prisoners well for a long time with all the hospitality they can think of, each man who has a prisoner calls a great assembly of his acquaintances. He ties a rope to one of the prisoner's arms by the end of which he holds him, a few steps away, for fear of being hurt, and gives his dearest friend the other arm to hold in the same

---

In Spain, the events in the Netherlands were treated for what they were: open rebellion. Despite the fact that Margaret had already restored order, Philip II was determined to punish the rebels and enforce the heresy laws. A large military force under the command of the Duke of Alba (1507–82)—whose record of success was matched only by his record of brutality—was sent from Spain as an army of occupation. As befit a warrior who had made his reputation leading imperial troops against the Lutherans, Alba gave no quarter to the Protestants of the Netherlands. "Everyone must be made to live in constant fear of the roof breaking down over his head," he wrote.

Alba lured Count Egmont and other Protestant noblemen to Brussels, where he publicly executed them in 1568. He also established a military court to punish participants in the rebellion, a court that came to be called the Council of Blood. The Council handed down over nine thousand convictions, a thousand of which carried the death penalty. As many as sixty thousand Protestants fled beyond Alba's jurisdiction. Alba next made an example of several small towns that had been implicated in the iconoclasm. He allowed his soldiers to pillage the towns at will before slaughtering their entire populations and razing them to the ground. By the end of 1568, royal policy had gained a sullen acceptance in the Netherlands, but the hostilities did not end. For the next eighty years, with only occasional truces, Spain and the Netherlands were at war.

way; and these two, in the presence of the whole assembly, kill him with their swords. This done, they roast him and eat him in common and send some pieces to their absent friends. This is not, as people think, for nourishment, as of old the Scythians used to do; it is to betoken an extreme revenge. And the proof of this came when they saw the Portuguese, who had joined forces with their adversaries, inflict a different kind of death on them when they took them prisoner, which was to bury them up to the waist, shoot the rest of their body full of arrows, and afterward hang them. They thought that these people from the other world, being men who had sown the knowledge of many vices among their neighbors and were much greater masters than themselves in every sort of wickedness, did not adopt this sort of vengeance without some reason, and that it must be more painful than their own; so they began to give up their old method and to follow this one.

I am not sorry that we notice the barbarous horror of such acts, but I am heartily sorry that, judging their faults rightly, we should be so blind to our own. I think there is more barbarity in eating a man alive than in eating him dead; and in tearing by tortures and the rack a body still full of feeling, in roasting a man bit by bit, in having him bitten and mangled by dogs and swine (as we have not only read but seen within fresh memory, not among ancient enemies, but among neighbors and fellow citizens, and what is worse, on the pretext of piety and religion), than in roasting and eating him after he is dead. . . .

So we may well call these people barbarians, in respect to the rules of reason, but not in respect to ourselves, who surpass them in every kind of barbarity.

Their warfare is wholly noble and generous, and as excusable and beautiful as this human disease can be; its only basis among them is their rivalry in valor. They are not fighting for the conquest of new lands, for they still enjoy that natural abundance that provides them without toil and trouble with all necessary things in such profusion that they have no wish to enlarge their boundaries. They are still in that happy state of desiring only as much as their natural needs demand; anything beyond that is superfluous to them. . . . Truly here are real savages by our standards, for either they must be thoroughly so, or we must be; there is an amazing distance between their character and ours.

From Montaigne, "Of Cannibals."

Alba's policies drove Protestants into rebellion. This forced the Spanish government to maintain its army by raising taxes from those provinces that had remained loyal. Soon the loyal provinces too were in revolt, not over religion, but over taxation and local autonomy. Tax resistance and fear of an invasion from France left Alba unprepared for the series of successful assaults Protestants launched in the northern provinces during 1572. Protestant generals established a permanent base in the northwestern provinces of Holland and Zeeland. By 1575 the Protestants had gained a stronghold that they would never relinquish. Prince William of Orange assumed the leadership of the two provinces that were now united against the tyranny of Philip's rule.

Spanish government was collapsing all over the Netherlands. William ruled in the north and the States-General, a parliamentary body composed of representatives from the separate provinces, ruled in the south. Margaret of Parma had resigned in disgust at Alba's tactics, and Alba had been relieved of his command when his tactics had failed. No one was in control of the Spanish army. The soldiers, who had gone years with only partial pay, now roamed the southern provinces looking for plunder. Brussels and Ghent both had been targets, and in 1576 the worst atrocities of all occurred when mutinous Spanish troops sacked Antwerp. One of the wealthiest cities in Europe, home to the most important mercantile and banking establishments in the world, Antwerp was torn apart like a roasted pig. The rampage

The troops of Philip II of Spain under the duke of Alba inflicted countless cruelties on the people of the Netherlands.

lasted for days. When it ended, over seven thousand people had been slaughtered and nearly a third of the city burned to the ground.

The "Spanish fury" in Antwerp effectively ended Philip's rule over his Burgundian inheritance. The Protestants had established a permanent home in the north. The States-General had established its ability to rule in the south, and Spanish policy had been totally discredited. To achieve a settlement, the Pacification of Ghent of 1576, the Spanish government conceded local autonomy in taxation, the central role of the States-General in legislation, and the immediate withdrawal of all Spanish troops from the Low Countries. Five southern provinces pledged to remain Catholic and to accept the authority of the king's regent. This rift between the provinces was soon followed by a permanent split. In 1581 one group of provinces voted to depose Philip II, while a second group decided to remain loyal to him.

Philip II refused to accept the dismemberment of his inheritance and refused to recognize the independent Dutch state that now existed in Holland. Throughout the 1580s and 1590s military expeditions attempted to reunite the southern provinces and to

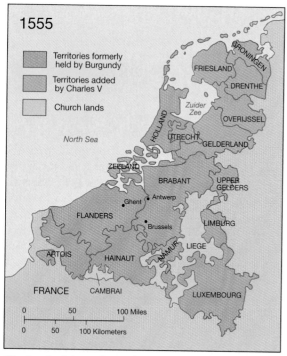

The Revolt of the Netherlands

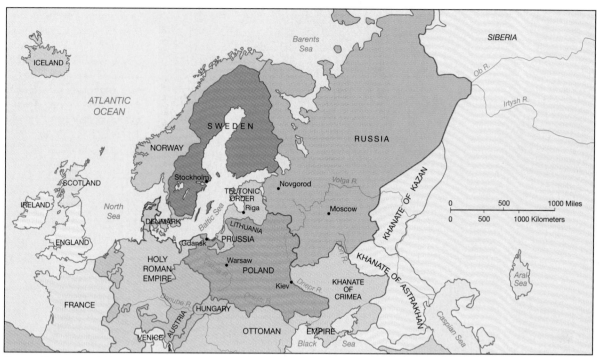

Eastern Europe, ca. 1550

conquer the northern ones. But Spanish military successes in the south were outweighed by the long-term failure of their objectives in the north. In 1609 Spain and the Netherlands concluded the Twelve Years' Truce, which tacitly recognized the existence of the state of Holland. By the beginning of the seventeenth century, Holland was not only an independent state, it was one of the greatest rivals of Spain and Portugal for the fruits of empire.

The Struggles in Eastern Europe

In eastern Europe dynastic struggles outweighed the problems created by religious reform. Muscovy remained the bulwark of Eastern Orthodox Christianity, immune from the struggles over the Roman faith. Protestantism did spread into Poland-Lithuania, but unlike its reception in the west, its presence was tolerated by the Polish state. The spread of dissent was checked not by repression, but by a vigorous Catholic reformation led by the Jesuits. The domestic crises in the east were crises of state rather than of church. In Muscovy, the disputed succession that followed the death of Ivan the Terrible plunged the state into anarchy and civil war. Centuries of conflict between

Poland-Lithuania and Muscovy came to a head with the Poles' desperate gamble to seize control of their massive eastern neighbor. War between Poland-Lithuania and Muscovy inevitably dominated the politics of the entire region. The Baltic states, of which Sweden was to become the most important, had their own ambitions for territory and economic gain. They soon joined the fray, making alliances in return for concessions and conquering small pieces of the mainland.

Kings and Diets in Poland

Until the end of the sixteenth century, Poland-Lithuania was the dominant power in the eastern part of Europe. It was economically healthy and militarily strong. Through its Baltic ports, especially Gdansk, Poland played a central role in international commerce and a dominant role in the northern grain trade. The vast size of the Polish state made defense difficult, and during the course of the sixteenth century it had lost lands to Muscovy in the east and to the Crimean Tartars in the south. But the permanent union with Lithuania in 1569 and the gradual absorption of the Baltic region of Livonia more than compensated for these losses. Matters of war and peace, of taxation and reform, were placed under the strict supervision of the

An assembly of the Polish Diet, the parliamentary body composed of the landed elite. On the throne is Sigismund III. Rivalry among the magnates weakened the Diet, and conflicts with the elected monarchs were frequent.

Polish Diet, a parliamentary body that represented the Polish landed elite. The Diet also carefully controlled religious policy. Roman Catholicism was the principal religion in Poland, but the state tolerated numerous Protestant and Eastern creeds. In the Warsaw Confederation of 1573, the Polish gentry vowed, "We who differ in matters of religion will keep the peace among ourselves."

The biological failure of the Jagiellon monarchy in Poland ended that nation's most successful line of kings. Without a natural heir, the Polish nobility and gentry, who officially elected the monarch, had to peddle their throne among the princes of Europe. When Sigismund III (1587–1632) was elected to the Polish throne in 1587, he was also heir to the crown of Sweden. Sigismund accepted the prohibitions against religious repression that were outlined in the Warsaw Confederation, but he actively encouraged the establishment of Jesuit schools, the expansion of monastic orders, and the strengthening of the Roman Catholic church.

All of these policies enjoyed the approval of the Polish ruling classes. But the Diet would not support Sigismund's efforts to gain control of the Swedish crown, which he inherited in 1592 but from which he was deposed three years later. If Sigismund triumphed in Sweden, all Poland would get was a part-time monarch. The Polish Diet consistently refused to give the king the funds necessary to invade Sweden successfully. Nevertheless, Sigismund mounted several unsuccessful campaigns against the Swedes that sapped Polish money and manpower.

Muscovy's Time of Troubles

The wars of Ivan the Great and Ivan the Terrible in the fifteenth and sixteenth centuries were waged to secure agricultural territory in the west and a Baltic port in the north; both objectives came at the expense of Poland-Lithuania. But following the death of Ivan the Terrible in 1584, the Muscovite state began to disintegrate. For years it had been held together only by conquest and fear. Ivan's conflicts with the boyars, the hereditary nobility, had created an aristocracy unwilling and unable to come to the aid of his successors. By 1601 the crown was plunged into a crisis of legitimacy known as the Time of Troubles. Ivan had murdered his heir in a fit of anger and left his half-witted son to inherit the throne. This led to a vacuum of power at the center as well as a struggle for the spoils of government. Private armies ruled great swaths of the state and pretenders to the crown—all claiming to be Dimitri,

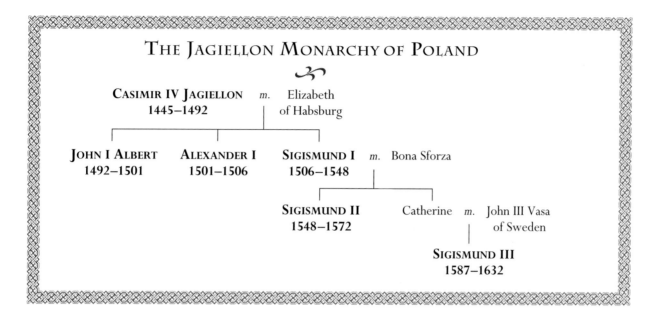

THE JAGIELLON MONARCHY OF POLAND

CASIMIR IV JAGIELLON *m.* Elizabeth
1445–1492   of Habsburg

JOHN I ALBERT   **ALEXANDER I**   **SIGISMUND I** *m.* Bona Sforza
1492–1501   1501–1506   1506–1548

SIGISMUND II   Catherine *m.* John III Vasa
1548–1572   of Sweden

SIGISMUND III
1587–1632

The Rise of Russia

of opportunity. While anarchy and civil war raged, Poland looked to regain the territory that it had lost to Muscovy over the previous century. Sigismund abandoned war with Sweden in order to intervene in the struggle for the Russian crown. Polish forces crossed into Muscovy and Sigismund's generals backed one of the strongest of the false Dimitris, but their plan to put him on the throne failed when he was assassinated. Sigismund used the death of the last false Dimitri as a pretext to assert his own claim to the Muscovite crown. More Polish forces poured across the frontier. In 1610 they took Moscow and Sigismund proclaimed himself tsar, intending to unite the two massive states.

The Russian boyars, so long divided, now rose against the Polish enemy. The Polish garrison in Moscow was starved into submission, and a native Russian, Michael Romanov (1613–45) was chosen tsar by an assembly of landholders, the Zemsky Sobor. He made a humiliating peace with the Swedes—who had also taken advantage of the Time of Troubles to invade Muscovy's Baltic provinces—in return for Swedish assistance against the Poles. Intermittent fighting continued for another twenty years. In the end, Poland agreed to peace and a separate Muscovite state, but only in exchange for large territorial concessions.

The Rise of Sweden

Sweden's rise to power during the seventeenth century was as startling as it was swift. Until the Reformation, Sweden had been part of the Scandinavian confederation ruled by the Danes. Although the Swedes had a

the lost brother of the last legitimate tsar—appeared everywhere. Ambitious groups of boyars backed their own claimants to the throne. So, too, did ambitious foreigners who eagerly sought to carve up Muscovite possessions.

Muscovy's Time of Troubles was Poland's moment

MICHAEL FEDEROWITS,
Czar ou Grand Duc de Moscovie.

Michael Romanov was chosen to be tsar in 1613. His father, the Patriarch Philaret of Moscow, acted as joint ruler with Michael until the patriarch's death in 1633.

found themselves no longer capable of ruling in Livonia, the Baltic seaports that had been under their dominion scrambled for new alliances. Muscovy and Poland-Lithuania were the logical choices, but the town of Reval, an important outlet for Russian trade near the mouth of the Gulf of Finland, asked Sweden for protection. After some hesitation, since the occupation of territory on the southern shores of the Baltic would involve great expense, Sweden fortified Reval in 1560. A decade later, Swedish forces captured Narva, farther to the east, and consolidated their hold on the Livonian coast. By occupying the most important ports on the Gulf of Finland, Sweden could control a sizable portion of the Muscovite trade.

Now only two obstacles prevented them from dominating trade with Muscovy: Archangel in the north and Riga in the south. In the 1580s, the Muscovites established a port at Archangel on the White Sea. With this new port they opened a trading route to the west, around northern Scandinavia. Sweden benefitted from the White Sea trade by claiming the northern portions of the Scandinavian peninsula necessary to make the trade secure. In all of their dealings with Muscovy the Swedes sought further privileges at Archangel while laying plans for its conquest. Riga was a problem of a different sort. As the Swedes secured the northern Livonian ports, more of the Muscovy trade moved to the south and passed through Riga, which would have to be captured or blockaded if the Swedes were to control commerce in the eastern Baltic.

Sigismund's aggressive alliance with the Polish Jesuits persuaded the Swedish nobility that he would undermine their Lutheran church. Sigismund was deposed in favor of his uncle Charles IX (1604–11). War with Poland resulted from Sigismund's efforts to regain the Swedish crown. The Swedes used the opportunity to blockade Riga and to occupy more Livonian territory. The Swedish navy was far superior to any force that the Poles could assemble, but on land Polish forces were masters. The Swedish invasion force suffered a crushing defeat and had to retreat to its coastal enclaves. The Poles now had an opportunity to retake all of Livonia but, as always, the Polish Diet was reluctant to finance Sigismund's wars. Furthermore, Sigismund had his eyes on a bigger prize. Rather than follow up its Swedish victory, Poland invaded Muscovy.

Meanwhile, the blockade of Riga and the assembly of a large Swedish fleet in the Baltic threatened Denmark. The Danes continued to claim sovereignty over Sweden and took the opportunity of the Polish-Swedish conflict to reassert it. In 1611, under the ener-

measure of autonomy, they were very much a junior partner in Baltic affairs. Denmark controlled the narrow sound that linked the Baltic with the North Sea, and its prosperity derived from the tolls it collected on imports and exports. When, in 1523, Gustav I Vasa led the uprising of the Swedish aristocracy that ended Danish domination, he won the right to rule over a poor, sparsely populated state with few towns or developed seaports. The Vasas ruled Sweden in conjunction with the aristocracy. Although the throne was hereditary, the part played by the nobility in elevating Gustav I Vasa (1523–60) gave the nobles a powerful voice in Swedish affairs. Through the council of state, known as the Rad, the Swedish nobility exerted a strong check on the monarch. Sweden's aggressive foreign policy began accidentally. When in the 1550s the Teutonic Knights

A Livonian peasant. Livonia was conquered by Ivan the Terrible in his campaign of 1563, but was soon reclaimed by the Poles. In 1660 Livonia became part of the Swedish empire. Livonia was originally inhabited by the Livs, a Finnish people.

getic leadership of the Danish king Christian IV (1588–1648), Denmark invaded Sweden from both the east and the west. The Danes captured the towns of Kalmar and Alvsborg and threatened to take Stockholm. To end the Danish war, Sweden accepted humiliating terms in 1613. Sweden renounced all claims to the northern coasts and recognized Danish control of the Arctic trading route.

Paradoxically, these setbacks became the springboard for Swedish success. Fear of the Danes led both the English and the Dutch into alliances with Sweden. The countries all shared Protestant interests, and the English were heavily committed to the Muscovy trade, which was still an important part of Swedish commerce. Fear of the Poles had a similar effect upon Muscovy. In 1609 the Swedes agreed to send five thousand

troops to Muscovy to help repel the Polish invasion. In return, Muscovy agreed to cede to Sweden its Baltic possessions. This was accomplished in 1617, giving Sweden complete control of the Gulf of Finland.

In 1611, during the middle of the Danish war, Charles IX died and was succeeded by his son Gustavus Adolphus (1611–32). Unlike his father and cousin before him, who had come by chance to the Swedish throne, Gustavus Adolphus was raised to be king. Gruff and affable by turns, he was one of the leading Protestant princes of his day, in every way a match for Christian IV of Denmark. Gustavus's greatest skills were military. He inherited an ample navy and an effective army. Unlike nearly every other European state, Sweden raised its forces from its own citizens. Gustavus's predecessors had made important innovations in the training of soldiers and in their battlefield tactics. These the new king improved upon. He introduced new weapons such as the light mobile gun and reshaped his army into standard-size squadrons and regiments, which were easier to administer and deploy.

The calamitous wars inherited from his father occupied Gustavus during the early years of his reign. He was forced to conclude the humiliating peace with the Danes in 1613 and to go to war with the Russians in 1614 in order to secure the Baltic coastal estates that had been promised in 1609. Gustavus's first military initiative was to resume war with Poland in order to force Sigismund to renounce his claim to the Swedish throne. In 1621 Gustavus landed in Livonia and within two weeks had captured Riga, the capstone of Sweden's Baltic ambitions. Occupation of Riga increased Swedish control of the Muscovy trade and deprived Denmark of a significant portion of its customs duties. Gustavus now claimed Riga as a Swedish port and successfully demanded that ships sailing from there pay tolls to Sweden rather than Denmark. The capture of Riga firmly established Sweden as a coequal Baltic power.

By the mid-seventeenth century, the Sweden of Gustavus Adolphus was well on its way to international prominence. The capture of Riga gave Sweden complete control of the eastern Baltic and ended Polish pretensions to the Swedish throne. A negotiated settlement with the Danes over the collection of tolls enhanced Swedish prestige and increased Sweden's commercial prosperity. Moreover, Gustavus's marriage into the family of the Protestant rulers of Prussia gave Sweden a presence in Germany as well. For the time being Sweden faced east. But the storm clouds of religious warfare were already bursting over the Holy

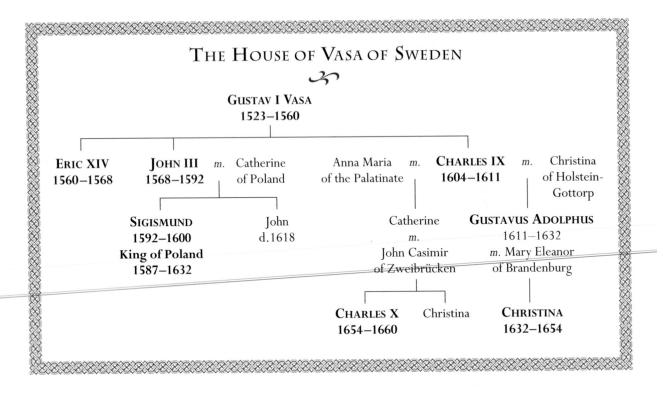

THE HOUSE OF VASA OF SWEDEN

GUSTAV I VASA
1523–1560

ERIC XIV
1560–1568

JOHN III *m.* Catherine
1568–1592 of Poland

Anna Maria *m.* **CHARLES IX** *m.* Christina
of the Palatinate **1604–1611** of Holstein-
Gottorp

SIGISMUND John
1592–1600 d.1618
King of Poland
1587–1632

Catherine
m.
John Casimir
of Zweibrücken

GUSTAVUS ADOLPHUS
1611–1632
m. Mary Eleanor
of Brandenburg

CHARLES X Christina
1654–1660

CHRISTINA
1632–1654

Map legend:
- Sweden, 1560
- Territory added by 1592
- Territory added by 1632

The Rise of Sweden

Roman Empire. Gustavus Adolphus now took his place among the Protestant princes of Europe, and Sweden ranked among the leading Protestant powers.

The Thirty Years' War, 1618–48

Perhaps it was just a matter of time before the isolated conflicts that dotted the corners of Europe were joined together. In 1609 Spain and the Dutch Republic had signed a truce that was to last until 1621. In over forty years of nearly continuous fighting, the Dutch had carved out a state in the northern Netherlands. They used the truce to consolidate their position and increase their prosperity, largely at the expense of Spain and Portugal. Thus, to the insult of rebellion was added the injury of commercial competition. Spain had reluctantly accepted Dutch independence, but Philip III (1598–1621) never abandoned the objective of recovering his Burgundian inheritance. By the opening of the seventeenth century, Philip had good reasons for hope. Beginning in the 1580s, Spanish forces had reconquered the southern provinces of the Nether-

THE THIRTY YEARS' WAR

1618	**Defenestration of Prague**
1619	**Ferdinand Habsburg elected Holy Roman Emperor; Frederick of the Palatinate accepts the crown of Bohemia**
1620	**Catholic victory at battle of White Mountain**
1621	**End of Twelve Years' Truce; war between Spain and Netherlands**
1626	**Danes form Protestant alliance under Christian IV**
1627	**Spain declares bankruptcy**
1630	**Gustavus Adolphus leads Swedish forces into Germany**
1631	**Sack of Magdeburg; Protestant victory at Breitenfeld**
1632	**Protestant victory at Lutzen; death of Gustavus Adolphus**
1635	**France declares war on Spain**
1640	**Portugal secedes from Spain**
1643	**Battle of Rocroi; French forces repel Spaniards**
1648	**Peace of Westphalia**

Bohemia Revolts

The Peace of Augsburg had served the German states well. The principle that the religion of the ruler was the religion of the state complicated the political life of the Holy Roman Empire, but it also pacified it. Although rulers had the right to enforce uniformity on their subjects, in practice many of the larger states tolerated more than one religion. By the beginning of the seventeenth century, Catholicism and Protestantism had achieved a rough equality within the German states, symbolized by the fact that of the seven electors who chose the Holy Roman Emperor, three were Catholic, three Protestant, and the seventh was the emperor him-

lands. The prosperous towns of Brussels, Antwerp, and Ghent were again under Spanish control, and they provided a springboard for another invasion.

The Twelve Years' Truce gave Spain time to prepare for the final assault. During this time Philip III attempted to resolve all of Spain's other European conflicts so that he could then give full attention to a resumption of the Dutch war. Circumstance smiled upon his efforts. In 1603 the pacific James I (1603–25) came to the English throne. Secure in his island state, James I desired peace among all Christian princes. He quickly concluded the war with Spain that had begun with the invasion of the Spanish Armada and entered into negotiations to marry his heir to a Spanish princess. In 1610 the bellicose Henry IV of France was felled by an assassin's knife. French plans to renew war with Spain were abandoned with the accession of the eight-year-old Louis XIII (1610–43). As the sands of the Twelve Years' Truce ran out, Spain and the Netherlands readied for war. But not even the greatest empire in Europe could control its own destiny. War was in the air all over the Continent, and not everyone could wait until 1621.

Marie de Médicis, the widow of Henry IV, with her son Louis XIII.

independent authority over their states, and the imperial diet, rather than the emperor, was empowered to settle disputes. Thus weakened, future emperors ruled in the Habsburg territorial lands with little ability to control, influence, or even arbitrate German affairs. The judgment that the Holy Roman Empire was neither holy, nor Roman, nor an empire was now irrevocably true.

• • •

The Peace of Westphalia put the pieces of the map of European states back together. Protestantism and Catholicism now coexisted and there was to be little further change in the geography of religion. The northwest of Europe—England, Holland, Scandinavia, and the north German states—was Protestant, while the south was Catholic. The empire of the German peoples was now at an end, the Austro-Hungarian empire at a beginning. Holland and Sweden had become international powers; Spain and Denmark faded from prominence. Muscovy began a long period of isolation from the west, attempting to restore a semblance of government to its people. But if the negotiators at Westphalia could resolve the political and religious ambitions that gave rise to a century of nearly continuous warfare, they could do nothing to eradicate the effects of war itself. The devastation of humanity in the name of God with which the reform of religion had begun was now exhausted. The costs were horrific. The population of Germany fell from 15 million in 1600 to 11 million in 1650. The armies brought destruction of all kinds in their wake. Plague again raged in Europe—the town of Augsburg lost 18,000 inhabitants in the early 1630s. Famine, too, returned to a continent that fifty years earlier had been self-sufficient in grain. The war played havoc with all of the economies that it touched. Inflation, devaluation of coinage, and huge public and private debts were all directly attributable to the years of fighting. And the toll taken on the spirit of those generations that never knew peace is incalculable.

Suggestions for Further Reading

General Reading

* J. H. Elliott, *Europe Divided, 1559–1598* (New York: Harper & Row, 1968). An outstanding synthesis of European politics in the second half of the sixteenth century.

* Geoffrey Parker, *Europe in Crisis, 1598–1648* (London: William Collins and Sons, 1979). An up-to-date study of European states in the early seventeenth century.

* Richard Bonney, *The European Dynastic States, 1494–1660* (Oxford: Oxford University Press, 1991.) The most up-to-date introduction to the period, by a noted historian of France.

* Jan de Vries, *The European Economy in an Age of Crisis* (Cambridge: Cambridge University Press, 1976). A comprehensive study of economic development, including long-distance trade and commercial change.

* Richard Dunn, *The Age of Religious Wars, 1559–1715* (New York: Norton, 1979). A well-written survey of early modern society.

* H. G. Koenigsberger, *Early Modern Europe* (London: Longman, 1987). A general overview designed for beginning students.

The Crises of the Western States

J. H. M. Salmon, *Society in Crisis* (New York: St. Martins, 1975). The best single-volume account of the French civil wars; difficult but rewarding.

N. M. Sutherland, *The Massacre of St. Bartholomew and the European Conflict* (London: Macmillan, 1973). Argues the case for the importance of Spanish influence on the massacre and the course of the wars of religion.

Robert Kingdon, *Myths about the St. Bartholomew's Day Massacres, 1572–76* (Cambridge, MA: Harvard University Press, 1988). A study of the impact of a central event in the history of France.

David Buisseret, *Henry IV* (London: George Allen & Unwin, 1984). A stylish biography of a problematic personality.

* Mark Greengrass, *France in the Age of Henri IV* (London: Longman, 1984). An important synthesis of French history in the early seventeenth century.

Geoffrey Parker, *Philip II* (Boston: Little, Brown, 1978). The best introduction.

* Garrett Mattingly, *The Armada* (Boston: Houghton Mifflin, 1959). Still the classic account, despite recent reinterpretations.

Colin Martin and N. G. Parker, *The Spanish Armada* (London: Hamilton Press, 1988). A recent study based on archaeological finds and a fresh look at the evidence.

John Lynch, *Spain, 1516–1598: From Nation State to World Empire* (Cambridge, MA: Blackwell, 1992). The most up-to-date survey.

* Henry Kamen, *Spain, 1469–1714* (London: Longman, 1983). A recent survey with up-to-date interpretations.

* Geoffrey Parker, *The Dutch Revolt* (London: Penguin Books, 1977). An outstanding account of the tangle of events that comprised the revolts of the Netherlands.

* Pieter Geyl, *The Revolt of the Netherlands* (London: Ernest Benn, 1962). Still worth reading for its passion and enthusiasm.

W. E. F. Reddawaay, et al., eds., *The Cambridge History of Poland to 1696* (Cambridge: Cambridge University Press, 1950). A difficult but thorough narrative of Polish history.

Michael Roberts, *Gustavus Adolphus and the Rise of Sweden* (London: English Universities Press, 1973). A highly readable account of Sweden's rise to power.

The Struggles in Eastern Europe

S. F. Platonov, *The Time of Troubles* (Lawrence: University Press of Kansas, 1970). A good narrative of the disintegration of the Muscovite state.

Stewart Oakley, *War and Peace in the Baltic, 1560–1790* (New York: Routledge, 1992). A solid account of military history during the period of Sweden's rise.

David Kirby, *Northern Europe in the Early Modern Period: The Baltic World, 1492–1772* (London: Longman, 1990). The best single volume on Baltic politics.

Michael Roberts, *The Swedish Imperial Experience* (Cambridge: Cambridge University Press, 1979). Reflections on Swedish history by the preeminent historian of early modern Sweden.

The Thirty Years' War

* C. V. Wedgwood, *The Thirty Years' War* (New York: Doubleday, 1961). An heroic account; the best narrative history.

Geoffrey Parker, ed., *The Thirty Years' War* (London: Routledge and Kagen Paul, 1984). A multiauthor account that views the war from a variety of vantage points.

* Peter Limm, *The Thirty Years' War* (London: Longman, 1984). An excellent brief survey with documents.

S. F. Platonov, *The Time of Troubles* (Lawrence: University Press of Kansas, 1970). A good narrative of the disintegration of the Muscovite state.

Stewart Oakley, *War and Peace in the Baltic, 1560–1790* (New York: Routledge, 1992). A solid account of military history during the period of Sweden's rise.

David Kirby, *Northern Europe in the Early Modern Period: The Baltic World,* 1492–1772 (London: Longman, 1990). The best single volume on Baltic politics.

Michael Roberts, *The Swedish Imperial Experience* (Cambridge: Cambridge University Press, 1979). Reflections on Swedish history by the preeminent historian of early modern Sweden.

J. H. Elliott, *Richelieu and Olivares* (Cambridge: Cambridge University Press, 1984). A comparison of statemen and statemanship in the early seventeenth century.

*Paperback edition available.

15 ~ THE EXPERIENCES OF LIFE IN EARLY MODERN EUROPE, 1500–1650

Haymaking

*I*t is summer in the Low Countries. The trees are full, the
meadows green; flowers rise in
clumps and bushes hang heavy
with fruit. The day has dawned
brightly for haymaking. Yesterday
the long meadow was mowed, and
today the hay will be gathered and
the first fruits and vegetables of
the season harvested. From
throughout the village families
come together to labor. Twice each
summer the grass is cut, dried, and

stacked. Some of it will be left in
the fields for the animals until
autumn; some will be carried into
large lofts and stored for the winter.

This scene of communal farming is repeated with little variation
throughout Europe in the early
modern era. The village we are
viewing is fairly prosperous. We
can see at least three horses and a
large wheeled cart. Horses are still
a luxury for farmers; they can be

used for transportation as well as
labor, but they are weaker than
oxen and must be fed on grain
rather than grass. The houses of
the village also suggest comfort.
The one at the far right is typical.
It contains one floor for living and
a loft for storage. The chimney
separates a kitchen in the back
from the long hall where the family works, sleeps, and entertains
itself. The bed—it is not uncommon for there to be only one for

the whole family—would be near the fireplace. It will be restuffed with straw after the harvest. The spinning wheel and whatever other machines the family possesses would be situated nearest the single window, which lets in light and air on good days and cold and rain on bad ones. The window is covered by oiled animal skin, since glass is still too expensive for use in rural housing. The long end of the hall, farthest from heat and light, will be home to the family's animals once winter sets in. But now, in summer, it is luxurious space where children can play or parents claim a little privacy.

The church is easily distinguished by its steeple and arched doorway and is made of brick. The steeple has 16 windows, probably all set with expensive glass and some even stained. The church would have been built over several generations at considerable cost to the villagers. Even the most prosperous houses in the far meadow are made of timber and thatch. The layout of the buildings shows us how the village must have grown. The original settlement was all on the rise

above the church. The houses nearer the center of the picture were undoubtedly added later, perhaps to allow the sons of the more prosperous village farmers to begin their own families before their parents' death.

In the center of the scene are a large number of laborers. Four men with pitchforks load the cart while two women sweep the hay that falls back into new piles. Throughout the field, men and women, distinguished only by their clothing, rake hay into large stacks for successive loadings of the cart. At least twenty-five individuals work at these tasks. Men perform the heaviest work of loading the haycart and hammering the scythes while men and women share all the other work. Although no children appear in the scene, some are undoubtedly at work picking berries and beans.

Perhaps the three women returning to work are of the same family, a young girl flanked by her grandmother and mother. The expression of the eldest woman tells a tale of lifelong exertion as she holds her rake loosely and balances it carefully on her shoulder

to lessen its weight. The woman on the other end has a look of determination. She is holding her hat rather than wearing it, and her thick, muscular shoulders suggest a regimen of heavy labor. She has made this journey many times before. The young girl seems almost serene, still invigorated rather than ground down by the day's exercise.

As a trio they remind us that the life of ordinary people in the early modern period was neither romantic nor despondent, neither quaint nor primitive. It had its own joys and sorrows, its own triumphs and failures, its own measures of progress and decay. Inevitably, we compare it to our experiences and contrast it to our comforts. By our standards, a sixteenth-century prince endured greater material hardships than a twentieth-century welfare recipient. There was no running water, no central heating, no lavatories, no electricity. There was no relief for toothache, headache, or numbing pain. Travel was dangerous and exhausting. There was no protection from the open air, and many nights were spent on the bare ground. Waiting for winds to sail was more tedious than waiting to board a plane. Entertainment was sparse, and the court jester was little match for stereo and video. But though we cannot help but be struck by these differences, we will not understand very much about the experiences of life in sixteenth-century Europe if we judge it by our own standard of living. We must exercise our historical imagination if we are to appreciate the conditions of early modern European society.

Economic Life

There was no typical sixteenth-century European. Travelers' accounts and ambassadors' reports indicate that contemporaries were constantly surprised by the habits and possessions of other Europeans. Language, custom, geography, and material conditions separated peoples in one place from those in another. Contrasts between social groups were more striking still. A Muscovite boyar had more in common with an English nobleman than either had with his country's peasants. A Spanish goldsmith and a German brass maker lived remarkably similar lives when compared to that of a shepherd anywhere in Europe. No matter how carefully historians attempt to distinguish between country and town life, between social or occupational groups, or between men and women, they are still smoothing out edges that are very rough, still turning individuals into aggregates, still sacrificing the particular for the general. No French peasant family ever had 3.5 children even if, on average, they all did. There was no typical sixteenth-century European.

But there were experiences that most Europeans shared and common structures through which their activities were channeled that separated them from their predecessors and their successors. There was a distinctive sixteenth-century experience that we can easily discern and that they could dimly perceive. Much of it was a natural progression in which one generation improved upon the situation of another. Agriculture increased: more land was cleared, more crops were grown, and better tools were crafted. Some of the experience was natural regression. Irreplaceable resources were lost: more trees were felled, more soil was eroded, and more fresh water was polluted. But some of what was distinctive about sixteenth-century life resulted from dynamic changes in economic and social conditions. The century-long population explosion and increase in commodity prices fundamentally altered people's lives. Not since the Black Death had Europe experienced so thorough a transformation in its economic development and its social organization. Change and reactions to change became dominant themes of everyday life.

Rural Life

In the early modern era, as much as 90 percent of the European population lived on farms or in small towns in which farming was the principal occupation. Villages were small and relatively isolated, even in densely populated regions like Italy and the Low Countries. They might range in size from a hundred families, as was common in France and Spain, to less than twenty families, which was the average size of Hungarian vil-

This picture, painted in 1530, shows farmworkers threshing grain. The figure at the door seems to be an overseer. He has just sold a sack of grain, indicating the transition from a system of self-sufficient manors to a market economy.

lages. These villages, large or small, prosperous or poor, were the bedrock of the sixteenth-century state. A surplus peasant population fed the insatiable appetite of towns for laborers and of crowns for soldiers. The manor, the parish, and the rural administrative district were the institutional infrastructures of Europe. Each organized the peasantry for its own purposes. Manorial rents supported the lifestyle of the nobility; parish tithes supported the works of the Church; local taxes supported the power of the state. Rents, tithes, and taxes easily absorbed more than half of the wealth produced by the land. From the remaining half, the peasant had to make provision for the present and the future.

To survive, the village community had to be self-sufficient. In good times there was enough to eat and some to save for the future. Hard times meant hunger and starvation. Both conditions were accepted as part of the natural order, and both occurred regularly. One in every three harvests was bad; one in every five was disastrous. Bad harvests came in succession. Depending upon the soil and crop, between one-fifth and one-half of the grain harvested had to be saved as seed for the next planting season. When hunger was worst, people faced the agonizing choice of eating or saving their seed corn.

Hunger and cold were the constant companions of the average European. In Scandinavia and Muscovy, winter posed as great a threat to survival as did starvation. There the stove and garments made from animal fur were essential requirements, as were the hearth and the woolen tunic in the south. Everywhere in Europe homes were inadequate shelter against the cold and damp. Most were built of wood and roofed in thatch. Inside walls were patched with dried mud and sometimes covered with bark or animal skins. Windows were few and narrow. Piled leaves or straw, which could be easily replaced, covered the ground and acted as insulation. The typical house was one long room with a stone hearth at the end. The hearth provided both heat and light and belched forth soot and smoke through a brick chimney.

People had relatively few household possessions. The essential piece of furniture was the wooden chest, which was used for storage. A typical family could keep all of its belongings in the chest, which could then be buried or carried away in times of danger. The chest had other uses as well. Its flat top served as a table or bench or as a sideboard on which food could be placed. Tables and stools were becoming more common during the sixteenth century, though chairs were still a great luxury. Most domestic activities, of which cooking, eat-

An illustration for the month of December from a sixteenth-century Book of Hours shows pig-killing and baking. The loaves were prepared in individual homes and baked in communal ovens.

ing, and sleeping were dominant, took place close to the ground, and squatting, kneeling, and sitting were the usual postures of family members. In areas in which spinning, weaving, and other domestic skills were an important part of the family's economy, a long bench was propped against the wall, usually beneath a window. Bedsteads were also becoming more common as the century wore on. They raised the straw mattresses off the ground, keeping them warmer and drier. All other family possessions related to food production. Iron spits and pots, or at least metal rings and clamps for wooden ones, were treasured goods that were passed from generation to generation. Most other implements were wooden. Long-handled spoons; boards known as trenchers, which were used for cutting and eating; and one large cup and bowl were the basic stock of the kitchen. The family ate from the long trencher and passed the bowl and cup. Knives were essential farm tools that doubled for kitchen and mealtime duty, but forks were still a curiosity.

LIVING BY ONE'S WITS

Lazarillo De Tormes (1554) is among the first modern novels, one of a variety of sixteenth-century Spanish stories that are called picaresque after the wandering beggars that are their heroes. Although the picaresque novel was a fictional account, much of the descriptive detail accurately portrays the social conditions for the vast majority of the Spanish population in the so-called Golden Age.

We began our journey, and in a few days he taught me thieves' jargon, and when he saw me to be of a good wit, was well pleased, and used to say: "Gold or silver I cannot give thee, but I will show thee many pointers about life." And it was so; for after God this man gave me my life, and although blind lighted and guided me in the career of living.

He used to carry bread and everything else in a linen sack which closed at the mouth with an iron ring and a padlock and key, and when he put things in and took them out, it was with so much attention, so well counted, that the whole world wouldn't have been equal to making it a crumb less. But I would take what stingy bit he gave me, and finish it in less than two mouthfuls. After he had fastened the lock and stopped worrying about it, thinking me to be engaged in other things, by a little seam, which I un-sewed and sewed up again many times in the side of the sack, I used to bleed the miserly sack, taking out bread—not measured quantities but good pieces—and slices of bacon and sausage; and thus would seek a convenient time to make good the devilish state of want which the wicked blind man left me in.

When we ate he used to put a little jug of wine near him. I would quickly seize it and give it a couple of silent kisses and return it to its place; but this plan didn't work long, for he noticed the deficiency in his draughts, and in order to keep his wine safe, he never after let go the jug, but kept hold of the handle. But there is no lode-stone that draws things to it so strongly as I with a long rye straw, which I had pre-pared for that purpose, and placing which in the mouth of the jug, I would suck up the wine to a fare-ye-well. But the villian was so clever that I think he

heard me; and from then on he changed procedure and set his jug between his legs and covered it with his hand, and thus drank secure.

We were at Escalona, town of the Duke of that ilk, in an inn, and he gave me a piece of sausage to roast. When he had basted the sausage and eaten the bast-ing, he took a maravedi from his purse and bade me fetch wine from the tavern. The devil put the occa-sion before my eyes, which, as the saying is, makes the thief; and it was this: there lay by the fire a small turnip, rather long and bad, and which must have been thrown there because it was not fit for the stew. And as nobody was there at the time but him and me alone, as I had an appetite whetted by having got the toothsome odour of the sausage inside me (the only part, as I knew, that I had to enjoy myself with), not considering what might follow, all fear set aside in order to comply with desire—while the blind man was taking the money out of his purse, I took the sausage, and quickly put the above-mentioned turnip on the spit, which my master grasped, when he had given me the money for the wine, and began to turn before the fire, trying to roast what through its demerit had escaped being boiled. I went for the wine, and on the way did not delay in despatching the sausage, and when I came back I found the sinner of a blind man holding the turnip ready between two slices of bread, for he had not yet recognized it, because he had not tried it with his hand. When he took the slices of bread and bit into them, thinking to get part of the sausage too, he found himself chilled by the chilly turnip.

From *Lazarillo De Tormes.*

The scale of life was small, and its pace was con-trolled by the limits that nature imposed. It was a civi-lization of daylight—up at dawn, asleep at dusk; long working hours in summer, short ones in winter. For most people, the world was bounded by the distance that could be traveled on foot. Those who stayed all their lives in their rural villages may never have seen more than a hundred other people at once or have heard any noise louder than a human voice and terrify-

ing thunder. Their wisdom—hard won and carefully preserved—was of the practical experience necessary to survive the struggle with nature. This was the most important legacy that parents left their children.

Peasant life centered on agriculture. Technology and technique varied little across the continent, but there were significant differences depending upon climate and soil. The lives of those who grew crops contrasted with the experiences of those who raised animals.

Across the great plain, the breadbasket that stretched from the Low Countries to Poland-Lithuania, the most common form of crop growing was still the three-field rotation system. In this method winter crops like wheat or rye were planted in one field; spring crops like barley, peas, or beans were planted in another; and the third field was left fallow. Over 80 percent of what was grown on the farm was consumed on the farm. In most parts of Europe, wheat was a luxury crop, sold at market rather than eaten at home. Wheat bread was prized for its taste, texture, and white color. Rye and barley were the staples for peasants. These grains were cheaper to grow, had higher yields, and could be brewed as well as baked. Most of this grain was baked into the coarse black bread that was the monotonous fare of the peasant diet. Two to three pounds a day for an adult male was an average allotment when grain was readily available. Beer and gruels of grain and skimmed milk or water flavored with fruit juice supplemented peasant fare. In one form or another, grain provided over 75 percent of the calories in a typical diet.

The warm climate and dry weather of Mediterranean Europe favored a two-crop rotation system. With less water and stronger sunlight, half the land had to be left fallow each year to restore its nutrients. Here fruit, especially grapes and olives, was an essential supplement to diet. With smaller cereal crops, wine replaced beer as a nutritious beverage. The fermentation of grapes and grain into wine and beer also provided convenient ways of storing foodstuffs, a constant problem during the winter and early spring. Wine and olive oil were also luxury products and were most commonly exchanged for meat, which was less plentiful on southern European farms.

Animal husbandry was the main occupation in the third agricultural area of Europe, the mountainous and hilly regions. Sheep were the most common animal that Europeans raised. Sheep provided the raw material for almost all clothing, their skins were used for parchment and as window coverings, and they were a ready source of inexpensive meat. They were bred in hundreds of thousands, migrating across large areas of grazing land, especially in western Europe, where their wool was the main export of both England and Spain. Pigs were domestic animals prevalent in woodland settlements. They foraged for food and were kept, like poultry, for slaughter. Cattle, on the other hand, were essential farm animals. "The fundamentals of the home," wrote the Spanish poet Luis de Leon (1527–91), "are the woman and the ox, the ox to plow and the woman to manage things." In the dairying areas of Europe, cattle produced milk, cheese, and butter; in Hungary and Bohemia, the great breeding center of the continent, they were raised for export; and most everywhere else they were used as beasts of burden.

Because agriculture was the principal occupation of Europeans, land was the principal resource. Most land was owned, not by those who worked it, but by lords who let it out in various ways. The land was still divided into manors, and the manor lord, or seigneur, was still responsible for maintaining order, administering

The marketplace at Antwerp by an unknown artist.

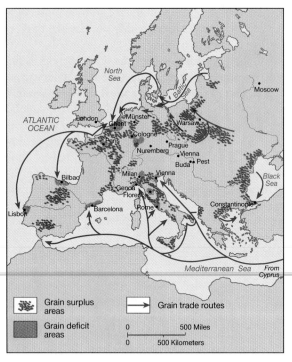

Grain Supply and Trade in Sixteenth-Century Europe

Although the land in each village was set out in large fields so that crops could be rotated, families owned their own pieces within the field, usually in scattered strips that they plowed, manured, and planted individually. There were also large common fields used as pasture, as well as common woodlands where animals foraged, fuel was gathered, and game hunted. Even the common fields and woodlands were not shared equally. Those who held the most land in the fields possessed greater shares of the commons. Villagers disputed frequently over rights to sticks and branches of trees and over the number of sheep or cows that could be grazed in the meadows, especially when resources were scarce.

Farm work was ceaseless toil. Six or seven times a year farmers tilled the fields to spread animal manure below the surface of the soil. While most villages possessed metal plows, the team of draught animals was the single essential component for farming. The births of foals and calves were more-celebrated events than the births of children; the death of an ox or horse was a catastrophe that could drive a family into debt or from the land entirely. Calamities lurked everywhere, from rain and drought to locusts and crows. Most farms could support only one family at subsistence level, and excess sons and daughters had to fend for themselves, either through marriage in the village or by migration to a town.

Town Life

In the country men and women worked to the natural rhythm of the day: up at the cock's crow, at work in the cooler hours, at rest in the hotter ones. Rain and cold kept them idle; sunlight kept them busy. Each season brought its own activity. In the town the bell tolled every hour. In the summer the laborers gathered at the town gates at four in the morning, in the winter at seven. The bell signaled the time for morning and afternoon meals as well as the hour to lay down tools and return home. Wages were paid for hours worked: seven in winter, as many as sixteen in June and July.

In all towns there was an official guild structure that organized and regulated labor. Rules laid down the requirements for training, the standards for quality, and the conditions for exchange. Only those officially sanctioned could work in trades, and each trade could perform only specified tasks. In the German town of Nuremberg a sword maker could not make knives, nor could a pin maker make thimbles. Specialization went even further in London, Paris, and other large cities.

While the life of the peasant community turned on self-sufficiency, that of the town turned on interdepen-

justice, and arbitrating disputes. Although the personal bonds between lords and tenants were gradually loosening, political and economic ties were as strong as ever. Lords were not necessarily individual members of the nobility; in fact, they were more commonly the Church or the State. In western Europe, peasants generally owned between a third and a half of the land they worked, while eastern European peasants owned little if any land. But by the sixteenth century, almost all peasants enjoyed security of tenure on the land they worked. In return for various forms of rents, they used the land as they saw fit and could hand it down to their children. Rents were only occasionally paid in coin, though money rents became more common as the century progressed. More frequently, the lord received a fixed proportion of the yield of the land or received labor from the peasant. Labor service was being replaced by monetary payments in northern and western Europe, but it continued in the east, where it was known as the *robot*. German and Hungarian peasants normally owed two or three days' labor on the lord's estate each week, while Polish peasants might owe as much as four days. Labor service tied the peasants to the land they worked. Eastern European peasants were less mobile than peasants in the west, and as a result towns were fewer and smaller in the east.

dence. Exchange was the medium that transformed labor and skill into food and shelter. The town was one large marketplace in which the circulation of goods dictated the survival of the residents. Men and women in towns worked as hard as did those on farms, but town dwellers received a more varied and more comfortable life in return. This is not to suggest that hunger and hardship were unknown in towns. Urban poverty was endemic and grew worse as the century wore on. In most towns, as much as a quarter of the entire population might be destitute, living from casual day labor, charity, or crime. But even for these people, food was more readily available in greater varieties than in the countryside, and the institutional network of support for the poor and homeless was stronger. In Lyon the overseers of the poor distributed a daily ration of a pound and a half of bread, more than half of what a farm laborer would consume. The urban poor fell victim more often to disease than to starvation.

Towns were distinguished by the variety of occupations that existed within them. The preparation and exchange of food dominated small market towns. Peasants would bring in their finest produce for sale and exchange it for vital manufactured goods like iron spits and pots for cooking or metal and leather tools for farm work. In smaller towns there was as much barter as sale; in larger places, money was exchanged for commodities. Women dominated the food trades in most market towns, trading, buying, and selling in the shop fronts that occupied the bottom story of their houses. Because of their skills in food preparation, they were better able to obtain the best prices and advantageously display the best goods. In these small towns, men divided their time between traditional agricultural pursuits—there were always garden plots and even substantial fields attached to towns—and manufacturing. Half of the households in the Spanish town of Ciudad Real derived their income entirely from farming. Almost every town made and distributed to the surrounding area some special product that drew to the town the wealth of the countryside.

In larger towns the specialization of labor was more intense and wage earning more essential. Large traders dominated the major occupations like baking, brewing, and cloth manufacture, leaving distribution in the hands of the family economy, where there might still be a significant element of bartering. Piecework handicrafts became the staple for less prosperous town families, who prepared raw materials for the large manufacturers or finished products before their sale. Occupations were normally organized geographically, with metal- or glassworking taking place in one quarter

of the town, brewing or baking in another. There was a strong family and kin network to these occupations, as each craft required long years of technical training, which was handed down from parents to children.

In large towns there were also specialized trades performed by women. There were 55 midwives in Nuremberg in the middle of the sixteenth century, and a board of women chosen from among the leading families of the town supervised their work. Nursing the sick was a logical extension of these services and also appears to have been an exclusively female occupation. So, too, was prostitution, which was an officially sanctioned occupation in most large towns in the early modern era. There were town brothels, situated in specified districts, subject to taxation and government control. Public bathhouses, which employed skilled women workers, served as unofficial brothels for the upper ranks of urban society. They too were regulated, especially after the first great epidemic of venereal disease in the early sixteenth century.

Most town dwellers, however, lived by unskilled labor. The most lucrative occupations were strictly controlled, so those who flocked to towns in search of employment usually hired themselves out as day labor-

A woodcut from De conceptu et generatione hominis *(1554), a famous handbook for midwives. During the birth, astrologers cast the infant's horoscope in the background.*

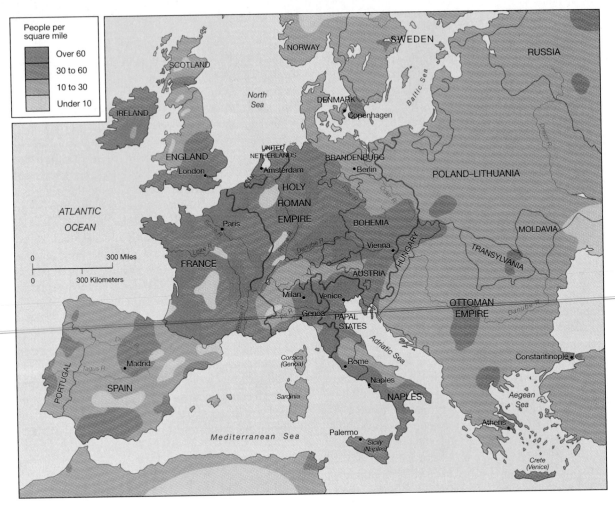

Population Density in Europe, ca. 1600

ers, hauling and lifting goods onto carts or boats, stacking materials at building sites, or delivering water and food. After the first decades of the century, the supply of laborers exceeded the amount of work to occupy them and town authorities were constantly attempting to expel them. The most fortunate might succeed in becoming servants.

Domestic service was a critical source of household labor. Even families on the margins of subsistence employed servants to undertake the innumerable household tasks, which allowed parents to pursue their primary occupations. Everything was done by hand and on foot, and extra pairs of each were essential. In Münster at mid-century there were four hundred servants for a thousand households. Domestics were not apprentices, though they might aspire to become apprentices to the trade followed in the family with whom they lived. If they had kinship bonds in the

town, apprenticeship was a likely outcome. But more commonly, domestics remained household servants, frequently changing employers in hope of more comfortable housing and better food. Their lives were always precarious. Any number of circumstances, from the death of their employer to allegations of misconduct, could cost them their places. Male servants were scapegoats for missing household items; female servants were vulnerable to sexual assaults.

Just as towns grew by the influx of surplus rural population, they sustained themselves by the import of surplus agricultural production. Most towns owned tracts of land, which they leased to peasants or farmed by hired labor. The town of Nuremberg controlled 25 square miles of forest and farmlands, while the region around Toledo was inhabited by thousands of peasants who paid taxes and rents to city landlords. Agriculture was the fourth largest occupation in the Spanish city of

Barcelona, which had a population of over 35,000 in the early sixteenth century. All towns had municipal storehouses of grain to preserve their inhabitants from famine during harvest failures. Grain prices were strictly regulated and frequently subsidized to ensure that laborers were adequately fed. The diet of even a casual laborer would have been envied by an average peasant. Male grape pickers in Stuttgart received meat, soup, vegetables, wine, and beer; females got soup, vegetables, milk, and bread. In addition they received their wages. It is hardly surprising that towns were enclosed by thick walls and defended by armed guards.

Economic Change

Over the course of the sixteenth century, the European population increased by about a third, with much of the growth taking place in the first fifty years. Rough estimates suggest the rise to have been from about 80 to 105 million. Patterns of growth varied by region. The population of the eastern part of Europe seems to have increased more steadily across the century, while western Europe experienced a population explosion in the early decades. The population of France may have doubled between 1450 and 1550, from 10 to 20 million. The population of England nearly doubled between 1500 and 1600, from over 2 million to over 4 million. Castile, the largest region in Spain, grew 50 percent in fifty years. Europe had finally recovered from the devastation of the Black Death, and by 1600 its population was greater than it had ever been. Demographic growth was even more dramatic in the cities. In 1500, only four cities had populations greater than 100,000; in 1600, there were eight. Naples grew from 150,000 to 280,000, and both Paris and London to more than 200,000 inhabitants. Fifteen large cities more than doubled their populations, with London experiencing a phenomenal 400 percent increase.

The rise in population dramatically affected the lives of ordinary Europeans. In the early part of the century, the first phase of growth brought prosperity. The land was still not farmed to capacity, and extra hands meant increased productivity. As there was uncultivated land that could be plowed, convenient room for new housing, and enough commons and woodlands to be shared, the population increase was a welcome development. Even when rural communities began to reach their natural limits as people's needs pressed against nature's resources, opportunity still existed in the burgeoning towns and cities. At first the cycle was beneficial. Surplus on the farms led to economic growth in the towns. Growth in the towns meant more opportunities for those on the farms. More food supported more workers, and more workers produced more goods and services, which were exchanged for more food.

The first waves of migrants to the towns found opportunity everywhere. Even the most lucrative textile and provisioning trades were recruiting new members, and apprenticeships were easy to find. A shortage of casual labor kept wages at a decent rate. Successful migrants encouraged kin from their villages to move to the towns and sponsored their start in trade or service. For a while, rural families did not have to make elaborate preparations to provide for their younger sons and daughters: they could be sent to the towns. Instead of saving every extra penny to give their children a start in life, farmers could purchase some luxury goods or expand their landholdings.

Such an opportunity could not last. With more mouths to feed, more crops had to be planted. Since the most productive land was already under the plow, new fields were carved from less fertile areas. In some villages land was taken from the common waste, the woodlands or scrublands that were used for animal forage and domestic fuel. This land was less suitable for crops, and it became unavailable for other important uses. In Spain, for example, the land that was reclaimed came at the expense of sheep grazing. This reduced the size of the flocks of sheep and damaged both the domestic and the foreign wool trade. It also reduced the amount of fertilizer available for enriching the soil. In England and the Low Countries, large drainage projects were undertaken to reclaim land for crops. In the east, so-called forest colonies sprang up, clearing space in the midst of woodlands for new farms. Colonization of areas in Poland-Lithuania, Muscovy, and the Ukraine can be compared to the overseas ventures of Spain and Portugal.

By mid-century there was a natural limit to the number of workers who could profitably engage in any given trade, and those safely in were pulling the ladder up behind them. Town governments came under pressure from the guilds to enforce apprenticeship requirements that had been relaxed during the period of growth. Guilds raised fees for new entrants and designated only a small number of places where their goods could be purchased. Most apprenticeships were limited to patrimony: one son for each full member. Such restrictions meant that newly arrived immigrants could enter only into the less profitable small crafts.

As workers continued to flood into the towns, real wages began to fall, not only among the unskilled but

The new money economy inspired this satirical portrait by Quentin Massys. It shows a moneylender counting his receipts while his wife is distracted from her Bible by the pile of coins. Many such merchants won fame and power and even titles.

throughout the work force. A black market in labor developed to take advantage of the surplus population. In terms of purchasing power, the wages of a craftsman in the building trade in England fell by one-half during the sixteenth century. A French stonemason, a highly paid skilled laborer, could buy 33 pounds of bread with his daily wage in 1480; by 1550 he could buy fewer than 10. Peasants in the French region of Languedoc who hired out for farm labor lost 56 percent of their purchasing power during the century. Only reapers, who were the physically strongest agricultural laborers, appear to have kept pace with inflation; grape pickers, among the least skilled, endured declines of up to 300 or 400 percent.

The fall in real wages took place against a backdrop of inflation that has come to be called the Price Revolution. Between 1500 and 1650, cereal prices increased between five- and sixfold, manufactured goods between two- and threefold. Most of the rapid increase came in the second half of the sixteenth century, a result of both population growth and the import of precious metals from the New World. Sixteenth-century governments understood little about the relationship between money supply and prices. Gold and silver

from America flooded the international economy, raising commodity prices. As prices rose so did the deficits of the state, which was the largest purchaser of both agricultural and manufactured goods. With huge deficits, states began to devalue their coins in the mistaken belief that this would lower their debt. But debased coinage resulted in still higher prices, and higher prices resulted in greater debt. The Price Revolution was felt throughout the Continent and played havoc with government finances, international trade, and the lives of ordinary people.

A 500 percent inflation in agricultural products over a century is not much by modern standards. Compounded, the rate averages less than 2 percent a year. But the Price Revolution did not take place in a modern society or within a modern market economy. In the sixteenth century, this level of rising prices disrupted everything. In the Spanish town of Seville, almost all buildings were rented on 99-year leases to the families who lived and worked in them. This was a fairly common practice throughout Europe. It meant that a landlord who rented a butcher shop and living quarters in 1501 could not raise the rent until 1600! Similarly, lords frequently held the right to purchase agricultural produce at specified prices. This system, similar to today's commodity market, helped both lords and peasants plan ahead. It assured the lord a steady supply and the peasant a steady market. But it assumed steady prices. Until the middle of the seventeenth century, the king of England had the right to purchase wheat at prices set 300 years earlier.

Thus an enduring increase in prices created profound social dislocation. Some people became destitute; others became rich beyond their dreams. The towns were particularly hard hit, for they exchanged manufactured goods for food and thus suffered when grain prices rose faster than those of other commodities. Landholders who derived their income from rents were squeezed; those who received payment in kind reaped a windfall of more valuable agricultural goods. Peasants were largely protected from the rise in food prices, but they were not insulated from its consequences. As long as they consumed what they raised, the nominal value of commodities was of no great matter. But if some part of their subsistence had to be obtained by labor, they were in grave peril.

There was now an enormous incentive to produce a surplus for market and to begin to specialize in particular grains that were in high demand. Every small scrap of land that individual peasant families could bring under cultivation would now yield foodstuffs that

An illumination from a sixteenth-century manuscript shows a prosperous Venetian merchant entertaining visitors at his mainland country estate.

could be exchanged for manufactured luxury goods. The tendency for all peasants to hold roughly equivalent amounts of land abruptly ceased. The fortunate could become prosperous by selling their surplus. The unfortunate found ready purchasers for their strips and common rights. Villagers began to be divided into those who held large amounts of land and sold their surplus at a profit and those who held small amounts of land and hired out as laborers to their more fortunate neighbors.

The beneficial cycle now turned vicious. Those who had sold out and left the land looking for prosperity in the towns were forced to return to the land as agrarian laborers. In western Europe they became the landless poor, seasonal migrants without the safety net of rooted communal life. In eastern Europe labor service enriched the landed nobility, who were able to sell stores of grain in the export market. They used the law to tie the peasants to the land in order to ensure that grain would be cultivated for the market. Poland-Lithuania became a major supplier of cereals to northern Europe, and Gdansk became the most important agricultural seaport in the world. But agricultural surplus from the east could not make up for the great shortfall in the west. By the beginning of the seventeenth century, the western European states faced a crisis of subsistence. Everyone was hungry; many were starving.

Social Life

Social organization combines elements of tradition, belief, and function, but these elements are so fused together that it is impossible to determine where one ends and the other begins. Society is a human construct, subject to the strengths and frailties of its creators. The basic assumption of sixteenth-century European society was inequality, and its basic form of social organization was stratification. The group, rather than the individual, was the predominant unit in society. The first level of the social order was the family and the household; then came the village or town community; and finally the gradations of ranks and orders of society at large. Elaborate rituals helped define membership in each of these groups, from the marriage ceremony to the initiation rites of citizens and to the processions and ceremonial displays of the nobility. All stressed the significance of the rights and obligations of different levels of society. Each group had its own place in the social order and each performed its own essential function. Society was the sum of its parts.

This traditional social organization was severely tested over the course of the early modern period. Economic change reshaped ideas of mobility and drew sharper distinctions between rural and urban life. The growth of towns and their domination of the countryside around them challenged beliefs about the primacy of agricultural production and the subordinate nature of trade and commerce. The rise to new wealth and prominence of some social groups challenged traditional elites' hold on power and prestige. The transformation of landholding patterns in the villages challenged the stability of rural communities. The rising numbers of both urban and rural poor challenged the institutions of charitable relief and posed the threat of crime and disorder. Eventually these developments led to bloody confrontations between social groups.

Social Constructs

Hierarchy was the dominant principle of social organization in the early modern era. Hierarchy existed at every level, from the basic distinction between lords and commoners to the fastidious complexity of the ranks of the nobility. The hierarchy of masters, journeymen, and apprentices dominated trades; trades themselves existed in a hierarchy. In the hierarchy of civic government, each official held a place in an ascending order, up to the elite of councilors and mayors. On the land was the hierarchy of freeholder, laborer, and leaseholder among the peasants. The family itself was hierarchically organized, with the wife subordinate to her husband, the children to their parents, and the apprentices and servants to their master and mistress. "All things observe degree, priority and place," Shakespeare wrote of both natural and human order in *Troilus and Cressida* (1601–02). "Take but degree away, untune that string, and hark what discord follows."

Hierarchy was a principle of orderliness that helped govern social relations. It is tempting to approach hierarchy through wealth, to divide groups and individuals into rich and poor. Many gradations in the sixteenth-century social hierarchy corresponded to levels of wealth, but they were threshold levels rather than absolute levels. Lords, by definition, did not engage in manual labor. They were wealthier than peasants. The governing elites of towns needed sufficient wealth to neglect their own affairs while occupied in public service. They were wealthier than wage earners. But the ranks of the nobility cannot be explained by gradations of wealth among nobles, and there were many rich town dwellers who were not members of the governing elite.

Status, rather than wealth, determined the social hierarchy. It conferred privileges and exacted responsibilities according to rank. Status was everywhere apparent. It was confirmed in social conventions like bowing and hat doffing. In towns and cities the clothing that people were allowed to wear—even the foods that they were allowed to eat—reflected status. Status was signified in titles: not just in the ranks of the nobility or between nobles and commoners, but even in ordinary communities masters and mistresses, goodmen and goodwives, squires and ladies, adopted the English equivalents of European titles. The acceptance of status was an everyday, uncomplicated, unreflective act, like stopping at a red light. Inequality was a fact of European social life that was as unquestioned as it was unquestionable.

Images that people used to describe both the natural world and their social world reinforced the functional nature of hierarchy. The first, and most elaborate image, was that of the Great Chain of Being. The Great Chain was a description of the universe in which everything had a place, from God at the top of the chain to inanimate objects like rocks at the bottom. Complex accounts of the chain listed the seven orders of angels, the multiple ranks of humans, even the degrees of animals and plants, from which lions emerged as kings of the jungle. Spanish botanists were dispatched to the New World to help identify the unknown flora and fauna in terms of their places in the chain. Native Americans were first thought to be the lost tribes of Israel, as these were the only humans missing from traditional accounts of the chain. For ordinary people, the Great Chain of Being expressed the belief that all life was interconnected, that every link was a part of a divinely ordered universe and was as necessary as every other.

The second metaphor used to describe society stressed this notion of interdependency even more strongly. This was the image of the Body Politic. In the Body Politic, the head ruled, the arms protected, the stomach nourished, and the feet labored. The image described a small community as well as a large state. In the state the king was the head, the Church the soul, the nobles the arms, the artisans the hands, and the peasants the feet. Each performed its own function, and each function was essential to the health of the body. The Body Politic was an organic unity of separate parts working harmoniously for a common goal. Like the Great Chain of Being, it was a profoundly conservative concept of social organization. Taken literally, it precluded the idea of social mobility, of people rising or falling from one group to another.

Social Structure

The Great Chain of Being and the Body Politic were static concepts of social organization. But in the early modern era, European society was in a state of dynamic change. Fundamentally, all European societies were divided into nobles and commoners. This was a basic distinction that existed throughout the Continent, though relationships between the two orders differed from place to place. Nobility was a legal status that conferred certain privileges upon its holders. The first was rank and title, a well-defined place at the top of the social order that was passed from one generation to the next. Each rank had its own privileges and each was clearly demarcated from the next by behavior, dress, and title. The escutcheon—the coat of arms—was a universally recognized symbol of rank and family connection. The coat of arms was woven in garments; emblazoned on windows, carriages, and household goods; and displayed on banners during formal processions. Although there were various systems of title in use across the Continent and the nobility of one state could not claim noble privileges in another state, the hierarchy of prince, duke, earl, count, and baron was roughly standard.

Because rulers conferred these titles on individuals, elevating some to higher ranks and others from commoner to noble, the nobility was a political order as well as a social one. Political privileges were among the nobility's most important attributes. In many countries, the highest offices of the state and the military were reserved for members of the nobility. In Poland, for example, all offices were held by noblemen. This was a privilege that could work both ways, either restricting officeholders to those already ennobled or, as in town councils in France and Spain, ennobling those who achieved certain offices. The nobility was also granted rights of political participation in the deliberative bodies of the state. In England the peerage was defined as all those who were summoned to the House of Lords. In most parts of central Europe, the nobility alone composed the diets that advised the monarch. In the empire, the rank of imperial free knights allowed the nobility to separate itself entirely from the jurisdiction of towns or individual principalities.

Finally, members of the nobility held economic privileges, a result both of their rank and of their role as lords on the lands they owned. In almost every state, the nobility was exempt from most taxation. This was an area in which the interests of the nobles conflicted directly with those of the ruler. The larger the number of tax exemptions for the nobility, the stronger was its power in relation to the monarch. Tax exemptions of the nobility were most extensive in eastern and central Europe. There the crowns were elective rather than hereditary, allowing the nobles to bargain their support.

The Polish nobility was exempt from the salt tax, the alcohol tax, and all internal tolls and customs. As Polish agriculture developed into an export industry, exemption from tolls gave the nobility a competitive advantage over merchants in the marketing of goods. The Hungarian nobility was exempt from all direct taxes, including the land tax. The nobility in western Europe enjoyed fewer immunities but not necessarily less valuable ones. French nobles were exempt from the taille, Spanish nobles from the hearth tax. As French nobles had vast incomes and Spanish nobles' houses had many hearths, both were important exclusions. The English nobility enjoyed no exemptions from direct taxation, but then there was little direct taxation from which to be exempted. The most important English taxes were on exports of wool and cloth, and thus fell on merchants rather than landholders.

Privileges implied obligations. Initially the nobility was the warrior caste of the state and its primary obligations were to raise, equip, and lead troops into battle. Much of the great wealth that nobles possessed was at the service of the ruler during times of war, and war was a perpetual activity. By the sixteenth century, the military needs of the state had far surpassed the military power of its nobility. Warfare had become a national enterprise that required central coordination. Nobles became administrators as much as warriors, though it is fair to say that many did both. The French nobility came to be divided into the nobility of the sword and the nobility of the robe—that is, warriors and officeholders. The old military nobility could hardly understand the new service nobility. "I have continually been astounded," one of them remarked, "that so many young men could thus amuse themselves in a law court, since ordinarily youthful blood is boiling." A glorious battlefield death was still an ideal for most of Europe's noblemen.

Nobles also had the obligation of governing at both the national and the local level. At the discretion of the ruler, they could be called to engage in any necessary occupation, no matter how disruptive to their economic or family affairs. On their land, they administered their estates and settled the disputes of their tenants. In times of want they were expected to provide for the needy, in times of dearth for the hungry. There was an obligation of good lordship that was implicitly understood, if not always explicitly carried out, between lord and peasant.

The principal distinction in sixteenth-century society was between lord and commoners, but it was not the only one. In both town and countryside a new social group was emerging. It had neither the legal nor the social privileges of nobility, but it performed many of the same functions. Over the course of the century this group carved out a place that was clearly distinct from that of the commoners, even if it was not clearly identical to the lords. It is easiest to describe in the towns, for the towns remained a separate unit of social organization in most states. Towns enjoyed many of the same political and economic privileges as the nobility. In many states, the towns sent representatives to meet with the nobles and the king and were the most important part of national deliberative assemblies such as the English Parliament, the French estates, or the Spanish Cortes. Towns were granted legal rights to govern their own citizens, to engage in trade, and to defend themselves by raising and storing arms. Although they paid a large share of most taxes, towns also received large tax concessions.

Yet, as individuals, members of the town elite held no special status in society at large. Some were among the richest people in the state—great bankers and merchants wealthier than dukes—but they had to devise their own systems of honor and prestige. In Venice, the *Book of Gold* distinguished the local elite from the ranks of ordinary citizens. Members of the "Old Families," who monopolized the highest civic offices, ruled Nuremberg. In France and Spain, some of the highest officers of leading towns were granted noble status, like the "honored citizens" of Barcelona who were ennobled by King Ferdinand of Aragon. German burghers, as prosperous townsmen were called, remained caught in a state between noble and common, despised from above because they worked with their hands, envied from below for their wealth and comfort. In Münster, many withdrew from urban affairs and sought the privileges of the lower nobility.

In rural society the transformation of agricultural holdings in many places also created a group that fit uncomfortably between lords and commoners. The accumulation of larger and larger estates through purchase from the nobility, the state, or the Church made lords—in the sense of landowners with tenants—out of many who were not lords in rank. They received rents and dues from their tenants, administered their estates, and preserved the so-called moral economy that sustained the peasants during hard times. In England this group came to be known as the gentry, and there were parallel groups in Spain, France, and the empire. The gentry aspired to the privileges of the nobility. In England members of the gentry had the right to have a coat of arms and could be knighted. But knighthoods were not hereditary and did not confer membership in the House of Lords. In Spain, the caballeros and hidalgos

gained noble privileges but were still of lower status than the grandees. The gentry aped the habits of the nobility, often outdoing nobles in lavish displays of wealth and spending.

Social stratification did not only apply to the wealthy groups within European societies. Although it is more difficult to reconstruct the principles upon which rural communities based their complicated systems of status and order, there can be no doubt that systems existed and that they helped create the bonds that tied communities together. In many German villages, a principal distinction was between those who held land in the ancient part of the settlement—the *Esch*—and those who held land in those areas into which the village had expanded. The *Esch* was normally the best land, and thus the distinction was likely to correlate with the relative wealth of the two groups. But interestingly, the holders of the *Esch* were tied to the lord of the estate, while holders of the less desirable lands were free peasants. Here freedom to move from place to place was less valued than the right to live in the heart of the village.

Just the opposite set of values prevailed in English villages, where freeholders were in the most enviable position. They led the movements to break up the common fields for planting and were able to initiate legal actions against their lord. They might not have the best lands in the village, but whenever village land was converted to freehold, unfree tenants would go into debt to buy it. Increasingly, French peasants came to own the land that they farmed. They protested against the very title of *villein,* claiming that its older association with serfdom discouraged others from trading with those so labeled. The relationship of free and unfree went even further in Muscovy, where thousands of starving laborers sold themselves into slavery. Perhaps as much as 10 percent of the population of Muscovy accepted their loss of freedom and became domestic slaves of the military and noble orders.

In towns, the order of rank below the elite pertained as much to the kind of work that one performed as it did to the level at which it was undertaken. The critical division in town life was between those who had the freedom of the city—citizens—and those who did not. Citizenship was restricted to membership in certain occupations and was closely regulated. It could be purchased, especially by members of learned professions whose services were becoming vital in the early modern era, but most citizenship was earned by becoming a master in one of the guilds after a long period of apprenticeship and training. Only males could be citizens. In Germany, the feminine equivalent for the word used to denote a male citizen in good standing meant "prostitute"! But women who were married to citizens enjoyed their husbands' privileges, and widows of citizens could pass the privileges to their new husbands when they remarried. In both town and countryside, the privileges and obligations of each social group was the glue that held communities together.

Social Change

In the sixteenth century, social commentators believed that change was transforming the world in which they lived. In 1600 a Spanish observer blamed the rise of the rich commoners for the ills of the world: "They have obtained a particular status, that of a self-made group; and since they belong neither to the rich nor to the poor nor to the middle, they have thrown the state into the confusion we now see it in." An Englishman commenting on the rise of the gentry could give no better definition of its status than to say that a gentleman was one who lived like a gentleman. The challenge that the new nobility of the robe posed to the old nobility of the sword poisoned relations between these two segments of the French ruling elite. The military service class in Muscovy, who were of more use to the Muscovite princes than were the traditional landed nobility, posed an even greater threat to the privileges of the boyars.

Pressures on the ruling elites of European society came from above as well as below. The expansion of the state and the power of the prince frequently came as a result of direct conflict with the nobility. Only in east-central Europe—in Hungary, Bohemia, and Poland-Lithuania—did the consolidation of the state actually enhance the privileges of the traditional noble orders, and these were areas in which towns were small and urban elites weak.

There were many reasons why the traditional European social hierarchy was transformed during the course of the early modern era. In the first place, population increase necessitated an expansion of the ruling orders. With more people to govern, there had to be more governors who could perform the military, political, and social functions of the state. The traditional nobility grew slowly, as titles could be passed to only one son and intermarriage within the group was very high. Second, opportunities to accumulate wealth expanded dramatically with the Price Revolution. Traditionally wealth was calculated in land and tenants rather than in the possession of liquid assets like gold and silver. But with the increase in commodity prices, surplus producers could rapidly improve their economic position. What previously might have taken a generation or two of good fortune to amass could now be gathered seemingly overnight. Moreover, state service became a source of unlimited riches. The profits to be made from tax collecting, officeholding, or administering the law could easily surpass those to be made from landholding, especially after the economic downturn at the end of the century. The newly rich clamored for privileges, and many were in a position to lobby rulers effectively for them. Across European society the nobility grew, fed from fortunes made on the land, in trade, and in office.

Social change was equally apparent at the bottom of the social scale, but here it could not be so easily absorbed. The continuous population growth created a group of landless poor who squatted in villages and clogged the streets of towns and cities. Although poverty was not a new development of the early modern era, its growth created new problems. Rough estimates suggest that as many as a quarter of all Europeans were destitute. This was a staggering figure in great cities. There were tens of thousands of destitute people in London or Paris, where, it was observed, "the crowds of poor were so great that one could not pass through the streets."

Feeding the Hungry *by Cornelius Buys, 1504. A maidservant is doling out small loaves to the poor and the lame at the door of a wealthy person's home. The poor who flocked to the towns were often forced to rely on charity to survive.*

Traditionally, local communities cared for their poor. Widows, orphans, and the handicapped, who would normally constitute over half of the poor in a village or town, were viewed as the "deserving poor," worthy of the care of the community through the Church or through private almsgiving. Catholic communities like Venice created a system of private charity that paralleled the institutions of the Church. Although Protestant communities took charity out of the control of the church, they were no less concerned about the plight of the deserving poor. In England a special tax, the poor rate, supported the poor and provided them with subsistence until they remarried or found employment. Perhaps the most elaborate system of all existed in the French town of Lyon. There all the poor were registered and given identity cards. Each Sunday they would receive a week's worth of food and money. Young girls were provided with dowries, and young boys were taught crafts. Vagrants from the surrounding countryside were given one week's allotment to enable them to travel on. But this enlightened system was only for the deserving poor, and as the century progressed it was overwhelmed.

Charity began at home—it was an obligation of the community. But as the sixteenth century progressed, the number of people who lived on the margins of subsistence grew beyond the ability of the local community to care for them. Perhaps more importantly, many of those who now begged for alms fell outside the traditional categories of the deserving poor. In England they were called the sturdy beggars, men and women capable of working but incapable of finding more than occasional labor. To support themselves and their families, they left their native communities in search of employment and thus forfeited their claims on local charity. Most wound up in the towns and cities, where they slept and begged in the streets. Some disfigured themselves to enhance their abilities as beggars. As strangers they had no claim on local charity; as able-bodied workers they had no claim on local sympathy. Poor mothers abandoned their newborn infants on the steps of foundling hospitals or the houses of the rich. It is estimated that 10 percent of all newborn babies in the Spanish city of Valladolid were abandoned.

The problem of crime complicated the problems of poverty and vagrancy. Increasing population and increasing wealth equaled increasing crime; the addition of the poor to the equation aggravated the situation. The poor, destitute outsiders to the community, without visible means of support, were the easiest targets of official retribution. Throughout the century, numerous European states passed vagrancy laws in an effort to alleviate the problem of the wandering poor. In England the poor were whipped from village to village until they were returned home. The sturdy beggars were branded with the letter V on their chests to identify them as vagrants, and therefore as potential criminals. Both Venetian and Dutch vagrants were regularly rounded up for galley service, while vagrants in Hungary were sold into slavery. Physical mutilation was used in an ineffective method of deterrence; thieves had fingers chopped off—which, of course, made it impossible for them to perform manual labor, and thus likely to steal again. Sexual offenses were criminalized—especially bastardy, since the birth of illegitimate children placed an immediate burden on the community. Prostitutes, who had long been tolerated and regulated in towns, were now persecuted. Rape increased. Capital punishment was reserved for the worst crimes—murder, incest, and grand larceny being most common—but, not surprisingly, executions were carried out mostly on outsiders to the community, single women, the poor, and the vagrant being the most frequent victims.

Peasant Revolts

The economic and social changes of the sixteenth century bore serious consequences. Most telling was the upswing of violent confrontations between peasants and their lords. There was more than one difference between rich and poor in sixteenth-century society, but when conflict arose between them the important difference was that the wealthy controlled the means of coercion: the military and the law. Across Europe, and with alarming regularity, peasants took up arms to defend themselves from what they saw as violations of traditional rights and obligations. Peasant revolts were not hunger riots. Although they frequently occurred in periods of want, after bad harvests or marauding armies had impoverished villages, peasant revolts were not desperate attacks against warehouses or grain silos. Nor did those who took part in them form an undisciplined mob. Most revolts chose leaders, drew up petitions of grievances, and organized the rank and file into a semblance of military order. Leaders were literate—usually drawn from the lower clergy or minor gentry rather than from the peasantry—political demands were moderate, and tactics were sophisticated. But peasant revolts so profoundly threatened the social order that they were met with the severest repression. Confronted with the execution of their estate agents, rent strikes, and confiscation of their property, lords responded as if they were at war. Veteran soldiers and trained merce-

Rebellious peasants carrying a standard called the Banner of the Shoe surround a knight.

naries were called out to fight peasant armies composed mostly of raw recruits. The results were horrifying.

It is essential to realize that while peasants revolted against their lords, fundamentally their anger and frustration were products of agrarian changes that could be neither controlled nor understood. As population increased and market production expanded, many of the traditional rights and obligations of lords and peasants became oppressive. One example is that of forest rights. On most estates, the forests surrounding a village belonged to the lord. Commonly the village had its own woodlands in which animals foraged and fuel and building material were available. As the population increased, more farms came into existence. New land was put under the plow, and grain fields pressed up against the forest. There were more animals in the village, and some of them were let loose to consume the young sprouts and saplings. Soon there was not enough food for the wild game that was among the lord's most valuable property. So the game began to feed on the peasants' crops, which were now placed so appetizingly close to the forests. It was a capital crime for a peasant to kill wild game, but peasants couldn't allow the game to consume their crops.

A similar conflict arose over enclosing crop fields. An enclosure was a device—normally a fence or hedge that surrounded an area—to keep a parcel of land separate from the planted strips of land owned by the villagers. The parcel could be used for grazing animals or raising a specialty crop for the market. But an enclosure destroyed the traditional form of village agriculture,

whereby decisions on which crops to plant were made communally. It became one of the chief grievances of the English peasants. But while enclosures broke up the old field system in many villages, they were a logical response to the transformation of land ownership that had already taken place. As more land was accumulated by fewer families, it made less sense for them to work widely scattered strips all over the village. If a family could consolidate its holdings by swaps and sales, it could gain an estate large enough to be used for both crops and grazing. An enclosed estate allowed wealthy farmers to grow more luxury crops for market or to raise only sheep on a field that had once been used for grain.

Enclosure was a process that both lord and rich peasant undertook, but it drove the smallholders from the land and was thus a source of bitter resentment for the poorer peasants. It was easy to protest the greed of the lords who, owning the most land, were the most successful enclosers. But enclosures were more a result of the process in which villages came to be characterized by a very small elite of large landholders and a very large mass of smallholders and landless poor. It was an effect rather than a cause.

From Hungary to England, peasant revolts brought social and economic change into sharp relief. A call for a crusade against Ottoman advances in 1514 provided the opportunity for Hungarian peasants to revolt against their noble landlords. Thousands dropped their plowshares and grasped the sword of a holy war. However, in fact, war against the Ottomans did not materi-

THE PEASANTS' REVOLT

In 1524 and 1525 a series of local protests over economic conditions coalesced into one of the largest concerted peasant uprisings in German history. The Peasants' Revolt was not a disorganized uprising of the hungry and dispossessed, but rather a carefully coordinated movement that attempted to win widespread social reforms. The Twelve Articles of the Peasants of Swabia show both the nature of the peasants' grievances and their ability to articulate them.

The First Article. First, it is our humble petition and desire, as also our will and resolution, that in the future we should have power and authority so that each community should choose and appoint a pastor, and that we should have the right to depose him should he conduct himself improperly. The pastor thus chosen should teach us the gospel pure and simple, without any addition, doctrine, or ordinance of man.

The Second Article. According as the just tithe is established by the Old Testament and fulfilled in the New, we are ready and willing to pay the fair tithe of grain. . . . We will that for the future our church provost, whomsoever the community may appoint, shall gather and receive this tithe. . . .

The Tenth Article. In the tenth place, we are aggrieved by the appropriation by individuals of meadows and fields which at one time belonged to a community. These we will take again into our own hands. . . .

Conclusion. In the twelfth place, it is our conclusion and final resolution that if any one or more of the articles here set forth should not be in agreement with the word of God, as we think they are, such article we will willingly retract if it is proved really to be against the word of God by a clear explanation of the Scripture.

From the Twelve Articles of the Peasants of Swabia.

---

alize. Instead, the mobilized peasants, under the leadership of disaffected army officers and clergymen, issued grievances against the labor service that they owed to their lords as well as numerous violations of customary agricultural practices. Their revolt turned into a civil war that was crushed with great brutality. In England, severe economic conditions led to a series of revolts in 1549. Participants in the Western Rising, who succeeded in storming the town of Exeter, also combined religious and economic grievances. Cornish rebels added a social dimension with their slogan "Kill the gentlemen." In eastern England, Ket's Rebellion arose from peasant opposition to enclosure. The rebels occupied Norwich, the second largest city in the realm, but their aspirations were for reform rather than revolution. They, like the Hungarian peasants, were crushed by well-trained forces.

The complexity of the peasants' problems is perhaps best revealed in the series of uprisings that are known collectively as the German Peasants' War. It was by far the most widespread peasant revolt of the sixteenth century, involving tens of thousands of peasants, and it combined a whole series of agrarian grievances with an awareness of the new religious spirit preached by Martin Luther. Luther condemned both lords and peasants: the lords for their rapaciousness, the peasants for their rebelliousness. Although he had a large following among the peasants, his advice that earthly oppression be passively accepted was not followed. The Peasants' War was directed against secular and ecclesiastical lords, and the rebels attacked both economic and religious abuses. Their combination of demands, such as the community's right to select its own minister and the community's right to cut wood freely, attracted a wide following in the villages and small towns of southern and central Germany. The printed demands of the peasantry, the most famous of which was the Twelve Articles of the Peasants of Swabia (1525), helped spread the movement far beyond its original bounds. The peasants organized themselves into large armies led by experienced soldiers. Initially they were able to besiege castles and abbeys and plunder lords' estates. Ultimately, those movements that refused compromise were ruthlessly crushed. By conservative estimates, over one hundred thousand peasants were slaughtered during and after the war, many to serve as warning against future uprisings.

At base the demands of the peasantry addressed the agrarian changes that were transforming German villages. Population growth was creating more poor villagers who could only hire out as laborers but who demanded a share of common grazing and woodlands. Because the presence of these poor increased the taxable wealth of the village, they were advantageous to the lord. But the strain they placed on resources was felt by both the subsistence and the surplus farmers. Tensions within the village were all the greater because the landless members were the kin of the landed—sons and daughters, brothers and sisters. If they were to be settled properly on the land, then the lord would have to let the village expand. If they were to be kept on the margins of subsistence, then the more prosperous villagers would have to be able to control their numbers and their conduct. In either case, the peasants needed more direct responsibility for governing the village than existed in their traditional relationship with their lord. Thus the grievances of the peasants of Swabia demanded release of the village peasantry from the status of serfs. They wanted to be allowed to move off the land, to marry out of the village without penalty, and to be free of the death taxes that further impoverished their children. These concessions would make it easier for the excess population to adjust to new conditions. They also wanted stable rents fixed at fair rates, a limit placed on labor service, and a return to the ancient customs that governed relations between lords and peasants. All of these proposals were backed by an appeal to Christian principles of love and charity. They were profoundly conservative.

The demands of the German peasants reflected a traditional order that no longer existed. In many places, the rents and tithes that the peasants wanted to control no longer belonged to the lords of the estates. They had been sold to town corporations or wealthy individuals who purchased them as an investment and expected to realize a fair return. Most tenants did enjoy stable and fixed rents, but only on their traditional lands. As they increased their holdings, perhaps to keep another son in the village or to expand production for the market, they were faced with the fact that rents were higher and land more expensive than it had been before. Marriage fines, death duties, and labor service were oppressive, but they balanced the fact that traditional rents were very low. In many east German villages, peasants willingly increased their labor service for a reduction in their money rents. It was hardly likely

that they could have both. If the peasants were being squeezed, and there can be little doubt that they were, it was not only the lords who were doing the squeezing. The Church took its tenth, the state increased its exactions, and the competition for survival and prosperity among the peasants themselves was ferocious. Peasants were caught between the jaws of an expanding state and a changing economy. When they rebelled, the jaws snapped shut.

Private Life

The great events of the sixteenth century—the discovery of the New World, the consolidation of states, the increasing incidence and ferocity of war, the reform of religion—all had profound impact on the lives of ordinary people. There could be no private life separate from these developments. However slowly they penetrated to isolated village communities, however intermittent their effect, they were inextricably bound up with the experiences and the world view of all Europeans. The states offered more protection and demanded more resources. Taxes increased, and tax collecting became more efficient. Wars took village boys and made them soldiers. Armies brought devastation to thousands of communities. The New World offered new opportunities, brought new products, and increased the wealth of the Continent. Religious reform, both Protestant and Catholic, penetrated into popular beliefs and personal piety. All these sweeping changes blurred the distinction between public and private life.

Still, the transformations wrought by political and intellectual developments were not necessarily the most important ones in people's lives. The lives of most Europeans centered on births and deaths, on the harvest, and on the social relations in their communities. For them, great events were the successful crop, the marriage of an heir, or the festivals that marked the progress of the year. Their beliefs were based as much on the customs they learned as children as on the religion they learned at church. Their strongest loyalties were to family and community rather than to church or state.

The Family

Sixteenth-century life centered on the family. The family was a crucial organizing principle for Europeans of all social ranks, and it served a variety of functions. In the most obvious sense, the family was the primary kin

Peasant Family (ca. 1640), a realistic scene of peasant life in France by the genre painter Louis Le Nain.

group. European families were predominantly nuclear, composed of a married couple and their children. In western Europe, a small number of families contained the adult siblings of the family head, uncles and aunts who had not yet established their own families. This pattern was more common in the east, especially in Hungary and Muscovy, where taxation was based on households and thus encouraged extended families. There several nuclear families might live under the same roof. Yet however families were composed, kinship had a wider orbit than just parents and children. In-laws, step-relations, and cousins were considered part of the kin group and could be called upon for support in a variety of contexts, from charity to employment and business partnerships. In towns such family connections created large and powerful clans.

In a different sense, family was lineage, the connections between preceding and succeeding generations. This was an important concept among the upper ranks of society, where ancient lineage, genuine or fabricated, was a valued component of nobility. This concept of family imparted a sense of stability and longevity in a world in which individual life was short. Even in peasant communities, however, lineage existed in the form of the family farm, that is, the strips in the field that were passed from generation to generation and named for the family that owned them. The village's fields and landmarks also bore the names of individual families, and membership in one of the ancient families of the village was a mark of social distinction.

The family was also an economic unit. Here family overlapped with the household—all those who lived under the same roof, including servants and apprentices. In its economic functions, the family was the basic unit for the production, accumulation, and transmission of wealth. Occupation determined the organization of the economic family. Every member of the household had his or her own functions that were essential to the survival of the unit. Tasks were divided by gender and by age, but there was far more intermixture than is traditionally assumed. On farms women worked at nearly every occupation with the exception of mowing and plowing. In towns they were vital to the success of shops and trades, though they were denied training in the skilled crafts. As laborers, they worked in the town fields—for little more than half the wages of men performing the same tasks—and in carrying and delivering goods and materials. Children contributed to the economic vitality of the household from an early age.

Finally, the family was the primary unit of social organization. In the family children were educated and the social values of hierarchy and discipline were taught. Authority in the family was strictly organized in a set of three overlapping categories. At the top was the husband, head of the household, who ruled over his wife, children, and servants. All members of the family owed obedience to the head. The family was like "a little commonwealth," as English writers put it, in which the adult male was the governor and all others the governed. But two other categories of relationships in the family dispersed this authority. Children owed obedience to their parents, male or female. In this role the wife and mother was governor as well as governed. Similarly, servants owed obedience to both master and mistress. Male apprentices were under the authority of the wife, mother, and mistress of the household. The importance of the family as a social unit was underscored by the fact that people unattached to families attracted suspicion in sixteenth-century society. Single men were often viewed as potential criminals; single women as potential prostitutes. Both lived outside the discipline and social control of families.

Although the population of Europe was increasing in the early modern era, families were not large. Throughout northern and western Europe, the size of the typical family was two adults and three or four children. Late marriages and breast-feeding helped control family size: the former restricted the number of childbearing years while the latter increased the space between pregnancies. Women married around age twenty-five, men slightly later. A woman could expect about fifteen fertile years and seven or eight pregnancies if neither she nor her husband died in the interim. Only three or four children were likely to survive beyond the age of ten. In her fertile years, a woman was constantly occupied with infants. She was either about to give birth or about to become pregnant. If she used a wet nurse rather than feed her own babies, as many women in the upper ranks of society did, then she was likely to have ten or twelve pregnancies during her fertile years and correspondingly more surviving children.

Constant pregnancy and child care may help explain some of the gender roles that men and women assumed in the early modern era. Biblical injunctions and traditional stereotypes help explain others. Pregnant or not, women's labor was a vital part of the domestic economy, especially until the first surviving children were strong enough to assume their share. The woman's sphere was the household. On the farm she was in charge of the preparation of food, the care of domestic animals, the care and education of children, and the manufacture and cleaning of the family's clothing. In towns women supervised the shop that was part of the household. They sold goods, kept accounts, and directed the work of domestics or apprentices. Mothers trained their daughters to perform these tasks in the same way that fathers trained their sons to work the fields or ply their craft.

The man's sphere was public—the fields in rural areas, the streets in towns. Men plowed, planted, and did the heavy reaping work of farming. They made and maintained essential farm equipment and had charge of the large farm animals. They marketed surplus produce and made the few purchases of equipment or lux-

In an age of high infant mortality and short life expectancy, women were expected to bear many children to ensure family continuity. This embroidery depicts a mother with her thirteen daughters.

A FEMININE PERSPECTIVE

Arcangela Tarabotti was born in Venice in the early seventeenth century. Her family did not have the means to provide her with a sufficient dowry, so she was sent to live in a Catholic convent, where she unhappily remained for the rest of her life. She wrote two major works. The first, Monastic Hell, *gives the flavor of her attitude toward her fate. The second was* Innocence Undone, *from which the following excerpt is taken.*

Since woman is the epitome of all perfections, she is the last of the works of God, as far as material creation is concerned, but otherwise she dates from the beginning, and is the first-generated of all creatures, generated by the breath of God himself, as the Holy Spirit inferred, through the mouth of Solomon in the Ecclesiastes where he introduces the Most Holy Virgin to sing of herself: *The Lord possessed me in the beginning of his ways, before he made any thing from the beginning.*

This creature, although a woman, did not need to be made with a rib taken from man, because, so to speak, she was born before the beginning of time as well as before men, who, blinded by their ambition to dominate the world alone, astutely fail to mention this infallible truth, that the woman has existed in the Divine mind from the beginning. *I was set up from eternity, and of old before the earth was made. The depths were not as yet, and I was already conceived.*

They cannot deny the fact, although their malice prevents them from speaking it openly; but let us try to make them admit, in accordance with the Holy Scriptures rather with some ill-informed preachers, that the woman made the man perfect and not vice versa.

After the Supreme Being created the world and all the animals (as I have said before), the text says *And God saw all the things that he had made; and they were very good.* Foreseeing that the man without woman would be the compendium of all imperfections, God said: *It is not good for man to be alone: let us make him a help like unto himself.* And therefore he created a companion for him that would be the universal glory of humanity and make him rich with merits.

ury goods. Men performed the labor service that was normally due the lord of the estate, attended the local courts in various capacities, and organized the affairs of the village. In towns men engaged in heavy labor, procured materials for craft work, and marketed their product if it was not sold in the household shop. Only men could be citizens of the towns or full members of most craft guilds, and only men were involved in civic government.

This separation of men and women into the public and the domestic spheres meant that marriage was a blending of complementary skills. Each partner brought to the marriage essential knowledge and abilities that were fundamental to the economic success of the union. Except in the largest towns, nearly everyone was married for at least a part of his or her life. Remar-riage was more common for men than women, however, because a man continued to control the family's property after the death of his wife, whereas a widow might have only a share of it after bequests to children and provisions for apprentices. In the French town of Nantes, a quarter of the annual weddings were remarriages.

While male roles were constant throughout the life cycle, as men trained for and performed the same occupations from childhood to death, female roles varied greatly depending upon the situation. While under the care of fathers, masters, or husbands, women worked in the domestic sphere; once widowed, they assumed the public functions of head of household. Many women inherited shops or farmland; most became responsible for the placement and training of their children. But

Almighty God, having kept the creation of the woman as the last act of his wonderful work, desired to bestow privileges upon her, reinforce her graces and gladden the whole world with her splendour. If the supreme Architect's greatness, wisdom and love towards us shone brightly in his other works, he planned to make the woman, this excellent last addition to his splendid construction, capable of filling with wonder whoever looked at her. He therefore gave her the strength to subdue and dominate the proudest and wildest hearts and hold them in sweet captivity by a mere glance or else by the power of her pure modesty. God formed Man, who is so proud, in the field of Damascus; and from one of his ribs he formed woman in the garden of Eden.

If I were not a female, I would deduce from this that the woman, both because of her composition and because of the place in which she was created, is nobler, gentler, stronger and worthier than the man.

What is true strength anyway, if not domination over one's feelings and mastery over one's passions? And who is better at this than the female sex, always virtuous and capable of resisting every temptation to commit or even think evil things? Is there anything more fragile than your head? Compare it to the strength of a rib, the hard bone that is the material from which we were created, and you will be disappointed. Anyone knows that women show more strength than men when they conceive and give birth, by tirelessly carrying all that weight around for nine months.

But you cruel men, who always go around preaching evil for good and good for evil, you pride yourselves in your strength because, like the inhuman creatures you are, you fight and kill each other like wild beasts. . . . Thus, if strength is the ability to bear misfortunes and insults, how can you call yourselves strong when you shed other people's blood sometimes for no reason at all and take the life of innocent creatures at the slightest provocation of a word or a suspicion?

Strength is not mere violence; it requires an indomitable soul, steadfast and constant in Christian fortitude. How can you, o most inconstant ones, ever boast of such virtù? Improperly and deceitfully you have called yourselves virtuous, because only those who fill the world with people and virtù can be called strong.

And those are women. Listen to Solomon, whose words about women reinforce my argument: *Strength and dignity are her clothing.*

From Tarabotti, *Innocence Undone.*

---

because of the division of labor upon which the family depended and because of the inherent social and economic prejudices that segregated public and domestic roles, widows were particularly disadvantaged. The most fortunate among them remarried—"The widow weeps with one eye and casts glances with the other," an English proverb held. Their financial and personal independence from men, prized today, was a millstone in the early modern world.

Communities

Despite its central place in all aspects of sixteenth-century life, the family was a fragile and impermanent institution. Even without divorce—permitted in Protestant communities, though never very common—marriages were short. The early death of one of the partners abbreviated the life of the natural family. New marriage partners or social welfare to aid the indigent were sought from within the wider community. On the farm, this community was the rural village; in the town, it was the ward, quarter, or parish in which the family lived. Community life must not be romanticized. Interpersonal violence, law suits, and feuds were extraordinarily common in both rural and urban communities. The community was not an idyllic haven of charity and love, where everyone knew and respected neighbors and worked toward a common goal. Like every other aspect of society, the community was socially and economically stratified, gender roles were segregated, and resources were inequitably divided. But the community was the place where people found their social identity. It provided marriage partners for its families, charity for its poor, and a local culture for all of its inhabitants.

The two basic forces that tied the rural community together were the lord and the priest. The lord set conditions for work and property ownership that necessitated common decision-making on the part of the village farmers. The lord's presence, commonly in the form of an agent, could be both a positive and a negative force for community solidarity. Use of the common lands, the rotation of labor service, and the form in which rents in kind were paid were all decisions that had to be made collectively. Village leadership remained informal, though in some villages headmen or elders bargained with the lord's agent or resolved petty disputes among the villagers. Communal agreement was also expressed in communal resistance to violations of custom or threats to the moral economy. All these forms of negotiation fused individual families into a community. So, too, in a different way did the presence of the parish priest or minister, who attended all the pivotal events of life—birth, marriage, and death. The church was the only common building of the community; it was the only space that was not owned outright by the lord or an individual family. The scene of village meetings and ceremonies, it was the center of both spiritual and social life. The parish priest served as a conduit for all the news of the community and the focal point for the village's festive life. In rural communities, the church was the only organization to which people belonged.

Communities were bound together by the authorities who ruled them and by their common activities. But they were also bound together by their own social customs. Early modern communities used a number of ceremonial occasions as opportunities for expressing solidarity and confirming, in one way or another, the values to which they adhered. In rural parishes there was the annual perambulation, a walk around the village fields that usually occurred before planting began. It was led by the priest, who carried with him any particularly sacred objects that the parish possessed. Behind him followed the village farmers, in some places all members of the village who were capable of walking the distance. The perambulation had many purposes. The priest blessed the fields and prayed for a bountiful crop; the farmers surveyed their own strips and any damage that had been done to the fields during the winter; the community defined its geographical space in distinction to the space of others; and all the individuals who took part reaffirmed their shared identity with others in the village.

In towns ceremonial processions were far more elaborate. Processions might take place on saints' days in Catholic communities or on anniversaries of town liberties. The order of the march, the clothing worn by the participants, and the objects displayed reflected the strict hierarchies of the town's local organizations. In Catholic towns the religious orders led the town governors in their robes of office. Following the governors were the members of guilds, each guild placed according to its rank of importance and each organized by masters, journeymen, and apprentices. In some towns the wives of citizens marched in procession; in others they were accorded special places from which to view the ceremony. Village and civic ceremonies normally ended with communal feasting and dancing, which were the most popular forms of recreation.

Not all ceremonial occasions were so formal. The most common ceremony was the wedding, a rite of passage that was simultaneously significant to the individual, the family, and the community. The wedding was a public event that combined a religious ceremony and a community procession with feasting and festivity. It took different forms in different parts of Europe and in different social groups. But whether eastern or western, noble or common, the wedding was celebrated as the moment when the couple entered fully into the community. Marriage involved more than just the union of bride and groom. Parents were a central feature in the event, both in arranging the economic aspects of the union—dowry and inheritance—and in approving the occasion. Many couples were engaged long before they were married, and in many places it was the engagement that was most important to the individuals and the wedding that was most important to the community. One German townsman described how he "had taken a wife but they have not held the wedding yet."

Traditional weddings involved the formal transfer of property, an important event in rural communities, where the ownership of strips of land or common rights concerned everyone. The bridal dowry and the groom's inheritance were formally exchanged during the wedding, even if both were small. The public procession—"the marriage in the streets" as it was sometimes called in towns—proclaimed the union throughout the community and was considered to be as important as the religious ceremony. It was followed by a feast as abundant as the families of bride and

Carnivals were occasions for games and feasting. A Carnival on the Feast Day of Saint George in a Village Near Antwerp, *painted around 1605 by Abel Grimmer, shows the revels of the villagers presided over by the religious figure on the banner at the right.*

groom could afford. In peasant communities, gifts of food for the feast were as common as were gifts to the couple. There were always provisions made that excess food should be sent to the poor or unfortunate after the wedding.

Weddings also legitimated sexual relations. Many of the dances and ceremonies that followed the feast symbolized the sexual congress. Among German burghers it was traditional for the bride to bring the bed to her new home, and bridal beds were passed from mothers to daughters. Among the nobility, the consummation of the marriage was a vital part of the wedding, for without it the union could be annulled. Finally, the marriage inaugurated both bride and groom into new roles in the community. Their place at the wedding table next to their parents elevated them to the status of adults.

Other ceremonies were equally important in creating a shared sense of identity within the community. In both town and countryside, the year was divided by a number of festivals that defined the rhythm of toil and rest. They coincided with both the seasonal divisions of agricultural life and the central events of the Christian calendar. There was no essential difference between the popular and Christian elements in festivals, however strongly the official church insisted upon one. Christmas and Easter were probably the most widely observed Christian holidays, but Carnival, which preceded Lent, was a frenzied round of feasts and parties

that resulted in a disproportionate number of births nine months later. The Twelve Days of Christmas, which inaugurated the slow, short days of winter, were only loosely attached to the birth of Jesus and were even abolished by some Protestant churches. The rites of May, which celebrated the rebirth of spring, were filled with sexual play among the young adults of the community. Youth groups went "a-Maying" by placing flowers at the homes of marriageable girls, electing a Queen of the May, and dancing and reveling before the hard work of planting. All Hallows' Eve was a celebration for the community's dead. Their spirits wandered the village on that night, visiting kin and neighbors.

Festivals helped maintain the sense of community that might be weakened during the long months of increased work or enforced indoor activity. They were first and foremost celebrations in which feasting, dancing, and play were central. But they also served as safety valves for the pressures and conflicts that built up over the year. There were frequently group and individual sports, like soccer or wrestling, which served to channel aggressions. Village elders would arbitrate disputes, and marriage alliances or property transactions would be arranged.

Festivals further cemented the political cohesion of the community. Seating arrangements reflected the hierarchy of the community, and public punishment of offenders reinforced deference and social and sexual mores. Youth groups, or even the village women, might

❧ Sex and the Married Man

On 27 May 1618 the peace of the small hamlet of Quemerford, in the west of England, was shattered by the appearance of a large crowd from the neighboring market town of Calne. Men marched with fowling pieces and muskets to a cacophony of drums, clanging pots, whistles, and shouts. Among them, on a red horse, rode an outlandishly costumed man—a smock covering his body; on his head a nightcap with two long shoehorns tied to his ears; and on his face a false beard made from a deer's tail. The crowd escorted the rider to the home of Thomas Mills, who worked in Calne as a cutler. There they stopped. Guns were discharged into the air; an even greater clamor of rough music arose from drums, pipes, and metal objects; and when Mills opened his door, members of the crowd waved aloft the horns of goats or rams mounted on sticks. Then a few strong men entered the house; seized hold of his wife, Agnes; and dragged her to a village mud hole where she was ducked and covered in filth. She was rescued from being set on the horse and ridden to Calne.

This event, known as a skimmington in the west of England, and a charivari in France, was a shaming ritual. It was an element of popular culture that took place against the wishes of local authorities and without their connivance. Its purpose was twofold: to identify and punish sexual misconduct and to maintain the male-dominated gender system. These shaming rituals resulted from conduct that the male members of the community believed threatened local order (few women are known to have taken part in these events). In France most charivaris were conducted against husbands who were beaten by their wives; in England many skimmingtons were directed against husbands whose wives had been unfaithful. In both they were designed to shame men into disciplining women and to warn women to remain obedient.

Athough skimmingtons and charivaris differed from place to place, they all contained similar elements. These were designed to invert normal behavior in one way or another. The rough music symbolized the disharmony of a household in which the woman dominated, either by her physical conduct—adultery or husband beating—or her verbal conduct—cursing or abusing her husband or other men. The music was made with everyday objects rather than instruments, and pots and pans were universally present. The "riding" of the husband was another common feature. In many rituals the "husband," played by a neighbor, was placed facing the tail of the horse or donkey to symbolize the backwardness of his behavior. In some, a "wife," also acted by a neighbor, rode behind the man and beat him with a stick or, in England, with the long-handled ladle used to skim cream that was known as a skimmington. In the end, the real husband or wife was captured, the man to ride in shame throughout the town, the woman to be sat on a cucking stool and dunked in water.

The presence of horns on the male riding the horse and on sticks carried by members of the crowd or worn atop their heads was the universal symbol of adultery. The cuckold—a word derived from the name of a promiscuous female bird—was an object of derision throughout European society. Codes of conduct from noble to peasant stressed the importance of female sexual fidelity in maintaining the purity of bloodlines and the order of the household. The cuckold was shorn of his masculinity; he had lost his "horns," in common parlance. His personal indignity was a cause for jest and insult, but the disorderliness implicit in the conduct of his wife was a cause for community concern. In local society, reputation was equated with personal worth, and no one had less reputation than the cuckold. Among the nobility, duels were fought over the slightest suggestion of a wife's unfaithfulness, while among ordinary folks the raising of the forefinger and pinkie—the sign of horns—initiated brawls.

The skimmington or charivari combined festive play with the enforcement of social norms. It was rough justice, as the objects of shame were allowed neither explanation nor defense. They were guilty by common fame, that is, by the report of their neighbors and the gossip of the local alehouse rather than by any examination of evidence. Women who yelled at their husbands were sometimes assumed to have beaten them; women who had beaten their husband were assumed to have cuckolded them. The crimes were all interrelated, and protestations

of innocence were useless. The crowds that gathered to perform the ceremony usually had bolstered their courage at the local tavern, and among them were village toughs and those who held grudges against the targeted family. Assault, property damage, and theft occasionally accompanied a skimmington. But most of the crowd was there to have a bit of sport and revel in the discomfort of the victims. Their conduct was the inverse of a legal procedure, as disorderly as the conduct of those to be punished. However, their purpose was not to turn the world upside down, but to set it right side up again by restoring the dominance of husbands over wives.

While shaming rituals like the charivari and the skimmington had a long history in Europe, they seem to have exploded into prominence in the late sixteenth and early seventeenth centuries. Population pressures and economic hardship are two conventional explanations for why there were greater local tensions during this period. Skimmingtons and charivari frequently had rough edges, with some participants motivated by hatred or revenge. But it is also likely that there were more inversion rituals because there was more inversion. Women were taking a larger role in economic affairs and were becoming increasingly literate and active in religion, especially in Protestant countries. Assertive, independent women threatened the male-dominated social order as much as demographic and social change. That these threats were most identified with sexual misconduct and with the stripping of a husband's masculinity was hardly surprising. The image of the obedient female was conventionally the image of chastity. Thus the image of the independent female had to become one of promiscuity. Through the use of skimmingtons and charivari, men attempted to restore norms of sexual conduct and gender relations that were increasingly under attack. As one English poet put it:

Ill fares the hapless family that shows
A cock that's silent, and a Hen that crows.
I know not which live more unnatural lives,
Obedient husbands, or commanding wives.

A reluctant witch rides off to hell with the devil while indifferent peasants go about their business. This woodcut is from Historia de gentibus septentrionalibus (History of the Northern Folk) by Olaus Magnus, published at Rome in 1555.

Witches were usually women, most often those unmarried or widowed. Although male sorcerers and wizards were thought to have powers over evil spirits, by the sixteenth century it was females who served as the mediators between humans and the diabolical. In a sample of more than seven thousand cases of witchcraft prosecuted in early modern Europe, over 80 percent of the defendants were women. There is no clear explanation why women fulfilled this important and powerful role. Belief in women's special powers over the body through their singular ability to give birth is certainly one part of the explanation, for many stories about the origins of witches suggest that they were children fathered by the devil and left to be raised by women. The sexual element of union with the devil and the common belief that older women were sexually aggressive combined to threaten male sexual dominance. Witches were also believed to have peculiar physical characteristics. A group of Italian witches, male and female, were distinguished by having been born with a caul (a membrane around their heads that was removed after birth). Accused witches were strip-searched to find the devil's mark, which might be any bodily blemish. Another strand of explanation lies in the fact that single women existed on the fringes of society, isolated and exploited by the community at large. Their occult abilities thus became a protective mechanism that gave them a function within the community while they remained outside it.

It is difficult to know how important black magical beliefs were in ordinary communities. Most of the daily magic that was practiced was the mixture of charms, potions, and prayers that mingled magical, medical, and Christian beliefs. But as the century progressed, more and more notice was taken of black magic. Misfortunes that befell particular families or social groups were blamed upon the activities of witches. The campaign of the established churches to root out magic was largely directed against witches. The churches transposed witches' supposed abilities to communicate with the devil into the charge that they worshiped the devil. Because there was such widespread belief in the presence of diabolical spirits and in the capabilities of witches to control them, Protestant and Catholic church courts could easily find witnesses to testify in support of the charges against individual witches. Yet wherever sufficient evidence exists to understand the circumstances of witchcraft prosecutions, it is clear that the community itself was under some form of social or economic stress. Sacrificing a marginal member of the community might be the means to restore village solidarity.

• • •

Population growth, economic diversification, and social change characterized life in early modern Europe. It was a century of extremes. The poor were getting poorer and the rich were getting richer. The

THE DEVIL'S DUE

Evidence of the supernatural world abounded for the people of premodern Europe. Natural disasters such as plague and human disasters such as war promoted fear of witchcraft. When the world seemed out of balance and the forces of good retreated before the forces of evil, people sought someone to blame for their troubles. Witches were an obvious choice. Accused witches were most commonly women on the margins of society. Once brought before the authorities, many admitted their traffic with Satan, especially under torture. The Witch Hammer *is a set of detailed instructions for the rooting out of witches, including procedures to induce their confessions.*

The method of beginning an examination by torture is as follows: First, the jailers prepare the implements of torture, then they strip the prisoner (if it be a woman, she has already been stripped by other women, upright and of good report). This stripping is lest some means of witchcraft may have been sewed into the clothing—such as often, taught by the Devil, they prepare from the bodies of unbaptized infants, [murdered] that they may forfeit salvation. And when the implements of torture have been prepared, the judge, both in person and through other good men zealous in the faith, tries to persuade the prisoner to confess the truth freely; but, if he will not confess, he bids attendants make the prisoner fast to the strappado or some other implement of torture. The attendants obey forthwith, yet with feigned agitation. Then, at the prayer of some of those present, the prisoner is loosed again and is taken aside and once more persuaded to confess, being led to believe that he will in that case not be put to death.

But if, neither by threats nor by promises such as these, the witch can be induced to speak the truth, then the jailers must carry out the sentence, and torture the prisoner according to the accepted methods, with more or less of severity as the delinquent's crime may demand. And, while he is being tortured, he must be questioned on the articles of accusation, and this frequently and persistently, beginning with the lighter charges—for he will more readily confess the lighter than the heavier. And, while this is being done, the notary must write down everything in his record of the trial—how the prisoner is tortured, on what points he is questioned, and how he answers.

And note that, if he confesses under the torture, he must afterward be conducted to another place, that he may confirm it and certify that it was not due alone to the force of the torture.

But, if the prisoner will not confess the truth satisfactorily, other sorts of tortures must be placed before him, with the statement that, unless he will confess the truth, he must endure these also. But, if not even thus he can be brought into terror and to the truth, then the next day or the next but one is to be set for a *continuation* of the tortures—not a *repetition,* for they must not be repeated unless new evidence be produced. . . .

And during the interval, before the day assigned, the judge, in person or through approved men, must in the manner above described try to persuade the prisoner to confess, promising her (if there is aught to be gained by this promise) that her life shall be spared.

The judge shall see to it, moreover, that throughout this interval guards are constantly with the prisoner, so that she may not be left alone; because she will be visited by the Devil and tempted into suicide.

From *The Witch Hammer.*

---

early part of the century has been called the golden age of the peasantry; the later part has been called the crisis of subsistence. At all levels of the social scale, the lives of grandparents and grandchildren were dramatically different. For surplus producers, the quality of life improved throughout the century. The market economy expanded. Agricultural surplus was exchanged for more land and a wider variety of consumer goods. Children could be provided with an education, and domestic and agricultural labor was cheap and plentiful. For subsistence producers, the quality of life eroded. In the first half of the century, their diet contained more meat than it would for the next three hundred years. Their children could be absorbed on new farms or sent to towns where there was a shortage of both skilled and unskilled labor. But gradually the outlook turned bleak. The land could support no more new families, and the towns needed no more labor. As wages fell and prices rose, peasants in western Europe were caught between the crushing burdens of taxation from lord, state, and church and the all-too-frequent catastrophes of poor harvests, epidemic disease, and warfare. In eastern Europe the peasantry was tied to the land in a new serfdom that provided minimum subsistence in return for the loss of freedom and opportunity. When peasants anywhere rose up against these conditions, they were cut down and swept away like new-mown hay.

Suggestions for Further Reading

General Reading

Henry Kamen, *European Society, 1500–1700* (London: Hutchinson, 1984). A general survey of European social history.

* Robert Mandrou, *Introduction to Modern France* (New York: Harper & Row, 1977). Explores a variety of subjects in French social history from the mental to the material world.

* Peter Laslett, *The World We Have Lost: Further Explored* (New York: Scribners, 1984). One of the pioneering works in the family and population history of England.

George Huppert, *After the Black Death* (Bloomington: Indiana Univerity Press, 1986). An up-to-date and detailed study of social history in all parts of the Continent.

Economic Life

* Fernand Braudel, *Civilization and Capitalism: The Structures of Everyday Life* (New York: Harper & Row, 1981). Part of a larger work filled with fascinating detail about the social behavior of humankind during the early modern period.

Le Roy Ladurie, Emmanuel, *The French Peasantry 1450–1660* (London: Scholar Press, 1987). A complex study of the lives of the French peasantry.

Gerald Strauss, *Nuremberg in the Sixteenth Century* (New York: John Wiley and Sons, 1966). A political and social history of a typical German town.

David Palliser, *Tudor York* (Oxford: Oxford University Press, 1979). A study of the second largest English urban area and its decline in the sixteenth century.

* Natalie Z. Davis, *Society and Culture in Early Modern France* (Stanford, CA: Stanford University Press, 1975). A collection of compelling essays drawn from the author's research on the French town of Lyon.

* Carlo Cipolla, ed., *Fontana Economic History of Europe.* Vol. 2, *The Sixteenth and Seventeenth Centuries* (London: Harvester Press, 1977). A multiauthored compendium of information and analysis on all aspects of European economic life.

* Peter Kriedte, *Peasants, Landlords and Merchant Capitalists* (Cambridge: Cambridge University Press, 1983). A Marxist interpretation of the transformations of the European economy.

Hermann Kellenbenz, *The Rise of the European Economy* (London: Weidenfeld and Nicolson, 1976). A general survey of economic life with good material from Scandinavian and German sources.

Social Life

* E. M. W. Tillyard, *The Elizabethan World Picture* (New York: Harper & Row, 1960). The classic account of the social constructs of English society.

* Arthur Lovejoy, *The Great Chain of Being* (New York: Random House, 1959). An intellectual history of an idea through its centuries of development.

Michael Bush, *Noble Privilege* (New York: Holmes & Meier, 1983). An analytic account of the types of privileges enjoyed by the European nobility, based on wide reading.

Antoni Maczak, Henryk Samsonowicz, and Peter Burke, eds., *East-Central Europe in Transition* (Cambridge: Cambridge University Press, 1985). Essays by leading historians of eastern Europe, most of which focus upon economic development.

Michael Weisser, *The Peasants of the Montes* (Chicago: University of Chicago Press, 1972). A study of the lives of the Spanish peasants who lived in the shadow of Toledo.

* Margaret Spufford, *Contrasting Communities* (Cambridge: Cambridge University Press, 1974). A detailed reconstruction of three English villages that explores social, economic, and religious life in the late sixteenth and early seventeenth centuries.

* R. Scribner and G. Benecke, *The German Peasant War, 1525* (London: Allen & Unwin, 1979). Essays by leading scholars on different aspects of the most important of all peasant revolts.

* Peter Blickle, *The Revolution of 1525* (Baltimore: Johns Hopkins University Press, 1981). A provocative interpretation of the causes and meaning of the German Peasants' War.

Yves-Marie Bercé, *Revolt and Revolution in Early Modern Europe* (New York: St. Martin's Press, 1987). A study of the structure of uprisings throughout Europe by a leading French historian.

Private Life

* Roger Chartier, ed., *A History of Private Life.* Vol. 3, *Passions of the Renaissance* (Cambridge, MA: Harvard University Press, 1989). A lavishly illustrated study of the habits, mores, and the structures of private life from the fifteenth to the eighteenth centuries.

* Michael Mitterauer and Reinhard Sieder, *The European Family* (Chicago: University of Chicago Press, 1982). A soci-

ological survey that presents the varying ways in which European families were structured.

* Ralph Houlbrooke, *The English Family, 1450–1700* (London: Longman, 1984). A thorough survey of family history for the society that has been most carefully studied.

* Jean-Louis Flandrin, *Families in Former Times* (Cambridge: Cambridge University Press, 1976). Studies of kinship, household, and sexuality by one of the leading French family historians.

* A. T. Van Deursen, *Plain Lives in a Golden Age* (Cambridge: Cambridge University Press, 1991). A study of Dutch popular culture and religious belief that makes excellent use of the visual arts.

Merry Wiesner, *Working Women in Renaissance Germany* (New Brunswick, NJ: Rutgers University Press, 1986). A survey of women's work in Germany and the ways in which it changed during the sixteenth century.

Brian Pullan, *Rich and Poor in Renaissance Venice* (Cambridge, MA: Harvard University Press, 1971). A massive history of social classes in Venice with a detailed account of poverty and vagrancy.

* Peter Burke, *Popular Culture in Early Modern Europe* (New York: Harper & Row, 1978). A lively survey of cultural activities among the European populace.

R. Muchembled, *Popular Culture and Elite Culture in France, 1400–1750* (Baton Rouge: Louisiana State University Press, 1985). A detailed treatment of the practices of two conflicting cultures.

* D. Underdown, *Revel, Riot and Rebellion* (Oxford: Oxford University Press, 1985). An engaging study of popular culture and its relationship to social and economic structures in England.

* Keith Thomas, *Religion and the Decline of Magic* (New York: Scribners, 1971). A gargantuan descriptive and anecdotal account of the forms of religious and magical practice in England.

* Jean Delumeau, *Sin and Fear* (New York: St. Martin's Press, 1990). A cultural history of emotion based on a dazzling study of mainly Catholic writers.

* Brian Levack, *The Witch-Hunt in Early Modern Europe* (London: Longman, 1987). A study of the causes and meaning of the persecution of European witches in the sixteenth and seventeenth centuries.

*Paperback edition available.

16 ✣ THE ROYAL STATE IN THE SEVENTEENTH CENTURY

Fit for a King

Behold Versailles: the greatest palace of the greatest king of the greatest state in seventeenth-century Europe. Everything about it was stupendous, a reflection of the grandeur of Louis XIV and of France. Sculptured gardens in dazzling geometric forms stretched for acres, scenting the air with exotic perfumes. Nearly as beautiful as the grounds were the 1400 fountains, especially the circular basins of Apollo and Latona, the sun god and his mother. The hundreds of water jets that sprayed at Versailles defied nature as well as the senses, for the locale was not well irrigated and water had to be pumped through elaborate mechanical works all the way from the Seine. Gardens and fountains provided the setting for the enormous palace with its hundreds of rooms for both use and show. Five thousand people, a tenth of whom served the king alone, inhabited the palace. Thousands of others flocked there daily. Most lived in the adjacent town, which had grown from a few hundred people to over forty thousand in a single generation. The royal stables quartered twelve thousand horses and hundreds of carriages. The cost of all of this magnificence was equally astounding. Fragmentary accounts indicate that construction costs were over 100 million French pounds. Louis XIV ordered the official receipts burned.

Like the marble of the palace, nature itself was chiseled to the requirements of the king. Forests were pared to make leafy avenues or trimmed to conform to the geometric patterns of the gardens. In spring and summer, groves of orange trees grown in tubs were everywhere; in winter and fall they were housed indoors at great expense. Life-size statues and giant carved urns lined the carefully planned walkways that led to breathtaking views or sheltered grottoes. A cross-shaped artificial canal, over a mile long, dominated the western end of the park. Italian gondolas skimmed along its surface, carrying visitors to the zoo and aviary on one side or to the king's private chateau on the other.

But this great pile of bricks and stone, of marble and precious metals, expressed the contradictions of its age as well as its grandeur. The seventeenth century was an era when the rich got richer and the poor got poorer. It was a time when the monarchical state expanded its power and prestige even as it faced grave challenges to its very existence. It was an epoch of unrelenting war amid a nearly universal desire for lasting peace. Thus it was fitting that this prodigious monument was uncomfortable to live in, so unpleasant that Louis had a separate chateau built on the grounds as a quiet retreat. His wife and his mistresses complained constantly of accommodations in which all interior comforts had been subordinated to the external facade of the building. Versailles was a seat of state as well as the home of the monarch, and it is revealing that the private was sacrificed to the public.

The duc de Saint-Simon, who passed much of his time at Versailles, was well aware of the contradictions: "The beautiful and the ugly were sown together, the vast and the constricted." Soldiers, artisans, and the merely curious clogged the three great avenues that led from Paris to the palace. When the king dined in public, hordes of Parisians drove out for the spectacle, filing past the monarch as if he were an exhibit at a museum. The site itself was poorly drained. "Its mud is black and stinking with a stench so penetrating that you can smell it for several leagues around." The orange groves and the stone urns filled with flower petals were more practical than beautiful: they masked the stench of sewage that was particularly noxious in the heat and the rain. Even the gardens were too vast to be enjoyed. In the planted areas, the smell of flowers was overpowering while the acres of mown lawn proved unattractive to an aristocracy little given to physical exercise. "The gardens were admired and avoided," Saint-Simon observed acidly. In these contrasts of failure amid achievement, Versailles stands as an apt symbol of its age: a gaudy mask to hide the wrinkles of the royal state.

The Rise of the Royal State

The religious and dynastic wars that dominated the early part of the seventeenth century had a profound impact upon the western European states. Not only did they cause terrible suffering and deprivation, but they also demanded efficient and better-centralized states to conduct them. War was both a product of the European state system and a cause of its continued development. As armies grew in size, the resources necessary to maintain them grew in volume. As the battlefield spread from state to state, defense became government's most important function. More and more power was absorbed by the monarch and his chief advisers; more and more of the traditional privileges of aristocracy and towns were eroded. At the center of these rising states, particularly in western Europe, were the king and his court. In the provinces were tax collectors and military recruiters.

Divine Kings

"There is a divinity that doth hedge a king," wrote Shakespeare. Never was that hedge more luxuriant than in the seventeenth century. In the early sixteenth century, monarchs treated their states and their subjects as personal property. Correspondingly, rulers were praised in personal terms: for their virtue, wisdom, or strength. By the early seventeenth century, the monarchy had been transformed into an office of state. Now rulers embodied their nation and, no matter what their personal characteristics, they were held in awe because they were monarchs.

Thus, as rulers lost direct personal control over their patrimony, they gained indirect symbolic control over their nation. This symbolic power was to be seen everywhere. By the beginning of the seventeenth century, monarchs had set permanent seats of government attended by vast courts of officials, place seekers, and servants. The idea of the capital city emerged, with Madrid, London, Paris, and Vienna as the models. Here the grandiose style of the ruler stood proxy for the wealth and glory of the nation. Great display bespoke great pride, and great pride was translated into great strength.

Portraits of rulers in action and repose conveyed the central message. Elizabeth I was depicted bestriding a map of England or clutching a rainbow and wearing a gown woven of eyes and ears to signify her power to see and hear her subjects. The Flemish painter Sir Anthony Van Dyck (1599–1641) created powerful images of

Queen Elizabeth I of England. This portrait was commissioned by Sir Henry Lee to commemorate the queen's visit to his estate at Ditchley. Here the queen is the very image of Gloriana—ageless and indomitable.

three generations of Stuart kings of England. He was court painter to Charles I, whose qualities he portrayed with great sympathy and not a little exaggeration. Diego Velázquez (1599–1660) was court painter to Philip IV of Spain. His series of equestrian portraits of the Habsburgs—kings, queens, princes, and princesses—exude the spirit of the seventeenth-century monarchy, the grandeur and pomp, the power and self-assurance. Peter Paul Rubens (1577–1640) represented 21 separate episodes in the life of Marie de Médicis, queen regent of France.

The themes of writers were no different than those of artists. Monarchy was glorified in a variety of forms of literary representation. National history, particularly of recent events, enjoyed wide popularity. Its avowed purpose was to draw the connection between the past and the present glories of the state. One of the most popular French histories of the period was entitled *On the Excellence of the Kings and the Kingdom of France*. Francis Bacon (1561–1626), who is remembered more as a philosopher and scientist, wrote a laudatory history of Henry VII, founder of the Tudor dynasty.

In England it was a period of renaissance. Poets, playwrights, historians, and philosophers by the dozens gravitated to the English court. One of the most remarkable of them was Ben Jonson (1572–1637). He began life as a bricklayer, fought against the Spanish in Flanders, and then turned to acting and writing. His wit and talent brought him to court, where he made his mark by writing and staging masques, light entertainment that included music, dance, pantomime, and acting. Jonson's masques were distinguished by their lavish productions and exotic costumes and the inventive set designs of the great architect Inigo Jones (1573–1652). They were frequently staged at Christmastime and starred members of the court as players. The masques took the grandeur of England and its rulers for their themes.

The role of William Shakespeare (1564–1616) in the celebration of monarchy was more ambiguous. Like Jonson, Shakespeare came from an ordinary family, had little formal education, and began his astonishing career as an actor and producer of theater. He soon began to write as well as direct his plays and his company, the King's Players, received royal patronage. He set many of his plays at the courts of princes, and even comedies like *The Tempest* (1611) and *Measure for Measure* (1604) centered on the power of the ruler to dispense justice and to bring peace to his subjects. Both plays were staged at court. Skakespeare's history plays focused entirely on the character of kings. In *Richard II* (1597) and *Henry VI* (three parts, 1591–94) Shakespeare exposed the harm that weak rulers inflicted on their states, while in *Henry IV* (two parts, 1598–1600) and *Henry V* (1599) he highlighted the benefits to be derived from strong rulers. Shakespeare's tragedies made this point in a different way. The tragic flaw in the personality of rulers exposed the world around them to ruin. In *Macbeth* (1606) this flaw was ambition. Macbeth killed to become a king and had to keep on killing to remain one. In *Hamlet* (1602) the tragic flaw was irresolution. The inability of the Prince of Denmark to act decisively and reclaim the crown that was his by right brought his state to the brink of collapse. Shakespeare's plays were viewed in London theaters by members of all social classes, and his concentration on the affairs of rulers helped reinforce their dominating importance in the lives of all of their subjects.

The political theory of the divine right of kings further enhanced the importance of monarchs. This theory held that the institution of monarchy had been created by God and that the monarch functioned as God's representative on earth. One clear statement of divine-right theory was actually written by a king, James VI of Scotland, who later became James I of England (1603–25). In *The True Law of Free Monarchies* (1598), James reasoned that God had placed kings on earth to rule and that he would judge them in heaven for their transgressions.

The idea of the divine origin of monarchy was uncontroversial, and it was espoused not only by kings. One of the few things that the French Estates-General actually agreed upon during its meeting in 1614—the last for over 175 years—was the statement "The king is sovereign in France and holds his crown from God only." This sentiment echoed the commonplace view of French political theorists. The greatest writer on the subject, Jean Bodin (1530–96), called the king "God's image on earth." In *The Six Books of the Commonwealth* (1576), Bodin defined the essence of the monarch's power: "The principal mark of sovereign majesty is essentially the right to impose laws on subjects generally without their consent."

Although at first glance the theory of the divine right of kings appears to be a blueprint for arbitrary rule, in fact it was yoked together with a number of principles that restrained the conduct of the monarch. As James I pointed out, God had charged kings with obligations: "to minister justice; to establish good laws; and to procure peace."

Kings were bound by the law of nature and the law of nations. They could not deprive their subjects of their lives, their liberties, or their property without due cause established by law. As one French theorist held, "While the kingdom belongs to the king, the king also belongs to the kingdom." Wherever they turned, kings were instructed in the duties of kingship. In tracts, letters, and literature they were lectured on the obligations of their office. "A true king should be first in government, first in council, and first in all the offices of state."

The Court and the Courtiers

For all of the bravura of divine-right theory, far more was expected of kings than they could possibly deliver. The day-to-day affairs of government had grown beyond the capacity of any monarch to handle them. The expansion in the powers of the western states absorbed more officials than ever. At the beginning of the sixteenth century, the French court of Francis I employed 622 officers; at the beginning of the seventeenth century, the court of Henry IV employed over 1500. Yet the difference was not only in size. Members of the seventeenth-century court were becoming servants of the state as well as of the monarch.

Expanding the court was one of the ways in which monarchs co-opted potential rivals within the aristocracy. In return, those who were favored enhanced their power by royal grants of titles, lands, and income. As the court expanded, so did the political power of courtiers. Royal councils—a small group of leading officeholders who advised the monarch on state business—grew in significance. Not only did the council assume the management of government, it also began to advocate policies for the monarch to adopt.

Yet, like everything else in seventeenth-century government, the court revolved around the monarch. The monarch appointed, promoted, and dismissed officeholders at will. As befit this type of personal government, most monarchs chose a single individual to act as a funnel for private and public business. This was the "favorite," whose role combined varying proportions of best friend, right-hand man, and hired gun. Some favorites, like Cardinal Richelieu of France and Spain's Count-Duke Olivares, were able to transform themselves into chief ministers with a political philosophy and a vision of government. Others, like the English duke of Buckingham, simply remained royal companions. Favorites walked a not very tight rope. They could retain their balance only as long as they retained their influence with the monarch. Richelieu claimed that it was "more difficult to dominate the four square feet of the king's study than the affairs of Europe." The parallel careers of Richelieu, Olivares, and Buckingham neatly illustrate the dangers and opportunities of the office.

Cardinal Richelieu (1585–1642) was born into a French noble family of minor importance. A younger son, he trained for the law and then for a position that his family owned in the Church; he was made a cardinal in 1622. After skillful participation in the meeting of the Estates-General of 1614, Richelieu was given a court post through the patronage of Queen Marie de Médicis, mother of Louis XIII. The two men made a good match. Louis XIII hated the work of ruling and Richelieu loved little else.

Although Richelieu received great favor from the king—he became a duke and amassed the largest private

porters, but he was more interested in establishing political policy than in building a court faction. His objective was to maintain the greatness of Spain, whose fortunes, like his moods, waxed and waned. Like Richelieu, Olivares attempted to further the process of centralizing royal power, which was not very advanced in Spain. Olivares's plans for a nationally recruited and financed army ended in disaster. His efforts at tax reform went unrewarded. He advocated the aggressive foreign policy that mired Spain in the Thirty Years' War and eighty years of war in the Netherlands. As domestic and foreign crises mounted, Philip IV could not resist the pressure to dismiss his chief minister. In 1643 Olivares was removed from office and two years later, physically exhausted and mentally deranged, he died.

This portrait of Richelieu by Philippe de Champaigne shows the cardinal's intellectual power and controlled determination.

fortune in France—his position rested on his managerial abilities. Richelieu never enjoyed a close personal relationship with his monarch, and he never felt that his position was secure. In 1630 Marie de Médicis turned against him and he very nearly was ousted from office. His last years were filled with suppressing plots to undermine his power or to take his life.

Count-Duke Olivares (1587–1645) was a younger son of a lesser branch of a great Spanish noble family. By the time he was twenty he had become a courtier with a title, a large fortune, and most unusually, a university education. Olivares became the favorite of King Philip IV (1621–65). He was elevated to the highest rank of the nobility and lost no time consolidating his position.

Olivares used his closeness to the monarch to gain court appointments for his relatives and political sup-

The Spanish master Diego Velázquez painted this portrait of the Count-Duke Olivares.

George Villiers, duke of Buckingham. The royal favorite virtually ruled the country between 1618 and 1628. The general rejoicing at his death embittered the king and helped bring about the eleven years' rule without Parliament.

The duke of Buckingham (1592–1628) was also a younger son, but not of the English nobility. He received the aimless education of a country gentleman, spending several years in France learning the graces of fashion and dancing. Reputedly one of the most handsome men in Europe, Buckingham hung about the fringes of the English court until his looks and charm brought him to the attention of Queen Anne, James I's wife. She recommended him for a minor office that gave him frequent access to the king. Buckingham quickly caught the eye of James I, and his rise was meteoric. In less than seven years he went from commoner to duke, the highest rank of the English nobility.

Along with his titles, Buckingham acquired political power. He assumed a large number of royal offices, among them Admiral of the Navy, and placed his relatives and dependents in many others. Buckingham took his obligations seriously. He began a reform of naval administration, for example, but his rise to power had been so sudden that he found enemies at every turn. These increased dramatically when James I died in 1625. But Buckingham succeeded where so many others had failed by becoming the favorite and chief minister of the new king, Charles I (1625–49). His accumulation of power and patronage proceeded unabated, as did the enmity he aroused. But Charles I stood firmly behind him. In 1628 a discontented naval officer finally accomplished what the most powerful men in England could not: Buckingham was assassinated. While Charles I wept inconsolably at the news, ordinary Londoners drank to the health of his killer.

The Drive to Centralize Government

Richelieu, Olivares, and Buckingham met very different ends. Yet in their own ways they shared a common goal: to extend the authority of the monarch over his state and to centralize his control over the machinery of governance.

One of the chief means by which kings and councilors attempted to expand the authority of the state was through the legal system. Administering justice was one of the sacred duties of the monarchy. The complexities of ecclesiastical, civil, and customary law gave trained lawyers an essential role in government. As legal experts and the demands for legal services increased, royal law courts multiplied and expanded. In France, the Parlement of Paris, the main law court of the state, became a powerful institution that contested with courtiers for the right to advise the monarch. The number of regional parlements increased, bringing royal justice to the farthest reaches of the realm. Members of the Parlement of Paris and of the expanding provincial parlements were known as nobility of the robe, because of the long gowns lawyers and judges wore. In Spain the *letrados*—university-trained lawyers who were normally members of the nobility—were the backbone of royal government. Formal legal training was a requirement for many of the administrative posts in the state. In Castile members of all social classes frequently used the royal courts to settle personal disputes. The expansion of a centralized system of justice thus joined the interests of subjects and the monarchy.

In England the legal system expanded differently. Central courts, situated in the royal palace of Westminster, grew and the lawyers and judges who practiced in them became a powerful profession. They were especially active in the House of Commons of the English Parliament, which, along with the House of Lords, had extensive advisory and legislative powers. More important than the rise of the central courts, however, was the rise of the local ones. The English Crown extended royal justice to the counties by granting legal authority to members of the local social elite. These justices of the peace, as they were known, became agents of the Crown in their own localities. Justices were given power to hear and settle minor cases and to imprison those who had committed serious offenses until the assizes, the semiannual sessions of the county court.

Assizes combined the ceremony of rule with its process. Royal authority was displayed in a great procession to the courthouse that was led by the judge and the county justices, followed by the grand and petty juries of local citizens who would hear the cases, and finally by the carts carrying the prisoners to trial. Along with the legal business that was performed, assizes were occasions for edifying sermons, typically on the theme of obedience. Their solemnity—marked by the black robes of the judge, the Latin of the legal proceedings, and the public executions with which assizes invariably ended—all served to instill a sense of the power of the state in the throngs of ordinary people who witnessed them.

Efforts to integrate center and locality extended to more than the exercise of justice. The monarch also needed officials who could enforce royal policy in those localities where the special privileges of groups and individuals remained strong. The best strategy was to appoint local leaders to royal office. But with so much of the aristocracy resident at court, this was not always an effective course. In France, the provincial governors were traditionally members of the ancient nobility who enjoyed wide powers in matters of military recruitment, revenue collection, and judicial administration. But many governors spent far more time in Paris than in the locality that they were to administer and often opposed the exactions demanded by the monarch. By the beginning of the seventeenth century, the French monarchy began to rely on new central officials known as intendants to perform many of the tasks of the provincial governors. Cardinal Richelieu expanded the use of the intendants, and by the middle of the century they had become a vital part of royal government.

The Lords Lieutenant were a parallel institution created in England. Unlike every other European state, England had no national army. Every English county was required to raise, equip, and train its own militia.

Lords Lieutenant were in charge of these trained bands. Since the aristocracy was the ancient military class in the state, the lieutenants were chosen from the greatest nobles of the realm. But they delegated their work to members of the gentry, large local landholders who took on their tasks as a matter of prestige rather than profit. Perhaps not surprisingly, the English military was among the weakest in Europe and nearly all its foreign adventures ended in disaster.

Efforts to centralize the affairs of the Spanish monarchy could not proceed so easily. The separate regions over which the king ruled maintained their own laws and privileges. Attempts to apply Castilian rules or implant Castilian officials always drew opposition from other regions. Olivares frequently complained that Philip IV was the king of Castile only and nothing but a thorough plan of unification would make him the king of Spain. He proposed such a plan in 1625 to attempt to solve the dual problems of military manpower and military finance. After 1621, Spain was again deeply involved in European warfare. Fighting in the Netherlands and in Germany demanded large armies and larger sums of money. Olivares launched a plan for a Union of Arms to which all the separate regions of the empire—including Mexico and Peru in the west, Italy in the east, and the separate regions in Iberia—would contribute. He envisioned an army of 140,000 but soon lowered his sights. Not all of the Iberian provinces were persuaded to contribute: Catalonia stood upon its ancient privileges and refused to grant either troops or funds. But Olivares was able to establish at least the principle of unified cooperation.

The Taxing Demands of War

More than anything else, war propelled the consolidation of the state. Whether offensive or defensive, continuous or intermittent, successful or calamitous, war was the irresistible force of the seventeenth-century monarchy. War taxation was its immovable object. Perhaps half of all revenue of the western states went to finance war. To maintain its armies and navies, its fortresses and outposts, the state had to squeeze every penny from its subjects. Old taxes had to be collected more efficiently; new taxes had to be introduced and enforced. As one Spanish jurist observed, in a familiar refrain, "There can be no peace without arms, no arms without money, and no money without taxation." However, the unprecedented demands for money by the state were always resisted. The privileged challenged the legality of levying taxes; the unprivileged did whatever they could to avoid paying them.

The claims and counterclaims of subjects and sovereigns were very strong. In the first place, armies had grown bigger and more expensive. In 1625 Philip IV had nearly three hundred thousand men in arms throughout his empire. The expense of maintaining Spanish fortresses alone had quintupled since the time of Philip II. Not only were there more men to pay, equip, and supply, but the cost of war materials continued to rise with inflation. Similarly, the cost of food and fodder rose. Marauding armies might be able to plunder sufficient grain during the spring and autumn, but they still consumed massive amounts of meat and drink that could not be supplied locally.

The economic hardships caused by the ceaseless military activity touched everyone. Those in the direct path of battle had little left to feed themselves, let alone to provide to the state. The disruption of the delicate cycle of planting and harvesting devastated local communities. Armies plundered ripened grain and trampled seedlings as they moved through fields. The conscription of village men and boys removed vital skills from the community and upset the gender-based division of labor. Peasants were squeezed by the armies for crops, by the lords for rents, and by the state for taxes.

In fact, the inability of the lower orders of European society to finance a century of warfare was clear from the beginning. In Spain and France, the principal problem was that so much of the wealth of the nation was beyond the reach of traditional royal taxation. The nobility and many of the most important towns had long achieved exemption from basic taxes on consumption and wealth. European taxation was regressive, falling most heavily on those least able to pay. Rulers and subjects alike recognized the inequities of the system. Regime after regime began with plans to overhaul the national system of taxation before settling for propping up new emergency levies against the rotting foundations of the old structure. Nevertheless, the fiscal crisis that the European wars provoked did result in an expansion of state taxation.

In France, for example, royal expenditures rose 60 percent during the first two decades of the seventeenth century, while the yield from the *taille,* the crown's basic commodity tax, remained constant. Thus the crown was forced to search for new revenues, the most important of which was the *paulette,* a tax on officeholding. To raise money, especially in emergencies, the crown had been forced to sell government offices, until by the seventeenth century a majority of offices had been obtained by direct purchase. The sale of an office provided a one-time windfall for the crown, but after that the cost of salaries and benefits was a perpetual drain. So, too, were the administrative costs of potentially inefficient officeholders. Many purchased their posts as an investment and treated them as personal property. For an annual payment of one-sixtieth of the value of the office, the paulette allowed the current holder to sell or bequeath it as desired. Henry IV instituted the paulette in 1604, and it became a vital source of royal revenue as well as an acute source of aristocratic and legal complaint. In the early 1620s, revenue from the sale of offices amounted to one-third of the crown's income. The purchase of office was inherently corrupt, but it was not necessarily inefficient. Sons who were to inherit offices could be trained for their posts, if for no other reason than to operate them profitably. The crown received money from classes in society that were generally beyond the reach of taxation, while members of these classes received power, prestige, and experience in public service. As long as profit and efficiency went hand in hand, both officeholder and monarch might be well served. Unfortunately, it was the king rather than his officers who had the greatest incentive to manipulate the system. The more offices that could be created, the larger the income from the paulette. During fiscal emergencies this was a temptation to which all French monarchs succumbed.

"Fiscal emergency" was just another name for the routine problems of the Spanish monarchy. As the greatest military power in Europe, Spain necessarily had the greatest military budget, and thus the most extensive system of taxation. The crown taxed both domestic and imperial trade and took a healthy share of the gold and silver that continued to be mined in America. But all these revenues fell short of the state's needs. In the 1590s Philip II established an important new source of internal taxation. In an agreement with the Cortes of Castile, he introduced the *milliones,* a tax on consumption that was to yield millions of ducats a year for war costs. An extremely regressive measure, the milliones taxed the sale of meat, wine, and oil—the basic elements of diet. This tax, which hit urban areas particularly hard, was originally designed to last only six years. But the crises that the crown pleaded in the 1590s were even deeper at the turn of the century. The milliones became a permanent tax and a permanent grievance throughout Castile.

By contrast, the English crown was never able to persuade Parliament to grant permanent additional revenues. Although uninvolved in European conflicts, England was not immune from military spending. War with Ireland in the 1590s and with Spain between 1588 and 1604 depleted the reserves that the crown had obtained when Henry VIII dissolved the monasteries. Disasterous wars against France and Spain in the 1620s provoked fiscal crisis for a monarchy that had few direct sources of revenue. While the great wealth of the kingdom was in land, the chief sources of revenue for the crown were in trade. In the early seventeenth century, customs duties, or impositions, became a lucrative source of income when the judges ruled that the king could determine which commodities could be taxed and at what rate. Impositions fell heavily upon the merchant classes and urban consumers, but unlike the milliones, impositions were placed on luxury import goods rather than on basic commodities.

Because so much of the crown's revenues derived from commerce and because foreign invasion could only come from the sea, the most pressing military need of the English monarchy was for naval defense. Even during the Armada crisis, the largest part of the English fleet had been made up of private merchant ships pressed into service through the emergency tax of Ship Money. This was a tax on each port town to hire a merchant ship and fit it out for war. In the 1630s Charles I revived Ship Money and extended it to all English localities. His innovation aroused much opposition from the gentry, especially after his refusal to call Parliament into session to have the tax confirmed.

War finance was like an all-consuming monster. No matter how much new revenue was fed into it, its appetite grew for more. New taxes and increased rates of traditional taxation created suffering and a sense of grievance throughout the western European states. Opposition to taxation was not based on greed: the state's right to tax was not yet an established principle. Monarchs received certain forms of revenue in return for grants of immunities and privileges to powerful groups in their state. The state's efforts to go beyond these restricted grants were viewed as theft of private property. In the case of Ship Money, challengers argued that the king had no right to what belonged to his subjects except in a case of national emergency. This was a claim that the king accepted, arguing that such an emergency existed in the presence of pirates who were attacking English shipping. But if Charles I did not make a convincing claim for national emergency, the monarchs of France and Spain, the princes of Germany, and the rulers of the states of eastern Europe all did.

Throughout the seventeenth century, monarchy solidified itself as a form of government. The king's authority came from God, but his power came from his people. By administering justice, assembling armies, and extracting resources through taxation, the monarch ruled as well as governed. The richer the king and the more powerful his might, the more potent was his state. Europeans began to identify themselves as citizens of a nation and to see themselves in distinction to other nations.

The Crises of the Royal State

The expansion of the functions, duties, and powers of the state in the early seventeenth century was not universally welcomed in European societies. The growth of central government came at the expense of local rights and privileges held by corporate bodies like the Church and the towns or by individuals like provincial officials and aristocrats. The state proved a powerful competitor, especially in the contest for the meager surplus produced on the land. As rents and prices stabilized in the early seventeenth century after a long period of inflation, taxation increased, slowly at first and then at a pace with the gathering momentum of the Thirty Years' War. State exactions burdened all segments of society. Peasants lost the small benefit that rising prices had conferred on producers. The surplus that parents had once passed on to children was now taken by the state. Local officials, never altogether popular, came to be seen as parasites and were easy targets for peasant rebellions. Larger landholders, whose prosperity depended on rents and services from an increasingly impoverished peasantry, suffered along with their tenants. Even the great magnates were appalled by the state's insatiable appetite.

Taxation was not the only thing that aroused opposition. Social and economic regulation meant more laws. More laws meant more lawyers and agents of enforcement. State regulation may have been more efficient (though many believed it was more efficient only for the state) but it was certainly disruptive. It was also expensive at a time when the fragile European economy was in a phase of decline. The early seventeenth century was a time of hunger in most of western Europe. Subtle changes in climate reduced the length of growing seasons and the size of crops. Bad harvests in the 1620s and 1640s left disease and starvation in their wake. And the wars ground on. Armies brought misery to those who were forcibly recruited to fight, those who were taxed into destitution, and those who simply had the misfortune to live in the path of destruction.

The oppression of the peasantry is the theme of this engraving published in the mid-seventeenth century: "This noble is the spider and the peasant the fly." The poor man is handing over goods and money to the fat milord, who says, "You must pay or serve." The peasant replies, "To all masters, all honors."

By the middle of the seventeenth century, a European crisis was taking shape, though its timing and forms differed from place to place. Rural protests, like grain riots and mob assaults on local institutions, had a long history in all of the European states. Popular revolt was not the product of mindless despair, but rather the natural form of political action for those who fell outside the institutionalized political process. Bread riots and tax revolts became increasingly common in the early seventeenth century. More significantly, as the focus of discontent moved from local institutions to the state, the forms of revolt changed. So, too, did the participants. Members of the political elite began to formulate their own grievances against the expansion of state power. A theory of resistance, first developed in the French wars of religion, came to be applied to political tyranny and posed a direct challenge to the idea of the divine right of kings. By the 1640s, all of these forces had converged, and rebellion exploded across the Continent. In Spain, the ancient kingdoms of Catalonia and Portugal asserted their independence from Castilian rule; in France, members of the aristocracy rose against a child monarch and his regent. In Italy, revolts rocked Naples and Sicily. In England, a constitutional crisis gave way to civil war, and then to the first political revolution in European history.

The Need to Resist

Europeans lived more precariously in the seventeenth century than in any period since the Black Death. One benchmark of crisis was population decline. In the Mediterranean, Spain's population fell from 8.5 to 7 million and Italy's population from 13 to 11 million. The ravages of the Thirty Years' War were most clearly felt in central Europe: Germany lost nearly a third of its people, Bohemia nearly half. Northwestern Europe—England, the Netherlands, and France—was hardest hit in the first half of the century, and only gradually recovered by 1700. Population decline had many caus-

The Plague in Milan, a painting by Caspar Crayer of the seventeenth-century Flemish school. The victims of the epidemic are being consoled by a priest.

European Population Data (in millions)

Year	1550	1575	1600	1625	1650	1675	1700
England	3		4	4.5		5.8	5.8
France		20					19.3
Italy	11	13	13	13	12	11.5	12.5
Russia	9		11	8	9.5	13	16
Spain	6.3		7.6		5.2		7
All Europe	85	95	100	100	80	90	100

es and, rather remarkably, direct casualties from warfare were a very small component. The indirect effects of war, the disruption of agriculture, and the spread of disease were far more devastating. Spain alone lost a half million people at the turn of the century and another half million between 1647 and 1652. Severe outbreaks of plague in 1625 and in 1665 hit England, while France endured three consecutive years of epidemics, from 1629 to 1631.

All sectors of the European economy, from agriculture to trade, stagnated or declined in the early seventeenth century. Not surprisingly, peasants were hardest hit. The surplus from good harvests did not remain in rural communities to act as a buffer for bad ones. Tens of thousands died during the two great subsistence crises in the late 1620s and the late 1640s. Predictably, acute economic crisis led to rural revolt. As the French peasants reeled from visitations of plague, frost, and floods, the French state was raising the taille, the tax that fell most heavily on the lower orders. A series of French rural revolts in the late 1630s focused on opposition to tax increases. The Nu-Pieds—"the barefooted"—rose against changes in the salt tax; others rose against new levies on wine. These revolts began in the same way: with the murder of a local tax official, the organization of a peasant militia, and the recruitment of local clergy and notables. The rebels forced temporary concessions from local authorities, but they never achieved lasting reforms. Each revolt ended with the reimposition of order by the state. In England the largest rural protests, like the Midland Revolt of 1607, centered on opposition to the enclosure of grain fields and their conversion to pasture.

The most spectacular popular uprisings occurred in Spanish-occupied Italy. In the spring of 1647 the Sicilian city of Palermo exploded under the pressure of a disastrous harvest, rising food prices, and relentless taxation. A city of 130,000 inhabitants, Palermo imported nearly all of its foodstuffs. As grain prices rose, the city government subsidized the price of bread, running up huge debts in the process. When the town governors could no longer afford the subsidies, they decided to reduce the size of the loaf rather than increase its price. This did not fool the women of the city, who rioted when the first undersized loaves were placed on sale. Soon the entire city was in revolt. "Long live the king and down with taxes!" became the rebel slogan. Commoners who were not part of the urban power structure led the revolt in Palermo. For a time they achieved the abolition of Spanish taxes on basic foodstuffs. Their success provided the model for a similar uprising in Naples, the largest city in Europe. The Neapolitan revolt began in 1647 after the Spanish placed a tax on fruit. A crowd gathered to protest the new imposition, burned the customs house, and murdered several local officials. The protesters were led first by a fisherman and then by a blacksmith, and again the rebels achieved the temporary suspension of Spanish taxation. But neither of the Italian urban revolts could attract support from the local governors or the nobility. Both uprisings were eventually crushed.

The Right to Resist

Rural and urban revolts by members of the lower orders of European society were doomed to failure. Not only did the state control vast military resources, but it could count on the loyalty of the governing classes to suppress local disorder. It was only when local elites rebelled and joined their social and political discontent to the economic grievances of the peasants that the state faced a genuine crisis. Traditionally, aristocratic rebellion focused on the legitimacy rather than the power of the state. Claimants to the throne initiated civil wars for the prize of the crown. By the early seventeenth century, however, hereditary monarchy was too firmly entrenched to be threatened by aristocratic rebellions. When Elizabeth I of England died without an heir, the throne passed to her cousin, James I, without even a murmur of discontent. The assassination of Henry IV in 1610 left a child on the French throne, yet it provoked little more than intrigue over which aristocratic faction would advise him. The principles of hereditary monarchy and the divine right of kings laid an unshakable foundation for royal legitimacy. But if the monarch's right to rule could no longer be challenged, was the method of rule equally unassailable? Were subjects bound to their sovereign in all cases whatsoever?

Luther and Calvin had preached a doctrine of passive obedience. Magistrates ruled by divine will and must be obeyed in all things, they argued. Both left a

The execution of François Ravaillac, the assassin of Henry IV of France.

tiny crack in the door of absolute submission, however, by recognizing the right of lesser magistrates to resist their superiors if divine law was violated. It was during the French civil wars that a broader theory of resistance began to develop. In attempting to defend themselves from accusations that they were rebels, a number of Huguenot writers responded with an argument that accepted the divine right of kings but limited royal power. They claimed that kings were placed on earth by God to uphold piety and justice. When they failed to do so, lesser magistrates were obliged to resist them. As God would not institute tyranny, oppressive monarchs could not be acting by divine right. Therefore, the king who violated divine law could be punished. In the most influential of these writings, *A Defense of Liberty Against Tyrants* (1579), Philippe Duplessis-Mornay (1549–1623) took the critical next step and argued that the king who violated the law of the land could also be resisted.

In the writings of both Huguenot and Dutch Protestants there remained strict limits to this right to resist. These authors accepted all the premises of divine-right theory and restricted resistance to other divinely ordained magistrates. Obedience tied society together at all levels, and loosening any of the knots might unravel everything. In fact, one crucial binding had already come loose when the arguments used to justify resistance in matters of religion came to be applied to matters of state. Logic soon drove the argument further. If it was the duty of lesser magistrates to resist monarchical tyranny, why was it not the duty of

all citizens to do so? This was a question posed not by a Protestant rebel, but by a Jesuit professor, Juan de Mariana (1536–1624). In *The King and the Education of the King* (1598), Mariana described how human government developed from the need of individuals to have leaders to act for their convenience and well-being. These magistrates were established by the people and then legitimated by God. Magistrates were nothing other than the people's representatives, and if it was the duty of magistrates to resist the tyranny of monarchs, then it must also be the duty of every individual citizen. "If the sacred fatherland is falling into ruins, he who tries to kill the tyrant will be acting in no ways unjustly."

Mariana was careful to specify that only the most willful and deliberate lawbreakers were actually tyrants. He also advocated the use of national assemblies rather than individual assassins to make the decision to punish them. But there was no escaping the implications of his argument. If anyone could judge the conduct of kings, then there would be no standards of judgment. As Cardinal Richelieu observed succinctly: "Tyranny is monarchy misliked." In 1605 a Catholic conspiracy to murder James I of England was foiled by government agents at the last moment. In 1610 a religious fanatic assassinated Henry IV of France. The right of individuals to resist tyrants was rapidly developing into the right of subjects to overthrow their monarchs.

In fact, there remained one more vital link in the chain. This was supplied by the great English poet John Milton (1608–74) in his defense of the English Revolution. Milton built upon traditional resistance theory as it had developed over the previous fifty years. Kings were instituted by the people to uphold piety and justice. Lesser magistrates had the right to resist monarchs. An unjust king forfeited his divine right and was to be punished as any ordinary citizen. In *The Tenure of Kings and Magistrates* (1649), Milton expanded upon the conventional idea that society was formed by a covenant, or contract, between ruler and ruled. The king in his coronation oath promised to uphold the laws of the land and rule for the benefit of his subjects. The subjects promised to obey. Failure by either side to meet obligations broke the contract.

By the middle of the seventeenth century, resistance theory provided the intellectual justification for a number of different attacks on monarchical authority. In 1640 simultaneous rebellions in the ancient kingdoms of Portugal and Catalonia threatened the Spanish monarchy. The Portuguese successfully dissolved the rather artificial bonds that had been created by Philip II and resumed their separate national identity. Catalonia, the easternmost province of Spain, which Ferdinand of Aragon had brought to the union of crowns in the fifteenth century, presented a more serious challenge. Throughout the 1620s Catalonia, with its rich Mediterranean city of Barcelona, had consistently rebuffed Olivares's attempts to consolidate the Spanish provinces. The Catalonian Cortes—the representative institution of the towns—refused to make even small contributions to the Union of Arms or to successive appeals for emergency tax increases. Catalonian leaders feared that these demands were only the thin edge of the wedge. They did not want their province to go the way of Castile, where taxation was as much an epidemic as plague.

Catalonia relied on its ancient laws to fend off demands for contributions to the Spanish military effort. But soon the province was embroiled in the French war, and Olivares was forced to bring troops into Catalonia. The presence of the soldiers and their conduct inflamed the local population. In the spring of 1640 an unconnected series of peasant uprisings took place. Soldiers and royal officials were slain, and the Spanish viceroy of the province was murdered. But the violence was not directed only against outsiders. Attacks on wealthy citizens raised the specter of social revolt.

At this point a peasant uprising broadened into a provincial rebellion. The political leaders of Barcelona not only decided to approve the rebellion, they decided to lead it. They declared that Philip IV had violated the fundamental laws of Catalonia and that as a consequence their allegiance to the crown of Spain was dis-

solved. Instead they turned to Louis XIII of France, offering him sovereignty if he would preserve their liberties. In fact, the Catalonians simply exchanged a devil they knew for one they did not. The French happily sent troops into Barcelona to repel a Spanish attempt to crush the rebellion, and now two armies occupied Catalonia. The Catalonian rebellion lasted for twelve years. When the Spanish finally took Barcelona in 1652, both rebels and ruler were exhausted from the struggle.

The revolt of the Catalonians posed a greater external threat to the Spanish monarchy than it did an internal one. In contrast, the French Fronde, an aristocratic rebellion that began in 1648, was more directly a challenge to the underlying authority of the state. It too began in response to fiscal crises brought on by war. Throughout the 1640s the French state had tottered on the edge of bankruptcy. It had used every means of creative financing that its ministers could devise, mortgaging as much of the future as anyone would buy. Still, it was necessary to raise traditional taxes and institute new ones. The first tactic revived peasant revolts, especially in the early years of the decade; the second led to the Fronde.

The Fronde was a rebellion against the regency government of Louis XIV (1643–1715), who was only four years old when he inherited the French throne. His mother, Anne of Austria (1601–66), ruled as regent with the help of her Italian advisor, Cardinal Mazarin (1602–61). In the circumstances of war, agricultural crisis, and financial stringency, no regency government was going to be popular, but Anne and Mazarin made the worst of a bad situation. They initiated new taxes on officeholders, Parisian landowners, and the nobility. Soon all three united against them, led by the Parlement of Paris, the highest court in the land, in which new decrees of taxation had to be registered. When the Parlement refused to register a number of the new taxes proposed by the government and soon insisted on the right to control the crown's financial policy, Anne and Mazarin struck back by arresting a number of leading members of the Parlement. But in 1648 barricades went up in Paris, and the court, along with the nine-year-old king, fled the capital. Quickly the Fronde—which took its name from the slingshots that children used to hurl stones at carriages—became an aristocratic revolt aimed not at the king, but at his advisers. Demands for Mazarin's resignation, the removal of the new taxes, and greater participation in government by nobles and Parlement were coupled with profuse statements of loyalty to the king.

The duc de Condé, leader of the Parisian insurgents, courted Spanish aid against Mazarin's forces, and the cardinal was forced to make concessions in order to prevent a Spanish invasion of France. The leaders of the Fronde agreed that the crown must overhaul its finances and recognize the rights of the administrative nobility to participate in formulating royal policy, but they had no concrete proposals to accomplish either aim. Nor could they control the deteriorating political situation in Paris and a number of provincial capitals where urban and rural riots followed the upper-class attack upon the state. The catastrophic winter of 1652, with its combination of harvest failure, intense cold, and epidemic disease, brought the crisis to a head. Louis XIV was declared old enough to rule and his forces recaptured Paris, where he was welcomed as a savior. Born of frustration, fear, and greed, the Fronde accomplished little. It demonstrated only that the French aristocracy remained an independent force in politics. Like the Catalonian revolt, it revealed the fragility of the absolute state on the one hand, yet its underlying stability on the other.

The English Civil War

On the surface, it is difficult to understand why the most profound challenge to monarchical authority took place in England. Among the nations of Europe, England alone enjoyed peace in the early seventeenth century. Except for a brief period around 1620, the English economy sputtered along. The monarchy itself was stable. James I had succeeded his cousin Elizabeth I without challenge and already had as many children as the Tudors had produced in nearly a century.

James I was not a lovable monarch, but he was capable, astute, and generous. In the eyes of his critics he had two great faults: he succeeded a legend and he was Scottish. There was little he could do about either. Elizabeth I had ruled England successfully for over forty years. As the economy soured and the state tilted toward bankruptcy in the 1590s, the queen remained above criticism. She sold off royal lands worth thousands of pounds and ran up huge debts at the turn of the century, yet the gleaming myth of the glorious virgin queen tarnished not the least bit. When she died, the general population wept openly and the governing elite breathed a collective sigh of relief. There was so much to be done to set things right.

At first James I endeared himself to the English gentry and aristocracy by showering them with the gift of social elevation. On his way to London from Scotland, the first of the Stuart kings knighted thousands of gentlemen who had waited in vain for favor from the queen. He promoted peers and created new titles to meet the pent-up demands of decades of stinginess. But he showered favor equally on his own countrymen, members of his royal Scottish court who accompanied him to England. A strong strain of ethnic prejudice combined with the disappointed hopes of English courtiers to generate immediate hostility to the new regime. If Elizabeth could do no wrong, James could do little right. Although he relied upon Elizabeth's most trusted ministers to guide state business, James was soon plunged into financial and political difficulties. He never escaped from either.

His financial problems resulted directly from the fact that the tax base of the English monarchy was undervalued. For decades the monarchy had staved off a crisis by selling lands that had been confiscated from the Church in the mid-sixteenth century. But this solution reduced the crown's long-term revenues and made it dependent on extraordinary grants of taxation from Parliament. Royal demands for money were met by parliamentary demands for political reform, and these differing objectives provoked unintentional political controversies in the 1620s. The most significant, in 1628, during the reign of Charles I, led to the formulation of the Petition of Right, which restated the traditional English freedoms from arbitrary arrest and imprisonment (habeas corpus), nonparliamentary taxation, and the confiscation of property by martial law.

Religious problems mounted on top of economic and political difficulties. Demands were made for thoroughgoing church reforms by groups and individuals who had little in common apart from the name given to them by their detractors: Puritans. One of the most contentious issues raised by Puritans was the survival in the Anglican church of the Catholic hierarchy of archbishops and bishops. They demanded the abolition of this episcopal form of government and its replacement with a presbyterial system similar to that in Scotland, in which congregations nominated their own representatives to a national assembly. As the king was the supreme head of the English church, an attack upon church structure was an attack upon the monarchy. "No bishop, no king," James I declared as he rejected the first formal attempts at reform. But neither James I nor his son, Charles I, opposed religious reform. They too wanted a better educated clergy, a plain and decorous worship service, and godly citizens. But to achieve their reforms they strengthened episcopal power. In the 1620s Archbishop William Laud (1573–1645) rose to power in the English church by espousing a Calvinism so moderate that many denied it was Calvinism at all. Laud preached the beauty of holiness and strove to reintroduce decoration in the church and a formal

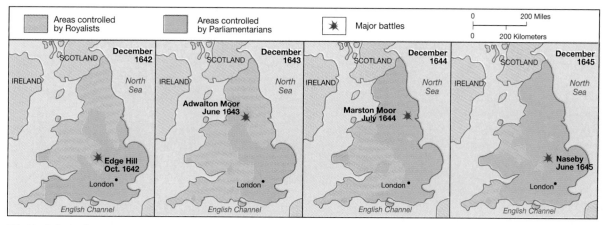

The English Civil War

decorum in the service. One of Laud's first projects after he was appointed archbishop of Canterbury was to establish a consistent divine service in England and Scotland by creating new prayer books.

It fell to the unfortunate dean of St. Giles Cathedral in Edinburgh to introduce the new Scottish prayer book in 1637. The reaction was immediate: someone threw a stool at his head and dozens of women screamed that "popery" was being brought to Scotland. There were riots by citizens and resistance to the use of the new prayer book by clergy and the nobility. To Charles I the opposition was rebellion, and he began to raise forces to suppress it. But Scottish soldiers were far more determined to preserve their religious practice than were English soldiers to impose the king's. By the end of 1640, a Scottish army had successfully invaded England.

Now the fiscal and political problems of the Stuart monarchs came into play. For eleven years Charles I had managed to do what he was in theory supposed to do: live from his own revenues. He had accomplished this by a combination of economy and the revival of ancient feudal rights that struck hard at the governing classes. He levied fines for unheard-of offenses, expanded traditional taxes, and added a brutal efficiency to the collection of revenue. While these expedients sufficed during peacetime, now that an army had to be raised and a war fought, Charles I was again dependent upon grants from Parliament, which he reluctantly summoned in 1640.

The Long Parliament, which met in November 1640 and sat for thirteen years, saw little urgency in levying taxes to repel the Scots. After all, the Scots were resisting Laud's religious innovations, and there were many Englishmen who believed that they should be resisted. More to the point, members of Parliament had

a host of political grievances to be redressed before they granted the king his money. Parliament proposed a number of constitutional reforms that Charles I reluctantly accepted. The Long Parliament would not be dismissed without its own consent. In the future, Parliaments would be summoned once every three years. Due process in common law would be observed, and the ancient taxes that the crown had revived would be abolished. To show its seriousness of purpose, Parliament, as the highest court in the land, tried and executed Charles's leading political adviser, the Earl of Strafford, and imprisoned Archbishop Laud.

At first Charles I could do nothing but bide his time and accept these assaults on his power and authority. Once he had crushed the Scots he would be able to bargain from a position of strength. But as the months passed, it became clear that Parliament had no intention of providing him with money or forces. Rather, the members sought to negotiate with the Scots themselves and to continue to demand concessions from the king as long as the Scottish threat remained. By the end of 1641, Charles's patience had worn thin. He bungled an attempt to arrest the leaders of the House of Commons, but he successfully spirited his wife and children out of London. Then he too left the capital and headed north where, in the summer of 1642, he raised the royal standard and declared the leaders of Parliament rebels and traitors. England was plunged into civil war.

Parliament had finally pushed too hard, and its members now found themselves in the unprecedented situation of having to fight a war against their sovereign, a war that few of them wanted and that hardly anyone believed they could win. One of the Parliament's generals summed up the futility of the situation: "If we defeat the king ninety-nine times, yet still he is king. But if he defeat us once we will all be hanged as

Charles I turning from his panic-stricken troops at the battle of Naseby. Cromwell's victory in the battle ended the civil war and sealed Charles's fate.

traitors." Nevertheless, there were strong passions on both sides. Parliamentarians believed that they were fighting to defend their religion, their liberties, and the rule of law. Royalists believed they were fighting to defend their monarch, their church, and social stability. After nearly three years of inconclusive fighting, in June 1645 Parliament won a decisive victory at Naseby and brought the war to an end the following summer. The king was in captivity, bishops had been abolished, a Presbyterian church had been established, and limitations were placed on royal power. All that remained necessary to end three years of civil war was the king's agreement to abide by the judgment of battle.

But Charles I had no intention of surrendering either his religion or his authority. Despite the rebels' successes, they could not rule without him, and he would concede nothing as long as opportunities to maneuver remained. In 1647 there were opportunities galore. The war had proved ruinously expensive to Parliament. It owed enormous sums to the Scots, to its own soldiers, and to the governors of London. Each of these elements had its own objectives in a final settlement of the war, and they were not altogether compatible. London feared the parliamentary army, unpaid and camped dangerously close to the capital. The Scots and the English Presbyterians in Parliament feared that the religious settlement already made would be sacrificed by those known as Independents, who desired a more decentralized church. The Independents feared that they would be persecuted just as harshly by the Presbyterians as they had been by the king. In fact, the war had settled nothing.

The English Revolution

Charles I happily played both ends against the middle until the army decisively ended the game. In June 1647 soldiers kidnaped the king and demanded that Parliament pay their arrears, protect them from legal retribution, and recognize their service to the nation. Those in Parliament who opposed the army's intervention were impeached, and when London Presbyterians rose up against the army's show of force, troops moved in to occupy the city. The civil war, which had come so close to resolution in 1647, had now become a military revolution. Religious and political radicals flocked to the army and encouraged the soldiers to support their programs and resist disbandment. New fighting broke out in 1648 as Charles encouraged his supporters to resume the war. But forces under the command of Sir Thomas Fairfax (1612–71) and Oliver Cromwell (1599–1658) easily crushed the royalist uprisings in England and Scotland. The army now demanded that Charles I be brought to justice for his treacherous conduct both before and during the war. When the major-

A Short, Sharp Shock

Charles I was executed at Westminster on a bitter January afternoon in 1649. This excerpt comes from an eyewitness account of his last moments. Charles, who was accompanied on the scaffold by the bishop of London, discovered that the chopping block was very short so that he could be held down if he resisted.

And to the executioner he said, "I shall say but very short prayers, and when I thrust out my hands—"

Then he called to the bishop for his cap, and having put it on, asked the executioner, "Does my hair trouble you?" who desired him to put it all under his cap; which, as he was doing by the help of the bishop and the executioner, he turned to the bishop, and said, "I have a good cause, and a gracious God on my side."

The bishop said, "There is but one stage more, which, though turbulent and troublesome, yet is a very short one. You may consider it will soon carry you a very great way; it will carry you from earth to heaven; and there you shall find to your great joy the prize you hasten to, a crown of glory."

The king adjoins, "I go from a corruptible to an incorruptible crown; where no disturbance can be, no disturbance in the world."

The bishop. "You are exchanged from a temporal to an eternal crown—a good exchange."

Then the king asked the executioner, "Is my hair well?" . . . and looking upon the block, said . . . "You must set it fast."

The executioner. "It is fast, sir."

King. "It might have been a little higher."

Executioner. "It can be no higher, sir."

King. "When I put out my hands this way, then—"

Then having said a few words to himself, as he stood, with hands and eyes lifted up, immediately stooping down he laid his neck upon the block; and the executioner, again putting his hair under his cap, his Majesty, thinking he had been going to strike, bade him, "Stay for the sign."

Executioner. "Yes, I will, an it please your Majesty."

After a very short pause, his Majesty stretching forth his hands, the executioner at one blow severed his head from his body; which, being held up and showed to the people, was with his body put into a coffin covered with black velvet and carried into his lodging.

His blood was taken up by divers persons for different ends: by some as trophies of their villainy; by others as relics of a martyr; and in some hath had the same effect, by the blessing of God, which was often found in his sacred touch when living.

---

ity in Parliament refused, still hoping against hope to reach an accommodation with the king, the soldiers again acted decisively. In December 1648 army regiments were sent to London to purge the two houses of Parliament of those who opposed the army's demands. The remaining members, contemptuously called the Rump Parliament, voted to bring the king to trial for his crimes against the liberties of his subjects. On 30 January 1649, Charles I was executed and England was declared to be a commonwealth. (See "'King Charles's Head,'" pp. 500–501.) The monarchy and the House of Lords were abolished, and the nation was to be governed by what was left of the membership of the House of Commons.

For four years the members of the Rump Parliament struggled with proposals for a new constitution while balancing the demands of moderate and radical reformers and an increasingly hostile army. It achieved little other than to raise the level of frustration. In 1653 Oliver Cromwell, with the support of the army's senior officers, forcibly dissolved the Rump and became the leader of the revolutionary government. At first he ruled along with a Parliament handpicked from among the supporters of the commonwealth. When Cromwell's Parliament proved no more capable of governing than had the Rump, a written constitution, The Instrument of Government (1653), established a new polity. Cromwell was given the title Lord Protector, and he was to rule along with a freely elected Parliament and an administrative body known as the Council of State.

Cromwell was able to hold the revolutionary cause together through the force of his own personality. A member of the lesser landed elite who had opposed the

"King Charles's Head"

They could have killed him quietly: the executioners slipping away silently in the night, unauthorized, unknown. It was the quickest way, and it would end all doubts. Since June 1647, Charles I had been prisoner of the parliamentary army, and there had been more than one moment in which his elimination would have settled so many vexing problems. They could have let him escape: a small boat, an unlocked door, a guard conveniently asleep. Let him take his chances on the open sea. Let him live out his life in exile. Dangerous, perhaps, but still he would be gone and a new government in the name of the people could get on with creating a new order. They could have done it quietly.

Instead, the leaders of Parliament and the army decided on a trial, a public presentation of charges against the king. A high court of justice, enforcing the laws of England, would try its king for treason against the state. The logic was simple: If Parliament had fought for the preservation of the liberties of all Englishmen, then they could only proceed against the king by law. If they followed any other course, then they were usurpers, ruling by might rather than law. But if the logic was simple, everything else was hopelessly complex. English law was a system of precedents, one case stacked upon another to produce the weighty judgments of what was lawful. Never had there been a treason case like this one. Indeed, how could the king commit treason? How could he violate his own allegiance?

Nor was it clear what court had jurisdiction over this unprecedented case. The royal judges would have no part of it; neither would the House of Lords. The House of Commons was forced to create its own high court of justice, 135 supporters of the parliamentary cause drawn from its own members, from the army, and from among the leading citizens of London. Barely half attended any of the sessions. Judge John Bradshaw, who presided over two provincial royal courts, was chosen to preside at the king's trial after several of his more distinguished colleagues tactfully declined the post. Bradshaw took the precaution of lining his hat with lead against the chance that he would be shot at from the galleries rather than the floor.

These shortcomings did not deter the leaders of the parliamentary cause. These were unprecedented times, and the ossified procedures of lawyers and law courts could not be allowed to detract from the undeniable justice of their cause. Charles I had committed treason against his nation. He had declared war on his people. He had brought Irish and Scottish armies into England to repress Parliament, and when that had failed he had negotiated with French, Danish, and Dutch troops for the same purpose. Even when he had been defeated in battle, when the judgment of God was clear for all to see: even then he plotted and he tricked. His lies were revealed by his own hand, his captured correspondence detailing how he intended to double-cross those to whom he swore he would be faithful. Cromwell called him "a man against whom the Lord had witnessed," and the prosecution needed no better testimony than that. If there were no precedents, then this trial would set one.

Nevertheless, the makeshift nature of the court provided the king with his line of attack. If there was to be a public display, then Charles I was determined to turn it to his advantage. Even as his royal palace was being converted into a courtroom and an execution platform was being hastily erected on one of its balconies, even now the king could not conceive that the nation could be governed without him. Royal government had guided England for a millennium, and for all he could see would do so for another.

About the trial itself, he worried not at all. There could be no court in the land that could try its king, no authority but his own that could determine a charge of treason. When it was read out that he was a tyrant and traitor, he burst out laughing: "Remember, I am your king, your lawful king and what sins you bring upon your heads and the judgment of God upon this land, think well upon it," he told his accusers.

The trial began on Saturday, 20 January 1649. Armed soldiers in battle dress cleared the floor of the large chamber. Curious onlookers packed the galleries. Despite the fact that all former royalists had been ordered out of the city before the trial began, the king had more than one supporter well placed to heckle the commissioners. The king wore the enormous golden star of the Order of the Garter on his cloak but was allowed no other symbol of royalty to overawe his accusers.

The charge of "treason and high misdemeanors"

had been carefully prepared. The king was accused of making war on his people "whereby much innocent blood of the free people of this nation hath been spilt." When the resounding indictment concluded, all eyes turned toward Charles I. Now he would have to answer the charge, guilty or not guilty, and in answering show the line of his defense. But the king chose a different strategy. Rather than answer the charge, he questioned the authority of the court. "I would know by what power I am called hither, a king cannot be tried by any superior jurisdiction here on earth." This was the weakest point of the parliamentary strategy. Judge Bradshaw could only assert that the court represented the free people of England. But Charles was relentless. He demanded precedents and refused to be silenced by the assertion that his objections were overruled.

The prosecutors had prepared a case against the king and were ready to call their witnesses. They hoped to place the king's evil conduct before the eyes of the nation. But in English law, a defendant who refused to plead was presumed to have pleaded guilty. Thus the king's trial ended as soon as it had begun. After three fruitless sessions and much behind-the-scenes maneuvering, it was decided that the king should be condemned and sentenced to die. On 27 January, Judge Bradshaw appeared in the scarlet robes of justice and issued the sentence. Charles had prepared a statement for maximum effect and waited patiently to deliver it. Now it was the king's turn to be surprised. After pronouncing sentence, Bradshaw and the commissioners rose from the bench. "Will you not hear me a word, Sir," called a flustered Charles I. "No," replied the judge. "Guards, withdraw your prisoner."

Tuesday, 30 January, dawned cold and clear. It had been a bitter winter. Charles put on two shirts so that if he trembled from the cold it would not be interpreted as fear. In fact, he made a very good end. He spoke briefly and to the point, denying that he had acted against the true interests and rights of his subjects. Then he lay down on the platform, placed his head upon the block, and prayed. As the axe fell, one witness recorded, "such a groan as I never heard before and hope never to hear again" broke forth from the crowd. The English Revolution had begun.

arbitrary policies of Charles I, he was a devout Puritan who believed in a large measure of religious toleration for Christians. As both a member of Parliament and a senior officer in the army, he had been able to temper the claims of each when they conflicted. Cromwell saw God's hand directing England toward a more glorious future, and he believed that his own actions were divinely ordained: "No man climbs higher than he that knows not whither he goes." Although many urged him to accept the crown of England and begin a new monarchy, Cromwell steadfastly held out for a government in which fundamental authority resided in Parliament. Until his death he defended the achievements of the revolution and held its conflicting constituents together.

But a sense that only a single person could effectively rule a state remained too strong for the reforms of the revolutionary regimes to have much chance of success. When Cromwell died in 1658 it was only natural that his eldest son, Richard, should be proposed as the

Allegorical view of Cromwell as savior of England. Babylon and Error are trampled under his feet. On the pillar at the right, England, Scotland, and Ireland pay him homage, and the left pillar enumerates the legal bases of his power.

new Lord Protector despite the fact that Richard had very little experience in either military or civil affairs. Nor did he have the sense of purpose that was his father's greatest source of strength. Without an individual to hold the movement together, the revolution fell apart. In 1659 the army again intervened in civil affairs, dismissing the recently elected Parliament and calling for the restoration of the monarchy to provide stability to the state. After a period of negotiation in which the king agreed to a general amnesty with only a few exceptions, the Stuarts were restored when Charles II (1649–85) took the throne in 1660.

Twenty years of civil war and revolution had had their effect. Parliament became a permanent part of civil government and now had to be managed rather than ignored. Royal power over taxation and religion was curtailed, though in fact Parliament proved more vigorous in suppressing religious dissent than the monarchy ever had. England was to be a reformed Protestant state, although there remained much dispute about what constituted reform. Absolute monarchy had become constitutional monarchy, with the threat of revolution behind the power of Parliament and the threat of anarchy behind the power of the crown.

Both threats proved potent in 1685 when James II (1685–88) came to the throne. A declared Catholic, James attempted to use his power of appointment to foil the constraints that Parliament imposed on him. He elevated Catholics to leading posts in the military and in the central government and began a campaign to pack a new Parliament with his supporters. This proved too much for the governing classes, who entered into negotiations with William, Prince of Orange, husband of Mary Stuart, James's eldest daughter. In 1688 William landed in England with a small force. Without support, James II fled to France, the English throne was declared vacant, and William and Mary were proclaimed king and queen of England. There was little bloodshed in England and little threat of social disorder, and the event soon came to be called the Glorious Revolution. Its achievements were set down in the Declaration of Rights (1689), which was presented to William and Mary before they took the throne. The Declaration reasserted the fundamental principles of constitutional monarchy as they had developed over the previous half-century. Security of property and the regularity of Parliaments were guaranteed. The Toleration Act (1689) granted religious freedom to nearly all groups of Protestants. The liberties of the subject and the rights of the sovereign were to be in balance.

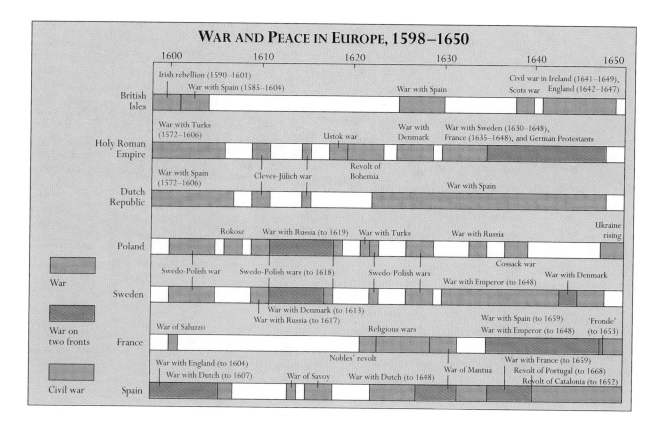

WAR AND PEACE IN EUROPE, 1598–1650

The events of 1688 in England reversed a trend toward increasing power on the part of the Stuarts. This second episode of resistance resulted in the development of a unique form of government that a century later would spawn dozens of imitators. John Locke (1632–1704) was the theorist of the Revolution of 1689. He was heir to the century-old debate on resistance, and he carried the doctrine to a new plateau. In *Two Treatises on Civil Government* (1690), Locke developed the contract theory of government. Political society was a compact that individuals entered into freely for their own well-being. It was designed to maintain each person's natural rights—life, liberty, and property. Natural rights were inherent in individuals; they could not be given away. The contract between rulers and subjects was an agreement for the protection of natural rights. "Arbitrary power cannot consist with the ends of society and government. Men would not quit the freedom of the state of nature were it not to preserve their lives, liberties, and fortunes and by stated rules to secure their peace and happiness."

When rulers acted arbitrarily, they were to be deposed by their subjects, preferably in the relatively peaceful manner in which James II had been replaced by William III.

The efforts of European monarchies to centralize their power came at the expense of the Church, the aristocracy, and the localities. It was a struggle that took place over decades and was not accomplished easily. In France, the Fronde was an aristocratic backlash; in Spain, the revolt of the Catalonians pitted the Castilian crown against a proud ethnic province. In England, a civil war fought to prevent the encroachments of the crown against the rights of the community gave way to a bloody revolution that combined religious and constitutional grievances—the excesses of monarchy were succeeded by the excesses of parliamentary rule. But the lesson learned by the English ruling elites was that for a nation to enjoy the benefits of a powerful central authority, it was necessary to restrain that authority. The Glorious Revolution of 1689 helped create a constitutional balance between ruler and ruled.

The Zenith of the Royal State

The crises of midcentury tested the mettle of the royal states. Over the long term, these crises had two different consequences. First, they provided a check to the exercise of royal power. Fear of recurring rebellions had a chilling effect upon policy, especially taxation. Reforms of financial administration, long overdue, were one of the themes of the later seventeenth century. Even as royal government strengthened itself, it remained concerned about the impact of its policies. Second, the memory of rebellion served to control the ambitions of factious noblemen and town oligarchs.

If nothing else, these episodes of opposition to the rising royal states made clear the universal desire for stable government, which was seen as the responsibility of both subjects and rulers. By the second half of the seventeenth century, effective government was the byword of the royal state. As Louis XIV proclaimed, rule was a trade that had to be constantly studied and practiced. The natural advantages of monarchy had to be merged with the interests of the state's citizens and their desires for wealth, safety, and honor. After so much chaos and instability, the monarchy had to be elevated above the fray of day-to-day politics; it had to become a symbol of the power and glory of the nation. Control no longer meant the greedy grasp of royal officials but rather their practiced guidance of affairs.

In England, Holland, and Sweden, a form of constitutional monarchy developed in which rulers shared power, in varying degrees, with other institutions of state. In England it was Parliament, in Holland the town oligarchies, and in Sweden the nobility. But in most other states in Europe there developed a pure form of royal government known as absolutism. Absolute monarchy revived the divine-right theories of kingship and added to them a cult of the personality of the ruler. Absolutism was practiced in states as dissimilar as Denmark, Brandenburg-Prussia, and Russia. It reached its zenith in France under Louis XIV, the most powerful of the seventeenth-century monarchs.

The Nature of Absolute Monarchy

Locke's theory of contract provided one solution to the central problem of seventeenth-century government: how to balance the monarch's right to command and the subjects' duty to obey. By establishing a constitutional monarchy in which power was shared between the ruler and a representative assembly of subjects, England found one path out of this thicket. But it was not a

The title page of the first edition of Thomas Hobbes's Leviathan, *published in 1651. The huge figure, composed of many tiny human beings, symbolizes the surrender of individual human rights to those of the state.*

path that many others could follow. The English solution was most suited to a state that was largely immune from invasion and land war. Constitutional government required a higher level of political participation of citizens than did an absolute monarchical one. Greater participation in turn meant greater freedom of expression, greater toleration of religious minorities, and greater openness in the institutions of government. All were dangerous. The price that England paid was a half-century of governmental instability.

The alternative to constitutional monarchy was absolute monarchy. It too found its greatest theorist in England. Thomas Hobbes (1588–1679) was one of many Englishmen who went into exile in France during the course of the English civil wars. In his greatest work, *Leviathan* (1651), Hobbes argued that before civil society had been formed, humans lived in a savage state of nature, "in a war of every man against every man." This was a ghastly condition without morality or law—"the notions of right and wrong, of justice and injustice have there no place." People came together to form a government for the most basic of all purposes: self-preservation. Without government they were condemned to a life that was "solitary, poor, nasty, brutish, and short." To escape the state of nature, individuals pooled their power and granted it to a ruler. The terms of the Hobbesian contract were simple. Rulers agreed to rule; subjects agreed to obey. When the contract was intact, people ceased to live in a state of nature. When it was broken, they returned to it. With revolts, rebellions, and revolutions erupting in all parts of Europe, Hobbes's state of nature never seemed very far away.

For most states of Europe in the later seventeenth century, absolute monarchy became not only a necessity but an ideal. The consolidation of power in the hands of the divinely ordained monarch who nevertheless ruled according to principles of law and justice was seen as the perfect form of government. Absolutism was an expression of control rather than of power. If the state was sometimes pictured as a horse, the absolute monarch gripped the reins more tightly than the whip. "Many writers have tried to confound absolute government with arbitrary government. But no two things could be more unlike," wrote Bishop Jacques Bossuet (1627–1704), who extolled absolutism

in France. The absolute ruler ruled in the interests of his people: "The prince is the public person, the whole state is included in him, the will of all the people is enclosed within his own."

The main features of absolute monarchy were all designed to extend royal control. As in the early seventeenth century, the person of the monarch was revered. Courts grew larger and more lavish in an effort to enhance the glory of the monarchy, and thereby of the state. "*L'état, c'est moi*"—"I am the state"—Louis XIV was supposed to have said. No idea better expresses absolutism's connection between governor and governed. As the king grew in stature, his competitors for power all shrank. Large numbers of nobles were herded together at court under the watchful eye of monarchs who now ruled rather than reigned. The king shed the cloak of his favorites and rolled up his own sleeves to manage state affairs. Representative institutions, especially those that laid claim to control over taxation, were weakened or cast aside for obstructing efficient government and endangering the welfare of the state. Monarchs needed standing armies, permanent forces that could be drilled and trained in the increasingly sophisticated arts of war. Thus the military was expanded and made an integral part of the machinery of government. The military profession developed within nations, gradually replacing mercenary adventurers who had fought for booty rather than for duty.

A CLOSE SHAVE

Peter the Great made many efforts to westernize Russia after his travels in Holland and England. He reformed the navy, built a great seaport at St. Petersburg, and instituted an array of governmental reforms. But nothing was so prominent as or affected ordinary people more than his edicts on beards and clothing.

The tsar labored at the reform of fashions, or, more properly speaking, of dress. Until that time the Russians had always worn long beards, which they cherished and preserved with much care, allowing them to hang down on their bosoms, without even cutting the moustache. With these long beards they wore the hair very short, except the ecclesiastics, who, to distinguish themselves, wore it very long. The tsar, in order to reform that custom, ordered that gentlemen, merchants, and other subjects, except priests and peasants, should each pay a tax of one hundred rubles a year if they wished to keep their beard; the commoners had to pay one kopeck each. Officials were stationed at the gates of the towns to collect that tax, which the Russians regarded as an enormous sin on the part of the tsar and as a thing which tended to the abolition of their religion.

These insinuations, which came from the priests, occasioned the publication of many pamphlets in Moscow, where for that reason alone the tsar was regarded as a tyrant and a pagan; and there were many old Russians who, after having their beards shaved off, saved them preciously, in order to have them placed in their coffins, fearing that they would not be allowed to enter heaven without their beards. As for the young men, they followed the new customs with the more readiness as it made them appear more agreeable to the fair sex.

From the reform in beards we may pass to that of clothes. Their garments, like those of the Orientals, were very long, reaching to the heel. The tsar issued an ordinance abolishing that costume, commanding all the boyars (nobles) and all those who had positions at the court to dress after the French fashion, and likewise to adorn their clothes with gold or silver according to their means. . . .

The same ordinance also provided that in the future women, as well as men, should be invited to entertainments, such as weddings, banquets, and the like, where both sexes should mingle in the same hall, as in Holland and England. It was likewise added that these entertainments should conclude with concerts and dances, but that only those should be admitted who were dressed in English costumes. His Majesty set the example in all these changes.

From De Missy's "Life of Peter."

Yet the absolute state was never as powerful in practice as it was in theory, nor did it ever exist in its ideal shape. Absolutism was always in the making, never quite made. Its success depended upon a strong monarch who knew his own will and could enforce it. It depended upon unity within the state and the absence or ruthless suppression of religious or political minorities. The absolute ruler needed to control information and ideas, to limit criticism of state policy. Ultimately, the absolute state rested upon the will of its citizens to support it. The seventeenth-century state remained a loose confederation of regions, many acquired by conquest, whose loyalty was practical rather than instinctive. There was no state police force to control behavior or attitudes, no newspapers or mass communication to spread propaganda. Censorship might restrict the flow of forbidden books, but it could do little to dam up the current of ideas.

Absolutism in the East

Frederick William, the Great Elector of Brandenburg-Prussia (1640–88), was one of the European princes who made the most effective use of the techniques of absolutism. In 1640 he inherited a scattered and ungovernable collection of territories that had been devastated by the Thirty Years' War. Brandenburg, the richest of his possessions, had lost nearly half of its population. The war had a lasting impact on Frederick William's character. As a child he had hidden in the woods to escape bands of marauding soldiers; as a teenager he had followed to its burial the corpse of Gustavus Adolphus, the man he most admired and wished to emulate. A long stay in Holland during the final stages of the Dutch Revolt impressed on him the importance of a strong army and a strong base of revenue to support it.

Frederick William had neither. In 1640 his forces totaled no more than 2500 men, most of them, including the officers, the dregs of German society. Despite the fact that he was surrounded by powerful neighbors—Sweden and Poland both claimed sovereignty over parts of his inheritance—the territories under his control had no tradition of military taxation. The nobility, known as the Junker, enjoyed immunity from almost all forms of direct taxation, and the towns had no obligation to furnish either men or supplies for military operations beyond their walls. When Frederick William attempted to introduce an excise—the kind of commodity tax on consumption that had so successfully financed the Dutch revolt and the English Revolution—he was initially rebuffed. But military emergency overcame legal precedents. By the 1650s Frederick William had established the excise in the towns, though not on the land.

With the excise as a steady source of revenue, the Great Elector could now create one of the most capable standing armies of the age. The strictest discipline was maintained in the new army, and the Prussian army developed into a feared and efficient fighting machine. Frederick William organized one of the first departments of war to oversee all of the details of the creation

of his army, from housing and supplies to the training of young officer candidates. This department was also responsible for the collection of taxes. By integrating military and civilian government, Frederick William was able to create an efficient state bureaucracy that was particularly responsive in times of crisis. The creation of the Prussian army was the force that led to the creation of the Prussian state.

The same materials that forged the Prussian state led to the transformation of Russia. Soon after the young tsar Peter I (1682–1725) came to the throne, he realized that he could compete with the western states only by learning to play their game. In 1697 Peter visited the West, ostensibly to build an alliance against the Turks but actually to learn as much as he could about Western military technology. He loved novelty and introduced new agricultural products like wine and potatoes to his subjects. When he determined that Russians should no longer wear beards, he took a hand in cutting them off. When he was persuaded of the benefits of dentistry, he practiced it himself on his terrified subjects. His campaign to westernize Russia frequently confused the momentous with the inconsequential, but it had an extraordinary impact at all levels of government and society.

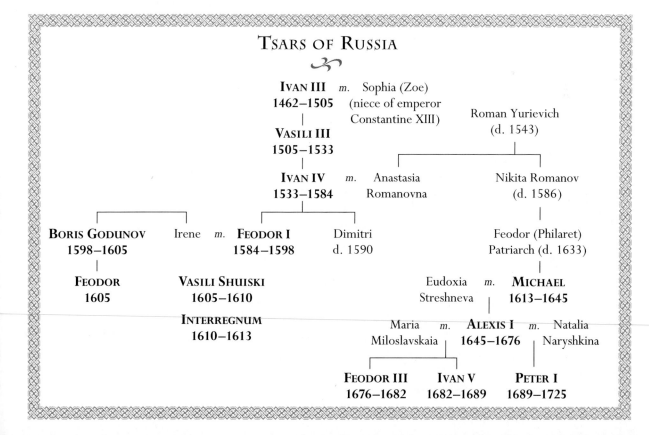

TSARS OF RUSSIA

In his campaign to modernize Russia, Peter the Great declared that the nobles should shear off their beards, which were a symbol of their status. In this illustration, a clean-shaven Peter wields the scissors himself.

Like those of Frederick William, Peter's greatest reforms were military. Peter realized that if Russia were to flourish in a world dominated by war and commerce, it would have to reestablish its hold on the Baltic ports. This meant dislodging the Swedes from the Russian mainland and creating a fleet to protect Russian trade. Neither goal seemed likely. The Swedes were one of the great powers of the age, constant innovators in battlefield tactics and military organization. Peter studied their every campaign. His first wars against the Swedes ended in humiliating defeats, but with each failure came a sharper sense of what was needed to succeed.

First Peter introduced a system of conscription that resulted in the creation of a standing army. Conscripts were branded to inhibit desertion, and a strict discipline was introduced to prepare the soldiers for battle. Peter unified the military command at the top and stratified it in the field. He established promotion based on merit. For the first time, Russian officers were given particular responsibilities to fulfill during both training and battle. Peter created military schools to train cadets for the next generation of officers.

Finally, in 1709, Peter realized his ambitions. At the battle of Poltava, the Russian army routed the Swedes, wounding King Charles XII, annihilating his infantry, and capturing dozens of his leading officers. That night

The battle of Poltava (1709). The defeat of King Charles XII led to the decline of Swedish power in the Baltic.

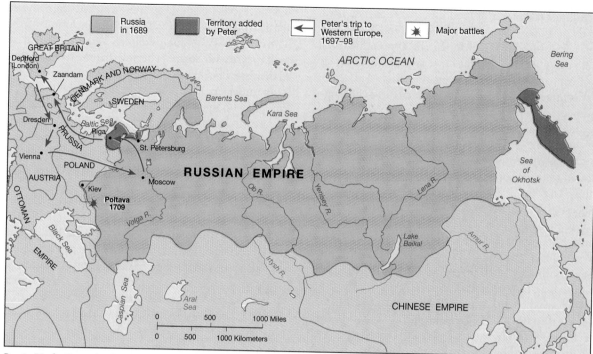

Russia Under Peter the Great

Peter toasted the captured Swedish generals. He claimed that everything he knew about warfare he had learned from them, and he congratulated them on their success as teachers. After the battle of Poltava, Russia gradually replaced Sweden as the dominant power in the Baltic.

Like everything else about him, Peter the Great's absolutism was uniquely his own. But though Peter's power was unlimited, it was not uncontested. He secularized the Russian Orthodox church, subjecting it to the control of state power and confiscating much of its wealth in the process. He broke the old military service class, which attempted a coup d'état when Peter was abroad in the 1690s. By the end of his reign, the Russian monarchy was among the strongest in Europe.

The Origins of French Absolutism

Nowhere was absolutism as successfully implanted as in France. Louis XIII (1610–43) was only eight years old when he came to the throne, and he grew slowly into his role under the tutelage of Cardinal Richelieu. It was Richelieu's vision that stabilized French government. As chief minister, Richelieu saw clearly that the prosperity and even the survival of France depended upon

strengthening royal power. He preached a doctrine of *raison d'état*—reason of state—in which he placed the needs of the nation above the privileges of its most important groups. Richelieu saw three threats to stable royal government: "The Huguenots shared the state, the nobles conducted themselves as if they were not subjects, and the most powerful governors in the provinces acted as if they were sovereign in their office."

Richelieu took measures to control all three. The power of the nobles was the most difficult to attack. The nobles' long tradition of independence from the crown had been enhanced by the wars of religion. Perhaps more importantly, the ancient aristocracy, the nobility of the sword, felt themselves in a particularly vulnerable position. Their world was changing and their traditional roles were becoming obsolete. Professional soldiers replaced them at war, professional administrators at government. Mercantile wealth threatened their economic superiority; the growth of the nobility of the robe—lawyers and state officials—threatened their social standing. They were hardly likely to take orders from a royal minister like Richelieu, especially when he attacked one of the great symbols of their power, the duel.

To limit the power of local officials, Richelieu used intendants to examine their conduct and to reform their administration. He made careful appointments of local governors and brought more regions under direct royal control. Against the Huguenots, Richelieu's policy was more subtle. He was less interested in challenging their religion than their autonomy. In 1627, when the English sent a force to aid the Huguenots against the government, Richelieu and Louis XIII abolished the Huguenots' privileges altogether. They were allowed to maintain their religion, but not their special status. They would have no privileges other than to be subjects of the king of France.

Richelieu's program was a vital prelude to the development of absolute monarchy in France. But the cardinal was not a king. While it is clear that Richelieu did not act without the full support of Louis XIII and clear that the king initiated many reforms for which the cardinal received credit, there can be no doubt that Richelieu was the power behind the throne. Louis XIII hated the business of government and even neglected his principal responsibility of providing the state with an heir. For years he and his wife slept in separate palaces, and only a freak rainstorm in Paris forced him to spend a night with the queen, Anne of Austria, in 1637. It was the night Louis XIV was conceived. Louis XIII and Richelieu died within six months of each other in 1642 and 1643, and the nation again endured the turmoil of a child king. Richelieu's aggressive policy to curb the nobility and his stringent financial program in the 1630s helped precipitate the Fronde. Louis XIV (1643–1715) was never to forget the terror of the aristocratic rebellion in Paris: how he was forced to flee the capital in the dead of night, how he endured the penury of exile, how he suffered the humiliation of being bossed about by the rebels. He would never forget, and he would have a long time to remember.

Louis le Grand

Not quite five years old when he came to the throne, Louis XIV was tutored by Cardinal Jules Mazarin (1602–61), Richelieu's successor as chief minister. If anything, Mazarin was more ruthless and less popular than his predecessor. An Italian from a modest background, Mazarin won the money to launch his career at the gaming table. Good fortune seemed to follow him everywhere. He gambled with his life and his career, and each time he raked in the stakes. He died with the largest private fortune that had ever been accumulated by a French citizen, easily surpassing the fortune of Richelieu. Like Richelieu, whom he emulated, Mazarin was an excellent administrator who had learned well the lessons of *raison d'état*. At the conclusion of the Thirty Years' War, for example, Mazarin refused to make peace with Spain, believing that the time was ripe to deliver a knockout blow to the Spanish Habsburgs.

In order to pacify the rebellious nobility of the Fronde, who opposed Mazarin's power, Louis XIV was declared to have reached his majority at the age of thirteen. But it was not until Mazarin died ten years later in 1661 that the king began to rule. Louis was blessed with able and energetic ministers. The two central props of his state—money and might—were in the hands of dynamic men, Jean-Baptiste Colbert (1619–83) and the Marquis de Louvois (1639–91). Colbert—to whom credit belongs for the building of the French navy, the reform of French legal codes, and the establishment of national academies of culture—was Louis's chief minister for finance. Colbert's fiscal reforms were so successful that in less than six years a debt of 22 million French pounds had become a surplus of 29 million. Colbert achieved this astonishing feat not by raising taxes but by increasing the efficiency of their collection. Until Louis embarked on his wars, the French state was solvent.

To Louvois, Louis's minister of war, fell the task of reforming the French army. During the Fronde, royal troops were barely capable of defeating the makeshift forces of the nobility. By the end of the reign, the army had grown to 400,000 and its organization had been thoroughly reformed. Louvois introduced new ranks for the field officers who actually led their men into battle, and promotions were distributed by merit rather than purchase. He also solved one of the most serious logistical problems of the age by establishing storehouses of arms and ammunition throughout the realm. The greatest achievements of the reign were built on the backs of fiscal and military reforms, which were themselves a product of the continuing sophistication of French administration.

Louis XIV furthered the practice of relying on professional administrators to supervise the main departments of state and offer advice on matters of policy. He created a separation between courtiers and officeholders and largely excluded the nobility of the sword from the inner circles of government, which were composed of ministers of departments and small councils that handled routine affairs. These councils were connected to the central advisory body of government, the secret council of the king. Within each department, ministers furthered the process of professionalization that led to the advancement of talented clerks, secretaries, and administrators. Although there still remained a large gulf between the promulgation of policy at Versailles and its enforcement in the provinces, it was now a gulf that could be measured and ultimately bridged. Louis XIV built on the institution of the intendant that Richelieu had developed with so much success. Intendants were now a permanent part of government, and their duties expanded from their early responsibilities as coordinators and mediators into areas of policing and tax collection. It was through the intendants that the wishes of central government were made known in the provinces.

Although Louis XIV was well served, it was the king himself who set the tone for French absolutism. "If he was not the greatest king, he was the best actor of majesty that ever filled the throne," wrote an English observer. The acting of majesty was central to Louis's rule. His residence at Versailles was the most glittering court of Europe, renowned for its beauty and splendor. It was built on a scale never before seen, and Louis took a personal interest in making sure it was fit for a king. When the court and king moved there permanently in 1682, Versailles became the envy of the Continent. But behind the imposing facade of Versailles stood a well-thought-out plan for domestic and international rule.

Louis XIV attempted to tame the French nobles by requiring their attendance at his court. Louis established a system of court etiquette so complex that constant study was necessary to prevent humiliation. While the nobility studied decorum they could not plot rebellion. At Versailles one never knocked on a door; one scratched with a fingernail. This insignificant custom had to be learned and remembered—it was useless anywhere else—and practiced if one hoped for the favor of the king. Leading noblemen of France rose at dawn so that they could watch Louis be awakened and hear him speak his first words. Dozens followed him from hall to gallery and from gallery to chamber as he washed, dressed, prayed, and ate.

This aura of court culture was equally successful in the royal art of diplomacy. During Louis's reign, France replaced Spain as the greatest nation in Europe. Massive royal patronage of art, science, and thought brought French culture to new heights. The French language replaced Latin as the universal European tongue. France was the richest and most populous European state, and Louis's absolute rule finally harnessed these resources to a single purpose. France became a commercial power rivaling the Netherlands, a naval power rivaling England, and a military power without peer. It was not only for effect that Louis took the image of the sun as his own. In court, in the nation, and throughout Europe everything revolved around him.

This Hyacinthe Rigaud portrait of Louis XIV in his coronation robes shows the splendor of Le Roi Soleil (the Sun King), who believed himself to be the center of France as the sun is the center of the solar system.

France's rise to preeminence in Europe was undoubtedly the greatest accomplishment of the absolute monarchy of Louis XIV. But it did not come without costs. Louis XIV made his share of mistakes, which were magnified by the awe in which his opinions were held. His aggressive foreign policy ultimately bankrupted the crown. But without doubt his greatest error was to persecute the Huguenots. As an absolute ruler, Louis believed that it was necessary to have absolute conformity and obedience. The existence of the Huguenots, with their separate communities and distinct forms of worship, seemed an affront to his authority. Almost from the beginning, Louis allowed the persecution of Protestants, despite the protection provided by the Edict of Nantes. Protestant churches were pulled down, conversions to Catholicism were bought with the lure of immunities from taxation, and children were separated from their families to be brought up in Catholic schools. Finally, in 1685 Louis

LE ROY DE FRANCE.
l'Home immortel Chef de la Ste Ligue.

Mon soleil parsa force eclaira l'heretique.
Il chassa tout d'un coup les brouillards de Calvin:
Non pas par un Zele divin,
Mais afin de cacher ma fine Politique.

A symbolic drawing shows how heretics will be driven from France by the Sun King. Such a policy proved shortsighted, however, as thousands of Huguenot émigrés enriched Louis's potential enemies with their valuable skills.

XIV revoked the Edict of Nantes. All forms of Protestant worship were outlawed, and the ministers who were not hunted down and killed were forced into exile. Despite a ban on Protestant emigration, over two hundred thousand Huguenots fled the country, many of them carrying irreplaceable skills with them to Holland and England in the west and Brandenburg in the east.

Supporters of the monarchy celebrated the revocation of the Edict of Nantes as an act of piety. Religious toleration in seventeenth-century Europe was still a policy of expediency rather than of principle. Even the English, who prided themselves on developing the concept of toleration, and the Dutch, who welcomed Jews to Amsterdam, would not officially tolerate Catholics. But the persecution of the Huguenots was a social and political disaster for France. Those who fled to other Protestant states spread the stories of atrocities that

stiffened European resolve against Louis. Those who remained became an embittered minority who pulled at the fabric of the state at every chance. Nor did the official abolition of Protestantism have much effect upon its existence. Against these policies, the Huguenots held firm to their beliefs. There were well over a million French Protestants, undoubtedly the largest religious minority in any state. Huguenots simply went underground, practicing their religion secretly and gradually replacing their numbers. No absolutism, however powerful, could succeed in eradicating religious beliefs.

• • •

Louis XIV gave his name to the age that he and his nation dominated, but he was not its only towering figure. The Great Elector, Peter the Great, Louis the Great: so they were judged by posterity, kings who had forged nations for a new age. Their style of rule showed the royal state at its height, still revolving around the king but more and more dependent upon permanent institutions of government that followed their own imperatives. The absolute state harnessed the economic and intellectual resources of the nation to the political will of the monarch. It did so to ensure survival in a dangerous world. But while monarchs ruled as well as reigned, they did so by incorporating vital elements of the state into the process of government. In England the importance of the landholding classes was recognized in the constitutional powers of Parliament. In Prussia the military power of the Junker was asserted through command in the army, the most important institution of the state. In France Louis XIV co-opted many nobles at his court while making use of a talented pool of lawyers, clergymen, and administrators in his government. A delicate balance existed between the will of the king and the will of the state, a balance that would soon lead these continental powers into economic competition and military confrontation.

Suggestions for Further Reading

General Reading

* Thomas Munck, *Seventeenth Century Europe, 1598–1700* (New York: St. Martin's Press, 1990). The most up-to-date survey.

* William Doyle, *The Old European Order* (Oxford: Oxford University Press, 1978). An important synthetic essay, bristling with ideas.

* Geoffrey Parker, *Europe in Crisis, 1598–1648* (London: William Collins and Sons, 1979). The best introduction to the period.

Perry Anderson, *Lineages of the Absolutist State* (London: NLB Books, 1974). A sociological study of the role of absolutism in the development of the western world.

The Rise of the Royal State

* Graham Parry, *The Golden Age Restor'd* (New York: St. Martin's Press, 1981). A study of English court culture in the reigns of James I and Charles I.

J. H. Elliott and Jonathan Brown, *A Palace for a King* (New Haven, CT: Yale University Press, 1980). An outstanding work on the building and decorating of a Spanish palace.

* J. N. Figgis, *The Divine Right of Kings* (Cambridge: Cambridge University Press, 1914). Still the classic study of this central doctrine of political thought.

* J. H. Elliott, *Richelieu and Olivares* (Cambridge: Cambridge University Press, 1984). A brilliant dual portrait.

* Roger Lockyer, *Buckingham* (London: Longman, 1984). A stylish biography of the favorite of two monarchs.

The Crises of the Royal State

* Quentin Skinner, *The Foundations of Modern Political Thought.* 2 vols.(Cambridge: Cambridge University Press, 1978). A seminal work on the history of ideas from Machiavelli to Calvin.

* Perez Zagoin, *Rebels and Rulers.* 2 vols. (Cambridge: Cambridge University Press, 1982). A good survey of revolutions, civil war, and popular protests throughout Europe.

* Trevor Aston, ed., *Crisis in Europe, 1600–1660* (Garden City, NY: Doubleday, 1967). Essays on the theme of a general crisis in Europe by distinguished historians.

G. Parker and L. Smith, eds., *The General Crisis of the Seventeenth Century* (London: Routledge & Kegan Paul, 1978). A collection of essays on the problem of the general crisis.

* Lawrence Stone, *The Causes of the English Revolution* (New York: Harper & Row, 1972). A vigorously argued explanation of why England experienced a revolution in the mid-seventeenth century.

* Ann Hughes, *The Causes of the English Civil War* (New York: St. Martin's Press, 1991). A lucid introduction to the scholarship of a vast subject.

* D. E. Underdown, *Pride's Purge* (London: Allen & Unwin, 1985). The most important work on the politics of the English Revolution.

The Zenith of the Royal State

* Geoffrey Parker, *The Military Revolution* (Cambridge: Cambridge University Press, 1988). A lucid discussion of how power was organized and deployed in the early modern state.

* H. W. Koch, *A History of Prussia,* (London: Longman, 1978). A comprehensive study of Prussian history, with an excellent chapter on the Great Elector.

* Paul Dukes, *The Making of Russian Absolutism* (London: Longman, 1982). A thorough survey of Russian history in the seventeenth and eighteenth centuries.

* Vasili Klyuchevsky, *Peter the Great* (London: Random House, 1958). A classic work, still the best study of Peter.

* W. E. Brown, *The First Bourbon Century in France* (London: University of London Press, 1971). A good introduction to French political history.

* William Beik, *Absolutism and Society in Seventeenth Century France* (Cambridge: Cambridge University Press, 1985). The single best study of the government of a French province in the seventeenth century.

Peter Burke, *The Fabrication of Louis XIV* (New Haven, CT: Yale University Press, 1992). A compelling account of a man and a myth.

* John Wolf, *Louis XIV* (New York: Norton, 1968). An outstanding biography of the Sun King.

*Paperback edition available.

17 ✌ SCIENCE AND COMMERCE IN EARLY MODERN EUROPE

Rembrandt's Lessons

By the early seventeenth century, interest in scientific investigation had spread out from narrow circles of specialists to embrace educated men and women. One of the more spectacular demonstrations of new knowledge was public dissection, by law performed only on the corpses of criminals. Here the secrets of the human body were revealed both for those who were training to be physicians and those who had the requisite fee and strong stomach. Curiosity about the human body was becoming a mark of education. New publications, both scientific and popular, spread ancient wisdom as well as the controversial findings of the moderns. Pictures drawn on the basis of dissections filled the new medical texts, like the one on the stand at the feet of the corpse in *The Anatomy Lesson of Dr. Nicolaes Tulp* (1632) by Rembrandt van Rijn (1606–69).

Dr. Tulp's anatomy lesson was not meant for the public. In fact, those gathered around him in various poses of concentration were not students at all. They were members of the Amsterdam company of surgeons, the physicians' guild of the early seventeenth century. The sitters had commissioned the picture, which was a celebration of themselves as well as of the noted Professor Tulp. They hired the young Rembrandt to compose the picture with the assurance that each of the sitters (whose names are written on the paper one of them holds in his hand) would appear as if he alone were the subject of a portrait. Rembrandt succeeded beyond expectation. Each individual was given his due. The expressions on their faces as much as their physical characteristics mark each one out from the group. Yet the portraits were only one part of the painting. The scene that Rembrandt depicted unified them. They became a group by their participation in the anatomy lesson. Rembrandt has chosen a moment of drama to stop the action. Dr. Tulp is demonstrating how the gesture he is making with his left hand would be made by the tendons in the arm of the gruesome cadaver. The central figures of the group are rapt in attention, though only one of them is actually observing the procedure of the dissection. Each listens to Tulp, comparing his own experience and knowledge to that of the professor and the text that stands open.

The *Anatomy Lesson* established the twenty-five-year-old Rembrandt as one of the most gifted and fashionable painters in Amsterdam. If any people could be said to be consumers of art in seventeenth-century Europe, it was the Dutch. Artists flourished and pictures abounded. Travelers were struck by the presence of artwork in both public and private places and in the homes of even moderately prosperous people. The group portrait, which Rembrandt brought to new levels of expression, was becoming a favorite genre. It was used to celebrate the leaders of Dutch society, who—unlike the leaders of most other European states—were not princes and aristocrats, but rather merchants, guild officials, and professionals. Rembrandt captured a spirit of civic pride in his group portraits. Here it was the surgeons' guild; later it would be the leaders of the cloth merchants' guild, another time a militia company.

Like the leaders of the surgeons' guild, who hung their commissioned portraits in their company's hall, the Dutch Republic swelled with pride in the seventeenth century. Its long war with Spain was finally drawing to a close, and it was time to celebrate the birth of a new state. The Dutch were a trading people, and their trade flourished as much in times of war as in times of peace. Their ships traveled to all parts of the globe, and they dominated the great luxury trades of the age. Bankers and merchants were the backbone of the Dutch Republic. Yet this republic of merchants was also one of the great cultural centers of the Continent. Intellectual creativity was cultivated in the same manner as was a trading partner. In the burgeoning port of Amsterdam, the fastest-growing city in Europe, artists, philosophers, and mathematicians lived cheek by jowl. The free exchange of ideas made Amsterdam home to those exiled for their beliefs. The Dutch practiced religious toleration as did no one else. Catholics, Protestants, and Jews all were welcomed to the Dutch Republic and found that they could pursue their own paths without persecution. Freedom of thought and freedom of expression helped develop a new spirit of scientific inquiry, like that portrayed in *The Anatomy Lesson of Dr. Nicolaes Tulp.*

The New Science

"And new Philosophy calls all in doubt,/ The element of fire is quite put out;/ The sun is lost and the earth, and no man's wit/ Can well direct him where to look for it." So wrote the English poet John Donne (1572–1631) about one of the most astonishing yet perplexing moments in the history of Western thought: the emergence of the new science. It was astonishing because it seemed truly new. The discoveries of the stargazers, like those of the sea explorers, challenged people's most basic assumptions and beliefs. Men dropping balls from towers or peering at the skies through a glass claimed that they had disproved thousands of years of certainty about the nature of the universe: "And new Philosophy calls all in doubt." But the new science was perplexing because it seemed to loosen the moorings of everything that educated people thought they knew about their world. Nothing could be more disorienting than to challenge common sense. One needed to do little more than wake up in the morning to know that the sun moved from east to west while the earth stood still. But mathematics, experimentation, and deduction were needed to understand that the earth was in constant motion and that it revolved around the sun—"And no man's wit/ Can well direct him where to look for it."

The scientific revolution was the opening of a new era in European history. After two centuries of classical revival, European thinkers had finally come against the limits of ancient knowledge. Ancient wisdom had served Europeans well, and it was not to be discarded lightly. But one by one, the certainties of the past were being called into question. The explanations of the universe and the natural world that had been advanced by Aristotle and codified by his followers no longer seemed adequate. There were too many contradictions between theory and observation, too many things that did not fit. Yet breaking the hold of Aristotelianism was no easy task. A full century was to pass before even learned people would accept the proofs that the earth revolved around the sun. Even then, the most famous of them—Galileo—had to recant these views or be condemned as a heretic.

The two essential characteristics of the new science were that it was materialistic and mathematical. Its materialism was contained in the realization that the universe is composed of matter in motion. This meant that the stars and planets were not made of some perfect ethereal substance but of the same matter that was found on earth. They were thus subject to the same rules of motion as were earthly objects. The mathematics of the new science was contained in the realization that calculation had to replace common sense as the basis for understanding the universe. Mathematics itself was transformed with the invention of logarithms, analytic geometry, and calculus. More importantly, scientific experimentation took the form of measuring repeatable phenomena. When Galileo attempted to develop a theory of acceleration, he rolled a brass ball down an inclined plane and recorded the time and distance of its descent 100 times before he was satisfied with his results.

The new science was also a Europe-wide movement. The spirit of scientific inquiry flourished everywhere. The main contributors to astronomy were a Pole, a Dane, a German, and an Italian. The founder of medical chemistry was Swiss; the best anatomist was Belgian. England contributed most of all—the founders of modern chemistry, biology, and physics. By and large, these scientists operated outside the traditional seats of learning at the universities. Although most were university trained and not a few taught the traditional Aristotelian subjects, theirs was not an academic movement. Rather, it was a public one made possible by the printing press. Once published, findings became building blocks for scientists throughout the Continent and from one generation to the next. Many discoveries were made in the search for practical solutions to ordinary problems, and what was learned fueled advances in technology and the natural sciences. The new science gave seventeenth-century Europeans a sense that they might finally master the forces of nature.

Heavenly Revolutions

There was much to be said for Aristotle's understanding of the world, for his cosmology. For one thing, it was harmonious. It incorporated a view of the physical world that coincided with a view of the spiritual and moral one. The heavens were unchangeable, and therefore they were better than the earth. The sun, moon, and planets were all faultless spheres, unblemished and immune from decay. Their motion was circular because the circle was the perfect form of motion. The earth was at the center of the universe because it was the heaviest planet and because it was at the center of the Great Chain of Being, between the underworld of spirits and the upper world of gods. The second advantage to the Aristotelian world view was that it was easily incorporated into Christianity. Aristotle's description of the heavens as being composed of a closed system of crystalline rings that held the sun, moon, and planets

This chart of the heavens was engraved by Andreas Cellarius in 1660. It portrays the heliocentric universe described by Nicolaus Copernicus and accepted by Galileo. Earth and Jupiter are shown with moons orbiting them.

in their circular orbits around the earth left room for God and the angels to reside just beyond the last ring.

There were, of course, problems with Aristotle's explanation of the universe as it was preserved in the work of Ptolemy, the greatest of the Greek astronomers. For one thing, if the sun revolved in a perfect circle around the earth, then why were the seasons not perfectly equal? If the planets all revolved around the earth in circles, then why did they look nearer or farther, brighter or darker at different times of year? To solve these problems, a host of ingenious hypotheses were advanced. Perhaps the sun revolved around the earth in an eccentric circle, that is, a circle not centered on the earth. This would account for the differing lengths of seasons. Perhaps the planets revolved in circles that rested on a circle around the earth. Then, when the planet revolved within the larger circle, it would seem nearer and brighter, and when it revolved outside it, it would seem farther away and darker. This was the theory of epicycles. Yet to account for the observable movement of all the known planets, there had to be 55 of these epicycles, these circles within circles. As ingeniously complex as they were, the modifications of Aristotle's views made by the theories of eccentric circles and epicycles had one great virtue: they accurately predicted the movements of the planets. Although they were completely hypothetical, they answered the most troubling questions about the Aristotelian system.

In the 1490s, Nicolaus Copernicus (1473–1543) came to the Polish University of Krakow, which had one of the leading mathematical faculties in Europe. There they taught the latest astronomical theories and vigorously debated the existence of eccentric circles and epicycles. Copernicus came to Krakow for a liberal arts

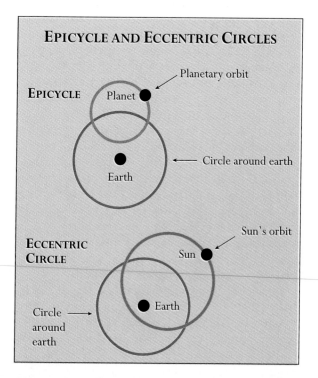

EPICYCLE AND ECCENTRIC CIRCLES

EPICYCLE

Planetary orbit

Planet

Earth

Circle around earth

ECCENTRIC CIRCLE

Sun's orbit

Sun

Earth

Circle around earth

STARGAZING

Nicolaus Copernicus was born in Poland and educated at the University of Krakow, which had one of the greatest mathematics faculties of the age. He prepared for a career in the church, but his abiding interest was the study of astronomy. Through observation and calculation, Copernicus worked out a heliocentric view of the universe in which the earth revolved on an axis and orbited the sun. His path-breaking work was not published until the year of his death, and he was fully aware of the implications of his discovery.

For, first, the mathematicians are so unsure of the movements of the Sun and Moon that they cannot even explain or observe the constant length of the seasonal year. Secondly, in determining the motions of these and of the other five planets, they use neither the same principles and hypotheses nor the same demonstrations of the apparent motions and revolutions. . . . Nor have they been able thereby to discern or deduce the principal thing—namely the shape of the Universe and the unchangeable symmetry of its parts. . . .

Thus assuming motions, which in my work I ascribe to the Earth, by long and frequent observations I have at last discovered that, if the motions of the rest of the planets be brought into relation with the circulation of the Earth and be reckoned in proportion to the circles of each planet, not only do their phenomena presently ensue, but the orders and magnitudes of all stars and spheres, nay the heavens themselves, become so bound together that nothing in any part thereof could be moved from its place without producing confusion of all the other parts of the Universe as a whole.

From Copernicus, *On the Revolutions of Heavenly Spheres* (1543).

education before pursuing a degree in Church law. He became fascinated by astronomy and puzzled by the debate over planetary motion. Copernicus believed, like Aristotle, that the simplest explanations were the best. If the sun was at the center of the universe and the earth simply another planet in orbit, then many of the most elaborate explanations of planetary motion were unnecessary. "At rest, in the middle of everything is the sun," Copernicus wrote in *On the Revolutions of the Heavenly Spheres* (1543). "For in this most beautiful temple who would place this lamp in another or better position than that from which it can light up the whole thing at the same time?" Because Copernicus accepted most of the rest of the traditional Aristotelian explanation, especially the belief that the planets moved in circles, his sun-centered universe was only slightly better at predicting the position of the planets than the traditional earth-centered one, but Copernicus's idea stimulated other astronomers to make new calculations.

Under the patronage of the king of Denmark, Tycho Brahe (1546–1601) built a large observatory to study planetary motion. In 1572 Brahe discovered a nova, a brightly burning star that was previously unknown. This discovery challenged the idea of an immutable universe composed of crystalline rings. In 1577 the appearance of a comet cutting through the supposedly impenetrable rings punched another hole into the old cosmology. Brahe's own views were a hybrid of old and new. He believed that all planets but the earth revolved around the sun and that the sun and the planets revolved around a fixed earth. To demonstrate this theory, Brahe and his students compiled the largest and most accurate mathematical tables of planetary motion yet known. From this research, Brahe's pupil Johannes Kepler (1571–1630), one of the great mathematicians of the age, formulated laws of planetary motion. Kepler discovered that planets orbited the sun in an elliptical rather than a circular path. This accounted for their movements nearer and farther from the earth. More importantly, he demonstrated that there was a precise mathematical relationship between the speed with which a planet revolved and its distance from the sun. Kepler's findings supported the view that the galaxy was heliocentric and that the heavens, like the earth, were made of matter that was subject to physical laws.

What Kepler demonstrated mathematically, the Italian astronomer Galileo Galilei (1564–1642) confirmed by observation. Creating a telescope by using magnify-

THE TELESCOPE

No single individual is as much associated with the Scientific Revolution as Galileo Galilei. He made formative contributions to mathematics, physics, and astronomy, but he also served as a lightning rod for the dissemination of the newest ideas. He popularized the work of Copernicus and was condemned by the Catholic church for his views and publications. He ended his life under house arrest. Among his other accomplishments, Galileo was the first to use a telescope to make scientific observations.

About ten months ago a report reached my ears that a certain Fleming had constructed a spyglass by means of which visible objects, though very distant from the eye of the observer, were distinctly seen as if nearby. Of this truly remarkable effect several experiences were related, to which some persons gave credence while others denied them. A few days later the report was confirmed to me in a letter from a noble Frenchman at Paris, Jacques Badovere, which caused me to apply myself wholeheartedly to inquire into the means by which I might arrive at the invention of a similar instrument. This I did shortly afterwards, my basis being the theory of refraction. First I prepared a tube of lead, at the ends of which I fitted two glass lenses, both plane on one side while on the other side one was spherically convex and the other concave. Then placing my eye near the concave lens I perceived objects satisfactorily large and near, for they appeared three times closer and nine times larger than when seen with the naked eye alone. Next I constructed another one, more accurate, which represented objects as enlarged more than sixty times. Finally, sparing neither labor nor expense, I succeeded in constructing for myself so excellent an instrument that objects seen by means of it appeared nearly one thousand times larger and over thirty times closer than when regarded with our natural vision.

It would be superfluous to enumerate the number and importance of the advantages of such an instrument at sea as well as on land. But forsaking terrestrial observations, I turned to celestial ones, and first I saw the moon from as near at hand as if it were scarcely two terrestrial radii. . . .

. . . Let us speak first of that surface of the moon which faces us. For greater clarity I distinguish two parts of this surface, a lighter and a darker; the lighter part seems to surround and to pervade the whole hemisphere, while the darker part discolors the moon's surface like a kind of cloud, and makes it appear covered with spots. . . . From observation of these spots repeated many times I have been led to the opinion and conviction that the surface of the moon is not smooth, uniform, and precisely spherical as a great number of philosophers believe it (and the other heavenly bodies) to be, but is uneven, rough, and full of cavities and prominences, being not unlike the face of the earth, relieved by chains of mountains and deep valleys.

From Galileo, *The Starry Messenger* (1610).

ing lenses and a long tube, Galileo saw parts of the heavens that had never been dreamed of before. In 1610 he discovered four moons of Jupiter, proving conclusively that all heavenly bodies did not revolve around the earth. He observed the landscape of the earth's moon and described it as full of mountains, valleys, and rivers. It was of the same imperfect form as the earth itself. He even found spots on the sun, which suggested that it, too, was composed of ordinary matter. Through the telescope, Galileo gazed upon an unimaginable universe: "The Galaxy is nothing else but a mass of innumerable stars," he wrote. Galileo's greatest scientific discoveries had to do with motion—he was the first to posit a law of inertia—but his greatest contribution to the new science was his popularization of the Copernican theory. He took the debate over the structure of the universe to the public, popularizing the discoveries of scientists in his vigorous Italian tracts.

As news of his experiments and discoveries spread, Galileo became famous throughout the Continent, and his support for heliocentrism became a celebrated cause. In 1616 the Roman Catholic church cautioned him against promoting his views. In 1633, a year after publishing his *A Dialogue Between the Two Great Systems of the World*, Galileo was tried by the Inquisition and forced specifically to recant the idea that the earth

didn't easily yield the secrets of life. Much of what was known about matters as common as reproduction was a combination of ancient wisdom and the practical experiences of midwives and doctors. Both were woefully inadequate.

One of the greatest mysteries was the method by which blood moved through the vital organs. It was generally believed that the blood originated in the liver, traveled to the right side of the heart, and then passed to the left side through invisible pores. Anatomical investigation proved beyond doubt that there was blood in both sides of the heart, but no one could discover the pores through which it passed. William Harvey (1578–1657), an Englishman who had received his medical education in Italy, offered an entirely different explanation. Harvey was employed as royal physician to both James I and Charles I and had one of the most lucrative medical practices in Europe. His real interest, however, was in studying the anatomy of the heart. Harvey examined hearts in more than forty species before concluding that the heart worked like a pump or, as he put it, a water bellows. Harvey observed that the valves of the heart's chambers allowed the blood to flow in only one direction. He thus concluded that the blood was pumped by the heart and circulated throughout the entire body.

The greatest of all English scientists was the mathematician and physicist Sir Isaac Newton (1642–1727). It was Newton who brought together the various strands of the new science. He merged the materialists and Hermeticists, the astronomers and astrologers, the chemists and alchemists. He made stunning contributions to the sciences of optics, physics, astronomy, and mathematics, and his magnum opus, *Mathematical Principles of Natural Philosophy* (1687), is one of a handful of the most important scientific works ever composed. Most important, Newton solved the single most perplexing problem: if the world was composed of matter in motion, what was motion?

Newton came from a moderately prosperous background and was trained at a local grammar school before entering Cambridge University. There was little in his background or education to suggest his unique talents, and in fact his most important discoveries were not appreciated until years after he had made them. Newton was the first to understand the composition of light, the first to develop a calculus, and the first to build a reflecting telescope. Newton became a professor at Cambridge, but he spent much of his time alone. He made a great study of Hermetic writings and from them revived the mystical notions of attraction and repulsion.

Although Galileo had developed a *theory of inertia,* the idea that a body at rest stays at rest, most materialists believed that motion was inherent in objects. In contrast, Newton believed that motion was the result of the interaction of objects and that it could be calculated mathematically. From his experiments he formulated the concept of force and his famous laws of motion: (1) that objects at rest or of uniform linear motion remain in such a state unless acted upon by an external force; (2) that changes in motion are proportional to force; and (3) that for every action there is an equal and opposite reaction. From these laws of motion, Newton advanced one step further. If the world was no more than matter in motion and if all motion was subject to the same laws, then the movement of the planets could be explained in the same way as the movement of an apple falling from a tree. There was a mathematical relationship between attraction and repulsion—a universal gravitation, as Newton called it— that governed the movement of all objects. Newton's theory of gravity joined together Kepler's astronomy and Galileo's physics. The mathematical, materialistic world of the new science was now complete.

Science Enthroned

By the middle of the seventeenth century, the new science was firmly established throughout Europe. Royal and noble patrons supported the enterprise by paying some of the costs of equipment and experimentation. Royal observatories were created for astronomers, colleges of physicians for doctors, and laboratories for chemists. Both England and France established royal societies of learned scientists to meet together and discuss their discoveries. The French Academie des Sciences (1666) was composed of 20 salaried scientists and an equal number of students, representing the different branches of scientific learning. They met twice weekly throughout the year, and each member worked on a project of his own devising. The English Royal Society (1662) boasted some of the greatest minds of the age. It was there that Newton first made public his most important discoveries. Scientific bodies were also formed outside the traditional universities. These were the so-called mechanics colleges, like Gresham College in London, where the practical applications of mathematics and physics were studied and taught. Navigation was a particular concern of the college, and the faculty established close ties with the Royal Navy and with London merchants.

The establishment of learned scientific societies and practical colleges fulfilled part of the program advocated by Sir Francis Bacon (1561–1626), one of the leading supporters of scientific research in England. In *The Advancement of Learning* (1605), Bacon had proposed a scientific method through inductive empirical experimentation. Bacon believed that experiments should be carefully recorded so that results were both reliable and repeatable. He advocated the open world of the scientist over the secret world of the magician. In his numerous writings, he stressed the practical impact of scientific discovery and even wrote a utopian work in which science appeared as the savior of humanity. Although he was not himself a scientific investigator, Bacon used his considerable influence to support scientific projects in England.

Bacon's support for the new science contrasts markedly with the stance taken by the Roman Catholic church. Embattled by the Reformation and the wars of religion, the Church had taken the offensive in preserving the core of its heritage. By the early seventeenth century, the missionary work of the Jesuits had won many reconversions and had halted the advance of Protestantism. Now the new science appeared to be another heresy. Not only did it confound ancient wisdom and contradict Church teachings, but it was also a lay movement that was neither directed nor controlled from Rome. The trial of Galileo slowed the momentum of scientific investigation in Catholic countries and starkly posed the conflict between authority and knowledge. But the stand taken by the Church was based on more than narrow self-interest. Ever since Copernicus had published his views, a new skepticism had emerged among European intellectuals. Every year new theories competed with old ones, and dozens of contradictory explanations for the most common phenomena were advanced and debated. The skeptics concluded that nothing was known and nothing was knowable. Their position led inevitably to the most shocking of all possible views: atheism.

There was no necessary link between the new science and an attack upon established religion: so Galileo had argued all along. Few of the leading scientists ever saw a contradiction between their studies and their faith. Sir Robert Boyle endowed a lectureship for the advancement of Christian doctrine and contributed money for the translation of the New Testament into Turkish. Still, by the middle of the century attacks on the Church were increasing, and some blamed the new science for them. Thus it was altogether fitting that one of the leading mathematicians of the day should also provide the method for harmonizing faith and reason.

René Descartes (1596–1650) was the son of a provincial lawyer and judge. He was trained in one of

René Descartes, the seventeenth-century French mathematician, philosopher, and scientist. He remained a faithful Catholic all his life while questioning the very foundations of Catholic philosophy.

the best Jesuit schools in France before taking a law degree in 1616. While it was his father's intention that his son practice law, it was René's intention that he become educated in "the school of life." He entered military service in the Dutch Republic, and after the outbreak of the Thirty Years' War served in the Duke of Bavaria's army. Descartes was keenly interested in mathematics, and during his military travels he met and was tutored by a leading Dutch mathematician. For the first time he learned of the new scientific discoveries and of the advances made in mathematics. In 1619 he dreamed that he had discovered the scientific principles of universal knowledge. After this dream, Descartes returned to Holland and began to develop his system. He was on the verge of publishing his views when he learned of the Church's condemnation of Galileo. Reading Galileo's *Dialogue Between the Two Great Systems of the World,* Descartes discovered that he shared many of the same opinions and had worked out mathematical proofs for them. He refrained from publishing until 1637 when he brought out his *Discourse on Method.*

In the *Discourse on Method,* Descartes demonstrated how skepticism could be used to produce certainty. He began by declaring that he would reject everything that could not be clearly proved beyond doubt. Thus he rejected his perception of the material world, the testimony of his senses—all known or imagined opinions. He was left only with doubt. But what was doubt, if not thought, and what was thought, if not the workings of his mind? The only thing of which he could be certain, then, was that he had a mind. Thus his famous formulation: "I think, therefore I am." From this first certainty came another: the knowledge of perfectibility. He knew that he was imperfect and that a perfect being had to have placed that knowledge within him. Therefore, a perfect being—God—existed.

Descartes's philosophy, known as Cartesianism, rested on the dual existence of matter and mind. Matter was the material world, subject to the incontrovertible laws of mathematics. Mind was the spirit of the creator. Descartes was one of the leading mechanistic philosophers, believing that all objects operated in accord with natural laws. He invented analytic geometry and made important contributions to the sciences of optics and physics on which Newton would later build. Yet it was in his proof that the new science could be harmonized with the old religion that Descartes made his greatest contribution to the advancement of learning. Despite the fact that his later work was condemned by the Catholic church and that he preferred the safety of Protestant Holland to the uncertainty of his Catholic homeland, Cartesianism became the basis for the unification of science and religion.

"I shall attempt to make myself intelligible to everyone," Descartes wrote. Like many of the new scientists, he preferred the use of vernacular languages to elite Latin, hoping that his work would reach beyond the narrow bounds of high culture. Descartes was one of many new scientists who saw the practical import of what they had learned and who hoped to bring that knowledge to the aid of the material well-being of their contemporaries. John Dee (1527–1608) translated the Greek geometrician Euclid into English so that ordinary people might "find out and devise new works, strange engines and instruments for sundry purposes in the commonwealth." Although many of the breakthrough discoveries of the new scientists would not find practical use for centuries, the spirit of discovery was to have great impact in an age of commerce and capital. The quest for mathematical certainty and prime movers led directly to improvements in agriculture, mining, navigation, and industrial activity. It also brought with it a sense of control over the material world that provided a new optimism for generations of Europeans.

Empires of Goods

Under the watchful eye of the European states, a worldwide marketplace for the exchange of commodities had been created. First the Dutch and then the English had established monopoly companies to engage in exotic trades in the East. First the Spanish and Portuguese, then the English and French had established colonial dependencies in the Atlantic that they carefully nurtured in hope of economic gain. Protected trade had flourished beyond the wildest dreams of its promoters. Luxury commodities became staples; new commodities became luxuries. Trade enhanced the material life of all Europeans, though it came at great cost to the Asians, Africans, and Latin Americans whose labor and raw materials were converted into the new crazes of consumption.

While long-distance trade was never as important to the European economy as inland and intracontinental trade, its development in the seventeenth and eigh-

The Geographer *by Jan Vermeer van Delft, 1669. A Dutch cartographer, holding dividers, is shown surrounded by charts, a globe, and other paraphernalia of his craft. Such cartographers combined the skills of artist and mathematician.*

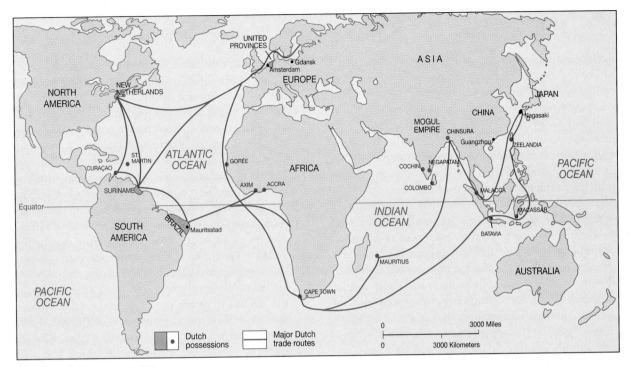

Dutch Trade Routes, ca. 1650

teenth centuries had a profound impact on lifestyles, economic policy, and ultimately, warfare. The Dutch became the first great commercial power. Their achievements were based on innovative techniques, rational management, and a social and cultural environment that supported mercantile activities. Dutch society was freer than any other; it was open to new capital, new ventures, and new ideas. The Dutch improved the organization of trade by developing the concept of the entrepôt, a place where goods were brought for storage before being exchanged. They pioneered in finance by establishing the Bank of Amsterdam. They led in shipbuilding by developing the flyboat, a long, flat-hulled vessel designed specifically to carry bulky cargoes like grain. They traded around the globe with the largest mercantile fleet yet known. It was not until the end of the seventeenth century that England and France surpassed the Dutch. This reversal owed less to new innovations than it did to restrictions on trade. Because the Dutch dominated the European economy, the French and English began to pass laws to eliminate Dutch competition. The English banned imports carried in Dutch ships; the French banned Dutch products. Both policies cut heavily into the Dutch superiority, and both ultimately resulted in commercial warfare.

The Marketplace of the World

By the sixteenth century, all the major trading routes had already been opened. The Spanish moved back and forth across the Atlantic; the Dutch and Portuguese sailed around the tip of Africa to the Indian Ocean. The Baltic trade connected the eastern and western parts of Europe as Danes, Swedes, and Dutch exchanged Polish and Russian raw materials for English and French manufactured goods. The Mediterranean, which had dominated world trade for centuries, was still a vital artery of intercontinental trade, but its role was diminishing. In 1600 almost three-quarters of the Asian trade was still land based, much of it carried through the Middle East to the Mediterranean. A century later, nearly all Asian trade was carried directly to western Europe by Dutch and English vessels. Commercial power was shifting to the northern European states just as dramatically as military and political power.

The technology associated with commerce achieved no breakthroughs to compare with the great transformations of the fifteenth century, when new techniques of navigation made transatlantic travel possible. It is certainly true that there continued to be improvements. The astronomical findings of the new science were a direct aid to navigation, as were the recorded experiences of so many practiced sea travelers. The materials used to make and maintain ships improved with the importation of pitch and tar from the east and with the greater availability of iron and copper from Scandinavia. It was the Dutch who made the single most important innovation in shipbuilding. To gain maximum profit from their journeys to the Baltic, the Dutch designed the so-called flyboats. Flyboats sacrificed speed and maneuverability, but they were cheap to build and could be manned by small crews. They carried no heavy armaments and were thus well adapted to the serene Baltic trade.

It was unspectacular developments like the flyboat that had such an impact on seventeenth- and eighteenth-century transcontinental trade. Innovation, organization, and efficient management were the principal elements of what historians have called the commercial revolution. Concerted efforts to maximize opportunities and advantages accounted for the phenomenal growth in the volume and value of commercial exchange. One of the least spectacular and most effective breakthroughs was the replacement of bilateral with triangular trade. In bilateral trade, the surplus commodities of one community were exchanged for those of another. This method, of course, restricted the range of trading partners to those with mutually desirable surplus production: England and Italy were unlikely to swap woolens or Sicily and Poland to trade grain. For those with few desirable commodities, bilateral trade meant the exchange of precious metals for goods, and throughout much of the sixteenth and early seventeenth centuries, bullion was by far the most often traded commodity. Triangular trade created a larger pool of desirable goods. British manufactured goods could be traded to Africa for slaves, the slaves could be traded in the West Indies for sugar, and the sugar could be consumed in Britain. Moreover, the merchants involved in shifting these goods from place to place could achieve profits on each exchange. Indeed, their motive in trading could now change from dumping surplus commodities to matching supply and demand.

Equally important were the changes made in the way trade was financed. As states, cities, and even individuals could stamp their own precious metal, there were hundreds of different European coins with different nominal and metallic values. The influx of American silver further destabilized an already unstable system of exchange. The Bank of Amsterdam was created in 1609 to establish a uniform rate of exchange for the various currencies traded in that city. From this useful function a second developed—transfer, or giro, banking, a system that had been invented in Italy. In giro banking, various merchant firms held money on account and issued bills of transfer from one to another. This transfer system meant that merchants in different cities did not have to transport their precious metals or endure long delays in having their accounts settled.

Giro banking also aided the development of bills of exchange, an early form of checking. Merchants could conclude trades by depositing money in a given bank or merchant house and then having a bill drawn for the sum they owed. Bills of exchange were especially important in international trade, as they made large-scale shipments of precious metals to settle trade deficits unnecessary. By the end of the seventeenth century bills of exchange had become negotiable; that is, they could pass from one merchant to another without being redeemed. Thus a Dutch merchant could buy French wines in Bordeaux with a bill of exchange drawn on an account in the Bank of Amsterdam. The Bordeaux merchant could then purchase Spanish oranges and use the same bill of exchange as payment. There were two disadvantages to this system: ultimately the bill had to return to Amsterdam for redemption; and when it did, the account on which it was drawn might be empty. The establishment of the Bank of England in 1694 overcame these difficulties. The Bank of England was licensed to issue its own bills of exchange, or bank notes, which were backed by the revenue from specific English taxes. This security of payment was widely sought after, and the Bank of England soon became a clearing house for all kinds of bills of exchange. The Bank would buy in bills at a discount, paying less than their face value, and pay out precious metal or their own notes in exchange.

The effects of these and many other small-scale changes in business practice helped fuel prolonged growth in European commerce. It was the European merchant who made this growth possible by accepting the risks of each individual transaction and building up small pools of capital from which successive transactions could take place. Most mercantile ventures were conducted by individuals or families and were based on the specialized trade of a single commodity. Trade offered high returns because it entailed high risks. The long delays in moving goods and their uncertain arrival; the unreliability of agents and the unscrupulousness of other traders; and the inefficiencies in transport and communication all weighed heavily against success. Those who succeeded did so less by luck than by hard work. They used family members to receive shipments. They lowered shipping costs by careful packaging. They lowered protection costs by securing their trade routes. Financial publications lowered the costs of information. Ultimately, lower costs meant lower prices. For centuries luxury goods had dominated intercontinental trade. But by the eighteenth century, European merchants had created a world marketplace in which the luxuries of the past were the common fare of the present.

Detail of an Indian textile from the Madras region, ca. 1650. Calicut gave its name to the cotton cloth called calico. This is an example of a "painted Calicut," a wall hanging that shows richly dressed Indian women.

Consumption Choices

As long-distance trade became more sophisticated, merchants became more sensitive to consumer tastes. Low-volume, high-quality goods like spices and silks could not support the growing merchant communities in the European states. These goods were the preserve of the largest trading companies and, more importantly, they had reached saturation levels by the early seventeenth century. The price of pepper, the most used of all spices, fell nearly continuously after 1650. Moreover, triangular trade allowed merchants to provide a better match of supplies and demands. The result was the rise to prominence of a vast array of new commodities, which not only continued the expansion of trade but also reshaped diet, lifestyles, and patterns of consumption. New products came from both East and West. Dutch and English incursions into the Asian trade provoked competition with the Portuguese and expanded the range of commodities that were shipped back to Europe. An aggressive Asian triangle was created in which European bullion bought Indonesian spices that were exchanged for Persian silk and Chinese and Japanese finished goods. In the Atlantic, the English were quick to develop both home and export markets for a variety of new or newly available products.

European trade with Asia had always been designed to satisfy consumer demand rather than to exchange surplus goods. Europeans manufactured little that was desired in Asia, and neither merchants nor governments saw fit to attempt to influence Asian tastes in the way they did those of Europeans. The chief commodity imported to the East was bullion: tons of South American silver, perhaps a third of all that was produced. In return came spices, silk, coffee, jewels, jade, porcelain, dyes, and a wide variety of other exotic goods. By the middle of the seventeenth century, the Dutch dominated the spice trade, obtaining a virtual monopoly over cinnamon, cloves, nutmeg, and mace and carrying the largest share of pepper. Each year Europeans consumed perhaps a million pounds of the four great spices and seven million pounds of pepper. Both Dutch and English competed for preeminence in the silk trade. The Dutch concentrated on Chinese silk, which they used mostly in trade with Japan. The English established an interest in lower-quality Indian silk spun in Bengal and even hired Italian silk masters to try to teach European techniques to the Indian spinners.

The most important manufactured articles imported from the East to Europe were the lightweight, brightly colored Indian cottons known as calicoes. The Dutch first realized the potential of the cotton market. Until the middle of the seventeenth century, cotton and cotton blended with silk were used in Europe only for wall hangings and table coverings. Colorful Asian chintz contained floral patterns that Europeans still considered exotic. But the material was also soft and smooth to the touch, and it soon replaced linen for use as underwear and close-fitting garments among the well-to-do. The fashion quickly caught on, and the Dutch began exporting calicoes throughout the Continent. The English and French followed suit, establishing their own trading houses in India and bringing European patterns and designs with them for the Asians to copy. The calico trade was especially lucrative because the piece goods were easy to pack and ship and, unlike consumables, could be stored indefinitely. When the English finally came to dominate the trade in the middle of the eighteenth century, they were shipping over a million cloths a year into London. The craze for calicoes was so great that both the English and French governments attempted to ban their import to protect their own clothing industries.

Along with the new apparel from the East came new beverages. Coffee, which was first drunk in northern Europe in the early seventeenth century, had become a fashionable drink by the end of the century. Coffeehouses sprang up in the major urban areas of northern

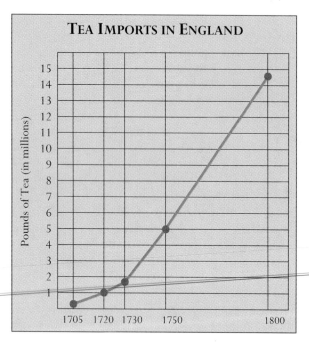

TEA IMPORTS IN ENGLAND

Europe. There political and intellectual conversation was as heady as the strong Middle Eastern brew that was served. The Dutch and English both established themselves in the coffee trade, which was centered in the Middle Eastern seaport of Mocha. By the beginning of the eighteenth century, the Dutch had begun to grow their own coffee for export from their island colony of Java, and the two different types of coffee competed for favor.

As popular as coffee became among the European elites, it paled in comparison to the importance of tea as both an import commodity and a basic beverage. While coffee drinking remained the preserve of the wealthy, tea consumption spread throughout European society. It was probably most prevalent in England, where the combination of China tea and West Indian sugar created a virtual revolution in nutrition. The growth in tea consumption was phenomenal. In 1706 England imported 100,000 pounds of tea. By the end of the century the number had risen to over 15 million pounds. The English imported most of this tea directly from China, where an open port had been established at Canton. Originally just one of a number of commodities that was carried on an Asian voyage, tea soon became the dominant cargo of the large English merchant ships. Some manufactured goods would be brought to India on the outward voyage in order to fill as much cargo space as possible, but once the ships had loaded the green and black teas, they sailed directly home. Almost all tea was purchased with bullion, as the Chinese had even less use for European goods than did

other Asians. It was not until the discovery that the Chinese consumed large quantities of opium, which was grown in India and Southeast Asia, that a triangular trade developed.

The success of tea was linked to the explosive growth in the development of sugar in Europe's Atlantic colonies. The Portuguese had attempted to cultivate sugar in the Azores at the end of the fifteenth century, but it was not until the settlement of Brazil, whose hot, humid climate was a natural habitat for the cane plants, that widespread cultivation began. The island of Barbados became the first English sugar colony. Barbados turned to sugar production accidentally, when its first attempts to market tobacco failed. The planters modeled their methods on those of Brazil, where African slaves were used to plant, tend, and cut the giant canes from which the sugar was extracted. For reasons that will never be fully understood, the English had an insatiable appetite for sugar's sweetness. It was taken plain, like candy; used in small quantities in almost all types of recipes; and diluted in ever-increasing quantities of tea. Hot, sweet tea became a meal for the lower orders of English society, a meal which—unlike beer—provided a quick burst of energy. By 1700 the English were sending home over 50 million pounds of sugar besides what they were shipping directly to the North American colonies. This quantity doubled by 1730, and still there was no slackening of demand. What might have become a valuable raw material in English trade instead became a staple of consumption.

The triangular trade of manufactures—largely reexported calicoes—to Africa for slaves, who were exchanged in the West Indies for sugar, became the dominant form of English overseas trade. Colonial production depended upon the enforced labor of hundreds of thousands of Africans. Gold and silver, tobacco, sugar, rice, and indigo were all slave crops. Africans were enslaved by other Africans and then sold to Europeans to be used in the colonies. Over six million black slaves were imported into the Americas during the course of the eighteenth century. While rum and calicoes were the main commodities exchanged for slaves, the African tribes that dominated the slave trade organized a highly competitive market. Every colonial power participated in this lucrative trade. Over three million slaves were imported into the Portuguese colony of Brazil; by the end of the eighteenth century, there were 500,000 slaves and only 35,000 French inhabitants on the sugar island of Saint Domingue. But it was the English, with their sugar colonies of Barbados and Jamaica and their tobacco colonies of Virginia

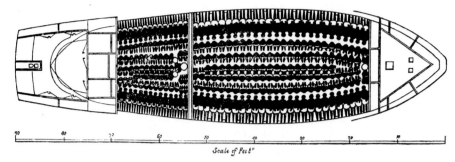

Scale of Feet

PLAN OF A SLAVE VESSEL.

This diagram shows how slaves were packed into cargo holds for the notorious Middle Passage to the Americas. The plan was a model of efficiency, for slave traders sought to maximize profits.

THE SLAVE TRADE.

The motion in the House of Lords made by Lord Denman, on Tuesday night, has naturally revived the interest of the measures for the extinction of this vile traffic of "man-selling and man-stealing." The close of the session is marked by these humane exertions, as was its commencement, in the comprehensive speech of Lord George Bentinck, in the House of Commons, on February 3. His Lordship then held in his hand a communication from Captain Pilkington, of the Royal Navy, on the subject of the slave-trade, accompanied with a plan of one of the slave vessels (which we now Engrave). They were sit-

Water Line

entertainment enlivened by some most exquisite performances on the nationa instrument, the harp, much to the delight of all assembled. From the dinner-table the company retired at an early hour to the School-rooms, where the *conversazioni* were held.

WEDNESDAY.

On Wednesday, as the Geological and Natural History Sections were unable to finish the business before them, they each held meetings ; but as a great number of members had left Swansea that morning by the *Lord Beresford* steamer, and others were examining the works in the neighbourhood, the Sections were very slightly attended, and the papers communicated were of small general interest.

A dinner, given by Lewis W. Dillwyn, Esq., who is himself one of the oldest members of the Royal Society, may be regarded as the close of the proceedings.

The last General Meeting was held in the afternoon, when it appeared, that, notwithstanding the inferiority of Swansea as respects population, this meeting has added considerably to the funds of the Association.

In concluding our notice of an Association which numbers among its members all the most eminent men in every department of physical and natural science, we cannot but express our satisfaction at the business-like character of this meeting. It is true that it has not startled the wor d by the announcement of any great discovery ; but it will be found, upon examination, to present a fair average rate of progress. The vulnerable points have been less apparent than hitherto ; and by the exclusion from the sections of all subjects which were not purely scientific, and by particularly avoiding those communications which have frequently been introduced as mere trading advertisements, of which we witnessed but one, that on gutta percha, which in our opinion should not have been received, the Association has placed itself upon exalted ground, and en-

and Maryland, who ultimately came to control the slave trade. The prosperity of Newport, Rhode Island, in North America and the port of Liverpool in Lancashire were built entirely on the slave trade, as were hundreds of plantation fortunes. The sweet tooth of Europe was fed by the sweat of black Africans.

Sugar was by far the dominant commodity of the colonial trade, but it was not the only one. Furs and fish had first driven Europeans toward North America, and both remained important commodities. Beaver and rabbit skins were the most common materials for making headgear in an age in which everyone wore a hat. The schools of cod in Canadian waters were among the richest in the world, and the catch was shipped back either salted or dried. The English established what amounted to a manufacturing industry on the Newfoundland coast, where they dried the tons of fish that they caught. In the eighteenth century, rice was grown for export in the southern American colonies, particularly South Carolina. Rice never achieved great popularity in England, though it was in constant demand in the German states. Tobacco was the first new American product to come into widespread use in Europe, and its popularity—despite various official efforts to ban its use as dirty and unhealthy—grew steadily. American tobacco was grown principally in the colonies of Virginia and Maryland and shipped across the ocean, where it was fre-

This illustration of a Caribbean tobacco plantation shows an overseer directing the planting of the tobacco shoots while slaves in the drying sheds roll the leaves for export.

quently blended with European varieties. Although the English were the principal importers, it was the Dutch who dominated the European tobacco trade, making the most popular blends.

The new commodities flooded into Europe from all parts of the globe. By the middle of the eighteenth century, tea, coffee, cocoa, gin, and rum were among the most popular beverages. These were all products that had been largely unknown a century earlier. Among the wealthy, tea was served from porcelain pots imported from China; among all classes it was drunk with sugar imported from America. Beaver hats and Persian silks were fashionable in the upper reaches of society, rabbit caps and calico prints in the lower. New habits were created as new demands were satisfied. Tea and sugar passed from luxury to staple in little more than a generation, and the demand for both products continued to increase. To meet it, the European trading powers needed to create and maintain a powerful and efficient mercantile system.

Dutch Masters

For the nearly eighty years between 1565 and 1648 that the Dutch were at war, they grew ever more prosperous. While the economies of most other European nations were sapped by warfare, the Dutch seemed to draw strength from their interminable conflict with the Spanish empire. They did have the advantage of fighting defensively on land and offensively on sea. Land war was terribly costly to the aggressor, who had to raise large armies, transport them to the site of battles or sieges, and feed them while they were there. The defender simply had to fortify strong places, keep its water routes open to secure supplies, and wait for the weather to change. Sea war—or piracy, depending on one's viewpoint—required much smaller outlays for men and material and promised the rewards of captured prizes. The Dutch became expert at attacking the Spanish silver fleets, hunting like a lion against a herd by singling out the slower and smaller vessels for capture. The Dutch also benefited from the massive immigration into their provinces of Protestants who had lived and worked in the southern provinces. These immigrants brought with them vital skills in manufacturing and large reserves of capital for investment in Dutch commerce.

The Dutch grounded their prosperity on commerce. Excellent craftsmen, they took the lead in the skilled occupations necessary for finishing cloth, refining raw materials, and decorating consumer goods. They were

The Fishmarket at Leiden *by Jan Steen (ca. 1626–79) illustrates the importance of the fishing industry to the Dutch economy.*

also successful farmers, especially given the small amounts of land with which they had to work and the difficult ecological conditions in which they worked it. But their greatest abilities were in trade.

Although the Dutch Republic comprised seven separate political entities, with a total population of about two million, the province of Holland was preeminent among them. Holland contained more than a quarter of this population, and its trading port of Amsterdam was one of the great cities of Europe. The city had risen dramatically in the seventeenth century, growing from a midsized urban community of 65,000 in 1600 to a metropolis of 170,000 fifty years later. The port was one of the busiest in the world, for it was built to be an entrepôt. Vast warehouses and docks lined its canals. Visitors were impressed by the bustle, the cleanliness, and the businesslike appearance of Amsterdam. There were no great public squares and few recognizable monuments. The central buildings were the Bank and the Exchange, testimony to the dominant activities of the residents.

The Dutch dominated all types of European trade. They carried more English coal than England, more French wine than France, more Swedish iron than Sweden. Dutch ships outnumbered all others in every important port of Europe. Goods were brought to Amsterdam to be redistributed throughout the world. Dutch prosperity rested first upon the Baltic trade. Even after it ceased to expand in the middle of the seventeenth century, the Baltic trade composed over one-quarter of all of Holland's commercial enterprise. The Dutch also were the leaders in the East Indian trade throughout the seventeenth century. They held a virtual monopoly on the sale of exotic spices and the largest share of the pepper trade. Their imports of cottons, and especially of porcelain, began new consumer fads that soon resulted in the development of European industries. Dutch potteries began to produce china, as lower-quality ceramic goods came to be known. Dutch trade in the Atlantic was of less importance, but the Dutch did have a colonial presence in the New World, controlling a number of small islands and the rapidly growing mainland settlement of New Netherland. Yet the Dutch still dominated the secondary market in tobacco and sugar, becoming the largest processor and refiner of these important commodities.

In all of these activities the Dutch acted as merchants rather than as consumers. Unlike most other Europeans, they regarded precious metal as a commodity like any other and took no interest in accumulating it for its own sake. This attitude enabled them to pioneer triangular trading and develop the crucial financial institutions necessary to expand their overseas commerce. The Dutch were not so much inventors as improvers. They saw the practical value in Italian accounting and banking methods and raised them to new levels of efficiency. They made use of marine insurance to help diminish the risks of mercantile activity. Their legal system favored the creation of small trading companies by protecting individual investments. The European stock and commodity markets were centered in Amsterdam. By the 1670s, over 500 commodities were traded on the Amsterdam exchange, and even a primitive futures market had evolved for those who wished to speculate.

There were many explanations for the unparalleled growth of this small maritime state into one of the greatest of European trading empires. Geography and climate provided one impetus, the lack of sufficient foodstuffs another. Yet there were cultural characteristics as well. One was the openness of Dutch society. Even before the struggle with Spain, the northern provinces had shown a greater inclination toward religious toleration than had most parts of Europe. Amsterdam became a unique center for religious and intellectual exchange. European Jews flocked there, as did Catholic dissidents like Descartes. These people brought with them a wide range of skills and knowledge, along with capital that could be invested in trade. There was no real nobility among the Dutch, and certainly no set of values that prized investment in land over investment in trade. The French and Spanish nobility looked with scorn upon their mercantile classes and shunned any form of commercial investment; and the English, though more open to industry and trade, sank as much of their capital as possible into landed estates and country houses. The Dutch economic elite invested in trade. By the middle of the seventeenth century, the Dutch Republic enjoyed a reputation for cultural creativity that was the envy of the Continent. A truly extraordinary school of Dutch artists led by Rembrandt celebrated this new state born of commerce with vivid portrayals of its people and its prosperity.

Mercantile Organization

Elsewhere in Europe, trade was the king's business. The wealth of the nation was part of the prestige of the monarch, and its rise or fall part of the crown's power.

Power and prestige were far more important to absolute rulers than was the profit of merchants. Indeed, in all European states except the Dutch Republic, the activities of merchants were scorned by both the landed elite and the salaried bureaucrats. Leisure was valued by the one and royal service by the other. The pursuit of wealth by buying and selling somehow lacked dignity, yet the activities of the mercantile classes took on increasing importance for the state for two reasons. First, imported goods, especially luxuries, were a non-controversial target for taxation. Customs duties and excise taxes proliferated all over Europe. Representative assemblies composed of landed elites were usually happy to grant them to the monarch, and merchants could pass them on to consumers in higher prices. Second, the competition for trade was seen as a competition between states rather than individual merchants. Trading privileges involved special arrangements with foreign powers, arrangements that recognized the sovereign power of European monarchs. In this way, trade could bring glory to the state.

The competition for power and glory derived from the theory of mercantilism, a set of assumptions about economic activity that were commonly held throughout Europe and that guided the policies of almost every government. There were two interrelated ideas. One was that the wealth of a nation resided in its stock of precious metal, and the other was that economic activity was a zero-sum game. There was thought to be a fixed amount of money, a fixed number of commodities, and a fixed amount of consumption. Thus, what one country gained, another lost. If England bought wine from France and paid £100,000 in precious metal for it, then England was £100,000 poorer and France £100,000 richer. If one was to trade profitably, it was absolutely necessary to wind up with a surplus of precious metal. Therefore, it was imperative that governments regulate trade so that the stocks of precious metal were protected from the greed of the merchants. The first and most obvious measure of protection, then, was to prohibit the export of coin except by license, a prohibition that was absolutely unenforceable and was violated more often by government officials than by merchants.

These ideas about economic activity led to a variety of forms of economic regulation. The most common was the monopoly, a grant of special privileges in return for both financial considerations and an agreement to abide by the rules set out by the state. In the context of the seventeenth-century economy, there were a number of advantages to monopolies. First, of course, were those that accrued to the crown. There were direct and indirect revenues: monopolists usually paid considerable fees for their rights, and their activities were easy to monitor for purposes of taxation. The crown could use the grant of monopoly to reward past favors or to purchase future support from powerful individuals. There were also advantages for the monopolists. They could make capital investments with the expectation of long-term gains. This advantage was especially important in attracting investors for risky and expensive ventures like long-distance trade. Indeed, there were even benefits for the economy as a whole, as monopolies increased productive investment at a time when most capital was being used to purchase land, luxury goods, or offices.

Two monopoly companies, the English and the Dutch East India companies, dominated the Asian trade. The English East India Company, founded in 1600 with a capital of £30,000, was given the exclusive right to the Asian trade and immediately established itself throughout the Indian Ocean. The Dutch East India Company was formed two years later with ten times the capital of its English counterpart. By the end of the century, the Dutch company employed over twelve thousand people. Both companies were known as joint-stock companies, an innovation in the way in which businesses were organized. Subscribers owned a percentage of the total value of the company, based on the number of shares they bought, and were entitled to a distribution of profits on the same basis. Initially, the English company determined profits on single voyages and was supposed to distribute all of its assets to its shareholders after a given period. But changes in legal practice gave the company an identity separate from the individuals that held the shares. Now shares could be exchanged without the breakup of the company as a whole. Both Amsterdam and London soon developed stock markets to trade the shares of monopoly companies.

Both East India companies were remarkably good investments. The Dutch East India Company paid an average dividend of 18 percent for over two hundred years. The value of English East India Company shares rose fivefold in the second half of the seventeenth century alone. Few other monopoly companies achieved a record comparable to that of the East India companies. The English Royal African Company, founded in 1672 to provide slaves for the Spanish colonies, barely recouped costs and was soon superseded by private trade. Even the French East Indian and African companies, which were modeled on the Dutch and Eng-

EASTERN TRADERS

The Dutch East India Company was the most important of the monopoly trading companies that were founded in the early seventeenth century. It was organized as a stock company and its shares traded on the Amsterdam bourse. Merchants could purchase portions of its ships for both imports and exports, and the company was given total control over the eastern spice trade. It was also given political and diplomatic powers in the areas in which it traded, and its overseas members behaved as much as foreign ambassadors as merchants. This excerpt, from an early history of the company, provides details of its original charter.

After various private merchants joined with others in the 1590s and after the turn of the century to form companies, first in Amsterdam and then in other cities of Holland and Zeeland, to open up and undertake travel and trade with the East Indies, and from time to time equipped and sent out many ships, which returned, on the average, with no small success, the States General came to the conclusion that it would be more useful and profitable not only for the country as a whole but also for its inhabitants individually, especially all those who had undertaken and shared in navigation and trade, that these companies should be combined and this navigation and trade be placed and maintained on a firm footing, with order and political guidance. After much argument and persuasion, this union was worked out by Their High Mightinesses [the government of the United Provinces], in their own words, to advance the prosperity of the United Netherlands, to conserve and increase its industry and to bring profit to the Company and to the people of the country.

. . . The Company's charter authorized it to make alliances with princes and potentates east of the Cape of Good Hope and beyond the Straits of Magellan, to make contracts, build fortresses and strongholds,

name governors, raise troops, appoint officers of justice, and perform other necessary services for the advancement of trade; to dismiss the said governors and officers of justice if their conduct was found to be harmful and disloyal, provided that these governors or officers could not be prevented from returning here to present such grievances or complaints as they think they might have. . . .

The inhabitants of this country were permitted to invest as much or as little as they pleased in shares of the Company.

The subscription had to be made before September 1, 1602. . . .

. . . When the time for this investment or subscription had expired, various competent persons in different places presented requests in person or by sealed letter to the assembly of the XVII, asking that they be permitted to join the Company with the investment of certain sums of money; it was decided that no one else should be permitted to join in violation of the charter and to the detriment of the shareholders who had paid in their subscriptions before the expiration of the date fixed, and that the subscribed capital should be neither increased nor reduced.

---

lish, were forced to abandon their monopolies. The Dutch and English companies were successful not because of their special privileges but because they were able to lower the costs of protecting their ships and cargoes.

Monopolies were not the only form of regulation in which seventeenth-century government engaged. For those states with Atlantic colonies, regulation took the form of restricting markets rather than traders. In the 1660s the English government, alarmed at the growth

of Dutch mercantile activity in the New World, passed a series of Navigation Acts designed to protect English shipping. Colonial goods—primarily tobacco and sugar—could be shipped to and from England only in English boats. If the French wanted to purchase West Indian sugar, they could not simply send a ship to the English colony of Barbados loaded with French goods and exchange them for sugar. Rather, they had to make their purchases from an English import-export merchant and the goods had to be unloaded in an English

DEFINING COMMERCE

Adam Smith was a Scottish political theorist whose work The Wealth of Nations *(1776) was the first great work of economic analysis in European history. Smith had wide-ranging interests and wrote with equal authority about manufacturing, population, and trade. He was the first to develop the doctrine of free trade, which he called* laissez-faire. *Smith argued that the government that governed least governed best, and he was an early critic of protective tariffs and monopolies.*

Every individual necessarily labours to render the annual revenue of the society as great as he can. He generally, indeed, neither intends to promote the public interest, nor knows how much he is promoting it. By preferring the support of domestic to that of foreign industry, he intends only his own security; and by directing that industry in such a manner as its produce may be of the greatest value, he intends only his own gain, and he is in this, as in many other cases, led by an invisible hand to promote an end which was no part of his intention. Nor is it always the worse for the society that it was no part of it. By pursuing his own interest he frequently promotes that of the society more effectually than when he really intends to promote it. I have never known much good done by those who affected to trade for the public good. . . .

. . . Each nation has been made to look with an invidious eye upon the prosperity of all the nations with which it trades, and to consider their gain as its own loss. Commerce, which ought naturally to be, among nations as among individuals, a bond of union and friendship, has become the most fertile source of discord and animosity. The capricious ambition of kings and ministers has not, during the present and the preceding century, been more fatal to the repose of Europe, than the impertinent jealousy of merchants and manufacturers. The violence and injustice of the rulers of mankind is an ancient evil, for which, I am afraid, the nature of human affairs can scarce admit of a remedy. But the mean rapacity, the monopolizing spirit of merchants and manufacturers, who neither are, nor ought to be, the rulers of mankind, though it cannot perhaps be corrected, may very easily be prevented from disturbing the tranquility of anybody but themselves. . . .

The natural advantages which one country has over another in producing particular commodities are sometimes so great, that it is acknowledged by all the world to be in vain to struggle with them. . . . Very good grapes can be raised in Scotland, and very good wine too can be made of them at about thirty times the expense for which at least equally good can be brought from foreign countries. Would it be a reasonable law to prohibit the importation of all foreign wines merely to encourage the making of claret and burgundy in Scotland?

From Adam Smith, *The Wealth of Nations* (1776).

port before they could be reloaded to be shipped to France. As a result, the English reexport trade skyrocketed. In the year 1700, reexports amounted to nearly 40 percent of all English commerce. With such a dramatic increase in trading, all moved in English ships, shipbuilding boomed. English coastal towns enjoyed heightened prosperity, as did the great colonial ports of Bristol and Liverpool. For a time, colonial protection proved effective.

French protectionism was as much internal as colonial. The French entered the intercontinental trade later than their North Atlantic rivals, and they were less dependent on trade for their subsistence. Of all the states of Europe, only France could satisfy its needs from its own resources. But to achieve such self-sufficiency required coordination and leadership. In the 1670s, Louis XIV's finance minister, Jean-Baptiste Colbert (1619–83), developed a plan to bolster the French economy by protecting it against European imports. First Colbert followed the English example of restricting the reexport trade by requiring that imports come to France either in French ships or in the ships of the country from which the goods originated. In addition, he used tariffs to make imported goods unattractive in France. He sponsored a drive to increase French manufacturing, especially of textiles, tapestries, linens, glass, and furniture. To protect the investments in French manufacturing, enormous duties were placed on the import of similar goods manufactured elsewhere. The Venetian glass industry, for example, suffered a serious blow from Colbert's tariffs. English woolen manufacturers were also damaged, and the English sought retaliatory measures. But in fact, the English had already begun to imitate this form of protection. In the early eighteenth century, England attempted to limit the importation of cotton goods from India to prevent the collapse of the domestic clothing industry.

The Navigation Acts and Colbert's program of protective tariffs were directed specifically against Dutch reexporters. The Dutch were the acknowledged leaders in all branches of commerce in the seventeenth century. There were many summers when there were more Dutch vessels in London Harbor than there were English ships. In the 1670s the Dutch merchant fleet was probably larger than the English, French, Spanish, Portuguese, and German fleets combined! Restrictive navigation practices were one way to combat an advantage that the Dutch had built through heavy capital investment and by breaking away from the prevailing theories about the relationship between wealth and precious metals. The English and French Navigation Acts cut heavily into the Dutch trade, and ultimately both the English and French overtook them. But protectionism had its price. Just as the dynastic wars were succeeded by the wars of religion, so the wars of religion were succeeded by the wars of commerce.

"The discovery of America and that of a passage to the East Indies by the Cape of Good Hope are the two greatest and most important events in the history of mankind." So wrote the great Scottish economist Adam Smith (1723–90) in *The Wealth of Nations* (1776). For Smith and his generation, the first great age of commerce was coming to an end. The innovations of the Dutch had given way to a settled pattern of international long-distance trade. States now viewed commerce as a part of their national self-interest. They developed overseas empires, which they protected as markets for their goods and sources for their raw materials. These were justified by the theory of mercantilism and the demands of a generation of consumers who saw the luxuries of the past as the necessities of the present.

The Wars of Commerce

The belief that there was a fixed amount of trade in the world was still strong in the late seventeenth century. One country's gains in trade were another's losses. There was not more than enough to go around, and it could not be easily understood how the expansion of one country's trade could benefit all countries. Competition for trade was the same as competition for territory or subjects, part of the struggle by which the state grew powerful. It was not inevitable that economic competition would lead to warfare, only that restrictive competition would.

Thus the scramble for colonies in the seventeenth century led to commercial warfare in the eighteenth. As the English gradually replaced the Dutch as the leading commercial nation, so the French replaced the English as the leading competitor. Hostility between the English and the French had existed for centuries, and it was not without cause that the commercial wars of the eighteenth century should be likened to the territorial wars of the Middle Ages. The greed of merchants and the glory of princes fueled a struggle for the dominance of world markets that brought European warfare to every corner of the globe.

The Mercantile Wars

Commercial warfare in Europe began between the English and the Dutch in the middle of the seventeenth century. Both had established aggressive overseas trading companies in the Atlantic and in Asia. In the early seventeenth century, the Dutch were the undisputed leaders, their carrying capacity and trade monopolies the greatest in the world. But the English were rising quickly. Their Atlantic colonies began to produce valuable new commodities like tobacco and sugar, and their Asian trade was expanding decade after decade. Conflict was inevitable, and the result was a series of three naval wars fought between 1652 and 1674.

The Dutch had little choice but to strike out against English policy, but they also had little chance of overall success. Their spectacular naval victory in 1667, when the Dutch fleet surprised many English warships at port and burned both ships and docks at Chatham, obscured the fact that Dutch commercial superiority was slipping. In 1664 the English conquered New Netherland on the North American mainland and renamed it New York. With this defeat, the Dutch lost their largest colonial possession. The wars were costly

Painter Jan Peter depicts an incident in the naval warfare caused by trade rivalry between the Dutch and the English. The Dutch fleet sailed up the Medway River and destroyed many English vessels, towing away a battleship.

to both states, nearly bankrupting the English Crown in 1672. Anglo-Dutch rivalry was finally laid to rest after 1688, when William of Orange, stadtholder of Holland, became William III (1689–1702), king of England.

The Anglo-Dutch commercial wars were just one part of a larger European conflict. Dutch commerce was as threatening to France as it was to England, though in a different way. Under Colbert, France pursued a policy of economic independence. The state supported internal industrial activity through the financing of large workshops and the encouragement of new manufacturing techniques. To protect French products, Colbert levied a series of punitive tariffs on Dutch imports, which severely depressed both trade and manufacture in Holland. Although the Dutch retaliated with restrictive tariffs of their own—in 1672 they banned the import of all French goods for an entire year—the Dutch economy depended on free trade. The Dutch had much more to lose than did France in a battle of protective tariffs.

But the battle that Louis XIV had in mind was to be more deadly than one of tariffs. Greedily he eyed the Spanish Netherlands—to which he had a weak claim through his Habsburg wife—believing that the Dutch stood in the way of his plans. The Dutch had entered into an alliance with the English and Swedes in 1668 to counter French policy, and Louis was determined to

crush them in retaliation. He successfully bought off both of Holland's supposed allies, providing cash pensions to the kings of England and Sweden in return for England's active participation and Sweden's passive neutrality in the impending war. In 1672 Louis's army, over one hundred thousand strong, invaded the Low Countries and swept all before them. Only the opening of the dikes prevented the French from entering the province of Holland itself.

The French invasion coincided with the third Anglo-Dutch war, and the United Provinces found themselves besieged on land and sea. Their international trade was disrupted, their manufacturing industries were in ruins, and their military budget skyrocketed. Only able diplomacy and skillful military leadership prevented total Dutch demise. A separate peace was made with England, and Spain, whose sovereign territory had been invaded, entered the war on the side of the Dutch, as did a number of German states. Louis's hope for a lightning victory faded, and the war settled into a series of interminable sieges and reliefs of fortified towns. The Dutch finally persuaded France to come to terms in the Treaty of Nijmegen (1678–79). While Louis XIV retained a number of the territories he had taken from Spain, his armies withdrew from the United Provinces and he agreed to lift most of the commercial sanctions against Dutch goods. The first phase of mercantile warfare was over.

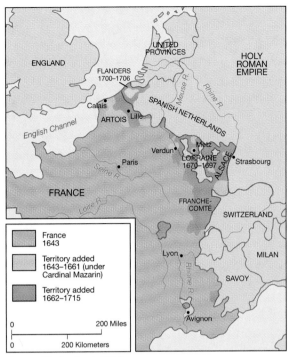

France Under Louis XIV

The Wars of Louis XIV

It was Louis XIV's ambition to restore the ancient Burgundian territories to the French crown and to provide secure northern and eastern borders for his state. Pursuit of these aims involved him in conflicts with nearly every other European state. Spain had fought for eighty years to preserve the Burgundian inheritance in the Low Countries. By the Peace of Westphalia (1648), the northern portion of this territory became the United Provinces, while the southern portion remained loyal to the crown and became the Spanish Netherlands. This territory provided a barrier between Holland and France that both states attempted to strengthen by establishing fortresses and bridgeheads at strategic places. In the east, Louis eyed the duchies of Lorraine and Alsace and the large swath of territory farther south known as Franche-Comté. The Peace of Westphalia had granted France control of a number of imperial cities in these duchies, and Louis aimed to link them together. All of these territories were ruled by Habsburgs: Alsace and Lorraine by the Austrian Holy Roman Emperor, Franche-Comté by the Spanish king.

In the late seventeenth century, ambassadors and ministers of state began to develop the theory of a balance of power in Europe. This was a belief that no state or combination of states should be allowed to become so powerful that its existence threatened the peace of the others. Behind this purely political idea of the balance of power lay a theory of collective security that knit together the European state system. French expansion in either direction not only threatened the other states directly involved but also posed a threat to European security in general.

Louis showed his hand clearly enough in the Franco-Dutch war that had ended in 1679. Although he withdrew his forces from the United Provinces and evacuated most of the territories he had conquered,

The ratification of the Treaty of Münster (1648). Under the treaty, Spain finally recognized Dutch independence.

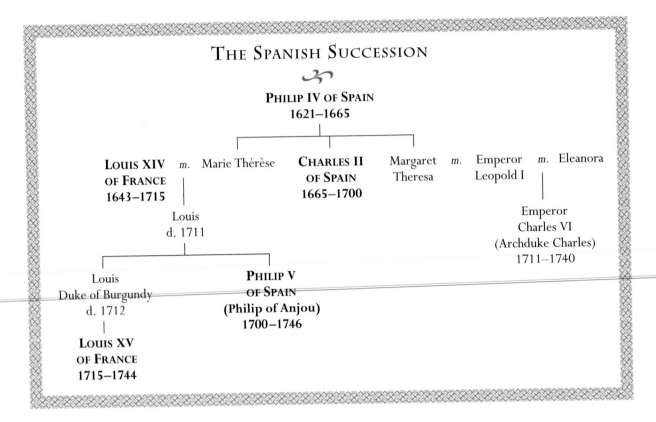

The Spanish Succession

Philip IV of Spain
1621–1665

Louis XIV   *m.*   Marie Thérèse   **Charles II**   Margaret   *m.*   Emperor   *m.*   Eleanora
of France   **of Spain**   Theresa   Leopold I
1643–1715   **1665–1700**

Louis   Emperor
d. 1711   Charles VI
                                                                                      (Archduke Charles)
                                                                                      1711–1740

Louis   **Philip V**
Duke of Burgundy   **of Spain**
d. 1712   **(Philip of Anjou)**
                            1700–1746

Louis XV
of France
1715–1744

France absorbed Franche-Comté by the Treaty of Nijmegen, as well as portions of the Spanish Netherlands. Louis began plotting his next adventure almost as soon as the treaty was signed. Over the next several years, French troops advanced steadily into Alsace, ultimately forcing the city of Strasbourg, a vital bridgehead on the Rhine, to recognize French sovereignty. Expansion into northern Italy was similarly calculated. Everywhere Louis looked, French engineers rushed to construct fortresses and magazines in preparation for another war.

It finally came in 1688 when French troops poured across the Rhine to seize Cologne. A united German empire led by Leopold I, archduke of Austria, combined with the maritime powers of England and Holland, led by William III, to form the Grand Alliance, the first of the great balance-of-power coalitions. In fact, the two sides proved so evenly matched that the Nine Years' War (1688–97) settled very little, but it demonstrated that a successful European coalition could be formed against France. It also signified the permanent shift in alliances that resulted from the Rev-

olution of 1688 in England. Although the English had allied with France against the Dutch in 1672, after William became king he persuaded the English Parliament that the real enemy was France. Louis's greatest objective, to secure the borders of his state, had withstood its greatest test. He might have rested satisfied but for the vagaries of births, marriages, and deaths.

Like his father, Louis XIV had married a daughter of the king of Spain. Philip IV had married his eldest daughter to Louis XIV and a younger one to Leopold I of Austria, who subsequently became the Holy Roman Emperor (1658–1705). Before he died, Philip finally fathered a son, Charles II (1665–1700), who attained the Spanish crown at the age of four but was mentally and physically incapable of ruling his vast empire. For decades it was apparent that there would be no direct Habsburg successor to an empire that, despite its recent losses, still contained Spain, South America, the Spanish Netherlands, and most of Italy. Louis XIV and Leopold I both had legitimate claims to an inheritance that would have irreversibly tipped the European balance of power.

As Charles II grew increasingly feeble, efforts to find a suitable compromise to the problem of the Spanish succession were led by William III, who, as stadtholder of Holland, was vitally interested in the fate of the Spanish Netherlands and, as king of England, in the fate of the Spanish American colonies. In the 1690s two treaties of partition were drawn up. The first achieved near universal agreement but was nullified by the death of the German prince who was to inherit the Spanish crown. The second, which would have given Italy to Louis's son and everything else to Leopold's son, was opposed by Leopold, who had neither naval nor commercial interests and who claimed most of the Italian territories as imperial fiefs.

War of the Spanish Succession

An eighteenth-century English playing card showing Philip of Anjou, the grandson of Louis XIV, stealing the Spanish crown.

All of these plans had been made without consulting the Spanish. If it was the aim of the European powers to partition the Spanish empire in order to prevent any one state from inheriting too much of it, it was the aim of the Spanish to maintain their empire intact. To this end, they devised a brilliant plan. Charles II bequeathed his entire empire to Philip of Anjou, the younger grandson of Louis XIV, with two stipulations: first, that Philip renounce his claim to the French throne; and second, that he accept the empire intact, without partition. If he—or more to the point, if his grandfather Louis XIV—did not accept these conditions, then the empire would pass to Archduke Charles, the younger son of Leopold I. Such provisions virtually assured war between France and the empire unless compromise between the two powers could be reached. But before terms could even be suggested, Charles II died and Philip V (1700–46) was proclaimed king of Spain and its empire.

Thus the eighteenth century opened with the War of the Spanish Succession (1702–14). Emperor Leopold rejected the provisions of Charles's will and sent his troops to occupy Italy. Louis XIV confirmed

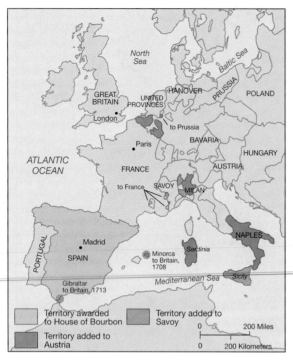

The Treaty of Utrecht, Europe 1714

Efforts to negotiate a peace settlement took longer than the war itself. The Austrians had taken control of Italy, the English and Dutch had secured the Spanish Netherlands, and the French had been driven back beyond the Rhine. The Allies believed that they could now enforce any treaty they pleased on Louis XIV and, along with concessions from France, attempted to oust his grandson, Philip V, from the Spanish throne. This proved impossible to achieve, though it took more than five years to learn the lesson. By then the European situation had taken another strange twist. Both Emperor Leopold and his eldest son had died. Now Leopold's younger son, Archduke Charles, inherited the empire as Charles VI (1711–40) and raised the prospect of an equally dangerous combined Austrian-Spanish state. Between 1713 and 1714, a series of treaties at Utrecht settled the War of the Spanish Succession. Spanish possessions in Italy and the Netherlands were ceded to Austria; France abandoned all its territorial gains east of the Rhine and ceded its North American territories of Nova Scotia and Newfoundland to England. England also acquired from Spain Gibraltar, on the southern coast of Spain, and the island of Minorca in the Mediterranean. Both were strategically important to English commercial interests. English intervention in the Nine Years' War and the War of the Spanish Succession did not result in large territorial gains, but it did result in an enormous increase in English power and prestige. Over the next thirty years England would assert its own imperial claims.

The Colonial Wars

The Treaty of Utrecht (1713–14) ushered in almost a quarter century of peace in western Europe. Austrian rule in the Netherlands and Italy remained a major irritant to the Spanish, but Spain was too weak to do more than sulk and snarl. The death of Louis XIV in 1715 quelled French ambitions for a time and even led to an Anglo-French accord that guaranteed the preservation of the settlement reached at Utrecht. Peace allowed Europe to rebuild its shattered economy and resume the international trade that had been so severely disrupted over the last forty years. The Treaty of Utrecht had resolved a number of important trading issues, all in favor of Great Britain (as England was known after its union with Scotland in 1707). In addition to receiving Gibraltar and Minorca from Spain, Britain was also

the worst fears of William III when he provided his grandson with French troops to "defend" the Spanish Netherlands. William III revived the Grand Alliance and initiated a massive land war against the combined might of France and Spain. The allied objectives were twofold: to prevent the unification of the French and Spanish thrones and to partition the Spanish empire so that both Italy and the Netherlands were ceded to Austria. The objective of Louis XIV was simply to preserve as much as possible of the Spanish inheritance for the house of Bourbon.

William III died in 1702 and was succeeded by Anne (1702–14). John Churchill (1650–1722), duke of Marlborough and commander in chief of the army, continued William's policy. England and Holland again provided most of the finance and sea power, but, in addition, the English also provided a land army nearly seventy thousand strong. Prussia joined the Grand Alliance, and disciplined Prussian troops helped offset the addition of the Spanish army to Louis's forces. In 1704 Churchill defeated French forces at Blenheim in Germany, and in 1706 at Ramillies in the Spanish Netherlands. France's military ascendancy was over.

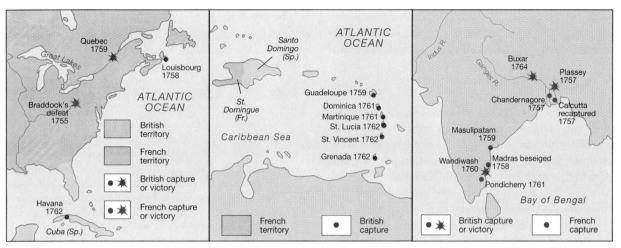

The Seven Years' War

granted the monopoly to provide slaves to the Spanish American colonies and the right to send one trading ship a year to them. In east and west, Britain was becoming the dominant commercial power in the world.

At least some of the reason for Britain's preeminence was the remarkable growth of the Atlantic colonies. The colonial economy was booming, and consumer goods that were in demand in London, Paris, and Amsterdam were also in demand in Boston, Philadelphia, and New York. Like every other colonial power, the British held a monopoly on their colonial trade. They were far less successful than the Spanish and French in enforcing the notion that colonies existed only for the benefit of the parent country, but the English Parliament continued to pass legislation aimed at restricting colonial trade with other nations and other nations' colonies. Like almost all other mercantile restrictions, these efforts were stronger in theory than in practice. Tariffs on imports and customs duties on British goods provided a double incentive for smuggling.

France emerged as Britain's true colonial rival. In the Caribbean, the French had the largest and most profitable of the West Indian sugar islands, Saint Domingue (modern-day Haiti). In North America, France held not only Canada but laid claim to the entire continent west of the Ohio River. The French did not so much settle their colonial territory as occupy it. They surveyed the land, established trading relations with the Native Americans, and built forts at strategic locations. The English, in contrast, had developed fixed communities, which grew larger and more prosperous by the decade. France determined to defend its colonies by establishing an overseas military presence. Regular French troops were shipped to Canada and installed in Louisbourg, Montreal, and Quebec. The British responded with troops of their own and sent an expeditionary force to clear the French from the Ohio River Valley. This action was the immediate cause of the Seven Years' War (1756–63).

Although the Seven Years' War had a bitter Continental phase, it was essentially a war for empire between the English and the French. There were three main theaters: the North American mainland, the West Indian sugar plantations, and the eastern coast of India. All over the globe, the British won smashing victories. The British navy blockaded the water route to Canada, inflicting severe hardship on French settlers in Montreal and Quebec. British forces ultimately captured both towns. After some initial successes, the French were driven back west across the Mississippi River, and their line of fortresses in the Ohio Valley fell into English hands. The English also succeeded in taking all the French sugar islands except Saint Domingue. British success in India was equally complete. The French were chased from their major trading zone and English dominance was secured.

By the end of the Seven Years' War, Britain had become a global imperial power. In the Peace of Paris (1763), France ceded all of Canada in exchange for the return of its West Indian islands. British dominion in the East Indian trade was recognized and led ultimately to British dominion of India itself. In less than a century, the ascendancy of France was broken and Europe's first modern imperial power had been created.

• • •

European commercial expansion was the first step in a long process that would ultimately transform the material life of all human beings. The quest for new commodities led to increased sophistication in transportation, marketing, and distribution—all vital developments for agricultural changes in the future. The ability to move large quantities of goods from place to place and to exchange them between different parts of the globe laid the foundation for organized manufacturing. The practical impact of scientific discovery, as yet only dimly glimpsed, would soon spur the transformation of handicrafts into industries. In the eighteenth century the material world was still being conquered, and the most unattractive features of this conquest were all too plainly visible. Luxuries for the rich were won by the labors of the poor. The pleasures of sugar and tobacco were purchased at the price of slavery for millions of Africans. The greed of merchants and the glory of princes was an unholy alliance that resulted in warfare around the globe. But it was a shrinking globe, one whose peoples were becoming increasingly interdependent, tied together by the goods and services that they could provide to each other.

Suggestions for Further Reading

General Reading

* A. Rupert Hall, *The Revolution in Science, 1500–1750* (London: Longman, 1983). The best introduction to the varieties of scientific thought in the early modern period. Detailed and complex.

* Jan de Vries, *The European Economy in an Age of Crisis* (Cambridge: Cambridge University Press, 1976). A comprehensive study of economic development, including long-distance trade and commercial change.

* K. H. D. Haley, *The Dutch in the Seventeenth Century* (London: Thames and Hudson, 1972). A well-written and well-illustrated history of the golden age of Holland.

* Derek McKay and H. M. Scott, *The Rise of the Great Powers, 1648–1815* (London: Longman, 1983). An outstanding survey of diplomacy and warfare.

* Jeremy Black, *The Rise of the European Powers, 1679–1793* (New York: Edward Arnold, 1990). A new look at diplomatic history from an English point of view.

The New Science

* Margaret C. Jacob, *The Cultural Meaning of the Scientific Revolution* (New York: Alfred A. Knopf, 1988). Scientific thought portrayed in its social context.

* Stillman Drake, *Galileo* (New York: Hill and Wang, 1980). A short but engaging study of the great Italian scientist.

* Allen Debus, *Man and Nature in the Renaissance* (Cambridge: Cambridge University Press, 1978). An especially good account of the intellectual roots of scientific thought.

* Richard Westfall, *The Construction of Modern Science: Mechanisms and Mechanics* (Cambridge: Cambridge University Press, 1977). A survey of scientific developments from Kepler to Newton. A good introduction to both mechanics and mathematics.

Charles Webster, *The Great Instauration: Science, Medicine, and Reform* (London: Duckworth, 1975). A complicated but rewarding analysis of experimental science and the origins of scientific medicine.

David Lindberg and Robert Westman, eds., *Reappraisals of the Scientific Revolution* (Cambridge: Cambridge University Press, 1990). A collection of essays that survey recent scholarship on the scientific revolution.

* Frank E. Manuel, *Sir Isaac Newton: A Portrait* (Cambridge, MA: Harvard University Press, 1968). A readable account of one of the most complex intellects in European history, from a psychoanalytic point of view.

* Richard Westfall, *The Life of Isaac Newton* (Cambridge: Cambridge University Press, 1993). The best short biography.

Empires of Goods

*Ralph Davis, *The Rise of the Atlantic Economies* (Ithaca, NY: Cornell University Press, 1973). A nation-by-nation survey of the colonial powers.

* J. N. Ball, *Merchants and Merchandize: The Expansion of Trade in Europe* (London: Croom Helm, 1977). A good overview of European overseas economies.

* K. N. Chaudhuri, *The Trading World of Asia and the English East India Company* (Cambridge: Cambridge University Press, 1978). A brilliant account of the impact of the Indian trade on both Europeans and Asians.

* Sidney Mintz, *Sweetness and Power* (New York: Viking Press, 1985). An anthropologist explores the lure of sugar and its impact on Western society.

* Philip Curtin, *The Atlantic Slave Trade* (Madison: University of Wisconsin Press, 1969). A study of the importation of African slaves into the new world, with the best estimates of the numbers of slaves and their destinations.

* Joseph Miller, *Way of Death: Merchant Capitalism and the Angolan Slave Trade, 1730–1830* (Madison: University of Wisconsin Press, 1988). An illuminating portrait of the eighteenth-century slave trade, with an unforgettable account of the slave voyages.

* Jonathan Israel, *Dutch Primacy in World Trade, 1585–1740* (Oxford: Oxford University Press, 1989). The triumph of Dutch traders and techniques written by the leading authority.

* Simon Schama, *The Embarassment of Riches* (New York: Alfred A. Knopf, 1987). A social history of the Dutch Republic that explores the meaning of commerce in Dutch society.

* Holden Furber, *Rival Empires of Trade in the Orient, 1600–1800* (Minneapolis: University of Minnesota Press, 1976). A comprehensive survey of the battle for control of the Asian trade in the seventeenth and eighteenth centuries.

The Wars of Commerce

A. C. Carter, *Neutrality or Commitment: The Evolution of Dutch Foreign Policy, 1667–1795* (London: Edward Arnold, 1975). A tightly written study of the objectives and course of Dutch diplomacy.

Charles Wilson, *Profit and Power* (London: Longman, 1957). Still the best study of the Anglo-Dutch wars of the mid-seventeenth century.

Herbert Rowan, *The Princes of Orange* (Cambridge: Cambridge University Press, 1988). An engrossing history of the family that ruled the Dutch Republic.

Paul Langford, *The Eighteenth Century, 1688–1815* (New York: St. Martin's Press, 1976). A reliable guide to the growth of British power.

Ragnhild Hatton, ed., *Louis XIV and Europe* (London: Macmillan, 1976). An important collection of essays on French foreign policy in its most aggressive posture.

Richard Pares, *War and Trade in the West Indies, 1739–63* (Oxford: Oxford University Press, 1936). A blow-by-blow account of the struggle for colonial supremacy in the sugar islands.

*Paperback edition available.

18 ⮞ The Balance of Power in Eighteenth-Century Europe

Calling the Tune

Frederick the Great loved music. During his youth it was one of his private passions that so infuriated his father. Mathematics; political economy; modern languages—even the dreaded French—these were the subjects that a future king of Prussia should learn. But music, never. Rather, the boy should be at the hunt watching the dogs tear apart a stag, or on maneuvers with the Potsdam guards, a troop of soldiers all nearly seven feet tall. This was the regimen King Frederick William I prescribed for his son. It was no longer enough to reign over one's subjects; to be a successful monarch in the power politics of the eighteenth century, a king had to be a soldier.

But Frederick the Great loved music. He secretly collected all the books and manuscripts he could find on the subject, outspending his tiny allowance in the process. He had Johann Quantz (1697–1773), the greatest flutist of the day, placed on his staff to teach him and to conspire with him against his father. At night, while the old king drank himself into a stupor—an activity he warmly recommended to his son—Frederick powdered his hair, put on a jacket of the latest French style, and regaled his friends with his newest compositions. A lookout guarded the door in case the king wandered by unexpectedly. Once the musicians were almost discovered and Frederick's fine new jacket was tossed on the fire, but the flutes and musical scores remained safely hidden.

After he became king, Frederick the Great could indulge his passion more openly. Yet he preferred to hold his concerts, usually small gatherings, at the Palace of San Souci, which he built in Potsdam. A special music room was designed for the king's use, and he lavished attention on it. The great chandelier, lit by a circle of candles, illuminated the center of the room and highlighted the soloist. The entire palace reflected Frederick's personal taste. Unlike most great palaces of state, it was small, functional, and beautiful. Here Frederick could escape the mounting cares of governing one of the most powerful states in Europe by reading, corresponding with eminent French intellectuals, and playing the flute. In this picture, *Das Flötenkonzert* (The Flute Concert), Frederick is portrayed performing in his great music room. Before a small audience of courtiers and intimates, he plays to the accompaniment of cello, violins, and piano.

Frederick's talent was real enough. A British visitor to Sans Souci, who had little reason to flatter the king, reported: "I was much pleased and surprised with the neatness of his execution. His performance surpassed anything I had ever heard among the dilettanti or even professors." This judgment is reinforced when one studies the expressions of the three men in the left corner of the painting. They are taking genuine pleasure in the music they are hearing (all the more genuine in that the king's back is to them). So, too, are the musicians who are accompanying the king. There is as much joy as concentration upon their faces.

Frederick's musical accomplishment was not unique among eighteenth-century monarchs: Joseph II of Austria was also a skilled flutist. But it was not so much music as accomplishment that was coming to be valued among the monarchs of the new European powers. Catherine the Great of Russia corresponded with philosophers; Frederick the Great brought the great French intellectual Voltaire (1698–1778) to his court—though they quickly took a dislike to each other. The acquisition of culture seemed to matter more and more as the century wore on. Museums, opera houses, and great art collections were established all over the Continent. The Hermitage in Saint Petersburg was stocked with the works of Dutch and English masters. The British Museum was founded in London with the support of King George II, who deposited his great library there. Whether this veneer of culture did anything to lessen the brutality of warfare and power politics is a matter of opinion. But as a veneer it was as highly polished as the flute that Frederick the Great is so delicately pressing to his mouth.

Europe in 1714

Europe in 1714

Within a relatively short span of time at the beginning of the eighteenth century, two treaties brought about a considerable reorganization of the political geography of Europe. The Treaty of Utrecht (1713–14) created a new Europe in the west. The Treaty of Nystad (1721) created a new Europe in the east. Both agreements reflected the dynamics of change that had taken place over the previous century. The rise of France on the Continent and Britain's colonial empire around the globe were facts that could no longer be ignored. The decline of Sweden and Poland and the emergence of Russia as a great power were the beginning of a long-term process that would continue to dominate European history.

All of this could be seen on a map of Europe in the early eighteenth century. France's absorption of Alsace and encroachments into Lorraine would be bones of contention between the French and the Germans for two centuries and would ultimately contribute to the outbreak of World Wars I and II. The political footballs of the Spanish Netherlands and Spanish Italy, now temporarily Austrian, continued to be kicked about until the nationalist movements of the nineteenth century gave birth to Belgium, Luxembourg, and a united Italy. The emergence of Brandenburg-Prussia on the north German coast and the gradual decline of the Holy Roman Emperor's power were both vital to the process that created a unified Germany and a separate Austria. In the southeast, the slow but steady reconquest of the Balkans from Ottoman dominion restored the historic southern border of the Continent. The inexorable expansion of Russia was also already apparent.

Expansion in the West

Perhaps the most obvious transformation in the political geography of western Europe was the expansion of European power around the globe. In the Atlantic, Spain remained the largest colonial power. Through its viceroyalty system it controlled all of Mexico and Central America; the largest and most numerous of the Caribbean islands; North America from Colorado to California (as well as Florida); and most of South America. The other major colonial power in the region was Portugal, which shared dominion over the South American continent. In the Portuguese colony of Brazil, production of sugar, dyestuffs, timbers, and exotic commodities amply repaid the meager investment the Portuguese had made.

In North America, the French and British shared the eastern half of the continent. The French controlled most of it. They had landed first in Canada and then slowly made their way down the Saint Lawrence River. New France, as their colonial empire was called, was a trading territory, and it expanded along the greatest of the waterways: the Great Lakes and the Ohio, Missouri, and Mississippi rivers. French settlements had sprung up as far south as the Gulf of Mexico. France also claimed the territory of Louisiana, named for Louis XIV, which stretched from New Orleans to Montana. The British settlements were all coastal, stretching from Maine to Georgia on the Atlantic seaboard. Unlike the French, the British settled their territory and were only interested in expansion when their population, which was doubling every twenty-five years, outgrew its resources. By the early eighteenth century, the ports of Boston, New York, Philadelphia, and Charleston were thriving commercial centers.

Europeans managed their eastern colonial territories differently than they did those in the Atlantic. Initially the Portuguese and the Dutch had been satisfied with establishing trading factories—coastal fortresses in Africa and Asia that could be used as warehouses and defended against attack. But in the seventeenth century, the European states began to take control of vital ports and lucrative islands. Here the Dutch were the acknowledged leaders, replacing the Portuguese, who had begun the process at the end of the sixteenth century. Holland held by force or in conjunction with local leaders all the Spice Islands in the Pacific. The Dutch also occupied both sides of the Malay Peninsula and nearly all the coastal areas of the islands in the Java Sea. Dutch control of Ceylon was strategically important for its Indian trade. Compared to the Dutch Republic, all other European states had only a minor

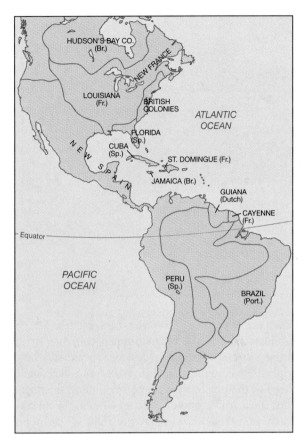

The Americas

territorial presence in the East, with the exception of Spain, which still controlled the Philippines. The British had limited their eastern outposts to trading establishments, and through these they maintained a significant presence in India. During the eighteenth century, the British began to colonize the Indian subcontinent directly.

Imperial expansion was the most obvious change in the geopolitical boundaries of Europe, but it was not the only one. A brief tour of the western states after the Treaty of Utrecht reveals some others. In 1707 England and Scotland formally joined together to form Great Britain. In addition to its eastern and western colonies, Britain had also gained control of Gibraltar at the foot of Spain and the island of Minorca in the Mediterranean. Both territories were strategically important to British commerce.

Across the English Channel were the Low Countries, now permanently divided between the United Provinces in the north, led by Holland, and those provinces in the south that had remained loyal to the Spanish crown in the sixteenth century. By 1714 the

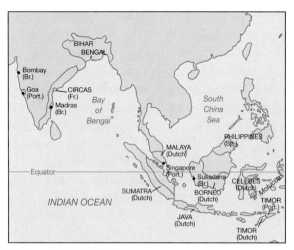

India and the East Indies

now being slowly dismembered. Since the accession of Louis XIV, France had plucked small pieces from the territories that had been contested between France and Spain since the fifteenth century. Between French aggression and the Dutch occupation of such important places as Ghent and Ypres, the ability of the southern provinces to maintain a separate identity suffered a grave blow. But not as grave as that formalized at Utrecht, when sovereignty over this territory was assigned to Austria, ostensibly because the emperor was a Habsburg, but really because the balance of power in western Europe demanded it.

To the south lay France, still the most powerful nation in Europe despite its losses in the War of the Spanish Succession. By 1714 Louis XIV had broken forever the danger of Spanish encirclement that had been the worry of every French king since Francis I in the early sixteenth century. Louis had methodically set out to occupy those territories that were strategically necessary to defend his state from invasion by the Dutch, the Spanish, the British, or the emperor. In the northeast he absorbed the Duchy of Bar. In the north he absorbed a healthy portion of Flanders, including Dunkirk on the English Channel and the prosperous clothing town of Lille. He pushed the eastern boundary of his state to the Rhine by overrunning Alsace and parts of Lorraine. Strasbourg remained French under the settlement of 1714, testimony to the fact that it was possible to hold France only at the western banks

golden age of the Dutch was over. Although the Dutch continued as a colonial and maritime power, their small numbers and meager natural resources eventually outweighed their abilities as innovators and managers. They lost their eastern empire to Britain and their predominance in European trade to France. What the Dutch gained at Utrecht was the right to maintain their forces in the towns along the border between France and the old Spanish Netherlands. The Spanish Netherlands, the original Burgundian inheritance, were

The Dutch East India Company's trading station on the Hooghly River in Bengal, 1665. The station was one of a network of bases the company established throughout its eastern trading empire.

Great Britain and the Low Countries

from interference in the internal administration of the large states, was less dominant in German affairs than he had been before the Thirty Years' War.

Increasingly, Habsburg power centered on Austria, Bohemia, and Hungary. This was especially true during the reign of Leopold I (1655–1705). Withstanding threats on all sides, Leopold was able to expand his state both to the west and to the south and to bring Austria into the ranks of the great European powers. Such an outcome could hardly have been foreseen in the middle of the seventeenth century, when the Ottomans made their last great thrust into the interior of Europe. In 1683 the Ottomans besieged Vienna itself, and only the arrival of seventy thousand Polish-led troops saved it from falling. But from that time forward, Austrian forces scored stunning victories. By 1699 almost all of Hungary had been retaken by Austria; with the Treaty of Passarowitz in 1718 Austria gained the rest of Hungary and Serbia. When the Treaty of Utrecht granted Austria control of the Netherlands, Lombardy, and Naples, the Austrian Habsburgs became rulers of a European empire.

Austria's Italian possessions included the vast southern territories of Naples (including Sicily after 1720) and the rich industrial area surrounding Milan in the

of the Rhine. Finally, farther to the south, Louis had won and held Franche-Comté, once the center of Burgundy. In 1714 France was larger, stronger, and better able to defend its borders than ever before. It was also exhausted.

As France expanded, so Spain contracted. Less than two centuries earlier, a Spanish king had dreamed of being monarch over all of Europe. Now a French Bourbon sat on the great Habsburg throne and Spain was slowly being sliced to pieces. By 1714 the European territories of the Spanish empire had been reduced to Iberia itself. But the loss of its European empire was to prove a blessing in disguise for Spain, which now entered upon a new and unexpected phase of growth and influence.

The center of Europe remained occupied by the agglomeration of cities, bishoprics, principalities, and small states known collectively as the Holy Roman Empire, but now more accurately called the German empire. There were still over three hundred separate jurisdictions, most of them vulnerable to preying neighbors such as Louis XIV. Bavaria in the south and Saxony, Brandenburg, and Hanover in the north were among the most important of the large states, with the added twist that Hanover was now ruled by the king of Great Britain. The emperor, now officially prohibited

France and Spain

north. Alongside the Austrian territories, a number of independent city-states continued to flourish on the Italian peninsula. Both Venice and Genoa remained prosperous and independent. The Grand Duchy of Tuscany, with its great city of Florence, and the Papal States had both expanded over the course of the seventeenth century, absorbing their smaller neighbors until both were large consolidated territories. To the west of the Italian states was the Duchy of Savoy. Savoy had pursued a flexible foreign policy, pleasing whichever of its powerful neighbors was most dangerous and accepting the patronage of whichever seemed most friendly. Client of the Spanish, French, and Austrians, Savoy grew and prospered. After the War of the Spanish Succession, Savoy was counted among the victors, though it had fought on both sides. Duke Victor Amadeus II became a king when he received the island of Sicily, which he exchanged with Austria for Sardinia in 1720.

Thus the Treaty of Utrecht signaled a new configuration of political power. England, France, Prussia, and Austria were the ascending powers, Holland and Spain the declining ones. Italy and the southern Netherlands were the bones over which the biggest dogs fought, sometimes playfully, sometimes in deadly earnest.

The siege of Vienna, 1683. The invading Turks were repelled in this, their last great advance in Europe.

Realignment in the East

This was western Europe in 1714. In the east, it was the Treaty of Nystad (1721), ending the Great Northern War (1700–21), that fixed the political geography. Here the emerging powers were Russia and Prussia, while those in decline were Sweden and Poland. The critical factor in eastern European politics remained access to the sea. Outlets to the Baltic Sea in the north and the Black Sea in the south were the vital lifeline for this part of the Continent, and control of these outlets was the central motivation for the long years of war fought among the eastern states.

The expansion of Russia is one of the central events in European history, and the early eighteenth century is its pivotal period. During the long years of social and economic recovery after the death of Ivan the Terrible

The Holy Roman Empire

in 1584, Russia had been easy prey for its powerful neighbors Sweden and Poland. Through a series of wars and political pacts, Russia had ceded most of its Baltic territories to Sweden, while it had relinquished land and population in the west to Poland. Peter the Great (1682–1725) set out to reclaim what had been lost. As a result of the Great Northern War, Russia regained the eastern Baltic coastline from the southeastern end of Finland to Riga in the west. Russia now controlled all of the vital Baltic ports in the east. Peter built a new capital on the Gulf of Finland. In this new city, named Saint Petersburg, he laid the foundation for the Russian navy.

What Russia gained, Sweden lost. At the height of its power in the middle of the seventeenth century, Sweden had dominated the Baltic. It occupied all of Finland, controlled the important eastern coast of Norway, and had gained a foothold in Germany. Most importantly, Sweden had captured the southern tip of its own peninsula from the Danes, making the mainland portion of its state whole. But Sweden's century-long rise to power was followed by a rapid period of decline. The small and relatively poor population could not long succeed in governing an empire. The Great Northern War ended whatever pretensions Sweden still had. It lost all of its German territories: those on the North Sea went to Hanover, those on the Baltic to Prussia. Livonia, Estonia,

and the eastern provinces were returned to Russia, but Sweden was able to hold on to its vital gains from the Danes. Sweden had built its own window to the west at Göteborg on the North Sea, and from there it could carry on a direct trade with Britain and the Netherlands.

Since the end of the Thirty Years' War, Brandenburg-Prussia had been steadily growing. A strange configuration of a state, with its geographical heart in Brandenburg, it was one of the domains of the Holy Roman Empire. From the capital at Berlin the princes of Brandenburg directed the accumulation of small neighboring German lands: Magdeburg and Halle to the southwest, a piece of Pomerania to the northeast. But while Brandenburg expanded in every direction, it could do little to join itself to the kingdom of Prussia. A huge swath of Poland, cutting between the two, stood in the way. This division of Brandenburg-Prussia was its most important geopolitical feature. In the eighteenth century, the determination to join together dominated Prussian history.

This aim, of course, meant eventual conflict with Poland. Despite its political weakness, Poland was one of the largest landmasses in Europe. On its southern border it held back Ottoman expansion; on its eastern border it held back the Russians. Its great port of Gdansk on the Baltic dominated the grain and timber trade with northern Europe as well as local Baltic commerce between Scandinavia and the mainland. Sweden and Russia, the eastern powers, controlled Poland politically, helping nominate its elected kings and ensuring that its decentralized form of aristocratic government kept Poland weak. Poland served as a useful counterweight in the balance of power in eastern Europe. Except for its Baltic territories, Poland was not yet seen as a great prize to be fought over. But by the beginning of the eighteenth century it was a helpless giant ready to be toppled.

Thus a potent Prussia and Russia and a prostrate Poland characterized the realignment of the eastern portion of Europe. Most importantly, the separation between east and west was narrowing. Prussia's German orientation and the westernization of Russia led to closer ties with the west.

Russia and Sweden

The Rise of Russia

At the beginning of the eighteenth century, Russia was scarcely known about or cared about in the rest of Europe. Peter the Great changed all that. The Treaty of Nystad had confirmed the magnitude of his victory over the Swedes in the Great Northern War, both in territory and prestige. The change created consternation in the courts of Europe. Just a quarter century before, no one had cared very much what the king of Russia called himself. In fact, little was known for sure about the Russian ruler or his state. What little mercantile contact there was between Russia and the West was conducted entirely by westerners. Foreign merchants were allowed to live in Moscow in a separate ghetto called "Germantown." Their letters were the main source of western knowledge about the vast Muscovite empire.

Peter the Great brought Europe to Russia and Russia to Europe. Twice he visited Europe to discover the secrets of western prosperity and might. He arranged marriages between the closest heirs to his throne, including his son Alexis, and the sons and daughters of German princes and dukes. By 1721 he had established 21 separate foreign embassies. The sons of the Russian gentry and nobility were sent west—sometimes forcibly—to further their education and to learn to adapt to western outlooks. Peter recruited Europeans to fill the most important skilled positions in the state: foreign engineers and gunners to serve in the army; foreign architects to build the new capital at Saint Petersburg; foreign scholars to head the new state schools; foreign administrators to oversee the new departments of state. Peter borrowed freely and adapted sensibly. If necessary, he would drag his countrymen kicking and screaming into the modern world.

By 1721 Russia was recognized all over Europe as an emerging power. The military defeat of the seemingly invincible Swedes had made monarchs from Louis XIV to William III sit up and take notice. And the great Russian victory over Sweden at Poltava in 1709 was no fluke. Peter's forces followed it up with several strong campaigns, which proved that Russia could organize, equip, finance, and train an up-to-date military force. Moreover, Peter's absorption of Sweden's Baltic territories made Russia a power in the north. The Russian navy, built mostly by foreigners, was now capable of protecting Russian interests and defending important ports such as Riga and Saint Petersburg. Even the Dutch, who had long plotted the decline of Swedish might, now became nervous. Thus it was unsettling that Peter wished to be recognized as emperor.

The Reforms of Peter the Great

Peter the Great was not the first Russian tsar to attempt to borrow from western developments. The process had been under way for decades. The opening of the northern port of Archangel in 1584 led to direct contact with British and Dutch traders, who brought with them new ideas and useful products, which were then adapted to Russian needs and conditions. Russia was a vast state, and Europe was only one of its neighbors. Its religion had come from Byzantium rather than Rome, thus giving Russian Christianity an eastern flavor. Its Asian territories mixed the influence of Mongols and Ottomans; its southern borders met Tartars and Cossacks. While most European states were racially and ethnically homogeneous, Russia was a loose confederation of diverse peoples. Yet it was the western states that posed the greatest threat to Russia in the seventeenth century, and it was to the west that Peter, like his father before him, turned his attention.

It would be wrong to see Peter's westernizing innovation as a systematic program. More to the point, nearly all of his reforms—economic, educational, administrative, social, military—were done to enhance military efficiency rather than civil progress. In his thirty years of active rule there was only one year—1724—during which he was not at war. Vital reforms like the poll tax (1724), which changed the basis of taxation from the household to the individual adult male, had enormous social consequences. The new policy of taxing individuals officially erased whole social classes. A strict census taken (and retaken) to inhibit tax evasion became the basis for further governmental encroachments on the tsar's subjects. Yet the poll tax was not designed for any of these purposes. It was instituted to increase tax revenue for war. Similarly, compulsory lifetime military service required of the landowning classes (the nobility and gentry) was established to provide officers and state servants for an expanding military machine.

Yet if Peter's reforms were not systematic and developed from little other than military necessity, nevertheless they constituted a fundamental transformation in the life of all Russian people. The creation of a gigantic standing army and an entirely new navy meant conscription of the Russian peasantry on a grand scale. In a ten-year period of the Great Northern War, the army absorbed 330,000 conscripts, most of whom never returned to their homes. Military service was not confined to the peasantry. Traditionally, the rural gentry raised and equipped the local conscript forces and gave them what training they could. Most gentry lived on estates that had been granted to them, along with the resident peasants, as a reward for their military contributions. Peter the Great intensified the obligations of

This portrait of Peter the Great by his court painter Louis Caravaque pays homage to Peter's intense interest in naval matters. Ships flying English, Dutch, Danish, and Russian flags prepare for maneuvers under his command.

the gentry. Not only were they to serve the state for life, but they were to accompany their regiments to the field and lead them in battle. When too old for active military service, they were to perform administrative service in the new departments of state.

The expansion of military forces necessitated an expansion of military administration as well. Peter's first innovation was the creation of the Senate, a group of nine senior administrators who were to oversee all aspects of military and civil government. The Senate became a permanent institution of government led by an entirely new official, the Procurator-General, who presided over its sessions and could propose legislation as well as oversee administration. From the Senate emanated five hundred officials known as the fiscals, who traveled throughout the state looking for irregularities in tax assessment and collection. They quickly developed into a hated and feared internal police force.

Peter's efforts to reorganize his government went a step further in 1722, when he issued the Table of Ranks. This was an official hierarchy of the state that established the social position or rank of individuals. It was divided into three categories—military service, civil service, and owners of landed estates. Each category contained 14 ranks, and it was decreed that every person who entered the hierarchy did so at the bottom and worked his way up. The creation of the Table of Ranks was significant in a number of ways. It demonstrated Peter's continued commitment to merit as a criterion for advancement. This standard had been shown in the military, where officers were promoted on the basis of service and experience rather than birth or background. Equally important was Peter's decision to make the military service the highest of the three categories. This reversed the centuries-old position of the landed aristocracy and the military service class. Although the old nobility also served in the military and continued to dominate state service, the Table of Ranks opened the way for the infusion of new elements into the Russian elite.

Many of those who were able to advance in the Table of Ranks did so through attendance at the new institutions of higher learning that Peter founded. His initial educational establishments were created to further the military might of the state. The Colleges of Mathematics, Engineering, and Artillery, which became the training grounds for his army officers, were all founded during the Great Northern War. But Peter was interested in liberal education as well. He had scores of western books translated into Russian. He had a press established in Moscow to print original works, including the first Russian newspaper. He decreed that a new, more westernized alphabet replace the one used by the Russian Orthodox church and that books be written in the language that the people spoke rather than in the formal literary language of religious writers. He also introduced Arabic numerals into official accounting records.

Peter's reforms of government and society were matched by his efforts to energize the economy. No state in Europe had as many natural resources as did Russia, yet manufacturing barely existed there. As with everything else he did, Peter took a direct hand in establishing factories for the production of textiles, glass, leather, and most importantly, iron and copper. The state directly owned about half of these establishments, most of them on a larger scale than any known in the west. By 1726, more than half of all Russian exports were manufactured goods and Russia had become the largest producer of iron and copper in the world.

Peter the Great was a precocious child. He began his education at the age of two, using a book similar to the illustrated Russian speller whose "Z" page is shown here.

In all of these ways and more, Peter the Great transformed Russia. But the changes Peter wrought did not come without cost. The traditions of centuries were not easily broken. Intrigue against Peter led first to confrontation with the old military elite, and later to conflict with his only son, Alexis. It remains unclear whether the plot with which Alexis was connected actually existed or whether it was a figment of Peter's imagination, but it is abundantly clear that Alexis's death from torture plunged the state into a succession crisis in 1725. Finally, the great costs of westernization were paid by the masses of people, who benefited little from the improvement in Russia's international standing or from the social and economic changes that affected the elites.

Life in Rural Russia

At the beginning of the eighteenth century, nearly 97 percent of the Russian people lived on the land and practiced agriculture. Farming techniques and agrarian lifestyles had changed little for centuries. Most of the country's soil was poor. Harsh climate and low yields characterized Russian agriculture. Thirty-four of the 100 Russian harvests during the eighteenth century can be termed poor or disastrous, yet throughout the century state taxation was making larger and larger demands upon the peasantry. During Peter's reign alone, direct taxation increased by 500 percent.

The theory of the Russian state was one of service, and the role of Russian peasants was to serve their master. Beginning in the mid-seventeenth century, the peasantry had undergone a change in status. The law code of 1649 formalized a process that had been under way for over a century whereby peasants were turned into the property of their landlords. During the next century, laws curtailed the ability of peasants to move freely from one place to another, eliminated their right to hold private property, and abolished their freedom to petition the tsar against their masters. At the same time that landlords increased their hold over peasants, the state increased its hold over landlords. They were made responsible for the payment of taxes owed by their peasants and for the military service due from them. By the middle of the eighteenth century, over half of all peasants—6.7 million adult males by 1782—had thus become serfs, the property of their masters, without any significant rights or legal protection.

Private landlords reckoned their wealth in the number of serfs they owned, but in fact most owned only a small number—fewer than fifty—in the middle of the eighteenth century. This resulted from the common practice whereby a father divided his estate among all of his surviving sons. Most gentry were small landholders, constantly in debt and rarely able to meet their financial and service obligations to the state. This life of poverty at the top was, of course, magnified at the bottom. The vast majority of serfs lived in small villages where they divided up their meager surplus to pay their taxes and drew lots to see who would be sent for military service. When the debts of their lords became too heavy, it was the serfs who were foreclosed.

If serfs made up the bottom half of the Russian peasantry, there were few advantages to being in the top half, among the state peasants. State peasants lived on lands owned by the monarchy itself. Like the serfs, they were subject to the needs of the state for soldiers and workers. The use of forced labor was a feature of each of Peter's grandiose projects. Saint Petersburg was built by the backbreaking labor of peasant conscripts. From 1709, when the project began, perhaps as many as forty thousand laborers a year were forced to work on the various sites. The unhealthy conditions of the swampy environment from which the new capital rose claimed the lives of thousands of these workers, as did the appalling conditions of overwork and undernourishment in which they lived.

Many Russian peasants developed a philosophy of submission and a rich folk culture that valued a stubborn determination to endure. For those who would no longer bend to the knout—the heavy leather whip that was the omnipresent enforcer of obedience—there was only flight or rebellion. Hundreds of thousands of serfs fled to state-owned lands in hope of escaping the cruelties of individual landlords. Although severe penalties were imposed for aiding runaway serfs, in fact most state overseers and many private landlords encouraged runaways to settle on their lands. In their social and economic conditions, eighteenth-century Russian peasants were hardly distinguishable from medieval European serfs.

The Enlightened Empress Catherine

Of all the legacies of Peter the Great, perhaps the one of most immediate consequence was that government could go on without him. During the next thirty-seven years, six tsars ruled Russia, "three women, a boy of twelve, an infant, and a mental weakling," as one commentator acidly observed. More to the point, each succession was contested, as there were no direct male heirs to the throne in this period. Nevertheless, despite turmoil at the top, government continued to function smoothly and Peter's territorial conquests were largely maintained. Russia also experienced a remarkable increase in numbers during this period. Between 1725 and 1762 the population increased from 13 to 19 million, a jump of nearly one-third in a single generation. This explosion of people dramatically increased the wealth of the landholding class, who reckoned their status by the number of serfs they owned.

The expansion of the economic resources of the nobility was matched by a rise in legal status and political power. This was the period sarcastically dubbed "the emancipation of the nobility," a phrase that captures not only the irony of the growing gap between rich and poor but also the contrast between the social structures of Russia and those of western Europe. In return for their privileges and status, Peter the Great extended the duties the landowning classes owed to the state. By granting unique rights, like the ownership of serfs, to the descendants of the old military service class, Peter had forged a Russian nobility. Lifetime service, however, was the price of nobility.

In order to gain and hold the throne, each succeeding tsar had to make concessions to the nobility to gain their loyalty. At first it was a few simple adjustments. The sons of wealthy landowners who completed a course of education at one of the state academies were allowed to enter the Table of Ranks in the middle of the hierarchy rather than at the bottom. Then life service was commuted to a term of twenty-five years, still a long time in a world of short lives and sudden deaths. But these concessions were not enough.

Twenty-five years of service did not solve the problem of estate management, especially as the tasks of management grew along with the population of serfs. Thus, the next capitulation was that a single son could remain on the estate and escape service altogether. The births of younger sons were concealed; owners of multiple estates claimed the exemption of one son for each. Most decisively, the talented remained at home to serve the family while the wastrels were sent to serve the state. Finally, in 1762, the obligation for state service by the nobility was abolished entirely.

The abolition of compulsory service was not the same as the abolition of service itself. In fact the end of compulsory service enabled Catherine II, "the Great" (1762–96), to enact some of the most important reforms of her reign. (See "Catherine Before She Was Great," pp. 558–559.) At first, Catherine's accession seemed nothing more than a continuation of monarchical instability—her first two acts were to have her husband, Peter III, murdered and to lower the salt tax. Each brought her a measure of security.

Catherine was a dynamic personality who alternately captivated and terrified those with whom she came into contact. Her policies were as complex as her personality, influenced on the one hand by the new French ideas of social justice and the nobility of the human race, and on the other hand by the traditional Russian ideas of absolute rule over an enserfed and subhuman population. Catherine handled these contrasting dimensions of her rule masterfully, gaining abroad the reputation as the most enlightened of European monarchs and at home the sincere devotion of her people.

The most important event in the early years of Catherine's reign was the establishment of a legislative commission to review the laws of Russia. Catherine

❧ Catherine Before She Was Great

Catherine the Great wasn't always called the Empress of All the Russias. In fact, she wasn't always called Catherine. Sophie of Anhalt-Zerbst was the daughter of a petty German prince whose estates were too poor to provide for his family. He hired out as a military officer to the kings of Prussia and became governor of the dreary Baltic port of Stettin. Here Sophie passed her childhood. The family lived comfortably, and Sophie was provided with a French governess, Babette Cardel. From Babette she learned not only the language of the French but their ways. Sophie was no easy child to handle. Her natural curiosity led to some narrow escapes, and she was nearly killed at the age of three when she pulled a cupboard down. To curiosity was added spirit, and the shouting matches in which she and Babette engaged were long remembered. Indeed, Babette took to bribing young Sophie with sweets, which in the long run did less to soften her temper than to ruin her teeth.

By far the most significant event of Sophie's childhood was the sudden sickness that overtook her at the age of seven. She was seized by coughing, fevers, and fits that incapacitated her for weeks. For a time her life was in danger. It was not unusual in those days for unexplained illness to appear and disappear with bewildering suddenness, and this is what happened to Sophie. One morning she awoke without fever and without the racking cough that had seared her body. But in its place had come a physical change. Weeks of lying on her side had deformed her physique: "I had assumed the shape of a letter Z. My right shoulder was much higher than the left, the backbone running in a zigzag and the left side falling in," she later recalled. Such a result was as mysterious as the illness that occasioned it. Doctors were sought for advice. None could help until at last a veterinarian who practiced on the limbs of horses and cows was found. He prescribed a useless concoction of medicines but also built a body frame for Sophie that was designed to reshape her deformity. She wore this for four years until she regained her former posture.

Sophie's father was a strict Lutheran who prescribed a regimen for the education of his children that was to be precisely followed. Just after her recovery, Sophie was told that she could no longer play with her toys but must behave as an adult. Tutors were brought to teach her history and geography, and a Lutheran minister was deputed to train her in religion. Sophie took delight in confounding her religion instructor, and in general showed the same high spirits as she had in childhood.

Although Sophie did not have a close relationship with her mother—in later years they quarreled incessantly—it was her mother who showed her the world outside Stettin. Joanna of Holstein-Gottorp had grown up surrounded by courtly pomp. While her family, too, came from the ranks of the minor princes of the Holy Roman Empire, marriages and inclination had brought them into the circle of German aristocratic life. This was a world for which Joanna longed, and every year she visited her relations in Brunswick. Sophie began to accompany her mother on these trips, and they became for her the means to escape the boredom of Stettin. On one visit to Berlin she was introduced to Frederick William I, king of Prussia. Her relatives included a future king of Sweden and a future queen of Britain. These trips to Brunswick and Berlin opened Sophie's eyes to the possibility of a different life, the possibility of life with one of the crown princes of Europe.

As it happened, Sophie had little need to wish. By a twist of fate, another of her mother's innumerable cousins had recently been declared heir to the throne of Russia. This was Peter, soon to be duke of Holstein-Gottorp and ultimately Peter III of Russia. Empress Elizabeth of Russia was childless, and Peter was her nearest relative. She determined to have him married to an eligible German princess, and after much casting about, the choice fell on Sophie. In 1744 Sophie was summoned to Russia. Joanna was thrilled with the prospect, not only because of the possibility of a successful marriage for her daughter, but also because she was to have a role in the affair. No one asked Sophie what she thought, since her opinion hardly mattered.

The journey to Russia was a trip that Sophie would never forget. Stettin was no tropical paradise, but the climate there had little prepared Sophie and her mother for the rigors of the east. Carriages gave way to sleighs, and her heavy cloth clothing to sable. Sophie and Joanna huddled together for warmth, covering their faces and hands from the bitter arctic winds. It took nearly four weeks to reach Saint Petersburg, and when they arrived they were informed that they must hurry to join the royal court at Moscow. There they were received with unusual warmth, as it was the sixteenth birthday of the new heir to the throne and all of Russian society was eager to see his bride-to-be.

Sophie's earliest meetings with her fiance were not entirely satisfactory. In a strange land she might have expected strange customs, but Peter was a German like herself. Thus she was unprepared for their first interview, in which Peter professed his passionate love for one of the ladies of the court. Sophie was only fifteen and, by her own account at least, innocent in sexual matters. Peter's frank confession,

which was accompanied by assurances that he would marry Sophie anyhow, caused her as much confusion as it did anger and resentment. She resolved to keep her own counsel and to attempt to please the empress, if not the heir. Sophie spent the days before her marriage learning both the Russian language and the Eastern Orthodox religion. She would have to convert to the old faith before she could be betrothed. As part of her conversion, she had to take a Russian name, and thus she came to be called Catherine. Whether her change of religion was sincere or not, it was required. Sophie was shrewd enough to realize the importance of the Church, and she won many admirers at court when, after being taken suddenly ill, she asked for an Orthodox priest rather than a Lutheran minister or a doctor.

Sophie's marriage took place in 1745 in one of the most magnificent ceremonies anyone could recall. By then she knew that she was alone in the world. She had fought bitterly with her mother. Sophie shared nothing with her new husband—including the marriage bed. The household set up for her was composed entirely of spies for the empress, and even her correspondence was monitored. She spent the next fifteen years supplementing the education that she had received as a child. She read everything she could get hold of. Her Russian improved dramatically as she read Russian and French or German versions of the same works. She devoured the classics, especially history and philosophy, and for the first time became acquainted with the works of the new European writers whose reputations had reached as far as Russia. Sophie indulged her enthusiasm for riding, an exercise not usually taken by women. She also developed a passion for the handsome guardsmen who inhabited the palace. Perhaps in revenge for her husband's conduct, perhaps in return for his neglect, she took the first of more than twenty lovers. When she became pregnant in 1754, it was almost certainly not with Peter's child. Eight years later, Empress Elizabeth died and the private life of Sophie of Anhalt-Zerbst ended. The half-mad Peter III acceded to the throne, and Sophie, now known to the world as Catherine, began her remarkable public career.

CHILDHOOD TRAUMAS

Catherine the Great left a fascinating account of her early years, which is in sharp contrast to her reputation for ruthlessness as a ruler.

My father, whom I saw very seldom, considered me to be an angel, my mother did not bother much about me. She had had, eighteen months after my birth, a son whom she passionately loved, whereas I was merely tolerated and often repulsed with violence and temper, not always with justice. I was aware of all this, but not always able to understand what I really felt about it.

At the age of seven I was suddenly seized with a violent cough. It was the custom that we should kneel every night and every morning to say our prayers. One night as I knelt and prayed I began to cough so violently that the strain caused me to fall on my left side, and I had such sharp pains in my chest that they almost took my breath away.

Finally, after much suffering, I was well enough to get up and it was discovered, as they started to put on my clothes, that I had in the meantime assumed the shape of the letter Z: my right shoulder was much higher than the left, the backbone running in a zigzag and the left side falling in.

From Catherine the Great, *Memoirs* (1755).

---

herself wrote the *Instruction* (1767), by which the elected commissioners were to operate. She borrowed her theory of law from the French jurist Baron de Montesquieu (1689–1755) and her theory of punishment from the Italian reformer Cesare Beccaria (1738–94). Among other things, Catherine advocated the abolition of capital punishment, torture, serf auctions, and the breakup of serf families by sale. Few of these radical reforms were ever put into practice.

But in 1775 Catherine did restructure local government. Russia was divided into 50 provincial districts, each with a population of between 300,000 and 400,000 inhabitants. Each district was to be governed by both a central official and elected local noblemen. This reform was modeled upon the English system of justices of the peace. Previous local reforms had failed because of the absence of a resident local nobility. The abolition of compulsory service finally made possible the establishment of local institutions. In 1785 Catherine issued the Charter of the Nobility, a formal statement of the rights and privileges of the noble class. The Charter incorporated all the gains the nobility had made since the death of Peter the Great, but it also instituted the requirements for local service that had been the basis of Catherine's reforms. District councils with the right to petition directly to the tsar became the centerpiece of Russian provincial government.

In order to train the local nobility for government service, Catherine introduced educational reforms. Peter had established military schools for the nobility and had staffed them with foreigners. The University of Moscow had been founded in 1755, and its faculty too was dominated by European emigrants. Catherine saw the need to broaden the educational system. Borrowing from the Austrian system, she established provincial elementary schools to train the sons and daughters of the local nobility. To staff these, Catherine created teachers' colleges so that the state would have its own educators. Although the program called for the equal education of women, except in Saint Petersburg and Moscow few women attended either elementary or high schools.

Catherine's reforms did little to enhance the lives of the vast majority of her people. Although she often spoke in the terms of the French philosophers who saw the enserfment of fellow humans as a blot on civilization, Catherine took no effective action either to end serfdom or to soften its rigors. In fact, by grants of state land Catherine gave away 800,000 state peasants, who became serfs. So, too, did millions of Poles who became her subjects after the partition of Poland in 1793 and 1795.

The most significant uprising of the century, Pugachev's revolt (1773–75), took place during Catherine's reign. Emelyan Pugachev (1726–75) was a Cossack who in his youth had been a military adventurer. Disappointed in his career, he made his way to the Ural mountains, where he recruited Asian tribesmen and laborers forced to work in the mines. By promising freedom and land ownership, he drew peasants to his cause. In 1773 Pugachev declared himself to be Tsar Peter III, the murdered husband of Catherine II. He began with small raiding parties against local landlords and military outposts and soon had gained the allegiance of tens of thousands of peasants. In 1774, with an army of nearly twenty thousand, Pugachev took the city of Kazan and threatened to advance on Moscow. It was another year before state forces could effectively control the rebellion. Finally, Pugachev was betrayed by his own followers and sent to Moscow, where he was executed.

During the reigns of Peter and Catherine the Great, Russia was transformed into an international power. Saint Petersburg, a window to the west, was a capital worthy of a potent monarch, and during the course of the eighteenth century it attracted many of Europe's leading luminaries. At court French was spoken, the latest fashions were worn, and the newest ideas for economic and educational reform were aired. The Russian nobility mingled comfortably with its European counterparts, while the military service class developed into bureaucrats and administrators. But if life glittered at court, it remained the same dull regimen in the country. Millions of peasants were owned either by the state or by private landlords, and their quality of life was no different at the end of the campaign of westernization than it had been at the beginning.

The Two Germanies

The Thirty Years' War, which ended in 1648, initiated a profound transformation of the Holy Roman Empire. Warfare had devastated imperial territory. It was decades before the rich imperial lands recovered, and then the political consequences of the war had taken effect. There were now two empires, a German and an Austrian, though both were ruled by the same person. In the German territories, whether Catholic or Protestant, the Holy Roman Emperor was more a constitutional monarch than the absolute ruler he was in Austria. The larger states like Saxony, Bavaria, and Hanover made their own political alliances despite the jurisdictional control that the emperor claimed to exercise. Most decisively, so did Brandenburg-Prussia. By the beginning of the eighteenth century, the electors of Brandenburg had become the kings of Prussia, and Prussia's military power and efficient administrative structure became the envy of its German neighbors.

The Austrian empire was composed of Austria and Bohemia, the Habsburg hereditary lands, and as much of Hungary as could be controlled. In Austria, the Habsburgs clung tightly to their power. For decades Austria was the center of the still-flourishing Counter-Reformation, and the power and influence of the Jesuits was as strong here as it was in Spain. The War of the Spanish Succession, which gave the Habsburgs control of the southern Netherlands and parts of Italy, brought Austria an enhanced role in European affairs. Austria remained one of the great powers of Europe and the leading power in the Holy Roman Empire despite the rise of Prussia. Indeed, from the middle of the eighteenth century, the conflict between Prussia and Austria was the defining characteristic of central European politics.

Chained but undaunted, Emelyan Pugachev awaits punishment for leading a peasant rebellion in the southern Urals.

The Rise of Prussia

The transformation of Brandenburg-Prussia from a petty German principality to a great European power was one of the most significant and least expected developments of the eighteenth century. Frederick William, the Great Elector (1640–88), had begun the process of forging Brandenburg-Prussia into a power in its own right by building a large and efficient military machine. At the beginning of the eighteenth century, Prussia was on the winning side in both the War of the Spanish Succession and the Great Northern War. When the battlefield dust had settled, Prussia found itself in possession of Pomerania and the Baltic port of Stettin. It was now a recognized power in eastern Europe.

Frederick William I (1713–40) and his son Frederick II, "the Great" (1740–86), turned this promising beginning into an astounding success. A devout Calvinist, Frederick William I deplored waste and display as much on moral as on fiscal grounds. The reforms he initiated were intended to subordinate both aristocracy and peasantry to the needs of the state and to subordinate the needs of the state to the demands of the military.

Because of its geographical position, Prussia's major problem was to maintain an efficient and well-trained army during peacetime. Defense of its exposed territories required a constant state of military preparedness, yet the relaxation of military discipline and the desertion of troops to their homes inevitably followed the cessation of hostilities. Frederick William I solved this problem by integrating the economic and military structures of his state. First he appointed only German officers to command his troops, eliminating the mercenaries who sold their services to the highest bidders. Then he placed these noblemen at the head of locally recruited regiments. Each adult male in every district was required to register for military service in the regiment of the local landlord. These reforms dramatically increased the effectiveness of the army by shifting the burden of recruitment and training to the localities.

Yet despite all the attention that Frederick William I lavished on the military—by the end of his reign nearly 70 percent of state expenditures went to the army—his foreign policy was largely pacific. In fact, his greatest achievements were in civil affairs, reforming the bureaucracy, establishing a sound economy, and raising state revenues. Through generous settlement schemes and by welcoming Protestant and Jewish

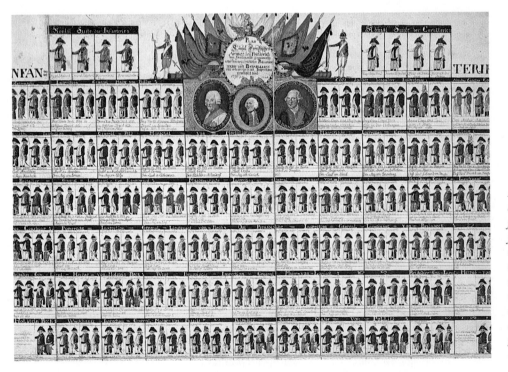

Prussian infantry officers display their uniforms in this painting from the late eighteenth century. Distinctive, colorful, and elaborate uniforms, different for each regiment, were common in European armies before the field-gray and khaki era of the twentieth century.

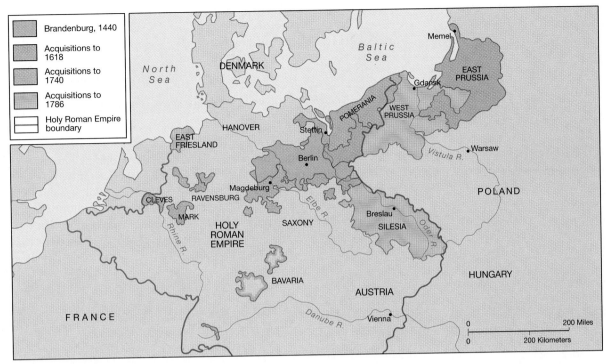

Brandenburg, 1440

Acquisitions to 1618

Acquisitions to 1740

Acquisitions to 1786

Holy Roman Empire boundary

The Expansion of Prussia

refugees, Frederick William was able to expand the economic potential of these eastern territories. Frederick William I pursued an aggressive policy of land purchase to expand the royal domain, and the addition of so many new inhabitants in Prussia further increased his wealth. While the major western European powers were discovering deficit financing and the national debt, Prussia was running a surplus.

Financial security was vital to the success of Frederick the Great. Father and son had quarreled bitterly throughout Frederick's youth—not only about music—and most observers expected that out of spite Frederick would tear down all that his father had built up. In fact father and son were cast in the same mold, with the unexpected difference that the son was more ruthless and ambitious. With his throne, Frederick II inherited the fourth largest army in Europe and the richest treasury. He wasted no time in putting both to use. His two objectives were to acquire the Polish corridor of West Prussia that separated his German and Prussian territories and to acquire the agriculturally and industrially rich Austrian province of Silesia to the southeast of Berlin. Just months after his coronation, Frederick conquered Silesia, increasing the size of Prussia by nearly a quarter. Within a decade the province dominated the Prussian economy, outproducing and outconsuming all other areas of Frederick's state.

It was Frederick's military prowess that earned him the title "the Great." But this was only a part of his achievement. More than his father, Frederick II forged an alliance with the Prussian nobility, integrating them into a unified state. A tightly organized central administration, which depended upon the cooperation of the local nobility, directed both military and bureaucratic affairs. At the center, Frederick worked tirelessly to oversee his government. Where Louis XIV had proclaimed, "I am the state," Frederick the Great announced, "I am the first servant of the state." He codified the laws of Prussia, abolished torture and capital punishment, and instituted agricultural techniques imported from the states of western Europe. By the end of Frederick's reign, Prussia had become a model for bureaucratic organization, military reform, and enlightened rule.

Austria Survives

Austria was the great territorial victor in the War of the Spanish Succession, acquiring both the Netherlands and parts of Italy. Austrian forces recaptured a large

A KING'S-EYE VIEW

Frederick the Great wrote philosophical and military tracts as well as composing dozens of compositions for the flute. Here is his definition of the enlightened despot.

The sovereign is attached by indissoluble ties to the body of the state; hence it follows that he, by repercussion, is sensible to all the ills which afflict his subjects; and the people, in like manner, suffer from the misfortunes which affect their sovereign. There is but one general good, which is that of the state. . . . The sovereign represents the state; he and his people form but one body, which can only be happy as far as united by concord. The prince is to the nation he governs what the head is to the man; it is his duty to see, to think, and act for the whole community, so that he may procure it every advantage of which it is capable. . . . Such are in general the duties imposed upon a prince, from which, in order that he may never depart, he ought often to recollect that he himself is but a man, like the least of his subjects. If he be the first general, the first minister of the realm, it is not so that he should shelter in the shadow of authority, but that he should fulfil the duties of such titles. He is only the first servant of the state, who is obliged to act with probity and prudence; and to remain as totally disinterested as if he were each moment liable to render an account of his administration to his fellow citizens.

From Frederick the Great, *An Essay on Forms of Government.*

---

part of Hungary from the Turks, thereby expanding their territory to the south and the east. Hereditary ruler of Austria and Bohemia, king of Hungary, and Holy Roman Emperor of the German nation, Charles VI (1711–40) was recognized as one of Europe's most potent rulers. But appearances were deceptive. The apex of Austrian power and prestige had already passed. Austria had benefited from balance-of-power politics, not so much from its own strength as from the leverage it could give to others. With the rise of Russia and Prussia, there was now more than one fulcrum to power in eastern Europe.

The difficulties facing Austria ran deep. The Thirty Years' War had made the emperor more an Austrian monarch than an imperial German ruler. On the Austrian hereditary estates, the Catholic Counter-Reformation continued unabated, bringing with it the benefits of Jesuit education, cultural revival, and the religious unity necessary to motivate warfare against the Ottomans. But these benefits came at a price. Perhaps as many as two hundred thousand Protestants fled Austria and Bohemia, taking with them their skills and capital. For centuries the vision of empire had dominated Habsburg rule. This meant that the Austrian monarchy was a multiethnic confederation of lands loosely tied together by loyalty to a single head. The

components preserved a high degree of autonomy: Hungary elected the Habsburg emperor its king in a separate ceremony. Local autonomy continually restricted the imposition of central policy, and never were the localities more autonomous than in the matter of taxation. Thus it was hard for Austria to centralize in the same way as had Prussia.

Austria was predominantly rural and agricultural. Less than 5 percent of the population lived in towns of ten thousand or more; less than 15 percent lived in towns at all. On the land, the local aristocracy, whether nobility or gentry, exploited serfs to the maximum. Not only were serfs required to give labor service three days a week (and up to six during planting and harvest times), but the nobility maintained a full array of feudal privileges, including the right to mill all grain and brew all beer. When serfs married, when they transferred property, even when they died, they paid taxes to their lord. As a result they had little left to give the state. In consequence, the Austrian army was among the smallest and the poorest of the major powers despite the fact that it had the most active enemies along its borders.

Lack of finance, human resources, and governmental control were the underlying problems of Austria, but they were not the most immediate difficulties fac-

MILITARY DISCIPLINE

Herman Maurice de Saxe was the illegitimate son of the king of Poland. He had extensive military experience in both eastern and western Europe. He ultimately achieved the office of Marshal of France, where he was celebrated as a military reformer. He modeled many of his reforms on the Prussian army.

Would it not be much better to establish a law obliging men of all conditions of life to serve their king and country for the space of five years? A law, which could not reasonably be objected against, as it is both natural and just for people to be engaged in the defense of that state of which they constitute a part, and in choosing them between the years of twenty and thirty, no manner of inconvenience can possibly be the result; for those are years devoted, as it were, to libertinism; which are spent in adventures and travels, and, in general, productive of but small comfort to parents. An expedient of this kind could not come under the denomination of a public calamity, because every man, at the expiration of his five years service, would be discharged. It would also create an inexhaustible fund of good recruits, and such as would not be subject to desertion. In course of time, every-

one would regard it as an honor rather than a duty to perform his task; but to produce this effect upon a people, it is necessary that no sort of distinction should be admitted, no rank or degree whatsoever excluded, and the nobles and rich rendered, in a principal manner, subservient to it. This would effectually prevent all murmur and repining, for those who had served their time, would look upon such, as betrayed any reluctance, or dissatisfaction at it, with contempt; by which means, the grievance would vanish insensibly, and every man at length esteem it an honor to serve his term. The poor would be comforted by the example of the rich; and the rich could not with decency complain, seeing themselves on a footing with the nobles.

From Marshal de Saxe, *Memoirs on the Art of War* (1757).

---

ing Charles VI. With no sons to succeed him, Charles feared that his hereditary and elective states would go their separate ways after his death and that the great Habsburg monarchy would end. For twenty years his abiding ambition was to gain recognition for the principle that his empire would pass intact to his daughter, Maria Theresa. He expressed the principle in a document known as the Pragmatic Sanction, which stated that all Habsburg lands would pass intact to the eldest heir, male or female. Charles VI made concession after concession to gain acceptance of the Pragmatic Sanction. But the leaders of Europe licked their lips at the prospect of a dismembered Austrian empire.

Maria Theresa (1740–80) inherited the imperial throne in 1740 and quickly discovered what it was like to be a woman in a man's world. In 1740 Frederick of Prussia invaded the rich Austrian province of Silesia and attracted allies for an assault upon Vienna. Faced with Bavarian, Saxon, and Prussian armies, Maria Theresa might well have lost her inheritance had she not shown her remarkable capacities so early in her reign. She appeared before the Hungarian estates,

accepted their crown, and persuaded them to provide her with an army capable of halting the allied advance. Although she was unable to reconquer Silesia, Hungarian aid helped her hold the line against her enemies.

The loss of Silesia, the most prosperous part of the Austrian domains, signaled the need for fundamental reform. The new eighteenth-century idea of building a state replaced the traditional Habsburg concern with maintaining an empire. Maria Theresa and her son Joseph II (1780–90) began the process of transformation. For Austria, state building meant first the reorganization of the military and civil bureaucracy to clear the way for fiscal reform. As in Prussia, a central directory was created to oversee the collection of taxes and the disbursement of funds. Maria Theresa personally persuaded her provincial estates both to increase taxation and to extend it to the nobles and the clergy. While her success was limited, she finally established royal control over the raising and collection of taxes.

The second element in Maria Theresa's reform program involved the condition of the Austrian peasantry. Maria Theresa established the doctrine that "the peas-

Maria Theresa and her family. Eleven of Maria Theresa's sixteen children are posed with the empress and her husband, Francis of Lorraine. Standing next to his mother is the future emperor Joseph II.

ant must be able to support himself and his family and pay his taxes in time of peace and war." She limited labor service to two days per week and abolished the most burdensome feudal dues. Joseph II ended serfdom altogether. The new Austrian law codes guaranteed peasants' legal rights and established their ability to seek redress through the law. Joseph II hoped to extend reform even further. In the last years of his life, he abolished obligatory labor service and ensured that all peasants kept one-half of their income before paying local and state taxes. Such a radical reform met a storm of opposition and was ultimately abandoned at the end of the reign.

The reorganization of the bureaucracy, the increase in taxation, and the social reforms that created a more productive peasantry revitalized the Austrian state. The efforts of Maria Theresa and Joseph II to overcome provincial autonomy worked better in Austria and Bohemia than in Hungary. The Hungarians declined to contribute at all to state revenues, and Joseph II took the unusual step of refusing to be crowned king of Hungary so that he would not have to make any concessions to Hungarian autonomy. He even imposed a tariff on Hungarian goods sold in Austria. More seriously, parts of the empire already had been lost before

the process of reform could begin. Prussia's seizure of Silesia was the hardest blow of all. Yet in 1740, when Frederick the Great and his allies swept down from the north, few would have predicted that Austria would survive.

The Politics of Power

Frederick the Great's invasion of Silesia in 1740 was callous and cynical. Since the Pragmatic Sanction bound him to recognize Maria Theresa's succession, Frederick cynically offered her a defensive alliance in return for which she would simply hand over Silesia. It was an offer she should not have refused. Although Frederick's action initiated the War of the Austrian Succession, he was not alone in his desire to shake loose parts of Austria's territory. Soon nearly the entire Continent became embroiled in the conflict.

The War of the Austrian Succession (1740–48) resembled a pack of wolves stalking its injured prey. It quickly became a major international conflict, involving Prussia, France, and Spain on one side and Austria, Britain, and Holland on the other. Spain joined the fighting to recover its Italian possessions, Saxony claimed Moravia, France entered Bohemia, and the Bavarians moved into Austria from the south. With France and Prussia allied, it was vital that Britain join with Austria to maintain the balance of power. Initially the British did little more than subsidize Maria Theresa's forces, but once France renewed its efforts to conquer the Netherlands, both Britain and the Dutch Republic joined in the fray. That the British cared little about the fate of the Habsburg empire was clear from the terms of the treaty that they dictated at Aix-la-Chapelle (Aachen) in 1748. Austria recognized Frederick's conquest of Silesia, as well as the loss of parts of its Italian territories to Spain. France, which the British had always regarded as the real enemy, withdrew from the Netherlands in return for the restoration of a number of colonial possessions. The War of the Austrian Succession made Austria and Prussia permanent enemies and gave Maria Theresa a crash course in international diplomacy. She learned firsthand that self-interest rather than loyalty underlay power politics. This lesson was reinforced in 1756 when Britain and Prussia entered into a military accord at the beginning of the Seven Years' War (1756–63). Prussian expansion and duplicity had already alarmed both Russia and France, and Frederick II feared that he would be squeezed from east and west. He could hardly expect help from Maria Theresa, so he extended overtures to the British, whose interests in protecting Hanover, the hereditary estates of their German-born king, outweighed their prior commitments to Austria. Frederick's actions drove France into the arms of both the Austrians and the Russians, and an alliance that included the German state of Saxony was formed in defense. Thus was initiated a diplomatic revolution in which France and Austria became allies after three hundred years as enemies.

Once again Frederick the Great took the offensive, and once again he won his risk against the odds. His attack on Saxony and Austria in 1756 brought a vigorous response from the Russians, who interceded on Austria's behalf with a massive army. Three years later, at the battle of Kunersdorf, Frederick suffered the worst military defeat of his career when the Russians shattered his armies. In 1760 his forces were barely a third of the size of those massed by his opponents, and it was only a matter of time before he was fighting defensively from within Prussia.

In 1762 Empress Elizabeth died. She was succeeded by her nephew, the childlike Peter III, a German by birth who worshiped Frederick the Great. When Peter came to the throne, he immediately negotiated peace with Frederick, abandoning not only his allies but also the substantial territorial gains that the Russian forces had made within Prussia. It was small wonder that the Russian military leadership joined in the coup d'état that brought Peter's wife, Catherine, to the throne in 1762. With Russia out of the war, Frederick was able to fend off further Austrian offensives and to emerge with his state, including Silesia, intact.

The Seven Years' War did little to change the boundaries of the German states, but it had two important political results. The first was to establish beyond doubt the status of Prussia as a major power and a counterbalance to Austria in central Europe. The existence of the dual Germanies, one led by Prussia and the other by Austria, was to have serious consequences for German unification in the nineteenth century and for the two world wars in the twentieth. The second result of the Seven Years' War was to initiate a long period of peace in eastern Europe. Both Prussia and Austria were financially exhausted from two decades of fighting. Both states needed a breathing spell to initiate administrative and economic improvements, and the period following the Seven Years' War witnessed the sustained programs of internal reforms for which Frederick the Great, Maria Theresa, and Joseph II were famous in the decades following 1763.

Peace among the eastern European powers did not mean that they abandoned their territorial ambitions. All over Europe, absolute rulers reformed their bureaucracies, streamlined their administrations, increased their sources of revenue, and built enormous standing armies. All over Europe except in Poland. There the autonomous power of the nobility remained as strong as ever. No monarchical dynasty was ever established, and each elected ruler not only confirmed the privileges of the nobility but usually was forced to extend them. In the Diet, the Polish representative assembly, small special-interest groups could bring legislative business

A satire on the Treaty of Paris, which ended the Seven Years' War.

This engraving by Le Mire is called "The Cake of the Kings: First Partition of Poland, 1773." The monarchs of Russia, Austria, and Prussia join in carving up Poland. The Polish king is clutching his tottering crown.

separated the Prussian and Brandenburg portions of Frederick's state.

By the 1770s the idea of carving up Poland was being actively discussed in Berlin, Saint Petersburg, and Vienna. Austria, too, had an interest in a Polish partition, especially to maintain its power and status with the other two states, and perhaps to use Polish territory as a potential bargaining chip for the return of Silesia. Finally, in 1772, the three great eastern powers struck a deal. Russia would take a large swath of the grain fields of northeast Poland, which included over one million people, while Frederick would unite his lands by seizing West Prussia. Austria gained both the largest territories, including Galicia, and the greatest number of people, nearly two million Polish subjects.

to a halt by exercising their veto power. Given the size of Poland's borders, its army was pathetically inadequate for the task it had to face. The Polish monarchy was helpless to defend its subjects from the destruction on all sides.

In 1764 Catherine the Great and Frederick the Great joined to place one of Catherine's former lovers on the Polish throne and to turn Poland into a weak dependent. Russia and Prussia had different interests in Poland's fate. For Russia, Poland represented a vast buffer state that kept the German powers at a distance from Russia's borders. It was more in Russia's interest to dominate Polish foreign policy than to conquer its territory. For Prussia, Poland looked like another helpless flower, "to be picked off leaf by leaf," as Frederick observed. Poland seemed especially appealing because Polish territory, including the Baltic port of Gdansk,

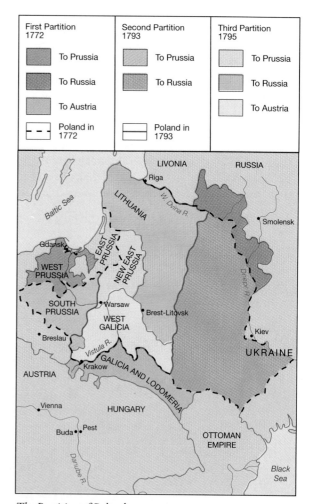

The Partition of Poland

In half a century the balance of power in central Europe had shifted decisively. Prussia's absorption of Silesia and parts of Poland made it a single geographical entity, as well as a great economic and military power. Austria, despite its lost territory, proved capable of surviving the accession of a female ruler and of fighting off an attempt to dismember its empire. Its participation in the partition of Poland strengthened its role in the politics of the eastern powers, while its alliance with France fortified its role in the west. From one empire there were now two states, and the relationship between Prussia and Austria would dominate central Europe for the next century.

The Greatness of Great Britain

By the middle of the eighteenth century, Great Britain had become the leading power of Europe. It had won its spurs in Continental and colonial wars. Britain was unsurpassed as a naval power, able to protect its far-flung trading empire and to make a show of force in almost any part of the world. Perhaps more impressively for a nation that did not support a large standing army, British soldiers had won decisive victories in the European land wars. Until the American Revolution, Britain came up a winner in every military venture it undertook. But might was only one part of British success. Economic preeminence was every bit as important. British colonial possessions in the Atlantic and Indian oceans poured consumer products into Britain for export to the European marketplaces. Growth in overseas trade was matched by growth in home production. British advances in agricultural technique had transformed Britain from an importer to an exporter of grain. The manufacturing industries that other European states attempted to create with huge government subsidies flourished in Britain through private enterprise.

British military and economic power was supported by a unique system of government. In Britain the nobility served the state through government. The British constitutional system, devised in the seventeenth century and refined in the eighteenth, shared power between the monarchy and the ruling elite through the institution of Parliament. Central government integrated monarch and ministers with chosen representatives from the localities. Such integration not only provided the Crown with the vital information necessary to formulate national policy, but it eased acceptance and enforcement of government decisions.

Government was seen as the rule of law which, however imperfect, was believed to operate for the benefit of all.

The parliamentary system gave Britain some of its particular strengths, but they came at a cost. Politics was a national pastime rather than the business of an elite of administrators and state servants. Decentralization of decision-making led to half-measures designed to placate competing interests. Appeals to public opinion, especially by candidates for Parliament, often played upon fears and prejudices that divided rather than united the nation. Moreover, the relative openness of the British system hindered diplomatic and colonial affairs, in which secrecy and rapid changes of direction were often the monarch's most potent weapons. These weaknesses came to light most dramatically during the struggle for independence waged by Britain's North American colonists. There the clash of principle and power was most extreme and the strengths and weaknesses of parliamentary rule were ruthlessly exposed.

The British Constitution

The British Constitution was a patchwork of laws and customs that was gradually sewn together to form a workable system of government. Many of its greatest innovations came about through circumstance rather than design, and circumstance continued to play an essential role in its development in the eighteenth century. At the apex of the government stood the king, not an absolute monarch like his European counterparts, but not necessarily less powerful for having less arbitrary power. The British people revered monarchy and the monarch. The theory of mixed government depended upon the balance of interests represented by the monarchy in the Crown, the aristocracy in the House of Lords, and the people in the House of Commons. Less abstractly, the monarch was still regarded as divinely ordained and a special gift to the nation. The monarch was the actual and symbolic leader of the nation as well as the Supreme Head of the Church of England. Allegiance to the Anglican church, whether as a political creed among the elite or as a simple matter of devotion among the populace, intensified allegiance to the king.

The partnership between Crown and representative body was best expressed in the idea that the British government was composed of King-in-Parliament. Parliament consisted of three separate organs: monarch, lords, and commons. Although each existed separately as a check upon the potential excesses of the others, it was only when the three functioned together that parliamentary government could operate. The king was charged with selecting ministers, initiating policy, and supervising administration. The two houses of Parliament were charged with raising revenue, making laws, and presenting the grievances of subjects to the Crown.

There were 558 members of the House of Commons after the union with Scotland in 1707. Most members of the lower house were nominated to their seats. The largest number of seats were located in small towns where a local oligarchy, or neighboring patron, had a customary right to make nominations that were invariably accepted by the electorate. Even in the largest cities, influential citizens made arrangements for nominating members in order to avoid the cost and confusion of an actual election. Campaigns were ruinously expensive for the candidates—an election in 1754 cost the losing candidates £40,000—and potentially dangerous to the local community, where bitter social and political divisions boiled just below the surface.

The British gentry dominated the Commons, occupying over 80 percent of the seats in any session. Most of these members also served as unpaid local officials in the counties, as justices of the peace, captains of the local militias, or collectors of local taxes. They came to Parliament not only as representatives of the interests of their class, but as experienced local governors who understood the needs of both Crown and subject.

Nevertheless, the Crown had to develop methods to coordinate the work of the two houses of Parliament and facilitate the passage of governmental programs. The king and his ministers began to use the deep royal pockets of offices and favors to bolster their friends in Parliament. Not only were those employed by the Crown encouraged to find a place in the House of Commons, but those who had a place in Parliament were encouraged to take employment from the Crown. Despite its potential for abuse, this was a political process that integrated center and locality, and at first it worked rather well. Those with local standing were brought into central offices. There they could influence central policy making while protecting their local constituents. These officeholders, who came to be called placemen, never constituted a majority of the members of Parliament. They formed the core around which eighteenth-century governments operated, but it was a core that needed direction and cohesion. It was such leadership and organization that was the essential contribution of eighteenth-century politics to the British Constitution.

Parties and Ministers

Although parliamentary management was vital to the Crown, it was not the Crown that developed the basic tools of management. Rather, these techniques originated within the political community itself, and their usefulness was only slowly grasped by the monarchy. The first and, in the long term, most important tool was the party system. Political parties initially developed in the late seventeenth century around the issue of the Protestant succession. Those who opposed James II because he was a Catholic attempted to exclude him from inheriting the crown. They came to be called by their opponents *Whigs,* which had come to mean "horse thieves" (the term originally derived from *Wiggamore,* a name for Western Isle Scots who cried "Whig, whig!" to spur their horses on). Those who supported James's hereditary rights but who also supported the Anglican church came to be called by their opponents *Tories,* which in Gaelic meant "cattle rustlers." The Tories cooperated in the Revolution of 1688 that placed William and Mary on the throne because James had threatened the Anglican church by tolerating Catholics and because Mary had a legitimate hereditary right to be queen. After the death of Queen Anne in 1714, the Tories supported the succession of James III, James II's Catholic son, who had been raised in France, rather than of George I (1714–27), prince of Hanover and Protestant great-grandson of James I. An unsuccessful rebellion to place James III on the throne in 1715 discredited the leadership of the Tory party, but did not weaken its importance in both local and parliamentary politics.

The Whigs supported the Protestant succession and a broad-based Protestantism. They attracted the allegiance of large numbers of dissenters, heirs to the Puritans of the seventeenth century who practiced forms of Protestantism different from that of the Anglican church. The struggle between Whigs and Tories was less a struggle for power than it was for loyalty to their opposing viewpoints. As the Tories opposed the Hanoverian succession and the Whigs supported it, it was no mystery which party would find favor with George I. Moreover, as long as there was a pretender to the British throne—another rebellion took place in Scotland in 1745 led by the grandson of James II—the Tories continued to be tarred with the brush of disloyalty.

The division of political sympathies between Whigs and Tories helped create a set of groupings to which parliamentary leadership could be applied. A national, rather than a local or regional outlook, could be used to organize support for royal policy as long as royal policy conformed to that national outlook. The ascendancy of the Whigs enabled George I and his son George II (1727–60) to govern effectively through Parliament, but at the price of dependence upon the Whig leaders. Although the monarch had the constitutional freedom to choose his ministers, realistically he could choose only Whigs, and practically none but the Whig leaders of the House of Commons. Happily for the first two Georges, they found a man who was able to manage Parliament but desired only to serve the Crown.

Sir Robert Walpole (1676–1745) came from a long-established gentry family in Norfolk. Walpole was an early supporter of the Hanoverian succession and an early victim of party warfare. But once George I was securely on the throne, Walpole became an indispensable leader of the House of Commons. His success rested upon his extraordinary abilities: he was an excellent public speaker; he relished long working days and the details of government; and he understood better than anyone else the intricacies of state finance. Walpole became First Lord of the Treasury, a post that he transformed into first minister of state. From his treasury post, Walpole assiduously built a Whig parliamentary party. He carefully dispensed jobs and offices, using them as bait to lure parliamentary supporters. Walpole's organization paid off both in the passage of legislation desired by the Crown and at the polls, where Whigs were returned to Parliament time and again.

From 1721 to 1742 Walpole was the most powerful man in the British government. He refused an offer of a peerage so that he could continue to lead the House of Commons. Walpole's long tenure in office was as much a result of his policies as of his methods of governing. He brought a measure of fiscal responsibility to government by establishing a fund to pay off the national debt. In foreign policy he pursued peace with the same fervor that both his predecessors and successors pursued war. The long years of peace brought prosperity to both the landed and merchant classes, but they also brought criticism of Walpole's methods. The way in which he used government patronage to build his parliamentary party was attacked as corruption. So, too, were the ways in which the pockets of Whig office-holders were lined. During his last decade in office, Walpole struggled to survive. His attempt to extend the excise tax on colonial goods nearly led to his loss of office in 1733. His refusal to respond to the clamor for continued war with Spain in 1741 finally led to his downfall.

Walpole's twenty-year rule established the pattern of parliamentary government. The Crown needed a "prime" minister who was able to steer legislation through the House of Commons. It also needed a patronage broker who could take control of the treasury and dispense its largess in return for parliamentary backing. Walpole's personality and talents had combined these two roles. Hereafter they were divided. Those who had grown up under Walpole had learned their lessons well. The Whig monopoly of power continued unchallenged for nearly another twenty years. The patronage network Walpole had created was vastly extended by his Whig successors. Even minor posts in the customs or the excise offices were now exchanged for political favor, and only those approved by the Whig leadership could claim them. The cries of corruption grew louder not only in the country houses of the long-disenfranchised Tories, but in the streets of London, where a popular radicalism developed in opposition to the Whig oligarchy. They were taken up as well in the North American colonies, where two million British subjects champed at the bit of imperial rule.

America Revolts

Britain's triumph in the Seven Years' War (1756–63) had come at great financial cost to the nation. At the beginning of the eighteenth century, the national debt stood at £14 million; by 1763 it had risen to £130 million, despite the fact that Walpole's government had been paying off some of it. Then, as now, the cost of world domination was staggering. George III (1760–1820) came to the throne with a taste for reform and a desire to break the Whig stranglehold on government. He was to have limited success on both counts, though not for want of trying. In 1763 the king and his ministers agreed that reform of colonial administration was long overdue. Such reform would have the twin benefit of shifting part of the burden of taxation from Britain to North America and of making the commercial side of colonization pay.

This was sound thinking all around, and in due course Parliament passed a series of duties on goods imported into the colonies, including glass, wine, coffee, tea, and, most notably, sugar. The so-called Sugar Act (1764) was followed by the Stamp Act (1765), a tax on printed papers such as newspapers, deeds, and court documents. Both acts imposed taxes in the colonies similar to those that already existed in Britain. Accompanying the acts were administrative orders

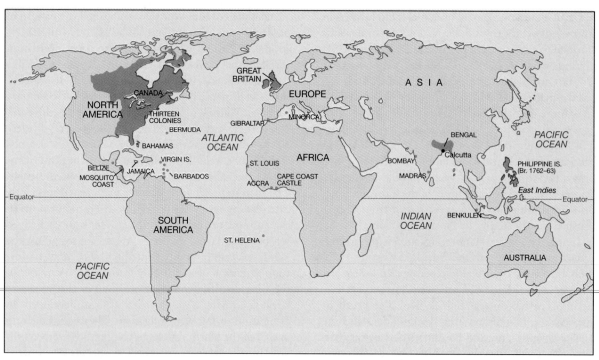

The British Empire, ca. 1763

designed to cut into the lucrative black market trade. The government instituted new rules for searching ships and transferred authority over smuggling from the local colonial courts to Britain's Admiralty courts. Although British officials could only guess at the value of the new duties imposed, it was believed that with effective enforcement £150,000 would be raised. All this would go to pay the vastly greater costs of colonial administration and security.

British officials were more than perplexed when these mild measures met with a ferocious response. Assemblies of nearly every colony officially protested the Sugar Act. They sent petitions to Parliament begging for repeal and warning of dire economic and political consequences. Riots followed passage of the Stamp Act. Tax collectors were hounded out of office, their resignations precipitated by threats and acts of physical violence. In Massachusetts, mobs that included political leaders in the colony razed the homes of the collector and the lieutenant-governor. However much the colonists might have regretted the violence that was done, they believed that an essential political principle was at stake. It was a principle of the freedom of an Englishman.

At their core, the protests of the American colonists underscored the vitality of the British political system. The Americans argued that they could not be taxed without their consent and that their consent could come only through representation in Parliament. Since there were no colonists in Parliament, Parliament had no jurisdiction over the property of the colonists. Taxation without representation was tyranny. There were a number of subtleties to this argument that were quickly lost as political rhetoric and political action heated up. In the first place, the colonists did tax themselves through their own legislatures and much of that money paid the costs of administration and defense. Second, as a number of pamphleteers pointed out, no one in the colonies had asked the British government to send regiments of the army into North America. The colonists had little reason to put their faith in British protection. Hard-fought colonial victories were tossed away at European negotiating tables, while the British policy of defending Indian rights in the Ohio Valley ran counter to the interests of the settlers. When defense was necessary, the colonists had proven themselves both able and cooperative in providing it. A permanent tax meant a permanent army, and a standing

THE NEW EUROPEAN POWERS

1707	England and Scotland unite to form Great Britain
1713–1714	Peace of Utrecht ends War of the Spanish Succession (1702–1714)
1714	British crown passes to House of Hanover
1721	Treaty of Nystad ends Great Northern War (1700–1721)
1721–1742	Sir Robert Walpole leads British House of Commons
1722	Peter the Great of Russia creates Table of Ranks
1740	Frederick the Great of Prussia invades Austrian province of Silesia
1748	Treaty of Aix-la-Chapelle ends War of the Austrian Succession (1740–1748)
1756–1763	Seven Years' War pits Prussia and Britain against Austria, France, and Russia
1773–1775	Pugachev's revolt in Russia
1774	Boston Tea Party
1775	American Revolution begins
1785	Catherine the Great of Russia issues Charter of the Nobility

army was as loathed in Britain as it was in the colonies.

In opposing the Stamp Act, colonists also tried to draw a distinction between internal and external taxation. They deemed regulation of overseas commerce a legitimate power of Parliament but argued that the regulation of internal exchange was not. But this distinction was lost once the issue of parliamentary representation was raised. If the colonists had not consented to British taxation, then it made no difference whether taxation was internal or external. The passion generated in the colonies was probably no greater than that generated in Britain. The British government also saw the confrontation as a matter of principle, but for Britain the principle was parliamentary sovereignty. This, above all, was the rock upon which the British constitution had been built over the last century. Parliament had entered into a partnership with the Crown.

The Crown had surrendered—willingly or not—many of its prerogatives. In return, Parliament had bound the people to obedience. There were well-established means by which British subjects could petition Parliament for redress of grievances against the monarch, but there were no channels by which they could question the sovereignty of Parliament.

Once the terms of debate had been so defined, it was difficult for either side to find a middle ground. Parliamentary moderates managed repeal of the Stamp Act and most of the clauses of the Sugar Act, but they also joined in passing the Declaratory Act (1766), which stated unequivocally that Parliament held sovereign jurisdiction over the colonies "in all cases whatsoever." This was a claim that became more and more difficult to sustain as colonial leaders began to cite the elements of resistance theory that had justified the Revolution of 1688. Then the protest had been against the tyranny of the king; now it was against the tyranny of Parliament. American propagandists claimed that a conspiracy existed to deprive the colonists of their property and rights and to enslave them for the benefit of special interests and corrupt politicians.

The techniques of London radicals who opposed parliamentary policy were imported into the colonies. Newspapers were used to whip up public support; boycotts brought ordinary people into the political arena; public demonstrations like the Boston Tea Party (1774) were carefully designed to intimidate; mobs were occasionally given free rein. Although the government had faced down these tactics when they were used in London to support John Wilkes (1725–97), an ardent critic of royal policy, they were less successful when the crisis lay an ocean away. When, in 1770, British troops fired on a Boston mob, American propagandists were provided with empirical evidence that Britain intended to enslave the colonies. Violence was met by violence, passion by passion. In 1775 full-scale fighting was under way. Eight years later Britain withdrew from a war it could not win, and the American colonies were left to govern themselves.

• • •

By the end of the third quarter of the eighteenth century, Europe had a new political configuration. A continent once dominated by a single power—Spain in the sixteenth century and France in the seventeenth—was now dominated by a state system in which alliances among several great powers held the balance. Despite

UNALIENABLE RIGHTS

The Declaration of Independence, written by Thomas Jefferson (1776), succinctly summarized the principles on which the American Colonists were to build a new form of democratic government.

We hold these truths to be self-evident, that all men are created equal, that they are endowed by their Creator with certain unalienable Rights, that among these are Life, Liberty and the pursuit of Happiness. That to secure these rights, Governments are instituted among Men, deriving their just powers from the consent of the governed. That whenever any Form of Government becomes destructive of these ends, it is the Right of the People to alter or to abolish it, and to institute new Government, laying its foundation on such principles and organizing its powers in such form, as to them shall seem most likely to effect their Safety and Happiness. Prudence, indeed, will dictate that Governments long established should not be changed for light and transient causes; and accordingly all experience hath shown, that mankind are more disposed to suffer, while evils are sufferable, than to right themselves by abolishing the forms to which they are accustomed. But when a long train of abuses and usurpations, pursuing invariably the same Object, evinces a design to reduce them under absolute Despotism, it is their right, it is their duty, to throw off such Government, and to provide new Guards for their future security.

From the Declaration of Indepencence.

---

the loss of its American colonies, Great Britain had proved the most potent of the states. Its victories over the French in the Seven Years' War and over France and Prussia in the War of the Austrian Succession secured its position. But it was a position that could be maintained only through alliances with the German states, either with Prussia or Austria. The rise of Prussia provided a counterweight to French domination of the Continent. Although these two states became allies in the middle of the century, the ambitions of their rulers made them natural enemies, and it would not be long before French and Prussian armies were again pitted against each other. France, still the wealthiest and most populous of European states, had slumbered through the eighteenth-century reorganization. The legacies of Louis XIV took a long time to reach fruition. He had claimed glory for his state, giving the French people a sense of national identity and national destiny, but making them pay an enormous price in social and economic dislocation. Thus the mid-eighteenth century was to be an age of the greatest literary and philosophical achievement for France, but the late eighteenth century was to be an age of the greatest social upheaval that Europe had ever known.

Suggestions for Further Reading

General Reading

* Olwen Hufton, *Europe: Privilege and Protest, 1730–1789* (Ithaca, NY: Cornell University Press, 1980). An excellent survey of the political and social history of the mid-eighteenth century.

* Leonard Krieger, *Kings and Philosophers, 1689–1789* (New York: Norton, 1970). A brilliant depiction of the personalities and ideas of eighteenth-century Europe.

* M. S. Anderson, *Europe in the Eighteenth Century, 1713/1783,* 3d ed. (London: Longman, 1987). A country-by-country survey of political developments.

Nicholas Riasanovsky, *A History of Russia* (New York: Oxford University Press, 1984). The best one-volume history of Russia.

David Kirby, *Northern Europe in the Early Modern Period* (London: Longman, 1990). Political history from a Baltic perspective, with excellent chapters on Sweden and Russia.

Europe in 1714

* Derek McKay and H. M. Scott, *The Rise of the Great Powers* (London: Longman, 1983). An outstanding survey of diplomacy and warfare.

The Rise of Russia

* Paul Dukes, *The Making of Russian Absolutism, 1613–1801* (London: Longman, 1982). An extensive survey of the Russian monarchy in its greatest period.

* B. H. Sumner, *Peter the Great and the Emergence of Russia* (New York: Collier Books, 1962). A short and readable study; the best introduction.

* M. S. Anderson, *Peter the Great* (London: Thames and Hudson, 1978). A well-constructed, comprehensive biography.

* Jerome Blum, *Lord and Peasant in Russia* (New York: Columbia University Press, 1961). The best work on the social life of Russians.

* Isabel de Madariaga, *Catherine the Great, a Short History* (New Haven, CT: Yale University Press, 1990). The best brief life.

The Two Germanies

* H. W. Koch, *A History of Prussia* (London: Longman, 1978). The most recent study of the factors that led to Prussian dominance of Germany.

* Gerhard Ritter, *Frederick the Great* (Berkeley: University of California Press, 1974). A classic biography, short and readable.

* Walther Hubatsch, *Frederick the Great of Prussia* (London: Thames and Hudson, 1975). A full account of the reign of Prussia's greatest leader.

* Ernst Wangermann, *The Austrian Achievement* (New York: Harcourt Brace Jovanovich, 1973). The most readable study of Austrian politics, culture, and society in the eighteenth century.

* T. C. W. Blanning, *Joseph II and Enlightened Despotism* (London: Longman, 1970). Displays the relationship between new ideas, reform policies, and the practical necessities of government.

C. A. Macartney, *Maria Theresa and the House of Austria* (Mystic, CT: Verry Inc., 1969). Still the best introductory study.

The Greatness of Great Britain

* J. C. D. Clark, *English Society, 1688–1832* (Cambridge: Cambridge University Press, 1985). A bold reinterpretation of the most important features of English society.

* J. H. Plumb, *The Origins of Political Stability, England 1675–1725* (Boston: Houghton Mifflin, 1967). The fullest of the contributions of Walpole to the establishment of the British constitution.

* Linda Colley, *Britons* (New Haven, CT: Yale University Press, 1992). A lively account of how a nation was forged from Welsh, Scots, and English and how unity and diversity intermixed.

Ragnhild Hatton, *George I Elector and King* (Cambridge, MA: Harvard University Press, 1978). An outstanding biography that shows the German side of a British monarch.

* John Brewer, *Party Ideology and Popular Politics at the Accession of George III* (Cambridge: Cambridge University Press, 1976). An important book about the pressures on the political system in the late eighteenth century.

* Ian Christie and Benjamin W. Labaree, *Empire or Independence, 1760–1777* (New York: Norton, 1977). The American troubles from the British point of view.

* Bernard Bailyn, *The Ideological Origins of the American Revolution* (Cambridge, MA: Harvard University Press, 1967). A brilliant interpretation of the underlying causes of the break between Britain and the North American colonies.

* Robert Middlekauff, *The Glorious Cause: The American Revolution, 1763–1789* (New York: Oxford University Press, 1982). A lively narrative account from the American perspective.

*Paperback edition available.

19 ✣ Culture and Society in Eighteenth-Century Europe

Happy Families

"Happy families are all alike," wrote Lev Tolstoy in the nineteenth century when the idea of a happy family was already a cliché. Such an idea would never have occurred to his eighteenth-century forebears. For them the happy family was new. Personal happiness was an invention of the Enlightenment, the result of novel attitudes about human aspirations and human capabilities. "Happiness is a new idea in Europe," wrote Louis de Saint-Just (1767–94). It emerged in response to the belief that what was good brought pleasure and what was evil brought pain. Happiness, both individual and collective, became the yardstick by which life was measured. This meant a reorientation in personal conduct, and most of all, a reorientation of family life. Especially for those with an economic cushion, a pleasurable family life became essential. Husbands and wives were to be companions, filled with romantic love for each other and devoted to domestic bliss. Children, the product of their affection, were to be doted on, treated not as miniature adults to be lectured and beaten, but as unfilled vessels into which was poured all that was good.

Were ever a couple more in love than the husband and wife depicted in *A Visit to the Wet Nurse* by Jean-Honoré Fragonard (1732–1806)? The man clasps his wife's arm to his cheek, she lays her hand on his shoulder. Their sighs are almost audible! Together they admire the fruit of their love, the baby asleep in the cradle. It is hard to guess which parent dotes more, the mother with her rapturous expression or the father with his intensity. He kneels on a cushion in almost religious devotion, his hands folded as if in prayer. Who can doubt their companionship or their love for their babe? They have come together to see how the wet nurse is caring for their child.

At the beginning of the eighteenth century, the use of a wet nurse was still common among the families of the French bourgeoisie, the class to which this couple belongs. As time passed, however, more and more families began to keep their children at home and more mothers began to nurse their babies themselves. In part this change was a response to the higher mortality rate among infants sent out to wet nurses. But a wet nurse who could be supervised, that is, one who lived near enough to be visited, but far enough away from the town to enjoy wholesome air, might be the best of both worlds. This is just what the couple here has found, and today they come, with their other child (the boy in the hat), to see their baby sleeping peacefully, the wet nurse sitting attentively at the infant's side.

But there are two families in this picture, and they are hardly alike. At first glance, the wet nurse looks like an old woman, perhaps even an aging nanny. She sits with her distaff in her hand, for the arrival of her clients has interrupted her spinning. It is shocking to realize that she cannot be much older than thirty, an age beyond which wealthy families would not hire her for fear either that she would not have much milk or that it would be sour. The two younger children are undoubtedly hers, the youngest probably just weaned so that all of the milk would go to the baby. No adoring husband sits beside the wet nurse. Her husband, if he is still alive, is hard at work with no leisure time for visits to the country. Not only does the wet nurse have to sell her milk, but she also spins, to keep her family clothed and to earn a little extra to put away for hard times.

The newest fads of the age have passed her family by. While the child in the cradle will be spoiled by toys manufactured especially for children—puzzles, games, rocking horses, and balls—the children of the wet nurse must make do with household objects and their own imagination. A ball of yarn thrown to the cat helps the elder child while away the hours. Like much else in the eighteenth century, the world of the family was divided between high and low.

Eighteenth-Century Culture

The eighteenth-century spawned a rich and costly culture. Decorative architecture, especially interior design, reflected the increasing sociability of the aristocracy. Entertainment became a central part of aristocratic life, losing its previous formality. In this atmosphere music became a cultural passion. The string quartet made its first appearance in the eighteenth century, and chamber music enjoyed unparalleled popularity. Only the wealthiest could afford to stage private operas, the other musical passion of the age. The Esterhazys of Hungary employed 22 musicians and a conductor, who for most of the late eighteenth century was Joseph Haydn (1732–1809), the father of the modern symphony. Haydn's post was not an honorary one. In addition to hiring and managing the orchestra, he was expected to direct two operas and two concerts a week, as well as the music for Sunday services. An aristocratic patron was essential for the aspiring composer. If he could not find one or if, like Wolfgang Amadeus Mozart (1756–91), he could not bend his will to one, he could not flourish. While Haydn lived comfortably in a palace, Mozart, probably the greatest musical genius in Western history, lived impoverished in a garret and died at age thirty-five from lack of medical attention.

Musical entertainments in European country houses were matched by the literary and philosophical entertainments of the urban salons. Papers on scientific and literary subjects were read at gala dinner parties and discussed with great seriousness in drawing rooms. In the salons, most of which were organized by the wives and daughters of the nobility, were to be found the most influential thinkers of the day presenting the ideas of the Enlightenment, a new European outlook on religion, society, and politics.

The seven-year-old musical prodigy Wolfgang Amadeus Mozart plays the harpsichord while his father Leopold plays the violin and his sister Nannerl sings. The boy won great ovations on concert tours throughout Europe.

The Enlightenment

The Enlightenment was less a set of ideas than it was a set of attitudes. At its core was criticism, a questioning of traditional institutions, customs, and morals. In 1762 the French philosopher Jean-Jacques Rousseau (1712–78) published one of the most important works on social theory, *The Social Contract,* which opened with the gripping maxim "Man is born free and everywhere he is in chains." But most of the great thinkers of the Enlightenment were not so much philosophers as savants, knowledgeable popularizers whose skills were in simplifying and publicizing a hodgepodge of new views.

In France, Enlightenment intellectuals were called *philosophes* and claimed all the arts and sciences as their purview. The *Encyclopedia* (35 volumes, 1751–80), edited by Denis Diderot (1713–84), was one of the greatest achievements of the age. Titled *Systematic Dictionary of the Sciences, Arts, and Crafts,* it attempted to summarize all acquired knowledge and to dispel all imposed superstitions. There was no better definition of a philosophe than that given them by one of their enemies: "Just what is a philosophe? A kind of monster in society who feels under no obligation towards its manners and morals, its proprieties, its politics, or its religion. One may expect anything from men of their ilk."

THE ALL-KNOWING

The Encyclopedia *was one of the great collaborative ventures of the new spirit of reason that so characterized the Enlightenment. Following is the* Encyclopedia's *entry on itself, the purpose of compiling human knowledge in book form.*

Encyclopedia . . . In truth, the aim of an *encyclopedia* is to collect all the knowledge scattered over the face of the earth, to present its general outlines and structure to the men with whom we live, and to transmit this to those who will come after us, so that the work of past centuries may be useful to the following centuries, that our children, by becoming more educated, may at the same time become more virtuous and happier, and that we may not die without having deserved well of the human race. . . .

I have said that it could only belong to a philosophical age to attempt an *encyclopedia;* and I have said this because such a work constantly demands more intellectual daring than is commonly found in [less courageous periods]. All things must be examined, debated, investigated without exception and without regard for anyone's feelings. . . . We must ride roughshod over all these ancient puerilities, overturn the barriers that reason never erected, give back to the arts and sciences the liberty that is so precious to them. . . . We have for quite some time needed a reasoning age when men would no longer seek the rules in classical authors but in nature. . . .

From Denis Diderot, *Encyclopedia* (1751–72).

The influence of French counterculture on enlightened thought was great, but the Enlightenment was by no means a strictly French phenomenon. Its greatest figures included the Scottish economist Adam Smith (1723–90), the Italian legal reformer Cesare Beccaria (1738–94), and the German philosopher Immanuel Kant (1724–1804). In France it began among antiestablishment critics; in Scotland and the German states it flourished in the universities; and in Prussia, Austria, and Russia it was propagated by the monarchy. The Enlightenment began in the 1730s and was still going strong a half century later when its attitudes had been absorbed into the mainstream of European thought.

No brief summary can do justice to the diversity of enlightened thought in eighteenth-century Europe. Because it was an attitude of mind rather than a set of shared beliefs, there are many contradictory strains to follow. In his famous essay *What Is Enlightenment?* (1784), Immanuel Kant described it simply as freedom to use one's own intelligence. "I hear people clamor on all sides: Don't argue! The officer says: Don't argue, drill! The tax collector says: Don't argue, pay. The pastor says: Don't argue, believe." To all of them Kant replied: "Dare to know! Have the courage to use your own intelligence."

The Spirit of the Enlightenment. In 1734 there appeared in France a small book titled *Philosophical Letters Concerning the English Nation.* Its author, Voltaire (1694–1778), had spent two years in Britain, and while there he had made it his business to study the differences between the peoples of the two nations. In a simple but forceful style, Voltaire demonstrated time and again the superiority of the British. They practiced religious toleration and were not held under the sway of a venal clergy. They valued people for their merits rather than their birth. Their political constitution was a marvel—"The English nation is the only one on earth that has succeeded in controlling the power of kings by resisting them." They made national heroes of their scientists, poets, and philosophers. In all of this Voltaire contrasted British virtue with French vice. He attacked the French clergy and nobility directly, the French monarchy implicitly. Not only did he praise the genius and accomplishments of Sir Isaac Newton above those of René Descartes, but he also graphically contrasted the Catholic church's persecution of Descartes with the British state's celebration of Newton. "England, where men think free and noble thoughts," Voltaire enthused.

It is difficult now to recapture the psychological impact that the *Philosophical Letters* had on the generation of educated Frenchmen who first read them. The book was officially banned and publicly burned, and a warrant was issued for Voltaire's arrest. The *Letters* dropped like a bombshell upon the moribund intellectual culture of the Church and the universities and burst open the complacent, self-satisfied Cartesian worldview. The book ignited in France a movement that would soon be found in nearly every corner of Europe.

Born in Paris in 1694 into a bourgeois family with court office, François-Marie Arouet, who later took the pen name Voltaire, was educated by the Jesuits, who encouraged his poetic talents and instilled in him an enduring love of literature. He was a difficult student, especially as he had already rejected the core of the Jesuits' religious doctrine. He was no less difficult as he grew and began a career as a poet and playwright. It was not long before he was imprisoned in the Bastille for penning verses that maligned the honor of the regent of France. Released from prison, he insulted a nobleman, who retaliated by having his servants publicly beat Voltaire. Voltaire issued a challenge for a duel, a greater insult than the first, given his low birth. Again he was sent to the Bastille and was only released on the promise that he would leave the country immediately.

Thus Voltaire found himself in Britain, where he spent two years learning English, writing plays, and enjoying his celebrity free from the dangers that celebrity entailed in France. When he returned to Paris in 1728, it was with the intention of popularizing Britain to Frenchmen. He wrote and produced a number of plays and began writing the *Philosophical Letters,* a work that not only secured his reputation but also forced him into exile at the village of Cirey, where he moved in with the Marquise du Châtelet (1706–49).

The Marquise du Châtelet, though only twenty-seven at the time of her liaison with Voltaire, was one of the leading advocates of Newtonian science in France. She built a laboratory in her home and introduced Voltaire to experimental science. While she undertook the immense challenge of translating Newton into French, Voltaire worked on innumerable projects: poems, plays, philosophical and antireligious tracts (which she wisely kept him from publishing), and histories. It was one of the most productive periods of his life, and when the Marquise du Châtelet died in 1749, Voltaire was crushed.

Now past fifty years old, Voltaire began his travels. He was invited to Berlin by Frederick the Great, who admired him most of all the intellectuals of the age. The relationship between these two great egotists was predictably stormy and resulted in Voltaire's arrest in Frankfurt. Finally allowed to leave Prussia, Voltaire eventually settled in Geneva, where he quickly became embroiled in local politics and was none too politely asked to leave. He was tired of wandering and tired of being chased. His youthful gaiety and high spirits, which remained in Voltaire long past youth, were dealt a serious blow by the tragic earthquake in Lisbon in 1755, when thousands of people attending church services were killed.

Painting of a lively dinner conversation among philosophes. Voltaire, with raised arm, is shown seated to the left of Diderot.

THE HUMAN CONDITION

More than anyone else, Voltaire symbolized the new thinking of the Enlightenment. Witty, ironic, irreverent, and penetrating, his writings provoked howls of protest and squeals of delight. Among the most widely read was his philosophical dictionary, from which this definition of evil is drawn

People clamor that human nature is essentially perverse, that man is born the child of the devil, and of evil. Nothing is more ill-advised; for, my friend, in preaching at me that everybody is born perverse, you warn me that you were born that way, that I must distrust you as I would a fox or a crocodile. . . . It would be much more reasonable, much nobler, to say to me: "You were all born good; see how frightful it would be to corrupt the purity of your being." We should treat mankind as we should treat all men individually. . . .

Man is not born evil; he becomes evil, as he becomes sick. . . . Gather together all the children of the universe; you will see in them nothing but innocence, gentleness, and fear. . . .

If men were essentially evil, if they were all born the subjects of a being as malevolent as it is unhappy, who inspired them with all this frenzy to avenge his own torment, we would see husbands murdered by their wives, and fathers by their children every morning. . . .

From Voltaire, *The Philosophical Dictionary* (1764)

Optimism in the face of such a senseless tragedy was no longer possible. His black mood was revealed in *Candide* (1759), which was to become his enduring legacy. *Candide* introduced the ivory-tower intellectual Dr. Pangloss, the overly optimistic Candide, and the very practical philosophy "We must cultivate our own garden." It was Voltaire's capacity to challenge all authority that was probably his greatest contribution to Enlightenment attitudes. He held nothing sacred. He questioned his own paternity and the morals of his mother; he lived openly with the Marquise du Châtelet and her husband; and he spoke as slightingly of kings and aristocrats as he did of his numerous critics. At the height of the French Revolution, Voltaire's body was removed from its resting place in Champagne and taken in great pomp to Paris, where it was interred in the Panthéon, where the heroes of the nation were put to rest. "Voltaire taught us to be free" was the slogan that the Parisian masses chanted during the funeral procession. It was an ending perhaps too solemn and conventional for one as irreverent as Voltaire. When the monarchy was restored after 1815, his bones were unceremoniously dumped in a lime pit.

Some enlightened thinkers based their critical outlook on skepticism, the belief that nothing could be known for certain. When the Scottish philosopher David Hume (1711–76) was accused of being an athe-

ist, he countered the charge by saying he was too skeptical to be certain that God did not exist. Hume's first major philosophical work, *A Treatise of Human Nature* (1739), made absolutely no impression upon his contemporaries. For a time he took a post as a merchant's clerk; then he served as a tutor; and finally he found a position as a private secretary. During the course of these various employments he continued to write, publishing a series of essays on the subject of morality and rewriting his treatise into *An Enquiry Concerning Human Understanding* (1748), his greatest philosophical work.

Hume made two seminal contributions to Enlightenment thought. He exploded the synthesis of Descartes by arguing that neither matter nor mind could be proved to exist with any certainty. Only perceptions existed, either as impressions of material objects or as ideas. If human understanding was based on sensory perception rather than on reason, then there could be no certainty in the universe. Hume's second point launched a frontal attack upon established religion. If there could be no certainty, then the revealed truths of Christian religion could have no basis. In his historical analysis of the origins of religion, Hume argued that "religion grows out of hope or fear." He attacked the core of Christian explanations based on either Providence or miracles by arguing that to anyone

David Hume.

two societies that he most admired were ancient Rome and present-day Britain, and he studied the forms of their government and the principles that animated them. *The Spirit of the Laws* was published in 1748, and despite its gargantuan size and densely packed examples, it was immediately recognized as a masterpiece. Catherine the Great of Russia kept it at her bedside, and it was the single most influential work for the framers of the United States Constitution.

In both *Persian Letters* and *The Spirit of the Laws* Montesquieu explored how liberty could be achieved and despotism avoided. He divided all forms of government into republics, monarchies, and despotisms. Each form had its own peculiar spirit: virtue and moderation

who understood the basis of human perception it would take a miracle to believe in miracles.

In 1749 Hume received in the mail a work from an admiring Frenchman, titled *The Spirit of the Laws.* The sender was Charles-Louis de Secondat, Baron Montesquieu (1689–1755). Born in Bordeaux, he ultimately inherited both a large landed estate and the office of president of the Parlement of Bordeaux. His novel *Persian Letters* (1721) was a brilliant satire of Parisian morals, French society, and European religion all bound together by the story of a Persian despot who leaves his harem to learn about the ways of the world. The use of the Persian outsider allowed Montesquieu to comment on the absurdity of European customs in general and French practices in particular. The device of the harem allowed him to titillate his audience with exotic sexuality.

After this success, Montesquieu decided to sell his office and make the grand tour. He spent nearly two years in England, for which, like Voltaire, he came to have the greatest admiration. Back in Bordeaux, Montesquieu began to assemble his thoughts for what he believed would be a great work of political theory. The

The frontispiece from Montesquieu's Spirit of the Laws *has a medallion of the author surrounded by allegorical figures, including the blind Justice. In the lower left corner are copies of the author's works.*

OF THE PEOPLE

Baron de Montesquieu's Spirit of the Laws *(1750) was one of the most important political works of the Enlightenment. It analyzed the various forms of government and estimated their strengths and weaknesses. Montesquieu provided inspiration for the American Declaration of Independence and the Constitution.*

In a democracy the people are in some respects the sovereign, and in others the subject. There can be no exercise of sovereignty but by their suffrages, which are . . . fundamental to this government. And indeed it is as important to regulate in a republic, in what manner, by whom, to whom, and concerning what suffrages are to be given, as it is in a monarchy to know who is the prince, and after what manner he ought to govern. . . .

The people are extremely well qualified for choosing those whom they are to intrust with part of their authority. . . . They can tell when a person has fought many battles, and been crowned with success; . . . They can tell when a judge is assiduous in his office, gives general satisfaction, and has never been charged with bribery. . . . But are they capable of conducting an intricate affair, of seizing and improving the opportunity and critical moment of action? No; this surpasses their abilities. . . .

As most citizens have sufficient ability to choose, though unqualified to be chosen, so the people, though capable of calling others to an account for their administration, are incapable of conducting the administration themselves. . . .

Again, there is no liberty if the judiciary power be not separated from the legislative and executive. Were it joined with the legislative, the life and liberty of the subject would be exposed to arbitrary control; for the judge would be then the legislator. Were it joined to the executive power the judge might behave with violence and oppression.

From Montesquieu, *Spirit of the Laws.*

---

in republics, honor in monarchies, and fear in despotisms. Like each form, each spirit was prone to abuse and had to be restrained if republics were not to give way to vice and excess, monarchies to corruption, and despotisms to repression. Montesquieu classified regimes as either moderate or immoderate, and through the use of extensive historical examples attempted to demonstrate how moderation could be maintained through rules and restraints, through the spirit of the law.

For Montesquieu, a successful government was one in which powers were separated and checks and balances existed within the institutions of the state. As befit a provincial magistrate, he insisted on the absolute separation of the judiciary from all other branches of government. The law needed to be independent and impartial, and it needed to be just. Montesquieu advocated that law codes be reformed and reduced mainly to regulate crimes against persons and property. Punishment should fit the crime but should be humane. Montesquieu was one of the first to advocate the abolition of torture. Like most Europeans of his age, he saw monarchy as the only realistic form of government, but

he argued that for a monarchy to be successful, it needed a strong and independent aristocracy to restrain its tendency toward corruption and despotism. He based his arguments on what he believed was the case in Britain, which he praised as the only state in Europe in which liberty resided.

Enlightened thinkers attacked established institutions, above all the Church. Most were deists who believed in the existence of God on rational grounds only. Following the materialistic ideas of the new science, deists believed that nature conformed to its own material laws and operated without divine intervention. God, in a popular Enlightenment image, was like a clockmaker who constructed the elaborate mechanism, wound it, and gave the pendulum its first swing. After that the clock worked by itself. Deists were accused of being anti-Christian, and they certainly opposed the ritual forms of both Catholic and Protestant worship. They also opposed the role of the Church in education, for education was the key to an enlightened view of the future. This meant, above all, conflict with the Jesuits. "Let's eat a Jesuit" was Voltaire's half-facetious comment.

Jean-Jacques Rousseau attacked the educational system. His tract on education, disguised as the romantic novel *Émile* (1762), argued that children should be taught by appealing to their interests rather than with strict discipline. Education was crucial because the Enlightenment was dominated by the idea of the British philosopher John Locke (1632–1704) that the mind was blank at birth, a *tabula rasa*—"white paper void of all characters"—and that it was filled up by experience. Contrary to the arguments of Descartes, Locke wrote in *An Essay Concerning Human Understanding* (1690) that there were no innate ideas and no good or evil that was not conditioned by experience. For Locke, as for a host of thinkers after him, good and evil were defined as pleasure and pain. We do good because it is pleasurable and we avoid evil because it is painful. Morality was a sense experience rather than a theological one. It was also relative rather than absolute. This was an observation that derived from increased interest in non-European cultures. The *Persian Letters* of Baron Montesquieu was the most popular of a genre describing non-European societies that knew nothing of Christian morality.

By the middle of the eighteenth century, the pleasure/pain principle enunciated by Locke had come to be applied to the foundations of social organization. If personal good was pleasure, then social good was happiness. The object of government, in the words of the Scottish moral philosopher Francis Hutcheson (1694–1746), was "the greatest happiness of the greatest number." This principle was at the core of *Crimes and Punishments* (1764), Cesare Beccaria's pioneering work of legal reform. Laws were instituted to promote happiness within society. They had to be formulated equitably for both criminal and victim. Punishment was to act as a deterrent to crime rather than as retribution. Therefore, Beccaria advocated the abolition of torture to gain confessions, the end of capital punishment, and the rehabilitation of criminals through the improvement of penal institutions. By 1776 happiness was established as one of the basic rights of man, enshrined in the American Declaration of Independence as "life, liberty, and the pursuit of happiness."

It was in refashioning the world through education and social reform that the Enlightenment revealed its orientation toward the future. *Optimism* was a word invented in the eighteenth century to express this feeling of liberation from the weight of centuries of traditions. "This is the best of all possible worlds and all things turn out for the best," was the satirical slogan of Voltaire's *Candide*. But if Voltaire believed that enlightened thinkers had taken optimism too far, others believed that it had to be taken further still.

Progress, an idea that not all enlightened thinkers shared, was another invention of the age. It was expressed most cogently by the French philosopher the Marquis de Condorcet (1743–94) in *The Progress of the Human Mind* (1795), in which he developed an almost evolutionary view of human development from a savage state of nature to a future of harmony and international peace.

The Impact of the Enlightenment. As there was no single set of Enlightenment beliefs, so there was no single impact of the Enlightenment. Its general influence was felt everywhere, even seeping to the lowest strata of society. Its specific influence is harder to gauge. Paradoxically, enlightened political reform took firmer root in eastern Europe, where the ideas were imported, than in western Europe, where they originated. It was absolute rulers who were most successful in borrowing Enlightenment reforms.

It is impossible to determine what part enlightened ideas and what part practical necessities played in the eastern European reform movement that began around mid-century. In at least three areas the coincidence between ideas and actions was especially strong: law, education, and the extension of religious toleration.

Jean-Jacques Rousseau.

THE GOOD OF ALL

The Social Contract (1762) was one of the greatest visionary tracts of the eighteenth century. In it Jean-Jacques Rousseau envisioned a harmonious society capable of eliminating want and controlling evil. Here he discusses his famous idea of the general will.

As long as men united together look upon themselves as a single body, they have but one will relating to the common preservation and general welfare. Then all the energies of the state are vigorous and simple: its maxims are clear and luminous; there are no mixed contradictory interests; the common prosperity shows itself everywhere, and requires only good sense to be appreciated. Peace, union, and equality are enemies of political subtleties. Upright, honest men are difficult to deceive, because of their simplicity: decoys and pretexts do not impose upon them, they are not cunning enough to be dupes. When we see among the happiest people in the world troops of peasants regulating the affairs of state under an oak, and conducting themselves wisely, can we help despising the refinements of other nations, who make themselves illustrious and miserable with so much art and mystery?

From Jean-Jacques Rousseau, *The Social Contract.*

Law was the basis of Enlightenment views of social interaction, and the influence of Montesquieu and Beccaria spread quickly. In Prussia and Russia the movement to codify and simplify the legal system did not reach fruition in the eighteenth century, but in both places it was well under way. The Prussian jurist Samuel von Cocceji (1679–1755) initiated the reform of Prussian law and legal administration. Cocceji's project was to make the enforcement of law uniform throughout the realm, to prevent judicial corruption, and to produce a single code of Prussian law. The code, finally completed in the 1790s, reflected the principles of criminal justice articulated by Beccaria. In Russia, the Law Commission summoned by Catherine the Great in 1767 never did complete its work. Nevertheless, profoundly influenced by Montesquieu, Catherine attempted to abolish torture and to introduce the Beccarian principle that the accused was innocent until proven guilty. In Austria, Joseph II presided over a wholesale reorganization of the legal system. Courts were centralized, laws codified, and torture and capital punishment abolished.

Enlightenment ideas also underlay the efforts to improve education in eastern Europe. The religious orders, especially the Jesuits, were the most influential educators of the age, and the Enlightenment attack upon them created a void that had to be filled by the state. Efforts at compulsory education were first undertaken in Russia under Peter the Great, but these were aimed at the compulsory education of the nobility. It was Catherine who extended the effort to the provinces, attempting to educate a generation of Russian teachers. She was especially eager that women

MAJOR WORKS OF THE ENLIGHTENMENT

1690	*An Essay Concerning Human Understanding* (Locke)
1721	*Persian Letters* (Baron Montesquieu)
1734	*Philosophical Letters Concerning the English Nation* (Voltaire)
1739	*A Treatise of Human Nature* (Hume)
1740	*Pamela* (Richardson)
1748	*An Enquiry Concerning Human Understanding* (Hume); *The Spirit of the Laws* (Baron Montesquieu)
1751–1780	*Encyclopedia* (Diderot)
1759	*Candide* (Voltaire)
1762	*Émile; The Social Contract* (Rousseau)
1764	*Crimes and Punishments* (Beccaria)
1784	*What Is Enlightenment?* (Kant)
1795	*The Progress of the Human Mind* (Marquis de Condorcet)
1798	*An Essay on the Principles of Population* (Malthus)

receive primary schooling, although the prejudice against educating women was too strong to overcome. Austrian and Prussian reforms were more successful in extending the reach of primary education, even if its content remained weak.

Religious toleration was the area in which the Enlightenment had its greatest impact in Europe, though again it was in the eastern countries that this was most visible. Freedom of worship for Catholics was barely whispered about in Britain, while neither France nor Spain were moved to tolerate Protestants. Nevertheless, within these parameters there were some important changes in the religious makeup of the western European states. In Britain, Protestant dissenters were no longer persecuted for their beliefs. By the end of the eighteenth century, the number of Protestants outside the Church of England was growing; and by the early nineteenth century discrimination against Protestants was all but eliminated. In France and Spain, relations between the national church and the papacy were undergoing a reorientation. Both states were asserting more independence—both theologically and financially—from Rome. The shift was symbolized by disputes over the role of the Jesuits, who were finally expelled from France in 1764 and from Spain in 1767.

In eastern Europe, enlightened ideas about religious toleration did take effect. Catherine the Great abandoned persecution of a Russian Orthodox sect known as the Old Believers. Prussia had always tolerated various Protestant groups, and with the conquest of Silesia it acquired a large Catholic population. Catholics were guaranteed freedom of worship, and Frederick the Great even built a Catholic church in Berlin to symbolize this policy. Austria extended enlightened ideas about toleration the furthest. Maria Theresa was a devout Catholic and had actually increased religious persecution in her realm, but Joseph II rejected his mother's dogmatic position. In 1781 he issued the Patent of Toleration, which granted freedom of worship to Protestants and members of the Eastern Orthodox church. The following year he extended this toleration to Jews. Joseph's attitude toward toleration was as practical as it was enlightened. He believed that the revocation of the Edict of Nantes—which had granted limited toleration to Protestants—at the end of the seventeenth century had been an economic disaster for France, and he encouraged religious toleration as a means to economic progress.

A science of economics was first articulated during the Enlightenment. A group of French thinkers known as the Physiocrats subscribed to the view that land was wealth and thus argued that agricultural activity, especially improved means of farming and livestock breeding, should take first priority in state reforms. As wealth came from land, taxation should be based only on land ownership, a principle that was coming into increased prominence despite the opposition of the landowning class. Physiocratic ideas combined a belief in the sanctity of private property with the need for the state to increase agricultural output. Ultimately the Physiocrats, like the great Scottish economic theorist Adam Smith, came to believe that government should cease to interfere with private economic activity. They articulated the doctrine *Laissez faire, laissez passer*—"Let it be, let it go." The ideas of Adam Smith and the Physiocrats ultimately formed the basis for nineteenth-century economic reform.

If the Enlightenment did not initiate a new era, it did offer a new vision, whether in Hume's psychology, Montesquieu's political science, Rousseau's sociology, or Smith's economic theory. All of these subjects, which have such a powerful impact on contemporary life, had their modern origins in the Enlightenment. As the British poet Alexander Pope (1688–1744) put it: "Know then thyself, presume not God to scan/ The proper study of mankind is man." Enlightened thinkers challenged existing ideas and existing institutions. A new emphasis on self and on pleasure led to a new emphasis on happiness. All three fed into the distinctively Enlightenment idea of self-interest. Happiness and self-interest were values that would inevitably corrode the old social order, which was based upon principles of self-sacrifice and corporate identity. It was only a matter of time.

Eighteenth-Century Society

Eighteenth-century society was a hybrid of old and new. It remained highly stratified socially, politically, and economically. Birth and occupation determined wealth, privilege, and quality of life as much as they had in the past. But in the eighteenth century the gulf between top and bottom was being filled by a thriving middle class, a *bourgeoisie*, as they were called in France. There were now more paths toward the middle and upper classes, more wealth to be distributed among those above the level of subsistence. It was bourgeois culture and bourgeois values that were new in the eighteenth century. At the bottom of society, poverty still gripped the mass of European people. Changes in agriculture allowed more to survive than ever before, but their survival was still perilous, dependent upon chance rather than effort.

The Nobility

Nobles were defined by their legal rights. They had the right to bear arms, the right to special judicial treatment, the right to tax exemptions. In Russia only nobles could own serfs; in Poland only nobles could hold government office. In France and Britain the highest court positions were always reserved for noblemen. Nobles dominated the Prussian army. In 1786, out of nearly 700 senior officers only 22 were not noblemen. The Spanish nobility claimed the right to live idly. Rich or poor, they shunned all labor as a right of their heritage. Swedish and Hungarian noblemen had their own legislative chambers, just as the British had the House of Lords. Noble privilege was as vibrant as ever.

Although all who enjoyed these special rights were noble, not all nobles were equal. In many states the noble order was subdivided into easily identifiable groups. The Spanish grandees, the upper nobility, were numbered in the thousands; the Spanish hidalgos, the lower nobility, in the hundreds of thousands. In Hungary, out of 400,000 noblemen only about 15,000 belonged to the landed nobility, who held titles and were exempt from taxes. The landed nobility were personally members of the upper chamber of the Hungarian Diet, while the lesser nobility sent representatives to the lower chamber. This was not unlike the situation in England, where the elite class was divided between the peerage and the gentry. The peerage held titles, were members of the House of Lords, and had a limited range of judicial and fiscal privileges. In the mid-eighteenth century, there were only 190 British peers. The gentry, which numbered over 20,000, dominated the House of Commons and local legal offices but were not strictly members of the nobility. The French nobility was informally distinguished among the small group of peers known as the Grandes, whose ancient lineage, wealth, and power set them apart from all others; a rather larger service nobility whose privileges derived in one way or another from municipal or judicial service; and what might be called the country nobility, whose small estates and local outlook made their fiscal immunities vital to their survival.

These distinctions among the nobilities of the European states masked a more important one: wealth. As the saying went, "All who were truly noble were not wealthy, but all who were truly wealthy were noble." In the eighteenth century, despite the phenomenal increase in mercantile activity, wealth was still calculated in profits from the ownership of land, and it was the wealthy landed nobility who set the tone of elite life in Europe.

All That Glitters. Eighteenth-century Europe was a society of orders gradually transforming itself into a society of classes. At the top, as vigorous as ever, was the nobility, the privileged order in every European state. In different parts of Europe the nobility used different methods to maintain their land-based wealth. In places like Britain, Spain, Austria, and Hungary, forms of entail were the rule. In simple terms, an entail was a restriction prohibiting the breakup of a landed estate either through sale or inheritance. The owner of the estate was merely a caretaker for his heir, and while he could add land, he could not easily subtract any. Entailed estates grew larger and larger and, like magnets, attracted other entailed estates through marriage. In Britain, where primogeniture—inheritance by the eldest son—accompanied entail, four hundred families owned one-quarter of the entire country. Yet this concentration of landed wealth paled into insignificance when compared to the situation in Spain, where just four families owned one-third of all the cultivable land. In the east, where land was plentiful, the Esterhazys of Hungary and the Radziwills of Poland owned millions of acres.

The second method by which the European nobility ensured that the wealthy would be noble was by absorption. There were several avenues to upward mobility, but by the eighteenth century the holding of state offices was the most common. In France, for example, a large number of offices were reserved for the nobility. Many of these were owned by their holders and passed on to their children, but occasionally an office was sold on the market and the new holder was automatically ennobled. The office of royal secretary was one of the most common routes to noble status. The number of secretaries increased from 300 to 900 during the course of the eighteenth century, yet despite this dilution the value of the offices continued to skyrocket. An office that was worth 70,000 French pounds at the beginning of the century was worth 300,000 by the 1780s. In fact, in most European societies there was more room for new nobles than there were aspiring candidates. This was because of the costs that maintaining the new status imposed. In Britain, anyone who could live like a gentleman was accounted one. But the practice of entail made it very difficult for a newcomer to purchase the requisite amount of land. Philip V increased the number of Spanish grandees in an effort to dilute their power, yet when he placed a tax on entrance into the lower nobility, the number of hidalgos dropped precipitously.

For the wealthy, aristocracy was becoming an international status. The influence of Louis XIV and the court of Versailles lasted for well over a century and spread to town and country life. Most nobles main-

Blenheim Palace, Oxfordshire, was built for the duke of Marlborough by a grateful nation and named after his famous victory.

tained multiple residences. The new style of aristocratic entertainment required more public space on the first floor, while the increasing demand for personal and familial privacy necessitated more space in the upper stories. The result was larger and more opulent homes. Here the British elite led all others. Over 150 country houses were built in the early eighteenth century alone, including Blenheim Palace, which was built for John Churchill, duke of Marlborough, at a cost of £300,000. To the expense of architecture was added the expense of decoration. New materials such as West Indian mahogany occasioned new styles, and both drove up costs. The high-quality woodwork and plastering made fashionable by the English Adam brothers was quickly imitated on the Continent. Only the Spanish nobility shunned country estates, preferring to reside permanently in towns.

The building of country houses was only one part of the conspicuous consumption of the privileged orders. Improvements in travel, both in transport and roads, permitted increased contact between members of the national elites. The stagecoach linked towns, and canals linked waterways. Both made travel quicker and more enjoyable. The grand tour of historical sites continued to be used as a substitute for formal education. Young men would pass from country house to country house buying up antiquities, paintings, and books along the way. The grand tour was a means of introducing the European aristocracies to each other, and also a means of communicating taste and fashion

among them. Whether it was a Russian noble in Germany, a Swede in Italy, or a Briton in Prussia, all spoke French and shared a cultural outlook.

Much of this was cultivated in the salons, a social institution begun in the seventeenth century by French women that gradually spread throughout the Continent. In the salons, especially those in Paris, the aristocracy and bourgeoisie mingled with the leading intellectuals of the age. Here wit and insight replaced polite conversation. At formal meetings, papers on scientific or philosophical topics were read and discussed. At informal gatherings new ideas were examined and exchanged. The British ambassador to Spain was appalled to discover that men and women were still kept separate in the salons of Madrid and that there was no serious conversation during evenings out. It was in the salons that the impact of the Enlightenment, the great European intellectual movement of the eighteenth century, first made itself felt.

The Bourgeoisie

Bourgeois is a French word, and it carried the same tone of derision in the eighteenth century that it does today. The bourgeois was a man on the make, scrambling after money or office or title. He was neither wellborn nor well-bred, or so said the nobility. Yet the bourgeoisie served vital functions in all European societies. They dominated trade, both nationally and internationally. They made their homes in cities and did much to improve the quality of urban life. They were the civilizing influence in urban culture, for unlike the nobility, they were the city's permanent denizens. Perhaps most importantly, the bourgeoisie provided the safety valve between the nobility and those who were acquiring wealth and power but lacked the advantages of birth and position. By developing their own culture and class identity, the bourgeoisie provided successful individuals with their own sense of pride and achievement and eased the explosive buildup of social resentments.

During the eighteenth century, the bourgeoisie grew in both numbers and importance. An active commercial and urban life gave many members of this group new social and political opportunities, and many of them passed into the nobility through the purchase of land or office. But for those whose aspirations or abilities were different, this social group began to define its own values, which centered on the family and the home. A new interest in domestic affairs touched both men and women of the European bourgeoisie. Their homes became social centers for kin and neighbors, and their outlook on family life reflected new personal relationships. Marriages were made for companionship as much as for economic advantage. Romantic love between husbands and wives was newly valued. So were children, whose futures came to dominate familial concern. Childhood was recognized as a separate stage of life and the education of children as one of the most important of all parental responsibilities. The image of the affectionate father replaced that of the hard-bitten businessman; the image of the doting mother replaced that of the domestic drudge.

Urban Elites. In the society of orders, nobility was the acid test. The world was divided into the small number of those who had it and the large number of those who did not. At the apex of the non-noble pyramid was the bourgeoisie, the elites of urban Europe whose place in the society of orders was ambiguous. *Bourgeois,* or *burgher,* simply meant "town dweller," but as a social group it had come to mean wealthy town dweller. The bourgeoisie was strongest where towns were strongest: in western rather than in eastern Europe and in northern rather than southern Europe, with the notable exception of Italy. Holland was the exemplar of a bourgeois republic. More than half of the Dutch population lived in towns, and there was no significant aristocratic class to compete for power. The Regents of Amsterdam were the equivalent of a European court nobility in wealth, power, and prestige, though not in the way in which they had accumulated their fortunes. The size of the bourgeoisie in various European states cannot be absolutely determined. At the end of the eighteenth century, the British middle classes probably constituted around 15 percent of the population, the French bourgeoisie less than 10 percent. By contrast, the Russian or Hungarian urban elites were less than 2 percent of the population in those states.

Like the nobility, the bourgeoisie constituted a diverse group. At the top were great commercial fami-

The Dutton Family *by John Zoffany. This eighteenth-century painting shows the comforts enjoyed by the British upper middle class.*

lies engaged in the expanding international marketplace and reaping the profits of trade. In wealth and power they were barely distinguishable from the nobility. At the bottom were the so-called petite bourgeoisie; shopkeepers, artisans, and small manufacturers. The solid core of the bourgeoisie was employed in trade, exchange, and service. Most were engaged in local or national commerce. Trade was the lifeblood of the city, for by itself the city could neither feed nor clothe its inhabitants. Most bourgeois fortunes were first acquired in trade. Finance was the natural outgrowth of commerce, and another segment of the bourgeoisie accumulated or preserved their capital through the sophisticated financial instruments of the eighteenth century. While the very wealthy loaned directly to the central government or bought shares in overseas trading companies, most bourgeois participated in government credit markets. They purchased state bonds or lifetime annuities and lived on the interest. The costs of war flooded the urban credit markets with high-yielding and generally stable financial instruments. Finally, the bourgeoisie were members of the burgeoning professions that provided services for the rich. Medicine, law, education, and the bureaucracy were all bourgeois professions, for the cost of acquiring the necessary skills could be borne only by those already wealthy.

During the course of the eighteenth century, this combination of occupational groups was expanding, both in numbers and in importance, all over Europe. So was the bourgeois habitat. The urbanization of Europe continued steadily throughout the eighteenth century. A greater percentage of the European population were living in towns, and a greater percentage were living in large towns of over 10,000 inhabitants, which, of necessity, were developing complex socioeconomic structures. In France alone there were probably over a hundred such towns, each requiring the services of the bourgeoisie and providing opportunities for their expansion. And the larger the metropolis, the greater the need. In 1600, only 20 European cities contained as many as 50,000 people; in 1700 that number had risen to 32; and by 1800 to 48. During the course of the eighteenth century, the number of cities with 75,000 inhabitants doubled. London, the largest city, had grown to 865,000, a remarkable feat considering that in 1665 over a quarter of the London population had died in the Great Plague. In such cities the demand for lawyers, doctors, merchants, and shopkeepers was almost insatiable.

Besides wealth, the urban bourgeoisie shared another characteristic: mobility. The aspiration of the bourgeoisie was to become noble, either through office or by acquiring rural estates. In Britain, a gentleman was still defined by lifestyle: "All are accounted gentlemen in England who maintain themselves without manual labor." Many trading families left their wharves and countinghouses to acquire rural estates, live off rents, and practice the openhanded hospitality of gentlemen. In France and Spain, nobility could still be purchased, though the price was constantly going up. For the greater bourgeoisie, the transition was easy; for the lesser, the failure to move up was all the more frustrating for being just beyond their grasp. The bourgeoisie did not only imagine their discomfort, they were made to feel it at every turn. They were the butt of jokes, theater, and popular songs. They were the first victims in the shady financial dealings of crown and court, the first casualties in urban riots. Despised from above and envied from below, the bourgeoisie were uncomfortable with the present yet profoundly conservative about the future. The one consolation to their perpetual misery was that as a group they got richer and richer. And as a group they began to develop a distinctive culture that reflected their qualities and aspirations.

Bourgeois Values. Many bourgeoisie viewed their condition as temporary and accepted the pejorative connotations of the word *bourgeois*. They had little desire to defend a social group out of which they fervently longed to pass. Others, whose aspirations were lower, were nevertheless uncomfortable with the status that they had already achieved. They had no ambition to wear the silks and furs reserved for the nobility or to attend the opening night at the opera decked in jewels and finery. In fact, such ostentation was alien to their existence and to the success that they had achieved. There was a real tension between the values of noble and bourgeois. The ideal noble was idle, wasteful, and ostentatious; the ideal bourgeois was industrious, frugal, and sober. Voltaire, who made his fortune as a financial speculator rather than as a man of letters, aped the lifestyle of the nobility. But he could never allow himself to be cheated by a tradesman, a mark of his origins. When Louis XVI tried to make household economies in the wake of a financial crisis, critics said that he acted "like a bourgeois."

Even if the bourgeoisie did not constitute a class, they did share certain attitudes that constituted a culture. The wealthy among them participated in the new world of consumption, whether they did so lavishly or frugally. For those who aspired to more than their birth allowed, there was a loosening of the strict codes of dress that reserved certain fabrics, decorative materials, and styles to the nobility. Merchants and bankers could now be seen in colored suits or with piping made of cloth of gold; their wives could be seen in furs and silks. They might acquire silverware, even if they did not go so far as the nobility and have a coat of arms engraved upon it. Coaches and carriages were also becoming common among the bourgeoisie, to take them on the Sunday rides through the town gardens or to their weekend retreats in the suburbs. Parisian merchants, even master craftsmen like clockmakers, were now acquiring suburban homes, although they could not afford to retire to them for the summer months.

But more and more, the bourgeoisie was beginning to travel. In Britain whole towns were established to cater to leisure travelers. The southwestern town of Bath, which was rebuilt in the eighteenth century, was the most popular of all European resort towns, famous since Roman times for the soothing qualities of its waters. Bath was soon a social center as notable for its marriage market as for its recreations. Brighton, a seaside resort on the south coast, quadrupled in size in the second half of the eighteenth century. Bathing—what we would call swimming—either for health or recreation, became a middle-class fad, displacing traditional fear of the sea.

The leisure that wealth bestowed on the bourgeoisie, in good bourgeois fashion, quickly became commercialized. Theater and music halls for both light and serious productions proliferated. By the 1760s an actual theater district had arisen in London and was attracting audiences of over twenty thousand a week. London was unusual, both for its size and for the number of well-to-do visitors who patronized its cultural events. The size of the London audiences enabled the German-born composer Georg Friedrich Handel (1685–1759) to earn a handsome living by performing and directing concerts. He was one of the few musicians in the eighteenth century to live without noble patronage. But it was not only in Britain that theater and music flourished. Voltaire's plays were performed before packed houses in Paris, with the author himself frequently in attendance to bask in the adulation of the largely bourgeois audiences who attended them. In Venice it was estimated that over 1200 operas were produced in the eighteenth century. Rome and Milan were even better known, and Naples was the center for Italian opera. Public concerts were a mark of bourgeois culture, for the court nobility was entertained at the royal palaces or great country houses. Public concerts began in Hamburg in the 1720s, and Frederick the Great helped establish the Berlin Opera House some decades later.

L'Amour au Théâtre Français *(Love in the French Theater) (ca. 1716), by Antoine Watteau. The painting is thought to portray a scene from* Les Fêtes de l'Amour et de Bacchus, *a comic opera composed in 1672.*

Theater and concert going were part of the new attitude toward socializing that was one of the greatest contributions of the Enlightenment. Enlightened thinkers spread their views in the salons, and the salons soon spawned the academies, local scientific societies which, though led and patronized by provincial nobles, included large numbers of bourgeois members. The academies sponsored essay competitions, built up libraries, and became the local centers for intellectual interchange. A less structured form of sociability took place in the coffeehouses and tearooms that came to be a feature of even small provincial towns. In the early eighteenth century, there were over two thousand London coffee shops where men—for the coffeehouse was largely a male preserve—could talk politics, read the latest newspapers and magazines, and indulge their taste for this still-exotic beverage. More exclusive clubs were also a form of middle-class sociability, some centering on political issues, some (like the chambers of commerce) centering on professional interests. Parisian clubs, called *sociétés,* covered a multitude of diverse interests. Literary *sociétés* were the most popular, maintaining their purpose by forbidding drinking, eating, and gambling on their premises.

Above all, bourgeois culture was literate culture. Wealth and leisure led to mental pursuits—if not always to intellectual ones. The proliferation of relatively cheap printed material had an enormous impact on the lives of those who were able to afford it. Holland and Britain were the most literate European societies and also, because of the absence of censorship, the centers of European printing. This was the first great period of the newspaper and the magazine. The first daily newspaper appeared in London in 1702; eighty years later, 37 provincial towns had their own newspapers, while the London papers were read all over Britain. Then as now, the newspaper was as much a vehicle for advertisement as for news. News reports tended to be bland, avoiding controversy and concentrating on general national and international events. Advertising, on the other hand, tended to be lurid, promising cures for incurable ills and the most exquisite commodities at the most reasonable prices. For entertainment and serious political commentary, the British reading public turned to magazines, of which there were over 150 separate titles by the 1780s. The most famous were *The Spectator,* which ran in the early part of the century and did much to set the tone for a cultured middle-class life, and *The Gentleman's Magazine,* which ran in mid-century and was said to have had a circulation of nearly fifteen thousand. The longest-lived of all British magazines was *The Ladies' Diary,* which continued in existence from 1704 to 1871 and doled out self-improvement, practical advice, and fictional romances in equal proportion.

The Ladies' Diary was not the only literature aimed at the growing number of leisured and lettered bourgeois women. Although enlightened thinkers could be ambivalent about the place of women in the new social order, they generally stressed the importance of female education and welcomed women's participation in intellectual pursuits. Whether it was new ideas about women or simply the fact that more women had leisure, a growing body of both domestic literature and light entertainment was available to them. This included a vast number of teach-yourself books aimed at instructing women how best to organize domestic life and how to navigate the perils of polite society. Moral instruction, particularly on the themes of obedience and sexual fidelity, was also popular. But the greatest output directed toward women was in the form of fanciful romances, from which a new genre emerged. The novel first appeared in its modern form in the 1740s. Samuel Richardson (1689–1761) wrote *Pamela* (1740), the story of a servant girl who successfully resisted the advances of her master until he finally married her. It was composed in long episodes, or chapters, that developed Pamela's character and told her story at the expense of the overt moral message that was Richardson's original intention. Richardson's novels were printed in installments and helped to drive up the circulation of national magazines.

Family Life. While the public life of the bourgeoisie can be measured in the sociability of the coffeehouse and the academy, private life must be measured in the home. There a remarkable transformation was under way, one that the bourgeoisie shared with the nobility. In the pursuit of happiness encouraged by the Enlightenment, one of the newest joys was domesticity. The image—and sometimes the reality—of the happy home, where love was the bond between husband and wife and care the bond between parents and children, came to dominate both the literary and visual arts. Only those wealthy enough to afford to dispense with women's work could partake of the new domesticity; only those touched by Enlightenment ideas could attempt to make the change. But where it occurred, the transformation in the nature of family life was one of the most profound alterations in eighteenth-century culture.

The Snatched Kiss, *or* The Stolen Kiss *(1750s), by Jean-Honoré Fragonard, was one of the "series paintings" popular in the late eighteenth century. A later canvas entitled* The Marriage Contract *shows the next step in the lives of the lovers.*

The first step toward the transformation of family relationships was in centering the conjugal family in the home. In the past, the family was a less important structure for most people than the social groups to which they belonged or the neighborhood in which they lived. Marriage was an economic partnership and a means to carry on lineage. Individual fulfillment was not an object of marriage, and this attitude could be seen among the elites in the great number of arranged marriages, the speed with which surviving spouses remarried, and the formal and often brutal personal relationships between husbands and wives.

Patriarchy was the dominant value within the family. Husbands ruled over wives and children, making all of the crucial decisions that affected both the quality of their lives and their futures. As late as the middle of the eighteenth century, a British judge established the "rule of thumb," which asserted that a husband had a legal right to beat his wife with a stick, but the stick should be no thicker than a man's thumb. It was believed that children were stained with the sin of Adam at birth and that only the severest upbringing could clean some of it away. In nearly two hundred child-rearing advice books published in England before the middle of the eighteenth century, only three did not advise the beating of children. John Wesley (1703–91), the founder of Methodism, remembered his own mother's dictum that "children should learn to fear the rod and cry softly." Children were sent out first for wet-nursing; then at around the age of seven for boarding, either at school or in a trade; and finally into their own marriages.

There can be no doubt that this profile of family life began to change, especially in western Europe, during the second half of the eighteenth century. Although the economic elements of marriage remained strong—newspapers actually advertised the availability of partners and the dowries or annual income that they would bring to the marriage—other elements now appeared. Fed by an unending stream of stories and novels and a new desire for individual happiness, romantic and sexual attraction developed into a factor in marriage. Potential marriage partners were no longer kept away from each other or smothered by chaperons. The social season of polite society, in which prospective partners could dance, dine, and converse with each other to determine compatibility, gave greater latitude to courtship. Perhaps more importantly, the role of potential spouses in choosing a partner appears to have increased. This was a subtle matter, for even in earlier centuries parents did not simply assign a spouse to their children. But by the eighteenth century, adolescents themselves searched for their own marriage partners and exercised a strong negative voice in identifying unsuitable ones.

The quest for compatibility, no less than the quest for romantic love, led to a change in personal relationships between spouses. The extreme formality of the past was gradually breaking down. Husbands and wives began spending more time with each other, developing common interests and pastimes. Their personal life began to change. For the first time, houses were built to afford a couple privacy from their children, servants, and guests. Rooms were designed for specific functions and were set off by hallways. Corridors were an important innovation in creating privacy. In earlier architecture, one walked through a room to the next one behind it. Now rooms were separated and doors could be closed. This new design allowed for an intimate life that earlier generations did not find necessary and that they could not, in any case, put into practice.

Couples had more time for each other because they were beginning to limit the size of their families. There were a number of reasons for this development, which again pertained only to the upper classes. For one thing, child mortality rates were declining among wealthy social groups. Virulent epidemic diseases like the plague, which knew no class lines, were gradually disappearing. Moreover, though there were few medical breakthroughs in this period, sanitation was improving. Bearing fewer children had an enormous impact on the lives of women, reducing the danger of death and disablement in childbirth and giving them leisure time to pursue domestic tasks. This is not to say that the early part of a woman's marriage was not dominated by children; in fact, because of new attitudes toward child rearing it may have been dominated more than ever. Many couples appear to have made a conscious decision to space births, though success was limited by the fact that the most common technique of birth control was coitus interruptus, or withdrawal.

The transformation in the quality of relationships between spouses was mirrored by an even greater transformation in attitudes toward children. There were many reasons why childhood now took on a new importance. Decline in mortality rates had a profound psychological impact. Parents could feel that their emotional investment in their children had a greater chance of fulfillment. But equally important were the new ideas about education, especially Locke's belief that the child enters the world a blank slate whose personality is created through early education. This view not only placed a new responsibility on parents but also gave them the concept of childhood as a stage through which individuals passed. This idea could be seen in the commercial sphere as well as in any other. In 1700 there was not a single shop in London that sold children's toys exclusively; by the 1780s there were toy shops everywhere, three of which sold nothing but rocking horses. Children's toys abounded: soldiers and forts, dolls and dollhouses. The jigsaw puzzle was invented in the 1760s as a way to teach children geography. There were also shops that sold nothing but clothes specifically designed for children, no longer simply adult clothes in miniature.

Most important of all was the development of materials for the education of children. This took place in two stages. At first so-called children's books were books whose purpose was to help adults teach children. Later came books directed at children themselves, with large print, entertaining illustrations, and nonsensical characters, usually animals who taught moral lessons. In Britain the Little Pretty Pocket Book series, created by John Newbery (1713–67), not only encompassed educational primers but also included books for the entertainment of the child. Newbery published a Mother Goose book of nursery rhymes and created the immortal character of Miss Goody Two-Shoes. Instruction and entertainment also lay behind the development of children's playing cards, in which the French specialized. Dice games, like one in which a child made a journey across Europe, combined geographical instruction with the amusement of competition.

The commercialization of childhood was, of course, directed at adults. The new books and games that were designed to enhance a child's education not only had to be purchased by parents, but had to be used by them as well. More and more mothers were devoting their time to their children. Among the upper classes, the practice of wet-nursing began to decline. Mothers wanted to nurture their infants—both literally, by breast-feeding, and figuratively, by teaching them. Children became companions to be taken on outings to the increasing number of museums or shows of curiosities, which began to discount children's tickets by the middle of the century.

The preconditions of this transformation of family life could not be shared by the population at large. Working women could afford neither the cost of instructional materials for their children nor the time to use them. Ironically, they now began using wet nurses, once the privilege of the wealthy, for increasingly a working woman's labor was the margin of survival for her family. Working women enjoyed no privacy in the hovels in which they lived, with large families in single rooms. Wives and children were still beaten by husbands and fathers, and were unacquainted with enlightened ideas of the worth of the individual and the innocence of the child. By the end of the eighteenth century, two distinct family cultures coexisted in Europe: one based on companionate marriage and the affective bonds of parents and children; the other based on patriarchal dominance and the family as an economic unit.

The Masses

The paradox of the eighteenth century was that for the masses, life was getting better by getting worse. More Europeans were surviving than ever before, and more food was available to feed them; there was more housing, better sanitation, and even better charities. Yet for all of this, there was more misery. Those who would have succumbed to disease or starvation a century before now survived from day to day, beneficiaries—or victims—of increased farm production and improved agricultural marketing. The market economy organized a more effective use of land, but it created a widespread social problem. The landless agrarian laborer of the eighteenth century was the counterpart of the sturdy sixteenth-century beggar, capable of working but incapable of finding work. In the cities, the plight of the poor was as desperate as ever. Men and women sold their labor or their bodies for a pittance, while beggars slept at every doorway. Even the most openhearted charitable institutions were unable to cope with the massive increase in the poor. By the thousands, mothers abandoned their children to the foundling hospitals, where it was believed they would have a better chance of survival, even though hospital death rates were nearly 80 percent.

Not all members of the lower orders succumbed to poverty or despair. In fact, many were able to benefit from existing conditions and lead a more fulfilling life than ever before. The richness of popular culture, signified by a spread of literacy into the lower reaches of European society, was one indication of this change. So too were the reforms urged by enlightened thinkers to improve basic education and the quality of life in the cities. For the segment of the lower orders that could keep its head above water, the eighteenth century offered new opportunities and new challenges.

Breaking the Cycle. Of all the legacies of the eighteenth century, none was more fundamental than the steady increase in European population that began around 1740. This was not the first time that Europe had experienced sustained population growth, but it was the first time that such growth was not checked by a demographic crisis. Breaking the cycle of population growth and crisis was a momentous event in European history, despite the fact that it went unrecorded at the time and unappreciated for centuries after.

The figures tell one part of the story. In 1700 European population is estimated to have been 120 million. By 1800 it had grown 50 percent, to over 180 million. And the aggregate hides significant regional variations. While France, Spain, and Italy expanded between 30 and 40 percent, Prussia doubled and Russia and Hungary may have tripled in number. Britain increased by 80 percent, from about 5 to 9 million, but the rate of growth was accelerating. In 1695 the English population stood at 5 million. It took 62 years to add the next million and 24 years to add the million after that. In 1781 the population was 7 million, but it took only 13 years to reach 8 million and only 10 more years to reach 9 million. Steady population growth had continued without significant checks for well over half a century.

Ironically, the traditional pattern of European population found its theorist at the very moment that it was about to disappear. In 1798 Thomas Malthus (1766–1834) published *An Essay on the Principles of Population*. Reflecting on the history of European population, Malthus observed the cyclical pattern by which growth over one or two generations was checked by a crisis that significantly reduced population. From these lower levels new growth began until it was checked and the cycle repeated itself. Because people increased more quickly than did food supplies, the land could only sustain a certain level of population. When that level was near, population became prone to a demographic check. Malthus divided population checks into two categories: positive and preventive. Positive checks were war, disease, and famine, all of which Malthus believed were natural, although brutal, means of population control. Famine was the obvious result of the failure of food supplies to keep pace with demand; war was the competition for scarce resources; and disease often accompanied both. It was preventive checks that most interested Malthus. These were the means by which societies could limit their growth to avoid the devastating consequences of positive checks. Celibacy, late marriages, and sexual abstinence were among the choices that Malthus approved, though abortion, infanticide, and contraception were also commonly practiced.

In the sixteenth and seventeenth centuries, the dominant pattern of the life cycle was high infant and child mortality, late marriages, and early death. All controlled population growth. Infant and child mortality rates were staggering: only half of all those born reached the age of ten. Late marriage was the only effective form of birth control—given the strong social taboos against sexual relations outside marriage—for a late marriage reduced a woman's childbearing years. Women in western Europe generally married between the ages of twenty-four and twenty-six; they normally ceased bearing children at the age of forty. But not all marriages lasted this fourteen- or sixteen-year span, as one or the other partner died. On average, the childbearing period for most women was between ten and twelve years, long enough to endure six pregnancies, which would result in three surviving children. (See "Giving Birth in the Eighteenth Century," pp. 598–599.)

Three surviving children for every two adults would, of course, have resulted in a 50 percent rise in population in every generation. Celibacy was one limiting factor; cities were another. Perhaps as much as 15 percent of the population in western Europe remained celibate, either by entering religious orders that imposed celibacy or by lacking the personal or financial attributes necessary to make a match. Religious orders that enforced celibacy were still central features of Catholic societies, and spinsters, as unmarried women were labeled, were increasing everywhere. Cities were like sticky webs, trapping the surplus rural population for the spiders of disease, famine, and exposure to devour. Throughout the early modern period, urban areas grew through migration. Settled town dwellers might have been able to sustain their own numbers despite the unsanitary conditions of cities, but it was migrants who brought about the cities' explosive growth. Rural migrants accounted for the appallingly high urban death rates. When we remember that the largest European cities were continuously growing— London from 200,000 in 1600 to 675,000 in 1750;

Paris from 220,000 to 576,000; Rome from 105,000 to 156,000; Madrid from 49,000 to 109,000; Vienna from 50,000 to 175,000—then we can appreciate how many countless thousands of immigrants perished before marriage. If urban perils were not enough, there were still the positive checks. Plagues carried away hundreds of thousands, wars halved populations of places in their path, and famine overwhelmed the weak and the poor. The worst famine in European history came as late as 1697, when one-third of the population of Finland starved to death.

The late seventeenth and early eighteenth centuries was a period of population stagnation, if not actual decline. It was not until the third or fourth decade of the eighteenth century that another growth cycle began. It rapidly gained momentum throughout the Continent and showed no signs of abating after two full generations. More important, this upward cycle revealed unusual characteristics. In the first place, fertility was increasing. This had several causes. In a few areas, most notably in Britain, women were marrying younger, thereby increasing their childbearing years. This pattern was also true in eastern Europe, where women traditionally married younger. In the late eighteenth century, the average age at marriage for Hungarian women had dropped to 18.6 years. Elsewhere, most notably in France, the practice of wet-nursing was becoming more common among the masses. As working women increasingly took jobs outside the house, they were less able to nurse their own children. Finally, sexual activity outside marriage was rising. Illegitimacy rates, especially in the last decades of the century, were spurting everywhere. Over the course of the century, they rose by 60 percent in France, more than doubled in England, and nearly quadrupled in Germany. So, too, were the rates of premarital pregnancy on the rise. The number of couples rushed to the altar in 1800 was nearly double that before 1750 in most of western Europe.

But increasing fertility was only part of the picture. More significant was decreasing mortality. The positive checks of the past were no longer as potent. European warfare not only diminished in scale after the middle of the century, it changed location as well. Rivalry for colonial empires removed the theater of conflict from European communities. So did the increase in naval warfare. The damage caused by war had always been more by aftershock than by actual fighting. The destruction and pillage of crops and the wholesale slaughter of livestock created food shortages that weakened local populations for the diseases that came in train with the armies. As the virulence of warfare abated, so did that of epidemic disease. The plague had all but disappeared from western Europe by the middle of the eighteenth century. The widespread practice of quarantine—especially in Hungary, which had been the crucial bridge between eastern and western epidemics—went far to eradicate the scourge of centuries.

Without severe demographic crises to maintain the cyclical pattern, the European population began a gentle but continuous rise. Urban sanitation, at least for permanent city dwellers, was becoming more effective. Clean water supplies, organized waste and sewage disposal, and strict quarantines were increasingly part of urban regulations. The use of doctors and trained midwives helped lower the incidence of stillbirth and decreased the number of women who died in childbirth. Almost everywhere levels of infant and child mortality were decreasing. More people were being born, more were surviving the first ten dangerous years, and thus more were marrying and reproducing. Increased fertility and decreased mortality could have only one result: renewed population growth. No wonder Malthus was worried.

Daily Bread. In the past, if warfare or epidemic diseases failed to check population growth, famine would have done the job. How the European economy conquered famine in the eighteenth century is a complicated story. There was no single breakthrough that accounts for the ability to feed the tens of millions of additional people who now inhabited the continent. Holland and Britain, at the cutting edge of agricultural improvement, employed dynamic new techniques that would ultimately provide the means to support continued growth, but most European agriculture was still mired in the time-honored practices that had endured for centuries. Still, not everyone could be fed or fed adequately. Widespread famine might have disappeared, but slow starvation and chronic undernourishment had not. It is certainly the case that hunger was more common at the end of the eighteenth century than at the beginning and that the nutritional content of a typical diet may have reached its lowest point in European history.

Nevertheless, the capacity to sustain rising levels of population can only be explained in terms of agricultural improvement. Quite simply, European farmers were now producing more food and marketing it better. In the most advanced societies, this was a result of conscious efforts to make agriculture more efficient. In traditional open-field agriculture, communities quickly

Agricultural techniques are illustrated in this plate from Diderot's Encyclopedia. *In the foreground, a man steers a high-wheeled horse-drawn plow while a woman operates a hopper device to sow seeds.*

ran up against insurmountable obstacles to growth. The three-field crop rotation system left a significant proportion of land fallow each year, while the concentration on subsistence cereal crops progressively eroded the land that was in production. Common farming was only as strong as the weakest member of the community. There was little incentive for successful individuals to plow profits back into the land, either through the purchase of equipment or the increase of livestock. Livestock was a crucial variable in agricultural improvement. As long as there was only enough food for humans to eat, only essential livestock could be kept alive over the winter. Oxen, which were still the ordinary beasts of burden, and pigs and poultry, which required only minimal feed, were the most common. But few animals meant little manure, and without manure the soil could not easily be regenerated.

It was not until the middle of the seventeenth century that solutions to these problems began to appear. The first change was consolidation of landholdings so that traditional crop rotations could be abandoned. A

Giving Birth in the Eighteenth Century

"In sorrow thou shalt bring forth children." Such was Eve's punishment for eating of the forbidden tree, and that sorrow continued for numberless generations. Childbirth was painful, dangerous, and all too often deadly. Although successful childbirth needed no outside intervention, without the accumulated wisdom of the ages, babies and mothers routinely perished. That wisdom was passed from mother to daughter and finally was collected by skilled women who practiced the craft of midwifery. Every village, no matter how small, had women who were capable of assisting others in childbirth. Midwives' skills ranged widely, from the use of herbal potions and strong drink to ease the pain of labor to a rudimentary understanding of how to assist a complicated delivery when the fetus was not in the proper position.

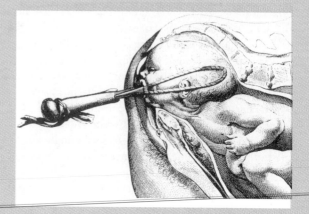

Midwives, who until the late seventeenth century were always women, were part of the support group that attended a woman during her labor. Typically, childbirth was a social occasion. Along with the midwife would be a wet nurse and female kin and neighbors, who would offer encouragement, bring refreshments, and tend to the chores that the pregnant woman would have performed herself. Without chemicals to induce contractions and without the ability to intervene in the delivery, labor was usually long. Ordinarily, it did not take place in bed, but rather in a room or a part of a room that had been set aside for the occasion. By the eighteenth century, at least in larger urban areas, poor women who had no separate space for labor could give birth in lying-in hospitals. Within the birthing room, the conclave of women was much like a social gathering. The pregnant woman was advised to adopt any position that made her feel comfortable; standing and walking were favored in the belief that the effects of gravity helped the baby move downward. The woman might sit on a neighbor's lap or on a birthing stool, a chair open at the bottom, during contractions and delivery.

Most midwives subscribed to the philosophy of letting nature take its course. Because the difficulties and length of labor differed markedly from woman to woman, the midwife's most important contribu-

tion was to offer comfort and reassurance based on her long experience. By the seventeenth century, manuals for midwives were being published, some of them written by women, but most by male doctors with surgical experience. Midwives and doctors were always at daggers drawn. Trained physicians increasingly saw childbirth as a process that could be improved by the application of new medical knowledge, but as childbirth was a female experience, midwives jealously guarded their role in it. No matter how skilled they were, they were denied access to medical training that might have enabled them to develop lucrative practices on their own. Thus they had no intention of letting male doctors into their trade. For a time the compromise was the handbooks, which contained guides to anatomy, descriptions of the most common complications, and the direst warnings to call trained physicians when serious problems arose.

By the beginning of the eighteenth century, the "man-midwife" had made his appearance in western Europe. Medically trained and usually experienced in other forms of surgery, the emergence of the man-midwife led to a number of breakthroughs in increasing the safety of childbirth. There can be no question that more mothers and children survived as a result of the man-midwives' knowledge and skills. But at the same time, the social experience of childbirth changed dramatically. What had been a female rite of passage, experienced by and with other women, now became a private event experienced by an individual woman and her male doctor. As female midwives were still excluded from medical training and licensing, their ability to practice their trade eroded in the face of new techniques and information to which they were denied access.

Although most man-midwives trained in hospitals where the poor came to give birth, they practiced among the rich. New attitudes toward marriage and children made the pain and danger of childbirth less acceptable to husbands, who sought every remedy they could afford. British and French man-midwives made fortunes practicing their trade. Their first task was to ascertain that the fetus was in the proper position to descend. In order to do this, however, they had to make an examination that was socially objectionable. Although advanced thinkers could face their man-midwife with the attitude that shame was better than death—"I considered that through modesty I was not to give up my life," as one English noblewoman reasoned—many women and more husbands were unprepared for the actual practice of a man. Thus students were taught as much about bedside manner as about medicine. They were not to examine the patient unless there was another person present in the room, they were not to ask direct questions, and they were not to face the patient during any of their procedures. They were taught to keep a linen cloth on top of the woman's abdomen and to make the examination only by touch—incredulous students were reminded that the most famous French man-midwife was blind! If the fetus was in the correct position, nothing further would be done until the delivery itself. It was only when the fetus was in what was labeled an "unnatural" position that the skill of the physician came into play.

For the most part, a child that could not be delivered head first, face down was in serious risk of being stillborn and the mother in serious risk of dying in labor. This was the problem to which the physicians addressed themselves in the eighteenth century and for which they found remarkable solutions. Most answers came from better understanding of female anatomy and a better visualization of the way in which the fetus moved during labor. The first advance was the realization that the fetus could be turned while still in the womb. Pressure applied on the outside of the stomach, especially in early stages of labor, could help the fetus drop down correctly. A

baby who emerged feet first had to be turned face down before it was pulled through the birth canal.

For babies who could not be manually manipulated, the greatest advance of the eighteenth century was the invention of the forceps, or the *tire-tête*, as the French called them. With forceps, the physician could pull the baby by force when the mother was incapable of delivery. Forceps were used mostly in breech births but were also a vital tool when the baby was too large to pass through the cervix by contraction. The forceps were invented in Britain in the middle of the seventeenth century but were kept secret for more than fifty years. During that time they were used by three generations of a single family of man-midwives. In the eighteenth century, they came into general use when the Scotsman William Smellie (1697–1765) developed a short, leather-covered instrument that enabled the physician to do as little damage as possible to either mother or child. Obstetrics now emerged as a specialized branch of medical practice. If neither the pain nor the sorrow of childbirth could be eliminated, its dangers could be lessened.

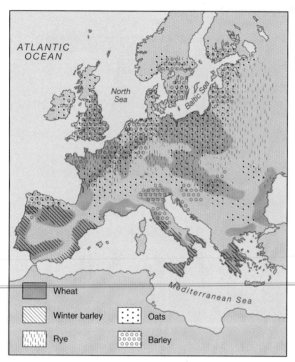

Cereal Crops

higher nutritional value than most other cereals, it also yielded more food per acre than traditional grains, reaching levels as high as forty to one. So, too, did the potato, which also entered the European diet from the New World. The potato grew in poor soil, required less labor, and yielded an abundant and nutritious harvest. It rapidly took hold in Ireland and parts of Prussia, from which it spread into eastern Europe. French and Spanish peasants reluctantly introduced it into their diet. Wherever it took root, the potato quickly established itself as survival food. It allowed families to subsist on smaller amounts of land and with less capital outlay. As a result, potato cultivation enabled people in some parts of Europe to marry younger, and thus to produce more children.

It must be stressed, however, that these new developments involved only a very narrow range of producers. The new techniques were expensive, and knowledge of the new crops spread slowly. Change had to overcome both inertia and intransigence. With more mouths to feed, profits from agriculture soared without landowners having to lift a finger. Only the most ambitious were interested in improvement. At the other end, peasant farmers were more concerned with failure than success. An experiment that did not work could devastate a community; one that did only meant higher taxes. Thus, the most important improvements in agricultural production were more traditional ones. Basically, there was an increase in the amount of land that was utilized for growing. In most of western Europe there was little room for agricultural expansion, but in the east there remained great tracts of uncultivated land. In Russia, Prussia, and Hungary, hundreds of thousands of new acres came under the plow, though it must be admitted that some of it simply went to replace land that had been wastefully exhausted in previous generations. In one German province, nearly 75 percent more land was in cultivation at the end of the eighteenth century than had been at the beginning. Even in the west, drainage schemes and forest clearance expanded productive capacity.

There was also an upswing in the efficiency with which agricultural products were marketed. From the seventeenth century onward, market agriculture was gradually replacing subsistence agriculture in most parts of Europe. Market agriculture had the advantage of allowing specialization on farms. Single-crop farming enabled farmers to benefit from the peculiarities of their own soil and climate. They could then exchange their surplus for the range of crops they needed to sub-

second innovation was the introduction of fodder crops, some of which—like clover—added nutrients to the soil, while others—like turnips—were used to feed livestock. Better grazing and better winter feed increased the size of herds, while new techniques of animal husbandry, particularly crossbreeding, produced hardier strains. It was quite clear that the key to increased production lay in better fertilization, and by the eighteenth century some European farmers had broken through the "manure barrier." Larger herds, the introduction of clover crops, the use of human waste from towns, and even the first experiments with lime as an artificial fertilizer were all part of the new agricultural methods. The impact of new farming techniques was readily apparent. In Britain and Holland, where they were used most extensively, grain yields exceeded ten kernels harvested for each one planted, while in eastern Europe, where they were hardly known, yields were less than five to one.

Along with the new crops that helped nourish both soil and animals came new crops that helped nourish people. Indian corn, or maize, was a staple crop for Native Americans and gradually came to be grown in most parts of western Europe. Maize not only had

sist. Market exchange was facilitated by improved transportation and communication, and above all by the increase in the population of towns, which provided demand. On a larger scale, market agriculture was able to respond to regional harvest failures in a way that subsistence agriculture could not. The most hated figure in the eighteenth century was the grain engrosser, a middleman who bought up local surplus and shipped it away. Engrossers were accused of driving up prices—which they did—and of creating famines—which they did not. In fact, the national and international trade in large quantities of grain evened out regional variations in harvests and went a long way toward reducing local grain shortages. The upkeep of roads, the building of canals, and the clearing of waterways created a national lifeline for the movement of grain.

Finally, it is believed that the increase in agricultural productivity owed something to a change in climate that took place in the late eighteenth century. This is very difficult to substantiate and impossible to explain. It is thought that the annual ring of growth inside tree trunks is an indicator of changes in climate. Hot years produce markedly different rings than cold ones; wet years are etched differently than dry ones. Examination of trees that are centuries old seems to indicate that the European climate was unusually cold and wet during the seventeenth century—some have even called it a little ice age—and that it gradually warmed during the eighteenth century. Even moderate climatic change, when combined with new techniques, new crops, expanded cultivation, and improved marketing, would go a long way toward explaining how so many more people were being fed at the end of the eighteenth century.

The Plight of the Poor.
"Of every ten men one is a beggar, five are too poor to give him alms, three more are ill at ease, embarrassed by debts and lawsuits, and the tenth does not represent a hundred thousand families." So observed an eighteenth-century Frenchman about the distribution of wealth in his country. There can be no doubt that the most serious social problem of the eighteenth century was the explosion of poor people throughout Europe. There was grim irony in the fact that advances in the production and distribution of food and the retreat of war and plague allowed more people to survive hand-to-mouth than ever before. Where their ancestors had succumbed to quick death from disease or starvation, they eked out a miserable existence of constant hunger and chronic pain, with death at the end of a seemingly endless corridor.

It is impossible to gauge the number of European poor or to separate them into categories of greater and greatest misery. The truly indigent, the starving poor, probably composed 10 to 15 percent of most societies, perhaps as many as 20 million people throughout the Continent. They were most prevalent in towns but were an increasing burden on the countryside, where they wandered in search of agricultural employment. The wandering poor had no counterpart in the east, where serfdom kept everyone tied to the land, but the hungry and unsheltered certainly did. Yet the problem of poverty was not only to be seen among the destitute. In fact, the uniqueness of the poor in the eighteenth century is that they were drawn from social groups that even in the hungry times of the early seventeenth century had been successful subsistence producers. Perhaps another 40 percent of the population in western Europe was described by contemporaries as those without a fixed interest: in the country, those without land; in the towns, those without steady jobs.

It was easy to see why poverty was increasing. The relentless advance of population drove up the price of food and drove down the price of wages. In the second half of the eighteenth century, the cost of living in France rose by over 60 percent while wages rose only by 25 percent. In Spain the cost of living increased by 100 percent while wages rose only 20 percent. Only in Britain did wages nearly keep pace with prices. Rising prices made land more valuable. At the beginning of the eighteenth century, as the first wave of population expansion hit western Europe, small holdings began to decrease in size. The custom of partible inheritance, by which each son received a share of land, shrank the average size of a peasant holding below that necessary to sustain an average-size family, let alone one that was growing larger. In one part of France it was estimated that 30 acres was a survival plot of land in good times. At the end of the seventeenth century 80 percent of the peasants there owned less than 25 acres.

As holdings contracted, the portion of the family income derived from wage labor expanded. In such circumstances, males were more valuable than females, both as farmers and laborers, and there is incontrovertible evidence that European rural communities practiced female infanticide. In the end, however, it became increasingly difficult for the peasant family to remain on the land. Mediterranean sharecroppers fell further and further into debt until they finally lost their land entirely. Small freeholders were forced to borrow against future crops until a bad harvest led to foreclosure. Many were allowed to lease back their own lands, on short terms and at high rents, but most swelled the ranks of agricultural laborers, migrating during the planting and harvest seasons and suffering cruelly during winter and summer. In Britain the rural landless outnumbered the landed by two to one. In France there were as many as 8 million peasants who no longer owned their own land.

Emigration was the first logical consequence of poverty. In places where rural misery was greatest, like Ireland, whole communities pulled up stakes and moved to America. Frederick the Great attracted hundreds of thousands of emigrants to Prussia by offering them land. But most rural migrants did not move to new rural environments. Rather, they followed the well-trodden paths to the cities. Many traditional domestic crafts were evolving into industrial activities. In the past, peasants had supplemented their family income by processing raw materials in the home. Spinning, weaving, and sewing were common cottage industries in which the workers took in the work, supplied their own equipment, and were paid by the piece. Now, especially in the cloth trades, a new form of industrial activity was being organized. Factories, usually located in towns or larger villages, assembled workers together, set them at larger and more efficient machines, and paid them for their time rather than for their output. Families unable to support themselves from the land had no choice but to follow the movement of jobs.

Urban poverty seemed more extreme to observers because there were more poor to observe. They crowded into towns in search of work or charity, though they were unlikely to find much of either. It was certainly true that urban areas were better equipped to assist the poor than were the rural communities from which they came. But the likelihood of finding aid only attracted more and more poor, straining and finally breaking the capacities of urban institutions. The death rate of these migrants and their children was staggering. It is perhaps best typified by the dramatic increase in the numbers of abandoned babies throughout western European cities. The existence of foundling hospitals in cities meant that unwed or poor mothers could leave their children in the hope that they would receive better care than the mother herself could provide. In fact, this was rarely the case. In the largest foundling hospital in Paris, only 15 percent of the children survived their first year of "care." But this did little to deter abandonment. In 1772 over 7500 babies were left in this charnel house, representing 40 percent of all the children born in Paris that year. The normal rates of abandonment of between 10 and 15 percent of all children born in such diverse cities as Madrid and Brussels were little better.

Neither state nor private charities could cope with the flood of poor immigrants. Although the English pundit Samuel Johnson (1709–84) opined that "a decent provision for the poor is the true test of civilization," what he meant was provision for the deserving poor, those unfortunates who were physically or mentally unable to support themselves. The distinction between the worthy and unworthy poor was one involved with changing definitions of charity itself. In earlier times, charity was believed to benefit the soul of the giver as much as the body of the recipient. Thus the poor were socially useful, providing the rich with the opportunity to do good works. But now the poor were coming to be viewed as a problem of social administration. Hospitals, workhouses, and more ominously, prisons were established or expanded to deal with them.

Hospitals were residential asylums rather than places for health care. They took in the old, the incapacitated, and increasingly, the orphaned young. Those in France were aptly named "Hotels of God," considering their staggering death rates. "There children dwell who know no parents' care/Parents who know no children's care dwell there," one poet lamented. Workhouses existed for those who were capable of work but incapable of finding it. They were supposed to improve the values of the idle by keeping them busy, though in most places they served only to improve the profits of the industrialists, who rented out workhouse inmates at below-market wages. Prisons grew with crime. There were spectacular increases in crimes against property in all eighteenth-century cities, and despite severe penalties that could include hanging for petty theft, more criminals were incarcerated than executed. Enlightened arguments for the reform of prisons and punishment tacitly acknowledged the social basis of most crime. As always, the victims of crime were mostly drawn from the same social backgrounds as the perpetrators. Along with all of their other troubles, it was the poor who were most commonly robbed, beaten, and abused.

Popular Culture. However depressing this story of the unrelieved misery of the poor is, we should not think of the masses of eighteenth-century society only

Der Pesthof *(The Plague Ward), 1746, illustrates the conditions in eighteenth-century medical facilities. The centerpiece is a gruesome amputation.*

as the downtrodden victims of social and economic forces beyond their control. For the peasant farmer about to lose his land or the urban artisan without a job, security was an overwhelming concern. While many were to endure such fates, many others lived comfortably by the standards of the age, and almost everyone believed that things were better now than they had ever been before. Popular culture was a rich mixture of family and community activities that provided outlets from the pressures of work and the vagaries of fortune. It was no less sustaining to the population at large than was the purely literate culture of the elite, no less vital as a means of explanation for everyday events than the theories of the philosophers or the programs of the philosophes.

In fact, the line between elite and popular culture in the eighteenth century is a thin one. For one thing, there was still much mixing of social classes in both rural and urban environments. Occasions of display such as festivals, village fairs, and religious holidays brought entire communities together and reinforced their collective identities. Moreover, there were many shared elements between the two cultures. All over Europe, literacy was increasing, the result of primary education, of new business techniques, and of the millions of books that were available in editions tailored to even the most modest purse. Nearly half of the inhabitants of France were literate by the end of the eighteenth century, perhaps 60 percent of those in Britain. Men were more likely to have learned to read than

A 1781 colored mezzotint by J. R. Smith shows a lady leaving a lending library with a book.

women, as were those who lived in urban areas. More than a quarter of French women could read, a number that had doubled over the century. As the rates of female literacy rose, so did overall rates, for women took the lead in teaching children.

Popular literacy spawned popular literature in remarkable variety. Religious works remained the most important, but they were followed by almanacs, romances, and (perhaps surprisingly) chivalric fiction. Religious tracts aimed at the populace were found throughout Europe. They contained stories of the saints in Catholic countries and of the martyrs in Protestant ones, proverbs intended to increase spirituality, and prayers to be offered for all occasions. Almanacs combined prophecies, home remedies, astrological tables, predictions about the weather, and advice

on all varieties of agricultural and industrial activities. In the middle of the century, just one of the dozens of British almanacs was selling over eighty thousand copies a year. Romances were the staple of lending libraries, which were also becoming a common feature of even small towns. These books were usually published in inexpensive installments spaced according to the time working families needed to save the pennies to purchase them. Written by middle-class authors, popular romances had a strong moral streak, promoting chastity for women and sobriety for men. Yet the best-selling popular fiction, at least in western Europe, was melodramatic tales of knights and ladies from the age of chivalry. These themes had seeped into popular consciousness after having fallen out of favor among the elites. But cultural tastes did not only trickle down. The masses kept the chivalric tradition alive during the eighteenth century; it would percolate up into elite culture in the nineteenth.

Nevertheless, literate culture was not the dominant form of popular culture. Traditional social activities continued to reflect the violent and even brutal nature of day-to-day existence. Village festivals were still the safety valve of youth gangs who enforced sexual morals by shaming husbands whose wives were unfaithful or women whose reputations were sullied. Many holidays were celebrated by sporting events that pitted the inhabitants of one village against those of another. These almost always turned into free-for-alls in which broken bones were common and deaths not unknown. In fact, the frequent breakdown of sporting activities into gang wars was the principal cause for the development of rules for soccer, as well as more esoteric games like cricket in Britain. Well-organized matches soon became forms of popular entertainment. Over twenty thousand spectators attended one eighteenth-century cricket match, and soccer and cricket soon became as popular for gambling as was horse racing among the wealthy.

Even more popular were the so-called blood sports, which continued to be the most common form of popular recreation. These were brutal competitions in which, in one way or another, animals were maimed or slaughtered. Dog- and cockfighting were among those that still survive today. Less attractive to the modern mind were blood sports like bearbaiting or bull running, in which the object was the slaughter of a large beast over a prolonged period of time. Blood sports were certainly not confined to the masses—foxhunting

The Cockpit *(ca. 1759)* by William Hogarth. *The central figure is a blind nobleman who was said never to have missed an important cockfight. The steel spurs on the birds' legs enabled them to inflict serious damage in the heat of battle.*

and bullfighting were pastimes for the very rich—but they formed a significant part of local social activity.

So too did the tavern or alehouse, which in town or country was the site for local communication and recreation. There women and men gossiped and gambled to while away the hours between sundown and bedtime. Discussions and games became animated as the evening wore on, for staggering amounts of alcohol were consumed. "Drunk for a penny, dead drunk for two pennies, straw for nothing," advertised one of the thousands of British gin mills that dominated the poorer quarters of towns. The increased use of spirits—gin, brandy, rum, and vodka—changed the nature of alcohol consumption in Europe. Wine and beer had always been drunk in quantities that we would find astounding, but these beverages were also an important part of diet. The nutritional content of spirits was negligible. People drank spirits to get drunk. The British reformer Francis Place (1771–1854), who grew up in a working-class family, commented that the British masses had only two pleasures, "sex and drinking. And drunkenness is by far the most desired." The level to which it rose in the eighteenth century speaks volumes about the changes in social and economic life that the masses of European society were now experiencing.

• • •

Eighteenth-century society was a hybrid of old and new. It remained highly stratified. Birth and occupation determined wealth, privilege, and quality of life as much as they had in the past, but there were now more paths toward the middle and upper classes, more wealth to be distributed among those above the level of subsistence. Opulence and poverty increased in step as the fruits of commerce and land enriched the upper orders while rising population impoverished the lower ones. Enlightenment ideas highlighted the contradictions. The attack on traditional authority, especially the Roman Catholic church, was an attack on a conservative, static world view. Enlightenment thinkers looked to the future, to a new world shaped by reason and knowledge, a world ruled benevolently for the benefit of all human beings. Government, society, the individual—all could be improved if only the rubble of the past was cleared away. These thinkers could hardly imagine how potent their vision would become.

Suggestions for Further Reading

General Reading

* Olwen Hufton, *Europe: Privilege and Protest, 1730–1789* (Ithaca, NY: Cornell University Press, 1980). An excellent survey of the political and social history of the mid-eighteenth century.

* Leonard Krieger, *Kings and Philosophers, 1689–1789* (New York: Norton, 1970). A brilliant depiction of the personalities and ideas of eighteenth-century Europe.

* Isser Woloch, *Eighteenth Century Europe, Tradition and Progress, 1715–89* (New York: Norton, 1982). Especially strong on social movements and popular culture.

* William Doyle, *The Old European Order, 1660–1800* (Oxford: Oxford University Press, 1978). An important essay on the structure of European societies and the ways in which they held together.

Raymond Birn, *Crisis, Absolutism, Revolution: Europe, 1648–91* (New York: Holt, Rinehart and Winston, 1977). A reliable survey with especially good chapters on the Enlightenment.

Eighteenth-Century Culture

* Norman Hampson, *The Enlightenment* (London: Penguin Books, 1982). The best one-volume survey.

* Peter Gay, *The Enlightenment: An Interpretation.* 2 vols. (New York: Alfred A. Knopf, 1966–1969). A difficult but rewarding study by one of the leading historians of the subject.

Carolyn Lougee, *Le Paradis des Femmes: Women, Salons, and Social Stratification* (Princeton, NJ: Princeton University Press, 1976). A study of the foundation of the French salons and the role of women in it.

* Judith Sklar, *Montesquieu* (Oxford: Oxford University Press, 1987). A concise, readable study of the man and his work.

Theodore Besterman, *Voltaire* (Chicago: University of Chicago Press, 1976). The best of many biographies of an all-too-full life.

* Peter Gay, *The Enlightenment: A Comprehensive Anthology* (New York: Simon & Schuster, 1985). The best single volume for selections of the major works of the Enlightenment.

* John G. Gagliardo, *Enlightened Despotism* (New York: Thomas Y. Crowell, 1967). A sound exploration of the impact of Enlightenment ideas on the rulers of Europe, with emphasis on the east.

John W. Yolton, ed., *The Blackwell Companion to the Enlightenment* (Cambridge, MA: Blackwell, 1992). A comprehensive dictionary that identifies major people, works, and events.

Eighteenth-Century Society: The Nobility

Michael Bush, *Noble Privilege* (New York: Holmes and Meier, 1983). A good analytic survey of the rights of European nobles.

J. V. Beckett, *The Aristocracy in England* (London: Basil Blackwell, 1986). A comprehensive study of a tightly knit national aristocracy.

* Albert Goodwin, ed., *The European Nobility in the Eighteenth Century* (New York: Harper & Row, 1967). Separate essays on national nobilities, including those of Sweden, Poland, and Spain.

Eighteenth-Century Society: The Bourgeoisie

Jan de Vries, *European Urbanization, 1500–1800* (Cambridge, MA: Harvard University Press, 1984). An important, though difficult, study of the transformation of towns into cities, with the most reliable estimates of size and rates of growth.

* P. J. Corfield, *The Impact of English Towns 1700–1800* (Oxford: Oxford University Press, 1982). A thorough survey of the role of towns in English social and economic life.

* Elinor Barber, *The Bourgeoisie in Eighteenth-Century France* (Princeton, NJ: Princeton University Press, 1955). Still the best study of the French bourgeoisie.

* Simon Shama, *The Embarrassment of Riches* (Berkeley: University of California Press, 1987). The social life of Dutch burghers, richly portrayed.

* Ian Watt, *The Rise of the Novel* (Berkeley: University of California Press, 1957). An important essay on the relationship between literature and society in the eighteenth century.

David Garrioch, *Neighborhood and Community in Paris, 1740–90* (Cambridge: Cambridge University Press, 1986). A good microstudy of Parisian neighborhoods and the people who inhabited them.

George Sussman, *Selling Mothers' Milk: The Wet-Nursing Business,* (Bloomington: Indiana University Press, 1982). A study of buyers and sellers in this important social marketplace.

Samia Spencer, *French Women and the Age of Enlightenment* (Bloomington: Indiana University Press, 1984). A survey of the role of women in French high culture.

* Lawrence Stone, *The Family, Sex and Marriage in England 1500–1800* (New York: Harper & Row, 1979). A controversial but extremely important argument about the changing nature of family life.

* Jean-Louis Flandrin, *Families in Former Times* (Cambridge: Cambridge University Press, 1979). Strong on family and household organization.

Eighteenth-Century Society: The Masses

* Michael W. Flinn, *The European Demographic System* (Baltimore, MD: Johns Hopkins University Press, 1981). The best single-volume study especially for the nonspecialist.

E. A. Wrigley and R. S. Schofield, *The Population History of England* (Cambridge, MA: Harvard University Press, 1981). The most important reconstruction of a national population, by a team of researchers.

Olwen Hufton, *The Poor in Eighteenth-Century France* (Oxford: Oxford University Press, 1974). A compelling study of the life of the poor.

* Roy Porter, *English Society in the Eighteenth Century* (London: Penguin Books, 1982). A breezy, entertaining survey of English social life.

* J. M. Beattie, *Crime and the Courts in England* (Princeton, NJ: Princeton University Press, 1986). A difficult but sensitive analysis of crime and criminal justice.

* Peter Burke, *Popular Culture in Early Modern Europe* (New York: Harper & Row, 1978). A wide survey of practices throughout the continent.

Robert Muchembled, *Popular Culture and Elite Culture in France, 1400–1750* (Baton Rouge: Louisiana State University Press, 1985). A complex but richly textured argument about the relationship between two cultures.

* Robert Malcolmson, *Popular Recreation in English Society, 1700–1850* (Cambridge: Cambridge University Press, 1973). Sport and its role in society.

*Paperback edition available.

20 ✦ THE FRENCH REVOLUTION AND THE NAPOLEONIC ERA, 1789–1815

"Let Them Eat Cake"

*T*he Queen of France was bored. Try as she might, Marie Antoinette (1755–93) found insufficient diversion in her life at the great court of Versailles. When she was fourteen, she had married the heir to the French throne, the future Louis XVI. By the age of nineteen, she was queen of the most prosperous state in continental Europe. Still, she was bored. Her life, she complained to her mother, Empress Maria Theresa of Austria, was futile and meaningless. Maria Theresa advised the unhappy queen to suffer in silence or risk unpleasant consequences.

Sometimes mothers know best. As head of the Habsburg Empire, Maria Theresa understood more about politics than her youngest child. She understood that people have little sympathy with the boredom of a monarch, especially a foreign-born queen. But Marie Antoinette chose to ignore maternal advice and pursued amusements and intrigues that had unpleasant consequences indeed.

Unpopular as a foreigner from the time she arrived in France, Marie Antoinette suffered a further decline in her reputation as gossip spread about her gambling and affairs at court. The public heard exaggerated accounts of the fortunes she spent on clothing and jewelry. In 1785 she was linked to a cardinal in a nasty scandal over a gift of a diamond necklace. In spite of her innocence, rumors of corruption and infidelity surrounded her name. Dubbed "Madame Deficit," she came to represent all that was considered decadent in royal rule.

She continued to insist, "I am afraid of being bored." To amuse

herself, she ordered a life-size play village built on the grounds of Versailles, complete with cottages, a chapel, a mill, and a running stream. Then, dressed in silks and muslins intended as the royal approximation of a milkmaid's garb, she whiled away whole days with her friends and children, all pretending they were inhabitants of this picturesque "hamlet." Her romantic view of country life helped pass the time, but it did little to bring her closer to the struggling peasants who made up the majority of French subjects.

Marie Antoinette's problems need not have mattered much. Monarchs before her had been considered weak and extravagant. The difference was that her foibles became public in an age when the opinion of the people affected political life. Rulers, even those believed to be divinely appointed, were subjected to a public scrutiny all the more powerful because of the growth of the popular press. Kings, their ministers, and their spouses were held accountable—a dangerous phenomenon for an absolute monarchy.

This Austrian-born queen may not have been more shallow or wastefully extravagant than other queens, but it mattered that people came to see her that way. The queen's reputation sank to its nadir when it was reported that she dis-

missed the suffering of her starving subjects with the haughty retort "Let them eat cake." What better evidence could there be of the queen's insensitivity than this heartless remark?

Marie Antoinette never said "Let them eat cake," but everyone thought she did. This was the kind of callousness that people expected from the monarchy in 1789. Marie Antoinette understood the plight of her starving subjects, as

her correspondence indicates. Probably a courtier at Versailles was the real source of the brutal retort, but the truth did not matter. Marie Antoinette and her husband were being indicted by the public for all the political, social, and fiscal crises that plagued France.

In October 1793, Marie Antoinette was put on trial by the Revolutionary Tribunal and found guilty of treason. She was stripped of all the trappings of monarchy and forced to don another costume. Dressed as a poor working woman, her hair shorn, the former queen mounted the guillotine, following in the footsteps of her husband, who had been executed earlier that year. The monarchy did not fall because of a spendthrift queen with too much time on her hands. Nor did it fall because of the mistakes of the well-meaning but inept king. The monarchy had ceased to be responsive to the profound changes that shook France. It fell because of a new concern among the people for royal accountability in words and deeds. A rising democratic tide carried with it ideas about political representation, participation, and equality. If a queen could change places with a milkmaid, why should not a milkmaid be able to change places with a queen?

The Crisis of the Old Regime in France, 1715–88

France in the eighteenth century, the age of the Enlightenment, was a state invigorated by new ideas. It was also a world dominated by tradition. The traditional institutions of monarchy, Church, and aristocracy defined power and status. Talk of reform, progress, and perfectibility coexisted with the social realities of privileges and obligations determined by birth. The eighteenth century was a time when old ways prevailed even as a new view of the world was taking shape.

At the end of the eighteenth century, a number of foreign visitors to France commented on the disparities that characterized French social and political life. One English visitor in particular—Arthur Young (1741–1820), an agronomist writing on his travels in France in the 1780s—observed that though a prosperous land, France was pocked with extreme poverty; though a land of high culture and great art, it was riddled with ignorance, illiteracy, and superstition; though a land with a centralized bureaucracy, it was also saddled with local pettiness and obsolete practices.

The tensions generated by the clash of continuity and change made this an exciting and complex period in France. Reformers talked of progress while peasants still used wooden plows. The philosophes glorified reason in a world of violence, superstition, and fear. The great crisis of eighteenth-century France, the French Revolution, destroyed the *ancien régime* (old regime). But the revolution was as much a product of continuities and traditions as it was a product of change and the challenge of new ideas.

Louis XV's France

When Louis XV (1715–74) died, he was a hated man. In his 59-year reign, he managed to turn the public against him. He was denounced as a tyrant who was trying to starve his people, a slave to the mistresses who ruled his court, and an indecisive sybarite dominated by evil ministers. Louis XV's apathy and ineptitude contributed to his poor image. The declining fortunes and the damaged prestige of the monarchy, however, reflected more than the personality traits of an ineffectual king: they reflected structural challenges to fiscal solvency and absolutist rule that the monarchy was unable to meet.

Louis XV, like his great-grandfather Louis XIV, laid claim to rule as an absolute monarch. He insisted that

"the rights and interests of the nation . . . are of necessity one with my own, and lie in my hands only." Such claims failed to mask the weaknesses of royal rule. Louis XV lacked a sufficiently developed bureaucracy to administer and tax the nation in an evenhanded fashion. By the beginning of the eighteenth century, the absolute monarchy had extended royal influence into the new areas of policing, administration, lawmaking, and taxation. But none of this proved sufficient to meet the growing needs of the state.

The heightened tensions between the monarch and the aristocracy found expression in various institutions, especially the parlements, the thirteen sovereign courts in the French judicial system, with their seats in Paris and a dozen provincial centers. The magistrates of each parlement were members of the aristocracy, some of them nobles of recent origin and others of long standing, depending on the locale. The king needed the parlements to record royal decrees before they could become law. This recording process conferred real political power on the parlements, which could withhold approval for the king's policies by refusing to register his decrees. When decrees involved taxation, the magistrates often refused to endorse them. By successfully challenging the king, the parlements became a battleground between the elite, who claimed that they represented the nation, and the king, who said the nation was himself.

The king repeatedly attempted to neutralize the power of the parlements by relying instead on his own state bureaucracy. His agents in the provinces, called intendants, were accountable directly to the central government. The intendants, as the king's men, and the magistrates who presided in the parlements represented contradictory claims to power. As the king's needs increased in the second half of the eighteenth century, the situation was becoming intolerable for those exercising power and those aspiring to rule in the name and for the good of the nation.

The nadir of Louis XV's reign came in 1763, with the French defeat in the Seven Years' War both on the Continent and in the colonies. In the Treaty of Paris, France ceded territory, including its Canadian holdings, to Great Britain. France lost more than lands: it lost its footing in the competition with its chief rival, Great Britain, which had been pulling ahead of France in international affairs since the mid-eighteenth century. The war was also a financial debacle, paid for by loans secured against the guarantee of victory. The defeat not only left France barren of funds, it also promoted further expenditures for strengthening the

French navy against the superior British fleet. New taxation was the way out of the financial trap in which the king now found himself.

Louis XV's revenue problem was not easily solved. In order to raise taxes, the king had to turn to the recording function of the parlements. Following the costly Seven Years' War, the parlements chose to exercise the power of refusal by blocking a proportional tax to be imposed on nobles and commoners alike. The magistrates resisted taxation, arguing that the king was attacking the liberty of his subjects by attempting to tax those who were exempt by virtue of their privileged status.

René Nicolas Charles Augustin de Maupeou (1714–92), Louis XV's chancellor from 1768 to 1774, decided that the political power of the parlements had to be curbed. In 1770, in an attempt to coerce the magistrates into compliance with the king's wishes, he engineered the overthrow of the Parlement of Paris, the most important of the high courts. Those magistrates who remained obdurate were sent into exile. New courts, whose membership was based on appointment instead of the sale of offices, took their place amid much public criticism. Ultimately, Maupeou's attempt failed. His action did nothing to improve the monarch's image, and it did even less to solve the fiscal problems of the regime. The conflict between Louis XV and the parlements revealed the dependent nature of the monarchy that claimed to be absolute and accountable only to God.

The dignity and prestige of the monarchy were seriously damaged in the course of Louis XV's long reign. His legacy was well captured in the expression erroneously attributed to him, *Après moi le deluge*—"After me, the flood." Continuing to live the good life at the court, he failed dismally to offset rising state expenditures—caused primarily by military needs—with new sources of revenue. In 1774 Louis XV died suddenly of smallpox. His unprepared twenty-year-old grandson, Louis XVI (1774–92), a young man who amused himself by hunting and pursuing his hobby as an amateur locksmith, was left to try to stanch the flood.

Louis XVI and the National Debt

Louis XV left to his heir Louis XVI the legacy of a disastrous deficit. From the beginning of his reign, Louis XVI was caught in the vicious circle of excessive state spending—above all, military spending—followed by bouts of heavy borrowing. Borrowing at high rates required the government to pay out huge sums in interest and service fees on the loans that were keeping it afloat. These outlays in turn piled the state's indebtedness ever higher, requiring more loans, and threatening to topple the whole financial structure of the state and the regime itself.

In inheriting this trouble-ridden fiscal structure, Louis XVI made his own contribution to it. Following in the footsteps of his grandfather, he involved France in a costly war, the War of American Independence (1775–83), by supporting the thirteen colonies in their revolt against Great Britain. This involvement brought the French monarchy to the brink of bankruptcy. Contrary to public opinion, most of the state's expenditures did not go toward lavishing luxuries on the royal court and the royal family at Versailles. They went to pay off loans. More than half of the state budget in the 1780s represented interest on loans taken to pay for foreign military ventures.

The king needed money, and he needed it fast. To those who could afford to purchase them, the king continued to sell offices that carried with them titles, revenues, and privileges. He also relied on the sale of annuities that paid high interest rates and that attracted speculators, large and small. The crown had leased out its rights to collect the salt tax in return for large lump-sum advances from the Royal General Farms, a syndicate of about one hundred wealthy financier families. The Royal General Farms reaped healthy profits on their annual transactions at the state's expense. The combined revenues collected by the king through these various stratagems were little more than a drop in the vast ocean of debt that threatened to engulf the state.

The existing tax structure proved hopelessly inadequate to meet the state's needs. The *taille*, a direct tax, was levied, either on persons or on land, according to region. Except for those locales where the taille was attached to land, the nobility was always exempt from direct taxation. Members of the bourgeoisie could also avoid the direct tax as citizens of towns enjoying exemption. That meant that the wealthy, those best able to pay, were often exempt. Indirect taxes, like those on salt (the *gabelle*) and on food and drink (the *aide*), and internal and external customs taxes were regressive taxes that weighed heavily on those least able to pay. The peasantry bore the brunt of the nation's tax burden, and Louis XVI knew all too well that he could not squeeze blood from a stone by increasing indirect taxes. A peasantry too weighted down would collapse—or rebel.

The privileged elite persisted in rejecting the crown's attempts to tax them. As one of the first acts of his

This cartoon from 1789 depicts Necker (at left) showing the king how to conceal the size of the deficit from the Estates. On the wall, a list of royal loans is headed "New ways to revive France"—but the total is "Deficit."

reign, in 1775 Louis XVI had restored the magistrates to their posts in the parlements, treating their offices as a form of property of which they had been deprived. In his conciliatory act, Louis XVI nevertheless stressed that the self-interest of the aristocracy was at odds with the common good of the nation and urged the approval of his programs. Nevertheless, by 1776 the Parlement of Paris was again obstructing royal decrees.

Louis XVI appointed Anne Robert Jacques Turgot (1727–1781) as his first controller-general. Turgot's reformist economic ideas were influenced by Enlightenment philosophes. In order to generate revenues, Turgot reasoned, France needed to prosper economically. The government was in a position to stimulate economic growth by eliminating regulations, economizing at court, and improving the network of roads through a tax on landowners. Each of Turgot's reforms

offended established interests, thereby ensuring his early defeat. Emphasis on a laissez-faire economy outraged the guilds; doing away with the forced labor of peasants on the roads (the *corvée*) threatened privileged groups who had never before been taxed. As the king was discovering, divine right did not bring with it absolute authority or fiscal solvency.

As he floundered about for a solution to his economic difficulties, the king turned to a new adviser, Jacques Necker (1732–1804), a Swiss-born Protestant banker. The king and the public expected great things from Necker, whose international business experience was counted on to save the day. Necker, a prudent man, applied his accounting skills to measuring—for the first time—the total income and expenditures of the French state. The budget he produced and widely circulated allayed everyone's fears of certain doom and assured the nation that no new taxes were necessary—an assurance based on disastrous miscalculations. Instead of raising taxes, Necker committed his ministry to eliminating costly inefficiencies. He promised to abolish the sale of offices that drained revenues from the crown. He next set his sights on contracts of the farmers-general, collectors of the indirect salt taxes, whom he likened to weeds sprouting in a swamp. Necker's aim was to reduce ordinary expenses of the realm in order to be ready for the extraordinary ones associated with waging a war. Such policies made him enemies in high places and numbered his days in office.

Necker and those who preceded him in controlling and directing the finances of the state under Louis XV and Louis XVI were committed to reforming the system. All the advisers recognized that the state's fiscal problems were structural and required enlightened solutions, but no two of them agreed on the same program of reforms. Necker had somehow captivated popular opinion, and there was widespread regret expressed over his forced resignation.

Charles Alexandre de Calonne (1734–1802), appointed controller-general in 1783, had his own ideas of how to bail out the ship of state. He authored a program of reforms that would have shifted the tax burden off those least able to pay and onto those best able to support the state. Specifically, he proposed a tax on land proportional to land values, a measure that would have most seriously affected the land-rich nobility. In addition, taxes that affected the peasantry were to be lightened or eliminated. Finally, Calonne proposed the sale of Church lands for revenues. In an attempt to bypass the recalcitrant parlements, Calonne advised the crown in 1787 to convene an Assembly of Notables made up of 150 individuals from the magistracy, the Church hierarchy, the titled nobility, and municipal bodies, for the purpose of enlisting their support for reforms. Louis listened to Calonne, who was denounced by the Assembly of Notables for attacking the rights of the privileged. He too was forced to resign.

All of Louis XVI's attempts to persuade the nobility to agree to tax reforms had failed. Louis was incapable of the effort required either to inspire or to manipulate the privileged classes to support his plans. Aristocratic magistrates insisted on a constitution, in which their own right to govern would be safeguarded and the accountability of the king would be defined. In opposing the royal reforms, nobles spoke of the "rights of man" and used the term *citizen*. They rebuffed the monarch with the cry "No taxation without consent." The nobility had no sympathy for tax programs that would have resulted in a loss of privilege and what some nobles were beginning to consider an attack on individual freedom. Louis XVI was met with passivity from the Assembly of Notables and resistance from the Parlement of Paris and the provincial parlements.

By the 1780s, almost 50 percent of annual expenditures went to servicing the accumulated national debt of 4 billion livres and to paying interest. The new controller-general, Archbishop Loménie de Brienne (1727–94) recommended emergency loans. The crown once again disbanded the Paris Parlement, which was now threatening to block loans as well as taxes.

The Three Estates

Louis XVI was a desperate man in 1788, so desperate that he yielded to the condition placed on him by the Paris Parlement: he agreed to convene the Estates-General, a medieval body that had not met since 1614 and that had been considered obsolete with the rise of a centralized bureaucratic government. However, eighteenth-century French society continued to be divided by law and custom into a pyramid of three tiers called orders or estates. At the top were those who prayed (the clergy), followed by those who fought (the nobility). The base of the pyramid was formed by the largest of the three estates, those who worked—the bourgeoisie, the peasantry, and urban and rural workers. The Estates-General included equal representation from these three estates of the clergy, nobility, and commoners. Yet only about two hundred thousand subjects belonged to the first two estates. The Third Estate was composed of all those members of the realm who enjoyed a common identity only in their lack of privilege—over 23 million French people. Traditionally

each of the three orders was equally weighted. This arrangement favored the nobility, who controlled the first two estates. The nobility, therefore, was understandably not worried about the prospect of having the Estates-General decide the tax-reform program.

In the second half of the eighteenth century, these traditional groups no longer reflected social realities—a situation that proved to be a source of serious problems for the Estates-General. The piety of the first order had been called into doubt as religious leaders were criticized for using the vast wealth of the Church for personal benefit instead of public worship. The protective military function of the second order had ceased to exist with the rise of the state and the changing nature of war. Some members of the bourgeoisie—those who worked with their heads, not their hands—shared privileges with the nobility and aspired to a noble lifestyle, in spite of their legal and customary presence in the ranks of the Third Estate alongside peasants and urban workers.

The vast majority of French subjects who constituted the Third Estate certainly were identified by work,

This cartoon depicts the plight of the French peasants. An old farmer is bowed down under the weight of the privileged aristocracy and clergy while birds and rabbits, protected by unfair game laws, eat his crops.

but the array of mental and physical labor—and lack of work—splintered the estate into a myriad of occupations, aspirations, and identities. All power flowed upward in this arrangement, with the First and Second Estates dominating the social and political universe. Women and men accepted this hierarchy as the natural organization of society in eighteenth-century France.

The king continued to stand at the pinnacle of the eighteenth-century social pyramid. Traditionally revered as the "father" of his subjects, he claimed to be divinely appointed by God. Kingship in this era had a dual nature. The king was both supreme overlord (a legacy from feudal times) and absolute monarch. As supreme overlord he stood dominant over the aristocracy and the court. As absolute monarch he stood at the head of the state and society. When the king equated himself with the state—*"L'état, c'est moi,"* as Louis XIV boasted—all problems—economic, social, and political—also came to be identified with the king. Absolutism required a weakened nobility and a bureaucracy strong enough to help the monarchy to adjust to changes. After the death of Louis XIV in 1715, Louis XV and Louis XVI faced a resurgent aristocracy without the support of a state bureaucracy capable of successfully challenging aristocratic privilege or of solving fiscal problems.

"To live nobly," that is, to live as a noble, was the social ideal to which one could aspire in the eighteenth century. While the system of orders set clear boundaries of social status, distinctions within estates created new hierarchies. The clergy, a privileged order, contained both commoners and nobles, but leadership in the Church depended on social rank. The aristocracy retained control of the bishoprics even as an activist element among the lower clergy agitated for reforms and better salaries. In a state in which the king claimed to rule by God's will, Catholicism, virtually the state religion, was important in legitimizing the divine claims of the monarchy.

The nobility experienced its own internal tensions, generated by two groups: the older nobility of the sword, who claimed descent from medieval times, and the more recent nobility of the robe, who had acquired their position through the purchase of offices that conferred noble status. By increasing the numbers of the nobility of the robe, Louis XIV had hoped to undermine the power of the aristocracy as a whole and to decrease its political influence. But aristocrats rallied and closed ranks against the dilution of their power. As a result, both Louis XV and Louis XVI faced a reviving rather than a declining aristocracy. One in four nobles had moved from the bourgeoisie to the aristocratic ranks in the eighteenth century; two out of every three had been ennobled during the seventeenth or eighteenth centuries. Nobles had succeeded in restoring their economic and social power. Furthermore, a growing segment of the aristocracy, influenced by Enlightenment ideas and the example of English institutions, was intent on increasing the political dominance of the aristocracy.

Generally, the nobility strengthened their powers in two ways. First, they monopolized high offices and closed access to non-nobles, thereby controlling posts in ministries, the Church, and the army. Second, the nobility benefited greatly from the doubling in land values brought on by the increase in the value of crops. Nobles enjoyed privileges, the greatest being, in most cases, exemption from taxes. Seeking ever higher returns from the land, some members of the aristocracy adopted new agricultural techniques to achieve greater crop yields. There were certainly poor aristocrats who lacked the lands to benefit from this trend, but those who did control sizable holdings profited greatly from higher dues paid to them and reaped increased incomes from crops. In addition, many aristocrats revived their feudal claims to ancient seigneurial, or lordly, privileges. They hired lawyers to unearth old claims and hired agents to collect dues.

A spirit of innovation characterized the values of certain members of the nobility. Although technically prevented from participating in trade by virtue of their titles and privileges, an active group among the nobility succeeded in making fortunes in metallurgy, glassmaking, and mining. Others participated in trade. These nobles were an economically dynamic and innovative segment of the aristocracy. In spite of the obsolete aspect of their privileges, aristocrats were often responsible for the introduction of modern ideas and techniques in the management of estates and in the bookkeeping involved with collection of rents. Capitalist techniques were not unknown to nobles adapting to the marketplace. These nobles formed an elite partnership with forward-looking members of the bourgeoisie.

Common people—that is, those who did not enjoy the privileges of the nobility—constituted a broad range of the French populace. The peasantry was by far the largest group of commoners. Most French peasants were free, no longer attached to the soil as serfs were in a feudal system. Yet all peasants endured common obligations placed on them by the crown and the privileged classes. A bewildering array of taxes afflicted peasants: they owed the tithe to the Church, land taxes to

"Brooms, Brooms," a plate from a volume on the cries of Paris, shows a woman hawking brooms. Most poor women were forced to do exhausting manual labor.

the state, and seigneurial dues and rents to the land-lord. In some areas, peasants repaired roads and drew lots for military service. Dues affected almost every aspect of rural life, including harvests and the sale of property. In addition, indirect taxes like that on salt were a serious burden for the peasantry. As if all this were not enough, peasants who were forced to take loans to survive from one harvest to another paid exorbitant interest rates. No matter how bad conditions were, peasants had to be sure to save the seed for next year's crop.

The peasants who staggered and collapsed under all these obligations were forced to work as itinerants or leave the land. The precariousness of rural life and the increase in population in the countryside contributed to the permanent displacement and destitution of a growing sector of rural society. Without savings and destroyed by poor harvests, impoverished rural inhabitants wandered the countryside looking for odd jobs and eventually begging to survive. The labor of women

was essential to the survival of the rural family. Peasant women sought employment in towns and cities as seamstresses and servants in order to send money back home to struggling relatives. Children, too, added their earnings to the family pot. In spite of various strategies for survival, more and more peasant families were disrupted by the end of the eighteenth century.

Another group of commoners in the Third Estate, the bourgeoisie, embraced within it a variety of professions, from bankers and financiers to businessmen, merchants, entrepreneurs, lawyers, shopkeepers, and artisans. Along with the nobility, wealthy bourgeois formed the urban elites that administered cities and towns. Prestigious service to the state or the purchase of offices that carried with them noble status enabled the wealthiest members of the bourgeoisie to move into the ranks of the nobility. Many bourgeois served as middlemen for the nobility by running estates and collecting dues.

Like the rest of the social universe, the world of artisans and workers was shaded with various gradations of wealth and status. Those who owned their own shops and perhaps employed other workers stood as an elite among the working class. In spite of their physical proximity, there was a vast difference between those who owned their own shops and those who earned wages or were paid by the piece. Wage earners represented about 30 percent of the population of cities and towns, and their numbers were swelling as artisans were pushed out of their guilds and peasants were pushed off their land.

Those who worked in crafts were a labor elite, and guilds were intended to protect the corporations of masters, journeymen, and apprentices through monopolistic measures. The king's attempt in 1775 to promote free trade resulted in the temporary abolition of guilds. Guilds insisted that they were best able to ensure the quality of goods, but the emphasis on free trade and the expansion of markets in the eighteenth century weakened their hold. Merchants often took guilds over and paid workers by the piece. The effect was a reduction in the wages of skilled workers. By the 1780s, most journeymen who hoped to be masters knew that their dream would never be realized. Frustration and discontent touched workers in towns and cities who may not have shared a common work experience. But they did share a common anger about the high cost of food—especially bread.

So, when Louis XVI announced in August 1788 that the Estates-General would meet at Versailles in May 1789, people from all walks of life hoped for some

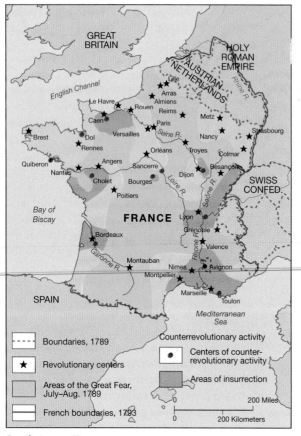

GREAT
BRITAIN

HOLY
ROMAN
EMPIRE

AUSTRIAN
NETHERLANDS

Rhine R.

English Channel

Lille
★★
Arras
★
Almiens
★
Le Havre
★
Rouen
★
Reims
★
Metz ★ ★
Caen ★
Paris
★★
Versailles
Seine R.
Nancy ★
Strasbourg
★
Dol
Brest ★
Rennes ●
Orléans
★
Troyes
★
Colmar
★
Angers
★
Sancerre
Dijon
Besançon
★★
SWISS
CONFED.
Quiberon
Nantes ●
Cholet ●
Bourges ●
Saône R.
Poitiers ●

Bay of
Biscay

FRANCE

Lyon ●
Grenoble ★

Loire R.

Rhône R.

Bordeaux ●
Garonne R.
Valence ●

Montauban ★
Nimes ★ ● Avignon
Montpellier ★
Marseille ●
Toulon ★

SPAIN

Mediterranean
Sea

- - - Boundaries, 1789

★ Revolutionary centers

□ Areas of the Great Fear,
July–Aug. 1789

□ French boundaries, 1793

Counterrevolutionary activity

● Centers of counter-
revolutionary activity

■ Areas of insurrection

0   200 Miles
0   200 Kilometers

Revolutionary France

redress of the miseries and abuses that beset their lives. When the king directed each of the three estates—clergy, nobility, and commoners—to elect their representatives, he promised that they would come together to discuss the fiscal and political problems plaguing the nation. Every social group, from the nobles to the poorest laborers, had its own grievances and concerns, but all greeted the news with fireworks, parades, and toasts to the best of all kings.

The First Stage of the French Revolution, 1789–92

Those who lived through it were sure that there had never been a time like it before. The French Revolution, or the Great Revolution, as it was known to contemporaries, was a time of creation and discovery. The ten years from 1789 to 1799 were punctuated by genuine euphoria and democratic transformations. From the privileged elites who initiated the overthrow of the existing order to the peasants and workers, men and

women, who railed against tyranny, the revolution touched every segment of society.

The revolution achieved most in the area of politics. The overthrow of absolutist monarchy brought with it new social theories, new symbols, and new behavior. The excitement of anarchy was matched by the terror of repression. Revolutionary France had to contend with war throughout Europe. The revolution had its dark side of violence and instability: in its wake came internal discord, civil war, and violent repression. In the search for a new order, political forms followed one after the other in rapid succession: constitutional monarchy, republic, oligarchy. The creation of Napoleon's dictatorship at the end of the century signified that the revolution had come to an end.

Revolutionary incidents flared up throughout Europe in the second half of the eighteenth century in the Netherlands, Belgium, and Ireland. Absolute authority was challenged and sometimes modified. Across the Atlantic, American colonists concerned with the principle of self-rule had thrown off the yoke of the British in the War of Independence. But none of these events, including the American Revolution, was so violent in breaking with the old order, so extensive in involving millions of men and women in political action, and so consequential for the political futures of other European states as was the French Revolution. The triumphs and contradictions of the revolutionary experiment in democracy mark the end of the old order and the beginning of modern history. Politics would never be the same again.

Taking Politics to the People

Choosing representatives for the Estates-General in March and April 1789 stirred up hope and excitement in every corner of France. From the very beginning, there were warning signs that a more astute monarch might have noticed. The call for national elections set in motion a politicizing process the king could not control. Members of the Third Estate, traditionally excluded from political and social power, were presented with the opportunity of expressing their opinions on the state of government and society. In an increasingly literate age, pamphlets, broadsides, and political tracts representing every political persuasion blanketed France. Those who could not read stood in marketplaces and city squares or sat around evening fires and had the political literature read to them. Farmhands and urban laborers realized that they were participating in the same process as their social betters, and they believed they had a right to speak and be heard.

This was a time of great hope, especially for people who had been buffeted by the rise in prices, decline in real wages, and the hunger that followed crop failures and poor harvests. Now there was the promise of a respite and a solution. Taxes could be discussed and changed, the state bureaucracy could be reformed—or better, abolished. Intellectuals discussed political alternatives in the salons of the wealthy. Nobles and bourgeois met in philosophical societies dedicated to enlightened thought. Commoners gathered in cafes to drink and debate. Although the poor often fell outside of this network of communication, they were not immune to the ideas that emerged. In the end, people of all classes had opinions and were more certain than ever of their right to express their ideas. Absolutism was in trouble, though Louis XVI did not know it, as people began to forge a collectively shared idea of politics. People now had a forum—the Estates-General—and a focus—the politics of taxation. But most important, they had the elections.

In competing for power, some members of the Third Estate were well aware of their vast numerical superiority over the nobility. Because of it, they demanded greater representation than the three hundred members per estate defined according to the practices of 1614. At the very least, they argued, the number of representatives of the Third Estate should be doubled to six hundred members, giving commoners equality in numbers with nobles and priests together. Necker, recalled as director-general of finance in August 1788, agreed to the doubling in the size of the Third Estate as a compromise but left unresolved the additional demand of vote by head rather than by order. If voting was to be left as it was, in accordance with the procedures of 1614, the nobility who controlled the First and Second Estates would determine all outcomes. With a voting procedure by head instead of by order, however, the deputies of the Third Estate could easily dominate the Estates-General, confident that they could count on parish priests and liberal nobles like the Marquis de Lafayette to defect from voting with the First and Second Estates and join their cause.

In conjunction with this political activity and in scheduled meetings, members of all three estates drew up statements of their problems. This took place in a variety of forums, including guilds and village and town meetings. The people of France set down their grievances in notebooks—known as *cahiers de doléances*—that were then carried to Versailles by the deputies elected to the Estates-General. The cahiers expressed the particular grievances of each estate. These notebooks contained a collective outpouring of problems and are important for two major reasons. First, they made clear the similarity of grievances shared throughout France. Second, they indicated the extent to which a common political culture, based on a concern with political reform, had permeated different levels of French society. Both the privileged and the nonprivileged identified a common enemy in the system of state bureaucracy to which the monarch was so strongly tied. Although the king was still addressed with respect, new concerns with liberty, equality, property, and the rule of law were voiced.

"If only the king knew!" In this phrase, French men and women had for generations expressed their belief in the inevitability of their fate and the benevolence of their king. They saw the king as a loving and wise father who would not tolerate the injustices visited on his subjects if only he knew what was really happening. In 1789 peasants and workers were questioning why their lives could not be better, but they continued to express their trust in the king. Combined with their old faith was a new hope. The peasants in the little town of Saintes recorded their newly formed expectations in their cahier:

> Our king, the best of kings and father of a great and wise family, will soon know everything. All vices will be destroyed. All the great virtues of industriousness, honesty, modesty, honor, patriotism, meekness, friendliness, equality, concord, pity, and thrift will prevail and wisdom will rule supreme.

Those who opposed the revolution later alleged that these notebooks proved the existence of a highly coordinated plot on the part of secret societies out to destroy the regime. They were wrong. Similarities in complaints, demands, and language proved the forging of a new political consciousness, not a conspiracy. Societies and clubs circulated "model" cahiers among themselves, resulting in the use of similar forms and vocabulary. People were questioning their traditional roles and now had elected deputies who would represent them before the king. In the spring of 1789, a severe economic crisis that heightened political uncertainty swept through France. For a king expected to save the situation, time was running out.

Convening the Estates-General

The elected deputies arrived at Versailles at the beginning of May 1789 carrying in their valises and trunks the grievances of their estates. The opening session of the Estates-General took place in a great hall especially constructed for the event. The 1248 deputies presented a grand spectacle as they filed to their assigned places to hear speeches by the king and his ministers. Contrasts among the participants were immediately apparent. Seated on a raised throne under a canopy at one end of the hall, Louis XVI was vested in full kingly regalia. On his right sat the archbishops and cardinals of the First Estate, strikingly clad in the pinks and purples of their offices. On his left were the richly and decorously attired nobility. Facing the stage sat the 648 deputies of the Third Estate, dressed in plain black suits, stark against the colorful and costly costumes of the privileged. It was clear, in the most visual terms, that "clothes make the man." Members of the Third Estate had announced beforehand that they would not follow the ancient custom for commoners of kneeling at the king's entrance. Fired by the hope of equal treatment and an equal share of power, they had come to Versailles to make a constitution. The opening ceremony degenerated into a moment of confusion over whether members of the Third Estate should be able to wear their hats in the presence of the king. Many saw in the politics of clothing a tense beginning to their task.

The tension between commoners and privileged was further aggravated by the unresolved issue of how the voting was to proceed. The Third Estate was adamant in its demand for vote by head. The privileged orders were equally firm in insisting on vote by order. Paralysis set in, as days dragged into weeks and the Estates were unable to act. The body that was to save France from fiscal collapse was hopelessly deadlocked.

Two men whose backgrounds made them unlikely heroes emerged as leaders of the Third Estate. One, Abbé Emmanuel Joseph Sieyès (1748–1836), was a member of the clergy who frequented Parisian salons. The other, the comte Honoré Gabriel Victor de Mirabeau (1749–91), a black sheep among the nobility, had spent time in prison because of his father's charges that he was a defiant son who led a misspent, debauched, and profligate youth. In spite of his nobility, Mirabeau appeared at Versailles as a deputy for Aix and Marseilles to the Third Estate. His oratory and presence commanded attention from the start. As a consummate politician, Mirabeau combined forces with Sieyès, who had already established his reputation as a firebrand reformer with his eloquent pamphlet "What Is the Third Estate?" published in January 1789.

Sieyès and Mirabeau reminded members of the Third Estate of the reformist consensus that character-

ized their ranks. Under their influence, the Third Estate decided to proceed with its own meetings. On 17 June 1789, the Third Estate, joined by some sympathetic clergy, changed its name to the National Assembly as an assertion of its true representation of the French nation. Three days later, members of the new National Assembly found themselves locked out of their regular meeting room by the king's guard. Outraged by this insult, they moved to a nearby indoor tennis court, where they vowed to stay together for the purpose of writing a constitution. This event, known as the Oath of the Tennis Court, marked the end of the absolutist monarchy and the beginning of a new concept of the state that power resided in the people. The revolution had begun.

The drama of Versailles, a staged play of gestures, manners, oaths, and attire, also marked the beginning of a far-reaching political revolution. Although it was a drama that took place behind closed doors, it was not one unknown to the general public. Throughout May and June 1789, Parisians trekked to Versailles to watch the deliberations. Then they brought news back to the capital. Deputies wrote home to their constituents to keep them abreast of events. Newspapers that reported daily on these wranglings and pamphleteers who analyzed them spread the news throughout the nation. Information, often conflicting, stirred up anxiety; news of conflict encouraged action.

The frustration and stalemate of the Estates-General threatened to put the spark to the kindling of urban unrest. The people of Paris had suffered through a harsh winter and spring under the burdens of high prices (especially of bread), limited supplies, and relentless tax demands. The rioting of the spring had for the moment ceased as people waited for their problems to be solved by the deputies of the Estates-General. The suffering of the urban poor was not new, but their ability to connect economic hardships with the politics at Versailles and to blame the government was. As hopes began to dim with the news of political stalemate, news broke of the creation of the National Assembly. It was greeted with new anticipation.

The Storming of the Bastille

The king, who had temporarily withdrawn from sight following the death of his son at the beginning of June, reemerged to meet with the representatives of each of the three estates and propose reforms, including a constitutional monarchy. But Louis XVI refused to accept the now popularly supported National Assembly as a

"What Is the Third Estate?"

As an ambitious clergyman from Chartres, Abbé Emmanuel-Joseph Sieyès was a member of the First Estate. Yet Sieyès was elected deputy to the Estates General for the Third Estate on the basis of his attacks on aristocratic privilege. He participated in the writing and editing of the great documents of the early revolution: the Oath of the Tennis Court and the Declaration of the Rights of Man and Citizen. The pamphlet for which he is immortalized in revolutionary lore was his daring "What Is the Third Estate?" Written in January 1789, it boldly confronted the bankruptcy of the system of privilege of the Old Regime and threw down the gauntlet to those who ruled France. In this document the revolution found its rallying point.

1st. What is the third estate? Everything.

2nd. What has it been heretofore in the political order? Nothing.

3rd. What does it demand? To become something therein. . . .

Who, then, would dare to say that the third estate has not within itself all that is necessary to constitute a complete nation? It is the strong and robust man whose one arm remains enchained. If the privileged order were abolished, the nation would not be something less but something more. Thus, what is the third estate? Everything; but an everything shackled and oppressed. What would it be without the privileged order? Everything; but an everything free and flourishing. Nothing can progress without it; everything would proceed infinitely better without the others. It is not sufficient to have demonstrated that the privileged classes, far from being useful to the nation, can only enfeeble and injure it; it is necessary, moreover, to prove that the nobility does not belong to the social organization at all; that, indeed, it may be a *burden* upon the nation, but that it would not know how to constitute a part thereof.

The third estate, then, comprises everything appertaining to the nation; and whatever is not the third estate may not be regarded as being of the nation. What is the third estate? Everything!

---

legitimate body, insisting instead that he must rely on the three estates for advice. He simply did not understand that the choice was no longer his to make. He summoned troops to Versailles and began concentrating soldiers in Paris. Civilians continually clashed with members of the military, whom they jostled and jeered. The urban crowds recognized the threat of repression that the troops represented. People decided to meet force with force. To do so, they needed arms themselves—and they knew where to get them.

On 14 July 1789, the irate citizens of Paris stormed the Bastille, a royal armory that also served as a prison for a handful of debtors. The storming of the Bastille has become the great symbol in the revolutionary legend of the overthrow of the tyranny and oppression of the old regime. But it is significant for another reason. It was an expression of the power of the people to take politics into their own hands. Parisians were following the lead of their deputies in Versailles. They had formed a citizen militia known as the National Guard, and they were prepared to defend their concept of justice and law.

The people who stormed the Bastille were not the poor, the unemployed, the criminals, or the urban rabble, as their detractors portrayed them. They were bourgeois and petit-bourgeois: shopkeepers, guild members, family men and women who considered it their right to seize arms in order to protect their interests. The Marquis de Lafayette (1757–1834), a noble beloved of the people because of his participation in the American Revolution, helped organize the National Guard. Under his direction, the militia adopted the tricolor flag as its standard. The tricolor combined the red and blue colors of the city of Paris with the white of the Bourbon royal family. It became the flag of the revolution, replacing the fleur-de-lis of the Bourbons. It is the national flag of France today.

The king could no longer dictate the terms of the constitution. By their actions, the people in arms had ratified the National Assembly. Louis XVI was forced

staple of their diet. Women responsible for managing the consumption of the household were most directly in touch with the state of provisioning the capital. When they were unable to feed their families, the situation became intolerable.

So it was, on the morning of 5 October 1789, that six thousand Parisian women marched out of the city and toward Versailles. They were taking their problem to the king with the demand that he solve it. Later in the day, Lafayette, sympathetic to the women's cause, led the Parisian National Guard to Versailles to mediate events. The women were armed with pikes, the simple weapon available to the poorest defender of the revolution, and they were prepared to use them. The battle came early the next morning, when the women, tired and cold from waiting all night at the gates of the palace, invaded the royal apartments and chased Marie Antoinette from her bedroom. Several members of the royal guards, hated by the people of Paris for alleged insults against the tricolor cockade, were killed by the angry women, who decapitated them and mounted their heads on pikes. A shocked Louis XVI agreed to return with the crowd to Paris. The crowd cheered Louis's decision, which briefly reestablished his personal popularity. But as monarch, he had been humiliated at the hands of women of the capital. Reduced to the roles of "the baker, the baker's wife, and the baker's son" by jeering crowds, the royal family was forced to return to Paris that very day. Louis XVI was now captive to the revolution, whose efforts to form a constitutional monarchy he purported to support.

The Revolution Threatened

The disciplined deliberations of committees intent on fashioning a constitutional monarchy replaced the passion and fervor of revolutionary oratory. The National, or Constituent, Assembly divided France into new administrative units—*départements*—for the purpose of establishing better control over municipal governments. Along with new administrative trappings, the government promoted its own rituals. On 14 July 1790, militias from each of the newly created 83 départements of France came together in Paris to celebrate the first anniversary of the storming of the Bastille. A new national holiday was born and with it a sense of devotion and patriotism for the new France liberated by the revolution. In spite of these unifying elements, however, the newly achieved revolutionary consensus began to show signs of breaking down.

In February 1790 legislation dissolved all monasteries and convents, except for those that provided aid to the poor or that served as educational institutions. As the French church was stripped of its lands, Pope Pius VI (1775–99) denounced the principles of the revolution. In July 1790 the government approved the Civil Constitution of the Clergy: priests now became the equivalent of paid agents of the state. By requiring an oath of loyalty to the state from all practicing priests, the National Assembly created a new arena for dissent. Catholics were forced to choose to embrace or reject the revolution. Many "nonjuring" priests who refused to take the oath went into hiding. The wedge driven

Depart des Heroines de Paris pour Versailles le 5 Octobre 1789.

A contemporary print of the women of Paris advancing on Versailles. The determined marchers are shown waving pikes and dragging an artillery piece. The women were hailed as heroines of the revolution.

The fleeing Louis XVI and his family were apprehended at Varennes in June 1791.

between the Catholic church and revolutionary France allowed a mass-based counterrevolution to emerge. Aristocratic émigrés who had fled the country because of their opposition to the revolution were languishing for lack of a popular base. From his headquarters in Turin, the king's younger brother, the comte d'Artois, was attempting to incite a civil war in France. When the revolutionaries decided to attack the Church not just as a landed and privileged institution but also as a religious one, the counterrevolution rapidly expanded.

The Constitution of 1791, completed after over two years of deliberations, established a constitutional monarchy with a ministerial executive power answerable to a legislative assembly. Louis XVI, formerly the divinely anointed ruler of France, was now "Louis, by the grace of God and the constitutional law of the state, King of the French." In proclaiming his acceptance of the constitution, Louis expressed the sentiments of many when he said, "The end of the revolution is come. It is time that order be reestablished so that the constitution may receive the support now most necessary to it; it is time to settle the opinion of Europe concerning the destiny of France, and to show that French men are worthy of being free." Louis, who had been wrong often enough in the past, could not have been more mistaken when he declared that the end of the revolution was at hand.

The Constitution of 1791 marked the triumph of the principles of the revolution. But it was at best a precarious political compromise. Months before the ink was dry on the final document, the actions of the king doomed the new constitution to failure. To be successful, constitutional monarchy required a king worthy of honor and respect. Louis XVI seemed to be giving the revolutionaries what they wanted by cooperating with the framers of the constitution. Yet late one night in June 1791, Louis XVI, Marie Antoinette, and their children disguised themselves as commoners, crept out of the royal apartments in the Tuileries Palace, and fled Paris. Louis intended to leave France to join foreign forces opposing the revolution at Metz. He got as far as Varennes, where he was captured by soldiers of the National Guards and brought back to a shocked Paris. The king had abandoned the revolution. Although he was not put to death for another year and a half, he was more than ever a prisoner of the revolution. The monarchy was effectively finished as part of a political solution; with its demise went liberal hopes for a constitutional settlement.

The defection of the king was certainly serious, but it was not the only problem facing the revolutionaries. Other problems plagued the revolutionary government, notably foreign war and the fiscal crisis, coupled with inflation. In order to establish its seriousness and legitimacy, the National Assembly had been willing in 1789 to absorb the debts of the old regime. The new government could not sell titles and offices, as the king had done to deal with financial problems, but it did confiscate Church property. In addition, it issued treasury bonds in the form of assignats in order to raise money. The assignats soon assumed the status of bank notes, and by the spring of 1790 they had become compulsory legal tender. Initially they were to be backed by land confiscated from the Church and now being sold by the state. But the need for money soon outran the value of the land available, and the government continued to print assignats according to its needs. Depreciation of French currency in international markets and inflation at home resulted. The revolutionary government found itself in a situation which in certain respects was worse than that experienced by Louis XVI before the calling of the Estates-General. Assignat-induced inflation produced a sharp decline in fortunes of bourgeois investors living on fixed incomes. Rising prices meant increased misery for workers and peasants.

New counterrevolutionary groups were becoming frustrated with revolutionary policies. Throughout the winter and spring of 1791–92, people rioted and demanded that prices be fixed, while the assignat dropped to less than half its face value. Peasants refused to sell crops for the worthless paper. Hoarding further drove up prices. Angry crowds turned to pillaging, rioting, and murder, which became more frequent as the value of the currency declined and prices rose.

Foreign war beginning in the fall of 1791 also challenged stability. Some moderate political leaders welcomed war as a blessing in disguise, since it could divert the attention of the masses away from problems at home and promote loyalty to the revolution. Others envisioned war as a great crusade to bring revolutionary principles to oppressed peoples throughout Europe. The king and queen, trapped by the revolution, saw war as their only hope of liberation. Louis XVI could be rightfully restored as the leader of a France defeated by the sovereigns of Europe. Some who opposed the war believed it would destabilize the revolution. France must solve its problems at home, they argued, before fighting a foreign enemy. Louis, however, encouraged those ministers and advisers eager for battle. In April 1792, France declared war against Austria.

Individuals, events, economic realities, and the nature of politics conspired against the success of the first constitutional experiment. The king's attempt to flee France in the summer of 1791 seriously wounded the attempt at compromise. Many feared that the goals of the revolution could not be preserved in a country at war and with a king of dubious loyalties.

The Revolution's Second Stage: Experimenting with Democracy, 1792–99

A political universe populated by individual citizens replaced the eighteenth-century world of subjects loyal to their king. This new construction of politics, in which all individuals were equal, ran counter to prevailing ideas about collective identities defined in guilds and orders. Before the revolution, public opinion had been voiced outside of traditional institutions—in cafes, salons, and philosophical societies. French provincial academies sponsored a dynamic intellectual life as centers for debate over capital punishment, civic virtue, and the best form of government. Nobles and bourgeois met in these academies to discuss government, power, and the means of social improvement.

New forms of social intercourse fostered the growth of democratic ideas and the emergence of a new political culture that was both progressive and democratic, and that considered individuals as perfectible. Political documents, like the Constitution of 1791, reflected these changes to some extent. But the revolutionaries intended to do more than reallocate political power: they aimed to change the ways people thought, talked, and lived. People needed new symbols to replace those that had been repudiated. They needed new words to talk about transformed political realities. The revolution created its own calendar, setting the beginning of accounted time in the revolutionary era. The first day of the first year of the rest of history was 22 September 1792—the beginning of the new revolutionary month Vendémiaire, Year I. New patterns of speech fostered a new way of looking at the world. People now addressed each other familiarly as *tu* instead of the more formal *vous,* as the vague concepts of liberty, equality, and fraternity took root in people's lives.

The French Revolution was a school for the French nation. People at all levels of society learned politics by doing it. In the beginning, experience helped. The elites, both noble and bourgeois, had served in government and administration. But the rules of the game under the old regime had been very different, with birth determining power. After 1789, all men were declared free and equal, in opportunity if not in rights. Men of ability and talent, who had served as middlemen for the privileged elite under the old regime, now claimed power as their due. Many of them were lawyers, educated in the rules and regulations of the society of orders. They experienced firsthand the problems of the exercise of power in the old regime, and they had their own ideas about reform. But the school of the revolution did not remain the domain of a special class. Women demanded their places but continued to be excluded from the political arena, though the importance of their participation in the revolution was indisputable. Workers talked of seizing their rights, but because of the inherent contradictions of representation and participation, experimenting with democracy led to outcomes that did not look very democratic at all.

Declaring Political Rights

"Liberty consists in the ability to do whatever does not harm another." So wrote the revolutionary deputies of 1789. Sounding a refrain similar to that of the American Declaration of Independence, the Declaration of the Rights of Man and Citizen appeared on 26 August 1789. The document amalgamated a variety of Enlightenment ideas drawn from the works of political philosophy, including those of Locke and Montesquieu. "Men are born and remain free and equal in rights. Social distinctions may be based only on common utility." Perhaps most significant of all was the attention given to property, which was declared a "sacred and inviolable," "natural," and "imprescriptible" right of man.

In the year of tranquillity that followed the violent summer of 1789, the new politicians set themselves the task of creating institutions based on the principle of liberty and others embodied in the Declaration of the Rights of Man and Citizen. The result was the Constitution of 1791, a documentary monument to the belief in a progressive constitutional monarchy. A king accountable to an elected parliamentary body would lead France into a prosperous and just age. The constitution acknowledged the people's sovereignty as the source of political power. It also enshrined the principle of property by making voting rights dependent on property ownership. All men might be equal before the law, but by the Constitution of 1791 only wealthy men had the right to vote for representatives and hold office. A new male elite, those who owned property and controlled wealth, was emerging within the revolution.

All titles of nobility were abolished. In the early period of the revolution, civil liberties were extended to Protestants and Jews, who had been persecuted under the old regime. Previously excluded groups were granted freedom of thought, worship, and full civil liberties. More reluctantly, deputies outlawed slavery in the colonies in 1794. Slave unrest in Saint Domingue (modern-day Haiti) had coincided with the political conflicts of the revolution and exploded in rebellion in 1791, driving the revolutionaries in Paris to support black independence although it was at odds with French colonial interests. Led by Toussaint L'Ouverture (1743–1803), black rebels worked to found an independent Haitian state, which was declared in 1804. But the concept of equality with regard to race remained incompletely integrated with revolutionary principles, and slavery was reestablished in the French colonies in 1802.

Men were the subject of these newly defined rights. No references to women or their rights appear in the constitutions or the official Declarations of Rights. Women's organizations agitated for an equitable divorce law, and divorce was legalized in September 1792. Women were critical actors in the revolution from its very inception, and their presence shaped and directed the outcome of events, as the women's march to Versailles in 1789 made clear. The marquis de Condorcet (1743–94), elected to the Legislative Assembly in 1791, was one of the first to chastise the revolutionaries for overlooking the political rights of women who, he pointedly observed, were half of the human race. "Either no individual of the human race has genuine rights, or else all have the same; and he who votes against the right of another, whatever the religion,

Slaves revolting against the French in Saint Domingue in 1791. Napoleon sent an army to restore colonial rule in 1799, but yellow fever decimated the French soldiers, and the rebels defeated the weakened French army in 1803.

DECLARATION OF THE RIGHTS OF MAN AND CITIZEN

Sounding a refrain similar to that of the American Declaration of Independence (1776), the Declaration of the Rights of Man and Citizen was adopted by the National Assembly on 26 August 1789. The document amalgamated a variety of Enlightenment ideas, including those of Locke and Montesquieu. The attention to property, which was defined as "sacred and inviolable," rivaled that given to liberty as a "natural" and "imprescriptible" right of man.

1. Men are born and remain free and equal in rights. Social distinctions may be founded only upon the general good.

2. The aim of all political association is the preservation of the natural and imprescriptible rights of man. These rights are liberty, property, security, and resistance to oppression.

3. The principle of all sovereignty resides essentially in the nation. No body nor individual may exercise any authority which does not proceed directly from the nation.

4. Liberty consists in the freedom to do everything which injures no one else; hence the exercise of the natural rights of each man has no limits except those which assure to the other members of the society the enjoyment of the same rights. These limits can only be determined by law.

5. Law can only prohibit such actions as are hurtful to society. Nothing may be prevented which is not forbidden by law, and no one may be forced to do anything not provided for by law.

6. Law is the expression of the general will. Every citizen has a right to participate personally, or through his representative, in its formation. It must be the same for all, whether it protects or punishes. All citizens, being equal in the eyes of the law, are equally eligible to all dignities and to all public positions and occupations, according to their abilities, and without distinction except that of their virtues and talents.

7. No person shall be accused, arrested, or imprisoned except in the cases and according to the forms prescribed by law. Any one soliciting, transmitting, executing, or causing to be executed, any arbitrary

---

color, or sex of that other, has henceforth abjured his own." Condorcet argued forcefully but unsuccessfully for the right of women to be educated and for state support of this right. Women's talents, he warned, were slumbering under the ignorance of neglect.

The revolutionaries had declared that liberty was a natural and inalienable right, a universal right that was extended to all with the overthrow of a despotic monarch and a privileged elite. The principle triumphed in religious toleration. Yet the revolutionary concept of liberty foundered on the divergent claims of excluded groups—workers, women, and slaves—who demanded full participation in the world of politics. In 1792 revolutionaries confronted the contradictions inherent in their political beliefs of liberty and equality now being challenged in the midst of social upheaval and foreign war. In response, the revolution turned to more radical measures to survive.

The Second Revolution: The Revolution of the People

The first revolution, from 1789 through the beginning of 1792 was based on liberty—the liberty to compete, to own, and to succeed. The second revolution, which began in 1792, took equality as its rallying cry. This was the revolution of the working people of French cities. The popular movement that spearheaded political action in 1792 was committed to equality of rights in a way not characteristic of the leaders of the revolution of 1789. Urban workers were not benefiting from the revolution, but they had come to believe in their own power as political beings. Organized on the local level into sections, artisans in cities identified themselves as *sans-culottes*—literally, those trousered citizens who did not wear knee breeches (*culottes*)—to distinguish themselves from the privileged elite.

order, shall be punished. But any citizen summoned or arrested in virtue of the law shall submit without delay, as resistance constitutes an offense.

8. The law shall provide for such punishments only as are strictly and obviously necessary. . . .

9. As all persons are held innocent until they shall have been declared guilty, if arrest shall be deemed indispensable, all harshness not essential to the securing of the prisoner's person shall be severely repressed by law.

10. No one shall be disquieted on account of his opinions, including his religious views, provided their manifestation does not disturb the public order established by law.

11. The free communication of ideas and opinions is one of the most precious of the rights of man. Every citizen may, accordingly, speak, write, and print with freedom, but shall be responsible for such abuses of this freedom as shall be defined by law.

12. The security of the rights of man and of the citizen requires public military forces. These forces are, therefore, established for the good of all and not for the personal advantage of those to whom they shall be instrusted.

13. A common contribution is essential for the maintenance of the public forces and for the cost of administration. This should be equitably distributed among all the citizens in proportion to their means.

14. All the citizens have a right to decide, either personally or by their representatives, as to the necessity of the public contribution; to grant this freely; to know to what uses it is put: and to fix the proportion, the mode of assessment and of collection and the duration of the taxes.

15. Society has the right to require of every public agent an account of his administration.

16. A society in which the observance of the law is not assured, nor the separation of powers defined, has no constitution at all.

17. Since property is an inviolable and sacred right, no one shall be deprived thereof except where public necessity, legally determined, shall clearly demand it, and then only on condition that the owner shall have been previously and equitably indemnified.

French towns and villages set up "Liberty Trees" to show their revolutionary fervor. The trees were hung with cockades and topped with red caps. This drawing shows a tree near the captured Bastille. In the background sans-culottes rout an Austrian army.

On 10 August 1792, the people of Paris stormed the Tuileries, chanting their demands for "Equality!" and "Nation!" The people tramped across the silk sheets of the king's bed and broke his fine furniture, reveling in the private chambers of the royal family. Love and respect for the king had vanished. What the people of Paris demanded now was universal manhood suffrage and participation in a popular democracy. Working people were acting independently of other factions, and the bourgeois political leadership became quickly aware of the need to scramble to maintain order.

Who constituted the popular movement? The self-designated sans-culottes were the working men and women of Paris. Some were wealthier than others, some were wage earners, but all shared a common identity as consumers in the marketplace. They hated the privileged (les gros), who appeared to be profiting at the expense of the people. The sans-culottes wanted government power to be decentralized, with neighborhoods ruling themselves through sectional organizations. As the have-nots, they were increasingly intent on pulling down the haves, and they translated this sense of vengeance into a new revolutionary justice. When they invaded the Tuileries Palace on the morning of 10 August, the sans-culottes did so in the name of the people. They saw themselves as patriots whose duty it was to brush the monarchy aside. The people were now a force to be reckoned with and feared.

"Terror Is the Order of the Day"

Political factions characterized revolutionary politics from the start. The terms *Left* and *Right*, which came to represent opposite ends of the political spectrum, originated in a description of where people sat in the Assembly in relation to the podium. Political designations were refined in successive parliamentary bodies. The Convention was the legislative body elected in September 1792 that succeeded the Legislative Assembly and had as its charge determining the best form of government after the collapse of the monarchy. On 21 September 1792, the monarchy was abolished in France; on the following day the Republic, France's first, came into being. Members of the Convention conducted the trial of Louis XVI for treason and pronounced his sentence: execution by the guillotine in January 1793.

The various political factions of the Convention were described in terms borrowed from geography. The Mountain, sitting on the upper benches on the left, was made up of members of the Jacobin Club (named for its meeting place in an abandoned monastery). The

THE FRENCH REVOLUTION

August 1788	Louis XVI announces meeting of Estates-General to be held May 1789
5 May 1789	Estates-General convenes
17 June 1789	Third Estate declares itself the National Assembly
20 June 1789	Oath of the Tennis Court
14 July 1789	Storming of the Bastille
20 July 1789	Revolution of peasantry begins
26 August 1789	Declaration of the Rights of Man and Citizen
5 October 1789	Parisian women march to Versailles; force Louis XVI to return to Paris
February 1790	Monasteries, convents dissolved
July 1790	Civil Constitution of the Clergy
June 1791	Louis XVI and family attempt to flee Paris; are captured and returned
April 1792	France declares war on Austria
10 August 1792	Storming of the Tuileries
22 September 1792	Revolutionary calendar implemented
January 1793	Louis XVI executed
July 1793	Robespierre assumes leadership of Committee of Public Safety
1793–1794	Reign of Terror
1794	Robespierre guillotined
1799	Napoleon overthrows the Directory and seizes power

Jacobins were the most radical element in the National Convention, supporting democratic solutions and speaking in favor of the cause of people in the streets. The Plain held the moderates, who were concerned with maintaining public order against popular unrest. Many members of the Plain came to be called Girondins in the mistaken belief that they originated in the département of the Gironde.

Both Girondins and Jacobins were from the middle ranks of the bourgeoisie, and both groups were dedicated to the principles of the revolution. Although they controlled the ministries, the Girondins began to lose their hold on the revolution and the war. The renewed

European war fragmented the democratic movement, and the Girondins, unable to control violence at home, saw political control slipping away. They became prisoners of the revolution when eighty thousand armed Parisians surrounded the National Convention in June 1793.

Girondin power had been eroding in the critical months between August 1792 and June 1793. A new leader was working quietly and effectively behind the scenes to weld a partnership between the popular movement of sans-culottes and the Jacobins. He was Maximilien Robespierre (1758–94), leader of the Mountain and the Jacobin Club. Robespierre was typical of the new breed of revolutionary politician. Only 31 years old in 1789, he wrote mediocre poems and attended the local provincial academy to discuss the new ideas when he was not practicing law in his hometown of Arras. Elected to the Estates-General, he joined the Jacobin Club and quickly rose to become its leader. He was willing to take controversial stands on issues: unlike most of his fellow members of the Mountain— including his rival, the popular orator Georges Danton (1759–94)—he opposed the war in 1792. Although neither an original thinker nor a compelling orator, Robespierre discovered with the revolution that he was an adroit political tactician. He gained a following and learned how to manipulate it. It was he who engineered the Jacobins' replacement of the Girondins as leaders of the government.

Robespierre's chance for real power came when he assumed leadership of the Committee of Public Safety in July 1793. Faced with the threat of internal anarchy and external war, the elected body, the National Convention, yielded political control to the 12-man Committee of Public Safety that ruled dictatorially under Robespierre's direction. The Great Committee, as it was known at the time, orchestrated the Reign of Terror (1793–94), a period of systematic state repression that meted out justice in the people's name. Summary trials by specially created revolutionary tribunals were followed by the swift execution of the guilty under the blade of the guillotine.

Influenced by *The Social Contract* (1762) and other writings of Jean-Jacques Rousseau, Robespierre believed that sovereignty resided with the people. For him, individual wills and even individual rights did not matter when weighed against the will of the nation. The king was dead; the people were the new source of political power. Robespierre saw himself in the all-important role of interpreting and shaping the people's will. His own task was to guide the people "to the summit of its destinies." As he explained to his critics, "I am defending not my own cause but the public cause." As head of the Great Committee, Robespierre oversaw a revolutionary machinery dedicated to economic regulation, massive military mobilization, and a punitive system of revolutionary justice characterized by the slogan "Terror Is the Order of the Day." Militant revolutionary committees and revolutionary tribunals were established throughout France to identify traitors and to mete out the harsh justice that struck hardest against those members of the bourgeoisie perceived as opponents of the government.

The guillotine became the symbol of revolutionary justice, but it was not the only means of execution. In Lyon, officials of the Reign of Terror had prisoners tied to stakes in open fields and fired on with cannon. In Nantes, a Parisian administrator of the new justice had enemies of the revolution chained to barges and drowned in the estuary of the Loire. The civil war, which raged most violently in the Vendée in the west of France, consisted often of primitive massacres that sent

A satirical print shows Robespierre, having executed everyone else ("Toute la France") during the Reign of Terror, turning the guillotine on the executioner.

Declaration of the Rights of Woman and Citizen

"Woman, wake up!" Thus did Olympe de Gouges (d. 1793), a self-educated playwright, address French women in 1791. Aware that women were being denied the new rights of liberty and property extended to all men by the Declaration of the Rights of Man and Citizen, Gouges composed her own Declaration of the Rights of Woman and Citizen, modeled on the 1789 document. Persecuted for her political beliefs, she foreshadowed her own demise at the hands of revolutionary justice in article 10 of her declaration. The Declaration of the Rights of Woman and Citizen became an important document in women's demands for political rights in the nineteenth century, and Gouges herself became a feminist hero.

Article I

Woman is born free and lives equal to man in her rights. Social distinctions can be based only on the common utility.

Article II

The purpose of any political association is the conservation of the natural and imprescriptible rights of woman and man; these rights are liberty, property, security, and especially resistance to oppression.

Article III

The principle of all sovereignty rests essentially with the nation, which is nothing but the union of woman and man; no body and no individual can exercise any authority which does not come expressly from it [the nation].

Article IV

Liberty and justice consist of restoring all that belongs to others; thus, the only limits on the exercise of the natural rights of woman are perpetual male tyranny; these limits are to be reformed by the laws of nature and reason.

Article V

Laws of nature and reason proscribe all acts harmful to society; everything which is not prohibited by these wise and divine laws cannot be prevented, and no one can be constrained to do what they do not command.

Article VI

The law must be the expression of the general will; all female and male citizens must contribute either personally or through their representatives to its formation; it must be the same for all: male and female citizens, being equal in the eyes of the law, must be equally admitted to all honors, positions, and public employment according to their capacity and without other distinctions besides those of their virtues and talents.

Article VII

No woman is an exception; she is accused, arrested, and detained in cases determined by law. Women, like men, obey this rigorous law.

---

an estimated quarter of a million people to their deaths. The bureaucratized Reign of Terror was responsible for about forty thousand executions in a nine-month period, resulting in the image of the republicans as "drinkers of blood." (See "The Guillotine and Revolutionary Justice," pp. 632–633.)

The Cult of the Supreme Being, a civic religion without priests or churches and influenced by Rousseau's ideas about nature, followed de-Christianization. The cathedral of Notre Dame de Paris was turned into the Temple of Reason, and the new religion established its own festivals to undermine the persistence of Catholicism. The cult was one indication of the Reign of Terror's attempt to create a new moral universe of revolutionary values.

Women remained conspicuously absent from the summit of political power. After 1793, Jacobin revolutionaries, who had been willing to empower the popular movement of workers, turned against women's participation and denounced it. Women's associations

ARTICLE VIII

The law must establish only those penalties that are strictly and obviously necessary. . . .

ARTICLE IX

Once any woman is declared guilty, complete rigor is [to be] exercised by the law.

ARTICLE X

No one is to be disquieted for his very basic opinions; woman has the right to mount the scaffold; she must equally have the right to mount the rostrum, provided that her demonstrations do not disturb the legally established public order.

ARTICLE XI

The free communication of thoughts and opinions is one of the most precious rights of woman, since that liberty assures the recognition of children by their fathers. Any female citizen thus may say freely, I am the mother of a child which belongs to you, without being forced by a barbarous prejudice to hide the truth; [an exception may be made] to respond to the abuse of this liberty in cases determined by the law.

ARTICLE XII

The guarantee of the rights of woman and the female citizen implies a major benefit; this guarantee must be instituted for the advantage of all, and not for the particular benefit of those to whom it is entrusted.

ARTICLE XIII

For the support of the public force and the expenses of administration, the contributions of woman and man are equal; she shares all the duties *[corvées]* and all the painful tasks; therefore, she must have the same share in the distribution of positions, employment, offices, honors and jobs *[industrie]*.

ARTICLE XIV

Female and male citizens have the right to verify, either by themselves or through their representatives, the necessity of the public contribution. This can only apply to women if they are granted an equal share, not only of wealth, but also of public administration, and in the determination of the proportion, the base, the collection, and the duration of the tax.

ARTICLE XV

The collectivity of women, joined for tax purposes to the aggregate of men, has the right to demand an accounting of his administration from any public agent.

ARTICLE XVI

No society has a constitution without the guarantee of rights and the separation of powers: the constitution is null if the majority of individuals comprising the nation have not cooperated in drafting it.

ARTICLE XVII

Property belongs to both sexes whether united or separate; for each it is an inviolable and sacred right; no one can be deprived of it, since it is the true patrimony of nature, unless the legally determined public need obviously dictates it, and then only with a just and prior indemnity.

---

were outlawed and the Society of Revolutionary Republican Women was disbanded. Olympe de Gouges, revolutionary author of the Declaration of the Rights of Woman and Citizen, was guillotined. Women were declared unfit for political participation, according to the Jacobins, because of their biological functions of reproduction and child-rearing. Rousseau's ideas about family policy were probably more influential than his political doctrines. His best-selling books *La Nouvelle Héloïse* (1761) and *Émile* (1762), which combined went into 72 editions before 1789, were moral works that transformed people's ideas about family life. Under his influence, the reading public came to value a separate and private sphere of domestic and conjugal values. Following Rousseau's lead, Robespierre and the Jacobins insisted that the role of women as mothers was incompatible with women's participation in the political realm.

By attacking his critics on both the Left and the Right, Robespierre undermined the support he needed

❧ The Guillotine and Revolutionary Justice

In the sultry summer days of 1792, Parisians found a new way to entertain themselves. They attended executions. French men, women, and children were long accustomed to watching criminals being tortured and put to death in public view. During the old regime, spectators could enjoy the variety of a number of methods: drawing and quartering, strangling, or hanging. Decapitation, reputedly a less painful death, was a privilege reserved for nobles sentenced for capital crimes. The French Revolution extended this formerly aristocratic privilege to all criminals condemned to death. What especially attracted people to public squares in the third year of the revolution was the introduction of a novel method of decapitation. In 1792 the new instrument of death, the guillotine, became the center of the spectacle of revolutionary justice.

The guillotine promised to eliminate the suffering of its victims. Axes, swords, and sabers—the tra-

ditional tools of decapitation and dismemberment—were messy and undependable, producing slow and bloody ordeals when inept or drunken executioners missed their mark or victims flinched at the fatal moment. The design of the guillotine took all of this into account. On its easel-like wooden structure, victims, lying on their stomachs, were held in place with straps and a pillory. Heavy pulleys guaranteed that the sharp blade would fall efficiently from its great height. A basket was placed at the base of the blade to catch the severed head; another was used to slide the headless body through the base of the scaffolding for removal. In place of unintended torture and gore, the guillotine was devised as a humanitarian instrument to guarantee swift and painless death.

It should have been called the Louisette, after its inventor, Dr. Antoine Louis. In what now seems a dubious honor, the new machine was named instead after its greatest supporter, Dr. Joseph Ignace Guillotin, a delegate to the National Assembly. Both Guillotin and Louis were medical doctors, men of science influenced by Enlightenment ideas and committed to the revolution's elimination of the cruelty of older forms of punishment. In the spirit of scientific experimentation, Louis's invention was tested on sheep, cadavers, and then convicted thieves. In 1792 it was used for the first time against another class of offenders: political prisoners.

Early in the revolution, the Marquis de Condorcet, philosophe and mathematician, had opposed capital punishment with the argument that the state did not have the right to take life. Ironically, Maximilien Robespierre, future architect of the Reign of Terror, was one of the few revolutionaries who agreed with Condorcet. Those who favored justice by execution of the state's enemies prevailed. The revolutionary hero and associate of the radical Jacobins Jean-Paul Marat (1743–93), who was himself stabbed to death in his bathtub, advocated the state's use of violence against its enemies: "In order to ensure public tranquillity, 200,000 heads must be cut off." By the end of 1792, as revolution and civil war swept over France, 83 identical guillotines were constructed and installed in each of the départements of France. For the next two years, the guillotine's great blade was rhythmically raised and lowered daily in public squares all over France. In the name of the revolution, the "axe of the people" dispatched over fifty thousand victims.

Although intended as a humanitarian instrument, the guillotine became the symbol of all that was arbitrary and repressive about a revolution run amok. Day and night, the Revolutionary Tribunal in Paris delivered the death sentence to the "enemies of the people." Most of those executed were members of what had been the Third Estate: members of the bourgeoisie, workers, peasants. Only 15 percent of the condemned were nobles and priests. During the Terror, the guillotine could be used to settle old scores. Sans-culottes turned in their neighbors, sometimes over long-standing grievances that owed more to spite than politics. The most fanatical revolutionaries had fantasies that guillotines were about to be erected on every street corner to dispense with hoarders and traitors. Others suggested that guillotines be made portable so that by putting justice on wheels, it could be taken directly to the people.

As usual, Paris set the style. The most famous of the guillotines stood on the Place du Carrousel, deliberately placed in front of the royal palace of the Tuileries. It was eventually moved to the larger Place de la Révolution in order to accommodate the growing numbers of spectators. Famous victims drew especially large crowds. The revolutionary drama took on the trappings of a spectacle as hawkers sold toy guillotines, miniature pikes, and liberty caps as souvenirs, along with the usual food and drink. Troops attended these events, but not to control the crowd. Members of the National Guard in formation, their backs to the people, faced the stage of the scaffold. They, like the citizenry, were there to witness the birth of a new nation and, by their presence, to give legitimacy to the event. The crowd entered into the ritual, cheering the victim's last words and demanding that the executioner hold high the severed head. In the new political culture, death was a festival.

For two centuries Western societies have debated the legitimacy of the death sentence and have periodically considered the relative merits of the guillotine, the gas chamber, and the electric chair. For the French, the controversy temporarily ceased in 1794, when people were convinced that justice had gotten out of hand and that they had had enough. For the time being, the government put an end to capital punishment. The guillotine would return. But at the height of its use, between 1792 and 1794, it had played a unique role in forging a new system of justice: the guillotine had been the great leveler. In the ideology of democracy, people were equal—in death as well as in life. The guillotine came to be popularly known as the "scythe of equality." It killed king and commoner alike.

to stay in power. He abandoned the alliance with the popular movement that had been so important in bringing him to power. Robespierre's enemies—and he had many—were able to break the identification between political power and the will of the people that Robespierre had established. As a result, he was branded a traitor by the same process that he had used against many of his own enemies. He saved France from foreign occupation and internal collapse, but he could not save democracy through terror. In the summer of 1794, Robespierre was guillotined. The Reign of Terror ceased with his death in the revolutionary month of Thermidor 1794.

The revolution did not end with the Thermidorian Reaction, as the fall of Robespierre came to be known, but his execution initiated a new phase. For some, democracy lost its legitimacy. The popular movement was reviled, and *sans-culotte* became a term of derision. Jacobins were forced underground. Price controls were abolished, resulting in extreme hardship for most urban residents. Out of desperation, in April 1795 the Jacobins and the sans-culottes renewed their alliance and united to demand "bread and the Constitution of 1793." The politics of bread had never been more accurately captured in slogan. Those who took to the streets in 1795 saw the universal manhood suffrage of the unimplemented 1793 constitution as the way to solve their economic problems. But their demands went unheeded; the popular revolution had failed.

The End of the Revolution

In the four years after Robespierre's fall, a new government by committee, called the Directory, appeared to offer mediocrity, caution, and opportunism in place of the idealism and action of the early years of the revolution. No successor to Robespierre stepped forward to command center stage. There were no heroes like Lafayette or the great Jacobin orator Georges-Jacques Danton (1759–94) to inspire patriotic fervor. Nor were there women like Olympe de Gouges to demand in the public arena equal rights for women. Most people, numbed after years of change, barely noticed that the revolution was over. Ordinary men in parliamentary institutions effectively did the day-to-day job of running the government. They tried to steer a middle path between royalist resurgence and popular insurrection. This nearly forgotten period in the history of the French Revolution was the fulfillment of the liberal hopes of 1789 for a stable constitutional rule.

However, the Directory continued to be dogged by European war. A mass army of conscripts and volunteers had successfully extended France's power and frontiers. France expelled foreign invaders and annexed territories, including Belgium, while increasing its control in Holland, Switzerland, and Italy. But the expansion of revolutionary France was expensive and increasingly unpopular. Military defeats and the corruption of the Directory undermined government control. The Directory might have succeeded in the slow accretion of a parliamentary tradition, but reinstatement of conscription in 1798 met with widespread protest and resistance. No matter what their political leanings, people were weary. They turned to those who promised stability and peace.

In the democratic experiment at the heart of the second stage of the French Revolution, the sovereign will of the people permanently replaced the monarch's claim to divine right to rule. Yet with democracy came tyranny. The severe repression of the terror revealed the pressures that external war and civil unrest created for the new Republic. The Thermidorian Reaction and the elimination of Robespierre as the legitimate interpreter of the people's will ushered in a period of conciliation, opportunism, and a search for stability. Ironically, the savior that France found to answer its needs for peace and a just government was a man of war and a dictator.

The Reign of Napoleon, 1799–1815

Napoleon is one of those individuals about whom one can say that if he had not lived, history would have been different. He left his mark on an age and a continent. The great debate about Napoleon that rages to this day revolves around the question of whether he fulfilled the aims of the revolution or perverted them. In his return to a monarchical model, Napoleon resembled the enlightened despots of eighteenth-century Europe. In a modern sense, he was also a dictator, manipulating the French people through a highly centralized administrative apparatus. He locked French society into a program of military expansionism that depleted its human and material resources. Yet in spite of destruction and war, he dedicated his reign to building a French state according to the principles of the revolution.

Bonaparte Seizes Power

In Paris in 1795 a young, penniless, and unknown military officer moved among the wealthy and the beautiful of Parisian society and longed for fame. Already

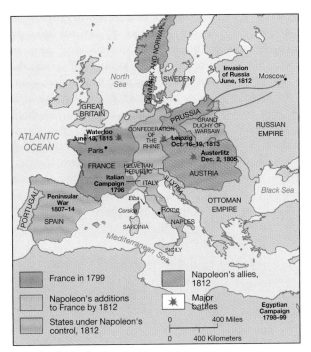

Napoleon's Empire

Foreign war and civil war required military leaders devoted to the revolution. Forced to flee Corsica because he had sided with the Jacobins, Napoleon and his troops crushed Parisian protesters who rioted against the Directory in 1795. His victories in the Italian campaign in 1796–97 launched his political career. As he extended French rule into central Italy, he became the embodiment of revolutionary values and energy.

The revolutionary wars had begun as wars to liberate humanity in the name of liberty, equality, and fraternity. Yet concerns for power, territory, and riches soon replaced earlier concerns with defense of the nation and of the revolution. This aggrandizement was nowhere more evident than in the Egyptian campaign of 1798, in which Napoleon Bonaparte headed an expedition whose goal was to enrich France by hastening the collapse of the Turkish empire, crippling British trade routes, and handicapping Russian interests in the region. With Napoleon's highly publicized campaigns in Egypt and Syria, the war left the European theater and moved to the East, leaving behind its original revolutionary ideals. The Egyptian campaign, which was in reality a disaster, made Napoleon a hero at home. Yet in 1799 he readily joined a conspiracy that pulled down the Directory, the government he had earlier preserved, and became the First Consul of a triumvirate of consuls.

Napoleon set out to secure his position of power by eliminating his enemies on the Left and weakening those on the Right. He guaranteed the security of property acquired in the revolution, a move that undercut royalists who wanted to return property to its original owners. Through policing forces and special criminal courts, law and order prevailed and civil war subsided. The First Consul promised a balanced budget and appeared to deliver it. Bonaparte spoke of healing the nation's wounds, especially those opened by de-Christianization during the revolution. Realizing the importance of religion in maintaining domestic peace, Napoleon reestablished relations with the pope in 1801 by the Concordat, which recognized Catholicism as the religion of the French and restored the Roman Catholic hierarchy.

Napoleon's popularity as First Consul flowed from his military and political successes and his religious reconciliation. He had come to power in 1799 by appealing for the support of the army. In 1802 Napoleon decided to extend his power by calling for a plebiscite in which he asked the electorate to vote him First Consul for life. Public support was overwhelming. An electoral landslide gave Napoleon greater political power than any of his Bourbon predecessors. Using revolu-

nicknamed at school "the Little Corporal" on account of his short stature, he was snubbed because of his background and ridiculed for his foreign accent. His story is typical of all stories of thwarted ambition. Yet the outcome of this story is unique: within four years this young man would become ruler of France. The story of his ascent to power is also a story of the demise of the revolution.

Napoleon Bonaparte (1769–1821) was a true child of the eighteenth century. He shared the philosophes' belief in a rational and progressive world. Born in Corsica, which until a few months before his birth was part of the Republic of Genoa, he received his training in French military schools. Even as a youth, he was arrogant and ambitious. But he could have never aspired to a position of leadership in the army during the old regime because he lacked the noble birth necessary for advancement. The highest rank Napoleon could hope to achieve was that of captain or major.

The revolution changed everything for him. First, it opened up careers previously restricted by birth, including those in the military, to talent. Second, the revolution made new posts available when aristocratic generals defected and crossed over to the enemy side, both before and after the execution of the king. Finally, the revolution created great opportunities for military men to test their mettle.

tionary mechanisms, Napoleon laid the foundation for a new dynasty.

War and More War

Napoleon was either at war or preparing for war during his entire reign. He certainly seemed up to the task of defeating the European powers. His military successes before 1799, real and apparent, had been crucial in his bid for political power. By 1802 he had signed favorable treaties with both Austria and Great Britain. He appeared to deliver a lasting peace and to establish France as the dominant power in Europe. But the peace was short-lived. In 1803 France embarked on an eleven-year period of continuous war. Under Napoleon's command, the French army delivered defeat after defeat to the European powers. Austria fell in 1805, Prussia in 1806, and the Russian armies of Alexander I were defeated at Friedland in 1807. In 1808 Napoleon invaded Spain to drive out British expeditionary forces intent on invading France. The great painter of the Spanish court, Francisco Goya (1746–1828), produced a series of etchings, *The Disasters of War,* that depicted the atrocities accompanying the Napoleonic invasion. Spain became a satellite kingdom of France, though the conflict continued.

Britain was the one exception to the string of Napoleonic victories. Napoleon initially considered sending a French fleet to invade the island nation. Lacking the strength necessary to achieve this, he turned to economic warfare, blockading European ports against British trade. Beginning in 1806, the Continental System, as the blockade was known, erected a structure of protection for French manufactures in all continental European markets. The British responded to the tariff walls and boycotts with a naval blockade that succeeded in cutting French commerce off from its Atlantic markets. The Continental System did not prove to be the decisive policy that Napoleon had planned: the British economy was not broken and the French economy did not flourish when faced with restricted resources and the persistence of a black market in smuggled goods.

Still, by 1810 the French leader was master of the Continent. French armies had extended revolutionary reforms and legal codes outside France and brought with them civil equality and religious toleration. They had also drained defeated countries of their resources and had inflicted the horrors of war with armies of occupation, forced billeting, and pillage. Napoleon's empire extended across Europe, with only a diminished Austria, Prussia, and Russia remaining independent. He placed his relatives and friends on the thrones of the new satellite kingdoms of Italy, Naples, Westphalia, Holland, and Spain. It was a fine empire, Napoleon later recalled in the loneliness of exile. Napoleon's

This engraving, from the series Disasters of War *by Francisco Goya, depicts the horrors of war. The series was inspired by Napoleon's invasion and occupation of Spain from 1808 to 1813.*

The 1804 coronation of Napoleon by Jacques-Louis David. Pope Pius VII is seated behind the emperor, who is about to place a crown on the head of Josephine. Napoleon later ordered David to alter the painting to show the pope's hand raised in blessing.

empire did not endure, but at its acme, it seemed as though it would never fall.

Peace at Home

Napoleon measured domestic prosperity in terms of the stability of his reign. Through the 1802 plebiscite that voted him First Consul for life, he maintained the charade of constitutional rule while he ruled as virtual dictator. In 1804 he abandoned all pretense and had himself proclaimed emperor of the French. Mimicking the rituals of kingship, he staged his own coronation and that of his wife Josephine at the cathedral of Notre Dame de Paris. Breaking the tradition set by Charlemagne, Napoleon took the crown from the hands of Pope Pius VII (1800–23) and placed it on his own head.

Secure in his regime, surrounded by a new nobility that he created based on military achievement and talent and that he rewarded with honors, Napoleon set about implementing sweeping reforms in every area of government. Like many of the men of the revolutionary assemblies who had received scientific educations in their youth, he recognized the importance of science for both industry and war. The revolution had removed an impediment to the development of a national market by creating a uniform system of weights and measures. The metric system was established by 1799. But

Napoleon felt the need to go further: France must be first in scientific research and application. To assure French predominance, Napoleon became a patron of science, supporting important work in the areas of physics and chemistry. Building for the future, Napoleon made science a pillar in the new structure of higher education.

The Directory had restored French prosperity through stabilization of the currency, fiscal reform, and support of industry. Napoleon's contribution to the French economy was the much needed reform of the tax system. He authorized the creation of a central banking system. French industries flourished under the protection of the state. The blockade forced the development of new domestic crops such as sugar beets and indigo, which became substitutes for colonial products. Napoleon extended the infrastructure of roads so necessary for the expansion of national and European markets.

Perhaps his greatest achievement was the codification of law, a task begun under the revolution. Many of the new articles of the Napoleonic Code were hammered out in Napoleon's presence, as he presided regularly over meetings with legal reformers. Combined with economic reforms, the Napoleonic Code facilitated trade and the development of commerce by regularizing contractual relations and protecting property rights and equality before the law.

THE REIGN OF NAPOLEON

1799	Napoleon establishes consulate, becomes First Consul
1801	Napoleon reestablishes relations with pope, restores Roman Catholic hierarchy
1802	Plebiscite declares Napoleon First Consul for life
1804	Napoleon proclaims himself Emperor of the French
1806	Continental System implemented
1808–1814	France engaged in Peninsular War with Spain
June 1812	Napoleon invades Russia
September 1812	French army reaches Moscow, is trapped by Russian winter
1813	Napoleon defeated at Battle of Nations at Leipzig
March 1814	Napoleon abdicates and goes into exile on island of Elba
March 1815	Napoleon escapes Elba and attempts to reclaim power
15 June 1815	Napoleon is defeated at Waterloo and exiled to island of Saint Helena

The civil laws of the new code carved out a family policy characterized by hierarchy and subordination. Married women were neither independent nor equal to men in ownership of property, custody of children, and access to divorce. Women also lacked political rights. In the Napoleonic Code, women, like children, were subjected to paternal authority. The Napoleonic philosophy of woman's place is well captured in an anecdote told by Madame Germaine de Staël (1766–1817), a leading intellectual of her day. As the daughter of Jacques Necker, the Swiss financier and adviser to Louis XVI at the time of the revolution, she had been taught Enlightenment ideas from an early age. On finding herself seated next to Napoleon at a dinner party, she asked him what was very likely a self-interested question: whom did he consider the greatest woman, alive or dead? Napoleon had no name to give her but

responded, without pausing: "The one who has had the most children."

Napoleon turned his prodigious energies to every aspect of French life. He encouraged the arts while creating a police force. He had monuments built but did not forget about sewers. He organized French administrative life in a fashion that has endured. In place of the popular democratic movement, he offered his own singular authority. In place of elections, clubs, and free associations, he gave France plebiscites and army service. To be sure, Napoleon believed in constitutions, but he thought they should be "short and obscure." For Napoleon the great problem of democracy was its unpredictability. His regime solved that problem by eliminating choices.

Decline and Fall

Militarily, Napoleon went too far. The first cracks in the French facade began to show in the Peninsular War (1808–14) with Spain, in which Spanish guerrilla tactics proved costly for French troops. Napoleon's biggest mistake, the one that shattered the myth of his invincibility, occurred when he decided to invade Russia in June 1812. Having decisively defeated Russian forces in 1807, Napoleon had entered into a peace treaty with Tsar Alexander I that guaranteed Russian allegiance to French policies. Alexander repudiated the Continental System in 1810 and appeared to be preparing for his own war against France. Napoleon seized the initiative, sure that he could defeat Russian forces once again. With an army of 500,000 men, Napoleon moved deep into Russia in the summer of 1812. The tsar's troops fell back in retreat. It was a strange war, one that pulled the French army to Moscow like a bird following bread crumbs. When Napoleon and his men entered Moscow in September, they found a city in flames. The people of Moscow had destroyed their own city to deprive the French troops of winter quarters.

Winter comes early in Moscow, Napoleon's men discovered. They had left France basking in the warmth of summer and sure of certain and early victory. They now found themselves facing a severe Russian winter without overcoats, supplies, or food. Russia's strategy has become legendary. The Russians destroyed grain and shelter that might be of use to the French. Napoleon and his starving and frostbitten troops were forced into retreat. The horses of the French cavalry died because they were not properly shod for cold weather. The French army was decimated. Fewer than 100,000 men made it back to France.

This 1835 painting by De Boisde-nier depicts the suffering of Napoleon's Grand Army on the retreat from Moscow. The Germans were to meet a similar fate over one hundred years later when they invaded Russia without adequate supplies for the harsh winter.

The empire began to crumble. Britain, unbowed by the Continental System, remained Napoleon's sworn enemy. Prussia joined Great Britain, Sweden, Russia, and Austria in opposing France anew. In the Battle of Nations at Leipzig in October 1813, France was forced to retreat. Napoleon refused a negotiated peace and fought on until the following March, when the victorious allies marched down the streets of Paris and occupied the French capital. Only then did Napoleon abdicate in favor of his young son, François, the titular king of Rome (1811–32).

Still it was not quite the end for Napoleon. While the European heads of state sat in Vienna trying to determine the future of Europe and France's place in it, Napoleon returned from his exile on the Mediterranean island of Elba. On 15 June 1815, Napoleon once again, and for the final time, confronted the European powers in one of the most famous military campaigns in history. With 125,000 loyal French forces, Napoleon seemed within hours of reestablishing the French empire in Europe.

He had underestimated his opponents. The defeat of Napoleon's forces at Waterloo was decisive. Napoleon later explained, "Everything failed me just when everything had succeeded!" He had met his Waterloo, and with his defeat a new expression entered the language to describe devastating, permanent, irreversible downfall. Napoleon's return proved brief—it

lasted only one hundred days. An era had come to an end. Napoleon was exiled to the inhospitable island of Saint Helena in the South Atlantic. For the next six years, Napoleon wrote his memoirs under the watchful eyes of his British jailors. He died a painful death from cancer on 5 May 1821.

• • •

The period of revolution and empire from 1789 to 1815 radically changed the face of France. A new, more cohesive elite of bourgeois and nobles emerged, sharing power based on wealth and status. Ownership of land remained a defining characteristic of both old and new elites. A new state bureaucracy, built on the foundations of the old, expanded and centralized state power.

The people as sovereign now legitimated political power. Napoleon at his most imperial never doubted that he owed his existence to the people. In this sense, Napoleon was the king of the revolution—an apparently contradictory fusion of old forms and new ideology. Napoleon channeled democratic forces into enthusiasm for empire. He learned his lessons from the failure of the Bourbon monarchy and the politicians of the revolution. For sixteen years Napoleon successfully reconciled the old regime with the new France. Yet he could not resolve the essential problem of democracy: the relationship between the will of the people and the exercise of political power. The picture in 1815 was not dramatically different from the situation in 1789. The revolution might be over, but changes fueled by the revolutionary tradition were just beginning. The struggle for a workable democratic government continued in France for another century, and elsewhere in Europe throughout the twentieth century.

Suggestions for Further Reading

The Crisis of the Old Regime in France

C. B. A. Behrens, *Society, Government, and the Enlightenment* (New York: Harper & Row, 1985). A comparative study of eighteenth-century France and Prussia, focusing on the relationship between government and the ruling classes, that explains how pressures for change in both countries led to different outcomes: revolution in France and reform in Prussia.

* Roger Chartier, *The Cultural Origins of the French Revolution,* tr. Lydia G. Cochrane (Durham, NC: Duke University Press, 1991). Argues for the importance of the rise of critical modes of thinking in the public sphere in the eighteenth century and of long-term de-Christianization in shaping the desire for change in French society and politics.

Olwen Hufton, *The Poor in Eighteenth-Century France, 1750–1789* (Oxford: Clarendon, 1974). Examines the lives of the poor before the revolution and the institutions that attempted to deal with the problem of poverty.

Olwen Hufton, *Europe: Privilege and Protest, 1730–1789* (Sussex, England: The Harvester Press, 1980). An overview of the impact of rapid social, ideological, and economic changes on the concept and exercise of privilege.

* Daniel Roche, *The People of Paris* (Berkeley: University of California Press, 1987). An essay on popular culture in the eighteenth century in which the author surveys the lives of the Parisian popular classes—servants, laborers, and artisans—and examines their housing, furnishing, dress, and leisure activities.

Isser Woloch, *Eighteenth-Century Europe: Tradition and Progress, 1715–1789* (New York: Norton, 1982). A discussion of eighteenth-century Europe comparing social, economic, political, and intellectual developments elsewhere on the Continent to the French experience, with special attention to cultural aspects such as popular beliefs and religion.

The First Stage of the French Revolution

François Furet and Denis Richet, *The French Revolution* (New York: Macmillan, 1970). Two experts on the French Revolution present a detailed overview of the period from 1789 to 1798, when Bonaparte returned to Paris.

* Georges Lefebvre, *The Great Fear of 1789* (New York: Pantheon Books, 1973). This classic study analyzes the rural panic that swept through parts of France in the summer of 1789. The Great Fear is presented as a distinct episode in the

opening months of the revolution, with its own internal logic.

Colin Lucas, ed., *Rewriting the French Revolution* (Oxford: Clarendon Press, 1991). Responding to the historiographic challenge of the bicentenary of the French Revolution, eight scholars present new interpretations in the areas of social development, ideas, politics, and religion.

* D. M. G. Sutherland, *France, 1789–1815: Revolution and Counter-Revolution* (New York: Oxford University Press, 1986). An interpretation of the revolutionary period that stresses the struggle against counterrevolution and presents the revolution as a complex and contradictory process of social and political conflict over incompatible rights and privileges enjoyed by significant portions of the population.

* Michel Vovelle, *The Fall of the French Monarchy* (Cambridge: Cambridge University Press, 1984). A social history of the origins and early years of the revolution, beginning with a brief examination of the old regime and paying special attention to social and economic changes initiated by the revolution, the role of the popular classes, and the creation of revolutionary culture.

The Revolution's Second Stage

* François Furet, *Interpreting the French Revolution* (Cambridge: Cambridge University Press, 1981). A series of essays challenging many of the assumptions about the causes and outcome of the revolution and reviewing its historiography. The author argues that political crisis, not class conflict, was the revolution's primary cause and that revolutionary ideas concerning democracy are central to an understanding of the Reign of Terror.

Carla Hesse, *Publishing and Cultural Politics in Revolutionary Paris, 1789–1810* (Berkeley: University of California Press, 1991). Reconstructs the publishing world that emerged from the revolutionary struggles of publishers and printers of Paris and examines the political, legal, and socioeconomic forces shaping the new cultural politics between 1789 and 1810.

* Lynn Hunt, *Politics, Culture, and Class in the French Revolution* (Berkeley: University of California Press, 1984). A study of the revolution as the locus of the creation of modern political culture. The second half of the book examines the social composition and cultural experiences of the new political class that emerged during the revolution.

Lynn Hunt, *The Family Romance of the French Revolution* (Berkeley: University of California Press, 1992). Studies recurrent images of the family in French revolutionary politics in order to understand the gendered nature of the revolution and republicanism.

* Joan B. Landes, *Women and the Public Sphere in the Age of the French Revolution* (Ithaca, NY: Cornell University Press, 1988). Landes examines the genesis of the modern notion of the public sphere from a feminist perspective and

argues that within the revolutionary process women were relegated to the private sphere of the domestic world.

* Sara E. Melzer and Leslie Rabine, eds., *Rebel Daughters: Women and the French Revolution* (New York: Oxford University Press, 1992). Contributors from a variety of disciplines examine the importance of women in the French Revolution, with special attention to the exclusion of women from the new politics.

Dorinda Outram, *The Body of the French Revolution: Sex, Class and Political Culture* (New Haven, CT: Yale University Press, 1989). Examines how images of the body in the late eighteenth century differed from class to class and how bourgeois attitudes toward physicality resulted in a gendered political discourse in which the hero replaced the king.

* Albert Soboul, *The Sans-Culottes* (New York: Anchor, 1972). An exhaustive study of the artisans who composed the core of popular political activism in revolutionary Paris. Soboul examines the political demands and ideology of the *sans-culottes,* as well as the composition, culture, and actions of the popular movement during the revolution.

The Reign of Napoleon

* Louis Bergeron, *France Under Napoleon* (Princeton, NJ: Princeton University Press, 1981). An analysis of the structure of Napoleon's regime, its social bases of support and its opponents.

* Felix Markham, *Napoleon* (New York: New American Library, 1963). This classic study treats both Napoleon's life and legend while giving a balanced account of the social and intellectual life of the period and the impact of the Napoleonic Empire on Europe.

Jean Tulard, *Napoleon: The Myth of the Saviour* (London: Weidenfeld and Nicolson, 1984). This biography of Napoleon situates his rise to power within the crisis of legitimacy created by the destruction of the monarchy during the revolution. The Napoleonic Empire is presented as a creation of the bourgeoisie, who desired to end the revolution and consolidate their gains and control over the lower classes.

*Paperback edition available.

21 ✤ INDUSTRIAL EUROPE

Claude Monet 77

Portrait of an Age

The Normandy train has reached Paris. The coast and the capital are once again connected. Passengers in their city finery disembark and are greeted by others who have awaited their scheduled arrival. Workmen stand ready to unload freight, porters to carry luggage. Steam billows forth from the resting engine, which is the object of all human activity. The engine stares at us as enigmatically as any character in a Renaissance portrait. We hardly think to ask what lies behind the round black face with its headlight for an eye and its chimney for a snout. Yet the train that has arrived in *La Gare Saint-Lazarre* by Claude Monet (1840–1926) is as much the central character in this portrait of the industrial age as was any individual in portraits of ages past.

The train's iron bulk dwarfs the people around it. Indeed, iron dominates our attention. Tons of it are in view. The rails, the lampposts, the massive frame of the station, no less than the train itself, are all formed from iron—pliable, durable, inexpensive iron—the miracle product of industrialization. The iron station with its glass panels became as central a feature of nineteenth-century cities as stone cathedrals were in the Middle Ages. Railway stations changed the shape of urban settings, just as railway travel changed the lives of millions of people.

There had never been anything like it before. Ancient Romans had hitched four horses to their chariots; nineteenth-century Europeans hitched four horses to their stage-coaches. The technology of overland transportation had hardly changed in two thousand years. Coach journeys were long, uncomfortable, and expensive. They were governed by the elements and the muddy, rutted roads, which caused injuries to humans and horses with alarming regularity. First-class passengers rode inside, where they were jostled against one another and breathed the dust that the horses kicked up in front of them. Second-class passengers rode on top, braving the elements and risking life and limb in an accident.

Railway travel was a quantum leap forward. It was faster, cheaper, and safer. Overnight it changed conceptions of time, space, and, above all, speed. People could journey to what once were distant places in a single day. Voyages became trips, and the travel holiday was born. Commerce was transformed, as was the way in which it was conducted. Large quantities of goods could be shipped quickly from place to place; orders could be instantly filled. The whole notion of locality changed, as salesmen could board a morning train for what only recently had been an unreachable market. Branch offices could be

overseen by regional directors, services and products could be standardized, and the gap between great and small cities and between town and countryside could be narrowed. Wherever they went, the railroads created links that had never been forged before. In Britain the railroad schedule became the source of the creation of official time. Trains that left London were scheduled to arrive at their destinations according to London time, which came to be kept at the royal observatory in Greenwich. Trains carried fresh fish inland from the coasts and fresh vegetables from rural farms to city tables. Mail moved farther and more quickly; news spread more evenly. Fashionable ideas from the capital cities of Europe circulated everywhere, as did new knowledge and discoveries. The railroads brought both diversity and uniformity.

They also brought wonderment. The engine seemed to propel itself with unimaginable power and at breathtaking speed. The English actress Fanny Kemble (1809–93) captured the sensation memorably: "You can't imagine how strange it seemed to be journeying on thus, without any visible cause of progress other than the magical machine, with its flying white breath and rhythmical, unvarying pace. I felt no fairy tale was ever half so wonderful as what I saw." For many the railroad symbolized the genius of the age in which they were living, an age in which invention, novelty, and progress were everywhere to be seen. It combined the great innovations of steam, coal, and iron that were transforming nearly

every aspect of ordinary life. But for others, the railway was just as centrally a symbol of disquiet, of the passing of a way of life that was easier to understand and to control. "Seated in the old mail-coach we needed no evidence out of ourselves to indicate the velocity," wrote the English author Thomas De Quincey (1785–1859) in his obituary for the passing of horse travel. "We heard our speed, we saw it, we felt it. This speed was not the product of blind, insensate agencies, that had no sympathy to give, but was incarnated in the fiery eyeballs of the noblest among brutes."

The fruits of the railways, like the fruits of industrialization, were not all sweet. As the nineteenth century progressed, there could be no doubt that, year by year, one way of life was being replaced by another. More and more laborers were leaving the farms for the factories; more and more products were being made by machines. Everywhere there was change, but it was not always or everywhere for the better. Millions of people poured into cities that mushroomed up without plan or intention. Population growth, factory labor, and ultimately the grinding poverty that they produced overwhelmed traditional means of social control. Families and communities split apart; the expectations of ordinary people were no longer predictable. Life was spinning out of control for individuals, groups, and even whole societies. It was an engine racing down a track that only occasionally ended as placidly as did the Normandy train at the Gare Saint-Lazarre.

The Traditional Economy

The curse of Adam and Eve was that they would earn their daily bread by the sweat of their brows. For generation after generation, age after age, economic life was dominated by toil. Man, woman, and child labored to secure their supply of food against the caprice of nature. There was nothing even vaguely romantic about the backbreaking exertion needed to crack open the hard ground, plant seeds in it, and protect the crops from the ravages of insects, birds, and animals long enough to be harvested. Every activity was labor intensive. Wood for shelter or fuel was chopped with thick, blunt axes. Water was drawn from deep wells by the long, slow turn of a crank or dragged in buckets from the nearest stream. Everything that was consumed was pulled or pushed or lifted. French women carried soil and water up steep terraces in journeys that could take as long as seven hours. "The women seemed from their persons and features to be harder worked than horses," Arthur Young (1741–1820), the English agricultural expert, observed with a combination of admiration and disgust. The capital that was invested in the traditional economy was human capital, and by the middle of the eighteenth century nearly eight out of every ten Europeans still tilled the soil, earning their bread by the sweat of their brow.

Although the traditional economy was dominated by agriculture, an increasing amount of labor was devoted to manufacture. The development of a secure and expanding overseas trade created a worldwide demand for consumer goods. In the countryside, small domestic textile industries grew up. Families would take in wool for spinning and weaving to supplement their income from agriculture. When times were good, they would expend proportionately less effort in manufacturing; when times were bad, they would expend more. Their tasks were set by an entrepreneur who provided raw materials and paid the workers by the piece. Wages paid to rural workers were lower than those paid to urban laborers because they were not subject to guild restrictions and because they supplemented farm income. Thus entrepreneurs could profit from lower costs, although they had to bear the risk that the goods produced in this fashion would be of lesser quality or that markets would dry up in the interval. Although domestic industry increased the supply of manufactured commodities, it demanded even more labor from an already overworked sector of the traditional economy.

Throughout the traditional economy, the limits on progress were set by nature. Good harvests brought prosperity, bad harvests despair. Over the long run, the traditional economy ran in all-too-predictable cycles. Sadly, the adage "Eat, drink, and be merry, for tomorrow we may die," was good advice. Prosperity was sure to bring misery in its train. The good fortune of one generation was the hard luck of the next, as more people competed for a relatively fixed quantity of food. No amount of sweat and muscle and, as yet, ingenuity could rescue the traditional economy from its pendulum swings of boom and bust.

By the eighteenth century, the process that would ultimately transform the traditional economy was already under way. It began with the agricultural revolution, one of the great turning points in human history. Before it occurred, the life of every community and of every citizen was always held hostage to nature. The struggle to secure an adequate food supply was the dominant fact of life to which nearly all productive labor was dedicated. After the agricultural revolution, an inadequate food supply was a political rather than an economic fact of life. Fewer and fewer farmers were required to feed more and more people. In Britain, where nearly 70 percent of the population was engaged in agriculture at the end of the seventeenth century, fewer than 2 percent now work on farms. By the middle of the nineteenth century, the most advanced economies were capable of producing vast surpluses of basic commodities. The agricultural revolution was not an event, and it did not happen suddenly. It would not deserve the label "revolution" at all were it not for its momentous consequences: Europe's escape from the shackles of the traditional economy.

Farming Families

Over most of Europe, agricultural activity in the eighteenth century followed methods of crop rotation that had been in place for over a thousand years. Fields were divided into strips of land, and each family "owned" a certain number of strips, which they cultivated for their livelihood. Between one-half and one-third of village land lay fallow each year so that its nutrients could be restored. Open-field farming, as this system was called, was communal rather than individual. Decisions about which crops to grow in the productive fields, where animals would be pastured, or how much wood could be cut from the common wastes affected everyone. Moreover, many activities, such as plowing, gleaning, and manuring, could not conveniently observe the distinctions of ownership of separate strips. Nor, given the realities of nature, could individual families be self-sustaining without the services of a village tanner or milk-

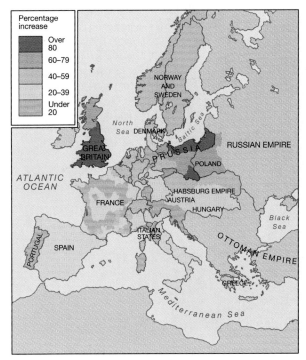

Population Growth in Europe, 1800–1850

and kind, could take as much as half of each year's output, while demands from the state and the Church might absorb another quarter. The surplus wealth produced by the European peasantry, whether free or unfree, was extracted by their lords.

This is not to say that European peasants were uninterested in bettering their immediate economic circumstances or that they obstructed agricultural change. Agriculture was a profoundly conservative occupation, for the risk of experimentation was nothing less than survival. Lords and peasants both practiced defensive innovation, introducing change only after its practical benefits were easily demonstrable. For example, in the mid-seventeenth century two French provincial parlements banned the cultivation of potatoes in the mistaken belief that they caused leprosy. Yet both potatoes and corn became peasant crops and spread rapidly throughout southern Europe, not least because as new commodities they were untaxed. Peasants bartered their surplus, hoarded their profits, and took what few advantages they could out of a system in which the deck was stacked against them.

As the European population entered a new cycle of growth in the second quarter of the eighteenth century, the traditional economy began to increase agricultural productivity in traditional ways. In the east, new lands were colonized and slowly brought under cultivation. Frederick the Great welcomed immigrants to Prussia, where land was plentiful, if not very fertile. In settled communities, less productive land, which had provided fodder for animals at the end of the seventeenth century, now had to provide food for humans. Scrubland was cleared and hillsides terraced. Dry ground was irrigated manually by women and children working in bucket brigades. As always, an increase in population initially meant an increase in productivity. For a time, more able-bodied workers produced more food. In the half century that ended in the 1770s, French peasants increased agricultural production by nearly 60 percent. The intensification of traditional methods rather than innovation accounted for the increase. The number of strips held by each family declined, but each strip was more carefully cultivated.

By the end of the eighteenth century, the European population was reaching the point at which another check on its growth might be expected. Between 1700 and 1800, total European population had increased by nearly 50 percent, and the rate of growth was continuing to accelerate. This vast expansion of rural population placed a grave strain on agricultural production. Decade by decade, more families attempted to eke out an existence from the same amount of land. The gains

maid or hog minder drawn from the closely intertwined group of kin and neighbors that constituted the community. Communal agriculture was effective, but it also limited the number of people that could survive on the produce from a given amount of land.

There were a number of reasons why this pattern of agricultural production remained unchanged century after century. In the first place, there was little incentive for the peasantry to change it. Although they worked hard to ensure their subsistence, they had little desire to create a surplus. For one thing, almost every commodity produced in the village was perishable, and unless it could be consumed or converted at market into durable goods or cash it was largely worthless. For another thing, peasants owed much of their productivity—in one form or another—to their lords. In eastern Europe, serfdom tied the peasantry to the land, where they were used as laborers for the production of foodstuffs for export. Peasants in central Europe were still obligated to perform labor service for their lords, though in parts of Germany in the eighteenth century this obligation was being commuted to money rents. In France and Scandinavia peasants "owned" much of their land in the sense that within the constraints imposed by the village, they could cultivate it as they saw fit and bequeath it to their heirs. But they paid dearly for these rights. Manorial taxes, in both money

Linen production is the subject of an engraving from Nuremberg by Franz Philipp Florin, 1705. The flax stems were soaked to soften the tough outer fibers, which were then removed by beating. The inner fibers were spun into linen on hand looms.

made by intensive cultivation were now lost to over-population. In areas that practiced partible inheritance, farms were subdivided into units too small to provide subsistence. Competition for these "morsels" of land, as the French called them, was intense. Older sons bought out younger brothers; better-off families purchased whatever came on the market to prevent their children from slipping into poverty. Even in areas in which primogeniture was the rule, portions for younger sons and daughters ate into the meager inheritance of the eldest son. Over much of Europe, it was becoming increasingly difficult to live by bread alone.

Rural Manufacture

The crisis of overpopulation meant that not only were there more mouths to feed, there were more bodies to clothe. This increased the need for spun and woven cloth, and thus for spinners and weavers. Traditionally, commercial cloth production was the work of urban artisans, but the expansion of the marketplace and the introduction of new fabrics, especially cotton and silk, had eroded the monopoly of most of the clothing guilds. Merchants could sell as much finished product as they could find, and the teeming rural population provided a tempting pool of inexpensive labor for anyone willing to risk the capital to purchase raw materials. Initially, farming families took manufacturing work into their homes to supplement their income. Spinning

and weaving were the most common occupations, and they were treated as occasional work, reserved for the slow times in the agricultural cycle. This was known as cottage industry. It was supplementary employment, less important and less valuable than the vital agricultural labor that all members of the family undertook.

But by the middle of the eighteenth century, cottage industry was developing in a new direction. As landholdings grew smaller, even good harvests did not promise subsistence to many families. This oversupply of labor was soon organized into the putting-out system, which mobilized the resources of the rural labor force for commercial production of large quantities of manufactured goods. The characteristics of the putting-out system were similar throughout Europe, whether it was undertaken by individual entrepreneurs or lords of the manor, or even sponsored by the state. The process began with the capital of the entrepreneur, which was used to purchase raw materials. These materials were "put out" to the homes of workers where the manufacture, most commonly spinning or weaving, took place. The finished goods were returned to the entrepreneur, who sold them at a profit, with which he bought raw materials to begin the process anew.

The simplicity of the putting-out system was one of its most valuable features. All of its essential elements were already present in rural communities. The small nest egg of a prosperous farmer or small trader was all the money needed to make the first purchase of raw materials. These raw materials could be put out to his kin or closest neighbors and the finished goods then delivered to market along with surplus crops. Not only could a small amount of cash begin the cycle of putting-out, but that capital continued to circulate to keep the process in motion.

The small scale of the initial enterprise can be seen in the fact that many entrepreneurs had themselves begun as workers. In Bohemia, for example, some of the largest putting-out operations were run by serfs who paid their lords fees for the right to engage in trade. At the end of the eighteenth century, there were over a quarter-million spinners in the Bohemian linen industry alone, most of them organized into small groups around a single entrepreneur, though one monastery employed over 650 women spinners. Putting-out also required only a low level of skill and common, inexpensive tools. Rural families did their own spinning and rural villages their own weaving. Thus, putting-out demanded little investment, either in plant, equipment, or education. Nor did it inevitably disrupt traditional gender-based tasks in the family economy. In most places spinning was women's work, weaving was done by men, and children helped at whichever task was under way. In fact, certain occu-

pations, like lacemaking in France, were so gender-based that men would not even act as entrepreneurs. In Austria, lacemaking was considered less honorable than other forms of clothmaking because of its association with women and household-based production. Performed at home, rural manufacture remained a traditional family-oriented occupation.

Because this form of manufacturing began as supplementary work, rural laborers were willing to accept low wages. In urban areas, guild restrictions regulated the number of laborers and ensured that they were paid a living wage. Lower labor costs were probably a necessary condition for the success of domestic-based manufacturing. It was vital that the finished goods could be readily sold at market, for it was that sale that allowed the purchase of more raw material. If the entrepreneur could not dispose of his product, his network of workers collapsed. On the other hand, piecework provided farmers with the cushion they needed to survive too-small harvests or too-small plots of land. In the Swiss highlands during the late eighteenth century, farmers prospered on farms one-eighth the size of those tilled by their grandfathers. But more of their time was now occupied in cloth production than in agriculture. As long as rural manufacture supplemented

This charcoal sketch shows an eighteenth-century cottage industry. The entire family participates in the preparation of the flax. Another cottager will weave the thread into linen cloth.

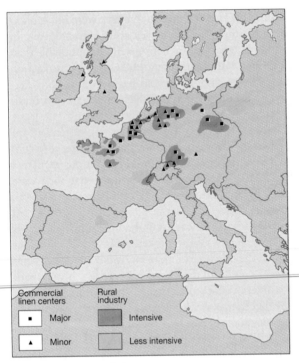

The European Linen Industry

agricultural income, it was seen as a benefit for everyone involved—the entrepreneur, the individual worker, and the village community.

Gradually, the putting-out system came to dominate the lives of many rural families. From small networks of isolated villages, domestic manufacture grew to cover entire regions. Perhaps as many as one-quarter of the inhabitants of the Irish province of Ulster were engaged in manufacturing linen by the end of the eighteenth century. Spinning and weaving became full-time occupations for families that kept no more than a small garden. But without agricultural earnings, piecework rates became starvation wages, and families unable to purchase their subsistence were forced to rely upon loans from the entrepreneurs who set them at work. Long hours in dank cottages performing endlessly repetitive tasks became the lot of millions of rural inhabitants, and their numbers increased annually. While the sons of farmers waited to inherit land before they formed their families, the sons of cottage weavers needed only a loom to begin theirs. They could afford to marry younger and to have more children, for children could contribute to manufacturing from an early age.

Consequently, the expansion of the putting-out system, like the expansion of traditional agriculture, fueled the continued growth of population. Like tradi-

tional agriculture, putting-out contained a number of structural inefficiencies. Both entrepreneur and worker were potential victims of unscrupulousness. Embezzlement of raw materials was a problem for the entrepreneur, arbitrary wage cuts for the laborers. Because the tasks were performed at home, the entrepreneur could not supervise the work. Most disputes in domestic manufacturing arose over specifications of quality. Workers would not receive full pay for poorly produced goods that could not be sold for full value. Inexperienced, aged, or infirm workers could easily spoil costly raw materials. One Bohemian nobleman created village spinning rooms on his estates so that young girls could be given four weeks of training before they set up on their own. Finally, the putting-out system was labor- rather than capital-intensive. As long as there were ready hands to employ, there was little incentive to seek better methods or more efficient techniques.

The Agricultural Revolution

The continued growth of Europe's population necessitated an expansion of agricultural output. In most places this was achieved by intensifying traditional practices, bringing more land into production and more labor to work the land. But in the most advanced European economies, first in Holland and then in England, traditional agriculture underwent a long but dynamic transformation, an agricultural revolution. It was a revolution of technique rather than technology. Humans were not replaced by machines nor were new forms of energy substituted for human and animal muscle. Indeed, many of the methods that were to increase crop yields had been known for centuries and practiced during periods of population pressure. But they had never been practiced as systematically as they came to be from the seventeenth century onward, and they were never combined with a commercial attitude toward farming. It was the willingness and ability of owners to invest capital in their land that transformed subsistence farming into commercial agriculture.

As long as farming was practiced in open fields, there was little incentive for individual landowners to invest in improvements to their scattered strips. While the community as a whole could enclose a small field or plant some fodder crops for the animals, its ability to change traditional practice was limited. In farming villages, even the smallest landholder had rights in common lands, which were jealously guarded. Rights in commons meant a place in the community itself. Commercial agriculture was more suited to large rather than

Surveyors measure a field for land enclosure. The enclosure movement eliminated large areas of what had formerly been communal land.

small estates and was more successful when the land could be utilized in response to market conditions rather than the necessities of subsistence.

The consolidation of estates and the enclosure of fields was thus the initial step toward change. This was a long-term process that took many forms. In England, where it was to become most advanced, enclosure was already under way in the sixteenth century. Prosperous families had long been consolidating their strips in the open fields, and at some point the lord of the manor and the members of the community agreed to carve up the common fields and make the necessary exchanges to consolidate everyone's lands. Perhaps as much as three-quarters of the arable land in England was enclosed by agreement before 1760. Enclosure by agreement did not mean that the breakup of the open-field community was necessarily a harmonious process. Riots preceding or following agreed enclosures were not uncommon.

Paradoxically, it was the middling rather than the poorest villagers who had the most to lose. The breakup of the commons initially gave the poor more arable land from which to eke out their subsistence, and few of them could afford to sacrifice present gain for future loss. These smallholders were quickly bought out. It was the middle-size holders who were squeezed hardest. Although prosperous in communal farming, these families did not have access to the capital necessary to make agricultural improvements such as con-

verting grass to grain land or purchasing large amounts of fertilizer. They could not compete in producing for the market, and gradually they, too, disappeared from the enclosed village. Their opposition to enclosure by agreement led, in the eighteenth century, to enclosure by act of Parliament. Parliamentary enclosure was legislated by government, a government composed for the most part of large landowners. A commission would view the community's lands and divide them, usually by a prescribed formula. Between 1760 and 1815, over one-and-a-half million acres of farmland were enclosed by act of Parliament. During the late eighteenth century, the Prussian and French governments emulated this practice by ordering large tracts of land enclosed.

The enclosure of millions of acres of land was one of the largest expenses of the new commercial agriculture. Hedging or fencing off the land and plowing up the commons required extra labor beyond that necessary for basic agrarian activities. Thus many who sold the small estates that they received on the breakup of the commons remained in villages as agricultural laborers or leaseholders. But now they practiced a different form of farming. More and more agricultural activity became market-oriented. Single crops were sown in large enclosed fields and exchanged at market for the mixture of goods that previously had been grown in the village. Market production turned attention from producing a balance of commodities to increasing the yield of a single one.

The first innovation was the widespread cultivation of fodder crops such as clover and turnips. Crops like clover restore nutrients to the soil as they grow, shortening the period in which land has to lie fallow. Moreover, farm animals grazing on clover or feeding on turnips return more manure to the land, further increasing its productivity. Turnip cultivation had begun in Holland and was brought to England in the sixteenth century. But it was not until the late seventeenth century that Viscount Charles "Turnip" Townsend (1675–1738) made turnip cultivation popular. Townsend and other large Norfolk landowners developed a new system of planting known as the four-crop rotation, in which wheat, turnips, barley, and clover succeeded one another. This method kept the land in productive use, and both the turnip and clover crops were used to feed larger herds of animals.

The ability of farmers to increase their livestock was as important as their ability to grow more grain. Not only were horses and oxen more productive than humans—a horse could perform seven times the labor of a man while consuming only five times the food—but the animals also refertilized the land as they worked. Light fertilization of a single acre of arable land required an average of 25,000 pounds of manure. But animals competed with humans for food, especially during the winter months when little grazing was possible. To conserve grain for human consumption, lambs were led to the slaughter and the fatted calf was killed in the autumn. Thus the development of the technique of meadow floating was a remarkable breakthrough. By flooding low-lying land near streams in the winter, English and Dutch farmers could prevent the ground from freezing during their generally mild winters. When the water was drained, the land beneath it would produce an early grass crop on which the beasts could graze. This meant that more animals could be kept alive during the winter.

The relationship between animal husbandry and grain growing became another feature of commercial agriculture. In many areas farmers could choose between growing grain and pasturing animals. When prices for wool or meat were relatively higher than those for grain, fields could be left in grass for grazing. When grain prices rose, the same fields could be plowed. Consolidated enclosed estates made this convertible husbandry possible. The decision to hire fieldworkers or shepherds could be taken only by large agricultural employers. Whatever the relative price of grain, the open-field village continued to produce grain as its primary crop. Farmers who could convert their

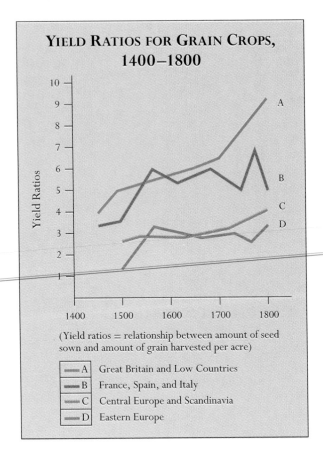

YIELD RATIOS FOR GRAIN CROPS, 1400–1800

(Yield ratios = relationship between amount of seed sown and amount of grain harvested per acre)

A	Great Britain and Low Countries
B	France, Spain, and Italy
C	Central Europe and Scandinavia
D	Eastern Europe

production in tune to the market could not only maximize their profits, they could also prevent shortages of raw materials for domestic manufacturers or of foodstuffs for urban and rural workers.

Convertible husbandry was but the first step in the development of a true system of regional specialization in agriculture. Different soils and climates favored different use of the land. In southern and eastern England the soil was thin and easily depleted by grain growing. Traditionally, these light soil areas had been used almost exclusively for sheep rearing. On the other hand, the clay soils of central England, though poorly drained and hard to work, were more suited to grain growing. The new agricultural techniques reversed the pattern. The introduction of fodder crops and increased fertilization rejuvenated thin soils, and southeastern England became the nation's breadbasket. Large enclosed estates provided a surplus of grain throughout the eighteenth century. By the 1760s, England was exporting enough grain to feed over half a million people. Similarly, the midland clays became the location of great sheep runs and cattle herds. Experiments in herd management, crossbreeding, and fattening all resulted in increased production of wool, milk, meat, leather, soap, and tallow for candles.

There can be no doubt about the benefits of the transformation of agricultural practices that began in Holland and England in the seventeenth century and spread slowly to all corners of the Continent over the next two hundred years. Millions more mouths were fed at lower cost than ever before. In 1700 each person engaged in farming in England produced enough food for 1.7 people; in 1800 each produced enough for 2.5. Cheaper food allowed more discretionary spending, which fueled the demand for consumer goods, which in turn employed more rural manufacturers. But there are no benefits without costs. The transformation of agriculture was also a transformation in a way of life. The open-field village was a community; the enclosed estate was a business. The plight of the rural poor was tragic enough in villages of kin and neighbors, where face-to-face charity might be returned from one generation to the next. With their scrap of land and their common rights, even the poorest villagers laid claim to a place of their own. But as landless laborers, either on farms or in rural manufacturing, they could no longer make that claim. They would soon be fodder for the factories, the "dark satanic mills" that came to disfigure the land once tilled in open-field villages. For the destitute, charity was now visited upon them in anonymous parish workhouses or in the good works of the comfortable middle class. In all of these ways the agricultural revolution changed the face of Europe.

The Industrial Revolution in Britain

Like the changes in agriculture, the changes in manufacturing that began in Britain during the eighteenth century were more revolutionary in consequence than in development. But their consequences were revolutionary indeed. A work force that was predominantly agricultural in 1750 had become predominantly industrial a century later. A population that for centuries had centered on the south and east was now concentrated in the north and west. Liverpool, Manchester, Glasgow, and Birmingham mushroomed into giant cities. While the population of England grew by 100 percent between 1801 and 1851, from about 8.5 million people to over 17 million, the populations of Liverpool and Manchester grew by over 1000 percent.

It was the replacement of animal muscle by hydraulic and mineral energy that made this continued population growth possible. Water and coal drove machinery that dramatically increased human productivity. In 1812, one woman could spin as much thread as two hundred women had in 1770. What was most revolutionary about the Industrial Revolution was the wave after wave of technological innovation, a constant tinkering and improving of the ways in which things were made, which could have the simultaneous effects of cutting costs and improving quality. It was not just the great breakthrough inventions like the steam engine, the smelting of iron with coke, and the spinning jenny that were important, but also the hundreds of adjustments in technique that applied new ideas in one industry to another, opened bottlenecks, and solved problems. Ingenuity rather than genius was at the root of the Industrial Revolution in Britain.

The Industrial Revolution was a sustained period of economic growth and change brought about by the application of mineral energy and technological innovations to the process of manufacturing. It took place during the century between 1750 and 1850, though different industries moved at different paces and sustained economic growth continued in Britain until the First World War. It is difficult to define the timing of the Industrial Revolution with any great precision because, unlike a political event, an economic transformation does not happen all at once. Nor are new systems and inventions ever really new. Coal miners had been using rails and wheeled carriages to move ore since the seventeenth century. In the sixteenth century, "Jack of Newbury" had housed his cloth workers in a large shed. The one was the precursor of the railroad and the other the precursor of the factory, but each preceded the Industrial Revolution by more than a century. Before 1750, innovations made their way slowly into general use, and after 1850 the pace of growth slowed appreciably. By then, Britain had a manufacturing economy: fewer than one-quarter of its labor force engaged in agriculture and nearly 60 percent were involved in industry, trade, and transport.

Britain First

The Industrial Revolution occurred first in Britain, but even in Britain industrialization was a regional rather than a national phenomenon. There were many areas of Britain that remained untouched by innovations in manufacturing methods and agricultural techniques, though no one remained unaffected by the prosperity that industrialization brought. This was the result of both national conditions and historical developments. When industrialization spread to the Continent, it took hold—as it had in Britain—in regions where mineral resources were abundant or where domestic manufacturing was a traditional activity. There was no single model for European industrialization, however often contemporaries looked toward Britain for the key to unlock the power of economic growth. There was as much technological innovation in France, as much capital for investment in Holland. Belgium was rich in coal, while eastern Europe enjoyed an agricultural surplus that sustained an increase in population. The finest cotton in the world was made in India; the best iron was made in Sweden. Each of these factors was in some way a precondition for industrialization, but none by itself proved sufficient. Only in Britain did these circumstances meld together.

Among Britain's blessings, water was foremost. Water was its best defense, protecting the island from foreign invasion and making it unnecessary to invest in a costly standing army. Rather, Britain invested heavily in its navy to maintain its commercial preeminence around the globe. The navy protected British interests in times of war and transported British wares in times of peace. Britain's position in the Asian trade made it the leading importer of cottons, ceramics, and teas. Its

colonies, especially in North America, not only provided sugar and tobacco, but also formed a rich market for British manufacturing.

But the commercial advantages that water brought were not confined to oceanic trade. Britain was favored by an internal water system that tied inland communities together. In the eighteenth century, no place in Britain was more than 70 miles from the sea or more than 30 miles from a navigable river. Water transport was far cheaper than hauling goods overland; a packhorse could carry 250 pounds of goods on its back but could move 100,000 pounds by walking alongside a river and pulling a barge. Small wonder that river transport was one of the principal interests of merchants and traders. Beginning in the 1760s, private concerns began to invest in the construction of canals, first to move coal from inland locations to major arteries and then to connect the great rivers themselves. Over the next fifty years several hundred miles of canals were built by authority of Navigation Acts, which allowed for the sale of shares to raise capital. In 1760 the Duke of Bridgewater (1736–1803) lived up to his name by completing the first great canal. It brought coal to Manchester and ultimately to Liverpool. It cost more than £250,000 and took fourteen years of labor to build, but it repaid the duke and his investors many times over by bringing an uneconomical coal field into

The Worsley-Manchester Canal, as shown in Arthur Young's Six Months' Tour Through the North of England, *1770. This view shows the mouth of the subterranean tunnel at Worsley, where the canal was driven underground to a coal mine. The crane was used to hoist blocks of stone onto canal boats.*

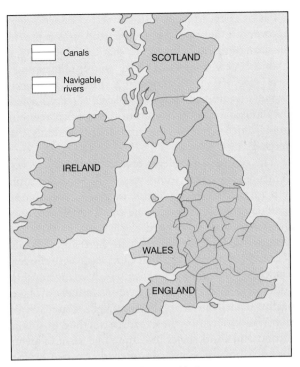

Great Britain—Canals and Navigable Rivers

Over the course of years, Britain had developed an infrastructure for economic advancement. The transformation of domestic handicrafts to industrial production depended as much on the abilities of merchants as on those of manufacturers. The markets for domestic manufacturing had largely been overseas, where British merchants built up relationships over generations. Export markets were vital to the success of industrialization as production grew dynamically and most ventures needed a quick turnaround of sales to reinvest their profits in continued growth. The flexibility of English trading houses would be seen in their ability to shift from reexporting eastern and North American goods to exporting British manufactures. Equally important, increased production meant increased demand for raw materials: Swedish bar iron for casting, Egyptian and American cotton for textiles, and Oriental silk for luxuries. The expansion of shipping mirrored the expansion of the economy, tripling during the eighteenth century to over 1 million tons of cargo capacity.

The expansion of shipping, agriculture, and investment in machines, plant, and raw material all required capital. Not only did capital have to exist, but it had to be made productive. Profits in agriculture, especially in the south and east, somehow had to be shifted to investment in industry in the north and west. The

production. Not the least of the beneficiaries were the people of Manchester, where the price of coal was halved.

Coal was the second of Britain's natural blessings on which it improved. Britain's reserves of wood were nearly depleted by the eighteenth century, especially those near centers of population. Coal had been in use as a fuel for several centuries, and the coal trade between London and the northern coal pits had been essential to the growth of the capital. Coal was abundant, much of it almost at surface level along the northeastern coast and easily transported on water. The location of large coalfields along waterways was a vital condition of its early use. As canals and roadways improved, more inland coal was brought into production for domestic use. Yet it was in industry rather than in the home that coal was put to its greatest use. Here again Britain was favored, for large seams of coal were also located near large seams of iron. At first this coincidence was of little consequence, since iron was smelted by charcoal made from wood and iron foundries were located deep in forests. But ultimately ironmakers learned to use coal for fuel, and then the natural economies of having mineral, fuel, and transport in the same vicinity were given full play.

The factors that contributed to Britain's early industrialization were not only those of natural advantage.

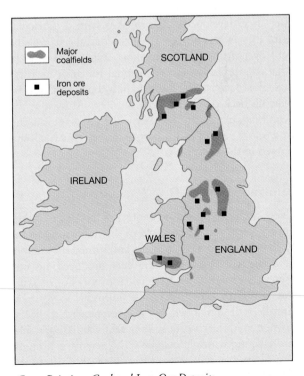

Great Britain—Coal and Iron Ore Deposits

wealth of merchants, which flowed into London, had to be redistributed throughout the economy. More importantly, short-term investments had to give way to long-term financing. At the end of the seventeenth century, the creation of the Bank of England had begun the process of constructing a reliable banking system. The Bank of England dealt almost entirely with government securities, but it also served as a bill broker. It bought the debts of reputable merchants at a discount in exchange for Bank of England notes. Bank of England notes could then be exchanged between merchants, and this increased the liquidity of the English economy, especially in London. It also became the model for provincial banking by the middle of the eighteenth century.

Private family banks also grew in importance in London, handling the accounts of merchants and buying shares in profitable enterprises, of which the canals were a favorite. Regional banks, smaller and less capitalized, began to use these private London banks as correspondents, that is, as extensions of their own banks in the city. This allowed local manufacturers and city merchants to do business with one another. The connections between the regional banks and London facilitated the flow of capital from one section of the nation to the other. In 1700 there were just twelve provincial banks; by 1790 there were nearly three hundred. Banks remained reluctant to invest for the long term, preferring to discount bills for a few months, but after they developed a relationship with a particular firm, they were usually willing to continue to roll the debt over. Although the banking system was vital to large enterprises, in fact the capital for most industry was raised locally, from kin and neighbors, and grew by plowing back profits into the business. At least at the beginning, manufacturers were willing to take risks and to work for small returns to ensure the survival and growth of their business.

Minerals and Metals

There could have been no Industrial Revolution without coal. It was the black gold of the eighteenth century, the fuel that fed the furnaces and turned the engines of industrial expansion. The coal produced by one miner generated as much energy as twenty horses. Coal was the first capital-intensive industry in Britain, already well developed by the seventeenth century. Owners paid the costs of sinking shafts, building roads, and erecting winding machines. Miners were brought to a pit and paid piecework for their labor. Only the very wealthy could afford to invest in coal mining, and

it was by chance that British law vested mineral rights in owners rather than users of the land, as was the case on the Continent. This meant that the largest English coalfields were owned by landed families of means who were able to invest agricultural profits in mining. Britain's traditional elites thus played a crucial role in the industrial transformation of the agrarian economy from which their wealth and social standing had derived.

The technical problems of coal mining grew with demand. As surface seams were exhausted it became necessary to dig deeper shafts, to lower miners farther underground, and to raise the coal greater heights to the surface. Men loosened the coal from the seam; women and children hauled it to the shaft. They also cleared the tons of debris that came loose with the coal. Underground mining was extremely dangerous. In addition to all-too-frequent cave-ins, miners struggled against inadequate ventilation and light. Better ventilation was achieved by the expensive method of sinking second and third shafts into the same seam, allowing for cross breezes. Candles and sparks created by flint wheels addressed the problem of light, though both methods suffered from the disadvantage that most pits contained combustible gases. Even after a fireman walked through the mine exploding gas with a long lighted stick, many miners preferred to work in total darkness, feeling the edges of the seam.

But by far the most difficult mining problem was water. As pits were sunk deeper they reached pools of groundwater, which enlarged as the coal was stripped away from the earth. Dripping water increased the difficulty of hewing, standing water the difficulty of hauling. The pit acted like a riverbed and filled quickly. Water drainage presented the greatest obstacle to deep-shaft mining. Women and children could carry the water out in large skin-lined baskets, which were attached to a winding wheel and pulled up by horses. Primitive pumps, also horse-powered, had been devised for the same purpose. Neither method was efficient or effective when shafts sank deeper. In 1709 Thomas Newcomen (1663–1729) introduced a steam-driven pump that enabled water to be sucked through a pipe directly from the pit bottom to the surface. Although the engine was expensive to build and needed tons of coal to create the steam, it could raise the same amount of water in a day as 2500 humans. Such economies of labor were enormous, and within twenty years of its introduction there were 78 engines draining coal and metal mines in England.

Innovations like Newcomen's engine helped increase output of coal at just the time that it became needed as

Women and children were the cheapest labor force in England during the Industrial Revolution. They were sometimes employed in heavy work such as mining. Here two children are shown being raised to ground level from the mine pit.

an industrial fuel. Between 1700 and 1830, coal production increased tenfold despite the fact that deeper and more difficult seams were being worked. Eventually, the largest demand for coal came from the iron industry. In 1793 just two ironworks consumed as much coal as the entire population of Edinburgh. Like mining coal, making iron was both capital- and labor-intensive, requiring expensive furnaces, water-powered bellows, and mills in which forged iron could be slit into rods or rolled into sheets. Ironmaking depended upon an abundance of wood, for it took the charcoal derived from ten acres of trees to refine one ton of iron ore. After the ore was mined, it was smelted into pig iron, a low-grade, brittle metal. Pig iron was converted to higher-quality bar iron in charcoal-powered forges that burned off some of its impurities. From bar iron came the rods and sheets used in casting household items like pots and nails or in making finer wrought-iron products like plows and armaments. Because each process in the making of iron was separate, furnaces, forges, and mills were located near their own supplies of wood. The shipping of the bulky ore, pig iron, and bar iron added substantially to its cost, and it was

cheaper to import bars from Sweden than to carry them twenty miles overland.

The great innovations in the production of iron came with the development of techniques that allowed for the use of coal rather than wood charcoal in smelting and forging. As early as 1709, Abraham Darby (1678?–1717), a Quaker nail maker, experimented with smelting iron ore with coke, coal from which most of the gas has been burned off. Iron coking greatly reduced the cost of fuel in the first stages of production, but because most ironworks were located in woodlands rather than near coal pits, the method was not widely adopted. Moreover, although coke made from coal was cheaper than charcoal made from wood, coke added its own impurities to the iron ore. Nor could it provide the intense heat needed for smelting without a large bellows. The cost of the bellows offset the savings from the coke until James Watt (1736–1819) invented a new form of steam engine in 1775.

Like most innovations of the Industrial Revolution, Watt's steam engine was an adaptation of existing technology made possible by the sophistication of techniques in a variety of fields. Although James Watt is credited with the invention of the condensing steam engine, one of the seminal creations in human history, the success of his work depended upon the achievements of numerous others. Watt's introduction to the steam engine was accidental. An instrument maker in Glasgow, he was asked to repair a model of a Newcomen engine and immediately realized that it would work more efficiently if there were a separate chamber for the condensation of the steam. Although his idea was sound, Watt spent years attempting to implement it. He was continually frustrated that poor-quality valves and cylinders never fit well enough together to prevent steam from escaping from the engine.

Watt was unable to translate his idea into a practical invention until he became partners with the Birmingham ironmaker and manufacturer Matthew Boulton (1728–1809). At Boulton's works, Watt found craftsmen who could make precision engine valves, and at the foundries of John Wilkinson (1728–1808) he found workers who could bore the cylinders of his engine to exact specifications. Watt's partnership with Boulton and Wilkinson was vital to the success of the steam engine. But Watt himself possessed the qualities necessary to ensure that his ideas were transformed into reality. He persevered through years of unsuccessful experimentation and searched out partners to provide capital and expertise. He saw beyond bare mechanics, realizing the practical utility of his invention long before it was perfected. Watt designed the mechanism to convert the traditional up-and-down motion of the pumping engine into rotary motion, which could be used for machines and ultimately for locomotion.

Watt's engine received its first practical application in the iron industry. Wilkinson became one of the largest customers for steam engines, using them for pumping, moving wheels, and ultimately increasing the power of the blast of air in the forge. Increasing the heat provided by coke in the smelting and forging of iron led to the transformation of the industry. In the 1780s, Henry Cort (1740–1800), a naval contractor, experimented with a technique for using coke as fuel in removing the impurities from pig iron. The iron was melted into puddles and stirred with rods. The gaseous carbon that was brought to the surface burned off, leaving a purer and more malleable iron than even charcoal could produce. Because the iron had been purified in a molten state, Cort reasoned that it could be rolled directly into sheets rather than first made into bars. He erected a rolling mill adjacent to his forge and combined two separate processes into one.

Puddling and rolling had an immediate impact upon iron production. There was no longer any need to use charcoal in the stages of forging and rolling. From mineral to workable sheets, iron could be made entirely with coke. Ironworks moved to the coalfields, where the economies of transporting fuel and finished product were great. Moreover, the distinct stages of production were eliminated. Rather than separate smelting, forging, and finishing industries, one consolidated manufacturing process had been created. Forges, furnaces, and rolling machines were brought together and powered by steam engines. Cort's rolling technique alone increased output 15 times. By 1808, output of pig iron had grown from 68,000 to 250,000 tons and of bar iron from 32,000 to 100,000 tons.

Cotton Is King

Traditionally, British commerce had been dominated by the woolen cloth trade, in which techniques of production had not changed for hundreds of years. Running water was used for cleaning and separating fleece; crude wooden wheels spun the thread; simple hand-looms wove together the long warp threads and the short weft ones. It took nearly four female spinners to provide the materials for one male weaver, the tasks having long been gender-specific. During the course of the seventeenth century, new fabrics appeared on the domestic market, particularly linen, silk, and cotton. It was cotton that captured the imagination of the eighteenth-century consumer, especially brightly colored, finely spun Indian cotton.

Spinning and weaving were organized as domestic industries. Work was done in the home on small, inexpensive machines to supplement the income from farming. Putters-out were especially frustrated by the difficulty in obtaining yarn for weaving in the autumn, when female laborers were needed for the harvest. Even the widespread development of full-time domestic manufacturers did not satisfy the increased demand for cloth. Limited output and variable quality characterized British textile production throughout the early part of the eighteenth century. The breakthrough came with technological innovation. Beginning in the mid-eighteenth century, a series of new machines dramatically increased output and, for the first time, allowed English textiles to compete with Indian imports.

The first innovation was the flying shuttle, invented by John Kay (1704–64) in the 1730s. A series of hammers drove the shuttle, which held the weft, through the stretched warp on the loom. The flying shuttle allowed weavers to work alone rather than in pairs, but it was adopted slowly because it increased the demand for spun thread, which was already in short supply. The

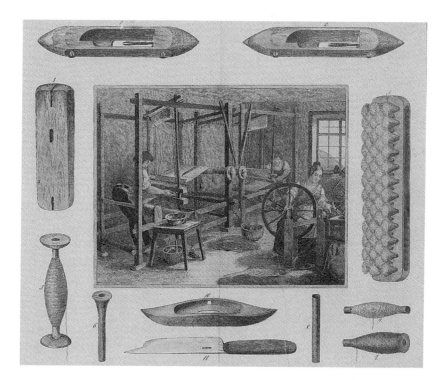

This hand-colored engraving shows the interior of a German weaver's shop around 1850. Two men are weaving at looms and two women are winding bobbins. The scene is bordered with details of tools such as shuttles and quills.

spinning bottleneck was opened by James Hargreaves (d. 1778), who devised a machine known as the jenny. The jenny was a wooden frame containing a number of spindles around which thread was drawn by means of a hand-turned wheel. The first jennies allowed for the spinning of eight threads at once, and improvements brought the number to over one hundred. Jennies replaced spinning wheels by the tens of thousands. The jenny was a crucial breakthrough in redressing the balance between spinning and weaving, though it did not solve all problems. Jenny-spun thread was not strong enough to be used as warp, which continued to be wheel spun. But the jenny could spin cotton in unimaginable quantities.

As is often the case with technological change, one innovation followed another. The problem set by improvements in weaving gave rise to solutions for increasing the output of spinners. The need to provide stronger warp threads posed by the introduction of the jenny was ultimately solved by the development of the water frame. It was created in 1769 by Richard Arkwright (1732–92), whose name was also to be associated with the founding of the modern factory system. Arkwright's frame consisted of a series of water-power-driven rollers that stretched the cotton before spinning. These stronger fibers could be spun into threads suitable for warp, and English manufacturers could finally

produce an all-cotton fabric. It was not long before another innovator realized that the water frame and the jenny could be combined into a single machine, one that would produce an even finer cotton yarn than that made in India. The mule, so named because it was a cross between a frame and a jenny, was invented by Samuel Crompton (1753–1827), who sold its rights for only £60. It was the decisive innovation in cotton production. By 1811, ten times as many threads were being spun on mules as on water frames and jennies combined.

The original mules were small machines that, like the jennies, could be used for domestic manufactures. But increasingly the mule followed the water frame into purposely built factories, where it became larger and more expensive. The need for large rooms to house the equipment and for a ready source of running water to power it provided an incentive for the creation of factories, but secrecy provided a greater one. The original factories were called "safe-boxes," and whether they were established for the manufacture of silk or cotton, their purpose was to protect trade secrets. Innovators took out patents to prevent their inventions from being copied and fought long lawsuits to prevent their machines from being used. Workers were sworn to secrecy about the techniques they were taught. Imitators practiced industrial espionage as sophisticated as

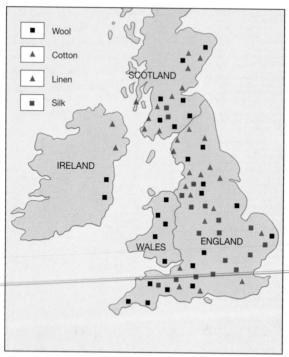

Great Britain—Textile Centers

the age would allow: enticing knowledgeable workers; employing spies; copying inventions. Although the factory was designed to protect secrets, its other benefits were quickly realized. Manufacturers could maintain control over the quality of products through strict supervision of the work force. Moreover, workers in shifts could keep the costly machines in continuous use.

Richard Arkwright constructed the first cotton factories in Britain, all of which were designed to house water frames. The first was established in 1769 at Cromford near Nottingham, which was the center of stocking manufacture. The site was chosen for its isolation, since stockings were an article of fashion in which secrecy was most important. The Cromford mill was a four-story building that ultimately employed over 800 workers. During the next quarter century, Arkwright built over a dozen other mills, most in partnership with wealthy manufacturers. Arkwright's genius lay in industrial management rather than mechanical innovation. As others switched from frames to mules, Arkwright stubbornly stuck to his own invention. When steam power began to replace water, he failed to make the shift. But his methods of constructing and financing factories were undeniably successful. From a modest beginning as a traveling salesman of wigs, Sir Richard

Arkwright died in possession of a fortune worth more than £500,000.

The organization of the cotton industry into factories was one of the pivotal transformations in economic life. Domestic spinning and weaving took place in agricultural villages; factory production took place in mill towns. The location of the factory determined movements of population, and from the first quarter of the eighteenth century onward a great shift toward northeast England was under way. Moreover, the character of the work itself changed. The operation of heavy machinery reversed the traditional gender-based tasks. Mule spinning became men's work, while handloom weaving was taken over by women. The mechanization of weaving took longer than that of spinning, both because of difficulties in perfecting a power loom and because of opposition to its introduction by workers known as Luddites, who organized machine-breaking riots in the 1810s. The Luddites attempted to maintain the traditional organization of their industry and the independence of their labor. For a time, handloom weavers managed to survive by accepting lower and lower piece rates. But their competition was like that of a horse against an automobile. In 1820 there were over 250,000 handloom weavers in Britain; by 1850 the number was less than 50,000. Weaving as well as spinning became factory work.

The transformation of cotton manufacture had a profound effect on the overall growth of the British economy. It increased shipping because the raw material had to be imported, first from the Mediterranean and then from America. American cotton—especially after 1794, when American inventor Eli Whitney (1765–1825) patented his cotton gin—fed a nearly insatiable demand. In 1750 Britain imported less than 5 million pounds of raw cotton; a century later the volume had grown to 588 million pounds. And to each pound of raw cotton, British manufacturers added the value of their technology and their labor. By the midnineteenth century, nearly half a million people earned their living from cotton, which alone accounted for over 40 percent of the value of all British exports. Cotton was undeniably the king of manufactured goods.

The Iron Horse

The first stage of the Industrial Revolution in Britain was driven by the production of consumer goods. Pottery, cast-iron tools, clocks, toys, and textiles, especially cottons—all were manufactured in quantities unknown in the early eighteenth century. These prod-

THE WEALTH OF BRITAIN

❧

Cotton was the first of the new industries that led to British economic domination in the nineteenth century. In producing cotton, new inventions like the spinning jenny and the water frame revolutionized manufacture and the factory system was born. Britain's domination of cotton production impressed contemporaries. In this excerpt, a contemporary tries to explain why Britain took the lead in industrialization.

In comparing the advantages of England for manufactures with those of other countries, we can by no means overlook the excellent commercial position of the country—intermediate between the north and south of Europe; and its insular situation, which, combined with the command of the seas, secures our territory from invasion or annoyance. The German ocean, the Baltic, and the Mediterranean are the regular highways for our ships; and our western ports command an unobstructed passage to the Atlantic, and to every quarter of the world.

A temperate climate, and a hardy race of men, have also greatly contributed to promote the manufacturing industry of England.

The political and moral advantages of this country, as a seat of manufactures, are not less remarkable than its physical advantages. The arts are the daughters of peace and liberty. In no country have these blessings been enjoyed in so high a degree, or for so long a continuance, as in England. Under the reign of just laws, personal liberty and property have been secure; mercantile enterprise has been allowed to reap its reward; capital has accumulated in safety; the workman has "gone forth to his work and to his labour until the evening;" and, thus protected and favoured, the manufacturing prosperity of the country has struck its roots deep, and spread forth its branches to the ends of the earth.

England has also gained by the calamities of other countries, and the intolerance of other governments. At different periods, the Flemish and French protestants, expelled from their native lands, have taken refuge in England, and have repaid the protection given them by practising and teaching branches of industry, in which the English were then less expert than their neighbours.

From Edward Baines, *The History of the Cotton Manufactures in Great Britain* (1835).

---

ucts fed a ravenous market at home and abroad. The greatest complaint of industrialists was that they could not get enough raw materials or fuel, nor could they ship their finished products fast enough to keep up with demand. Transportation was becoming a serious stumbling block to continued economic growth. Even with the completion of the canal network that linked the major rivers and improvement in highways and tollways, raw materials and finished goods moved slowly and uncertainly. It was said that it took as long to ship goods from Manchester to Liverpool on the Duke of Bridgewater's canal as it did to sail from New York to Liverpool on the Atlantic Ocean. Furthermore, once the canals had a monopoly on bulk cargo, transportation costs began to rise.

It was the need to ship increasing amounts of coal to foundries and factories that provided the spur for the development of a new form of transportation. Ever since the seventeenth century, coal had been moved from the seam to the pit on rails, first constructed of wood and later of iron. Broad-wheeled carts hitched to horses were as much dragged as rolled, but this still represented the most efficient form of hauling, and these railways ultimately ran from the seam to the dock. By 1800 there was perhaps as much as three hundred miles of iron rail in British mines.

In the same year, Watt's patent on the steam engine expired, and inventors began to apply the engine to a variety of mechanical tasks. Richard Trevithick (1771–1833), whose father managed a tin mine in Cornwall, was the first to experiment with a steam-driven carriage. George Stephenson (1781–1848), who is generally recognized as the father of the modern railroad, made two crucial improvements. In mine railways the wheels of the cart were smooth and the rail was grooved. Stephenson reversed this construction to provide better traction and less wear. Perhaps more importantly, Stephenson made the vital improvement in engine power by increasing the steam pressure in the boiler and exhausting the smoke through a chimney. In 1829 he won a £500 prize with his engine "The Rocket," which pulled a load three times its own weight at a speed of 30 miles per hour and could actually outrun a horse.

In 1830 the first modern railway, the Manchester-to-Liverpool line, was opened. Like the Duke of Bridgewater's canal, it was designed to move coal and bulk goods, but surprisingly its most important function came to be moving people. In its first year, the Manchester-Liverpool line carried over 400,000 passengers, which generated double the revenue derived from freight. The railway was quicker, more comfortable, and ultimately cheaper than the coach. Investors in the Manchester-Liverpool line, who pocketed a comfortable 9.5 percent when government securities were paying 3.5 percent, learned quickly that links between population centers were as important as those between industrial sites. The London-to-Birmingham and London-to-Bristol lines were both designed with passenger traffic in mind.

Railway building was one of the great boom activities of British industrialization. Since it came toward the end of the mechanization of factories, investors and industrialists were psychologically prepared for the benefits of technological innovation. By 1835 Parliament had passed 54 separate acts to establish over 750 miles of railways. Ten years later, over 6000 miles had been sanctioned and over 2500 miles built; by 1852 over 7500 miles of track were in use. The railways were built on the model of the canals. Private bills passed through Parliament, which allowed a company to raise money through the sale of stock. Most railways were trunk lines, connecting one town to another or joining two longer lines together. They were run by small companies, and few ultimately proved profitable. Only because of the dominant influence of George Stephenson and his son Robert (1803–59) was there an attempt to establish a standard gauge for tracks and engines. Britain was the only country in which the government did not take a leading role in building the railways. Hundreds of millions of pounds were raised privately, and in the end it is calculated that the railroads cost £40,000 a mile to build, more than three times the cost per mile of railroads on the Continent and in the United States.

Nevertheless, the investment paid huge dividends. By the 1850s, the original purpose of the railways was being realized as freight revenues finally surpassed passenger revenues. Coal was the dominant cargo shipped by rail, and the speedy, efficient service continued to drive down prices. The iron and steel industries were modernized on the back of demand for rails, engines, and cast-iron seats and fittings. In peak periods—and railway building was a boom-and-bust affair—as much

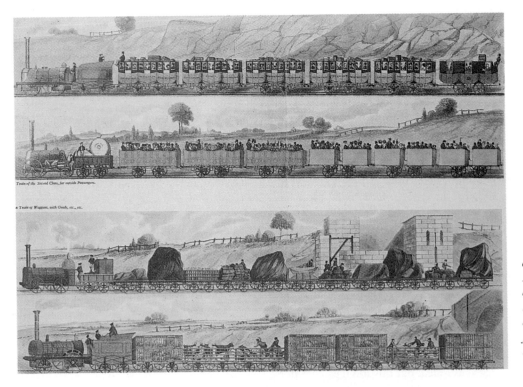

This representation of travel on the Liverpool and Manchester railway illustrates the great difference between first-class (top) and second-class (bottom) travel conditions.

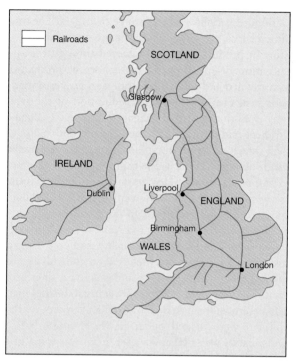

Great Britain—Railroads, ca. 1850

because it was time-consuming. Ordinary people could not take off the days necessary to complete relatively short round-trip journeys. When passenger rail service began, there was even a debate over whether provision should be made for third-class passengers, a class unknown on the coaches, where the only choices were riding inside for comfort or outside for savings. Third-class passengers quickly became the staple of railroad service. The cheap excursion was born to provide short holidays or even day trips. The career of Thomas Cook (1808–92), who became the world's first travel agent, began after he took a short excursion. Over 6 million people visited London by train to view the Crystal Palace exhibition in 1851, a number equivalent to one-third of the population of England and Wales. The railways did more than link places; they brought people together and helped develop a sense of national identity by speeding all forms of communication.

Entrepreneurs and Managers

The Industrial Revolution in Britain was not simply invented. Too much credit is given to a few breakthroughs and too little to the ways in which they were improved and dispersed. The Industrial Revolution was an age of gadgets when people believed that new was better than old and that there was always room for improvement. "The age is running mad after innovation," the English moralist Dr. Johnson wrote. "All the business of the world is done in a new way; men are hanged in a new way." Societies for the advancement of knowledge sprang up all over Britain. Journals and magazines promoted new ideas and techniques. Competitions were held for the best invention of the year; prizes were awarded for agricultural achievements. Practical rather than pure science was the hallmark of industrial development.

Yet technological innovation was not the same as industrialization. A vital change in economic activity took place in the organization of industry. Putters-out with their circulating capital and hired laborers could never make the economies necessary to increase output and quality while simultaneously lowering costs. This was the achievement of industrialists, producers who owned workplace, machinery, and raw materials and invested fixed capital by plowing back their profits. Industrial enterprises came in all sizes and shapes. A cotton mill could be started with as little as £300 or as much as £10,000. As late as 1840, fewer than 10 percent of the mills employed over 500 workers. Most were family concerns with under 100 employees, and

as a quarter of the output of the rolling mills went into domestic railroads, and much more into Continental systems. The railways were also a massive consumer of bricks for beddings, sidings, and especially bridges, tunnels, and stations. Finally, the railways were a leading employer of labor, surpassing the textile mills in peak periods. Hundreds of thousands worked in tasks as varied as engineering and ditch digging, for even in this most advanced industry, sophisticated mechanized production went hand in hand with traditional drudgery. Over 60,000 workers were permanently engaged in the industry to run trains, mind stations, and repair track. Countless others were employed in manufacturing engines, carriages, boxcars, and the thousands of components that went into making them.

Most of all, the railroads changed the nature of people's lives. Whole new concepts of time, space, and speed emerged to govern daily activities. As Henry Booth, an early railroad official, observed, "Notions which we have received from our ancestors and verified by our own experience are overthrown in a day. What was slow is now quick; what was distant is now near." Coach travel had ordinarily been limited to those with means, not only because it was expensive, but also

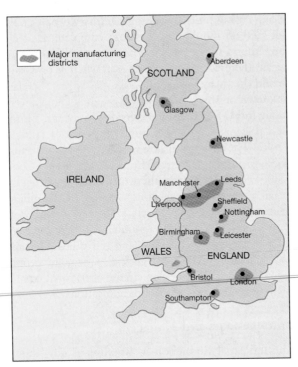

Major manufacturing districts

SCOTLAND

Aberdeen

Glasgow

Newcastle

IRELAND

Manchester　Leeds

Liverpool　Sheffield

Nottingham

Birmingham　Leicester

WALES　ENGLAND

Bristol

London

Southampton

Great Britain—Manufacturing Centers

many of them failed. For every story with a happy ending, there was another with a sad one. When Major Edmund Cartwright (1740–1824) erected a cotton mill, he was offered a Watt steam engine built for a distiller who had gone bankrupt. He acquired his machinery at the auction of another bankrupt. Cartwright's mill, engine, and machinery ended on the auction block less than three years later. There were over 30,000 bankruptcies in the eighteenth century, testimony both to the risks of business and to the willingness of entrepreneurs to take them.

To survive against these odds, successful industrialists had to be both entrepreneur and manager. As entrepreneurs they raised capital, almost always locally from relatives, friends, or members of their church. Quakers were especially active in financing each other's enterprises. The industrial entrepreneur also had to understand the latest methods for building and powering machinery and the most up-to-date techniques for performing the work. One early manufacturer claimed "a practical knowledge of every process from the cotton-bag to the piece of cloth." Finally, entrepreneurs had to know how to market their goods. In these functions, industrial entrepreneurs developed logically from putters-out.

But industrialists also had to be managers. The most difficult task was organization of the workplace. Most gains in productivity were achieved through the specialization of function. The processes of production were divided and subdivided until workers performed a basic task over and over. The education of the work force was the industrial manager's greatest challenge. Workers had to be taught how to use and maintain their machines and disciplined to apply themselves continuously. At least at the beginning, it was difficult to staff the factories. Many employed children as young as seven from workhouses or orphanages, who, though cheap to pay, were difficult to train and discipline. It was the task of the manager to break old habits of intermittent work, indifference to quality, and petty theft of materials. Families were preferred to individuals, for then parents could instruct and supervise their children. There is no reason to believe that industrial managers were more brutal masters than farmers or that children were treated better in workhouses than in mills. Labor was a business asset, what was sometimes called "living machinery," and its control with carrots and sticks was the chief concern of the industrial manager.

Who were the industrialists who transformed the traditional economy? Because British society was relatively open, they came from every conceivable background: dukes and orphans, merchants and salesmen, inventors and improvers. Though some went from rags to riches—like Richard Arkwright, who was the thirteenth child of a poor barber—it was extremely difficult for a laborer to acquire the capital necessary to set up a business. Wealthy landowners were prominent in capital-intensive aspects of industries—for example, owning ironworks and mines—but few established factories. Most industrialists came from the middle classes, which, while comprising one-third of the British population, provided as much as two-thirds of the first generation of industrialists. These included lawyers, bankers, merchants, and those already engaged in manufacturing, as well as tradesmen, shopkeepers, and self-employed artisans. The career of every industrialist was different, as a look at two—Josiah Wedgwood and Robert Owen—will show.

Josiah Wedgwood (1730–95) was the thirteenth child of a long-established English potting family. He worked in the potteries from childhood, but a deformed leg made it difficult for him to turn the wheel. Instead he studied the structure of the business. His head teemed with ideas for improving ceramic manufacturing, but it was not until he was thirty that he could set up on his own and introduce his innovations. These encompassed both technique and organization, the entrepreneurial and managerial sides of his business.

Wedgwood developed new mixtures of clays that took brilliant colors in the kiln and new glazes for both useful and ornamental ware. His technical innovations were all the more remarkable in that he had little education in mineral chemistry and made his discoveries by simple trial and error. But there was nothing of either luck or good fortune in Wedgwood's managerial innovations. He was repelled by the disorder of the traditional pottery, with its waste of materials, uneven quality, and slow output. When he began his first works, he divided the making of pottery into distinct tasks and assigned separate workers to them. One group did nothing but throw the pots on the wheel; another painted designs; a third glazed. To achieve this division of function, Wedgwood had to train his own workers almost from childhood. Traditional potters performed every task from molding to glazing and prized the fact that no two pieces were ever alike. Wedgwood wanted each piece to replicate another, and he stalked the works breaking defective wares on his wooden leg. He invested in schools to help train young artists, in canals to transport his products, and in London shops to sell them. Wedgwood was a marketing genius. He named his famed cream-colored pottery Queen's Ware and made special coffee and tea services for leading aristocratic families. He would then sell replicas by the thousands. In less than twenty years, Wedgwood pottery was prized all over Europe and Wedgwood's potting works were the standard of the industry.

Robert Owen (1771–1858) did not have a family business to develop. The son of a small tradesman, he was apprenticed to a clothier at the age of ten. As a teenager he worked as a shop assistant in Manchester, where he audaciously applied for a job as a manager of a cotton mill. At nineteen he was supervising five hundred workers and learning the cotton trade. Owen was immediately successful, increasing the output of his workers and introducing new materials to the mill. In 1816 he entered a partnership to purchase the New Lanark mill in Scotland. Owen found conditions in Scotland much worse than those in Manchester. Over five hundred workhouse children were employed at New Lanark, where drunkenness and theft were endemic. Owen believed that to improve the quality of work one had to improve the quality of the workplace. He replaced old machinery with new,

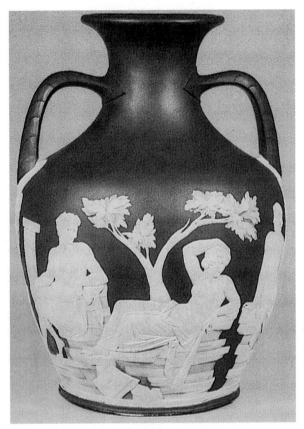

Jasperware copy of the Portland vase by Josiah Wedgwood. The Portland vase is one of the most famous ancient vases. It was found near Rome in the seventeenth century in a tomb believed to be that of Alexander Severus.

reduced working hours, and instituted a monitoring system to check theft. To enhance life outside the factory, he established a high-quality company-run store, which plowed its profits into a school for village children.

Owen was struck by the irony that in the mills, machines were better cared for than were humans. He thought that with the same attention to detail that had so improved the quality of commodities he could make even greater improvements in the quality of life. He prohibited children under ten from mill work and instituted a ten-hour day for child labor. His local school took infants from one year old, freeing women to work and ensuring each child an education. Owen instituted old-age and disability pensions, funded by

THE SIN OF WAGES

Robert Owen was both a successful manufacturer and a leading philanthropist. He believed that economic advance had to take place in step with the improvement of the moral and physical well-being of the workers. He organized schools, company shops, and ultimately utopian communities in an effort to improve the lives of industrial laborers. Owen was one of the first social commentators to argue that industrialism threatened the fabric of family and community life.

The acquisition of wealth, and the desire which it naturally creates for a continued increase, have introduced a fondness for essentially injurious luxuries among a numerous class of individuals who formerly never thought of them, and they have also generated a disposition which strongly impels its possessors to sacrifice the best feelings of human nature to this love of accumulation. To succeed in this career, the industry of the lower orders, from whose labour this wealth is now drawn, has been carried by new competitors striving against those of longer standing, to a point of real oppression, reducing them by successive changes, as the spirit of competition increased and the ease of acquiring wealth diminished, to a state more wretched than can be imagined by those who have not attentively observed the changes as they have gradually occurred. In consequence, they are at present in a situation infinitely more degraded and miserable than they were before the introduction of these manufactories, upon the success of which their bare subsistence now depends. . . .

The inhabitants of every country are trained and formed by its great leading existing circumstances, and the character of the lower orders in Britain is now formed chiefly by circumstances arising from trade, manufactures, and commerce; and the governing principle of trade, manufactures, and commerce is immediate pecuniary gain, to which on the great scale every other is made to give way. All are sedulously trained to buy cheap and to sell dear; and to succeed in this art, the parties must be taught to acquire strong powers of deception; and thus a spirit is generated through every class of traders, destructive of that open, honest sincerity, without which man cannot make others happy, nor enjoy happiness himself.

From Robert Owen, *Observations on the Effect of the Manufacturing System* (1815).

---

mandatory contributions from workers' wages. Taverns were closed and workers were fined for drunkenness and sexual offenses. In the factory and the village, Owen established a principle of communal regulation to improve both the work and the character of his employees. New Lanark became the model of the world of the future, and each year thousands made an industrial pilgrimage to visit it.

The Wages of Progress

Robert Owen ended his life as a social reformer. His efforts to improve the lot of his workers at New Lanark led to experiments to create ideal industrial communities throughout the world. He founded cooperative societies, in which all members shared in the profits of the business, and supported trade unions in which workers could better their lives. His followers planted colonies where goods were held in common and the fruits of labor belonged to the laborers. Owen's agitation for social reform was part of a movement that produced results of lasting consequence. The Factory Act (1833) prohibited factory work by children under nine, provided two hours of daily education, and effectively created a 12-hour day in the mills until the Ten Hours Act (1847). The Mines Act (1842) prohibited women and children from working underground.

Nor was Owen alone in dedicating time and money to the improvement of workers' lives. The rapid growth of unplanned cities exacerbated the plight of those too poor and overworked to help themselves. Conditions of housing and sanitation were appalling even by nineteenth-century standards. The *Report on the Sanitary*

Condition of the Laboring Population in Britain (1842), written by Edwin Chadwick (1800–1890), so shocked Parliament and the nation that it helped to shift the burden of social reform to government. The Public Health Act (1848) established boards of health and the office of medical examiner, while the Vaccination Act (1853) and the Contagious Diseases Act (1864) attempted to control epidemics. (See "Industry and the Environment," pp. 666–667.)

The movement for social reform began almost as soon as industrialization. The Industrial Revolution initiated profound changes in the organization of British society. Cities sprang up from grain fields almost overnight. The lure of steady work and high wages prompted an exodus from rural Britain and spurred an unremitting boom in population. In the first half of the nineteenth century, the population of England doubled from 9 to 18 million, with growth most rapid in the newly urban north and west. In 1750, about 15 percent of the population lived in urban areas; by 1850, about 60 percent did. Industrial workers married younger and produced more chil-

dren than their agricultural counterparts. For centuries women had married in their middle twenties, but by 1800, age at first marriage had dropped to twenty-three for the female population as a whole and to nearly twenty in the industrial areas. This was in part because factory hands did not have to wait until they inherited land or money, and in part because they did not have to serve an apprenticeship. But early marriage and large families were also a bet on the future, a belief that things were better now and would be even better soon, that the new mouths would be fed and the new bodies clothed. This was an investment on the part of ordinary people similar to that made by bankers and entrepreneurs when they risked their capital in new businesses. Was it an investment that paid off?

It is difficult to calculate the benefits of the Industrial Revolution or to weigh them against the costs. What is certain is that there was a vast expansion of wealth as well as a vast expansion of people to share it. Agricultural and industrial change made it possible to support comfortably a population over three times

Dudley Street, Seven Dials, London, *by Gustave Doré, is a scene of life in the London slums of the early nineteenth century.*

✑ Industry and the Environment

The Industrial Revolution changed the landscape of Britain. Small villages grew into vast metropolises seemingly overnight. The rates of growth were absolutely staggering: in 1801 there were 75,000 people in Manchester; by 1851 the number had more than quadrupled. This unremitting boom in population did more than strain the resources of local authorities: it broke them apart. It was not that the new industrial cities were unplanned; they were beyond the capacity of planning. Every essential requirement for human survival became scarce and expensive. Shortages of food, water, and basic accommodation were commonplace.

Shantytowns sprang up wherever space would allow, making the flimsily built habitations of construction profiteers seem like palaces. There was loud complaint about these nineteenth-century rip-off artists, but in truth the need for housing was so desperate that people willingly lived anywhere that provided shelter. Houses were built back to back and side by side, with only narrow alleyways to provide

sunlight and air. In Edinburgh one could step through the window of one house into the window of the adjoining one. Whole families occupied single rooms where members slept as they worked, in shifts. In Liverpool over 38,000 people were estimated to be living in cellars—windowless underground accommodations that flooded with the rains and the tides.

Most cities lacked both running water and toilet facilities. Districts were provided with either pumps or capped pipes through which private companies ran water for a few hours each day. The water was collected in buckets and brought to the home, where it would stand for the rest of the day and serve indifferently for washing, drinking, and cooking. Outhouse toilets were an extravagant luxury; in one Manchester district 33 outhouses had to accommodate 7095 people. They were a mixed blessing even in the middle-class districts where they were more plentiful, as there was no system of drainage to flush away the waste. It simply accumulated in cesspools, which were emptied manually about every two years. The thing that most impressed visitors as they approached an industrial city was the smoke; what impressed them most when they arrived was the smell.

The quality of life experienced by most of the urban poor who lived in these squalid conditions has been recorded by a number of contemporary observers. Friedrich Engels was a German socialist who was sent to England to learn the cotton trade. He lived in Manchester for two years and spent much of his time exploring the working-class areas of the city. "In this district I found a man, apparently about sixty years old, living in a cow stable," Engels recounted from one of his walking tours in *The Condition of the Working Class in England in 1844*. "He had constructed a sort of chimney for his square pen, which had neither windows, floor, nor ceiling, had obtained a bedstead and lived there, though the rain dripped through his rotten roof. This man was too old and weak for regular work, and supported himself by removing manure with a hand-cart; the dungheaps lay next door to his palace!" From his own observations Engels concluded that "in such dwellings only a physically degenerate race, robbed of all humanity, degraded, reduced morally and physically to bestiality, could feel comfortable and at home." And as he was quick to point out, his own observations were no different from those of parliamentary commissioners, medical officers, or civic authorities who had seen conditions firsthand.

Among these observers, the most influential by far was Sir Edwin Chadwick, who began his government career as a commissioner for the poor law and ended it as the founder of a national system of public health. Chadwick wrote the report of a parliamentary commission, *The Sanitary Condition of the Laboring Population of Britain* (1842), which caused a sensation among the governing classes. Building on the work of physicians, overseers of the poor, and the most technical scholarship available, Chadwick not only painted the same grim picture of urban life as Engels did, he proposed a comprehensive solution to one of its greatest problems, waste management.

Chadwick was a civil servant, and he believed that problems were solved by government on the basis of conclusions of experts. He had heard doctors argue their theories about the causes of disease, some believing in fluxes that resulted from combinations of foul air, water, and refuse; others believing disease was spread by the diseased, in this case Irish immigrants who settled in the poorest parts of English industrial towns. Although medical research had not yet detected the existence of germs, it was widely held that lack of ventilation, stagnant pools of water, and the accumulation of human and animal waste in proximity to people's dwellings all contributed to the increasing incidence of disease. Chadwick fixed upon this last element as crucial. Not even in middle-class districts was there any effective system for the remov-al of waste. Chamber pots and primitive toilets were emptied into ditches, which were used to drain rain off into local waterways. The few underground sewers that existed were square containers without outlets that were simply emptied once filled. Chadwick's vision was for a sanitation system, one that would carry waste out of the city quickly and deposit it in outlying fields where it could be used as fertilizer.

Chadwick realized that the key to disposing of waste was a constant supply of running water piped through the system. Traditionally, only heavy rainstorms cleared the waste ditches in most cities, and these were too infrequent to be effective. The river had to be the beginning of the sewerage system as well as its end. River water had to be pumped through an underground construction of sewage pits that were built to facilitate the water's flow. Civil engineers had already demonstrated that pits with rounded rather than angular edges were far more effective, and Chadwick advocated the construction of a system of oval-shaped tunnels, built on an incline beneath the city. Water pumped from one part of the river would rush through the tunnels, which would empty into pipes that would carry the waste to nearby farms.

Chadwick's vision took years to implement. He had all of the zeal of a reformer and none of the tact of a politician. He offended nearly everyone with whom he came into contact, because he believed that his program was the only workable one and because he believed that it must be implemented whatever the price. He was uninterested in who was to pay the enormous costs of laying underground tunnel and building pumping stations and insisted only that the work begin immediately. In the end, he won his point. Sanitation systems became one of the first great public-works projects of the industrial age.

EXPLOITING THE YOUNG

The condition of child laborers was a concern of English legislators and social reformers from the beginning of industrialization. Most of the attention was given to factory workers, and most legislation attempted to regulate the age at which children could begin work, the number of hours they could be made to work, and the provision of schooling and religious education during their leisure. It was not until the mid-1840s that a parliamentary commission was formed to investigate the condition of child labor in the mines. In this extract the testimony of the child is confirmed by the observations of one of the commissioners.

Ellison Jack, 11-years-old girl coal-bearer at Loanhead colliery, Scotland: I have been working below three years on my father's account; he takes me down at two in the morning, and I come up at one and two next afternoon. I go to bed at six at night to be ready for work next morning: the part of the pit I bear in the seams are much on the edge. I have to bear my burthen up four traps, or ladders, before I get to the main road which leads to the pit bottom. My task is four or five tubs: each tub holds 4¼ cwt. I fill five tubs in twenty journeys.

I have had the strap when I did not do my bidding. Am very glad when my task is wrought, as it sore fatigues. I can read, and was learning the writing; can do a little; not been at school for two years; go to kirk occasionally, over to Lasswade: don't know much about the Bible, so long since read.

R. H. Franks, Esq., the sub-commissioner: A brief description of this child's place of work will illustrate her evidence. She has first to descend a nine-ladder pit to the first rest, even to which a shaft is sunk, to draw up the baskets or tubs of coals filled by the bearers; she then takes her creel (a basket formed to the back, not unlike a cockle-shell flattened towards the neck, so as to allow lumps of coal to rest on the back of the neck and shoulders), and pursues her journey to the wall-face, or as it is called here, the room of work. She then lays down her basket, into which the coal is rolled, and it is frequently more than one man can do to lift the burden on her back. The tugs or straps are placed over the forehead, and the body bent in a semicircular form, in order to stiffen the arch.

"Child Labor in the Coal Mines," Testimony to the Parliamentary Investigative Committee, 1842.

---

larger than that of the seventeenth century, when it was widely believed that England had reached the limits of expansion. Despite the fact that population doubled between 1801 and 1851, per capita income rose by 75 percent. That means that had the population remained stable, per capita income would have increased by a staggering 350 percent. At the same time, untold millions of pounds had been sunk into canals, roads, railways, factories, mines, and mills.

But the expansion of wealth is not the same as the improvement in the quality of life, for wealth is not equally distributed. An increase in the level of wealth may mean only that the rich are getting richer more quickly than the poor are getting poorer. Similarly, economic growth over a century involved the lives of sev-

eral generations, each of which experienced different standards of living. One set of parents may have sacrificed for the future of their children; another may have mortgaged it. Moreover, economic activity is cyclical. Trade depressions, like those induced by the War of 1812 and the American Civil War, which interrupted cotton supplies, could have disastrous short-term effects. The "Great Hunger" of the 1840s was a time of agrarian crisis and industrial slump. The downturn of 1842 threw 60 percent of the factory workers in the town of Bolton out of work at a time when there was neither unemployment insurance nor a welfare system. Finally, quality of life cannot be measured simply in economic terms. People with more money to spend may still be worse off than their ancestors, who may have preferred leisure to wealth or independence to the discipline of the clock.

Thus there are no easy answers to the quality-of-life question. In the first stages of industrialization, it seems clear that only the wealthy benefited economically, though much of their increased wealth was reinvested in expansion. Under the impact of population growth, the Napoleonic wars, and regional harvest failure, real wages seem to have fallen from the levels reached in the 1730s. Industrial workers were not substantially better off than agricultural laborers when the high cost of food and rent is considered. But beginning around 1820, there is convincing evidence that the real wages of industrial workers were rising despite the fact that more and more work was semi- and unskilled machine-minding and more of it was being done by women, who were generally paid only two-thirds the wages of men. Although this increase in real wages was still subject to trade cycles, like the Great Hunger of the 1840s, it continued nearly unabated for the rest of the nineteenth century. Thus, in the second half of the Industrial Revolution, both employers and workers saw a bettering of their economic situation. This was one reason why rural workers flocked to the cities and Irish peasants emigrated in the hundreds of thousands to work the lowest paid and least desirable jobs in the factories.

But economic gain had social costs. The first was the decline of the family as a labor unit. In both agricultural and early industrial activity, families labored together. Workers would not move to mill towns without the guarantee of a job for all members of their family, and initially they could drive a hard bargain. The early factories preferred family labor to workhouse conscripts, and it was traditional for children to work beside their parents, cleaning, fetching, or assisting in minding the machines. Children provided an essential part of family income, and youngest children were the agency of care for infirm parents. Paradoxically, it was agitation for improvement in the conditions of child labor that spelled the end of the family work unit. At first young children were barred from the factories and older ones allowed to work only a partial adult shift. Although reformers intended that schooling and leisure be substituted for work, the separation of children from parents in the workplace ultimately made possible the substitution of teenagers for adults, especially as machines replaced skilled human labor. The individual worker now became the unit of labor, and during economic downturns it was adult males with their higher salaries who were laid off first.

The decline of the family as a labor unit was matched by other changes in living conditions when rural dwellers migrated to cities. Many rural habits were unsuited to both factory work and urban living. The tradition of "Saint Monday," for example, was one that was deeply rooted in the pattern of agricultural life. Little effort was expended at the beginning of the work week and progressively more at the end. Sunday leisure was followed by Monday recovery, a slow start to renewed labor. The factory demanded constant application six days a week. Strict rules were enforced to keep workers at their stations and their minds on their jobs. More than efficiency was at stake. Early machines were not only crude, they were dangerous, with no safety features to cover moving parts. Maiming accidents were common in the early factories, and they were the fault of both workers and machines. Similarly, industrial workers entered a world of the cash economy. Most agricultural workers were used to being paid in kind and to barter exchange. Money was an unusual luxury that was associated with binges of food, drink, and frivolities. This made adjustment to the wage packet as difficult as adjustment to the clock. Cash had to be set aside for provisions, rent, and clothing. On the farm, the time of a bountiful harvest was the time to buy durable goods; in the factory, "harvest time" was always the same.

Such adjustments were not easy, and during the course of the nineteenth century a way of life passed forever from England. For some its departure caused profound sorrow; for others it was a matter of rejoicing. A vertically integrated society in which lord of the manor, village worthies, independent farmers, workers, and servants lived together interdependently was replaced by a society of segregated social classes. By the middle decades of the nineteenth century, a class of capitalists and a class of workers had begun to form and had begun to clash. The middle classes abandoned the city centers, building exclusive suburban communities in which to raise their children and insulate their families. Conditions in the cities deteriorated under the pressure of overcrowding, lack of sanitation, and the absence of private investment. The loss of interaction between these different segments of society had profound consequences for the struggle to improve the quality of life for everyone. Leaders of labor saw themselves fighting against profits, greed, and apathy; leaders of capital against drunkenness, sloth, and ignorance. Between these two stereotypes there was little middle ground.

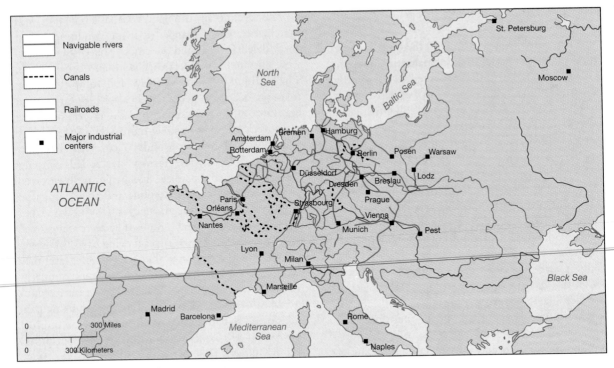

The Industrial Revolution on the Continent

The Industrialization of the Continent

Although Britain took the first steps along the road to an industrial economy, it was not long before other European nations followed. There was intense interest in "the British miracle," as it was dubbed by contemporaries. European ministers, entrepreneurs, even heads of state, visited British factories and mines in hope of learning the key industrial secrets that would unlock the prosperity of a new age. The Crystal Palace exhibition of manufacturing and industry held in London in 1851 was the occasion for a Continent-wide celebration of the benefits of technology and a chance for ambitious Europeans to measure themselves against the mighty British. By then many European nations had begun the transformation of their own economies and had entered a period of sustained growth.

There was no single model for the industrialization of the Continental states. Contemporaries continually made comparisons with Britain, but in truth the process of British industrialization was not well suited to any but the coal-rich regions in Belgium and the Rhineland. Nevertheless, all of Europe benefited from the British experience. No one else had to invent the jenny, the mule, or the steam engine. Although the British government banned the export of technology, none of these path-breaking inventions remained a secret for long. Britain had demonstrated a way to make cheap, durable goods in factories, and every other state in Europe was able to skip the long stages of discovery and improvement. Thus, while industrialization began later on the Continent, it could progress more quickly. France and Germany were building a railroad system within years of Britain despite the fact that they had to import most of the technology, raw materials, and engineers.

Britain shaped European industrialization in another way. Its head start made it very difficult for follower nations to compete against British commodities in the world market. This meant that European industrialization would be directed first and foremost to home markets, where tariffs and import quotas could protect fledgling industries. Although European states were willing to import vital British products, they placed high duties on British-made consumer goods and encouraged higher-cost domestic production. Britain's competitive advantage demanded that European governments become involved in the industrialization of their countries, financing capital-intensive industries, backing the railroads, and favoring the establishment of factories.

European industrialization was therefore not the thunderclap it was in Britain. In France it was a slow, accretive development that took advantage of traditional skills and occupations and gradually modernized the marketplace. In Germany industrialization had to overcome the political divisions of the empire, the economic isolation of the petty states, and the wide dispersion of vital resources. Regions rather than states industrialized in the early nineteenth century, and parts of Austria, Italy, and Spain imported machinery and techniques and modernized their traditional crafts. But most of these states and most of the eastern part of Europe remained tied to a traditional agrarian-based economy that provided neither labor for industrial production nor purchasing power for industrial goods. These areas quickly became sources for raw materials and primary products for their industrial neighbors.

Industrialization Without Revolution

The experience of France in the nineteenth century demonstrates that there was no single path to industrialization. Each state blended together its natural resources, historical experiences, and forms of economic organization in unique combinations. While some mixtures resulted in explosive growth, as in Britain, others made for steady development, as in France.

French industrialization was keyed to domestic rather than export markets and to the application of new technology to a vast array of traditional crafts. The French profited, as did all of the Continental states, from British inventions, but they also benefited from the distinct features of their own economy. France possessed a pool of highly skilled and highly productive labor, a manufacturing tradition oriented toward the creation of high-quality goods, and consumers who valued taste and fashion over cost and function. Thus while the British dominated the new mass market for inexpensive cottons and cast-iron goods, a market with high sales but low profit margins, the French were producing luxury items whose very scarcity kept both prices and profits high.

Two decisive factors determined the nature of French industrialization: population growth and the French

Revolution. From the early eighteenth to the mid-nineteenth centuries, France grew slowly. In 1700, the French population stood at just under 20 million; in 1850 it was just under 36 million, a growth rate of 80 percent. In contrast, Germany grew 135 percent, from 15 to 34 million, and England 300 percent, from 5 to 20 million, during the same period. Nevertheless, France remained the most populous nation in western Europe, second on the Continent only to Russia. There is no simple explanation for France's relatively sluggish population growth. The French had been hit particularly hard by subsistence crises in the seventeenth century, and there is reliable evidence that the rural population consciously attempted to limit family size by methods of birth control as well as by delaying marriages. Moreover, France urbanized slowly at a time when city dwellers were marrying younger and producing larger families. As late as the 1860s, a majority of French workers were farmers. Whatever the cause of this moderate population growth, its consequences were clear. France was not pressured by the force of numbers to abandon its traditional agricultural methods, nor did it face a shortage of traditional supplies of energy. Except during crop failures, French agriculture could produce to meet French needs, and there remained more than enough wood for domestic and industrial use.

The consequences of the French Revolution are less clear. Throughout the eighteenth century, the French economy performed at least as well as the British, and in many areas better. French overseas trade had grown spectacularly until checked by military defeat in the Seven Years' War (1756–63). French agriculture steadily increased output, while French rural manufactures flourished. A strong guild tradition still dominated urban industries, and although it restricted competition and limited growth, it also helped maintain the standards for the production of high-quality goods that made French commodities so highly prized throughout the world. The Revolution disrupted every aspect of economic life. Some of its outcomes were unforeseen and unwelcome. For example, Napoleon's Continental System, which attempted to close European markets to Britain, resulted in a shipping war, which the British won decisively and which eliminated France as a competitor for overseas trade in the mid-nineteenth century. But other outcomes were the result of direct policies, even if their impact could not have been entirely predicted. Urban guilds and corporations were abolished, opening trades to newcomers but destroying the close-knit groups that trained skilled artisans and

This engraving shows a French steelworks, Manufacture Nationale, in Paris, 1800. At that time this was the only French steelworks that compared with those in Sheffield, England.

introduced innovative products. Similarly, the breakup of both feudal and common lands to satisfy the hunger of the peasantry had the effect of maintaining a large rural population for decades.

Despite the efforts of the central government, there had been little change in the techniques used by French farmers over the course of the eighteenth century. French peasants clung tenaciously to traditional rights that gave even the smallest landholder a vital say in community agriculture. Landlords were predominantly absentees, less interested in the organization of their estates than in the dues and taxes that could be extracted from them. Thus the policies of successive revolutionary governments strengthened the hold of small peasants on the land. With the abolition of many feudal dues and with careful family planning, smallholders could survive and pass a meager inheritance on to their children. Even prosperous farmers could not grow into the large-scale proprietors that had enclosed English fields, for little land came on the market, and many parts of France practiced partible inheritance, which, over time, tended to even out the size of holdings. French agriculture continued to be organized in its centuries-old patterns. While it was able to supply the nation's need for food, it could not release large numbers of workers for purely industrial activity.

Thus French industrial growth was constrained on the one hand by the relatively small numbers of workers who could engage in manufacturing and on the other by the fact that a large portion of the population remained subsistence producers, cash-poor and linked only to small rural markets. Throughout the eighteenth century, the French economy continued to be regionally segregated rather than nationally integrated. The size of the state inhibited a highly organized internal trade, and there was little improvement of the infrastructure of transportation. Although some British-style canals were built, it must be remembered that canals in Britain were built to move coal rather than staple goods and France did not have much coal to move. Manufacturing concerns were still predominantly family businesses whose primary markets were regional rather than international. Roads that connected the short distances between producers and consumers were of greater importance to these producers than arterial routes that served the markets of others. Similarly, there was no national capital market until the mid-nineteenth century, and precious few regional ones. French producers were as thrifty and profit-oriented as any others, but they found it more difficult to raise the large amounts of capital necessary to purchase the most expensive new machinery and build the most up-to-date factories.

Ironworks, coal mines, and railroads, the three capital-intensive ventures of industrialization, were financed either by government subsidy or by foreign investment.

All of these factors determined the slow, steady pace of French industrialization. Recovery after 1815 came in fits and starts. British inventors, manufacturers, and entrepreneurs were enticed to France to demonstrate new machinery and industrial techniques, but in most places the real engine of growth was skilled workers' steady application of traditional methods. By 1820 only 65 French factories were powered by steam engines, and even water-powered machinery was uncommon. Industrial firms remained small and were frequently a combination of putting-out and factory production. It was not until midcentury that sustained industrial growth became evident. This was largely the result of the construction of railroads on a national plan, financed in large part by the central government. Whereas in Britain the railways took advantage of a national market, in France they created one. They also gave the essential stimulation to the modernization of the iron industry, in which much refining was still done with charcoal rather than coke; of machine making; and of the capital markets. Imported steel and foreign investment were vital ingredients in a process that took several decades to reach fruition.

The disadvantages of being on the trailing edge of economic change were mitigated for a time by conventional practices of protectionism. Except in specialty goods, agricultural produce, and luxury products, French manufactures could not compete with either British or German commodities. Had France maintained its position as a world trader, this comparative disadvantage would have been devastating. But defeat in the wars of commerce had led to a drawing inward of French economic effort. Marseille and Bordeaux, once bustling centers of European trade, became provincial backwaters in the nineteenth century. But the internal market was still strong enough to support industrial growth, and domestic commodities could be protected by prohibitive tariffs, especially against British textiles, iron, and ironically, coal. Despite the fact that France had to import over 40 percent of its meager requirements of coal, it still insisted upon slapping high import duties on British supplies. This was in part to protect French mine owners, who had never integrated their operations with iron production and therefore had no interest in keeping fuel costs low. Moreover, the slow pace of French industrialization allowed for the skipping of intermediate stages of development. France had hardly entered the canal age when it began to build its railways. Ultimately, industry moved from hand power to steam power in one long step.

While France achieved industrialization without an industrial revolution, it also achieved economic growth within the context of its traditional values. Agriculture may not have modernized, but the ancient village communities escaped the devastation modernization would bring. The orderly progression of generations of farming families characterized rural France until the shattering experiences of the Franco-Prussian War (1870) and the First World War (1914–18). Nor did France experience the mushroom growth of new cities with all of their problems of poverty, squalor, and homelessness. Slow population growth ameliorated the worst of the social diseases of industrialization while traditional rural manufacturing softened the transformation of a way of life. If France did not reap the windfall profits of the Industrial Revolution, neither did it harvest the bitter crop of social, economic, and spiritual impoverishment that was pulled in its train.

Industrialization and Union

The process of industrialization in Germany was dominated by the historic divisions of the empire of the German peoples. Before 1815 there were over three hundred separate jurisdictional units within the empire, and after 1815 there were still more than thirty. These included large advanced states like Prussia, Austria, and Saxony as well as small free cities and the personal enclaves of petty nobles who had guessed right during the Napoleonic wars. Political divisions had more than political impact. Each state clung tenaciously to its local laws and customs, which favored its citizens over outsiders. Merchants who lived near the intersection of separate jurisdictions could find themselves liable for several sets of tolls to move their goods and several sets of customs duties for importing and exporting them. These would have to be paid in different currencies at different rates of exchange according to the different regulations of each state. Small wonder that German merchants exhibited an intense localism, preferring to trade with members of their own state and supporting trade barriers against others. Such obstacles had a depressing effect on the economies of all German states, but pushed with greatest weight against the manufacturing regions of Saxony, Silesia, and the Rhineland.

THE SLAVERY OF LABOR

Though born in Germany, Friedrich Engels witnessed industrialization in England firsthand. His father owned a factory in Manchester of which Engels was put in charge. By day he oversaw industrial production, and by night he wandered the city streets overwhelmed by the suffering of the working classes. His analysis of industrialization developed from his own observations. He became first a socialist and then, with Karl Marx, a founder of the Communist party.

Capital is the all-important weapon in the class war. Power lies in the hands of those who own, directly or indirectly, foodstuffs and the means of production. The poor, having no capital, inevitably bear the consequences of defeat in the struggle. Nobody troubles about the poor as they struggle helplessly in the whirlpool of modern industrial life. The working man may be lucky enough to find employment, if by his labour he can enrich some member of the middle classes. But his wages are so low that they hardly keep body and soul together. If he cannot find work, he can steal, unless he is afraid of the police; or he can go hungry and then the police will see to it that he will die of hunger in such a way as not to disturb the equanimity of the middle classes. . . .

The only difference between the old-fashioned slavery and the new is that while the former was openly acknowledged the latter is disguised. The worker *appears* to be free, because he is not bought and sold outright. He is sold piecemeal by the day, the week, or the year. Moreover he is not sold by one owner to another, but he is forced to sell himself in this fashion. He is not the slave of a single individual, but of the whole capitalist class. As far as the worker is concerned, however, there can be no doubt as to his servile status. It is true that the apparent liberty which the worker enjoys does give him some *real* freedom. Even this genuine freedom has the disadvantage that no one is responsible for providing him with food and shelter. His real masters, the middle-class capitalists, can discard him at any moment and leave him to starve, if they have no further use for his services and no further interest in his survival. . . .

From Friedrich Engels, *The Condition of the Working Class in England in 1844* (1845).

Most of imperial Germany was agricultural land suited to a diversity of uses. The mountainous regions of Bavaria and the Austrian alpine communities practiced animal husbandry; there was a grain belt in Prussia, where the soil was poor but the land plentiful, and one in central Germany in which the soil was fertile and the land densely occupied. The Rhine Valley was one of the richest in all of Europe and was the center of German wine production. The introduction of the potato was the chief innovation of the eighteenth century. While English farmers were turning farms into commercial estates, German peasants were learning how to make do with less land.

Agricultural estates were organized differently in different parts of Germany. In the east, serfdom still prevailed. Peasants were tied to the land and its lord and were responsible for labor service during much of the week. Methods of cultivation were traditional, and neither peasants nor lords had much incentive to adopt new techniques. The vast agricultural domains of the Prussian Junkers, as these landlords were called, were built on the backs of cheap serf labor, and the harvest was destined for the Baltic export trade, where world grain prices rather than local production costs would determine profits. In central Germany, the long process of commuting labor service into rents was nearly completed by the end of the eighteenth century. The peasantry was not yet free, as a series of manorial relationships still tied them to the land, but they were no longer mere serfs. Moreover, western Germany was dominated by free farmers who either owned or leased their lands and who had a purely economic relationship with their landlords. The restriction of peasant mobility in much of Germany posed difficulties for the creation of an industrial work force. As late as 1800, over 80 percent of the German population was engaged in agriculture, a proportion that would drop slowly over the next half century.

Although Germany was well endowed with natural resources and skilled labor in a number of trades, it had not taken part in the expansion of world trade during the seventeenth century, and the once bustling Hanseatic ports had been far outdistanced by the rise of the Atlantic economies. The principal exported manufacture was linen, which was expertly spun and woven in Saxony and the Prussian province of Silesia. The linen industry was organized traditionally, with a mixture of domestic production managed on the putting-out system and some factory spinning, especially after the introduction of British mechanical innovations. But even the most advanced factories were still being powered by water, and thus they were located in mountainous regions where rapidly running streams could turn the wheels. In the 1840s there were only 22 steam-driven spinning mills in Germany, several of them established by the Prussian government, which imported British machines and technicians to run them. Neither linens nor traditional German metal crafts could compete on the international markets, but they could find a wider market within Germany if only the problems of political division could be resolved.

These were especially acute for Prussia after the reorganization of European boundaries in 1815 (see chapter 22). Prussian territory now included the coal- and iron-rich Rhineland provinces, but a number of smaller states separated these areas from Prussia's eastern domain. Each small state exacted its own tolls and customs duties whenever Prussian merchants wanted to move goods from one part of Prussia to the other. Such movement became more common in the nineteenth century as German manufacturing began to grow in step with its rising population. Between 1815 and 1865, the population of Germany grew by 60 percent to over 36 million people. This was an enormous internal market, nearly as large as the population of France, and the Prussians resolved to make it a unified trading zone by creating a series of alliances with smaller states known as the Zollverein (1834). The Zollverein was not a free-trade zone, as was the British empire, but rather a customs union in which member states adopted the liberal Prussian customs regulations. Every state was paid an annual portion of receipts based upon its population, and every state—except Prussia—increased its revenues as a result. The crucial advantage the Prussians received was the ability to move goods and materials from east to west, but Prussia reaped political profits as well. It forced Hanover and Saxony into the Zollverein and kept its powerful rival Austria out. Prussia's economic union soon proved to be the basis for the union of the German states.

The creation of the Zollverein was vital to German industrialization. It permitted the exploitation of natural advantages, like plentiful supplies of coal and iron, and it provided a basis for the building of railroads. Germany was a follower nation in the process of industrialization. It started late and it self-consciously modeled its success on the British experience. British equipment and engineers were brought to Germany to attempt to plant the seeds of an industrial economy. German manufacturers sent their children to England to learn the latest techniques in industrial management. Friedrich Engels (1820–95) worked in a Manchester cotton factory, where he observed the appalling conditions of the industrial labor force and wrote *The Condition of the Working Class in England* (1845). Steam engines were installed in coal mines, if not in factories, and the process of puddling revolutionized ironmaking, though most iron was still smelted with charcoal rather than coke. Although coal was plentiful in Prussia, it was to be found at the eastern and western extremities of Germany. Even with the lowering of tolls and duties, it was still too expensive to move over rudimentary roads and an uncompleted system of canals.

Thus the railroads were the key to tapping the industrial potential of Germany. Here they were a cause rather than a result of industrialization. The agreements hammered out in the creation of the Zollverein made possible the planning necessary to build single lines across the boundaries of numerous states. Initially German railroads were financed privately, with much foreign investment. But ultimately governments saw the practical advantages of rail transport and took an active part in both planning and financing the system. Over a quarter of the track constructed in Prussia before 1870 was owned directly by the government, and most of the rest had been indirectly financed by the government, which purchased land and guaranteed interest on stock issues.

Germany imported most of its engines directly from Britain and thus adopted standard British gauge for its system. As early as 1850 there were over 3500 miles of rail in Germany, with important roads linking the manufacturing districts of Saxony and the coal and iron deposits of the Ruhr. Twenty years later Germany

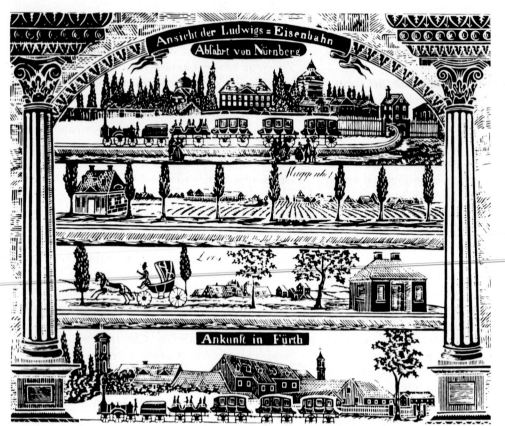

An engraving of the train from Nuremberg to Fürth. This Bavarian train ran for the first time in 1835. Passengers rode the seven kilometers between Nuremberg and Fürth in coaches that closely resembled their horse-drawn predecessors.

was second only to Britain in the amount of track that had been laid and opened. By then it was no longer simply a follower. German engineers and machinists, trained in Europe's best schools of technology, were turning out engines and rolling stock second to none. And the railroads transported a host of high-quality manufactures, especially durable metal goods that came to carry the most prestigious trademark of the late nineteenth century: "Made in Germany."

The Lands That Time Forgot

Nothing better demonstrates the point that industrialization was a regional rather than a national process than a survey of those states that did not develop industrial economies by the middle of the nineteenth century. These states ranged from the Netherlands, which was still one of the richest areas in Europe, to Spain and Russia, which were the poorest. Also included were Austria-Hungary, the states of the Italian peninsula,

and Poland. In all of these nations there was some industrial progress. The Bohemian lands of Austria contained a highly developed spinning industry; the Spanish province of Catalonia produced more cotton than did Belgium; and the Basque region was rich in iron and coal. Northern Italy mechanized its textile production, particularly silk spinning, while in the regions around both Moscow and Saint Petersburg, factories were run on serf labor. Nevertheless, the economies of all these states remained nonindustrial and, with the exception of the Netherlands, dominated by subsistence agriculture.

There were many reasons why these states were unable to develop their industrial potential. Some, like Naples and Poland, were simply underendowed with resources; others, like Austria-Hungary and Spain, faced difficulties of transport and communications that could not easily be overcome. Spain's modest resources were located on its northern and eastern edges, while a vast, arid plain dominated the center. To move raw materials and finished products from one end of the country to the other was a daunting task, made more difficult by lack of waterways and the rudimentary condition of Spanish roads. Two-thirds of Austria-Hungary is either mountains or hills, a geographic feature that presented obstacles not even the railroads could easily solve. But there was far more than natural disadvantage behind the failure of these parts of Europe to move in step with the industrializing states. Their social structure, agricultural organization, and commercial policies all hindered the adoption of new methods, machines, and modes of production.

Despite the fact that industrialization created new and largely unmanageable social problems, the follower states were eager for its benefits. All imported the latest products of technology, and the ruling elites in even the most traditional economies lived a material life similar to those in the most advanced. British entrepreneurs and artisans were courted by heads of state and their ministers and were offered riches in exchange for their precious knowledge. British industrialists set up textile factories in Moscow, built spinning machines in Bohemia, and taught Spanish miners how to puddle iron. Railroad pioneer George Stephenson himself surveyed the prospect of creating a passenger rail system in Spain, though he concluded pessimistically, "I have not seen enough people of the right sort to fill a single train." In the later part of the nineteenth century, French, Belgian, and German industrialists served similar roles. There were no traditional economies by choice. Industrialization was seen as a miracle, and the latecomers worshiped avidly at its shrine.

It was work rather than faith that would produce economic salvation. The most common characteristic of the latecomers was a traditional agrarian structure that consumed the lion's share of labor and capital while producing little surplus for any but a small dominant class. In areas as dissimilar as Spain, Italy, and Russia, agriculture was organized in vast estates, which kept the mass of peasants perpetually poor. Sharecropping systems in the west and serfdom in the east differed only in formal organization. Both conditions made it impossible for peasants to accumulate the land necessary to invest in capital improvements or to send their children to towns to engage in industrial occupations. In Hungary, Poland, and Russia it was illegal for people to change occupations, and serfs who engaged in industrial activity paid their lords for the privilege. Though a number of serfs amassed considerable fortunes in organizing domestic or factory spinning, legal constraints restricted the efforts of potential entrepreneurs.

Similarly, the leaders of traditional economies maintained tariff systems that insulated their own producers from competition. Austrian tariffs were not only artificially high, they were accompanied by import quotas to keep all but the smallest fraction of foreign products from Austrian consumers. The Spanish government prohibited the importation of grain, forcing its eastern provinces to pay huge transport costs for domestic grain despite the fact that cheaper Italian grain was readily available. Such policies sapped much-needed capital from industrial investment. There were many reasons for so-called protective tariffs, and it was not only the follower states that imposed them. France and the Zollverein protected domestic industry while Britain was converted to free trade only in the 1840s. But protection was sensible only when it protected rather than isolated. Inefficiently produced goods of inferior quality were the chief results of the protectionist policies of the follower nations. Failure to adopt steam-powered machines made traditionally produced linens and silks so expensive that smuggling occurred on an international scale. Although these goods might find buyers in domestic markets, they could not compete in international trade, and one by one the industries of the follower nations atrophied. Such nations became exporters of raw materials and foodstuffs. The export of Russian linen was replaced by the export of Russian flax. Spain, once the largest exporter of woolen cloth in Europe, now exported mainly wines and fruits. Those economies that remained traditionally organized came to be exploited for their resources by those that had industrialized.

This international situation was not all that different from the dual system that came into effect within the nonindustrialized states. In Austria-Hungary, for example, it was Hungary that was kept from industrializing, first by the continuation of serf-based agriculture, then by the high internal tariffs that favored Austrian over Hungarian manufactures. In Italy the division was between north and south. In Lombardy and Tuscany, machine-based manufacturing took hold alongside mining and metallurgy; in 1860 northern Italy contained 98 percent of the railways and 87 percent of the roads that existed on the entire peninsula. In Naples and Sicily, half-starved peasants eked out a miserable existence on once-rich soil that was now depleted from overuse. It was estimated that of the 400,000 people living in Naples, over 100,000 were destitute beggars. In Spain, Catalonia modernized while Castile stagnated. Until the loss of its Latin American empire in the first half of the nineteenth century, Spain had a ready market for Catalonian textiles and handicrafts. But since Castile remained the cultural and administrative center of the state, it did little to encourage change, and much government policy was actually counterproductive. The chief problem faced by these dual economies was that neither part could sustain the other. Traditional agriculture could not produce the necessary surplus of either labor or capital to support industry, and industry could not economize sufficiently to make manufactured goods cheap enough for a poor peasantry.

Thus the advantages of being a follower were all missed. Technology could not be borrowed or stages skipped because the ground was not prepared for widespread industrial activity to be cultivated. Even by standing still, followers fell behind. While over the course of the nineteenth century male illiteracy dropped dramatically in the industrialized states—to 30 percent in Britain and France and 10 percent in Prussia—it remained at 75 to 80 percent in Spain and Italy and over 90 percent in Russia. There was more than irony in the fact that one of the first railroads built on the Continent was built in Austria but was built to be powered by horses rather than engines. The first railways in Italy linked royal palaces to capital cities. Those in Spain radiated from Madrid and bypassed most centers of natural resources. In these states, the railroads were built to move the military rather than passengers or goods. They were state-financed, occasionally state-owned, and almost always lost money. They were symbols of the industrial age, but in these states they were symbols without substance.

· · ·

The industrialization of Europe in the eighteenth century was an epochal event in human history. The constraints on daily life imposed by nature were loosened for the first time. No longer did population growth in one generation mean famine in the next; no longer was it necessary for the great majority of people to toil in the fields to earn their daily bread. Manufacture replaced agriculture as humanity's primary activity, though the change was longer and slower than the burst of industrialization that took place in the first half of the nineteenth century. For the leaders, Britain especially, industrialization brought international eminence. British achievements were envied, British inventors celebrated, Britain's constitutional and social organization lauded. A comparatively small island nation had become the greatest economic power in Europe. Industrialization had profound consequences

for economic life, but its effects ran deeper than that. The search for new markets would result in the conquest of continents; the power of productivity unleashed by coal and iron would result in the first great arms race. Both would reach fruition in World War I, the first industrial war. For better or worse, we still live in the industrial era that began in Britain in the middle of the eighteenth century.

Suggestions for Further Reading

General Reading

* Carlo Cipolla, ed., *The Fontana Economic History of Europe: The Emergence of Industrial Societies.* 2 vols. (London: Fontana Books, 1973). A country-by-country survey of Continental European industrialization.

* David Landes, *The Unbound Prometheus* (Cambridge: Cambridge University Press, 1969). A vigorously argued study of the impact of technology on British and European society from the eighteenth to the twentieth century.

* E. L. Jones, *The European Miracle,* 2d ed. (Cambridge: Cambridge University Press, 1987). A comparative study of the acquisition of technology in Europe and Asia and the impact that industrialization had upon the two continents.

* T. S. Ashton, *The Industrial Revolution* (Oxford: Oxford University Press, 1969). A compelling brief account of the traditional view of industrialization.

The Traditional Economy

* E. A. Wrigley, *Continuity, Chance and Change* (Cambridge: Cambridge University Press, 1988). Explores the nature of the traditional economy and the way in which Britain escaped from it.

* L. A. Clarkson, *Proto-Industrialization: The First Phase of Industrialization?* (London: Macmillan, 1985). A study of domestic manufacturing and its connection to the process of industrialization.

J. D. Chambers and G. E. Mingay, *The Agricultural Revolution* (London: Batsford, 1966). The classic survey of the changes in British agriculture.

E. L. Jones, *Agriculture and the Industrial Revolution* (New York: John Wiley and Sons, 1974). A detailed study of the relationship between agricultural innovations and the coming of industrialization in Britain.

The Industrial Revolution in Britain

* Peter Mathias, *The First Industrial Nation,* 2d ed. (London: Methuen, 1983). An up-to-date general survey of British industrialization.

* Phyllis Deane, *The First Industrial Revolution,* 2d ed. (Cambridge: Cambridge University Press, 1979). The best introduction to the technological changes in Britain.

A. E. Musson, *The Growth of British Industry* (New York: Holmes & Meier, 1978). An in-depth survey of British industrialization that is especially strong on technology.

* John Rule, *The Vital Century: England's Developing Economy, 1714–1815* (London: Longman, 1992). The most up-to-date survey on the British economy.

N. F. R. Crafts, *British Economic Growth During the Industrial Revolution* (Oxford: Oxford University Press, 1985). A highly quantitative study by a new economic historian arguing the case that economic growth was slow in the early nineteenth century.

T. S. Ashton, *Iron and Steel in the Industrial Revolution* (Manchester: Manchester University Press, 1963). A lucid account of the transformation of ironmaking, including the story of James Watt.

Philip Bagwell, *The Transport Revolution from 1770* (London: Batsford, 1974). A thorough survey of the development of canals, highways, and railroads in Britain.

* François Crouzet, *The First Industrialists* (Cambridge: Cambridge University Press, 1985). An analysis of the social background of the first generation of British entrepreneurs.

* Harold Perkin, *The Origins of Modern English Society, 1780–1880* (London: Routledge & Kegan Paul, 1969). An outstanding survey of British social history in the industrial era.

* E. P. Thompson, *The Making of the English Working Class* (New York: Random House, 1966). A brilliant and passionate study of the ways laborers responded to the changes brought about by the industrial economy.

Friedrich Engels, *The Condition of the Working Class in England in 1844* (London: Allen and Unwin, 1952). The classic eyewitness account of the horrors of the industrial city.

The Industrialization of the Continent

* Tom Kemp, *Industrialization in Nineteenth-Century Europe,* 2d ed. (London: Longman, 1985). Survey of the process of industrialization in the major European states.

* Clive Trebilcock, *The Industrialization of the Continental Powers, 1780–1914* (London: Longman, 1981). A complex study of Germany, France, and Russia.

Sidney Pollard, *Peaceful Conquest* (Oxford: Oxford University Press, 1981). Argues the regional nature of industrialization throughout western Europe.

Roger Price, *The Economic Transformation of France* (London: Croom Helm, 1975). A study of French society before and during the process of industrialization.

W. O. Henderson, *The Rise of German Industrial Power* (Berkeley: University of California Press, 1975). A chronological study of German industrialization that centers on Prussia.

Herbert Kisch, *From Domestic Manufacture to Industrial Revolution: The Case of the Rhineland Textile Districts* (New York: Oxford University Press, 1989). A scholarly study of the slow pace of industrialization in Germany.

* Wolfgang Schivelbusch, *The Railway Journey* (Berkeley: University of California Press, 1986). A social history of the impact of railways, drawn from French and German sources.

*Paperback edition available.

22 ⁓ SOCIAL TRANSFORMATIONS AND POLITICAL UPHEAVALS, 1815–1850

Potato Politics

*V*egetables have histories too. But none has a more interesting history in the West than the humble potato. First introduced to northern Europe from the Andean highlands in South America at the end of the sixteenth century, it rapidly became a staple of peasant diets from Ireland to Russia. The potato's vitamins, minerals, and high carbohydrate content provided a rich source of energy to Europe's rural poor. It was simple to plant, required little or no cultivation, and did well in damp, cool climates. Best of all, it could be grown successfully on the smallest plots of land. One acre could support a peasant family of four for a year. Potato peelings helped sustain the family cow and pig, further supplementing family income.

The French painter Jean-François Millet (1814–75) provides a view of the peasant labor involved in *Planting Potatoes*. Millet, the son of a wealthy peasant family, understood well the importance of the potato crop in the peasant diet. The man and woman in this canvas plant their potatoes as a reverent act, bowing as field laborers might in prayer (laborers actually do pray in Millet's more sentimental work *The Angelus*). The primitive nature of the process is striking: the man uses a short hoe to scrape at what seems to be unyielding soil. The peasants seem part of the nature that surrounds them, patient as the beast that waits in the shade, bent and gnarled and lovely as the tree that arches in the background.

The fleshy root not only guaranteed health, it also affected social relations. Traditionally, peasants had delayed marrying and starting families because of the unavailability of land. The potato changed that behavior. Now the potato allowed peasants with only a little land to marry and have children earlier. Millet's depiction of the man and woman working together in the field resonates with the simple fact that potato cultivation aided in the formation of the couple. Millet's couple are parents whose baby sleeps swaddled in a basket and shaded by the tree. In those peasant homes where family members did putting-out work for local entrepreneurs, potato cultivation drew little labor away from the spinning wheel and loom. It permitted prosperous farmers to devote more land to cash crops, since only a small portion of land was required to feed a family. As the sole item of diet, it provided life-sustaining nutrients and a significant amount of the protein so necessary for heavy labor. The Irish adult male ate an average of 12 to 14 pounds of potatoes a day—a figure that may seem preposterous to us today.

Proverbs warned peasants against putting all their eggs in one basket, but no folk wisdom prepared the Irish, many of whom relied on the potato as a single crop, for the potato disaster that struck them. In 1845 a fungus from America destroyed the new potato crop. Although peasants were certainly accustomed to bad harvests and crop failures, they had no precedent for the years of blight that followed. From 1846 to 1850, famine and the diseases resulting from it—scurvy, dysentery, cholera, and typhus fever—killed over a million people in what became known as the Great Hunger. Another million people emigrated, many to the United States. Total dependence on the potato reaped its grim harvest, devastating all levels of Irish society. Within five years the Irish population was reduced by almost 25 percent.

The Irish potato famine has been called the "last great European *natural* disaster," to distinguish it from the man-made horrors of war and revolution. But it was as much a social disaster as a natural one. Food was the most political issue in the United Kingdom, the political entity created in 1801 consisting of England, Scotland, Ireland, and Wales. Governing one of the world's most prosperous states, British statesmen expected that the free market would solve the problems caused by famine in Ireland once trade barriers were removed in 1847. But the famine had hit the Irish so hard that they simply did not have the means to take advantage of tariff-free grains. Emergency work relief was established and soup kitchens were opened in the spring of 1847, but this meager assistance was withdrawn because the famine coincided with a banking crisis in England. In 1847 the problem was handed over to the Irish Poor Law system imposed on Ireland in 1838. The workhouses created by the recent law were not intended to deal with disasters of such proportions. Mass deaths and mass graves were the inevitable result.

As the wealth of European societies expanded in the nineteenth century, so did the number of those who lived on the edge, poised between unemployment and starvation. The Irish Great Hunger was the most striking example of the problem that plagued all Western societies in the first half of the nineteenth century: what to do with the poor.

Poverty was by no means a new social phenomenon, but the scale of impoverishment in both rural and urban areas and the perceived threat that it could disrupt whole societies were. In the case of the Irish famine, the British government was unable to handle an extreme crisis that was different in degree from the economic crises that periodically challenged other European nations. The question of poverty, the social question, lay at the heart of social experience and influenced new ideas about the role of government in solving social problems. It also fueled the firestorm of protest and revolution that swept across Europe after 1830 and, most notably, in 1848. In the context of poverty and the politics of food, Millet's melancholy painting of planting potatoes is not after all a pretty picture.

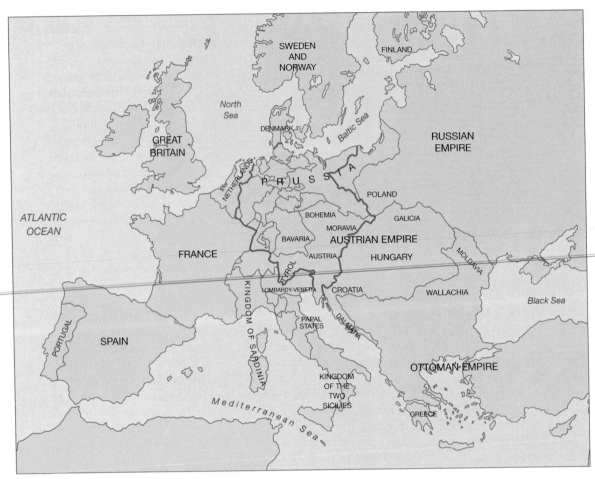

Europe in 1815

Europe After 1815

In his quest for empire, Napoleon had given Europe a geography lesson. Because no one state had been able to defeat him, Napoleon had made clear the territorial and political interdependence of the European powers. This lesson was not lost on the Great Powers as they sat down to redraw the map of Europe in 1815. The leaders of Russia, Austria, Prussia, and France shared with the British foreign secretary Lord Castlereagh (1769–1822) the vision of Europe as a machine that must be kept in running order. They looked on the whole of Europe as one entity and conceived of peace in terms of a general European security.

The primary goal of the European leaders who met in 1815 was to devise the most stable territorial arrangement possible. The settlement that emerged from their meeting was not simply a reaction to the ideological challenges of the French Revolution, nor was it a restoration of the European state system that had existed before Napoleon. During the negotiations, traditional claims of the right to rule came head to head with new ideas about stabilization. The equilibrium established in 1815 made possible a century-long European peace. Conflicts erupted, to be sure, but they took on the characteristics of the new system that was constructed at Vienna in 1815.

The Congress of Vienna

Because of the concern with establishing harmony at the time of Napoleon's defeat, the peace enforced against France was not a punitive one. After Napoleon's abdication in 1814, the victorious powers of Great Britain, Russia, Prussia, and Austria decided that leniency was the best way to support the restored Bourbon monarchy. After 1793, royalist émigrés referred to the young son of the executed Louis XVI as Louis XVII, although the child died in captivity and never reigned. In 1814 the four powers designated the elder of the two surviving brothers of Louis XVI as the appropriate candidate for the restored monarchy. Because of the circumstances of his restoration, the new king, Louis XVIII (1814–15; 1815–24), bore the ignominious image of returning "in the baggage car of the Allies." Every effort was made not to weigh down Louis XVIII with a harsh settlement. The First Peace of Paris, signed by the Allies with France in May 1814, had reestablished the French frontiers at the 1792 boundaries, which included Avignon, Venaissin, parts of Savoy, and German and Flemish territories—none of which had belonged to France in 1789.

After the hundred-day return of Napoleon, the "Usurper," the Second Peace of Paris of November 1815 somewhat less generously declared French frontiers restricted to the boundaries of 1790 and exacted from France an indemnity of 700 million francs. An army of occupation consisting of 150,000 troops was also placed on French soil at French expense, but was removed ahead of schedule in 1818. Contrary to the terms of the first treaty, the second treaty also required France to return plundered art treasures to their countries of origin.

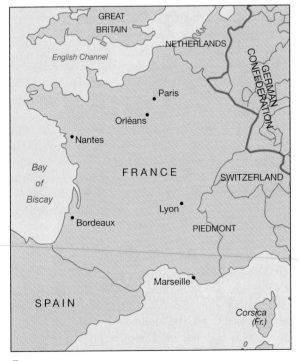

France

Representatives of the victorious Allies agreed to convene in the Austrian capital of Vienna for the purposes of mopping up the mess created in Europe by French rule and restoring order to European monarchies. On the surface, the Congress of Vienna, which began its deliberations in September 1814, seemed to be no more than an excuse for endless partying among Europe's royalty. Glittering balls as costly as battles gave critics the impression that statesmen were waltzing their way through treaty arrangements. The survival of an old system of precedence and etiquette hobbled negotiations. Issues of who should sign a treaty first and who should have the preferred places at the dinner table were the subjects of endless debates and fatal duels. But the image of bewigged men arguing over which criterion should be used to determine who would enter a room first belied the reality of the diplomats' serious negotiations as they sought to fashion a lasting peace by redrawing the map of Europe.

The central actors whose personalities dominated the Congress were Austrian minister of foreign affairs Prince Klemens von Metternich (1812–22), British foreign secretary Viscount Castlereagh, French minister of foreign affairs Charles Maurice de Talleyrand (1814–15), the Russian tsar Alexander I (1801–25), and the Prussian king Frederick William III (1797–1840). In spite of personal eccentricities, animosities, and occasionally outright hostilities among Europe's leaders, all shared a common concern with reestablishing harmony in Europe.

The dominant partnership of Austria and Britain at the Congress of Vienna resulted in treaty arrangements that served to restrain the ambitions of Russia and Prussia. No country was to receive territory without giving up something in return, and no one country was to receive enough territory to make it a present or future threat to the peace of Europe. To contain France, some steps taken prior to the Congress were ratified or expanded. In June 1814, the Low Countries had been set up as a unitary state to serve as a buffer against future French expansion on the Continent and a block to the revival of French sea power. The new Kingdom of the Netherlands, created out of the former Dutch Republic and the Austrian Netherlands, was placed under the rule of William I (1815–40). The Catholic southern provinces were thus uneasily reunited with the Protestant northern provinces, regions that had been separated since the Peace of Westphalia in 1648. Lest there be any doubt about the intended purpose of this new kingdom, Great Britain gave William I of the Netherlands £2 million to fortify his frontier against France. A reestablished monarchy that united the island kingdom of Sardinia with Piedmont and included Savoy, Nice, and part of Genoa contained France on its southeast border. To the east, Prussia was given control of the left bank of the Rhine. Switzerland was reestablished as an independent confederation of cantons. Finally, Bourbon rule was restored in Spain on France's southwestern border.

Austria's power was firmly established in Italy, either through outright territorial control or influence over independent states. The Papal States were returned to Pope Pius VII (1800–23), along with territories that had been Napoleon's Cisalpine Republic and the Kingdom of Italy. The Republic of Venice was absorbed into the Austrian empire. Lombardy and the Illyrian provinces on the Dalmatian coast were likewise restored to Austria. The Italian duchies of Tuscany, Parma, and Modena were placed under the rule of Habsburg princes.

After the fall of Napoleon, the Allies made no attempt to restore the Holy Roman Empire. Napoleon's Confederation of the Rhine, which organized the majority of German territory under French auspices in 1806, was dissolved. In its place, the German Confederation was created by reorganizing the 300 petty states into 38. The German Confederation

Italy

was intended as a bulwark against France, not to serve any nationalist or parliamentary function. The 38 states, along with Austria as the thirty-ninth, were represented in a new Federal Diet at Frankfurt, dominated by Austrian influence.

All of these changes were the result of carefully discussed but fairly uncontroversial negotiations. The question of Poland was another matter indeed. Successive partitions by Russia, Austria, and Prussia in 1772, 1793, and 1795 had completely dismembered the land that had been Poland. Napoleon had reconstituted a small portion of Poland as the Grand Duchy of Warsaw. The Congress faced the dilemma of what to do with this Napoleonic creation and with Polish territory in general. Fierce debate over Poland threatened to shatter congressional harmony.

Tsar Alexander I of Russia argued for a large Poland that he intended to be fully under his influence, thus extending Russian-controlled territories to the banks of the Oder. He also envisioned extending Russian dominance farther into central and eastern Europe. He based his claim on the significant contribution the Russian army had made to Napoleon's defeat. But such thinking conflicted with the Austrian minister Metter-

United Netherlands

The German Confederation

Poland

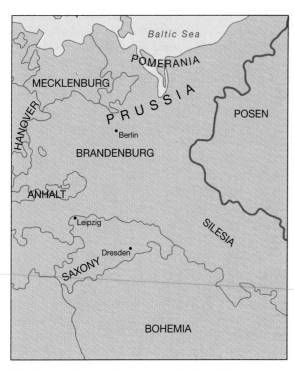

Saxony

nich's pursuit of equilibrium. Frederick William III of Prussia contended that if a large Poland was to be created, Prussia would expect compensation by absorbing Saxony. Both Great Britain and France distrusted Russian and Prussian territorial aims.

Negotiating for the French, Talleyrand was a man who knew something about survival and taking advantage of opportunities. A bishop under the old regime, a revolutionary who managed to keep his head, an exile in America during the Terror, Napoleon's chief minister, and then the representative of the restored Bourbon monarchy at the Congress, he was a shrewd and experienced diplomat who managed to convince the Allies to accept France, their defeated enemy, as an equal partner in negotiations. In the midst of the crisis over Poland, he persuaded Britain and Austria to sign a secret treaty with France in order to preserve an independent Polish territory. He then deliberately leaked news of the secret agreement of these powers to go to war, if necessary, to block Russian and Prussian aims. Alexander I and Frederick William III immediately backed down. Talleyrand's private opinion of the other four powers was acidic: "Too frightened to fight each other, too stupid to agree."

In this French cartoon satirizing the Congress of Vienna, left to right, Talleyrand is watching and waiting as Castlereagh balks, Metternich leads the "dancing," the king of Saxony clutches his crown in fear, and Genoa jumps up and down on the sidelines.

But under Talleyrand's manipulation, agree they did. In the final arrangement, Prussia retained the Polish territory of Posen and Austria kept the Polish province of Galicia. Krakow, with its population of 95,000, was declared a free city. Finally, a kingdom of Poland, nominally independent but in fact under the tutelage of Russia, emerged from what remained of the Grand Duchy of Warsaw. It was a solution that benefited no one in particular and disregarded Polish wishes.

In addition to receiving Polish territories, Prussia gained two-fifths of the kingdom of Saxony. Prussia also received territory on the left bank of the Rhine, the Duchy of Westphalia, and Swedish Pomerania. With these acquisitions, Prussia doubled its population to around 11 million people. The Junkers, the landed class of east Prussia, reversed many of the reforms of the Napoleonic period. The new territories that Prussia gained were rich in waterways and resources but geographically fragmented. The dispersal of holdings that was intended to contain Prussian power in central Europe spurred Prussia to find new ways of uniting its markets. In this endeavor, Prussia constituted a future threat to Austrian power over the German Confederation.

In Scandinavia, Russia's conquest of Finland was acknowledged by the members of the Congress, and in return Sweden acquired Norway from Denmark. Unlike Austria, Prussia, and Russia, Great Britain made no claim to territories at the Congress. Having achieved its aim of containing France, its greatest rival for dominance on the seas, Britain returned the French colonies it had seized in war. For the time being, the redrawing of the territorial map of Europe had achieved its pragmatic aim of guaranteeing the peace. It was now left to a system of alliances to preserve that peace.

The Alliance System

Only by joining forces had the European powers been able to defeat Napoleon, and the necessity of a system of alliances was recognized even after the battles were over. Two alliance pacts dominated the post-Napoleonic era: the renewed Quadruple Alliance and the Holy Alliance. The Quadruple Alliance, signed by the victorious powers of Great Britain, Austria, Russia, and Prussia in November 1815, was intended to protect Europe against future French aggression and to preserve the status quo. In 1818 France, having completed its payment of war indemnities, joined the pact, which now became the Quintuple Alliance. The five powers promised to meet periodically over the next twenty years to discuss common problems and to ensure the peace.

The Holy Alliance, very different in tone and intent, was the brainchild of Alexander I and was heavily influenced by his mystical and romantic view of international politics. In this pact, the monarchs of Prussia, Austria, and Russia agreed to renounce war and to protect the Christian religion. The Holy Alliance spoke of "the bonds of a true and indissoluble brotherhood . . . to protect religion, peace, and justice." Russia was able

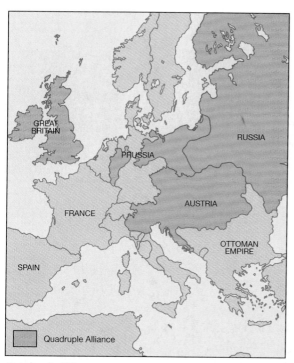

Quadruple Alliance

THE ALLIANCE SYSTEM

May 1814	**First Peace of Paris**
23 September 1814–	**Congress of Vienna**
9 June 1815	
26 September 1815	**Formation of the Holy Alliance**
20 November 1815	**Second Peace of Paris; Formation of the Quadruple Alliance**
November 1818	**Quadruple Alliance expands to include France in Quintuple Alliance**
1823	**French restoration of Bourbon Monarchy in Spain**

to give some credibility to the alliance with the sheer size of its army. Career diplomats were aware of its hollowness as a treaty arrangement, but it did indicate the willingness of Europe's three eastern autocracies to intervene in the affairs of other states.

The concept of Europe acting as a whole, through a system of periodic conferences, marked the emergence of a new diplomatic era. Conflict, however, was inherent in the commitment of parliamentary governments to open consultation and the need for secrecy in diplomacy. Dynastic regimes sought to intervene in smaller states to buoy up despots, as was the case in 1822, when European powers met to consider restoring the Bourbon monarchy in Spain. The British acted as a counterbalance to interventionist tendencies, refused to cooperate, and blocked united action by the Alliance. France took military action on its own in 1823, restored King Ferdinand VII, and abolished the Spanish constitution.

Both in the Congress of Vienna and the system of alliances that succeeded it, European nations aimed to establish a balance of power that recognized legitimate rulers and preserved the peace. The upheaval of the French Revolution and the revolutionary and Napoleonic wars had made clear the interdependence of one nation on another as a guarantee of survival. By maintaining an international equilibrium, Europe's statesmen hoped—erroneously, as it turned out—that by keeping the peace abroad, domestic peace would follow.

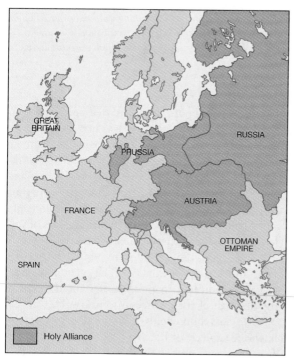

Holy Alliance

The New European Society

The peace that emerged from the Congress of Vienna did not restore the old order, although it did preserve principles of rule that a property-owning elite held dear. The search for stability and a reaction against political changes brought about by French rule characterized national and international affairs after 1815. Social structure and the world of production were undergoing dramatic transformations, and European states had to reckon with the fact that the daily lives of growing numbers of their subjects were transformed between 1815 and 1850. The demands of an international balance of power stood poised against the internal assaults on old social values in new arenas of conflict. Urbanization, industrialization, and economic uncertainties challenged Europeans in new ways in their search for stability.

Urban Miseries

In 1800, two of every one hundred Europeans lived in a city. By 1850 the number of urban dwellers per hundred had jumped to five and was rising rapidly. In England, the shift was more concentrated than the general European pattern. With one of every two people living in a city, England had become an urban society by midcentury. London was the fastest-growing city in Europe, followed at some distance by Paris and Berlin. The numbers of smaller urban centers were also multiplying.

Massive internal migrations caused most urban growth. People from the same rural areas often lived together in the same urban neighborhoods, and even in the same boardinghouses. Irish emigrants crowded together in the "Little Dublin" section of London. Similarly, districts in other cities were set off by regional accents and native provincial dress. Workers from the same hometowns gravitated to their favorite cafes. These social networks helped make the transition from rural to urban life bearable for the tens of thousands of people who poured into Europe's cities in search of jobs and opportunity. Until midcentury, many migrants returned to their rural homes for the winter when work, especially in the building trades, was scarce in the city. Young migrant women who came to the city to work as servants sent money home to support rural relatives, or worked to save a nest egg—or dowry—with the plan of returning to the village permanently. Before 1850, 20 percent of the workers in London were domestics, and most of them were women.

The Awakening Conscience (1854) by William Holman Hunt. The painting captures a moment in the relationship of a London man of means and the young woman he has set up in a suburban flat. Such arrangements were common in an era when some women resorted to prostitution to eke out a living.

Despite the support networks that migrants constructed for themselves, the city was not always a hospitable place. Workers were poorly paid, and women workers were more poorly paid than men. When working women were cut free of the support of home and family, uncounted numbers were forced into part-time prostitution to supplement meager incomes. More and more women resorted to prostitution as a means of surviving in times of unemployment. It is conservatively estimated that in 1850 there were 34,000 prostitutes in Paris and 50,000 in London. The phenomenon of prostitution indicated changing mores about sexuality in the first half of the nineteenth century. The "angel" of middle-class households and the "whore" of the streets were subjects of fascination in fiction and nonfiction. Increased prostitution created a veritable epidemic of venereal diseases, especially syphilis, for which there was no known cure until the twentieth century.

Urban crime also grew astronomically, with thefts accounting for the greatest number of crimes. Social reformers identified poverty and urban crowding as causes of the increase in criminal behavior. In 1829, both Paris and London began to create modern urban police forces to deal with the challenges to law and order. Crime assumed the character of disease in the minds of middle-class reformers. Statisticians and social scientists, themselves a new urban phenomenon, produced massive theses on social hygiene, lower-class immorality, and the unworthiness of the poor. The pathology of the city was widely discussed. Always at the center of the issue was the growing problem of what to do with the poor.

The "Social Question"

State-sponsored work relief expanded after 1830 for the deserving poor: the old, the sick, and children. Able-bodied workers who were idle were regarded as undeserving and dangerous, regardless of the causes of their unemployment. Performance of work became an indicator of moral worth as urban and rural workers succumbed to downturns in the economic cycle. Those unable to work sought relief from the state as a last resort. What has been called a "revolution in government" took place in the 1830s and 1840s as legislative bodies increased regulation of everything from factories and mines to prisons and schools.

Poverty was not just an urban problem, though it was both more conspicuous and more feared in urban areas. Politicians, social reformers, religious thinkers, and revolutionaries all had different solutions that followed one of two general orientations. There were those who argued, as in the case of the Irish famine, that the government must do nothing to intervene because the problem would correct itself, as Thomas Malthus had predicted forty years earlier. Malthus argued that the "natural" means of famine and death would keep population from outgrowing available resources and food supplies. The Irish population, one of the poorest in Europe, had indeed doubled between 1781 and 1841, and for Malthusians the Irish famine was the fulfillment of their vision that famine was the only way to correct overpopulation. This first group insisted that poverty was a social necessity; by interfering with it, governments could only make matters worse.

A second group contended that poverty was society's problem, and perhaps society's creation, and not a law of nature. Thus it was the social responsibility of the state to take care of its members. The question of how

Child labor in the textile factories. The meager wages of children were often necessary for the survival of their families.

to treat poverty—or the "social question," as it came to be known among contemporaries—underlay many of the protests and reforms of the two decades before 1850 and fueled the revolutionary movements of 1848. Parliamentary legislation attempted to improve the situation of the poor, especially the working class, during the 1830s and 1840s.

In 1833 British reformers turned their attention to the question of child labor. Against the opposition of those who argued for a free market for labor, Parliament passed the Factory Act of 1833, which prohibited the employment of children under nine years of age and restricted the workweek of children aged nine to thirteen to 48 hours. No child in this age group could work more than 9 hours a day. Teenagers between thirteen and eighteen years could work no more than 69 hours a week. By modern standards, these "reformed" workloads present a shocking picture of the heavy reliance on child labor. The British Parliament commissioned investigations, compiled in the "Blue Books," that reported the abusive treatment of men, women, and children in factories. Similar studies existed for French and Belgian industry.

RECALLING A CHILDHOOD IN THE FACTORY

In the early 1830s, philanthropists and reformers demanded that the British government do something about the appalling abuses of children laboring in textile factories. In response to public outcry, parliamentary commissions interviewed thousands of women and children workers and compiled a record of horrifying exploitation and abuse.

These investigations resulted in legislation that limited the work hours of children, provided for inspection of work conditions by state agents, and required that young workers receive educational instruction.

Eliza Marshall, who was eighteen at the time she gave the following testimony before the commission, recalled her childhood in the factory, beginning at age nine. Crippled by the tasks she performed and beaten frequently by her employer, she endured a grueling life of factory discipline typical of that legion of children who helped Britain maintain its industrial dominance.

I was turned ten when I began to work from five [a.m.] to nine [p.m.]. My sister was nine. There were older than me at Burgess'. Mr. Warburton picked us out, I suppose, because I was sharp at my work, a good hand: so was my sister. I was forced to go to work. I had no father, and my mother could not keep us without working. My mother is dead now. She died about half a year ago, since I was in London. I worked on at Warburton's till better than a year ago. I worked those hours all the time. We sometimes worked from six [a.m.] to seven [p.m.], but it was mostly from five to nine. He has got nearly two rooms full now; when I left him, there were about fifteen hands or so. I went from there to the Infirmary. . . .

It was the work and hours together that hurt me, and always having to stop the flies with my knee. I could stop it with my hand, but I had to hold it with my knee while I pieced it. It was having to crook my knee to stop the spindle that lamed me as much as any thing else.

From Great Britain's *Parliamentary Papers,* 1833, XX, Factory Inquiry Commission, 1st Report.

British legislation marked an initial step in state intervention in the workplace. Additional legislation over the next three decades further restricted children's and women's labor in factories and concerned itself with improving conditions in the workplace. Fundamentally, the "social question" was the question of what the state's role and responsibility was in caring for its citizens.

Smaller Families, Higher Hopes

Industrialization profoundly altered the structure of daily life within the family during the first half of the nineteenth century. Changes affected both middle-class and working-class families, though to varying degrees. With the rise of the state and a growing emphasis on education, the socializing role of the family was gradually transformed. By midcentury, population growth was beginning to slow down throughout Europe as people chose to restrict the size of their families. Europeans of earlier times had delayed marriage, practiced birth control, and employed abortion to limit family size. But the nineteenth century marks the first time in history that the majority of Europeans saw having fewer children as a value and acted on it.

Why decisions about limiting family size were made and how they were implemented are among the most intimate and private of questions; the answers can never really be known. But there is no doubt about the outcome of these decisions: people began having two or three children per family instead of five or six. Economic motivation appears to have been primary. In the nineteenth century, children had little economic value when they were eliminated from the workplace. The hope of a better life for one's progeny required that existing resources be concentrated on fewer children. The middle-class pattern of small families became the dominant one in western Europe in the nineteenth century as middle-class culture became more self-conscious.

Jane Austen (1775–1817), one of Europe's great novelists, created a picture of middle-class life in nineteenth-century England and of women's place in it. In *Pride and Prejudice* (1813) and *Emma* (1815), parents and guardians wait helplessly on the sidelines, hoping their charges will marry well. Young people, freed from the arranged marriages of the previous century, choose mates on the basis of affection and affinity. The couple is a locus for personal fulfillment. Yet the middle-class family exists in a network of value and status. In Austen's novels, families are ranked according to their furniture, carriages, and pianofortes; the numbers of their servants; and the frequency of their trips to London. Austen chronicles the importance of income for marriage and status in a money-oriented society. The family is the primary arena of consumption.

The privacy of family life intensified with the transfer of paid work to a public workplace. Middle-class Europeans, whether French, German, or British, shared with Austen's families a taste for decorated interiors and material comforts in the home. In Germany, the Biedermeier style, named after a popular furniture maker, appeared in 1815 and remained popular until midcentury. Biedermeier stressed coziness, intimacy, and domesticity in the furnishings, clothes, and paintings of the German middle class. To its critics, the style was sentimental and vulgar. During this era, middle-class consumers began collecting on a mass scale. They filled their homes with knickknacks, curios, and mass-produced art. By accumulating these objects, the middle class asserted its right to be arbiter of its own style. At the same time, middle-class collectors aped the great aristocratic connoisseurs of a previous age.

A vast gulf separated working-class families from these middle-class consumers. Factory owner and social critic Friedrich Engels (1820–95) left a bleak but accurate account of working-class life in Manchester in *The Condition of the Working Class in England in 1844.* Working women, unsupervised children, and unemployed husbands figured prominently in his brutal tale of misery and immorality. Western culture redefined family life as the seat of solace, comfort, and consumption, but for the majority of the population that ideal remained out of reach.

Reformers confronted the disparities in family life and placed the blame squarely on women's absence from the home. Women had made industrialization possible as they poured into the British and Continental textile factories and became the primary work force. Employers found women more adept and more dexterous than men in running the intricate new looms. Women worked for cheaper wages and generally were more docile than men in accepting the routinization of the factory. Men were considered more likely to organize, riot, or become rowdy. Women and children worked long hours under dire conditions. The number of women in factories was expanding rapidly in the 1830s and 1840s. The solution to the perceived decline in the working-class family was found in legislation to restrict women from working away from home and return them to care for their husbands and children.

Children were an even cheaper work force than women. Some proponents of child labor argued that the choice was to have children running wild in the streets and unsupervised at home or in the disciplined

Cloakroom of the Clifton Assembly Rooms *(1817–18) by Rolinda Sharples is an example of the popular genre scenes that dealt with sentimental romanticized subjects.*

Seneca Falls Resolutions

One of the most influential meetings in furthering the claims of women to full participation in civil life occurred at Seneca Falls, New York, in 1848 where the assembled women declared their rights as individuals equal to men and full members of the body politic. The women present—many of them active in the antislavery and temperance movement—included Elizabeth Cady Stanton (1815–1902) and Susan B. Anthony (1820–1906). In 1840, eight years before Seneca Falls, Stanton and other abolitionists had attended an international antislavery convention in London. The exclusion of the women delegates from the floor of the London convention shocked Stanton and her female colleagues and served as a turning point in their own political consciousness. Their resolutions at Seneca Falls, especially those demanding the right to vote, influenced burgeoning women's movements in Europe and the United States.

Resolved, That such laws as conflict, in any way, with the true and substantial happiness of woman, are contrary to the great precept of nature and of no validity, for this is "superior in obligation to any other."

Resolved, That all laws which prevent woman from occupying such a station in society as her conscience shall dictate, or which place her in a position inferior to that of man, are contrary to the great precept of nature, and therefore of no force or authority.

Resolved, That woman is man's equal—was intended to be so by the Creator, and the highest good of the race demands that she should be recognized as such.

Resolved, That the women of this country ought to be enlightened in regard to the laws under which they live, that they may no longer publish their degradation by declaring themselves satisfied with their present position, nor their ignorance, by asserting that they have all the rights they want.

Resolved, That inasmuch as man, while claiming for himself intellectual superiority, does accord to woman moral superiority, it is pre-eminently his duty to encourage her to speak and teach, as she has an opportunity, in all religious assemblies.

Resolved, That the same amount of virtue, delicacy, and refinement of behavior that is required of woman in the social state, should also be required of man, and the same transgressions should be visited with equal severity on both man and woman.

Resolved, That the objection of indelicacy and impropriety, which is so often brought against woman when she addresses a public audience, comes with a very ill-grace from those who encourage, by their attendance, her appearance on the stage, in the concert, or in feats of the circus.

Resolved, That woman has too long rested satisfied in the circumscribed limits which corrupt customs and a perverted application of the Scriptures have marked out for her, and that it is time she should move in the enlarged sphere which her great Creator has assigned her.

Resolved, That it is the duty of the women of this country to secure to themselves their sacred right to the elective franchise.

Resolved, That the equality of human rights results necessarily from the fact of the identity of the race in capabilities and responsibilities.

Resolved, therefore, That, being invested by the Creator with the same capabilities, and the same consciousness of responsibility for their exercise, it is demonstrably the right and duty of woman, equally with man, to promote every righteous cause by every righteous means; and especially in regard to the great subjects of morals and religion, it is self-evidently her right to participate with her brother in teaching them, both in private and in public, by writing and by speaking, by any instrumentalities proper to be used, and in any assemblies proper to be held; and this being a self-evident truth growing out of the divinely implanted principles of human nature, any custom or authority adverse to it, whether modern or wearing the hoary sanction of antiquity, is to be regarded as a self-evident falsehood, and at war with mankind.

Resolved, That the speedy success of our cause depends upon the zealous and untiring efforts of both men and women, for the overthrow of the monopoly of the pulpit, and for the securing to woman an equal participation with men in the various trades, professions, and commerce.

From Declaration of Sentiments and Resolutions, Seneca Falls Convention of 1848.

A family portrait of Queen Victoria, the Prince Consort, and their eldest children, painted by Franz Xavier Winterhalter in 1846. Their first daughter, Victoria, would become the mother of Kaiser Wilhelm II of Germany.

environment of the factories. The situation at its worst was reflected in one eyewitness account of French silk manufacture. For 18 hours a day, six-year-old girls were harnessed to mechanical wheels to work.

Women's rights, little affected by industrialization, were increasingly disputed in public forums after 1815. In France, the equality of citizens before the law did not extend to women. Women's subservience in marriage was clearly defined: "A husband owes protection to his wife, a wife obedience to her husband." The law preserved a double standard for judging the behavior of women and men. In English law, men could terminate their marriages but their wives had no such access to divorce. Agitation for the right to divorce, converging with notorious public scandals over abused married women, achieved nothing before 1850. Critics blamed the decline in sexual mores on women's refusal to "know their place." By the mid-nineteenth century, women were organizing to demand equal political rights, political representation, assistance in caring for children, and better living conditions. Through their own newspapers, journals, and pamphlets, bourgeois women publicized their political demands for all women. John Stuart Mill, the leading liberal theorist, joined with women reformers in demanding full equality for British women. These movements achieved little in solid reforms before 1850, but they made clear the tensions within the family and within the law.

The growing emphasis on public education added its own special twist to the debate over family life and women's rights. Few agreed with French labor leader Flora Tristan (1801–44) and the utopian reformer Charles Fourier that women had the capacity and the right to receive an equal education with men. Most argued that women should be educated only to fulfill better their natural responsibilities as mothers. Napoleon's dictum "The hand that rocks the cradle rules the nation" became the chief justification for educating girls as mothers.

In 1837, in Great Britain, an eighteen-year-old became queen. Reigning until her death in 1901, Victoria gave her name to an age and its morals. Girls became queens of Portugal and Spain. They, like the young Victoria, were little more than political figureheads, protecting the survival of dynastic claims and contributing little to the growing debate about women's proper place in society. Although the presence of women on European thrones may have provided inspiration for disenfranchised women, it did not affect the broader reality that everywhere women were deprived of the vote and equal protection before the law, that married women could not own property or claim custody of their own children. Victoria, ruler of one of the world's great nations, became the model for domestic bliss. The changing expectations about the emotional rewards of family life, reflected in the publicity of the queen's marriage to Prince Albert of Saxe-Coburg-Gotha in 1840, created a new image of proper womanhood that had little relation to the lives that most women led.

To European societies that had remained stable, if not stagnant, for centuries, the changes in the first half of the nineteenth century were undoubtedly startling and disruptive. More people than ever before lived in cities, and national populations faced the prospect of becoming urban. Industrialization reshaped how people worked, how people lived, and how they consumed. But change did not necessarily mean improvement. Urban congestion brought crime and disease; new factories created the arena for exploitation and misery; and patterns of consumption demonstrated beyond dispute that people were not created equal. New expectations were attached to the family as its size changed and gender roles underwent redefinition. A new European society that challenged existing political ideas and demanded new political formulations was in the process of emerging.

The New Ideologies

Early industrialization had been accomplished without a dramatically new technology. Wood, water, wind, and muscle—animal and human—the sources of energy in the preindustrial period, fueled the early stages of industrialization. Practices began to change slowly as crises in energy supply—deforestation and drought, for example—encouraged the use of coal as a more reliable and eventually more efficient fuel. After 1815, steam-driven mechanical power in production and transportation steadily replaced human and animal power. In deference to what it was replacing, the new mechanical force was measured in units of horsepower. The new technology challenged old values; new definitions of worth emerged from the changing world of work. The fixed, castelike distinctions of the old aristocratic world were under attack or in disarray. Western intellectuals struggled with the changes of the new age as they sought to make sense of the way in which Europeans lived, looked at the world, and defined their place in it.

The political and economic upheavals of the first half of the nineteenth century encouraged a new breed of thinkers to search for ways to explain the transformations of the period. During this period, Europeans witnessed one of the most intellectually fertile periods in the history of the West. The search for understanding during this era gave birth to new ideologies—liberalism, nationalism, romanticism, conservatism, and socialism—that would shape the ideas and institutions of the present day.

Liberalism

The term *liberal* was first used in a narrow political sense to indicate the Spanish party of reform that supported the constitution modeled on the French document of 1791. But the term assumed much broader connotations in the first half of the nineteenth century as its appeal spread among the European middle classes. The two main tenets of belief that underlay liberalism were the freedom of the individual and the corruptibility of authority. As a political doctrine, liberalism built on Enlightenment rationalism and embraced the right to vote, civil liberties, legal equality, constitutional government, parliamentary sovereignty, and a free-market economy. Liberals firmly believed that less government was better government and that noninterference would produce a harmonious and well-ordered world. They also believed that human beings were basically good and reasonable and needed freedom in which to flourish. The sole end of government should be to promote that freedom.

No single representative thinker embodied all the tenets of liberal thought, but many shared similar ideas and beliefs. Liberal thinkers tried to make sense of the political conflicts of the revolutionary period and the economic disruptions brought on by industrialization. The Great Revolution at the end of the eighteenth century spawned a vast array of liberal thought in France. Republicans, Bonapartists, and constitutional monarchists cooperated as self-styled "liberals" who shared a desire to preserve the gains of the revolution while ensuring orderly rule. Not the least influenced by liberal ideas were a variety of political movements in the United States, including those demanding the liberation of slaves and the extension of legal and political rights to women. Abolitionists justified their opposition to slavery on humanitarian Christian grounds and on the liberal principles of freedom and equality. American women who were active in antislavery societies extended their liberal crusade against oppression to their own legal and political status.

By the mid-nineteenth century, liberal thinking constituted a dominant strain in British politics. Jeremy Bentham (1748–1832), trained in British law, fashioned himself into a social philosopher. He founded utilitarianism, a fundamentally liberal doctrine that argued for "the greatest happiness of the greatest number" in such works as *Introduction to the Principles of Morals and Legislation*. Bentham believed that government could achieve positive ends through limited and "scientific" intervention. Only the pursuit of social har-

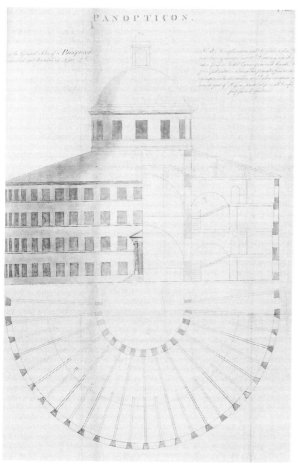

This model prison, called the Panopticon, was designed by Jeremy Bentham. The circular arrangement allowed a centrally located guard to monitor all outside cells. The prison was never built, but the design influenced later prison builders.

mony justified interference with individual liberty. He found the best testing grounds for his theories in prisons, among convicted criminals. By supporting the reform of penal codes and prison regulations in *Rationale of Punishments and Rewards* (1825), he hoped that rewards and punishments could be meted out to convicts in a measurable "geometry" of pain and pleasure. He was sure that behavior could be improved and that prisoners could be rehabilitated and returned as honest citizens to society.

The Scottish philosopher, economist, and historian James Mill (1773–1836) met Jeremy Bentham in 1808 and dedicated the rest of his life to promulgating Bentham's utilitarian philosophy. James Mill's son John Stuart Mill (1806–73) reacted to his early and intense education in Benthamite ideas by rejecting the tenets of utilitarianism. Forging his own brand of classical liberalism in his treatise *On Liberty* (1859), the younger Mill became the greatest liberal thinker of the age. John Stuart Mill criticized Bentham for ignoring human emotions and for the mass tyranny implicit in his ideas. Mill went beyond existing political analyses by applying economic doctrines to social conditions in *Principles of Political Economy* (1848). With Harriet Taylor (d. 1858), who married him after years of intellectual collaboration, he espoused social reform for the poor and championed the equality of women and the necessity of birth control. By 1848 his writings on liberty and equality were questioning the sacredness of private property. In later life, John Stuart Mill came to believe that a more equitable distribution of wealth was both necessary and possible.

David Ricardo (1772–1823) was a stockbroker prodigy who by the age of twenty had made his fortune. In *Principles of Political Economy and Taxation* (1817), Ricardo outlined his opposition to government intervention in foreign trade and elaborated his "iron law of wages," which contended that wages would stabilize at the subsistence level. Increased wages would cause the working classes to grow, and the resulting competition in the labor market would drive wages down to the level of subsistence. Other liberals, more concerned with social welfare than Ricardo, argued that state intervention was unavoidable but could be limited.

Nationalism

In its most basic sense, nationalism before 1850 was the political doctrine that glorified the people united against the absolutism of kings and the tyranny of foreign oppressors. The success of the French Revolution and the spread of Napoleonic reforms boosted nationalist doctrines, which were most fully articulated on the Continent. In Germany, Johann Gottfried von Herder (1744–1803) rooted national identity in German folk culture. The *Fairy Tales* (1812–14) of the brothers Jacob Ludwig Grimm (1785–1863) and Wilhelm Carl Grimm (1786–1859) had a similar national purpose. The brothers painstakingly captured in print the German oral tradition of peasant folklore. The philosophers Johann Fichte (1762–1814) and Georg Wilhelm Friedrich Hegel (1770–1831) emphasized the importance of the state. Nationalism gave birth to a search for new symbols, just as the tricolor flag replaced the fleur-de-lis and the image of Marianne replaced the monarch as a result of the Great Revolu-

YOUNG ITALY (1832)

Giuseppe Mazzini, an Italian patriot and revolutionary, was the principal theorist of national revolution in Europe in the first half of the nineteenth century. He claimed that his strong commitment to equality and democratic principles stemmed from his readings on the French Revolution of 1789 and his study of the Latin classics. As a young man, he resolved to dress always in black as a sign of mourning for his country, disunited and under foreign oppressors. In 1832 he founded the secret society Young Italy. The goal of this revolutionary group was the unification of Italy under a republican form of government through direct popular action.

We have beheld Italy—Italy, the purpose, the soul, the consolation of our thoughts, the country chosen of God and oppressed by men, twice queen of the world and twice fallen through the infamy of foreigners and the guilt of her citizens, yet lovely still though she be dust, unmatched by any other nation whatever fortune has decreed; and Genius returns to seek in this dust the word of eternal life, and the spark that creates the future. . . .

Young Italy: but we chose this term because the one term seems to marshal before the youth of Italy the magnitude of its duties and the solemnity of the mission that circumstances have entrusted to it, so that it will be ready when the hour has struck to arise from its slumber to a new life of action and regeneration. And we chose it because we wanted to show ourselves, writing it, as what we are, to do battle with raised visors, to bear our faith before us, as the knights of medieval times bore their faith on their shields. For while we pity men who do not know the truth, we despise men who, though they know the truth, do not dare to speak it.

tion in France. There was a new concern with history as nationalists sought to revive a common cultural past.

In the period between 1830 and 1850, many nationalists were liberals and many liberals were nationalists. The nationalist yearning for liberation meshed with the liberal political program of overthrowing tyrannical rule. Giuseppe Mazzini (1805–72) represented the new breed of liberal nationalist. A less-than-liberal nationalist was political economist Georg Friedrich List (1789–1846), who formulated a statement of economic nationalism to counter the liberal doctrines of David Ricardo. Arguing that free trade worked only for the wealthy and powerful, List advocated a program of protective tariffs for developing German industries. He perceived British free trade as merely economic imperialism in disguise. List was one of the few nationalists who did not wholeheartedly embrace liberal economic doctrines. Beyond ideology and political practices, nationalism began to capture the imagination of groups who resented foreign domination. Expanding state bureaucracies did little to tame the centrifugal forces of nationalist feeling and probably exacerbated a desire for independence in eastern and central Europe, especially in the Habsburg-ruled lands.

Romanticism

Unlike liberalism and nationalism, which were fundamentally political ideologies, romanticism designated a variety of literary and artistic movements throughout Europe that spanned the period from the late eighteenth century to the mid-nineteenth century. One could be a nationalist and a romantic or a liberal and a romantic just as easily as one could be a conservative and a romantic. Above all, and in spite of variations, romantics shared similar beliefs and a common view of the world. Among the first romantics were the English poets William Wordsworth (1770–1850) and Samuel Taylor Coleridge (1772–1834), whose collaborative *Lyrical Ballads* (1798) exemplified the iconoclastic romantic idea that poetry was the result of "the spontaneous overflow of powerful feelings" rather than a formal and highly disciplined intellectual exercise. Romantics, in general, rebelled against the confinement of classical forms and refused to accept the supremacy of reason over emotions.

The English gardens designed at the end of the eighteenth century provide one of the best visual examples of the new romanticism. The formal gardens that surrounded the castles and manor houses of Europe's wealthy elite throughout the eighteenth century relied on carefully drawn geometric patterns, minutely trimmed hedges and lawns, and symmetrically arranged flowers planted in rows by size and color to achieve the effect of total mastery of nature. The gardens at the great palace of Versailles are a good example of the formal landscaping chosen by France's kings and emulated by the wealthy everywhere in Europe. The romantic or English garden was, by contrast, a rebellious profusion of color in which the landscaper rejected the carefully drawn geometric patterns then in vogue and set out instead, deliberately and somewhat paradoxically, to imitate nature. The romantic aesthetic, whether in landscape gardening or in literature, recognized the beauty of untamed nature and the inspiration produced by the release of human emotions.

By rooting artistic vision in spontaneity, romantics endorsed a concept of creativity based on the supremacy of human freedom. The artist was valued in a new way as a genius through whose insight and intuition great art was created. Intuition, as opposed to scientific learning, was endorsed as a valid means of knowing. Building on the work of the eighteenth-century philosopher Immanuel Kant (1724–1804), romanticism embraced subjective knowledge. Inspiration and intuition took the place of reason and science in the romantic pantheon of values.

Germaine de Staël (1766–1817), often hailed as the founder of French romanticism, was an extraordinary woman whose writings influenced French liberal political theory after 1815. Madame de Staël's mother had followed the principles of education spelled out by Jean Jacques Rousseau in *Émile* (1762), according to which the child was allowed to follow his or her own path of intellectual development. De Staël authored histories, novels, literary criticism, and political tracts that opposed what she judged to be the tyranny of Napoleonic rule. She, like many other romantics, was greatly influenced by the writings of Rousseau, and through him she discovered that "the soul's elevation is born of self-consciousness." The recognition of the subjective meant for de Staël that women's vision was as essential as men's for the flowering of European culture.

"It is within oneself that one must look at what lies outside." Following de Staël's lead, Victor Hugo (1802–85), one of the great French writers of the nineteenth century, identified another essential ingredient in romanticism. The turning "within oneself" so apparent in Hugo's poetry was profoundly influenced by the political events of the French Revolution and its principles of liberty and equality. His greatest novels, including *Notre-Dame de Paris* (1831) and *Les Misérables* (1862), offer bold panoramic sweeps of the social universe of Paris across the ages.

Nationalists in the first half of the nineteenth century were often romantics who valued the authenticity of the vernacular and folklore over the language and customs imposed by a foreign ruler. Herder and the brothers Grimm were German examples of the romantic appreciation of the roots of German culture. While French romantics emphasized the glories of their revolutionary heritage, German romantics stressed the importance of history as the source of one's identity. By searching for the self in a historic past, and especially in the Middle Ages, they glorified their collective cultural identity and national origins. Medievalism in Germany was at the heart of *Sturm und Drang* (Storm and Stress), a literary movement founded in the 1770s. A founder of the *Sturm und Drang* movement, Johann Wolfgang von Goethe (1749–1832), hailed as the greatest of modern German writers, inspired generations with his dramatic poem *Faust* (Part I, 1808; Part II, 1832). In the poem, Goethe recounts the traditional legend of a man who sells his soul to the devil in exchange for greater knowledge. Faust, who achieves mystical salvation in the poem's final scene, symbolizes for Goethe the spiritual crisis plaguing European civilization in the early nineteenth century.

Whether in words or in music or on canvas, romanticism conveyed a new way of understanding the world. The supremacy of the emotions over reason found its way into the works of the great romantic composers of the age. Liberation from the forms that dominated the classical era could be heard in the works of French composer Louis Hector Berlioz (1803–69), who set Faust's damnation to music; Polish virtuoso Frédéric Chopin (1810–49), who created lyric compositions for the piano; and Hungarian concert pianist Franz Liszt (1811–86), who composed symphonic poems and Hungarian rhapsodies.

Artists as different as J. M. W. Turner (1775–1851), the English landscape painter, and Eugène Delacroix (1798–1863), the leader of the French romantic school in painting, shared a commitment to their iconoclastic art. Turner's intense and increasingly abstract vision of an often turbulent natural world and Delacroix's epic historical and political masterpieces shared a rebellious experimentation with color and a rejection of classical

Liberty Leading the People (1831) *by Eugène Delacroix captures the spirit of the French romantics, who looked upon revolutionary action as a way to achieve union with the spirit of history.*

conventions and forms. Characteristic of a particular strain within romanticism was the political message of Delacroix's art. In the magnificent painting *Liberty Leading the People* (1831), for example, Delacroix immortalized the revolutionary events that swept Paris in 1830 in his moving portrayal of valiant revolutionaries of different social classes led into battle by a female Liberty.

In the postrevolutionary years between 1815 and 1850, romanticism claimed to be no more than an aesthetic stance in art, letters, and music, a posture that had no particular political intent. Yet its validation of the individual as opposed to the caste or the estate was the most revolutionary of doctrines, just as its justification of subjective knowledge threatened to erode the authority of classical learning. Artists did not make revolutions, but they supported them. Some stood by on the sidelines; others mounted the barricades; but all romantics, no matter how political or apolitical, helped shape a new way of looking at the world and helped define a new political consciousness.

Conservatism

Conservatism was not a rejection of political, economic, or social change. Like liberalism, conservatism rep-

resented a dynamic adaptation to a social system in transition. In place of individualism, conservatives stressed the corporate nature of European society; in place of reason and progress, conservatives saw organic growth and tradition. Liberty, argued British statesman Edmund Burke (1729–97) in *Reflections on the Revolution in France* (1790), must emerge out of the gradual development of the old order, and not its destruction. On the Continent, conservatives Louis de Bonald (1754–1840) and Joseph de Maistre (1753–1821) defended the monarchical principle of authority against the onslaught of revolutionary events.

Conservatism took a reactionary turn in the hands of the Austrian statesman Metternich. The Carlsbad decrees of 1819 are a good example of the "Metternich system" of espionage, censorship, and repression in central Europe, which sought to eliminate any constitutional or nationalist sentiments that had arisen during the Napoleonic period. The German Confederation approved decrees against free speech and civil liberties and set up mechanisms to root out "subversive" university students. Students who had taken up arms in the Wars of Liberation (1813–15) against France had done so in hopes of instituting liberal and national reforms. Metternich's system aimed at uprooting these goals. Student fraternities were closed, and police became a regular fixture in the university. Political expression was driven underground for at least a decade. Metternich set out to crush liberalism, constitutionalism, and parliamentarianism in central Europe. His goals, though tolerated, were certainly not shared by more liberal regimes such as Great Britain's.

Socialism

Socialists and conservatives shared one point of view: both rejected the world as it was. Socialism, like other ideologies of the first half of the nineteenth century, grew out of changes in the structure of daily life and the structure of power. There were as many stripes of socialists as there were liberals, nationalists, and conservatives. Socialists as a group shared a concern with "alienation," though they may not all have used the term.

Henri de Saint-Simon (1760–1825) rejected liberal individualism in favor of social organization, and for this reason has been called the father of French socialism. To Saint-Simon, the accomplishments and potential of industrial development represented the highest stage in history. In a perfect and just society, productive work would be the basis of all prestige and power. The elite of society would be organized according to the hierarchy of its productive members, with industrial

leaders at the top. Work was a social duty. The new industrial society that Saint-Simon foresaw would be both efficient and ethical, based on a religion similar to Christianity.

Like Saint-Simon, the French social theorist Pierre-Joseph Proudhon (1809–65) recognized the social value of work. But unlike Saint-Simon, Proudhon refused to accept the dominance of industrial society. A self-educated typesetter of peasant origin, Proudhon gained national prominence with his ideas about a just society, free credit, and equitable exchange. In his famous pamphlet *What Is Property?* (1840), Proudhon answered, "Property is theft." This statement was not, however, an argument for the abolition of private ownership. Proudhon reasoned that industrialization had destroyed workers' rights, which included the right to the profits of their own labor. In attacking "property" in the form of profits amassed from the labor of others, Proudhon was arguing for a socialist concept of limited possession—people had the right to own only what they had earned from their own labor. Proudhon, who did not himself participate in political agitation, held a profoundly anarchistic view of society, hated government, and favored instead small self-ruling communities of producers. Proudhon's ideal world would be one of comfort but not great wealth.

Proudhon and His Children *(1865) by Gustave Courbet. Proudon's literary and political activities often led to trouble with the authorities. He spent a number of years in prison or in exile.*

At least one socialist believed in luxury. Charles Fourier (1772–1837), an unsuccessful traveling salesman, devoted himself to the study and improvement of society and formulated one of the most trenchant criticisms of industrial capitalism. In numerous writings between 1808 and his death, this eccentric, solitary man put forth his vision of a utopian world organized into units called phalanxes that took into account the social, sexual, and economic needs of their members. With a proper mix of duties, everyone in the phalanx would work only a few hours a day. In Fourier's scheme, work was not naturally abhorrent, but care had to be taken to match temperaments with tasks. Women and men fulfilled themselves and found pleasure and gratification through work. People would be paid according to their contributions in work, capital, and talent. In his vision of a better world, Fourier's phalanxes were always rural and were organized communally, though neither poverty nor property would be eliminated. Education would help alleviate discord, and rich and poor would learn to live together in perfect harmony.

Charles Fourier's work, along with that of Saint-Simon and Proudhon, became part of the tradition of utopian thinking that can be traced back to Thomas More in the sixteenth century. Because he believed in the ability of individuals to shape themselves and their world, Fourier intended his critique of society to be a blueprint for living. Fourier's followers set up communities in his lifetime—40 phalanxes were established in the United States alone—but because of financial problems and petty squabbling, all of them failed.

Women active in demanding their own emancipation were often joined by men who espoused utopian socialist and liberal views. The issue of increased civil liberties for women, tied as it often was to talk of freeing the slaves, was both a moral and political question for social reformers and utopian thinkers, including Fourier, who put the issue of women's freedom at the center of their plans to redesign society. Saint-Simonians argued for woman's social elevation and searched for a female messiah. Other social reformers joined with conservative thinkers in arguing that women must be kept in their place and that their place was in the home. Proudhon, for example, saw women's only choices as working at home as housewives or working in the streets as prostitutes.

Socialists, along with other ideologues in the decades before the middle of the nineteenth century, were aware of how rapidly their world was changing. Many felt that a revolution that would eliminate poverty and the sufferings of the working class was at hand. Followers of Saint-Simon, Fourier, and Proudhon all hoped that their proposals and ideas would change the world and prevent violent upheaval. Not all social critics were so sanguine. In January 1848, two young men, one a philosopher living in exile and the other a businessman working for his father, began a collaboration that would last a lifetime with the publication of a short tract entitled *The Communist Manifesto*. Karl Marx (1818–83) and Friedrich Engels described the dire situation of the European working classes throughout the 1840s. The growing poverty and alienation of the proletariat, the authors promised, would bring to industrialized Europe a class war against the capitalists. Exploited workers must prepare themselves for the moment of revolution by joining with each other across national boundaries: "Workers of the world unite. You have nothing to lose but your chains." In light of subsequent events, the *Manifesto* appears to be a work of great predictive value. But neither Marx nor Engels realized that the hour of revolution was at hand.

Intellectuals and reformers hoped to reshape the world in which they lived with the force of their ideas. Yet the new ideologies were themselves the consequence of the changing role of government and the changing practices of daily life. The technology of industrial production informed people's values and required a new way of looking at the world. Liberals, nationalists, romantics, conservatives, and socialists addressed the challenges of a changing economy in a political universe buffeted by democratic ideas. The new ideologies did not provide easy answers, but they did serve to incite their followers to take up arms in protests and revolutions throughout Europe.

Protest and Revolution

Few Europeans alive in 1830 remembered the age of revolution that spanned the period from 1789 to 1799. Yet the legends were kept alive from one generation to the next. Secret political organizations perpetuated Jacobin republicanism. Mutual-aid societies and artisans' associations preserved the rituals of democratic culture. A revolutionary culture seemed to be budding in the student riots in Germany and in the revolutionary waves that swept across southern and central Europe in the early 1820s. Outside Manchester, England, in August 1819 a crowd of 80,000 people gathered in St. Peter's Field to hear speeches for parliamentary reform and universal male suffrage. The cavalry swept down on them in a bloody slaughter that

Massacre at St. Peters or "BRITONS STRIKE HOME"!!!

A savage satire of the Peterloo Massacre by cartoonist George Cruikshank. One soldier urges the others on by telling them that the more poor people they kill, the fewer taxes they will have to pay for poor relief.

came to be known as the "Peterloo" massacre, a bitter reference to the Waterloo victory four years before.

The fabric of stability began unraveling throughout Europe in the 1820s. The forces of order reacted to protest with repression everywhere in Europe. In the more industrialized countries of England and France, the army was joined by the newly created peacekeeping forces of the police. Yet armed force proved inadequate to contain the demands for political participation and the increased political awareness of whole segments of the population. Workers, the middle class, and women's political organizations now demanded, through the vote, the right to govern themselves.

The Revolutions of 1830

Poor harvests in 1829 followed by a harsh winter left people cold, hungry, and bitter. Misery fueled social protest, and political issues of participation and representation commanded a new attention. The convergence of social unrest with long-standing political demands touched off apparently simultaneous revolutions all over Europe. Governmental failure to respond to local grievances sparked the revolutions of 1830. Highly diverse groups of workers, students, lawyers, professionals, and peasants rose up spontaneously to demand a voice in the affairs of government.

In France, the late 1820s were a period of increasing political friction. Charles X (1824–30), the former comte d'Artois, had never resigned himself to the constitutional monarchy accepted by his brother and predecessor, Louis XVIII. When Charles assumed the throne in 1824, he dedicated himself to a true restoration of kingship as it had existed before the revolution. To this end, he realigned the monarchy with the Catholic church and undertook several unpopular measures, including approval of the death penalty for those found guilty of sacrilege. The king's bourgeois critics, heavily influenced by liberal ideas about political economy and constitutional rights, sought increased political power through their activities in secret organizations and in public elections. The king responded to his critics by relying on his ultraroyalist supporters to run the government. In May 1830, the king dissolved the Chamber of Deputies and ordered new elections. The elections returned a liberal majority unfavorable to the king. Charles X retaliated with what proved to be his last political act, the Four Ordinances, in which he censored the press, changed the electoral law to favor his own candidates, dissolved the newly elected Chamber, and ordered new elections.

Opposition to Charles X might have remained at the level of political wrangling and journalistic protest, if it had not been for the problems plaguing the people of Paris. A severe winter in France had driven up food prices by 75 percent. Most urban dwellers were barely subsisting. The king had erred in hoping that France's recent conquest of Algeria in North Africa would keep the populace quiet. He underestimated the extent of hardship and the political volatility of the population. Throughout the spring of 1830, prices continued to rise and Charles continued to blunder. In a spontaneous uprising in the last days of July 1830, workers took to the streets of Paris. The revolution they initiated spread rapidly to towns and the countryside as people throughout France protested the cost of living, hoarding by grain merchants, tax collection, and wage cuts. In "three glorious days," the restored Bourbon regime was pulled down and Charles X fled to England.

The people fighting in the streets demanded a republic, but they lacked organization and political experience. Liberal bourgeois politicians quickly filled the power vacuum. They presented Charles's cousin Louis-Philippe, formerly the duc d'Orléans, as the savior of France and the new constitutional monarch. This July Monarchy, born of a revolution, put an end to the Bourbon Restoration. Louis-Philippe became "king of the French." The charter that he brought with him was, like its predecessor, based on restricted suffrage, with property ownership a requisite for voting. The voting age was lowered from 30 to 25, and the tax requirement was also lowered. The electorate nearly doubled, from 90,000 to 170,000, but nevertheless voting remained restricted to a small fraction of the population.

Popular disturbances did not always result in revolution. In Britain, rural and town riots erupted over grain prices and distribution, but no revolution followed. German workers broke their machines to protest low wages and loss of control of the workplace, but no prince was displaced. In Switzerland, reformers found strength in the French revolutionary example. Ten Swiss cantons granted liberal constitutions and established universal manhood suffrage, freedom of expression, and legal equality.

In southern Europe, Greece had languished as a subjugated country for centuries. Turkish overlords ruled Greece as part of the Ottoman Empire. The longing for independence smoldered in Greece throughout the 1820s as public pressure to support the Greeks mounted in Europe. Greek insurrections were answered by Turkish retaliations throughout the Ottoman Empire. In 1822 a Turkish fleet captured the island of Chios in the Aegean Sea off the west coast of Turkey and massa-cred or enslaved the population. The atrocities committed by the Turks against Greeks in Constantinople provoked international reaction in the form of a Philhellenic (literally, "lover of Greece") movement supported by two of Britain's great romantic poets, Lord Byron (1788–1824) and Percy Bysshe Shelley (1792–1822). Byron sailed to the besieged Greek city of Missolonghi in 1824 to help coordinate the military effort, and there he contracted malaria and died. The sultan of Turkey had been able to call upon his vassal, the pasha of Egypt, to subdue Greece. In response, Great Britain, France, and Russia signed the Treaty of London in 1827, pledging intervention on behalf of Greece. In a joint effort, the three powers defeated the Egyptian fleet. Russia declared war on Turkey the following year, seeking territorial concessions from the Ottoman Empire. Following the Russian victory, Great Britain and France joined Russia in declaring Greek independence.

The concerted action of the three powers in favor of Greek independence was neither an endorsement of liberal ideals nor a support of Greek nationalism. The British, French, and Russians were reasserting their commitment made at the Congress of Vienna to territorial stability. Yet beneath the veneer of their commitment, the Russians intervened, hoping for territorial gains in the Ottoman Empire. The British favored Ottoman stability while distrusting Russian ambitions in the area. The Turks had been unable to maintain stability on their own. Finally, the three powers abandoned their policy of propping up the Ottoman Empire and supported instead the movement for Greek independence. But they did so on their own terms by creating a monarchy in Greece and placing a German-born prince on the new throne.

The overthrow of the Bourbon monarch in France served as a model for revolution in other parts of Europe. Following the French lead, in the midst of the Greek crisis the Belgian provinces revolted against the Netherlands. The Belgians' desire for their own nation struck at the heart of the Vienna settlement. Provoked by a food crisis similar to that in France, Belgian revolutionaries took to the streets in August 1830. As a symbol of their solidarity with the successful French Revolution, they flew the tricolor in defiance of their Dutch rulers. Belgians protested the deterioration of their economic situation and made demands for their own Catholic religion, their own language, and constitutional rights. Bitter fighting on the barricades in Brussels ensued, and the movement for freedom and independence spread to the countryside.

'Gentlemen,' says Nicholas I, the bear, to the Polish revolutionaries of 1830, 'I know that you wish to address me; but to spare you from delivering a pack of lies, I desire that you hold your tongues.' The Polish rebellion of 1830–31 was brutally suppressed by the Russians. However, this brutality reinforced Polish national sentiment (the Poles rebelled again in 1863) and engaged the sympathy of the West for the Poles—as this English cartoon shows. (2)

This English cartoon of 1832 is titled "The Clemency of the Russian Monster." It shows Nicholas I in the guise of a bear with menacing teeth and claws addressing the Poles after crushing their rebellion against Russian rule.

The Great Powers disagreed on what to do. Russia, Austria, and Prussia were all eager to see the revolution crushed. France, having just established the new regime of the July Monarchy, and Great Britain, fearing the involvement of the central and eastern European powers in an area where Britain had traditionally had interests, were reluctant to intervene. A provisional government in Belgium set about the task of writing a constitution. All five great powers recognized Belgian independence, with the proviso that Belgium was to maintain the status of a neutral state.

Russia, Prussia, and Austria were convinced to accept Belgian independence because they were having their own problems in eastern and southern Europe. Revolution erupted to the east, in Warsaw, Poland. Driven by a desire for national independence, Polish army cadets and university students revolted in November 1830, demanding a constitution. Landed aristocrats and gentry helped establish a provisional government but soon split over how radical reforms should be. Polish peasants refused to support either landowning group. Within the year, Russia brought in 180,000 troops to crush the revolution and reassert its rule over Poland. All pretext of constitutional rule ended. Thousands of Poles were executed; others fled to exile in western Europe, including the five thousand who settled in France. Inspired by the poetry of Adam Mickiewicz (1798–1855) and the music of Frédéric

Chopin, many of them dedicated themselves to the cause of Polish nationalism and to resurrecting an independent Polish kingdom. The Poles remained a captive people of the Habsburg, Hohenzollern, and Romanov empires until 1918–19.

In February 1831, the Italian states of Modena and Parma rose up to throw off Austrian domination of northern Italy. The revolutionaries were ineffective against Austrian troops. Revolution in the Papal States resulted in French occupation that lasted until 1838 without serious reforms. Nationalist and republican yearnings were driven underground, kept alive there in the Young Italy movement under the leadership of Giuseppe Mazzini.

Although the revolutions of 1830 are called "the forgotten revolutions" of the nineteenth century, they are important for several reasons. First, they made clear to European states how closely tied together were their fates. The events of 1830 were a test of the Great Powers' commitment to stability and a balance of power in Europe. True to the principles of the Vienna settlements of 1815, European leaders preserved the status quo. Revolutions in Poland and Italy were contained by Russia and Austria without interference from the other powers. Where adaptation was necessary, as in Greece and Belgium, the Great Powers were able to compromise on settlements, though the solutions ran counter to previous policies. Heads of state were willing to use the forces of repression to stamp out protest. Although each revolution followed its own pattern of development, all shared origins in domestic crises unsuccessfully addressed by those in power.

The international significance of the revolutions reveals a second important aspect of the events of 1830: the vulnerability of international politics to domestic instability. No state could practice diplomacy in a vacuum. Grain prices and demands for democratic participation had direct impact on the balance of power of European states. The five Great Powers broke down into two ideological camps. On the one hand were the liberal constitutional states of Great Britain and France; on the other stood the autocratic monarchies of Russia, Austria, and Prussia. Yet ideological differences were always less important than the shared desire for internal stability as a prerequisite for international peace.

Finally, the 1830 revolutions exposed a growing awareness of politics at all levels of European society. If policies in 1830 revealed a shared consciousness of events and shared values among ruling elites, the revolutions disclosed a growing awareness among the lower classes of the importance of politics in their daily lives. The cry for "liberty, equality, and fraternity" transcended national borders and the French language. The demands for constitutions, national identity, and civic equality resounded from the Atlantic to the Urals. In a dangerous combination of circumstances, workers and the lower classes throughout Europe were politicized, yet they continued to be excluded from political power.

Reform in Great Britain

The right to vote had been an issue of contention in the revolutions of 1830 in western Europe. Only the Swiss cantons enforced the principle of "one man, one vote." The July Revolution in France had doubled the electorate, but still only a tiny minority of the population (less than 1 percent) enjoyed the vote. Universal male suffrage had been mandated in 1793 during the Great Revolution but not implemented. This exclusion of the mass of the population from participation in electoral politics was no oversight. Those in power believed that the wealthiest property owners were best qualified to govern, in part because they had the greatest stake in politics and society. One also needed to own property to hold office. Because those who served in parliaments received no salary, only the wealthy had the resources and the leisure to represent the electorate. When confronted by his critics, François Guizot (1787–1874), French prime minister and chief

spokesman for the July Monarchy, offered this glib advice to an aspiring electorate: "Get rich!"

Landowners ruled Britain too. There the dominance of a wealthy elite was strengthened by the geographic redistribution of population resulting from industrialization. Migration to cities had depleted the population of rural areas. Yet the electoral system did not adjust to these changes: large towns had no parliamentary representation, while dwindling county electorates maintained their parliamentary strength. Areas that continued to enjoy representation greater than that justified by their population were dubbed "rotten" or "pocket" boroughs to indicate a corrupt and antiquated electoral system. In general, urban areas were grossly underrepresented and the wealthy few controlled county seats.

Liberal reformers attempted to rectify the electoral inequalities by reassigning parliamentary seats on the basis of density of population, but vested interests balked at attempted reforms and members of Parliament wrangled bitterly. Popular agitation by the lower classes provoked the fear of civil war, which helped break the parliamentary deadlock. The Great Reform Bill of 1832 proposed a compromise. Although the vast majority of the population still did not have the vote, the new legislation strengthened the industrial and commercial elite in the towns, enfranchised most of the middle class, opened the way to social reforms, and encouraged the formation of political parties.

Years of bad harvests, unemployment, and depression, coupled with growing dissatisfaction with the government's weak efforts to address social problems, put the spur to a new national reform movement in the 1830s. Radical reformers, disillusioned with the 1832 Reform Bill because it strengthened the power of a wealthy capitalist class, argued that democracy was the only answer to the problems plaguing British society. In 1838, a small group of labor leaders, including representatives of the London Working Men's Association, an organization of craft workers, drew up a document known as the People's Charter. The single most important demand of the charter was that all men must have the vote. In addition, Chartists petitioned for a secret ballot, salaries for parliamentary service, elimination of the requirement that one must own property in order to run for office, equal electoral districts, and annual elections. The proposal favored direct democracy, guaranteed by frequent elections that would ensure maximum accountability of officials to their constituents.

Chartist appeal was greatest in periods of economic hardship. A violent mood swept through the move-

THE REFORM BILL.

The Reform Bill of 1832 is praised by a contemporary cartoonist. "Rotten boroughs" and political corruption are put through a meat grinder by Whig leaders, and a triumphant Britannia emerges.

ment in 1839. The Irish Chartist leader Feargus O'Connor (1794–1855) and the Irish journalist and orator James Bronterre O'Brien (1805–64) urged an unskilled and poorly organized working class to protest inequities through strikes that on occasion became violent. O'Brien thrilled his working-class listeners by haranguing "the big-bellied, little-brained, numbskull aristocracy." Chartism blossomed as a communal phenomenon in working-class towns and appeared to involve all members of the family: "Every kitchen is now a political meeting house; the little children are members of the unions and the good mother is the political teacher," one Chartist organizer boasted. Chartist babies were christened with the names of Chartist heroes. When Mrs. King of Manchester, England, attempted to register the birth of her son, James Feargus O'Connor King, her choice of names was challenged. The registrar demanded, "Is your husband a Chartist?" Mrs. King replied, "I don't know, but his wife is." Women organized Chartist schools and Sunday schools in radical defiance of local church organizations. Many middle-class observers were sure that the moment for class war and revolutionary upheaval had arrived. The government responded with force to the perceived threat of arm-

ed rebellion and imprisoned a number of Chartist leaders.

Throughout the 1840s, bad harvests and economic hardships continued to fan the flames of discontent. National petitions signed by millions were submitted to the House of Commons, which stubbornly resisted the idea of universal manhood suffrage. Strikes and attacks on factories spread throughout England, Scotland, and Wales in 1842. Increased violence served to make the Parliament intransigent and caused the movement to splinter and weaken as moderates formed their own factions. The final moment for Chartism occurred in April 1848 when 25,000 Chartist workers, inspired by revolutionary events on the Continent, assembled in London to march on the House of Commons. They carried with them a newly signed petition demanding the enactment of the terms of the People's Charter. In response, the government deputized nearly 200,000 "special" constables in the streets. These deputized private citizens were London property owners and skilled workers intent on holding back a revolutionary rabble. Tired, cold, and rain-soaked, the Chartist demonstrators disbanded. No social revolution took place in Great Britain, and the dilemma of democratic representation was deferred.

THE COMMUNIST MANIFESTO

The Communist Manifesto is one of the most important documents in world history. Translated into many languages in countless editions, it inspired worker organizations throughout Europe in the second half of the nineteenth century and fired the imagination of Communist leaders in Asia, Latin America, Africa, and Europe well into the twentieth century.

The pamphlet, which in its entirety consists of no more than twelve thousand words, was written at the beginning of 1848 by Karl Marx, founder of modern communism, and his collaborator and friend, Friedrich Engels. Their intention was to urge exploited workers throughout Europe to prepare themselves for the coming revolution by uniting across national boundaries. The Communist Manifesto is a concise statement of the basic tenets of Marxism. Although mistaken in most of its predictions about the future development of capitalism, it accurately distilled some of the most salient inequities of industrial economies whose remedies, Marx and Engels asserted, could only be found through the revolutionary overthrow of the capitalist system.

BOURGEOIS AND PROLETARIANS*

The history of all hitherto existing society is the history of class struggles.

Freeman and slave, patrician and plebeian, lord and serf, guild-master and journeyman, in a word, oppressor and oppressed, stood in constant opposition to one another, carried on an uninterrupted, now hidden, now open fight, a fight that each time ended, either in a revolutionary reconstitution of society at large, or in the common ruin of the contending classes. . . .

The modern bourgeois society that has sprouted from the ruins of feudal society has not done away with class antagonisms. It has but established new classes, new conditions of oppression, new forms of struggle in place of the old ones.

Our epoch, the epoch of the bourgeoisie, possesses, however, this distinctive feature: it has simplified the class antagonisms. Society as a whole is more and more splitting up into two great hostile camps, into two great classes directly facing each other: Bourgeoisie and Proletariat. . . .

The bourgeoisie cannot exist without constantly revolutionizing the instruments of production, and thereby the relations of production, and with them the whole relations of society. Conservation of the old modes of production in unaltered form, was, on the contrary, the first condition of existence for all earlier industrial classes. Constant revolutionizing of production, uninterrupted disturbance of all social conditions, everlasting uncertainty and agitation distinguish the bourgeois epoch from all earlier ones. All fixed, fast-frozen relations, with their train of ancient and venerable prejudices and opinions are swept away, all new-formed ones become antiquated before they can ossify. All that is solid melts into air, all that is holy is profaned, and man is at last com-

Workers Unite

The word *proletariat* entered European languages before the mid-nineteenth century to describe those workers afloat in the labor pool who owned nothing, not even the tools of their labor, and who were becoming "appendages" to the new machines that dominated production. To workers, machines could mean the elimination of jobs or the deskilling of tasks; almost always machines meant a drop in wages. Mechaniza-

tion deprived skilled craft workers of control of the workplace. In Great Britain, France, and Germany, groups of textile workers destroyed machines in protest. Workers demanding a fair wage smashed cotton power looms, knitting machines, and wool carding machines. Sometimes the machines were a bargaining point for workers who used violence against them as a last resort. Machine-breakers tyrannized parts of Great Britain from 1811 to 1816 in an attempt to frighten masters. The movement was known as Luddism after

pelled to face with sober senses, his real conditions of life, and his relations with his kind.

The need of a constantly expanding market for its products chases the bourgeoisie over the whole surface of the globe. It must nestle everywhere, settle everywhere, establish connexions everywhere. . . .

The proletariat goes through various stages of development. With its birth begins its struggle with the bourgeoisie. At first the contest is carried on by individual labourers, then by the work-people of a factory, then by the operatives of one trade, in one locality, against the individual bourgeois who directly exploits them. They direct their attacks not against the bourgeois conditions of production, but against the instruments of production themselves; they destroy imported wares that compete with their labour, they smash to pieces machinery, they set factories ablaze, they seek to restore by force the vanished status of the workman of the Middle Ages.

PROLETARIANS AND COMMUNISTS

In what relation do the Communists stand to the proletarians as a whole?

The Communists do not form a separate part opposed to other working-class parties.

They have no interests separate and apart from those of the proletariat as a whole. . . .

You are horrified at our [Communists'] intending to do away with private property. But in your existing society, private property is already done away with for

nine-tenths of the population; its existence for the few is solely due to its non-existence in the hands of those nine-tenths. You reproach us, therefore, with intending to do away with a form of property the necessary condition for whose existence is the non-existence of any property for the immense majority of society. . . .

In short, the Communists everywhere support every revolutionary movement against the existing social and political order of things.

In all these movements they bring to the front, as the leading question in each, the property question, no matter what its degree of development at the time.

Finally, they labour everywhere for the union and agreement of the democratic parties of all countries.

The Communists disdain to conceal their views and aims. They openly declare that their ends can be attained only by the forcible overthrow of all existing social conditions. Let the ruling classes tremble at a Communistic revolution. The proletarians have nothing to lose but their chains. They have a world to win.

WORKING MEN OF ALL COUNTRIES, UNITE!

*By bourgeoisie is meant the class of modern Capitalists, owners of the means of social production and employers of wage labour. By proletariat, the class of modern wage-labourers who, having no means of production of their own, are reduced to selling their labour power in order to live. [Note by Engels to the English edition of 1888.]

---

its mythical leader, Ned Ludd. Workers damaged and destroyed property for more control over the work process, but such destruction met with severe repression. From the 1820s to the 1850s, sporadic but intense outbursts of machine-breaking occurred in continental Europe. Suffering weavers in Silesia and Bohemia resorted to destroying their looms in 1844.

Craft production continued to deteriorate with the rise in industrial competition. Skilled workers, fearing that they would be pulled down into the new proletari-

at because of mechanization and the increased scale of production, began organizing in new ways after 1830 by forming associations to assert their control over the workplace and to demand a voice in politics.

In Britain, skilled craft workers built on a tradition of citizenship. They resisted the encroachments of factory production, and some channeled their political fervor into the Chartist movement. Skilled workers in France also built on a cultural heritage of shared language and values to create a consciousness of themselves as an exploited class. Uprisings and strikes in France, favoring the destruction of the monarchy and the creation of a democratic republic, increased dramatically from 1831 to 1834. Many French craft workers grew conscious of themselves as a class and embraced a socialism heavily influenced by their own traditions and contemporary socialist writings. Republican socialism spread throughout France by means of a network of traveling journeymen and tapped into growing economic hardship and political discontent with the July Monarchy. Government repression drove worker organizations underground in the late 1830s, but secret societies proliferated. Increasingly, workers saw the validity of the slogan of the silk workers of Lyon: "Live Working or Die Fighting!"

Women were an important part of the work force in the industrializing societies. Working men were keenly aware of the competition with cheaper female labor in the factories. Women formed a salaried work force in the home too. In order to turn out products cheaply and in large quantities, some manufacturers turned to subcontractors to perform the simpler tasks in the work process. These new middlemen contracted out work like cutting and sewing to needy women who were often responsible for caring for family members in their homes. This kind of subcontracting, called "sweated labor" because of the exertion and long hours involved in working in one's own home, was always poorly paid.

Cheap female labor paid by the piece allowed employers to profit by keeping overhead costs low and by driving down the wages of skilled workers. Trade unions opposed women's work, both in the home and in the factories. Women's talents, union leaders explained, were more properly devoted to domestic chores. Unions argued that their members should earn a family wage "sufficient to support a wife and children." Unions consistently excluded women workers from their ranks.

French labor leader Flora Tristan, herself a wife and mother, had a very different answer for those who wanted to remove women from the workplace and assign them to their "proper place" in the home. She recognized that working women needed to work in order to support themselves and their families. Tristan told audiences in Europe and Latin America that the emancipation of women from their "slave status" was essential if the working class as a whole was to enjoy a better future. She deplored the economic competition between working men and women and denounced the degradation of women in both the home and the workplace. A working woman earned one-third or less of the

All over Europe, workers reacted to industrialization with outbursts of violence against the factory machines. Here Bohemian weavers destroy their "most immediate enemy" in 1848.

average working man's wages, and women's working conditions were often deplorable. In the 1840s, British parliamentary commissions heard the horrifying testimony of one young London dressmaker from the country who was forced to work grueling hours—often 20 hours a day—under unhealthy working conditions that had destroyed her health. She concluded that "no men could endure the work enforced from the dressmakers."

Working women's only hope, according to Tristan, lay in education and unionization. She urged working men and women to join together to lay claim to their natural and inalienable rights. In some cases, working women formed their own organizations, like that of the Parisian seamstresses who joined together to demand improved working conditions. On the whole, however, domestic workers in the home remained isolated from other working women, and many women in factories feared the loss of their jobs if they engaged in political activism. The wages of Europe's working women remained low, often below the level of subsistence. In the absence of a man's income, working women and their children were the poorest of the poor in European society in the middle of the nineteenth century.

For some men and women of the working class, the 1840s were a time of mounting unrest, increased organization, and growing protest. Workers used their unity in associations, unions, and mutual-aid societies to press for full political participation and government action in times of economic distress. (See "Fear in Paris," pp. 710–711.)

The Revolutions of 1848

Europeans had never experienced a year like 1848. Beginning soon after the ringing in of the New Year, revolutionary fervor swept through nearly every European country. By year's end, regimes had been created and destroyed. France, Italy, the German states, Austria, Hungary, and Bohemia were shaken to their foundations. Switzerland, Denmark, and Romania experienced lesser upheavals. Great Britain had survived reformist agitation, and famine-crippled Ireland had endured a failed insurrection. No one was sure what had happened. Each country's conflict was based on a unique mix of issues, but all were connected in their conscious emulation of a revolutionary tradition.

Hindsight reveals warning signs in the two years before the 1848 cataclysm. Beginning in 1846, a severe famine—the last serious food crisis Europe would experience—racked Europe. Lack of grain drove up prices. An increasing percentage of disposable income was spent on food for survival. Lack of spending power severely damaged markets and forced thousands of industrial workers out of their jobs. The famine hurt everyone—the poor, workers, employers, and investors—as recession paralyzed the economy.

The food crisis took place in a heavily charged political atmosphere. Throughout Europe during the 1840s, the middle and lower classes had intensified their agitation for democracy. Chartists in Great Britain argued for a wider electorate. Bourgeois reformers in France campaigned for universal manhood suffrage. Known as the "banquet" campaign because its leaders attempted to raise money by giving speeches at subscribed dinners, the movement for the vote appeared to be developing a mass following by taking its cause directly to the people. In making demands for political participation, those agitating for suffrage necessarily criticized those in power. Freedom of speech and freedom of assembly were demanded as inalienable rights. The food crisis and political activism provided the ingredients for an incendiary situation.

In addition to a burgeoning democratic culture, growing demands for national autonomy based on linguistic and cultural claims spread through central, southern, and eastern Europe. The revolts in Poland in 1846, though failures, encouraged similar movements for national liberation among Italians and Germans. Even in the relatively homogeneous nation of France, concerns with national mission and national glory grew among the regime's critics. National unity was primarily a middle-class ideal. Liberal lawyers, teachers, and businessmen from Dublin to Budapest to Prague agitated for separation from foreign rule. Austria, with an empire formed of numerous ethnic minorities, had the most to lose. Since 1815, Metternich had been ruthless in stamping out nationalist dissent. However, by the 1840s, national claims were assuming a cultural legitimacy that was difficult to dismiss or ignore.

The events in France in the cold February of 1848 ignited the conflagration that swept Europe. Bourgeois reformers had arranged for their largest banquet to date in support of extension of the vote, to take place in Paris on 22 February. City officials became nervous at the prospect of thousands of workers assembling for political purposes and canceled the scheduled banquet. This was the spark that touched off the powder keg. In a spontaneous uprising, Parisians demonstrated against the government's repressive measures. Skilled workers took to the streets, not only in favor of the banned banquet but also with the hope that the government would recognize the importance of labor to the social order. Shots were fired; a demonstrator was killed. The French Revolution of 1848 had begun.

Events moved quickly. The National Guard, a citizen militia of bourgeois Parisians, defected from Louis-Philippe. Many army troops garrisoned in Paris crossed the barricades to join revolutionary workers. The king attempted some reform, but it was too little and too late. Louis-Philippe fled. The Second Republic was proclaimed at the insistence of the revolutionary crowds on the barricades. The Provisional Government, led by the poet Alphonse de Lamartine (1790–1869), included members of both factions of political reformers of the July Monarchy: moderates who sought constitutional reforms and an extension of the suffrage; and radicals who favored universal manhood suffrage and social programs to deal with poverty and work. Only the threat of popular violence held together this uneasy alliance.

The people fighting in the streets had little in common with the bourgeois reformers who assumed power on 24 February. Workers made a social revolution out

❧ Fear in Paris

At the height of his power, in 1810, Napoleon envisioned Paris as the capital of Europe, a mecca of art, style, and learning, "the most beautiful city that could ever exist." He never achieved his dream. Paris in 1840 was certainly a center of fashion and culture, but it was far from the extravagant beauty Napoleon dreamed of. Dark, dirty, ugly, rat-infested slums dominated the "city of light." It is reported that General Blücher, commander of the victorious Prussian forces that entered Paris in 1814, stood on the heights overlooking the city and predicted that Paris would achieve what invading armies could not: the destruction of France.

Problems arose because early-nineteenth-century Paris was physically a medieval city, yet it housed a modern population. By 1840 Paris held one million people, twice as many as it had only forty years earlier. The fastest growth occurred between 1830 and 1850, when 350,000 new residents were recorded. One out of every two Parisians had not been born in the city but had migrated to it. The city acted like a magnet, attracting provincials in search of employment and opportunity. The artisan Martin Nadaud was typical of many immigrants who came to the capital expecting to find its streets literally paved with gold. He found instead raw sewage, inadequate water supplies, overcrowded housing, disease, and poverty. Sixty-five percent of all Parisians were so poor that they paid no taxes. Fifty percent officially qualified as "indigents" and were eligible for humiliating and inadequate poor relief. Eighty percent of the people who died in Paris were buried in paupers' graves.

A bad situation got worse when a cholera epidemic ravaged the city for 189 days in 1832, leaving 18,000 people dead and 30,000 others afflicted. The vast majority of those stricken were from the lower classes. City dwellers knew nothing about the etiology of cholera, but they understood that the poor were dying and the rich were not. To explain their apparent immunity, many bourgeois citizens decided that the cholera epidemic was the fault of the poor, whose decadent lifestyles had created the disease and caused it to spread. Moralists railed that godlessness and sexual excess were taking their toll. Outraged bourgeois demanded sanitation—but of the spiritual sort.

If the bourgeoisie blamed the epidemic on immorality, workers attributed it to a conspiracy. The wealthy, they argued, were poisoning the water supply of the poor in order to limit their numbers. Such collective delusions gave rise to fear and general panic. Wealthy bourgeois fled the city to sit out the disease in rural peace. Among the lower classes, vigilante groups proliferated for the purpose of eliminating bourgeois villains. Several well-dressed gentlemen who strayed into working-class neighborhoods were killed for no greater offense than carrying suspicious-looking bottles that might contain contaminated fluids.

Urban life was further polarized by a rising crime rate that many felt portended the end of civilization. Gangs of homeless youths roamed city streets, fanning bourgeois fears. Gavroche, a character in Victor Hugo's *Les Misérables,* was one such fictional child of the streets who participated in the uprising of 1832. Hugo was sympathetic to the child's plight; many of his bourgeois readers were not. The title of a minor police official's best-selling account of urban life, *On the Dangerous Classes,* said it all to a terrified bourgeoisie. Crime was everywhere. In his *Human Comedy,* a vast collection of novels and short stories appearing between 1830 and 1850, Honoré de Balzac (1799–1850) created gangsters and thieves who were not only part of the criminal underworld but also ran the police force, commerce, and finance.

During the July Monarchy, social-scientific studies presented the city as a giant laboratory. Misery was measured. The hair color, height, and birthplaces of prostitutes were recorded. Infanticides and suicides were tallied. The studies concluded that poverty caused demoralization, violence, and crime. Reformers argued for low-cost housing, mass sanitation, and lighting. Yet the regime did little to address urban problems. Instead, the government undertook what seemed to many a curious public-works project of building a ring of fortifications around the city of Paris.

As other European cities began dismantling fortifications, Paris was the only city in the nineteenth century to enclose itself behind a fortified wall. Fortifications aggravated urban problems as thousands of workers flocked to the city to compete for the new jobs. Police complained about crime on the work sites and the increase in prostitution that they were unable to control. Fortifying the city played on people's fears. Why, it was asked, were troops, supplies, and equipment pulled back from the French-German border and concentrated in the capital? If France feared a foreign war, why was it preparing for one at the expense of its national frontiers?

Public debate raged over the excessive costs of the program. When it was discovered that the gun turrets on the forts could swivel inward and be aimed at the city as well as outward at an invading enemy, critics were sure they knew what was happening. The government, they charged, was preparing itself for a defensive action against its own capital and against its own citizens. There was reason for suspicion. After 1840 the government relied increasingly on the military as a repressive police force, spurning the National Guard, a citizen militia, as unreliable and its own municipal police as inefficient. Troops were the monarchy's solution to problems of law and order. Paris in 1840 had been turned into an armed camp.

The fortifications were never used against Parisians. When the revolution came in February 1848, the troops refused to fire on the people. The problems of the city of Paris were so severe that people from all classes shared an apocalyptic vision. At the end of June 1848, thousands of Parisian bourgeois joined the army in pitched battle against the city's revolutionary workers. Fifteen hundred people died in the fighting. Three thousand more insurgents were ruthlessly put to death. Most of the 12,000 arrested were deported to Algeria. The worst fears of urban life had come to pass.

711

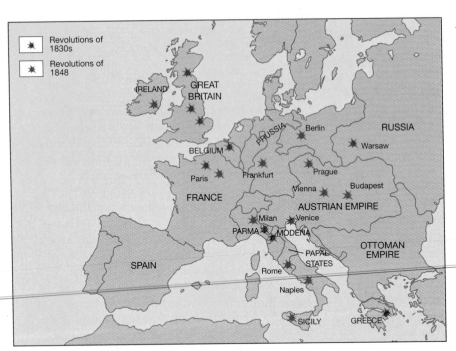

Revolutions of 1830 and 1848

of a commitment to their "right to work," which would replace the right to property as the organizing principle of the new society. Only one member of the new Provisional Government was a worker, and he was included as a token symbol of the intentions of the new government. He was known as "Albert, the worker," and was not addressed by his surname, Martin. The government acknowledged the demand of the "right to work" and set up two mechanisms to guarantee workers' relief. First, a commission of workers and employers was created to act as a grievance and bargaining board and settle questions of common concern in the workplace. Headed by the socialist Louis Blanc (1811–82) and known as the Luxembourg Commission, the worker-employer parliament was an important innovation, but accomplished little other than deflecting workers' attention away from the problems of the Provisional Government. The second measure was the creation of "national workshops" to deal with the problems of unemployment in Paris. Although the name was taken from Blanc's plan for worker control of production, the national workshops were no more than an inefficient charity program that paid men minimal wages. The national workshops quickly proved disastrous. Workers from all over France poured into Paris with the hope of finding jobs. However, the workshops had a residency requirement that even Parisians had difficulty meeting. As a result, unemployment skyrock-

eted. Furthermore, the government was going bankrupt trying to support the program. The need to raise taxes upset peasants in the provinces. National pressure mounted to repudiate the programs of the revolution.

French workers were too weak to dominate the revolution. The government dissolved the workshops and recalled General Louis Cavaignac (1802–57) from service in Algeria to maintain order. In a wave of armed insurrection, Parisian workers rebelled in June. Using provincial troops having no identification with the urban population and employing guerrilla techniques he had mastered in Algeria, Cavaignac put down the uprising. The June fighting was the bloodiest that Paris had ever seen. The Second Republic was placed under the military dictatorship of Cavaignac until December, when presidential elections were scheduled.

The overthrow of the July Monarchy at the end of February set off shock waves of protest in central and eastern Europe. Long-suppressed desires for civil liberties and constitutional reforms erupted in widespread popular disturbances throughout Prussia and the German states. Fearing a war with France and unable to count on Austria or Russia for support, the princes who ruled Baden, Württemberg, Hesse-Darmstadt, Bavaria, Saxony, and Hanover followed the advice of moderate liberals and acceded quickly to revolutionary demands. In Prussia, Kaiser Friedrich Wilhelm IV (1840–61) preferred to use military force to respond to popular demonstrations. Only in mid-March 1848 did the Prussian king yield to the force of the revolutionary crowds building barricades in Berlin by ordering his troops to leave the city and by promising to create a national Prussian assembly. The king was now a prisoner of the revolution.

Meanwhile, the collapse of absolute monarchy in Prussia gave further impetus to a constitutional movement among the liberal leaders of the German states. The governments of all the German states were invited to elect delegates to a national parliament in Frankfurt. The Frankfurt Assembly, which was convened in May 1848, had as its dual charge the framing of a constitution and the unification of Germany. It was composed for the most part of members of the middle class, with civil servants, lawyers, and intellectuals predominating. In spite of the principle of universal manhood suffrage, no members of the working class served among the eight hundred men elected. To most of the delegates, who had been trained in universities and shared a social and cultural identity, nationalism and constitutionalism were inextricably related.

As straightforward as the desire for a German nation appeared to be, it was complicated by two important facts. First, there were non-German minorities living in German states. What was to be done with the Poles, Czechs, Slovenes, Italians, and Dutch in a newly constituted and autonomous German nation? Second, there were Germans living outside the German states under Habsburg rule in Austria, in Danish Schleswig and Holstein, in Posen (Poznan), in Russian Poland, and in European Russia. How were they to be included within the linguistically and ethnically constituted German nation? No matter how small the circle was drawn, it included non-Germans; no matter how wide, it excluded Germans. After much wrangling over a "small" Germany that excluded Austrian Germans and a "large" Germany that included them, the Frankfurt Assembly opted for the small-Germany solution in March 1849. The crown of the new nation was offered to the unpredictable Friedrich Wilhelm IV of Prussia, head of the largest and most powerful of the German states. Unhappy with his capitulation to the revolutionary crowd in March 1848, the Prussian king refused to

A woodcut depicting a session of the Frankfurt Assembly. The assembly was doomed to failure, and with it the hopes of German liberals for a representative democracy.

A satiric cartoon shows Pope Pius IX removing the mask of a liberal "savior" to reveal his true countenance after he failed to support the revolution in Italy.

accept a "crown from the gutter." He had his own plans to rule over a middle-European bloc, but not at the behest of a liberal parliament. The attempt to create a German nation crumbled with his unwillingness to lead.

Revolution in Austrian-dominated central Europe was concentrated in three places: Vienna, where German-speaking students, workers, and middle-class liberals were agitating for constitutional reform and political participation; Budapest, where the Magyars, the dominant ethnic group in Hungary, led a movement for national autonomy; and Prague, where Czechs were attempting self-rule. By April 1848, Metternich had fallen from power and the Viennese revolutionaries had set up a constituent assembly. In Budapest, the initial steps of the patriot Lajos Kossuth

(1802–94) toward establishing a separate Hungarian state seemed equally solid as the Magyars defeated Habsburg troops. Habsburg armies were more successful in Prague, where they crushed the revolution in June 1848.

The Habsburg empire was also under siege in Italy, where the Kingdom of the Two Sicilies, Tuscany, and Piedmont declared new constitutions in March 1848. Championed by Charles Albert of Piedmont, Venice and Lombardy rose up against Austria. Italian middle-class intellectuals and professionals championed the idea of national unification and the expulsion of the hated Austrian overlords. Nationalist sentiments had percolated underground in the Young Italy movement, founded in 1831 by Giuseppe Mazzini. Mazzini, a tireless and idealistic patriot, favored a democratic revolution. In spite of his reputation as a liberal, Pope Pius IX (1846–78) lost control of Rome and was forced to flee the city. Mazzini became head of the Republic of Rome, created in February 1849.

The French government decided to intervene to protect the pope's interests and sent in troops to defeat the republicans. One of Mazzini's disciples, Giuseppe Garibaldi (1807–82), returned from exile in South America to undertake the defense of Rome. Garibaldi was a capable soldier who had learned the tactics of guerrilla warfare by joining independence struggles in Brazil and Argentina. Although his legion of poorly armed patriots and soldiers of fortune, known from their attire as the Red Shirts, waged a valiant effort to defend the city from April to June 1849, they were no match for the highly trained French army. French troops restored Pius IX as ruler of the Papal States.

Meanwhile, from August 1848 to the following spring, the Habsburg armies fought and finally defeated each of the revolutions. Austrian success can be explained in part because the various Italian groups of Piedmontese, Tuscans, Venetians, Romans, and Neapolitans continued to identify with their local concerns and lacked coordination and central organization. Both Mazzini and Pius IX had failed to provide the focal point of leadership necessary for a successful national movement.

In December 1848, Emperor Ferdinand I (1835–48), whose authority had been weakened irreparably by the overthrow of Metternich, abdicated in favor of his eighteen-year-old nephew, Franz Josef I (1848–1916). By the fall of 1849, Austria had solved the problems in its own capital and with Italy and Hungary by military

PROTEST AND REVOLUTION

August 1819	**Peterloo Massacre**
1824	**Charles X assumes French throne**
1827	**Treaty of London to support liberation of Greece**
July 1830	**Revolution in Paris; creation of July Monarchy under Louis-Philippe**
August 1830	**Revolution in Belgium**
November 1830	**Revolution in Poland**
1831–1838	**Revolutions in Italian states**
1831–1834	**Labor protests in France**
1832	**Britain's Great Reform Bill**
1838	**Drawing up the first People's Charter in Britain**
1846	**Beginning of food crisis in Europe; revolts in Poland**
1846–1848	**Europe-wide movements for national liberation**
February 1848	**Revolution in France; overthrow of the July Monarchy; proclamation of the French Second Republic and creation of Provisional Government**
March 1848	**Uprisings in some German states; granting of a constitution in Prussia**
March 1848–June 1849	**Revolutions in Italy**
April 1848	**Revolutions in Vienna, Budapest, Prague**
May 1848	**Frankfurt Assembly**
June 1848	**Second revolution in Paris, severely repressed by army troops under General Cavaignac**
December 1848	**Presidential elections in France; Louis Napoleon wins**

dominance. Austria understood that a Germany united under Friedrich Wilhelm IV of Prussia would undermine Austrian dominance in central Europe. In 1850 Austrians threatened the Prussians with war if they did not give up their plans for a unified Germany. In November of that year, Prussian ministers signed an agreement with their Austrian counterparts in the Moravian city of Olmütz. The convention became known as "the humiliation of Olmütz" because Prussia was forced to accept Austrian dominance or go to war. In every case, military force and diplomatic measures prevailed to defeat the national and liberal movements within the German states and the Austrian Empire.

Europe in 1850

By 1850 a veneer of calm had spread over central Europe. In Prussia, the peasantry were emancipated from feudal dues, and a constitution, albeit conservative and based on a three-class system, was established. Yet beneath the surface, there was the deeper reality of Austrian decline and Prussian challenge. The great Habsburg empire needed to call on outside help from Russia to defeat its enemies within. The imperial giant was again on its feet, but for how long? In international relations, Austria's dominance in the German Confederation had diminished, while Prussia assumed greater political and economic power.

The 1848 revolutions spelled the end to the concert of Europe as it had been defined in the peace settlement of 1815. The European powers were incapable of united action to defend established territorial interests. Perhaps France would have provoked united action if it had attempted to extend its revolution throughout Europe, as in 1792. Instead, pragmatism prevailed. The British failed to support independence for Hungary, for example, because they feared the consequences of Russian ambitions that would be unchecked with a weaker Austria.

The revolutions of 1848 failed in part because of the irreconcilable split between moderate liberals and radical democrats. The participation of the masses had frightened members of the middle classes, who were committed to moderate reforms that did not threaten property. In France, working-class revolutionaries had attempted to replace property with labor. Property triumphed. In the face of more extreme solutions, members of the middle class were willing to accept the increased authority of existing rule as a bulwark against anarchy. In December 1848, Prince Louis Napoleon, nephew of the former emperor, was elected president of the Second Republic by a wide margin. The first truly modern French politician, Louis Napoleon managed to appeal to everyone—workers, bourgeois, royalists, and peasants—by making promises that were vague or unkeepable. Severe repression forced radical protest into hiding. The new Bonaparte bided his time, apparently as an ineffectual ruler, until the moment in 1851 when he seized absolute power.

Similar patterns emerged elsewhere in Europe. In Germany, the bourgeoisie accepted the dominance of the old feudal aristocracy as a guarantee of law and order. Repressive government, businessmen were sure, would restore a strong economy. The attempts in 1848 to create new nations based on ethnic identities were in shambles by 1850.

Nearly everywhere throughout Europe, constitutions had been systematically withdrawn with the recovery of the forces of reaction. With the French and Swiss exceptions, the bid for the extension of the franchise failed. The propertied classes remained in control of political institutions. Radicals willing to use violence to press electoral reforms were arrested, killed, or exiled. The leadership of the revolutionary movements had been decapitated, and there seemed no effective opposition to the rise and consolidation of state power. The 1848 revolutions have been called a turning point at which modern history failed to turn. Contemporaries wondered how so much action could have produced so few lasting results.

Yet the perception that nothing had changed was wrong. The revolutions of 1848 and subsequent events galvanized whole societies to political action. Conservatives and radicals alike turned toward a new realism in politics. Everywhere governments were forced to adapt to new social realities. No longer could the state ignore economic upheavals and social dislocations if it wanted to survive. Revolutionaries also learned the lesson of repression. The state wielded powerful forces of violence against which nationalists, socialists, republicans, and liberals had all been proven helpless. Organizing, campaigning, and lobbying were newly learned political skills, as was outreach across class lines—from bourgeoisie to peasantry—around common political causes. In these ways, 1848 was a turning point in the formation of a modern political culture.

Suggestions for Further Reading

Europe After 1815

* Robert Gildea, *Barricades and Borders, Europe 1800–1914* (Oxford: Oxford University Press, 1987). A synthetic overview of economic, demographic, political, and international trends in European society.

* Harold Nicolson, *The Congress of Vienna: A Study in Allied Unity, 1812–1822* (New York: Viking Press, 1965). Dissects the maneuverings of the Allied diplomats and analyzes their cooperation in reconstructing Europe.

* Alan Sked, *The Decline and Fall of the Habsburg Empire, 1815–1918* (London: Longman, 1989). A revisionist interpretation that demonstrates the strength and viability of Europe's greatest dynasty throughout the nineteenth century.

The New European Society

* Leonore Davidoff and Catherine Hall, *Family Fortunes: Men and Women of the English Middle Class, 1750–1850* (Chicago: University of Chicago Press, 1991). Through the stories of families during the Industrial Revolution, the authors explain the development of middle-class identity and the role that gender played in the development of property relations, the construction of family life, and the differentiation of the world of the home from the public world of production.

* Gertrude Himmelfarb, *The Idea of Poverty: England in the Early Industrial Age* (New York: Vintage Books, 1983). Traces the concept of poverty in Britain from the mid-eighteenth to the mid-nineteenth century through a discussion of inadequate solutions, changing material conditions of industrialism, and new modes of thought and sensibility.

* Joel Mokyr, *Why Ireland Starved: A Quantitative and Analytical History of the Irish Economy, 1800–1850* (London: Allen & Unwin, 1983). An analysis of the structural factors that produced poverty in pre-famine Ireland and a thorough examination of the impact of the famine.

* Redcliffe N. Salaman, *The History and Social Influence of the Potato,* revised impression edited by J. G. Hawkes (Cambridge: Cambridge University Press, 1985). The classic study of the potato. A major portion of the work is devoted to the potato famine.

* Louise A. Tilly and Joan W. Scott, *Women, Work and Family* (New York: Holt, Rinehart and Winston, 1978). An overview of the impact of a wage economy on the family and on women's work.

The New Ideologies

* Jonathan Beecher, *Charles Fourier: The Visionary and His World* (Berkeley: University of California Press, 1986).

An intellectual biography that traces the development of Fourier's theoretical perspective and roots it firmly in the social context of nineteenth-century France.

* Craig Calhoun, *The Question of Class Struggle: Social Foundations of Popular Radicalism During the Industrial Revolution* (Chicago: University of Chicago Press, 1982). Presents popular protest of eighteenth- and early-nineteenth-century England as the reaction of communities of artisans defending their traditions against encroaching industrialization.

* William H. Sewell, Jr., *Work and Revolution in France: The Language of Labor from the Old Regime to 1848* (Cambridge: Cambridge University Press, 1980). Traces nineteenth-century working-class socialism to the corporate culture of Old Regime guilds through traditional values, norms, language, and artisan organizations.

Gareth Stedman Jones, *Languages of Class: Studies in English Working Class History, 1832–1982* (Cambridge: Cambridge University Press, 1983). A series of essays, on topics such as working-class culture and Chartism, that examine the development of class consciousness.

* Edward P. Thompson, *The Making of the English Working Class* (New York: Pantheon Books, 1963). Spans the late eighteenth to mid-nineteenth centuries in examining the social, political, and cultural contexts in which workers created their own identity and put forward their own demands.

Protest and Revolution

* Maurice Agulhon, *The Republican Experiment, 1848–1852* (Cambridge: Cambridge University Press, 1983). Traces the Revolution of 1848 from its roots to its ultimate failure in 1852 through an analysis of the republican ideologies of workers, peasants, and the bourgeoisie.

Clive Church, *Europe in 1830: Revolution and Political Change* (London: Allen & Unwin, 1983). Considers the origins of the 1830 revolutions within a wider European crisis through a comparative analysis of European regions.

* Peter N. Stearns, *1848: The Revolutionary Tide in Europe* (New York: Norton, 1974). Surveys the causes, impact, and legacy of the revolutions in France, Germany, the Habsburg Empire, and Italy, which shattered the diplomatic framework established at the Congress of Vienna and served as a transition to a new society.

* Dorothy Thompson, *The Chartists: Popular Politics in the Industrial Revolution* (New York: Pantheon Books, 1984). Thompson demonstrates that Chartism was an extraordinary coalition of women, laborers, artisans, and alehouse keepers whose goals were transforming public life and forging a new political culture.

*Paperback edition available.

23 ❧ STATE-BUILDING AND SOCIAL CHANGE IN EUROPE, 1850–1871

The Birth of the German Empire

Secret fancies bubbled in Otto von Bismarck's brain. As he explained in long letters to his wife, he imagined that the Russian king and German princes crowding around him were pregnant women seized by "strange cravings." In the next moment, he imagined himself a midwife assisting at a momentous birth. In spite of his remarkable train of thought, Otto von Bismarck (1815–98) was not a fanciful man. The birth in his daydream was the proclamation of the German Empire on 21 January 1871. The building was the palace of Versailles outside of Paris. As the Prussian statesman stood in the great Hall of Mirrors on that fateful day, surrounded by German aristocrats, he could not forget the years of struggle and planning that preceded this event. His tension and anticipation provoked his birthing fantasies.

The newly established Second Reich, successor to the Holy Roman Empire (962–1806), united the German states into a single nation. The unification process had been a precarious pregnancy, with years of foreign wars and a Herculean labor of diplomatic maneuverings. The placid, glossy scene painted by Anton von Werner (1843–1915) hardly suggests Bismarck's violent emotions on this momentous day. Bismarck saw his task in terms of the female metaphor of birth. Yet this warrior group was the most masculine of gatherings. Look at the painting. The richly marbled and mirrored room, the site of the birth, figures as prominently in the tableau as the uniformed princes and aristocrats who, with sabers, helmets, and standards raised, cheer the new emperor. The massive mirrors reflect more than this soldier society standing before the long windows of the opposite wall; they reflect a humiliation. This is, after all, the great hall built by Louis XIV at Versailles, one of Europe's greatest palaces, designed to reflect and glorify the power of absolutist France. Here the kings of France presided over lavish ceremonies and opulent receptions. Here Napoleon I honored his generals, victorious in conquering central Europe. Here, not long ago, Napoleon III had danced on the parqueted floors with Queen Victoria of Britain. The choice of the Hall of Mirrors as the meeting place for the German princes, who had successfully combined forces to defeat the French Second Empire in only six weeks of war in the fall of 1870, was intended as an assertion of German superiority in Europe.

In less than a decade, German unity had been achieved through military victories over Denmark, Austria, and France. The gilded moldings that commemorate the age of the Sun King are matched by the glitter of golden ribbons, medals, buttons, and cuffs of German uniforms, by the soft glow of burnished Prussian helmets. France is about to be stripped of its territories of Alsace and Lorraine; now the French are to be stripped of their dignity as the Prussian king stands on luxuriant French carpeting to assert his claim. There is an arrogance here in the details on which Werner dwells. The French understood and promised to avenge their humiliation.

Look at the painting again. There on the dais is King Wilhelm I of Prussia, flanked by his son, Crown Prince Friedrich Wilhelm, and his son-in-law, Friedrich I, the Grand Duke of Baden, whose upraised hand signals a cheer for the new emperor. At the foot of the steps, like a loyal retainer, stands the self-described midwife, Otto von Bismarck. Yet there is something amiss here. The new German emperor, the person for whom the event has been orchestrated, stands to one side of the canvas. Bismarck commands its center. If the eyes of most of the cheering princes turn to the emperor, ours are pulled to the chancellor of the new Reich, who is singled out in his pure white uniform. Werner is telling us that this is the

statesman's event, for it is he who has crafted a united Germany. Bismarck got what he wanted: a German Empire under the leadership of the Prussian king.

In both hands Bismarck clasps the proclamation of empire, the document wrested out of endless wrangling among the heads of the 38 German states. The kings of Saxony, Bavaria, and Württemberg refused to attend the ceremony. Some who did attend were disgruntled and resentful. Even Bismarck's sovereign was not happy with the document, nor did he like the title assigned to him. He would have preferred to be "emperor of Germany" rather than "German emperor." Before the ceremony, Wilhelm I had refused to speak to Bismarck. Yet the artist reveals none of this in the impassive faces and the sturdy stances of the two men.

Bismarck understood that symbols forge unity. The artist Werner also attends to symbol. Beneath the red-encased document, Bismarck firmly grasps his Prussian military helmet. Military victories had ensured Prussian predominance over a united Germany. To Bismarck's left, in profile facing the emperor, stands Count Helmuth von Moltke (1800–1891), head of the Prussian General Staff and the man responsible for reorganizing the Prussian army with Bismarck's support. Medals for bravery and service to his sovereign adorn Moltke's chest. With one foot forward, Moltke is a man of action, almost caught in mid-stride, a man ready to move into the future.

The unification of Germany was not achieved by democratic means. Bismarck understood the new age. As he explained in a speech to the Prussian Diet, "The great questions of the time are not decided by speeches and majority decisions—that was the error of 1848 and 1849—but by iron and blood." The new Reich was a "state of princes," an empire born of the union of force and military conquest. A century earlier, Voltaire, the French philosopher of the Enlightenment, had his own theory of creation: God gave the English the seas, the French the land, and the Germans the clouds. Fragmented and without a state, Germans could claim a rich, if ethereal, culture of philosophy, music, and literature in the previous century. In 1871, with the proclamation of the German Empire, Germans had put their feet on the ground. The struggle for land and sea, so easily assigned by Voltaire, lay ahead.

Building Nations: The Politics of Unification

The revolutions of 1848 had occurred in a period of experimentation from below. Radicals enlisting popular support had tried and failed to reshape European states for their own nationalist, liberal, and socialist ends. Governments in Paris, Vienna, Berlin, and a number of lesser states had been swept away. The revolutions had created a power vacuum but no durable solutions. To fill that vacuum, a new breed of politician emerged in the 1850s and 1860s, men who understood the importance of the centralized nation-state and saw the need of reforms from above. They also had an appreciation of the importance of foreign policy successes as a means of furthering domestic programs. Cavour of Italy, Bismarck of Germany, and Louis Napoleon of France shared a new realism about means and ends.

National unification had escaped the grasp of liberals and radicals between 1848 and 1850 with the failure of revolutionary and reform movements. In the 1850s and 1860s, those committed to radical transformations worked from within the existing system. The new realists subordinated liberal nationalism to the needs of conservative state-building. Military force validated what intellectuals and revolutionaries had not been able to legitimate through ideological claims.

The Crimean War

After 1815 Russia, as the greatest military power in Europe, honored its commitment to preserving the status quo by acting as policeman of Europe. It supported Austria against Hungary and Prussia in 1849 and 1850. But Russia sought greater power to the south, in the Balkans. The Bosporus, the narrow strait connecting the Black Sea with the Sea of Marmara, and the strait of the Dardanelles, which connects the Sea of Marmara with the Aegean Sea, were controlled by the Ottoman Empire. Russia hoped to benefit from Ottoman weakness caused by internal conflicts and gain control of these straits, which were the only outlet for the Russian fleet to the warm waters of the Mediterranean, Russia's southern outlet to the world.

At the center of the hope for Ottoman disintegration lay the "Eastern question," the term used to refer to the disputes over the European territories controlled by the Ottoman Empire. Each of the Great Powers—including Russia, Great Britain, Austria, Prussia, and France—hoped to benefit territorially from the collapse of Ottoman control. In 1853, Great Power rivalry over the "Eastern question" created an international situation that led to war.

In 1853 the Russian government demanded that the Turkish government recognize Russia's right to protect Greek Orthodox believers in the Ottoman Empire. The Russian action was a response to measures taken by the French government during the previous year, which had gained from the Turkish government rights for Roman Catholic religious orders in certain sanctuaries in the Holy Land. In making its claims as protector, Russia demanded that the rights granted Roman Catholic orders also be rescinded. The Turkish government refused Russian demands and the Russians, feeling that their prestige had been damaged, ordered troops to enter the Danubian Principalities held by the Turks. In October 1853, the Turkish government, counting on support from Great Britain and France, declared war on Russia.

Russia easily prevailed over its weaker neighbor to the south. In a four-hour battle, a Russian squadron destroyed the Turkish fleet off the coast of Sinope. Tsar Nicholas I (1825–55) drew up the terms of a settlement with the Ottoman Empire and submitted them to Great Britain and France for review. The two western European powers, fearing Russian aggrandizement at Turkish expense, responded by declaring war on Russia on 28 March 1854, a date that marked a new phase in the Crimean War. Both Great Britain and France, like Russia, had ambitions in the Balkans and the eastern Mediterranean. Great Britain feared Russian expansion as a threat to its trade and holdings in India and had a vested interest in an independent but weak Turkey presiding over the straits. The French hoped that by entering into a partnership with the British to defeat the Russians, they would be able to lay claim to greater power and status in European international politics. The Austrian Empire, frightened by Russia's seizure of the Danubian Principalities of Moldavia and Walachia, remained neutral but threatened to enter the war with Britain and France on the side of Turkey. The Italian kingdom of Piedmont-Sardinia joined the war on the side of the western European powers in January 1855, hoping to make its name militarily and win recognition for its aim to unite Italy into a single nation. Without explicit economic interests, the Great Powers and the lesser Italian state of Piedmont-Sardinia were motivated by ambition, prestige, and rivalry in the Balkans.

British and French troops landed in the Crimea, the Russian peninsula extending into the Black Sea, in September 1854, with the intention of capturing Sevastopol, Russia's heavily fortified chief naval base on the Black Sea. In March 1855, Nicholas I died and was succeeded by his son Alexander II (1855–81), who wanted to bring the war to a speedy end. His attempts to negotiate a peace in the spring of 1855 repeatedly failed. In battle, the Russians continued to resist as the allies laid siege to the fortress at Sevastopol, which fell only after 322 days of battle, on 11 September 1855. The defeated Russians abandoned Sevastopol, blew up their forts, and sank their own ships.

Russia, now facing the threat of Austrian entry into the war, agreed to preliminary peace terms. In the Peace of Paris of 1856, Russia relinquished its claim as protector of Christians in Turkey. The British gained the neutralization of the Black Sea. The mouth of the Danube was returned to Turkish control, and an international commission was created to oversee safe navigation on the Danube. The Danubian Principalities were placed under joint guarantee of the powers, and Russia gave up a small portion of Bessarabia. In 1861 the Principalities were united in the independent nation of Romania.

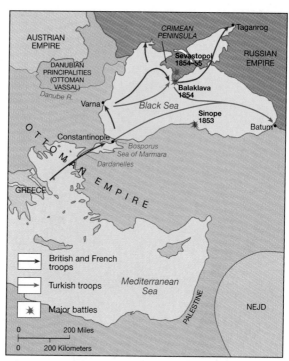

The Crimean War

Lithograph of the charge of the Light Brigade at the battle of Balaklava, 1854. The charge was one of the most controversial events in military history. Public opinion blamed the commanders, Lord Lucan and Lord Raglan, but the confusion of battle caused their orders to be misinterpreted, leading to disaster.

The Crimean War had the highest casualty rate of any European war between 1815 and 1914. Three-quarters of a million soldiers—Russian, French, British, and Turkish—died. Because no sanitary practices were observed in caring for the wounded, four out of five succumbed to disease, especially typhus and cholera. The English nurse Florence Nightingale (1820–1910) brought medical reforms to the theater of war, introduced sanitation, and organized barracks hospitals, all of which saved the lives of countless British soldiers. (See "A Working Woman," pp. 722–723.) Russians suffered disproportionately, claiming two-thirds of all dead and wounded; 450,000 Russian soldiers died. Of those who died in battle, many died needlessly, under poorly prepared leaders. A typical example occurred during the battle of Balaklava when six hundred troops of the British Light Brigade were ordered into battle by incompetent and confused commanders. British soldiers charged down a narrow valley flanked by Russian guns on the heights on both sides and into the teeth of yet another battery at the head of the valley. The battlefield became known as the Valley of Death. When the dust of the fighting had settled, the battlefield lay strewn with the bodies of nearly two-thirds of the soldiers of the Light Brigade. Their horses, slain too, lay beside them.

✣ A Working Woman

Women have always worked, but how society has valued women's work has changed over time. After 1850, women of all income levels, not just the wealthy, were expected to retire from the workplace upon marrying. Woman's proper role was that of wife and mother in the home, caring for her husband and family, watching over her children. Young women worked before they married to help their parents and to save for dowries. There is no doubt that many women continued to work for wages because they had to; they were too poor to live by society's norms. But mid-nineteenth-century European culture reinforced the idea that woman's place was in the separate domestic sphere of private pleasures and unpaid labor. To be a "public" man was a valued trait. The same adjective applied to a woman meant that she was a harlot.

Yet it is this culture that immortalized Florence Nightingale, a woman who valued what she called "my work" above home and family. She was a single woman in an age when more and more women were making the choice to remain unmarried; but it was also an age in which *spinster* was a term of derision

and a sign of failure. Miss Nightingale, as she was known, received the British Empire's Order of Merit for her achievements. Queen Victoria, the most maternal and domestic of queens, hailed her as "an example to our sex." Nightingale was widely regarded as the greatest woman of her age, among the most eminent of Victorians. A highly visible and outspoken reformer, Nightingale deviated from woman's unpaid role as nurturer in the private sphere. How could she be an example to the women of her time?

Florence Nightingale was hailed as a national heroine because of her work during the Crimean War in organizing hospital care at Scutari, a suburb outside Constantinople on the Asiatic side of the Bosporus. In the Crimea, she entered her own field of battle, attacking the mismanagement, corruption, and lack of organization characteristic of medical treatment for British soldiers. She campaigned for better sanitation, hygiene, ventilation, and diet, and in 1855 the death rate plummeted from 42 percent to 2 percent thanks to her efforts. The *London Times* declared, "There is not one of England's proudest and purest daughters who at the moment stands on as high a pinnacle as Florence Nightingale."

It was a pinnacle not easily scaled. Blocked by her family and publicly maligned, Nightingale struggled against prevailing norms to carve out her occupation. She was the daughter of a wealthy gentry family, and from her father she received a man's classical education. Women of her milieu were expected to be educated only in domestic arts. The fashion of the day emphasized woman's confinement to the home: crinolines, corsets, and trains restricted movement and suggested gentility. This was the life of Nightingale's older sister, one that "the Angel of the Crimea" fiercely resisted. Nightingale railed at the inequity of married life: "A man gains everything by marriage: he gains a 'helpmate,' but a woman does not." Her memoirs are filled with what she called her "complaints" against the plight of women.

Nightingale was not a typical working woman. She struck out on her career as a rebel. Because of her wealth, she did not need to work, yet she felt driven to be useful. Her choice of nursing much alarmed her family, who considered the occupation to be on a level with domestic service. For them, nursing was worse, in fact, because nurses worked with the naked bodies of the sick. Thus nurses were either shameless or promiscuous, or both. Nightingale shattered these taboos. She visited nursing establishments throughout Europe, traveling alone—another feat unheard of for women in her day—and studied their methods and techniques. She conceived of her own mission to serve God through caring for others.

As with any exceptional individual, character and capabilities must figure in an explanation of achievements. Nightingale was a woman of drive and discipline who refused to accept the limited choices available to Victorian women. She possessed, in her sovereign's words, "a wonderful, clear and comprehensive head." Yet her unique talents are not enough to explain her success. In many ways, Nightingale was not a rebel, but rather an embodiment of the changing values of her age. In 1860, she established a school to train nurses, just as similar institutions were being created to train young women as teachers. These occupations were extensions of women's roles from the arena of the home into society. In keeping with their domestic roles, women remained nurturers in the classroom and at the sickbed.

These new female professions were also poorly paid. Significantly, Florence Nightingale, honored as she was in her lifetime, received no salary for her contributions to the British state. Her work was supported by donations from the benefactors and administrative protectors she referred to as her "masters." She and other women of her class, including Elizabeth Fry (1780–1845), who was a Quaker minister, prison reformer, banker's wife, and mother of ten, and the English writer and political reformer Harriet Martineau (1802–76), were regarded as philanthropists, women who donated their time and expertise to the public good. Theirs was the moral obligation of the wealthy toward the poor. It also sprang out of the nature of women, contemporary moralists asserted, to mother and to heal. The definition of women's proper role did not need to be dis-

mantled to accommodate these activities. It needed merely to be stretched.

Florence Nightingale spent a good part of the last forty-five years of her life in a sickbed suffering from what she called "nervous fever." During this period she wrote incessantly and continued to lobby for her programs, benefiting, one of her biographers claimed, from the freedom to think and write provided by her illness. It may well be true that her invalidism protected her from the claims on her time made by her family and by society. It may also be true that she, like many of her middle-class female contemporaries, experienced debilitation or suffered from hypochondria in direct proportion to the limitations they experienced.

Midcentury Europe had witnessed a series of failed protests on behalf of women against social and political restrictions. In spite of reform movements, women did not enjoy the franchise or equal property rights. Access to divorce was available only to women wealthy enough to afford it. Yet women did participate in new activities and enter new occupations justified by their role as nurturers. Nightingale herself believed that the right to vote was less important than financial independence for women. New occupations labeled "women's work" were essential to the expansion of industrial society. A healthy and literate population guaranteed a strong citizenry, a strong army, and a strong work force. As helpmeets, women entered a new work sector identified by the adjective *service*. Women were accepted as clerical workers, performing the "housekeeping" of business firms and bureaucracies.

After midcentury, gender differences, socially defined virtues for men and women, became more set. Individualism, competition, and militarism were the values of the world of men. Familial support, nurturance, and healing were female virtues. These were the separate and unequal worlds created by the factory and the battlefield. The virtues of the private sphere were extended into the public world with the creation of new forms of poorly paid female labor. In this sense, Florence Nightingale was not a rebel. This "Lady with the Lamp," whom fever-ridden soldiers called their mother, was another working woman.

"The Charge of the Light Brigade"

Alfred, Lord Tennyson (1809–92) described the bravery of the British Light Brigade in the Crimean War as they charged, hopelessly outnumbered, into the "valley of Death" at the Battle of Balaklava. His poem brought home to the British public both the glory of their troops and the tragedy brought on by a commander's "blunder."

1

Half a league, half a league,
Half a league onward,
All in the valley of Death
   Rode the six hundred.
"Forward the Light Brigade!
Charge for the guns!" he said.
Into the valley of Death
   Rode the six hundred.

2

"Forward, the Light Brigade!"
Was there a man dismay'd?
Not tho' the soldier knew
   Some one had blunder'd.
   Theirs not to make reply,
   Theirs not to reason why,
   Theirs but to do and die.
   Into the valley of Death
      Rode the six hundred.

3

Cannon to right of them,
Cannon to left of them,
Cannon in front of them
   Volley'd and thunder'd;
Storm'd at with shot and shell,
Boldly they rode and well,
Into the jaws of Death,
Into the mouth of hell
   Rode the six hundred.

4

Flash'd all their sabres bare,
Flash'd as they turn'd in air

Sabring the gunners there,
Charging an army, while
   All the world wonder'd.
Plunged in the battery-smoke
Right thro' the line they broke;
Cossack and Russian
Reel'd from the sabre-stroke
   Shatter'd and sunder'd.
Then they rode back, but not,
   Not the six hundred.

5

Cannon to right of them,
Cannon to left of them,
Cannon behind them
   Volley'd and thunder'd;
Storm'd at with shot and shell,
While horse and hero fell,
They that had fought so well
Came thro' the jaws of Death,
Back from the mouth of hell,
All that was left of them,
   Left of six hundred.

6

When can their glory fade?
O the wild charge they made!
   All the world wonder'd.
Honor the charge they made!
Honor the Light Brigade,
   Noble six hundred!

This was a war no one really won, a war over obscure disagreements in a faraway peninsula in the Black Sea. Nevertheless, it had dramatic and enduring consequences. Russia ceased playing an active role in European affairs and turned toward expansion in central Asia. Its withdrawal opened up the possibility for a move by Prussia in central Europe. The rules of the game had changed. The concert of Europe so carefully crafted by European statesmen in 1815 came to an end with the Crimean War. With the Peace of Paris of 1856, the hope that goals could be achieved by peaceful means also died. Piedmont-Sardinia, an empty-handed victor, realized that only the force of the cannon could achieve the unification of Italy.

Unifying Italy

Italy had not been a single political entity since the end of the Roman Empire in the West in the fifth century. The movement to reunite Italy culturally and politically was known as the Risorgimento (literally, "resurgence") and had its roots in the eighteenth century. Hopes for unification encouraged by reorganization during the Napoleonic era had been repeatedly crushed throughout the first half of the nineteenth century. Revolutionary movements had failed to cast out foreign domination by Austria in 1848.

Both Giuseppe Mazzini's Young Italy movement and Giuseppe Garibaldi's Red Shirts had as their goal in 1848 a united republican Italy achieved through direct popular action. But both movements had failed. It took a politician of aristocratic birth to recognize that Mazzini's and Garibaldi's model of revolutionary action was doomed against the powerful Austrian military machine. Mazzini was a moralist; Garibaldi was a fighter. But Camillo Benso di Cavour (1810–61) was an opportunistic politician and a realist. He knew that only as a unified nation could Italy lay claim to status as a great power in Europe. And he saw that a united Italy could be achieved only through the manipulation of diplomacy and military victory. He understood that international events could be made to serve national ends.

As premier for Piedmont-Sardinia from 1852 to 1859 and again in 1860–61, Cavour was well placed to launch his campaign for Italian unity. The kingdom of Piedmont-Sardinia had made itself a focal point for unification efforts. Piedmont-Sardinia's king, Carlo-Alberto (1831–49) had stood alone among Italian rulers in opposing Austrian domination of the Italian peninsula in 1848 and 1849. Severely defeated by the Austrians, he was forced to abdicate. With his death in exile, Carlo-Alberto became a saint martyred for the cause of unification. He was succeeded by his son Victor Emmanuel II (1849–61), who had the good sense to appoint Cavour as his first minister. From the start, Cavour undertook liberal administrative reforms that included tax reform, stabilization of the currency, improvement of the railway system, the creation of a transatlantic steamship system, and the support of private enterprise. With these programs Cavour created for Piedmont-Sardinia the dynamic image of progressive change. He involved Piedmont-Sardinia in the Crimean War, thereby securing its status among the European powers.

Most important, however, was his successful pursuit of an alliance with France against Austria in 1858. Cavour shrewdly secured the French pledge of support, including military aid if necessary, against Austria in

This Italian tricolor flag echoes the tricolor banner of the French Revolution. First used in an uprising against the pope in 1794, it soon became the standard of Italian unity.

the Treaty of Plombières, signed by Napoleon III in 1858. The treaty was quickly followed by an arranged provocation against the Habsburg monarchy. Austria declared war in 1859 and was easily defeated by French forces in the battles of Magenta and Solferino. The peace, signed in November 1859 at Zurich, joined Lombardy to Piedmont-Sardinia. Cavour wielded the electoral weapon of the plebiscite—a method of direct voting that gives to electors the choice of voting for or against an important public question—to unite Tuscany, Parma, and Modena under Piedmont's king.

Cavour's approach was not without its costs. His partnership with a stronger power meant sometimes following France's lead. French bullying provoked fits of rage and forced Cavour to resign from office temporarily in 1859 over a war ended too early by Napoleon III. The need to solicit French support meant enriching France with territorial gain in the form of Nice and Savoy. However, Piedmont-Sardinia got more than it gave up. In the summer of 1859, revolutionary assemblies in Tuscany, Modena, Parma, and the Romagna, wanting to eject their Austrian rulers, voted in favor of union with the Piedmontese. By April 1860 these four areas of central Italy were under Victor Emmanuel's rule. Piedmont-Sardinia had doubled in size to become the dominant power on the Italian peninsula.

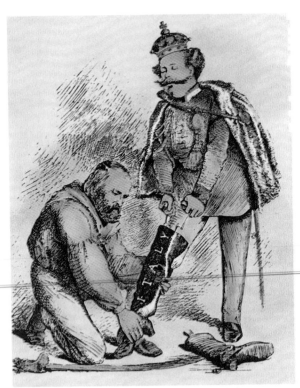

In this British cartoon of 1860, Garibaldi surrenders his power to Victor Emmanuel II, king of Piedmont-Sardinia (soon to be king of a united Italy). The caption reads "Right Leg in the Boot at Last."

Southern Italians took their lead from events in central Italy and in the spring of 1860 initiated disturbances against the rule of King Francis II (1859–61) of Naples. Uprisings in Sicily inspired Giuseppe Garibaldi to return from his self-imposed exile to organize his own army of Red Shirts, known as the Thousand, with whom he liberated Sicily and crossed to the Italian mainland to expel Francis II from Naples. Garibaldi next turned his attention to the liberation of the Holy City, where a French garrison protected the pope. After his defeat in Rome in 1849, Garibaldi had never lost sight of his mission to free all of Italy from foreign rule, even in the 1850s when he had lived on New York's Staten Island as a candle maker and had become a naturalized citizen of the United States.

As Garibaldi's popularity as a national hero grew, Cavour became alarmed by his competing effort to unite Italy and took secret steps to block the advance of the Red Shirts and their leader. To seize the initiative, Cavour directed the Piedmontese army into the Papal States. After defeating the pope's troops, Cavour's men crossed into the Neapolitan state and scored important

victories against forces loyal to the king of Naples. Cavour proceeded to annex southern Italy for Victor Emmanuel, using plebiscites to seal the procedure. At this point, in 1860, Garibaldi yielded his own conquered territories to the Piedmontese ruler, making possible the declaration of a united Italy under Victor Emmanuel II, who reigned as king of Italy from 1861 to 1878.

The new king of Italy was now poised to acquire Venetia, still under Austrian rule, and Rome, still ruled by Pope Pius IX, and he devoted much of his foreign policy in the 1860s to these ends. In 1866, when Austria lost a war with Prussia, Italy struck a deal with the victor and gained control of Venetia. When Prussia prevailed against France in 1870, Victor Emmanuel II took over Rome. The boot of Italy, from top to toe, was now a single nation. The pope remained in the Vatican, opposed to an Italy united under King Victor Emmanuel II. The new national government sought to impose centralization with a heavy hand and had little interest in preserving regional differences and regional cultures. Cavour's liberal constitutional principles, combined with moderately conservative stands on social issues, produced alienation, especially in southern Italy, among both the peasantry and the nobility.

The Unification of Italy

Cavour did not live to see the united Italy that he had worked so hard to fashion. He had succeeded where poets and revolutionaries had failed in preparing the ground for unification because he understood that the world had changed dramatically in the first half of the nineteenth century. He appreciated the relationship between national and international events and was able to manipulate it for his own ends. Both Cavour and his counterpart in Germany, Otto von Bismarck, considered themselves realists who shared a recognition of diplomacy as an instrument of domestic policy.

Unifying Germany

Seldom in modern history does an individual emerge as a chess master, overseeing international politics and domestic affairs as if the world were a great board game with movable pieces. Otto von Bismarck (1815–98) was aware that he was playing a game of high risks and high stakes. His vision was limited to the pragmatic pursuit of preserving the power of his beloved Prussia. For him the empire was not an end in itself but a means of guaranteeing Prussian strength. In an age of realistic politicians, he emerged as the supreme practitioner of *Realpolitik*, the ruthless pursuit by any means, including illegal and violent ones, to advance the interests of his country.

Bismarck was a Junker, an aristocratic estate owner from east of the Elbe River, who entered politics in 1847. As a member of the United Diet of Prussia, he made his reputation as a reactionary when he rose to speak in favor of hunting privileges for the nobility: "I am a Junker and I want to enjoy the advantages of it." In the 1850s, he became aware of Prussia's future in the center of Europe: he saw that the old elites must be allied with the national movement in order to survive. The problem was that nationalism was the property of the liberals, who had been defeated in 1848. Bismarck appropriated it. Liberals and Junkers shared an interest in unification, but for different political ends. As a politician, Bismarck learned how to exploit their common ground.

In 1850 Prussia had been forced to accept Austrian dominance in central Europe; the alternative was going to war. Throughout the following decade, however, Prussia systematically undermined Austrian power by wielding the trade agreements of the Zollverein as a tool to exclude Austria from German economic affairs. In 1862, at the moment of a crisis provoked by the new king, Wilhelm I, over military reorganization, Bismarck became minister-president

of the Prussian cabinet as well as foreign minister. He overrode the parliamentary body, the Diet, by reorganizing the Prussian army without a formally approved budget. In 1864 he constructed an alliance between Austria and Prussia for the purpose of invading Schleswig, a predominantly German-speaking territory controlled by the king of Denmark, whose population hoped to become part of the German Confederation. Within five days of invasion, Denmark yielded the duchies of Schleswig and Holstein, now to be ruled jointly by Austria and Prussia.

Ascertaining that he had a free hand in central Europe, Bismarck skillfully provoked a crisis between Austria and Prussia over management of the territories. Counting on the neutrality of France and Great Britain, the support of Piedmont-Sardinia, and good relations with Russia, Bismarck led his country into war with Austria in June 1866. In this Seven Weeks' War—the war took its name from its short duration—Austrian forces proved to be no match for the better-equipped and better-trained Prussian army. Bismarck dictated the terms of the peace, which demonstrated that he had no desire to cripple Austria, only to exclude it from a united Germany in which Prussia would be the dominant force. Austria's exclusion from Germany forced the Austrian government to deal with its own internal problems of imperial organization. In 1867, in response to pressures from the subject nationalities, the Habsburg Empire transformed itself into a dual monarchy of two independent and equal states under one ruler, who would be both the emperor of Austria and the king of Hungary. In spite of the reorganization, the problem of nationalities persisted, and ethnic groups began to agitate for total independence from imperial rule.

Bismarck's biggest obstacle to German unification was laid to rest with Austria's defeat. The south German states, however, continued to resist the idea of Prussian dominance. Prussia's militarism, Protestant religion, and economic strength threatened antimilitarists, Catholics, and the ruling elites of the southern states. Liberals, democrats, and socialists from the south feared the political consequences of Prussian conservatism. But growing numbers of people in Baden, Württemberg, Bavaria, and the southern parts of Hesse-Darmstadt recognized the necessity of uniting under Prussian leadership.

Many French observers were troubled by the Prussian victory over Austria and were apprehensive over what a united Germany might portend for the future of French dominance in Europe. Napoleon III made

The Unification of Germany

clear his opposition to further Prussian growth and attempted unsuccessfully to contain Prussian ambitions through diplomatic maneuverings. Instead, France found itself stranded without important European allies. In the spring of 1870, Bismarck decided to seize the initiative and provoke a crisis with France.

Bismarck recognized that war with France could be the dramatic event needed to forge cooperation and unity among all German states. The issue of succession to the Spanish throne gave him the opportunity he sought. Bismarck skillfully created the impression that the French ambassador had insulted the Prussian king, then leaked news of the incident to the press in both countries. Enraged and inflamed French and Prussian publics both demanded war.

As a direct result of this misunderstanding deliberately manufactured by Bismarck, France declared war on Prussia in July 1870. The southern German princes, as Bismarck hoped, immediately sided with the Prussian king. For years before hostilities broke out, the Prussians had been preparing for war. They had been sending Prussian army officers disguised as landscape painters into France to study the terrain of battle. French troops carried maps of Germany but were ignorant of the geography of their own country, where the battles were waged. Sent into battle against the Germans, French troops roamed around in search of their commanders and each other. The Germans had learned new deployment strategies from studying the use of railroads in the American Civil War of 1861–65. Unlike the Germans, the French had not coordinated deployment with the new technology of the railroad. Although French troops had the latest equipment, they were sent into battle without instructions on how to use it. Finally, the Prussian-led German army was superior, outnumbering French troops 450,000 to 260,000. All these factors combined to spell disaster for the French. Within a matter of weeks, it was clear that France had lost this Franco-Prussian War. The path was now clear for the declaration of the German Empire in January 1871.

The newly established Second Reich, successor to the Holy Roman Empire, united the German states into a single nation. After years of foreign wars and endless wrangling among the heads of the 38 German states, Bismarck got what he wanted: a German Empire under the leadership of the Prussian king. The Proclamation of Empire was signed on 21 January 1871 in a ceremony in the French palace of Versailles. Bismarck, always the pragmatist, understood clearly that Europe was not the same place that it had been a decade or two earlier. "Anyone who speaks of Europe is wrong—it is nothing but a set of national expressions." This understanding was the key to his success. In unifying Germany, Bismarck built on the constitution of the North German Confederation formed in 1867, which guaranteed Prussian dominance. Bismarck used the bureaucracy as a mainstay of the emperor. The new Reichstag—the national legislative assembly—was to be elected by means of universal male suffrage, a concession to the liberals. Yet the constitution was not a liberal one, since the Reichstag was not sovereign and the chancellor was accountable only to the emperor. Policy was made outside the domain of electoral politics. The federal structure of the constitution, especially with regard to taxation, also kept the central parliament weak. Most liberals supported the constitution, but a minority persisted in a tradition of radical dissent. Critics felt that true constitutional government had been sacrificed to the demands of empire. As one liberal remarked, "Unity without freedom is a unity of slaves." Bismarck spoke in confidence of his aim "to destroy parliamentarianism by parliamentarianism." According to this formula, Bismarck hoped that a weak Reichstag would undermine parliamentary institutions better than any dictatorial ruler.

During the 1860s, another great crisis in state-building had been resolved across the Atlantic. The United States had cemented political unity through the

Im Etappenquartier vor Paris, 1871. *This 1894 painting by Anton von Werner shows Prussian troops making themselves at home in a French drawing room on their way to victory in Paris. The Prussians occupied the city for only 48 hours.*

use of force in its Civil War. Just as Bismarck had resolved his crisis through "blood and iron," so did the president of the United States, Abraham Lincoln (1809–65), mobilize the greater human and industrial resources of the North against the agrarian, slave-owning South. Republican democracy triumphed in the United States, while a neo-absolutism emerged in Germany. Yet there is a remarkable similarity between the two events. In both countries, wars eventually resulted in a single national market without internal tariffs. The wars made possible a single financial system through which capital could be raised. In both countries, unified national economies paved the way for the expansion of industrial power.

Nationalism and Force

It is commonplace in the Western historical tradition to speak of nations as if they were individuals possessing emotions, making choices, taking actions, having ideas. "Russia turned inward"; "Germany chose its enemies as well as its friends"; "France vowed revenge"; "Great Britain took pride in its achievements." On one level, to attribute volition, feeling, and insight to an abstract entity like a nation is nonsense. But on another level, the personification of nation-states was one of the great achievements of statesmen throughout

Europe between 1850 and 1870. The language and symbols they put in place created the nation itself, a new political reality whose forms contain modern political consciousness. The nation-state became an all-knowing being whose rights had to be protected, whose destiny had to be assured. Before the nineteenth century, the person of the king had embodied the nation. With the political upheavals of the midcentury revolutions and the creation of new states, symbols took the place of monarchs to communicate a single undivided entity. A female form, whether it was that of Britannia of Great Britain or Marianne of France, could be used to capture the purity, strength, and vulnerability of the new nationalist concept.

The nation was above all a creation that minimized or denied real differences in dialect and language, regional loyalties, local traditions, and village identities. The crises in state-building in Italy and Germany had been resolved finally by violence. No power was acknowledged to exist above the nation-state. No power could sanction the nation's actions but itself. Force was an acceptable alternative to diplomacy. War was a political act and a political instrument, a continuation of political relations. Violence and nationalism were inextricably linked in the unification of both Italy and Germany in the third quarter of the nineteenth century.

Reforming European Society

The revolutions of 1848 had failed to deal with social problems, just as they had failed to realize nationalist aspirations. After the revolutions, government repression silenced radical movements throughout Europe. But repression could not maintain social harmony and promote growth and prosperity. In the third quarter of the nineteenth century, Europe's leaders recognized that reforms were needed to build dynamic and competitive states.

Three different models for social and political reform developed in Europe after 1850. One model is that of France, where the French emperor worked through a highly centralized administrative structure and with a highly valued elite of specialists to achieve social and economic transformation. The French model was a technocratic one that emphasized the importance of specialized knowledge to achieve material progress. Reform in France relied on both autocratic direction and liberal participation.

Great Britain provides another model, in which reform was fostered through liberal parliamentary democracy. In government by "amateurs," with local rather than a highly centralized administration, British legislation alternated between a philosophy of freedom and one of protection. But reforms were always hammered out by parliamentary means with the support of a gradually expanding electorate.

Finally, Russia offers a third model for reform. Like Britain, Russia had avoided revolution at midcentury. Like Britain, it hoped to preserve social peace. Yet the Russian model for reform stands in dramatic contrast to Britain's. Russia was still a semifeudal society in the 1850s. Beginning in the late 1850s, Russia embarked on a radical restructuring of society by autocratic means. Reforms in the three societies had little in common ideologically, but all reflected a commitment to progress and an awareness of the state's role and responsibility in achieving it.

The Second Empire in France, 1852–70

Napoleon III ruled France from the middle of the century until 1870. His apprenticeship for political leadership had been an unusual one. Louis Napoleon (1808–73) was a nephew of the emperor Napoleon I. The child Louis, born at the peak of French glory, was old enough to remember the devastation of his uncle's defeat in 1815. He dedicated his exiled youth to preparing for his family's restoration as rulers of France.

With the death of Napoleon's son, the duc de Reichstadt, in 1832, Louis was aware that the mantle of future power and the family destiny fell to him.

In comparing Louis Napoleon with his uncle, Napoleon I, Karl Marx said that history happens the first time as tragedy and the second time as farce. There was much that passed as farcical before Louis Napoleon established France's Second Empire in 1852, as one attempt after another to seize power failed. Yet those who viewed Louis Napoleon as a figure of derision were misled: by 1848 he understood the importance of shaping public opinion to suit his own ends. He wielded the Napoleonic legend to play on the dissatisfaction of millions. He understood that to succeed in an electoral system, he had to promise something to everyone. That is exactly what he did in the fall of 1848 when he spoke of prosperity, order, and the end of poverty, slogans that sent different and incompatible messages to a bourgeoisie who wanted social peace, workers who wanted jobs and social justice, and peasants who wanted land and freedom from taxes. Universal manhood suffrage was for the first time employed in a French national election. Recognizing its legitimating power, Louis Napoleon swept the field, the only candidate supported by all social classes.

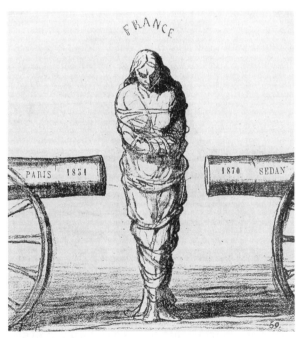

The cartoon "History of a Reign" by Honoré Daumier depicts the Second Empire as a captive France caught between the violent episodes of Louis Napoleon's Paris coup of 1851 and the humiliating defeat of the French army at Sedan in 1870.

View of the Champs-Elysées after the rebuilding of Paris. The renovations were carried out under the direction of Baron Georges Haussmann, who was called "the Attila of the Straight Line" for the ruthless manner in which his pencil cut through city neighborhoods on the map.

In spite of his awareness of his own importance, nobody took Louis Napoleon very seriously, even when as the dark-horse candidate he was elected president of the Second Republic in December 1848. The politicians were sure that he could be managed, so insignificant did he seem. They and the rest of France were literally caught sleeping before dawn on 2 December 1851 when the nephew of the great Napoleon seized power in a coup d'état and became dictator of France. Exactly one year later, he proclaimed himself Emperor Napoleon III and set about the tasks of establishing his dynasty and reclaiming French imperial glory.

Napoleon III's regime has been condemned for its decadence and its spectacle. On the surface, the world of the Second Empire glittered like a fancy-dress ball, with men in sparkling uniforms and women in full-skirted, low-necked gowns waltzing to gay tunes. Courtesans in open carriages, parading through the newly landscaped Bois de Boulogne, became as famous as cabinet members. But to judge the empire on superficial criteria alone would be a mistake. The Second Empire achieved significant successes in a variety of areas. Napoleon III supported economic expansion and industrial development. During his reign, the French economy prospered and flourished. The discovery of gold in California and Australia fueled a demand for French products in international markets and initiated a period of sustained economic growth that lasted beyond Napoleon III's reign into the 1880s. A new private banking system, founded in 1852 by financiers and key political figures, enabled the pooling of investors'

resources, small and large, to finance industrial expansion. Stable authoritarian government encouraged increased investment in state public-works programs.

Napoleon III surrounded himself with advisers who saw in prosperity the answer to all social problems. Between 1852 and 1860, the government supported a massive program of railroad construction. Jobs multiplied and investment increased. Agriculture expanded as railroad lines opened new markets. The rich got richer, but the extreme poverty of the first half of the nineteenth century was diminishing. Brutal misery in city and countryside did not disappear, but on the whole, the standard of living increased as wages rose faster than prices.

The best single example of the energy and commitment of the imperial regime was the rebuilding of the French capital. As Sir Edwin Chadwick (1800–1890), Britain's leading public health reformer, put it, Napoleon III found Paris stinking and left it sweet. Before midcentury, Paris was one of the most unsanitary, crime-ridden, and politically volatile capitals in Europe. Within fifteen years it had been transformed into a city of lights, wide boulevards and avenues, monumental vistas, parks, and gardens. Napoleon III was the architect of the idea for a new Paris, something his uncle never had the time or resources to accomplish. But the real credit for carrying through these municipal improvements goes to Baron Georges Haussmann (1809–91).

As Prefect of the Seine from 1853 to 1870, Baron Haussmann typified the technocrat in power. He was called "the Attila of the Straight Line" for the ruthless manner in which his protractor cut through city neighborhoods, destroying all that lay in his pencil's path. Poor districts were turned into rubble to make way for the elegant apartment buildings of the Parisian bourgeoisie. The new housing was too expensive for workers, who were pushed out of Paris into the suburbs. The boundaries of the city expanded. As workers from all over France migrated to the capital in search of jobs, the population nearly doubled, increasing by just under one million in the 1850s and 1860s. A poor and volatile population encircled the city of monuments and museums. Paris as the radical capital of France was being physically dismantled and a new, more conservative political entity rose in its place as the middle classes took over the heart of the city. This process was very different from the development of other urban areas like London, where the middle class fled to the suburbs, leaving behind the problems of urban life.

Much has been made of the policing benefits of rebuilding the city of Paris. Wider streets facilitated the movement of troops, which could more easily crush revolutionary disturbances. While the control aspect of urban reconstruction was not lost on Haussmann and Napoleon III, it was not the primary purpose of the vast public-works project that lasted for the whole regime. Napoleon wanted Paris to be the center of Western culture and the envy of the world. Its wide, straight avenues served as the model for other French cities. The new Paris became an international model copied in Mexico City, Brussels, Madrid, Rome, Stockholm, and Barcelona between 1870 and 1900. American city planners of the City Beautiful movement were also influenced by the "Haussmannization" of Paris. In spite of financial scandals that plagued the reconstruction near the end of the regime, few disputed that Napoleon III had transformed Paris into one of the world's most beautiful cities.

Just as a new Paris would make France the center of culture, Napoleon III intended his blueprint for foreign policy to restore France to its pre-1815 status as the greatest European power. French governments after 1815 had been forced to abandon adventurous foreign policies. By involving France in both the Crimean War and the war for Italian unification, Napoleon III reversed this pattern. The emperor had undertaken both wars with the hope of further increasing French economic and diplomatic prominence on the Continent. Napoleon III supported Piedmont-Sardinia not out of any sense of altruism, in spite of his claim that he was "doing something for Italy." The accession of Nice and Savoy increased French territory—and reversed the settlements of 1815.

The Italian campaign complicated relations with Great Britain, which feared a resurgent French militarism. French construction of the Suez Canal between the Red Sea and the Mediterranean also created tensions with Great Britain, protective of its own dominance in the Mediterranean and the Near East. Nevertheless, the free-trade agreement between the British and the French in 1860—the Chevalier-Cobden Treaty—was a landmark in overseas policy and a commitment to liberal economic policies.

The Second Empire's involvement in Mexico was another matter. It was simply a fiasco. The Mexican government had been chronically unable to pay its foreign debts, and France was Mexico's largest creditor. Napoleon III hoped that by intervening in Mexican affairs he could strengthen ties with Great Britain and Spain, to whom the Mexicans also owed money. The emperor planned to turn Mexico into a satellite empire that would be economically profitable to France. The United States, occupied with civil war, did not interfere in 1861 when Napoleon III sent a military expedition to "pacify" the Mexican countryside. With the backing of Mexican conservatives who opposed Mexican president Benito Juárez (1806–72), Napoleon III supported the Austrian archduke Maximilian (1832–67) as emperor of Mexico. The reasons for the choice of Maximilian are obscure, although the gesture was probably intended to win favor in the Viennese court. Max, as he was known, was well-meaning but inept. After he was crowned in 1863, the new Mexican emperor struggled to rule in an enlightened manner, but he was stymied from the beginning by the lack of popular support. Napoleon III recalled the 34,000 French troops that, at considerable expense, were keeping Maximilian's troubled regime in place. Abandoned, Maximilian was captured and executed by a firing squad in the summer of 1867. The Mexican disaster revealed the weaknesses of Napoleon III's regime and damaged French prestige in the international arena. Intensely aware of public criticism, the emperor undertook the reorganization of the army and a series of liberal reforms, including increasing parliamentary participation in affairs of state, and granting to trade unions the right of assembly.

The Prussian victory over Austria in the Seven Weeks' War had dramatically changed the situation on the Continent. Pundits in Paris were fond of saying that the Austrian loss really marked the defeat of France. France's position within Europe was threatened, and Napoleon III knew it. In 1870, the humiliatingly rapid defeat of French imperial forces in the Franco-Prussian War brought to an end the experiment in liberal empire.

In 1870 France remained a mixture of old and new. Although industrial production had doubled between 1852 and 1870, France was still an agricultural nation. Foreign trade expanded by 300 percent, growing faster than that of any other nation in Europe. Six times as many miles of railroad track crisscrossed France at the time Napoleon III went into exile as when he came into power. Napoleon III did not create the economic boom from which all of Europe benefited between 1850 and 1880, but he did build on it, using the state to stimulate and enhance prosperity. His policies favored business and initiated a financial revolution of enduring benefits. However, the technocratic model of rule by specialists was not applied to the army in forcing it to modernize. Nor had foreign policy benefited from the careful calculations employed in domestic administration. The empire had become the victim of its own myth of invincibility.

The Victorian Compromise

Contemporaries were aware of two facts of life about Great Britain in 1850: first, that Britain had an enormously productive capitalist economy of sustained growth; and second, that Britain enjoyed apparent social harmony without revolution and without civil war. As revolutions ravaged continental Europe in 1848, the British took pride in a parliamentary system that valued a tradition of freedom. British statesmen were not reluctant to point out to the rest of the world that Great Britain had achieved industrial growth without rending the social fabric.

The political rhetoric of stability and calm was undoubtedly exaggerated. Great Britain at midcentury had its share of serious social problems. British slums rivaled any in Europe. Poverty, disease, and famine ravaged the kingdom. Many feared that British social protests of the 1840s would result in upheavals similar to those in continental Europe. Yet Great Britain avoided a revolution. One explanation for Britain's relative calm lay in the shared political tradition that emphasized liberty as the birthright of English citizens. Building on an established political culture, the British Parliament was able to adapt to the demands of an industrializing society. Adaptation was gradual, but as slow as it seemed, a compromise was achieved among competing social interests. The great compromise of Victorian society was the reconciliation of industrialists' commitment to unimpeded growth with workers' need for the protection of the state. The British political system was democratized slowly after 1832.

The Reform Bill of that year gave increased political power to the industrial and manufacturing bourgeoisie,

William Gladstone rides in an omnibus in this painting titled One of the People *by Alfred Morgan. This mode of transport was thought of as a social leveler because all classes of people could afford the fares.*

who joined a landed aristocracy and merchant class. The property qualification meant that only 20 percent of the population was able to vote. The next step toward democracy was not taken for another thirty-five years. In 1867, under conservative leadership, a second Reform Bill was introduced. Approval of this bill doubled the electorate, giving the vote to a new urban population of shopkeepers, clerks, and workers. In 1884, farm laborers were enfranchised. Women, however, remained disenfranchised; they were not granted the vote until after World War I. Through parliamentary cooperation between Liberals and Conservatives, the male franchise was slowly implemented without a revolution.

The lives and careers of two men, William Ewart Gladstone (1809–98) and Benjamin Disraeli (1804–81), exemplify the particular path the British government followed in maintaining social peace. Rivals and political opponents, both men served as prime ministers and both left their mark on the age. From different political perspectives, they contributed to British reform in the second half of the nineteenth century.

William Gladstone was an example of a British statesman with no counterpart elsewhere in Europe: he was a classical liberal who believed in free enterprise and was opposed to state intervention. Good government, according to Gladstone, should remove obstacles to talent, competition, and individual initiative but should interfere as little as possible in economy and society. Surprisingly, this leader of the Liberal party began his long parliamentary career at the other end of the political spectrum, as a Tory. The son of a successful merchant and slave trader, Gladstone enjoyed the benefits of wealth and attended Eton and Oxford, where he studied classics and mathematics. Discouraged by his father from a career in the Church of England, Gladstone used his connections to launch a parliamentary career in 1832. He gradually left behind his conservative opposition to parliamentary reform and his support of protective tariffs. In 1846, as a member of the government, Gladstone broke with Tory principles and voted in favor of free trade. The best government, he affirmed in true liberal fashion, was the one that governed least.

Those who knew Gladstone in these early years were struck not by his brilliance but by his capacity for hard work and assiduous application to the task at hand. He chopped wood for relaxation. In his spare time he wrote a three-volume study on Homer and the Homeric age. He practiced an overt morality, targeting prostitutes in the hope of convincing them to change their lives. Gladstone was not blind to social problems, but he considered private philanthropy the best way to correct them.

Many of the significant advances of the British liberal state were achieved during Gladstone's first term as prime minister (1868–74). Taking advantage of British prosperity, Gladstone abolished tariffs, cut defense expenditures, lowered taxes, and sponsored sound budgets. He furthered the liberal agenda by disestablishing the Anglican church in Ireland in 1869. The Church had been the source of great resentment to the vast majority of Irish Catholics, who had been forced to pay taxes to support the Protestant state church.

Gladstone reformed the army, in disrepute after its poor performance in the Crimea, so that one could no longer purchase a commission. Training and merit would justify all future advancements. Similarly, Gladstone reformed the civil service system by separating it from political influence and seniority. A merit system and examinations were intended to ensure the most efficient and effective government administration. The secret ballot was introduced to prevent coercion in voting. Finally, the Liberals stressed the importance of education for an informed electorate and passed an education act that aimed to make elementary schooling available to everyone.

These reforms added up to a liberal philosophy of government. Liberal government was, above all, an attack on privilege. It sought to remove restraints on individual freedom and to foster opportunity and talent. Liberal government sought to protect democracy through education. Voting men must be educated men. As one Liberal put it, "We must educate our masters." Liberals governed in the interests of the bourgeoisie and with the belief that what was good for capitalism was good for society. Tariffs, therefore, were kept low or eliminated to promote British commerce. Gladstone believed that all political questions were moral questions and that fairness and justice could solve political problems. In spite of his moral claims, his programs made him enemies among special interests, including farmers and the Church of England, because his policies undermined their security and privileges.

During these years, another political philosophy also left its mark on British government. This was conservatism. Under the flamboyant leadership of Benjamin Disraeli, the Conservative party supported state intervention and regulation on behalf of the weak and disadvantaged. Disraeli sponsored the Factory Act of 1875, which set a maximum of 56 hours for the factory work week. The Public Health Act established a sanitary code. The Artisans Dwelling Act defined minimum housing standards. Probably the most important conservative legislation was the Trade Union Act, which permitted picketing and other peaceful labor tactics.

Disraeli's personal background and training were very different from Gladstone's and made him unique in British parliamentary politics. He was known primarily as a novelist, social critic, and failed financier before he entered the political arena in 1837. His father was a Jewish merchant descended from a family of Spanish refugees in Venice. The senior Disraeli became a British subject in 1801, three years before Benjamin's birth. In embracing English culture, the senior Disraeli had his children baptized in the Anglican church.

The split between Disraeli and Gladstone was clearly apparent in 1846 when they, both Tories, disagreed over the issue of free trade versus tariffs. Disraeli moved on to champion protection, and throughout the early 1860s consistently opposed Gladstone's financial system. Unlike the Liberals, Disraeli insisted on the importance of traditional institutions like the monarchy, the House of Lords, and the Church of England. Queen Victoria named him the First Earl of Beaconsfield for his strong foreign policy and social reforms. "Dizzy's" real cleverness and contribution to British politics was in an area that few contemporaries appreciated at the time. Disraeli's work in organizing a national party machinery facilitated the adaptation of the parliamentary system to mass politics. His methods of campaigning and building a mass base of support were used by successful politicians regardless of political persuasion.

The terms *liberal* and *conservative* hold none of the meaning today that they did for men and women in the nineteenth century. Classical liberalism has little in common with its twentieth-century counterpart, which favors an active interventionist state. Disraeli is a far more likely candidate for the twentieth-century liberal label than is Britain's leading nineteenth-century liberal statesman, Gladstone. Disraeli placed value in the ability of the state to correct and protect. Because of his interventionist philosophy, he may be compared with Continental statesmen like Bismarck and Napoleon III.

In spite of Liberal hopes, Great Britain never had a purely laissez-faire economy. As the intersecting careers of Gladstone and Disraeli demonstrate, the British model combined free enterprise with intervention and regulation. The clear issues and the clear choices of the two great parties—Liberal and Conservative—dominated parliamentary life after midcentury. In polarizing parliamentary politics, these parties also invigorated it.

Political rivals William Gladstone (left) and Benjamin Disraeli prepare to sling mud at each other in a Punch *cartoon.*

Reforming Russia

In 1850 Russia was an unreformed autocracy, a form of government in which the tsar held absolute power. Without a parliament, a constitution, or civil liberties for its subjects, the Russian ruler governed through a bureaucracy and a police force. Economically, Russia was a semifeudal agrarian state with a class of privileged aristocrats supported by serf labor on their estates.

For decades—since the reign of Alexander I (1801–25)—the tsars and their advisers realized that they were out of step with developments in western Europe. An awareness was growing that serfdom was uncivilized and morally wrong. The remnants of feudalism had been swept away in France in the Great Revolution at the end of the eighteenth century. Prussia had abolished hereditary serfdom beginning in 1806. Among the European powers, only Russia remained a serf-holding nation. Russian serfs were tied to the land and owed dues and labor services in return for the lands they held. Peasant protests mounted, attracting public attention to the plight of the serfs. A

Russian aristocrat, Baron N. Wrangel (1847–1920), recounted in his memoirs a story from his childhood in the 1850s, when he was about ten years old, that exemplifies the growing social awareness of the problem:

One day we were sitting quietly on the terrace listening to the reading aloud of *Uncle Tom's Cabin*, a recently translated book that was then in fashion. My sisters could not get over the horrors of slavery and wept at the sad fate of poor Uncle Tom. "I cannot conceive," said one of them, "how such atrocities can be tolerated. Slavery is horrible." "But," said Bunny, in her shrill little voice, "we have slaves too."

In spite of growing moral concern, there were many reasons to resist the abolition of serfdom. Granting freedom to all serfs was a vastly complicated affair. How were serf-holders to be compensated for the loss of labor power? What was to be the freed serf's relationship to the land? Personal freedom would be worthless without a land allotment. Yet landowners opposed loss of land as strongly as loss of their work force. A landless work force would be a serious social threat, if western European experience could be taken as an example.

Hesitation about abolition evaporated with the Russian defeat in the Crimean War. The new tsar, Alexander II (1855–81), viewed Russia's inability to repel an invasion force on its own soil as proof of its backwardness. Russia had no railroads and was forced to transport military supplies by carts to the Crimea. It took Moscow three months to provision troops, whereas the enemy could do so in three weeks. Alexander II believed in taking matters into his own hands. Russia must be reformed. Abolition of serfdom would permit a well-trained reserve army to exist without fear of rebellion. Liberating the serfs would also create a system of free labor so necessary for industrial development. Alexander interpreted rumblings within his own country as the harbinger of future upheavals similar to those that had rocked France and the Austrian Empire. He explained to the Muscovite nobility, "It is better to abolish serfdom from above than to wait until the serfs begin to liberate themselves from below."

In March 1861 the tsar signed the emancipation edict that liberated the serfs. Serfdom was eliminated in

Poland three years later. Alexander II, who came to be known as the "Tsar-Liberator," compromised between landlord and serf by allotting land to freed peasants, while requiring from the former serfs redemption payments that were spread out over a period of forty-nine years. The peasant paid the state in installments; the state reimbursed the landowner in lump sums. To guarantee repayment, the land was not granted directly to individual peasants but to the village commune *(mir),* which was responsible for collecting redemption payments.

Emancipation of the serfs, Alexander's greatest achievement, was a reform of unprecedented scale. It affected 52 million peasants, over 20 million of them enserfed to private landowners. By comparison, Abraham Lincoln's Emancipation Proclamation less than two years later freed 4 million American slaves. However, beneath the surface of the Russian liberation, peasants soon realized that the repayment schedule increased their burdens and responsibilities. The peasants resented being forced to pay for land they considered rightfully theirs. An old peasant saying reflected this belief: "We are yours"—they acknowledged to the landlords—"but the land is ours." It was not an accident that the *mir* arrangement prevented mobility; Alexander had no intention of creating a floating proletariat similar to that of western Europe. He wanted his people closely tied to the land, but freed from the servility of feudal obligations.

The abolition of serfdom did not solve the problem of Russian backwardness. Farming methods and farming implements remained primitive. Russian agriculture did not become more productive. Nor did emancipation result in a contented and loyal peasantry. Frustrations festered. A large proportion of peasants received too little land to make their redemption payments. Many peasants in the south received smaller plots of land than they had farmed under serfdom. The commune replaced the landowner in a system of peasant bondage. Redemption payments were finally abolished in 1907, but not before exacerbating social tensions in the countryside.

The real winner in the abolition of serfdom was not the landowners, and certainly not the peasantry, but the state. A bureaucratic hierarchy and a financial infrastructure were expanded. Other reforms in the system of credit and banking contributed significantly to rapid economic growth. With the help of foreign—especially French—investment, railway construction increased dramatically, from 660 miles of track in 1855 to 14,000 by 1880. Thanks in large part to the new trans-

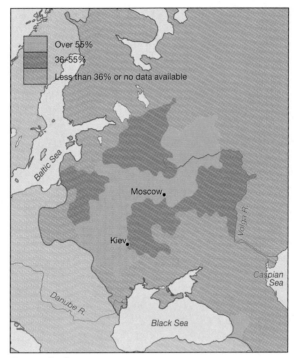

Russian Serfs

portation network, Russia became a world grain supplier during this period, with exports increasing threefold. But development was uneven and remained uncoordinated. The coexistence of the old alongside the new, combined with the speed of change, created friction and promised future unrest.

Alexander II, a man conservative by temperament but aware that Russia must move forward, did not stop here. In 1864 he introduced *zemstvos,* local elected assemblies on the provincial and county levels, to govern local affairs. The three classes of landowners, townspeople, and peasants elected representatives who were responsible for implementing educational, health, and other social welfare reforms. Similar statutes governing towns were passed in 1870. In the spirit of modernization, the state also undertook judicial reforms. New provincial courts were opened in 1866. Corporal punishment was to be eliminated. Separate courts for peasants still endured, however, preserving the impression that peasants were a lower class of citizens subject to different jurisdiction.

With the military triumph of Prussia over France in 1870–71, the tsar found the excuse he had been looking for in the 1860s to push through fundamental military reforms. Alexander II had admired the Prussian

Russian peasants at a village meeting. With the abolition of serfdom in 1861, village leaders gained considerable power.

military model since his childhood. In 1874 he used that model to require that all young men on reaching the age of twenty be eligible for conscription "in defense of the fatherland." Fifteen years of service were specified, but only six were served in active duty. This was a significant reduction from the twenty-five years of active service that peasant and lower-class conscripts had formerly served. Although length of service was reduced according to educational level, the military reforms were, on the whole, democratizing because they eliminated an important privilege of the wealthy.

In spite of this vast array of "Great Reforms"—emancipating the serfs, creating local parliamentary bodies, reorganizing the judiciary, modernizing the army—Russia was not sufficiently liberalized or democratized to satisfy the critics of autocracy. Between 1860 and 1870, a young generation of intelligentsia, radical intellectuals who benefited from the democratization of education and were influenced by the rhetoric of revolution in the West, assumed a critical stance in protest against the existing order. Although not itself a class, many members of the intelligentsia shared a similar background as the student sons and daughters of petty officials or priests. Young women, who often sought the education in Switzerland that was denied to them at home, were especially active in supporting ideas of emancipation.

In 1873 the imperial government considered the Western liberal and socialist ideas of the intelligentsia so threatening that it ordered Russian students studying in Switzerland to return home. Many returning students combined forces with radical intellectuals in Russia and decided to "go to the people." About 2500 educated young men and women traveled from village to village to educate, to help, and, in some cases, to attempt to radicalize the peasants. These populist crusaders sought to learn from what they considered to be the source of all morality and justice, the Russian peasantry. They paid dearly for what proved to be a fruitless commitment to populism in the mass trials and repression of the late 1870s.

Some of the tsarist regime's critics fled into exile to reemerge as revolutionaries in western Europe, where they continued to oppose the tsarist regime and helped shape the tradition of revolution and dissent in Western countries. Other educated men and women who remained in Russia chose violence as the only effective weapon against absolute rule. Terrorists who called themselves "Will of the People" decided on assassination as the best strategy and condemned the tsar to death. In the "emperor hunt" that followed, numerous attempts were made on the tsar's life. Miraculously, Alexander II escaped even the bombing of his own living quarters in the Winter Palace. The tsarist state responded with stricter controls, but repression only fanned the flames of discontent.

In response to attempts on his life and the assassination of public officials intended to cripple the central regime, Alexander II put the brakes on reform in the second half of his reign. The Great Reforms could not be undone, however, and had set in motion sweeping economic and social changes. The state encouraged capitalist growth and witnessed the rise of a professional middle class and the formation of an embryonic factory proletariat. Serfdom was dead forever. Yet reforms had increased expectations for an equally dramatic political transformation that failed to materialize. In the end, the "Will of the People" movement succeeded in its mission. A terrorist bomb killed Alexander II, the "Tsar-Liberator," in St. Petersburg in 1881.

The Politics of Leadership

Modern politics emerged in Europe only after 1850. Until that time, traditional political categories had prevailed. When faced with revolutionary upheavals, regimes aimed for stability and permanence. Only after 1850 did a new breed of political leader appear who understood the world of politics and directed it to their own ends. Three statesmen typify the new approach to the public world of power: Camillo di Cavour, Otto von Bismarck, and Louis Napoleon.

In old-regime Europe, power flowed downward from the monarch, who was perched atop a hierarchically organized social system often depicted as a pyramid. The source of royal power was both timeless and historic. As God's appointed agents, the sovereigns of Europe reinforced their right to rule with the continuity of their dynasties. Men of great political acumen ministered to their royal masters and were legitimated by royal power. In the years between 1789 and 1850, this system was challenged as kings were displaced—sometimes restored to power, sometimes executed. In the Austrian Empire, Spain, France, the Low Countries, Italy, and the German states, kingship, even when accepted, no longer went unquestioned. Divine authority was an archaic idea to the growing numbers of those who spoke of democratic principles and rallied to banners that represented new concepts of liberty and equality.

In the first half of the nineteenth century, men and women had learned that those in power could be questioned. The good of the people was the primary justification for government. Power now flowed upward from the citizenry to their appointed and elected representatives. The new power brokers were those who could control and direct the flow, not merely be carried along or swept away by it. These new political men were realists in the same tradition as Machiavelli and reflected the new political culture of the nineteenth century.

Political realists like Cavour, Bismarck, and Louis Napoleon understood the importance of public opinion. Public opinion had been a central fact of political life from the eighteenth century, but as revolutionary events in France demonstrated, public opinion proved unreliable building material for a stable government. The new political leaders appreciated public opinion for what it was—an unreliable guide for policy-making, often a dangerous beast that must be controlled and tamed. But above all, it was a tool for the shaping of consensus, the molding of support. The new political realists also understood the power of the press. Cavour achieved first prominence and then power by founding his own newspaper, *Il Risorgimento*. Louis Napoleon ran Europe's first modern political campaign, manipulating the printed word to shape his image and tailor his message to different audiences. Bismarck used public opinion and fashioned an image of German power that served his political ends.

The new political men also shared, to varying degrees, a disregard for traditional morality in decision-making. They were often politically amoral, willing to

This cartoon from the London News, *1848, shows newsboys selling election broadsides for Louis Napoleon and his opponent, General Cavaignac. The boys are fighting over the merits of their respective candidates.*

use whatever methods guaranteed success. As Bismarck succinctly put it at the end of his long career in public life, "Politics ruins the character." Machiavelli, too, shared this disregard for traditional morality. The new political men forged their own standards by which they judged the correctness of decisions and policies.

The nation-state was the supreme justification for all actions. Cavour, Bismarck, and Louis Napoleon saw struggle as the central fact of life. Nation-states were inherently competitive, with conflicting objectives. *Realpolitik* meant that statesmen had to think in terms of military capability, technological dominance, and the acceptable use of force. Without a traditional morality of right and wrong, these leaders recognized that there could be no arbiter outside the interests of the nation-state. From exile in England following his military defeat and his abdication, Napoleon III placed the welfare of France above his failed ambitions. At the former emperor's funeral, his son led a cheer, not for the empire but for France.

Modern European statesmen did not, however, share a common ideological outlook. Cavour leaned toward liberal ideas, while Bismarck was unquestionably conservative and Louis Napoleon held a blend of liberal and conservative views. Yet these leaders willingly enacted similar policies and sponsored similar legislation, not from any shared political commitment, but because of their desire to strengthen and promote their nations. In order to maintain power, they adapted to circumstance; they did not insist on principle. As Bismarck explained it, he always had more than one arrow in his quiver.

Finally, the new political men were risk takers. They acted without the safety net of tradition or political legitimacy under them. Bismarck saw himself on a tightrope, but one he felt prepared to walk. Just as Jeremy Bentham, earlier in the century, had figured the relationship between actions and outcomes in terms of profits and losses, the new statesmen were calculators; they weighed levels of risk appropriate for the ends they sought to achieve. *Realpolitik* was less the invention of a particular statesman and more a characteristic of the new age of gamesmanship in statecraft.

Changing Values and the Force of New Ideas

Like the political world, the material world was changing rapidly after 1850. The world of ideas that explained the place of women and men in this new universe was rapidly changing as well. The railroad journey became the metaphor for the new age. The locomotive hurtling forward signified the strength, power, and progress of materialism. Yet the passenger was strangely dislocated, the landscape between one point and another a blur seen through a carriage window. New points of reference must be found; new roots must be put down. In the period between 1850 and 1870, a materialist system of values emerged as behaviors changed. This was as true for the private world of the home as it was for the public world of high politics.

In any age, changes in material life find their way into literature, philosophy, science, and art. Changes in the environment affect the way people look at the world. In turn, intellectuals can have a profound effect on values and behavior. Truly great thinkers not only reflect their times, they also shape them. The third quarter of the nineteenth century was especially rich in both the creativity and critical stance that shaped modern consciousness. Amid the tumult of new ideas in the period after 1850, two titans stand out. Not artists, but scientists—one of biology, the other of society—they sought regularity and predictability in the world they observed and measured. The ideas of Charles Darwin and Karl Marx both reflected and changed the world they lived in.

People alive during the third quarter of the nineteenth century called themselves "modern." They were, indeed, "modern," since in their values and view of the world they were closer to their twentieth-century progeny than they were to their eighteenth-century grandparents.

The Politics of Homemaking

At the Great Exhibition of 1851 held in London, the achievements of modern industry were proudly displayed for all the world to see. Engineering marvels and mechanistic wonders dwarfed the thousands of visitors who came to the Crystal Palace to view civilization at its most advanced. In the midst of the machinery of the factory, household items took their place. Modern kitchens with coal-burning stoves were showcased, and the artifacts of the ideal home were carefully displayed. Predictably, mechanical looms, symbols of the new age, were exhibited; but inkstands, artificial flowers, thermostats, and cooking utensils were also enshrined. Visitors did not find strange this juxtaposition of the public world of production with the private world of the home in an exhibition celebrating British superiority.

The world of the home, not immune to changes in society and the economy, was invested with new power and meaning in mid-nineteenth-century Europe. Home was glorified as the locus of shelter and comfort where the harsh outside world could be forgotten. In 1870, an article in a popular Victorian magazine explained that the home functioned as a haven: "Home is emphatically man's place of rest, where his wife is his friend who knows his mind, where he may be himself without fear of offending, and relax the strain that must be kept out of doors: where he may feel himself safe, understood, and at ease."

Throughout Europe, the home served another function, as a symbol of status and achievement. Objects of a proper sort indicated wealth, upward mobility, and taste. In the belief that the more objects that could be displayed the better, the middle-class home of the third quarter of the nineteenth century was usually overdecorated. Drapes hung over doors and windows, pictures and prints covered the walls, and overstuffed furniture filled the rooms. All were intended to convey gentility and comfort.

Industrialization had separated the workplace from the home. Protective legislation before midcentury attempted to ease women out of the work force. Middle-class women were expected to assume primary responsibility for the domestic goals of escape and status. Just as the workplace was man's world, the private world of the home was woman's domain. After 1850, magazines, handbooks, and guidebooks that instructed women on how to fulfill their domestic duties proliferated. The most famous of the instruction manuals in Britain was Mrs. Beeton's *Book of Household Management* (1861). The title is instructive. The business concept of management could now be applied to the home. Mrs. Beeton told her readers, "The functions of the mistress of the house resemble those of the general of an army or the manager of a great business concern." "Home economics" was invented during this period. As the marketplace had its own rules and regulations that could be studied in the "dismal science" of economics, so too, women were told, the domestic sphere could benefit from the application of rational principles of organization.

Women were also well-informed by popular literature on how to get a man and keep him. Manuals cautioned women not to be too clever, since women with opinions were not popular with men. Mrs. Beeton's advice centered on food as the way to a man's heart. A wife's duty, she explained, was above all to provide her husband with a hot meal, prepared well and served punctually. Meals became elaborate occasions of several courses requiring hours of work. Women's magazines bombarded a growing readership with menus and recipes for the careful housewife. Status was communicated not by expensive foods, but by extravagant preparation. Meal-planning was an art, women learned, one whose practice required and assumed the assistance of household servants.

Before this time, women had produced in the home products they could now buy in the marketplace. Purchases of bread, beer, soap, and candles saved housewives hours of labor every week. But with rising expectations about the quality of life in the home, women had more rather than less to do each day. Handbooks prescribed rules on etiquette and proper manners. The rituals of domestic life, from letter-writing to afternoon visits and serving tea, were minutely detailed for middle-class audiences. The woman of the house was instructed in the care and education of her children; in health, cleanliness, and nutrition; and in the management of resources. Thrift, industry, and orderliness, the virtues of the business world, had their own particular meaning in the domestic sphere.

To the Victorian mind, gentility and morality were inextricably interwoven. A woman who failed in her duty to maintain a clean and comfortable home threatened the safety of her family. An 1867 English tract warned:

> The man who goes home on a Saturday only to find his house in disorder, with every article of furniture out of its place, the floor unwashed or sloppy from uncompleted washing, his wife slovenly, his children untidy, his dinner not yet ready, or spoilt in the cooking, is much more likely "to go on a spree" than the man who finds his house in order, the furniture glistening from the recent polishing, the burnished steel fire-irons looking doubly resplendent from the bright glow of the cheerful fire, his well-cooked dinner laid on a snowy cloth, and his wife and children tidy and cheerful.

The ideal was very far from the experiences of most families throughout Europe after the middle of the century. The "science" of homemaking presupposed a cushion of affluence out of reach to the men, women, and children who made up the vast majority of the population. Working-class wives and mothers often had to earn wages if their families were to survive. One Englishwoman, Lucy Luck (1848–1922), began her working career in a silk mill at the age of eight. By law allowed to work only half a day, the child Lucy returned to her foster home at the end of her shift to labor late into the night plaiting straw for baskets. In her reminiscences, she looked back over her life: "I have been at work for forty-seven years, and have never missed one season, although I have a large family of seven surviving children." Lucy, who married at the age of eighteen, learned that on her own she could not survive without a man's income or without resorting to the "bad life" of crime and prostitution. In the marriage, the couple could not survive without Lucy's wages.

Like Lucy Luck, many women held jobs outside the home or did piecework to supplement the meager family incomes. In 1866 women constituted a significant percentage of the French labor force, including 45 percent of all textile workers. At the height of the rhetoric about the virtues of domesticity, as many as two married Englishwomen in five worked in the mills in industrial areas like Lancashire. Working women often chose the "sweated labor" that they could perform in their home because it allowed them to care for their children while being paid by the piece. Home workers labored in the needle trades, shoemaking, and furniture making in their cramped living quarters under miserable conditions; and they worked for a third or less of what men earned.

The "haven" of the home was not insulated from the perils of the outside world. Nor was every home a happy one. Venereal diseases rose dramatically in Western nations, belying the image of the devoted couple. By the end of the nineteenth century, 14 to 17 percent of all deaths in France were attributable to sexually transmitted diseases. These diseases were blind to class distinctions. Illegitimacy rates rose in the first half of the nineteenth century and remained high after 1850 among the working classes, defying middle-class standards of propriety. Illegitimate births were highest in urban areas, where household life assumed its own distinctive pattern among working-class families, with couples often choosing free union instead of legal marriage.

Because virtue was defined in terms of woman's roles as wife and mother, working women were regarded as immoral. Social evils were, according to this reasoning, easily attributed to the "unnatural" phenomenon of women leaving the home to work in a man's world. Women continued to work and, in some cases, to organize to demand their rights. Women like Lucy Luck did not and could not accept the prescription that good mothers should not work, since their wages fed their children. The politics of homemaking defined women as mothers and hence legitimated the poor treatment and poor pay of women as workers. Yet the labor of women outside as well as inside the home remained the norm.

Nor did all middle-class women accept approved social roles. Increasing numbers of middle-class women

This female aboveground coal-mine worker was photographed in 1864 by Arthur J. Munby. Such women, who sorted the coal, had low status and no prospects.

in western Europe protested their circumscribed sphere. Critics argued that designating the home as woman's proper domain stifled individual development. Earlier in the century, Jane Austen, one of Britain's greatest novelists, had to keep a piece of muslin work on her writing table in the family drawing room to cover her papers lest visitors detect evidence of literary activity. In the next generation, Florence Nightingale refused to accept the embroidery and knitting to which she was relegated at home. This period in Western society witnessed both the creation of the cult of domesticity and the stirrings of feminism among middle-class women, whose demand for equal treatment for women was to become more important after 1870. Patterns of behavior changed within the family, and they were not fixed immutably in social practice. Woman's place and woman's role proved to be much-disputed questions in the new politics of homemaking.

The New World of Realism in the Arts

The term *realism* was first used in 1850 to describe the paintings of Gustave Courbet (1819–77), but the spirit of realism characterized a wide array of artistic endeavors. Realism in the arts and literature was a rejection of romantic idealism and subjectivity. Realists responded to the disillusionment with the political failures of midcentury by withdrawing from politics. And they responded directly to the challenges of urban and industrial growth by confronting the alienation of modern existence. In *The Artist's Studio* (1855), Courbet portrayed himself surrounded by the intellectuals and political figures of his day. He may have been painting a landscape, but contemporary political life crowded in; a starving Irish peasant and her child crouch beneath his easel. Of his unrelenting canvases, none more fittingly portrays the harsh realism of bourgeois life than the funeral ceremony depicted in *Burial at Ornans* (1849–50) or better depicts the brutality of workers' lives than *Stone Breakers* (1849).

After midcentury, idealization in romantic literature yielded to novels depicting the objective and unforgiving social world. Through serialization in journals and newspapers, fiction reached out to mass audiences, who got their "facts" about modern life through stories that often cynically portrayed the monotony and boredom of daily existence. In *Hard Times* (1854), set in the imaginary city of Coketown, Charles Dickens (1812–70) creates an allegory that exposes the sterility and soullessness of industrial society through "fact, fact, fact everywhere in the material aspect of the town; fact, fact, fact everywhere in the immaterial."

Gustave Flaubert (1821–80), the great French realist novelist, critiqued the Western intellectual tradition in his unfinished *Dictionary of Accepted Ideas* (1881). In the novel *Bouvard et Pécuchet* (1881), Flaubert satirized modern man's applications of Enlightenment ideas about the environment and progress by showing that they are foolish and often at odds with common sense. The main characters of the novel know everything there is to know about theories and applied sciences, but they know nothing about life. His best-known work, *Madame Bovary* (1856), recounts the story of a young country doctor's wife whose desire to escape from the boredom of her provincial existence leads her into adultery and eventually results in her destruction. Flaubert was put on trial for obscenity and violating public morality with his tale of the unrepentant Emma Bovary. This beautifully crafted novel is marked by an ironic detachment from the hypocrisy of bourgeois life. Mary Ann Evans (1819–80), writing under the pseudonym George Eliot, was also concerned with moral choices and responsibilities in novels like *Middlemarch* (1871–72), a tale of idealism disappointed by the petty realities of provincial English life.

The problem of morality in the realist novel is nowhere more apparent than in the works of the Russian writer Fyodor Dostoyevsky (1821–81). Dostoyevsky's protagonists wrestle with a universe where God no longer exists and where they must shape their own morality. The impoverished student Raskolnikov in *Crime and Punishment* (1866) justifies his brutal murder of an old woman that occurs in the opening pages of the novel. Realist art and literature addressed an educated elite public but did not flinch before the unrelenting poverty and harshness of contemporary life. The morality of the realist vision lay not in condemning the evils of modern life and seeking their political solutions, as an earlier generation of romantics did, but in depicting social evils for what they were, failures of a smug and progressive middle class.

Charles Darwin and the New Science

Science had a special appeal for a generation of Europeans disillusioned with the political failures of idealism in the revolutions of 1848. This was not an age of great scientific discovery, but rather one of synthesis of previous findings and their technological applications. Science was, above all, to be useful in promoting material progress.

Charles Darwin (1809–82), the preeminent scientist of the age, was a great synthesizer. Darwin began his scientific career as a naturalist with a background in geology. As a young man, he sailed around the world on the *Beagle* (1831–36). He collected specimens and fossils as the ship's naturalist, with his greatest finds in South America, especially the Galapagos Islands. He spent the next twenty years of his life taking notes of his observations of the natural world. In chronically poor health, Darwin produced five hundred pages of what he called "one long argument." *On the Origin of Species by Means of Natural Selection* (1859) was a book that changed the world.

Darwin's argument was a simple one: life forms originated in and perpetuated themselves through struggle. The outcome of this struggle was determined by "natural selection," or what came to be known as "survival of the fittest." Better-adapted individuals survived, while others died out. Competition between species and within species produced a dynamic model of organic evolution. Darwin did not use the word *evolution* in the original edition, but a positivist belief in an evolutionary process permeated the 1859 text.

Evolutionary theory was not new, nor was materialism a new concept in organic biology. In the 1850s, others were coming forward with similar ideas about natural selection, including most notably A. R. Wallace (1823–1913), who stressed geographic factors in biological evolution. Darwin's work was a product of discoveries in a variety of fields—philosophy, history, and science. He derived his idea of struggle from Malthus's *Essay on Population* and borrowed across disciplines to construct a theory of "the preservation of favored races in the struggle for life" (part of the book's subtitle). The publication of *Origin of Species* made Darwin immediately famous. Scientific theory was the stuff of front-page headlines. Like Samuel Smiles, a businessman who published the best-seller *Self-Help* in 1860, Darwin spoke of struggle and discipline, though in nature, not in the marketplace. In the world of biology, Darwin's ideas embodied a new realist belief in progress based on struggle. Force explained the past and would guarantee the future as the fittest survived. These were ideas that a general public applied to a whole range of human endeavors and to theories of social organization.

Karl Marx and the Science of Society

"Just as Darwin discovered the law of development of organic nature, Marx discovered the law of development of human history." So spoke Friedrich Engels (1820–95), longtime friend of and collaborator with Karl Marx (1818–83), over Marx's grave. Marx would have been pleased with Engels's eulogy: he called himself the Darwin of sociology. Marx footnoted as corroborating evidence Darwin's "epoch-making work on the origin of species" in his own masterwork, *Das Kapital*, the first volume of which appeared in 1867. As the theorist of the socialism that he called "scientific," Marx viewed himself as an evolutionist who demonstrated that history is the dialectical struggle of classes.

Engels first encountered Marx in Paris. It was a meeting of kindred spirits: each had been seeking out the other. Engels had just written *The Condition of the Working Class in England in 1844*. Marx was an iconoclast. The son of a Prussian lawyer who had converted from Judaism to Christianity, Marx had rejected the study of the law and belief in a deity. In exile because of his political writings, Marx was the most brilliant of the German young Hegelians, intellectuals heavily influenced by the ideas of Georg Friedrich Hegel (1770–1831), which held sway over the German intellectual world of the 1830s and 1840s. By the mid-

1840s, Marx was in rebellion against Hegel's idealism and was developing his own materially grounded view of society. When Engels and Marx first met, they talked daily for two weeks about their common concern with social injustice and the struggles of the poor. Their momentous encounter was the beginning of a lifelong collaboration.

Engels was a wealthy German businessman whose father owned factories in Manchester, England. When Marx was expelled from France in 1847 at the request of the Prussian government, Engels financed his move to London, where he eventually took up permanent residence in 1849. While Karl Marx studied in the main reading room of the British Museum, Engels paid for the Marx family's expenses, bailed them out in hard times, and even assumed responsibility for Marx's illegitimate son, whose mother was the family maid. Karl Marx, who was to become the foremost critic of the capitalist system, joked self-disparagingly that he could not survive without Engels, since he did not know how to manage money.

The philosophy that evolved in these years of collaboration with Engels was built on a materialist view of society. Human beings were defined not by their souls but by their labor. Labor was a struggle to transform nature by producing commodities useful for survival. Their ability to transform nature by work differentiated men and women from animals. Building on this fundamental concept of labor, Marx and Engels saw society as divided into two camps: those who own property and those who do not. Nineteenth-century capitalist society was divided into two classes: the bourgeoisie, those who owned the means of production as its private property, and the proletariat, the propertyless working class.

This materialist perspective on society was the engine driving Marx's theory of history. For Marx, every social system based on a division into classes carries within it the seeds of its own destruction. Marx and Engels used a biological metaphor to explain this destruction. The growth of a plant from a seed is a dialectical process in which the germ is destroyed by its opposite, the plant. The mature plant produces seed while continuing its form. The different stages of history are determined by different forms of the ownership of production. In a feudal-agrarian society, the aristocracy controlled and exploited the unfree labor of serfs. In a world of commerce and manufacturing, the capitalist bourgeoisie are the new aristocracy exploiting free labor for wages.

Marx was more than an observer: he was a critic of capitalism. His labor theory of value was the wedge he

This illustration by Gustave Doré appeared in The Condition of the Working Class in England in 1844 *by Friedrich Engels. Small and cramped industrial working-class houses with their tiny walled backyards are framed by railway lines.*

drove into the self-congratulatory rhetoric of the capitalist age. Labor is the source of all value, he argued, and yet the bourgeois employer denies workers the profit of their work by refusing to pay them a decent wage. Instead, he pockets the profits. Workers are separated, or alienated, from the product of their labor. But more profoundly, in a capitalist system all workers are alienated from the creation that makes them human; they are alienated from their labor.

Marx predicted that capitalism would produce more and more goods but would continue to pay workers the lowest wages possible. By driving out smaller producers, the bourgeoisie would increase the size of the proletariat. Yet Marx was optimistic. As workers were slowly pauperized, they would become conscious of their exploitation and would revolt. The force of these ideas mobilized thousands of contemporaries aware of the injustices of capitalism. Few thinkers in the history of the West have left a more lasting legacy than Karl Marx. The legacy has survived the fact that much of Marx's analysis rested on incorrect predictions about the increasing misery of workers and the inflexibility of the capitalist system.

Karl Marx was a synthesizer who combined economics, philosophy, politics, and history in a wide-ranging critique of industrial society. Marxism spread across Europe as workers responded to its message. Marx did not cause the increase in the organization of workers that took place in the 1860s, but his theories did give shape and focus to a growing critique of labor relations in the second half of the nineteenth century. Political parties throughout Europe coalesced around Marxist beliefs and programs. Marxists were beginning to be heard in associations of workers, and in 1864 they helped found the International Working Men's Association in London, an organization of French, German, and Italian workers dedicated to "the end of all class rule." The promise of a common association of workers transcending national boundaries became a compelling idea to those who envisioned the end of capitalism. The importance of the international exchange of ideas and information cannot be underestimated as a means of promoting labor organization in western Europe. In 1871 Marx and his followers turned to Paris for proof that the revolution was at hand.

A New Revolution?
The Siege of Paris and the Commune

Soundly defeated on 2 September 1870, Napoleon III and his fighting force of 100,000 men became Prussia's prisoners of war. With the emperor's defeat, the Second Empire collapsed. But even with the capture of Napoleon III, the French capital city of Paris refused to capitulate. The dedication of Parisians to the ongoing war with the Prussians was evident from the first. The regime's liberal critics in Paris seized the initiative to proclaim France a republic. If a corrupt and decadent empire could not save the nation, then France's Third Republic could.

In mid-September 1870, two German armies surrounded Paris and began a siege that lasted for over four months. Only carrier pigeons and balloon-transported passengers linked Paris with the rest of France. In the beginning, Parisian heroism, unchallenged by battle, seemed festive and unreal. Bismarck's troops were intent on bringing the city to its knees not by fighting but by cutting off its vital supply lines. By November, food and fuel were dwindling and Parisians were facing starvation. Undaunted, they began to eat dogs, cats, and rats. By December, famine threatened to become a reality. Most people had no vegetables and no meat. Rationing was ineffective, and a black market

prevailed in which the wealthy could buy whatever was available. Horses disappeared from the streets and the zoo was emptied as antelope, camel, donkey, mule, and elephant became desirable table fare. The Bois de Boulogne, the city's largest park, was leveled for timber to build barricades and for fuel. But the wood was too green and would not burn. The bitter cold of one of the century's most severe winters heightened the horror.

Yet the population was committed to fighting on. Men and women became part of the city's citizen militia, the National Guard, and trained for combat against the Germans. "Siege fever" swept the city. In spite of dire conditions, there were moments of euphoria. Collective delusions, perhaps intensified by empty stomachs, convinced Parisians that they were invincible against the enemy. Citizens joined clubs to discuss politics and preparedness, and probably to keep warm. Patents on inventions to defeat the Germans proliferated. Most of them were useless and silly, like the musical machine gun that was intended to lure its victims within firing range. The enemy at their gates absorbed the total attention of the urban population. There was no life other than the war.

Apparently with the goal of terrorizing the population, the Germans began a steady bombardment of the city at the beginning of January 1871. The shells fell

Interior of a meat market in Paris during the siege of 1870–71. Food shortages were taking their toll, as the sign advertising dog and cat meat attests.

RED WOMEN IN PARIS

Louise Michel, a schoolteacher and a member of the Paris Commune, was one of the many women and men who took up arms to defend the Commune against the forces of the government in Versailles. Men's and women's vigilance committees (Michel attended both) met to ensure that the Commune set up by the people would survive. The Communards believed that the Versailles government would limit their hard-won freedoms by creating a new king of France. When the Versailles government attacked Paris, the Communards fought back.

Learning that the Versailles soldiers were trying to seize the cannon, men and women of Montmartre swarmed up the Butte in a surprise maneuver. Those people who were climbing believed they would die, but they were prepared to pay the price.

The Butte of Montmartre was bathed in the first light of day, through which things were glimpsed as if they were hidden behind a thin veil of water. Gradually the crowd increased. The other districts of Paris, hearing of the events taking place on the Butte of Montmartre, came to our assistance.

The women of Paris covered the cannon with their bodies. When their officers ordered the soldiers to fire, the men refused. The same army that would be used to crush Paris two months later decided now that it did not want to be an accomplice of the reaction. They gave up their attempt to seize the cannon from the National Guard. They understood that the people were defending the Republic by defending the arms that the royalists and imperialists would have turned on Paris in agreement with the Prussians. When we had won our victory, I looked around and noticed my poor mother, who had followed me to the Butte of Montmartre, believing that I was going to die.

On this day, the eighteenth of March, the people wakened. If they had not, it would have been the triumph of some king; instead it was a triumph of the people. The eighteenth of March could have belonged to the allies of kings, or to foreigners, or to the people. It was the people's.

From Louise Michel, *The Red Virgin: Memoirs of Louise Michel* (1981).

---

for three weeks, but Parisian resistance prevailed. However, the rest of France wanted an end to the war. The Germans agreed to an armistice at the end of January 1871 in order that French national elections could be held to elect representatives to the new government. In the elections, French citizens outside Paris repudiated the war and returned an overwhelmingly conservative majority to seek peace.

Thus the siege came to an end. Yet it left deep wounds that still festered. Parisians felt they had been betrayed by the rest of France. Through four months as a besieged city, they had sacrificed, suffered, and died. Parisians believed that they were defenders of the true republic, the true patriots. Among Parisians, disparities of wealth were more obvious than ever before. Some wealthy citizens had abandoned the city during the siege. The wealthy who stayed ate and kept warm. Poor women who stood in food lines from before dawn every day to provision their families knew that there was food—but not for them.

The war was over, but Paris was not at peace. The new national government, safely installed outside Paris at Versailles, attempted to reestablish normal life. The volatility of the city motivated the government's attempt in March 1871 to disarm the Parisian citizenry by using army troops. In the hilly neighborhood of northern Paris, men, women, and children poured into the streets to protect their cannons and to defend their right to bear arms. In the fighting that followed, the Versailles troops were driven from the city. Paris was in a state of siege once again.

The spontaneity of the March uprising was soon succeeded by organization. Citizens rallied to the idea of the city's self-government and established the Paris Commune, as other French cities followed the capital's lead. Karl Marx hailed this event as the beginning of the revolution that would overthrow the capitalist system and saw in it the beginning of the dictatorship of the proletariat. But what occurred between March and May 1871 was not a proletarian revolution. Rather, it was a continuation of the state of siege that had held Paris through the fall and early winter months. Parisians were still at war. It was not war against a foreign enemy, nor was it a class war. It was a civil war against the rest of France.

The social experiment of self-defense in the Commune lasted for 72 days. Armed women formed their own fighting units, the city council regulated labor relations, and neighborhoods ruled themselves. In May 1871, government troops reentered the city and brutally crushed the Paris Commune. In one "Bloody Week," 25,000 Parisians were massacred and 40,000 others were arrested and tried. Of the 10,000 rebels convicted, 5,000 were sent to a penal colony in the southwestern Pacific Ocean. Such reprisals inflamed radicals and workers all over Europe. The myth of the Commune became a rallying cry for revolutionary movements throughout the world and inspired the future leaders of the Russian revolutionary state.

The Commune was important at the time, but not as a revolution. It offered two lessons to men and women at the end of the third quarter of the nineteenth century. First, it demonstrated the power of patriotism. Competing images of the nation were at stake, one Parisian and the other French, but no one could deny the power of national identity to inspire a

STATE-BUILDING AND SOCIAL CHANGE

1853–1856	Crimean War
1859	Austria declares war on Kingdom of Sardinia; France joins forces with Italians
1860	Piedmont-Sardinia annexes duchies in central Italy; France gains Nice and Savoy
3 March 1861	Emancipation of Russian serfs
14 March 1861	Kingdom of Italy proclaimed with Victor Emmanuel II as king
1861–1865	American Civil War
1863	Maximilian crowned emperor of Mexico
1863	Prussians and Austrians at war with Denmark
1866	Seven Weeks' War between Austria and Prussia; Italy acquires Venetia
1867	Emperor Maximilian executed
July 1870	Franco-Prussian War begins
2 September 1870	French Second Empire capitulates with Prussian victory at Sedan
20 September 1870	Italy annexes Rome
18 January 1871	German Empire proclaimed
March–May 1871	Paris Commune

whole city to suffer and to sacrifice. Second, the Commune made clear the power of the state. No revolutionary movement could succeed without controlling the massive forces of repression at the state's command. The Commune had tried to recapture a local, federal view of the world but failed to take sufficient account of the power of the state that it opposed. In writing of this episode two decades later, Friedrich Engels wondered if revolution would ever again be possible in the West.

• • •

Western societies had crossed the threshold into the modern age in the third quarter of the nineteenth cen-

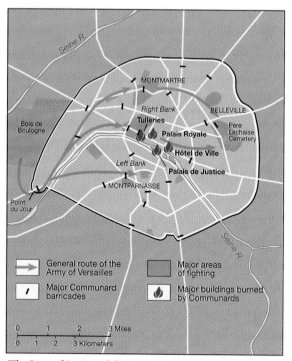

The Siege of Paris and the Paris Commune

tury. Strong states from Great Britain to Russia were committed to creating and preserving the conditions of industrial expansion. The machine age, railroads, and metallurgy were spreading industrial development much more widely through western and central Europe than had been possible before 1850. Italians and Prussians, in attempting to join the ranks of nation-states, realized that the road to a strong nation could only be achieved with industrial development and social reforms.

State-building in Western societies went hand in hand with growth in the social responsibilities of government. The national powers that would dominate world politics and economy in the twentieth century all underwent modernizing transitions in the 1860s. These included the United States, France, Great Britain, and Germany. The Austrian Empire, too, undertook programs to modernize its government and economy; and the Russian Empire established social reforms of unparalleled dimensions. New nations came into existence in this period through the limited use of armed force. With the establishment of the German Empire, Otto von Bismarck, the most realistic of politicians, was intent on preserving the peace in Europe by balancing the power of the great European states. Europeans prided themselves on being both modern and realistic in the third quarter of the nineteenth century. Peace was possible if it was armed and vigilant. Reform, not revolution, many were sure, was the key to the future progress of European societies.

Suggestions for Further Reading

Building Nations: The Politics of Unification

Derek Beales, *The Risorgimento and the Unification of Italy* (London: Allen & Unwin, 1982). Drawing a distinction between unification and national revival, Beales situates the period of unification within the larger process of the cultural and political revival.

* Gordon A. Craig, *Germany, 1866–1945* (New York: Oxford University Press, 1978). This synthetic view of German history provides a thorough examination of German unification. Craig analyzes all aspects of imperial development, with special attention to the institutional framework, its politics, economy, and diplomacy.

James J. Sheehan, *German Liberalism in the Nineteenth Century* (Chicago: University of Chicago Press, 1978). Sheehan explores the problems of transferring Western liberalism to Germany by examining the origins of German liberalism, the revolutions of 1848, and the politics of the Bismarckian state.

Denis Mack Smith, *Cavour* (London: Weidenfeld and Nicolson, 1985). Smith contrasts Cavour and his policies to Garibaldi and Mazzini and considers the challenge of regionalism to the unification process.

Reforming European Society

* David Pinkney, *Napoleon III and the Rebuilding of Paris* (Princeton, NJ: Princeton University Press, 1972). Describes how Paris was transformed into the monumental city that became not only a manifestation of French culture, but also a symbol of European culture as a whole. The planning, financing, and building of Napoleon III's Paris are analyzed, as is the impact of the rebuilding on the city's residents.

* Alain Plessis, *The Rise and Fall of the Second Empire, 1852–1871,* tr. Jonathan Mandelbaum (Cambridge: Cambridge University Press, 1985). Discusses the Second Empire as an important transitional period in French history, when the conflict was between traditional and modern values in political, economic, and social transformations.

* W. H. C. Smith, *Second Empire and Commune: France, 1848–1871* (London: Longman, 1985). Places the reign of Louis Napoleon in its domestic and international context and argues that the Empire was destroyed by external forces.

H. Seton Watson, *The Russian Empire, 1801–1917* (Oxford: Clarendon Press, 1967). This narrative history describes the social and economic background of late imperial Russia, with attention to intellectual trends and political ideologies.

Changing Values and the Force of New Ideas

* Jacques Barzun, *Darwin, Marx, Wagner: Critique of a Heritage* (Garden City, NY: Doubleday Anchor, 1958). A classic study of mid-nineteenth-century intellectual and cultural trends that situates the roots of the modern heritage in the science and art of this period.

Jenni Calder, *The Victorian Home* (London: B. T. Batsford, 1977). A cultural and social history of Victorian domestic life in which the author describes both bourgeois and working-class domestic environments.

* Bonnie G. Smith, *Ladies of the Leisure Class: The Bourgeoises of Northern France in the Nineteenth Century* (Princeton, NJ: Princeton University Press, 1981). Explores the impact of industrialization on the lives of bourgeois women in northern France and demonstrates how the cult of domesticity emerged in a particular community.

Edith Thomas, *The Women Incendiaries,* tr. James and Starr Atkinson (New York: George Braziller, 1966). One of the few studies that examines the prominent role played by women in the Paris Commune, this book considers how instrumental women were in the burning of Paris and also examines contemporary feminist debates.

* Martha Vicinus, *Independent Women: Work and Community for Single Women, 1850–1920* (Chicago: University of Chicago Press, 1985). Chronicles the choices that Victorian women made to live outside the norms of marriage and domesticity in various women's communities, including sisterhoods, nursing communities, colleges, boarding schools, and settlement houses.

*Paperback edition available.

24 ✍ THE CRISIS OF EUROPEAN CULTURE, 1871–1914

Speeding to the Future

"We want to demolish museums and libraries." These are not the words of an anarchist or a terrorist but of a poet. The Italian writer Emilio Marinetti (1876–1944) endeavored—symbolically, at least, through the power of his pen—to destroy the citadels of Western culture at the beginning of the twentieth century. Marinetti was not alone in wanting to pull down all that preserved art and learning in the West. Joined by other artists and writers who called themselves futurists, Marinetti represented a desire to break free of the past. By shocking complacent bourgeois society with their art, futurists hoped to fashion a new and dynamic civilization. Although they were a small group with limited influence, their concerns were shared by a growing number of intellectuals who judged European culture to be in the throes of a serious moral and cultural crisis. Futurist ideas also reflected the growing preoccupation with the future common among European men and women who spurned the value of tradition.

The futurist painter Umberto Boccioni (1882–1916) captures an aspect of the dynamic intensity of this changing world in his *Riot in the Galleria* (1910). Look at the painting. The setting is a galleria, the equivalent of a modern shop-ping mall, in front of a respectable *caffè* (an Italian coffee shop), this one frequented by well-dressed men and women, clearly members of the middle class. Here is a modern urban scene, a public space in every way characteristic of the new age of enjoyment and consumption.

There is a story here. In a flurry of light and shadow, a rush of figures moves toward the middle ground of the canvas. At the center of this movement are two women engaged in a brawl that seems to pull the figures of shoppers and strollers toward it. The fact that the brawlers are female is intended to underscore the irrationality of the incident. Yet the brawl itself is not compelling our attention. It is rather the movement of the crowd, like moths to a flame, that Boccioni intends us to see. This is a painting about movement. These objects in motion are little more than vibrations in space, faceless and indistinguishable as individuals. The crowd does not walk or run; it appears instead to be in flight. In his studies for the canvas, Boccioni reduces movement to a series of lines both swirling and directed.

The riot Boccioni depicts here is an irrational event. This is no ordinary rabble: it is a well-dressed mob, as the blurred but sumptuously flowered hats and the occasional yellow straw boaters make clear. Movement is taking place without forethought, fueled by the attraction of violence and the possibility of participating in it. There are those on the periphery who have not joined the frenzy, but we as spectators are confident that they will be swept up in the action as the energy of the brawl sucks everything to its center, like the vortex of a tornado. European society seemed to many contemporaries to be moving into an abyss, a world of tumultuous change but without values.

In the violence of the riot we are shown beauty of movement that surpasses that of an orderly waltz. Boccioni uses the warm glow of the electric lights, symbol of the modern age, to illuminate a "new reality." Golden tones, warm oranges and rosy hues, shadowed in delicate purples, create a mosaic whose beauty in the play of color is strangely at odds with the theme of the two brawling figures who activate the crowd. There is no meaning beyond the movement.

Riot in the Galleria reflects the preoccupation with change in the early twentieth century. Life was moving so fast that European society seemed to have outrun its own heritage by 1900. Technology was transforming Europe with a breakneck speed unmatched in human history. Science undermined the way people thought about themselves by challenging moral and religious values as hollow and meaningless. The natural sciences threw into doubt the existence of a creator. New forms of communication and transportation—the telephone, the wireless telegraph, the bicycle, the automobile, the airplane—were obliterating traditional understandings of time and space. The cinema and the X ray altered visual perception and redefined the ways people saw the world around them. This was a period of intense excitement and vitality in the history of the West, one which traditional values did not always explain.

Like the political revolutionaries of an earlier age, futurist artists issued "manifestoes." They sought the liberation of the human spirit from a world that could no longer be understood or controlled. Liberation could only be achieved through immersion in mass society and rapid change. Boccioni's goal was a revolutionary one: "Let's turn everything upside down. . . . Let's split open our figures and place the environment inside them."

Not all contemporary artists went as far in embracing the new age as Marinetti, Boccioni, and the other futurists. Many of Europe's intellectuals understood the attempt to break free of the stranglehold of Western tradition. In the arts, French impressionists, including Édouard Manet (1832–83), Claude Monet (1840–1926), Edgar Degas (1834–1917), and Pierre-Auguste Renoir (1841–1919) experimented with capturing the nature of light on canvas. They painted scenes from modern life, including urban subjects, that broke with traditional forms by emphasizing the private, individual lives of the middle class.

The moral dimensions of the cultural crisis affecting the West were grasped early by the German philosophers Arthur Schopenhauer (1788–1860), who made pessimism into a philosophical category, and Friedrich Nietzsche (1844–1900), who argued against all religion and glorified the superman. Georges Sorel (1847–1922) in France reflected on the importance of violence, and his countryman Alfred Jarry (1873–1907) used the stage to show that nonsense and irrationality ruled everywhere.

The futurists went beyond the radical cultural critique of European intellectuals when they proclaimed, "A speeding automobile is more beautiful than *The Victory of Samothrace.*" By declaring that modern mechanical invention surpassed the beautiful ancient Greek statue enshrined in the Louvre museum in Paris, Boccioni intended to establish the supremacy of contemporary achievement.

Boccioni has been recognized as one of the great artists of the twentieth century. In his sculpture and painting, he aimed to capture the vitality and excitement of the new age. The desire to destroy all traditional values led Boccioni and the futurists to embrace violence and war as "hygienic." Futurism glorified the masses and rejected traditional elites as sterile. The individual was no longer at the center of the new culture. Change, technology, and, above all, violence were exalted. As the First Futurist Manifesto urged, "Let us leave Wisdom behind. . . . Let us throw ourselves to be devoured by the Unknown." With the figures in his canvas swept up into an irrational mass, Boccioni emphasizes the rush and unpredictability of daily life. Beauty was a speeding car swallowing up the landscape, and it was a crowd sucked into the whirlwind of collective irrationality. Boccioni met his own death in 1916 as a soldier in the war that he welcomed as a purifying event.

The "whirling life of steel, of pride, of fever and of speed" identified by the futurists in their 1910 Manifesto suggested a new universe of continuous upheaval. Futurists were not alone in their confusion over what to keep and what to reject in Western culture or in their inability to break entirely with the past. But they were single-minded in their rebellion against constraints. Before 1914 a new generation of Europeans rushing forward abandoned the lessons of the past for the promise of the future.

European Economy and the Politics of Mass Society

Between 1871 and 1914, the scale of European life was radically altered. Industrial society had promoted largeness as the norm, and growing numbers of people worked under the same roof. Large-scale heavy industries fueled by new energy sources dominated the economic landscape. Great Britain, the leader of the first phase of the industrial revolution of the eighteenth century, slipped in prominence as an industrial power at the end of the nineteenth century, as Germany and the United States devised successful competitive strategies of investment, protection, and control.

The organization of factory production throughout Europe and the proximity of productive centers to distribution networks meant ever greater concentration of populations in urban areas. Like factories, cities were getting bigger at a rapid rate and were proliferating in numbers. Berlin, capital of the new German nation, mushroomed in size in the last quarter of the nineteenth century. In the less industrialized parts of eastern Europe, cities also underwent record growth. Warsaw, St. Petersburg, and Moscow all expanded by at least 400,000 inhabitants each. Budapest, the city created by uniting the towns of Buda and Pest in 1872, tripled in size between 1867 and 1914 and was typical of the booming growth of provincial cities throughout Europe. With every passing year proportionately fewer people remained on the land. Those who did stay in the agricultural sector were linked to cities and tied into national cultures by new transportation and communications networks.

Changes in the scale of political life paralleled the rise of heavy industry and the increasing urbanization of European populations. Great Britain experienced the transformation in political organization and social structure before other European nations. But after 1870, changes in politics influenced by the scale of the new industrial society spread to every European country. Mass democracy was on the rise and was pushing aside the liberal emphasis on individual rights valued by parliamentary governments everywhere.

In spite of dramatic changes in politics and society, the old order still persisted. Throughout Europe, monarchy remained the dominant form of government, whether in the small German dynasties or the great Habsburg holdings. The progeny of Britain's Queen Victoria married the sons and daughters of Europe's other royal houses, seeming to make Europe's aristocrats one extended family network. But the age of royal influence was in twilight. In 1901, Victoria, Britain's longest-reigning monarch, died; her son and successor Edward VII (1901–11) died ten years later. Their obsequies symbolized the end of an era. New industrial and financial leaders assumed positions of power among Europe's ruling elite. A new style of politics brought new political actors into the public arena at the beginning of the twentieth century.

Women were excluded from national political participation, although the right to vote was gradually being extended to all men in western Europe, regardless of property or social rank. Paradoxically, the extension of the suffrage worked to undermine the significance of parliaments. Political parties developed as interest groups with single issues that were at odds with the liberal policies of the nineteenth century. Demagogues appealing to anti-Semitic, antiliberal, and antilabor voters attracted mass followings. Extraparliamentary groups—lobbies, trade unions, and cartels—grew in influence and power and came to exert pressure on the political process. The politics of mass society made

Berlin street scene, 1909.

clear the contradictions inherent in democracy. Propaganda, the ability to control information, became the avenue to success.

Great Britain, Germany, France, and Austria-Hungary, all with very different political traditions, had to adapt to the new realities of mass politics. The challenges of trade unions in England, socialism in Germany, political scandals in France, and anti-Semitic politics in Austria provide strikingly different vantage points on a common phenomenon: the crisis in European liberalism and the new politics of mass society.

Regulating Boom and Bust

Between 1873 and 1895, an epidemic of slumps battered the economies of European nations. These slumps, characterized by falling prices, downturns in productivity, and declining profits, have been called the "Great Depression" of the nineteenth century. In reality, the economic downturn of this period was not a great depression like the one that followed the crash of 1929. It did not strike European nations simultaneously, nor did it affect all countries with the same degree of severity. But the so-called Great Depression of the late nineteenth century and the boom period of intense economic expansion from 1895 to 1914 did teach

industrialists, financiers, and politicians one important lesson: alternative booms and busts in the business cycle were dangerous and had to be regulated.

Too much of a good thing brought on the steady deflation of the last quarter of the nineteenth century. In the world economy, there was an overproduction of agricultural products—a sharp contrast to the famines that had ravaged Europe only fifty years earlier. Overproduction resulted from two new factors in the world economy: technological advances in crop cultivation, and the low cost of shipping and transport, which had opened up European markets to cheap agricultural goods from the United States, Canada, and Argentina. The absolute numbers of those employed in agriculture remained more or less constant, but world output soared. Cheap foreign grains, especially wheat, flooded European markets and drastically drove down agricultural prices. The drop in prices affected purchasing power in other sectors and resulted in long-term deflation and unemployment.

Financiers, politicians, and businessmen dedicated themselves to eliminating the boom-and-bust phenomenon, which they considered dangerous. Why were cyclic downturns considered so dangerous at the end of the nineteenth century when they had not been before? Earlier in the century, manufacturers of textiles could endure "bust" periods of depressed prices and declining profits without great hardship. Small family firms requiring little capital could move in and out of production to meet demand. But by the last quarter of the nineteenth century that situation had changed dramatically. The application of science and technology to industrial production required huge amounts of capital. The two new sources of power after 1880, petroleum and electricity, could only be developed with heavy capital investment. Large mechanized steel plants were costly and out of reach for small family firms of the scale that had industrialized textiles so successfully earlier in the century. Heavy machinery, smelting furnaces, buildings, and transport were all beyond the abilities of the small entrepreneur. In order to raise the capital necessary for the new heavy industry at the end of the nineteenth century, firms had to look outside themselves to the stock market, banks, or the state to find adequate capital resources.

But investors, especially banks, refused to invest without guarantees on their capital. Bankers all over Europe were intent on minimizing risks, and they certainly wanted to avoid the uncertainties of the business cycle. Because investment in heavy industry meant tying up capital for extended periods of time, banks insisted on safeguards against falling prices. The solu-

A cartoon from a pamphlet published in Britain by the Tariff Reform League in 1903. The tree represents Britain's free-trade policy. The other nations of the world are harvesting the benefits of the British policy.

tion they demanded was the elimination of uncertainty through the regulation of markets.

Regulation was achieved through the establishment of cartels, combinations of firms in a given industry united to fix prices and to establish production quotas. Not as extreme as the monopolies that appeared in the United States in the same period and for the same purpose, cartels were agreements among big firms intent on controlling markets and guaranteeing profits. Trusts were another form of collaboration that resulted in the elimination of unprofitable businesses. Firms joined together horizontally within the same industry—for example, all steel producers agreed to fix prices and set quotas. Or they combined vertically by controlling all levels of the production process, from raw materials to the finished product, and all other ancillary products necessary to or resulting from the production process. This type of cartel was exemplified by a single firm that controlled the entire production process and the marketing of a single product, from raw materials and fuel through sales and distribution.

Firms in Great Britain, falling behind in heavy industry, failed to form cartels and for the most part remained in private hands. But heavy industry in Germany, France, and Austria, to varying degrees, sought regulation of markets through cartels. International cartels appeared that regulated markets and prices across national borders within Europe. Firms producing steel, chemicals, coke, and pig iron all minimized the effects of competition through the regulation of prices and output.

Banks, which had been the initial impetus behind the transformation to a regulated economy, in turn formed consortia to meet the need for greater amounts of capital. A consortium—paralleling a cartel—was a partnership among banks, often international in character, in which interest rates and the movement of capital were regulated by mutual agreement. The state, too, played an important role in directing the economy. In capital-poor Russia, the state used indirect taxes on the peasantry to finance industrialization and railway construction at the end of the nineteenth century. Russia industrialized with the sweat of its peasants. Russia also needed to import capital, primarily from France after 1887. The state had to guarantee foreign loans and regulate the economy to pay interest on foreign capital investment. Foreign investors were not willing to leave the export of capital to chance or the vagaries of the business cycle. The state must intervene.

Throughout Europe, nation-states protected domestic industries by erecting tariff barriers that made foreign goods noncompetitive in domestic markets. Only Great Britain among the major powers stood by a policy of free trade. Europe was split into two tiers, the haves and the have-nots—those countries with a solid industrial core and those that had remained unindustrialized. This division had a geographic character, with the north and west of Europe heavily developed and capitalized and the southern and eastern parts of Europe remaining heavily agricultural. For both the haves and the have-nots, tariff policies were an attractive form of regulation by the state to protect established industries and to nurture those industries struggling for existence.

Economic regulation was not a twentieth-century creation, as critics of the welfare state contend. Intervention and control began in the late nineteenth century, very much under the impetus of bankers, financiers, and industrialists. Capitalists looked on state intervention not as an intrusion but as a welcome corrective to the ups and downs of the business cycle. Regulation did not emerge from any philosophical or ideological assumption about government but came about as a result of the very real need for capital to enable heavy industry to expand and the equally compelling need to protect profits in order to encourage financiers to invest.

Challenging Liberal England

Great Britain had avoided revolution and social upheaval in the nineteenth century. It prided itself on the progress achieved by a strong parliamentary tradition. One writer caught the self-congratulatory spirit of the age in an 1885 book on popular government: "We Englishmen pass on the Continent as masters of the art of government." Parliamentary government was based on a homogeneous ruling elite. Aristocrats and businessmen and financial leaders shared a common educational background in England's elitist educational system of the public schools and the universities of Oxford or Cambridge. Schooling produced a common outlook and common attitudes toward parliamentary rule, whether in Conservative or Liberal circles, and guaranteed a certain stability in policies and legislation.

In the 1880s, issues of unemployment, housing, public health, and education challenged the attitudes of Britain's ruling elite and fostered the advent of an independent working-class politics. Between 1867 and 1885, extension of the suffrage increased the electorate fourfold. Protected by the markets of its empire, the British economy did not experience the roller-coaster effect of recurrent booms and busts after 1873. Nor did Britain experience severe economic crisis between 1890 and 1914, a period of growing labor unrest. But after 1900, wages stagnated, while prices continued to rise. Traditional parliamentary politics had little to offer those workers whose standard of living suffered a real decline. The quality of urban housing deteriorated, as exemplified by the severe overcrowding of London's East End.

Workers responded to their distress by supporting militant trade unions. Trade unions, drawing on a long tradition of working-class associations, were all that stood between workers and the economic dislocation

An election poster of 1895 exhorts voters to send Keir Hardie to Parliament. His positions on labor issues are succinctly stated.

caused by unemployment, sickness, or old age. In addition, new unions of unskilled and semiskilled workers flourished, beginning in the 1880s and 1890s. A Scottish miner, James Keir Hardie (1856–1915), attracted national attention as the spokesman for a new political movement, the Labour party, whose goal was to represent workers in Parliament. In 1892 Hardie was the first independent working man to sit in the House of Commons. Hardie and his party convinced trade unions that it was in their best interests to support Labour candidates instead of Liberals in parliamentary elections after 1900. Unions, as extraparliamentary groups, worked successfully toward achieving a parliamentary voice. By 1906, the new Labour party had 29 seats in Parliament.

Yet Parliament seemed to be failing the poor. So argued a group of intellectuals concerned with social welfare who called themselves Fabians. They named themselves after the Roman dictator Fabius, who was noted for his delaying tactics, which enabled him to avoid decisive battle with Hannibal in the Punic Wars. Fabius believed in cutting off the supplies of his enemies and engaging in skirmishes. Following his lead, the Fabians were socialists, not in a Marxist sense of ultimate revolutionary confrontation, but in a gradualist sense of a reformist commitment to social justice. Led by Beatrice Webb (1858–1943) and Sidney Webb (1859–1947), and including in their number playwright and critic George Bernard Shaw (1856–1950), theosophist Annie Besant (1847–1943), and novelist H. G. Wells (1866–1946), the Fabians proved to be successful propagandists who were able to keep issues

A union leader addresses striking British coal miners in 1912. Labor unions became increasingly militant after the turn of the century as rising unemployment and declining real wages cut into the gains of the working class.

of social reform in the public eye. They advocated collective ownership of factories and workshops and state direction of production through gradual reform. At the turn of the century, the Fabian Society threw its support and the power of its tracts on social issues behind Labour party candidates. Intellectuals now joined with trade unionists in demanding public housing, better public sanitation, municipal reforms, and improved pay and benefits for working people.

The existence of the new Labour party pressured Conservatives and Liberals to develop more enlightened social policies and programs. After 1906, under threat of losing votes to the Labour party, the Liberal party heeded the pressures for reform. The "new" Liberals supported legislation to strengthen the right of unions to picket peacefully. Led by David Lloyd George (1863–1945), who was chancellor of the exchequer, Liberals sponsored the National Insurance Act of 1911. Modeled after Bismarck's social welfare policies, the act provided compulsory payments to workers for sickness and unemployment benefits. In order to gain approval to pay for this new legislation, Lloyd George

recognized that Parliament itself had to be renovated. The Parliament Bill of 1911 reduced the House of Lords, dominated by Conservatives resistant to proposed welfare reforms, from its status as equal partner with the House of Commons. Commons could and now did raise taxes without the consent of the House of Lords to pay for new programs that benefited workers and the poor.

Social legislation did not silence unions and worker organizations. To the contrary, protest increased in the period up to the beginning of World War I in 1914. There was little doubt about the ability of militant trade unions to mobilize workers. In 1910, three of every ten manual workers belonged to a union, and this figure doubled to 60 percent of the work force between 1910 and 1914. In these years, waves of strikes broke over England. Unions threatened to paralyze the economy. Coal miners, seamen, railroad workers, and dockers protested against stagnant wages and rising prices.

The high incidence of strikes was a consequence of growing distrust of Parliament and distrust, too, of a regulatory state bureaucracy responsible for the social welfare reforms. Workers felt manipulated by a system unresponsive to their needs. Labour's voice grew more strident. The Trade Unions Act of 1913 granted unions legal rights to settle their grievances with management directly. In the summer of 1914, a railway worker boasted, "We are big and powerful enough to fight our own battle without the aid of Parliament or any other agency. There could be no affection between the robber and the robbed." Only the outbreak of war in 1914 ended the possibility of a general strike by miners, railwaymen, and transport workers.

The question of Irish Home Rule also plagued Parliament. In Ulster in northern Ireland, army officers of Protestant Irish background threatened to mutiny. In addition, women agitating for the vote shattered parliamentary complacence. The most advanced industrial nation in the world, with its tradition of peaceful parliamentary rule, had entered the age of mass politics.

Political Struggles in Germany

During his reign as chancellor of the German Empire (1871–90), Otto von Bismarck formed shrewd alliances that hampered the development of effective parliamentary government. He repeatedly and successfully blocked the emergence of fully democratic participation. In Germany, all males had the right to vote, but the German parliament, the Reichstag, enjoyed only restricted powers in comparison to the British Parliament. Bismarck's objective remained always the suc-

Zwischen Berlin und Rom.

The struggle between Bismarck and the pope is symbolized in this cartoon. Bismarck's chessmen include "Germania," the press, and antimonastic legislation. The pope marshals encyclicals, interdicts, and the Syllabus of Errors.

cessful unification of Germany, and he promoted cooperation with democratic institutions and parties only so long as that goal was enhanced.

Throughout the 1870s, the German chancellor collaborated with the German liberal parties in constructing the legal codes, the monetary and banking system, the judicial apparatus, and the railroad network that pulled the new Germany together. Bismarck backed German liberals in their antipapal campaign, in which the Catholic church was declared the enemy of the German state. He suspected the identification of Catholics with Rome, which the liberals depicted as an authority in competition with the nation-state. The anti-Church campaign, launched in 1872, was dubbed the *Kulturkampf,* the "struggle for civilization," because its supporters contended that it was a battle waged in the interests of humanity.

The legislation of the *Kulturkampf* expelled Jesuits from Germany, removed priests from state service, attacked religious education, and instituted civil marriage. Bishops and priests who followed the instructions of Pope Pius IX (1846–78) not to obey the new laws were arrested and expelled from Germany. Many Germans grew concerned over the social costs of such widespread religious repression, and the Catholic Center party increased its parliamentary representation by rallying Catholics as a voting bloc in the face of state repression. With the succession of a new pontiff, Leo XIII (1878–1903), Bismarck took advantage of the opportunity to negotiate a settlement with the Catholic church, cutting his losses and bringing the *Kulturkampf* to a halt. Bismarck had grown wary of the demands of the National Liberal party for an increasing share of political power.

Bismarck's repressive policies also targeted the Social Democratic party. The Social Democrats were committed to a Marxist critique of capitalism and to international cooperation with other socialist parties. Seeing them as a threat to stability in Germany and in Europe as a whole, he set out to smash them. In 1878, using the opportunity for repression presented by two attempts on the emperor's life, Bismarck outlawed the fledgling Socialist party. The Anti-Socialist Law forbade meetings among Socialists, fund-raising, and distribution of printed matter. The law relied on expanded police powers and was a fundamental attack on civil liberties and freedom of choice within a democratic electoral system. Nevertheless, individual Social Democratic candidates stood for election in this period and quickly learned how to work with middle-class parties in order to achieve electoral successes. By 1890 Social Democrats had captured 20 percent of the electorate and controlled 35 Reichstag seats, in spite of Bismarck's anti-Socialist legislation.

Throughout the 1880s, as his ability to manage Reichstag majorities declined and as Socialist strength steadily mounted, Bismarck grew disenchanted with universal manhood suffrage. Beginning in 1888, the chancellor found himself at odds with the new emperor, Wilhelm II (1888–1918), over his foreign and domestic policies. The young emperor dismissed Bismarck in March 1890 and abandoned the chancellor's anti-Socialist legislation. The Social Democratic party became the largest Marxist party in the world and, by 1914, the largest single party in Germany.

The socialism of the German Social Democrats was modified in the 1890s. Although it had never been violent or insurrectionary, social democracy moved away from a belief in a future revolution and toward a democratic "revisionism" that favored gradual reform through parliamentary participation. Those who continued to maintain a more orthodox Marxist position, such as August Bebel (1840–1913) and Karl Kautsky (1854–1938), believed capitalism would destroy itself, as Karl Marx had predicted, without any violent action by German Social Democrats. Bebel confided to Friedrich Engels in 1885 that he went to bed every night with the confidence that "the last hour of bourgeois society strikes soon."

Revisionism was both practical and democratic. Its leading advocate, Eduard Bernstein (1850–1932), introduced aspects of Fabian state socialism into the German movement. This grass-roots transformation favored evolutionary rather than revolutionary political action. Workers were the primary force behind the shift away from the catastrophe theory of Bebel and Kautsky. Their standard of living had been improving in Germany, and the prospect of the imminent collapse of capitalism seemed slight to workers intent on achieving further gains. Union membership grew dramatically among unskilled workers after 1895. Working-class organizations, tolerated earlier by Social Democrats for their future potential, now became centers of power and pressed for practical benefits for their members.

During the period when the Social Democratic movement had been outlawed, Bismarck had employed carrot-and-stick methods to woo the working class away from the Marxists. The stick with which Bismarck beat back the political opposition had been the Anti-Socialist Law. The carrot that he and then Wilhelm II used to win mass support was social welfare legislation, including accident insurance, sick benefits, and old age and disability benefits introduced by the state. But such legislation did not undermine the popularity of socialism, nor did it attract workers away from Marxist political programs, as the mounting electoral returns demonstrated. Social democracy built its rank-and-file union membership by employing sophisticated organizational techniques in order to expand its mass base of support.

The success and popularity of the Social Democratic party cemented a stronger alliance on the Right among Conservatives. Realizing that they could not beat the Left, right-wing groups decided to copy it. Unable to defeat social democracy by force or by state-sponsored welfare policies, Bismarck's successors set out to organize mass support. Agrarian and industrial interests united strongly behind state policies. An aggressive foreign policy was judged as the surest way to win over the masses. Leagues were formed to exploit nationalism and patriotism among the electorate over issues of naval and military expansion and colonial development.

In the end, the Reichstag failed to defy the absolute authority of Emperor Wilhelm II, who was served after 1890 by a string of ineffectual chancellors. Despite its constitutional forms, Germany was ruled by a state authoritarianism in which the bureaucracy, the military, and various interest groups exercised influence over the emperor. A high-risk foreign policy that had a mass appeal was one way to circumvent a parliamentary system incapable of decision-making. Constitutional solutions had been short-circuited in favor of authoritarian rule.

Political Scandals and Mass Politics in France

The Third Republic in France had an aura of accidental origins and precarious existence. Founded in 1870 with the defeat of Napoleon III's empire by the Germans, the Third Republic claimed legitimacy by placing itself squarely within the revolutionary democratic tradition. Yet its early days were marked by bloody social conflict and its existence was plagued by ongoing struggles among contenders on the Right and Left who sought to control it.

In spite of surface indications of political conflict, the Third Republic successfully worked toward the creation of a national community based on a common identity for its citizens. Compulsory schooling, one of the great institutional transformations of French government in 1885, socialized French children by implanting in them common values, patriotism, and identification with the nation-state. Old ways, local dialects, superstitious practices, and peasant insularity dropped away or were modified under the persistent pressure of a centralized curriculum of reading, writing, arithmetic, and civics. Compulsory service in the army for the generation of young men of draft age served the same end of communicating national values to a predominantly peasant population.

Technology also accelerated the process of shaping a national citizenry as railroad lines tied people together and the infrastructure of roads made distances shrink. People could now travel back and forth between village and city, town and countryside, with ease and frequency. Common expectations for a better life and upward mobility moved through rural populations that for most of the nineteenth century had not looked beyond the horizon of the village. Young working women were particularly influential in transferring values from urban to rural areas as they moved from villages to towns in search of domestic and industrial jobs and then returned to their villages with new outlooks and new goals for their families.

Information was controlled at the center—Paris—and distributed on a national scale. Villagers in southern France read Parisian newspapers over their morning bowls of coffee and learned—with a previously unimaginable immediacy—about French foreign exploits and parliamentary wrangles. A truly national mass culture emerged in the period between 1880 and 1914. Common symbols like the bust of Marianne appeared in every city hall in France, and a common vocabulary of patriotism spread across the land. French people were not necessarily more political, but they were political in a new way that enabled them to identify their own local interests with national issues.

Two events in particular that occurred in the three decades before World War I indicate the extent of the transformation of French political life. The first, the Boulanger Affair, involved the attempt of a French general to seize power. The second, the Dreyfus Affair, involved all of French society in the treason conviction of a Jewish army captain.

General Georges Boulanger (1837–91) was a popular and romantic figure who captured the imagination of the French press. As minister of war, Boulanger became a hero to French soldiers when he undertook needed reforms of army life. He won over businessmen by leading troops against strikers. Above all, he cultivated the image of a patriot ready to defend France's honor at any cost. Known as "the Man on Horseback" because of his ability to look dashing in public appearances astride his black horse, Boulanger was a shallow man whose success and national popularity were created by a carefully orchestrated publicity campaign that made him the most popular man in France by 1886.

Boulanger's potential in the political arena attracted the attention of right-wing backers, including monarchists who hoped eventually to restore kingship to France. Supported by big-money interests who favored a strengthened executive and a weaker parliamentary system, Boulanger undertook a nationwide political campaign, hoping to appeal to those unhappy with the Third Republic and promising vague constitutional reforms. General Boulanger's 1889 campaign managers successfully manipulated images that were recognizable to a rural electorate. Religious lithographs carried likenesses of the modern "messiah," the blond-bearded general, in place of Jesus. Campaign workers were recruited at the local level. Boulangists hoped that through universal suffrage an authoritarian government could be established. By 1889 Boulanger was able to amass enough national support to frighten the defenders of parliamentary institutions. The charismatic general ultimately failed in his bid for power and fled the country because of allegations of treason. But he left in his wake an embryonic mass movement on the Right that operated outside the channels of parliamentary institutions. Boulanger's success was due to a new nationalism that flexed its muscles after 1880. Cultural symbols like the flag and the nation-in-arms moved from the revolutionary tradition of the Left to become part of the appeal of the new right-wing groups that were growing in importance.

A very different type of crisis began to take shape in 1894 with the controversy surrounding the trial of Captain Alfred Dreyfus (1859–1935) that came to be known simply as "the Affair." Dreyfus was an Alsatian Jewish army officer accused of selling military secrets to the Germans. His trial for treason served as a lightning rod for xenophobia—the hatred of foreigners, especially Germans—and anti-Semitism, the hatred of Jews. Dreyfus was stripped of his commission and honors and sentenced to solitary confinement for life on Devil's Island, a convict colony off French Guiana in South America.

Illegal activities and outright falsifications by Dreyfus's superiors in order to secure a conviction came to light in the mass press. The nation was soon divided. Those who supported Dreyfus's innocence, the pro-Dreyfusards, were for the most part on the left of the political spectrum and spoke of the Republic's duty to uphold justice and freedom. The anti-Dreyfusards were associated with the traditional institutions of the Catholic church and the army and considered themselves to be defending the honor of France. Among those who upheld the conviction were right-wing groups, monarchists, and virulent anti-Semites.

Dreyfus was eventually exonerated and granted a full pardon in 1905. On the personal level, the Affair represented the ability of an individual to seek redress against injustice. On the national level, the Affair represented an important transformation in the nature of French political life. Existing parliamentary institutions had been found wanting and unable to cope with the

Captain Alfred Dreyfus, accused of treason, marches with a "guard of dishonor." After Dreyfus was declared innocent, he became a lieutenant colonel in the French army and was enrolled in the Legion of Honor.

mass politics stirred up by Dreyfus's conviction. New groups entered public life after 1894, coalescing around the question of the guilt or innocence of an individual man. The newspaper press vied with parliament and the courts as a forum for investigation and decision-making. Intellectuals, too, organized. Leagues on the left and on the right took shape; unions, cooperatives, and professional societies all raised their voices. These organizations manipulated propaganda around issues of national defense and republican justice.

The crises provoked by Boulanger's attempt at power and the Dreyfus Affair demonstrated the major role of the press and the importance of public opinion in exerting pressure on the system of government. The press emerged as a myth-maker in shaping and channeling public opinion. Émile Zola (1840–1902), the great French novelist, spearheaded the pro-Dreyfusard movement with his damning article "I Accuse!" in which he pointed to the military and the judiciary as the "spirits of social evil" for persecuting an innocent man. The article appeared in a leading French newspaper and was influential in securing Dreyfus's eventual exoneration and the discovery of the real culprit, one of Dreyfus's colleagues in the General Staff. The Third Republic had never been in danger of collapsing, but it

was transformed. The locus of power in parliament was challenged by pressure groups outside of it.

Defeating Liberalism in Austria

In the 1870s, the liberal values of the bourgeoisie dominated the Austro-Hungarian Empire. The Habsburg monarchy had adjusted to constitutional government, which was introduced throughout Austria in 1860. Faith in parliamentary government based on a restricted suffrage had established a tenuous foothold. After the setbacks of 1848 and the troublesome decade of the 1860s, when Prussia had trounced Austria and Bismarck had routed the hope of an Austrian-dominated German Empire, the Austrian bourgeoisie counted on a peaceful future with a centralized multinational state dedicated to order and progress.

There is no better symbol of middle-class political and cultural aspirations in this period than the monumental rebuilding of the city of Vienna that took place after 1860. The belt of public and private buildings on the Ringstrasse, or "Ring Street," girding the old central city and separating it from its suburbs was dramatic testimony to bourgeois self-confidence. Grandiose buildings, likened to "cakes on platters," glorified constitutional government, economic vitality, the fine arts, and educational values. Monumental architecture was intended to legitimize bourgeois claims to power and to link Austrian institutions with the great cultural heritage of the West. The buildings were blatant copies of past architectural styles—massive Gothic for the city hall, Renaissance for the university, and early baroque for the theater. Yet this was more than a self-confident statement of Austria's inheritance of a rich cultural tradition. Vienna's ruling class was fortifying itself behind the edifices of Western politics and culture against the onslaught of the new age.

In reality, the Austrian bourgeoisie was weaker than its French or British counterparts. The Austrian ruling class was heavily dependent on the Habsburg emperor and identified itself with the values of the aristocracy. Rapid economic growth had strengthened bourgeois status between 1840 and 1870, but it had also unleashed new social forces that existing institutions were unable to control. Liberal values of constitutional monarchy, centralization, restricted suffrage, and multinational government came up against new and threatening forces of anti-Semitism, socialism, nationalism, and mass politics.

By 1900 liberal politicians were being eliminated as a directing force in national politics. The new politicians who replaced them rejected the liberal-rational

"J'Accuse"

The central role of the press during the Dreyfus Affair is nowhere more apparent than in the impact of the novelist Émile Zola's front-page letter to the president of the Third Republic in Le Figaro, *one of France's leading newspapers, on 13 January 1898.*

"J'Accuse" was an impassioned appeal to the French nation for justice in which Zola pointed to those truly guilty of betraying France in a cascade of ringing accusations. This letter, which was ultimately instrumental in freeing Captain Dreyfus, resulted in Zola's own prosecution for libel.

I accuse Lieutenant-Colonel du Paty de Clam of having been the diabolical artisan of the judicial error, without knowing it, I am willing to believe, and then of having defended his nefarious work for three years throughout the most grotesque and culpable machinations.

I accuse General Mercier of having become an accomplice, out of mental weakness at the least, in one of the greatest iniquities of the century. . . .

I accuse the three handwriting experts, Mssrs. Belhomme, Varinard, and Couard, of having composed deceitful and fraudulent reports, unless a medical examination declares them to be stricken with an impairment of vision or judgment.

I accuse the offices of War of having conducted in the press, particularly in *L'Éclair* and in *L'Echo de Paris,* an abominable campaign designed to mislead public opinion and to conceal their wrongdoing.

Finally, I accuse the first Court Martial of having violated the law in convicting a defendant on the basis of a document kept secret, and I accuse the second Court Martial of having covered up that illegality on command by committing in turn the juridical crime of knowingly acquitting a guilty man.

In bringing these accusations, I am not without realizing that I expose myself in the process to Articles 30 and 31 of the press law of July 29, 1881, which punishes offenses of slander. And it is quite willingly that I so expose myself.

As for those whom I accuse, I do not know them, I have never seen them, I have neither rancor nor hatred for them. They are for me no more than entities, spirits of social malfeasance. And the act that I hereby accomplish is but a revolutionary means of hastening the explosion of truth and justice.

I have but one passion, one for seeing the light, in the name of humanity which has so suffered and which is entitled to happiness. My fiery protest is but the cry of my soul. Let me be brought then before a criminal court and let the investigation be conducted in the light of day!

I am waiting.

---

values of progress and order and moved into a realm colored by charisma, fantasy, and demagoguery. A new Right wielded mass political strategies that embraced the irrational and the violent.

The new groups laying claim to political power and displacing a weak Austrian bourgeoisie were peasants, workers, urban artisans and shopkeepers, and the colonized Slavic peoples of the empire. Bourgeois politics and laissez-faire economics had offered little or nothing to these varied groups, who were now claiming the right of participation. Mass parties were formed based on radical pan-Germanic feeling; anticapitalism, which appealed to peasants and artisans; hatred of the Jews, shared by students and artisans; and nationalist aspirations that attracted the lower middle classes. In 1895 Karl Lueger (1844–1910) used anti-Semitism in his successful campaign for the office of mayor of Vienna. Lueger's election was the first serious sign of the collapse of Austrian liberalism. Jews were identified with

capitalists, and the irrational hatred directed at them unified different groups and helped to sweep Lueger into office.

Austrian poet and playwright Hugo von Hofmannsthal (1874–1929) understood the rejection of bourgeois politics in the age of expanded suffrage: "Politics is magic. He who knows how to summon the forces from the deep, him will they follow." The creation of a scapegoat by means of anti-Semitism and racism became the means of uniting the masses against a common foe and in favor of a common nationalist program. In Austria, antiliberal politics grew stronger in the years before 1914. The great buildings on the Ringstrasse that had attempted to connect Austrian political life with the glories of the European past were mocked as relics of a dead age. Centrifugal forces of pan-Germanism and nationalism were pulling the parliamentary system apart. An urban and capitalist middle class that ruled Austria by virtue of a limited suffrage based on property had lost ground to new groups that were essentially anticapitalist and antiliberal in their outlook and for whom parliamentary deliberations held no promise. The rejection of liberalism was a "revolt against the fathers." A new style of leader had emerged in Vienna at the end of the century, charismatic in style and violent in appeal. The "politics of fantasy" based on a new electorate was fast becoming the nightmare of parliamentary disintegration.

The political experiences of Great Britain, Germany, France, and Austria between 1871 and 1914 make clear the common challenges confronting Western parliamentary systems in a changing era of democratic politics. In spite of variations, each nation experienced its own challenge to liberal parliamentary institutions, and each shaped its own variety of responses to a new international phenomenon—the rise of the masses as a political force.

Outsiders in Mass Politics

By the end of the nineteenth century, the masses were replacing the individual in political culture. A faceless, nameless electorate became the basis of new political strategies and a new political rhetoric. A concept of class identification of workers was devalued in favor of interest-group politics in which lobbies formed around single issues to pressure European governments. But the apparently all-inclusive concept of mass society continued to exclude some groups. Women, ethnic minorities, and Jews were pushed to the margins. Outsiders in mass politics had little in common with one another except for the common experience of repression by the state. But they did not remain quietly on the periphery. Women and ethnic minorities learned to incorporate strategies and techniques of politics and organization that permitted them to challenge the existing political system. Others, including anarchists, rejected both the organizational techniques of mass society and the values of the nation-state. Outsiders, then, were both those intent on being integrated into mass politics and those who sought its destruction.

Feminists and Politics

Women's emancipation had been a recurrent motif of European political culture throughout the nineteenth century. In the areas of civil liberties, legal equality with men, and economic autonomy, only the most limited reforms had been enacted. The cult of domesticity, important throughout the nineteenth century, assigned women to a separate sphere, that of the home. Glorifying domesticity was a recognition of women's unique contribution to society in the home, but it may itself have been a means of controlling women who protested the separation between public and private space.

European women were paid at most one-third to one-half of what men earned for the same work. In Great Britain, women did not enjoy equal divorce rights until the twentieth century. In France, married women had no control over their own incomes: all their earnings were considered their husbands' private property. From the Atlantic to the Urals, women were excluded from economic and educational opportunities. Serfs had been liberated. Working-class men had gained the right to vote. But the new electoral politics that emerged in the last quarter of the nineteenth century explicitly excluded women.

Growing numbers of women, primarily from the middle classes, began calling themselves "feminist," a term coined in France in the 1830s. The new feminists throughout western Europe differed from earlier generations in their willingness to organize mass movements and to appropriate the techniques of interest-group politics. The first international congress of women's rights, held in Paris in 1878, initiated an era of international cooperation and exchange among women's organizations. Women's groups now positioned themselves for sustained political action.

Feminism as a historic term is worth pondering. Like liberalism, which had pulled down kings and destroyed privilege, feminism aimed at eliminating social inequalities. Like socialism, feminism was a set of principles for action whose purpose was to build a better world. At its base, feminism recognized the equality of the sexes, without denying difference. As John Stuart Mill in Great Britain and Ernest Legouvé (1807–1903), a French dramatist and leading proponent of women's rights, had demonstrated, one need not be female to be a feminist. Most feminists, however, were women, and the leadership of the movement for equal rights was in women's hands. The converse—that most women were feminists—was not true. Contemporary critics often dismissed feminism on the grounds that it represented no more than a tiny minority of women. The same minority status characterized the trade union movement—which in France, for example, had a smaller membership at the end of the nineteenth century than did feminist organizations.

European feminist organizations did not share a common agenda, but instead grouped themselves around a series of related concerns for legal, educational, economic, and political emancipation. Rather than speaking of a single feminism, it is more appropriate to speak of different feminisms. The General German Women's Association agitated for educational opportunities and democratic participation for women. In France, women working for the vote were a minority of the women's organizations. Many French feminists defended a "maternal politics," by which they sought protection for women's responsibilities in the home. Other feminists were involved in abortion reform, birth control issues, and repeal of state control of prostitution. The French League for the Rights of Women stood steadfastly against the vote as an end in itself and worked instead for legal and economic reforms. On the whole, however, feminist organizations were divided into two camps. In the first group were those who agitated for the vote; the second included those who thought that the vote was beside the point and that the central issues were economic, social, and legal reforms of women's status. Constituting the left wing of the second group were socialist women who were dedicated to needs of women of the working class.

The lessons of the new electoral politics were not lost on feminists seeking women's emancipation through the vote. Leaders like Hubertine Auclert (1848–1914) in France and Emmeline Pankhurst (1858–1928) in Great Britain recognized the need for a mass base of support. If women's organizations were to survive as competing interest groups, they needed to form political alliances, control their own newspapers and magazines, and keep their cause before the public eye. Just as cartels, trade unions, and political parties had learned the game of influence and leverage so important for survival in the modern political milieu, so too did feminists rely on organization to achieve their ends. There was a growing willingness by a variety of women's organizations to hold mass demonstrations and rallies and to use violent tactics.

No movement operated more effectively in this regard than the British suffrage movement. In 1903 the Women's Social and Political Union (WSPU) was formed by a group of eminently respectable middle-class and aristocratic British women. At the center of the movement was Emmeline Pankhurst, an attractive middle-aged woman with a frail appearance but a will of iron and a gift for oratory. Emmeline Pankhurst and her two daughters—Christabel (1880–1958), a lawyer by training, and Sylvia (1882–1960), an artist—succeeded in keeping women's suffrage before the British public and brought the plight of British women to international attention. Over the next seven years, the WSPU made considerable progress, attracting a grow-

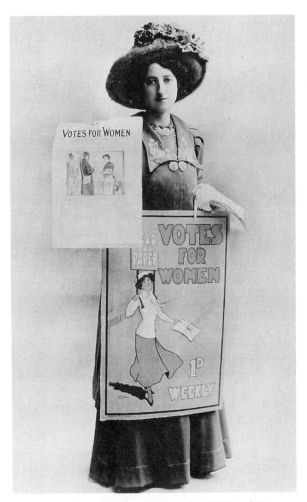

A young member of the Women's Social and Political Union sells copies of the paper Votes for Women.

ing number of followers and successfully aligning itself with parliamentary supporters.

Women's demands for political power were the basis of an unheralded revolution in Western culture. In Great Britain, the decade before the Great War of 1914 was a period of profound political education for women seeking the vote. An unprecedented 250,000 women gathered in Hyde Park in 1908 to hear more about female suffrage. Laughed at by men, ridiculed in the press, taunted in public demonstrations, women activists refused to be quiet and to "know their place." If respectable women would never demonstrate for their rights, then the suffragists were willing to cease being respectable. Because they spoke out for voting rights, feminists were demeaned, humiliated, and accused of not being *real* women by their detractors. One of the best examples of the rebellion of women against the limitations of their social roles took place

CONSTANCE LYTTON

Civil disobedience by British women demanding the right to vote often led to their arrest. In protest, incarcerated suffragettes went on hunger strikes to publicize their cause. The British government responded with a brutal policy of force-feeding of prisoners. Constance Lytton, a British aristocrat and suffragette, recounts here the agony of being forcibly fed in prison. Her own health was seriously weakened by the experience.

[The prison's senior medical officer] urged me to take food voluntarily. I told him that was absolutely out of the question, that when our legislators ceased to resist enfranchising women then I should cease to resist taking food in prison. . . . I offered no resistance to being placed in position, but lay down voluntarily on the plank bed. Two of the wardresses took hold of my arms, one held my head and one my feet. One wardress helped to pour the food. The doctor leant on my knees as he stooped over my chest to get at my mouth. I shut my mouth and clenched my teeth. . . . The doctor offered me the choice of a wooden or steel gag; he explained elaborately, as he did on most subsequent occasions, that the steel gag would hurt and the wooden one not, and he urged me not to force him to use the steel gag. But I did not speak nor open my mouth, so that after playing about for a moment or two with the wooden one he finally had recourse to the steel. He seemed annoyed at my resistance and he broke into a temper as he plied my teeth with the steel implement. . . . The pain of it was intense and at last I must have given way for he got the gag between my teeth, when he proceeded to turn it much more than necessary until my jaws were fastened wide apart, far more than they could go naturally. Then he put down my throat a tube which seemed to me much too wide and was something like four feet in length. The irritation of the tube was excessive. I choked the moment it touched my throat until it had got down. Then the food was poured in quickly; it made me sick a few seconds after it was down and the action of the sickness made my body and legs double up, but the wardresses instantly pressed back my head and the doctor leant on my knees. The horror of it was more than I can describe. I was sick over the doctor and wardresses, and it seemed a long time before they took the tube out. As the doctor left he gave me a slap on the cheek, not violently, but, as it were, to express his contemptuous disapproval, and he seemed to take for granted that my distress was assumed. . . . I had been sick over my hair, which, though short, hung on either side of my face, all over the wall near my bed, and my clothes seemed saturated with it, but the wardresses told me they could not get me a change that night as it was too late, the office was shut. I lay quite motionless, it seemed paradise to be without the suffocating tube, without the liquid food going in and out of my body and without the gag between my teeth. Before long I heard the sounds of the forced feeding in the next cell to mine. It was almost more than I could bear, it was Elsie Howey, I was sure. When the ghastly process was over and all quiet, I tapped on the wall and called out at the top of my voice, which wasn't much just then, "No surrender," and there came the answer past any doubt in Elsie's voice. "No surrender."

From Constance Lytton, *Prisons and Prisoners* (1914).

---

on 18 November 1910, a day that came to be known among feminists as Black Friday. On that day, suffragists marched on Parliament, which had failed to support the vote for women. In a confrontation that lasted six hours, unarmed women battled with police to hold their ground. Rather than returning home as they were ordered, the women relentlessly pushed forward, meeting the blows and the wrath of London's bobbies. Many women were injured and many arrested.

The year 1910 marked the beginning of an era of increased militancy among women, who were derisively called "suffragettes" in the press in order to distinguish them from the nonmilitant suffragists. A basic element in the new militancy was the willingness to use violence to achieve political emancipation. As Emmeline Pankhurst explained it, "The argument of the broken window pane is the most valuable argument in modern politics." Militant women set mailboxes on fire or poured glue and jam over their contents, threw bombs into country houses, and slashed paintings in the National Gallery. All over London the tinkling of thousands of shattered windowpanes ushered in a new age of women's political action. Mrs. Pankhurst was not naive about what her followers were doing: "There is something which governments care for more than human life and that is the security of property, and so it is through property that we shall strike the enemy." Suffragettes set fires in public buildings, churches, and hotels. As frustration grew, some assaulted members of the cabinet. One suffragette, Emily Wilding Davison (1872–1913), probably intent on suicide as an act of protest, was trampled to death when she threw herself under the king's horse on Derby Day at Epsom Downs in 1913. Mrs. Pankhurst and others advocated violence against personal property to highlight the violence done to women by denying them their rights. These tactics seemed to accomplish little before the war, although they certainly kept the issue of woman suffrage in the public eye until the outbreak of war in 1914. It was not until 1918 that British women were granted limited suffrage, and not until 1928 that women gained voting rights equal to those of men.

Women suffered for their militancy, for civil disobedience evoked harsh repressive measures from the British government. Previous benevolence toward middle-class female prisoners arrested for attacks on property gave way to a new harshness that included the force-feeding of convicted suffragettes. Using tubes, hoses, and metal jaw clamps, prison guards and doctors poured gruel down the throats of imprisoned women who, as a form of protest, refused to eat. Such repressive measures only increased the solidarity within the women's movement and won the suffragettes international sympathy and support. Stymied, the government passed the Cat and Mouse Act in 1913. Imprisoned women who refused to eat were released, then reincarcerated once they had resumed eating and regained their strength. This "cat-and-mouse" pattern of release and reimprisonment could double or extend indefinitely a three-year sentence served in three-day segments. Many of the more dramatic tactics of the suffragettes, including getting arrested, were not available to working-class activists, who could not put aside their family responsibilities to serve jail sentences.

European women did not easily gain the right to vote. In France and Germany, moderate and left-wing politicians opposed extension of the vote to women because they feared that women would strengthen conservative candidates. Many politicians felt that women were not "ready" for the vote and that they should receive it only as a reward—an unusual concept in democratic societies. Queen Victoria condemned women's agitation for the vote as a "mad, wicked folly." Only after war and revolution was the vote extended to women in the West—in Germany in 1918, in the United States in 1920, and in France at the end of World War II.

Not all activist women saw the right to vote as the solution to women's oppression. Those who agitated for social reforms for poor and working-class women parted ways with the militant suffragettes. Sylvia Pankhurst, for example, left her mother and sister to their political battles in order to work for social reform in London's poverty-stricken East End. Differing from those who focused on woman's right to vote as a primary goal, women socialists were concerned with working-class women's "double oppression" in the home and in the workplace. The largest women's socialist movement existed in Germany, with 175,000 members by 1914. With its own newspaper, it operated independently of the men's socialist movement. German socialist women were opposed to suffrage on the grounds that giving middle-class women the vote did not address social issues.

Socialist women's lot was not an easy one, since union members often denied women's right to work and saw women's employment as a threat to men in the workplace. In Germany, socialist men opposed women industrial workers. Unions supported the concept of separate spheres for men and women and based their demands for a family wage on the need to maintain a separate private domain of the home. Socialist men argued that women's work often resulted in the neglect of children and could lead to the physical degeneration of the family. Working women, socialist men argued, undermined existing wage scales and aided the exploitation of workers by their willingness to work for lower wages. Class oppression, countered German socialist leader and theorist Clara Zetkin (1857–1933), was the basis of women's oppression. For militants like Zetkin, socialism offered the only means to eliminate sexual inequalities.

The women's movements of the period from 1871 to 1914 differed socially and culturally from nation to nation. Yet there is a sense in which the women's movements constituted an international phenomenon. The rise in the level of women's political consciousness occurred in the most advanced Western countries almost simultaneously and had a predominantly middle-class character. Working-class women, most notably in Germany, united feminism with socialism in search of a better life. In spite of concerted efforts, women remained on the outside of societies that excluded them from political participation, access to education, and social and economic equality.

The Jewish Question and Zionism

The term *anti-Semitism,* meaning hostility to Jews, was first used in 1879 to give a pseudoscientific legitimacy to bigotry and hatred. Persecution was a harsh reality for Jews in eastern Europe at the end of the nineteenth century. In Russia, Jews could not own property and were restricted to living in certain territories. Organized massacres, or *pogroms,* in Kiev, Odessa, and Warsaw followed the assassination of Tsar Alexander II in 1881 and recurred after the failed Russian revolution of 1905. Russian authorities blamed the Jews, seen as perennial outsiders, for the assassination and revolution and the social instability that followed them. Pogroms resulted in the death and displacement of tens of thousands of Russian and eastern European Jews.

Two million eastern European Jews migrated westward between 1868 and 1914 in search of peace and refuge. Seventy thousand settled in Germany. Others continued westward, stopping in the United States. Another kind of Jewish migration took place in the nineteenth century—the movement of Jews from rural to urban areas within nations. In eastern Europe, Jewish migrations coincided with downturns in the economic cycle, and Jews became scapegoats for the high rates of unemployment and high prices that seemed to follow in their wake. Most migrants were peddlers, artisans, or small shopkeepers who were seen as threatening to small businesses. Differing in language, culture, and dress, they were viewed as alien in every way.

In western Europe, Jews considered themselves "assimilated" into their national cultures, identifying with their nationality as much as with their religion. Austrian and German Jews were granted full civil rights in 1867 on the principle that citizens of all religions enjoyed full equality. In France, Jews had been legally emancipated since the end of the eighteenth century. But western and central European politics of the 1890s had a strong dose of anti-Semitism. Demagogues like Georg von Schönerer (1842–1921) of Austria were capable of whipping up a frenzy of riots and violence against Jews. They did not distinguish between assimilated and immigrant Jewish populations in their irrational denunciations.

Western and central European anti-Semitism assumed a new level of virulence at the end of the nineteenth century. Fear of an economic depression united aristocrat and worker alike in blaming a Jewish conspiracy. German anti-Semitism proliferated in the 1880s. "It is like a horrible epidemic," the scholar Theodor Mommsen (1817–1903) observed. "It can neither be explained nor cured."

Fear of the Jews was connected with hatred of capitalism. In France and Germany, Jews controlled powerful banking and commercial firms that became the targets of blame in hard times. Upwardly mobile sons of Jewish immigrants entered the professions of banking, trading, and journalism. They were also growing in numbers as teachers and academics. In the 1880s, more than half of Vienna's physicians (61 percent in 1881) and lawyers (58 percent of barristers in 1888) were Jewish. Their professional success only heightened tensions and condemnations of Jews as an "alien race." Anti-Semitism served as a violent means of mobilizing mass support, especially among those groups who felt threatened by capitalist concentration and large-scale industrialization. For anti-Semitic Europeans, Jews embodied the democratic, liberal, and cosmopolitan tendencies of the culture that they were consciously rejecting in their new political affiliations.

A Jewish leadership emerged in central and western Europe that treated anti-Semitism as a problem that could be solved by political means. For their generation at the end of the nineteenth century, the assimilation of their fathers and mothers was not the answer. Jews needed their own nation, it was argued, since they were a people without a nation. Zionism was the solution to what Jewish intellectuals called "the Jewish problem." Zion, the ancient homeland of Biblical times, would provide a national territory, and a choice, to persecuted Jews. Zionism became a Jewish nationalist movement dedicated to the establishment of a Jewish state. Although Zionism did not develop mass support in western Europe among assimilated Jews, its program for national identity and social reforms appealed to a large following of eastern European Jews in Galicia (Poland), Russia, and the eastern lands of the Habsburg Empire—those directly subjected to the extremes of persecution.

Theodor Herzl (1860–1904), an Austrian Jew born in Budapest, was the founder of Zionism in its political form. As a student in Vienna he had encountered discrimination, but his commitment to Zionism developed as a result of his years as a journalist in Paris. Observing the anti-Semitic attacks in republican France provoked by the scandals surrounding the misappropriation of funds by leading French politicians and businessmen during the construction of the Panama Canal and the divisive conflict over the Dreyfus Affair in the 1890s, Herzl came to appreciate how deeply imbedded anti-Semitism was in European society. He despaired of the ability of corrupt parliamentary governments to solve the problem of anti-Semitism. In *The Jewish State* (1896), Herzl concluded

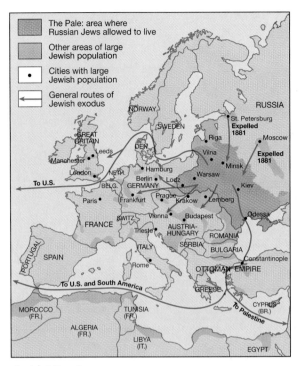

The Pale: area where
Russian Jews allowed to live

Other areas of large
Jewish population

Cities with large
Jewish population

General routes of
Jewish exodus

Jewish Migration

zens of their respective nation-states and would exacerbate hostilities toward Jews as outsiders. Yet Zionism had much in common with the European liberal tradition because it sought in the creation of a nation-state for Jews the solution to social injustice. Zion, the Jewish nation in the Middle East, was a liberal utopia for the Jewish people. Zionism learned from other mass movements of the period the importance of a broad base of support. By the time of the First Zionist Congress, held in Basel, Switzerland, in 1897, it had become a truly international movement. Herzl was also well aware of the necessity for a charismatic leader and cast himself in the role of messiah for his people.

Zionism did not achieve its goals before World War I, and the Jewish state of Israel was not recognized by the world community until 1948. Before World War I, anti-Semitism and antifeminism were strongly linked in nationalist political programs, which insisted that the place for Jews was on the periphery and the place for women was in the home. Through the Zionist movement, Jews victimized by nationalism planned for their own nation-state as a solution.

Workers and Minorities on the Margins

In 1892 the Parisian trial of a bomb-throwing anarchist named Ravachol attracted great public attention. He and other French anarchists had captured the popular imagination with their threats to destroy bourgeois society by bombing private residences, public buildings, and restaurants. Ravachol's terrorist deeds represented the extreme rejection of participation in electoral politics. The public was frightened—but also fascinated. Ravachol opposed the state and the capitalist economy as the dual enemy that could only be destroyed through individual acts of random physical violence. For his crimes he was condemned to death and publicly executed.

The best-known anarchists of the late nineteenth century were those, like Ravachol, who engaged in terrorist assassinations and bombings. Although not all anarchists were terrorists intent on destruction, all shared a desire for a revolutionary restructuring of society. Most anarchists were loners. They dreamed of the collapse of the capitalist system with its exploitation and inequality and of the emergence of a society based on personal freedom, autonomy, and justice. Anarchists spurned the Marxist willingness to organize and participate in parliamentary politics. They disdained the tyranny of new organizations and bureaucracies that worked for gradual reforms at the expense of principles of justice.

that Jews must have a state of their own. Under his direction, Zionism developed a worldwide organization and its own newspaper with the aim of establishing a Jewish homeland in Palestine.

Jews began emigrating to Palestine. With the financial backing of Jewish donors like the French banker Baron de Rothschild, nearly 90,000 Jews had established settlements there by 1914. Calculated to tap a common Jewish identification with an ancient heritage, the choice of Palestine as a homeland was controversial from the beginning. The problems arising from the choice have persisted through the twentieth century.

The promised land of the Old Testament, Zion is a holy place in Judaism. The Austrian psychoanalyst Sigmund Freud (1856–1939), who described himself as "a Jew from Moravia," was sympathetic to the Zionist cause but critical of the idea of Palestine as a Jewish state. He considered the idea unworkable and one bound to arouse Christian and Islamic opposition. Freud feared that Palestine would arouse the suspicions of the Arab world and challenge "the feelings of the local natives." He would have preferred a "new, historically unencumbered soil."

Some Jewish critics of Zionism felt that a separate Jewish state would prove that Jews were not good citi-

There was no single anarchist doctrine, but the varieties of anarchism all shared a hope in a future free from constraints. Mikhail Bakunin (1814–76), a member of the Russian nobility, absorbed the works and the message of the French social critic Pierre-Joseph Proudhon. Bakunin became Europe's leading anarchist spokesman. Unlike Proudhon, Bakunin was a man of revolutionary action who espoused the use of violence to achieve individual liberation. All existing institutions must be swept away before ownership of production could be collectivized. Bakunin broke with Marx, whom he considered a "scientific bourgeois socialist" out of touch with the mass of workers.

Bakunin's successor in international anarchist doctrine was also a Russian of aristocratic lineage—Prince Petr Kropotkin (1842–1921). Kropotkin joined together communism and anarchism, arguing that goods should be communally distributed, "from each according to his ability, to each according to his needs." On the basis of his own empirical observations, Kropotkin argued that competition and dominance were not laws of nature and instead stressed human interdependence.

It is difficult to measure the extent of Bakunin's or Kropotkin's influence, since whatever followers they might have inspired were not overtly or formally organized. Anarchism's greatest appeal was in the less industrialized countries of southern Europe: Spain, Italy, and southern France. In these countries, grass-roots anarchism germinated in working-class communities. In the second half of the nineteenth century, Russia too had developed a strong populist tradition similar to anarchism in its opposition to state tyranny. But anarchism was primarily a western European phenomenon.

Anarchism had special appeal to workers in trades staggering under the blows of industrial capitalism. Calling themselves anarcho-syndicalists, artisans—especially in France—were able to combine local trade union organization with anarchist principles. Alienation from the political process was strong among the French working class, who had recent bitter memories of repression during the Paris Commune in 1871 and who rejected the sterility and corruption of the party politics of the Third Republic. Most of these workers were in skilled trades that suffered from high rates of unemployment and chronically depressed wages.

Unlike union movements in the industrialized countries of Great Britain and Germany, French trade unions remained small, weak, and local, without the resources to undertake sustained action. French unions had gained legal recognition in 1884, eight years after Great Britain but six years before Germany. Workers

Mikhail Bakunin.

who combined trade unionism with anarchism shared an apocalyptic vision of social transformation. The contrast between the Labour party in Great Britain and the German Social Democrats on the one hand and the French anarcho-syndicalists on the other highlighted the split between advanced industrial countries and less-developed areas of Europe, where an artisan class was attempting to preserve autonomy and control.

The journalist and social thinker Georges Sorel (1847–1922) captured the philosophy of anarcho-syndicalism in his book *Reflections on Violence* (1908). Sorel described the "myth," or shared belief, in the "general strike," a kind of final judgment day when justice would prevail. Unlike the trade unions of other western European states, anarcho-syndicalist unions were militantly opposed to issues of improved wages and better working conditions. In order to be ready for the collapse of bourgeois society, anarcho-syndicalists must not collaborate with the existing system by accepting benefits and improvements from it. Instead, workers were to hold themselves ready by employing a technique of "direct action" to maintain worker solidarity. "Direct action" was a symbolic gesture that did not advance the revolution but did help workers remain aware of their exploitation. A typical example of "direct action" was the agreement among the militantly revolutionary barbers' union to nick their customers periodically with the razor while shaving them. Acts such as this were meaningless in themselves—except perhaps to those who experienced them—but were intended to raise the level of commitment to a common cause.

The problems of disaffected groups in general intensified before 1914. Anarchists and anarcho-syndicalist workers deplored the centralization and organization of mass society. Yet anarchism posed no serious threat to social stability because of the effectiveness of policing in most European states. As Friedrich Engels observed at the turn of the century, random violence directed against politics and the economy was no match for the repressive forces at the command of the nation-state. The politics of mass society excluded diverse groups—including women, Jews, and ethnic minorities—from participation. Yet the techniques, values, and organization of the world of politics remained available to all these groups. It was the outbreak of war in 1914 that silenced, temporarily at least, the challenge of these outsiders.

Shaping the New Consciousness

Imagine a world that discovered how to eliminate the difference between night and day. Imagine further a civilization that could obliterate distance or shrink it. Imagine a people who could see for the first time into solid mass, into their own bodies, and send images through space. These are the imaginings of fable and fantasy that can be traced back to prehistory. But what had always been the stuff of magic became reality between 1880 and 1914. The people of the West used science and technology to reshape the world and their understanding of it.

The discoveries of science had ramifications that extended beyond the laboratory, the hospital, and the classroom. Science changed the way people thought and the way they lived. It improved the quality of life by defeating diseases, improving nutrition, and lengthening life span. But scientific knowledge was not without its costs. Scientific discoveries led to new forces of destruction. Scientific ideas challenged moral and religious beliefs. Science was invoked to justify racial and sexual discrimination. Traditional values and religious belief also did combat with the new god of science, with philosophers proclaiming that God was dead. New disciplines claimed to study society scientifically with methods similar to those applied to the study of bacilli and the atom. A traditional world of order and hierarchy gave way to a new reality in which the center

was no longer holding and the limits were constantly expanding.

The Authority of Science

What may seem commonplace at the end of the twentieth century was no less than spectacular at the end of the nineteenth. Scientific discoveries in the last quarter of the century pushed out the frontiers of knowledge. In physics, James Clerk Maxwell (1831–79) discovered the relationship between electricity and magnetism. Maxwell showed mathematically that an oscillating electric charge produces an electromagnetic field and that such a field radiates outward from its source at a constant speed—the speed of light. His theories led to the discovery of the electromagnetic spectrum, comprising radiation of different wavelengths, including X rays, visible light, and radio waves. This discovery had important practical applications for the development of the electrical industry and led to the invention of radio and television. Within a generation, the names of Edison, Westinghouse, Marconi, Siemens, and Bell entered the public realm.

Discoveries in the physical sciences succeeded one another with great rapidity. The periodic table of chemical elements was formulated in 1869. Radioactivity was discovered in 1896. Two years later, Marie Curie (1867–1934) and her husband Pierre (1859–1906) discovered the elements radium and polonium. At the end of the century, Ernest Rutherford (1871–1937) identified alpha and beta rays in radioactive atoms. Building on the new discoveries, Max Planck (1858–1947), Albert Einstein (1879–1955), and Niels Bohr (1885–1962) dismantled the classical physics of absolute and determined principles and left in its place modern physics based on relativity and uncertainty. In 1900, Planck propounded a theory that renounced the emphasis in classical physics on energy as a wave phenomenon in favor of a new "quantum theory" of energy as emitted and absorbed in minute, discrete amounts.

The name Einstein has become synonymous with genius in the twentieth century. In 1905 Albert Einstein formulated his special theory of relativity, in which he established the relationship of mass and energy in the famous equation $E = mc^2$. In 1916 he published his general theory of relativity, a mathematical formulation that created a new conception of space and time. Einstein disproved the Newtonian view of gravitation as a force and instead saw it as a curved field in the time-space continuum created by the presence of mass. No one at the time foresaw that the application

∾ *Sigmund Freud, Explorer of Dreams*

Sigmund Freud was a disciplined man, precise and punctual in his habits. In many ways, his life was typical of the life of a Viennese bourgeois professional at the end of the nineteenth century. His day was like a railway timetable, scheduled to the minute—whether seeing patients, dining with his family, or taking his daily constitutional. He even calculated his pleasures, counting as his only indulgence the twenty cigars he smoked every day

The order in Freud's life seemed curiously at odds with his dedication to the study of disorder. He was a man of science, a medical doctor specializing in organic diseases of the nervous system. Early in his career, he began to question physiological explanations for certain nervous disorders and to search for another reason for the disorders of the mind. His exploration took him to Paris in 1885 to study with the leading French neurologist, Jean Martin Charcot (1825–93), whose work on hysteria had won him an international reputation.

Surrounded by hysterics in Charcot's clinic, Freud wondered whether organic physical illnesses could be traced to psychological problems. Freud explored the value of hypnosis as a technique for uncovering the secret workings of the mind. He learned that emotions alone could produce physical symptoms like blindness and paralysis. By hypnotizing patients, Freud caught glimpses of the world of the unconscious as a vast and hidden terrain. He approached this new territory as an explorer.

Freud created a new science of the unconscious, psychoanalysis, when he rejected physiological causes for nervous disorders in favor of psychological ones. He intended psychoanalysis as a theory of personality and a method of treatment or therapy. This was a dramatic break with existing theories of madness and mental disorder. On his seventieth birthday, Freud looked back over his own career and described his achievement: "The poets and philosophers before me discovered the unconscious; what I discovered was the scientific method by which the unconscious can be studied."

The hostile reaction to Freud's break with existing ideas about mental disorders was further aggravated by the importance he attributed to sexuality.

Colleagues in Vienna were shocked by the direction that his work was taking. Freud began by hypothesizing that disturbed patients developed neurotic symptoms because of the repression of memories of actual sexual abuse as children. He moved away from this theory of sexual abuse to one in which the subject had *fantasized* about sex as a child and then had repressed the desire. In searching for the root of psychological disorders, Freud argued that sexual conflicts originating in early childhood were the cause of adult neuroses. Repressed sexual desire therefore became the key to understanding human behavior.

Freud's self-described scientific method, which allowed him to probe the unconscious, was free association. Patients were encouraged to talk, or "associate," in a relaxed atmosphere. The couch in the doctor's office has become the enduring symbol of the psychoanalytic method. Patients were particularly encouraged to talk about their dreams. The unconscious, Freud argued, manifests itself in dreams. The role of the psychoanalyst is to examine the content of the dream and interpret it, facilitating recognition and hence a cure in the patient.

Freud's first major work, and probably the most important study of his career, *The Interpretation of Dreams* (1900), heralded the new century. Working with his own dreams and those of his patients, Freud posited that a dream is the fulfillment of a wish. Dreams are not literal in their meaning; their symbols and context must always be interpreted. The experiences of our conscious lives are rearranged in dreams. For Freud, nothing was accidental. Jokes, obsessions, and even slips of the tongue ("Freudian slips") as well as dreams were indicators of unconscious desires. In later life, Freud was supposed to have said, "Sometimes a cigar is just a cigar." But in his dream theory, every object— cigar, banana, flight of stairs, or broken candle—had meaning in the context of the patient's associations. Freud used his own dreams and his relationship with his parents to describe the neurotic personality and the Oedipus complex, so important to his later work on childhood sexuality. Here the child's unresolved desire for the parent of the opposite sex formed the basis for all ego development. In famous case studies such as "Dora," "The Wolf Man," and "The Rat Man," Freud described the symptoms and histories of patients to whom he assigned fictitious names. In subsequent works, Freud went on to detail the uncharted land of the unconscious he discovered in his work on dreams, using designations for the components of personality—the "ego," the "superego," and the "id."

Sigmund Freud gave to Western culture a new vocabulary. His lexicon has survived throughout the twentieth century and has entered common parlance as a way of explaining our daily lives in psychological terms that range from "anal-retentive stage" to "sublimation." He bequeathed to Western men and women a new way of looking at the world. Freud's work sounded the death knell for the nineteenth century's blind faith in reason. For Freud, human beings were driven by subterranean instincts and desires. The horrors of war and destruction in the twentieth century confirmed for Freud his belief in the irrationality of Western civilization.

Freud died in exile in London in 1939, having fled from the Nazi occupation of his beloved Vienna. During his lifetime and ever since, his theories have been refuted, with critics saying that they explain nothing more than the psychic world in which Freud lived—the world of European middle-class men at the beginning of the twentieth century. But there can be no denying that Freud's exploration of the land of dreams in the world of the unconscious was a revolutionary event in the history of Western thought.

The new social science of criminology claimed scientific veracity after 1880. In 1885, Sir Francis Galton (1822–1911), a cousin of Charles Darwin, proved the individuality of fingerprints through scientific study and thereby initiated an important method of identifying criminals. Criminologists joined psychiatrists as expert witnesses in criminal trials for the first time at the end of the nineteenth century. Galton also propagated pseudoscientific ideas about eugenics, the improvement of the human race through selective breeding. Anthropological studies of primitive cultures influenced eugenic assumptions about racial inferiority.

The new specialties of forensic medicine and criminal anthropology came into being at the end of the century. *The Criminal Man* (1876), written by Italian criminologist Cesare Lombroso (1836–1909), claimed to be a scientific study of the physical attributes of convicted criminals. Through observation and statistical compilation, Lombroso discovered "born criminals," individuals whose physical characteristics proved their deviance. Criminals, he claimed, could be identified by their looks. With statistics Lombroso demonstrated, for example, that left-handed, redheaded people with low foreheads were naturally disposed to a life of crime. Even during his lifetime, Lombroso's ideas were widely disputed, and subsequently they were discredited, but their temporary legitimacy was a good indication of how scientific claims justified prejudicial assumptions. Opposing Lombroso's ideas, the French school of criminology stressed the social determinants of crime, seeing poverty and malnutrition as explanations for the different physical appearance of criminals.

The psychology of crowd behavior originated in the work of the French physician Gustave Le Bon (1841–1931). In *Psychology of Crowds* (1895), Le Bon argued that the masses were instinctively irrational. Through his "science" he arrived at the political judgment that democracy was a despicable and dangerous form of government. Émile Durkheim (1858–1917) is regarded as the founder of modern sociology. In his famous study of suicide as a social phenomenon, Durkheim pitted sociological theory against psychology and argued that deviance was the result not of psychic disturbances but of environmental factors and hereditary forces.

Heredity became a general explanation for behavior of all sorts. The novels of Émile Zola presented a popular view of biological determinism. Zola's protagonists were doomed by self-destructive characteristics they inherited from their parents. Everything from poverty, drunkenness, and crime to a declining birthrate could be attributed to biologically determined causes. For some theorists, this reasoning teetered on the edge of racism and ideas about "better blood." Intelligence was now measured "scientifically" for the first time with IQ tests developed at the Sorbonne by the psychologist Alfred Binet (1857–1911) in the 1890s. The tests did not acknowledge the importance of cultural factors in the development of intelligence, and they scientifically legitimated a belief in natural elites. Not least of all, science was also invoked in support of a particular system of gender relations, one that itself was undergoing assault and upheaval between 1871 and 1914.

The "New Woman" and the New Consciousness

New scientific ideas had a formative impact on prevailing views of gender relations and female sexuality. The natural sciences were employed to prove the inferiority of women in the species. In *The Descent of Man* (1871), Charles Darwin, the giant of evolutionary theory, concluded that the mental power of man was higher than that of woman. The female's need for male protection, the father of evolution reasoned, had increased her dependence over time while at the same time increasing the competition of natural selection among men. The result, Darwin argued, was inequality between the sexes. Darwin went on to reject women's emancipation as out of step with biological realities. What Darwin presented was a vicious circle in which women's dependence had made them inferior and their inferiority kept them dependent. These attitudes toward gender and race marked the advent of biological "proofs" to justify social policies. Those of Darwin's disciples who applied biological principles to society came to be known as "social Darwinists," specialists who claimed that "survival of the fittest" was a concept that could be applied to all social interactions between races and the sexes.

Darwin was not the only man of science who had ideas about a woman's proper place. Others made a dubious case for brain size as an index of superiority. The French physiologist Paul Broca (1824–80), a contemporary of Darwin's, countered in 1873 that the skull capacity of the two sexes was very similar and that a case for inferiority could not be based on measurement. But Broca was atypical. Most scientific opinion argued in favor of female frailty and outright inferiority. Social Darwinists adapted evolutionary biology to the debate over inequality between the sexes. They complemented their race theories with evolutionary theories of sexual division: "What was decided among the prehistoric Protozoa cannot be annulled by an Act of Parliament." Sexless prehistoric protozoa held the message for social Darwinists that women should not enjoy the right to vote.

In general, the natural sciences worked to reinforce the idea of women as reproducers whose proper role was nurturing and whose proper domain was the home. The social sciences, in particular sociology, echoed these findings by asserting that the male-dominated household was a proof of social progress.

These "scientific" arguments justified the exclusion of women from educational opportunities and from professions like medicine and law. Biology became destiny as women's attempts at equal education came up against closed doors. Stalwarts broke the prohibitions, but women who gained higher education in these decades were the exception that proved the rule. Those women who were able to get an education were blocked from using it. There was a generalized fear in Western societies that women who attempted to exceed their "natural" abilities would damage their reproductive functions and neglect their nurturing roles. The specter of sickly children and women with nervous disorders was invoked as grounds for opposing demands for coeducation. Women's education was assigned to the church and was intended to meet the needs of the family. The creation of the first separate women's colleges in the late 1860s marked the beginning of the pioneering era of higher education for women.

In this age of scientific justification of female inferiority, the "new woman" emerged. All over Europe the feminist movement had demanded social, economic, and political progress for women. But the "new woman" phenomenon exceeded the bounds of the feminist movement and can be described as a general cultural phenomenon. The search for independence was overwhelmingly a middle-class phenomenon that had a psychological as well as a political significance in the years between 1880 and 1914. Victorian stereotypes of the angel at the hearth were crumbling. The "new woman" was a woman characterized by intelligence, strength, and sexual desire—in every way man's equal. The Norwegian playwright Henrik Ibsen (1828–1906) created a fictional embodiment of the phenomenon in Nora, the hero of *A Doll's House* (1879), who was typical of the restive spirit for independence among wives and mothers confined to suffocating households and relegated to the status of children. Contemporary opinion condemned Nora as immoral for abandoning her home, her husband, and her children.

The "new woman's" pursuit of independence included control over her own body. The term *birth control* was first used by an American, Margaret Sanger (1879–1966), although the reality itself was not new.

Margaret Sanger led the birth control movement in the United States. She was arrested several times for her activities but helped get laws passed that allowed doctors to disseminate birth control information.

Women had always known of and employed contraceptive and abortive techniques to limit family size. What was different in the period before 1914 was the militant public discussion of ways to prevent conception and an awareness of the death and debilitation that resulted from primitive methods. The development of a process of vulcanizing rubber in the mid-nineteenth century had made condoms available to a mass market, but they were little employed. A growing number of women, among whom were medical doctors, decided to take information to the public. A common result was state repression of their activities. Annie Besant, advocating birth control in Great Britain, was charged with corrupting youth by distributing books that dealt with contraception. Aletta Jacobs (1849–1929), the first woman to practice medicine in Holland, opened a contraceptive clinic in 1882. Leagues for distributing contraceptive information were formed elsewhere in Europe. Birth-control advocates aimed to preserve women's health and to give them some control over their reproductive lives.

Discussions of contraception brought into the public arena the premise that women, like men, were sexual beings. This was reinforced by the frank discussions of sexuality in the works of Sigmund Freud. The first English translation of Freud's *The Interpretation of Dreams* appeared in 1913 with a warning note from the publisher that its sale should be limited to doctors, lawyers, and clerics. Richard von Krafft-Ebing (1840–1902) and Havelock Ellis (1859–1939) also con-

"ANGEL" OR WOMAN?

Victorian domestic ideals viewed woman as an "Angel in the House" (the title of a poem by Coventry Patmore) who created a paradise of love and nurturance for her husband and children. By the end of the nineteenth century, many women recognized that this description, however rosy, kept women in the home and out of public life. Here Maria Desraismes, a French feminist and republican, rebuts republican and historian Jules Michelet for his popular books that romanticized women and marriage.

Of all woman's enemies, I tell you that the worst are those who insist that woman is an angel. To say that woman is an angel is to impose on her, in a sentimental and admiring fashion, all duties, and to reserve for oneself all rights; it is to imply that her specialty is self-effacement, resignation, and sacrifice; it is to suggest to her that woman's greatest glory, her greatest happiness, is to immolate herself for those she loves; it is to let her understand that she will be *generously* furnished with every opportunity for exercising her aptitudes. It is to say that she will respond to absolutism by submission, to brutality by meekness, to indiffer-

ence by tenderness, to inconstancy by fidelity, to egotism by devotion.

In the face of this long enumeration, I decline the honor of being an angel. No one has the right to force me to be both dupe and victim. Self-sacrifice is not a habit, a custom; it is an *extra!* It is not on the program of one's duties. No power has the right to impose it on me. Of all acts, sacrifice is the freest, and it is precisely because it is free that it is so admirable.

From Maria Desraismes, "La Femme et le droit" public address published in *Eve dans l'humanité* (1891).

---

tributed to the public discussion of sex in their works on sexuality and sexual deviance. By 1900 sexuality and reproduction were openly connected to discussions of women's rights.

The new sciences had worked to change the world. At the same time, those intent on preserving traditional values invoked scientific authority. But as the uncertainty over gender roles at the beginning of the twentieth century makes clear, science was a way of thinking as well as a body of doctrine. Traditional ideas might be scientifically justified, but they would not go unchallenged.

The New Consumption

The great Russian novelist Lev Tolstoy (1828–1910) was an astute observer of the world in which he lived. In 1877 he condemned the materialism that characterized European society: "Money is a new form of slavery, and distinguishable from the old simply by the fact that it is impersonal—that there is no human relation between master and slave." Although he was speaking as a moral philosopher, Tolstoy had put his finger on something that economists were just beginning to understand—the extension of a money economy. Tol-

stoy was aware of how peasants freed from the land became entangled in a web of financial obligations that constituted a new form of serfdom.

At the end of the nineteenth century, the role of money changed in ways affecting all of Western society. Workers were beginning to share in the benefits of industrial prosperity. This prosperity differed dramatically by geographic region and occupation. But the expansion in the ranks of a salaried working class augured a shift in patterns of behavior. Lagging behind the industrial revolutions but no less important was a revolution in consumption patterns among European populations. The new consumer age is best illustrated by the creation of the big department stores of the last quarter of the nineteenth century. The Bon Marché Department Store in Paris occupied over 52,000 square feet and contained a vast selection of goods. Everything from initialed toilet paper to household furniture was now located under a single roof. The department store was intended to satisfy every need. Advertising and the art of display became industries in themselves, whose goal was to encourage people to buy things they did not need. The promise of the good life, epitomized in the department store and preached by advertising, now seemed accessible to everyone.

Leisure time also became a consumer item in the late nineteenth century. In 1899, the American economist Thorstein Veblen (1857–1929) published a pathbreaking work that was little appreciated at the time. *The Theory of the Leisure Class* argued that leisure was a form of "conspicuous consumption," a term Veblen coined. More than a theory, his work constituted a critique of the values of Western culture. Women and the family were, for Veblen, the primary vehicles for conspicuous consumption. Elegant dress, for example, conveyed status and served as a sign of leisure just as it had done in aristocratic society. Expensive clothing was designed to show that the wearer had no need to earn wages. For this purpose, women were actually "mutilated," in Veblen's term, by the corset that constricted their vitality and rendered them unfit for work. Women immobilized by their clothes and shoes became the ultimate symbols of social status.

The middle and upper classes controlled sufficient disposable income to allow them to spend time in such leisure pursuits as flocking to seaside resorts in Great Britain and on the Continent. However, resort vacations remained out of the financial reach of most working-class people. Instead, in pursuit of leisure-time activities, working-class men congregated in cafes and pubs. Starting in the 1880s, vaudeville and music halls rose in popularity, their low admission price attracting ever larger crowds. There were at least thirty striptease shows in Paris in the 1890s. These activities fostered fear among the middle classes that working-class leisure was degenerate. The newly invented cinema also exercised a growing appeal for European men and women of all ages and classes.

Not least important in the new leisure was the rise of organized sports. The strict organization of work life in mature industrial societies may have made sports an attractive way of organizing leisure. Men—there were few organized sports for women—worked by the clock and now played by the clock as well. Sports also promoted national and regional identification. Beginning in the 1860s, men began playing the games they had learned as boys in English public schools. Rugby, football (soccer), and cricket soon developed national followings. Golf originated in Scotland in this period and spread throughout Europe and to the United States. Spectator sports grew in importance, with audiences of over 100,000 people at British soccer matches at the beginning of the twentieth century. Victorians saw the necessity of recreation and endorsed the renewing, relaxing, and entertaining aspects of organized play.

Scouting also originated at the end of the nineteenth century as another form of organized leisure. Uniformed boys were taught "manly" virtues of self-reliance and teamwork. Team spirit was tied to patriotism. Scouting organizations for girls emphasized domestic virtues and household tasks.

Amateur athletics and track-and-field events grew in popularity, especially after the establishment of an international Olympics competition, modeled on the ancient Greek games. The first modern Olympiad was

Middle-class and working-class excursionists to the seaside are shown in this scene from Yarmouth, England. The era of special bathing attire was yet to come.

The Eiffel Tower under construction. The huge wrought-iron tower rises 944 feet above the city of Paris. For many years, it was the highest structure in the world.

held in Athens in 1896, and—except for upheavals caused by war—the Olympic Games have been held at four-year intervals throughout the twentieth century.

Cycling became a popular competitive sport on the Continent with the establishment of the Tour de France at the beginning of the twentieth century. Some saw in the new pastime of bicycling a threat to the social order. Women, attracted by the exercise and mobility afforded by this new means of transportation, altered their costumes in favor of freedom of movement. For eminently practical reasons, they discarded their corsets and bustles and shortened their skirts. As women gained greater mobility, some observers saw in the "new woman" on the bicycle seat the decline of true womanhood and Western values.

The engineering marvel of the Eiffel Tower, built in 1889 for the World Exposition held in Paris, became a symbol not only of the French capital but of the values

of the new age. New artifacts of European culture proliferated. Photography, motorcars, bicycles, motion-picture cameras, and X rays all created sensations when they appeared. London's Inner Circle underground railway was completed in 1884, and other lines soon followed, forming a vast urban subterranean network. In 1898, the miracle of underground transportation became a reality in Paris with the opening of the Métro, or subway. Yet some observers saw in this new age only upheaval and disruption of traditional liberal values. The Eiffel Tower was criticized more than it was praised. It was a building, yet it was not. Its inside and its outside were confused. The admirers of classic architecture lamented the ugliness of this girdered monument whose main function was to demonstrate structural innovation for its own sake. The Eiffel Tower—like the values of the new age, critics warned— was hollow and would not endure.

Suggestions for Further Reading

European Economy and the Politics of Mass Society

Michael Burns, *Rural Society and French Politics: Boulangism and the Dreyfus Affair, 1886–1900* (Princeton, NJ: Princeton University Press, 1984). Examines the impact on rural France of two political watersheds of the Third Republic in order to gauge the importance of national politics in nonurban settings.

* Albert S. Lindemann, *A History of European Socialism* (New Haven, CT: Yale University Press, 1983). Surveys socialist thought in the nineteenth and twentieth centuries and examines the relationships between ideology, institutions, and workers in their historical context.

* Carl E. Schorske, *Fin-de-Siècle Vienna: Politics and Culture* (New York: Alfred A. Knopf, 1980). A series of essays describing the break with nineteenth-century liberal culture in one of Europe's great cities as artists, intellectuals, and politicians responded to the disintegration of the Habsburg Empire.

* Eugen Weber, *Peasants into Frenchmen: The Modernization of Rural France* (Stanford, CA: Stanford University Press, 1976). Views the integration of the French peasantry into national political life through agents of change, including the railroads, schools, and the army. The author contends that a national political culture took the place of traditional beliefs and practices between 1870 and 1914 in France.

* Hans-Ulrich Wehler, *The German Empire, 1871–1918* (Leamington Spa, England: Berg Publishers, 1985). Stresses the institutional continuities of German society and links pre-World War I Germany to the rise of Nazism.

Outsiders in Mass Politics

* Richard J. Evans, *The Feminist Movement in Germany, 1894–1933* (London: Sage Publications, 1976). Considers two conflicting approaches to bourgeois feminism—one radical and the other conservative and authoritarian—and discusses the role of social Darwinism in the women's movement and the place of feminism in political life.

* Steven C. Hause and Anne R. Kenney, *Women's Suffrage and Social Politics in the French Third Republic* (Princeton, NJ: Princeton University Press, 1984). Examines the women's suffrage movement from its origins through its defeat after World War I in the Senate. Aims, tactics, and leadership of the women's movement receive special attention.

* William M. Reddy, *The Rise of Market Culture: The Textile Trade and French Society, 1750–1900* (Cambridge: Cambridge University Press, 1984). A cultural interpretation of the textile trade in the era of industrialization. Reddy examines the creation of market culture and workers' resistance to it through a study of collective action, workers' songs, bourgeois attitudes, and factory organization.

* Richard Stites, *The Women's Liberation Movement in Russia: Feminism, Nihilism, and Bolshevism, 1860–1930* (Princeton, NJ: Princeton University Press, 1978). Situates the Russian women's movement within the contexts of both nineteenth-century European feminism and twentieth-century communist ideology and traces its development from the early feminists through the rise of the Bolsheviks to power. Includes a discussion of the Russian Revolution's impact on the status of women.

Shaping the New Consciousness

* Stephen Kern, *The Culture of Time and Space, 1880–1918* (Cambridge, MA: Harvard University Press, 1983). Describes how late-nineteenth-century technological advances created new modes of thinking about and experiencing time and space.

* Michael B. Miller, *The Bon Marché: Bourgeois Culture and the Department Store, 1869–1920* (Princeton, NJ: Princeton University Press, 1981). A social and cultural history of the department store as the creation and reflection of bourgeois culture.

Robert A. Nye, *Crime, Madness, and Politics in Modern France: The Medical Concept of National Decline* (Princeton, NJ: Princeton University Press, 1984). Nye shows how the medical concept of deviance was linked to a general cultural crisis in fin-de-siècle France.

* William M. Reddy, *Money and Liberty in Modern Europe: A Critique of Historical Understanding* (Cambridge: Cambridge University Press, 1987). This essay on the role of money in modern Europe contends that its widespread use in exchange influenced social structure. Arguing that monetary exchange intensified existing social inequities, Reddy examines the expansion of commerce in France, Germany, and England.

* Martin Wiener, *English Culture and the Decline of the Industrial Spirit, 1850–1980* (Cambridge: Cambridge University Press, 1981). A cultural history of growth and decline from Victoria to Thatcher. By drawing on literature, art, architecture, politics, and economics, the author describes the ambiguous attitude of the elite toward industry and argues that English culture was never conducive to sustained industrial growth.

* Rosalind H. Williams, *Dream Worlds: Mass Consumption in Late Nineteenth-Century France* (Berkeley: University of California Press, 1982). A historical overview of attitudes toward consumption and an examination of the creation of the consumer mentality in terms of the consumer revolution and its consequences.

*Paperback edition available.

25 ❧ EUROPE AND THE WORLD, 1870–1914

The Power of Words

European conquest of African territories often involved sizable military expeditions and resulted in high death tolls among native populations. But imperial domination also took forms other than those reflected in battles and conquest. Language was an important tool of domination often overlooked in favor of more tangible indicators of control. Imperialist powers were able to extract natural wealth, employ native labor, and administer and control millions of Africans—not with bullets but with the power of words.

For certain kinds of profit, words were not necessary—terror and repression were enough. In the Congo rubber trade, for example, early Belgian adventurers could simply steal from or blackmail whole villages until they were stopped by the force of international opinion. But for other enterprises, like mining, that required organization, technology, and discipline, communication between the colonized and the colonizer was essential. Hierarchies of power and authority had to be established on the basis of orders given and orders understood. A shared language was the only means of moving beyond a state of siege to ongoing economic activity and, ideally, efficiency and profitability.

Europeans did not always choose simply to impose their own languages on colonized populations. Nor did they take the time and trouble to learn the numerous languages and countless dialects of the tribes with whom they came into contact. The politics of language was more complicated than either of these alternatives and varied from region to region.

Particularly instructive is the adoption of Swahili as a lingua franca, or common language, in the Congo Free State (later the Belgian Congo, and now Zaire). Nineteenth-century missionaries had identified Swahili, a Bantu language heavily influenced by Arab traders on the eastern coast of Africa in the seventeenth century, as the easiest language for Europeans to learn. Belgians widely believed that Congolese natives were incapable of learning French, which the Belgians considered to be a superior language. In an area stretching 1300 miles along the Congo River from the west coast of Africa to Stanley Falls, missionaries and explorers encountered at least eight principal languages. Both Catholic priests and various Protestant missionaries, intent on converting natives, recognized the utility of Swahili and set about codifying vocabularies and training manuals for their own missionaries. Priests were sent home if they were not properly trained in Swahili. In the same manner, the Belgian government required basic language instruction in Swahili for administrators before they left Belgium.

Trade with agricultural areas populated by Swahili-speaking natives contributed to the spread of Swahili among African workers moving into newly created urban areas like Elizabethville and into the towns around the Belgian-owned copper mines of the Katanga area of the Congo Free State. Unlike European settlers, Africans showed a willingness to learn new languages quickly. Through the influence of urban migration and the encouragement of Belgian overseers, Swahili became the common tongue of growing numbers of workers and urban dwellers.

While Belgians and other Westerners used Swahili to control native workers, they did not speak the language. This is an important distinction. Many Europeans had access to vocabularies—they used words rather than explained ideas or expressed feelings. In their pidgin Swahili, Europeans knew only

how to give orders. Nouns were limited to concrete objects. True signs of language mastery—concern for syntax and grammar—were absent from Belgian training manuals. Verbs were listed only in their imperative forms—including the verb for love, *penda*. Most verbs referred to movements connected with employer-employee relations and domestic and agricultural work. In much the same way that modern-day tourists learn enough of a foreign language to order a meal or ask the location of a restroom, Belgian managers and work bosses often learned how to channel labor and increase output with pidgin-language skills that excluded the possibility of discussion and exchange of ideas. This was also true of the British in east Africa, in the area that is now Tanzania, Uganda, Kenya, and Zanzibar. Natives identified the limited dialect the British spoke as *kisetla* Swahili—the dialect of the settlers.

This situation reinforced stereotypes and prevented communication between Europeans and Africans. Europeans concluded from their limited exchanges that natives were childlike and simple. And what did Africans think of the Europeans? The novelist George Orwell, the pseudonym of Eric Arthur Blair (1903–50), experienced the reverse of the stereotyping phenomenon in his early career as a British police officer in Burma. Forced against his better judgment to kill an elephant, Orwell concluded, "The imperialist wears a mask and his face grows to fit it." In the mask of authority, Orwell became the violent and destructive imperialist that the natives saw. This was a process

without words, in what Orwell described as "the utter silence" experienced by every European in the colonies.

The hierarchy of languages reinforced the silence. The 1908 Charter of the Belgian Congo specified that French was the official language to be used at all state ceremonies. Native Africans, however, had no advanced training in French. Elementary French taught in the mission schools was intended to help the Congolese serve their Belgian masters as servants and low-level clerks. Furthermore, all decrees and regulations were to be published in French and Flemish, but not Swahili. As a result, Africans could not read the laws that governed them. But they could hear the laws translated for them into their regional languages by their own people.

Swahili, promoted by the state as the common language of work, expanded from a few hundred speakers in what is now central Zaire to become the first language of millions, including entire urban populations and a great majority of rural dwellers. Just as the French language was an effective barrier to Congolese participation in public life, Swahili—in its variety of dialects—effectively excluded Europeans from the private lives and popular customs of the Congolese. Within two generations, the Congolese were also able to use Swahili, encouraged as a language of deference and labor, as a bond of common identity and political resistance against their imperial rulers. Such was the power of words that the language imposed by the conqueror became the language of liberation.

The New Imperialism

The concept of empire was certainly not invented by Europeans in the last third of the nineteenth century: European states had controlled empires before 1870. The influence of Great Britain stretched beyond the limits of its formal holdings in India and South Africa. Russia held Siberia and central Asia, and France ruled Algeria and Indochina. Older empires—Spain, for example—had survived from the sixteenth century but as hollow shells. What, then, was new about the "new imperialism" practiced by England, France, and Germany after 1870? In part, the new imperialism was the acquisition of territories on an intense and unprecedented scale. Industrialization created the tools of transportation, communication, and domination that permitted the rapid pace of global empire-building. Above all, what distinguished the new imperialism was the domination by the industrial powers over the non-industrial world. The United States also participated in the new imperialism, less by territorial acquisition and more by developing an "invisible" empire of trade and influence in the Pacific. The forms of imperialism may have varied from nation to nation, but the basically unequal relationship between an industrial power and an undeveloped territory did not.

Only nation-states commanded the technology and resources necessary for the new scale of imperialist expansion. Rivalry among a few European nation-states—notably Great Britain, France, and Germany—was a common denominator that set the standards by which these nations and other European nation-states gained control of the globe by 1900. Why did the Europeans create vast empires? Were empires built for economic gain, military protection, or national glory? Questions about motives may obscure common features of the new imperialism. Industrial powers sought to take over nonindustrial regions, not in isolated areas but all over the globe. In the attempt they necessarily competed with one another, successfully adapting the resources of industrialism to the needs of conquest.

The Technology of Empire

For Europeans at the end of the nineteenth century, the world had definitely become a smaller place. Steam, iron, and electricity—the great forces of Western industrialization—were responsible for seemingly shrinking the globe. Technology not only allowed Europeans to accomplish tasks and to mass-produce goods efficiently, but also altered the previous conception of time and space.

Steam, which powered factories, proved equally efficient as an energy source in transportation. Great iron steamships fueled by coal replaced the smaller, slower, wind-powered wooden sailing vessels that had ruled the seas for centuries. Steam-powered vessels transported large cargoes of people and goods more quickly and more reliably than the sailing ships. Iron ships were superior to wood in their durability, lightness, water-tightness, cargo space, speed, and fuel economy. For most of the nineteenth century, British trading ships and the British navy dominated the seas, but after 1880 other nations, especially Germany, challenged England by building versatile and efficient iron steamers. In a society in which time was money, steamships were important because, for the first time, ocean-going vessels could meet schedules as precisely and as predictably as railroads could. Just as the imperial Romans had used their network of roads to link far-flung territories to the capital, Europeans used sea-lanes to join their colonies to the home country.

Until 1850, Europeans had ventured no farther on the African continent than its coastal areas. The installation of coal-burning boilers on smaller boats permitted navigation of previously uncharted and unnavigable rivers. Steam power made exploration and migration possible and greatly contributed to knowledge of terrain, natural wealth, and resources. Smaller steam-powered vessels also increased European inland trade with China, Burma, and India.

While technology improved European mobility on water, it also literally moved the land. Harbors were deepened to accommodate the new iron- and then steel-hulled ships. One of the greatest engineering feats of the century was the construction of a hundred-mile-long canal across the Isthmus of Suez in Egypt. The Suez Canal, completed in 1869, joined the Mediterranean and Red seas and created a new, safer trade route to the East. No longer did trading vessels have to make the long voyage around Africa's Cape of Good Hope. The Suez Canal was built by the French under the supervision of Ferdinand de Lesseps (1805–94), a diplomat with no technical or financial background who was able to promote construction because of concessions he received from Said Pasha, the viceroy of Egypt. The canal could accommodate ships of all sizes. Great Britain purchased a controlling interest in the Suez Canal in 1875 to benefit its trade with India.

De Lesseps later oversaw the initial construction of the Panama Canal in the Western Hemisphere. The combination of French mismanagement, bankruptcy, and the high incidence of disease among work crews enabled the United States to acquire rights to the Pana-

The Suez Canal was opened with appropriate ceremony in 1869 by the Egyptian ruler Said Pasha. He sold his canal shares to Great Britain in 1875.

ma project and complete the canal by 1914. Fifty-one miles long, the Panama Canal connected the world's two largest bodies of water, the Atlantic and Pacific oceans, across the Isthmus of Panama by a waterway containing a series of locks. Now the passage from the Atlantic Ocean to the Pacific Ocean took less than eight hours—much less time than it took using the various overland routes or voyaging around the tip of South America. Both the Suez and Panama canals were built in pursuit of speed. Shorter distances meant quicker travel, which in turn meant higher profits.

Technology also altered time by increasing the speed with which Westerners communicated with other parts of the world. In 1830, for example, it took about two years for a person sending a letter from Great Britain to India to receive a reply. In 1850, steam-powered mail boats shortened the time required for the same round-trip correspondence to about two or three months. But the real revolution in communication came through electricity. Thousands of miles of copper telegraph wire laced countries together; insulated underwater cables linked continents to each other. By the late nineteenth century, a vast telegraph network connected Europe to every area of the world. In 1870 a telegram from London to Bombay arrived in a matter of hours, instead of months, and a response could be received back in London on the same day. Faster communications extended power and control throughout empires. Europeans could communicate immediately with their distant colonies, dispatching troops, orders, and supplies. This communication network eliminated the problem of overextension that had plagued Roman imperial organization in the third century. For the first time, continents discovered by Europeans five centuries earlier were brought into daily contact with the West.

Technological advances in other areas helped foster European imperialism in the nineteenth century. Advances in medicine permitted European men and women to penetrate disease-ridden swamps and jungles. After 1850, European explorers, traders, missionaries, and adventurers carried quinine pills. Quinine, the bitter-tasting derivative of cinchona-tree bark, was discovered to be an effective treatment for malaria. This treatment got its first important test during the French invasion of Algeria in 1830, and it allowed the French to stay healthy enough to conquer that North African country between 1830 and 1847. David Livingstone (1813–73) and Henry M. Stanley (1841–1904) were just two of the many explorers who crossed vast terrains and explored the waterways of Africa, after malaria—the number one killer of European travelers—had been controlled.

Europeans carried the technologies of destruction as well as survival with them into less-developed areas of the world. New types of firearms produced in the second half of the nineteenth century included breech-loading rifles, repeating rifles, and machine guns. The new weapons gave the advantages of both accurate aim and rapid fire. The spears of African warriors and the primitive weaponry of Chinese rebels were no match

The transatlantic telegraph cable was the first intercontinental communications link of the electric age. This illustration shows the Great Eastern, *the largest ship afloat, which finally succeeded in laying the cable in 1866.*

for sophisticated European arms, which permitted their bearers to lie down while firing and to remain undetected at distances of up to half a mile.

The new technology did not cause the new imperialism. The Western powers used technological advances as a tool for establishing their control of the world. Viewed as a tool, however, the new technology does explain how vast areas of land and millions of people were conquered so rapidly.

Motives for Empire

If technology was not the cause but only a tool, what explains the new imperialism of the late nineteenth century? Were wealthy financiers, searching for high-yielding opportunities for investments, the driving force? Was profit the main motive? Were politicians and heads of state in the game for the prestige and glory that territorial expansion could bring them at home?

There are no easy or simple explanations for the new imperialism. Individuals made their fortunes overseas, and heavy industries like the Krupp firm in Germany prospered with the expansion of state-protected colonies. Yet many colonies were economically worthless. Tunisia and Morocco, acquired for their strategic and political importance, constituted an economic loss for the French, who poured more funds into their administration than they were able to extract. Each imperial power held one or more colonies whose costs outweighed the return. Yet this does not mean that some Europeans were simply irrational in their pursuit

of empire or that they were driven by an atavistic desire to recapture the glories of a precapitalist past and willing to incur financial losses in order to do so.

Economics. The test for economic motivation cannot simply be reduced to a balance sheet of debits and credits because, in the end, an account of state revenues and state expenditures provides only a static picture of the business of empire. Even losses cannot be counted as proof against the profit motive in expansion. In modern capitalism, profits, especially great profits, are often predicated on risks. Portugal and Italy, as smaller nations with limited resources, failed as players in the game in which the great industrial powers called the shots. Prestige through the acquisition of empire was one way of keeping alive in the game. Imperialism was influenced by business interests, market considerations, and the pursuit of individual and national fortunes. Not by accident did the great industrial powers control the scramble and dictate the terms of expansion. Nor was it merely fortuitous that Great Britain, the nation that provided the model for European expansion, dedicated itself to the establishment of a profitable worldwide network of trade and investment. Above all, the search for investment opportunities—whether railroads in China or diamond mines in South Africa—lured Europeans into a world system that challenged capitalist ingenuity and imagination. Acquiring territory was only one means of protecting investments. But there were other benefits associated with the acquisition of territory that cannot be reduced to economic terms, and those too must be considered.

LEOPOLD II OF BELGIUM, SPEECH TO AN INTERNATIONAL CONFERENCE OF GEOGRAPHERS, 12 SEPTEMBER 1876

~

Leopold II reigned as king of the Belgians from 1865 until his death in 1909. Although the ruler of a small European country, he had vast territorial aspirations in Africa. As the personal ruler of the Congo Free State, Leopold amassed an immense fortune until abuses of African workers forced him to hand over his authority of what is now Zaire to the Belgian government. In addressing geographers, Leopold evinced some of the self-serving goals that made him the architect of the scramble for territory.

The matter which brings us together today is one most deserving the attention of the friends of humanity. For bringing civilization to the only part of the earth which it has not yet reached and lightening the darkness in which whole peoples are plunged, is, I venture to say, a crusade worthy of this century of progress, and I am glad to find how favourable public opinion is to the accomplishment of this task. We are swimming with the tide. Many of those who have closely studied Africa have come to realise that it would be in the interest of the object they are all seeking to achieve for them to meet and consult together with a view to regulating the course to be taken, combining their efforts and drawing on all available resources in a way which would avoid duplication of effort. . . . Among the matters which remain to be discussed, the following may be mentioned:

1. Deciding exactly where to acquire bases for the task in hand . . . on the Zanzibar coast and near the mouth of the Congo, either by means of conventions with chiefs or by purchasing or renting sites from individuals.

2. Deciding on the routes to be successively opened up into the interior, and on the medical, scientific and peace-keeping stations which are to be set up with a view to abolishing slavery, and bringing about good relations between the chiefs by providing them with fair-minded, impartial persons to settle their disputes, and so forth.

3. Setting up—once the task to be done has been clearly defined—a central, international committee with national committees, each to carry out this task in the aspects of it which concern them, to explain the object to the public of all countries, and to appeal to the feeling of charity to which no worthy cause has ever appealed in vain.

These are some of the points which seem worthy of your attention. . . . My wish is to serve the great cause for which you have already done so much, in whatever manner you may suggest to me. It is with this object that I put myself at your disposal, and I extend a cordial welcome to you.

Geopolitics. Geopolitics, or the politics of geography, is based on the recognition that certain areas of the world are valuable for political reasons. The term, first used at the end of the nineteenth century, described a process well under way in international relations. Statesmen influenced by geopolitical concerns recognized the strategic value of land. Some territory was considered important because of its proximity to acquired colonies or to territory targeted for takeover. France, for example, occupied thousands of square miles of the Sahara Desert to protect its interests in Algeria.

Other territory was important because of its proximity to sea routes. Egypt had significance for Great Britain not because of its inherent economic potential but because it permitted the British to protect access to

lucrative markets in India through the Suez Canal. Beginning in 1875, the British purchased shares in the canal. By 1879 Egypt was under the informal dual rule of France and Great Britain. The British used the deterioration of internal Egyptian politics to justify their occupation of the country in 1882. Protected access to India also accounted for Great Britain's maintenance of Mediterranean outposts, its acquisition of territory on the east coast of Africa, and its occupation of territory in southern Asia.

A third geopolitical motive for annexation was the necessity of fueling bases throughout the world. Faster and more reliable than wind-powered vessels, coal-powered ships were nonetheless dependent on guaranteed fueling bases in friendly ports of call. Islands in the South Pacific and the Indian Ocean were acquired primarily to serve as coaling stations for the great steamers carrying manufactured goods to colonial ports and returning with foodstuffs and raw materials. Ports along the southern rim of Asia served the same purpose. The need for protection of colonies, fueling ports, and sea-lanes led to the creation of naval bases like those on the Red Sea at Djibouti by the French, along the South China Sea at Singapore by the British, and in the Pacific Ocean at Honolulu by the Americans.

In turn, the acquisition of territories justified the increase in naval budgets and the size of fleets. Britain still had the world's largest navy, but by the beginning of the twentieth century, the United States and Germany had entered the competition for dominance of sea-lanes. Japan joined the contest by expanding its navy as a vehicle for its own claims to empire in the Pacific.

The politics of geography was land- as well as sea-based. As navies grew to protect sea-lanes, armies expanded to police new lands. Between 1890 and 1914, military expenditures of Western governments grew phenomenally, with war machines doubling in size. In both its impact on domestic budgets and its protection of markets and trading routes, geopolitics had a strong economic component. Governments became consumers of heavy industry; their predictable participation in markets for armaments and military supplies helped control fluctuations in the business cycle and reduce unemployment at home. A side effect of the growing importance of geopolitics was the increased influence of military and naval leaders in foreign and domestic policy-making.

Nationalism. Many European statesmen in the last quarter of the nineteenth century gave stirring speeches about the importance of empire as a means of enhancing national prestige. In his Crystal Palace speech of 1872, Benjamin Disraeli, British prime minister in 1868 and 1874–80, put the challenge boldly to the British:

> I appeal to the sublime instinct of an ancient people. . . . The issue is not a mean one. It is whether you will be content to be a comfortable England, modelled and moulded upon Continental principles and meeting in due course an inevitable fate, or whether you will be a great country, an imperial country, a country where your sons, when they rise, rise to paramount positions and obtain not merely the esteem of their countrymen but command the respect of the world.

National prestige was not an absolute value but one weighed relatively. Possessing an empire may have meant "keeping up with the Joneses," as it did for smaller countries like Italy. Imperial status was important to a country like Portugal, which was willing to go bankrupt to maintain its territories. But prestige without economic power was the form of imperialism without its substance. Nation-states could, through the acquisition of overseas territories, gain bargaining chips to be played at the international conference table. In this way, smaller nations hoped to be taken seriously in the system of alliances that preserved "the balance of power" in Europe.

Western newspapers deliberately fostered the desire for the advancement of national interests. Newspapers competed for readers, and their circulation often depended on the passions they aroused. Filled with tales calculated to titillate and entertain, and with advertisements promising miracle cures, newspapers wrested foreign policy from the realm of the specialist and transformed politics into another form of entertainment. The drama and vocabulary of sporting events, whose mass appeal as a leisure activity also dates from this era, were now applied to imperialist politics. Whether it was a rugby match or a territorial conquest, readers backed the "home" team, disdained the opposition, and competed for the thrill of victory. This marked quite a change for urban dwellers whose grandparents worked the land and did not look beyond the horizon of their home villages. Newspapers forged a national consciousness whereby individuals learned to identify with collective causes they often did not fully comprehend. Some observed what was happening with a critical eye, identifying a deep-seated need in modern men and women for excitement in their otherwise dull and dreary lives.

Information conveyed in newspapers shaped opinion, and opinion, in turn, could influence policy. Leaders had to reckon with this new creation of "public opinion." In a typical instance, French newspaper editors promoted feverish public outcry for conquest of the Congo by pointing out the need to revenge British advances in Egypt. "Colonial fever" in France was so high in the summer of 1882 that French policymakers were pressured to pursue claims in the Congo Basin without adequate assessment or reflection. As a result, the French government evicted Belgians and Portuguese from the northern Congo territory and enforced questionable treaty claims rather than risk public censure for appearing weak and irresolute.

Public opinion was certainly influential, but it also could be manipulated. In Germany, the government

JOSEPH CHAMBERLAIN'S SPEECH
TO THE BIRMINGHAM RELIEF ASSOCIATION

Joseph Chamberlain (1836–1914) was an English businessman and statesman and, from 1873 to 1876, the mayor of one of Great Britain's leading industrial cities, Birmingham. He was a national advocate for an expansionist colonial policy as the means of keeping his country strong. On 22 January 1894, with no regard for African people, he spoke before a community group to convince them that British imperialism helped the working class.

Believe me, if in any one of the places [in Africa] to which I have referred any change took place which deprived us of that control and influence of which I have been speaking, the first to suffer would be the working-men of this country. Then, indeed, we should see a distress which would not be temporary, but which would be chronic, and we should find that England was entirely unable to support the enormous population which is now maintained by the aid of her foreign trade. If the working-men of this country understand, as I believe they do—I am one of those who have had good reason through my life to rely upon their intelligence and shrewdness—if they understand their own interests, they will never lend any countenance to the doctrines of those politicians who never lose an opportunity of pouring contempt and abuse upon the brave Englishmen, who, even at this moment, in all parts of the world are carving out new dominions for Britain, and are opening up fresh markets for British commerce, and laying out fresh fields for British labour. [Applause.] If the Little Englanders[1] had their way, not only would they refrain from taking the legitimate opportunities which offer for extending the empire and for securing for us new markets, but I doubt whether they would even take the pains which are necessary to preserve the great heritage which has come down to us from our ancestors. [Applause.]

When you are told that the British pioneers of civilisation in Africa are filibusters,[2] and when you are asked to call them back, and to leave this great continent to the barbarism and superstition in which it has been steeped for centuries, or to hand over to foreign countries the duty which you are unwilling to undertake, I ask you to consider what would have happened if 100 or 150 years ago your ancestors had taken similar views of their responsibility? Where would be the empire on which now your livelihood depends? We should have been the United Kingdom of Great Britain and Ireland; but those vast dependencies, those hundreds of millions with whom we keep up a mutually beneficial relationship and commerce would have been the subjects of other nations, who would not have been slow to profit by our neglect of our opportunities and obligations. [Applause.]

[1.] Britain's anti-imperialists.
[2.] A person engaged in a private military action against a foreign government.

From Joseph Chamberlain, M.P., *Foreign and Colonial Speeches* (1897).

often promoted colonial hysteria through the press in order to advance its own political ends. Chancellor Otto von Bismarck used his power over the press to support imperialism and to influence electoral outcomes in 1884. His successors were deft at promoting the "bread and circuses" atmosphere that surrounded colonial expansion in order to direct attention away from social problems at home and to maintain domestic stability.

The printed word was also manipulated in Britain, critics asserted, by business interests during the Boer War (1899–1902) to keep public enthusiasm for the war effort high. J. A. Hobson (1858–1940), a journalist and theorist of imperialism, denounced the "abuse of the press" in his hard-hitting *Psychology of Jingoism* (1901), which appeared while the war was still being waged. Hobson recognized jingoism as the appropriate term for the "inverted patriotism whereby the love of one's own nation is transformed into hatred of another nation, and into the fierce craving to destroy the individual members of that other nation."

Certainly jingoism was not a new phenomenon in 1900, nor was it confined to Britain. Throughout Europe a mass public appeared increasingly willing to support conflict to defend national honor. Xenophobia (hatred of foreigners) melded with nationalism, both nurtured by the mass press, to put new pressures on the determination of foreign policy. Government elites, who formerly had operated behind closed doors far removed from public scrutiny, were now accountable in new ways to faceless masses. Even in autocratic states like Austria-Hungary, the opinion of the masses was a powerful political force that could destroy individual careers and dissolve governments.

Every nation in Europe had its jingoes, those willing to risk war for national glory. Significantly, the term *jingo* was coined in 1878 during a British showdown with the Russians over Turkey. The sentiment that "the Russians shall not have Constantinople" was so strong that the acceptability of war was set to music:

> *We don't want to fight,*
> *But, by Jingo, if we do,*
> *We've got the men,*
> *We've got the ships,*
> *We've got the money too.*

This was the most popular music-hall song in Britain that year, and long after the crisis had faded the tune and its lyrics lingered.

To varying degrees, all of these factors—economics, geopolitics, and nationalism—motivated the actions of the three great imperialist powers—Britain, France, and Germany—and their less-powerful European neighbors. The same reasons account for the global aspirations of non-European nations like the United States and Japan. Each of the powers was aware of what the others were doing and tailored its actions accordingly. Imperialism followed a variety of patterns but always had a built-in component of emulation and acceleration. It was both a cause and a proof of a world system of states in which the actions of one nation affected the others.

The European Search for Territory and Markets

Most western Europeans who read about the distant regions that their armies and statesmen were bringing under their national flags tended to regard these new territories as no more than entries on a great tally sheet or as colors on a map. The daily press recorded the numbers of square miles gained and the captive populations taken, and for readers that was often the end of the story. Few Europeans looked on imperialism as a relationship of power between two parties and, like all relationships, one influenced by both partners. Fewer still understood or appreciated the distinctive qualities of the conquered peoples.

The areas European imperialism affected varied widely in their political organization. Throughout Africa, states were generally small or even nonexistent, and Europeans considered their governmental institutions too ineffectual to produce the economic changes and growth of trade Europe wanted. Military takeover and direct rule by European officials seemed the only feasible way to establish empire there. In Asia, on the other hand, societies such as China and India were territorially large and possessed efficient institutions of government dominated by established political hierarchies. Although they were more difficult to conquer, their leaders were also more likely to cooperate with the imperial powers because their own interests were often similar to those of the Westerners. For these reasons, European empire builders pursued a variety of models: formal military empires (as in Africa), informal empires (as in China), or formal but indirect rule over hierarchical societies (as in India).

The Scramble for Africa: Diplomacy and Conflict

In the mid-1860s, a committee of the British Parliament recommended that Britain withdraw from the scattering of small colonies it possessed in West Africa, arguing that they were costly anachronisms in an era of free trade. In 1898 the president of France, when commenting on French policies of the previous twenty

British General Horatio H. Kitchener (1850–1916) reviewing the troops. Kitchener, who served in colonial theaters from India to Africa, personified nineteenth-century British imperial expansion.

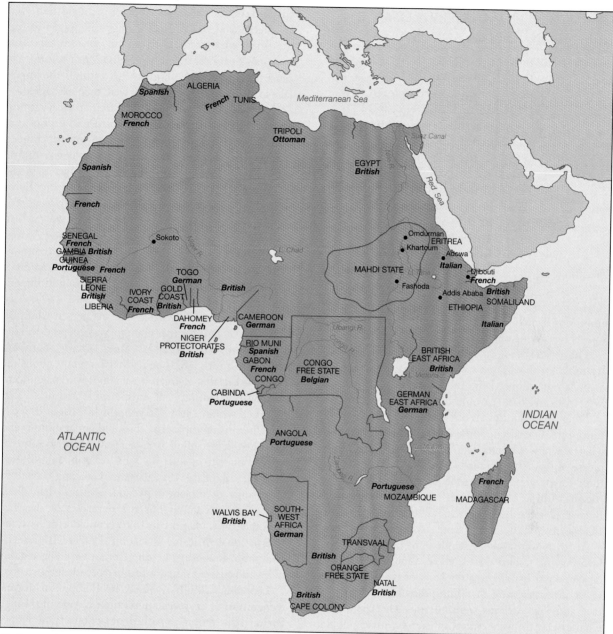

Beginning the Partition of Africa

years, remarked, "We have behaved like madmen in Africa, having been led astray by irresponsible people called the 'colonialists.'" The "mad" event that had altered the political landscape in Africa was the so-called "scramble for Africa" that is usually considered as extending from around 1875 to around 1912. By its end, virtually all Africa was under European control.

Africa is a large and complex continent, and the reasons which Europeans pursued specific pieces of African territory were similarly complex. The explanations for the acquisition of a particular colony, therefore, depend largely on the historical context of that particular case. In certain areas, such as the West African desert zones of the Sudan and the Sahara,

THE NEW IMPERIALISM IN AFRICA AND ASIA

1837–1844	**Great Trek**
1839–1842	**Opium War**
1869	**Suez Canal completed**
1884	**Berlin Conference held to regulate imperialism in Africa**
1886	**Gold discovered in the Transvaal Republic**
1894–1895	**Sino-Japanese War**
1896	**Battle of Adowa**
1899–1902	**Boer War**
1900	**Boxer Rebellion**
1904–1905	**Russo-Japanese War**

ambitious French military men sought to advance their careers by carving out grand colonies.

The existence of valuable minerals motivated the scramble for the area now called Zimbabwe, the Zambian-Zairian copper belt, and other areas. Along the West African coast, chronic disputes between traders working in a souring economy seemed to demand European annexation. Some colonies, such as those in what are now Uganda and Malawi, were created to please missionaries already working there. Britain took Egypt and France took Djibouti for strategic reasons. And in Mozambique, Tanzania, Namibia, and Botswana, some Europeans seized areas to keep other Europeans from doing the same.

Yet there were also basic underlying historical factors favoring the scramble as a whole. One was the rapid development in Europe after 1870 of pseudoscientific racist ideas asserting that Europeans were a superior race and that Africans were inferior. The writings of Charles Darwin were critical in gaining broad popular acceptance for the concept of a racial hierarchy governed by natural laws and operating within an evolutionist dynamic. This was not merely because Darwin's *Origin of Species* (1859) and *The Descent of Man* (1871) "scientifically" legitimated the concept of evolution, but also because he himself explicitly suggested its applicability to humanity. His suggestion was quickly taken up by intellectuals such as Herbert Spencer (1820–1903) and subsequently popularized as social Darwinism. According to this notion, the various racial groups not only occupied distinct positions in a staged sequence of "development" over time, with whites the most advanced and blacks the least so, but were also

engaged in a natural conflict or struggle with one another. Social Darwinism's strongest message was that the fittest were destined to prevail, an idea especially welcome to racists of the later nineteenth century because it could be used to justify as "natural" the imperial expansion upon which they were then embarked.

A second underlying historical factor was the atmosphere created by an economic downturn in Europe that lasted from 1873 until 1896. This downturn, coupled with Germany's rapid rise to economic power during the second phase of the Industrial Revolution in the 1870s and 1880s, was deeply unsettling to many Europeans. Protectionist policies springing from new economic anxieties eroded the earlier European faith in free trade. Many Europeans favored acquiring African territory just in case it should turn out to be economically useful. Even Britain, long the major champion of free trade, became ever more protectionist and imperialistic as the century neared its end.

Historians generally agree that the person who provided the catalyst for the scramble was Leopold II, king of Belgium (1835–1909). Sheer greed motivated Leopold. In early 1876 he had read a report about the Congo Basin that claimed it was "mostly a magnificent and healthy country of unspeakable richness" that promised within "30 to 16 months [to] begin to repay any enterprising capitalist." Leopold, an ambitious and frustrated king ruling over a small country, went to work at once to acquire the Congo Basin, an area one-third the size of the United States. Cloaking himself in the mantle of philanthropy and asserting that all he desired was to stamp out the remnants of the East African slave trade, in late 1876 Leopold organized the International African Association. Leopold II's association soon established trading stations on the region's rivers and coerced much valuable ivory from the people.

Leopold skillfully lobbied in Europe for formal recognition of his association's right to rule the Congo Basin. This action provoked objections from France and Portugal, and, after much diplomatic wrangling, an international conference was finally held in Berlin in late 1884 to decide who should rule the Congo. The Berlin Conference was important, not only because it yielded the Congo Basin to Leopold as the Congo Free State, but also because it laid down the ground rules for all other colonial acquisitions in Africa. For international recognition of a claim, "effective occupation" would be required. This meant that no longer would planting a flag in an area be considered adequate for establishing sovereignty; instead, a real presence calculated to produce "economic development" would be needed. If Leopold's actions began the scramble by panicking the European states, the Berlin Conference organized it. However, it is clear in retrospect that the scramble would have occurred even without Leopold II's greedy intervention.

In their disputes over apportioning Africa, the Europeans were remarkably pacific. Although Britain threatened Portugal with war in 1890 in a conflict over the area around Lake Malawi, and although it appeared for a while that Britain and France were headed toward armed conflict in 1898 at Fashoda, in a dispute over the Nile headwaters, peaceful diplomatic settlements that satisfied the imperial powers were always worked out. Deals where states traded territory were common, and peace was maintained. Africa was not worth a war to Europeans. Yet in every instance of expansion in Africa, Europeans were ready to shoot Africans. With Hiram Maxim's invention in 1884 of a machine gun that could fire eleven bullets per second, and with the sale of modern weapons to Africans banned by the Brussels Convention of 1890, the military advantage passed overwhelmingly to the imperialists. As the British poet Hillaire Belloc tellingly observed,

Whatever happens, we have got
The Maxim gun, and they have not.

The conquest of "them" became more like hunting than warfare. In 1893, for example, in Zimbabwe, 50 Europeans, using only six machine guns, killed 3000 Ndebele people in under two hours. In 1897, in northern Nigeria, a force of 32 Europeans and 500 African mercenaries defeated the 31,000-man army of the emir of Sokoto. The nature of such warfare is well summed up in a report by Winston Churchill about the battle at Omdurman, in the Sudan, in 1898:

> The [British] infantry fired steadily and stolidly, without hurry or excitement, for the enemy were far away and the officers careful. Besides the soldiers were interested in the work and took great pains. . . . And all the time out on the plain on the other side bullets were shearing through flesh, smashing and splintering bone: blood spouted from terrible wounds; valiant men were struggling on through a hell of whistling metal, exploding shells, and spurting dust—suffering, despairing, and dying.

After five hours of fighting, the number killed were 20 Britons, 20 Egyptian allies, and over 11,000 Sudanese. Technology had made bravery and courage obsolete for the majority of Africans.

The sole exception to the general rule of easy conquest was Ethiopia. The history of this country illustrates the overriding importance of guns in understanding the essential dynamic of the scramble. In the

The explorer Henry M. Stanley experiments with the Maxim gun, a rapid-fire machine gun, in the field in Africa.

middle of the nineteenth century, the emperor of Ethiopia possessed little more than a grand title. The empire had broken down into its ethnic and regional components, each of which was fueled by its own "big men," local rulers with little regard for the emperor. Yet the dream of a united empire was alive and pursued by the emperors of the time, Amharic-speaking "big men" with their political base on the fertile plateau that constituted the heartland of the country. In their campaigns to rebuild the empire, they relied increasingly on modern weapons imported from Europe. Their work went forward with some success.

By the early 1870s, however, the emperor realized that his accomplishments in re-creating the Ethiopian empire were endangered by the resistance of the people whom he was then trying to force into his empire and, more ominously, by interference from the outside world, especially Egypt to the north and the Sudan to the west. An expansionary Egypt actually invaded Ethiopian territory, and it was only the Egyptian government's bankruptcy in 1876 that gave the emperor breathing room. The opening of the Suez Canal in 1869 had made the Red Sea and its surroundings attractive not only to Egypt, but also to European countries eager to ensure their trade routes to Asia. By the end of the 1870s, when the scramble for Africa was getting seriously under way, Britain, France, and Italy were all contemplating acquiring land in the region. Soon thereafter, Britain occupied Egypt (1882), France took Djibouti (1884), and Italy seized Eritrea (1885).

The Ethiopian emperor, Menelik II (1889–1913), realized that he could exploit rival European interests in the area by playing off one European power against the others to obtain the weapons he needed for expanding his empire's boundaries. Thus he gave certain concessions to France in return for French weapons. Italy, upset by the growing French influence in Ethiopia, offered weapons as well, and Menelik accepted them. Russia and Britain joined in. More and more modern weapons flowed into Ethiopia during the 1870s and 1880s and into the early 1890s, and Menelik steadily strengthened his military position, both to stop internal unrest and to block encroachment from without. Because each European power feared its rivals' influence in Ethiopia, each sold arms to Menelik, and Ethiopia remained largely unaffected by the scramble going on around it.

In the early 1890s, Menelik's stratagems began to unravel. In 1889 he had signed the Treaty of Wichale with Italy, granting it certain concessions in return for more arms shipments. Italy then claimed that Ethiopia had become an Italian protectorate and moved against Menelik when he objected. By 1896 Italy was ready for a major assault on the Ethiopian army. The Italians were heady with confident racism, believing that their forces could defeat the "primitive" Ethiopians with ease. However, General Oreste Baratieri (1841–1901), the commander of the 18,000-man Italian army in Eritrea, was wisely cautious. He understood that modern weapons functioned the same, whether they were fired by Africans or by Italians. Baratieri knew that Menelik's army of some 100,000 troops had very long supply lines, and his strategy was to wait until Menelik could no longer supply his troops with food. Then, he assumed, the soldiers would simply disappear and the Italians would walk in. But the prime minister of Italy, Francesco Crispi (1819–1901), wanted a quick, glorious victory to enhance his political reputation. Crispi ordered Baratieri to send his army of 18,000 men into battle at once. Hopelessly outnumbered, the Italians lost over 8,000 at the decisive battle of Adowa on 1 March 1896. With its army destroyed and its artillery lost to the Ethiopians, Italy had no choice but to sue for peace.

Italy's acceptance of Ethiopia as a sovereign state with greatly expanded imperial boundaries was soon ratified by France and Britain. As a consequence of its victory at Adowa—and attesting to the crucial importance of modern weaponry for survival in late-nineteenth-century Africa—Ethiopia was the only African country aside from the United States' quasi-colony of Liberia not to be occupied in the scramble for Africa. After 1896 Menelik, with his access to modern weapons assured by his country's international recognition, continued his campaign to extend his control forcefully over the Ethiopian empire's subordinate peoples.

Gold, Empire-Building, and the Boer War

Europeans fought white African settlers as well as black Africans during the scramble, as they seized their lands and resources. In South Africa, for example, the British engaged in a long war over access to the world's largest supply of gold with a group of "Afrikaners"—white settlers who had emigrated, mostly from the Netherlands, and settled in South Africa during the eighteenth and early nineteenth centuries.

After the Great Trek (1837–44), in which a large number of Afrikaners had withdrawn from the British-controlled Colony of the Cape of Good Hope (or Cape

THE RHODES COLOSSUS

This cartoon shows Cecil Rhodes astride the continent of Africa like a colossus, fulfilling his dream of a British Africa from the Cape to Cairo.

Colony), the British had grudgingly recognized the independence of the Orange Free State and the Transvaal—the Afrikaner republics in the interior—in a series of formal agreements. The British complacently believed that the Afrikaners, economically weak and geographically isolated, could never challenge British preeminence in the region. Two events of the mid-1880s shattered British complacency. First, in 1884, Germany—Britain's greatest rival—inserted itself into the region by annexing Namibia as a colony as part of its imperial adventures. The British, aware that the Germans and the Afrikaners were as sympathetic to one another as both were hostile to them, worried about the German threat to their regional hegemony and economic prospects.

British fear of the Germans redoubled in 1886 when, in the Witwatersrand area of the Transvaal Republic, huge deposits of gold were discovered. A group of rich British diamond-mine owners moved in quickly to develop the gold mines in the Witwatersrand area, for the gold lay deep in the ground and could be mined only with a large capital investment, which the Afrikaners lacked. The best known of the British investors was Cecil Rhodes (1853–1902), a politician and financier intent upon expanding his wealth through an expansion of British power. Rhodes and his colleagues quickly recognized that Afrikaner governmental policies on agriculture, tariffs, and labor control were major impediments to profitable gold production. Therefore, in 1895, with the connivance of members of the British government, they organized an attempt to overthrow the Afrikaner government. This attempt was led by Dr. L. S. Jameson (1853–1917), Rhodes's lieutenant. It involved the invasion of Transvaal by British South African police and came to be known as the Jameson Raid. It was faultily executed, however, and to Rhodes's utter humiliation, it failed.

The failure of the Jameson raiders prompted the British government to send a new agent, Alfred Milner (1854–1925), to the area. He was an ardent advocate of expanding the British Empire and of keeping German influence in the region to a minimum. Well aware of the importance of gold to Britain's financial position in the world, Milner was determined to push the Afrikaners into uniting with the British in South Africa, either through diplomacy or war. By 1899 war had become inevitable, and in October it broke out. The British confidently expected to win the war by Christmas, but the Afrikaners did not cooperate. Inept British commanders opposed by skillful Afrikaner guerrilla-warfare leaders guaranteed that the so-called Boer War would drag on and on. (See "African Political Heroes and Resistance to the Scramble," pp. 796–797.)

The British eventually sent 350,000 troops to South Africa, but these forces could not decisively defeat the 65,000 Afrikaner fighting men. Casualties were high, not merely from the fighting, but because typhus epidemics broke out in the concentration camps in which the British interred Afrikaner women and children as they pursued their scorched-earth policies. By the war's end in April 1902, 25,000 Afrikaners, 22,000 British imperial troops, and 12,000 Africans had died. Britain had also been widely criticized for having treated white Afrikaners as if they were black Africans.

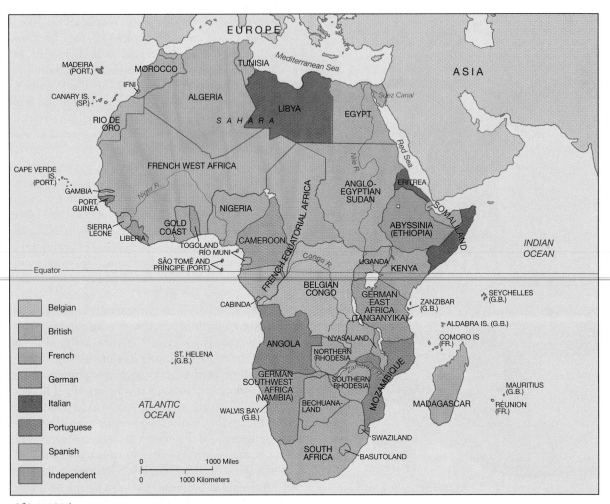

Africa, 1914

In April 1902, the British accepted the conditional surrender of the Afrikaners. The British annexed the Afrikaners to the empire and had the opportunity of making the gold industry efficient. However, they had to promise the Afrikaners that no decisions regarding the political role of the black African majority in a future South Africa would be made before returning political power to the Afrikaners. This crucial concession ensured that segregation would remain the model for race relations in South Africa throughout the twentieth century.

By the time World War I broke out in 1914, the scramble for Africa was over and the map of the continent was colored in imperial inks. France had secured the largest chunk of the continent—some 4 million square miles—but it was mostly desert and tropical forest. Britain had the second-largest empire, but it was richer in minerals and agricultural potential than France's. Germany was the proud possessor of two West African colonies, Togo and Cameroon, as well as Namibia and Tanganyika. Belgium had inherited Leopold II's Congo in 1908. Portugal had finally consolidated its feeble hold on Angola, Mozambique, and Portuguese Guinea. Italy and Spain held unimportant bits of coastal territory. Only Ethiopia and Liberia were politically independent. Now that the colonial powers had conquered Africa, they had to face the issue of how their new colonies could be made to pay off. Now that Africa had been conquered, Africans had to face the issue of how they might regain their political independence.

Imperialism in Asia

The British Parliament proclaimed that on New Year's Day, 1877, Queen Victoria (1837–1901) would add the title of Empress of India to her many honors. India, the great jewel in the imperial crown, was a land Victoria had never seen. The queen's new title, not universally popular in Britain and unnoticed by most famine-stricken Indian peasants, in fact changed nothing about the way the British ruled India. Yet it was more than merely a symbolic assertion of dominance over a country long controlled by the British.

India was the starting point of all British expansion, and it stood at the center of British foreign policy. To protect its sea routes to India and to secure its Indian markets, Britain acquired territories and carved out concessions all over the world. Devised by Prime Minister Benjamin Disraeli to flatter an aging monarch, the new title of empress was really a calculated warning to Russia—present on India's northern frontier in Afghanistan—and to France, busily pursuing its own interests in Egypt.

Formal British rule in India began in 1861 with the appointment of a viceroy, assisted by legislative and executive councils. Both of these bodies included some Indian representatives. British rule encountered the four main divisions of the highly stratified Hindu society. At the top were Brahmans—the learned and priestly class—followed by warriors and rulers, then by farmers and merchants, and finally by peasants and laborers. On the outside of Hindu society were the "untouchables"—a fifth division relegated to performing society's most menial tasks. Rather than disrupt this divisive caste system, the British found it to their advantage to maintain the status quo.

Britain's relationship with India originated in the seventeenth century, when the British East India Company—a joint-stock venture free of government control—began limited trading in Indian markets. The need for regulation and protection firmly established British rule by the end of the eighteenth century. Conquest of the Punjab in 1849 brought the last independent areas of India under British control. Throughout this period, Britain invested considerable overseas capital in India, and in turn India absorbed one-fifth of the total of British exports. The market for Indian cotton, for centuries exported to markets in Asia and Europe, collapsed under British tariffs, and India became a ready market for cheap Lancashire cotton. The British also exploited India's agricultural products, salt, and opium.

The Boer War and Queen Victoria. This Dutch caricature is from an album titled "John Bull in Africa," published in 1900. The war aroused much criticism among the British liberal opposition.

At the end of the eighteenth century, the British were trading English wool and Indian cotton for Chinese tea and textiles. But Britain's thirst for Chinese tea grew, while Chinese demand for English and Indian textiles slackened. Britain discovered that Indian opium could be used to balance the trade deficit created by tea. British merchants and local Chinese officials, especially in the entry port of Canton, began to expand their profitable involvement in a contraband trade in opium. The British East India Company held a monopoly over opium cultivation in Bengal. Opium exports to China mounted phenomenally: from 200 chests in 1729 to 40,000 chests in 1838. By the 1830s, opium was probably Britain's most important crop in world markets. The British prospered as opium was pumped into China at rates faster than tea was flowing out. Chinese buyers began paying for the drug with silver.

African Political Heroes and Resistance to the Scramble

Often a country's political heroes are its generals and kings, its presidents and statesmen—men of power and accomplishment. Paintings and photographs of them emphasize grandeur and majesty, reflecting their larger-than-life importance. Two of the political heroes of contemporary Zimbabwe are very different, however. One is a short, aging woman of about sixty whose name was Nehanda. The other is a short middle-aged man of about forty-five called Kagubi. Both appear undistinguished: scruffy, unkempt, and barefoot. Yet both were executed on 27 April 1898 and buried with utmost secrecy. And although they died almost a century ago, their memory is alive in Zimbabwe and students are taught about them in history books. Why?

In 1889 Cecil Rhodes, the South African financier and politician, convinced that large deposits of gold existed in Zimbabwe, persuaded the British government to support his efforts to seize Zimbabwe and Zambia. He established a private chartered company known as the British South Africa Company (BSAC) and in 1890 invaded the eastern part of Zimbabwe. The people who lived there were Shona people, and conquering them seemed easy because they were politically fragmented into myriad little states with neither strong chiefs nor a military tradition. So easy was the conquest, indeed, that the settlers came to view the Shona with utter contempt.

One of the frequently stated purposes of European imperialism during the scramble for Africa was to carry "civilization" to the "primitive" peoples of Africa—to "bear the White Man's burden" so that the people could improve their lives. For the Shona, however, Rhodes's agents displayed little perceptible civilization and much to be lamented. The Shona soon had a mass of grievances against the BSAC. Some of their land had been taken. They were forced to work for the settlers for little or no pay. They were compelled to pay taxes. Europeans took Shona women as concubines. Shona grievances grew steadily. Then, in 1896, their cattle herds were almost wiped out by a new disease, rinderpest, which the Italians who were occupying Eritrea had accidentally imported into Africa in the late 1880s and which was spreading southward. This seemed the last straw.

The Shona got the chance to make their complaints felt. At the end of 1895, most of the BSAC police force had gone over the border into the Transvaal to participate in the Jameson Raid on the Afrikaner state, and in 1896 they were still languishing in jail. With few police around, the Shona reasoned, the time was ripe for revolt against the BSAC. In June, the Shona rose in rebellion, and one hundred settlers were slain before the government knew what was occurring.

The BSAC could not believe that the disorganized Shona for whom they had such contempt were capable of such an uprising. But despite their lack of chiefs or a military tradition, they were. And when the company's officials investigated more closely, they were astounded to discover that the uprising, which came to be known as the *chimurenga,* was being organized and directed by the Shona religious leaders known as mediums. These were people who became possessed by spirits of Shona ancestors and articulated what the ancestors wanted the living to do. These people—obscure and seemingly unthreatening—were able not only to mobilize

the attack on the company, but, because of their very lack of notoriety in British eyes, to sustain it by spying on the company, distributing intelligence regarding company troop movements, and relaying messages across Shona country.

The result of the work of the spirit mediums was that the BSAC was unable to conquer the Shona quickly. The effort against the guerrilla war waged by the Shona took over fifteen months, almost bankrupting the company. Only in October 1897 did the company track down the leader of the rebellion, Kagubi, and his colleagues, including the important Nehanda. By then, however, the uprising had attracted so much negative publicity in Britain that the company was brought under greater control by the British government. Many of the abuses that had provoked the Shona to rebel were forbidden, and greater regularity in administration was instituted. The Shona had demonstrated to the company that there was a point beyond which the British could not go.

Seven decades later, in the 1970s, the African people again rose up, this time against the white government of Ian Smith, political heir to Cecil Rhodes, and this time successfully. They called their rebellion the "second *chimurenga.*" When they finally won, the Africans needed a new group of patriotic heroes from their past about whom to teach in independent Zimbabwe's schools. Two of those chosen were Kagubi and Nehanda, scruffy and unkempt to be sure, but remembered as early patriots and martyrs, the memory of whose work against Rhodes was able to travel across the years and inspire Zimbabweans during the 1970s.

A British gunboat, the Nemesis, *fires on Chinese junks during the Opium War.*
The Nemesis *was one of the first ironclad warships ever built.*

Concerned with the sharp rise in opium addiction, the accompanying social problems, and the massive exporting of silver, the Chinese government reacted. As Chinese officials saw it, they were exchanging their precious metal for British poison. Addicts were threatened with the death penalty. In 1839, the Chinese government destroyed British opium in the port of Canton, touching off the so-called Opium War (1839–42). British expeditionary forces blockaded Chinese ports, besieged Canton, and occupied Shanghai. In protecting the rights of British merchants engaged in illegal trading, Great Britain became the first Western nation to use force to impose its economic interests on China. The Treaty of Nanking (1842) initiated a series of unequal treaties between Europeans and the Chinese and set the pattern for exacting large indemnities.

Between 1842 and 1895, China fought five wars with foreigners and lost all of them. Defeat was expensive, as China had to pay costs to the winners. Before the end of the century, Britain, France, Germany, and

Japan had managed to establish major territorial advantages in their "spheres of influence," sometimes through negotiation and sometimes through force. By 1912, over fifty major Chinese ports had been handed over to foreign control as "treaty ports." British spheres included Shanghai, the lower Yangzi, and Hong Kong. France maintained special interests in South China. Germany controlled the Shandong peninsula. Japan laid claim to the northeast.

Spheres of influence grew in importance at the beginning of the twentieth century, when foreign investors poured capital into railway lines, which needed treaty protection from competing companies. Railways necessarily furthered foreign encroachment and opened up new territories to the claims of foreigners. As one Chinese official explained it, the railroads were like scissors that threatened to cut China into many pieces. As a result, China lost control of its trade and was totally unable to protect its infant industries. Foreigners established no formal empires in China, but the treaty ports certainly were evidence of both informal rule and indisputable foreign dominance.

Treaty ports were centers of foreign residence and trade, where rules of extraterritoriality applied. This meant that foreigners were exempt from Chinese law enforcement and that, though present on Chinese territory, they could be judged only by officials of their own countries. Extraterritoriality, a privilege not just for diplomats but one shared by every foreign national, implied both a distrust of Chinese legal procedures and a cultural arrogance about the superiority of Western institutions. These arrangements stirred Chinese resentment and contributed considerably to growing antiforeign sentiment.

In order to preserve extraterritoriality and maintain informal empires, the Western powers appointed civilian representatives known as consuls. Often merchants themselves and in the beginning unpaid in their posts, consuls acted as the chieftains of resident merchant communities, judges in all civil and criminal cases, and spokesmen for the commercial interests of the home country. They clearly embodied the commercial intentions of Western governments. Initially they stood outside the diplomatic corps; later they were consigned to its lower ranks. Consuls acted as brokers for commerce and interpreted the international commercial law being forged. Consulates spread beyond China as Western nations used consuls to protect their own interests elsewhere. In Africa, consuls represented the trading concerns of European governments and were instrumental in the transition to formal rule.

The rise of Western influence in China coincided with and benefited from Chinese domestic problems, including dynastic decline, famine, and successive rebellions. The European powers were willing to prop up the crumbling structure for their own ends, but the Boxer Rebellion of 1900 made clear to the Western powers their limited ability to control social unrest in China. The Boxers—peasants so named by Westerners because of the martial rites practiced by their secret society, the Harmonious Fists—rose up against the foreign and Christian exploitation in north China. At the beginning of the summer of 1900, the Boxers—with the concealed encouragement of the Chinese government—killed Europeans and seized the foreign legations in Beijing. An international expeditionary force of 16,000 well-armed Japanese, Russian, British, American, German, French, Austrian, and Italian troops entered Beijing in August to defend the treaty interests of their respective countries. Led by a German general,

The claims of the Boxer troops to invulnerability were believed by millions of Chinese. In this Chinese print, the Boxer forces use cannon, bayonets, dynamite, and sabers to drive the Western "barbarians" from the Middle Kingdom.

the international force followed Kaiser Wilhelm II's urging to remember the Huns: "Show no mercy! Take no prisoners!" Systematic plunder and slaughter followed. Beijing was sacked.

Abandoning earlier discussions of partitioning China, the international powers accepted the need for a central Chinese government—even one that had betrayed their interests—that would police a populace plagued by demographic pressures, famine, discrimination against minorities, excessive taxation, exorbitant land rents, and social and economic dislocations created by foreign trade. During the previous year (1899), the United States had asserted its claims in China in the Open Door policy. This policy, formulated by U.S. Secretary of State John Hay, was as much concerned with preserving Chinese sovereignty as it was with establishing equal economic opportunity for foreign competition in Chinese markets. Europeans and Americans wanted to send bankers to China, not gunboats. A stable central government facilitated their aims. By operating within delineated spheres of influence and using established elites to further their own programs, Westerners protected their financial interests without incurring the costs and responsibilities of direct rule.

European nations pursued imperialist endeavors elsewhere in Asia, acquiring territories on China's frontiers and taking over states that had formerly paid tribute to the Chinese empire. The British acquired Hong Kong (1842), Burma (1886), and Kowloon (1898). The Russians took over the Maritime Provinces in 1858. The French made gains in Indochina (Annam and Tonkin) in 1884, and in 1893 extended control over Laos and Cambodia.

The Sino-Japanese War of 1894–95 revealed Japan's intentions to compete as an imperialist power in Asia. The modernized and westernized Japanese army easily defeated the ill-equipped and poorly led Chinese forces. As a result, Japan gained the island of Taiwan. Pressing its ambitions on the continent, Japan locked horns with Russia over claims to the Liaotung peninsu-

la, Korea, and South Manchuria. Following its victory in the Russo-Japanese War of 1904–05, Japan expanded into all of these areas, annexing Korea outright in 1910. The war sent a strong message to the West about the ease with which the small Asian nation had defeated the Russian giant and contributed to the heightening of anti-imperialist sentiments in China.

Results of a European-Dominated World

Europeans fashioned the world in their own image, but in doing so, Western values and Western institutions underwent profound and unintended transformations. Family values were articulated in an imperialist context, and race emerged as a key factor in culture. The discovery of new lands, new cultures, and new peoples

A British family in India poses with their domestic staff in front of their bungalow. An 1878 handbook on upper-class life in India recommended 27 servants per family.

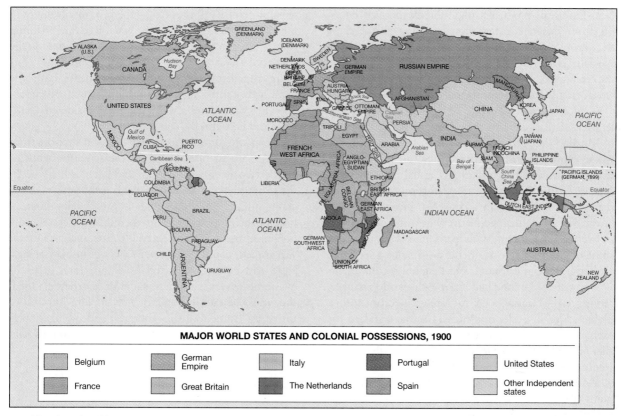

World Colonial Holdings, ca. 1914

altered the ways in which European women and men regarded themselves and viewed their place in the world. With the rise of new contenders for power—the United States and Japan—and growing criticism about the morality of capitalism, the Western world was not as predictable in 1914 as it had appeared to be in 1870.

A World Economy

Imperialism produced an interdependent world economy, with Europe at its center. Industrial and commercial capitalism linked together the world's continents in a communications and transportation network unimaginable in earlier ages. As a result, foreign trade increased from 3 percent of world output in 1800 to 33 percent by 1913. The greatest growth in trade occurred in the period from 1870 to 1914 as raw materials, manufactured products, capital, and men and women were transported across seas and continents by those seeking profits.

Most trading in the age of imperialism still took place among European nations and North America. But entrepreneurs in search of new markets and new resources saw in Africa and Asia opportunities for protected exploitation. Opportunities were not seized but created in nonindustrialized areas of the world as new markets were shaped to meet the needs of Western producers and consumers. European landlords and managers trained Kenyan farmers to put aside their traditional agricultural methods and grow more "useful" crops like coffee, tea, and sugar. The availability of cheaper British textiles of inferior quality drove Indian weavers away from their handlooms. Chinese silk producers changed centuries-old techniques to produce silk thread and cloth that was suited to the machinery and mass-production requirements of the French.

Non-European producers undoubtedly derived benefits from this new international trading partnership, but those benefits were often scarce. Trade permitted specialization, but at the choice of the colonizer, not the colonized. World production and consumption were being shaped to suit the needs of the West.

Capital in search of profits flowed out of the wealthier areas of Europe into the nonindustrialized regions of Russia, the Balkans, and the Ottoman Empire, where capital-intensive expenditures (on railways, for instance) promised high returns. Capital investment in overseas territories also increased phenomenally as railroads were built to gain access to primary products. Great Britain maintained its overwhelming dominance in overseas investment, with loans abroad greater than those of its five major competitors—France, Germany, Holland, the United States, and Belgium—combined.

The City of London had become the world's banker, serving as the clearinghouse for foreign investment on a global scale. The adoption of gold as the standard for exchange for most European currencies by 1874 further facilitated the operation of a single interdependent trading and investment system. Britain remained the world's biggest trading nation, with half of its exports going to Asia, Africa, and South America and the other half to Europe and the United States. But Germany was Britain's fastest-growing competitor, with twice as many exports to Europe and expanding overseas trade by 1914. The United States had recently joined the league of the world's great trading nations and was running a strong third in shares of total trade.

Foreign investments often took the form of loans to governments or to enterprises guaranteed by governments. Investors might be willing to take risks, but they also expected protection, no less so than merchants and industrialists trading in overseas territories. Together, trade and investment interests exerted considerable pressure on European states for control through acquisition and concessions. The vast amounts of money involved help explain the expectations of state involvement and the reasons why international competition, rivalry, and instability threatened to lead to conflict and war.

Race and Culture

The West's ability to kill and conquer as well as to cure was, as one Victorian social observer argued, proof of its cultural superiority. Every colonizing nation had its spokesmen for the "civilizing mission" to educate and to convert African and Asian "heathens." Cultural superiority was only a short step from arguments for racial superiority. Prompted by the U.S. involvement in the Philippines, the British poet Rudyard Kipling (1865–1936) characterized the responsibilities of the advanced West as "the White Man's burden." The smug and arrogant attitude of his poem about the white man's mission revealed a deep-seated and unacknowledged racism toward peoples considered "half-devil and half-child."

Views of cultural superiority received support from evolutionary theories based on the scientific work of Herbert Spencer (1820–1903) and Charles Darwin. In the 1880s, popularizers applied evolutionary ideas about animal and plant life to the development of human society. Just as animals could be hierarchically organized according to observable differences, so too, it was argued, could the different races of human beings. Race and culture were collapsed into each other. If Westerners were culturally superior, as they claimed, they must be racially superior as well. The "survival of the fittest" came to justify conquest and subjugation as "laws" of human interaction and, by extension, of relations among nations.

Women and Imperialism

Ideas about racial and cultural superiority were not confined to books by pseudoscientists and to discussions among policymakers. Public discussions about marriage, reproduction, motherhood, and child-rearing reflected new concerns about furthering "the imperial race"—the racial identity of white Westerners. Women throughout Western societies were encouraged by reformers, politicians, and doctors to have more children and instructed to take better care of them. "Children are the most valuable of imperial assets," one British doctor instructed his readers. Healthy young men were needed in the colonies, they were told, to defend Western values. State officials paid new attention to infant mortality at the end of the nineteenth century, set up health programs for children, and provided young women with training in home management, nutrition, and child care. These programs were no coincidence in an age of imperialism. Their rhetoric was explicitly imperialist and often racist in urging women to preserve the quality of the white race.

In the poem "White Man's Burden," Kipling advised, "Send forth the best ye breed." All over Europe, newly formed associations and clubs stressed the need for careful mate selection. In Britain, Francis Galton (1822–1911) founded eugenics, the study of genetics for the purpose of improving inherited characteristics of the race. Imperialism, the propagandists proclaimed, depended on mothers—women who would nurture healthy workers, strong soldiers and sailors, and intelligent and capable leaders. High infant mortality and poor health in children were attributed directly to maternal failings and not to environmental factors or poverty. Kaiser Wilhelm II stressed that German women's attention to the "three Ks"—*Kinder, Küche, Kirche* (children, kitchen, church)—would guarantee a race of Germans who would rule the world. British generals and French statesmen publicly applied similar sentiments to their own countries and stressed that the future depended on the devotion of women to their family obligations.

Some European women participated directly in the colonizing experience. As missionaries and nurses, they supported the civilizing mission. As wives of officials and managers, they were expected to embody the gentility and values of Western culture. Most men who traded and served overseas did so unaccompanied by women. But when women were present in any numbers, as they were in India before 1914, they were expected to preserve the exclusivity of Western communities and to maintain class and status differentiations as a proof of cultural superiority.

Ecology and Imperialism

Ecology—the relationship and adjustment of human groups to their environment—was affected by imperial expansion, which dislocated the societies that it touched. Early explorers had disrupted little as they arrived, observed, and then moved on. The missionaries, merchants, soldiers, and businessmen who came later required that those with whom they came into contact must change their thought and behavior. In some cases, dislocation resulted in material improvements, better medical care, and the introduction of modern technology. For the most part, however, the initial ecological impact of the imperialist was negative. Western men and women carried diseases to people who did not share the Westerners' immunity. Traditional village life was destroyed in rural India, and African tribal societies disintegrated under the European onslaught. Resistance existed everywhere, but only the Ethiopians, with their defeat of the Italians at Adowa in 1896, managed to have any success in keeping out foreigners.

Education of native populations had as its primary goal the improvement of administration and productivity in the colonies. When foreigners ruled indirectly through existing indigenous hierarchies, they often created corrupt and tyrannical bureaucracies that exploited natives. The indirect rule of the British in India was based on a pragmatic desire to keep British costs low.

When Asian and African laborers started producing for the Western market, they became dependent on its fluctuations. Victimized for centuries by the vagaries of weather, they now had to contend with the instability and cutthroat competition of cash crops in world markets. Individuals migrated from place to place in the countryside and from the countryside to newly formed cities. The fabric of tribal life unraveled. Such migrations necessarily affected family life, with individuals marrying later because they lacked the resources to set up households. The situation paralleled similar disruptions in English society at the beginning of the Industrial Revolution. Women as well as men migrated to find jobs. Many women, cut free of their tribes (as was the case in Nairobi), turned to prostitution—literally for pennies—as a means of survival.

In an extreme example of the colonizers' disdain for the colonized, some European countries used their overseas territories as dumping grounds for hardened and incorrigible convicted criminals. Imitating the earlier example of the British in Australia, the French developed Guiana and New Caledonia as prison colonies in the hope that they could solve their social problems at home by exporting them.

The United States provided another variation on imperial expansion. Its westward drive across the North American continent, beginning at the end of the eighteenth century, established the United States as an imperial power in the Western Hemisphere. By 1848, the relatively young American nation stretched over three thousand miles from one ocean to the other. It had met the opposition and resistance of the Native Americans with armed force, decimated them, and "concentrated" the survivors in assigned territories, and later on reservations.

At the end of the nineteenth century, the United States, possessing both the people and the resources for rapid industrial development, turned to the Caribbean and the Pacific islands in pursuit of markets and investment opportunities. By acquiring stepping stones of islands across the Pacific Ocean in the Hawaiian Islands and Samoa, it secured fueling bases and access to lucrative east Asian ports. And by intervening repeatedly in Central America and building the Panama Canal, the United States had established its

KARL PEARSON

The following is an excerpt from a lecture titled "National Life from the Standpoint of Science," given by a British professor of mathematics, Karl Pearson (1857–1936), in 1900. Pearson held the first chair in eugenics at the University of London, where he applied statistical methods to the study of heredity and evolution. The term eugenics *was introduced by Francis Galton, of whom Pearson was a follower. Pearson was heavily influenced by the pseudoscientific assumptions of social Darwinism and combined prejudices about race and nationalism to justify British imperialism as a proof of "survival of the fittest."*

The . . . great function of science in national life . . . is to show us what national life means, and how the nation is a vast organism subject as much to the great forces of evolution as any other gregarious type of life. There is a struggle of race against race and of nation against nation. In the early days of that struggle it was a blind, unconscious struggle of barbaric tribes. At the present day, in the case of the civilized white man, it has become more and more the conscious, carefully directed attempt of the nation to fit itself to a continuously changing environment. The nation has to foresee how and where the struggle will be carried on; the maintenance of national position is becoming more and more a conscious preparation for changing conditions, an insight into the needs of coming environments. . . .

If a nation is to maintain its position in this struggle, it must be fully provided with trained brains in every department of national activity, from the government to the factory, and have, if possible, a *reserve of brain and physique* to fall back upon in times of national crisis. . . .

You will see that my view—and I think it may be called the scientific view of a nation—is that of an organized whole, kept up to a high pitch of internal efficiency by insuring that its numbers are substantially recruited from the better stocks, and kept up to a high pitch of external efficiency by contest, chiefly by way of war with inferior races, and with equal races by the struggle for trade-routes and for the sources of raw material and of food supply. This is the natural history view of mankind, and I do not think you can in its main features subvert it. . . .

Is it not a fact that the daily bread of our millions of workers depends on their having somebody to work for? that if we give up the contest for trade-routes and for free markets and for waste lands, we indirectly give up our food supply? Is it not a fact that our strength depends on these and upon our colonies, and that our colonies have been won by the ejection of inferior races, and are maintained against equal races only by respect for the present power of our empire? . . .

We find that the law of the survival of the fitter is true of mankind, but that the struggle is that of the gregarious animal. A community not knit together by strong social instincts, by sympathy between man and man, and class and class, cannot face the external contest, the competition with other nations, by peace or by war, for the raw material of production and for its food supply. This struggle of tribe with tribe, and nation with nation, may have its mournful side; but we see as a result of it the gradual progress of mankind to higher intellectual and physical efficiency. It is idle to condemn it; we can only see that it exists and recognise what we have gained by it—civilization and social sympathy. But while the statesman has to watch this external struggle, . . . he must be very cautious that the nation is not silently rotting at its core. He must insure that the fertility of the inferior stocks is checked, and that of the superior stocks encouraged; he must regard with suspicion anything that tempts the physically and mentally fitter men and women to remain childless.

From Karl Pearson, *National Life from the Standpoint of Science* (1905).

hegemony in the Caribbean by 1914. Growing in economic power and hegemonic influence, both Japan and the United States had joined the club of imperial powers and were making serious claims against European expansion.

Critiquing Capitalism

Not least significant of the consequences of imperialism was the critique of capitalism it produced. Those who condemned capitalism as exploitative and racist saw imperialism as an expression of problems inherent in it. In 1902 J. A. Hobson (1858–1940) published *Imperialism, A Study,* a work that has remained in print ever since. In his book, Hobson argued that underconsumption and surplus capital at home drove Western industrial countries overseas in search of a cure for these economic ills. Rather than solving the problems by raising workers' wages, and thereby increasing their consumption power and creating new opportunities for investment in home markets, manufacturers, entrepreneurs, and industrialists sought higher profits abroad. Hobson considered these business interests "economic parasites," making large fortunes at the expense of national interests.

In the midst of world war, the future leader of the Russian Revolution, Vladimir Ilich Ulyanov (1870–1924)—or to use his revolutionary name, Lenin—added his own critique of capitalism. He did not share Hobson's belief that capitalism was merely malfunctioning in its imperialist endeavors. Instead, Lenin argued in *Imperialism, the Highest Stage of Capitalism* (1916) that capitalism is inherently and inevitably imperialistic. Because he was sure that Western capitalism was in the process of destroying itself, Lenin called World War I the final "imperialist war."

Critics, historians, and economists have since pointed out that these works by Hobson and Lenin are marred by errors and omissions. Yet the works usher in almost a century of debate over the morality and economic feasibility of imperialism. Hobson as a liberal and Lenin as a Marxist highlighted the connections between social problems at home—whether in late Victorian England or in prerevolutionary Russia—and economic exploitation abroad.

Yet if electoral results and the popular press are any indication, Europeans not only accepted but warmly embraced the responsibilities of empire. Criticism of

the backwardness of captive peoples prevailed. Victorian social scientist Walter Bagehot (1826–77) told the story of an aged savage who, upon returning to his tribe, informed them that he had "tried civilization for forty years and it was not worth the trouble." No matter how intelligent the judgment of this African might seem with hindsight, the possibility of returning to areas of the world not influenced by the civilization of the West was rapidly disappearing in the years before World War I.

Conflict at Home: The European Balance of Power

In addition to mounting conflicts in colonized areas, European states were locked in a competition within Europe for dominance and control. The politics of geography combined with rising nationalist movements in southern Europe and the Ottoman Empire to create a mood of increasing confrontation among Europe's great powers. The European balance of power so carefully crafted by Germany's Otto von Bismarck began to disintegrate with his departure from office in 1890. By 1914 a Europe divided into two camps was no longer the sure guarantee of peace that it had been a generation earlier.

The Geopolitics of Europe

The map of Europe had been redrawn in the two decades after 1850. By 1871 Europe consisted of five great powers, known as the Big Five—Britain, France, Germany, Austria-Hungary, and Russia—and a handful of lesser states. The declaration of a German Empire in 1871 and the emergence of Italy, with Rome as its capital, in 1870 unified numerous disparate states. Although not always corresponding to linguistic and cultural differences among Europe's peoples, national boundaries appeared fixed, with no country aspiring to territorial expansion at the expense of its neighbors. But the creation of the two new national units of Germany and Italy had legitimized nationalist aspirations and the militarism necessary to enforce them.

Under the chancellorship of Otto von Bismarck, Germany led the way in forging a new alliance system

THE SOCIETY FOR NATIONAL DEFENSE, SERBIA, 1911

The Society for National Defense (Narodna Odbrana) was a secret society formed by Serb national-ists. This group sought the liberation of Slavs through propaganda and subversive activities against Austria-Hungary, which had annexed Bosnia-Herzegovina in 1908. The Society for National Defense was a terrorist group, one of whose members was responsible for the assassination of the Austrian Archduke Ferdinand on 28 June 1914. Here the group spells out its program and speaks of a new kind of nationalism, one that is a "holy cause."

The Serbian people has endured during its existence many difficult and bitter days. Among these days is September 24, 1908, when Austria-Hungary illegally annexed Bosnia and Herzegovina. This day can be compared to the worst days of our past. It was especially painful for the Serbian people in that it came at a time when more fortunate peoples had already completed their national unification and had created large states, and when culture and freedom were presumed to be at their peak.

At such a time Austria-Hungary oppressed along with other peoples several million Serbs, whom she penalizes and seeks to alienate from us. They may not openly call themselves Serbs, and may not adorn their homes with the Serbian flag; they may not trade freely, cultivate their soil, erect Serbian schools, openly celebrate the feast of the patron saint [Slava], and may not sing of Kossowo or of Prince Marko and Milosch Obilitsch. Only such a state, only an Austria-Hungary, could carry through such an annexation. . . .

Today everywhere a new concept of nationalism has become prevalent. Nationalism (the feeling of nationality) is no longer a historical or poetical feeling, but the true practical expression of life. Among the French, Germans, and English, and among all other civilized peoples, nationalism has grown into something quite new; in it lies the concept of bread, space, air, commerce, competition in everything. Only among us is it still in the old form; that is, it is the fruit of spiritual suffering rather than of reasonable understanding and national advantage. If we speak of freedom and union, we parade far too much the phrases "breaking our chains" and "freeing the slaves"; we call far too much upon our former Serbian glory and think too little of the fact that the freeing of subjected areas and their union with Serbia are neces-sary to our citizens, our merchants, and our peasants on the grounds of the most elementary needs of culture and trade, of food and space. If one were to explain to our sharp-eyed people our national task as one closely connected with the needs of everyday life, our people would take up the work in a greater spirit of sacrifice than is today the case. We must tell our people that the freedom of Bosnia is necessary, not just because of their feeling of sympathy with their brothers who suffer there, but also because of commerce and its connection with the sea; national union is necessary because of the stronger development of a common culture. The Italians welcome the conquest of Tripoli not just because of the glory to be won by the success of their arms, but especially because of the advantage they hope to gain by annexing Tripoli. Our people must adopt a more realistic attitude toward politics. We must show them how we would stand culturally and economically if we were united into one state and were in as favorable a position commercially as that of Timok in relation to the Adriatic. . . .

Along with the task of explaining to our people the danger threatening us from Austria, the *Narodna Odbrana* has also the other important tasks of explaining to them, while preserving our holy national memories, this new, healthy, fruitful conception of nationalism, and of convincing them to work for national freedom and unity. . . .

All in all, the *Narodna Odbrana* aims through its work to advance upon the enemy on the day of reckoning with a sound, nationally conscious, and internally reconciled Serbian people, a nation of Sokols, rifle clubs, heroes—in fact, the fear and terror of the enemy—reliant front-rank fighters and executors of Serbia's holy cause.

If this succeeds, all will be well for us; woe to us if we fail.

based on the realistic assessment of power politics within Europe. In 1873 Bismarck joined together the three most conservative powers of the Big Five—Germany, Austria-Hungary, and Russia—into the Three Emperors' League. Consultation over mutual interests and friendly neutrality were the cornerstones of this alliance. Identifying one's enemies and choosing one's friends in this new configuration of power came in large part to depend on geographic weaknesses. The Three Emperors' League was one example of the geographic imperatives driving diplomacy. Bismarck was determined to banish the specter of a two-front war by isolating France on the Continent.

Each of the Great Powers had a vulnerability, a geographic Achilles' heel. Germany's vulnerability lay in its North Sea ports. German shipping along its only coast could be easily bottlenecked by a powerful naval force. Such an event, the Germans knew, could destroy their rapidly growing international trade. What was worse, powerful land forces could "encircle" Germany. As Britain's century-old factories slowly became obsolete under peeling coats of paint, Germany enjoyed the advantages of a latecomer to industrialization—forced to start from scratch by investing in the most advanced machinery and technology. The German Reich was willing to support industrial expansion, scientific and technological training, and social programs for its workers. Yet as Germany surged forward to seize its share of world markets, it was acutely aware that it was hemmed in on the Continent. Germany could not extend its frontiers the way Russia had to the east. German gains in the Franco-Prussian War in Alsace and Lorraine could not be repeated without risking greater enmity. German leaders saw the threat of encirclement as a second geographic weakness. Bismarck's awareness of these geographic facts of life prompted his engineering of the Three Emperors' League in 1873, two years after the founding of the German Empire.

Austria-Hungary was Europe's second largest nation in land and the third largest in population. The same factors that had made it a great European power—its size and its diversity—now threatened to destroy it. The ramshackle empire of Europe, it had no geographical unity. Its vulnerability came from within, from the centrifugal forces of linguistic and cultural diversity. Weakened by nationalities clamoring for independence and self-rule and by an unresponsive political system, Austria-Hungary remained backward agriculturally and unable to respond to the Western industrial challenge. It seemed most likely to collapse from social and political pressures.

Another feature must be added to the picture of Europe in the late nineteenth century. To the southeast lay the Ottoman Empire, a great decaying conglomeration that bridged Europe and Asia. Politically feeble and on the verge of bankruptcy, the Ottoman Empire, with Turkey at its core, comprised a vast array of ethnically, linguistically, and culturally diverse peoples. In the hundred years before 1914, increasing social unrest and nationalist bids for independence had plagued the Ottoman Empire. As was the case with the Habsburgs in Austria-Hungary, the Ottomans maintained power with increasing difficulty over these myriad ethnic groups struggling to be free. The Ottoman Empire, called "the sick man of Europe" by contemporaries, found two kinds of relations sitting at its bedside: those who would do anything to ensure its survival, no mat-

THE BOILING POINT.

A Punch cartoon shows European leaders trying to keep the lid on the simmering kettle of Balkan crises.

ter how weak; and those who longed for and sought to hasten its demise. Fortunately for the Ottoman Empire, its enemies were willing to preserve it in its weakened state rather than see one of the other rival European powers benefit from its collapse.

The Ottomans had already seen parts of their holdings lopped off in the nineteenth century. Britain, ever conscious of its interests in India, had acquired Cyprus, Egypt, Aden, and Sudan from the Ottomans. Germany insinuated itself into Turkish internal affairs and financed the Baghdad Railway in the attempt to link the Mediterranean to the Persian Gulf. Russia acquired territories on the banks of the Caspian Sea and had plans to take Constantinople. But it was the volatile Balkan Peninsula that threatened to upset the European power balance. The Balkans appeared to be a territory that begged for dismemberment. Internally, the Slavs sought independence from their Habsburg and Turkish oppressors. External pressures were equally great, with each of the major powers following its own geopolitical agenda.

The Instability of the Alliance System

The system of alliances formed between and among European states was guided by two realities of geopolitics. The first was the recognition of tension between France and Germany. France had lost its dominance on the Continent in 1870–71, when it was easily defeated by Prussia at the head of a nascent German Empire. With its back to the Atlantic, France faced the smaller states of Belgium, Luxembourg, Switzerland, and Italy and the industrially and militarily powerful Germany. It had suffered the humiliation of losing territory to Germany—Alsace and Lorraine in 1871—and was well aware of its continued vulnerability. Geopolitically, France felt trapped and isolated and in need of powerful friends as a counterweight to German power.

The second reality guiding alliances was Russia's preoccupation with maintaining free access to the Mediterranean Sea. Russia, clearly Europe's greatest landed power, was vulnerable because it could be landlocked by frozen or blockaded ports. The ice that crippled its naval and commercial vessels in the Baltic Sea drove Russia east through Asia to secure another ice-blocked port on the Sea of Japan at Vladivostok in 1860 and to seek ice-free Chinese ports. Russia was equally obsessed with protecting its warm-water ports

on the Black Sea. Whoever controlled the strait of the Bosporus controlled Russia's grain export trade, on which its economic prosperity depended. All diplomatic arrangements, especially after the turn of the century, took into account these two geopolitical realities.

Ostensibly, Russia had the most to gain from the extension of its frontiers and the creation of pro-Russian satellites. It saw that by championing Pan-Slavic nationalist groups in southeastern Europe, it could greatly strengthen its own position at the expense of the two great declining empires, Ottoman Turkey and Austria-Hungary. Russia hoped to draw the Slavs into its orbit by fostering the creation of independent states in the Balkans. A Serbian revolt began in two Ottoman provinces, Bosnia and Herzegovina, in 1874. International opinion pressured Turkey to initiate reforms. Serbia declared war on Turkey on 30 June 1876; Montenegro did the same the next day. Britain, supporting the Ottoman Empire because of its trading interests in the Mediterranean, found itself in a delicate position of perhaps condemning an ally when it received news of Turkish atrocities against Christians in Bulgaria. Prime Minister Disraeli insisted that Britain was bound to defend Constantinople because of British interests in the Suez Canal and India. While Britain stood on the sidelines, Russia, with Romania as an ally, declared war against the Ottoman Empire. The war was quickly over, with Russia capturing all of Armenia, forcing the Ottoman sultan, Abdul Hamid II (1842–1918) to sue for peace on 31 January 1878.

Bismarck, a seemingly disinterested party acting as an "honest broker," hosted the peace conference that met at Berlin. The British succeeded in blocking Russia's intentions for a Bulgarian satellite and keeping the Russians from taking Constantinople. Russia abandoned its support of Serbian nationalism, and Austria-Hungary occupied Bosnia and Herzegovina. The peace concluded at the 1878 Congress of Berlin disregarded Serbian claims, thereby promising continuing conflict over the nationalities question.

The Berlin Congress also marked the emergence of a new estrangement among the Great Powers. Russia felt betrayed by Bismarck and abandoned in its alliance with Germany. Bismarck in turn cemented a Dual Alliance between Austria-Hungary and Germany in 1879 that survived until the collapse of the two imperial regimes in 1918. The Three Emperors' League was renewed in 1881, now with stipulations regarding the division of the spoils in case of a war against Turkey.

In 1882 Italy was asked to join the Dual Alliance with Germany and Austria-Hungary, thus converting it into the Triple Alliance, which prevailed until the Great War of 1914. Germany, under Bismarck's tutelage, signed treaties with Italy, Russia, and Austria-Hungary and established friendly terms with Great Britain. A new Balkan crisis in 1885, however, shattered the illusion of stable relations.

Hostilities erupted between Bulgaria and Serbia. Russia threatened to occupy Bulgaria, but Austria stepped in to prevent Russian domination of the Balkans, thus threatening the alliance of the Three Emperors' League. Russia was further angered by German unwillingness to support its interests against Austrian actions in the Balkans. Germany maintained relations with Russia in a new Reinsurance Treaty drawn up in 1887, which stipulated that each power would maintain neutrality should the other find itself at war. Bismarck now walked a fine line, balancing alliances and selectively disclosing the terms of secret treaties to nonsignatory countries with the goal of preserving the peace. He was described by his successor as the only man who could keep five glass balls in the air at the same time.

After Bismarck's resignation in 1890, Germany found itself unable to juggle all the glass balls. Germany allowed the arrangement with Russia to lapse. Russia, in turn, allied itself in 1894 with France. Also allied with Great Britain, France had broken out of the isolation that Bismarck had intended for it two decades earlier. The Triple Entente came into existence following the Anglo-Russian understanding of 1907. Now it was the Triple Entente of Great Britain, France, and Russia against the Triple Alliance of Germany, Austria-Hungary, and Italy.

There was still every confidence that these two camps could balance each other and preserve the peace. But in 1908–09, the unresolved Balkan problem threatened to topple Europe's precarious peace. Against Russia's objections, Austria-Hungary annexed Bosnia and Herzegovina, the provinces it had occupied since 1878. Russia supported Serbia's discontent over Austrian acquisition of these predominantly Slavic territories that Serbia felt should be united with its own lands. Unwilling to risk a European war at this point, Russia was ultimately forced to back down under German pressure. Germany had to contend with its great geopolitical fear—hostile neighbors, France and Russia, on its western and eastern frontiers.

EUROPEAN CRISES AND THE BALANCE OF POWER

1871	German Empire created
1873	Three Emperors' League: Germany, Austria-Hungary, and Russia
1874	First Balkan crisis: Serbian revolt in Bosnia and Herzegovina
1875	Russo-Turkish War
1876	Serbia declares war on Turkey; Montenegro declares war on Turkey
1878	Congress of Berlin
1879	Dual Alliance: Germany and Austria-Hungary
1881	Three Emperors' League renewed
1882	Triple Alliance: Germany, Austria-Hungary, and Italy
1885	Second Balkan crisis: Bulgaria vs. Serbia
1887	Reinsurance Treaty between Germany and Russia
1894	Russia concludes alliance with France
1907	Triple Entente: Great Britain, France, and Russia
1908	Austria-Hungary annexes Bosnia and Herzegovina
1912	Third Balkan crisis: Italy vs. Turkey
1913	War erupts between Serbia and Bulgaria

A third Balkan crisis erupted in 1912 when Italy and Turkey fought over the possession of Tripoli in North Africa. The Balkan states took advantage of this opportunity to increase their holdings at Turkey's expense. This action quickly involved Great Power interests once again. A second war broke out in 1913 over Serbian interests in Bulgaria. Russia backed Serbia against Austro-Hungarian support of Bulgaria. The Russians and Austrians prepared for war while the British and Germans urged peaceful resolution. Although hostilities ceased, Serbian resentment toward Austria-Hungary over its frustrated nationalism was greater than ever. Britain, in its backing of Russia, and Germany, in its support of Austria-Hungary, were enmeshed in alliances that could involve them in a military confrontation.

Great Britain did not share Germany's and Russia's fears of strangulation by blockade. And although the question of Irish home rule was a nationalities problem for Britain, it paled in comparison with Austria-Hungary's internal challenge. As an island kingdom, however, Great Britain relied on imports for its survival. The first of the European nations to become an urban and industrial power, Britain was forced to do so at the expense of its agricultural sector. It could not feed its own people without importing foodstuffs. Britain's geographic vulnerability was its dependence on access to its empire and the maintenance of open sea-lanes. Britain saw its greatest menace coming from the rise of other sea powers—notably Germany.

• • •

From the very beginning of the competition for territories and concessions, no European state could act in Africa or Asia without affecting the interests and actions of its rivals at home. The African scramble made clear how interlocking the system of European states was after 1870. The development of spheres of influence in China underlined the value of world markets and international trade for the survival and expansion of western nations.

A "balance of power" among states guaranteed national security and independence until the end of the nineteenth century. But between 1870 and 1914, industrialization, technology, and accompanying capital formation created vast economic disparities. Conflict and disequilibrium challenged European stability and balance. Ultimately, it was the politics of geography on the European continent, not confrontations in distant colonies, that polarized the European states into two camps. Despite the unresolved conflicts behind all of these crises, European statesmen prided themselves on their ability to settle disputes through reason and negotiation. That was not to be the case with the last and final Balkan crisis that exploded in the summer of 1914.

Suggestions for Further Reading

The New Imperialism

* Michael W. Doyle, *Empires* (Ithaca, NY: Cornell University Press, 1986). Nineteenth-century imperialism is placed in a broad historical context that emphasizes a comparative perspective of the European imperial experience.

* Daniel R. Headrick, *The Tools of Empire: Technology and European Imperialism in the Nineteenth Century* (New York: Oxford University Press, 1981). By focusing on technological innovations in the nineteenth century, the author demonstrates how Europeans were able to establish control over Asia, Africa, and Oceania rapidly and at little cost.

* Daniel R. Headrick, *The Tentacles of Progress: Technology Transfer in the Age of Imperialism, 1850–1940* (New York: Oxford University Press, 1988). Argues that the transfer of technology to Africa and Asia by the Western imperial powers produced colonial underdevelopment.

The European Search for Territory and Markets

* Winfried Baumgart, *Imperialism: The Idea and Reality of British and French Colonial Expansion, 1880–1914* (New York: Oxford University Press, 1982). Principally concerned with the motives that led to imperial expansion, the author argues that motives were many and that each action must be studied in its specific social, political, and economic context.

Raymond F. Betts, *The False Dawn: European Imperialism in the Nineteenth Century* (Oxford: Oxford University Press, 1976). Explores the ideology of empire and the process of cultural transmission through colonial institutions.

* Eric Hobsbawm, *The Age of Empire, 1875–1914* (New York: Pantheon, 1987). A wide-ranging interpretive history of the late nineteenth century that spans economic, social, political, and cultural developments.

Thomas Pakenham, *The Scramble for Africa* (New York: Random House, 1991). A narrative history of how Europeans subdivided Africa among themselves.

Ronald Robinson and John Gallagher, with Alice Denny, *Africa and the Victorians: The Official Mind of Imperialism* (London: Macmillan, 1961). A classic, though controversial, analysis of British motivations during the scramble.

G. N. Uzoigwe, *Britain and the Conquest of Africa* (Ann Arbor: University of Michigan Press, 1975). An interpretation of the scramble by an African that disagrees with that of Robinson and Gallagher.

Results of a European-Dominated World

Anna Davin, "Imperialism and Motherhood," *History Workshop* (Spring 1978), no. 5: 9–65. Davin's article links imperialism and economic expansion with the increasing intervention of the state in family life. The author offers an analysis of an ideology that focused on the need to increase population in support of imperial aims and that led to the social construction of motherhood, domesticity, and individualism.

Johannes Fabian, *Language and Colonial Power: The Appropriation of Swahili in the Former Belgian Congo* (Cambridge: Cambridge University Press, 1986). Demonstrates how colonial power was exercised in the Belgian Congo through the study of the growth of Swahili as a lingua franca. The author pays particular attention to the uses of Swahili in industrial and other work situations.

* Paul B. Rich, *Race and Empire in British Politics* (Cambridge: Cambridge University Press, 1986). An intellectual history of ideas about race in the imperial tradition. Focusing on the years between 1890 and 1970, the author examines the political dimensions of race and race ideology in British society.

Conflict at Home:
The European Balance of Power

* George F. Kennan, *The Decline of Bismarck's European Order: Franco-Russian Relations, 1875–1890* (Princeton, NJ: Princeton University Press, 1979). A diplomatic history of the origins of the 1894 military alliance between Russia and France, Kennan's book views the alliance as a critical factor in the breakdown of the European balance of power established by Bismarck's diplomacy.

* Alan Sked, *The Decline and Fall of the Habsburg Empire, 1815–1918* (London: Longman, 1989). An overview of the Habsburg Empire's history from Metternich to World War I. The author interprets the various historiographical debates over the collapse of Habsburg rule. Rather than treating the late empire as a case of inevitable decline, the book examines the monarchy as a viable institution within a multinational state.

*Paperback edition available.

26 ❧ War and Revolution, 1914–1920

Selling the Great War

Advertising is a powerful influence in modern life. Some feel that it makes us buy goods we do not need. Others insist that advertising is an efficient way of conveying information, on the basis of which people make choices. The leaders of Western nations discovered the power of advertising during the years of World War I, from 1914 to 1918. Advertising did not create the conflict that became known as the Great War. Nor did it produce the enthusiasm that excited millions of Europeans when war was declared in 1914. But when death counts mounted, prices skyrocketed, food supplies dwindled, and the frenzy and fervor for the war flagged, governments came to rely more heavily on the art of persuasion. Survival and victory required the support and coordination of the whole society. For the first time in history, war had to advertise.

By the early decades of the twentieth century, businessmen had learned that it was not enough to develop efficient technologies and to mass-produce everything from hair oil to corsets—they had to sell their goods to the public. People would not buy goods they did not know about and whose merits they did not understand. Modern advertising pioneered sales techniques that convinced people to buy. Now political leaders came to realize that the advertising tech-

niques of the marketplace could be useful. Governments took up the "science" of selling—not products but the idea of war. It was not enough to have a well-trained and well-equipped army to ensure victory. Citizens had to be persuaded to join, to fight, to work, to save,

and to believe in the national war effort. Warring nations learned how to organize enthusiasm and how to mobilize the masses in support of what proved to be a long and bloody conflict.

Look at the poster on the facing page. Here is a dramatic appeal to

German women to support war work. A stern soldier whose visage and bearing communicate strength and singleness of purpose is backed up by an equally determined young woman. She is in the act of handing him a grenade as she stands with him, her arm on his shoulder, facing the unseen enemy. Grenades hang from his belt and from his left hand, giving us the sense that he is able to enter battle properly armed, thanks to this dedicated woman's efforts. The poster is a good representation of the centrality of women's work to the waging of a new kind of war in the twentieth century. The battlefront had to be backed up by a "home front"—the term used for the first time in the Great War—of working men, women, and even children. The poster communicates the dignity and worth that lay in the concerted partnership of soldiers and civilians to defeat the enemy.

Early war posters stressed justice and national glory. Later, as weariness with the war spread, the need for personal sacrifice became the dominant theme. Look at the sad female figure rising from a sea of suffering and death on the facing page. The woman, both goddesslike and vulnerable, symbolizes Great Britain. She is making a strong visual plea for action, seeking soldiers for her cause. This appeal for volunteers for the armed forces was unique to Great Britain, where conscription was not established until 1916. Yet the image is typical of every nation's reliance on a noble female symbol to emphasize the justice of its cause. The dark suffering and death in the waters lapping at her robes are reflected in her eyes. She evinces a

fierce determination as she exhorts, "Take up the sword of justice." In February 1915, Germany declared the waters around the British Isles to be a war zone. All British shipping was subject to attack, as were neutral merchant vessels, which were attacked without warning. In May 1915 the *Lusitania* was sunk, taking with it over a thousand lives, including those of 128 Americans. The poster frames an illuminated horizon where a ship that is probably the *Lusitania* is sinking. We need not read a word to understand the call to arms against the perfidy of an enemy who has killed innocent civilians. The female figure's determined jaw, clenched fist, and outstretched arms communicate the nobility of the cause and the certainty of success.

Civilians had to be mobilized for two reasons. First, it became evident early in the fighting that the costs of the war were high in human lives. Soldiers at the front had to be constantly replenished from civilian reserves. Second, the

costs of the war in food, equipment, and productive materials were so high that civilian populations had to be willing to endure great hardships and to sacrifice their own well-being to produce supplies for soldiers at the front. Advertising was used by nations at war to coordinate civilian and military contributions to a common cause.

The European governments proudly "selling" war to their citizens in 1914 expected quick victories and the triumph of their cause. Instead, what they got was a prolonged global war, costly in human life and material destruction, stretching out over four miserable years. Military technology and timetables called the tune in a defensive war fought from the trenches with sophisticated weapons capable of maiming and killing in new ways. Selling the Great War required selectively communicating information and inspiring belief and a commitment to total victory, no matter how high the cost.

European Alliances on the Eve of World War I

The War Europe Expected

In 1914 Europe stood confidently at the center of the world. Covering only 7 percent of the earth's surface, it dominated the world's trade and was actively exporting both European goods and European culture all over the globe. Proud of the progress and prosperity of urban industrial society, Europeans had harnessed nature to transform their environment. They extended their influence beyond their continent, sure that their achievements marked the pinnacle of civilization.

The values of nineteenth-century liberalism permeated the self-confident worldview of European men and women in 1914. Liberalism assured the middle classes that the world was at peace, governed by rules that could be known. Europeans assumed that they could discover these rules and fashion a better world. Science and industry were their tools for controlling nature and shaping institutions. If life was not yet perfect, it could become so.

Westerners assumed they could discover the rules that governed the world and use them to fashion a better civilization. They took stability and harmony for granted as preconditions for progress. Yet they also recognized the utility of war. In recent times, local con-frontations between European states in Africa had been successfully contained in bids for increased territory. While warfare was accepted as an instrument of policy, no one expected or wanted a general war. Liberal values served the goals of limited war, just as they had justified imperial conquest. Statesmen decided there were rules to the game of war that could be employed in the interests of statecraft. Science and technology also served the goals of limited war. Modern weapons, statesmen and generals were sure, would prevent a long war. Superiority in armed force became a priority for European states seeking to protect the peace.

The beginning of the modern arms race resulted in "armed peace" as a defense against war. Leaders nevertheless expected and planned for a war, short and limited, in which the fittest and most advanced nation would win. Planners believed that their rivals could not triumph. War was acceptable because it would be quick and decisive. Previous confrontations among European states had been limited in duration and destruction, as in the case of Prussia and France in 1870, or confined to peripheries, as squabbles among the Great Powers in Africa indicated. The alliance system was expected to defend the peace by defining the conditions of war.

As international tensions mounted, the hot summer days of 1914 were a time of hope and glory. The hope

Question wheth
Liège, should also b
At any rate Belgi
exist as a state, must
allow us to occupy
must place her coa
spects, must becom
ince. Given such
advantages of ann
domestic political
with Dunkirk, Cala
the population is
attached to this un
quarters will have t
position against Eng
3. *Luxemburg.*
state and will recei
province of Luxem
Longwy.
4. We must cre
association through
include France, Be
tria-Hungary, Polan
and Norway. This a
mon constitutional
members will be fo

pulled into a war wi
would be vulnerable t
The Schlieffen Plan re
be defeated in the wes
forces to the task of c
Plan thus committed
regardless of particula
the plan, with its strate
tries of Belgium, Holla
defeat France in six w
neutral countries.
Germany was not a
timetables when confli
gists planned full mo
Austria-Hungary, whic
Russia's ally Serbia. Ri
Germany would come
Russia knew, too, that
network it would be u
In order to compensate
ers planned to mobili

was that war, when it came, would be "over by Christmas." The glory was the promise of ultimate victory in the "crusade for civilization" that each nation's leaders held out to their people. Declarations of war were greeted with songs, flowers, wild enthusiasm, and dancing in the streets. Crowds welcomed the battles to come with the delirium of cheering a favorite team in a sports match. Some embraced war as a test of greatness, a purification of a society that had become lazy and complacent. When war did come in 1914, it was a choice, not an accident. Yet it was a choice that Europeans did not understand, one whose limits they could not control. Their unquestioned pride in reason and progress, which ironically had led them to this war, did not survive the four years of barbaric slaughter that followed.

Separating Friends from Foes

At the end of the nineteenth century, the world appeared to be coming together in a vast international network linked by commerce and finance. A system of alliances based on shared interests also connected states to one another. After 1905, the intricate defensive alliances between and among the European states maintained the balance of power between two blocs of nations and helped prevent one bloc from dominating the other. Yet by creating blocs, alliances identified foes as well as friends. On the eve of the war, France, Great Britain, and Russia stood together in the Triple Entente. Since 1882, Germany, Austria-Hungary, and Italy had joined forces in the Triple Alliance. Other states allied with one or the other of these blocs in pacts of mutual interest and protection. Throughout the world, whether in North Africa, the Balkans, or Asia, the power of some states was intended to balance the power of others. Yet the balance of power did not exist simply to preserve the peace. It existed to preserve a system of independent national societies—nation-states—in a precarious equilibrium. Gains in one area by one bloc had to be offset by compromises in another to maintain the balance. Nations recognized limited conflict as a legitimate means of preserving equilibrium.

The alliance system of blocs reflected the growing impact of public opinion on international relations. Statesmen had the ability to manipulate the newspaper images of allies as good and rivals as evil. But controlling public opinion served to lock policymakers into permanent partnerships and "blank checks" of support for their allies. Western leaders understood that swings in public opinion in periods of crisis could hobble their efforts in the national interest. Permanent military

Linguistic Groups in Austria-Hungary

alliances with clearly identified "friends," therefore, took the place of more fluid arrangements.

Although alliances that guaranteed military support did not cause war, they did permit weak nations to act irresponsibly, with the certainty that they would be defended by their more powerful partners. France and Germany were publicly committed to their weaker allies Russia and Austria-Hungary, respectively, in supporting imperialist ambitions in the Balkans from which they themselves derived little direct benefit. Because of treaty commitments, no country expected to face war alone. The interlocking system of defensive alliances was structured to match strength against strength—France against Germany, for example—thereby making a prolonged war more likely than would be the case if a weak nation confronted a strong enemy.

Military Timetables

As Europe soon discovered, military timetables restricted the choices of leaders at times of conflict. The crisis of the summer of 1914 revealed the extent to which politicians and statesmen had come to rely on military expertise and strategic considerations in making decisions. Military general staffs assumed increasing impor-

*The
as a
1914
mer
as s
kep
fror*

BETHMANN-
ON THE DIR
CLUSION OF

[The] general
man Reich in
For this purp
make her rev
time. Russia
from German
over the non-
1. *France.*
should demar
of the Vosge
coastal strip f
The ore-fi

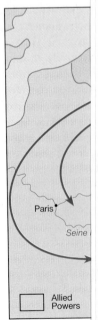

The Schlieffen Pla

A typical World War I trench. Millions of soldiers lived amid mud, disease, and vermin, awaiting death from enemy shells. After the French army mutiny in 1916, the troops wrung this concession from their commanders: they did not have to charge German machine guns while armed only with rifles.

Technology and the Trenches

In the history of nineteenth-century European warfare, armies had relied on mobile cavalry and infantry units whose greatest asset was speed. Rapid advance had been decisive in the Prussian victory over the French in 1870, which had resulted in the formation of the German Empire. Soldiers of the twentieth century were also trained for a war of movement, high maneuverability, and maximum territorial conquest. But after the first six weeks of battle, soldiers were ordered to do something unimaginable to strategists of European warfare: they were ordered to dig ditches and fight from fixed positions. Soldiers on both sides shoveled out trenches four feet deep, piled up sandbags, mounted their machine guns, and began to fight an unplanned defensive war.

The front lines of Europe's armies in the west wallowed in the 400 miles of trenches that ran from the English Channel to the Swiss frontier. The British and French on one side and the Germans on the other fought each other with machine guns and mortars, backed up by heavy artillery to the rear. Strategists on both sides believed they could break through enemy lines. As a result, the monotony of trench warfare was

punctuated periodically by infantry offensives in which immense concentrations of artillery caused great bloodshed. Ten million men were killed in this bizarre and deadly combination of old and new warfare. The glamour of battle that had attracted many young men disappeared quickly in the daily reality of living in mud with rats and constantly facing death. The British poet Wilfred Owen (1893–1918), shortly before his own death in battle, wrote about how the soldier next to him had been shot in the head, soaking Owen in blood: "I shall feel again as soon as I dare, but now I must not."

The invention of new weaponry and heavy equipment had transformed war into an enterprise of increasing complexity. Military and naval staffs expanded to meet the new needs of warfare, but old ways persisted. In their bright blue coats and red trousers, French and Belgian infantrymen made easy targets. Outmoded cavalry units survived despite more efficient mechanization. The railroad made the mobilization, organization, and deployment of mass armies possible. Specialists were needed to control the new war machines that heavy industry had created.

The shovel and the machine gun had indeed transformed war. The machine gun was not new in 1914, but its strategic value had not been fully appreciated before then. The Maxim machine gun had been used

The British invented the tank, which made its combat debut in 1916. The new weapon terrified the German troops when first used on the Western Front. The British had developed it in heavy secrecy under the pretext of constructing water tanks; hence the name.

"ALL QUIET ON THE WESTERN FRONT"

Eyewitness accounts described the horrors of the new trench warfare. But no one captured the war better than the German novelist Erich Maria Remarque (1898–1970) who drew on his own wartime experiences in All Quiet on the Western Front. *Published in 1928 and translated subsequently into 25 languages, this powerful portrayal of the transformation of a school boy into a soldier indicts the inhumanity of war and pleads for peace. Stressing the camaraderie of fighting men and sympathy for the plight of the enemy soldier, Remarque also underscored the alienation of a whole generation—the lost generation of young men who could not go home again after the war.*

Attack, counter-attack, charge, repulse—these are words, but what things they signify! We have lost a good many men, mostly recruits. Reinforcements have again been sent up to our sector. They are one of the new regiments, composed almost entirely of young fellows just called up. They have had hardly any training, and are sent into the field with only a theoretical knowledge. They do know what a hand-grenade is, it is true, but they have very little idea of cover, and what is most important of all, have no eye for it. A fold in the ground has to be quite eighteen inches high before they can see it.

Although we need reinforcement, the recruits give us almost more trouble than they are worth. They are helpless in this grim fighting area, they fall like flies. Modern trench-warfare demands knowledge and experience; a man must have a feeling for the contours of the ground, an ear for the sound and character of the shells, must be able to decide beforehand where they will drop, how they will burst, and how to shelter from them.

The young recruits of course know none of these things. They get killed simply because they hardly can tell shrapnel from high-explosive, they are mown down because they are listening anxiously to the roar of the big coal-boxes falling in the rear, and miss the light, piping whistle of the low spreading daisy-cutters. They flock together like sheep instead of scattering, and even the wounded are shot down like hares by the airmen.

Their pale turnip faces, their pitiful clenched hands, the fine courage of these poor devils, the desperate charges and attacks made by the poor brave wretches, who are so terrified that they dare not cry out loudly, but with battered chests, with torn bellies, arms and legs only whimper softly for their mothers and cease as soon as one looks at them.

Their sharp, downy, dead faces have the awful expressionlessness of dead children. . . .

I am young, I am twenty years old; yet I know nothing of life but despair, death, fear, and fatuous superficiality cast over an abyss of sorrow. I see how peoples are set against one another, and in silence, unknowingly, foolishly, obediently, innocently slay one another. I see that the keenest brains of the world invent weapons and words to make it yet more refined and enduring. And all men of my age, here and over there, throughout the whole world see these things; all my generation is experiencing these things with me. What would our fathers do if we suddenly stood up and came before them and proffered our account? What do they expect of us if a time ever comes when the war is over? Through the years our business has been killing;—it was our first calling in life. Our knowledge of life is limited to death. What will happen afterwards? And what shall come out of us?

From Erich Maria Remarque, *All Quiet on the Western Front.*

---

by the British in Africa. Strategists regarded the carnage that resulted as a stunning achievement but failed to ask how a weapon of such phenomenal destructive power would work against an enemy armed with machine guns instead of spears. Military strategists drew all the wrong conclusions. They continued to plan an offensive strategy when the weaponry developed for massive destruction had pushed them into fighting a defensive war from the trenches. Both sides

resorted to concentration of artillery, increased use of poison gas, and unrestricted submarine warfare in desperate attempts to break the deadlock caused by meeting armed force with force.

The necessity of total victory drove the Central Powers and the Allies to grisly new inventions. Late in the war, the need to break the deadlock of trench warfare ushered in the airplane and the tank. Neither was decisive in altering the course of the war, though the

By late 1914, the sight of marching soldiers was no longer a novelty in France. These vineyard workers do not even look up as a military column passes.

airplane was useful for reconnaissance and for limited bombing and the tank promised the means of breaking through defensive lines. Chlorine gas was first used in warfare by the Germans in 1915. Mustard gas, which was named for its distinctive smell and which caused severe blistering, was introduced two years later. The Germans were the first to use flamethrowers, especially effective against mechanized vehicles with vulnerable fuel tanks. Barbed wire, invented in the U.S. Midwest to contain farm animals, became an essential aspect of trench warfare, as it marked off the no-man's-land between combatants and prevented surprise attacks.

The technology that had been viewed as a proof of progress was now channeled toward engineering new instruments of death. Yet technology itself produced a stalemate. New weapons sometimes produced their antidotes. For example, the invention of deadly gas was followed soon after by gas masks. Each side was capable of matching the other's ability to devise new armaments. Deadlocks caused by technological parity forced both sides to resort to desperate concentrations of men and weaponry that resulted not in decisive battles but in ever-escalating casualty rates. By improving their efficiency at killing, the European powers were not finding a way to end the war.

The Battle of the Marne

German forces seized the offensive in the west and invaded neutral Belgium at the beginning of August 1914. The Belgians resisted stubbornly but unsuccess-

fully. Belgian forts were systematically captured, and the capital of Brussels fell under the German advance on 20 August. After the fall of Belgium, German military might swept into northern France with the intention of defeating the French in six weeks.

In the years preceding the war, the German General Staff, unwilling to concentrate all of their troops in the west, had modified the Schlieffen Plan by committing divisions to its eastern frontier. The absence of the full German fighting force in the west did not appreciably slow the German advance through Belgium. Yet the Germans had underestimated both the cost of holding back the French in Alsace-Lorraine and the difficulty of maneuvering German forces and transporting supplies in an offensive war. Eventually, unexpected Russian advances in the east also siphoned off troops from the west. German forces in the west were so weakened by the offensive that they were unable to swing west of Paris, as planned, and instead chose to enter the French capital from the northeast by crossing the Marne River. This shift exposed the German First Army on its western flank and opened up a gap on its eastern flank.

Despite an initial pattern of retreat and a lack of coordination of forces, Allied French and British troops were ready to take advantage of the vulnerabilities in the German advance. In a series of battles between 6 and 10 September 1914 that came to be known as the First Battle of the Marne, the Allies counterattacked and advanced into the gap. The German army was forced to drop back. In the following months, each army tried to outflank the other in what has been called "the race to the sea." By late fall it was clear that the battles from the Marne north to the border town of Ypres in northwest Belgium near the English Channel had ended an open war of movement on the western front. Soldiers now dug in along a line of battle that changed little in the long three and a half years until March 1918.

The Allies gained a strategic victory in the First Battle of the Marne by resisting the German advance in the fighting that quickly became known as the "miracle of the Marne." The legend was further enhanced by true stories of French troops being rushed from Paris to the front in taxicabs. Yet the real significance of the Marne lay in the severe miscalculations of military leaders and statesmen on both sides, who had expected a different kind of war. They did not understand the new technology that made a short war unlikely. Nor did they understand the demands that this new kind of warfare would make on civilian populations. Those Parisian taxi drivers foreshadowed how European civilians would be called upon again and again to support the war in the next four years. The Schlieffen Plan was dead. But it was no more a failure than any of the other military timetables of the Great Powers.

"I don't know what is to be done—this isn't war." So spoke Lord Horatio Kitchener (1850–1916), one of the most decorated British generals of his time. He was not alone in his bafflement over the stalemate of trench warfare at the end of 1914. By that time, Germany's greatest fear, a simultaneous war on two fronts, had become a grim reality. The Central Powers were under a state of siege, cut off from the world by the great battlefront in the west and by the Allied blockade at sea. The rules of the game had changed, and the European powers settled in for a long war.

War on the Eastern Front

War on Germany's eastern front was a mobile war, unlike its western counterpart, because there were relatively fewer men and guns in relation to the vast distances. The Russian army was the largest in the world. Yet it was crippled from the outbreak of the war by inadequate supplies and poor leadership. At the end of August 1914, the smaller German army, supported by divisions drawn from the west, delivered a devastating defeat to the Russians in the one great battle on the eastern front. At Tannenberg, the entire Russian Second Army was destroyed, and about 100,000 Russian soldiers were taken prisoner. Faced with this humiliation, General Aleksandr Vasilievich Samsonov (1859–

1914), head of the Russian forces, committed suicide on the field of battle.

The German general Paul von Hindenburg (1847–1934), a veteran of the Franco-Prussian war of 1870, had been recalled from retirement to direct the campaign against the Russians because of his intimate knowledge of the area. Assisted by Quartermaster General Erich Ludendorff (1865–1937), Hindenburg followed the stunning victory of Tannenberg two weeks later with another devastating blow to Russian forces at the Masurian Lakes.

The Russians were holding up their end of the bargain in the Allied war effort, but at great cost. They kept the Germans busy and forced them to divert troops to the eastern front, weakening the German effort to knock France out of the war. In the south, the tsar's troops defeated the Austro-Hungarian army at Lemberg in Galicia in September. This Russian victory gave Serbia a temporary reprieve. But by mid-1915, Germany had thrown the Russians back and was keeping Austria-Hungary propped up in the war. By fall, Russia had lost most of Galicia, the Polish lands of the Russian empire, Lithuania, and parts of Latvia and Byelorussia to the advancing enemy. These losses amounted to 15 percent of its territory and 20 percent of its population. The Russian army staggered, with over one million soldiers taken as prisoners of war and at least as many killed or wounded.

The Russian army, as one of its own officers described it, was being bled to death. Russian soldiers were poorly led into battle, or not led at all because of the shortage of officers. Munitions shortages meant that soldiers often went into battle without rifles, armed only with the hope of scavenging arms from their fallen comrades. Despite these difficulties, the Russians, under the direction of General Aleksei Brusilov (1853–1926), commander of the Russian armies in the southern part of the eastern front, remarkably managed to throw back the Austro-Hungarian forces in 1916 and almost eliminated Austria as a military power. But this was the last great campaign on the eastern front and Russia's last show of strength in the Great War.

Russia's near destruction of the Austrian army tremendously benefited Russia's allies. In order to protect its partner, Germany was forced to withdraw eight divisions from Italy—alleviating the Allied situation in the Tyrol—and twelve divisions from the western front, providing relief for the French at Verdun and the British at the Somme. In addition, Russia sent troops to the aid of a new member of the Allied camp, Roma-

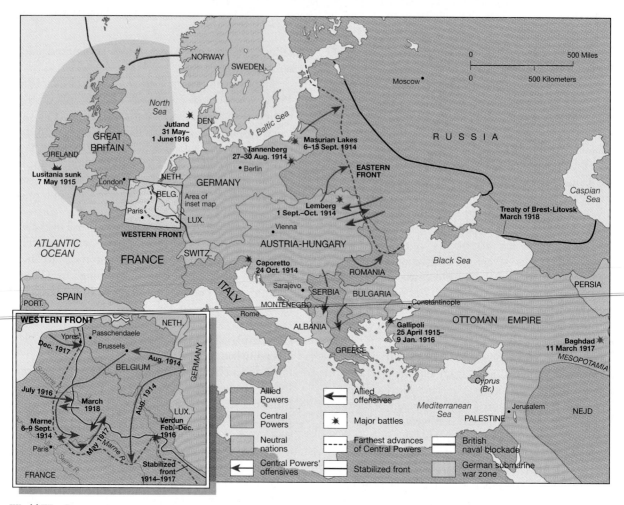

World War I

nia, an act which probably further weakened Brusilov's efforts. In response to Brusilov's challenge, the Germans established control over the Austrian army, assigning military command of the coalition to General Ludendorff.

By the summer of 1917, the tsardom had been overthrown and a provisional government ruled Russia. Tens of thousands of Russian soldiers were walking away from the war. Russia withdrew from the war and in March 1918 signed a separate peace by which Germany gained extensive territorial advantages and important supply bases for carrying on the war in the west. To protect these territories and their resources, the Germans had to maintain an army on the eastern front. No longer fighting in the east, however, Germany could release the bulk of its forces to fight in the west.

War on the Western Front

Along hundreds of miles of trenches, the French and British tried repeatedly to expel the Germans from Bel-

gium. Long periods of inactivity were punctuated by orgies of heavy bloodletting. The German phrase "All quiet on the western front," used in military communiqués to describe those periods of silence between massive shellings and infantry attacks, reported only the uneasy calm before the next violent storm.

Military leaders on both sides cherished the dream of a decisive offensive, the breakthrough that would win the war. In 1916 the Allies planned a joint strike at the Somme, a river in northern France flowing west into the English Channel, but the Germans struck first at Verdun, a small fortress city in northeast France. By concentrating great numbers of troops, the Germans outnumbered the French five to two. As General Erich von Falkenhayn (1861–1922), chief of the General Staff of the German army from 1914 to 1916, explained it, the German purpose in attacking Verdun was "to bleed the French white by virtue of our superiority in guns."

On the first day of battle, one million shells were fired. The battlefield was a living hell as soldiers stum-

A painting by François Flameng of Verdun in flames. This city on the Meuse River in northern France has played an important role in resisting enemy invasion since the time of Attila the Hun in the fifth century.

bled across corpse after corpse. Against the German onslaught, French troops were instructed to hold out, though they lacked adequate artillery and reinforcements. General Joseph Joffre (1852–1931), commander in chief of the French army, was unwilling to divert reinforcements to Verdun.

The German troops advanced easily through the first lines of defense. But the French held their position for ten long, horrifying months of continuous mass slaughter from February to December 1916. General Henri Philippe Pétain (1856–1951), a local commander who had been planning an early retirement before the war, bolstered morale by constantly rotating his troops to the point that most of the French army—259 of 330 infantry battalions—saw action at Verdun. Nearly starving and poorly armed, the French stood alone in the bloodiest offensive of the war. Attack strategy backfired on the Germans as their own death tolls mounted.

Pétain and his flamboyant general Robert Georges Nivelle (1856–1924) were both hailed as heroes for fulfilling the instruction to their troops: "They shall not pass." Falkenhayn fared less well and was dismissed from his post. Yet no real winners emerged from the scorched earth of Verdun, where observers could see the nearest thing to a desert created in Europe. Verdun was a disaster. The French suffered over half a million total casualties. German casualties were almost as high. A few square miles of territory had changed hands back and forth. In the end, no military advantage was

British machine gunners wearing gas masks at the battle of the Somme in 1916.

gained, and almost 700,000 lives had been lost. Legends of the brilliant leadership of Pétain and Nivelle, who both went on to greater positions of authority, and the failed command of Falkenhayn, who retired in disgrace, obscured the real lesson of the battle: an offensive war under these conditions was impossible.

Still, new offensives were devised. The British went ahead with their planned offensive on the Somme in July 1916. For an advance of seven miles, 400,000 British and 200,000 French soldiers were killed or wounded. The American writer F. Scott Fitzgerald (1896–1940), who had served as an army officer in World War I, wrote of the battle of the Somme in his novel *Tender Is the Night* (1934). One of his characters describes a visit to the Somme Valley after the war: "See that little stream. We could walk to it in two minutes. It took the British a whole month to walk to it—a whole empire walking very slowly, dying in front and pushing forward behind. And another empire walked very slowly backward a few inches a day, leaving the dead like a million bloody rugs." German losses brought the total casualties of this offensive to one million men. Despite his experience at Verdun, French general Robert Nivelle planned his own offensive in the Champagne region in spring 1917, sure that he could succeed where others had failed in "breaking the crust." The Nivelle offensive resulted in 40,000 deaths, and Nivelle was dismissed. The French army was falling apart, with mutiny and insubordination everywhere.

The British believed they could succeed where the French had failed. Under General Douglas Haig (1861–1928), the commander in chief of British expeditionary forces on the Continent, the British launched an attack in Flanders through the summer and fall of 1917. Known as the Passchendaele offensive for the village and ridge in whose "porridge of mud" much of the fighting took place, this campaign resulted in the slaughter of almost 400,000 British soldiers for insignificant territorial gain. The Allies and the Germans finally recognized that "going over the top" in offensives was not working and could not work. The war must be won by other means.

War on the Periphery

Recognizing the stalemate in the west, the Allies attempted to open up other fronts where the Central Powers might be vulnerable. In the spring of 1915, the Allies were successful in convincing Italy to enter the war on their side by promising that it would receive, at the time of the peace, the South Tyrol, the southern part of Dalmatia, and key Dalmatian islands, which would assure Italy's dominance over the Adriatic Sea. By thus capitalizing on Italian antagonism toward Austria-Hungary over control of this territory, the Allies gained 875,000 Italian soldiers for their cause. Although these Italian troops were in no way decisive in the fighting that followed, Great Britain, France, and Russia saw the need to build up Allied support in southern Europe in order to reinforce Serbian attempts to keep Austrian troops beyond its borders. The Allies also hoped that by pulling Germans into this southern front, some relief might be provided for British and French soldiers on the western front.

Germany, in turn, was well aware of the need to expand its alliances beyond Austria-Hungary if it was to compete successfully against superior Allied forces. Trapped as they were to the east and west, the Central Powers established control over a broad corridor stretching from the North Sea through central Europe and down through the Ottoman Empire to the Suez Canal so vital to British interests. In the Balkans, where the war had begun, the Serbs were consistently bested by the Austrians. By late 1915, the Serbs had been knocked out of the war in spite of Allied attempts to assist them. Serbia paid a heavy price in the Great War: it lost one-sixth of its population through war, famine, and disease. The promise of booty persuaded Bulgaria to join Germany and Austria-Hungary. Over the next year and a half, the Allies responded by convincing Romania and then Greece to join them.

The theater of war continued to expand. Although the Ottoman Empire had joined the war in late 1914 on the side of the Central Powers, its own internal difficulties attenuated its fighting ability. As a multinational empire consisting of Turks, Arabs, Armenians, Greeks, Kurds, and other ethnic minorities, it was plagued by Turkish misrule and Arab nationalism. Hence the Ottoman Empire was the weakest link in the chain of German alliances. Yet it held a crucial position. The Turks could block shipping of vital supplies to Russia through the Mediterranean and the Black seas. Coming to the aid of their Russian ally, a combined British and French fleet attacked Turkish forces at the straits of the Dardanelles in April 1915. In the face of political and military opposition, First Lord of the Admiralty Winston Churchill (1874–1965) supported the idea of opening a new front by sea. Poorly planned and mismanaged, the expedition was a disaster. When the naval effort in the German-mined strait failed, the British foolishly decided to land troops on the Gallipoli Peninsula, which extends from the southern coast of European Turkey. There British soldiers

Crew on the deck of a German World War I submarine at sea.

were trapped on the rocky terrain, unable to advance against the Turks and unable to fall back. Gallipoli was the first large-scale attempt at amphibious warfare. The Australian and New Zealand forces (ANZACs) showed great bravery in some of the most brutal fighting of the war. Critics in Britain argued that the only success of the nine-month campaign was the Allied evacuation.

Britain sought to protect its interests in the Suez Canal. Turkish troops menaced the canal effectively enough to terrify the British into maintaining an elaborate system of defense in the area and concentrating large troop reinforcements in Egypt. War with the Ottoman Empire also extended battle into the oil fields of Mesopotamia and Persia. This attempt at a new front was initially a fiasco for the British and Russian forces that threatened Baghdad. The Allies proceeded not only without plans, but also without maps. They literally did not know where they were going. Eventually, British forces recovered and took Baghdad in 1917, while Australian and New Zealand troops captured Jerusalem. The tentacles of war spread out, following the path of Western economic and imperial interests throughout the world.

Most surprising of all was the indecisive nature of the war at sea. The great battleships of the British and German navies avoided confrontation on the high seas. The only major naval battle of the Great War, the Battle of Jutland in the North Sea, took place in early 1916. Each side inflicted damage on the other but, through careful maneuvering, avoided a decisive outcome to the battle. Probably the enormous cost of replacing battleships deterred both the British and the Germans from risking their fleets in engagements on the high seas. With the demands for munitions and equipment on the two great land fronts of the war, neither side could afford to lose a traditional war at sea. Instead, the British used their seapower as a policing force to blockade German trade and strangle the German economy.

The German navy, much weaker than the British, relied on a new weapon, the submarine, which threatened to become decisive in the war at sea. Submarines were initially used in the first months of the war for reconnaissance. Their potential for inflicting heavy losses on commercial shipping became apparent in 1915. Undergoing technological improvements throughout the war, U-boats *(Unterseebooten),* as German submarines were called, torpedoed 6 million tons of Allied shipping in 1917. With cruising ranges as high as 3600 miles, German submarines attacked Allied and neutral shipping as far away as off the shore of the United States and the Arctic supply line to Russia. German insistence on unrestricted use outraged neutral powers, who considered the Germans in violation of international law. The Germans rejected the requirements of warning an enemy ship and boarding it for investigation as too dangerous for submarines, which were no match for battleships above water. The Allies invented depth charges and mines capable of blowing German submarines out of the water. These weapons, combined with the use of the convoy system in the Atlantic Ocean and the Mediterranean Sea, produced a successful blockade and antisubmarine campaign that put an end to the German advantage.

Adjusting to the Unexpected: Total War

The war that Europe got differed from all previous experiences and expectations of armed conflict. Technological advances, equally matched on both sides, introduced a war of attrition, defensive and prolonged. Nineteenth-century wars that lasted six to eight weeks, were confined to one locale, and were determined by a handful of battles marked by low casualties had nothing in common with the long, dirty, lice-infested reality of trench warfare. Warring European nations faced enemies to the west, to the east, and on the periphery with no end to the slaughter in sight.

The period from 1914 to 1918 marked the first time in history that the productive activities of entire populations were directed toward a single goal: military victory. The Great War became a war of peoples, not just of armies. Wars throughout history have involved noncombatants caught in the cross fire or standing in the wrong place at the wrong time. But this unexpected war of attrition required civilian populations to adjust to a situation in which what went on at the battlefront transformed life on the home front. For this reason, the Great War became known as history's first *total* war.

Adjusting to the unexpected war of 1914, governments intervened to centralize and control every aspect of economic life. Technology and industrial capacity made possible a war of unimaginable destruction. The scale of production and distribution of war-related materials required for victory was unprecedented. To persuade civilians to suffer at home for the sake of the war, leaders pictured the enemy as evil villains who must be defeated at any cost. The sacrifice required for a total war made total victory necessary. And total victory required an economy totally geared to fighting the war.

Mobilizing the Home Front

While soldiers were fighting on the eastern and western fronts, businessmen and politicians at home were creating bureaucracies to control wages and prices, distribute supplies, establish production quotas, and mobilize human and material resources. Just as governments had conscripted the active male population for military service, the Allies and the Central Powers now mobilized civilians of all ages and both sexes to work for the war.

Women played an essential role in the mobilization of the home front. They had never been isolated from the experiences and hardships of war, but they now found new ways to support the war effort. In cities, women went to work in munitions factories and war-related industries that had previously employed only men. Women filled service jobs, from fire fighting to

Women working in a munitions factory in England during World War I

WAR AT HOME

❧

The total character of World War I meant it changed life for noncombatants as much as it did for those at the front. Women had to fend for themselves, organizing relief societies, working the fields, and manufacturing weapons and war goods. They often took jobs men had held before. In London, taxi driving had been a male monopoly before the war. Articles from 16 March 1917 in the The Manchester Guardian show what could happen when both women and men shared jobs. Conflicts could break out when men felt threatened by women's new positions.

WOMEN TAXI-CAB DRIVERS

The taxi-cab drivers of London threaten to try to bring about a strike, which will include motor-'bus drivers and conductors, if the London County Council does not abandon its intention to license women to drive taxi-cabs. To be successful a strike must in the ultimate event be in defence of a principle that commands a measure of public assent. The only principle for which the men stand in this strike is that even where women are fitted to do men's work they should be debarred from it. It is a principle never tenable in justice, and utterly discredited in the popular mind by the war. If the employment of women as motor-drivers meant a decrease in the general level of skill in the trade, a worsening of conditions, or a lowering of wages a real principle would be involved. Stress of war might make the setting aside of it temporarily necessary, but the point would be at least arguable. In this matter such considerations do not arise. Hundreds of women have taken the place of men as motor-drivers for the army and the Red Cross at home and abroad, thousands more are employed in driving commercial motors. They have proved, if proof were needed, that this work is well within their compass. The woman who can take a man's place fully in the harder sort of tasks involved in work on the railways or in agriculture is an exception, and the employment of women for such work is a war-time necessity that may not to any great extent survive when peace comes. But the woman motor-driver has come to stay, and a strike of taxi-men could be no more than a vain and selfish protest against her arrival.

"DOWN CABS" AGAIN

The London taxi-drivers are again threatening trouble—this time because the Home Office refuses to give way on the question of licensing women drivers. Sir George Cave told a deputation of the Licensed Vehicle Workers the other day that there is no intention at present of licensing women as tram and 'bus drivers, but that competent women will certainly be licensed for taxi-driving. The men are holding indignation meetings on Sunday, and threaten to bring all the cab, 'bus, and tram drivers of London out on strike—about 20,000 workers, inclusive of garage men.

---

trolley-car conducting—jobs that were essential to the smooth running of industrial society and that had been left vacant by men. On farms, women literally took up the plow after both men and horses had been requisitioned for the war effort.

By 1918, 650,000 French women were working in war-related industries and in clerical positions in the army, and they had counterparts all over Europe. In Germany, two out of every five munitions workers were women. Women became more prominent in the work force as a whole, as the case of Great Britain makes clear: there the number of women workers jumped from 250,000 at the beginning of the war to 5 million by the war's end. Women also served in the auxiliary units of the armed services, in the clerical and medical corps, in order to free men for fighting at the front. In eastern European nations, women entered combat as soldiers. Although most women were displaced from their wartime jobs with the return of men after the armistice, they were as important to the war effort as the men fighting at the front.

In the first months of the war, the private sector had been left to its own devices with nearly disastrous results. Shortages, especially of shells, and bottlenecks in production threatened military efforts. Governments were forced to establish controls and to set up state monopolies in order to guarantee the supplies necessary to wage war. In Germany, industrialists

Walther Rathenau (1867–1922) and Alfred Hugenberg (1865–1951) worked with the government. By the spring of 1915, they had eliminated the German problem of munitions scarcity. France was in trouble six weeks after the outbreak of the war: it had used up half of its accumulated munitions supplies in the First Battle of the Marne. German occupation of France's northern industrial basin further crippled munitions production. Through government intervention, France improvised and relocated its war industries. The British government got involved in production, too, by establishing in 1915 the first Ministry of Munitions under the direction of David Lloyd George (1863–1945). Distinct from the Ministry of War, the Ministry of Munitions was to coordinate military needs with the armaments industry.

In a war that leaders soon realized would be a long one, food supplies assumed paramount importance. Germany, dependent on food imports to feed its people and isolated from the world market by the Allied blockade, introduced rationing five months after the outbreak of the war. Other Continental nations followed suit. Government agents set quotas for agricultural producers. Armies were fed and supplied at the expense of domestic populations. Great Britain, which enjoyed a more reliable food supply by virtue of its sea power, did not impose food rationing until 1917.

Three factors put food supplies at risk. First, the need for large numbers of soldiers at the front pulled farmers and peasants off the land. The resultant drop in the agricultural work force meant that land was taken out of production and what remained was less efficiently cultivated, so that productivity declined. A second factor was fear of requisitioning and the general uncertainties of war that caused agricultural producers to hoard supplies. What little was available was traded on black markets. Finally, because all European countries depended to some extent on imports of food and fertilizers, enemies successfully targeted trade routes for attack.

Silencing Dissent

The strains of total war were becoming apparent. Two years of sacrificing, scrimping, and, in some areas, starving began to take their toll among soldiers and civilians on both sides. With the lack of decisive victories, war weariness was spreading. Work stoppages and strikes, which had virtually ceased with the outbreak of war in 1914, began to climb rapidly in 1916. Between 1915 and 1916 in France, the number of strikes by dissatisfied workers increased by 400 percent. Underpaid

and tired workers went on strike, staged demonstrations, and protested exploitation. Labor militancy also intensified in the British Isles and Germany. Women, breadwinners for their families, were often in the forefront of these protests throughout Europe. Social peace between unions and governments was no longer held together by patriotic enthusiasm for war.

Politicians, too, began to rethink their suspension of opposition to government policies as the war dragged on. Dissidents among European socialist parties regained their prewar commitment to peace. Most socialists had enthusiastically supported the declarations of war in 1914. By 1916, the united front that political opponents had presented against the enemy was crumbling under growing demands for peace.

In a total war, unrest at home guaranteed defeat. Governments knew that all opposition to war policies had to be eliminated. In a dramatic extension of the police powers of the state, whether among the Allies or the Central Powers, criticism of the government became treason. Censorship was enforced and propaganda became more virulent. Those who spoke for peace were no better than the enemy. The governments of every warring nation resorted to harsh measures. Parliamentary bodies were stripped of power, civil liberties were suspended, democratic procedures were ignored. The civilian governments of Premier Georges Clemenceau (1841–1929) in France and Prime Minister Lloyd George in Great Britain resorted to rule by emergency police power to repress criticism. Under Generals von Hindenburg and Ludendorff in Germany, military rule became the order of the day. Nowhere was "government as usual" possible in total war.

Every warring nation sought to promote dissension from within the societies of its enemies. Germany provided some aid for the Easter Rebellion in Ireland in 1916 in the hope that the Irish demand for independence that predated the war would deflect British attention and undermine fighting strength and morale. Germany also supported separatist movements among minority nationalities in the Russian empire and was responsible for returning the avowed revolutionary V. I. Lenin under escort to Russia in April 1917. The British engaged in similar tactics. The British foreign secretary Arthur Balfour (1848–1930) worked with Zionist leaders in 1917 in drawing up the Balfour Declaration, which promised to "look with favor" on the creation of a Jewish homeland in Palestine. The British thereby encouraged Zionist hopes among central European Jews, with the intent of creating difficulties for German and Austrian rulers. Similarly, the British encouraged

Arabs to rebel against Turks with the same promise of Palestine. Undermining the loyalties of colonized peoples and minorities would be at minimum a nuisance to the enemy. Beyond that, it could erode war efforts from within.

Turning Point and Victory, 1917–18

For the Allies, 1917 began with a series of crises. Under the hammering of one costly offensive after another, French morale had collapsed and military discipline was deteriorating. A combined German-Austrian force had eliminated the Allied states of Serbia and Romania. The Italians experienced a military debacle at Caporetto and were effectively out of the war.

The year 1917 was "the blackest year of the war" for the Allies. At the beginning of the year, the peril on the sea had increased with the opening of unrestricted U-boat warfare against Allied and neutral ships. The greatest blow came when Russia, now in the throes of domestic revolution, withdrew. Germany was able to concentrate more of its resources in the west and fight a one-front war. Perhaps more significantly, it was able to utilize the foodstuffs and raw materials of its newly acquired Russian territories to buoy its home front.

Yet in spite of Allied reversals, it was not at all the case that the war was turning in favor of the Central Powers. Both Austria-Hungary and the Ottoman Empire teetered on the verge of collapse, with internal difficulties increasing as the war dragged on. Germany suffered from labor and supply shortages and economic hardship resulting from the blockade and an economy totally dedicated to waging war.

The war had gone from a stalemate to a state of crisis for both sides. Every belligerent state was experiencing war weariness that undermined civilian and military morale. Pressures to end the war increased everywhere. Attrition was not working; attacks were not working. Every country suffered on the home front and battlefront from strikes, food riots, military desertions, and mutinies. Defeatism was everywhere on the rise.

The Allies longed for the entry of the United States into the war. Although the United States was a neutral country, from the beginning of the war it had been an important supplier to the Allies. U.S. trade with the Allies had jumped from $825 million in 1914 to $3.2 billion in 1916. American bankers also made loans and extended credit to the Allies to the amount of $2.2 billion. The United States had made a sizable investment in the Allied war effort, and its economy was prospering.

Beginning with the sinking of the *Lusitania* in 1915, German policy on the high seas had incensed the American public. Increased U-boat activity in 1916 led U.S. president Woodrow Wilson (1856–1924) to issue a severe warning to the Germans to cease submarine warfare. The Germans, however, were driven to desperate measures. The great advantage of submarines was in sneak attacks—a procedure against international rules, which required warning. Germany initiated a new phase of unrestricted submarine warfare on 1 February 1917, when the German ambassador informed the U.S. government that U-boats would sink on sight all ships including passenger ships—even those neutral and unarmed.

German machinations in Mexico were also revealed on 25 February 1917, with the interception of a telegram from Arthur Zimmermann (1864–1940), the German foreign minister. The telegram communicated Germany's willingness to support Mexico's recovery of "lost territory" in New Mexico, Arizona, and Texas in return for Mexican support of Germany in the event of U.S. entry into the war. U.S. citizens were outraged. On 2 April 1917, Wilson, who had won the presidential election of 1916 on the promise of peace, asked the U.S. Congress for a declaration of war against Germany.

The entry of the United States was the turning point in the war, tipping the scales dramatically in favor of the Allies. The United States contributed its naval power to the large Allied convoys formed to protect shipping against German attacks. In a total war, control and shipment of resources had become crucial issues, and it was in these areas that the U.S. entry gave the Allies indisputable superiority. The United States was also able to send "over there" tens of thousands of conscripts fighting with the American Expeditionary Forces under the leadership of General John "Black Jack" Pershing (1860–1948). They reinforced British and French troops and gave a vital boost to morale.

However, for such a rich nation, the help that the United States was able to give at first was very little. The U.S. government was new to the business of coordinating a war effort, but it displayed great ingenuity in creating a wartime bureaucracy that increased a small military establishment of 210,000 soldiers to 9.5 million young men registered before the beginning of summer 1917. By July 1918, the Americans were sending a phenomenal 300,000 soldiers a month to Europe. By the end of the war, 2 million Americans had traveled to Europe to fight in the war.

The U.S. entry is significant not just because it provided reinforcements, fresh troops, and fresh supplies to the beleaguered Allies. From a broader perspective, it marked a shift in the nature of international politics: Europe was no longer able to handle its own affairs and settle its own differences without outside help.

U.S. troops, though numerous, were not well trained, and they relied on France and Great Britain for their arms and equipment. But the Germans correctly understood that they could not hold out indefinitely against this superior Allied force. Austria-Hungary was effectively out of the war. Germany had no replacements for its fallen soldiers, but it was able to transfer troops from Russia, Romania, and Macedonia to the west. It realized that its only chance of victory lay in swift action. The German high command decided on a bold measure: one great, final offensive that would knock the combined forces of Great Britain, France, and the United States out of the war once and for all by striking at a weak point and smashing through enemy lines. The great surprise was that it almost worked.

Known as the Ludendorff offensive, after the general who devised it, the final German push began in March 1918. Secretly amassing tired troops from the eastern front pulled back after the Russian withdrawal, the Germans counted on the element of surprise to enable them to break through a weak sector in the west. On the first day of spring, Ludendorff struck. The larger German force gained initial success against weak-ened British and French forces. Yet in spite of breaches in defense, the Allied line held. Allied Supreme Commander General Ferdinand Foch (1851–1929) coordinated the war effort that withstood German offensives throughout the spring and early summer of 1918.

The final drive came in mid-July. More than one million German soldiers had already been killed, wounded, or captured in the months between March and July. German prisoners of war gave the French details of Ludendorff's plan. The Germans, now exposed and vulnerable, were placed on the defensive. The German army was rapidly disintegrating. On the other side, tanks, plentiful munitions, and U.S. reinforcements fueled an Allied offensive that began in late September. The German army retreated, destroying property and equipment as it went. With weak political leadership and indecision in Berlin, the Germans held on until early November. The end came finally after four years of war. On 11 November 1918, an armistice signed by representatives of the German and Allied forces took effect.

Thus came to an end a war of slightly more than four years in duration that had consumed the soldiers, material, and productive resources of the European nations on both sides. Europeans had prided themselves on representing the pinnacle of civilization against the barbarism of other continents. Yet nothing

Allied flags are paraded on Armistice Day in Vincennes, France. The long ordeal was over, but relief and joy soon faded as the bitterness of the peace terms corroded postwar Europe.

Fighting the Great War

1905	Development of the Schlieffen Plan
28 June 1914	Assassination of Archduke Franz Ferdinand and his wife, Sophie
28 July 1914	Austria-Hungary declares war on Serbia
30 July–4 August 1914	Russia, France, Britain, and Germany declare war in accordance with system of alliances
August 1914	Germany invades Belgium
6–10 September 1914	First Battle of the Marne
1915	Germany introduces chlorine gas
April 1915–January 1916	Gallipoli Campaign
May 1915	Sinking of the *Lusitania*
February–December 1916	Battle at Verdun
1917	First use of mustard gas
2 April 1917	United States enters war
March 1918	Russia withdraws
11 November 1918	Armistice

matched the destructiveness of the Great War. Of the 70 million who were mobilized, about one in eight were killed. Battlefields of scorched earth and mud-filled ditches, silent at last, scarred once-fertile countrysides as grim memorials to history's first total war. Home fronts, too, served as battlefields, with those who demanded peace silenced as traitors. In the end, only the entry of the United States into the war on the side of the Allies brought an end to the human misery and staggering bloodletting. The war to end all wars was over; the task of settling the peace now loomed.

Reshaping Europe: After War and Revolution

In the aftermath of war, the task of the victors was to define the terms of a settlement that would guarantee peace and stabilize Europe. Russia was the ghost at the conference table, excluded from the negotiations because of its withdrawal from the Allied camp in 1917 and its separate peace with Germany in March 1918. The Bolsheviks were dealing with problems of their own following the revolution, including a great civil war lasting through 1920. Much of what happened in the peace settlements reflected the unspoken concern with the challenge of revolution that the new Soviet Russia represented. A variety of goals marked the peace talks: the idealistic desire to create a better world, the patriotic pursuit of self-defense, a commitment to the self-determination of nations, and the desire to fix blame for the outbreak of the war. In the end, the peace treaties satisfied none of these goals. Meanwhile, Russia's new leaders carefully watched events in the west, looking for opportunities that might permit them to extend their revolution to central Europe.

Settling the Peace

From January to June 1919, an assembly of nations convened in Paris to draw up the new European peace. Although the primary task of settling the peace fell to the Council of Four—Premier Georges Clemenceau of France, Prime Minister David Lloyd George of Great Britain, Prime Minister Vittorio Emanuele Orlando of Italy, and President Woodrow Wilson of the United States—small states, newly formed states, and non-European states, Japan in particular, joined in the task of forging the peace. The states of Germany, Austria-Hungary, and Soviet Russia were excluded from the negotiating tables where the future of Europe was to be determined.

President Wilson, who captured international attention with his liberal views on the peace, was the central figure of the conference. He was firmly committed to the task of shaping a better world: before the end of the war he had proclaimed the "Fourteen Points" as a guideline to the future peace and as an appeal to the people of Europe to support his policies. Believing that secret diplomacy and the alliance system were responsible for the events leading up to the declaration of war in 1914, he put forward as a basic principle "open covenants of peace, openly arrived at." Other points included the reduction of armaments, freedom of commerce and trade, self-determination of peoples, and a general association of nations to guarantee the peace that became the League of Nations. The Fourteen Points were, above all, an idealistic statement of the principles for a good and lasting peace. Point 14, which stipulated "mutual guarantees of independence and territorial integrity" through the establishment of the

Europe After World War I

Georges Clemenceau of France represented a different approach to the challenge of the peace, one motivated primarily by a concern for his nation's security. France had suffered the greatest losses of the war in both human lives and property destroyed. In order to prevent a resurgent Germany, Clemenceau supported a variety of measures to cripple it as a military force on the Continent. Germany was disarmed. The territory west of the Rhine River was demilitarized, with occupation by Allied troops to last for a period of fifteen years. With Russia unavailable as a partner to contain Germany, France supported the creation of a series of states in eastern Europe carved out of former Russian, Austrian, and German territory. Wilson supported these new states out of a concern for the self-determination of peoples. Clemenceau's main concern was self-defense.

Much time and energy were devoted to redrawing the map of Europe. New states were created out of the lands of three failed empires. To allow self-determination, Finland, Latvia, Estonia, Lithuania, Poland, Czechoslovakia, Austria, Hungary, and Yugoslavia were all granted status as nation-states. However, the rights of ethnic and cultural minorities were violated in some cases because of the impossibility of redrawing the map of Europe strictly according to the principle of self-determination. In spite of good intentions, every new nation had its own national minority, a situation that held the promise of future trouble.

League of Nations, was endorsed by the peace conference. The League, which the United States refused to join in spite of Wilson's advocacy, was intended to arbitrate all future disputes among states and to keep the peace.

The representatives of the victorious Allies at Versailles: (left to right) David Lloyd George of Great Britain, Vittorio Orlando of Italy, Georges Clemenceau of France, and Woodrow Wilson of the United States.

A German cartoon, titled "The Mask Falls," depicts German reaction to the terms of the Treaty of Versailles and to the Allies' brand of justice.

The peace conference produced five separate treaties with each of the defeated nations: Austria, Hungary, Turkey, Bulgaria, and Germany. The treaty signed with Germany on 28 June 1919, known as the Treaty of Versailles because it was signed in the great Bourbon palace, was the first and most important. In that treaty, the Allies imposed blame for the war on Germany and its expansionist aims in the famous War Guilt Clause. If the war was Germany's fault, then Germany must be made to pay. Reparations, once the price of defeat, were now exacted as compensation for damages inflicted by a guilty aggressor.

The principle of punitive reparations was included in the German settlement. By 1920 the German people knew that Germany had to make a down payment of $5 billion against a future bill; had to hand over a significant proportion of their merchant ships, including all vessels of more than 1600 tons; had to lose all German colonies; and had to deliver coal to neighbor-

ing countries. These harsh clauses, more than any other aspect of the peace settlement, came to haunt the Allies in the succeeding decades.

In the end, no nation got what it wanted from the peace settlement. The defeated nations felt that they had been badly abused. The victorious nations were aware of the compromises they had reluctantly accepted. Cooperation among nations was essential if the treaty was to work successfully. It had taken the combined resources, not only of France and the British Empire but also of Russia with its vast population and the United States with its great industrial and financial might to defeat the power of Germany and the militarily ineffective Austro-Hungarian Empire. A new and stable balance of power depended on the participation of Russia, the United States, and the British Empire. But Russia was excluded from and hostile to the peace settlement, the United States was uncommitted to it, and the British Empire declined to guarantee it. All three Great Powers backed off from their European responsibilities at the end of the war. By 1920 all aspects of the treaty, but especially the reparations clause, had been questioned and criticized by the very governments that had written and accepted them. The search for a lasting peace had just begun.

Revolution in Russia, 1917–20

Every country has its prophets. So too did Russia in 1914 when a now-forgotten former government minister advised Tsar Nicholas II (1894–1917) to avoid war or else face a social revolution. Other advisers prevailed: they said that Russia must go to war because it was a Great Power with interests beyond its borders. But within its empire, the process of modernization was widening social divisions. Nicholas preferred to listen to those who promised that a short, successful war would strengthen his monarchy against the domestic forces of change. Little did Nicholas know, when he committed Russia to the path of war instead of revolution, that he had guaranteed a future of war *and* revolution. He was delivering his nation up to humiliating defeat in global war and a devastating civil war. His own days were numbered, with his fate to be determined at the hands of a Marxist dictatorship.

The Last Tsar. The Romanov dynasty surely needed strengthening. In 1914 Russia was considered backward by the standards of Western industrial society. Russia still recalled a recent feudal past. The serfs had been freed in the 1860s, but the nature of the emancipation exacerbated tensions in the countryside and

Russian imperial troops fire on demonstrators outside the Winter Palace in St. Petersburg. The people were asking for better working conditions and a more responsive government. This day, 22 January 1905, is known in Russian history as Bloody Sunday.

peasant hunger for land. Russia's limited, rapid industrialization in the 1880s and 1890s was an attempt to catch up with Great Britain, France, and Germany as a world industrial power. But the speed of such change brought with it severe dislocation, especially in the industrial city of Moscow and the capital, St. Petersburg.

Twelve years earlier, in 1905, the workers of St. Petersburg protested hardships due to cyclical downturns in the economy. On a Sunday in January 1905, the tsar's troops fired on a peaceful mass demonstration in front of the Winter Palace, killing and wounding scores of workers, women, and children, who were appealing to the tsar for relief. The event, which came to be known as Bloody Sunday, set off a revolution that spread to Moscow and the countryside. In October 1905, the regime responded to the disruptions with a series of reforms that legalized political parties and established the Duma, or national parliament. Peasants, oppressed with their own burdens of taxation and endemic poverty, launched mass attacks on big landowners throughout 1905 and 1906. The government met workers' and peasants' demands with a return to repression in 1907. In the half-decade before the Great War, the Russian state stood as an autocracy of parliamentary concessions blended with severe police controls.

What workers had learned in 1905 was the power and the means of independent organization. Factory committees, trade unions, and "soviets," or workers'

councils, proliferated. Despite winning a grant of legal status after 1906, unions gained little in terms of ability to act on behalf of their members. Unrest among factory workers revived on the eve of the Great War, a period of rapid economic growth and renewed trade-union activity. Between January and July 1914, Russia experienced 3500 strikes in a six-month period. Although economic strikes were considered legal, strikes deemed political were not. With the outbreak of war, all collective action was banned. Protest stopped, but only momentarily. The tsar certainly weighed the workers' actions in his decision to view war as a possible diversion from domestic problems.

Russia was less prepared for war than any of the other belligerents. Undoubtedly it had more soldiers than other countries, but it lacked arms and equipment. Problems of provisioning such a huge fighting force placed great strains on the domestic economy and on the work force. Under government coercion to meet the needs of war, industrial output doubled between 1914 and 1917, while agricultural production plummeted. The tsar, who unwisely insisted on commanding his own troops, left the government in the hands of his wife, the Tsarina Alexandra, a German princess by birth, and her eccentric peasant adviser, Rasputin. Scandal, sexual innuendo, and charges of treason surrounded the royal court. The incompetence of a series of unpopular ministers further eroded confidence in the regime. (See "The Women Who Started the Russian Revolution," pp. 838–839.)

In the end, the war sharpened long-standing divisions within Russian society. Led by exhausted and starving working women, poorly paid and underfed workers toppled the regime in the bitter winter of March 1917. This event was the beginning of a violent process of revolution and civil war. The tsar abdicated, and all public symbols of the tsardom were destroyed. The banner bearing the Romanov two-headed eagle was torn down, and in its place the red flag flew over the Winter Palace.

Dual Power. With the tsar's abdication, two centers of authority replaced autocracy. One was the Provisional Government, appointed by the Duma and made up of progressive liberals led by Prince Georgi Lvov (1861–1925), prime minister of the new government, who also served as minister of the interior. Aleksandr Kerenski (1881–1970), the only socialist in the Provisional Government, served as minister of justice. The members of the new government hoped to establish constitutional and democratic rule. The other center of authority was the soviets—committees or councils elected by workers and soldiers and supported by radical lawyers, journalists, and intellectuals in favor of socialist self-rule. The Petrograd Soviet was the most prominent among the councils. This duality of power was matched by duality in policies and objectives, which guaranteed a short-lived and unstable regime.

The problems facing the new regime soon became apparent as revolution spread to the provinces and the battlefront. Peasants, who made up 80 percent of the Russian population, accepted the revolution and demanded land and peace. Without waiting for government directives, peasants began seizing the land. Peasants tried to alleviate some of their suffering by hoarding what little they had. The food crisis of winter persisted throughout the spring and summer as breadlines lengthened and prices rose. Workers in cities gained better working conditions and higher wages. But wage increases were invariably followed by higher prices that robbed workers of their gains. Real wages declined.

In addition to the problems of land and bread, the war itself presented the new government with other insurmountable difficulties. Hundreds of thousands of Russian soldiers at the front deserted the war, having heard news from home of peasant land grabs and rumors of a new offensive planned for July. The Provisional Government, concerned with Russia's territorial integrity and its position in the international system, continued to honor the tsar's commitments to the Allies by participating in the war. By spring 1917, 6 to 8 million Russian soldiers had been killed, wounded, or captured. The Russian army was incapable of fighting.

The Provisional Government tried everything to convince its people to carry on with the war. In the summer of 1917, the Women's Battalion of Death, composed exclusively of female recruits, was enlisted into the army. Its real purpose, officials admitted, was to "shame the men" into fighting. The all-female unit, like its male counterparts, experienced high losses: 80 percent of the force suffered casualties. The Provisional Government was caught in an impossible situation: it could not withdraw from the war, but neither could it fight. Continued involvement in the lost cause of the war blocked any consideration of social reforms.

As late as August 1917, the provisional government of Aleksandr Kerenski was determined to carry on the war, but the war-weary troops began to quit. In this scene from Galicia, demoralized Russian soldiers throw down their arms and flee after hearing that German cavalry has broken through the lines.

The Women Who Started the Russian Revolution

Women in Russia, like their counterparts all over Europe in 1914, took over new jobs in the workplace as men marched off to war. Four out of every ten Russian workers were women, up from three of ten on the eve of the war. The situation was more dramatic in Petrograd, Russia's capital and principal industrial center, where by 1917 women constituted 55 percent of the labor force. Russian working women faced greater hardships than their sisters in the west. Most women workers in Petrograd held unskilled, poorly paid jobs in the textile industries and worked grueling twelve- and thirteen-hour days. They left work only to stand for hours in long bread lines and then returned home to care for their elderly relatives and often sick children. Infant mortality was alarmingly high, with as many as half of all children dying before the age of three. Factory owners reported that nothing could be done. "The worker mother drudges and knows only need, only worry and grief," one commentator observed. "Her life passes in gloom, without light."

Russia was suffering badly in the war, with over 2 million soldiers killed by the beginning of 1917. News of disasters at the front reached mothers, wives, and sisters at home in spite of the government's efforts to hide the defeats. In the less than three years since the war had begun, prices had increased 400 percent and transport lines for food and coal had broken down. Bread was the main staple of meager diets. Supplies of flour and grain were not reaching towns and cities. People were starving and freezing to death. Young children were now working eleven-and-a-half-hour days in the factories. The situation was dire, and working women knew that something must be done if their families were to survive.

The working women of Petrograd correctly understood that the intolerable state of affairs had come about because the government was unable to control distribution and to ration limited supplies. Carrying a double burden of supporting those at home unable to work and of producing in the factory the armaments essential for the war effort, women workers began demanding that labor organizations take action to alleviate the situation. In the winter of 1916–17, labor leaders advised exhausted and starving workers to be cautious and patient: workers must wait to strike until the time was ripe. Women workers did not agree. On 8 March 1917 (23 February by the Russian calendar), over 7000 women went on strike in acknowledgment of International Women's Day, an event initiated in the United States in 1909 to recognize the rights of working women. These striking women were angry, frustrated, hungry, and tired of watching their families starve while their husbands, brothers, and sons were away at the battlefront. The week before, the city had been placed on severe rationing because Petrograd was down to its last few days' supply of flour. Although the principal concern of the striking women was bread, their protest was more than just a food riot. Women left their posts in the textile mills to demand an end to the war and an end to the reign of Tsar Nicholas II. They were responding not to revolutionary propaganda but to the politics of hunger. Singing songs of protest, they marched through the streets to take their cause to the better-paid and more radical male metalworkers. Women appealed to working men to join the strike. By the end of the day, 100,000 workers had left their jobs to join demonstrations against the government.

The women did not stop there. They took justice into their own hands and looted bakeries and grocery shops in search of food. In the street demonstrations of the next several days, women and men marched by the thousands, attracting growing support from workers throughout the city and the suburbs. Forty demonstrators were killed when government troops fired into a crowd. Still the women were not deterred. Bolshevik leader Leon Trotsky recalled women's bravery in going up to detachments of soldiers: "More boldly than men, they take hold of the rifles and beseech, almost command: 'Put down your bayonets—join us!'" Stories abound of how poor working women persuaded officers and soldiers of the Cossacks—the tsar's privileged fighting force—to lay down their arms. It was rumored that soldiers abandoned the tsar because they would not fire on the crowds of women. A participant in one confrontation reported how women workers stood without flinching as a detachment of Cossacks bore down upon them. Someone in the crowd shouted out that these were the wives and sisters of soldiers at the front. The Cossacks lowered their rifles and turned their horses around. Troops like these, tired of the war, mutinied all over Petrograd. Within four days of the first action taken by women textile operatives, the government had lost the support of Petrograd workers, women and men, and its soldiers, who had joined the demonstrators. The tsar was forced to abdicate. From this point on, the Romanov monarchy and the Russian war effort were doomed.

In those first days of protest, the women of Petrograd took action into their own hands, pouring into the streets to call for bread, peace, and the end of tsardom. They rejected autocracy and war in defense of their communities and their families. The Russian Revolution had begun.

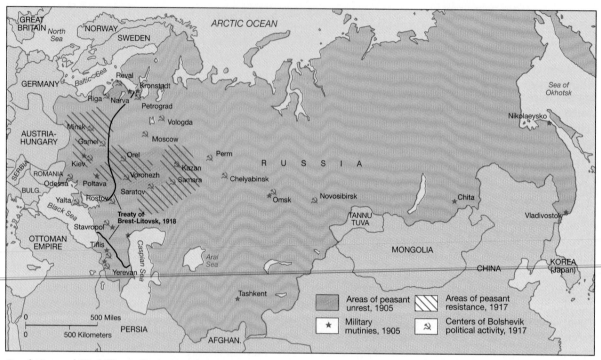

Revolution and Civil War in Russia, 1914–20

While the Provisional Government was trying to deal with the calamities, many members of the intelligentsia—Russia's educated class, who had been exiled by the tsar for their political beliefs—now rushed back from western Europe to take part in the great revolutionary experiment. Theorists of all stripes put their cases before the people. Those who were in favor of gradual reform debated the relative merits of various government policies with those who favored violent revolution. The months between February 1917 and July 1917 were a period of great intellectual ferment. It was the Marxists, or Social Democrats, who had the greatest impact on the direction of the revolution.

The Social Democrats believed that there were objective laws of historical development that could be discovered. Russia's future could be understood only in terms of the present situation in western Europe. Like Marxists in the West, the Russian Social Democrats split over how best to achieve a socialist state. The more moderate Mensheviks (the term means "minority") wanted to work through parliamentary institutions and

were willing to cooperate with the Provisional Government. A smaller faction—despite its name—calling themselves Bolsheviks (meaning "majority") dedicated themselves to preparation for revolutionary upheaval. After April 1917, the Bolsheviks refused to work with the Provisional Government and organized themselves to take control of the Petrograd Soviet.

The leader of the Bolsheviks was Vladimir Ilich Ulyanov (1870–1924), best known by his revolutionary name, Lenin. Forty-seven years old at the time of the revolution, Lenin had spent most of his life in exile or in prison. More a pragmatist than a theoretician, he argued for a disciplined party of professional revolutionaries, a vanguard that would lead the peasants and workers in a socialist revolution against capitalism. In contrast to the Mensheviks, he argued that the time was now ripe for a successful revolution and that it could be achieved through the soviets.

Immediately upon his arrival in Petrograd from Switzerland, Lenin threw down the gauntlet to the Provisional Government. In his April Theses, he promised the Russian people peace, land, and bread. The war must be ended immediately, he argued, because it represented an imperialist struggle that was benefiting capitalists. Russia's duty was to withdraw and wait for a world revolution. This was more than rhetoric on Lenin's part. His years in exile in the west and news of mutinies and worker protests convinced him that revolution was imminent. His revolutionary policies on land were little more than endorsements of the seizures already taking place all over Russia. Even his promises of bread had little substance. But on the whole, the April Theses constituted a clear critique of the policies of the Provisional Government.

Dissatisfaction with the Provisional Government increased as the war dragged hopelessly on and bread lines lengthened. In the midst of these calamities, a massive popular demonstration erupted in July 1917 against the Provisional Government and in favor of the soviets, which excluded the upper classes from voting. The Provisional Government responded with repressive force reminiscent of the tsardom. The July Days were proof of the growing influence of the Bolsheviks among the Russian people. Although the Bolshevik leadership had withdrawn support for the demonstrations at the last moment, Bolshevik rank-and-file party members strongly endorsed the protest. Indisputably, Bolshevik influence was growing in the soviets despite repression and the persecution of its leaders. Lenin was forced to flee to Finland.

As a result of the July Days, Kerenski, who had been heading the Ministry of Justice, was named prime minister and continued the Provisional Government's moderate policies. In order to protect the government from a coup on the right, Kerenski permitted the arming of the Red Guards, the workers' militia units of the Petrograd Soviet. The traditional chasm between the upper and the lower classes was widening as the policies of the Provisional Government conflicted with the demands of the soviets.

Lenin and the Bolsheviks Seize Power.
The second revolution came in November (October according to the Russian calendar). This time it was not a spontaneous street demonstration by thousands of working women that triggered the revolution, but rather the seizure of the Russian capital by the Red Guards of the Petrograd Soviet. The revolution was carefully planned and orchestrated by Lenin and his vanguard of Bolsheviks, who now possessed majorities in the soviets in Moscow and Petrograd and other industrial centers.

Returning surreptitiously from Finland, Lenin moved through the streets of Petrograd disguised in a curly wig and head bandages, watching the Red Guards seize centers of communication and public buildings. The military action was directed by Lev Bronstein, better known by his revolutionary name, Leon Trotsky (1879–1940). The Bolshevik chairman of the Petrograd Soviet, Trotsky used the Red Guards to seize political control and arrest the members of the Provisional Government. Kerenski escaped and fled the city.

The takeover was achieved with almost no bloodshed and was immediately endorsed by an All-Russian Congress of Soviets, which consisted of representatives of local soviets from throughout the nation who were in session amid the takeover of the capital. A Bolshevik regime under Lenin now ruled Russia. Tsar Nicholas II and the royal family were executed by the Bolshevik revolutionaries in July 1918.

The Russian Civil War, 1917–20.
Lenin immediately set to work to end the war for Russia. After months of negotiation, Russia signed a separate peace with the Germans in March 1918 in the Treaty of Brest-Litovsk. By every measure, the treaty was a bitter humiliation for the new Soviet regime. The territorial losses sustained were phenomenal. In a vast amputation, Russia was reduced to the size of its Muscovite period: it recognized the independence of the Ukraine, Georgia, and Finland; it relinquished its Polish territories, the Baltic States, and part of Byelorussia to Germany and Austria-Hungary; and it handed over other territories on the Black Sea to Turkey. Lenin felt that he had no choice: he needed to buy time in order to consolidate the revolution at home, and he hoped for a socialist revolution in Germany that would soften the results of the treaty.

The Treaty of Brest-Litovsk was judged a betrayal, not only outside Russia among the Allied powers, but also inside Russia among some army officers who had sacrificed much for the tsar's war. To these military men, the Bolsheviks were no more than German agents who held the country in their sway. Lacking sufficient organization, unable to coordinate their movements because the Bolsheviks dominated the country's center, and torn apart by different political goals, the White Armies ultimately failed to challenge successfully the Bolshevik hold on the reins of state. But in the three years of civil war between Whites and Reds, the Whites posed a serious threat to Bolshevik policies.

PROCLAMATION OF THE "WHITES," 8 JULY 1918

In the summer of 1918, opponents of the Bolsheviks organized their own volunteer army with the hope of destroying the communist Red Army and eliminating Bolshevik rule. Dissatisfied military officers, Cossacks who feared the loss of their lands and privileges under a Bolshevik state, moderate republicans, socialist revolutionaries, and detachments of workers, students, and intellectuals rallied together. The only thing they had in common was their enemy. In this proclamation, they paint the Bolsheviks as the enemy of the people.

To the Workers and Peasants:

Citizens! The events of the last few days compel all those who love their country and the Russian people, all true defenders of freedom, to take up arms against the Soviet Government and defeat the usurpers who are disguising their nefarious acts by using the name of the people.

The Soviet of People's Commissars has brought ruin to Russia. . . . Instead of bread and peace it has brought famine and war. The Soviet of People's Commissars has made of mighty Russia a bit of earth dripping with the blood of peaceful citizens doomed to the pangs of hunger. In the name of the people the self-styled commissars have given the most fertile land to the enemies of Russia—the Austrians and Germans. There have been wrested from us the Ukraine, the Baltic and Vistula regions, the Kuban, the Don, and the Caucasus, which fed and supplied us with bread. That bread now goes to Germany. With that bread they are feeding those who, step by step, are conquering us and with the help of the Bolsheviks are placing us in the power of the German Kaiser. With that bread they are feeding the German army, which is slaughtering our people in cities and villages of the Ukraine, on the banks of the Don, in the mountains of the Caucasus, and in the fields of Great Russia.

The Soviet of People's Commissars is a plaything in the hands of the German Ambassador, Count Mirbach.

The Soviet of People's Commissars dictates decrees in the name of the people but Kaiser Wilhelm writes those decrees. Spurning agreement with the best citizens of the country, the Soviet of People's Commissars is not only in complete accord with the German imperialists but is carrying out unhesitatingly all their orders and demands.

By its treacherous policy of executing the orders of Count Mirbach the Soviet of People's Commissars forced the rising of the Czechoslovak army, which was marching to the Western front to fight the Germans. . . .

The Czechoslovaks are true republicans and serve the same sublime cause that we do. They are making war on the usurpers and will not permit the strangling of liberty. The People's Commissars, having long since betrayed the cause of the working class and knowing that the wrath of the people is terrible, now depend upon the bayonets of the Germans and the duped Letts to save their own lives and to keep in power.

The People's Commissars have brought about a terrible fratricidal war, sending detachments of Red Guards and Letts against the peasants to take their grain. The People's Commissars are arresting and shooting workers who do not agree with their policies, are manipulating the elections, and are strangling all civil liberties. . . .

To arms all! Down with the Soviet of People's Commissars! Only by overthrowing it shall we have bread, peace, and freedom! Long live unity and order in Russia! When we put an end to the Soviet power we shall at the same time end civil war and return once more to our former strength and power.

And then the enemies of our country will not be terrifying to us. Down with the hirelings—the People's Commissars and their tools! Long live the coming Constituent Assembly!

Long live the free mighty fatherland!

Anti-Bolshevik forces were supplied with materials by the Allies, who intended to keep the eastern front viable. The Allies sent over 100,000 troops and supplies for the purpose of overthrowing the Bolshevik regime by supporting its enemies. Allied support for the White Armies came primarily from the United States, Great Britain, France, and Japan and continued beyond the armistice that ended the Great War in 1918. Although Allied support was not crucial to the outcome of the civil war, it played a significant role in shaping Soviet perceptions of the outside world. For generations of Soviet citizens, anti-Bolshevik assistance has been viewed as an indication that a hostile and predatory capitalist world intended to destroy the fledgling Soviet state for its own ends.

THE RUSSIAN REVOLUTION

January–July 1914	**Protests and strikes**
30 July 1914	**Russia enters World War I**
March 1917	**First Russian Revolution: abdication of Tsar Nicholas II**
March 1917	**Creation of Provisional Government**
April 1917	**Bolsheviks take control of Petrograd**
July 1917	**Massive demonstration against Provisional Government; Lenin is forced to flee Russia**
November 1917	**Bolsheviks and Red Guards seize political control in what comes to be known as the October Revolution**
March 1918	**Russia withdraws from World War I and signs Treaty of Brest-Litovsk**
July 1918	**Tsar Nicholas II and family are executed**

In this poster from 1922, Lenin points to a utopian future as he proclaims, "Let the ruling class tremble before the Communist revolution." The rising sun in the background symbolizes the dawn of the socialist era.

The civil war had another legacy for the future of the Soviet state. To deal with the anarchy caused by the fratricidal struggle, Lenin had to strengthen the government's dictatorial elements at the expense of its democratic ones. The new Soviet state used state police to suppress all opposition. The dictatorship of the proletariat yielded to the dictatorship of the repressive forces.

In the course of the civil war, Lenin was no more successful than Kerenski and the Provisional Government had been in solving the problems of food supplies. Human costs of the civil war were high, with over 800,000 soldiers dead on both sides and 2 million civilian deaths from dysentery and diseases caused by poor nutrition. Industrial production ceased, and people fled towns to return to the countryside. In 1920 it seemed that Russia could drop no lower. Millions had been killed in war or had died from famine. Stripped of territories and sapped of its industrial strength, Russia was a defeated nation. Yet Bolshevik idealism about the success of the proletarian revolution prevailed. No longer sure that a world socialist revolution would come to their aid, Bolshevik leaders set out to build the future.

• • •

By every measure, the Great War was disastrously expensive. Some European nations suffered more than others, but all endured significant losses of life, property, and productive capacity. The cost in human lives was enormous. In western Europe, 8.5 million were dead; total casualties amounted to 37.5 million. France lost 20 percent of its men between the ages of 20 and 44, Germany lost 15 percent, and Great Britain 10 percent. The war also resulted in huge losses in productive capacity. National economies buckled under the weight of foreign debts and resorted to a variety of methods to bail themselves out, including taxes, loans, and inflations. The people of Europe continued to pay for the war long after the fighting had ended.

The big winner in the war was the United States, now a creditor nation owed billions of dollars of loans from the Allies and operating in new markets established during the war. The shift was not a temporary move but a structural change. The United States now took its place as a great power in the international system. The world that had existed before 1914 was gone, and what was to replace it was still very much in flux. To the east, Russia was engaged in the vast experiment of building a new society. In the West, the absence of war was not peace.

Suggestions for Further Reading

The War Europe Expected

Marc Ferro, *The Great War, 1914–1918* (London: Routledge & Kegan Paul, 1973). The origins of World War I within a broad social and cultural context. Stressing the importance of an imagined war and patriotism as two factors that precipitated actual conflict, Ferro shows how the gulf between imagination and reality led to domestic conflict and social unrest once war broke out.

* James Joll, *The Origins of the First World War* (New York: Longman, 1984). In an examination of the decisions that brought about war in 1914, importance is placed on the limited options available to decision-makers. The July crisis, the international system, the arms race, domestic politics, the international economy, imperial rivalries, and cultural and psychological factors are considered in terms of their contributions to the outbreak of war.

* Keith Robbins, *The First World War* (Oxford: Oxford University Press, 1984). The major cultural, political, military, and social developments between 1914 and 1918. Includes a discussion of the course of the land war and modes of warfare.

The War Europe Got

* Gerd Hardach, *The First World War, 1914–1918* (Berkeley: University of California Press, 1977). Describes the changes in the world economy leading up to the war, the war's impact on trade, wartime monetary and fiscal policies, and the war's impact on labor. Each major power is included in an analysis of wartime economic history.

B. E. Schmitt and H. C. Vedeler, *The World in a Crucible, 1914–1919* (New York: Harper & Row, 1984). A broad survey of the military and political history of World War I; the war is viewed here as a period of revolution in both warfare and politics. Includes considerable discussion of the Russian Revolution and a section on the entry of the United States into European affairs.

* Denis Winter, *Death's Men: Soldiers of the Great War* (London: Penguin, 1979). Rather than being an account of military strategy and battlefield tactics, *Death's Men* goes inside the infantrymen's war to convey the experience of war in the trenches.

Adjusting to the Unexpected: Total War

John Williams, *The Homefronts: Britain, France and Germany, 1914–1918* (London: Constable, 1972). A comparative study of the home fronts, their impact on the course of the war, and the war's impact on civilian life.

Reshaping Europe: After War and Revolution

* Sheila Fitzpatrick, *The Russian Revolution, 1917–1932* (Oxford: Oxford University Press, 1982). An analysis of the October Revolution of 1917 from the perspective of Stalinist society. The February and October revolutions of 1917, the civil war, and the economic policies of the 1920s are treated as various aspects of a single revolutionary movement.

Tsuyoshi Hasegawa, *The February Revolution: Petrograd, 1917* (Seattle: University of Washington Press, 1981). A thorough examination of the effects of World War I on Russian workers, liberals, and revolutionary parties leads to an interpretation of the February Revolution as the outcome of a conflict between the state and its citizens. Particular attention is given to events leading to the abdication of the tsar, the establishment of the Provisional Government, and the early stages of the Russian Revolution.

Arno J. Mayer, *The Politics and Diplomacy of Peacemaking* (New York: Knopf, 1967). A comprehensive examination of the role of internal political concerns and the foreign policy of the warring nations, as well as a thorough analysis of the struggles between Bolshevism, Wilsonian liberalism, and counterrevolution.

* David Stevenson, *The First World War and International Politics* (Oxford: Oxford University Press, 1988). A study of the global ramifications of World War I, this work traces the development of war aims on both sides, the reasons peace negotiations failed, and why compromise proved elusive.

*Paperback edition available.

27 ❧ THE EUROPEAN SEARCH FOR STABILITY, 1920–1939

The Screams from Guernica

Rarely does a piece of art scream out. The mural *Guernica* is different. Listen to the painting shown here. It is a painting whose images convey sounds: the shrieks of terror, fear, suffering, and death. There is a chaos of noise here that seems at odds with the drab greys, black, and white, the monochromatic colorlessness of the artist's palette. But no, the lack of color only heightens the noise and allows us to focus on the sound, the screams that come from open mouths of human and beast on the canvas. Death and brutality reverberate throughout the painting. The open mouths of the dead baby's mother, the bull standing behind her, the small bird to the right of the bull, and the

wounded horse at the center of the canvas emit fear like projectiles—beak and tongues thrusting forth in pointed daggers.

Pablo Picasso (1881–1973) painted this great mural in May and June 1937 for the Spanish Pavilion of the International Exhibition to be held in Paris. He called it *Guernica* in commemoration of the bombing of the small Basque town in Spain by German planes at the end of April 1937. The destruction of Guernica was an event that shocked the world and devastated the Spanish artist, then living in France. Working in collaboration with the insurgent forces of Francisco Franco (1892–1975), German planes dropped bomb after bomb on the ancient city, destroying it in three and a half hours. Their purpose was to cut off the retreat of loyalist government troops and to terrorize civilians through saturation bombing. Picasso demonstrates vividly that noncombatants, represented by the women and child, were no longer just hapless bystanders but were, in fact, the very targets of indiscriminate killing.

Guernica is a huge canvas, measuring over 11 feet high and 25 feet long. It dwarfs spectators who stand before it, enveloping them in a modern-day apocalypse of contorted bodies. We do not look at war directly in the mural but at the terror it creates in this vision of needless slaughter. Picasso deliberately used the traditional religious symbols of the Madonna and Child and the Pietà as models for his terrifying image of maternity. The lips of the baby, who hangs like a rag doll in the arms of its despairing mother on the far left of the canvas, are sealed in the silence of death. The mother finds her counterpoint in the figure of the limping woman in the right foreground, who drags behind her a wounded arm and a swollen knee. Above her a woman, gaping in disbelief and clutching her breasts in anguish, raises a lamp over the scene. On the far right, a fourth woman, trapped in the flames of a burning building, appears to be exploding upward in terrified petition. On the ground under the horse lies a dead man with his head and arm severed from his body, clutching a broken sword and flower whose petals wait to be picked in his right hand. The presentation of his head as a piece of statuary fallen from its pedestal reinforces the bloodless horror of his death. His left palm is crisscrossed with the lines of fate, or perhaps marked with the toil of heavy labor. Suspended over the scene like a huge eye is a naked light bulb, a modern image illuminating the timelessness of the theme of the horror of war.

In one of his rare moments of self-interpretation, Picasso explained to a public eager to grasp the mural's symbolism that the horse whose side is opened by a terrible gash is "the people," victimized by incomprehensible cruelty. The bull is an enigmatic figure symbolizing, Picasso tells us, darkness and brutality. The horned beast appears as a powerful and vulnerable witness to this scene of needless destruction.

Guernica has been hailed as the most significant painting of the twentieth century. His greatness as an artist, Picasso claimed, derived from his ability to understand his time. In the stripped down, almost cartoonlike figures of *Guernica,* Picasso presents us with a picture of European society that is brutal and horrible. Here is a condemnation of the modern technological war that targets civilian populations; here on this horrifying canvas are portrayed the consequences of totalitarianism and the failure of democracy that characterized the European search for stability between 1920 and 1939. Subsequent events made Germany's actions in the Spanish Civil War seem like a dress rehearsal for atrocities against the population centers of Warsaw, Rotterdam, and London and made this canvas seem a prophesy of horrors to come. Some years later, during the Second World War, a Nazi official challenged Picasso with a photograph of the great mural, "So it was you who did this." The artist answered, "No, you did."

Europe in 1918

International Politics and Economic Nationalism

The armistice that ended World War I in 1918 did not stop the process of social upheaval and transformations challenging attempts to restore order throughout Europe. In 1918, parts of war-torn Europe faced the possibility of revolution. Russia, where revolution had destroyed tsardom, expectantly watched revolutionary developments in countries from the British Isles to eastern Europe. The Bolshevik leaders of Russia's revolution counted on the capitalist system to destroy itself. That did not happen. By 1921, revolutions had been brutally crushed in Berlin, Munich, and Budapest. The Soviets, meanwhile, had won the civil war against the Whites and survived the intervention of the British, French, Japanese, and Americans. But the new Russian regime was diplomatically isolated and in a state of almost total economic collapse.

In 1917–18, the United States had played a significant and central role in the waging of war and in the pursuit of peace. Under U.S. president Woodrow Wilson, who urged his country to guarantee European security and guide Europe's future, the American nation seemed promising as an active and positive force in international politics. By 1921, however, the United States had retreated to a position, not of isolation, but of selective involvement. With one giant, Russia, devastated and isolated, and the other, the United States, reluctant, Europeans faced an uncertain future.

New Nation-States, New Problems

Before World War I, east-central Europe was a region divided among four great empires—the Ottoman, the Habsburg, the Russian, and the German. Under the pressure of defeat, those empires collapsed into their component national parts, and when the dust of the peace treaties had settled, the region had been molded into a dozen sovereign states. The victorious Allies hoped that independent states newly created from fragments of empire would buffer Europe from the spread of communism westward and the expansion of German power eastward.

A swath of new independent states cut through the center of Europe. Finland had acquired its independence from Russia in 1917. Estonia, Latvia, and Lithuania, also formerly under Russian rule, comprised the now independent Baltic states. After more than a century of dismemberment among three empires, Poland became a single nation again. Czechoslovakia was carved out of former Habsburg lands. Austria and Hungary shriveled to small independent states. Yugoslavia was pieced together from a patchwork of territories. Romania swelled, fed on a diet of settlement concessions. These new nations assured the victorious powers and especially France that the new political geography of east-central Europe would guarantee the peace.

World War I victor nations hoped that these new states would stabilize European affairs; they could not have been more wrong. They erred in three important ways in their calculations. First, many of the new states were internally unstable precisely because of the principle of national self-determination, the idea that nationalities had the right to rule themselves. Honoring the rights of nationalities was simple in the abstract, but application of the principle proved complicated and at times impossible. Religious, linguistic, and ethnic diversity abounded in the newly formed nations, and recognizing nationality often meant ignoring the rights of minorities. In Czechoslovakia, for example, the Czechs dominated the Slovaks and the Germans even though the Czechs were fewer in number. Ethnic unrest plagued all of eastern Europe. Minority tensions weakened and destabilized the fragile governments.

Second, the struggle for economic prosperity further destabilized the new governments. East-central Europe was primarily agricultural, and the existence of the great empires had created guaranteed markets. The war disrupted the economy and generated social unrest. The peace settlements only compounded the economic problems of the region. When the Habsburg Empire disintegrated, the Danube River basin ceased to be a cohesive economic unit. New governments were saddled with borders that made little economic sense.

Creating cohesive economic units proved an insurmountable task for newly formed governments and administrations that lacked both resources and experi-

East-Central Europe

ence. Low productivity, unemployment, and overpopulation characterized most of east-central Europe. Attempts to industrialize and to develop new markets confronted many obstacles. Much of the land was farmed on a subsistence basis. What agricultural surplus was created was difficult to sell abroad. East-central Europeans—including Poles, Czechs, Yugoslavs, and Romanians, all tied to France through military and political commitments—were excluded from western European markets and were isolated economically from their treaty allies. Economic ties with Germany endured in ways that perpetuated economic dependence and threatened future survival.

Finally, common borders produced tensions over territories. The peace settlements made no one happy. Poland quarreled with Lithuania, and Czechoslovakia vied with Poland over territorial claims. Poland actually went to war with Russia for six months in 1920 in an effort to reclaim the Ukraine and expand its borders to what they had been more than a century earlier. The Bolsheviks counterattacked and tried to turn the conflict into a revolutionary war in order to spread communism to central Europe. French military advisers came to the aid of the Poles and turned the Russians back. The Treaty of Riga, signed in March 1921, gave Poland much but not all of the territory it claimed.

Hungary, having lost the most territory in World War I, held the distinction of having the greatest number of territorial grievances against its neighbors—Czechoslovakia, Romania, and Yugoslavia. Yugoslavia made claims against Austria. Bulgaria sought territories controlled by Greece and Romania. Ethnicity, strategic considerations, and economic needs motivated claims for territory. Disputes festered, fed by the intense nationalism that prevented the cooperation necessary for survival.

Germany, the Soviet Union, and Italy further complicated the situation with their own territorial claims against their east-central European neighbors. The new German government refused to accept the loss of the "corridor" controlled by Poland that severed East Prussia from the rest of Germany. Nor was Germany resigned to the loss of part of Silesia to Poland. Russia refused to forget its losses to Romania, Poland, Finland, and the Baltic states. Italy, too weak to act on its own, nevertheless dreamed of expansion into Yugoslavia, Austria, and Albania. The redefined borders of eastern and central Europe produced animosity and the seeds of ongoing conflict. The new states of eastern Europe stood as a picket fence between Germany and Russia, a fence that held little promise of guaranteeing the peace or of making good neighbors.

German Recovery

Germany, the most populous nation in western Europe with 60 million people, emerged strong from defeat. In 1919 the German people endorsed a new liberal and democratic government, the Weimar Republic, so named for the city in which its constitution had been written. The constitution of the new government was unusually progressive, with voting rights for women and extensive civil liberties for German citizens. Because World War I had not been fought in Germany, German transportation networks and industrial plants had escaped serious damage. Its industry was fed by raw materials and energy resources unsurpassed anywhere in Europe outside Russia.

In east-central Europe, Germany had actually benefited from the dismantling of the Habsburg Empire and the removal of Poland and the Baltic states from

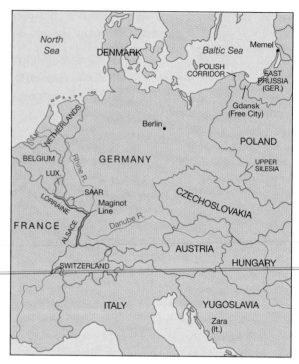

Germany

Russian control. Replacing its formerly large neighbor to the east were weak states potentially susceptible to Germany's influence. Because the governments of east-central Europe feared communism, they were not likely to ally themselves with the Soviet state. The existence of the small buffer states left open the possibility of German collaboration with Russia, since the two large nations might be able to negotiate their interests in the area.

On its western frontier, Germany's prospects were not so bright. Alsace and Lorraine had been returned to France. From German territory, a demilitarized zone had been created in the Rhineland. The Saar district was under the protection of League of Nations commissioners, and the Saar coal mines were transferred to French ownership until 1935, when a plebiscite returned the region to Germany. Humiliated and betrayed by the geographic consequences of its defeat, Germany looked to recover its status.

Germany's primary foreign policy goal was revision of the treaty settlements of World War I. German politicians and military leaders perceived disarmament, loss of territory, and payment of reparations as serious obstacles in restoring Germany's position as a great power. German statesmen sought liberation of the Rhineland from foreign military occupation; return of the Saar basin; and recovery of the Corridor and Upper Silesia from Poland.

German leaders set economic recovery as the basis of their new foreign policy. In 1922, Germany signed the Treaty of Rapallo with Russia, a peacetime partnership that shocked the western powers. Economics motivated the new Russo-German alliance: German industry needed markets and the Russians needed loans to reconstruct their economy. Both states wanted to break out of the isolation imposed on them by the victors of World War I. However, Germany quickly learned that markets in Russia were limited and that hopes for recovery depended on financial cooperation with western Europe and the United States. At the end of 1923, Gustav Stresemann (1878–1929) assumed direction of the German Foreign Ministry and began to implement a conciliatory policy toward France and Britain. By displaying peaceful intentions he hoped to secure American capital for German industry and win the support of the West for the revision of the peace settlement.

Stresemann joined his French and British counterparts, Aristide Briand (1862–1932) and Austen Chamberlain (1863–1937), in fashioning a series of treaties at Locarno, Switzerland, in 1925. In a spirit of cooperation, Germany, France, and Belgium promised never again to go to war against each other and to respect the demilitarized zone that separated them. Britain and Italy "guaranteed" the borders of all three countries and assured the integrity of the demilitarized zone. The treaties initiated an atmosphere of goodwill, a "spirit of Locarno," that heralded a new age of security and nonaggression.

However, Germany did not renounce its ambitions in eastern Europe. Stresemann expected Germany to recover the territory lost to Poland. He also knew that Germany must rearm and expand to the east. From the early 1920s until 1933, Germany secretly rearmed in violation of Versailles. Undercover, Germany rebuilt its army and trained its soldiers and airmen on Russian territory. In violation of Versailles treaty agreements, Germany planned to be once again a great power with the same rights as other European countries.

France's Search for Security

Having learned the harsh lessons of 1870–71 and 1914–18, France understood well the threat posed by a united, industrialized, and well-armed Germany. During the years immediately following World War I, France deeply distrusted Germany. France had a smaller population at 40 million people and lower industrial production than Germany. France had been devastated by the war, and Germany had not been. But France did have certain advantages in 1921. It had the best-equipped army in the world. Germany was disarmed. The Rhineland was demilitarized and occupied. But France knew that without the support of Great Britain and the United States it could not enforce the Treaty of Versailles and keep Germany militarily weak.

The Americans and the British refused to conclude a long-term peacetime alliance with the French. In search of allies on the Continent, therefore, France committed itself to an alliance in the east with Poland and the Little Entente nations of Czechoslovakia, Romania, and Yugoslavia. Treaties with these four states of east-central Europe gave France some security in the event of an attack. But the treaties were also liabilities because France would have to fight to defend east-central Europe.

To keep Germany militarily and economically weak, the French attempted to enforce the Treaty of Versailles fully and completely in 1921–23. They were willing to do so alone if necessary. In 1923 the French army invaded the Ruhr district of Germany and occupied it with the intention of collecting reparations payments. But the Ruhr invasion served only to isolate France further from its wartime allies. France depended on loans from American banks to balance its budget, and the Americans disapproved of the French use of military might to enforce the treaty.

In 1924–25, France decided to cooperate with the United States and Great Britain rather than continue a policy of enforcing the treaty alone and attempting to keep Germany weak. France withdrew its army from the Ruhr and some troops from the Rhineland. It agreed to lower German reparations payments. In addition, by signing the Locarno treaties, France cooperated with the Anglo-American policy that rejected the use of military force against Germany and promoted German economic recovery.

French anxiety about security continued. Nothing indicated the nature of this anxiety more clearly than the construction, beginning in the late 1920s, of the Maginot Line, a system of defensive fortifications between Germany and France.

Throughout the 1920s, French political leaders tried to engage Great Britain in guaranteeing the security of France and Europe. The British agreed to defend France and Belgium against possible German aggression. They stopped short, however, of promising to defend Poland and Czechoslovakia. After settling this matter at Locarno, Britain largely reverted to its prewar pattern of withdrawing from continental Europe and concentrating its attention on the demands of its global empire.

Western Europe

The United States in Europe

The Treaty of Versailles marked the demise of European autonomy. American intervention had boosted French and British morale during the crucial months of 1917. In providing financial help, ships, troops, and supplies, the United States had rescued the Allied powers. After the war, a balance of power in Europe could not be maintained without outside help. Germany had been defeated, but if it recovered, France and Britain alone would probably not be able to contain it. Security and peace now depended on the presence of the United States to guarantee a stable balance of power in Europe and to defend Western hegemony in the world.

However, the United States was unwilling to assume a new role as political leader of Europe and mediator of European conflict. It refused to sign a joint peace, arranging instead a separate peace with Germany. It also refused to join the League of Nations. Following the war, the League had been devised as an international body of nations committed, according to article 10 of its covenant, to "respect and preserve as against external aggression the territorial integrity and existing political independence" of others. Germany was excluded from membership until 1926, and the USSR (Union of Soviet Socialist Republics) was denied entry

until 1934. Otherwise, the League of Nations claimed a global membership. But the absence of U.S. support and the lack of any machinery to enforce its decisions undermined the possibility of the League's long-term effectiveness. Hopes that the international body could serve as a peacekeeper collapsed in 1931 with the League's failure to deal with the crisis of Japanese aggression against Manchuria.

The United States persisted in avoiding political and military obligations in Europe, with the idea of protecting its own freedom and autonomy. Instead, it sought to promote German economic recovery and reasoned that a peaceful and stable Europe would be reestablished without a real balance of power in Europe and without a commitment from the United States.

Many feared that territorial settlements of the peace held the promise of another war. Even efforts at comprehensive international cooperation like the League of Nations did not overcome the problem of competitive nations, nor did the Kellogg-Briand Pact, signed by 23 nations in 1928. Named for U.S. Secretary of State Frank B. Kellogg (1856–1937) and French foreign minister Aristide Briand, who devised the plan, the pact renounced war. In the atmosphere of the 1920s, a time of hope and caution, the agreement carried all the weight of an empty gesture.

Crisis and Collapse in a World Economy

In 1918 the belligerent nations—winners and losers alike—had big bills on their hands. Although nations at war had borrowed from their own populations through the sale of war bonds, private citizens could not provide all the money needed to finance four years of war. France borrowed from Great Britain. Both Great Britain and France took loans from the United States. When all else failed, belligerent nations could and did print money not backed by productive wealth. Because more money had claims on the same amount of national wealth, the money in circulation was worth less. When the people who had purchased war bonds were then paid off with depreciated currency, they lost real wealth. Inflation had the same effect as taxation. The people had less wealth and the government had less debt.

The United States, for the first time in history the leading creditor nation in the world, had no intention of wiping the slate clean by forgiving war debts. Nor did it intend to accept repayment in less-valuable postwar currencies: loans were tied to gold. Britain, France, and Belgium counted on reparations from Germany to pay their war debts and to rebuild their economies.

MARRIED AGAIN

IRELAND, *THE COLUMBUS DISPATCH*

"Married Again." This 1928 cartoon shows the wicked world once again pledging eternal fidelity to peace with the signing of the Kellogg-Briand pact. The cynical attitude of the artist was vindicated by the events of the later twentieth century.

Reparations were calculated on the basis of the damages Germany had inflicted on the Allies. The postwar Reparations Commission determined that Germany owed the victors 132 billion gold marks ($33 billion), to be paid in annual installments of 2 billion gold marks ($500 million), plus 26 percent of the value of German exports.

For the German people and for German leaders, reparations were an unacceptable punitive levy that mortgaged the prosperity of future generations. Germany, too, wanted to recover from the years of privation of the war. Substantial reparations payments would have transferred real wealth from Germany to the Allies. Transferring wealth would have cut into any increase in the German standard of living in the 1920s, and it would have diminished the investment needed to make the German economy grow.

When French and Belgian troops entered the Ruhr district of Germany in order to exact overdue reparations payments, the German government recommended that German miners, trainmen, and civil servants

respond with passive resistance. To pay these idle employees and employers, the German government printed huge amounts of currency. The mark collapsed and world currencies were endangered. With financial disaster looming, the British and Americans decided to intervene. A plan had to be devised that would permit Germany to prosper while funneling payments to France, so dependent on reparations for its own recovery and for its war debt payments to the United States. In 1924 the American banker Charles G. Dawes (1865–1951), along with a group of international financial experts appointed by the Allied governments, devised a solution to the reparations problem. The Dawes Plan aimed to end inflation and restore economic prosperity in Germany by giving Germany a more modest and realistic schedule of payments and by extending a loan from American banks to get payments started.

As important as reparations and war debts are in any understanding of the Western world in the 1920s, they cannot be considered in isolation. Debtor nations,

The runaway inflation of the 1920s is dramatized by this photo of a German housewife who is lighting the cooking fire with millions of marks. She declared that it was cheaper to use the worthless currency for kindling than to buy wood with it.

whether Allies paying back loans to the United States or defeated nations paying reparations to the victors, needed to be able to sell their goods in world markets. They saw trade as the principal way to accumulate enough national income to pay back what they owed and to prosper domestically without burying their citizens under a mountain of new taxes.

If trade was to be the stepladder out of the financial hole of indebtedness, open markets and stable currencies were its rungs. The United States recognized that a stable Europe would give it a market for its own agricultural and industrial products and provide a guarantee for recovery of its loans and investments. Yet the proverbial monkey wrench in a smoothly functioning international economy was the trade policy of the United States. Republican political leaders in the United States insisted on high tariffs to protect domestic

goods against imports. But high tariffs prevented Europeans from selling in the United States and earning the dollars they needed to repay war debts.

While blocking imports, the United States planned to expand its own exports to world markets, especially to Europe. The problem for American exporters, however, was the instability of European currencies in the first half of the 1920s. All over Europe, governments allowed inflation to rise with the expectation that depreciating currencies would make their goods cheaper in world markets and hence more saleable.

Depreciating European currencies on the one hand meant an appreciating dollar on the other. For the "grand design" of U.S. trade expansion, a strong dollar was no virtue. More and more German marks, British pounds, and French francs had to be spent to purchase American goods. The result was that fewer American exports were sold in European markets. Because two-thirds of Germany's long-term credits came from the United States, Germany's fate was directly linked to the fortunes of American financial centers. Conversely, the soundness of American banks depended on a solvent Germany, which now absorbed 18 percent of U.S. capital exports.

Despite the scaled-down schedule of the Dawes Plan, reparations remained a bitter pill for German leaders and the German public to swallow. In 1929, American bankers devised another plan under the leadership of the American businessman Owen D. Young (1874–1962), chairman of the board of General Electric. Although the Young Plan initially transferred $100 million to Germany, Germans saw the twentieth century stretching before them as year after year of nothing but humiliating reparations payments. To make matters worse, after 1928 American private loans shriveled in Germany as American investors sought the higher yields of a booming stock market at home.

Europe as a whole made rapid progress in manufacturing production during the second half of the decade, and by 1929 it had surpassed its prewar (1913) per capita income. Yet structural weaknesses were present, though they went almost unnoticed. The false security of a new gold standard masked the instability and interdependence of currencies. Low prices prevailed in the agricultural sector, keeping the incomes of a significant segment of the population depressed. But the low rate of long-term capital investment was obscured in the flurry of short-term loans, whose disappearance in 1928 spelled the beginning of the end for European recovery. The protectionist trade policy of the United States conflicted with its insistence on repayment of war debts. Germany's resentment over reparations was in no way alleviated by the Dawes and Young repayment plans. The irresponsibility of American speculation in the stock market pricked the bubble of prosperity. None of these factors operated in isolation to cause the collapse that began in 1929. Taken together, however, they caused a depression of previously unimagined severity in the international economic system.

The Great Depression

In the history of the Western world, the year 1929 has assumed mythic proportions. During one week in October of that year, the stock market in the United States collapsed. This crash set off the Great Depression in an international economic system already plagued with structural problems. It also marked the beginning of a long period of worldwide economic stagnation and depression.

A confluence of factors made Europe and the rest of the world vulnerable to reversals in the American economy. Heavy borrowing and reliance on American investment throughout the 1920s contributed to the inherent instability of European economies. Even Great Britain, itself a creditor, relied on short-term loans; "borrowing short and lending long" proved to be disastrous when loans were recalled. Excessive lending and leniency were fatal mistakes of creditor nations, especially the United States. When in the summer of 1929 American investors turned off the tap of the flow of capital to search for higher profits at home, a precarious situation began to get worse.

A depression is a severe downturn marked by sharp declines in income and production as buying and selling slow down to a crawl. Depressions were not new in the business cycles of modern economies, but what happened in October 1929 was more serious in its extent and duration than any depression before or since. The bottom was not reached until three years after the Great Depression began. In 1932 one in four American workers was without a job. One in three banks had closed its doors. People lost their homes, unable to pay their mortgages; farmers lost their land, unable to earn enough to survive. The great prosperity of the 1920s had vanished overnight.

The plight of the United States rippled through world markets. Americans stopped buying foreign goods. The Smoot-Hawley Tariff Act, passed by the U.S. Congress in 1930, created an impenetrable tariff fortress against agricultural and manufactured imports

Lining up for the dole in London, 1931. During the Great Depression, private charity and public relief offered hope to the unemployed.

WINIFRED HOLTBY

Winifred Holtby (1898–1935) was a British novelist, journalist, and social reformer who covered European political events throughout the interwar period. In this selection from her writings she chronicles the differential impact that war and depression had on women's lives. Expectations about woman's proper role, whether of housewife and mother or serving her country in the workplace, were profoundly political and hotly contested.

The effect of the slump upon women's economic position is most obvious, not only in the problems of unemployment among both industrial and professional women, but still more in the bitterness surrounding the question of married women's paid employment, "pin money" office girls, unorganised casual female factory labour, and claims to alimony, maintenance and separation allowances. These are the dilemmas of scarcity. It is here that the shoe pinches when national purchasing power has failed to distribute adequately the products of industry.

During the War, women entered almost every branch of industry and most of the professions. . . . In transport, engineering, chemicals, textiles, tailoring and woodwork, women took the places which, ever since the sorting-out process which followed the first disorganised scramble of the Industrial Revolution, had been reserved to men. They took and they enjoyed them.

Then the men returned, and on demobilisation demanded again the jobs which they had left. The position was not simple.

Some of the men had received promises that their work should be kept for them; but of these, some did not return. Some women surrendered their shovels, lathes and hoes without a grievance. Their work had been "for the duration of the war" and they had no desire to retain it.

But others thought differently. Women, they told themselves, had been excluded from the more highly-skilled and better-paid industrial posts for two or more generations. They had been told that certain processes were beyond their power. It was a lie. During the war they had proved it to be so, by their own skill and efficiency. Why surrender without a word opportunities closed to them by fraud and falsehood? They had as much right to wheel, loom or cash-register as any man. Why then pretend that they were

intruders in a world which was as much their own as their brothers'? . . .

After 1928, jobs became not duties which wartime propaganda taught girls that it was patriotic to perform, but privileges to be reserved for potential bread-winners and fathers of families. Women were commanded to go back to the home.

The bitterness began which has lasted ever since— the women keeping jobs and the men resenting it— the men regaining the jobs and the women resenting it. . . .

In Italy, Germany and Ireland a new dream of natural instinctive racial unity was arising, which designed for women a return to their "natural" functions of house-keeping and child-bearing; while in the English-speaking countries a new anti-rational philosophy combined with economic fatalism, militated against the ebullient hopes which an earlier generation had pinned to education, effort, and individual enterprise.

All generalisations are false. In every civilised country are little groups of older women with memories of suffrage struggles, and young women who grew up into the post-war optimism, and whose ideas remain unchanged by the fashions of the hour. It is they who still organise protests against reaction; who in national and international societies defend the political, civil, and economic equality of men and women; who invade new territories of achievement; who look towards a time when there shall be no wrangling over rights and wrongs, man's place and woman's place, but an equal and co-operative partnership, the individual going unfettered to the work for which he is best suited, responsibilities and obligations shared alike.

From Winifred Holtby, *Women in a Changing Civilization* (1934).

and hampered foreign producers. The major trading nations of the world, including Great Britain, enacted similar protectionist measures. American investment abroad dried up as the lifelines of American capital to Europe were cut.

European nations tried to staunch the outward flow of capital and gold by restricting the transfer of capital abroad. Large amounts of foreign-owned gold ($6.6 billion from 1931 to 1938) nevertheless were deposited in American banks. In 1931 President Herbert Hoover (1874–1964) supported a moratorium on the payment of reparations and war debts. The moratorium, combined with the pooling of gold in the United States, led to a run on the British pound sterling in 1931 and the collapse of Great Britain as one of the world's great financial centers.

The gold standard disappeared from the international economy, never to return. So too did reparations payments and war debts when the major nations of Europe met without the United States at a special conference held in Lausanne, Switzerland, in 1932. Something else died at the end of the 1920s: confidence in a self-adjusting economy, an "invisible hand" by which the business cycle would be righted. In 1932–33, the Great Depression, showing no signs of disappearing, reached its nadir and became a global phenomenon. Economic hardship transformed political realities. The Labour cabinet in Great Britain was forced to resign, and a new national government composed of Conservative, Liberal, and Labour leaders was formed to deal with the world economic emergency. Republican government was torn by bitter divisions in France. In the United States, the Republican party, which had been in power since 1920, was defeated in 1932. Franklin D. Roosevelt (1882–1945), a Democrat, was elected president in a landslide victory with a mandate to transform the American economy. German democratic institutions were pulled down in favor of fascist dictatorship.

In the decade following the Great War, peace settlements did not promote a stable international community. Instead, self-determination of peoples created new grounds for national rivalries in eastern Europe, and the lack of any effective means of guaranteeing the peace only exacerbated prewar animosities. The economic interdependence of nation-states through an international system of reparations payments and loans increased the vulnerability of governments to external pressures. With the collapse of the international finance system in 1929, political stability and international cooperation seemed more elusive than ever.

INTERNATIONAL POLITICS

1919	Creation of the League of Nations
1920	War between Poland and Russia
1921	Treaty of Riga
1922	Germany and Russia sign Treaty of Rapallo
1923	French and Belgian troops invade the Ruhr district
1924	Dawes Plan
1925	Locarno Treaties
1928	Kellogg-Briand Pact
1929	Young Plan
October 1929	Collapse of the United States stock market; beginning of the Great Depression
1935	Saar region returned to German control
1936	Germany stations troops in the Rhineland in violation of the Versailles Treaty

The Soviet Union's Separate Path

In the decade following war, revolution, and civil war, the Soviet state committed its people to a program of rapid industrial growth in order to ensure its survival as a great power. The costs of Russia's rapid industrialization were wasted resources, enormous human suffering, and millions of lost lives. Lenin's successor, Joseph Stalin (1879–1953), obliged the Soviet people to achieve in a single generation what it had taken the West a century and a half to accomplish.

The Soviet Regime at the End of the Civil War

Echoing Karl Marx, the Bolshevik leader Lenin declared that the revolution and the civil war had been won in the name of "the dictatorship of the proletariat." The hammer and sickle on the Soviet flag represented the united rule of workers and peasants and were symbolic reminders of the commitment to rule from below. But at the end of the civil war in 1921, the Bolsheviks, not the people, were in charge.

❧ Buildings for the Future

Buildings tell tales. Archaeologists, trying to understand other civilizations, excavate ancient dwellings in order to reconstruct past lives. Family life, social values, the nature of work, technology, and progress are all embodied in the structures in which people live and work. If future generations had only traces of the buildings of the twentieth century, they would nonetheless hold a key to understanding our civilization and values.

The twentieth-century architecture that we call "modern" was the child born from the union of technology and art in the aftermath of the Great War of 1914–18. In reaction to the horrors of the battlefront, a new generation of architects, many of them ex-soldiers, committed themselves to the creation of buildings as works of art that answered the needs of modern society. Those who followed the lead of the prewar avant-garde disdained imitating past masters. They saw their task as "starting from zero"—that is, striking out in a new direction unencumbered by the cultural baggage of a past that had proven itself to be morally bankrupt. In building for the future, the postwar generation felt that the present must create a new style of its own.

The battle cry for a new architectural style arose from defeated Germany and in particular from a single man, Walter Gropius (1883–1969). In 1919, only a few months after the Treaty of Versailles ended World War I, Gropius, a recent veteran of the front, founded the Bauhaus, a school based on the collaborative efforts of architects, sculptors, artists, and artisans. The untranslatable name Bauhaus (resulting from joining the German words for "building" and "house") soon characterized a new movement in the arts and architecture. As director of the Bauhaus until 1928, Gropius attracted some of Europe's leading artists to the school, including the architects Marcel Breuer (1902–1981) and Ludwig Mies van der Rohe (1886–1969). Russian abstract artist Vasili Kandinski (1866–1944) and his Swiss colleague Paul Klee (1879–1940) were also members of the teaching staff at the Bauhaus. Characterized by intense activity, exciting experimentation, and enthusiastic collaboration, the men and women who assembled at the Bauhaus pioneered new designs in everything from kitchen utensils and furniture to lighting fixtures and skyscrapers.

Gropius was a utopian dreamer who saw in buildings and in the humble objects of daily life the means of creating human happiness. Beauty in design was defined by the fit between form and function. Rather than rejecting industrial society, Gropius sought a new way of uniting art with it. Unlike other arts-and-crafts movements, the Bauhaus was willing to make use of the machine to produce for the masses, whether the production was of prefabricated houses or teacups. Gropius knew well that architecture does not move faster than the society it seeks to serve, but he also knew that it must keep pace with the world around it. The school's motto, one that Gropius considered realistic and responsible, proclaimed: "Art and technology—a new unity!"

Pictured here is one of the first Bauhaus models of a skyscraper. Modest by subsequent standards, its 32 stories dwarf the traditional buildings at its base. Steel and glass were expressly used to liberate the structure from supporting walls. With new engineering knowledge about support, loads, stress, and mass, sheer facades of glass opened up inside space to the outside world. Interior walls were eliminated. Gropius admired the new functional factory structures and early skyscrapers in the United States and Canada for their starkness and simplicity and sought to introduce their "majesty" to residential architecture.

The architects of the Bauhaus were in the right place at the right time. Germany needed new buildings, and in the period from 1924 to 1929 the return of economic prosperity allowed them to be built. Under Gropius's direction, working-class apartment blocks with open floor plans, unadorned facades, clean lines, and a stark simplicity spread across the German landscape. Office buildings of reinforced concrete with little to distinguish them from the new residential housing also mushroomed. By the end of the decade, Bauhaus architects had left their mark on German towns and cities. Then, seeking refuge from Hitler (eventually in the United States), Gropius and some of his associates transformed the skylines of America's great cities within a decade. In the second half of the twentieth century, the Bauhaus style of architecture spread throughout the world.

The architects of the Bauhaus changed the appearance of the modern world, and with it the twentieth-century experience. Critics who longed for a traditional architecture of decoration and classical emulation judged the Bauhaus style to be barren and ugly, but its emphasis on design and function prevailed. The skyscrapers of the twentieth century are products of the lessons of war and technology and the idealistic pursuit of a better world that took shape very visibly in the 1920s.

Leon Trotsky

Nikolai Bukharin

Joseph Stalin

The industrial sector, small as it was, was in total disarray by 1921. Famine and epidemics in 1921–22 killed and weakened more people than the Great War and the civil war combined. The countryside had been plundered to feed the Red and White armies. The combination of empty promises and a declining standard of living left workers and peasants frustrated and discontented. Urban strikes and rural uprisings defied short-term solutions. The proletarian revolutionary heroes of 1917 were rejecting the new Soviet regime. The Bolshevik party now faced the task of restoring a country exhausted by war and revolution, its resources depleted, its economy destroyed.

At the head of the Soviet state was Lenin, the first among equals in the seven-man Politburo. The Central Committee of the Communist party decided "fundamental questions of policy, international and domestic," but in reality the Politburo, the inner circle of the Central Committee, held the reins of power.

Among seven members of the Politburo, three in particular attempted to leave their mark on the direction of Soviet policy: Leon Trotsky, Nikolai Bukharin (1888–1938), and Joseph Stalin. The great drama of Soviet leadership in the 1920s revolved around how the most brilliant (Trotsky) and the most popular (Bukharin) failed at the hands of the most shrewdly political (Stalin).

The two extremes in the debate over the direction of economic development were, on the one hand, a planned economy totally directed from above and, on the other hand, an economy controlled from below. In 1920–21, Leon Trotsky, at that time people's commissar of war, favored a planned economy based on the militarization of labor. Trade unions opposed such a proposal and argued for a share of control over production. Lenin, however, favored a proletarian democracy and supported unions organized independently of state control.

The controversy was resolved in the short run at the Tenth Party Congress in 1921, when Lenin chose to steer a middle course between trade-union autonomy and militarization by preserving the unions and at the same time insisting on the state's responsibility for economic development. His primary goal was to stabilize Bolshevik rule in its progress toward socialism. He recognized that nothing could be achieved without the peasants. As a result, Lenin found himself embracing a new economic policy that he termed a "temporary retreat" from Communist goals.

The New Economic Policy, 1921–28

In 1921 Lenin ended the forced requisitioning of peasant produce that had been in effect during the civil war. In its place, peasants were to pay a tax in kind, that is, a fixed portion of their yield, to the state. Peasants in turn were permitted to reinstate private trade on their own terms. Party leaders accepted this dramatic shift in economic policy because it held the promise of prosperity so necessary for political stability. The actions of

Lenin to return the benefits of productivity to the economy, combined with those of the peasants to reestablish markets, created the New Economic Policy (NEP) that emerged in the spring and summer of 1921.

It remained for Nikolai Bukharin to give shape and substance to the economic policy that permitted Russian producers to engage in some capitalist practices. As one of the founding fathers of the Soviet state and the youngest of the top Bolshevik leaders, Bukharin took his place on the Central Committee of the Communist party and on the Politburo as well.

Bukharin set about solving Russia's single greatest problem: how could Russia, crippled by poverty, find enough capital to industrialize? Insisting on the need for long-term economic planning, Bukharin counted on a prosperous and contented peasantry as the mainstay of his policy. Bukharin was also strongly interested in attracting foreign investment to Soviet endeavors as a way of ensuring future productivity.

Bukharin appreciated the importance of landholding to Russian peasants and defended a system of individual farms and private accumulation. Agriculture would operate through a market system, and the peasants would have the right to control their own surpluses. Rural prosperity would generate profits that could be used for gradual industrial development. Bukharin's policy stood in stark contrast to Stalin's later plan to feed industry by starving the agricultural sector.

Collective and large-scale farming had to be deferred indefinitely in order to reconcile the peasantry to the state—a policy profoundly at odds with the programs of the Communist state to pull down the capitalist system and establish socialism. In 1924 the tax in kind was replaced with a tax in cash. With this shift the state now procured grain through commercial agencies and cooperative organizations instead of directly from the peasants. The move toward Western capitalist models seemed more pronounced than ever to critics of the NEP.

Beginning in 1922, Lenin suffered a series of strokes, which virtually removed him from power by March 1923. When he died on 21 January 1924, the Communist leadership split over the ambiguities of the NEP. The backward nature of agriculture did not permit the kind of productivity that the NEP policymakers had anticipated. Cities demanded more food as their populations swelled with the influx of unskilled workers from rural areas. In 1927 peasants held back their grain. The Soviet Union was then experiencing a series of foreign policy setbacks in the West and in China, and Bolshevik leaders spoke of an active anti-

Soviet conspiracy by the capitalist powers, led by Great Britain. The Soviet state lowered the price of grain, thereby squeezing the peasantry. The war scare, combined with the drop in food prices, soon led to an economic crisis.

By 1928 the NEP was in trouble. Stalin, general secretary of the Communist party of the Soviet Union, saw his chance. Under his supervision, the state intervened to prevent peasants from disposing of their own grain surpluses. The peasants responded to requisitioning by hoarding their produce and violently rioting. Bukharin and the NEP were in danger. Stalin exploited the internal crisis and external dangers to eliminate his political rivals. Stalin's rival Trotsky had been expelled from the Communist party in November 1927 on charges that he had engaged in antiparty activities. Banished from Russia in 1929, he eventually found refuge in Mexico, where he was assassinated in 1940 at Stalin's command.

Bukharin's popularity in the party also threatened Stalin's aspirations. Bukharin was dropped from the Politburo in 1929. Tolerated through the early 1930s, he was arrested in 1937, and tried and executed for alleged treasonous activities the following year. The fate that befell Trotsky and Bukharin was typical of what happened to those who stood in the way of Stalin's pursuit of dictatorial control. Stalin was, in a colleague's words, "a grey blur." Beneath his apparently colorless personality, however, was a dangerous man of great political acumen, a ruthless, behind-the-scenes politician who controlled the machinery of the party to his own ends and was not averse to employing violence in order to achieve them.

Stalin's Rise to Power

Joseph Stalin was born Iosif Vissarionovich Dzhugashvili in 1879. His self-chosen revolutionary name, Stalin, means "steel" in Russian and is as good an indication as any of his opinion of his own personality and will. Stalin, the man who ruled the Soviet Union as a dictator from 1928 until his death in 1953, was not a Russian. He was from Georgia, an area between the Black and Caspian seas, and spoke Russian with an accent. Georgia, with its land occupied and its people subjugated by invading armies for centuries, was annexed to the expanding Russian empire in 1801.

As the youngest of four and the only surviving child of Vissarion and Ekaterina Dzhugashvili, Stalin endured a childhood of brutal misery. Stalin's father was a poor and often unemployed shoemaker who

THE RESULTS OF THE FIRST FIVE-YEAR PLAN

Under Joseph Stalin the Soviet Union embarked on rapid industrialization that transformed the peasant-based economy into a leading iron and steel producer. The Five-Year Plan achieved in four years what the western industrialized nations took 150 years to accomplish. The Soviet leader did not tally the cost in human lives or the impact on the quality of life that such brutal economic transformation entailed.

The fundamental task of the Five-Year Plan was to transfer our country, with its backward, and in part medieval, technique, to the lines of new, modern technique.

The fundamental task of the Five-Year Plan was to convert the USSR from an agrarian and weak country, dependent upon the caprices of the capitalist countries, into an industrial and powerful country, fully self-reliant and independent of the caprices of world capitalism.

The fundamental task of the Five-Year Plan was, in converting the USSR into an industrial country, fully to eliminate the capitalist elements, to widen the front of socialist forms of economy, and to create the economic base for the abolition of classes in the USSR, for the construction of socialist society. . . .

The fundamental task of the Five-Year Plan was to transfer small and scattered agriculture to the lines of large-scale collective farming, so as to ensure the economic base for socialism in the rural districts and thus to eliminate the possibility of the restoration of capitalism in the USSR.

Finally, the task of the Five-Year Plan was to create in the country all the necessary technical and economic prerequisites for increasing to the utmost the defensive capacity of the country, to enable it to organize determined resistance to any and every attempt at military intervention from outside, to any and every attempt at military attack from without. . . .

What are the results of the Five-Year Plan in four years in the sphere of *industry*?

Have we achieved victory in this sphere?

Yes, we have. . . .

We did not have an iron and steel industry, the foundation for the industrialization of the country. Now we have this industry.

We did not have a tractor industry. Now we have one.

We did not have an automobile industry. Now we have one.

We did not have a machine-tool industry. Now we have one.

We did not have a big and up-to-date chemical industry. Now we have one.

We did not have a real and big industry for the production of modern agricultural machinery. Now we have one.

We did not have an aircraft industry. Now we have one.

In output of electric power we were last on the list. Now we rank among the first.

In output of oil products and coal we were last on the list. Now we rank among the first.

We had only one coal and metallurgical base—in

intended that his son be apprenticed in the same trade. Under his mother's protection, young Iosif received an education and entered a seminary against his father's wishes. Iosif's schooling, extraordinary for someone of his poverty-stricken background, gave him the opportunity to learn about revolutionary socialist politics. At the turn of the century, Georgia had a strong Marxist revolutionary movement that opposed Russian exploitation. Iosif dropped out of the seminary in 1899 to engage in underground Marxist activities, and he soon became a follower of Lenin.

Stalin's association with Lenin kept him close to the center of power after the October Revolution of 1917. First as people's commissar for nationalities (1920–23) and then as general secretary of the Central Committee of the Communist party (1922–53), Stalin showed

the Ukraine—which we barely managed to keep going. We have not only succeeded in improving this base, but have created a new coal and metallurgical base—in the East—which is the pride of our country.

We had only one center of the textile industry—in the North of our country. As a result of our efforts we will have in the very near future two new centers of the textile industry—in Central Asia and Western Siberia.

And we have not only created these new great industries, but have created them on a scale and in dimensions that eclipse the scale and dimensions of European industry.

And as a result of all this the capitalist elements have been completely and irrevocably eliminated from industry, and socialist industry has become the sole form of industry in the U.S.S.R.

And as a result of all this our country has been converted from an agrarian into an industrial country; for the proportion of industrial output, as compared with agricultural output, has risen from 48 per cent of the total in the beginning of the Five-Year Plan period (1928) to 70 per cent at the end of the fourth year of the Five-Year Plan period (1932). . . .

The object of the Five-Year Plan in the sphere of agriculture was to unite the scattered and small individual peasant farms, which lacked the opportunity of utilizing tractors and modern agricultural machinery, into large collective farms, equipped with all the modern implements of highly developed agriculture, and to cover unoccupied land with model state farms. . . .

The party has succeeded, in a matter of three years,

in organizing more than 200,000 collective farms and about 5,000 state farms specializing mainly in grain growing and livestock raising, and at the same time it has succeeded, in the course of four years, in enlarging the crop area by 21,000,000 hectares.

The party has succeeded in getting more than 60 per cent of the peasant farms, which account for more than 70 per cent of the land cultivated by peasants, to unite into collective farms, which means that we have *fulfilled* the Five-Year Plan *threefold*.

The party has succeeded in creating the possibility of obtaining, not 500,000,000 to 600,000,000 poods[1] of marketable grain, which was the amount purchased in the period when individual peasant farming predominated, but 1,200,000,000 to 1,400,000,000 poods of grain annually.

The party has succeeded in routing the kulaks as a class, although they have not yet been dealt the final blow; the laboring peasants have been emancipated from kulak bondage and exploitation, and a firm economic basis for the Soviet government, the basis of collective farming, has been established in the countryside.

The party has succeeded in converting the U.S.S.R. from a land of small peasant farming into a land where agriculture is run on the largest scale in the world.

Such, in general terms, are the results of the Five-Year Plan in four years in the sphere of agriculture.

[1.] Pood—a unit of weight equivalent to 36.1 lbs.

From Joseph Stalin, *Selected Writings* (1942).

natural talent as a political strategist. His familiarity with non-Russian nationalities was a great asset in his dealings with the ethnic diversity and unrest in the vast Soviet state. Unlike party leaders who had lived in exile in western Europe before the revolution, Stalin had little knowledge of the West.

After Lenin's death in 1924, Stalin shrewdly bolstered his own reputation by orchestrating cult worship

of Lenin. In 1929 Stalin used the occasion of his fiftieth birthday to fashion for himself a reputation as the living hero of the Soviet state. Icons, statues, busts, and images of all sorts of both Lenin and Stalin appeared everywhere in public buildings, schoolrooms, and homes. He systematically began eliminating his rivals so that he alone stood unchallenged as Lenin's true successor.

The First Five-Year Plan

The cult of Stalin coincided with the First Five-Year Plan (1929–32), which launched Stalin's program of rapid industrialization. Between 1929 and 1937, the period covered by the first two five-year plans (truncated because of their proclaimed success), Stalin laid the foundation for an urban industrial society in the Soviet Union. By brutally squeezing profits out of the agricultural sector, Stalin managed to increase heavy industrial production between 300 and 600 percent.

Stalin committed the Soviet Union to rapid industrialization as the only way to preserve socialism. The failure of revolutionary movements in western Europe meant that the Soviet Union must preserve "socialism in one country," the slogan of the political philosophy that justified Stalin's economic plans. Stalin made steel the idol of the new age. The Soviet state needed heavy machinery to build the future. An industrial labor force was created virtually overnight as peasant men and women were placed at workbenches and before the vast furnaces of modern metallurgical plants. The number of women in the industrial work force tripled in the decade after 1929. The reliability of official indices varied, but there is little doubt that heavy industrial production soared between 1929 and 1932. The Russian people were constantly reminded that no sacrifice could be too great in producing steel and iron.

When he first began to deal with the grain crisis of 1928, Stalin did not intend collective agriculture as a solution. But by the end of 1929, the increasingly repressive measures instituted by the state against the peasants had led both to collectivization and to the deportation of *kulaks,* the derisive term for wealthy peasants that literally means "the tight-fisted ones." Stalin achieved forced collectivization by confiscating land and establishing collective farms run by the state. Within a few months, half of all peasant farms were collectivized. By 1938 private land had been virtually eliminated. The state set prices, controlled distribution, and selected crops with the intention of ensuring a steady food supply and freeing a rural labor force for heavy industry. More as a publicity ploy than a statement of fact, the First Five-Year Plan was declared a success after only three years. It was a success in one important sense: it did lay the foundations of the Soviet planned economy, in which the state bureaucracy made all decisions about production, distribution, and prices.

Collectivization meant misery for the 25 million peasant families who suffered under it. At least 5 million peasants died between 1929 and 1932. Collectivization ripped apart the fabric of village life, destroyed families, and sent homeless peasants into exile. Peasants who resisted collectivization retaliated by destroying their own crops and livestock. Rapid industrial development shattered the lives of millions of people. In attempting to develop an industrial sector overnight, Stalin, as tsars before him, saw that Russia could be carried into the future only on the backs of its peasants.

The Comintern, Economic Development, and the Purges

In addition to promoting its internal economic development, the Soviet Union had to worry about survival in a world political system composed entirely of capitalist countries. After the Bolshevik revolution in 1917, Lenin had fully expected that other socialist revolutions would follow throughout the world, especially in central and western Europe. These revolutions would

A Soviet propaganda poster shows a fat capitalist dismissing the Five-Year Plan as "fantasy." Later, the smug capitalist turns green with envy as Soviet industrial might amazes the world.

Soviet women were mobilized into the labor force. Here a female tractor driver heads toward the fields.

destroy capitalism and secure Russia's place in a new world order. But as the prospects for world proletarian revolution evaporated, Soviet leaders sought to protect their revolutionary country from what they saw as a hostile capitalist world. They used diplomacy to this end. The end of the Allied intervention in Russia allowed the Bolshevik state to initiate diplomatic relations with the West, beginning with the Treaty of Rapallo signed with Germany in 1921. By 1924 all the major countries of the world—with the exception of the United States—had established diplomatic relations with the Soviet Union. In 1928 the USSR cooperated in the preparation of a world disarmament conference to be held in Geneva and joined western European powers in a commitment to peace. The United States and the Soviet Union exchanged ambassadors for the first time in 1933.

In addition to diplomatic relations, the Soviet state in 1919 encouraged various national Communist parties to form an association for the purpose of promoting and coordinating the coming world revolution. This Communist International, or Comintern, was based in Moscow and included representatives from 37 countries by 1920. As it became clear that a world revolution was not imminent, the Comintern concerned itself with the ideological purity of its member parties. Under Lenin's direction, the Soviet Communist party determined policy for all the member parties.

Bukharin and Stalin shared a view of the Comintern that prevailed from 1924 to 1929: since the collapse of capitalism was not imminent, the Comintern should work to promote the unity of working classes everywhere and should cooperate with existing worker organizations. In 1929, however, Stalin argued that advanced capitalist societies were teetering on the brink of new wars and revolutions. As a result, the Comintern must seek to sever the ties between foreign Communist parties and social democratic parties in order to prepare for the revolutionary struggle. Stalin purged the Comintern of dissenters, and he decreed a policy of noncooperation in Europe from 1929 to 1933. As a result, socialism in Europe was badly split between Communists and democratic socialists.

The Second Five-Year Plan, announced in 1933, succeeded in reducing the Soviet Union's dependence on foreign imports, especially in the areas of heavy industry, machinery, and metal works. The basic physical plant for armaments production was in place by 1937, and resources continued to be shifted away from consumer goods to heavy industrial development. This industrial development, and the collectivization of agriculture, brought growing urbanization. By 1939 one in three Soviet people were living in cities, compared to one in six in 1926. In his commitment to increased production, Stalin introduced into the workplace incentives and differential wage scales at odds with the principles and programs of the original Bolshevik revolution. Stricter discipline was enforced; absenteeism was punished with severe fines or loss of employment. Workers who exceeded their quotas were rewarded and honored.

Amid this rapid industrialization, Stalin inaugurated the Great Purge, actually a series of purges lasting from 1934 through 1938. Those whom Stalin believed to be his opponents—real and imagined; past, present, and future—were labeled "class enemies." The most prominent of them, including leaders of the Bolshevik revolution who had worked with Stalin during the 1920s, appeared in widely publicized "show trials." They were intimidated and tortured into false confessions of crimes against the regime, humiliated by brutal prosecutors, and condemned to death or imprisonment. Stalin wiped out the Bolshevik old guard, Communist party members whose first loyalty was to the international Communist movement rather than to Stalin himself, and all potential opposition within the Communist party. Probably 300,000 people were put to death, among them engineers, managers, technical specialists, and officers of the army and navy. In addition, 7 million people were placed in labor camps. Stalin now had unquestioned control of the Communist party and the country.

The purges dealt a severe blow to the command of the army and resulted in a shortage of qualified industrial personnel, slowing industrial growth. The Great Purge coerced the Soviet people into making great sacrifices in the drive for industrialization. It prevented any possible dissension or opposition within the USSR at a time when the "foreign threat" posed by Nazi Germany was becoming increasingly serious.

The human suffering associated with the dislocation and heavy workloads of rapid coerced industrialization cannot be measured. Planned growth brought with it a top-heavy and often inefficient bureaucracy, and that bureaucracy ensured that the Soviet Union was the most highly centralized of the European states. The growing threat of foreign war meant an even greater diversion of resources from consumer goods to war industries beginning with the Third Five-Year Plan in 1938.

Women and the Family in the New Soviet State

The building of the new Soviet state exacted particularly high costs from women. Soviet women had been active in the revolution from the beginning. Lenin and the Bolshevik leaders were committed to the liberation of women, who, like workers, were considered to be oppressed under capitalism. Lenin denounced housework as "barbarously unproductive, petty, nerve-wracking, stultifying, and crushing drudgery." In its early days, the Soviet state pledged to protect the rights of mothers without narrowing women's opportunities or restricting women's role to the family.

After the October Revolution of 1917, the Bolsheviks passed a new law establishing equality for women within marriage. In 1920 abortion was legalized. New legislation established the right to divorce and removed the stigma from illegitimacy. Communes, calling themselves "laboratories of revolution," experimented with sexual equality. Russian women were enfranchised in 1917, gaining the right to vote before women in the industrialized countries of western Europe. The Russian revolution went further than any revolution in history toward the legal liberation of women within such a short span of time.

These advances, as utopian as they appeared to admirers in western European countries, did not deal with the problems faced by the majority of Russian women. Bolshevik legislation did little to address the special economic hardships of peasant and factory women. Although paid maternity leaves and nursing breaks were required by law, these guarantees became a source of discrimination against women workers, who were the last hired and first fired by employers trying to limit expenses. Divorce legislation was hardly a blessing for women with children, since men incurred no financial responsibility toward their offspring in terminating a marriage. Even as legislation was being passed in the early days of the new Soviet state, women were losing ground in the struggle for equal rights and independent economic survival.

By the early 1930s, reforms affecting women were in trouble due in large part to a plummeting birthrate. This decline created special worries for Soviet planners, who forecast doom if the trend was not reversed. In 1936, a woman's right to choose to end a first pregnancy was revoked. In the following decade, all abortions were made illegal. Homosexuality was declared a criminal offense. The family was glorified as the mainstay of the socialist order and the independence of women was challenged as a threat to Soviet productivity. While motherhood was idealized, the Stalinist drive to industrialize could not dispense with full-time women workers.

Women's double burden in the home and workplace became heavier during Stalin's reign. Most Russian women held full-time jobs in the factories or on the farms. They also worked what they called a "second

THE LAW ON THE ABOLITION OF LEGAL ABORTION, 1936

In his drive to industrialize the Soviet Union as rapidly as possible, Stalin recognized the economic importance of women's roles both as workers and as mothers. At the height of the Second Five-Year Plan, many women's rights were revoked, including the right to an abortion. The "New Woman" of the revolutionary period gave way to the post-1936 woman, depicted by the state as the perfect mother who matched her husband's productivity in the workplace, ran the household, and raised a large family.

When we speak of strengthening the Soviet family, we are speaking precisely of the struggle against the survivals of a bourgeois attitude towards marriage, women and children. So-called "free love" and all disorderly sex life are bourgeois through and through, and have nothing to do with either socialist principles or the ethics and standards of conduct of the Soviet citizen. Socialist doctrine shows this, and it is proved by life itself.

The elite of our country, the best of the Soviet youth, are as a rule also excellent family men who dearly love their children. And vice versa: the man who does not take marriage seriously, and abandons his children to the whims of fate, is usually also a bad worker and a poor member of society.

Fatherhood and motherhood have long been virtues in this country. This can be seen at the first glance, without searching enquiry. Go through the parks and streets of Moscow or of any other town in the Soviet Union on a holiday, and you will see not a few young men walking with pink-cheeked, well-fed babies in their arms. . . .

The toilers of our land have paid with their blood for the right to a life of joy, and a life of joy implies the right to have one's own family and healthy, happy children. Millions of workers beyond the frontiers of our land are still deprived of this joy, for there unemployment, hunger and helpless poverty are rampant. Old maids and elderly bachelors, a rare thing in our country, are frequent in the West, and that is no accident.

We alone have all the conditions under which a working woman can fulfil her duties as a citizen and as a mother responsible for the birth and early upbringing of her children.

A woman without children merits our pity, for she does not know the full joy of life. Our Soviet women, full-blooded citizens of the freest country in the world, have been given the bliss of motherhood. We must safeguard our family and raise and rear healthy Soviet heroes!

---

shift" in running a household and taking care of children. In the industrialized nations of western Europe, the growth of a consumer economy lightened women's labor in the home to some extent. In the Soviet Union, procuring the simplest necessities was woman's work that required waiting in long lines for hours. Lack of indoor plumbing meant that women spent time hauling water for their families at the end of a working day. In such ways, rapid industrialization exacted its special price from Soviet women.

In the 1920s and 1930s, the Soviet search for stability and prosperity took the Soviet Union down a path very different from the states of western Europe. Rejecting an accommodation with a market economy, Stalin committed the Soviet people to planned rapid industrialization that was accomplished through mass repression and great human suffering. Insulated from

world markets and the devastation of the Great Depression, the Soviet Union relied on a massive state bureaucratic system to achieve socialism in one country and to make the Soviet state into an industrial giant.

The Promise of Fascism

Throughout western Europe, parliamentary institutions, representative government, and electoral politics offered no ready solutions to the problems of economic collapse and the political upheaval on the Left and the Right. Fascism promised what liberal democratic societies failed to deliver—a way out of the economic and political morass. Fascist rule—dictatorship by a charismatic leader—promised an escape from parlia-

THE SOVIET UNION'S SEPARATE PATH

November 1917	**Bolsheviks and Red Guard seize power**
1919	**Creation of the Communist International (Comintern)**
1920	**Legalization of abortion and divorce**
1921	**End of the civil war**
1921	**Introduction of the New Economic Policy**
3 April 1922	**Stalin becomes secretary general of the Communist party**
21 January 1924	**Lenin dies**
1924–1929	**Comintern policy of "Unity of the Working Classes"**
1927	**Dissatisfied peasants hoard grain**
November 1927	**Trotsky expelled from Communist party**
1928	**Stalin introduces grain requisitioning**
November 1929	**Bukharin expelled from Politburo**
1929	**Introduction of First Five-Year Plan and the collectivization of agriculture**
1929–1933	**Comintern policy of noncooperation with social democratic parties**
1933–1937	**Second Five-Year Plan**
1934–1938	**Great Purge**
1936	**Abortion declared illegal**
1938	**Third Five-Year Plan**

appealed to middle classes who feared loss of their property to socialists and loss of their money to the vagaries of international markets. The move toward dictatorship appeared relentless in the period between the wars. In 1920, of the 28 states in Europe, 26 were parliamentary democracies. By the end of 1940, only 5 democracies remained: the United Kingdom, Ireland, Sweden, Finland, and Switzerland. The rest of Europe was under dictatorial rule. The European dictatorships of the 1930s displayed a variety of forms. On the left, the "dictatorship of the proletariat" in the Soviet Union was in fact a regime driven by the ruthless brutality of Joseph Stalin toward the goal of building socialism. Other dictatorships were on the right. Italy and Germany each constructed fascist dictatorships that regarded Soviet communism as their mortal enemy. The Soviet Union, in turn, saw fascism as a serious threat.

War and postwar hardships were the catalysts for the emergence of the new mass movements of fascism in Europe. The Great War had created a political vacuum caused by the crisis in liberal values. In condemning the war and its costs, new fascist leaders, who tended to start their political careers as social reformers and even socialists, proposed a radical reformation of the status quo.

Fascism sounded very like socialism. In the Soviet Union, Bolshevik leaders reassured their people that socialism was the only way of dealing with the weaknesses and inequities of the world capitalist system laid bare in the world war. In its initial condemnations of the capitalist economy and liberal political institutions and values, fascists employed revolutionary language similar to that of the Left, while manipulating in radically new ways the political symbols of the Right—the nation, the flag, and the army. Fascism promised to steer a course between the uncertainties and exploitation of a liberal capitalist system and the revolutionary upheaval and expropriation of a socialist system. Fascism was ultranationalist, and the use of force was central to its appeal.

The word *fascism* is derived from the Latin *fasces,* the name for the bundle of rods with ax head carried by the magistrates of the Roman Empire. Fascism was rooted in the mass political movements of the late nineteenth century, which emphasized nationalism, antiliberal values, and a politics of the irrational. The electoral successes of the German variant—National Socialism, or Nazism—were just beginning in the late 1920s. In the same period, fascist movements were making their appearance in England, Hungary, Spain, and France.

mentary chaos, party wranglings, and the threat of communism. Fascism promised more: by identifying ready enemies—scapegoats for failed economic and national ambitions—fascism promised that it held the answer for those who sought protection and security.

The Rise of Dictatorships

Dictatorships became the most prevalent form of government in Europe between the wars. Dictatorships

But none was more successful and none demanded more attention than the fascist experiment in Italy, which inspired observers throughout Europe to emulate it.

Mussolini's Italy

Italy was a poor nation. Although Italy was one of the victorious Allies in World War I, Italians felt that their country had been betrayed by the peace settlement of 1919 by being denied the territory and status it deserved. A recently created electoral system based on universal manhood suffrage had produced parliamentary chaos and ministerial instability. The lack of coherent political programs only heightened the general disapproval with government that accompanied the peace negotiations. People were beginning to doubt the parliamentary regime's hold on the future. It was under these circumstances that the Fascist party, led by Benito Mussolini (1883–1945), entered politics in 1920 by attacking the large Socialist and Popular (Catholic) parties.

Mussolini had begun his prewar political career as a Socialist. The young Mussolini was arrested numerous times for Socialist political activities and placed under state surveillance. An ardent nationalist, he volunteered for combat in World War I and was promoted to the rank of corporal. Injured in early 1917 by an exploding shell detonated during firing practice, he returned to Milan to continue his work as editor of *Il Populo d'Italia* ("The People of Italy"), the newspaper he founded in 1914 to promote Italian participation in the war.

Mussolini yearned to be the leader of a revolution in Italy comparable to that directed by Lenin in Russia. Although his doctrinal allegiance to socialism was beginning to flag, Mussolini, like Lenin, recognized the power of the printed word to stir political passions. Emphasizing nationalist goals and vague measures of socioeconomic transformation, Mussolini identified a new enemy for Italy—bolshevism. He organized his followers into the Fascist party, a political movement that by utilizing strict party discipline quickly developed its own national network.

Many Fascists were former Socialists and war veterans like Mussolini who were disillusioned with postwar government. They dreamed of Italy as a great world power, as it had been in the days of ancient Rome. Their enemies were not only Communists with their international outlook but also the big businesses, which they felt drained Italy's resources and kept its people poor and powerless. Panicky members of the lower middle classes sought security against the economic uncertainties of inflation and were willing to endorse violence to achieve it. Unions were to be feared because they used strikes to further their demands for higher salaries and better working conditions for their members while other social groups languished. Near civil war erupted as Italian Communists and Fascists clashed violently in street battles in the early 1920s. The Fascists entered the national political arena and succeeded on the local level in overthrowing city governments. In spite of its visibility on the national political scene, the Fascist party was still very much a minority party when Mussolini refused to serve as a junior minister in the new government in 1922.

His refusal to serve as representative of a minority party reflected Mussolini's belief that the Fascists must be in charge. On 28 October 1922, the Fascists undertook their famous March on Rome, which followed similar Fascist takeovers in Milan and Bologna. Mussolini's followers now occupied the capital. This event marked the beginning of the end of parliamentary government and the emergence of Fascist dictatorship and institutionalized violence. Rising unemployment and severe inflation contributed to the politically deteriorating situation that helped bring Mussolini to power.

Destruction and violence, not the ballot box, became fascism's most successful tools for securing political power. *Squadristi*—armed bands of Fascist thugs—attacked their political enemies (both Catholic and Socialist), destroyed private property, dismantled the printing presses of adversary groups, and generally terrorized both rural and urban populations. By the end of 1922, Fascists could claim a following of 300,000 members endorsing the new politics of intimidation.

The Fascists achieved their first parliamentary majority by using violent tactics of intimidation to secure votes. One outspoken Socialist critic of Fascist violence, Giacomo Matteotti (1885–1924), was murdered by Mussolini's subordinates. The deed threatened the survival of Mussolini's government as 150 Socialist, Liberal, and Popular party deputies resigned in protest. Mussolini chose this moment to consolidate his position by arresting and silencing his enemies to preserve order. Within two years, Fascists were firmly in control, monopolizing politics, suppressing a free press, creating a secret police force, and transforming social and economic policies. Mussolini destroyed political parties and made Italy into a one-party dictatorship.

In 1925 the Fascist party entered into an agreement with Italian industrialists that gave industry a position of privilege protected by the state in return for its support. Mussolini presented this partnership as the end to class conflict, but in fact it ensured the dominance of capital and the control of labor and professional groups. A corrupt bureaucracy filled with Mussolini's cronies and run on bribes orchestrated the new relationship between big business and the state.

Mussolini, himself an atheist, recognized the importance of the Catholic church in securing his regime. In 1870, when Italy had been unified, the pope had been deprived of his territories in Rome. This event, which became known as the "Roman Question," proved to be the source of ongoing problems for Italian governments. In February 1929, Mussolini settled matters with Pope Pius XI in the Lateran Treaty and the accompanying Concordat, which granted to the pope sovereignty over the territory around St. Peter's Basilica and the Vatican. The treaty also protected the role of the Catholic church in education and guaranteed that Italian marriage laws would conform to Catholic dogma.

By 1929 *Il Duce* (the leader), as Mussolini preferred to be called, was at the height of his popularity and his power. Apparent political harmony had been achieved by ruthlessly crushing fascism's opponents. The agreement with the pope, which restored harmony with the Church, was matched by a new sense of order and accomplishment in Italian society and the economy.

Mussolini's Plans for Empire

In spite of official claims, Fascist Italy had not done well in riding out the Great Depression. A large rural sector masked the problems of high unemployment by absorbing an urban work force without jobs. Corporatism, a system of economic self-rule by interest groups promoted on paper by Benito Mussolini, was a sham that had little to do with the dominance of the Italian economy by big business. By lending money to Italian businesses on the verge of bankruptcy, the government acquired a controlling interest in key industries, including steel, shipping, heavy machinery, and electricity.

As fascism failed to initiate effective social programs, Mussolini's popularity plummeted. In the hope of boosting his sagging image, *Il Duce* committed Italy to a foreign policy of imperial conquest. Italy had con-

Intolerance for ideas was one of the main features of fascist regimes. This photograph of Mussolini's Italy shows the burning of books considered subversive.

Ethiopian soldiers march to meet the invading Italian forces.

quered Ottoman-controlled Libya in North Africa in 1911. Now, in the 1930s, Mussolini targeted Ethiopia for his expansionist aims and ordered Italian troops to invade that east African kingdom in October 1935. Using poison gas and aerial bombing, the Italian army defeated the native troops of Ethiopian emperor Haile Selassie (1892–1975). European democracies, under the pressure of public opinion, cried out against the wanton and unwarranted attack, but Mussolini succeeded in proclaiming Ethiopia an Italian territory.

The invasion of Ethiopia exposed the ineffectiveness of the League of Nations to stop such flagrant violations. Great Britain and France took no action other than to express their disapproval of Italy's conquest. Yet a rift opened up between these two western European nations and Italy. Mussolini had distanced himself from the Nazi state in the first years of the German regime's existence, and he was critical of Hitler's plans for rearmament. Now, in light of disapproval from Britain and France, Mussolini turned to Germany for support. In October 1936, Italy aligned itself with Germany in what Mussolini called the "Rome-Berlin Axis." This alliance was little more than a pledge of friendship. However, less than three years later, in May 1939, Germany and Italy agreed to offer support in any offensive or defensive war. The agreement, known as the Pact of Steel, in fact bound Italy militarily to Germany.

Mussolini pursued other imperialist goals within Europe. The small Balkan nation of Albania entered into a series of agreements with Mussolini beginning in the mid-1920s that made it dependent financially and militarily on Italian aid. By 1933 Albanian independence had been undermined by this "friendship" with its stronger neighbor. In order not to be outdone by Hitler, who was at the time dismantling Czechoslovakia, Mussolini invaded and annexed Albania in April 1939, ending the fiction that Albania was an Italian protectorate.

The Beginnings of the Nazi Movement in Germany

Repeated economic, political, and diplomatic crises of the 1920s buffeted Germany's internal stability. Most Germans considered reparations to be an unfair burden, so onerous that payment should be evaded and resisted in every way possible. The German government did not promote inflation in order to avoid paying reparations, but rather to avoid a postwar recession,

In this satirical painting, The Pillars of Society, *George Grosz caricatures the society of the Weimar Republic as composed of corrupt judges, petty bourgeoisie, militarists, and hypocritical pacifists.*

revive industrial production, and maintain high employment. But the moderate inflation that stimulated the economy spun out of control into destructive hyperinflation.

The Germans blamed the French, with their reparations demands and their invading troops, for the economic plight of Germany. Rampant inflation had negative repercussions for democracy as extremist political groups on both right and left attracted growing numbers of followers by blaming the liberal and democratic Weimar Republic. Because of the horrors of inflation, German governments thereafter were committed to balanced budgets. When the Great Depression hit the German economy in 1929, the fear of a new inflation prevented the government from using deficit spending to bring back prosperity. The Great

Depression in turn contributed to the burgeoning appeal of Hitler and the National Socialists. People grew cynical and defiant through suffering and sought security in extraordinary extrademocratic solutions.

The fiscal problems of the Weimar Republic obscure the fact that, in the period after World War I, Germany experienced real economic growth. German industry advanced, productivity was high, and German workers flexed their union muscles to secure better wages. Weimar committed itself to large expenditures for social welfare programs, including unemployment insurance. By 1930 social welfare was responsible for 40 percent of all public expenditures, compared to 19 percent before the war. All these changes, apparently fostering the well-being of the German people, aggravated the fears of German big businessmen, who resented the trade unions and the perceived trend toward socialism. The lower middle classes also felt cheated and economically threatened by inflation. They were a politically volatile group, susceptible to the antidemocratic appeals of some of Weimar's critics.

Constitutional provisions that allowed for the constant wrangling of a multiparty system divided the Weimar Republic. Political parties formed and destroyed cabinet after cabinet while Germany's real problems remained—the humiliating peace treaty, reparations, and a weak economic structure. As a result, growing numbers of Germans expressed disgust with parliamentary democracy. The Great Depression dealt a staggering blow to the Weimar Republic in 1929 as American loans were withdrawn and German unemployment skyrocketed. By 1930 the antagonisms among the parties were so great that the parliament was no longer effective in ruling Germany. As chancellor from 1930 to 1932, Centrist leader Heinrich Brüning (1885–1970) attempted to break this impasse by overriding the Weimar constitution. This move opened the door to enemies of the republic, and Brüning was forced to resign.

Hitler and the Third Reich

One man in particular knew how to exploit the Weimar Republic's weaknesses for his own political ends. Adolf Hitler was that man. He denounced the betrayal of reparations. He made a special appeal to Germans who saw their savings disappearing, first in inflation and then in the Great Depression. He promised a way out of economic hardship and the reassertion of Germany's claim to status as a world power.

Hitler's Rise to Power

Just as Stalin was born a Georgian and not an ethnic Russian, Adolf Hitler (1889–1945) was born an Austrian outside the German fatherland he came to rule. Hitler, the son of a customs agent who worked on the Austrian side of the border with Germany, came from a middle-class family with social pretensions. Aimlessness and failure marked Hitler's early life. Denied admission to architecture school, he took odd jobs to survive. Hitler welcomed the outbreak of war in 1914, which put an end to his self-described sleepwalking. He volunteered immediately for service in the German army. Wounded and gassed at the front, he was twice awarded the Iron Cross for bravery in action.

Hitler later described what he had learned from war in terms of the solidarity of struggle against a common enemy and the purity of heroism. The army provided him with a sense of security and direction. What he learned from the peace that followed was an equally powerful lesson that determined his commitment to a career in politics. Hitler profoundly believed in the stab-in-the-back legend: Germany had not lost the war, he insisted, it had been defeated from within—or stabbed in the back by communists, socialists, liberals, and Jews. The Weimar Republic signed the humiliating Treaty of Versailles and continued to betray the German people by taxing wages to pay reparations. His highly distorted and false view of the origins of the Republic and its policies was the basis for his demand that the "Weimar System" must be abolished and replaced by a Nazi regime.

For his failed attempt to seize control of the Munich municipal government in 1923, in an event that became known as the Beer Hall Putsch because of the locale in which Hitler attempted to initiate "the national revolution," he served nine months of a five-year sentence in prison. There he began writing the first volume of his autobiography, *Mein Kampf* ("My Struggle"). In this turgid work he condemned the decadence of Western society and singled out for special contempt Jews, Bolsheviks, and middle-class liberals. From his failed attempt to seize power, Hitler learned the important lesson that he could succeed against the German republic only from within, by coming to power legally. By 1928 he had a small party of about 100,000 Nazis. Modifying his anticapitalist message, Hitler appealed to the discontented small farmers and tailored his nationalist sentiments to a frightened middle class.

Adolf Hitler became chancellor of Germany in January 1933 by legal, constitutional, and democratic means. The Nazi party was supported by farmers, small businessmen, civil servants, and young people. In the elections of 1930 and 1932, the voters made the Nazi party the largest party in the country—although not the majority one. President Paul von Hindenburg (1925–34) invited Hitler to form a government. Hitler claimed that Germany was on the verge of a Communist revolution and persuaded Hindenburg and the Reichstag to consent to a series of emergency laws, which the Nazis used to establish themselves firmly in power. Legislation outlawed freedom of the press and public meetings, and approved of the use of violence against Hitler's political enemies, particularly the Socialists and the Communists. Within two months after Hitler came to office, Germany was a police state and Hitler was a "legal" dictator who could issue his own laws without having to gain the consent of either the Reichstag or the president. After carrying out this "legal revolution" incapacitating representative institutions and ending civil liberties, the Nazis worked to consolidate their position and their power. They abolished all other political parties, established single-party rule, dissolved trade unions, and put their own people into state governments and the bureaucracy.

Many observers at the time considered the new Nazi state to be a monolithic structure, ruled and coordinated from the center. This was not, however, an accurate observation. Hitler actually issued few directives. Policy was set by an often chaotic jockeying for power among rival Nazi factions. Hitler's political alliance with traditional conservative and nationalist politicians, industrialists, and military men helped give the state created by Adolf Hitler a claim to legitimacy based on continuity with the past. Hitler called this state the Third Reich. (The first Reich was the medieval German empire; the second Reich was the German Empire created by Bismarck in 1871.)

The first of the paramilitary groups so important in orchestrating violence to eliminate Hitler's enemies was the SA (Sturmabteilung), or the storm troopers, under Ernst Röhm (1887–1934). Röhm helped Hitler achieve electoral victories by beating up political opponents on the streets and using other thuglike tactics. SA followers, also known as Brownshirts, adopted a military appearance for their terrorist operations. By the beginning of 1934, there were 2.5 million members of the SA, vastly outnumbering the regular army of 100,000 soldiers.

Heinrich Himmler (1900–45) headed an elite force of the Nazi party within the SA called the SS (Schutzstaffel, or protection squad), a group whose members wore black uniforms and menacing skull-and-crossbones insignia on their caps. Himmler seized control of political policing and emerged as Röhm's chief rival. In 1934, with the assistance of the army, Hitler and the SS purged the SA and executed Röhm, thereby making the SS Hitler's exclusive elite corps, entrusted with carrying out his extreme programs and responsible later for the greatest atrocities of the Second World War.

Nazi Goals

Hitler identified three organizing goals for the Nazi state: *Lebensraum* (living space); rearmament; and economic recovery. These goals were the basis of the new foreign policy Hitler forged for Germany, and they served to fuse that foreign policy with the domestic politics of the Third Reich.

Key to Hitler's worldview was the concept of *Lebensraum,* in which he considered the right and the duty of the German master race to be the world's greatest empire, one that would endure for a thousand years. Hitler first stated his ideals about living space in *Mein Kampf,* where he argued that superior nations had the right to expand into the territories of inferior states. Living space meant for him German domination of central and eastern Europe at the expense of Slavic peoples. The Aryan master race would dominate inferior peoples. Colonies were unacceptable because they weakened rather than strengthened national security; Germany must annex territories within continental Europe. Hitler's primary target was what he called "Russia and her vassal border states."

Hitler continued the secret rearmament of Germany begun by his Weimar predecessors in violation of the restrictions of the Treaty of Versailles. He withdrew Germany from the League of Nations and from the World Disarmament Conference, signaling a new direction for German foreign policy. In 1935 he publicly renounced the Treaty of Versailles and announced that Germany was rearming. The following year he openly defied the French and moved German troops into the Rhineland, the demilitarized security zone that separated the armed forces of the two countries. Hitler also reversed the cooperative relationship his nation had established with the Soviet Union in the 1920s. In 1933 the German state was illicitly spending 1 billion Reichsmarks on arms. By 1939 annual expenditures to prepare Germany for war had climbed to 30 billion.

Hitler knew that preparation for war meant more than amassing weapons; it also required full economic recovery. One of Germany's great weaknesses in World

National Income of the Powers in 1937 and Percentage Spent on Defense

	National Income (billions of dollars)	Percentage on Defense
United States	68	1.5
British Empire	22	5.7
France	10	9.1
Germany	17	23.5
Italy	6	14.5
USSR	19	26.4
Japan	4	28.2

War I had been its dependence on imports of raw materials and foodstuffs. To avoid a repetition of this problem, Hitler instituted a program of autarky, or economic self-sufficiency, by which Germany aimed to produce everything that it consumed. He encouraged the efforts of German industry to develop synthetics for petroleum, rubber, metals, and fats.

The state pumped money into the private economy, creating new jobs and achieving full employment after 1936, an accomplishment unmatched by any other European nation. Recovery was built on armaments as well as consumer products. The Nazi state's concentration of economic power in the hands of a few strengthened big businesses. The victims of corporate consolidation were the small firms that could no longer compete with government-sponsored corporations like the chemical giant I. G. Farben.

In 1936 Hitler introduced his Four-Year Plan, dedicated to the goals of full-scale rearmament and economic self-sufficiency. Before the third year of the Four-Year Plan, however, Hitler was aware of the failure to develop synthetic products sufficient to meet Germany's needs. But if Germany could not create substitutes, it could control territories that provided fuel, metals, and foodstuffs. Germany had been importing raw materials from southeastern Europe and wielding increasing economic influence over the Balkan countries. Hitler now realized that economic self-sufficiency could be directly linked to the main goal of the Nazi state: *Lebensraum.*

Thus Hitler was committed to territorial expansion from the time he came to power. He rearmed Germany for that purpose. When economists and generals cautioned him, he refused to listen. Instead, he informed them of his commitment to *Lebensraum* and of his intention to use aggressive war to acquire it. He removed his critics from their positions of power and replaced them with Nazis loyal to him.

Propaganda, Racism, and Culture

To reinforce his personal power and to sell his program for the "total state," Hitler created a Ministry of Propaganda under Joseph Goebbels (1897–1945), a former journalist and Nazi party district leader in Berlin. Goebbels was a master of manipulating emotions in mass demonstrations held to whip up enthusiasm for Nazi policies. Flying the flag and wearing the swastika signified identification with the Nazi state. With his magnetic appeal, Hitler inspired and manipulated the devotion of hundreds of thousands of those who heard him speak. Leni Riefenstahl, a young filmmaker working for Hitler, made a documentary of a National Socialist party rally at Nuremberg. In scenes of swooning women and cheering men, her film, called *Triumph of the Will*, recorded the dramatic force of Hitler's rhetoric and his ability to move the German people. Hitler's public charisma masked a profoundly troubled

and incomplete individual capable of irrational rage and sick hatred of his fellow human beings. His warped views of the world were responsible for the greatest outrages ever committed in the name of legitimate power. Yet millions, including admirers in western Europe and the United States, succumbed to his appeal.

Family life, too, was carefully regulated through the propaganda machinery. Loyalty only to the state meant less loyalty to the family. In 1939, 82 percent of all German boys and girls between the ages of ten and eighteen were members of Nazi-controlled organizations. Special youth organizations, including the Hitler Youth, indoctrinated boys with nationalistic and military values. Organizations for girls were intended to mold them into worthy wives and mothers. Teenage girls were required to join a Nazi organization called Faith and Beauty, which taught them etiquette, dancing, fashion consciousness, and beauty care. Woman's natural function, Hitler argued, was to serve in the home. Education for women beyond the care of home and family was a waste. Adult women had their own organizations to serve the Nazi state. The German Women's Bureau under Gertrud Scholtz-Klink instructed women in their "proper" female duties. In an

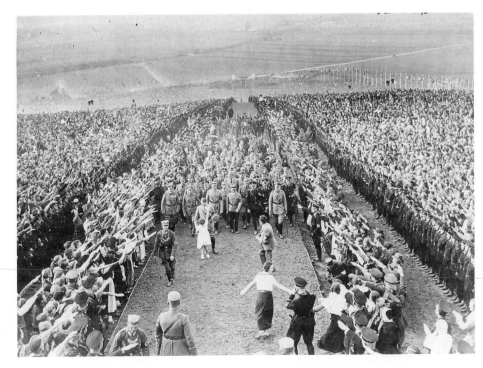

Hitler at a Nazi rally. These mass meetings were used by the Nazi mythmakers to enhance Hitler's image as the savior of Germany.

ADOLF HITLER ON "RACIAL PURITY"

The purity of German blood was a recurrent theme in Hitler's speeches and writings from the beginning of his political career. In attacking both liberalism and socialism, Hitler offered racial superiority as the essence of the National Socialist "revolution." This speech, delivered in Berlin on 30 January 1937, lays out his attack on the concept of individual rights and humanity in favor of the "folk community."

The most important plank in the National Socialist program is to abolish the liberal idea of the individual and the Marxist idea of humanity and to substitute for them the folk community rooted in the soil and held together by the bond of common blood. This sounds simple, but it involves a principle which has great consequences.

For the first time and in the first country our people are being taught to understand that, of all the tasks we have to face, the most noble and the most sacred for all mankind is the concept that each racial species must preserve the purity of blood which God has given to it.

The greatest revolution won by National Socialism is that it has pierced the veil which hid from us the knowledge that all human errors may be attributed to the conditions of the time and hence can be remedied, but there is one error that cannot be set right once it has been made by men—that is, the failure to understand the importance of keeping the blood and the race free from intermingling, and in this way to alter God's gift. It is not for human beings to discuss why Providence created different races. Rather it is important to understand the fact that it will punish those who pay no attention to its work of creation. . . .

I hereby prophesy that, just as knowledge that the earth moves around the sun led to a revolutionary change in the world picture, so will the blood-and-race doctrine of the National Socialist movement bring about a revolutionary change in our knowledge. . . . It will also change the course of history in the future.

This will not lead to difficulties between nations. On the contrary, it will lead to a better understanding between them. But at the same time it will prevent the Jews, under the mask of world citizenship, from thrusting themselves among all nations as an element of domestic chaos. . . .

The National Socialist movement limits its domestic activities to those individuals who belong to one people. It refuses to permit those of a foreign race to have any influence whatever on our political, intellectual, or cultural life. We refuse to give any members of a foreign race a dominant position in our national economic system.

In our folk community, which is based on ties of blood, in the results which National Socialism has obtained by training the public in the idea of this folk-community, lies the deepest reason for the great success of our Revolution.

---

effort to promote large families, the state paid allowances to couples for getting married, subsidized families according to their size, and gave tax breaks to large families. Abortion and birth control were outlawed, and women who sought such measures risked severe penalties and imprisonment.

By 1937 the need for women workers conflicted with the goals of Nazi propaganda. With the outbreak of war in 1939, women were urged to work, especially in jobs like munitions manufacture formerly held by men. For working women with families, the double burden was a heavy one, as women were required to work long shifts—sixty-hour workweeks were not unusual—for low wages. Many women resisted entering the work force if they had other income or could live on the cash payments they received as the wives of soldiers. At the beginning of 1943, the German people were ordered to make sacrifices for a new era of "total

Women receiving German Mother Iron Cross decorations in Berlin, October 1939. Such awards made role models of women who tended to the traditional concerns of Kinder, Küche, Kirche *(children, kitchen, church).*

war." Female labor became compulsory and women were drafted into working for the war.

Propaganda condemned everything foreign, including Mickey Mouse, who was declared an enemy of the state in the 1930s. Purging foreign influences meant purging political opponents, especially members of the Communist party, who were rounded up and sent to concentration camps in Germany. Communism was identified as an international Jewish conspiracy to destroy the German *Volk,* or people. Nazi literature also identified "asocials," those who were considered deviant in any way, including homosexuals, who were

likewise to be expelled. Euthanasia was used against the mentally ill and the mentally disabled in the 1930s. Concentration camps were expanded to contain enemies of the state. Later, when concentration camps became sites of extermination and forced labor, gypsies, homosexuals, criminals, and religious offenders had to wear insignia of different colors to indicate the reason for their persecution. The people who received the greatest attention for exclusion from Nazi Germany, and then from Europe, were the Jews.

The first measures against the German Jews—their exclusion from public employment and higher education—began almost immediately in 1933. In 1935 the Nuremberg Laws were enacted to identify Jews, to deprive them of their citizenship, and to forbid marriage and extramarital sexual relations between Jews and non-Jews. On the night of 9 November 1938, synagogues were set afire and books and valuables owned by Jews were confiscated throughout Germany. Jews were beaten, about 91 were killed, and 20,000 to 30,000 were imprisoned in concentration camps. The night came to be called *Kristallnacht,* meaning "night of broken glass," which referred to the Jewish shop windows smashed by the Brownshirts under orders

A propaganda-laden German beer coaster of the Nazi era informs the world that "who buys from the Jews is a traitor."

from Goebbels. The government claimed that *Kristallnacht* was an outpouring of the German people's will. An atmosphere of state-sanctioned hate prevailed.

Racism was nothing new in European culture, nor was its particular variant, anti-Semitism—hatred of Jews—the creation of the Third Reich. The link the Nazis cultivated between racism and politics was built on cultural precedents. In the 1890s, in France and Austria and elsewhere in Europe, anti-Semitism was espoused by political and professional groups that formed themselves around issues of militant nationalism, authoritarianism, and mass politics. Hitler was a racist and an anti-Semite and he placed theories of race at the core of his fascist ideology. "Experts" decided sterilization was the surest way to protect "German blood." In 1933 one of the early laws of Hitler's new Reich decreed compulsory sterilization of "undesirables" in order to "eliminate inferior genes." The Nazi state decided who these "undesirables" were and forced the sterilization of 400,000 men and women.

The Third Reich was a government that delivered on its promises to end unemployment, to improve productivity, to break through the logjam of parliamentary obstacles, and to return Germany to the international arena as a contender for power. Yet Hitler's Nazi state ruled by violence, coercion, and intimidation. With a propaganda machine that glorified the leader and vilified groups singled out as scapegoats for Germany's problems, Hitler undermined democratic institutions and civil liberties in his pursuit of German power.

Democracies in Crisis

Democracies in the 1930s turned in on themselves in order to survive. In contrast to the fascist mobilization of society and the Soviet restructuring of the economy, European democracies took small, tentative steps to respond to the challenges of the Great Depression. Democratic leaders lacked creative vision, or even clear policy. Both democratic France and Great Britain were less successful than Nazi Germany in responding to the challenges of the Great Depression. France paid a high price for parliamentary stalemate and was still severely depressed on the eve of war in 1938–39. Great Britain maintained a stagnant economy and stable politics under Conservative leadership. Internal dissension ripped Spain apart. Its civil war assumed broader dimensions as the Soviet Union, Italy, and Germany struggled over Spain's future while Europe's democratic nations stood by and accepted defeat.

Europe: Types of Government

The Failure of the Left in France

France's Third Republic, like most European parliamentary democracies in the 1930s, was characterized by a multiparty system. Genuine political differences often separated one party from another. The tendency to parliamentary stalemate was aggravated by the Great Depression and by the increasingly extremist politics on both the left and the right in response to developments in the Soviet Union and Germany.

The belief of the French people in a private enterprise economy was shaken by the Great Depression, but no new unifying belief replaced it. Some felt that state planning was the answer; others were sure that state intervention had caused the problem. Distrusting both the New Deal model of the United States and the Nazi response to depression politics, the Third Republic followed a haphazard, wait-and-see policy of insulating the economy, discouraging competition, and protecting favored interests in both industry and agriculture. Stimulating the economy by deficit spending was considered anathema. Devaluation of the franc, which might have helped French exports, was regarded by policymakers as an unpatriotic act. France stood fast as a bastion of liberal belief in the self-adjusting mechanism of the market, and it suffered greatly for it. Party politics worked to reinforce the defensive rather than offensive response to the challenges of depression and a sluggish economy.

In 1936 an electoral mandate for change swept the Left into power. The new premier, Léon Blum (1872–1950), was a Socialist. Lacking the votes to rule with an exclusively Socialist government, Blum formed a coalition of Left and Center parties intent on economic reforms known as the Popular Front. Before Blum's government could take power, a wave of strikes swept France. Though reluctant to intervene in the economy, the Popular Front nevertheless was pushed into some action. It promised wage increases, paid vacations, and collective bargaining to French workers. The reduced workweek of 40 hours caused a drop in productivity, as did the short-lived one-month vacation policy. The government did nothing to prevent the outflow of investment capital from France. Higher wages failed to generate increased consumer demand because employers raised prices to cover their higher operating costs.

German rearmament, now publicly known, forced France into rearmament, which France could ill afford. Blum's government failed in 1937, with France still bogged down in a sluggish and depressed economy. The last peacetime government of the 1930s represented a conservative swing back to laissez-faire policies that put the needs of business above those of workers and brought a measure of revival to the French economy.

The radical Right drew strength from the Left's failures. Right-wing leagues and organizations multiplied, appealing to a frightened middle class. The failure of the Socialists, in turn, drove many sympathizers further to the left to join the Communist party. A divided France could not stand up to the foreign policy challenges of the 1930s posed by Hitler's provocations.

Muddling Through in Great Britain

Great Britain was hard hit by the Great Depression of the 1930s; only Germany and the United States experienced comparable economic devastation. The socialist Labour government of the years 1929 to 1931 under Prime Minister Ramsay MacDonald (1866–1937) was unprepared to deal with the 1929 collapse and lacked the vision and the planning to devise a way out of the morass. It took a coalition of moderate groups from the three parties—Liberal, Conservative, and Labour—to address the issues of high unemployment, a growing government deficit, a banking crisis, and the flight of capital. The National Government (1931–35) was a centrist nonpartisan coalition whose members included Ramsay MacDonald, retained as prime minister, and Stanley Baldwin (1867–1947), a Conservative with a background in iron and steel manufacturing.

In response to the endemic crisis, the National Government took Britain off the international gold standard and devalued the pound. In order to protect domestic production, tariffs were established. The British economy showed signs of slow recovery, probably due less to these government measures than to a gradual improvement in the business cycle. The government had survived the crisis without resorting to the kind of creative alternatives devised in the Scandinavian countries, where, for example, consumer and producer cooperatives provided widespread economic relief. Moderates and classical liberals in Great Britain persisted in defending the nonintervention of the government in the economy, despite new economic theories such as that of John Maynard Keynes (1883–1946), who urged government spending to stimulate consumer demand as the best way to shorten the duration of the Great Depression.

In 1932 Sir Oswald Mosley (1896–1980) founded the British Union of Fascists (BUF), consisting of goon squads and bodyguards. The BUF was opposed to free-trade liberalism and communism alike. Mosley developed a corporate model for economic and political life in which interest groups rather than an electorate would be represented in a new kind of parliament. He favored, above all, national solutions by relying on imperial development; he rejected the world of international finance as corrupt.

The BUF shared similarities with European fascist organizations. BUF squads beat up their political opponents and began attacking Jews, especially the eastern European émigrés living in London. The British fascists struck a responsive chord among the poorest working-class people of London's East End; at its peak the group claimed a membership of 20,000. Public alarm over increasingly inflammatory and anti-Semitic rhetoric converged with parliamentary denunciation. Popular support for the group was already beginning to erode when the BUF was outlawed in 1936. By this time, anti-Hitler feeling was spreading in Great Britain.

Mosley's response to harsh economic times had proven to be no match for the steady and reassuring strength of Stanley Baldwin's National Government, which seemed to be in control of an improving economic situation. The traditional party system prevailed not because of its brilliant solutions to difficult economic problems but because of the willingness of mod-

THE RISE OF FASCISM AND DEMOCRACY IN CRISIS

28 October 1922	Italian Fascists march on Rome
November 1923	Beer Hall Putsch in Munich
1924	Fascists achieve parliamentary majority in Italy
1929	Lateran Treaty between Mussolini and Pope Pius XI
1932	Nazi party is single largest party in German parliament
January 1933	Hitler becomes Chancellor of Germany
30 June 1934	Purge of the SA leaves Hitler and the SS in unassailable position
15 September 1934	Enactment of Nuremberg Laws against Jews and other minorities
March 1935	Hitler publicly rejects Treaty of Versailles and announces German rearmament
3 October 1935	Italy invades Ethiopia
1936	Popular Front government elected in Spain
July 1936	Beginning of Spanish Civil War
October 1936	Rome-Berlin Axis Pact, an Italo-German accord
1936–1937	Popular Front government in France
27 April 1937	Bombing of the Spanish town of Guernica
9 November 1938	*Kristallnacht* initiates massive violence against Jews
March 1939	Fascists defeat the Spanish Republic
April 1939	Italy annexes Albania
May 1939	Pact of Steel between Germany and Italy

erate parliamentarians to cooperate and adapt, however slowly, to the new need for economic transformation.

The Spanish Republic as Battleground

In 1931 Spain became a democratic republic after centuries of Bourbon monarchy and almost a decade of military dictatorship. In 1936 the voters of Spain elected a Popular Front government. The Popular Front in Spain was more radical than its French counterpart. The property of aristocratic landlords was seized; revolutionary workers went on strike; the Catholic church and its clergy were attacked. This social revolution initiated three years of civil war. On one side were the Republicans, the Popular Front defenders of the Spanish Republic and of social revolution in Spain. On the other side were the Nationalists, those who sought to overthrow the Republic—aristocratic landowners, supporters of the monarchy and the Catholic church, and much of the Spanish army.

The Spanish Civil War began in July 1936 with a revolt against the Republic from within the Spanish army. It was led by General Francisco Franco (1892–

The Spanish Civil War

*Spanish refugees stream into France after the Republican defeat and the fall of Barcelona.
More than two hundred thousand refugees and troops were interned in France.*

1975), a tough, shrewd, and stubborn man, a conservative nationalist allied with the Falange, the fascist party in Spain. The conflict soon became a bloody military stalemate, with the Nationalists led by Franco controlling the more rural and conservative south and west of Spain and the Republicans holding out in the cities of the north and east—Madrid, Valencia, and Barcelona.

Almost from the beginning, the Spanish Civil War was an international event. Mussolini sent ground troops, "volunteers," to fight alongside Franco's forces. Hitler dispatched technical specialists, tanks, and the Condor Legion, an aviation unit, to support the Nationalists. The Germans regarded Spain as a testing ground for new equipment and new methods of warfare, including aerial bombardment. The Soviet Union intervened on the side of the Republic, sending armaments, supplies, and technical and political advisers. Because the people of Britain and France were deeply divided in their attitudes toward the war in Spain, the British government stayed neutral, and the government of France was unable to aid its fellow Popular Front

government in Spain. Although Americans volunteered to fight with the Republicans, the American government did not prevent the Texas Oil Company from selling 1.9 million tons of oil to Franco's insurgents, nor did it block the Ford Motor Company, General Motors, and Studebaker from supplying them with trucks.

The Spanish government pleaded, "Men and women of all lands! Come to our aid!" In response, 2800 American volunteers—among them college students, professors, intellectuals, and trade unionists—joined the loyalist army and European volunteers in defense of the Spanish Republic. Britons and antifascist émigrés from Italy and Germany also joined international brigades, which were vital in helping the city of Madrid hold out against the Nationalist generals. The Russians withdrew from the war in 1938, disillusioned by the failure of the French, British, and Americans to come to the aid of the Republicans. Madrid fell to the Nationalists in March 1939. The government established by Franco sent one million of its enemies to prison or concentration camps.

• • •

The fragile postwar stability of the 1920s crumbled under the pressures of economic depression, ongoing national antagonisms, and insecurity in the international arena. Europe after 1932 was plagued by the consequences of economic collapse, fascist success, and the growing threat of armed conflict. Parliamentary institutions were fighting and losing a tug-of-war with authoritarian movements. A fascist regime was in place in Italy. Political and electoral defeats eroded democratic and liberal principles in Germany's Weimar Republic. Dictatorships triumphed in Spain and in much of eastern and central Europe. Liberal parliamentary governments were failing to solve the economic and social challenges of the postwar years. In the democratic nations of France, Great Britain, and, during the brief period from 1931 to 1936, Spain, parliamentary institutions appeared to be persevering. But even here, polarization and increasing intransigence on both the left and the right threatened the future of democratic politics.

The exclusion of the Soviet Union from Western internationalism in the 1920s both reflected and exacerbated the crisis. The Bolshevik revolution had served as a political catalyst among workers in the West, attracting them to the possibility of radical solutions. That potential radicalization aggravated class antagonisms in the 1930s, when mass politics prevailed and drove political leaders to seek conservative solutions as a means of stabilizing class politics.

Suggestions for Further Reading

International Politics and Economic Nationalism

* Derek H. Aldcroft, *From Versailles to Wall Street, 1919–1929* (Berkeley: University of California Press, 1977). Traces the recovery of the international economy and the systemic forces of its disintegration in the 1920s, with special attention to such areas as war debts, reparations, the gold standard, the agricultural sector, and patterns of international lending.

Jon Jacobson, *When the Soviet Union Entered World Politics* (Berkeley: University of California Press, 1994). Deals with the revolutionary and diplomatic aspects of early Soviet foreign relations and demonstrates the central importance of foreign relations to Soviet economic development and the struggle for leadership.

Marshall M. Lee and Wolfgang Michalka, *German Foreign Policy, 1917–1933: Continuity or Break?* (Leamington Spa, England: Berg, 1987). A solid and synthetic treatment of Weimar diplomacy that takes into account the historiographical debates over revisionism and expansion.

* Melvyn P. Leffler, *The Elusive Quest: America's Pursuit of European Stability and French Security, 1919–1933* (Chapel Hill: University of North Carolina Press, 1979). Examines the economic and financial imperatives guiding U.S. foreign policy after World War I and identifies a particular Republican party approach labeled "economic diplomacy." Special attention is paid to European stabilization, French security, and Germany's rehabilitation.

* Joseph Rothschild, *East Central Europe Between the Two World Wars* (Seattle: University of Washington Press, 1983). A balanced survey of interwar developments in Poland, Czechoslovakia, Hungary, Yugoslavia, Romania, Bulgaria, Albania, and the Baltic states highlighting internal weaknesses and external vulnerabilities. A concluding chapter covers cultural contributions.

* Stephen A. Schuker, *The End of French Predominance in Europe: The Financial Crisis of 1924 and the Adoption of the Dawes Plan* (Chapel Hill: University of North Carolina Press, 1976). Locates the decline of France as a great power in the financial crisis of 1924 and the diplomacy of reparations and examines the domestic bases for French powerlessness.

The Soviet Union's Separate Path

* Stephen F. Cohen, *Bukharin and the Bolshevik Revolution: A Political Biography, 1888–1938* (Oxford: Oxford University Press, 1980). This milestone work is a general history of the period as well as a political and intellectual biography of Bukharin, "the last Bolshevik," who supported an evolutionary road to modernization and socialism and whose policies were an alternative to Stalinism.

* Sheila Fitzpatrick, *The Russian Revolution, 1917–1932* (Oxford: Oxford University Press, 1985). Arguing from the premise that the revolutionary upheaval did not end with the Bolshevik seizure of power in November 1917, Fitzpatrick interprets the developments of the 1920s and early 1930s, including the NEP and the first Five-Year Plan, as stages in a single revolutionary process.

* Robert C. Tucker, *Stalin as Revolutionary, 1879–1929: A Study in History and Personality* (New York: Norton, 1973). Traces Stalin's development from his Georgian childhood to his fiftieth year, when he established himself as the new hero of the Soviet state. Tucker uses Freudian terms of analysis in considering Stalin's hero-identification with Lenin.

The Promise of Fascism

* Volker R. Berghahn, *Modern Germany: Society, Economy and Politics in the Twentieth Century* (Cambridge: Cambridge University Press, 1987). Considers the particular challenges of rapid industrialization faced by Germany and how they interacted with social tensions and political conflict.

Eberhard Kolb, *The Weimar Republic*, tr. P. S. Falla (London: Unwin Hyman, 1988). An introduction to the history of Germany's first republic both as a historic survey and as an examination of the basic problems and trends in research.

* MacGregor Knox, *Mussolini Unleashed, 1939–1941: Politics and Strategy in Fascist Italy's Last War* (Cambridge: Cambridge University Press, 1982). Argues that Mussolini had a consistent foreign policy in the Mediterranean and a genuine program for living space in the Mediterranean and the Middle East. In his bid for power and prestige, Mussolini was willing to risk war and short-term instability at home.

* Adrian Lyttelton, *The Seizure of Power: Fascism in Italy, 1919–1929* (New York: Scribners, 1973). Addresses the question of why fascism first took root in Italy.

Hitler and the Third Reich

* Ian Kershaw, *The "Hitler Myth": Image and Reality in the Third Reich* (New York: Oxford University Press, 1987). Examines the power of the "Hitler myth" created by the German Propaganda Ministry, the German people, and Hitler. The myth accounted for the stability of the Third Reich throughout the thirties and in the first years of the war.

* Detlev Peukert, *Inside Nazi Germany: Conformity, Opposition, and Racism in Everyday Life* (New Haven, CT: Yale University Press, 1987). Discusses the informal modes of resistance among the German people.

Democracies in Crisis

M. S. Alexander and H. Graham, *The French and Spanish Popular Fronts: Comparative Perspectives* (Cambridge: Cambridge University Press, 1989). Contributions by specialists on the interwar period.

Herschel B. Chipp, *Picasso's* Guernica: *History, Transformations, Meanings* (Berkeley: University of California Press, 1988). Documents the creation of Picasso's *Guernica,* rooting it firmly in the context of the Spanish Civil War, and discusses the painting's reception in Spain and abroad.

* John Hiden and Patrick Salmon, *The Baltic Nations and Europe: Estonia, Latvia, and Lithuania in the Twentieth Century* (London and New York: Longman, 1991). Surveys the development of the Baltic states in this century, discussing Baltic independence, the period between the wars, and the states' incorporation into the Soviet Union as well as renewed efforts toward independence in the Gorbachev era.

* Julian Jackson, *The Popular Front in France: Defending Democracy, 1934–1938.* (Cambridge: Cambridge University Press, 1988). The first in-depth study of Leon Blum's government, with a special emphasis on cultural transformation and the legacy of the Popular Front.

Maurice Larkin, *France Since the Popular Front: Government and People, 1936–1986* (Oxford: Clarendon Press, 1988). A work of total history that situates French political developments in the history, traditions, social structure, and economy of France. Separates the legend from the legacy of the Popular Front.

*Paperback edition available.

28 ❧ GLOBAL CONFLAGRATION: WORLD WAR II, 1939–1945

Building Bombs

Scientists in the twentieth century participate in an international community of ideas and discoveries. In the first half of the twentieth century, as is the case now, academic scientists dedicated themselves to basic research—the pursuit of scientific knowledge for its own sake—and published their findings in scholarly scientific journals read only by specialists in their own fields throughout the world. It was not unusual for public-minded critics to accuse scientists and other academicians of living in an ivory tower, producing work without relevance or social value. For that matter, scientists themselves did not dispute the accusation that they gave little thought to the practical and applied scientific outcomes of their research. The transfer of basic research to useful technology was not a primary motivator for the great discoveries in physics and chemistry in the first half of the twentieth century. Einstein's theory of relativity or Heisenberg's uncertainty principle, both meriting the Nobel Prize in physics, seemed to offer little to the average citizen to change the world.

While international in their exchange of information, scientists worked very much within national scientific communities. Because of the demands for interdisciplinary

knowledge and highly specialized control, however, scientists began to abandon more individualistic models of doing research in favor of team approaches. In Italy, for example, the creation of a research center at the University of Rome brought together an outstanding and creative research team headed by the physicist Enrico Fermi and dedicated to collaboration on atomic physics. In France, the team led by J. F. Joliot and his wife Irene Curie Joliot, daughter of Nobel physicists Marie and Pierre Curie, trailblazed new directions in atomic physics with their discovery of artificial radioactivity. In 1932 the team of J. D. Cockcroft and E. T. S. Walton attracted pub-

lic attention by doing the unimaginable: they split the atom, which hitherto had been considered invisible and indivisible. Few at the time considered that this accomplishment held more than a curiosity value.

The leading national "factories" garnering Nobel Prizes in the sciences were the United States and Germany. Most of the important theoretical breakthroughs in physics were published first in the German language and spread quickly to the research teams of other nations, leading to new perspectives and new insights in pushing back the frontier of scientific knowledge. All of this, while interesting, seemed of little value to people concerned with improving depression economies or keeping the world safe from war.

But politics changed everything. Beginning in 1933, the racial policies directed against the Jews in Germany and Nazi political repression provoked a diaspora of leading chemists and physicists, who fled central Europe for the safer havens of Great Britain and the United States. Enrico Fermi traveled to Stockholm in 1938 to claim his Nobel Prize in physics, but did not return home to Italy. Instead, he fled to the United States with his wife, Laura, who was Jewish, because he feared for her safety in Fascist Italy. Two other refugee scientists, Otto Frisch and Rudolf

Peierls, left Germany and settled in Great Britain, where, because of their work on Uranium-235, they were able to persuade the British government to sponsor the first work on atomic weapons.

And here is where the story of science changed. In 1939 German scientists began to consider the possibility of applying all of the accumulated knowledge about atomic physics to the task of building the ultimate weapon, a new kind of bomb with explosive force unimaginable before the discovery of fission in 1939. The Allies feared that Germany would achieve exactly that goal. Building the ultimate bomb required a great commitment of resources and highly coordinated management of science, technology, and military needs. We now know that the German scientific community in Germany never really believed that building a massive bomb was possible, nor was it feasible for the Nazi state to dedicate sufficient resources to accomplish the task.

German leaders were sure that the war would be long over before such a weapon could be manufactured, and in the meantime, they had more pressing needs for weapons creation and production.

The Allies lacked neither resources nor scientific brainpower to address the task. The U.S. government joined forces with the British in an endeavor known by the code name of the Manhattan Project. By 1945 the budget of the project, entirely underwritten by the United States government, was estimated to be equal to that of the entire U.S. auto industry. Refugee scientists from central Europe and their British and American colleagues joined together in a collaboration unique in the annals of scientific culture.

The speed with which the scientists of the Manhattan Project moved from basic to applied research was staggering. Discoveries were made and applied almost instantaneously. Plutonium, an artificial material used in the bomb's explosive chain reaction, had to be manufactured. Detonation of a nuclear core was an especially knotty problem, since the materials comprising the bomb had to be compressed to critical volume in less than one-millionth of a second. The head of the Manhattan Project, Robert Oppenheimer (1904–67), a physicist who managed the scientific side of the project, spoke of the successive challenges of the production of the atomic bomb as "technically sweet." He explained that the scientists of the Manhattan Project continued to do what they did best—make discoveries, albeit in a highly focused and applied environment. "You go ahead and do it and you argue about what to do about it only after you have had your technical success. This is the way it was with the atomic bomb. I do not think anybody opposed making it; there were some debates about what to do with it after it was made."

The atomic bomb resulting from this new kind of scientific collaboration changed the world. In acknowledging the impact of this product of scientific expertise, it is easy to overlook the culture that itself had changed in order to build bombs. Governments entered laboratories as key players in supporting the research agenda. Scientists, perhaps not for the first time but certainly dramatically, were forced to confront the ethical consequences of their actions in a world where no form of knowledge could be considered innocent.

The Coming of World War II

The years between 1933 and 1939 marked a bleak period in international affairs when the British, the French, and the Americans were unwilling or unable to recognize the dire threat to world peace of Hitler and his Nazi state. The leaders of these countries did not comprehend Hitler's single-minded goal to extend German living space eastward as far as western Russia. They failed to understand the seriousness of the Nazi process of consolidation at home. They took no action against Hitler's initial acts of aggression. The war that began in Europe in 1939 eventually became a great global conflict that pitted Germany, Italy, and Japan—the Axis Powers—against the British Empire, the Soviet Union, and the United States—the Grand Alliance.

Even before war broke out in Europe, there was armed conflict in Asia. The rapidly expanding Japanese economy depended on Manchuria for raw materials and on China for markets. Chinese boycotts against Japanese goods and threats to Japanese economic interests in Manchuria led to a Japanese military occupation of Manchuria and the establishment of a Japanese puppet state there in 1931–32. When the powers of the League of Nations, led by Great Britain, refused to recognize this state, Japan withdrew from the League. Fearing that the Chinese government was becoming strong enough to exclude Japanese trade from China, Japanese troops and naval units began an undeclared war in China in 1937. Many important Chinese cities—Peking, Shanghai, Nanking, Canton, and Hankow—fell to Japanese forces. Relentless aerial bombardment of Chinese cities and atrocities committed by Japanese troops against Chinese civilians outraged Europeans and Americans. The governments of the Soviet Union, Great Britain, and the United States, seeking to protect their own ideological, economic, and security interests in China, gave economic, diplo-matic, and moral support to the Chinese government of Chiang Kai-shek. Thus the stage was set for major military conflicts in Asia and in Europe.

Hitler's Foreign Policy and Appeasement

For Hitler a war against the Soviet Union for living space was inevitable. It would come, he told some of his close associates, in the years 1943–45. However, he wanted to avoid refighting the war that had led to Germany's defeat in 1914–18. World War I was a war fought on two fronts—in the east and in the west. It was a war in which Germany had to face many enemies at the same time, and a war that lasted until German soldiers, civilians, and resources were exhausted. In the next war, Hitler wanted above all to avoid fighting Great Britain while battling Russia for living space. He convinced himself that the British would remain neutral if Germany agreed not to attack the British Empire. Would they not appreciate his willingness to abolish forever the menace of communism? Were they not Aryans too?

Beginning in 1938, with the non-Nazi conservatives removed from positions of power in Germany, Hitler alone determined foreign policy. He was becoming increasingly impatient, considering time his greatest enemy. He feared that Germany could fail to achieve its destiny as a world power by waiting too long to act. And he became more aggressive and willing to use military force as he set out to remove the obstacles to German domination of central Europe—Austria, Czechoslovakia, and Poland. In March he annexed Austria to the German Reich. Many Austrians wished to be united with Germany; others had no desire to be led by Nazis. Using the threat of invasion, he intimidated the Austrian government into legalizing the Nazi party, which thereby brought pro-Nazis into the Austrian cabinet and German troops into the country. Encouraged by his success, Hitler provoked a crisis in Czechoslovakia in the summer of the same year. He demanded "freedom" for the German-speaking people of the Sudetenland area of Czechoslovakia. His main objective, however, was not to protect the Germans of Czechoslovakia but to smash the Czech state, the major obstacle in central Europe to the launching of an attack on living space farther east.

Western statesmen did not understand Hitler's commitment to destroying Czechoslovakia or his willingness to fight a limited war against the Czechs to do so. Hitler did everything possible to isolate Czechoslovakia from its neighbors and its treaty partners. France, an ally of Czechoslovakia, appeared distinctly unwilling to

A triumphant Hitler enters Austria in 1938. The union of his native country with the German Reich had long been a cherished goal of the Nazi Führer.

defend it against Germany's menaces. Britain, seeking to avoid a war that the government did not think was necessary and for which the British were not prepared, sent Prime Minister Neville Chamberlain (1869–1940) to reason with Hitler. Believing that transferring the Sudetenland, the German-speaking area of Czechoslovakia, to Germany was the only solution—and one that would redress some of the wrongs done to Germany after World War I—Chamberlain convinced France and Czechoslovakia to yield to Hitler's demands.

Chamberlain's actions were the result of British self-interest. British leaders agreed that their country could not afford another war like the Great War of 1914–18. Defense expenditures had been dramatically reduced to devote national resources to improving domestic social services, protecting world trade, and fortifying Britain's global interests. Britain understood well its weakened position in its dominions. In the British hierarchy of priorities, defense of the British Empire ranked first, above defense of Europe; and Britain's commitment to western Europe ranked above the defense of eastern and central Europe.

Hitler's response to being granted everything he requested was to renege and issue new demands. His desire for war could not have been more transparent, nor could his unwillingness to play by the rules of diplomacy have been clearer. One final meeting was held at Munich to avert war. On 29 September 1938, one day before German troops were scheduled to invade Czechoslovakia, Mussolini and the French prime minister, Édouard Daladier (1884–1970), joined Hitler and Chamberlain at Munich to discuss a peaceful resolution to the crisis.

At Munich, Chamberlain and Daladier again yielded to Hitler's demands. The Sudetenland was ceded to Germany and German troops quickly moved to occupy the area. The policy of the British and French was dubbed *appeasement* to indicate the willingness to concede to demands in order to preserve peace. *Appeasement* has become a dirty word in twentieth-century European history, taken to mean weakness and cowardice. Yet Chamberlain was neither weak nor cowardly. His great mistake in negotiating with Hitler was in assuming that Hitler was a reasonable man, who like all reasonable persons wanted to avoid another war.

Chamberlain thought his mediation at Munich had won for Europe a lasting peace—"peace for our time," he reported. The people of Europe received Chamberlain's assessment with a sense of relief and shame—relief over what had been avoided, shame at having deserted Czechoslovakia. In fact, the policy of appeasement further destabilized Europe and accelerated Hitler's plans for European domination. Within months, Hitler cast aside the Munich agreement by annihilating Czechoslovakia. German troops occupied

A German motorized detachment rides through a bomb-shattered town during the Nazi invasion of Poland in 1939. The invasion saw the first use of the blitzkrieg—lightning war—in which air power and rapid tank movement combined for swift victory.

the western, Czech part of the state, including the capital of Prague. The Slovak eastern part became independent and a German satellite. At the same time, Lithuania was pressured into surrendering Memel to Germany, and Hitler demanded that Germany control Gdansk and the Polish Corridor. No longer could Hitler be ignored or appeased. No longer could his goals be misunderstood.

Hitler's War, 1939–41

In the tense months that followed the Munich meeting and the occupation of Prague, Hitler readied himself for war in western Europe. To strengthen his position, in May 1939 he formed a military alliance, the Pact of Steel, with Mussolini's Italy. Then Hitler and Stalin, previously self-declared enemies, shocked the West by joining their two nations in a pact of mutual neutrality, the Non-Aggression Pact of 1939. Opportunism lay

behind Hitler's willingness to ally with the Communist state that he had denounced throughout the 1930s. A German alliance with the Soviet Union would, Hitler believed, force the British and the French to back down and to remain neutral while Germany conquered Poland—the last obstacle to a drive for expansion eastward—in a short, limited war. Stalin recognized the failure of the western European powers to stand up to Hitler. There was little possibility, he thought, of an alliance against Germany with the virulently anti-Communist Neville Chamberlain. The best Stalin could hope for was that the Germans and the Western powers would fight it out while the Soviet Union waited to enter the war at the most opportune moment. As an added bonus, Germany promised not to interfere if the Soviet Union annexed eastern Poland, Bessarabia, and the Baltic republics of Latvia and Estonia.

Finally recognizing Hitler's intent, the British and the French also signed a pact in the spring of 1939 promising assistance to Poland in the event of aggression. Tensions mounted throughout the summer as Europeans awaited the inevitable German aggression. On 1 September 1939, Germany attacked Poland, which was ill-prepared to defend itself. By the end of the month, in spite of valiant resistance, the vastly outnumbered Poles surrendered. Although the German army needed no assistance, the Russians invaded Poland ten days before its collapse, and Germany and Russia divided the spoils. Almost immediately, Stalin took measures to defend Russia against a possible German attack. The Soviet Union assumed military control in the Baltic states and demanded of Finland territory and military bases from which the city of Leningrad could be defended. When Finland refused, Russia invaded. In the snows of the "Winter War" of 1939–40, the Finns initially fought the Russian army to a standstill, much to the encouragement of the democratic West. The Finns, however, were eventually defeated in March 1940.

Hitler's war, the war for German domination of Europe, had begun. But it had not begun the way he intended. Great Britain and France, true to their alliance with Poland and contrary to Hitler's expectations, declared war on Germany on 3 September 1939, even though they were unable to give any help to Poland. In the six months after the fall of Poland, no military action took place between Germany and the Allies because Hitler postponed offensives in northern and western Europe because of poor weather conditions. This strange interlude, which became known as "the phony war," was a period of suspended reality in which France and Great Britain waited for Hitler to

Legend:
- Axis powers, August 1939
- Extent of Axis control, May 1941
- Allies
- Neutral nations
- Axis offenses
- Allied offenses
- ★ Major battles

Battle of Britain
1 Aug.–12 Oct. 1940

D-Day
6 June 1944

Paris liberated
25 Aug. 1944

Battle of the Bulge
16 Dec. 1944–31 Jan. 1945

VICHY FRANCE
(occupied Nov. 1942)

Rome liberated
4 June 1944

Germany invades Soviet Union
June 1941

Leningrad besieged
Sept. 1941–Jan. 1944

Stalingrad
21 Aug. 1942–
31 Jan. 1943

El Alamein
June–Nov. 1942

0 ——— 400 Miles
0 ——— 400 Kilometers

World War II in Europe

make his next move. Civilian morale in France deteriorated among a population that still remembered the death and destruction that France had endured in the Great War. An attitude of defeatism germinated and grew before the first French soldier fell in battle.

With the arrival of spring, Germany attacked Denmark and Norway in April 1940. Then, on 10 May 1940, Hitler's armies invaded the Netherlands, Belgium, and Luxembourg. By the third week of May, German mechanized forces were racing through northern France toward the English Channel, cutting off the British and Belgian troops and 120,000 French forces

from the rest of the French army. With the rapid defeat of Belgium, these forces were crowded against the Channel and had to be evacuated from the beaches of Dunkirk. France, with a large and well-equipped army, nevertheless relied on Allied support and was in a desperate situation without it.

In France, the German army fought a new kind of war called a blitzkrieg, or "lightning war," so named because of its speed. The British and the French had expected the German army to behave much as it had in World War I, concentrating its striking forces in a swing through coastal Belgium and Holland in order to

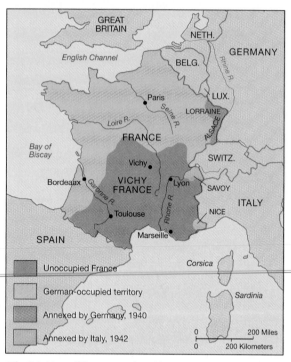

The Division of France, 1940–44

armistice, fled to London, where he set up a Free French government in exile.

French capitulation in June 1940 followed Italian entry into the war on the side of Germany in the same month. The British were now alone in a war against the two Axis powers as Germany made plans for an invasion of the British Isles from across the English Channel. To prepare the way, the German air force, under Reichsmarshal Hermann Göring (1893–1946), launched a series of air attacks against England—the Battle of Britain. The German air force first attacked British aircraft, airfields, and munitions centers and then shifted targets to major population centers like London and industrial cities like Coventry. Between 7 September and 2 November 1940, the German air force bombed the city of London every night, inflicting serious damage on the city and killing 15,000 people.

The British resisted these attacks under the leadership of Winston Churchill, who had succeeded Chamberlain as prime minister in 1940. Churchill was a master public speaker who, in a series of radio broadcasts, inspired the people of Britain with the historic greatness of the task confronting them—holding out against Nazism until the forces of the overseas British Empire and the United States could be marshaled to liberate Europe. The British Royal Air Force inflicted serious losses on German aircraft while British industry was able to maintain steady production of planes, bombs, and armaments. Civilians endured the nightly destruction and air raids in what Churchill termed Britain's "finest hour." Recognizing his lack of success in establishing air superiority over the Channel or in breaking the will of the British people, Hitler abandoned the Battle of Britain and canceled the invasion.

It was not in Great Britain but in the Balkans that Hitler was able to engage the British enemy and inflict serious losses. The British had a presence in the Greek Peloponnese, where their air units were deployed to support the valiant resistance of the Greeks against Italian aggression. In his original plans for a limited war, Hitler hoped to establish control over the Balkans by peaceful diplomatic means. But Mussolini's disastrous attempt to achieve military glory by conquering Greece impelled Hitler to make his own plans to attack Greece in Operation Marita. Using Bulgaria as the base of operations, Germany invaded Yugoslavia, whose government had been weakened by a recent military coup. The capital of Belgrade fell in April 1941. Internal ethnic enmity between the Croats and the Serbs led to the mutiny of Croatian soldiers and to the formation of an autonomous Croatian government favorably disposed to the Germans in Zagreb.

capture Paris. French strategists believed that France was safe because of hilly and forested terrain they thought was impassable. They also counted on the protection of the fortress wall known as the Maginot Line that France had built in the period between the wars. The Maginot Line stretched for hundreds of miles but was useless against mobile tank divisions, which outflanked it. With stunning speed, Germany drove its tanks—panzers—through the French defenses at Sedan in eastern France.

The French could have pinched off the advance of the overextended panzers, but the French army, suffering from severe morale problems, collapsed and was in retreat. On 17 June 1940, only weeks after German soldiers had stepped on French soil, Marshal Henri-Philippe Pétain, the great hero of the Battle of Verdun in World War I, petitioned the Germans for an armistice. Three-fifths of France, including the entire Atlantic seaboard, was occupied by the German army and placed under direct German rule. In the territory that remained unoccupied, Pétain created a collaborationist government that resided at Vichy—a spa city in central France—and worked in partnership with the Germans for the rest of the war. Charles de Gaulle (1890–1970), a brigadier general opposed to the

The reaction of this Frenchman watching the Axis powers take over his country was repeated across Europe as defending armies laid down their arms or escaped into exile.

The London Underground was pressed into service as a bomb shelter during the Battle of Britain.

German troops then crossed the Yugoslav border into Greece. Moving quickly down the Greek mainland, German soldiers captured the capital of Athens on 27 April 1941. German forces then turned their attention to the Greek island of Crete, where fleeing British soldiers sought refuge. In the first mass paratroop attack in history, Crete was rapidly subdued, forcing the British to evacuate to Egypt. The British were routed and experienced humiliating defeat by the German blitzkrieg.

The Balkans were important to Hitler for a number of reasons. Half of Germany's wheat and livestock came from the countries of southeastern Europe. Romanian and Hungarian oil fields supplied Germany's only non-Russian oil. Greece and Yugoslavia were important suppliers of metal ores, including aluminum, tin, lead, and copper so necessary for industry and the war effort.

The necessity of protecting resources, especially the oil fields in Romania, also gave the area geopolitical importance for Germany. In launching an attack against the Soviet Union, Hitler was well aware of the strategic significance of controlling the straits linking the Mediterranean and Black seas. The British lifeline to its empire could also be cut by control of the eastern Mediterranean.

Collaboration and Resistance

No one nation has ever controlled the Balkans, and Hitler understood that he must rule not by occupation but by collaboration. Some Balkan collaborators joined puppet governments out of an ideological commitment to fascism. They were hostile to communism and believed that Hitler's Nazism was far preferable to Stalin's communism. They saw in the German victory the chance to put their beliefs into practice.

Some governments collaborated with the Germans out of national self-interest. Just as the government of Hungary allied with Germany in the hope of winning back territory lost at the end of World War I, so did Romania ally with Russia. The government of Slovakia was loyal to the Third Reich because Hitler had given it independence from the Czechs. A German puppet state was set up in the Yugoslav province of Croatia. Other collaborators were pragmatists who believed that by taking political office they could negotiate with the German conquerors and soften the effects of the Nazi conquest on their people. Hitler had little affection for local ideological fascists and sometimes smashed their movements. He preferred to work with local generals and administrators. Pragmatic collaborators often could not or would not negotiate with the German authorities very well. The help they gave in rounding up opponents of Nazi Germany—resistance fighters and Jews—resulted in their punishment after the war.

Resistance against German occupation and collaborationist regimes took many forms. Resisters wrote subversive tracts, distributed them, gathered intelligence information for the Allies, sheltered Jews or other enemies of the Nazis, committed acts of sabotage or assassination or other violent acts, and carried on guerrilla warfare against the German army. Resisters ran the risk of endangering themselves and their families, who, if discovered, would be tortured and killed. Resistance movements developed most strongly after the German attack on the Soviet Union in 1941, when the Communist parties of occupied Europe formed the core of the violent resistance against the Nazi regime. Resistance grew stronger when the Germans began to draft young European men for work on German farms and in German factories. Many preferred to go underground rather than to Germany.

One of the great resistance fighters of the Second World War was Josip Broz (1892–1980), alias Tito. He was a Croatian Communist and a Yugoslav nationalist. Instead of waiting to be liberated by the Allies, his partisans fought against Italian and German troops. Ten or more German divisions that might otherwise have fought elsewhere were tied up combating Tito's forces. He gained the admiration and the support of Churchill, Roosevelt, and Stalin. After liberation, Tito's organization won 90 percent of the vote in the Yugoslav elections, and he became the leader of the

A Yugoslav partisan bayonetting a Nazi soldier.

THE WHITE ROSE

Resistance to Hitler's rule in Germany was a limited and isolated phenomenon, unable to claim, as the French resistance did, any coordinated leadership or mass following. On 22 February 1943, two students at the University of Munich and their professor were executed for distributing pamphlets that criticized Hitler's regime. The students, Sophie and Hans Scholl, were brother and sister, and along with Professor Kurt Huber they belonged to a small group of students, faculty, scientists, and intellectuals who called their society the White Rose.

APPEAL TO ALL GERMANS!

The war goes on to its certain conclusion. As in the year 1918, the German Government tries to tell us that the U-boat campaign is succeeding, while in the East our armies are retreating without stopping and in the West an Allied invasion is expected momentarily. America has yet to reach the height of its arming for war, and today it is already armed beyond anything like it in the past. With mathematical certainty Hitler is leading the German people to destruction.

Hitler cannot win the war, he can only prolong it. His guilt and that of those who helped him have already gone beyond the point of no return. A just punishment comes nearer and nearer!

What must the German people do? It sees nothing and it hears nothing. Blinded, it staggers on to its destruction. "Victory at any cost!" are the words written on its banners. "I shall fight to the last man," says Hitler—even though the war has already been lost.

Germans! Do you want yourself and your children to suffer the same fate as the Jews? Do you want to be judged the same way your mis-leader will be judged? Shall we forever be the most hated and rejected people in the world? Separate yourself, therefore, from the National Socialist subhumanity! Show by your deeds that you think otherwise!

This is the beginning of a new War of Liberation. The most decent of our people fight on our side! Tear up the cloak of indifference which you have placed around your hearts! *Decide yourself, before it is too late!*

Don't fall for that National Socialist propaganda that has put the fear of Bolshevism in your bones! Do you really think that the salvation of Germany is bound up for better or worse with National Socialism? A criminal conspiracy cannot possibly win a German victory. Abandon *immediately and in time* anything to do with National Socialism! There is going to be a terrible and just verdict for those who have shown themselves to be cowardly and irresolute.

This war was never a national one. What will be its lesson for us?

The imperialist concept of power, no matter from which side it comes, must have its teeth drawn for all time. One-sided Prussian militarism must never again be allowed to win power. Only in noble cooperation with other Europeans can the ground be prepared for a new political structure. Any centralized power, such as that the Prussian state sought to exercise inside Germany and in Europe, must be stifled in its germinal stage. The future Germany can be only a federal state. Only a sound federal state order can give Europe a new life. Workers must be freed by a rational socialism from their condition of abject slavery. The phantom of an autarchic economy must disappear in Europe. Every single person has the right to the good things of the world!

Freedom of speech, freedom of conscience, protection of the individual from despotism of the criminal power-state, these will be the foundation of the new Europe.

Support the Resistance! Distribute these leaflets!

---

country in the postwar era. Resistance entailed enormous risks and required secrecy, moral courage, and great bravery. On the whole, however, the actions of resistance fighters seldom affected military timetables and did little to change the course of the war and Hitler's domination of Europe.

By the middle of 1941, Hitler controlled a vast continental empire that stretched from the Baltic to the Black Sea and from the Atlantic Ocean to the Russian border. The German army occupied territories and controlled satellites, or Hitler relied on collaborationist governments for support. Having destroyed the democracies of western Europe, with the exception of Great Britain, Hitler's armies absorbed territory and marched across nations at rapid speed with technical and strategic superiority. Military conquest was not the only horror that the seemingly invincible Hitler inflicted on European peoples.

Racism and Destruction

War, as the saying goes, is hell. But the horrors perpetrated in World War II exceeded anything ever experienced in Western civilization. Claims of racial superiority were invoked to justify inhuman atrocities. The Germans and Japanese used spurious arguments of racial superiority to fuel their war efforts in both the European and Asian theaters of battle. In Asia the subjugation of inferior peoples became a rallying cry for conquest. But the Germans and the Japanese were not alone in using racist propaganda. The United States employed racial stereotypes to depict the inferiority of the enemy, and the government interned Japanese-Americans living on the West Coast in camps and seized their property.

Nowhere, however, was the use of racism by the state more virulent than in Germany. German racist ideology distorted pseudoscientific theories for the purpose of separating those they deemed racially superior from the racially inferior. The phrase "the master race" was used to identify those human beings worthy of living; those not worthy were designated "subhuman." Hatred of certain groups fueled both politics and war. Hitler promised the German people a purified Reich of Aryans "free of the Jews" and the racially and mentally inferior. Slavic peoples—Poles and Russians—were designated as subhumans who could be displaced in the search for *Lebensraum* and German destiny. With the war in eastern Europe, anti-Semitism changed from a policy of persecution and expropriation in the 1930s into a program of systematic extermination beginning in 1941.

Enforcing Nazi Racial Policies

Social policies erected on horrifying biomedical theories discriminated against a variety of social groups in the Third Reich. Gypsies were a case in point of "outsiders" who were labeled racially and genetically inferior. Gypsy ancestors had migrated to Germany in the fifteenth century, originating in the Punjab region of northern India and converting to the Christian religion in the course of their travels through Persia, Asia Minor, and the Balkans. As German itinerants with their own language, customs, and lifestyle, they were viewed by many other Germans during the Weimar period as a nuisance threatening the morals and hygiene of local communities. Beginning in 1933, police harassment against those identified as gypsies intensified. In 1936 the Nazi bureaucracy expanded to include the Reich Central Office Against the Gypsy Nuisance, where files on gypsies were assiduously maintained. They were subject to all racialist legislation and could be sterilized because of their "inferiority" without any formal hearing process. In September 1939, even as the war was beginning, high-ranking Nazis planned the removal of 30,000 gypsies to Poland. Over 200,000 German, Russian, Polish, and Balkan gypsies were killed in the course of the war by internment in camps and by systematic extermination. Discrimination against gypsies, however, did not begin with the Nazis, nor did it end with them. Not until 1982 were gypsies officially recognized by the German government as a persecuted group subject to Nazi genocidal policies. In 1989, as East Germans were welcomed in West Germany, gypsies from East Germany were either summarily deported to Yugoslavia or subject to attacks and discrimination in the newly united Germany.

Mixed-race children were also singled out for special opprobrium under Nazi racial policies. Children born of white German mothers and black fathers were a consequence of the presence in the Rhineland of French colonial troops from Senegal, Morocco, and Malaga as part of the French occupation forces during the 1920s and 1930s. The press during both the Weimar Republic and the Nazi regime attacked the children of these unions, probably numbering no more than 500 to 800 individuals, as "Rhineland bastards." In 1937 the Nazis decided to sterilize them without any legal proceedings.

Those suffering from hereditary illnesses were also labeled as a biological threat to the racial purity of the German people. Illegitimate medical tests were devised by state doctors to establish who was feeble-minded and genetically defective. By treating the society of the Third Reich as one huge laboratory for the production of the racially fit and the "destruction of worthless life," categories were constructed according to subjective criteria that claimed scientific validation. Medical officials examined children, and those judged to be deformed were separated from their families and transferred to special pediatric clinics where they were either starved to death or injected with lethal drugs. In the summer of 1939, euthanasia programs for adults were organized, and 65,000 to 70,000 Germans were identified for death. Asylums were asked to rank patients according to their race, state of health, and ability to work. These rankings were used to determine candidates for death. In Poland mental patients were simply shot; in other places they were starved to death. The uncooperative,

Schreibers rassenkundliche Anschauungstafel: Deutsche Rassenköpfe

Bearbeitet von Dr Alfred Eydt

Nordisch

Westisch

Fälisch

Dinarisch

Ostbaltisch

Ostisch

The Nazis attempted to cloak their self-serving racial theories in scientific respectability. A Nazi "race-identification table" displays what were asserted to be the typical heads of different German "races"—a classification that has no basis in anthropology.

the sick, and the disabled were purged as racially undesirable.

The umbrella covering hereditary illnesses was broad but not broader than the category covering the "asocial." In this designation, asocial behavior itself came to be interpreted as a hereditary trait. Criminals, beggars, vagrants, and the homeless could be compulsorily sterilized. Alcoholics, prostitutes, and people with sexually transmitted diseases could be labeled asocial and treated accordingly. These forms of behavior were considered to be hereditary and determined by blood.

Homosexuals were likewise treated as "community aliens" by Nazi social policies. The persecution of homosexual men intensified after 1934, when any form of "same-sex immorality" became subject to legal persecution. "Gazing and lustful intention" were left to the definition of the police and the courts. Criminal sentences could involve a term in a concentration camp. But because homosexuality was judged to be a sickness rather than an immutable biological trait, gays did not become the primary object of Nazi extermination policies that began to be enforced against the "biologically inferior." Instead, Nazi treatment of homosexuality might involve castration or indefinite incarceration in a concentration camp.

Gay men in Nazi concentration camps during the war were singled out with the badge of a pink triangle. Although it is not clear how many gay men were actually killed by the Nazis, estimates run as high as 200,000. Gay men rather than lesbian women were singled out by officials of the Third Reich because their behavior was considered a greater threat to the perpetuation of the German race.

The Destruction of Europe's Jews

Although anti-Semitism was an integral part of Hitler's view of the world, he did not think the peoples of Germany and Europe were ready for harsh measures against the Jews. When they came to power in 1933, the Nazis did not have a blueprint for the destruction of Europe's Jews; the anti-Semitic policies of the Third Reich evolved incrementally in the 1930s and 1940s.

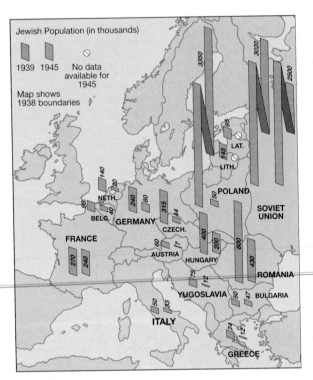

The Holocaust

sidered the possibility of deporting the more than 3 million Jews under German control to Madagascar, an island off the southeast coast of Africa. Until 1941, Nazi policies against the Jews were often uncoordinated and unfocused.

The "Final Solution." Confinement in urban ghettos was the beginning of a policy of concentration that ended in annihilation. After having identified Jews, seized their property, and then confined them to ghettos, German authorities began to implement a step-by-step plan for extermination. There appears to have been no single order from Hitler that decreed what became known to German officials as the "Final Solution"—the total extermination of European Jews. But Hitler's recorded remarks make it clear that he knew and approved of what was being done to the Jews. A spirit of shared purpose permeated the entire administrative system, from the civil service through the judiciary. Administrative agencies competed to interpret the Führer's will. SS guards in the camps and police in the streets embraced Hitler's "mission" of destruction. Those involved in carrying out the plan for extermination understood what was meant by the Final Solution and what their responsibilities were for enforcing it. To assure that the whole process operated smoothly, a planning conference for the Final Solution was conducted by Reinhard Heydrich (1904–42), leader of the Sicherheitsdienst (SD), or Security Service of the SS, for the benefit of state and party officials at Wannsee, a Berlin suburb, in January 1942.

After 1938, German civil servants expropriated Jewish property as rightfully belonging to the state. When the war began, Jews were rounded up and herded into urban ghettos in Germany and in the large cities of Poland. For a time the German foreign ministry con-

Seizing Jews in Warsaw. Nazi soldiers rounded up men, women, and children for "resettlement" in the east.

This scene from a German film found after the war shows women prisoners at an extermination camp.

Mass racial extermination began with the German conquest of Poland, where both Jews and non-Jews were systematically killed. It continued when Hitler's army invaded the Soviet Union in 1941. This campaign, known as Operation Barbarossa, set off the mass execution of eastern Europeans declared to be enemies of the Reich. The tactics of the campaign pointed the way to the Final Solution. To the Nazi leadership, Slavs were "subhuman." Russian Jews were, by extension, the lowest of the low, even more despised than German Jews. Nazi propaganda had equated Jews with Communists, and Hitler had used the expression "Judeo-communist" to describe what he considered to be the most dangerous criminal and enemy of the Third Reich, the enemy who must be annihilated at any cost.

The executions were the work of the SS, the elite military arm of the Nazi party. Special mobile murder squads of the SD under Heydrich were organized behind the German lines in Poland and Russia. Members of the army were aware of what the SS squads were doing and participated in some of the extermination measures. In the spring of 1941, Hitler ordered a massive propaganda campaign to be conducted among the armed forces. The army was indoctrinated to believe that the invasion of the Soviet Union was more than a military campaign: it was a "holy war," a crusade that

Germany was waging for civilization. SS chief Heinrich Himmler, probably responding to oral orders from Hitler, set about to enforce the Führer's threats with concrete extermination policies. Fearful that the SS would be outstripped by the regular army in the Führer's favor, Himmler exhorted his men to commit the worst atrocities.

Firing squads shot Russian victims en masse, then piled their bodies one on top of the other in open graves. Reviewing these procedures for mass killings, Himmler—ever competitive with other Nazi agencies—suggested a more efficient means of extermination that would require less manpower and would enhance the prestige of the SS. As a result, extermination by gas was introduced, using vans whose exhaust fumes were piped into the enclosed cargo areas that served as portable gas chambers. In Poland, Himmler replaced the vans with permanent buildings housing gas chambers using Zyklon B, a gas developed by the chemical firm I. G. Farben for the purpose. The chambers could annihilate thousands at a time.

The Third Reich began erecting its vast network of death in 1941. The first extermination camp was created in Chelmno, Poland, where 150,000 people were killed between 1941 and 1944. The camps practiced systematic extermination for the savage destruction of those groups deemed racially inferior, sexually deviant, or politically dangerous. The terms *genocide, judeocide,* and *holocaust* have been used to describe the mass slaughter of the Jewish people, most of which took place in the five major killing centers in what is now Polish territory—Chelmno, Belzec, Sobibor, Treblinka, and Auschwitz.

Many victims died before ever reaching the camps, transported for days in sealed railroad cars, without food, water, or sanitation facilities. Others died within months as forced laborers for the Reich. People of all ages were starved, beaten, and systematically humiliated. Guards taunted their victims verbally, degraded them physically, and tortured them with false hope. Promised clean clothes and nourishment, camp internees were herded into "showers" that dispensed gas rather than water. Descriptions of life in the camps reveal a systematized brutality and inhumanity on the part of the German, Ukrainian, and Polish guards toward their victims. In all, 11 million people died by the extermination process—6 million Jews and almost as many non-Jews, including children, the aged, homosexuals, Slavic slave laborers, Soviet prisoners of war, Communists, members of the Polish and Soviet leadership, various resistance elements, gypsies, and Jehovah's Witnesses.

"Work Makes You Free." The words ARBEIT MACHT FREI ("Work Makes You Free") were emblazoned over the main gate at Auschwitz, the largest of the concentration camps. It was at Auschwitz that the greatest number of persons died in a single place, including more than one million Jews. The healthy and the young were kept barely alive to work. Hard labor, starvation, and disease—especially typhus, tuberculosis, and other diseases that spread rapidly because of the lack of sanitation—claimed many victims.

On entering the camps, the sick and the aged were automatically designated for extermination because of their uselessness as a labor force. Many children were put to work, but some were designated for extermination. Many mothers chose to accompany their children to their deaths to comfort them in their final moments. Pregnant women were considered useless in the forced labor camps and were sent immediately to the "showers." The number of German Jewish women who died in the camps was 50 percent higher than the number of German Jewish men. Starvation diets meant that women stopped menstruating. Because the Nazis worried that women of childbearing age would continue to reproduce, women who showed signs of menstruation

were killed immediately. Women who were discovered to have given birth undetected in the camp were killed, as were their infants. Family relations were completely destroyed, as inmates were segregated by sex. It soon became clear that even those allowed to live were only intended to serve the short-term needs of the Nazis.

Resisting Destruction. Could the victims of extermination have effectively resisted? The answer is no. The impossibility of any effective resistance was based on two essential characteristics of the process of extermination. First, the entire German state and its bureaucratic apparatus were involved in the policies, laws, and decrees of the 1930s that singled out victims, while most Germans stood silently by. There was no course of appeal and no place to hide. Those who understood early what was happening and who had enough money to buy their way out emigrated to safer places, including Palestine and the United States. But most countries blocked the entry of German and eastern European refugees with immigration quotas. Neither Britain nor the United States was willing to deal with the mass influx of European Jews. Jews in the occupied countries and the Axis nations had virtually no chance to escape. They were trapped in a society where all forces of law and administration worked against them.

A second reason for the impossibility of effective resistance was the step-by-step nature of the process of extermination, which meant that few understood the final outcome until it was too late. Initially, in the 1930s, many German Jews believed that things could get no worse and obeyed the German state as good citizens. Even the policy of removing groups from the ghetto militated against resistance because the hope was that sending one thousand Jews to "resettlement" would allow ten thousand Jews remaining behind to be saved. The German authorities deliberately controlled information to cultivate this misunderstanding of what was happening.

Isolated instances of resistance in the camps—rioting at Treblinka, for example—only highlight how impossible rebellion was for physically debilitated people in these heavily guarded centers. In the Warsaw ghetto, a resistance movement was organized with a few firearms and some grenades and homemade Molotov cocktails in April 1943. Starvation, overcrowding, and epidemics made Warsaw, the largest of the ghettos, into an extermination camp. As news reached the ghetto that "resettlement" was the death warrant of tens of thousands of Polish Jews, armed rebellion erupted. It did not succeed in blocking the completion of the Final

MANIFESTO OF THE JEWISH RESISTANCE IN VILNA, SEPTEMBER 1943

In May 1943, in spite of the valiant resistance of Jewish fighting groups, the Warsaw ghetto was destroyed by the German SS. In August of the same year, inmates revolted in the concentration camp at Treblinka in the face of insurmountable odds. News of the Warsaw ghetto revolt had spread to the camp, where it inspired Jews to rise up and fight against their captors. Few survived the revolt, although considerable damage was done to the gas chambers, the railway station, and the barracks by the armed inmates. The Jews of the ghetto of Vilna (Vilnius) organized active resistance to the Nazis with the rallying cry, "Jews, we have nothing to lose!"

Offer armed resistance! Jews, defend yourselves with arms!

The German and Lithuanian executioners are at the gates of the ghetto. They have come to murder us! Soon they will lead you forth in groups through the ghetto door.

Tens of thousands of us were despatched. But we shall not go! We will not offer our heads to the butcher like sheep.

Jews, defend yourselves with arms!

Do not believe the false promises of the assassins or believe the words of the traitors.

Anyone who passes through the ghetto gate will go to Ponar! [Death Camp]

And Ponar means death!

Jews, we have nothing to lose. Death will overtake us in any event. And who can still believe in survival when the murderer exterminates us with so much determination? The hand of the executioner will reach each man and woman. Flight and acts of cowardice will not save our lives.

Active resistance alone can save our lives and our honor.

Brothers! It is better to die in battle in the ghetto than to be carried away to Ponar like sheep. And know this: within the walls of the ghetto there are organized Jewish forces who will resist with weapons.

Support the revolt!

Do not take refuge or hide in the bunkers, for then you will fall into the hands of the murderers like rats.

Jewish people, go out into the squares. Anyone who has no weapons should take an ax, and he who has no ax should take a crowbar or a bludgeon!

For our ancestors!

For our murdered children!

Avenge Ponar!

Attack the murderers!

In every street, in every courtyard, in every house within and without the ghetto, attack these dogs!

Jews, we have nothing to lose! We shall save our lives only if we exterminate our assassins.

Long live liberty! Long live armed resistance! Death to the assassins!

Vilna, the Ghetto, September 1, 1943.

Solution against the Warsaw ghetto the following year, when the SS commandant proclaimed, "The Jewish Quarter of Warsaw is no more!" Polish and Russian Jews account for 70 percent of the total Jewish deaths.

Who Knew?

It is impossible that killing on such a scale could have been kept secret. Along with those who ordered extermination operations, the guards and camp personnel involved in carrying out the directives were aware of what was happening. Those who brought internees to the camps, returning always with empty railroad cars, knew it too. People who saw their neighbors disappearing believed for a time that they were being resettled in the east. But as news got back to central and western Europe, it was more difficult to sustain belief in this ruse. People who lived near the camps could not ignore the screams and fumes of gas and burning bodies that permeated the environs.

THE ATROCITY AT LIDICE

Lidice was a small village in Czechoslovakia. The Nazis decided to raze the village to the ground in retaliation for the assassination of Reinhard Heydrich, Nazi head of the Secret Police and the Security Service of the SS. On 10 June 1942, all 173 men of the village were executed by German soldiers and the women and children were deported to concentration camps. Only 15 of Lidice's 101 children survived the war. So outraged was world opinion by this atrocity that memorials were created everywhere and many towns and cities changed their name to Lidice as a commemoration. The first extract is from a letter written by a Nazi official by the name of Krumey in charge of the camp at Lodz, Poland, where 38 of Lidice's children had been sent, to his superior, Adolf Eichmann, asking for direction. The second, from a letter addressed to the villagers of Lidice, is from five children in the camp.

In a telegram dated 17 June 1942 I asked the Commander of the Security Police and the Security Service . . . what was to be done with the Czech children. In the meantime, the Race and Resettlement Office has found seven of the children fit to be Germanized. [Note: these seven children were adopted by German families.]

Since I have no word on further disposition of the children and since the children were transferred here without any luggage, I urgently ask you to decide on the further use of the children.

• • •

Here it is always cold. We feel homesick for Lidice. We would like to beg you to send us some clothing because we don't own anything beyond what we are wearing, or especially something to eat. . . . Do you know anything about our parents? Send the things as soon as possible because we don't know how long we will remain in this place. Let us know what has become of Lidice. Send something that does not go bad for a long time. We are all here, all the children of the town. We don't know where our parents are. Send also some dresses and shoes. Above all, if you can, at least a bit of bread.

Signed Vera, Marenka, Mila, Anicka, and Valek

Although never publicly announcing its extermination program, the German government convinced its citizens that the policies of the Nazi state could not be judged by ordinary moral standards. The benefits to the German state were justification enough for the annihilation of 11 million people. Official propaganda successfully convinced millions that the Reich was the supreme good. Admitting the existence of the extermination program carried with it a responsibility on which few acted, perhaps out of fear of reprisals. There were some heroes like Raoul Wallenberg of Sweden, who interceded for Hungarian Jews and provided Jews in the Budapest ghetto with food and protection. The king of Denmark, when informed that the Nazis had ordered Danish Jews to wear the yellow star, stated that he and his family would also wear the yellow star as a "badge of honor." Heroic acts, however, were isolated and rare.

Collaborationist governments and occupied nations often cooperated with Nazi extermination policies. The French government at Vichy introduced and implemented a variety of anti-Jewish measures. All of this was done without German orders and without German pressure. By voluntarily identifying and deporting Jews, the Vichy government sent 75,000 men, women, and children to their deaths.

As the war dragged on for years, internees of the camps hoped and prayed for rescue by the Allies. But such help did not come. The U.S. State Department and the British Foreign Office had early and reliable information on the nature and extent of the atrocities. But they did not act. American Jews were unable to convince President Franklin D. Roosevelt to intercede to prevent the slaughter. Appeals to bomb the gas chambers at Auschwitz and the railroad lines leading to them were rejected by the United States on strategic grounds. Those trying to survive in the camps and the ghettos despaired at their abandonment.

The handful of survivors found by Allied soldiers who entered the camps after Germany's defeat presented a haunting picture of humanity. A British colonel who entered the camp at Bergen-Belsen in April 1945 gave a restrained account of what he found:

> As we walked down the main road of the camp, we were cheered by the internees, and for the first time we saw their condition. A great number were little more than living skeletons. There were men and women lying in heaps on both sides of the track. Others were walking slowly and aimlessly about, vacant expressions on their starved faces.

The sight of corpses piled on top of one another lining the roads and the piles of shoes, clothing, underwear, and gold teeth extracted from the dead shocked those who came to liberate the camps. One of the two survivors of Chelmno summed it all up: "No one can understand what happened here."

The Final Solution was a perversion of every value of civilization. The achievements of twentieth-century industry, technology, state, and bureaucracy in the West were turned against millions to create, as one

Jewish Population Loss, 1939–45

	1939	1945
Austria	60,000	7,000
Belgium	90,000	40,000
Bulgaria	50,000	47,000
Czechoslovakia	315,000	44,000
Denmark	6,500	5,500
France	270,000	200,000
Germany	240,000	80,000
Greece	74,000	12,000
Hungary	400,000	200,000
Italy	50,000	33,000
Luxembourg	3,000	1,000
Netherlands	140,000	20,000
Norway	2,000	1,000
Poland	3,350,000	50,000
Romania	800,000	430,000
USSR	3,020,000	2,500,000
Estonia	4,500	
Latvia	95,000	
Lithuania	145,000	
Yugoslavia	75,000	12,000

German official called it, murder by assembly line. Mass killing was not prompted by military or security concerns. Nor was the elimination of vital labor power consistent with the needs of the Nazi state. The international tribunal for war crimes that met in 1945 in the German city of Nuremberg attempted to mete out justice to the criminals against humanity responsible for the destruction of 11 million Europeans labeled as demons and racial inferiors. History in the end must record, even if it cannot explain, such inhumanity.

Allied Victory

The situation at the end of 1941 appeared grim for the British and their dominions and the Americans who were assisting them with munitions, money, and food. Hitler had achieved control of a vast land empire covering all of continental Europe in the west, north, south, and center. This empire, which Hitler called his "New Order," included territories occupied and directly administered by the German army, satellites, and collaborationist regimes. It was fortified by alliances with Italy, the Soviet Union, and Japan. Hitler commanded the greatest fighting force in the world, one that had

A British soldier listens to the story of an inmate of Bergen-Belsen as the camp is liberated by the Allies.

knocked France out of the war in a matter of weeks, brought destruction to British cities, and conquered Yugoslavia in twelve days. Much of the world was coming to fear German invincibility.

Then, in June 1941, Hitler's troops invaded the Soviet Union, providing the British with an ally. In December the naval and air forces of Japan attacked American bases in the Pacific, providing the British and the Russians with still another ally. What was a European war became a world war. This was the war Hitler did not want and that Germany could not win—a long, total war to the finish against three powers with inexhaustible resources: the British Empire, the Soviet Union, and the United States.

The Soviet Union's Great Patriotic War

Hitler had always considered the Soviet Union Germany's primary enemy. His hatred of communism was all-encompassing: Bolshevism was an evil invention of the Jewish people and a dangerous ideological threat to the Third Reich. The 1939 Non-Aggression Pact with Stalin was no more than an expedient for him. Hitler rebuked a Swiss diplomat in 1939 for failing to grasp the central fact of his foreign policy:

> Everything I undertake is directed against Russia. If those in the West are too stupid and too blind to understand this, then I should be forced to come to an understanding with the Russians to

beat the West, and then, after its defeat, turn with all my concentrated force against the Soviet Union.

That is exactly what happened on 22 June 1941, when German armies marched into Russia. They found the Soviet army larger but totally unprepared for war. In contrast to German soldiers, who had fought in Spain, Poland, and France, Soviet troops had no first-hand battle experience. Nor were they well led. Stalin's purges in the late 1930s removed 35,000 officers from their posts by dismissal, imprisonment, or execution. Many of the men who replaced them were unseasoned in the responsibilities of leadership.

Russian military leaders were sure they would be ready for a European war against the capitalist nations by 1942, and Stalin refused to believe that Hitler would attack the Soviet Union before then. British agents and Stalin's own spies tried to warn him of German plans for an invasion in the spring of 1941. When the Germans did invade Russian territory, Stalin was so overwhelmed that he fell into a depression and was unable to act for days.

In his first radio address after the attack on 3 July 1941, Stalin identified his nation with the Allied cause: "Our struggle for the freedom of our country will merge with the struggle of the peoples of Europe and America for their independence, for democratic liberties." He accepted offers of support from the United States and Great Britain, the two nations that had

Men and women on a Ukrainian collective farm labor to erect huge antitank traps during the German invasion of the Soviet Union. The steadfast courage of the civilian population contributed greatly to the defeat of Hitler's quest for Lebensraum in the east.

Russian villagers search for loved ones among civilians slain by German troops. Noncombatants were frequent victims of the Nazi policy of enslavement or annihilation.

worked consistently to exclude the Soviet Union from European power politics since the Bolshevik Revolution in 1917. With France defeated and Great Britain crippled, the future of the war depended on the Soviet fighting power and American supplies.

Hitler's invasion of Russia involved 3 million soldiers from Germany and Germany's satellites, the largest invasion force in history. It stretched along an immense battlefront from the Baltic to the Black Sea. Instead of exclusively targeting Moscow, the capital, the German army concentrated first on destroying Soviet armed forces and capturing Leningrad in the north and the oil-rich Caucasus in the south. In the beginning the German forces advanced rapidly in a blitzkrieg across western Russia, where they were greeted as liberators in the Ukraine. The Germans took 290,000 prisoners of war and massacred tens of thousands of others in their path through the Jewish settlements of western Russia.

Within four months, the German army had advanced to the gates of Moscow, but they concentrated their forces too late. The Red Army rallied to defend Moscow as thousands of civilian women set to work digging trenches and antitank ditches around the city. The Soviet people answered Stalin's call for a scorched-earth policy by burning everything that might be useful to the advancing German troops. German troops had also burned much in their path, depriving themselves

of essential supplies for the winter months ahead. The German advance was stopped, and the best ally of the Red Army—the Russian winter—settled in. The first snow fell at the beginning of October. By early November, German troops were beginning to suffer the harsh effects of an early and exceptionally bitter Russian winter.

Hitler promised the German people that "final victory" was at hand. So confident was Hitler of a speedy and decisive victory that he sent his soldiers into Russia wearing only light summer uniforms. Hitler's generals knew better and tried repeatedly to explain military realities to the Führer. General Heinz Guderian (1888–1954), commander of the tank units, reported that his men were suffering frostbite, that tanks could not be started, and that automatic weapons were jamming in the subzero temperatures. Back in Germany, the civilian population received little accurate news of the campaign. They began to suspect the worst when the government sent out a plea for woolen blankets and clothing for the troops.

By early December, the German military situation was desperate. The Soviets, benefiting from intelligence information about German plans and an awareness that Japan was about to declare war on the United States, recalled fresh troops from the Siberian frontier and the border with China and Manchuria and launched a powerful counterattack against the poorly outfitted German army outside Moscow. Under the command of General Gyorgi Zhukov (1896–1974), Russian troops, dressed and trained for winter warfare, pushed the Germans back in retreat across the snow-covered expanses. By February, 200,000 German troops had been killed, 46,000 were missing in action, and 835,000 were casualties of battle and the weather. Thus the campaign cost the German army over a million casualties. It probably cost the Soviets twice that number of wounded, missing, captured, and dead soldiers. At the end of the Soviet counterattack in March, the German army and its satellite forces were in a shambles reminiscent of Napoleon's troops, who 130 years earlier had been decimated in the campaign to capture Moscow. An enraged Hitler dismissed his generals for retreating without his permission, and he himself assumed the position of commander in chief of the armed forces.

Hitler was not daunted by the devastating costs of his invasion of Russia. In the summer of 1942, he initiated a second major offensive, this time to take the city of Stalingrad. Constant bombardment gutted the city, and the Soviet army was forced into hand-to-hand combat with the German soldiers. But the German troops, once again inadequately supplied and unprepared for the Russian winter, failed to capture the city. The Battle of Stalingrad was over in the first days of February 1943. Of the original 300,000 members of the German Sixth Army, fewer than 100,000 survived to be taken prisoner by the Soviets. Of those, only 5,000 returned to Germany in 1955, when German prisoners of war were repatriated.

The Soviets succeeded by exploiting two great advantages in their war against Germany: the large Soviet population and their knowledge of Russian weather and terrain. There was a third advantage that Hitler ignored: the Soviet people's determination to sacrifice everything for the war effort. In his successive Five-Year Plans, Stalin had mobilized Soviet society with an appeal to fulfill and surpass production quotas. In the summer of 1941, as Hitler's troops threatened Moscow, he used the same rhetoric to appeal to his Soviet "brothers and sisters" to join him in waging "the Great Patriotic War." The Russian people shared a sense of common purpose, sacrifice, and moral commitment in their loyalty to the nation.

The advancing Germans themselves intensified Soviet patriotism by torturing and killing tens of thousands of peasants who might have willingly cooperated against the Stalinist regime. Millions of Soviet peasants joined the Red Army. Young men of high school age were drafted into the armed forces. Three million

women became wage earners for the first time as they replaced men in war industries. Women who remained on the land worked to feed the townspeople and the soldiers. Because the Red Army had requisitioned horses and tractors for combat, grain had to be sown and harvested by hand—and this often meant women's hands. Tens of thousands of Russians left their homes in western Russia to work for relocated Soviet industries in the Urals, the Volga region, Siberia, and Central Asia. More than 20 million Soviet people, soldiers and civilians, men, women, and children, died in the course of World War II. In addition to those killed in battle, millions starved as a direct result of the hardships of war. In 1943 food was so scarce that seed for the next year's crops was eaten. One in every three men born in 1906 died in the war. But Soviet resistance did not flag. The Great Patriotic War had a profound impact on Soviet views of the world and the Soviet Union's place in it. The war left the Soviet people with an enduring fear of invasion. The official falsification of all published maps of the Soviet Union in order to mislead spies and foreign armies was just one indication of the Russian expectation of treachery. (This practice was as recent as 1988.) Today, a visitor to Stalingrad, renamed Volgograd, can still find old tanks in city parks and on streets as reminders of the front line of the Red Army in the Great Patriotic War. Ruins of buildings have been left standing as grim monuments to the need for continued preparedness. The few remaining trees that endured through the war's devastation bear plaques that make their survival a memorial.

The Soviet Union sacrificed 10 percent of its population to the war effort, incurring well over 50 percent of all the deaths and casualties of the war. Few families escaped the death of members in the defense of the nation. Soviet citizens correctly considered that they had given more than any other country to defeat Hitler. For the Soviet people, their suffering in battle made World War II the Soviet Union's war and their sacrifice made possible the Allied victory. But victory still eluded the Allies in western Europe, where now another nation, the United States, had entered the fray.

The United States Enters the War

Although a neutral power, the United States began extending aid to the Allies after the fall of France in 1940. Since neither Britain nor the Soviet Union could afford to pay all the costs of defending Europe against Hitler, the United States Congress passed the Lend-Lease Act in 1941. This act authorized President Roosevelt to provide armaments to Great Britain and the

The battleship USS West Virginia *in flames at Pearl Harbor. The attack was carried out entirely by carrier-based aircraft—a sign of things to come in naval warfare.*

Soviet Union without payment. America became "the arsenal of democracy." The United States and Britain sent 4,100 airplanes and 138,000 motor vehicles as well as steel and machinery to the Soviet Union for the campaign of 1943. In all, America pumped $11 billion worth of equipment into the Soviet war effort between 1941 and 1945. Stalin later told Roosevelt that the USSR would have lost the war with Germany without the help of the Americans and the British.

President Roosevelt and his advisers considered Germany, not Japan, to be America's primary target for a future war. Japan nevertheless had been threatening American trade interests in Asia and had embroiled the United States in disputes over Japanese imperialist expansion in the late 1930s. The United States understood Japan to be an aggressive country determined to expand its control over China and southeast Asia, which it opposed initially through economic embargoes. The presence of the Soviet Union pressing eastward across Asia, coupled with the colonial presences in Asia of Great Britain, France, and the United States, severely constrained Japan's capacity to expand its frontiers and ensure its security. The war in western Europe and the German invasion of the Soviet Union in June 1941 meant that the Japanese could concentrate their attention farther south in China, Indochina, and Thailand. Japan's limited reserves of foreign currency and raw materials made it increasingly vulnerable to economic disruptions. Japanese leaders accepted the necessity of grasping oil and raw materials in southeast Asia.

In September 1940, Japan joined forces with the Axis powers of Germany and Italy in the Tripartite Pact, in which the signatories, promising mutual support against aggression, acknowledged the legitimacy of each other's expansionist efforts in Europe and Asia. Japanese-American relations deteriorated following the Japanese invasion of southern Indochina in July 1941. The United States insisted that Japan vacate China and Indochina and reestablish the open door for trade in Asia. The United States knew, however, that it was only a matter of time until Japan attacked U.S. interests but was uncertain about where that attack would take place.

On Sunday morning, 7 December 1941, Japan struck at the heart of the American Pacific Fleet stationed at Pearl Harbor, Hawaii. The fleet was literally caught asleep at the switch: 2300 people were killed, and eight battleships and numerous cruisers and destroyers were sunk or severely damaged. The attack crippled American naval power in the Pacific as the American navy suffered its worst loss in history in a single engagement. The attack on Pearl Harbor led to the United States' immediate declaration of war against Japan. In President Roosevelt's words, 7 December 1941 was "a date which will live in infamy." In the next three months, Japan captured Hong Kong, Malaya,

PRESIDENT FRANKLIN ROOSEVELT'S REQUEST FOR A DECLARATION OF WAR ON JAPAN, 8 DECEMBER 1941

On 7 December 1941, the Japanese naval and air forces attacked the American naval base at Pearl Harbor in Hawaii, killing and wounding 3457 military personnel and civilians. Most of the U.S. Pacific fleet was moored in Pearl Harbor, and it sustained severe destruction of its naval vessels, battleships, and aircraft. U.S. military and political leaders were taken completely by surprise by the Japanese attack. Roosevelt's declaration of war reflects the outrage over this "infamy."

To the Congress of the United States:

Yesterday, December 7, 1941—a date which will live in infamy—the United States of America was suddenly and deliberately attacked by naval and air forces of the Empire of Japan.

The United States was at peace with that Nation and, at the solicitation of Japan, was still in conversation with its Government and its Emperor looking toward the maintenance of peace in the Pacific. Indeed, one hour after Japanese air squadrons had commenced bombing in Oahu, the Japanese Ambassador to the United States and his colleague delivered to the Secretary of State a formal reply to a recent American message. While this reply stated that it seemed useless to continue the existing diplomatic negotiations, it contained no threat or hint of war or armed attack.

It will be recorded that the distance of Hawaii from Japan makes it obvious that the attack was deliberately planned many days or even weeks ago. During the intervening time the Japanese Government has deliberately sought to deceive the United States by false statements and expressions of hope for continued peace.

The attack yesterday on the Hawaiian Islands has caused severe damage to American naval and military forces. Very many American lives have been lost. In addition American ships have been reported torpedoed on the high seas between San Francisco and Honolulu.

Yesterday the Japanese Government also launched an attack against Malaya.

Last night Japanese forces attacked Hong Kong.

Last night Japanese forces attacked Guam.

Last night Japanese forces attacked the Philippine Islands.

Last night the Japanese attacked Wake Island.

This morning the Japanese attacked Midway Island.

Japan has, therefore, undertaken a surprise offensive extending throughout the Pacific area. The facts of yesterday speak for themselves. The people of the United States have already formed their opinions and well understand the implications to the very life and safety of our Nation.

As Commander-in Chief of the Army and Navy I have directed that all measures be taken for our defense.

Always will we remember the character of the onslaught against us.

No matter how long it may take us to overcome this premeditated invasion, the American people in their righteous might will win through to absolute victory. . . .

With confidence in our armed forces—with the unbounded determination of our people—we will gain the inevitable triumph—so help us God.

I ask that the Congress declare that since the unprovoked and dastardly attack by Japan on Sunday, December seventh, a state of war has existed between the United States and the Japanese Empire.

FRANKLIN D. ROOSEVELT

and the important naval base at Singapore from the British, taking 60,000 prisoners. Like their earlier march into China, the Japanese invasion of southeast Asia moved swiftly to establish control, outstripping the Japanese military's own timetables for advance. In December 1941, the Japanese landed in Thailand and secured immediate agreement for Japanese occupation of strategic spots in the country. They then turned to the Malayan peninsula, decisively defeating the British fleet off Malaya and pushing on the ground toward Singapore, which they conquered in February 1942. They conquered British Borneo in January, drove the

JAPAN'S DECLARATION OF WAR ON THE UNITED STATES AND GREAT BRITAIN, 8 DECEMBER 1941

Japan's sense of its mission in East Asia is embodied in Emperor Hirohito's declaration of war against the United States and Great Britain on 8 December 1941, the day after Japanese forces attacked the American fleet in Hawaii. Interestingly, the Japanese declaration speaks of "world peace" and "friendship among nations." In spite of marked cultural differences in the form of the two declarations, both the Japanese and the American leaders make clear their country's dependence on the total support of their people to win the war.

We, by grace of heaven, Emperor of Japan, seated on the Throne of the line unbroken for ages eternal, enjoin upon ye. Our loyal and brave subjects.

We hereby declare war on the United States of America and the British Empire. The men and officers of Our Army and Navy shall do their utmost in prosecuting the war, Our public servants of various departments shall perform faithfully and diligently their appointed tasks, and all other subjects of Ours shall pursue their respective duties; the entire nation with a united will shall mobilize their total strength so that nothing will miscarry in the attainment of our war aims.

To insure the stability of East Asia and to contribute to world peace is the far-sighted policy which was formulated by Our Great Illustrious Imperial Grandsire and Our Great Imperial Sire succeeding Him, and which We have constantly to heart. To cultivate friendship among nations and to employ prosperity in common with all nations has always been the guiding principle of Our Empire's foreign policy. It has been truly unavoidable and far from Our wishes that Our Empire has now been brought to cross swords with America and Britain. More than four years have passed since the government of the Chinese Republic, failing to comprehend the true intentions of Our Empire, and recklessly courting trouble, disturbed the peace of east Asia and compelled Our Empire to take up arms. . . .

Patiently have We waited and long have We endured, in the hope that Our Government might retrieve the situation in peace. But our adversaries, showing not the least spirit of conciliation, have unduly delayed a settlement; and in the meantime, they have intensified the economic and military pressure to compel thereby Our Empire to submission. This trend of affairs would, if left unchecked, not only nullify Our Empire's efforts of many years for the sake of the stabilization of east Asia, but also endanger the very existence of Our nation. The situation being such as it is, Our Empire for its existence and self-defence has no other recourse but to appeal to arms and to crush every obstacle in its path.

The hallowed spirits of Our Imperial Ancestors guarding Us from above, We rely upon the loyalty and courage of Our subjects in Our confident expectation that the task bequeathed by Our Forefathers will be carried forward, and that the sources of evil will be speedily eradicated and an enduring peace immutably established in East Asia, preserving thereby the glory of Our Empire.

The 8th day of the 12th month of the 16th year of Showa.

HIROHITO

Dutch from all of Indonesia but New Guinea, pushed American forces in the Philippines into the Bataan Peninsula, occupied Burma, and inflicted severe defeats on British, Dutch, and American naval power in East Asia. U.S. general Douglas MacArthur (1880–1964) surrendered the Philippines to the Japanese on 2 January 1942 with the promise to return. With the armies of Germany deep in Russian territory, Australia now faced the threat of a Japanese invasion.

Hitler praised the Japanese government for its action against the British Empire and against the United States and its "millionaire and Jewish backers." Germany, with its armies retreating from Moscow, nevertheless declared war against the United States on 11 December 1941. Hitler, in fact, considered that the United States was already at war with Germany because of its policy of supplying the Allies. Within days the United States, a nation with an army smaller than Belgium's, had gone from neutrality to a war in two theaters. Although militarily weak, the United States was an economic giant, commanding a vast industrial capacity and access to resources. America grew even

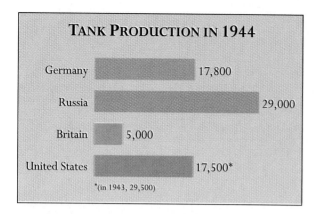

TANK PRODUCTION IN 1944

Germany   17,800
Russia   29,000
Britain   5,000
United States   17,500*

*(in 1943, 29,500)

stronger under the stimulus of war, increasing its production by 400 percent in two years. It now devoted itself to the demands of a total war and the unconditional surrender of Germany and then Japan.

Winning the War in Europe

The Allies did not always share the same strategies or concerns. President Roosevelt and Prime Minister Churchill had already discussed common goals in the summer of 1941 before U.S. entry into the war. The United States embraced the priority of the European war and the postponement of war in the Pacific. Stalin pleaded for the Anglo-Americans to open up a second front against Germany in western Europe to give his troops some relief and save Soviet lives. Anglo-American resources were committed to the Pacific to stop the Japanese advance, and the Americans and the British disagreed as to where a second front in Europe might be opened.

Because of British interests in the Mediterranean, Churchill insisted on a move from North Africa into Sicily and Italy. This strategy was put into effect in 1942. The Italian government withdrew from the war in September, but German troops carried on the fight in Italy. The Anglo-American invasion of Italy did little to alleviate Russian losses, and the Soviet Union absorbed almost the entire force of German military power until 1944. Stalin's distrust of his allies increased. Churchill, Roosevelt, and Stalin met for the first time in late November 1943 at Teheran, Iran. Roosevelt and Churchill made a commitment to Stalin to open a second front in France within six months. Stalin, in turn, promised to attack Japan to aid the United States in the Pacific. The great showdown of the global war was at hand.

On 6 June 1944, Allied troops under the command of American general Dwight D. Eisenhower (1890–1969) came ashore on the beaches of Normandy in the largest amphibious landing in history. In a daring operation identified by the code name Operation Overlord, 2.2 million American, British, and Free French forces, 450,000 vehicles, and 4 million tons of supplies poured into northern France. Allied forces broke through German lines to liberate Paris in late August. The Germans launched a last-ditch counterattack in late December 1944 in Luxembourg and Belgium. This Battle of the Bulge only slowed the Allied advance; in March 1945, American forces crossed the Rhine into Germany. Hitler, meanwhile, refused to surrender and insisted on a fight to the death of the last German soldier. Members of his own High Command had attempted unsuccessfully to assassinate Hitler in July 1944. The final German defeat came in April 1945, when the Russians stormed the German capital of Berlin. Hitler, living in an underground bunker near the Chancellery building, committed suicide on 30 April 1945.

Soldiers raise the hammer-and-sickle flag over the ruins of the Reichstag as Soviet troops occupy Berlin in May 1945. At war's end, the Soviets occupied most of eastern Europe, which gave Stalin an advantage at the Yalta Conference.

Supplies for the Allied forces pour ashore at the beachheads of Normandy during Operation Overlord in 1944. The invasion began the opening of the second front that Stalin had been urging on the Allies since the German armies thrust into Russia in 1941.

Japanese War Aims and Assumptions

Japan and the United States entered the Pacific War with very different understandings of what was at stake. Initially, the Japanese appealed to southeast Asian leaders as the liberators of Asian peoples from Western colonialism and imperialism. The approach struck a responsive chord as the Japanese established what they called the Greater East Asia Co-Prosperity Sphere. Ba Maw, Burma's leader, said at the Assembly of the Greater East Asiatic Nations held in Tokyo in November 1943, "My Asiatic blood has always called to other Asiatics. . . . This is not the time to think with our minds; this is the time to think with our blood, and it is thinking with the blood that has brought me all the way from Burma to Japan." But the passionate and positive welcome Ba Maw extended to the Japanese liberators did not last long. As he bluntly explained in his memoirs, "The brutality, arrogance, and racial pretensions of the Japanese militarists in Burma remain among the deepest Burmese memories of the war years; for a great many people in southeast Asia these are all they remember of the war."

The Greater East Asia Co-Prosperity Sphere began in 1940 and lasted until the summer of 1945. This reorganization of east and southeast Asia under Japanese hegemony constituted a redefinition of world geography, with Japan at the center. The Japanese fashioned a romanticized vision of the family living in harmony, each member knowing his place and enjoying the complementary division of responsibilities and reciprocities that made family life work smoothly. Behind this pleasant image lurked the reality of a brutal power structure forcing subject peoples to accept massively inferior positions in a world fashioned exclusively for Japanese desires and needs. The Japanese viewed southeast Asia principally as a market for Japanese manufactured goods, a source of raw materials, and a source of profits for Japanese capital invested in mining, rubber, and raw cotton. Plans were made for hydroelectric power and aluminum refining facilities.

Wartime Japanese nakedly displayed their disdain for the people they conquered in southeast Asia. All subject peoples were to bow on meeting a Japanese, while at public assemblies a ritual bow in the direction of the Japanese emperor was required, to the dismay of

❧ The Atomic Wasteland

Yasuko Yamagata

The sixth of August 1945 was a typical summer day in southwestern Japan. In the city of Hiroshima at 8:15 A.M., people were walking to work, sitting down at office desks, riding buses, weeding gardens, and clearing away breakfast dishes. Suddenly a noiseless flash lit the sky over the city and its environs for miles. A mammoth column of smoke in the shape of a mushroom cloud ballooned up. The United States had dropped history's first atomic bomb.

The explosion had the intensity of a huge blast furnace. In some areas, the brilliant light created by the explosion bleached everything it touched. Near the epicenter of the blast, human bodies were charred to cinders or turned into frightening statues. Flesh melted and bones fused. Buildings were reduced to ashes. Stones bled. The world had never seen a bomb like this. Hiroshima, a city renowned in prewar Japan for its relaxed and agreeable atmosphere, was leveled in an instant by the terrifying force of a single atomic bomb.

There were 78,000 dead in Hiroshima on 6 August. By December the number had reached 140,000 as the sickness caused by radioactive poisoning continued to take its toll. Rescue workers inhaled the dense dust and became contaminated by radioactivity. Surviving victims often lost their hair and eyebrows and experienced nausea, vomiting, diarrhea, and bleeding. Others suffered from internal hemorrhaging, blindness, chronic weakness, and fatigue. Many developed cancers like leukemia, sometimes years later. The bomb scarred and disfigured. Atomic radiation released by the bomb caused unseen damage by attacking the lungs, heart, bone marrow, and internal organs. It poisoned the lymph glands. It worked unobserved to alter genetic structure, deforming unborn babies and those not yet conceived.

Harry Truman, who became president of the United States on 12 April 1945, following the death of Franklin D. Roosevelt, later spoke of his decision to drop the atomic bomb to bring the war to a speedy end. In July 1945, Truman issued an ultimatum to Japan to surrender immediately or face dire consequences. The Japanese ignored the warning. Hiroshima was targeted, according to Truman, to make a point to the Japanese, to demonstrate the unimaginable force of this new American weapon. The city was a military center, a major storage and assembly point that supplied the armed forces. Nagasaki, bombed three days after Hiroshima with an experimental plutonium bomb, was targeted as an industrial center and the place where the torpedoes that had destroyed American ships were manufactured.

It is undoubtedly true that the bombings were responsible for the Japanese surrender that followed a few days later. The atomic bomb did bring the Asian war to an immediate end. But critics of the bombings pointed out that Japan was already close to defeat. Secret U.S. intelligence studies that came to light in the 1980s indicate that American leaders knew that Japan had been weakened by intense American incendiary bombing of its cities. Twenty-six square miles of the working-class and industrial section of Tokyo had been burned at the cost of well over 100,000 lives. Many refugees from other Japanese cities had fled to Hiroshima to live with relatives. The Sea of Japan had been heavily mined, cutting off Japan from its armies on the Asian mainland. Some radical young officers of the Japanese army were preparing to kidnap Emperor Hirohito to keep him from capitulating. The planned American landing on Japan was expected to be costly. U.S. forces had already suffered over 100,000 casualties in the conquest of the Japanese island of Okinawa in April. Truman and his advisers were now prepared to use any means possible to prevent further American casualties. Defenders of the decision have argued that any responsible American leader would have made the same decision to use the atomic bomb. Modern total wars acquire a life of their own, and desperate nations use the science, technology, and weapons available to them.

In the summer of 1945, General Dwight D. Eisenhower, then the victorious Supreme Allied Commander in the European theater of war, was informed by U.S. Secretary of War Henry L. Stimson of what was about to take place in Hiroshima. Eisenhower voiced his "grave misgivings" based on his "belief that Japan was already defeated and that the dropping of the bomb was completely unnecessary" to end the war. He was not alone among military men in questioning the use of nuclear force on strategic and moral grounds. Strong opposition to nuclear weapons began to surface among scientists working on the bomb. In opposition to many of their colleagues, they warned that the atomic bomb was an undiscriminating weapon that could not pinpoint supply depots and military targets but would destroy entire civilian populations. The peace movement based on banning nuclear weapons actually began among horrified scientists who were aware, before the rest of the world could know, of the terrible force that they had helped to create.

At the Potsdam Conference in July 1945, Stalin had informed President Truman and Prime Minister Winston Churchill that the Soviet Union was about to invade Manchuria, honoring the promise Stalin had made at Teheran in 1943 to join the war against Japan after Germany was defeated. The Soviet Union would now play a role in determining the future of Asia. Truman told Stalin of the powerful new weapon America had developed. Stalin seemed unimpressed. Secretary of War Stimson was aware that the atomic bomb would be an important weapon to have in the American arsenal when the time came to negotiate a postwar world settlement with the Russians. Truman and his advisers, however, never deviated from their insistence that saving the lives of thousands of American and Japanese soldiers was their only consideration in dropping the bomb.

An American observer called the bombing of Hiroshima "the immersion in death." Survivors repeatedly described Hiroshima after the "flash" as what hell must be like. Photographs of the city record the total destruction of buildings and vegetation. Japanese photographers avoided taking pictures of the devastation the bomb had done to human bodies, believing that what they saw was too horrible to record. Yet the brutality of nuclear war could not be ignored. It has become a central issue of international politics in the second half of the twentieth century. The decision to drop the atomic bomb has had enduring moral and political consequences. On that August morning in 1945, the world had its first terrifying glimpse of the power of total annihilation. In an instant—0.3 second—Hiroshima became an atomic wasteland. The world now lived with the knowledge that it could happen again.

southeast Asians such as Indies Muslims or Philippine Catholics who regarded Japanese emperor worship as pagan and presumptuous. Japanese holidays, such as the emperor's birthday, were enforced as Co-Prosperity Sphere holidays, and the calendar was reset to the mythical founding of the Japanese state in 660 B.C.

The Japanese were less brazen toward the Chinese in their rhetoric, in part because so much of east Asian civilization had its roots in China. But even if more temperate in their pronouncements, the realities of Japanese aggression in China included one of the worst periods of destruction in modern warfare. When they took over the Nationalist capital of Nanjing in December 1937, 20,000 women were raped, 30,000 soldiers killed, and another 12,000 civilians died in the more than six weeks of wanton terror inflicted by Japanese soldiers.

With regard to Westerners, Japanese propaganda avoided labeling them as inferior. In part this reflected Japan's economical and political emulation of the West since the late nineteenth century. Rather than denigrating Western people, the Japanese chose to elevate themselves as a people descended from divine origins. Stressing their unique mythical history gave the Japanese a strong sense of superiority neither intellectual nor physical, but moral. They believed that virtue was on their side in their mission to stop Western expansion in Asia and to take their "proper place" as the leading people in Asia by tyrannizing the Co-Prosperity Sphere.

To achieve their moral superiority, the Japanese government urged their people to "purify" themselves. Although purification rituals occur in the world's great religions, rarely do governments urge people to cleanse their souls. For the average wartime Japanese citizen, purification meant accepting extreme material poverty and scarcities, rejecting foreign influences, and if called upon, dying for the emperor. The Japanese elevation of patriotism to the level of human sacrifice lay outside Western sensibilities of the time; to expect the spirit to become more purified made little sense to large numbers of Westerners. A bit more comprehensible, perhaps, were Japanese wartime views of Americans as beasts because of the atrocities that American soldiers committed. The grotesque quality of the American soldier's desire for war trophies was captured by a *Life* magazine photograph of a blond young American woman holding a Japanese skull sent to her by her GI sweetheart. What *Life* magazine considered "human interest," the Japanese found racist. However reasonable this assessment may be, Japanese impressions of Westerners definitely proved fatally false in another

matter. The Japanese assumed that individual selfishness and egoism would make Americans and Europeans incapable of mobilizing for a long fight.

Winning the War in the Pacific

The tide in the Pacific War began to turn when the planned Japanese invasion of Australia was thwarted. Fighting in the jungles of New Guinea, Australian and American troops under the command of General Douglas MacArthur turned back the Japanese army. U.S. Marines did likewise with a bold landing at Guadalcanal and months of bloody fighting in the Solomon Islands. In June 1942, within six months of the attack at Pearl Harbor, American naval forces commanded by Admiral Chester Nimitz (1885–1966) inflicted a defeat on the Japanese navy from which it could not recover. In the battle of Midway, Japan lost 4 aircraft carriers, a heavy cruiser, over 300 airplanes, and 5000 men. Midway was the Pacific equivalent of the Battle of Stalingrad.

In the summer of 1943, as the Soviet Union launched the offensive that was to defeat Germany, America began to move across the Pacific toward Japan. Nimitz and MacArthur conceived a brilliant plan in which American land, sea, and air forces fought in a coordinated effort. With a series of amphibious landings, they hopped from island to island. Some Japanese island fortresses like Tarawa were taken; others like Truk were bypassed and cut off from Japanese home bases. With the conquest of Saipan in November 1944 and Iwo Jima in March 1945, the United States Air Force acquired bases from which B-29 bombers could strike at the Japanese home islands. In the summer of 1945, in the greatest air offensive in history, American planes destroyed what remained of the Japanese navy, crippled Japanese industry, and mercilessly firebombed major population centers. The attack ended with the dropping of atomic bombs on the cities of Hiroshima and Nagasaki. (See "The Atomic Wasteland," pp. 910–911.) The Japanese government accepted American terms for peace and surrendered unconditionally on 2 September 1945 on the battleship *Missouri* in Tokyo Bay. Four months after the defeat of Germany the war in Asia was over.

The Fate of Allied Cooperation: 1945

The costs of World War II in terms of death and destruction were the highest in history. Fifty million lives were lost. Most of the dead were Europeans, and

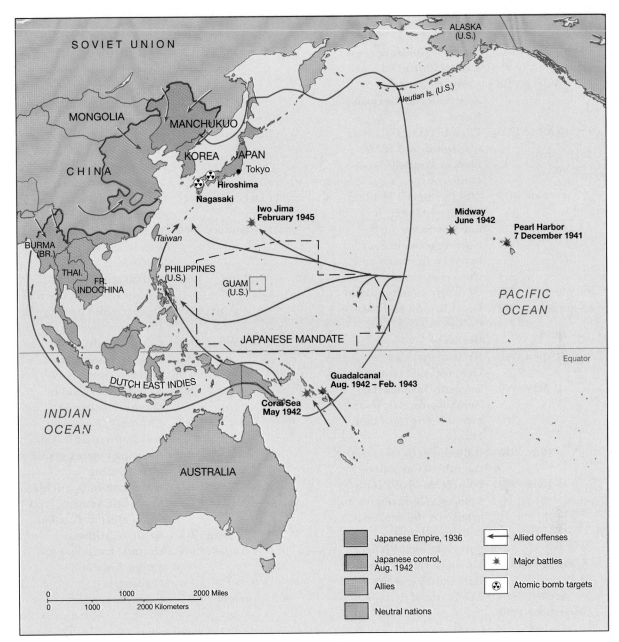

World War II in the Pacific, 1941–45

most of the Europeans were Russians and Poles. The high incidence of civilian deaths distinguished the Second World War from previous wars—well over 50 percent of the dead were noncombatants. Deliberate military targeting of cities explains this phenomenon only in part. The majority of civilian deaths were the result of starvation, enslavement, massacre, and deliberate extermination.

The psychological devastation of continual violence, deprivation, injury, and rape of survivors cannot be measured. Terrorizing citizens became an established means of warfare in the modern age. Another phenomenon not matched in the First World War emerged in 1945: mass rape. The Soviet officer corps encouraged the advancing Russian army to use sexual violence against German women and girls. The Rus-

WORLD WAR II

1937	Japan begins undeclared war on China	22 June 1941	Germany invades the Soviet Union
March 1938	Germany annexes Austria to the German Reich	1941	First extermination camp created in Chelmno, Poland
29 September 1938	Chamberlain, Daladier, Mussolini, and Hitler meet at Munich conference	7 December 1941	Japan attacks Pearl Harbor; the following day, the United States declares war on Japan
May 1939	"Pact of Steel": Military alliance between Italy and Germany	11 December 1941	Germany declares war on the United States
1939	Non-Aggression Pact between Germany and the Soviet Union	January 1942	Wannsee Conference, where the Final Solution is planned
1 September 1939	Germany attacks Poland	September 1942	Italian government withdraws from the war
3 September 1939	Great Britain and France declare war on Germany	April 1943	Unsuccessful uprising in the Warsaw ghetto
April 1940	Germany attacks Denmark and Norway	November 1943	Churchill, Roosevelt, and Stalin meet at Teheran conference
May 1940	Germany invades the Netherlands, Belgium, Luxembourg, and then France	6 June 1944	Allied forces land in northern France–D-Day
June 1940	Italy enters the war on the side of Germany	February 1945	Churchill, Roosevelt, and Stalin meet at Yalta
17 June 1940	French Marshal Pétain petitions Germany for an armistice and creates a collaborationist government at Vichy	March 1945	American forces march into Germany
		30 April 1945	Hitler commits suicide
		July and August 1945	Churchill, Truman, and Stalin meet at Potsdam
September 1940	Japan, Germany, and Italy sign Tripartite Pact	June 1945	Battle of Midway
September–November 1940	The Battle of Britain	6 August 1945	United States drops atomic bomb on Hiroshima
		2 September 1945	Japan surrenders

sians, brutally treated by Hitler's army, returned the savagery in their advance through eastern and central Europe. Collective rape became a means of direct retaliation. Victorious Japanese soldiers raped Chinese women as part of the spoils of war. Regardless of what country was involved, victorious armies practiced rape against civilian populations as one of the unspoken aspects of conquest.

Material destruction was great. Axis and Allied cities, centers of civilization and culture, were turned into wastelands by aerial bombing. The Germans bombed Rotterdam and Coventry. The British engineered the firebombing of Dresden. Warsaw and Stalingrad were destroyed by the German army. Hiroshima and Nagasaki were leveled by the United States. The nations of Europe were weakened after World War I;

"GLITTERING FRAGMENTS"

Hara Tamiki (1905–51) was a Japanese poet who was living in Hiroshima when the atomic bomb exploded there on 6 August 1945. His poem "Glittering Fragments" tells about what he saw. A victim of the bomb's radioactivity, he committed suicide in 1951.

> Glittering fragments
> Ashen embers
> Like a rippling panorama,
> Burning red then dulled.
> Strange rhythm of human corpses.
> All existence, all that could exist
> Laid bare in a flash. The rest of the world
> The swelling of a horse's corpse
> At the side of an upturned train,
> The smell of smouldering electric wires.

after World War II, they were crippled. Europe was completely displaced from the position of world dominance it had held for centuries. The United States alone was undamaged and stronger after the war than before, its industrial capacity and production greatly improved by the war.

What would be the future of Europe? The leaders of the United States, Great Britain, and the Soviet Union—the Big Three as they were called—met three times between 1943 and 1945: first at Teheran; then in February 1945 at Yalta, a Russian Black Sea resort; and finally in July and August 1945 at Potsdam, a suburb of Berlin. They coordinated their attacks on Germany and Japan and discussed their plans for postwar Europe. After Allied victory, the governments of both Germany and Japan would be totally abolished and completely reconstructed. No deals would be made with Hitler or his successors; no peace would be negotiated with the enemy; surrender would be unconditional. Germany would be disarmed and denazified, and its leaders would be tried as war criminals. The armies of the Big Three occupied Germany, each with a separate zone, but the country would be governed as a single economic unit. The Soviet Union, it was agreed, could collect reparations from Germany. With Germany and Japan defeated, a United Nations organiza-

tion would provide the structure for a lasting peace in the world.

Stalin expected that the Soviet Union would decide the future of the territories of eastern Europe that the Soviet army had liberated from Germany. This area was vital to the security of the war-devastated Soviet Union; Stalin saw it as a protective barrier against another attack from the west. Romania, Bulgaria, Hungary, Czechoslovakia, and Poland, the Big Three decided, would have pro-Soviet governments. Since Soviet troops occupied these countries in 1945, there was little that the Anglo-Americans could do to prevent Russian control unless they wanted to go to war against the USSR. Churchill realistically accepted this. But for Americans who took seriously the proclamations of President Roosevelt that their country had fought to restore freedom and self-determination to peoples oppressed by tyranny, Soviet power in eastern Europe proved to be a bitter disappointment.

• • •

The presence of Soviet armies in eastern Europe guaranteed that communism would prevail there after 1945. In western Europe, the American and British presence fostered the existence of parliamentary

Churchill, Roosevelt, and Stalin—the Big Three—at the Yalta Conference. Stalin invoked the Yalta agreements to justify the Soviet Union's control over eastern Europe after the war.

democracies. Germany was divided. A similar pattern emerged in Asia. The United States forces of occupation in Japan oversaw the introduction of democratic institutions. The USSR controlled Manchuria. Korea was divided. The celebration of victory after a war in which 50 million people died did not last long. Nor did the Anglo-American cooperation with the Soviet Union endure. With the defeat of Germany and Japan, the United States and the Soviet Union were the undisputed giants in world politics. Two ideological systems stood facing each other suspiciously across a divided Europe and a divided Asia.

Suggestions for Further Reading

The Coming of World War II

* Paul Kennedy, *The Realities Behind Diplomacy: Background Influences on British External Policy, 1865–1980*

(London: Allen & Unwin, 1981). Essays dealing with the continuity of appeasement in British foreign policy across two centuries.

* Ian Kershaw, *The Nazi Dictatorship* (London: Edward Arnold, 1985). A fine synthesis of key problems of interpretation regarding the Third Reich. Special attention is paid to the interdependence of domestic and foreign policy and the inevitability of war in Hitler's ideology.

* Donald Cameron Watt, *How War Came: The Immediate Origins of the Second World War* (London: Heinemann, 1989). An international historian chronicles the events leading to the outbreak of the war.

Racism and Destruction

* Renate Bridenthal, Atina Grossmann, and Marion Kaplan, eds., *When Biology Became Destiny: Women in Weimar and Nazi Germany* (New York: Monthly Review Press, 1984). A volume of essays pursuing common themes on the relation between sexism and racism in interwar and wartime Germany.

* Raul Hilberg *The Destruction of the European Jews*. 3 vols. (New York: Holmes and Meier, 1985). An exhaustive study of the annihilation of European Jews beginning with cultural precedents and antecedents. Examines step-by-step developments that led to extermination policies and contains valuable appendixes on statistics and a discussion of sources.

* Charles S. Maier, *The Unmasterable Past: History, Holocaust, and German National Identity* (Cambridge, MA: Harvard University Press, 1988). A thoughtful discussion of the historical debate over the Holocaust and the comparative dimensions of the event. Especially valuable in placing the Holocaust within German history.

* Michael R. Marrus, *The Holocaust in History* (New York: New American Library, 1987). A comprehensive survey of all aspects of the Holocaust, including the policies of the Third Reich, the living conditions in the camps, and the prospects for resistance and opposition.

Allied Victory

John Campbell, ed., *The Experience of World War II* (New York: Oxford University Press, 1989). This richly illustrated work provides an overview of the Second World War in both the Asian and European theaters, in terms of origins, events, and consequences.

* Akira Iriye, *The Origins of the Second World War in Asia and the Pacific* (London: Longman, 1987). Examines the events of the 1930s leading up to hostilities in the Pacific theaters with a special focus on Japanese isolation and aggression.

* John Keegan, *The Second World War* (New York: Viking, 1990). Provides a panoramic sweep of "the largest single event in human history," with special attention to warfare in all its forms and the importance of leadership.

*Paperback edition available.

29 ✤ Postwar Recovery and Crisis: From the Cold War to the New Europe, 1945–1968

Sex, Drugs, and Rock 'n' Roll

I Wanna Hold Your Hand" seems an unlikely anthem for a generation. Yet this song, performed by the British rock group the Beatles, was known around the world in the early 1960s by an entire generation of the young. Youths screamed and swooned and danced to it. Parents and educators screamed, too, but out of fear that

"Beatlemania" signaled the ruination of the younger generation in Western society. Adults worried that young people were being caught up in hedonism, sexual pleasure, and mind-numbing drugs, all because of this loud, cacophonous music.

Young people of the fifties and sixties saw the advent of rock 'n'

roll differently. Rock 'n' roll emerged as a national phenomenon in the United States in the mid-1950s. It was firmly rooted in the black music of rhythm and blues. White country and western music was also influential in shaping the new sound. Titles like "Rock Around the Clock," "Shake, Rattle, and Roll," "Keep

A-Knockin'," and "Blue Suede Shoes" captured the attention of a generation. The experiences of teenagers were at the center of the new rhythms, confronted in the lyrics and amplified with electric guitars. Rock 'n' roll appealed to the young because it dealt openly with the issues of sex and young love and was aimed at the hypocrisy of the adult white world. Even the sound was revolutionary. It became "the music of the young," something that accentuated their differences from the adult world and their commonalities with one another.

Babies born after World War II, who began entering adolescence at the end of the 1950s, constituted a new audience for mass entertainment. They were also an important international mass market for music: popular recordings began selling in the millions for the first time in history. Music was now an important consumer product. Elvis Presley, a country blues singer from Memphis, Tennessee, emerged as the greatest figure on the rock 'n' roll scene in the late 1950s. His overt androgynous sexuality, gyrating hips, and explicit lyrics made him an object of adult fears about losing control of their children. He quickly developed a worldwide following of devoted fans, who hailed him as "the King" and who continue to honor his memory years after his death.

In the 1960s, British groups such as the Beatles from Liverpool entered the international rock scene. Dubbed "the Mop-Tops" because of their long hair, they were condemned for transgressing sex roles in their appearance. Mil-

lions of boys copied their idols as hair became a political issue, a symbol of rebellion. Billboards appeared across the United States that proclaimed: "Beautify America—Get a Haircut!" With the new music came a new style of dressing, what adults saw as a uniform of disrespect for traditional values and parental authority. The British group the Rolling Stones were considered more outrageously sexual, vulgar, and lewd than their countrymen the Beatles. Antirock movements cited "specialists" who warned that the new amplified music caused deafness, drug addiction, and excessive sexual activity.

The gap between the generations yawned into a gulf as rock music became political in the mid-1960s. Bob Dylan, an American rock performer, introduced folk music to the genre with songs of social protest like "Blowin' in the Wind" and "Only a Pawn in Their Game." Rock music was denounced as a communist plot, with performers urging their audiences to "Make Love, Not War." Dylan's "Subterranean Homesick Blues" targeted the hypocrisy of his society:

Ah get born, keep warm
Short pants, romance, learn to dance
Get dressed, get blessed
Try to be a success
Please her, please him, buy gifts
Don't steal, don't lift
Twenty years of schoolin'
And they put you on the day shift
Look out kid
They keep it all hid . . .

Although rock music served as a rallying cry for a generation who opposed war and exploitation, its frankness about sexuality did not

result in a reformulation of gender roles. Woman's place in rock music was usually as an object of desire. Few of the major rock stars were women. The American singer Janis Joplin was a striking exception. What was known in the rock world as "girl groups"—the Ronettes and the Shangri-Las are two examples—reinforced predominantly male views of sexuality, both by their dress and by the lyrics of their songs. The female body was treated as a commodity itself in the fashions associated with the new youth culture, such as the miniskirt and the bikini. Girls and young women were important consumers of the new music and the values it communicated.

Rock music quickly became an international phenomenon, spreading from the United States and Great Britain to appeal to the young throughout the world. Rock stars were the new self-made millionaires, often from working-class backgrounds, who were able to benefit from advertising and mass-marketing techniques in a new age of consumption. The postwar generation that grew into adulthood in the late 1960s shared a common musical culture. Student protest movements spread throughout Europe and the United States, and in the same period rock music gained acceptance as a legitimate and important musical genre. Through radio, television, and the international distribution of recordings, an international youth culture linked European and American youth together with common symbols and a common language of protest.

Regulating the Cold War

With the cessation of the "hot" war that had ripped Europe apart from 1939 to 1945, the armies of the United States and the Soviet Union met on the banks of the Elbe River in 1945. Greeting each other as victors and allies, the occupying armies waited for direction on how to conduct the peace. Europe and Japan had been destroyed, leaving the United States and the Soviet Union as indisputably the two richest and strongest nations in the world. The Soviets understood that they ran a sorry second to American military superiority—the United States was alone in possessing the atomic bomb—and to American wealth, which, measured in GNP, was 400 percent greater than that of the Soviet Union. War had made these two superpowers allies; now the peace promised to make them once again into wary foes. In the three years that followed the war, a new kind of conflict emerged between the two superpower victors, a war deemed "cold" because of its lack of military violence, but a bitter war nonetheless.

The Cold War emerged as ideological opposition between communism and capitalist democracies, dominated by the two superpowers, the Soviet Union and the United States. It affected the entire world. Drawing on three decades of distrust between the East and the West, the Cold War was related to the economic and foreign policy goals of both superpowers.

Cold War conflict initially developed because of differing Russian and American notions regarding the economic reconstruction of Europe. The Soviet Union realized that American aid to Europe was not primarily a humanitarian program; it was part of an economic offensive in Europe that would contribute to the dominance of American capital in world markets. The United States recognized that the Soviet Union hoped to achieve its own recovery through outright control of Eastern Europe. Needing the stability of peace, the Soviets saw in Eastern Europe, hostile as the area may have been to forced integration, a necessary buffer against Western competition. The Soviet Union feared U.S. intentions to establish liberal governments and capitalist markets in these states bordering its own frontiers and viewed such attempts as inimical to Soviet interests. For these reasons, Stalin refused to allow free elections in Poland and, by force of occupying armies, annexed neighboring territories that included eastern Finland, the Baltic States, East Prussia, eastern Poland, Ruthenia, and Bessarabia. With the exception of East Prussia, these annexations were all limited to territories that had once been part of tsarist Russia.

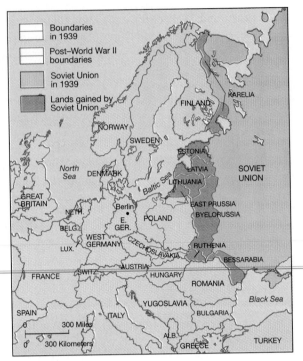

Territorial Gains of the USSR

Winston Churchill captured the drama of the new international order in a speech he delivered in Missouri in 1946: "From Stettin in the Baltic to Trieste in the Adriatic an iron curtain has descended across the Continent." The term *iron curtain* described graphically for many the new fate of Europe, rigidly divided between East and West, a pawn in the struggle of the superpowers.

Atomic Politics

The nuclear arms race began in earnest during World War II, well before the first atomic bomb was dropped in August 1945. The Germans, the Russians, and the British all had teams exploring the destructive possibilities of nuclear fission during the war, but the Americans had the edge in the development of the bomb. Stalin understood the political significance of the weapon and committed the Soviet Union to a breakneck program of development following the war. The result was that the USSR ended the American monopoly and tested its first atomic bomb in 1949. Both countries developed the hydrogen bomb almost simultaneously in 1953. Space exploration by satellite was also deemed important in terms of the detection and deployment of bombs, and the Soviets pulled ahead in this area with the launching of the first satellite, *Sput-*

THE IRON CURTAIN

Winston Churchill (1874–1965), prime minister of England during World War II, captured the drama of the postwar international order in a speech he delivered in Missouri in 1946. Churchill had long been suspicious of the political motives of the Soviet Union, though he welcomed Stalin as an ally in defeating Hitler. The term that he coined, iron curtain, described graphically the fate of Europe that many feared, a Europe rigidly divided between East and West, no more than a pawn in the struggle of the superpowers.

From Stettin in the Baltic to Trieste in the Adriatic, an iron curtain has descended across the Continent. Behind that line lie all the capitals of the ancient states of Central and Eastern Europe. Warsaw, Berlin, Prague, Vienna, Budapest, Belgrade, Bucharest and Sofia, all these famous cities and the populations around them lie in what I must call the Soviet sphere, and all are subject in one form or another, not only to Soviet influence but to a very high and, in many cases, increasing measure of control from Moscow. Athens alone—Greece with its immortal glories—is free to decide its future at an election under British, American and French observation. The Russian-dominated Polish Government has been encouraged to make enormous and wrongful inroads upon Germany, and mass expulsions of millions of Germans on a scale grievous and undreamed-of are now taking place. The Communist parties, which were very small in all these Eastern States of Europe, have been raised to preeminence and power far beyond their numbers and are seeking everywhere to obtain totalitarian control. Police governments are prevailing in nearly every case, and so far, except in Czechoslovakia, there is no true democracy.

The safety of the world requires a new unity in Europe, from which no nation should be permanently outcast. It is from the quarrels of the strong parent races in Europe that the world wars we have witnessed, or which occurred in former times, have sprung. Twice in our own lifetime we have seen the United States, against their wishes and their traditions, against arguments, the force of which it is impossible not to comprehend, drawn by irresistible forces, into these wars in time to secure the victory of

the good cause, but only after frightful slaughter and devastation had occurred. Twice the United States has had to send several millions of its young men across the Atlantic to find the war; but now war can find any nation, wherever it may dwell between dusk and dawn. Surely we should work with conscious purpose for a grand pacification of Europe, within the structure of the United Nations and in accordance with its Charter. That I feel is an open cause of policy of very great importance.

In front of the iron curtain which lies across Europe are other causes for anxiety. In Italy the Communist Party is seriously hampered by having to support the Communist-trained Marshal Tito's claims to former Italian territory at the head of the Adriatic. Nevertheless the future of Italy hangs in the balance. Again one cannot imagine a regenerated Europe without a strong France. All my public life I have worked for a strong France and I never lost faith in her destiny, even in the darkest hours. I will not lose faith now. However, in a great number of countries, far from the Russian frontiers and throughout the world, Communist fifth columns are established and work in complete unity and absolute obedience to the directions they receive from the Communist centre. Except in the British Commonwealth and in the United States where Communism is in its infancy, the Communist parties or fifth columns constitute a growing challenge and peril to Christian civilization. These are somber facts for anyone to have to recite on the morrow of a victory gained by so much splendid comradeship in arms and in the cause of freedom and democracy; but we should be most unwise not to face them squarely while time remains.

---

nik I, in 1957. Intercontinental ballistic missiles (ICBMs) followed, further accelerating the pace of nuclear armament.

The atomic bomb and thermonuclear weapons contributed greatly to the shape of Cold War politics. The incineration of Hiroshima and Nagasaki sent a clear message to the world about the power of total annihila-

tion available to those who controlled the bombs. The threat of such total destruction made full and direct confrontation with an equally armed enemy impossible. Both the United States and the Soviet Union, the first two members of the "nuclear club," knew that they had the capability of obliterating their enemy, but not before the enemy could respond in retaliation.

Sputnik I *on its support stand before launching. The news of the Soviet breakthrough galvanized the Western nations. The United States redoubled its efforts to enter the space age and reorganized school curricula to stress math and science.*

They also knew that the technology necessary for nuclear arms was available to any industrial power. By 1974 the "nuclear club" included Great Britain, France, the People's Republic of China, and India. These countries joined the United States and the Soviet Union in spending the billions of dollars necessary every year to expand nuclear arsenals and to develop more sophisticated weaponry and delivery systems.

A new vocabulary transformed popular attitudes and values. "Missile gaps," "deterrence," "first strike," "second strike," "radioactive fallout," and "containment" were all terms that heightened popular fears. Citizens in the Soviet Union learned of American weapons stockpiling and American deployment of military forces throughout the world. Americans learned that the Russians had the ability to deliver bombs that could wipe out major U.S. cities. Paranoia on both sides was encouraged by heads of state in their public addresses throughout the fifties. Traitors were publicly tried while espionage was being sponsored by the state.

The first nuclear test-ban treaty, signed in 1963, banned tests in the atmosphere. Arms limitation and nonproliferation were the subjects of a series of conferences between the United States and the Soviet Union in the late 1960s and pointed the way to limitations eventually agreed on in the next decade. The United Nations, created by the Allies immediately following World War II to take the place of the defunct League of Nations, established international agencies for the purpose of harnessing nuclear power for peaceful uses. On the whole, however, the arms race persisted as a continuing threat in Cold War politics. The race required the dedication of huge national resources to maintain a competitive stance. Conventional forces, too, were expanded to protect Eastern and Western bloc interests. With the aim of containing the USSR, the United States entered into a series of military alliances around the world. In order to provide mutual assistance should any member be attacked, the United States joined with Belgium, Britain, Canada, Denmark, France, Iceland, Italy, the Netherlands, Norway, and Portugal in 1949 to form the North Atlantic Treaty Organization (NATO). Greece and Turkey became members in 1952, West Germany in 1955, and Spain in 1982. The potential military threat of the Soviet Union in Western Europe prompted this peacetime military alliance. The Southeast Asia Treaty Organization (SEATO) in 1954 and the Baghdad Pact of 1955 (known as CENTO after 1959) followed. The United States strengthened its military presence throughout the period by acquiring 1400 military bases in foreign countries for its own forces. The Soviet Union countered developments in the West with its own alliances and organizations. In 1949 the USSR established the Council for Mutual Economic Assistance, or Comecon, with bilateral agreements between the Soviet Union and Eastern European states. Comecon was Stalin's response to the U.S. Marshall Plan in Western Europe. Rather than providing aid, however, Comecon benefited the Soviet Union at the expense of its partners, seeking to integrate and control the economies of Eastern Europe for Soviet gain. In 1955, Albania, Bulgaria, Romania, Czechoslovakia, Hungary, Poland, and East Germany—all Comecon members—joined with the Soviet Union to form a defensive alliance organization known as the Warsaw Pact. The USSR intended its Eastern European allies to serve as a strategic buffer zone against the NATO forces.

Atomic politics encouraged brinksmanship, a term coined by John Foster Dulles (1888–1959), U.S. secretary of state from 1953 to 1959. *Brinksmanship*

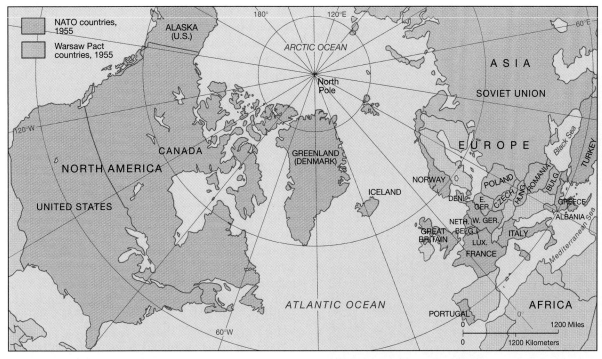

The Cold War: U.S. and Soviet Alliances

referred to a confrontationist foreign policy that brought the superpowers repeatedly to the edge of armed conflict. It also encouraged a new kind of global politics in which the superpowers vied with each other to find new partners, especially in formerly colonized areas, to join their camps.

Decolonization

By the end of the Second World War, European colonial empires had been weakened or destroyed by the ravages of battle, occupation, and neglect. The United States, committed to free and open markets, pushed its advantage at the conclusion of the peace by insisting on the dismantling of its allies' empires as well as those of its enemies. The Soviets, preoccupied with their own recovery, were in no position to assert a global policy at the end of the war.

Nationalist movements had been growing in power in the 1930s, and many nationalist leaders saw the war as a catalyst for independence, especially in Asia. Great Britain knew that it no longer commanded the resources to control India, historically its richest colony, which under the leadership of Mohandas Gandhi (1869–1948) had been agitating for independence since 1920. Given the title of "Mahatma," or "great-souled," by his people, Gandhi advocated passive resistance to achieve independence. He sought by means of civil disobedience, boycotts, and public fasts instead of violence to bring pressure on the colonizers. The British granted self-government to India in 1946 with the proviso that if the bitter conflict between Hindus and Muslims was not settled by mutual agreement, Great Britain would decide on the division of power. As a result, Muslim and Hindu representatives agreed to the division of British India into the independent states of India and Pakistan in 1947. Ceylon (now Sri Lanka) and Burma (now Myanmar) achieved full independence in 1948.

In its march through Asia during the war, Japan had smashed colonial empires. Japan's defeat created a power vacuum that nationalist leaders were eager to fill. Civil wars erupted in China, Burma, Korea, and Indochina. Anticolonial resistance opened the way to Communist insurgence. Indochina declared its independence in 1945 and waged war with France until 1954. South Vietnam was declared a republic, and the United States sponsored a regime that was considered favorable to Western interests. The North Vietnamese state was established under the French-educated leader Ho Chi Minh. The civil war continued, with the North Vietnamese backing the National Liberation Front in

Jubilant Algerians celebrate the granting of independence to their country on 3 July 1962, after a bloody seven-year war. Many Europeans whose families had been settled in Algeria for generations fled during the fighting or left after independence was won.

"the winds of change" in 1960, the year that proved to be a turning point in African politics. Britain and Belgium yielded their colonies. In 1960 Patrice Lumumba (1925–61) became the first prime minister of the Republic of the Congo (present-day Zaire). White European rule continued in Rhodesia (now Zimbabwe) and South Africa, despite continued world pressure.

The French, having faced what its officer corps considered a humiliating defeat in Indochina, held on against the winds of change in North Africa. France's problems in Algeria began in earnest in 1954 when Muslims seeking independence and self-rule revolted. Although the Algerian rebels successfully employed terrorist and guerrilla tactics, European settlers and the French army in Algeria refused to accept defeat. The Fourth Republic was on the verge of collapse when General Charles de Gaulle, leader of the Free French resistance in World War II, stepped in to establish the Fifth Republic with a strong executive branch. He ended the war and agreed to Algeria's independence, which was achieved in 1962.

One supporter of the Algerian revolution, Frantz Fanon (1925–61), was working as a French-trained psychiatrist in Algeria when the revolution began. In his writings, especially his book *The Wretched of the Earth* (1961), he argued in favor of national liberation movements and for the necessity of violence. Fanon described the trap of dependence of colonized countries: "We go on sending out raw materials; we go on being Europe's small farmers; we specialize in unfinished products."

Decolonization meant continued dependence for many third world countries, as they were now known. First world nations were identified as the advanced industrial countries; second world countries were those whose lower level of prosperity indicated a transition from agricultural to industrial production. Third world nations were suppliers of raw materials and food to the countries of the first world. These countries were no longer directly controlled as colonies but continued to be dominated by the Western capitalist powers and Japan, on whom they relied for their markets and trade. As Frantz Fanon had described it, these newly independent countries had to continue doing what they had done as colonies: supplying raw materials to their former masters.

African leader Kwame Nkrumah (1909–72) of Ghana denounced this situation of dependence as "neocolonialism" and called for a united Africa as the only means of resistance. Nkrumah argued that "aid" was merely a "revolving credit" plan that returned

the South. After almost two decades of escalating involvement, in 1973 American troops were finally withdrawn from a war they could not win. Cold War politics had enmeshed the United States in Southeast Asia and Cold War imperatives had kept it there.

The first wave of decolonization after 1945 had been in Asia. A second wave crested and crashed in the late 1950s and early 1960s in Africa, another ready battleground for Cold War dominance. During the Second World War, North Africa had served as a theater of military action, while South Africa was a source of supplies and troops. Wartime experiences and rapid economic development fed existing nationalist aspirations and encouraged the emergence of mass political demands for liberation. A new generation of leaders, many of them educated in European institutions, moved from cooperation with home rule to demands for independence by the early 1960s. British prime minister Harold MacMillan (1894–1986) spoke of

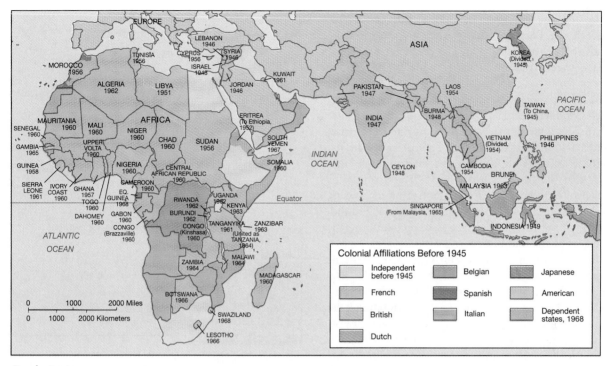

Decolonization

increased profits to the former colonial masters while extracting wealth from African nations. He led Ghana in a policy of nonalignment in the Cold War. With Jomo Kenyatta (1894–1978) of Kenya, he founded the Pan-African federation, which promoted African nationalism.

Soviet leader Joseph Stalin limited the Soviet Union's foreign involvement following the Second World War to communist regimes that shared borders with the USSR in Eastern Europe and Asia. After Stalin's death in 1953, the Soviet Union turned to the third world. Former colonies played an important new role in the Cold War strategies with the accession to power of Nikita Khrushchev (1894–1971) in the mid-1950s. The Soviet Union abandoned its previous caution and assumed a global role in offering "friendship treaties," military advice, trade credits, and general support for attempts at national liberation in Asia, Africa, and Latin America. Cold warriors took advantage of tribalism and regionalism, which mitigated against the establishment of strong central governments. Military rule and fragmentation often resulted. Instability and acute poverty continued to characterize former colonies after emancipation, regardless of which camp the new leaders joined.

The Two Germanys and the World in Two Blocs

In central Europe, Cold War tensions first surfaced over the question of how to treat Germany. The United States and the Soviet Union had very different ideas about the future of their former enemy. In fostering economic reconstruction in Europe, the United States counted on a German economy transfused with American funds that would be self-supporting and stable. To the contrary, the Soviet Union, blaming Germany for its extreme destruction, was explicit in its demands: German resources must be siphoned off for Soviet reconstruction. Stricken as the Soviets were with 20 million dead, millions of homeless refugees in dire poverty, and 1700 cities in ruins, commandeering German labor and stripping Germany of its industrial plant seemed to them only fair.

With Germany's defeat, its territory had been divided into four zones, occupied by American, Soviet, British, and French troops. An Allied Control Commission consisting of representatives of the four powers was to govern Germany as a whole in keeping with the decisions made at Yalta before the end of the war. As Soviet and American antagonisms over Germany's future deepened, however, Allied rule polarized between the East and the West, with the internal politics of each area determined by the ideological conflicts between communism and capitalist free enterprise.

Allied attempts to administer Germany as a whole faltered and failed in 1948 over a question of economic policy. The zones of the Western occupying forces (the United States, Great Britain, and France), now administered as a single unit, issued a uniform and stable currency that the Russians accurately saw as a threat to their own economic policies in Germany. The Soviets blockaded the city of Berlin, which, though behind the frontier of the Russian sector, was being administered in sectors by the four powers and whose western sector promised to become a successful enclave of Western capitalism. With the support of the people of West Berlin, the Allies responded by airlifting food and supplies into West Berlin for almost a year, defending it as an outpost that must be preserved from the advance of communism. The Russians were forced to withdraw the blockade in the spring of 1949. The Berlin blockade hardened the commitment on both sides to two Germanys.

The two new states came into existence in 1949, their founding separated by less than a month. The Federal Republic of Germany, within the American orbit, was established as a democratic parliamentary regime. Free elections brought the Christian Democrat Konrad Adenauer to power as chancellor. The German Democratic Republic was ruled as a single-party state under Walter Ulbricht, who took his direction from the Soviet Union.

The division of Germany became a microcosm of the division of the world into two armed camps. With the support of local Communist parties, Soviet-dominated governments were established in Poland, Hungary, Bulgaria, and Romania in 1947. The following year Czechoslovakia was pulled into the Soviet orbit. Czechoslovakia serves as a significant marker in the development of Cold War confrontation. The tactics of the Communists in Czechoslovakia taught the West that coalition governments were unacceptable and undoubtedly hardened the resolve of U.S. policymakers in support of two Germanys.

In 1953 the man who had ruled the Soviet Union in his own image for almost three decades died. The death of Joseph Stalin unleashed a struggle for power among the Communist party leadership. It also initiated almost immediately a process of de-Stalinization and the beginnings of a thaw in censorship and repres-

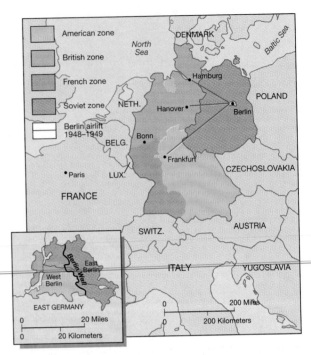

The Division of Germany

sion. A growing urban and professional class expected improvements in the quality of life and greater freedoms after years of war and hardship. In 1956, at the Twentieth Party Congress, Nikita Khrushchev, as head of the Communist party, denounced Stalin as incompetent and cruel. After five years of jockeying for power among Stalin's former lieutenants, Khrushchev emerged victorious and assumed the office of premier in 1958.

De-Stalinization also took place in Eastern Europe. Discontent over collectivization, low wages, and the lack of consumer goods fueled a latent nationalism among Eastern European populations resentful of Soviet control and influence. Violence erupted in 1953 in East Berlin as workers revolted over conditions in the workplace, but it was quickly and effectively suppressed. Demands for reforms and liberalization in Poland also produced riots and changes in Communist party leadership. Wladislaw Gomulka (1905–82), a Communist with a nationalist point of view who had survived Stalin's purges, aimed to take advantage of the power vacuum created by the departure of Stalinist leaders. Gomulka refused to back down in the face of severe Soviet pressure and the threat of a Soviet invasion to keep him from power. Elected as the first secretary of the Communist party in Poland, Gomulka sought to steer his nation on a more liberal course.

Hungarians followed suit with their demands for the withdrawal of Hungary from the Warsaw Pact. On 23 October 1956, inspired by the events in Poland, Hungarians rose up in anger against their old-guard Stalinist rulers. Imre Nagy (1896–1958), a liberal Communist, took control of the government, attempted to introduce democratic reforms, and relaxed economic controls. The Soviets, however, were unwilling to lose control of their sphere of influence in Eastern Bloc nations and to jeopardize their system of defense in the Warsaw Pact. Moscow responded to liberal experimentation in Hungary by sending tanks and troops into Budapest. Brutal repression and purges followed. The Hungarian experience in 1956 made clear that too much change too quickly would not be tolerated by the Soviet rulers. The thaw following Stalin's death had promoted expectations among Eastern Europeans that a new era was dawning. The violent crushing of the Hungarian revolution reminded everyone of the realities of Soviet control and the Soviet Union's defense priorities in Eastern Europe.

East Berlin in the late 1950s and early 1960s posed a particular problem for Communist rule. Unable to compete successfully in wages and standard of living with the capitalist western sector of the city, East Berlin saw increasing numbers of its population, especially the educated and professional classes, crossing the line to a more prosperous life. In 1961 the Soviet Union responded to this problem by building a wall that cordoned off the part of the city that it controlled. The Berlin Wall eventually stretched for 103 miles, with heavily policed crossing points, turrets, and troops and tanks facing each other across the divide that came to symbolize the Cold War.

The process of liberalization that had begun after Stalin's death and continued under Khrushchev certainly experienced its setbacks and reversals in the case of Budapest and Berlin. But in 1968 the policy of de-Stalinization reached a critical juncture in Czechoslovakia. Early in 1968, Alexander Dubcek, Czech party secretary and a member of the educated younger generation of technocrats, had supported liberal reforms in Czechoslovakia that included decentralization of planning and economic decision-making, market pricing, and market incentives for higher productivity and innovation. He acted on popular desire for nationalism, the end of censorship, and better working conditions. Above all, he called for democratic reforms in the political process that would restore rule to the people. Dubcek spoke of "socialism with a human face,"

The Berlin Wall, symbol of the Cold War era, skirted the historic Brandenburg Gate on the dividing line between East and West in the heart of Berlin.

although, unlike the Hungarians in 1956, he made no move to withdraw his country from the Warsaw Pact or to defy Soviet leadership. Moscow nevertheless feared the erosion of obedience within the Eastern Bloc and the collapse of one-party rule in the Czech state and sent in thousands of tanks and hundreds of thousands of Warsaw Pact troops to Prague and other Czech cities to reestablish control. The Czechs responded with passive resistance in what became known as the Prague Spring uprising. The Soviet invasion made clear that popular nationalism was intolerable in an Eastern Bloc nation.

Alone among Eastern European leaders, Marshal Tito of Yugoslavia resisted Soviet encroachment. As a partisan leader of the Communist resistance during World War II, Tito had heroically battled the Germans. Ruling Yugoslavia as a dictator after 1945, he refused to accede to Soviet directives to collectivize agriculture and to participate in joint economic ventures. For its defiance of Soviet supremacy, in 1948 Yugoslavia was expelled from the Cominform, the Soviet-controlled information agency that replaced the Comintern after 1943.

No part of the globe escaped the tensions generated by the Cold War. Asia was the next arena for the development of Cold War antagonisms. In 1950 the United States and the United Nations intervened when North Korea attacked South Korea. Korea, formerly controlled by Japan, had been divided following the war as a result of the presence of Russian and American troops. Communist-dominated North Korea refused to accept the artificial boundary between it and Western-dominated South Korea. China, a Communist state following the victory of Mao Zedong (1893–1976) in 1949, intervened in the Korean conflict when American troops advanced on Chinese frontiers in October 1950. After three years of military stalemate, Korea was partitioned on the 38th parallel in 1953. The Soviet Union was not party to the conflict in Korea, but the United States considered China to be in the Soviet camp rather than an independent contender for power.

The Middle East was another theater of confrontation between the superpowers. The United States and the Soviet Union used aid to win support of "client" states. The withdrawal, sometimes under duress, of British and French rule in the Middle East and North Africa and the creation of the state of Israel in 1948 destabilized the area and created the opportunities for new alliances. Egypt and Syria, for example, sought Soviet support against the new Israeli state, which had been formed out of the part of Palestine under British mandate from 1920 and was dependent on U.S. aid.

Oil, an essential resource for rapid industrialization, was the object of Soviet politicking in Iran after the war. Western oil companies, long active in the area, had won oil concessions in Iran in 1946, but such rights eluded the Soviets. In 1951 a nationalist Iranian government sought to evict Westerners by nationalizing the oil fields. The British blockaded Iranian trade in the Persian Gulf, and the newly formed American espionage organization, the Central Intelligence Agency (CIA), subverted the nationalist government and placed in power the shah of Iran, a leader favorable to American interests.

A crisis came in 1956 in Egypt. Egyptian president Gamal Abdel Nasser (1918–70), a nationalist in power by virtue of a military coup d'état in 1952, oversaw the nationalization of the Suez Canal. British and French military forces attacked and were forced to withdraw by pressure from both the Soviet Union and the United States, which cooperated in seeking to avert a disaster. The Middle East, however, remained a Cold War powder keg, with Israeli and Arab nationalist interests and Soviet and American aid running on a collision course. The expansion of the Israeli state at the expense of its Arab neighbors further exacerbated tensions.

The United States was heavily committed as a military presence in Southeast Asia after the French withdrawal from Indochina after the French defeat at Dien Bien Phu in 1954. Arguing the domino theory—that one Southeast Asian country after another would fall like a row of dominoes to Communist takeover—the United States also intervened in Laos and Cambodia. Between 1961 and 1973, the United States committed American troops to a full-scale war—though officially termed only a military action—against Communist guerrilla forces throughout the region.

The United States was also experiencing Cold War problems closer to home. In 1954 the CIA plotted the overthrow of Guatemala's leftist regime to keep Soviet influence out of the Western Hemisphere. In 1958 President Dwight D. Eisenhower sent his vice-president, Richard M. Nixon, on a tour of Latin American countries. Crowds everywhere jeered the American vice-president and hurled stones and eggs at his motorcade in response to U.S. policies. In 1959 a revolution in Cuba, an island nation only 90 miles off the American coast, resulted in the ejection of U.S. interests and the establishment of a Communist regime under the leadership of a young middle-class lawyer, Fidel Castro. In 1962 a direct and frightening confrontation occurred between the United States and the USSR over Soviet missile installations in Cuba. Following the Russian withdrawal from the island, both U.S. president John F. Kennedy and Soviet leader Nikita Khrushchev pursued policies of "peaceful coexistence," intent on averting nuclear confrontation. Both sides recognized how close they had come to mutual annihilation in the showdown over Cuba.

Another kind of challenge to Cold War power politics came from within the NATO alliance. General Charles de Gaulle, as president of the French Fifth Republic, rejected the straitjacket of American dominance in Western Europe and asserted his country's independent status by exploding the first French atomic bomb in 1960. Refusing to place the French military under an American general who served as Supreme Allied Commander for NATO, de Gaulle completely withdrew France from participation in NATO in 1966. He forged an independent French foreign policy, taking advantage of the loosening of bloc politics around the mid-1960s.

In May 1965, U.S. Secretary of State Dean Rusk observed, "This has become a very small planet. We have to be concerned with all of it—with all of its land, waters, atmosphere, and with surrounding space." Atomic politics in the Cold War era had helped to shrink the globe by bringing the threat of destruction closer to home. In the mid-1960s, leaders of the two great blocs of East and West began to realize that peaceful coexistence was the only reasonable strategy in the atomic age and that alternatives to the arms race must be found.

Reconstructing Europe

Europe faced peace in 1945 politically disorganized and economically crippled. Allied and Soviet occupation forces carved Germany into zones and its capital, Berlin, into sectors. In the international arena, growing antagonism marked relations between the United States and the Soviet Union, the two nations that controlled the future of Europe.

When the dust from the last bombs settled over Europe's cities, the balance sheets of destruction were tallied. Millions of survivors found themselves homeless, having lost their loved ones, often all of their personal belongings, and the roofs over their heads. Millions returned home from battlefronts and concentration camps to rubble, with wounds beyond healing. There were no jobs; there was nothing to eat. Peacetime rationing dipped below wartime levels. What was not measured in the statistics on physical and human destruction, at least immediately, was the psychological

devastation that succeeded such loss. There could be no returning to life as normal. For many the war was far gentler than the peace. For these combatants of peacetime, often women and children, digging out and surviving were the greatest battles of all.

The Problem: Europe in Ruins

An American military observer reported to his superiors in 1947: "Europe is steadily deteriorating. The political position reflects the economic. One political crisis after another merely denotes the existence of economic distress. Millions of people in the cities are slowly starving." Even the winners were losers as survivors faced a level of human and material destruction unknown in the history of warfare. Economists judged that Europe would need at least twenty-five years to regain its prewar economic capacity. The worst was also feared: that Europe would never recover as a world economic power.

A brother and sister on the way home from school walk down a deserted street in a bombed-out section of Berlin. They carry tin cans for the hot meals they receive in school.

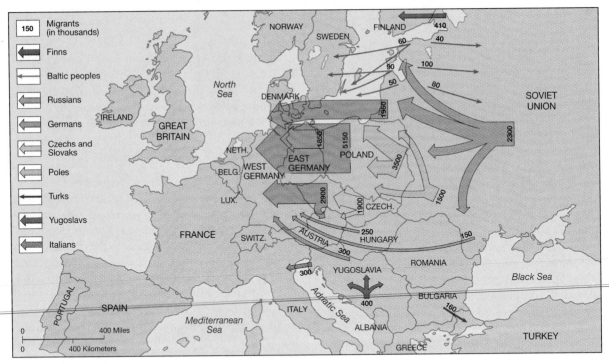

European Migrations After World War II

Large-scale population movements made matters worse. Displaced persons by the millions moved across Europe. The release of prisoners of war and slave workers imprisoned during the Third Reich strained already weak economies. Germans were expelled from territories that Germany had controlled before the war. Soviet expansionist policies forced others to flee Estonia, Latvia, and Lithuania. Jews who survived the concentration camps resettled outside Europe, primarily in Palestine and the United States.

Industrial production in 1945 was one-third of its level in 1938. Housing shortages existed everywhere. France had lost one-fifth of its housing during the war years; Germany's 50 largest cities had seen two-fifths of their buildings reduced to rubble. Frankfurt, Düsseldorf, Dresden, Warsaw, and Berlin were virtually destroyed. The transportation infrastructure was severely damaged: railways, roads, and bridges were in shambles all over Europe. Communications networks were in disarray. In some cases, industrial plants had not been as adversely affected as urban centers. Yet machinery everywhere had been worn out in wartime production and replacement parts were nonexistent. German equipment was dismantled and seized by Soviet soldiers to be used in Russia in place of what the Germans had destroyed.

Agriculture, too, suffered severe reversals in wartime economies and was unable to resume prewar production in 1945. In general, European agriculture was producing at 50 percent of its prewar capacity. Livestock had been decimated during the war years—in France, for example, 50 percent of all farm animals had been killed—and it was estimated that restoring herds would take decades. Italy suffered greatly, with one-third of its overall assets destroyed. The scarcity of goods converged with ballooning inflation. Black markets with astronomical prices for necessities flourished, while currency rates plummeted. Everywhere the outlook was bleak. Yet in less than a decade, the situation had been reversed. The solution came from outside of Europe.

The Solution: The Marshall Plan

The Soviet Union implemented an expansion of its territorial boundaries as a way of reversing some of its drastic losses in the war. Above all, it wanted a protective ring of satellite states as security from attack from the west. Stalin also was eager to see the Soviet Union surrounded by "friendly" governments in Eastern Europe to replace the hostile regimes with which the Soviets had had to contend in the period between the wars. Picking up territory from Finland, Poland, and parts of East Prussia and eastern Czechoslovakia; forcibly reincorporating the Baltic states of Estonia, Latvia, and Lithuania; and recovering Bessarabia, the Soviet Union succeeded in acquiring sizable territories.

In addition, the Soviet state dedicated itself to economic reconstruction behind a protective buffer of satellite states—Poland, East Germany, Czechoslovakia, Hungary, Romania, and Bulgaria—over which Soviet leaders exercised strong control. Yugoslavia and Albania chose to follow a more independent Communist path. Lacking the capital necessary to finance recovery, the Soviets sought compensation from Eastern and central European territories.

In contrast to the Soviet Union, the United States had incurred relatively light casualties in World War II. Because the fighting had not taken place on the North American continent, U.S. cities, farmlands, and factories were intact. As the chief producer and supplier for the Allied war effort, even before its entry into the conflict, the United States had benefited from the conflict in Europe and actually expanded its economic productivity during the war. In 1945 the United States was producing a full 50 percent of the world's gross national product—a staggering fact to a displaced Great Britain, whose former trade networks were permanently destroyed. Furthermore, the United States held two-thirds of the world's gold. A United States bursting with energy and prosperity was a real threat to the Soviet Union viewing the rubble of its destroyed cities and counting the bodies of its dead.

The United States knew that it lacked one important guarantee to secure its growth and its future prosperity: adequate international markets for its goods. After World War I, American officials and businessmen understood that America's productive capacity was outpacing its ability to export goods. In the 1920s, the United States had exported capital to Europe in the form of private loans with the hope that trade would flourish as a result. The decade following the Great Depression of 1929 witnessed the search for a policy to expand U.S. markets. Both Europe and Japan were recognized as potential buyers for American goods, but both areas parried with protectionism to foster their own postdepression recovery.

World War II facilitated the success of an international economic policy consistent with international economic goals identified by U.S. policymakers as early as 1920. In both Europe and Japan, the United States intervened to aid reconstruction and recovery of war-torn nations. These economies, hungry for capital, no longer opposed U.S. intervention or erected trade barriers against American goods. The prospect of a Europe in chaos economically, socially, and politically and on the verge of collapse justified immediate action by the United States.

By the spring of 1947 it was clear to American policymakers that initial postwar attempts to stabilize European economies and promote world recovery were simply not working. The United States had, earlier in the same year, engineered emergency aid to Turkey and Greece, both objects of Soviet aspirations for control. President Truman articulated a doctrine bearing his name: "I believe that it must be the policy of the United States to support free people who are resisting attempted subjugation by armed minorities or by outside pressures." The aid emerged in an atmosphere of opposition between the United States and the Soviet Union over issues of territorial control in Eastern and southern Europe. The Cold War coincided with and reinforced the U.S. need to reconstruct Western Europe.

On 5 June 1947, Secretary of State George C. Marshall (1880–1959) delivered the commencement address at Harvard University. In his speech, Marshall introduced the European Recovery Act, popularly known as the Marshall Plan, through which billions of

This West German poster says "Clear the road for the Marshall Plan." The truck is flying the flags of many of the European nations that were recipients of Marshall Plan aid.

THE MARSHALL PLAN

In the rituals that are part of graduation ceremonies, guest speakers often address the challenges of the future awaiting graduates. Not many of these commencement addresses change the world. The speech given by U.S. Secretary of State George C. Marshall at Harvard University in June 1947 was different. By pledging gifts in aid, the United States helped rebuild war-torn Europe and transform the world's economy.

The truth of the matter is that Europe's requirements for the next three or four years of foreign food and other essential products—principally from America—are so much greater than her present ability to pay that she must have substantial additional help or face economic, social, and political deterioration of a very grave character.

The remedy lies in breaking the vicious circle and restoring the confidence of the European people in the economic future of their own countries and of Europe as a whole. The manufacturer and the farmer throughout wide areas must be able and willing to exchange their products for currencies the continuing value of which is not open to question.

Aside from the demoralizing effect on the world at large and the possibilities of disturbances arising as a result of the desperation of the people concerned, the consequences to the economy of the United States should be apparent to all. It is logical that the United States should do whatever it is able to do to assist in the return of normal economic health in the world, without which there can be no political stability and no assured peace. Our policy is directed not against any country or doctrine but against hunger, poverty, desperation, and chaos. Its purpose should be the revival of a working economy in the world so as to permit the emergence of political and social conditions in which free institutions can exist. Such assistance, I am convinced, must not be on a piecemeal basis as various crises develop. Any assistance that this Government may render in the future should provide a cure rather than a mere palliative. Any government that is willing to assist in the task of recovery will find full cooperation, I am sure, on the part of the United States Government. Any government which maneuvers to block the recovery of other countries cannot expect help from us. Furthermore, governments, political parties, or groups which seek to perpetuate human misery in order to profit therefrom politically or otherwise will encounter the opposition of the United States.

From *Department of State Bulletin*, 15 June 1947.

---

dollars in aid would be made available to European states, both in the east and in the west, provided that two conditions were met: (1) the recipient states must cooperate with one another in aligning national economic policies and improving the international monetary system; and (2) they must work toward breaking down trade barriers.

Participating countries included Austria, Belgium, Denmark, France, West Germany, Great Britain, Greece, Iceland, Italy, Luxembourg, the Netherlands, Norway, Sweden, Switzerland, and Turkey. Russia and Eastern European countries were also eligible for aid under the original formulation. But Russia opposed the plan from the first, wary of U.S. intentions to extend the influence of Western capitalism. Soviet opposition encouraged members of the U.S. Congress, afraid of a Communist takeover in Europe, to support the plan.

Like the United States, the Soviet Union had its own economic imperatives that dictated its attitudes toward European economic development. Under Stalin's direction, the Soviet Union concentrated all its efforts on reconstructing its devastated economy and, to this end, sought integration with Eastern European states, whose technology and resources were needed for the rebuilding of the Soviet state. U.S. dominance threatened the vital connection with Eastern Europe that the Soviet Union was determinedly solidifying in the postwar years.

The amount of U.S. aid to Europe was massive. Over $23 billion was pumped into Western Europe between 1947 and 1952. By every measure, the Marshall Plan was judged a success in the West. American foreign aid restored Western European trade and production, while at the same time controlling inflation. Dean Acheson (1893–1971), Marshall's successor as secretary of state, described the plan in terms of "our duty as human beings" but nevertheless considered it "chiefly as a matter of national self-interest." Soviet critics and Western observers differed dramatically in describing the relationship between self-interest and philanthropy as motives for the plan.

Administering the Plan

As significant as the gift of funds to European states undoubtedly was, no less important was the whole administrative apparatus that the American money brought in its wake. In order to expend available monies most effectively and comply with stipulations for cooperation and regulation, the states of Western Europe resorted to intensified planning and limited nationalization. These ideas were not new in the experience of European states: Vichy France, for example, had emphasized the importance of planning and specialization in its corporatist approach to economic development and social-welfare policies. Regulation and state intervention dominated the formulation of economic policy. Special attention was given to workers' welfare through unemployment insurance, retirement benefits, public health, and housing policies. European states recognized the need to provide a safety net for their citizens in order to avoid reexperiencing the disastrous depression and stagnation of the 1930s while attempting to rebuild their shattered economies. These were lessons that had been learned as much from the attempts at recovery before 1939 as from the experiences of running wartime economies.

The economic theory of John Maynard Keynes, applied successfully by neutral Sweden to its economic policies during the war, came into vogue throughout Europe in 1945, and the postwar era saw the triumph of Keynesian economics. Keynes favored macroeconomic policies to increase productivity and argued for an active role for government in "priming the pump" of economic growth. The government should be responsible, according to Keynes, for the control and regulation of the economy with the goal of ensuring full employment for its people. Governments could and should check inflation and eliminate boom-and-bust cycles, incurring deficits by spending beyond revenues if necessary.

U.S. foreign aid contributed mightily to the extension of central planning and the growth of the welfare state throughout Western Europe. But money alone could not have accomplished the recovery that took place. The chief mechanism for administering Marshall Plan aid was the Office of European Economic Cooperation (OEEC). This master coordinating agency made the requirements for recovery clear. European states had to stabilize their own economies. Cooperation between the public and private sectors was intended to free market forces, modernize production, and raise productivity. Planning mechanisms, including transnational organizations and networks, resulted in the modernization of production and the assimilation of new techniques, new styles of management, and innovative business practices from the United States. This modernization of economies through centrally coordinated planning made Europe once again a major contender in the international economic arena.

The major exception to the establishment of central planning agencies and the nationalization of key industries was West Germany. Deciding against the British and French models of planned growth, the West Germans endorsed a free-market policy that encouraged private enterprise while providing state insurance for all workers. What has been described as "a free enterprise economy with a social conscience" produced the richest economy in Western Europe by the mid-1950s. Some West German industries had been dismantled, but much of West Germany's productive capacity remained intact in the late 1940s. The wealth of great industrialists such as Krupp serving prison sentences as war criminals had not been expropriated, and their commercial empires stood ready to direct the economic revival. The Krupp and I. G. Farben empires were successfully broken up into smaller units. Industries forced to start afresh benefited from the latest technology.

Japanese economic challenges in the postwar era were similar to those of Western Europe. As a defeated and occupied nation in 1945, Japan faced a grim future. U.S. aims for Asia were similar to those for Europe: American policymakers sought to create a multilateral system of world trade and preserve America's sphere of influence against communist encroachment. The American general Douglas MacArthur was appointed the Supreme Commander for the Allied Powers and the head of occupation forces in Japan. His mission in Japan was to impose rapid economic change from above. The occupation government set out to erect institutions to promote political democratization and to eliminate militaristic institutions, official patronage, and censorship. Planning, both formal and informal, reshaped the economy as U.S. aid flowed into Japan during the late forties and early fifties. These changes in Japan, as in Western Europe, took place alongside growing American fears of communism in the region.

Japan turned its wartime devastation into an advantage by replacing destroyed factories with the latest technology, obtained by license from foreign firms. Through a combination of bureaucracy and patronage devoted to planned growth, Japan's GNP reached prewar levels by 1956. By 1968 Japan had turned defeat into triumph and stood as the third largest industrial nation in the world. Japanese growth paralleled the "economic miracle" of West Germany, with the Japanese economy growing at a rate three times faster than that of the United States between 1954 and 1967.

The abolition of the army and navy was a boon for the Japanese economy, since 16 percent of prewar GNP had been devoted to support of the military. Postwar demilitarization freed Japan of the financial exigencies of the arms race. Funds formerly used for arms now flowed into investment and new technology. Slowed population growth after 1948 and increased volume in foreign trade contributed to Japanese prosperity. In the 1960s, Japan emerged as an affluent society undergoing a revolution in consumer durables, including televisions, washing machines, refrigerators, and automobiles.

The United States had succeeded in exporting aspects of its own economy abroad. Through management and planning, recipients of American aid surpassed U.S. goals. A multilateral system of world trade emerged out of the ashes of war. The effects of the Great Depression, which the world had been unable to shake throughout the 1930s, had been laid to rest by global war and its consequences.

A train carrying iron ore crosses the Franco-Luxembourg border, celebrating the joint community in coal and steel that became effective in 1953. The European Coal and Steel Community was the first step in the economic integration of Europe.

Western European Economic Integration

European integration, discussed before and during the war, received added impetus in the postwar period. The Marshall Plan reconciled Western Europe with West Germany through economic cooperation, although that was by no means its original purpose. Realizing that Europe as a region needed the cooperation of its member states if it was to contend in world markets, associations dedicated to integration began to emerge alongside economic planning mechanisms. The Council of Europe dealt with the "discussion of questions of common concern and by agreements and common action in economic, social, cultural, scientific, legal,

and administrative matters and in the maintenance and further realization of human rights and fundamental freedoms." Although not itself a supranational institution with its own authority, the Council of Europe urged a federation among European states. Britain alone rejected all attempts to develop structures of loose intergovernmental cooperation.

Belgium, the Netherlands, and Luxembourg were the first European states to establish themselves as an economic unit—Benelux. Internal customs duties among the three states were removed and a common external tariff barrier was erected. The Schuman Plan joined France and West Germany in economic cooperation by pooling all coal and steel resources, beginning in 1950. The creators of the plan, Jean Monnet (1888–1979) and Robert Schuman (1886–1963) of France, saw it as the first step toward the removal of all economic barriers among European states and as a move toward eventual political integration. In 1951 the Netherlands, Belgium, Luxembourg, France, Italy, and West Germany formed the European Coal and Steel Community (ECSC). While constantly confronting domestic opposition on nationalist grounds, the ECSC succeeded in establishing a "common market" in coal and steel among its member states. In 1957 the same six members created the European Economic Community (EEC) and committed themselves to broadening the integration of markets. This was the beginning of what became known as the Common Market.

The Common Market aimed to establish among its member states a free movement of labor and capital, the elimination of restrictions on trade, common investment practices, and coordinated social-welfare programs. National agricultural interests were to be protected. Great Britain was initially a vocal opponent of the Common Market and continued to defend its own trading relationship with its Commonwealth countries, eventually founding its own free trade association in 1959. In 1973 Great Britain became a member of the Common Market and joined with other European nations in defining common economic policies. The EEC meanwhile achieved the support of the United States in its transitional period, in which it had fifteen years to accomplish its aims.

European union was a phenomenon of exclusion as much as inclusion. It sharpened antagonisms between the West and the East by its very success. While promoting prosperity, European economic unification favored concentration and the emergence of large corporations. Vast individual fortunes flourished under state sponsorship and the rule of the experts. National parliaments were sometimes eclipsed by superfluous new economic decision-making organizations that aimed to make Western Europe into a single free-trade area. The Soviet Union, too, relied on state planning to foster rapid economic growth, but it was central planning emanating from Moscow, based on different assumptions and directed toward different ends.

Creating the Welfare State

The welfare state, a creation of the post–World War II era throughout Europe, grew out of the social welfare policies of the interwar period and out of the war itself. Welfare programs aimed to protect citizens through the establishment of a decent standard of living available for everyone. The experiences of the Great Depression

had done much to foster concern for economic security. In France, the primary concern of the welfare state was the protection of children and the issue of family allowances. In Great Britain, as in Germany, emphasis was placed on unemployment insurance and health care benefits. Everywhere, however, the welfare state developed a related set of social programs and policies whereby the state intervened in the cycles of individual lives to provide economic support for the challenges of birth, sickness, old age, and unemployment. (See "Utopia Lost," pp. 936–937.)

Protection of citizenry took varied forms according to Cold War politics. In the Warsaw Pact countries, the need to industrialize rapidly and to dedicate productive wealth to armament and military protection resulted in a nonexistent consumer economy in which the issues of quality of life and protection took a very different direction. Based on a concept of equal access to a minimum standard of living, welfare states did not treat all its members equally. Women were often disadvantaged in social welfare programs as family needs, men's rights, and the protection of children led to different national configurations.

Prosperity and Consumption in the West

Despite the different paths toward reconstruction following World War II, every Western European nation experienced dramatic increases in total wealth. Per capita income was clearly on the rise through the mid-1960s, and there was more disposable wealth than ever before. Prosperity encouraged new patterns of spending based on confidence in the economy. This new consumerism, in turn, was essential to economic growth and future productivity.

The social programs of the welfare state played an important role in promoting postwar consumption. People began to relax about their economic futures, more secure because of the provisions of unemployment insurance, old-age pensions, and health and accident insurance. The state alleviated the necessity of saving for a rainy day by providing protection that had formerly been covered by the savings of workers. In the mid-1950s, all over Western Europe, people began to spend their earnings, knowing that accidents, disasters, and sicknesses would be taken care of by the state.

The main items in the new consumption were consumer durables, above all televisions and automobiles. Refrigerators and washing machines also developed mass markets, as did the increased consumption of liquor and cigarettes. Increased leisure resulted in a boom in vacation travel. In addition to spending their

✂ *Utopia Lost*

The pig's name is Napoleon. The farmer who drinks too much and loses control of his animals is named Jones. In his "fairy tale" titled *Animal Farm,* George Orwell gives us a deceptively simple but frightening tale of rebellion and tyranny. The barnyard animals of Farmer Jones know they are exploited by their human masters. When they can stand it no longer, they rise up against their oppression. Their revolution succeeds only when one animal, a pig, emerges as the revolutionary leader, the consolidator of revolutionary aims. He is named Napoleon.

The animals' cause is just: they want equality and fair treatment for their labors. They dream of a utopian world, a place free of care and filled with comforts. But in the process of wresting power and consolidating it, their paradise is lost, their utopia distorted. The seven commandments of the animal revolution are rewritten in such a way that all power resides in the dictator pig. All principles are reduced to one commandment: "All animals are equal, but some animals are more equal than others." A desire for a better life has produced a dictatorship that is far worse than the human tyranny the animals overthrew.

George Orwell created a dystopia, a utopia turned inside out, a dream that ends as a nightmare, a paradise lost in a new hell of oppression. In the same tradition as Thomas More's sixteenth-century masterpiece *Utopia,* Orwell's story uses fable to criticize contemporary institutions and events. In his parable of farmyard life, Orwell intended to "fuse political purpose and artistic purpose into one whole" in an assault on totalitarianism. Orwell's novel appeared in 1946. *Animal Farm* is recognizably an indictment of the Russian Revolution, an event that Orwell thought had soured under Stalinist rule and one that had colored the politics of the twentieth century with false hope. It served as a fitting herald to Cold War politics in the West.

Yet *Animal Farm* indicts more than communist rule in one country. It is a fairy tale without a moral, a profoundly cynical appreciation of the advances of civilization in the twentieth century. The civilization that Orwell judged so negatively had made important advances in science, technology, state organization, and a rhetoric of equality and welfare. For the donkeys, horses, and chickens of the farmyard—as for people in his own society—liberal and democratic values shrivel when squared off against the realities of power and force. In the end, the farm grows richer but the animals do not. The dreams of a better life, of the luxuries that electric power could bring, fade. The pigs become the ruling class, controlling information in mysterious files, memoranda, and reports. Neither technology nor government bureaucracy has improved animal life. The animals now work harder to support a greedy and parasitic ruling class.

Most unsettling of all, the animals lack their own history, remembering only what they are told was their past. In the concluding pages of the work, an old donkey by the name of Benjamin, who has lived through the prerevolutionary and revolutionary periods and is now under the yoke of the new tyrant pig, declares that things are little different from the old days: hunger, hardship, and disappointment are the unalterable laws of life. His memory serves as the only historical record. Napoleon now lives in Farmer Jones's house, sleeps in his bed, wears his clothes, and drinks his whiskey. In the greatest perversion of the transfer of power, the pig now walks on his two hind legs, terrifyingly humanized.

Orwell's fusion of politics and art did not stop with *Animal Farm.* In *Nineteen Eighty-Four* (1949), he created an equally horrifying picture of the future, one that does not resort to animal parables but instead portrays a mechanized kind of inhuman tyranny, that of Big Brother, a force that sees all and controls all, down to what people think. Both works were banned in the Soviet Union and in communist Eastern Europe. Many intellectuals of the postwar period shared Orwell's concern for what they saw as the erosion of personal freedom. For Orwell, the liberal traditions of the West were as hollow as the socialist promises of the Soviet world were dangerous. The great principle of equality, the cornerstone of the Western political tradition, served as the instrument of a new oppression. Standing on the edge of the abyss of war, revolution, and human suffering in the twentieth century, Orwell peered into the future and saw ahead only what he was trying to leave behind.

A traffic jam on the Place de la Concorde in Paris in 1962. Western Europeans learned that prosperity has its price as nineteenth-century cities were thrust into the automobile age.

salaries, Western Europeans began to buy on credit, spending money they had not yet earned. This, too, was an innovation in postwar markets. People sought immediate gratification through consumption by means of delayed payment against future earnings.

Welfare programs could be sustained only in an era of prosperity and economic growth, since they depended on taxation of income for their funds. Such taxation did not, however, result in a redistribution of wealth. Wealth remained in the hands of a few and became even more concentrated as a result of phenomenal postwar economic growth. In West Germany, for example, 1.7 percent of the population owned 35 percent of the society's total wealth.

Just as the welfare state did not redistribute wealth, neither did it provide equal pay for equal work. In France, women who performed the same jobs as men received less pay. In typesetting, for example, women, who on average set 15,000 keystrokes per hour at the keyboards as compared to 10,000 by men, earned 50 percent of men's salaries and held different titles for their jobs. Separate wage scales for women drawn up during the Nazi period remained in effect in West Germany until 1956. The skills associated with occupations performed by women were downgraded, as were their salaries. Women earned two-thirds or less of what men earned throughout Western Europe. Welfare state revenues were a direct result of pay-scale inequities. Lower salaries for women meant higher profits and helped make economic recovery possible.

The Eastern Bloc and Recovery

In the years before his death in 1953, Joseph Stalin succeeded in making the Soviet Union a vital industrial giant second only to the United States. The Soviet economy experienced dramatic recovery after 1945, in spite of the severe damage inflicted on it during the war. The production of steel, coal, and crude oil skyrocketed under state planning. Heavy industry was the top priority of Soviet recovery, in keeping with prewar commitments to rapid modernization. In addition, the postwar Soviet economy assumed the new burdens of the development of a nuclear arsenal and an expensive program for the exploration of space. Stalin maintained the Soviet Union on the footing of a war economy, restricting occupational mobility and continuing to rely on forced-labor camps.

The Soviet Union's standard of living remained relatively low in these years when Western Europe was undergoing a consumer revolution. Soviet consumption was necessarily stagnant, since profits were plowed back as investments in future heavy industrial expansion. In the Soviet Union and throughout the Eastern Bloc countries, women's full participation in the labor force was essential for recovery. In spite of their presence in large numbers in highly skilled sectors like medicine, Soviet and Eastern Bloc women remained poorly paid, as did women in the West. Soviet men received higher salaries for the same work on the grounds that they had to support families.

REPORT TO THE TWENTIETH PARTY CONGRESS

Like Stalin before him, the Soviet leader Nikita Khrushchev perceived that the Soviet Union was locked in a worldwide struggle with the United States and Western capitalist nations. The experiences of the Korean War and the escalation of the nuclear arms race prompted him to proceed with wariness in foreign policy. In his now famous speech before the Twentieth Party Congress in February 1956, Khrushchev, as first secretary of the Communist party, accused the United States, England, and France of imperialism and pleaded for the peaceful coexistence of communism and capitalism, confident that, in the end, communism would win the day.

Soon after the Second World War ended, the influence of reactionary and militarist groups began to be increasingly evident in the policy of the United States of America, Britain, and France. Their desire to enforce their will on other countries by economic and political pressure, threats, and military provocation prevailed. This became known as the "positions of strength" policy. It reflects the aspiration of the most aggressive sections of present-day imperialism to win world supremacy, to suppress the working class and democratic and nation-liberation movements; it reflects their plans for military adventures against the socialist camp.

The international atmosphere was poisoned by war hysteria. The arms race began to assume more and more monstrous dimensions. Many big U.S. military bases designed for use against the USSR and the People's Democracies [East European countries under Soviet control] were built in countries thousands of miles from the borders of the United States. "Cold war" was begun against the socialist camp. International distrust was artificially kindled, and nations set against one another. A bloody war was launched in Korea; the war in Indochina dragged on for years. . . . The Leninist principle of peaceful co-existence of states with different social systems has always been and remains the general line of our country's foreign policy. . . . To this day the enemies of peace allege that the Soviet Union is out to overthrow capitalism in other countries by "exporting" revolution. It goes without saying that among us Communists there are no supporters of capitalism. But this does not mean that we have interfered or plan to interfere in the internal affairs of countries where capitalism still exists.

When we say that the socialist system will win in the competition between the two systems—the capitalist and the socialist—this by no means signifies that its victory will be achieved through armed interference by the socialist countries in the internal affairs of the capitalist countries. Our certainty of the victory of communism is based on the fact that the socialist mode of production possesses decisive advantages over the capitalist mode of production. Precisely because of this, the ideas of Marxism-Leninism are more and more capturing the minds of the broad masses of the working people in the capitalist countries, just as they have captured the minds of millions of men and women in our country and the People's Democracies. [*Prolonged applause.*] We believe that all working men in the world, once they have become convinced of the advantages communism brings, will sooner or later take the road of struggle for the construction of socialist society.

With Stalin's death, new leaders recognized the need for change, especially with regard to the neglected sectors of agricultural production and consumer products. The Soviet population was growing rapidly, from 170 million in 1939 to 234 million in 1967. Khrushchev promised the Russian people lower prices and a shorter workweek, but in 1964, when he fell from power, Russians were paying higher prices for their food than before. With a declining rate of development, the Soviet economy lacked the necessary capital to advance the plans for growth in all sectors. Defense spending nearly doubled in the short period between 1960 and 1968.

The nature of planned Soviet growth exacted heavy costs in the Eastern Bloc countries. Adhering to the Soviet pattern of heavy industrial expansion at the expense of agriculture and consumer goods, East Germany nearly doubled its industrial output by 1955, despite having been stripped of its industrial plants by the Soviet Union before 1948. Czechoslovakia, Bulgaria, Romania, and Yugoslavia all reported significant industrial growth in this period. Yet dislocations caused by collectivization and heavy defense expenditures stirred up social unrest in East Germany, Czechoslovakia, Poland, and Hungary. The Soviet Union respond-

THE COLD WAR

1947	Marshall Plan starts U.S. aid to European countries
1947	Pro-Soviet governments established in Poland, Hungary, Bulgaria, and Romania
1948	Pro-Soviet government established in Czechoslovakia
1949	European states and United States form North Atlantic Treaty Organization (NATO)
1949	Federal Republic of Germany and German Democratic Republic established
1949	Soviet Union creates Council for Mutual Economic Assistance (Comecon)
1949	Soviet Union tests its first atomic bomb
1950–1953	Korean War, ending with the partition of Korea
1953	United States and Soviet Union develop hydrogen bombs
1955	Formation of Warsaw Pact
1956	Hungarian uprising and subsequent repression by Soviet military forces
1957	The Netherlands, Belgium, Luxembourg, France, Italy, and West Germany form the European Economic Community (EEC), also called the Common Market
1957	Soviet Union launches first satellite, *Sputnik I*
1961	Berlin Wall built
1961–1973	U.S. troops engaged in Vietnam
1962	Cuban missile crisis
1963	Soviet Union and United States sign Nuclear Test-Ban Treaty
1968	Prague Spring uprising in Czechoslovakia, quelled by Soviet Union

ed with some economic concessions but on the whole stressed common industrial and defense pursuits, employing ideological persuasion and military pressure to keep its reluctant partners in line. The slowed growth of the 1960s, the delay in development of consumer durables, and the inadequacy of basic foodstuffs,

housing, and clothing were the costs that Eastern Bloc citizens paid for their inefficient and rigid planned economies dedicated to the development of heavy industry. In Eastern Europe and the Soviet Union, poverty was virtually eliminated, however, as the state subsidized housing, health care, and higher education, which were available to all.

Family Strategies

The pressures on European women and their families in 1945 were often greater than in wartime. Severe scarcity of food, clothes, and housing required careful management. Women who during the war held jobs in industry and munitions plants earned their own money and established their own independence. After the war, in victorious and defeated nations alike, women were moved out of the work force to make room for returning men. Changing social policies affected women's lives in the home and in the workplace and contributed to the politicization of women within the context of the welfare state.

Demography and Birth Control. Prewar concerns with a declining birthrate intensified after World War II. In some European countries, the birthrate climbed in the years immediately following the war, an encouraging sign to observers who saw in this trend an optimistic commitment to the future after the cessation of the horrors of war. The situation was more complicated in France and the United States, where the birthrates began to climb even before the war was over. Nearly everywhere throughout Europe, however, the rise in the birthrate was momentary, with the United States standing alone in experiencing a genuine and sustained "baby boom" until about 1960. In Germany and in Eastern Europe (Poland and Yugoslavia, for example), the costs of the war exacted heavy tolls on families long after the hostilities ended. On average, women everywhere were having fewer children by choice.

Technology had expanded the range of choices in family planning. In the early 1960s, the birth control pill became available on the European and American markets, primarily to middle-class women. Europeans were choosing to have smaller families. The drop in the birthrate had clearly preceded the new technological interventions that included intrauterine devices (IUDs), improved diaphragms, sponges, and more effective spermicidal creams and jellies. The condom, invented a century earlier, was now sold to a mass market. Controversies surrounded the unhealthy side effects of the pill and the dangerous Dalkon shield, an IUD that had not been adequately tested before marketing and that resulted in the death or sterilization of thousands of women. Religious leaders spoke out on the moral issues surrounding sexuality without reproduction. Information about their reproductive lives became more accessible to young women. Illegal abortions continued to be an alternative for women. In France and Italy, birth control information was often withheld from the public. Abortion was probably the primary form of birth control in the Soviet Union in the years following the war.

The Family and Welfare. Concurrent with a low birthrate was a return to family life and family values in the years after the war. Those who had lived through the previous twenty years were haunted by the memories of the Great Depression, severe economic hardships, destructive war, and the loss of loved ones. Women and men throughout Western Europe and the United States embraced family values and a return to normal life, even if they did not opt for large families. Expectations for improved family life placed new demands on welfare state programs. They also placed increased demands on mothers, whose presence in the home was now seen as all-important for the proper development of the child. Handbooks for mothers proliferated, instructing them in the "science" of child-rearing. The best-seller *Baby and Child Care* by Dr. Benjamin Spock was typical of such guides.

European states implemented official programs to encourage women to have more children and to be better mothers. "Pronatalism," as this policy was known, resulted from an official concern over low birthrates and a decline in family size. It is unlikely that "pronatalism" was caused by a fear of a decline in the labor force, since the influx of foreign workers, refugees from Eastern Europe, and migrant laborers from poorer southern European nations provided an expanding labor pool. Other considerations about racial dominance and woman's proper role seem to have affected the development of policies. In 1945, Lord Beveridge (1879–1960), the architect of the British welfare state, emphasized the importance of women's role "in ensuring the adequate continuance of the British race" and argued that women's place was in the home: "During marriage most women will not be gainfully employed. The small minority of women who undertake paid employment or other gainful employment or other gainful occupations after marriage require special treatment differing from that of single women."

Welfare state programs differed from country to country as the result of a series of different expectations of women as workers and women as mothers. Konrad Adenauer, chancellor of West Germany, spoke of "a will to children" as essential for his country's continued economic growth and prosperity. In Great Britain, the welfare system was built on the ideal of the mother at home with her children. With the emphasis on the need for larger families—four children was considered "desirable" in England—English society focused on the importance of the role of the mother. Family allowances determined by the number of children were tied to men's participation in the work force; women were defined according to their husbands' status. The state welfare system strengthened the financial dependence of English wives on their husbands.

In Great Britain, anxiety over the low birthrate was also tied to the debate over equal pay for women. Opponents of the measure argued that equal pay would cause women to forgo marriage and motherhood and

Many basic needs are provided for under Britain's cradle-to-grave social welfare system. Here mothers and children line up to receive orange juice. Vitamins and milk are also provided for growing children.

THE SECOND SEX

Simone de Beauvoir, one of France's leading intellectuals, wrote philosophical treatises, essays, and novels that drew on a wide variety of cultural traditions and synthesized philosophy, history, literary criticism, and Freudian psychoanalysis in her studies of the human condition. The Second Sex, which first appeared in French in 1949, has subsequently been translated into many languages and has appeared in numerous editions throughout the world. It has served as a call to arms for the feminist movement, provoking debate, controversy, and a questioning of the fundamental gender arrangements of modern society.

A man never begins by presenting himself as an individual of a certain sex; it goes without saying that he is a man. The terms *masculine* and *feminine* are used symmetrically only as a matter of form, as on legal papers. In actuality the relation of the two sexes is not quite like that of two electrical poles, for man represents both the positive and the neutral, as is indicated by the common use of *man* to designate human beings in general; whereas woman represents only the negative, defining by limiting criteria, without reciprocity. In the midst of an abstract discussion it is vexing to hear a man say: "You think thus and so because you are a woman"; but I know that my only defense is to reply: "I think thus and so because it is true," thereby removing my subjective self from the argument. It would be out of the question to reply: "And you think the contrary because you are a man," for it is understood that the fact of being a man is no peculiarity. A man is in the right in being a man; it is the woman who is in the wrong. It amounts to this: just as for the ancients there was an absolute vertical with reference to which the oblique was defined, so there is an absolute human type, the masculine. Woman has ovaries, a uterus; these peculiarities imprison her in her subjectivity, circumscribe her within the limits of her own nature. It is often said that she thinks with her glands. Man superbly ignores the fact that his anatomy also includes glands, such as the testicles, and that they secrete hormones. He thinks of his body as a direct and normal connection with the world, which he believes he apprehends objectively, whereas he regards the body of woman as a hindrance, a prison, weighed down by everything peculiar to it. "The female is a female by virtue of certain *lack* of qualities," said Aristotle; "we should regard the female nature as afflicted with a natural defectiveness." And Saint Thomas for his part pronounced woman to be an "imperfect man," an "inci-

should therefore be avoided. There was a consensus about keeping women out of the work force and paying them less in order to achieve that end.

The French system of *sécurité sociale* defined all women, whether married or single, as equal to men; unlike the British system, all French women had the same rights of access to welfare programs as men. This may well have reflected the different work history of women in France and the recognition of the importance of women's labor for reconstruction of the economy. As a result, family allowances, pre- and postnatal care, maternity benefits, and child care were provided on the assumption that working mothers were a fact of life. French payments were intended to encourage large families and focused primarily on the needs of children. More and more women entered the paid labor force after 1945, and they were less financially dependent on their husbands than were their British counterparts.

Both forms of welfare state—the British that emphasized women's role as mothers, and the French that accepted women's role as workers—were based on different attitudes about the nature of gender difference and equality. Women's political consciousness developed in both societies. The women's liberation movements of the late sixties and early seventies found their roots in the contradictions of differing welfare policies.

The Beginnings of Women's Protest. The 1960s was a period of protest in Western countries as people demonstrated for civil rights and free expression. The movement against U.S. involvement in Vietnam was fueled by the activism of the black civil rights movement. Pacifist and antinuclear groups united to "Ban the Bomb." Women participated in all of these movements, and by the end of the 1960s had begun to question their own place in organizations that did not

dental" being. This is symbolized in Genesis where Eve is depicted as made from what Bossuet called "a supernumerary bone" of Adam.

Now, woman has always been man's dependent, if not his slave; the two sexes have never shared the world in equality. And even today woman is heavily handicapped, though her situation is beginning to change. Almost nowhere is her legal status the same as man's, and frequently it is much to her disadvantage. Even when her rights are legally recognized in the abstract, long-standing custom prevents their full expression in the mores. In the economic sphere men and women can almost be said to make up two castes; other things being equal, the former hold the better jobs, get higher wages, and have more opportunity for success than their new competitors. In industry and politics men have a great many more positions and they monopolize the most important posts. In addition to all this, they enjoy a traditional prestige that the education of children tends in every way to support, for the present enshrines the past—and in the past all history has been made by men. At the present time, when women are beginning to take part in the affairs of the world, it is still a world that belongs to men—they have no doubt of it at all and women have scarcely any. To decline to be the Other, to refuse to be a party to the deal—this would be for women to renounce all the advantages conferred upon them by their alliance with the superior caste. Man-the-sovereign will provide women-the-liege with material protection and will undertake the moral justification of her existence; thus she can evade at once both economic risk and the metaphysical risk of a liberty in which ends and aims must be contrived without assistance. Indeed, along with the ethical urge of each individual to affirm his subjective existence, there is also the temptation to forgo liberty and become a thing. This is an inauspicious road, for he who takes it—passive, lost, ruined—becomes henceforth the creature of another's will, frustrated in his transcendence and deprived of every value. But it is an easy road; on it one avoids the strain involved in undertaking an authentic existence. When man makes of woman the *Other*, he may, then, expect her to manifest deep-seated tendencies toward complicity. Thus, woman may fail to lay claim to the status of subject because she lacks definite resources, because she feels the necessary bond that ties her to man regardless of reciprocity, and because she is often very well pleased with her role as the *Other*.

From Simone de Beauvoir, *The Second Sex* (1949).

acknowledge their claims to equal rights, equal pay, and liberation from the oppression of male society. A new critique began to form within the welfare state that indicated there were cracks in the facade.

One book in particular, written after World War II, captured the imagination of many women who were aware of the contradictions and limitations placed on them by state and society. *The Second Sex* (1949), written by Simone de Beauvoir (1908–86), a leading French intellectual, analyzed women's place in the context of Western culture. By examining the assumptions of political theories, including Marxism, in the light of philosophy, biology, history, and psychoanalysis, de Beauvoir uncovered the myths governing the creation of the female self. By showing how the male is the center of culture and the female is "other," de Beauvoir urged women to be independent and to resist male definitions. *The Second Sex* became the handbook of the women's movement in the 1960s.

French novelist and feminist Simone de Beauvoir participated in demonstrations for women's issues such as family planning.

A very different work, *The Feminine Mystique,* appeared in 1963. In this work author Betty Friedan voiced the grievances of a previously politically quiescent group of women. Friedan was an American suburban homemaker and the mother of three children when she wrote about what she saw as the schizophrenic split in her own middle-class world between the reality of women's lives and the idealized image of the perfect homemaker. After World War II, women were expected to find personal fulfillment in the domestic sphere. Instead, Friedan found women suffering from "the sickness with no name" and the "nameless desperation" of a profound crisis in identity.

A new politics centering on women's needs and women's rights slowly took root. The feminist critique did not emerge as a mass movement until the 1970s. Youth culture and dissent among the young further informed growing feminist discontent. But the agenda of protest in the sixties, reinforced by social policies, accepted gender differences as normal and natural.

Youth Culture and the Generation Gap

Youth culture was created by outside forces as much as it was self-created. Socialized together in an expanding educational system from primary school through high school, the young came to see themselves as a social force. They were also socialized by marketing efforts that appealed to their particular needs as a group.

The prosperity that characterized the period from the mid-fifties to the mid-sixties throughout the West provided a secure base from which radical dissenters could launch their protests. The young people of the 1960s were the first generation to come of age after World War II. Although they had no memory themselves of the destruction of that war, they were reminded daily of the imminence of nuclear destruction in their own lives. The combination of the security of affluence and the insecurity of Cold War politics created a widening gap between the world of decision-making adults and the idealistic universe of the young. To the criticisms of parents, politicians, and teachers, the new generation responded that no one over thirty could be trusted.

New styles of dress and grooming were a rejection of middle-class culture in Europe and the United States. Anthropologists and sociologists in the 1960s began studying youth as if they were a foreign tribe. The

"generation gap" appeared as the subject of hundreds of specialized studies. Adolescent behavior was examined across cultures. Sexual freedom and the use of drugs were subjected to special scrutiny. But, above all, it was the politics of the young that baffled and enraged many observers. When the stable base of economic prosperity began to erode as a result of slowed growth and inflation in the second half of the sixties—first in Western Europe and then in the United States—frustrated expectations and shrinking opportunities for the young served as a further impetus for political action.

Sex, Drugs, and Protest

Increased emphasis on fulfillment through sexual pleasure was one consequence of the technological revolution in birth control devices, and it led to what has been called a revolution in sexual values in Western societies in the 1960s. The sexual revolution drew attention to sexual fulfillment as an end in itself. Women's bodies were displayed more explicitly than

The Beatles were the icons of the sixties—the era of pacifism, when young people experimented with sexual liberation, the drug culture, and Eastern mysticism.

"SUBTERRANEAN HOMESICK BLUES"

The gap between the generations yawned into a gulf as rock music became political in the mid-1960s. Bob Dylan, an American rock performer, introduced folk music to the genre with songs of social protest like "Blowin' in the Wind" and "Only a Pawn in Their Game." Rock music was denounced as a communist plot, as performers urged their audiences to "Make Love, Not War." Dylan's "Subterranean Homesick Blues" targeted the hypocrisy of his society.

SUBTERRANEAN HOMESICK BLUES

Bob Dylan

Johnny's in the basement
Mixing up the medicine
I'm on the pavement
Thinking about the government
The man in the trench coat
Badge out, laid off
Says he's got a bad cough
Wants to get it paid off
Look out kid
It's somethin' you did
God knows when
But you're doin' it again
You better duck down the alley way
Lookin' for a new friend
The man in the coon-skin cap
In the big pen
Wants eleven dollar bills
You only got ten

Maggie comes fleet foot
Face full of black soot
Talkin' that the heat put
Plants in the bed but
The phone's tapped anyway
Maggie says that many say
They must bust in early May
Orders from the D.A.
Look out kid
Don't matter what you did
Walk on your tip toes
Don't try "No Doz"
Better stay away from those
That carry around a fire hose
Keep a clean nose
Watch the plain clothes
You don't need a weather man
To know which way the wind blows

Get sick, get well
Hang around a ink well
Ring bell, hard to tell
If anything is goin' to sell
Try hard, get barred
Get back, write braille
Get jailed, jump bail
Join the army, if you fail
Look out kid
You're gonna get hit
But users, cheaters
Six-time losers
Hang around the theaters
Girl by the whirlpool
Lookin' for a new fool
Don't follow leaders
Watch the parkin' meters

Ah get born, keep warm
Short pants, romance, learn to dance
Get dressed, get blessed
Try to be a success
Please her, please him, buy gifts
Don't steal, don't lift
Twenty years of schoolin'
And they put you on the day shift
Look out kid
They keep it all hid
Better jump down a manhole
Light yourself a candle
Don't wear sandals
Try to avoid the scandals
Don't wanna be a bum
You better chew gum
The pump don't work
'Cause the vandals took the handles

ever before in mass advertising in order to sell products from automobiles to soap. Sex magazines, sex shops, and movies were part of an explosion in the marketing of male sexual fantasies in the 1960s.

Sweden experienced the most far-reaching reforms of sexual mores in the 1960s. Sex education became part of every school's curriculum, contraceptive information was widely available, and homosexuality was decriminalized. Technology allowed women and men to separate pleasure from reproduction, but did nothing to alter men's and women's domestic roles. Pleasure was also separated from familial responsibilities, yet the domestic ideal of the woman in the home remained. Some women were beginning to question their exploitation in the sexual revolution. In the early 1970s, this issue became the basis of mass feminist protest.

Just as sexuality was invested with new meaning within the context of protest, so was the use of drugs. Drug use was not new in history: through the ages drugs have been taken as painkillers or pleasure enhancers and used in religious and cultural rituals. Soldiers in nineteenth-century wars in Europe and America returned home addicted to opium and morphine, which they were given when treated for their wounds. In the 1960s American soldiers in Vietnam turned to drugs as an escape from the horrors of war.

Drugs began to pervade Western cultures in apparently harmless ways. At the end of the nineteenth century in the United States, the newly created Coca-Cola was actually made with cocaine, a drug derived from the coca shrub. Another ingredient in the soft drink formula was the kola nut, which contains the stimulant caffeine. In the 1950s and 1960s, chemical technology made possible the manufacture of synthetic drugs. Pharmaceutical industries in Europe and the United States expanded by leaps and bounds with the mass marketing of amphetamines, barbiturates, and tranquilizers. Doctors prescribed these new drugs for a variety of problems from obesity to depression to sleeplessness. People discovered that these drugs had additional mood-altering effects.

Marijuana grew in popularity as a safe "recreational" drug, especially among college and university students in the 1960s. In fact, young people were the primary users of drugs of all sorts, including synthetic drugs like the hallucinogen LSD (lysergic acid diethylamide). Hallucinogens were considered by their proponents to be mind-expanding drugs that permitted the achieve-

ment of new levels of consciousness. Drugs used by young people affluent enough to afford them served to widen the gap between the generations still further.

The Protests of 1968

Student protest, which began at the University of California at Berkeley in 1964 as the Free Speech movement, by the spring of 1968 had become an international phenomenon that had spread to other American campuses and throughout Europe and Japan. A common denominator of protest, whether in New York, London, or Tokyo, was opposition to the war in Vietnam. Growing numbers of intellectuals and students throughout the world condemned the U.S. presence in Vietnam as an immoral violation of the rights of the Vietnamese people and violent proof of U.S. imperialism.

Student protesters shared other concerns in addition to opposition to the war in southeast Asia. The growing activism on American campuses was aimed at social reform, student self-governance, and a recognition of the responsibilities of the university in the wider community. In West Germany, highly politicized radical activists, a conspicuous minority among the students at the Free University of Berlin, directed protest out into the wider society. Student demonstrations met with brutal police repression and violence, and rioting was common.

European students, more than their American counterparts, were also experiencing frustration in the classroom. European universities were unprepared to absorb the huge influx of students in the 1960s. The student-teacher ratio at the University of Rome, for example, was 200 to 1. In Italian universities in general, the majority of over half a million students had no contact with their professors. The University of Paris was similarly overcrowded.

For the most part, student protest was primarily a middle-class phenomenon. In France, for example, only 4 percent of university students came from below the middle class. Higher education had been developed after World War II to serve the increased needs of a technocratic society. Instead of altering the social structure, which politically committed student protesters thought it should do, mass education served as a certifying mechanism for bureaucratic and technical institutions. Many of the occupations that students could look forward to were in dead-end service jobs or in bureaucratic posts.

Students riot in Paris in 1968. The student protests of the late 1960s were sparked by the war in Vietnam and by disillusionment with the present and uncertainty about the future.

Student dissent reflected the changing economy of the late 1960s. Inflation, which earlier in the decade had spurred prosperity, was spiraling out of control in the late sixties. In the advanced industrial countries of Western Europe and later in the United States, the growth of the postwar period was slowing down. Economic opportunity was evaporating and jobs were being eliminated. One survey estimated that only one in three Italian university graduates in 1967 was able to find a job. The dawning awareness of shrinking opportunities in the workplace for students who had attained their degrees and been properly certified further aggravated student frustration and dissent. Anger about the uncertainties of their future mixed with the realization of the boredom of the careers that awaited them upon graduation.

By the late sixties, universities and colleges provided the students a forum for expressing their discontent with advanced industrial societies. In their protests, student activists rejected the values of consumer society. The programs and politics of the student protesters aimed to transform the world in which they lived. Student protesters in France chanted *"Métro, boulot, dodo,"* a slang condemnation of the treadmill-like existence of those who spent their lives in a repetitive cycle of subway riding *(Métro)*, mindless work *(boulot)*, and sleep *(dodo)*. The spirit of protest was expressed in the graffiti and posters that seemed to appear overnight on the walls of Paris:

"Action must not be a reaction—but a creation"

"Power to the Imagination"

"The revolution will be won when the last bureaucrat is strangled in the entrails of the last cop"

"The state is each one of us"

In May 1968, French protest spread beyond the university when workers and managers joined students in paralyzing the French economy and threatening to topple the Fifth Republic. Between 7 and 10 million people went on strike in support of worker and student demands. White-collar employees and technicians joined blue-collar factory workers in the strike. Student demands, based on a thoroughgoing critique of the whole society, proved to be incompatible with the wage and consumption issues of workers. But the unusual, if short-lived, alliance of students and workers shocked those in power and induced reforms.

• • •

The division of the world into two camps framed the recovery of combatant nations dealing with the losses of World War II. The Cold War instilled fear and terror in the populations who lived on both sides of the divide. Yet the Cold War also created the terms for stability following the upheaval of war. It promoted prosperity that preserved the long-term policies of both the United States and the Soviet Union in the twentieth century. The Soviet Union had buffered itself from the West by creating a ring of friendly nations on its borders and had continued its race to industrialize. The belief that the USSR had won the war for the Allies and the sense of betrayal that followed the war determined the outlook of grim distrust shared by postwar Soviet leaders who had survived the years from 1939 to 1945.

The United States, on the other hand, found itself playing the role of rich uncle in bankrolling the European recovery. Its long-term commitment to promoting its own economic interests by helping future trading partners led it also into playing the role of policeman throughout the world. The escalating war in Vietnam made America vulnerable to growing world criticism and to growing domestic discontent.

The gains of economic recovery began to unravel in the mid-1960s. In the West, rising expectations of consumer societies came up against the harsh realities of slowed growth. In the East, frustrated nationalism, the lack of consumer goods, and repressive conditions resulted in low morale, demonstrations, and outright conflict. After Stalin's death, resources were diverted to consumer goods, but there was little measurable improvement in the quality of life.

The nations of Europe and the United States sensed that they stood at a crossroads in 1968. Whether the future inspired confidence or fear remained to be seen. The threat of nuclear annihilation had considerably diminished. The euphoria of students in the West and the Prague Spring in the East seemed to be more an interlude than a turning point. If the rivalry between East and West no longer dominated the international arena, what lay ahead?

Suggestions for Further Reading

Regulating the Cold War

* Franz Ansprenger, *The Dissolution of the Colonial Empires* (London: Routledge, 1989). An analysis of Europe's withdrawal from Asia and Africa following the Second World War, beginning with an examination of post–World War I imperialism.

* Walter Lafeber, *America, Russia, and the Cold War, 1945–1966* (New York: John Wiley and Sons, 1978). A Cold War revisionist interpretation of American foreign policy in the two decades after World War II. Lafeber examines the influence of Soviet and American domestic policies on the two nations' foreign policies.

* William Roger Louis and Roger Owen, eds., *Suez 1956: The Crisis and Its Consequences* (New York: Oxford University Press, 1989). A series of essays resulting from new research into the origins and consequences of the Suez crisis.

Charles S. Maier, ed., *The Origins of the Cold War and Contemporary Europe* (New York: Franklin Watts, 1978). A series of essays considering the origins of the Cold War and its impact on the political economy of Europe.

* Charles S. Maier, *In Search of Stability: Explorations in Historical Political Economy* (Cambridge: Cambridge University Press, 1987). Covers a wide variety of issues affecting twentieth-century Europe, including the foundation of American international economic policy after World War II and the conditions for stability in Western Europe after 1945.

* Bruce D. Porter, *The USSR in Third World Conflicts: Soviet Arms and Diplomacy in Local Wars, 1945–1980* (Cambridge: Cambridge University Press, 1984). A case study approach to the Soviet Union's changing postwar policies toward the third world that centers on local wars in Africa and the Middle East.

* Tony Smith, ed., *The End of the European Empire: Decolonization After World War II* (Lexington, MA: Heath, 1975). A collection of articles dealing with the rapid decolonization of the overseas holdings of Great Britain, France, the Netherlands, and Belgium and the growing agitation and organization of nationalist movements.

Reconstructing Europe

* Stanley Hoffman and Charles Maier, *The Marshall Plan: A Retrospective* (Boulder, CO: Westview Press, 1984). Based on a commemorative conference held at Harvard University thirty-five years after George C. Marshall's address there, this collection combines the work of specialists and actual participants in the plan's implementation.

* Michael J. Hogan, *The Marshall Plan: America, Britain, and the Reconstruction of Western Europe* (Cambridge: Cambridge University Press, 1987). A thoroughly researched argument on the continuity of U.S. economic policy in the twentieth century. Hogan counters the belief that the Marshall Plan was merely a response to the Cold War.

* Derek W. Urwin, *Western Europe Since 1945: A Political History,* 4th ed. (London: Longman, 1989). An updated general survey of postwar politics, with a special focus on the problems of reconstruction and the role of the resistance after 1945.

Creating the Welfare State

* Simone de Beauvoir, *The Second Sex* (New York: Knopf, 1963). The author, one of France's leading intellectuals in

the twentieth century, describes the situation of women's lives in the postwar West by placing them within the context of the history and myths governing Western culture.

* Betty Friedan, *The Feminine Mystique* (New York: Norton, 1963). Captures the essence of the fifties image of American middle-class women as perfect mothers and homemakers and chronicles the high social and emotional costs for women of the new feminine ideal.

* Jane Jenson, "Both Friend and Foe: Women and State Welfare," *Becoming Visible: Women in European History,* ed. Renate Bridenthal, Claudia Koonz, and Susan Stuard (Boston: Houghton Mifflin, 1987). This essay illuminates the mixed blessing of the welfare state for women after 1945 by focusing on the experiences of women in Great Britain and France.

* Walter Laqueur, *Europe Since Hitler: The Rebirth of Europe* (New York: Penguin Books, 1982). Surveys politics, economy, society, and culture in order to explain Europe's postwar resurgence.

* Denise Riley, *War in the Nursery: Theories of the Child and Mother* (London: Virago Press, 1983). Treats social policies of postwar "pronatalism" within the context of the popularization of developmental and child psychologies in Europe, with special attention to Britain and the United States and an emphasis on the postwar period as a turning point in attitudes toward women and the family.

* Mary Ruggie, *The State and Working Women: A Comparative Study of Britain and Sweden* (Princeton, NJ: Princeton University Press, 1984). A sociological study comparing the economic status of women in two European welfare states.

Youth Culture and the Generation Gap

* David Caute, *The Year of the Barricades: A Journey Through 1968* (New York: Harper & Row, 1988). More than its title suggests, this work is an overview of postwar youth culture on three continents. The politics of 1968 is featured, although other topics regarding the counterculture, lifestyles, and cultural ramifications are considered.

John R. Gillis, *Youth and History: Tradition and Change in European Age Relations, 1770–Present* (New York: Academic Press, 1981). Connects the history of European youth to broad trends in economic and demographic modernization over the last two hundred years.

* Margaret Mead, *Culture and Commitment: The New Relationships Between the Generations in the 1970s* (New York: Columbia University Press, 1978). This series of essays, written by one of America's premier anthropologists, explores the origins and the consequences of the generation gap, with special attention to Cold War politics, historical conditions, and technological transformations.

*Paperback edition available.

30 ✺ Europe Faces the Future: Hope and Uncertainty, 1968 to the Present

Toppling Communism

"Nothing Lasts Forever." This is what the sign hanging from the battered bust of the Communist dictator Joseph Stalin says in the picture. Such was the wisdom of Western women and men at the end of the twentieth century as they faced cataclysmic changes in their world. After over forty years of relative postwar stability, the year 1989 marked a period of rapid political transformation. In February, the Soviet Union withdrew its troops from an increasingly unpopular war in Afghanistan, paralleling the U.S. experience in Vietnam in the 1970s. In the spring of 1989, the Soviet people participated in elections and open debate as part of a new democratic process challenging Communist party rule. Reformers ousted by party leaders appealed directly to the electorate; one such reformer, Boris Yeltsin, dismissed as the head of the Moscow Communist party in 1987, garnered 89 percent of the popular vote in the elections for the Congress of People's Deputies. Soviet citizens looked forward to democratic reforms. Soviet leader Mikhail Gorbachev took the measure of popular opinion and channeled it by championing free enterprise, individual initiative, an open market, and the self-determination of peoples.

The apparent democratization of Soviet political

life in 1989 was matched by dramatic transformations in central and Eastern Europe among the Warsaw Pact nations that had been allied with the Soviet Union since 1955. In April, Hungarians disinterred the body of Imre Nagy, leader of the 1956 anti-Soviet uprising. He was declared a state hero and reburied with full honors. The Western world was stunned, but this was just the beginning. In June, after a number of political reversals in the 1980s, democratic rule was established in Poland. Symbols of freedom and democratic cooperation appeared everywhere in 1989. One million people joined hands to form a 370-mile-long human chain that stretched across the Soviet Baltic republics of Estonia, Latvia, and Lithuania in protest against Soviet annexation in 1940. In September 1989, East German citizens flooded into Hungary at the rate of 300 people an hour with the hope of escaping to West Germany and political and economic freedom. Soon thereafter, the German borders were opened to the free movement of people. The 35-year reign of Todor Zhivkov, dictator of Bulgaria, was ended as Bulgarians endorsed parliamentary government. In 1990 Germany was reunifed.

Throughout central and Eastern Europe, people were successfully rejecting Communist values in favor of democratic free institutions. In November 1989, Czechoslovakia embraced pluralist politics and democratic rule. Tens of thousands of Czech demonstrators in the capital city of Prague sang songs about freedom and cheered their new heroes, dissidents persecuted and jailed under the former Communist regime. Communism itself had been toppled by a mass movement reminiscent of the Prague Spring of 1968, when demands for greater freedom, national autonomy, and improved economic conditions were heard and brutally repressed.

In the illustration here, a nicked and battered bust of Stalin is being carried through the streets of Prague. Stalinism had been long dead by 1989, even within the Soviet Union, where it was criticized and buried by Stalin's successors. Yet the bust of Stalin was an easily recognizable symbol of the worst aspects of Communist rule: dictatorship, repression, and denial of individual liberties and civil rights. To the Czech people, the bust stood for communism controlled from the center by a bureaucratic elite that they were intent on overthrowing.

For many, the most dramatic moment in the collapse of communism came in November 1989 as bulldozers moved against the Berlin Wall, the tangible symbol of Cold War politics that had been erected through the center of Berlin in 1961. As the barrier came down, so too did the 18-year-old government of Communist leader Erich Honecker, who was forced to resign. The East German Communist party, confronted with popular discontent and charges of corruption, decided to change both its tune and its name.

Poland, Hungary, Bulgaria, Czechoslovakia, and East Germany all underwent what were considered to be "velvet revolutions," characterized by a lack of violence and smooth passage to a new order. The year 1989 did not end, however, without bloody upheaval. In December 1989, Nicolae Ceauşescu, Communist dictator of Romania, ordered his troops to fire on demonstrators. Thousands of men, women, and children were killed and buried unceremoniously in mass graves. The slaughter set off a revolution in which Ceauşescu and his wife and co-ruler Elena were captured, tried, and executed by a self-identified revolutionary tribunal. Their declared crimes were genocide—the slaughter of 64,000 people—and the mismanagement of the economy. In the days that followed, Romanians interviewed by the international media spoke of their newly won freedom as videotaped images of the slain leaders were broadcast to the world.

Any one of these events by itself could have commanded world attention and shocked international opinion. Combined, they spelled the end of an era. The Eastern Bloc under Soviet control was disintegrating and communism as an ideology was crumbling. No one was sure what the future held, as changes brought instability and cut central and Eastern European states free of their Soviet protector. "Nothing Lasts Forever" was a sign of the times. It reflected the optimism of hundreds of thousands of people who saw democracy, nationalism, and free markets as guarantees of a better future. Few recognized that the aphorism was a double-edged one that contained also the cynical recognition, perhaps forgotten in the euphoria of the moment, that change, even the toppling of communism, did not guarantee stability.

Ending the Cold War

The Soviet action against Czechoslovakia and other expressions of dissent in Eastern Europe in 1968 reminded the world of the power of Communist unity in the Eastern Bloc. The use of military intervention to resolve the Czech crisis opened a new era governed by what came to be known as the Brezhnev Doctrine. Leonid Brezhnev (1906–82), General Secretary of the Communist party and head of the Soviet Union from 1966 to 1982, established a policy whereby the Soviet Union claimed the right to interfere in the internal affairs of its allies in order to prevent counterrevolution. Brezhnev was responsible for the decision to intervene in Czechoslovakia, arguing that a socialist state was obliged to take action in another socialist state if the survival of socialism was at stake. The Brezhnev Doctrine influenced developments in Eastern Europe through the next decade. After 1968, rigidity and stagnation characterized the Soviet, East German, and Czechoslovak governments, as well as rule in other East European states.

With repression came protest. At first weak but growing in volume, it commanded international attention in the mid-1970s. Criticism of the Soviet Union had been strongly repressed in Eastern Bloc nations. In 1985 the accession to power of Mikhail Gorbachev as general secretary ushered in a new age of openness. A strong critique of domestic and foreign policy aims infused movements for reform throughout the Eastern Bloc, undermining communism and Cold War politics.

Soviet Dissent

In December 1989, Andrei Sakharov was buried with full state honors in the Soviet Union. Soviet president Gorbachev hailed him as a hero, "a man of conviction and sincerity." In terms of Sakharov's early career, such a description would hardly have been surprising. Much decorated as the father of the Soviet hydrogen bomb, Sakharov was a Russian scientist of great eminence. But he was also one of the leading dissidents of the Soviet Union.

During the Brezhnev years, dissent took on new forms in response to state repression. Growing numbers of Soviet Jews sought to emigrate to Israel in an attempt to escape anti-Semitism within the Soviet Union and to embrace their own cultural heritage. Some of the 178,000 who were allowed to emigrate found their way to Western Europe and the United States.

In May 1976, a number of Soviet dissidents, many of them Jewish, declared themselves united for the purpose of securing human rights. Some of the leading organizers were charged with anti-Soviet propaganda

The funeral of Andrei Sakharov. The scientist-dissenter was eulogized at a public service held in Lenin Stadium in Moscow.

and given harsh prison sentences. Outside the Soviet Union, protest against Soviet repression and violations of civil liberties began to mount.

Samizdat—the Russian word for self-published, privately circulated manuscripts—became the chief vehicle of dissident information. For the most part, dissidents came from an educated elite with professional and university training. Sakharov was joined by other figures of stature, including the novelist Alexander Solzhenitsyn and the historian Roy Medvedev. In his novels, such as *The Gulag Archipelago* and *One Day in the Life of Ivan Denisovich,* Solzhenitsyn showed the abuses of Soviet bureaucracy. For his writings he was forced into exile in the West. Medvedev criticized Stalinism and continued to speak out in favor of peace and democratic principles in the Gorbachev years.

For three decades Sakharov and other dissidents waged a lonely battle within the Soviet Union for civil liberties, democratic rights, and the end of the nuclear arms race. For his efforts, Sakharov won international acclaim abroad and was awarded the Nobel Peace Prize in 1975. But at home he was a prophet without honor. Sakharov endured internal exile for six years in the closed city of Gorki, one of Russia's great industrial cities east of Moscow, where inhabitants were not allowed freedom to enter or leave without permission and from which members of the foreign press corps were excluded. He never stopped agitating for peace and human rights. He continued his campaign against Soviet policies when he returned to Moscow in 1986.

In the few years before his death, Andrei Sakharov was reinstated as a public figure. He took his seat as a member of the Soviet Parliament. At his death, public opinion polls showed him to be the most respected individual in the Soviet Union. The changing fate of dissidents like Sakharov was one of the best barometers of the social revolution that was transforming Soviet politics in the late 1980s.

Détente: The Soviets and the West

The Nuclear Test Ban Treaty of 1963 inaugurated a period of lessening tension between the Eastern and Western Blocs. By the early 1970s, both the United States and the Soviet Union recognized the importance of a rapprochement between the superpowers. The USSR and the United States had achieved nuclear parity: from positions of equality, both sides expressed a willingness to negotiate. The 1970s became a decade of détente, a period of cooperation between the two superpowers. The Strategic Arms Limitation Treaty

(known as SALT I), signed in Moscow in 1972, limited defensive antiballistic missile systems.

The refusal in 1979 of the United States to sign SALT II to limit strategic nuclear weapons ushered in "the dangerous decade" of the 1980s, when the possibility of peaceful coexistence seemed slim. U.S. president Ronald Reagan, during his first term in office, revived traditional Cold War posturing. In many of his speeches, he pitted capitalism against communism and denounced the Soviet Union as "an evil empire." Nuclear strategists on both sides were once again talking about nuclear war as possible and winnable. Popular concern over the nuclear arms race intensified in the United States, the Soviet Union, and throughout Europe. U.S. plans for the Strategic Defense Initiative (SDI), popularly called the "Star Wars" defense system, promised an escalation in nuclear defense spending in an attempt to end the parity between the United States and the Soviet Union.

On balance, however, East-West relations after 1983 were characterized by less confrontation and more attempts at cooperation between the Soviet Union and the United States. The world political system itself appeared to have stabilized, with a diminution of conflict in the three main arenas of superpower competition—the third world, China, and Western Europe. At the end of 1989, leaders in the East and the West declared that the Cold War was over and that a new and permanent détente was now possible.

New Leadership and New Values in the Soviet State

By the mid-1980s, Soviet leaders faced the costs of increasing internal dissent and the promise of benefits from improved relations with the West. During the forty years following World War II, a new leadership was being forged in the ranks of the Communist party among a generation who favored more open political values and dynamic economic growth. Typical of the new generation of political leaders was Mikhail Gorbachev (born 1931), who was above all a technocrat, someone who could apply specialized knowledge to the problems of the Soviet economy.

Gorbachev was born on a collective farm near Stavropol, on the plains north of the Caucasus Mountains. At the age of nineteen he traversed the great social distance from the collective farm to Moscow and entered Moscow University to study law. At the unusually young age of thirty-nine, he was elected to the Central Committee; he became the Central Commit-

PERESTROIKA

In describing what he called "New Thinking for Our Country and the World" in his subtitle to his book Perestroika, *Soviet leader Mikhail Gorbachev offered a cogent explanation of the need for peaceful competition as the means of avoiding a third world war. He justifies perestroika historically by alluding to the history of war and revolution in the West since the nineteenth century.*

In developing our philosophy of peace, we have taken a new look at the interdependence of war and revolution. In the past, war often served to detonate revolution. One may recall the Paris Commune which came as an echo of the Franco-Prussian war, or the 1905 Russian Revolution triggered by the Russo-Japanese war. The First World War provoked a real revolutionary storm which culminated in the October Revolution in our country. The Second World War evoked a fresh wave of revolutions in Eastern Europe and Asia, as well as a powerful anti-colonial revolution.

All this served to reinforce the Marxist-Leninist logic that imperialism inevitably generates major armed confrontations, while the latter naturally creates a "critical mass" of social discontent and a revolutionary situation in a number of countries. Hence a forecast which was long adhered to in our ountry: a third world war, if unleashed by imperialism, would lead to new social upheavals which would finish off the capitalist system for good, and this would spell global peace.

But when the conditions radically changed so that the only result of nuclear war could be universal destruction, we drew a conclusion about the disappearance of the cause-and-effect relationship between war and revolution. The prospects of social progress "coincided" with the prospects of the prevention of nuclear war. At the 27th CPSU Congress we clearly "divorced" the revolution and war themes, excluding from the new edition of the Party Program the following two phrases: "Should the imperialist aggressors nevertheless venture to start a new world war, the peoples will no longer tolerate a system which drags them into devastating wars. They will sweep imperialism away and bury it." This provision admitting, in theory, the possibility of a new world war was removed as not corresponding to the realities of the nuclear era.

Economic, political and ideological competition between capitalist and socialist countries is inevitable. However, it can and must be kept within a framework of peaceful competition which necessarily envisages cooperation. It is up to history to judge the merits of each particular system. It will sort out everything. Let every nation decide which system and which ideology is better. Let this be decided by peaceful competition, let each system prove its ability to meet man's needs and interests. The states and peoples of the Earth are very different, and it is actually good that they are so. This is an incentive for competition. This understanding, of a dialectical unity of opposites, fits into the concept of peaceful coexistence.

From Mikhail Gorbachev, *Perestroika* (1987).

---

tee's secretary in charge of agriculture and then, in 1980, a voting member of the Politburo.

When Yuri Andropov (1914–84)—head of the KGB, the Soviet secret police controlled by the Communist party and responsible for internal intelligence-gathering and surveillance—succeeded Brezhnev as General Secretary in 1983, he recognized Gorbachev's abilities as a problem-solver. Gorbachev became Andropov's principal deputy and, following the brief regimes of Andropov and then Konstantin Chernenko (1911–85), assumed party leadership in 1985.

However, Gorbachev's story is more than simply a tale of an individual of exceptional ability and ambition making it to the top. His rise to political power was part of a general phenomenon in which social changes—urbanization, education, and increased communication—fostered the emergence of a generation of leaders committed to finding new and better ways of building Soviet prosperity. Gorbachev's life also reflects the changing outlook and experiences of an educated urban elite. Highly educated groups of professionals and managers constituted a significant 22 percent of the population by the 1980s.

In 1985, when Gorbachev came to power as Communist party General Secretary and the youngest Soviet leader since Stalin, he set in motion bold plans for increased openness, which he called *glasnost,* and a program of political and economic restructuring, which he

Mikhail Gorbachev, General Secretary of the Communist party of the Soviet Union, meets with potato farmers in the Ramanskoye District of the Moscow Region in 1987. A persistent shortage of food was one of the most recalcitrant problems of the troubled Soviet economy.

dubbed *perestroika.* Appointing men who shared his vision to key posts, especially in the foreign ministry, Gorbachev extended the olive branch to the West and met in Geneva for his first superpower summit with U.S. president Ronald Reagan. By 1989 many observers inside and outside the Soviet Union felt that a new age was at hand as the Soviet leader loosened censorship, denounced Stalin, and held the first free elections in the Soviet Union since 1917.

The Changing Soviet Economy.

The Soviet Union had undergone dramatic changes after Stalin's death in 1953, and many Stalinist policies were repudiated. The sixties were a period of increasing prosperity during which the population became more urban (180 million people lived in cities by mid-1970) and more literate (the majority of the population remains in school until the age of seventeen or eighteen). Soviet citizens of the 1960s and 1970s were better fed, better educated, and in better health than their parents and grandparents had been. When people grumbled over food shortages and long lines, the Soviet state reminded its citizens of how far they had come and told them that Soviet economic planning was not a failure. Yet while growth continued throughout the postwar years, by the 1970s the rate of growth was slowing down. Some planners feared that the Soviet Union would never catch up to the economies of the United States, Japan, and West Germany. Soviet citizens were increasingly aware of the

sacrifices and suffering that economic development had cost them in the twentieth century and of disparities between the standards of living in the capitalist and communist worlds. Outmoded technology, declining older industries, pollution, labor imbalances, critical shortages of foodstuffs and certain raw materials, and a significant amount of hidden unemployment in unproductive industries caused mounting discontent.

Consumer products were either of poor quality or unavailable. People queued an average of two hours every day to purchase food and basic supplies. Housing, when available, was inadequate, and there were long waiting lists for vacancies. The black market flourished, with high prices for everything from Western blue jeans to Soviet automobiles. People could look around them and see corruption in their ruling elite, who wore Western clothes, had access to material goods not available to the general population, and lived in luxury.

Workers were well paid, with more disposable income than ever before, and ironically that was a key to the problem. People had money to spend. In fact, purchasing power far outstripped supplies. The state system of production, which emphasized quantity over quality, resulted in overproduction of some goods and underproduction of others. The state kept prices low in order to control the cost of living, but low prices did not provide incentives for the production of better-quality goods.

The Big Mac comes to Moscow. McDonald's opened its first Soviet fast-food outlet in 1990, just a few blocks from the Kremlin. Muscovites stood in long lines for milkshakes, fries, and the "Bolshoi Mak."

Programs between 1985 and 1988 promised more than they delivered. Modest increases in output were achieved, but people's expectations regarding food and consumer goods were rising faster than they could be met. The Soviet Union did not increase imports of consumer durables or food to meet demand, nor did quality improve appreciably. Rising wages only gave workers more money that they could not or would not spend on Soviet products. The black market was a symbol, both of the economic failures of the state and of the growing consumerism of Soviet citizens. Rather than purchase poor-quality goods, Soviets purchased foreign products at vastly inflated prices.

Although his economic reforms broke sharply with the centralized economy established by Stalin in the 1930s, Gorbachev candidly warned that there would be no consumption revolution in the near future. Many critics, including Boris Yeltsin, felt that he did not go far or fast enough. In place of a controlled economy, Gorbachev proposed a limited open market free of state controls for manufacturing enterprises organized on a cooperative basis and for light industry. He loosened restrictions on foreign trade, encouraged the development of a private service sector, and decentralized economic decision-making for agriculture and the service sector.

Price increases and the importation of foreign goods, the two essential measures necessary for progress in the

Soviet consumer economy, had been resisted by Gorbachev's predecessors as politically explosive. The state kept prices down in order to maintain the low cost of living. But prices of raw materials and energy were kept so low that they discouraged increased productivity, efficiency, and quality. In both the economy and politics, Gorbachev wanted to usher in a period of change and greater freedom. In contrast to the ingrained conservatism of his predecessors, Gorbachev represented experimentation, innovation, and vitality. For him, economic and political reforms had to be accomplished in concert; the economy could only be restructured by "a democratization of our society at all levels."

Gorbachev's foreign policy also served his economic goals. Military participation in decision-making declined while state expenditures on defense were decreased. Moscow had always borne larger military costs than Washington. Gorbachev recognized that Cold War defense spending must decline if the Soviet Union was to prosper. Consumer durables had to take the place of weapons on the production lines.

The Final Crisis of Soviet Politics

From the beginning of the twentieth century, Soviet leaders had dealt with a vast array of crises: civil war, world war, collectivization, rapid industrialization, purges, and massive social dislocations. Stalin's plan-

CAREER ADVANCEMENT, COMMUNIST-STYLE

Interviewed in 1990, Klara Paramova, a Soviet lecturer who taught English language in Moscow, told of her decision to join the Communist party as a means of upward mobility. Although fluent in English and "the best pupil in the class," she realized that membership in the Party was the only way of getting the job she wanted in higher education. Her disillusionment with the tenets of communism was typical of many Soviet citizens of her generation and younger.

I'm thirty-nine and I joined the Party at twenty-four so that means fifteen years as a member in, what is the phrase, good standing—paying my dues, sometimes going to a meeting to elect a delegate to this conference or a representative for that occasion, but not much else. I'm not an active member, I don't take my share of responsibilities. Why? Well, because I am not a good Party member, as I told you. And I'm not a good Party member because I don't believe in Communism, it is as simple as that. Nor do a lot of Party members, does that surprise you? It should not. . . . Joining the Party was for me entirely a calculated way of furthering my career. It had nothing at all to do with ideals. . . .

But . . . I am still a member of the Party and I shall remain one. At its simplest it is because if I was to do something that would draw attention to me, like not continuing my membership and stepping down from it—well, then I think, almost certainly, I would lose my present job as senior lecturer. I got it because of those who were in contention for the vacancy, I was the only one who was in the Party—and from this it is correct to deduce, yes, the members of the appointments committee were nearly all themselves members of the Party. . . .

I am not a Communist, and don't believe in Communism, for the simple reason that I think it takes too rosy a view of human beings and it doesn't work. You could say I am not a Christian either, for almost the same reasons. I know there are good Communists and bad Communists, and not all the bad things done in the name of Communism are the fault of the system of itself. But I think it lacks things, and some of the things it lacks are serious. First I would put self-respect or a feeling of the value of people as individuals. I have never been to the West, but of course at the place where I work I have met a lot of people from the West—and there is something about their manner, their self-assurance, which is unlike that of Russian people. I think this can only be the fault of Communism: it may have done, it has done, many good things, but it has never somehow built up dignity in people. There are many catch-phrases, 'the dignity of labour' and such sayings; but there isn't one for the dignity of a person as a person, it's an idea which doesn't even exist.

I think I will not change in my views very much now, not at the age of forty: I think I will remain as I am, a Party member but not a good one because I don't share its beliefs.

---

ning had created a rigidly centralized bureaucracy that had proven itself incapable of meeting the consumer needs of the Soviet people in the late twentieth century. By the time Gorbachev came to power, Soviet citizens had enjoyed forty years of peace and were demanding a change from the decades of sacrifice for defense.

The Communist party, set in place as a disciplined body of cadres by Lenin, operated on the principle that power must flow from the top in order to preserve and advance the revolution. In the late 1980s, grass-roots movements responding to Gorbachev's rhetoric of reform and democracy asserted that they should have a political voice. On coming to power, Gorbachev could blame his predecessors for the Soviet Union's problems, but this defense had its limits as people began demand-

ing results. Tensions became most apparent over how Party rule and centralization could be coordinated with the demands for freedom and autonomy that Gorbachev's own reforms fostered.

To gain credibility and backing, Gorbachev supported the formation of new parliamentary bodies, including a 2250-member Congress of People's Deputies in 1988. The new Congress soon became the forum for attacks on the Communist party and the KGB. In March 1989, in the first free elections held in the Soviet Union since 1917, Communist party officials suffered further reversals. Early in 1990, Gorbachev ended the Party's constitutional monopoly of power; the Party now no longer played a leading role in Soviet political life.

Below a statue of Lenin, Mikhail Gorbachev addresses the Congress of People's Deputies in May 1989.

New parties proliferated, some defending the old order but many demanding a total break with the past and with Communist ideology and programs. Among Gorbachev's harshest critics was his former ally and supporter, the former Moscow Party leader Boris N. Yeltsin, who began in 1987 to criticize Gorbachev's caution in implementing reforms. Later, as the popularly elected president of the Russian republic in 1990, Yeltsin called for a true democracy and decisive economic action.

Aware of his precarious political position, Gorbachev appeared to retrench by increasing control over the media and by attempting to consolidate his own political position. (See "Television and Revolutions," pp. 960–961.) Many felt that the regime was becoming authoritarian. Gorbachev was clearly walking a fine line in attempting to maintain stability, yet neither Communist party hard-liners nor Western-oriented supporters of capitalism and democracy were happy.

In August 1991, the world watched in shock as a quasi-military council of hard-liners usurped power in order to restore Communist rule and reverse democratic reforms. Soviet citizens from the Baltic republics to Siberia protested the takeover, and tens of thousands of Muscovites poured into the streets to defy the tanks and troops of the rebel government. Three people were killed outside Russia's parliament building, which had become a rallying point for the protesters. Meanwhile, Gorbachev was held prisoner in his vacation home in the Crimea. The timing of the coup was probably determined by the fact that Gorbachev was scheduled to sign a new union treaty with nine of the republics the day following his house arrest.

Boris Yeltsin publicly defied the plotters, rallying popular support behind him and helping convince Soviet army troops to disobey orders to attack the White House, as the parliament building is called. After only two days, the coup d'état had failed; Gorbachev returned to Moscow and banned the Communist party. Although Gorbachev retained his title of Soviet president, his prestige had been seriously damaged by the coup and by the challenge of Yeltsin's new dominance as a popular hero.

The End of the Soviet Union

In 1979 the Soviet Union listed 102 nationalities in its census. Twenty-two of those nationalities had populations of a million or more people. Some Western observers predicted that this diversity would destroy the Soviet Union, that the Soviet empire was crumbling from within. Others wondered how Gorbachev could support the demands for self-determination in Eastern European states and deny it in the Soviet republics. For many, the nationalities problem posed the single greatest threat to Gorbachev's regime, even more challenging than the establishment of a free-market economy.

The nationalities problem in the Soviet Union was in fact shaped by the very social forces that brought Gorbachev to power. The three major areas of nationalist conflict—Central Asia, Armenia, and the Baltic states—had had grievances against the Soviet state since the 1920s. What was different about the protests of the 1980s was the emergence of a new and educated urban elite, formed after World War II, as the driving

Legend:
- Slavic
- Baltic
- Turkic
- Uralian
- Romance
- Armenian
- Caucasian
- Iranian
- Other languages or sparsely populated areas

ARCTIC OCEAN
PACIFIC OCEAN
Bering Sea
Sea of Okhotsk
Mediterranean Sea
Black Sea
Caspian Sea

Komi, Latvian, Karelian, Lithuanian, Estonian, Byelorussian, Ukrainian, Romanian, Komi, Russian, Russian, Yakut, Russian, Georgian, Armenian, Azerbaijani, Kazakh, Kazakh, Kirghiz, Tukmen, Uzbek, Tajik

Republics

1 Russia S.F.S.R.	9 Armenia
2 Estonia	10 Azerbaijan
3 Latvia	11 Kazakhstan
4 Lithuania	12 Turkmenia
5 Byelorussia	13 Uzbekistan
6 Ukraine	14 Tajikistan
7 Moldavia	15 Kirghizia
8 Georgia	

0   500   1000 Miles
0   500   1000 Kilometers

Republics of the Soviet Union

force behind nationalist reform. Moscow relied on these groups of university-educated and upwardly mobile professionals to further economic reforms. Gorbachev's challenge was to harness nationalist protest without undermining the Party's authority in favor of local organizations. The challenge before him was to make the Party responsible to these new social groups and to local needs.

Ethnic minorities—especially in the Soviet Baltic republics of Latvia, Lithuania, and Estonia—threatened the dominance of Party rule in favor of immediate self-determination. Large-scale riots erupted in Lithuania over demands for nationalist rights. Nationalist awareness was not unprecedented in the Baltic states in the 1980s, but the context of perestroika in which nationalist demands were now being voiced posed a serious challenge to Gorbachev's democratic reforms. In 1988 Estonians demanded the right of veto over any law passed in Moscow. Russians, who were a minority in Estonia, protested attacks and prejudicial treatment at the hands of Estonians.

Endorsing diversity of opinion, individual rights, and freedom as the bases of good government, Gor-

bachev now had to deal with vocal nationalist awareness in the Baltic states and the republic of Georgia and with outright violence in Azerbaijan. In 1988 tens of thousands of Armenians took to the streets to demand the return of the Armenian enclave of Nagorno-Karabakh, incorporated into Azerbaijan in 1921. In the Azerbaijan capital of Baku, the center of Russia's oil-producing region, demonstrators demanded greater autonomy for their republic and the accountability of their deputies in Moscow. Violence between Azerbaijanis and Armenians resulted in 32 deaths and the displacement of tens of thousands. The state of upheaval climaxed in December 1988 when an earthquake in Armenia killed 25,000 people. Soviet troops were placed in the area, ostensibly to deal with the aftermath of the natural disaster.

In 1986 university students in the Central Asian republic of Kazakhstan incited two days of demonstrations and rioting over the removal of a corrupt local leader who was replaced with a Russian. The Soviet government's attempt to clean up politics in the area betrayed a clumsy disregard for ethnic issues and seemed at odds with Gorbachev's commitment to

ꝏ Television and Revolutions

Television became the principal means of communicating current events to mass populations in the second half of the twentieth century. It was one of the chief consumer durables purchased by the newly prosperous populations of Europe and the United States beginning in the 1950s. Many intellectuals in the West feared that television, because of its uninspired programming, would dull the sensibilities of the masses and serve as a kind of opiate to cloud political judgment. Yet the role of television in politics was more complex, as events after 1968 made clear.

As East Germans in large numbers began buying televisions in the 1960s and 1970s, they faced a dilemma. Should they heed the prohibition of the East German government against watching West German television programs, whose signals were easily accessible to them, or should they disobey the law and take advantage of the varied entertainment that West German television afforded? East German leaders feared that the "corrupt" and "decadent" images of West Germany might attract their citizens. The East German head of state, Walter Ulbricht, warned ominously in 1961 that "the enemy of the people stands on the roof." He was talking about television antennas. However, the East German ban was impossible to enforce. Millions of East German viewers tuned in daily to West German programs and were able to compare the different standards of living in the two German nations and to learn of their own deprivation. The irony of awareness was that as East Germans achieved a higher standard of living and were able to buy more televisions, they became more and more discontented over their relatively low standard of living. Television contributed to rising expectations and the exodus of East Germans to the West.

Television played a central role in the Romanian revolution of 1989, spreading information and encouraging coordinated action throughout the country. One of the first acts of the Bucharest revolutionaries was to seize the headquarters of the state television station in order to transmit their own view of the conflict. When Nicolae and Elena Ceauşescu were executed, the event was videotaped for broadcast to the Romanian nation and the world (the photograph here shows Ceauşescu's corpse as it appeared on television). In a still heavily rural society undergoing modernization, television provided the essential link between city and countryside. Television promoted concerted action. Romanians in Timosoara, a small city near the Hungarian border, and Bucharest, the nation's capital, simultaneously espoused the same revolutionary program and adopted the same symbols, as similarly doctored national flags made clear. The new regime governed by means of the television screen.

Politicians on both the left and the right used television for political ends. The political utility of television was exploited in France, where 60 percent of the population owned TV sets in 1968. Charles de Gaulle, president of the Fifth Republic, used the medium to appeal directly to the French people against the student-worker revolt that began in Paris in May 1968. Television was decisive in maintaining de Gaulle in power and mobilizing conservatives against the activists.

No one in the late twentieth century was better at grasping the power of the televised image than the Soviet leader Mikhail Gorbachev, who from the very beginning used the small screen to appeal directly to the Soviet people. He carefully cultivated his own image and used television to build a personal power base outside of the Communist party. Gorbachev was so successful in creating his own televised publicity that he became a popular figure within the Western capitalist world as well as within Soviet Bloc countries. Crowds everywhere greeted him with the affectionate nickname "Gorby"; he was as easily recognizable in the streets of New York and Paris as in the streets of Moscow. Even the new revolutionaries in Eastern Europe, who were intent on breaking their bonds with the Soviet state and who espoused democracy and capitalism, saw in Gorbachev the guarantee of their aspirations. Romanians chanted his name in public squares as they set about pulling down the Communist regime that ruled them.

Above all, television contributed to the revolution in expectations in Communist countries in the last quarter of the twentieth century. The contrast between the quality of life in the East and the West became inescapable for many educated East European and Soviet men and women who had access to travel and to television. Modern video technology did not cause revolutions, but it did convey information and provide political platforms. Television also publicized revolutions and, in some cases, sold dreams.

Lithuanians in the capital city of Vilnius demonstrated for independence from the Soviet Union throughout the late 1980s.

decentralization. Crimean Tatars, who had been exiled in Islamic fundamentalist Kazakhstan since World War II, agitated for return home.

One by one, all fifteen of the Soviet republics proclaimed their independence, following the lead of the breakaway Baltic republics of Estonia, Lithuania, and Latvia. Having failed to agree on a new plan for union, in September 1991 Gorbachev and the leaders of ten republics transferred authority to an emergency State Council until a plan could be devised. By the end of the year, the Soviet Union was faced with serious food shortages and was bankrupt, unable to pay its employees and dependent on the financial backing provided by Yeltsin. Rejecting all Soviet authority, Russia, Belarus, and Ukraine joined together in December 1991 to form the Commonwealth of Independent

Russian president Boris Yeltsin talks to Muscovites on his way to the Kremlin on 22 September 1993. The country was in a governmental crisis after Yeltsin suspended parliament.

THE CRUMBLING
OF THE EASTERN BLOC

1972	East and West Germany normalize relations with the Basic Treaty
1980	Polish non-communist labor union Solidarity established under the leadership of Lech Walesa
1985	Mikhail Gorbachev assumes leadership of the Soviet Communist party, introducing glasnost (increased openness) and perestroika (political and economic restructuring)
1989	Free elections in Poland lead to the ouster of the Communist regime
September 1989	Hungary opens its borders to the West
November 1989	German Democratic Republic lifts travel restrictions between East and West Germany
1990	Boris Yeltsin elected president of the Russian Republic
1990	Gorbachev ends the Communist party's monopoly of power
1990	Lech Walesa elected president of Poland
October 1990	Federal Republic of Germany and German Democratic Republic reunited
December 1991	Eleven former Soviet Republics form Commonwealth of Independent States (CIS); Mikhail Gorbachev resigns and the Soviet Union is dissolved

States (CIS). Eight other republics followed their lead. The Soviet Union came to an end on 25 December 1991 with the resignation of Mikhail Gorbachev, who had become a man without a country to rule. Russian president Yeltsin moved into Gorbachev's presidential offices at the Kremlin.

Many issues remained unresolved. The new political organization did not address the endemic problems of economic hardship and left unanswered the question of who would control the former Soviet Union's vast military machine, including its nuclear arsenal. How would the strong nationalist demands for autonomy accord with the need for cooperation to establish a stable monetary policy, market economies, and effective trade networks? The Soviet Union, which had ruled as a world power for over seven decades, no longer existed, communism had been totally discredited, and the new nations of the former Soviet Union faced an uncertain future.

Eastern and Central Europe Since 1968

The dramatic upheavals in Eastern Europe in the late 1980s had been in the making for over two decades. Czechoslovakia's attempt in 1968 to strike out on a more independent path to socialism only strengthened the Soviet Union's hold on Warsaw Pact nations. The Soviet Union's use of troops had sent a clear message that it would not tolerate deviation. When the dust of tens of thousands of Soviet-led troops settled in the Czech capital of Prague, one-party rule was reestablished and a more democratic socialism based on freer markets and individual initiative had failed.

The demands for consumer goods and national autonomy voiced during the protests of 1968 were effectively quelled in the seventies by the memory of Soviet invasion, but they did not disappear. The recurrent crises over oil prices and the hardships inflicted on Eastern European consumers fanned the embers of discontent in the 1980s. Incidents of protest and resistance began to mount.

Solidarity in Poland

Poland was especially important to the Soviet Bloc, both because it was Eastern Europe's most populous country and because of its strategic location. Poland provided a corridor for supplies to the Soviet Union's 380,000 troops in East Germany. In Poland, as in Czechoslovakia, demonstrations against Soviet dominance and one-party rule by the Communists had been brutally repressed. Poland entered the 1970s economically handicapped. In December 1970, the Polish government instituted major price increases for food.

Lech Walesa, the leader of the Solidarity labor movement, was elected president of a newly independent Poland in 1990.

Workers spontaneously struck in protest, with demonstrations beginning in the shipyards of Gdansk, the Baltic seaport in northern Poland, and spreading to other cities. The Polish government responded by sending the militia to tear-gas the workers. People were killed and injured, but protest was not silenced.

Wladislaw Gomulka, who had been head of the Polish government since 1956, was replaced by Edward Gierek in hopes of improving the economic situation. More protests followed before prices were rolled back and the Soviet Union provided economic aid. Throughout the 1970s, one-party rule prevailed as workers attempted to maintain forms of permanent organization. The Polish government drew loans from abroad for investment in technology and industrial expansion. The government increased its foreign

indebtedness rather than raise prices at home. In 1976, however, Gierek could no longer avoid price increases. A new wave of spontaneous strikes erupted, forcing the government to rescind the increases.

Poland's indebtedness to the West rose from $2.5 billion in 1973 to $17 billion in 1980. Poland was sinking into the mire of ever higher interest payments that absorbed the country's export earnings. At the beginning of July 1980, the government was forced once again to raise food prices. Shipyard workers in Gdansk were ready, solidly organized in a new non-communist labor union called Solidarity under the leadership of a politically astute electrician named Lech Walesa. The union staged a sit-down strike that paralyzed the shipyards. Union committees coordinated their activities from one factory to the next and succeeded in shutting down the entire economy. The government agreed to a series of union-backed reforms known as the Gdansk Accords, which, among other measures, increased civil liberties and acknowledged Solidarity's right to exist.

Within a year Solidarity had an astounding 8 million members out of a population of 35 million. The Catholic church lent important support to those who opposed Communist rule. Dissident intellectuals also cast their lot with the organized workers in demanding reforms. General Wojciech Jaruzelski became prime minister in February 1981, but the situation of shortages did not change appreciably. Jaruzelski attempted to curb the union's demands for democratic government and participation in management by harsh measures: he declared martial law on 13 December 1981. Jaruzelski was trying to save the Polish Communist party by using the Polish military to crack down on the dissidents. The Soviet response was to do nothing. Poland was left to Polish rule. Soviet leaders knew that the size of Polish protest required a massive retaliation, which they were unwilling to undertake—especially since to do so would fly in the face of Western opinion that supported the Solidarity movement. In addition, the Soviet Union had other problems in this period: in 1979 it began a war in Afghanistan to secure Communist rule. Moscow feared that the Islamic fundamentalism at its border threatened to stir up the rapidly growing Muslim populations in six Soviet republics—Azerbaijan, Kazakhstan, Uzbekistan, Tadzhikistan, Turkmenistan, and Kirgizia.

Martial law in Poland produced military repression. Solidarity was outlawed and Walesa was jailed. The West did not lose sight of him: in 1983 the union leader was awarded the Nobel Peace Prize for his

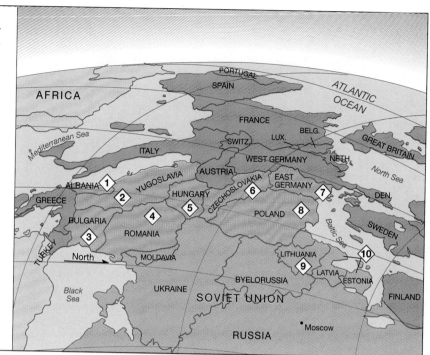

1. **Albania.** Communist party still retains Leninist orientation, Jan. 1990. Parliament backs liberal reforms, May 1990.

2. **Yugoslavia.** Government decides to hold free elections, Dec. 1989.

3. **Bulgaria.** Government disavows "dominant role" for Communist party; pledges free elections and new constitution in 1990.

4. **Romania.** Communist dictator Ceauşescu overthrown and executed, Dec. 1989; Salvation Front led by dissident former Communists wins elections, May 1990.

5. **Hungary.** Free election sweeps non-Communists into power, April 1990.

6. **Czechoslovakia.** Communist leadership ousted, Nov. 1989; Vaclav Havel named president, Dec. 1989.

7. **Germany.** Berlin Wall breached, Nov. 1989. Reunification of East and West Germany, Oct. 1990.

8. **Poland.** Solidarity party sweeps elections, June 1989.

9. **Lithuania** declares independence, March 1990; Moscow calls move illegal.

10. **Latvia and Estonia** begin process of separation from Soviet Union, April 1990.

Events in Eastern Europe, 1989–90

efforts. After years of negotiations and intermittent strikes, Solidarity was legalized once again in 1989. The economy was in dire straits, and Jaruzelski knew that he needed Solidarity's cooperation: he agreed to open elections. At the polls, Solidarity candidates soundly defeated the Communist party. Poland was the first country anywhere to turn a Communist regime out of office peacefully. Yet Poland did not pull out of the Warsaw Pact. As Lech Walesa explained it in 1989 on West German television, "Poland cannot forget where it is situated. You know we are in the Warsaw Pact. That cannot be changed." Poland needed above all its own perestroika, its own restructuring of its economy and administration.

The great challenge before the new Solidarity government, as for the Communist regime that preceded it, was economic recovery. Inflation drove food prices up at the rate of 50 percent a month. The Polish government committed itself to freeing the zloty from state control and making it a convertible currency, one that could be bought and sold for other currencies on the international currency market, so that Polish goods could compete on world markets. Poland faced the task of earning enough foreign trade credits to alleviate its indebtedness and to justify foreign investment. This was the challenge that Lech Walesa took up when he was elected president of Poland in 1990.

Emancipation in Eastern Europe

In the 1970s, Hungarians began to experiment cautiously with free markets and private control. Romania under Nicolae Ceauşescu appeared to be successful in evading its military responsibilities in the Warsaw Pact; it alone of the member states had refused to participate in the Czechoslovak intervention of 1968. The East German government tolerated the Lutheran church's criticism of the Soviet military presence in East Germany in the 1970s. The Soviets did not punish deviation, but quietly and carefully tolerated it while pursuing détente with the West.

The Soviet example and Gorbachev's calls for reforms and openness gave the lead to Eastern Europe. In 1988 Gorbachev, speaking before the United Nations, assured the West that he would not prevent Eastern European satellites from going their own way: "Freedom of choice is a universal principle," the Soviet head of state declared. Poland's first free elections in

Czech students wearing headbands proclaiming "democracy" hold a solidarity march in support of the ill-fated Chinese pro-democracy movement, which was crushed when the tanks of the Communist government rolled into Tiananmen Square in Beijing.

forty years were part of a vast mosaic of protest from which a pattern began to emerge in the spring of 1989. Hungary dismantled the barbed-wire fences on its Austrian border; all of its borders to the West were opened in September 1989. East German vacationers in Hungary poured across the frontiers, creating an international crisis. People wanted freedom of movement and freedom of expression. Everywhere East Europeans demanded democratic institutions modeled on those of Western nations. "People power" swept away Communist leaders and ousted the Communist party, many believed for good. The leader of the New Socialist party in Hungary, Imre Pozsgay, declared: "Communism does not work. We must start again at zero."

Czechoslovakia's revolution began with angry university students. Singing Czech versions of protest songs like "We Shall Overcome," student protesters were reminiscent of the student activists of 1968. They tried to give flowers to police, who responded by bludgeoning the protesters. This spark touched off a mass movement that within days drove out the Czech Communist party. Idealism and growing public sympathy were on the side of the protestors. The dissident playwright Vaclav Havel, released from jail just before the demonstrations began, emerged as the leader of the democratic opposition and was elected president of the new government.

The iceberg of communism was melting. As dictators were replaced by democrats, some observers wondered if counterrevolution was waiting in the wings, should the new capitalist experiments fail. Proto-fascist and anti-Semitic groups became more vocal in the early 1990s amidst the economic chaos. Festering ethnic differences erupted in civil war, beginning in 1991 in Yugoslavia with fighting between the Serbs and the secessionist Slovenes and Croats. Other Eastern European states were riddled with ethnic troubles, including conflicts between the Czechs and Slovaks in Czechoslovakia; the Hungarians and Romanians over the border region of Transylvania; and the Bulgarians and Turks in Bulgaria. Western nations stood helplessly by, divided in their policies for dealing with ethnic slaughter. As British prime minister Margaret Thatcher had warned earlier, when ice begins to break up, it can be very dangerous.

The Two Germanys Since 1968

The German Democratic Republic (East Germany) and the Federal Republic of Germany (West Germany) continued to develop after 1968 as two separate countries with different social, economic, and political institutions. On the surface, their differences seemed insurmountable. The Berlin Wall, erected in 1961, divided the former German capital; the Wall served its intended purpose of keeping East Germans confined behind it. German leaders in the West continued to voice their long-term commitment to reunification, while East German leaders insisted on the independence and autonomy of their state.

From the 1960s through the 1980s, East Germany underwent a series of economic transformations. Under the leadership of Walter Ulbricht (1893–1973), East Germans achieved their own version of recovery, the "other economic miracle," and overcame their severe economic handicaps after World War II. Ulbricht committed the German Democratic Republic to an economic policy in which performance was measured in terms of profits rather than quotas. Individual initiative and market incentives replaced Soviet-style central planning and bureaucratic decision-making. Ulbricht's programs were out of step with Soviet directives, though they foreshadowed the changing emphasis on local control that took place in the late 1980s in Eastern Bloc countries. By 1969 East Germany's economy was the strongest among Eastern Bloc nations and East Germans enjoyed the highest per capita output.

In spite of his economic successes, Ulbricht fell from power in 1971. An important factor in his removal was his support for rule by government bodies rather than Communist party control. Party members eagerly seized on economic reversals in 1970 to promote Moscow's disfavor with Ulbricht. In addition to his arrogance toward Soviet leaders, Ulbricht's opposition to improved relations between the Soviet Union and West Germany after 1969 gave Soviet leaders cause for complaint. Ulbricht felt that such a Soviet course of détente would only retard East Germany's chance for full recognition in the West.

Erich Honecker, who succeeded Ulbricht, had the mission of bringing the German Democratic Republic back into the fold of Soviet economic policy. Honecker rejected Ulbricht's emphasis on profitability and committed East Germany to centralized planning. By 1972 virtually all privately held businesses had been converted to state enterprises. Private enterprise was also eliminated in agriculture. Honecker's policies were not a return to Stalinism, but rather were built on an awareness of the consumer expectations of the East German population. Honecker's "consumer socialism" gave top priority to consumer goods and housing. But the oil crisis of the 1970s undermined this policy by driving up the costs of production, so dependent on foreign fuel, and thereby driving up consumer prices. Trade deficits soared and consumer industries slowed.

In West Germany, politics took a new direction in 1969. For the first time since 1930, the Social Democrats were back in power, displacing the more conservative Christian Democrats. An era of social-liberal cooperation between the leftist Social Democrats and the centrist Free Democrats began. Under the chancellorship of Social Democrat Willy Brandt, the new government promised to make the welfare state more responsive to social needs, to involve labor more directly in economic decision-making, and to attend to feminist demands regarding abortion, divorce, and pornography.

Brandt was equally committed to changes in foreign policy. From the first, he set out to improve relations with Eastern Europe and the Soviet Union. Repudiating the policy that refused recognition to any Eastern European country having diplomatic relations with East Germany, West Germany established trade missions in Poland, Hungary, Bulgaria, and Romania—everywhere in Eastern Europe except Albania.

While maintaining West Germany's commitment to NATO and Western European integration, Brandt pursued a new cooperation with the Soviet Union through a nonaggression pact. Negotiated in 1970, the pact renounced territorial claims and the use of force. A treaty with Poland accepted the status quo of existing borders in return for Polish exit visas for ethnic Germans. In a dramatic gesture of reconciliation, Brandt traveled to Warsaw and knelt before a memorial to Jewish victims of Nazi atrocities in World War II. Still without the official recognition of East Germany, West Germany agreed to normalized relations in 1972 in the Basic Treaty, which permitted West German citizens easier movement to visit relatives in East Germany. In 1973 both Germanys successfully applied for membership in the United Nations.

Willy Brandt captured international acclaim with his bold foreign policy of *Ostpolitik,* the establishment of cooperative politics with the East, for which he was awarded the Nobel Peace Prize in 1971. Brandt reminded Germans that they could once again be proud of their country. *Ostpolitik* was a clear break with superpower hegemony, as Brandt, in his own version of détente, seized the initiative without waiting for directions from the United States. At home, however, he was not always a hero: his domestic policies underwent reversals and the fabric of the social-liberal coalition began to fray. The 1973 oil crisis brought about rising unemployment and a decline in consumer demand. Shrinking tax revenues undermined Brandt's plans to expand the welfare state. Expenditures on existing state programs placed a heavy burden on the state's budget and contributed to the highest inflation rate in West Germany since 1948.

Added to these challenges at home was an espionage scandal in which a close aide of Chancellor Brandt's was discovered to be an East German spy. Cold War paranoia flared. Brandt resigned in 1974 and was succeeded by Social Democrat Helmut Schmidt, who continued Brandt's policies of rapprochement with the East. In 1981 Honecker, head of the East German state, and Schmidt, head of the West German state, sat down together to discuss common concerns. Bonn and East Berlin were engaging in their own détente.

When he came to power in 1974, Schmidt found that he had inherited a recession that became more severe over the next year. Necessary compromises with the Free Democrats in the 1970s produced growing dissension within the Social Democratic party and eroded Schmidt's support as chancellor. Taking advantage of the split between the Free Democrats and the Social Democrats and growing concern over the economic situation, the Christian Democrats displaced the Social Democrats with their candidate, Helmut Kohl, in 1982. Kohl stressed the importance of individual enterprise and competition and ran a winning campaign with the slogan "Less State, More Market."

Germany Reunified

East and West Germany were linked economically, if not politically, throughout most of the postwar period. When the Federal Republic of Germany entered the European Community in 1957, it insisted that in matters related to trade, the two Germanys were to be treated as one country. As a result, the German Democratic Republic benefited from its free-trade relationship with West Germany. This advantage provided an important part of East Germany's prosperity from the 1960s on. West Germany, in turn, achieved much of its prosperity through export-led growth, and it found markets in the German Democratic Republic.

In the 1980s, West Germany stood as an economic giant, second only to the United States in foreign trade and far ahead of Japan. With its economic opportunities and advanced social welfare programs, West Germany exerted considerable attraction for East Germans. East Germany, too, established itself as an important trading nation—fifteenth in the world in 1975. East Germany's number one problem in the 1950s was the exodus of skilled workers and professionals in search of a better life in the West. The flow of emigration throughout the 1950s turned into a torrent

"There Are No Better-Fed Refugees"

East Germany built the strongest economy in the Soviet Bloc, but its standard of living lagged far behind that of West Germany.

Federal Republic of Germany (West)	**German Democratic Republic (East)**
Population	
61 million	17 million
Life Expectancy	
For men, 71.2 years; for women, 78.1 years	For men, 69.5 years; for women, 75.4 years
Gross National Product	
$1.12 trillion	$207.2 billion
Public Spending on Education	
9.4% of all government expenditures	5.5% of all government expenditures
New Books Published	
50,903 volumes	5,636 volumes

Source: Statistical Yearbook, Unesco 1988; Demographic Yearbook, United Nations; CIA World Factbook, 1988

in the first eight months of 1961, when the number of refugees fleeing from East to West Germany reached 160,000 people. The Berlin Wall was, more than anything else, an effort to keep the labor force, so expensive to train and so necessary for economic recovery, in the German Democratic Republic.

Applications for authorized immigration increased in the 1980s, and in 1984 East Germany allowed 30,000 citizens to emigrate to the West. Throughout the late 1980s the emigration rate remained high, with an average exodus of 20,000 a year. With Hungary's refusal to continue to block the passage of East Germans into West Germany, the floodgates were opened. Within a matter of weeks, 57,000 East Germans had migrated. In the face of angry demonstrations, Honecker was forced to resign. The new government opened the Berlin Wall on 9 November 1989, ending all restrictions on travel between East and West. An East Germany with open borders could no longer survive as its citizens poured into the promised land of the West in record numbers. The Federal Republic intervened to assist East Germany in shoring up its badly faltering economy; the West German deutsche mark

In a scene that symbolizes the end of the Cold War, people dance atop the Berlin Wall in November 1989. Soon pieces of the demolished wall were being sold as souvenirs.

was substituted for East German currency. Monetary union prefigured political unification. In October 1990, Germany became a single united nation once again.

Germans represent the largest nationality in Europe west of Russia. Other Europeans, particularly the French, feared the prospect of a united Germany, though publicly they endorsed the principle of the self-determination of peoples. In addition, Western Europeans were troubled by the impact a united Germany might have on plans for European unification in the European Community. Not least of all, Germans themselves feared their new identity as citizens of a single nation: former East Germans were wary about marginalization and second-class citizenship, while those in the West worried that their poor cousins from the East would be a brake on the sustained economic expansion that had made West Germany one of the world's leading export economies.

Unity and Diversity in Western Europe

The protest and repression of 1968 in Eastern Europe sent a negative message to Western European Communists, who were intent on adopting a more liberal and cooperative stance with both parliamentary institutions and capitalism. By the end of the 1960s the fate of Communist parties in the West appeared uncertain. The events of the Prague Spring catalyzed a new kind of communism, dubbed Eurocommunism, among Western European Communist parties in the 1970s.

Western European nations had met the challenges of wartime devastation with miraculous economic recoveries in the 1950s and 1960s. A key component in achieving growth was the availability to Western European economies of a floating labor pool of work-

Reunified Germany, October 1990

ers from southern Europe and from former colonies in Asia and Africa. The phenomenal growth and prosperity of Western Europe came up against a new set of harsh realities in the 1970s with skyrocketing oil prices, inflation, and recession. The permanent presence of foreign workers, many of them unemployed or erratically employed during the economic downturns of the 1970s and 1980s, came to be seen as a problem by welfare-state leaders and politicians of the New Right. Europe's new working class became the brunt of racist antagonism.

With the goal of reviving the economy, in the 1980s the twelve member states of the European Economic Community devoted themselves to making Western Europe competitive as a bloc in world markets. At the same time that Russian satellites in Eastern Europe were breaking free of Soviet control and attempting to strike out on their own, the nations of Western Europe were negotiating a new unity based on a single market and centralized policy-making.

Eurocommunism

Divisions among the Left excluded the Western European Communists from wielding political power in the early 1970s. Then, in 1973, the international politics

of oil prices provoked an economic crisis, followed by a recession. The Organization of Petroleum Exporting Countries (OPEC) raised prices and cut back production. Western European countries depended heavily on imported oil, which they used to fuel their prosperity through the early 1970s. Poor Soviet economic performance in the postwar era offered no model for action, especially for dealing with Western economies after 1973. European Communists decided to cooperate with other leftists and moderates in a new electoral politics.

The Italian Communist party, the largest in Europe, led the way under the leadership of Enrico Berlinguer, who became the spearhead for Eurocommunism in Western Europe. Eurocommunism, a designation resisted by its practitioners, was a response to the dual influences of democratic institutions and Western economies that combined free enterprise and state control. It was above all a recognition that revolution was not likely—at least in the near future—in Western Europe. Eurocommunists accepted the European Community and membership in NATO. After 1973, Communists, first in Italy and then in Spain and France, moved from a position of opposition to partnership with liberal and left-wing reformers. With the move, Communists became Eurocommunists, rejecting unquestioned allegiance to Soviet policies and trying to become a mainstream electoral party.

In Spain, the death of General Francisco Franco in November 1975 ended the authoritarian regime set in place in the 1930s. The Spanish Communist party was granted legal status in 1977 and its leader, Santiago Carrillo, returned from exile in France to establish a Spanish version of Eurocommunism under a constitutional monarchy headed by King Juan Carlos. Moderates prevailed, with reformist Socialists coming to power in 1982.

Eurocommunism also helped to bring a Socialist president to power in France in 1981. The French Communist party had maintained its loyalty to Moscow longer than had its counterparts in Italy and Spain. Conservatives had controlled French politics since 1958, when Charles de Gaulle became president of the Fifth Republic. De Gaulle's successors, Georges Pompidou and Valéry Giscard d'Estaing, made it clear to the Left that they needed to cooperate with each other if they were to wrest power from the conservatives. In the late 1970s, the Communist party threw in its lot with the French Socialists, and their coalition resulted in the election of Socialist François Mitterrand as president. Yet at the moment of victory, the Communist party was in decline and a reformist Left was taking its place in electoral politics.

Eurocommunism's influence diminished in the 1980s as moderate politics maintained its appeal to voters. Eurocommunism had been a creative attempt to meet the challenge of preserving socialist goals in capitalist democracies. It paralleled attempts at democratic reforms in Czechoslovakia and Poland in the 1960s, except that the Eastern Bloc revisionists were met with repression and control rather than with electoral failures. Eurocommunism's attempt at adaptation actually marked the demise of communism's appeal in Western Europe. By criticizing Soviet actions, Western Communists had abandoned their self-imposed isolation within Western democracies. There appeared to be no turning back. But either in isolation or in cooperation, it appeared that the power of Western European Communist parties was on the decline.

A New Working Class: Foreign Workers

Foreign workers played an important role in the industrial expansion of Western Europe beginning in the 1950s. Western European nations needed cheap unskilled laborers. Great Britain, France, and West Germany were the chief labor-importing countries; their economic growth in the fifties and sixties had been made possible by readily available pools of cheap foreign labor. The chief labor-exporting countries included Portugal, Turkey, Algeria, Italy, and Spain, whose sluggish economic performance spurred workers to seek employment opportunities beyond national borders. Great Britain imported workers from the West Indies, Ireland, India, Pakistan, Africa, and southern Europe. Migrant employment was by definition poorly paid unskilled or semiskilled manual work. Italian workers in West Germany, for example, commonly worked factory night shifts that German workers refused. France employed a high number of foreign laborers in agriculture, public works, commerce, and engineering. Foreign male workers found employment on construction sites all over Western Europe. Foreign women worked in domestic service, personal care, and factories.

Commonly, married men migrated without their families with the goal of earning cash to send home to those left behind. Switzerland actually discouraged family migration with restrictions on income and housing. Nevertheless, prosperous and underpopulated Switzerland had Europe's highest percentage of foreign workers—16 percent of the total Swiss population in 1975. The inability of people to put down roots, however, hampered assimilation among this sizable percentage of foreign workers.

Most immigrants who came looking for jobs carried with them the "myth of return," the belief that they

Indian immigrants in France sewing in a sweatshop. Immigrant workers in European countries took low-paying menial jobs. They faced resentment from xenophobic native Europeans.

Demonstrating German youths give the neo-Nazi salute in a chilling reminder of the Hitler era.

would someday go back home. For the most part, however, foreign workers stayed in the host country. Irish workers were alone in following the pattern of return to the home country.

The lot of foreign workers was difficult and sometimes dangerous. Onerous and demanding labor was common. Foreign workers were often herded together in crowded living quarters, socially marginalized, and identified with the degrading work they performed. Street cleaning and refuse collection in France were jobs typically performed by black Africans. Foreign workers were frequently denied the rights of citizenship and subjected to the vagaries of legislation. In economic downturns they were the first to be laid off. Yet the obligations of foreign workers to send money back home to aged parents, spouses, children, and siblings persisted. The children who resided in the host country with their foreign-worker parents could suffer from severe identity problems, experiencing discrimination in schools in the countries in which they were born and with which they identified. A rising incidence of violence among second-generation Algerian adolescents in France, for example, indicated tensions and a new kind of rebellion among migrant populations in the 1970s and 1980s. Third and fourth generations of foreign workers born on West German soil were refused the rights of citizenship and denied the possibility of naturalization.

Women endured special problems within the foreign work force. Between 1964 and 1974, the majority of Portuguese immigrants to France came with families, but there was little in the way of social services to support them on their arrival. Dependable child care was either too expensive or unavailable to female workers with children. Increasing numbers of single women began migrating to Western Europe independently of their households. Like men, they worked in order to send money back home. Often housed in dormitories provided by their employers, Spanish and Portuguese women factory workers in Germany and France were isolated from the communities of their compatriots.

Opposition to the presence of foreign workers was often expressed in an ultranationalist rhetoric and usually flared up in periods of economic reversals. Right-wing politicians sometimes complained that foreign workers deprived native workers of jobs. This argument seemed baseless, since many of the jobs filled by migrants were spurned by native workers as too menial, too poorly paid, or too physically demanding. Opposition to foreign workers nonetheless became virulent. In 1986 in France, the xenophobic National Front campaigned on a platform of "France for the French" and captured 10 percent of the vote in national elections. Racism was out in the open in Western countries that had depended on a foreign labor force for their prosperity. Arab and black African workers in France resort-

THE RETURN OF FASCISM?

In the following two excerpts from the New York Times (2 December 1992), neo-Nazi attacks in Germany by gangs of skinheads gave rise to renewed fears about the resurgence of racism in Europe. Attacks on foreigners—gypsies, Cambodians, Turks, and other ethnic groups—are not unique to Germany in the last decade of the twentieth century. With renewed emphasis on nationalism, extremist groups have designated enemies based on racist terms throughout central, Eastern, and Western Europe.

MUSIC OF HATE RAISES THE VOLUME IN GERMANY

Were it not for the lyrics, it might be just another teen-age rock show. But this is a concert in Zwickau, in eastern Germany, by Störkraft, a Düsseldorf-based skinhead band whose name means "destructive force." They are performing hits like their 1990 song "Kraft für Deutschland," or "Strength for Germany," and the lead singer, Jörg Petrisch, howls the words:

> We fight shaved, our fists are hard as steel,
> Our heart beats true for our Fatherland.
> Whatever may happen, we will never leave you,
> We will stand true for our Germany,
> Because we are the strength for Germany,
> That makes Germany clean.
> *Germany awake!*

"Germany awake!" is a slogan the Nazis used during their rise to power in the early 1930's. When the concert ends, the audience of about 1,000 young people begins chanting "Sieg Heil." Some give the stiff-armed Fascist salute. Several young men unfurl a black-white-and-red Third Reich battle flag emblazoned with the swastika.

TWO GERMANS ADMIT ARSON ATTACK THAT KILLED THREE TURKISH NATIONALS

BERLIN, Dec. 1 (AP)—German officials said today that two men arrested in connection with the firebombing that killed a Turkish grandmother and two girls had confessed to their part in the attack, the country's worst case of neo-Nazi violence.

The two right-wing radicals have been charged with murder, attempted murder and arson after confessing to the attack on November 23 in the northern town of Mölln, Alexander von Stahl, the chief federal prosecutor, said.

Moving to counter a wave of violence by right-wing groups, officials have banned a neo-Nazi political party and expanded federal antiterrorist operations over the last week.

Justice Minister Sabine Leutheusser-Schnarrenberger said in Bonn today that dozens of neo-Nazi and skinhead hate-music bands would be investigated under the new ban. Critics say that the bands' racist lyrics, set to a derivative of punk and metal music, may have inspired some attacks.

Rightists have made nearly 1,800 attacks that have killed 16 people in Germany this year.

Officials are worried that the violence is hurting Germany's image abroad and could harm the export-dependent economy, leading to boycotts of German products or declining foreign investment.

In a statement issued in Cologne today, the Federation of German Industries said the world must know that "Germany is not an anti-foreigner country."

In the Mölln firebombing case, Lars Christiansen, 19 years old, and Michael Peters, 25, confessed to carrying out two bombings on houses where Turks lived, Mr. von Stahl said.

After each attack, the prosecutor said, Mr. Peters called the police from a telephone booth to claim responsibility, closing each call by shouting "Heil Hitler!"

---

ed to work stoppages to protest police discrimination and identity controls that they likened to the yellow Stars of David that Jews had been required to wear in Nazi Germany. Riots in Great Britain in 1980 and 1981, particularly in the London ghetto of Brixton, were motivated by racial discrimination against blacks,

severe cuts in social welfare spending, and deteriorating working conditions.

Before 1973 most countries in Western Europe, including Great Britain, had actively encouraged foreign labor. After that date, restrictions became the order of the day. It is no coincidence that restrictions on foreign labor followed the 1973 oil crisis. Western governments enforced new conservative policies throughout the 1970s and 1980s aimed at keeping out third world refugees. Exceptions were made for political refugees from Eastern Europe. Racial considerations lay beneath the surface of discussions about political asylum. In 1989 the British government sent back to Vietnam the "boat people" who had escaped to Hong Kong in search of a better life. Britain earned the condemnation of other Western governments and humanitarian groups for its refusal to provide a haven for Asian refugees, many of whom were children.

On the whole, restrictions failed to achieve what they set out to do—remove foreign workers from Western countries by repatriation. Foreign workers in West Germany learned to get around the restrictions and sent for their families to join them. British laws also had the effect of converting temporary migration by single men into permanent family migration, actually increasing the total annual rate of immigration. In 1974 the French government halted immigration altogether. The state withdrew subsidies from businesses employing large numbers of foreign workers and instituted police identity checks two years later. In 1977 foreign workers were offered cash incentives to encourage them to return to their home countries, but to little avail. Governments refused to acknowledge the reality of the plight of foreign workers.

By the end of the 1970s, there were 10 million foreign workers settled in Europe. Their presence heightened racism and overt antagonism from a resurgent extreme Right. At the moment in the late 1980s when movements for democratic freedom and human rights were being endorsed in Eastern Europe, the problem of permanent resident "aliens" was without a solution in Western Europe. Those who advocated extreme measures of removal seemed to be gaining ground in European states.

Women's Changing Lives

During the last quarter of the twentieth century, the lives of Western women reflected dramatic social changes. Women were more educated than ever before. Access to institutions of higher learning and professional schools had allowed women to participate in the work force in the areas of education, law, medicine, and business throughout the world, whether in France, the United States, or the Soviet Union. Women had been active in calling for the liberation of peoples in the 1960s. These activities served to heighten women's collective awareness of the disparities between their own situations and those of men in Western societies: women worked at home without pay; in the workplace women received less than men for the same work.

In this period of increased educational and work opportunities, an international women's movement emerged. International conferences about issues related to women were media events in the 1970s. In 1975 the United Nations Conference on the Decade for Women was convened in Mexico City. Women activists felt that something more was needed than this conference, which was accused of seeking only to integrate women into existing social structures dominated by men. On 8 March 1976—International Women's Day—the International Tribunal of Crimes Against Women was convened in Brussels.

Modeling the conference on tribunals like the Nuremberg Commission, which dealt with Nazi atrocities in World War II, the feminists who convened in Brussels concentrated on crimes against women for the purpose of promoting greater political awareness and action. Fertility and sexuality were at the center of the new politics of the women's movement, justified in the slogan "The personal is political." Rape and abortion were problems of international concern. "Sisterhood Is Powerful!" gave way to a new organizing slogan, "International Sisterhood is *More* powerful!"

In Italy, political action by women yielded a new law in 1970 that allowed divorce under very restricted circumstances. Italian feminists used the legal system as a public forum. In France, the sale of contraceptives was legalized in 1968. French feminists, like their Italian counterparts, worked through the courts to make abortion legal: they achieved their goal in 1975. Important in the victory were two manifestos: one signed in 1971 by 343 French women, many of them prominent, who acknowledged having had an abortion; the other signed in 1975 by 345 French doctors who acknowledged having performed abortions. Widespread opposition from religious and conservative groups did not reverse the legal gains.

The feminist movement also created a new feminist scholarship that sought to incorporate women's experiences and perspectives into the disciplines of the humanities and the social sciences. Women's studies courses, which emphasized the history of women and their contributions to civilization, became part of university and college curricula throughout Europe and the United States. Reformers also attempted to transform language, which, they argued, had served as a tool of oppression.

French women demonstrate for the right to contraception and abortion. The sign says, "A baby, no baby, ten babies if I wish."

In addition to promoting political action throughout Europe, issues of domestic violence, incest, and heterosexuality entered the political arena. In 1970 Western feminism was discovering that "socialism was not enough," and that women had to address problems of discrimination in terms of gender as much as class. As two French feminists explained it in 1974: "If we maintain that our sex unites us across all class differences because we are oppressed as women, regardless of class, race, and age, then even those men who serve the revolution start to react violently and brutally against us. Since we conceive of ourselves as an oppressed sex, we naturally resist those who oppress us." This was a declaration of war between the sexes. In its most radical form, lesbian separatism meant a total rejection of men

as enemies. Separatists provoked a rift in the women's movement.

Feminists continued to be politically active in the 1970s and 1980s in the peace movement, in antinuclear protests, and in ecological groups concerned with protecting the environment. As Petra Kelly, the West German leader of the Green party, an ecological and pacifist coalition, described it: "Women all over the world are rising up, infusing the antinuclear, peace, and alternative movements with a vitality and creativity never seen before."

The women's movement recognized that women in socialist and capitalist countries alike shared similar problems. Increasingly, well-educated Soviet women demanded reforms, and the beginnings of a women's protest literature in the 1970s indicated an awakening concern for women's issues. Soviet women enjoyed more representation in parliamentary bodies than women in the West. More than half of the 2.3 million deputies to the local Soviets in the 1980s were women. One-third of the 1500 members of the Supreme Soviet were women. Gorbachev appointed a woman as one of the twelve Central Committee secretaries—the most politically influential people in the country. In spite of greater participation, women enjoyed little real authority in the higher echelons of political life and most Soviet women rejected feminism as a political movement.

The same pattern held true for women in the work force. Over 85 percent of Soviet women worked, compared to about 60 percent of women in the West. Although 70 percent of doctors and 73 percent of teachers were women, women held few positions of authority. Both their pay and status were lower than men's, as the example of primary school teaching reveals: 80 percent of primary school teachers were women, two out of three head teachers were men.

Unlike Western women, many Soviet women—two out of three on average, according to censuses in the 1970s—performed heavy manual labor. Older women, for example, still chopped ice from Soviet streets. This practice had begun forty years earlier, because of the heavy losses of men in World War II—15 million had died in the war. In her doctoral dissertation on the sociology of the rural village of Stavropol, Raisa Gorbachev, wife of the Soviet leader, argued that while men were trained to run machines and tractors, women were expected more and more to perform the heavy physical labor associated with farm work.

Birthrates fell in the Soviet Union as in Western countries; women were bearing fewer children. Technology had made controlled fertility possible in safer, more dependable ways, but most birth control devices remained unavailable to Soviet women, and what was available was often unreliable. Abortion continued to be a common form of birth control in the Soviet Union, with two abortions for every live birth. Women were also choosing to have their children later, often because of work and financial considerations, with a growing percentage delaying childbearing until their thirties. Women complained of lack of quality in maternity hospital care. As one young mother explained, "The only experience worse than an abortion is having a baby in a Soviet hospital."

In the late 1980s, Soviet president Mikhail Gorbachev made direct appeals for women's support by promising preschool nurseries and kindergartens for every child. Gorbachev also committed himself to supporting increased sick leave for mothers of sick children, paid maternity leave for a period of eighteen months, increased child-care allowances, and shorter workdays for women who worked at home. In support of women's voice in the workplace, women's councils were to be revived.

Women's work experience in the East and the West varied in degree, but a startlingly similar pattern of home and work life prevailed in the late twentieth century. Neither state institutions nor the law met the needs of women.

Terrorism and Contemporary Society

Terrorism persisted as a force of political violence in the second half of the twentieth century. The creation of the state of Israel in part of the land of Palestine in 1948 led to conflict between the Israelis and the Palestinian Arabs, who refused to accept the new Jewish state. Israel's Arab neighbors went to war to support the Palestinians but were defeated by Israel in late 1948. Hundreds of thousands of Palestinians became refugees in neighboring Arab states, and Palestinian guerrillas decided that the best way to attack Israel and its protectors was with a global strategy of terrorist violence.

The first Palestinian highjacking took place in the summer of 1968. Ejected from Jordan, Palestinian guerrillas set up their headquarters in Syria and Lebanon in order to continue their terrorist activities. By the late 1970s, terrorism had become a tool of European revolutionaries and its use had intensified with political killings in Western Europe. A small group of left-wing radicals known as the Red Army Faction executed key industrial, financial, and judicial leaders in West Germany. The Red Army Faction was also responsible for a number of bombings, including that of the West German embassy in Stockholm. In Italy, a small group known as the Red Brigades, which claimed to represent the masses, was responsible for violent incidents, including the "kneecapping"—that is, crippling people by shooting them in the knees—of leading Italian businessmen and the kidnapping and murder of the former Italian prime minister Aldo Moro. In 1981 the Red Brigades targeted the United States for their terrorist reprisals when they abducted an American general, James Dozier.

Terrorism was heir to an anarchist tradition in Western society. Anarchism in nineteenth-century Europe fought against the rise of the state and in favor of an older way of life that existed before central control and industrialization. Anarchism was also a tool of oppressed nationalist minorities. The assassination of the Archduke Ferdinand in 1914 was the single most consequential act of an anarchist-nationalist—it started World War I. Although modern-day terrorists did not agree on a unified political program, they were alike in their desperation, as evidenced by graffiti scrawled on the wall of a French university in the late 1970s: "Hope betrayed arrays itself in bombs." Terrorists lacked access to channels of peaceful change and shared a utopian vision of a better world that could be achieved only by the use of violence for political ends. Groups as disparate as the Provisional Wing of the Irish Republican Army (IRA), the West German Baader-Meinhof gang, and the Palestine Liberation Organization (PLO) shared these common features.

An ancient Chinese proverb captures terrorism's strategic rationale: "Kill one, frighten ten thousand." Terrorism meant politically motivated violence performed by groups claiming to represent some greater political cause. Victims were targeted by terrorists not because they merited any punishment themselves but as a means of attracting international attention to the terrorists' cause. Victims—whether American tourists or German capitalists—were considered symbols of a greater oppression.

Western Europe served as an important arena for terrorist acts. In order to succeed—that is, to terrify—terrorism had to be publicized: terrorists relied on media exposure and claimed responsibility for their acts after they had been successfully completed. In Septem-

A hooded Arab terrorist stands on a balcony during the attack on the Israeli Olympic team headquarters at the Munich Olympics in 1972.

ber 1972, members of the Palestinian Black September movement kidnapped eleven Israeli athletes at the Olympic Games in Munich. An estimated 500 million people watched in horror as all eleven were slaughtered during an American sports broadcast. In a dramatic televised shoot-out, five of the terrorists also died. Later in the decade, OPEC oil ministers were held hostage in Vienna.

A recurrent pattern of terrorism prevailed throughout the 1980s, highlighted by international media coverage. In 1981 a Turkish fascist attempted to kill the pope. In 1983 a Lebanese Shiite guerrilla blew up the American garrison in Beirut, taking hundreds of American lives along with his own. In October 1985, the cruise ship *Achille Lauro* was highjacked by a Palestinian ultranationalist group. One aged American passenger, confined to a wheelchair, was killed. In 1985 Palestinian terrorists bombed the airports in Vienna and Rome. All of these highly publicized acts of violence were part of a larger pattern of terrorism throughout the 1980s.

The Provisional Wing of the IRA justified its bombing of Christmas crowds in London with the need to unite Northern Ireland with the independent Irish Republic. Like the Provisional Wing of the IRA and the Palestine Liberation Organization, many terrorists saw themselves as representing nationalist liberation movements: "One man's freedom fighter is another man's terrorist." Resistance fighters in World War II had used bombs and assassinations as their means of fighting a more powerful enemy. Seeing themselves engaged in wars of liberation, revolution, and resistance, terrorists argued that they used the only weapons at their disposal against the great imperialist powers. Plastic explosives in suitcases, nearly impossible to detect by available technology in the 1980s, became the weapon of choice. If all was fair in war—and World War II demonstrated that both sides had bombed innocent civilian victims in pursuit of victory—then, terrorists countered, they were fighting the war with the only weapons and in the only arena at their disposal.

Terrorism was not a single movement but a variety of groups and organizations on both the left and the right. Some organizations were Marxist, as was the Popular Front for the Liberation of Palestine (PFLP); some were nationalist, as was the PLO. All defined the enemy as an imperialist and a colonizer. Western capitalist nations, especially the United States and Israel,

The crash site at Lockerbie, Scotland, where a terrorist bomb brought down an airliner, killing all on board. Many people on the ground were also killed.

were common targets of terrorist attacks. Terrorists all shared a utopian vision of the world based on the commonly held belief that the destruction of the existing order was the only way of bringing about a more equitable system. The Japanese Red Army, in support of the PLFP, massacred 24 passengers at Lod Airport in Israel in 1972.

By 1990 terrorism challenged the tranquility of Western capitalist nations in effective ways. One reason for terrorism's success was the vulnerability of advanced industrial societies to random terror. Modern terrorists were able to evade police detection. Surveillance had not prevented terrorists from striking at airplanes and cruise ships. In December 1988 hundreds of people died when a Pan American flight was bombed over Lockerbie, Scotland, probably in retaliation for the accidental downing of an Iranian passenger airliner by the U.S. Navy in the Persian Gulf. Yet terrorism accomplished little by way of bringing about political change or solutions to problems like the question of a Palestinian homeland in the Middle East.

Western European governments often refused to bargain with terrorists. Yet at times European nations have been willing to negotiate for the release of kid-

napped citizens. They have also been willing to use violence themselves against terrorists. Israel led the way in creating antiterror squads. In 1976 Israeli commandos succeeded in freeing captives in Entebbe in Uganda. The following year, specially trained West German troops freed Lufthansa passengers and crew held hostage at Mogadishu in Somalia, on the east coast of Africa. The Arab kidnappers had hoped to bargain for the release of the imprisoned leaders of the Red Army Faction; the West German government refused. In 1986 the United States bombed Libya, long recognized as a training ground for international terrorist recruits, in retaliation for the bombing of a discotheque frequented by American service personnel in West Germany. Israel bombed refugee camps to retaliate against Palestinian nationalists. The goal of this "counter-terrorism" was the undermining of support for terrorists among their own people, which made it very similar in tactics and ends to the terrorism it was opposing.

Toward a Single European Community

In 1957 the founders of the European Economic Community, Robert Schuman and Jean Monnet, envisioned the idea of a United States of Europe. Both men perceived that Europe's only hope of competing in a new world system was through unity. The European Community had been created in 1967 by merging the three transnational European bodies—the European Coal and Steel Community, the European Economic Community, and the European Atomic Energy Community. It operated with its own commission, parliament, and council of ministers, though it had little real power over the operations of member states. In 1974 a "European Council" was created within the European Community, made up of heads of government who met three times a year. Almost since its inception, the European Community has been committed to European integration.

The oil crisis of the 1970s encouraged isolationism among the members of the EEC and eroded foreign markets, causing growing dependence on national suppliers and thereby undercutting the goals of the Common Market. As the crisis abated, competition and efficiency reemerged as priorities within the European Community. Europeans were well aware that the United States and Japan had surged ahead after the 1973 crisis. They also recognized that the Common Market had been successful in promoting European growth and integration since 1958. They now realized that

integration was the only defense against the permanent loss of markets and dwindling profits. In unity there was strength, as the aggregate economic indicators for 1987 made clear.

In 1985 the European Community negotiated the Single European Act, which by 1987 had been ratified by the parliamentary bodies of all the member nations. Final steps were initiated to establish a fully integrated market by 31 December 1992. The twelve members of the European Community intended to eliminate internal barriers and to create a huge open market among the member states with common external tariff policies. In addition, the elimination of internal frontier controls with a single-format European Community passport was intended to make travel easier and to avoid shipping delays at frontiers, thereby lowering costs. An international labor market based on standardized requirements for certification and interchangeable job qualifications would result. The easier movement of capital to areas where profitability was greatest was encouraged. All aspects of trade and communication, down to electrical plugs and sockets, had to be standardized. The goal behind the planning was to make the European Community think and act as a single country. Supporters compared it to the fifty individual American states participating in one nation.

Citizens of France attend a rally in support of the treaty on European economic and political union, which came out of the Maastricht Conference. French voters approved the treaty by a narrow margin.

Europe 1994

In 1989 there were 320 million European citizens of the twelve countries of the European Community: the original Common Market six of France, West Germany, Belgium, the Netherlands, Luxembourg, and Italy were joined by Britain, Denmark, and Ireland in 1973, Greece in 1981, and Portugal and Spain in 1986.

Plans for European economic integration moved dramatically forward in October 1991 when the twelve-nation European Community and the seven nations of the European Free Trade Association (EFTA) joined forces to form a new common market to be known as the European Economic Area. The EFTA countries that joined forces with the EC include Austria, Finland, Iceland, Liechtenstein, Norway, Sweden, and Switzerland. Several of the EFTA nations announced plans to join the EC as well. The European Economic Area constituted the world's largest trading bloc, stretching from the Arctic Circle to the Mediterranean and consisting of about 380 million consumers. The nations of the EFTA agreed to abide by the EC's plans for economic integration and adopted the vast array of laws and regulations that governed the European Community.

The European Community plan has had at its core the adoption of a single currency (based on the European Currency Unit, or ECU) by the member nations. Meeting in Maastricht, The Netherlands, in December 1991, the heads of the twelve EC countries agreed that a common currency, the ECU, would replace the national currencies of eligible nations as early as 1997 and no later than 1999. A single central banking system, known as the European Monetary Institute, would begin operations on 1 January 1994 for the purpose of guiding member nations in reducing inflation rates and budget deficits. Economic union would be reinforced by political union, with member states sharing a common European defense system and common social policies regulating immigration and labor practices. At the end of 1988 President François Mitterrand of France endorsed the goals of the 1992 integration: "One currency, one culture, one social area, one environment." Many worried, however, that the long histories, traditions, and national identifications of the individual member states would stand in the way of a fully integrated Europe.

Britain was the most reluctant of the member states at the prospect of European integration. British negotiators strongly resisted plans for monetary union because of fear of losing national sovereignty rights. Nonetheless, Prime Minister Margaret Thatcher and her successor John Major solidly committed Great Britain to the European Community. As Thatcher explained it, "Britain does not dream of an alternative to the European Community, of some cozy isolated existence on its fringes. Our destiny is in Europe, as part of the Community." In addition to resisting monetary union, British public opinion polls reflected cynicism over the 1991 Maastricht negotiations and a social policy affecting working hours, minimum wages, and conditions of employment throughout Europe.

Some planners were wary about the prospect of including all of eastern Europe, whose troubled economies, they feared, would dilute the economic strength of the European Community. Others predicted a fully integrated Europe, including the eastern European nations, by the year 2014. Three of the new regimes—Poland, Czechoslovakia, and Hungary—were admitted with the status of associate members.

The plan for a single European market affected more than just economics. Education, too, faced standardization of curricula and requirements for degrees. There were proposals for a common European history textbook that, in place of national perspectives, would emphasize the values of a single political entity in its discussion of battles, wars, social change, and culture.

Export-producing nations, including Japan and the United States, expressed concerns over "Fortress Europe," that is, Europe as a global trading bloc with a common external tariff policy that would exclude them. A united Europe, with the world's largest volume of trade and the highest productivity, would constitute a formidable presence in the world arena. With the thawing of the Cold War and the bloc politics of East versus West no longer dominating the international system, the move might easily place Europe at the center of world politics. However, by the mid-1990s roadblocks slowed the move toward European integration. These obstacles included economic recession, ethnic strife, resurgent nationalism, the popularity of conservative policies, and the power of entrenched interest groups.

●●●

The advanced industrial states of Western Europe and the United States were vulnerable to an invisible terrorist enemy who could terrorize populations and incapacitate the smooth functioning of the modern industrial state. More serious threats to stability and demands for some kind of armed response came from the ethnic unrest in central and Eastern Europe. Nationalist feelings and war were intensifying within Eastern Europe at the very moment that integration appeared to accelerate in the West. Demands for autonomy lay behind the revolutionary events in Poland, the Baltic Soviet states, Hungary, Bulgaria, and Romania. Talk of ethnic purity ominously echoed the despicable racial policies of Nazi Germany. Meanwhile, in Western Europe, planners spoke of a European Community in which national differences would be muted for the common good.

At the end of the twentieth century, Western women and men faced a future filled with uncertainty.

Jacques Delors, president of the European Community's Executive Commission, stated simply: "I don't want to live in a Europe that is like it was in 1914." Yet comparisons with Europe on the eve of the Great War seemed salient to some observers. Commentators warned of new nationalist conflicts on the horizon. Social change threatened to wither without producing fruit as governments cut free of the security of old ways grappled with new political challenges and economic chaos. Yet there was hope, too, as leaders of democratic and former communist states that had once been enemies spoke of a common European destiny based on security, freedom, and democratic principles.

Suggestions for Further Reading

Ending the Cold War

* Patrick Cockburn, *Getting Russia Wrong: The End of Kremlinology* (London: Verso, 1989). A Moscow correspondent takes the measure of the politics of the Gorbachev era while attempting to correct Western misconceptions about the Soviet Union.

* Stephen F. Cohen, *Rethinking the Soviet Experience: Politics and History Since 1917* (New York: Oxford University Press, 1985). Offers a revisionist analysis of the historiographical debates in Soviet studies, with the intention of casting light on contemporary Soviet politics.

Geoffrey Hosking, *The Awakening of the Soviet Union* (Cambridge, MA: Harvard University Press, 1990). Published in the midst of the dramatic changes taking place in the Soviet Union, this study emphasizes the social bases of reform and the challenges to Soviet leadership.

* Brian McNair, *Images of the Enemy: Reporting the New Cold War* (London: Routledge, 1988). Focuses on the importance of television in conveying the East-West debate to a mass audience in the 1980s. McNair demonstrates that the Soviets learned in the 1980s to manage communication techniques to their own advantage.

* Adam B. Ulam, *Dangerous Relations: The Soviet Union in World Politics, 1970–1982* (New York: Oxford University Press, 1983). Discusses the making of détente and the relationship between internal developments in the Soviet Union and their impact on foreign policy.

Eastern and Central Europe Since 1968

Timothy Garton Ash, *In Europe's Name: Germany and the Divided Continent* (London: Jonathan Cape, 1993). An original and complex thesis that looks at German reunification from its origins in the 1970s.

* Teresa Rakowska-Harmstone and Andrew Gyorgy, eds., *Communism in Eastern Europe* (Manchester, England: Manchester University Press, 1984). Provides a comprehensive country-by-country approach, with consideration of nationalism and shared regional problems.

* Joseph Rothschild, *Return to Diversity: A Political History of East Central Europe* (New York: Oxford University Press, 1989). A historical and analytical survey of Poland, Czechoslovakia, Hungary, Yugoslavia, Romania, Bulgaria, and Albania that appeared just before the great changes that swept through Eastern Europe in 1989. Rothschild highlights the tensions between nationalist aspirations and Communist rule.

Henry Ashby Turner, Jr., *The Two Germanies Since 1945* (New Haven, CT: Yale University Press, 1987). A political history of the postwar division of Germany until 1987 that bridges a period the author contends was one of increasing involvement and underlying mutual interests between the two nations.

Unity and Diversity in Western Europe

* J. Bowyer Bell, *Transnational Terror* (Washington, DC: American Enterprise Institute, 1975). Presents a compelling argument about the social revolutionary origins of terror and its threat to Western democracies.

* Richard Clutterbuck, *Guerrillas and Terrorists* (London: Faber and Faber, 1977). Clutterbuck considers terrorism as a kind of war rooted in historical experience and global in nature. His purpose is to consider protection against terrorists by examining the roles of the media, the police, and the public.

* Michael Emerson, et al., *The Economics of 1992: The E.C. Commission's Assessment of the Economic Effects of Completing the Internal Market* (Oxford: Oxford University Press, 1988). A work replete with empirical data that give a comprehensive assessment of the potential impact of establishing a single internal market in the European Economic Community.

Wolfgang Mommsen and Gerhard Hirschfeld, eds., *Social Protest, Violence and Terror in Nineteenth- and Twentieth-Century Europe* (London: MacMillan, 1982). Places terrorism within a historical context in Europe over the last century and a half in a series of articles that take a national case-history approach.

Richard E. Rubinstein, *Alchemists of Revolution: Terrorism in the Modern World* (New York: Basic Books, 1987). Examines the local root causes of terrorism in historical perspective and argues that terrorism is the social and moral crisis of a disaffected intelligentsia.

*Paperback edition available.

CREDITS

Document Credits

CHAPTER 1

p. 2, "The Code of Hammurabi," and p. 20, "A Homesick Egyptian": From James B. Pritchard, *The Ancient Near East: An Anthology of Texts and Pictures*. Copyright © 1958 by Princeton University Press. Reprinted by permission of Princeton University Press.

p. 28, "The Kingdom of Israel": Excerpts from 1 Samuel 8:9–10. Scripture quotations are from the Revised Standard Version of the Bible. Copyright 1946, 1952, 1971 by the Division of Christian Education of the National Council of Churches in Christ in the USA. Used by permission.

CHAPTER 2

p. 42, "Hector and Andromache": From *The Iliad of Homer*, translated by Richmond Lattimore. Copyright 1951 by the University of Chicago. Reprinted by permission of the University of Chicago Press.

p. 53, "All Things Change": Excerpts from Heraclitus in John Burnet, *Early Greek Philosophy*.

p. 57, "Two Faces of Tyranny": Excerpts from Herodotus translated by A. D. Godley; excerpts from Aristotle's *Athenian Constitution* translated by H. Rackham.

CHAPTER 3

p. 70, "The Two Faces of Athenian Democracy": Excerpts from Thucydides' *History of the Peloponnesian War*, translated by Rex Warner.

p. 79, "Socrates the Gadfly": From Plato's *Apology*, translated by F. J. Church.

p. 88, "Greeks and Barbarians": From Herodotus, Book III, translated by A. D. Godley.

p. 91, "Alexander Calls a Halt": From Arrian's *Campaigns of Alexander*, translated by Aubrey de Selincourt.

CHAPTER 4

p. 110, "The Twelve Tables": From *Roman Civilization*, Volume I, by Naphtali Lewis and Meyer Reinhold. Copyright 1951 by Columbia University Press, New York. Reprinted with the permission of the publisher.

p. 116, "Polybius Describes the Sack of New Carthage": From Polybius's *Rise of the Roman Empire*, translated by Ian Scot-Kilvert.

p. 125, "Cato's Slaves": From Plutarch's *Lives of the Noble Grecians and Romans*, translated by John Dryden and revised by Arthur Hugh Clough.

CHAPTER 5

p. 133, "The Reforms of Tiberius Gracchus": From *Roman Civilization*, Volume I, by Naphtali Lewis and Meyer Reinhold. Copyright 1951 by Columbia University Press, New York. Reprinted with the permission of the publisher.

p. 136, "Cicero on Justice and Reason": From Cicero's *De Re Publica de Legibus*.

p. 153, "Peter Announces the Good News": Excerpts from Acts 3:17–26. Scripture quotations are from the Revised Standard Version of the Bible. Copyright 1946, 1952, 1971 by the Division of Christian Education of the National Council of Churches in Christ in the USA. Used by permission.

CHAPTER 6

p. 167, "Tacitus on the Germans": From Tacitus's *Germany*.

p. 173, "Religious Toleration and Persecution": Excerpts from *Roman Civilization*, Volume II, by Naphtali Lewis and Meyer Reinhold. Copyright 1951 by Columbia University Press, New York. Used with the permission of the publisher. Excerpt from the Theodosian Code translated by Clyde Pharr.

p. 179, "Love in the Two Cities": From Saint Augustine, *The City of God* (Garden City, NY: Image Books, 1958), pp. 321–322.

CHAPTER 7

p. 192, "The Justinian Code": From Justinian's *Digest of Roman Law*, translated by C. F. Kolbert. Copyright © C. F. Kolbert, 1979. Reproduced by permission of Penguin Books Ltd.

p. 201, "The Qur'an": From the Qur'an, sura 2.

p. 212, "An Arab's View of Western Medicine": From *Arab Historians of the Crusades*, selected and translated from the Arabic sources by Francesco Gabrielli, translated from the Italian by E. J. Costello (Berkeley: University of California Press, 1969), pp. 76–77.

CHAPTER 8

p. 227, "From Slave to Queen": From *Sainted Women of the Dark Ages* by Jo Ann McNamara and John E. Halborg. Copyright © 1992 Duke University Press. Reprinted with permission of the publisher.

p. 228, "Two Missionaries": From Bede, *A History of the English Church and People*, translated by Leo Sherley-Price, revised by R. E. Latham. Copyright © Leo Sherley-Price, 1955, 1968. Reproduced by permission of Penguin Books Ltd.

p. 257, "Charlemagne and the Arts": From Einhard's *Life of Charlemagne*.

CHAPTER 9

p. 258, "Saint Francis of Assisi on Humility and Poverty": From *The Rule of St. Francis of Assisi,* in E. F. Henderson, ed., *Select Historical Documents.*

p. 267, "Word from the Fair": From *Medieval Trade in the Mediterranean World,* edited by Robert S. Lopez and Irving W. Raymond. Reprinted by permission of Columbia University Press.

p. 269, "Visions Like a Flame": From *Hildegard of Bingen: Mystical Writings.* edited by Fiona Bowie and Oliver Davies, with new translations by Robert Carver. Copyright © 1990 by Bowie, Davies, and Carver. Reprinted by permission of The Crossroad Publishing Company.

p. 285, "The Great Charter": Excerpt from Magna Carta, in Stephenson and Marcham, eds., *A Selection of Documents from A.D. 600 to the Interregnum.*

CHAPTER 10

p. 300, "The Black Death in Florence": From Boccaccio's *Decameron.*

p. 309, "A Woman Before the Inquisition": From "Jacques Fournier, Inquisition Records," in *Readings in Medieval History,* edited by Patrick J. Geary. Copyright © 1989 by Broadview Press Ltd. Reprinted by permission.

p. 312, "A Letter to Babbo": From *Babylon on the Rhone: A Translation of Letters by Dante, Petrarch, and Catherine of Siena on the Avignon Papacy* by Robert Coogan. Copyright © 1983 Robert Coogan. Reprinted by permission of José Porrue Turanzas, S.A.

CHAPTER 11

p. 326, "On the Family": From Leon Battista Alberti, "On the Family," in *The Family in Renaissance Florence* by Renee Watkins. Reprinted by permission of Renee Watkins.

p. 332, "The Renaissance Man": From Giorgio Vasari, "Life of Leonardo da Vinci," in *Lives of the Most Eminent Painters, Sculptors, and Architects.,* translated by Gaston DuC. De Vere (London: Warner, 1912–14).

p. 338, "The Lion and the Fox": From *The Prince* by Niccolò Machiavelli, translated and edited by Robert M. Adams (New York: Norton, 1977).

p. 345, "The Siege of Constantinople": From Kritovoulos, *The History of Mehmed the Conquerer,* pp. 324–325.

CHAPTER 12

p. 354, "A Momentous Discovery": From Christopher Columbus, *Letter from the First Voyage* (1493), in *Letters of Christopher Columbus,* trans. R. H. Major (London: Hakluyt Society, 1947).

p. 359, "The Halls of Montezuma": From Bernal Diaz, *The True History of the Conquest of Mexico,* in *The Bernal Diaz Chronicles,,* translated and edited by Albert Idell, pp. 169–171.

p. 373, "Last Words": From Anne Boleyn, scaffold speech.

p. 374, "The Kingdom of France": From Claude de Seyssel, *The Monarchy of France,* translated by J. H. Hexter and edited by Donald R. Kelley. Copyright © 1981 by Yale University Press. All rights reserved. Reprinted by permission.

CHAPTER 13

p. 389, "A Dutch Wit": From Desiderius Erasmus, *In Praise of Folly* (London: Reeves & Turner, 1876).

p. 396, "Luther on Marriage": From Martin Luther, *On Good Works,* translated and edited by William Hazlitt (London: George Bell and Sons, 1895).

p. 401, "The Eternal Decree": From John Calvin, *Institutes of the Christian Religion,* in *John Calvin, Selections from His Writings,* edited and with an introduction by John Dillenberger.

p. 409, "Heavenly Vision": From *The Life of St. Teresa of Avila* (1611), translated by David Lewis.

CHAPTER 14

p. 425, "Catholics and Huguenots": From the Edict of Nantes, translated by James Harvey Robinson, in *Readings in European History.* Volume II: *From the Opening of the Protestant Revolt to the Present Day* (Boston: Ginn & Company, 1906).

pp. 430–431, "Cannibals": From Montaigne, "Of Cannibals." Reprinted from *The Complete Essays of Montaigne,* translated by Donald M. Frame, with the permission of the publishers, Stanford University Press. © 1958 by the Board of Trustees of the Leland Stanford Junior University.

p. 440, "War Is Hell": From Hans Jacob Cristoph Von Grimmelshausen, *The Adventurous Simplicissimus ,* translated by A. T. S. Goodrick (1912).

p. 443, "Fire and Sword": From *The Destruction of Magdeburg.*

CHAPTER 15

p. 452, "Living by One's Wits": From *The Life of Lazarillo des Tormes,* translated and edited by Louis How, with an introduction by Charles Philip Wagner (New York: Mitchell Kennerly, 1917).

p. 466, "The Peasants' Revolt": From the Twelve Articles of the Peasants of Swabia, in *Readings in European History.* Volume II: *From the Opening of the Protestant Revolt to the Present Day,* edited by James Harvey Robinson (Boston: Ginn & Company, 1906).

pp. 470–471, "A Feminine Perspective": From Arcangela Tarabotti, *Innocence Undone,* translated by Brendan Dooley. Reprinted by permission of Brendan Dooley.

p. 479, "The Devil's Due": From "Medieval Witchcraft," in *Translations and Reprints from the Original Sources of European History,* Volume III. Reprinted by permission of The University of Pennsylvania Press.

CHAPTER 16

p. 486, "A Glimpse of a King": From *Memoirs of the Duke of Saint-Simon,* translated by Bayle St. John (London: Swan Sonnonschein & Co., 1900).

p. 499, "A Short, Sharp Shock": From an eyewitness account of the execution of Charles I.

p. 505, "Fathers Know Best": From Sir Robert Filmer, *Patriarcha.*

p. 506, "A Close Shave": From "De Missy's Life of Peter" in *Readings in European History.* Volume II: *From the Opening of the Protestant Revolt to the Present Day,* edited by James Harvey Robinson (Boston: Ginn & Company, 1906).

CHAPTER 17

p. 518, "Stargazing": From Copernicus, *On the Revolution of Heavenly Spheres* (1543), in *Movement of the Earth* by Thomas S. Kuhn.

p. 519, "The Telescope": From Galileo, *The Starry Messenger,* in *Discoveries and Opinions of Galileo* by Galileo Galilei. Copyright © 1957 by Stillman Drake. Used by permission of Doubleday, a division of Bantam Doubleday Dell Publishing Group, Inc.

p. 535, "Eastern Traders": From *The Low Countries in Early Modern Times: A Documentary History* by Herbert H. Rowen, p. 353. Copyright © 1972 by Herbert H. Rowen. Reprinted by permission of HarperCollins Publishers, Inc.

p. 537, "Defining Commerce": From Adam Smith, *The Wealth of Nations,* ed. James E. Thorold Rogers. Volume I, 2d ed. (Oxford: Clarendon Press, 1880).

Writings (New York: International Publishers, 1942). Reprinted by permission of International Publishers Company.

p. 867, "The Law on the Abolition of Legal Abortion, 1936": Excerpt from Rudolph Schlesinger, *The Family in the USSR: Documents and Readings* (London: Routledge & Kegan Paul, 1949), pp. 251–254. Reprinted by permission of the publisher.

p. 876, "Adolf Hitler on 'Racial Purity' ": From "Racial Purity: Hitler Reverts to the Dominant Theme of the National Socialist Program, January 30, 1937," in *Hitler's Third Reich,* edited by Louis L. Snyder. Copyright © 1981 by Louis L. Snyder. Reprinted by permission of Nelson-Hall, Inc.

CHAPTER 28

p. 893, "The White Rose": From "Opposition: Students of the 'Weisse Rose' Distribute a Leaflet Denouncing Nazism and Pay for It with Their Lives, February 22, 1943," translated by Louis L. Snyder, editor of *Hitler's Third Reich.* Copyright © 1981 by Louis L. Snyder. Reprinted by permission of Nelson-Hall, Inc.

p. 899, "Manifesto of the Jewish Resistance in Vilna, September 1943": From *An Anthology of Holocaust Literature,* edited by J. Glatstein, I. Knox, and S. Margoshes. Reprinted by permission of the Jewish Publication Society.

p. 900, "The Atrocity at Lidice": From Robert Battaglia, *La Seconda Guerra Mondiale: Problemice nodi cruciali* (1971).

p. 906, "President Franklin Roosevelt's Request for a Declaration of War on Japan, 8 December 1941": From *World War II: Policy and Strategy* by Hans Adolf Jacobsen and Arthur J. Smith, Jr. Reprinted by permission.

p. 907, "Japan's Declaration of War on the United States and Great Britain (8 December 1941)": From *World War II: Policy and Strategy* by Hans Adolf Jacobsen and Arthur J. Smith, Jr. Reprinted by permission.

p. 915, " 'Glittering Fragments' ": "Glittering Fragments" by Hara Tamiki from *The Penguin Book of Japanese Verse,* translated by Geoffrey Brownas and Anthony Thwaite (Penguin Books, 1964), translation copyright © Geoffrey Brownas and Anthony Thwaite, 1964. Reprinted by permission.

CHAPTER 29

p. 921, "The Iron Curtain": From "The Sinews of Peace" by Winston Churchill, in *Winston Churchill: His Complete Speeches, Volume VII: 1943–1949,* edited by Robert Rhodes James. Reprinted by permission.

pp. 932, "The Marshall Plan": From Department of State Bulletin, 15 June 1947.

p. 939, "Report to the Twentieth Party Congress": From "Report to the Twentieth Party Congress" by Nikita S. Khrushchev, reprinted from *Current Society Policies II. The Documentary Record of the Twentieth Party Congress and Its Aftermath,* published by *The Current Digest of the Soviet Press,* Columbus, Ohio. Used by permission.

pp. 942–943, "The Second Sex": From *The Second Sex* by Simone de Beauvoir, trans. H. M. Parshley. Copyright 1952 and renewed 1980 by Alfred A. Knopf, Inc. Reprinted by permission of the publisher.

p. 945, "Subterranean Homesick Blues": "Subterranean Homesick Blues" by Bob Dylan. Copyright © 1965 by Warner Bros. Music, Copyright renewed 1993 by Special Rider Music. All rights reserved. International copyright secured. Reprinted by permission.

CHAPTER 30

p. 954, "Perestroika": From *Perestroika* by Mikhail Gorbachev. Copyright © 1987 by Mikhail Gorbachev. Reprinted by permission of HarperCollins Publishers, Inc.

p. 957, "Career Advancement, Communist-Style": From *Russian Voices* by Tony Parker. Copyright © 1991 by Tony Parker. Reprinted by permission of Henry Holt and Company, Inc.

p. 973, "The Return of Fascism?": From "Two Germans Admit Arson Attack That Killed Three Turkish Nationals," as appeared in *The New York Times,* December 2, 1992. Reprinted by permission of the Associated Press. From "Music of Hate Raises the Volume in Germany" by Ferdinand Protzman in *The New York Times,* December 2, 1992. Copyright © 1992 by The New York Times Company. Reprinted by permission.

Photo Credits

Unless otherwise acknowledged, all photographs are the property of Scott, Foresman. Page abbreviations are as follows: T (top), C (center), B (bottom), L (left), R (right).

CHAPTER 1

2 European Space Agency 4 The Cleveland Museum of Natural History 5 Kazuyoshi Nomachi/Pacific Press Service 7 Kathleen M. Kenyon/Jericho Excavations 9 Copyright the British Museum 10 Staatliche Museen Preussischer Kulturbesitz, Berlin 11 Copyright the British Museum 12 Hirmer Fotoarchiv, Munich 14 Scala/Art Resource, New York 16 Hirmer Fotoarchiv, Munich 19 Copyright the British Museum 22 The Metropolitan Museum of Art, Rogers Fund, 1931 (31.3.157) 23 Hirmer Fotoarchiv, Munich 24 Bridgeman/Art Resource, New York 25 Lee Boltin 27 Erich Lessing/Art Resource, New York 29T Oriental Institute, the University of Chicago 29B Erich Lessing/Art Resource, New York 31 Erich Lessing/Art Resource, New York

CHAPTER 2

34 Courtesy, Museum of Fine Arts, Boston, William Francis Warden Fund 36 The Metropolitan Museum of Art, Rogers Fund, 1947(47.100.1) 38 Scala/Art Resource, New York 39 Hirmer Fotoarchiv, Munich 40 Ronald Sheridan/Ancient Art & Architecture Collection 41 Hirmer Fotoarchiv, Munich 43 Copyright the British Museum 44 Copyright the British Museum 45 Scala/Art Resource, New York 47 Bibliothèque Nationale, Paris 48 Scala/Art Resource, New York 49 Antikenmuseum, Berlin/Staatliche Museen Preussischer Kulturbesitz, Berlin 50 Alexander Tsiaras/Stock Boston 54 Scala/Art Resource, New York 55 Hirmer Fotoarchiv, Munich 56 Hirmer Fotoarchiv, Munich 58 Giraudon/Art Resource, New York 62 Lee Boltin

CHAPTER 3

66 Scala/Art Resource, New York 67 Scala/Art Resource, New York 68 © 1989 Raymond V. Schoder, S.J., Loyola University of Chicago 69 American Museum of Classical Studies at Athens: Agora Excavations 73 Antikensammlung, Berlin/Staatliche Museen Preussischer Kulturbesitz, Berlin 74T The Metropolitan Museum of Art, Fletcher Fund, 1931(31.11.10); photograph by Schecter Lee 74B Staatliche Antikensammlungen und Glyptothek, Munich 75 Michael Holford 78 Copyright the British Museum 82 The Metropolitan Museum of Art, Rogers Fund, 1952 (52.11.4) 83 SuperStock, Inc. 85 Alinari/Art Resource, New York 86 Alinari/Art Resource, New York 90 Copyright the British Museum 94 Giraudon/Art Resource, New York 95 The Metropolitan Museum of Art, Bequest of Walter C. Baker, 1971 (1972.118.95)

CHAPTER 15

448 National Gallery, Prague   449 National Gallery, Prague   450 Scala/Art Resource, New York   451 The British Library   453 Musées Royaux des Beaux-Arts de Belgique, Brussels   455 Philadelphia Museum of Art, Smith, Kline and French Collection   458 Giraudon/Art Resource, New York   459 Bibliothèque Nationale, Paris   463 Rijksmuseum Foundation, Amsterdam   465 Foto Kilian, Stuttgart   468 Scala/Art Resource, New York   469 Victoria & Albert Museum/Art Resource, New York   473 Bridgeman/Art Resource, New York   476 By permission of the Astronomer Royal of Scotland, Crawford Collection, © Royal Observatory, Edinburgh

CHAPTER 16

482 Service Photographique de la Réunion des Musées Nationaux   484 National Portrait Gallery, London   487T The National Gallery, London   487B Courtesy of the Hispanic Society of America, New York   488 National Portrait Gallery, London   492B Bettmann Archive   494 Bettmann Archive   498 The Parker Gallery, London   500 By permission of the Earl of Rosebery, on loan to the Scottish National Portrait Gallery   508T Mondadori Photo Archives   508B John Freeman   511 Scala/Art Resource, New York   512 Mansell Collection

CHAPTER 17

514 Photograph © Mauritshuis, The Hague   517 The British Library   521 National Library of Medicine, Bethesda, Maryland   522 Biblioteca Nazionale Centrale, Florence   525 Erich Lessing/Art Resource, New York   526 Städelsches Kunstinstitut, Frankfurt Am Main; photo: Blauel-Gnamm Artothek   529 The Metropolitan Museum of Art, Gift of Mrs. Albert Blum, 1920 (20.79)   531B Bibliothèque Nationale, Paris   532 Städelsches Kunstinstitut, Frankfurt Am Main; photo: Ursula Edelmann   538 National Maritime Museum, Greenwich, England   539 The National Gallery, London   541 Copyright the British Museum

CHAPTER 18

546 Nationalgalerie, Berlin/Staatliche Museen Preussischer Kulturbesitz, Berlin   550 Rijksmuseum Foundation, Amsterdam   552 Sonia Halliday Photographs   555 Central Naval Museum, St. Petersburg   558 State Russian Museum, St. Petersburg   562 Kunstbibliothek, Berlin/Staatliche Museen Preussischer Kulturbesitz, Berlin   566 Kunsthistorisches Museum, Vienna

CHAPTER 19

576 The Visit to the Nursery by Jean-Honoré Fragonard, painted before 1784. Samuel H. Kress Collection/National Gallery of Art, Washington, D.C.   578 Copyright the British Museum   580 Ets J. E. Bulloz   582T Scottish National Portrait Gallery   588 Mary Evans Picture Library   589 private collection   591 Gemäldegalerie, Berlin/Staatliche Museen Preussischer Kulturbesitz, Berlin   593 Scala/Art Resource, New York   603 Germanisches Nationalmuseum, Nuremberg   604 Copyright the British Museum   605 The Metropolitan Museum of Art, Harris Brisbane Dick Fund, 1932 (32.35.129)

CHAPTER 20

608 Giraudon/Art Resource, New York   609 Giraudon/Art Resource, New York   613 Ets J. E. Bulloz   620 Ets J. E. Bulloz   621 Musée Carnavalet, Paris   622 Ets J. E. Bulloz   623 Mansell Collection   625 Library of Congress   627 Bibliothèque Nationale, Paris   632 Giraudon/Art Resource, New York   636 Francisco José de Goya y Lucientes, Spanish, 1746–1828. Neither Do These (Ni por Esas), etching, 1863, 16 x 21 cm. Gift of J. C. Cebrian, 1920.1316, photograph © 1990, The Art Institute of Chicago. All Rights Reserved.   637 Scala/Art Resource, New York   639 Musée des Beaux-Arts, Rouen

CHAPTER 21

642 Saint-Lazare Train Station, The Normandy Train (La Gare Saint-Lazare, Le Train de Normandie) by Claude Monet, 1877, oil on canvas. 59.6 x 80.2 cm. Mr. and Mrs. Martin A. Ryerson Collection, 1933.1158. Photograph © 1990, The Art Institute of Chicago. All Rights Reserved.   647 Copyright the British Museum   649 Reproduced from the original in Bedfordshire Record Office   652 The British Library   655 Mansell Collection   657 Museum of American Textile History, North Andover, Mass.   660 Mansell Collection   663 Victoria & Albert Museum/Art Resource, New York   665 Mansell Collection   666 Fotomas Index/John Freeman   672 Ets J. E. Bulloz   676 Ullstein Bilderdienst

CHAPTER 22

680 Gift of Quincy Adams Shaw through Quincy A. Shaw, Jr., and Mrs. Marian Shaw Haughton. Courtesy, Museum of Fine Arts, Boston.   686 Bibliothèque Nationale, Paris   688 Tate Gallery, London/Art Resource, New York   689 The British Library   691 Bridgeman/Art Resource, New York   693 Windsor Castle, Royal Library; © Her Majesty Queen Elizabeth II   695 The British Library   698 Giraudon/Art Resource, New York   699 Giraudon/Art Resource, New York   701 Copyright the British Museum   708 Sachsische Landesbibliothek   710 Scala/Art Resource, New York   714 Copyright the British Museum

CHAPTER 23

718 Staatliche Museen Preussischer Kulturbesitz, Berlin   721 Copyright the British Museum   722 Weidenfeld Archives   725 Museo Resorgimento   729 Nationalgalerie/Staatliche Museen Preussischer Kulturbesitz, Berlin   730 Copyright the British Museum   731 Roger-Viollet   733 Bridgeman/Art Resource, New York   738 By courtesy of the Victoria & Albert Museum   742 Masters and Fellows of Trinity College, Cambridge

CHAPTER 24

750 Bridgeman/Art Resource, New York   753 Markisches Museum   755 Hulton Deutsch Collection Ltd.   758 Bibliothèque Nationale, Paris   763 The Museum of London   768 Bettmann Archive   770 AP/Wide World   771 U.S. Information Agency/The National Archives   772 Bettmann Archive   775 The Sophia Smith Collection (Womens History Archive)/ Smith College, Northampton, Mass.   777 By courtesy of the Victoria & Albert Museum   778 Photo Chevojon, Paris

CHAPTER 25

780 Bettmann Archive   783 Hulton Deutsch Collection Ltd.   788 René Dazy, Paris   791 Bettmann Archive   795 R. B. Fleming   796 The National Archives, Zimbabwe   798 National Maritime Museum, Greenwich, England   799 Copyright the British Museum   800 The British Library

CHAPTER 26

812 "Take Up the Sword of Justice" by Sir Bernard J. Partridge, England, 1915. From copy in Bowman Gray Collection, Rare Book Collection, University of North Carolina Library, Chapel Hill   813 "Deutsche Frauen Arbeitet im Heimat-Heer! Kriegsamtstelle

INDEX

᠕